The End of the Party

ANDREW RAWNSLEY

The End of the Party

VIKING
an imprint of
PENGUIN BOOKS

VIKING

Published by the Penguin Group

Penguin Books Ltd, 80 Strand, London WC2R 0RL, England

Penguin Group (USA) Inc., 375 Hudson Street, New York, New York 10014, USA

Penguin Group (Canada), 90 Eglinton Avenue East, Suite 700, Toronto, Ontario, Canada M4P 2Y3
(a division of Pearson Penguin Canada Inc.)

Penguin Ireland, 25 St Stephen's Green, Dublin 2, Ireland (a division of Penguin Books Ltd)

Penguin Group (Australia), 250 Camberwell Road, Camberwell, Victoria 3124, Australia
(a division of Pearson Australia Group Pty Ltd)

Penguin Books India Pvt Ltd, 11 Community Centre, Panchsheel Park, New Delhi – 110 017, India

Penguin Group (NZ), 67 Apollo Drive, Rosedale, North Shore 0632, New Zealand
(a division of Pearson New Zealand Ltd)

Penguin Books (South Africa) (Pty) Ltd, 24 Sturdee Avenue, Rosebank,
Johannesburg 2196, South Africa

Penguin Books Ltd, Registered Offices: 80 Strand, London WC2R 0RL, England

www.penguin.com

First published 2010

1

Copyright © Andrew Rawnsley, 2010

The moral right of the author has been asserted

Set in Sabon LT Std 9.75/13pt
Typeset by Palimpsest Book Production Limited, Grangemouth, Stirlingshire
Printed in Great Britain by Clays Ltd, St Ives plc

A CIP catalogue record for this book is available from the British Library

HARDBACK ISBN: 978–0–670–91851–5
TRADE PAPERBACK ISBN: 978–0–670–91852–2

www.greenpenguin.co.uk

Penguin Books is committed to a sustainable future
for our business, our readers and our planet.
The book in your hands is made from paper
certified by the Forest Stewardship Council.

Contents

PART TWO: THE PRICE OF AMBITION

Introduction

Bliss was it in that dawn to be alive, but to be New Labour was very heaven. Tony Blair, Gordon Brown and Peter Mandelson seized the commanding heights of their party in 1994 and three years later they captured the country with a parliamentary landslide of unprecedented scale in modern times. Whether you like New Labour, as so many millions did during the euphoric early period in power, or whether you loathe them, as so many millions do today, this has been a remarkable phenomenon. If New Labour now seems pretty old, that is a consequence of both its failing and its success. It is a formidable fact, which is usually overlooked, that this has been the longest-lasting non-Tory government since 1762. New Labour's story is all of our stories.

Since the publication of *Servants of the People*, which described the making of the project and its first term in office, I have continued to chronicle the victories and the tribulations of New Labour through television documentaries, in the *Observer* and on radio. It was around the time that Tony Blair reluctantly handed power to Gordon Brown that I decided I wouldn't be content until I had brought the story up to date between covers. Only the scope provided by a book could fully explain the characters who have governed us, comprehensively explore how they have wrestled with the dilemmas and events that have confronted them, and properly reveal the arguments which have divided and convulsed them.

I hope to bridge the gap between instantaneous journalism, which is inevitably forced to sacrifice deep research for immediacy, and the future historian who gains a longer perspective at the cost of delay. Historians will have the benefit of access to official papers that are today concealed, as well as memoirs and diaries that are as yet unpublished. The disadvantage of the future historian is that he or she will have to wait for a very long time – in some cases, we will all be dead first – to get sight of many Whitehall documents. Experience suggests that official papers will often mask as much as they reveal. It is also the case that many of the most crucial conversations at the heart of power have taken place without civil servants present to record a note. The literary output of New Labour's dramatis personae, as we know from some of the memoirs and diaries already published, is written from single and self-serving perspectives. At best, they offer only a partial account of what really happened. They often seek to shade, sanitise or conceal.

The unpartisan writer has the advantage of being able to seek answers from all the pivotal players and to ask any question to tease out the truth about how we have been ruled.

As I have revisited the seminal episodes of this Government's life, I have once again found that neither the claims made for themselves nor daily media coverage have told anything like the full story.

Part One of this book opens on the day after the election triumph in 2001. That victory was a remarkable achievement. New Labour was the product of repeated and traumatic failures: the party's four serial defeats in the seventies, eighties and nineties at the hands of the Conservatives. Now it had achieved a rare consecutive landslide victory. Within months, though, the seismic event of 9/11 utterly altered the trajectory of Tony Blair's premiership. The master consensualist of the first term became the conviction-driven lone warrior of the second. The early campaign against the Taliban and al-Qaeda in Afghanistan, which made regime change look so easy, was followed by the invasion of Iraq and another deceptively swift victory in the conventional war. I explore the fatal dynamics of the relationship between Blair and George Bush, how the Prime Minister overcame the apprehensions of the majority of both his Cabinet and senior aides to take Britain to war, and why the allies were so catastrophically unprepared for what would happen after the fall of Saddam. At his lowest point, Blair came very close to resigning as Prime Minister. It was also during this term that his dream of taking Britain into the euro died.

Another large theme of the second term is the battle to reform health, education and other public services to try to extract levels of performance commensurate with the huge extra resources that began to flow into them. This was enmeshed with the increasingly toxic power struggle between Tony Blair and Gordon Brown. To try to contain Brown and deal with his incessant demands that he should hand over power, Blair responded by making promises that he would do so. When he then reneged, Brown was driven even more demented. The two men managed to agree a brittle truce which just got them through the next campaign. Part One ends on election night 2005, when they secured a bittersweet victory: a third term with a solid parliamentary majority, but won with a miserably reduced share of the vote.

Part Two tells the story of the third term, beginning with Tony Blair's final two years at Number 10. Among the events addressed are 7/7, the Olympics bid, the Gleneagles Summit, the 'cash-for-coronets' affair and final battles on school reform. I also look at the Government's sharpening authoritarianism. A late pinnacle is the peace process in Northern Ireland, a shining achievement of Blair's premiership. He is ultimately forced to leave Number 10 earlier than he desired as a result of a coup orchestrated from the heart of the camp of Gordon Brown and with his knowledge.

The short honeymoon at Number 10 enjoyed by Brown proves, on closer inspection, to have mainly served to conceal many of the flaws that would undermine him as Prime Minister. After the phantom election, the revolt over 10p tax and a sequence of other debacles, Brown was regarded as such a liability by key Cabinet ministers that they were poised to remove him. Two things saved his premiership in the autumn of 2008. One was the greatest financial crisis since 1929, to which Brown responded with a boldness and imagination that impressed even those colleagues and civil servants who were otherwise in utter despair about him. The bursting of the bubble raised many questions about his stewardship of the boom years, but it also gave him a purpose for his premiership and a temporary political bounce. The other lifeline was provided by his remarkable reconciliation with Peter Mandelson, the man with whom Brown had waged a titanic feud for more than a decade. They were bound back together by a joint and desperate ambition to try to save the project they founded as the Government was engulfed by the parliamentary expenses scandal and slid into an unpopularity so profound that it looks terminal.

I offer a broad summary about why New Labour went from triumph to disaster in the final chapter. Conclusions about particular events, issues and personalities are woven throughout the book, which broadly unfolds in chronological sequence.

This work draws on multiple sources. The account is informed by the thousands of confidential conversations that I have had with the principal figures and many other witnesses over some two decades. Another source is the on-camera interviews that I have conducted for a series of documentaries on the governments of Tony Blair and Gordon Brown. These are supplemented by other interviews for the *Observer* as well as television and radio programmes. I have further conducted a very large number of additional interviews specifically for this book. In all, more than 500 witnesses contribute to this account.

In both the text and the notes, I almost always give to people the title or status they had at the time of the episode being described. As well as detailing dialogue, I sometimes describe what someone is thinking or feeling. This is not because I claim to possess psychic powers. It is because I have had a reliable account either from the person or from witnesses to whom they have directly expressed what they were thinking or feeling.

It will not be suprising if there are attempts to deny some of the revelations in this book, especially those which tell uncomfortable truths about our rulers. Many of the previously undisclosed incidents and arguments exposed in *Servants of the People* were denied when that book was first published only to be later confirmed by memoirs, diaries, documentaries and the release of official papers.

I apologise in advance to readers who are distressed by profanities and blasphemies. I am afraid politicians and those who work with them do swear when they are under stress or angry with each other.

A project of this scope would not have been possible without the assistance of a large cast of people at all levels of politics right up to the absolute apex. I am grateful to both Tony Blair and Gordon Brown for making the time over the years to talk to me in both private conversation and on-the-record interviews. I have not always accepted their versions of events. Nor have I always agreed with their analysis of issues. It has nevertheless been a great advantage to be able to understand the thinking of the two leading men at different stages of the New Labour story. I say the same about my interviews and conversations with Peter Mandelson, the third side of the eternal New Labour triangle.

In a way which wasn't possible with *Servants of the People*, I have been able to put many more witnesses on the record. I have been pleasantly stunned by the candour with which so many who saw history in the making are now prepared to speak. It remains the case, though, that some interviewees, especially serving civil servants, diplomats, and intelligence and military officers, are only willing to be frank if they are interviewed partially or wholly off the record. This is also the case with sensitive interviews with serving ministers and their aides. I have tried to be as open and comprehensive in the notes as is consistent with obligations to sources.

I feel I can express public gratitude to Robin Butler, Richard Wilson and Andrew Turnbull, successive Cabinet Secretaries of the New Labour years. I also owe particular thanks to the former Permanent Secretaries: Terry Burns of the Treasury; Michael Jay of the Foreign Office; John Gieve of the Home Office and later deputy Governor of the Bank of England; and Steve Robson, Second Permanent Secretary at the Treasury.

I have had enormous help in understanding the Iraq war from David Manning, Tony Blair's senior adviser on foreign affairs and then British ambassador in Washington. I would equally like to thank his predecessor as ambassador, Christopher Meyer. I am grateful to Jeremy Greenstock, ambassador to the UN during the build-up to the invasion and later British envoy in Baghdad, whose own account was hypocritically gagged by the Government. My thanks are also due to General Charles Guthrie and his successor as Chief of the Defence Staff, Admiral Michael Boyce, and to the former head of the army, General Mike Jackson, and to Stephen Lander, Director-General of MI5 at the time of 9/11 and later executive chairman of the Serious Organised Crime Agency.

I have also drawn on interviews with key actors from other countries, including Andrew Card and Condoleezza Rice, Chief of Staff and Secretary of State to George Bush; William Cohen, Richard Haas and George Mitchell; and Christine Lagarde, finance minister of France.

I have enjoyed the benefit of talking, both on the record and confidentially, to pivotal players and key witnesses in the Cabinet over the New Labour years. In an alphabetic order which may be potentially misleading, I am grateful to Andrew Adonis, Douglas Alexander, Hilary Armstrong, Ed Balls, Margaret Beckett, Hilary Benn, Hazel Blears, David Blunkett, Ben Bradshaw, Nick Brown, Des Browne, Andy Burnham, Stephen Byers, Liam Byrne, David Clark, Charles Clarke, the late Robin Cook, Jack Cunningham, Alistair Darling, John Denham, the late Donald Dewar, Frank Dobson, Charlie Falconer, Peter Hain, Harriet Harman, Patricia Hewitt, Geoff Hoon, John Hutton, Derry Irvine, Margaret Jay, Alan Johnson, Tessa Jowell, Ruth Kelly, Michael Meacher, Estelle Morris, the late Mo Mowlam, Alan Milburn, David Miliband, Ed Miliband, Paul Murphy, John Prescott, James Purnell, John Reid, George Robertson, Clare Short, Andrew Smith, Chris Smith, Jacqui Smith, Gavin Strang, Jack Straw, Ann Taylor, the late Gareth Williams and Shaun Woodward.

Many more ministers, MPs and other crucial witnesses have been generous with their time. I am particularly grateful to Jon Cruddas, Frank Field, Philip Gould, Stan Greenberg, Bruce Grocott, Roy Hattersley, Keith Hill, Neil Kinnock, Michael Levy, Ken Livingstone, Paul Myners, Geoffrey Robinson, Shriti Vadera and Michael Wills.

I also thank three of Gordon's 'GOATS': Digby Jones, Mark Malloch-Brown and Alan West, the last being the only one who has not torn away from his tether.

Special advisers – often crudely shorthanded as 'spin doctors' – get a bad press even though many journalists rely on them. At their worst, they can be malevolent and mendacious operators. At their best, I have found them candid and insightful. Two outstanding examples are Huw Evans, aide to David Blunkett, and Ed Owen, aide to Jack Straw.

I have also drawn on the perspectives and knowledge of non-Labour politicians, including Paddy Ashdown, Vince Cable, David Cameron, Menzies Campbell, Ken Clarke, Nick Clegg, David Davis, Iain Duncan Smith, Michael Gove, William Hague, Michael Heseltine, Michael Howard, the late Roy Jenkins, Charles Kennedy, George Osborne, David Trimble and David Willetts.

Jonathan Powell, Tony Blair's Chief of Staff throughout his time at Number 10 and his crucial right hand on the Northern Ireland peace process, has been of invaluable assistance. So too has been another absolutely key aide of the Blair years, Sally Morgan. From Blair's Number 10, I also thank Tim Allan, Michael Barber, Alastair Campbell, Hilary Coffman, Phil Collins, David Hill, Robert Hill, Anji Hunter, Peter Hyman, Tom Kelly, Steve Morris, Geoff Mulgan, Matthew Taylor, Stephen Wall and Ben Wegg-Prosser. There is a similar tally of people from Brown's Number 10 and Treasury to whom I would like to express gratitude, but many of them might not thank me for thanking them in print when they are still serving in close proximity to the Prime Minister or have only recently left. For their own protection, it is probably best to preserve their anonymity for the moment.

For helping me to develop my understanding of the personalities of the men who have occupied Number 10, I am especially grateful to Barry Cox and Nick Ryden, friends to Tony Blair, and to Murray Elder, friend since childhood to Gordon Brown. My assessment of Peter Mandelson and the tormented relationships between the three founding fathers of New Labour has been assisted by his friend Robert Harris.

I thank all the busy people who made space in extremely crowded diaries to be interviewed, quite often more than once, and were prepared to answer my follow-up requests for further information and amplification without complaint. I am also grateful for the inexhaustible patience of the many secretaries and personal assistants who have been so helpful in accommodating my demands.

During the period covered by this book, I have been exceptionally lucky to thrive on the encouragement of two fantastic editors of the *Observer*, Roger Alton and John Mulholland, and a first among deputy editors, Paul Webster. My gratitude for being such good people goes to all the friends I have made at the *Observer* and especially to my colleagues on the comment pages and political staff: Kamal Ahmed, Rafael Behr, Martin Bright, Barbara Gunnell, Toby Helm, Gaby Hinsliff, Bill Keegan, Ruaridh Nicoll, Jo Revill, Ned Temko, Nick Watt, Robert Yates and Patrick Wintour, Prince among Political Editors.

Chris Riddell has graced the cover of the book with one of his superlative cartoons.

I owe a huge amount to my friends at BrookLapping with whom I have made a series of documentaries about the governments of Blair and Brown. My thanks to Anne Lapping, warrior queen of executive producers, directors Rob Coldstream and Mick Gold, researcher Lucy Bell, consultant Jane Bonham Carter, production managers Bella Barr and Carrie Pennifer, and Sally Brindle, brilliant star among producers.

Gill Coleridge, my agent, was a wonderfully persistent voice telling me I had to complete the story. I could not have wished for Penguin to give me a more pleasurable editor to work with than Tony Lacey. My thanks also to his colleagues Venetia Butterfield, Amelia Fairney, Helen Fraser, Alex Hippisley-Cox, Joanna Prior, Ellie Smith and Tom Weldon. A big hat tip for his impeccable copy-editing to Mark Handsley.

My three daughters, Olivia, Jessica and Cordelia, have cheerfully sustained both their parents through a project which has often seemed all-consuming.

Nothing would have been possible without Jane, my closest collaborator, my wife and my best friend. Shoulder to shoulder, she was there at the first step and there to the last.

Andrew Rawnsley
November 2009

PART ONE

The Cost of Conviction
Second Term
2001–2005

1. Twice Promised Land

Tony Blair was sprawled on the sofa in his small office next door to the Cabinet Room on the ground floor of Number 10. The Prime Minister's den, the most modest working quarters of any leader of a major country, was where he took virtually all the crucial decisions. He sat there looking absolutely exhausted as he tackled a bacon, lettuce and tomato sandwich.

The Cabinet Secretary, Sir Richard Wilson, sat on the opposite side of the coffee table. Britain's most senior civil servant was a faintly Trollopian figure whose catchphrase was 'God bless'. The traditionalist Sir Richard often wrangled with Blair and his team about the way they ran government from the sofa, but it was hard to argue today when he was looking at a leader who had just won a second landslide election victory.

'Congratulations,' Sir Richard said to the charcoal-eyed Prime Minister. 'You are now at the peak of your powers.' He then added a caution: 'You may never be as strong again as you are now.'[1]

Blair took a bite out of the BLT, munched and nodded in a way that suggested he agreed.

Shortly after he first won power in 1997, Blair told me that 'the most important thing' was to get re-elected.[2] From the day that they took office, both he and Gordon Brown were fixated with keeping it. Blair because no previous Labour Prime Minister had secured a second full term in a century of the party's existence; Brown because he expected to take over the premiership. That ambition was a spur and a burden to both men during their first four years in power. That goal was now triumphantly realised. The second term was not only secure; it was won with a second landslide, a rare result in British politics. The enormous majority won in 1997, a feat which most thought unrepeatable, was reduced in 2001 by a mere dozen seats to 167. They seemed to have realised Harold Wilson's dream to make Labour 'the natural party of government'.

There was the occasional scare during the first term. The foot and mouth epidemic, which filled the nation's nostrils with the acrid smell of burning

3

cattle, was so severe that it delayed the election by a month. Even more alarming was the shorter and sharper shock of the refinery blockades when a few hundred protestors throttled the nation's fuel supplies in the autumn of 2000.[3] The Government came 'very close to asking the army to come in'.[4] A panic-struck Downing Street also tried to use MI5 against the protestors. Sir Stephen Lander, the head of the service, was asked: 'Why aren't you doing the farmers for us like you did the miners for Margaret Thatcher?'[5] For a few highly stressed days, Blair feared that he might live out his nightmare of being yet another one-term Labour Prime Minister overwhelmed by crisis. 'They could finish us off,' he shivered to his senior staff. 'If we don't get this back to normal soon, they will finish us off.'[6]

Office exposed some of the flaws in New Labour and its dominant personalities. Blair was easily seduced by poorly conceived glamour projects. The Millennium Dome was a *folie de bombast* which became symbolic of a compulsion to emphasise marketing over content, hype over substance.[7] Self-defeating control-freakery led to humiliation in London at the hands of Ken Livingstone when New Labour's *bête rouge* was elected as an independent for the post of Mayor, which had been Blair's personal invention.[8] The twin-headed beast of sleaze and spin ate into public trust for a Prime Minister who once piously claimed that he would be 'purer than pure'. The Ecclestone Affair was an unheeded early warning about dangerous liaisons with plutocrats. 'They'll get me for this,' Blair despaired to one intimate at the height of the furore about the £1 million donation secretly taken from the boss of Formula One. As it occurred during his honeymoon period with the voters, 'the pretty straight kind of guy' escaped from that with his premiership intact, but not all of his integrity. His halo was now stained with nicotine.[9]

New Labour often gave the impression of being government by soap opera and psychodrama because of the intensity of the emotions and the hysteria of the feuds between its leading characters. That was most true of the complex bonds between its founding triangle: Tony Blair, Gordon Brown and Peter Mandelson. Brown and Mandelson, once so close they could have been siblings, became 'poisoned with lack of trust' and 'utterly destructive' towards each other.[10] It was Brown's acolytes who destroyed Mandelson's first Cabinet career by triggering the revelations about the Geoffrey Robinson home loan.[11] Between Blair and Brown, there was another blood brother relationship disfigured by mistrust as they wrestled for control over the Government. The bond between Blair and Mandelson was also traumatised during the first term. In the estimation of Barry Cox, a television executive who had known both men for years, Mandelson had an 'almost homoerotic admiration' for Blair. 'It was almost embarrassing the terms in which Peter spoke to me about Tony.'[12] Yet that had not spared Mandelson when his career was crunched by scandal. Blair ruthlessly sacked his co-architect of New Labour from the Cabinet in Christmas 1998. He resurrected him in the autumn of 1999 only to dispatch this closest of allies for a second time in early 2001. On the second occasion, over the Hinduja Affair, a shroud-white Mandelson sat in Blair's den and miserably pleaded for his life. 'Are you really telling me you are going to end my political career over this?' 'Yes,' responded Blair bleakly but firmly. 'I'm afraid I am.'[13] Speaking many years later, Mandelson agreed that Blair was 'a ruthless bastard' who had sacked him with remarkable ease.[14] Mandelson's friend, the novelist Robert Harris, thought it 'the most brutal thing I have ever seen'.[15] For all his undoubted charm and general decency towards colleagues, there was a splinter of ice in Blair's heart. Even one of his oldest friends was not safe from sacrifice if there was a threat to his grip on power. Mandelson's second dismissal illustrated the 'incredibly unsentimental' face of Blair.[16] Most assumed that the double defenestration meant that there could never be a return to the front line of British politics for Peter Mandelson. Even Jesus Christ was only resurrected the once.

Of Blair's gifts, the most self-evident was a flair for performance. He was the most accomplished communicator of his era, a talent not to be dismissed in the age of 24/7 media where a leader is constantly on show. At times of national drama or international crisis, he displayed a high facility for capturing public sentiment and weaving it into a political narrative. When the royal family froze in self-endangering silence after the death of Diana, Blair took on the role of spokesman for national emotion, stepping into the position vacated by the mute head of state, and helping to save the royal family from itself. With his word wreath about a 'people's princess', he expressed the feelings that Britain – or at least a large part of it – wanted to hear. It was a significant episode in his early development as Prime Minister.[17] His personal pollster, Stan Greenberg, reported that Blair's approval ratings surged to such stratospheric levels that they exceeded even those manufactured in totalitarian regimes. 'Even Saddam doesn't get that,' joked Greenberg.[18]

That episode established Blair as more than a popular Prime Minister. It projected him as a leader of the nation.

Charles Kennedy quipped that Blair was so popular for a while that he could have won a referendum compelling the slaughter of the first born.[19] William Hague, Leader of the Opposition during the first term, was totally outclassed against what he acknowledged to be a 'truly formidable' opponent who had the country 'bedazzled'. Hague could never compete with Blair's 'mastery of the trembling lip and the watery eye'.[20] Successive Tory leaders scorned him as an actor while they floundered trying to compete with the potency of the act. Blair's real rival for power, Gordon Brown, privately derided all that 'touchy-feely stuff' only later to try to learn to do it himself when he realised that he suffered from the comparison.

Blair was 'a natural thespian', in the estimation of Jack Straw, 'a very, very good actor, which had its downsides as well as its upsides'.[21] That mastery of political stagecraft was combined with artful political positioning. On the map of public opinion, he would try to put himself at the median point. Asked by pollsters to place politicians on the left–right spectrum, voters put Blair in the same centrist position where most of the public located themselves. 'All policy issues were basically about political positioning,' thought Jon Cruddas, the most left-wing of Blair's advisers at Number 10 during the first term. 'Detail didn't really get in the way. Policies were a way of enabling him to get where he wanted to be in terms of his opponents and the electorate. He had a genius for that.'[22] Matthew Taylor, who joined Blair's senior staff in the second term, correctly noted that having 'a centrist Prime Minister leading a left-of-centre party' was 'a very powerful mix'.[23] Paddy Ashdown, though the leader of a rival party, saw 'extraordinary talents as a politician. He has a tremendous facility with words and an innate sense of where the erogenous zones of the British people are and how to get at them.'[24]

The Cabinet was biddable, the parliamentary party generally pliable, and his political opponents were entirely disorientated. Though the voter and media coalition that brought New Labour to power was frayed around the edges after four years in government, it was generally sustained. Memories of the Winter of Discontent and the economic calamities that swamped previous Labour governments were effaced by the image of a mainstream and basically competent, albeit flawed, administration. Bar the brief and scary blip during the fuel blockades, the Government polled comfortably ahead of the ridiculed and marginalised Tories for the entire four years.

Ideologically, Blair appeared to be of no fixed abode. One of his senior advisers, Sir Stephen Wall, thought 'he didn't have a socialist bone in his body'.[25] To his ally Alan Milburn, Blair once remarked: 'The job of being Labour leader is to save the Labour Party from itself.'[26] He rarely talked in terms of left and right. The past versus the future was his preferred dichotomy with himself as the personification of modernity. His most consistent trait was an impatience to shake up traditional British institutions, whether they be the House of Lords, the Labour Party or the NHS. He would tell staff that his favourite conference speech of the first term was the attack on 'the forces of conservatism' of both left and right.[27] That lack of anchoring on the ideological spectrum meant that he struggled to give solid definition to his project. Attempts to do so were either mildly comic or faintly sinister, as when he called New Labour 'the political arm of the British people'. The 'Third Way' was debated at earnest summits abroad and giggled to death at home. Blairism often seemed more about style than content.

The core idea was quite uncomplicated. The key political insight was that Labour had to enjoy the backing of aspirational voters as well as the party's heartland to win and retain power. Both he and Gordon Brown wanted to show that economic efficiency could be combined with social justice and decent public services. New Labour was a hybrid of both right-wing and left-wing. It accepted the Thatcherite economic settlement. Markets were unrestrained, the money-changers lightly regulated, and the rich indulged. The animal spirits of the City were allowed to let rip. New Labour believed this was necessary to sustain the consumer boom that kept voters content and produced the tax revenues for investment in public services and quiet redistribution of resources to the poor.

Blair was instinctively a constitutional conservative yet he had already presided over a radical redistribution of power within the United Kingdom. More than a hundred years after William Gladstone first attempted to introduce Home Rule, New Labour delivered where all previous progressive governments failed. Scotland gained its first parliament since the reign of Queen Anne, and its first elected parliament ever. Wales had its first representative body since Owain Glyndwr, and its first elected assembly ever.[28] The Good Friday Agreement, brokered over intense days and sleepless nights in Easter 1998, was the most promising attempt to bring lasting peace to Northern Ireland since partition, even if there was a tortuous struggle ahead to bring it to full implementation.[29] The House of Lords was finally dragged into the twentieth century by expelling most of the hereditary peers, though it would not be fit for the twenty-first until reform was complete.[30]

Blair's ambition to place Britain at the heart of Europe by joining the single currency was a goal he was dedicated to fulfilling in the second term. He did succeed in repairing Britain's relations with its continental partners after the isolation and division of the Conservative years.

He was acquiring an increasingly large appetite for the global arena, which would prove to have huge significance for what came next. Abroad he was free of the chafing shackles imposed on him at home by his power-sharing agreement with Gordon Brown. The world stage gave Blair a sensation of high drama, great adventure and clarity of moral purpose that he didn't feel when grappling with the duller graft of grinding out domestic reform. There was a glimpse of the messianic dimension of his character during the Kosovo conflict in 1999, which he proclaimed to be 'A battle between good and evil'. When his hawkish stance left him dangerously exposed, he told one intimate: 'This could be the end of me.' That amplified his sense of vindication when his bold and risky position proved decisive in saving the Muslim Kosovars from ethnic cleansing and defeating the Serbian dictator, Slobodan Milosevic.[31]

Both he and Brown had to learn on the job. Shortly before the 1997 election, Blair confided that he had two recurring nightmares: one that he would lose the election, the second that he would win only to find that he was no good at being Prime Minister.[32] A side of him was boyishly thrilled to find himself in Number 10, the youngest Prime Minister since the early nineteenth century. Shortly after the first victory, he visited Michael Levy at that wealthy friend's mansion in north London. After checking that his security detail weren't looking, Blair cried: 'I really did it! Can you believe it?' He started to jump up and down on the tennis court yelling: 'I'm the Prime Minister! I'm the Prime Minister! I'm the Prime Minister!'[33]

He was almost childishly exuberant about getting power, but also intimidated by office. He was a complete novice to government, as also was Gordon Brown. Neither of them had managed anything except a political party before they became the two most powerful men in Britain.

Despite their huge parliamentary majority and dominance in the polls, in the first term they displayed nervy under-confidence. This generation of centre-left politicians was deeply scarred by Labour's four consecutive defeats and eighteen years in Opposition between 1979 and 1997. They often behaved as if they were squatters in government from whom power could be snatched at any moment.

In the early years in office, the unexpected scale of his landslide did not thrill Blair as much as it daunted him.[34] They all had 'a sense of vertigo'.[35] Blair was 'very shocked' by the size of his first majority.[36] The towering scale of the majority excited expectations of a revolution when the New Labour prospectus was designed to be reassuringly modest about how much would change. Blair's 'driving mission' was 'modernisation of the institutions of the country' with himself as 'the fresh, young embodiment of this ideal.'[37] Yet his blue sky ambitions often lacked detailed and practical definition. 'Because the communication and campaign side of New Labour was so strong, so dominant, the task of winning elections took precedence over the task of thinking through how to use power,' regretted Geoff Mulgan, director of strategy and policy at Number 10 for seven years.[38] On the account of David Blunkett, they had come to office 'pretty sparse about what the policies were going to be' across large areas of government.[39] While Blair had 'a fairly clear idea' about what he wanted to do with schools, 'in areas like health it was far more sketchy', says one of his senior staff.[40]

Labour's first term successes mainly came from incremental reforms based on simple ideas such as numeracy and literacy classes or target-driven objectives like reducing hospital waiting lists. The gap between a cautious prospectus and great public expectations was too often filled by hyperbolic rhetoric which dressed up modest reforms as breathtaking revolutions, with the inevitable disappointment when expectations were not met. Blair's speech-writer, Peter Hyman, reflects that 'grandiose rhetoric about A Young Country and An Age of Achievement now seems far too overblown'.[41] Spending announcements were recycled or exaggerated – a trait for which Brown became especially notorious. 'It sounded enormous' when he announced £40 billion extra for public services in the summer of 1998, but the Cabinet knew that it was 'funny money'[42] confected by an accountancy trick. The result was that the voters and the media started to discount all the claims the Government made for itself as spin.

That four-letter word became the shorthand for the techniques of manipulating public opinion and the media that Labour perfected in Opposition. The personification of spin was Alastair Campbell, who began the second term with the grandiloquent title of Director of Strategic Communications. Few in Britain had heard of a spin doctor before New Labour; hardly anyone had not by now. A style of communication that served them brilliantly in Opposition was carried into government for far too long, as Blair, Campbell and Mandelson would all eventually acknowledge. Mandelson subsequently lamented: 'There was great emphasis on managing the media at the expense of managing policy. There was a sense that if you'd got the story right, you'd achieved something and that is not how government is.'[43]

Not a day, even an hour, was allowed to go by without the proclamation of a review, an initiative or a summit. New Labour appointed more tsars than all the Russias and launched more five-year plans than Stalin. This was a tactic designed to impress the country that its dynamic government was up and doing. It ultimately bred media cynicism and public disenchantment. The operation excelled at the daily firefight with the media. It was not so good at sustaining public trust. Geoff Mulgan says they 'often confused announcements for reality' and made the mistake of 'believing that if you were getting a success in the newspapers that meant you were getting a success on the ground'.[44]

Ridicule of Blair's feverish headline-chasing came to a peak when a leaked memo revealed him to be obsessing about manufacturing 'two or three eye-catching initiatives' to present himself as tough on crime.[45]

He initially rejected the critique that he was too mesmerised by opinion polling and media manipulation. By the end of the four years, though, he privately accepted the force of that analysis. He agreed that he had been too obsessive about hoarding popularity and not focused enough on using power to achieve lasting change. He wanted history to remember him as more than a skilful opportunist with a fluent tongue.

The largest frustration was the failure to make more progress towards giving the British the 'world class' public services he promised the voters in 1997. 'Education, education, education' was a slogan not a strategy; '24 hours to save the NHS' was a sound-bite not a plan.

The most important decision was to broadly stick to the painfully tight spending plans inherited from the Conservatives for the first two years. Every previous Labour government started with a spending splurge, ran out of money and then crashed into reverse gear with dire economic and political results. He and Gordon Brown opted for the opposite approach. One Cabinet minister later observed to me: 'We should have rebelled against Gordon over spending.'[46] A year into the second term, one of Blair's senior advisers was of the view: 'We are still feeling the pain of that.'[47]

The Prime Minister got an earful of public discontent during the election campaign, most bruisingly when he was ambushed at a hospital by Sharon Storer, a postmistress who was angry about the cancer care given to her partner. 'I'm sorry,' Blair feebly tried to assuage her scorn. His embarrassment at her hands would have played even bigger in the media had John Prescott not on the same day dealt with a discontented voter by thumping him.[48]

Most of those closest to Blair came to regard the first term as a wasted opportunity in which they had not moved fast enough on domestic reform.[49] Blair thought so himself. 'Part of the problem is we led such a charmed life in the first term,' he observed to me. 'It was unnatural, in a sense, to be just coasting along.'[50] He talked a lot about reform before he had worked out what precisely he meant by it. When he railed about the 'scars in my back' inflicted by grappling with the bureaucracy, it was as much an expression of his confusion about what to do as it was a howl of frustration with the civil service and vested interests.[51]

The Blair re-elected in 2001 was less naive and more experienced, tougher, older, clearer and, he liked to think, much wiser. A second thumping majority removed all excuses for failing to deliver the radical change that he relentlessly promised. He now realised he would be judged not only by the scale of his electoral victories, but by what he did with them. He promised himself that his second term was going to be very different. 'He thought he hadn't achieved enough in the first term,' notes Sir Andrew Turnbull, who observed Blair at close quarters as Cabinet Secretary during the second term:

For the first four years, he was a Bill Clinton: power comes from popularity. Every week you must identify why you are not popular and deal with it. In 2001, Blair joins the Margaret Thatcher camp and says: I am going to lead. I don't mind being unpopular so long as you respect me enough to re-elect me.[52]

The first Cabinet of the second term was fashioned with the intent of giving him a top team dedicated to delivering his agenda. The Home Office, transport, health and education, the four key delivery ministries, were put in the hands of David Blunkett, Stephen Byers, Alan Milburn and Estelle Morris, loyalists whom Blair assumed shared his instincts. He called them together for a dinner in Downing Street shortly after the election. 'Look,' he said. 'We've won the most phenomenal second term.' But voters were dissatisfied with the speed of delivery. That had to be accelerated. 'I really want this team to be the team in these departments for the rest of this parliament,' he told them.[53] As it turned out, not one of the quartet would last the course.

Jack Straw, another presumed loyalist, was made Foreign Secretary, displacing a surprised and distraught Robin Cook into the lesser role of Leader of the House. Straw went into Blair's den for his reshuffle interview that morning with no idea what was about to happen. He'd been briefing himself on the environment and transport, having been led to expect they would be his new responsibilities.[54] He emerged from Number 10 agreeably amazed to be the new master of the most gilded department in Whitehall. Blair's cavalier attitude towards Cabinet-making was typical of his haphazard and often impetuous way of taking decisions, one of his significant flaws as a Prime Minister.

'I'm going to tell you something you won't like,' the Prime Minister told Sir Richard Wilson during their brief chat in his study the day after the election. 'I've got to tell you that I want to move John Prescott to the Cabinet Office.' There had been no planning at all to create a role for the Deputy Prime Minister at the Cabinet Office. 'What's he going to do?' asked a bewildered Wilson. Blair shrugged: 'You'll think of something.'[55]

The most critical decision made by Blair on the day after the election victory was not to appoint a new Chancellor. Gordon Brown had combined the force of his personality with the might of the Treasury to turn himself into an unprecedentedly powerful Chancellor and a rival seat of power to Number 10. Brown was, by any standards, one of the most successful Chancellors of the post-war era in his first four years at Great George Street. His decision to hand control over interest rates to the Bank of England was hailed as a masterstroke which built confidence in Labour's ability to run the economy while freeing Brown to concentrate on building his dominance over White-hall. It was also typical of him that he conducted the negotiations about the Bank's future in such a brutal and corkscrew manner that he pushed the Governor, Eddie George, to the edge of resignation. 'Jesus, what has Gordon done?' exclaimed Blair, who had to intervene to help pull George back from the brink.[56] The Governor was made incandescent by the manner in which Brown stripped the Bank of its regulatory powers and handed them to a new Financial Services Authority. The regime's inadequacies would only be exposed many years later.

Almost alone among major economies, Britain was enjoying uninterrupted prosperity. Brown presented himself as the man who had discovered the holy grail of low inflation, low interest rates, sustained growth and full employment. So rosy did the outlook seem that it became Brown's boast that he had transcended the economic cycle. 'No return to Tory boom and bust' was a brag he trumpeted every time he presented a Budget, a financial statement or a spending review. Brown also projected himself as the real achiever of the Government who was delivering Labour programmes to combat child poverty and youth unemployment while stealthily redistribut-ing from the affluent to the less well-off. It was insinuated by his propagandists that Brown was the chief executive of New Labour plc while Blair was merely the titular chairman. The implication was that Blair was the grinning, travelling salesman of the Government while Brown was the man of true substance and action.[57]

They were struggling for control of the Government from the moment New Labour arrived in office on that sunny May Day in 1997. 'From day one, it was terrible,' says Jonathan Powell, Blair's Chief of Staff.[58] The tensions within this turbulent partnership were, by and large, skilfully concealed from the media in their early period in office. The more credulous commentators swallowed the fiction that never before had a Prime Minister and Chancellor worked in such sweet harmony. The first major indication that this was untrue came in early 1998. Some weeks of especially provoc-ative behaviour by Brown and his camp provoked intense anger in Blair and his team. That January I had a long private discussion with one of the most senior figures in Number 10. For the first five minutes of this conversation, I was spun the usual line that all was well between the neighbours of Down-ing Street. The Prime Minister still esteemed his Chancellor as 'a great talent' and 'a great force'. Then a little prodding produced an entirely different account of the relationship and a litany of complaint about the way in which Brown was obstructing the Prime Minister and destroying relationships with senior colleagues. The rest of the Cabinet, I was told, 'just don't trust Gordon. There's so much venom against him.' I asked why he was so difficult and received the reply: 'You know Gordon, he feels so vulnerable and so insecure. He has these psychological flaws.'[59]

That vivid phrase appeared in my *Observer* column that Sunday and was projected on to the paper's front page. There was a great media excitement at this revelation that the friction between Number 10 and the Treasury was much more inflamed than was previously appreciated. 'Psychological flaws' has echoed down the years since and been raised whenever the character of Brown or his relationship with Blair have been in debate. Brown confronted Blair that week demanding that the culprit be identified and sacked. Blair denied that anyone at Number 10 authored the phrase, a denial that the hurt and furious Brown rightly regarded as a lie.[60] Some have conjectured that it was Blair himself who first spoke of Brown's 'psychological flaws'. Though we did have many conversations about the relationship, it was not him on that occasion, though he was entirely in agreement with the assessment. Blair told a close friend that 'psychological flaws' wasn't 'the half of it'.[61]

'Psychological flaws' did not first come from the lips of Peter Mandelson, though he too agreed with it. He once remarked to Blair that he should put a sign up on his desk with the inscription: 'Remember: the Chancellor is mad.'[62]

Alastair Campbell always publicly denied that it was he who called Brown 'psychologically flawed', on one occasion denying it to a committee of MPs. He had to maintain this line to remain in his job. The edited version of his diaries published in 2007 was sanitised of all the most damaging references to Brown. Campbell cut out any reference to this episode and the fierce fall-out from it even though it dominated the headlines for several days and then reverberated down the years after. He has redacted the entry for Friday, 16 January 1998, the day I was told about Brown's 'psychological flaws', and all the days following until Thursday, 22 January.

Sir Richard Wilson came to believe he was the inadvertent inspiration. During a private conversation about Brown with Campbell, Wilson made a general remark about all politicians having 'psychological flaws' of one sort or another. Campbell, who once had a nervous breakdown and had since suffered severe bouts of depression, seemed excited by a phrase that could equally well describe himself.[63]

Despite all the official denials that anyone at Number 10 was responsible for telling me that Brown had 'psychological flaws', some inside the building privately reported that Blair was 'secretly pleased' because the episode 'put Gordon back in his box'.[64] The two warring courts became progressively more compulsive in their use of briefings to the media to prosecute the rivalry. This added to the corrosive impression that New Labour was addicted to the darker arts of spin at the expense of governing.

The most violent rows were usually about spending. In the New Year of 2000, a time when the NHS was buckling under the pressure of a flu outbreak, Blair was frantic to show that he was responding to mounting public pressure and terrible headlines. He pledged a huge increase in NHS funding, doing so to bounce Brown into making a larger commitment than the Chancellor intended. 'You've stolen my fucking Budget!' raged Brown when he confronted Blair. He was most infuriated because the other man was going to rob him of the credit for an increase.[65]

Many of his closest counsellors cautioned Tony Blair that he would never control his destiny until he dealt with the rival government across the road at the Treasury. So long as Brown remained there, gripping the rest of Whitehall with his power over money and jealously guarding the economic tests for membership of the euro, he wielded a veto over Blair's ambitions.

In the run-up to the 2001 election and its immediate aftermath, the option of moving Brown was debated deep within the Blair circle. Cherie, Anji Hunter, Sally Morgan and Jonathan Powell were most vehemently of the opinion that it had to be done. The Chief of Staff so often argued within Number 10 for the removal of Brown that Powell likened himself to Cato, the Roman who went to the Senate every day to cry: 'Carthage must be destroyed!'[66] Peter Mandelson, too, argued for dealing with the Chancellor, though he was warier of the consequences of Brown quitting and marauding from the backbenches.

Blair seriously contemplated trying to persuade him to go to the Foreign Office, the only alternative job with sufficient status that Brown might conceivably have accepted. 'He nearly did it,' says Sally Morgan and other close allies agree. 'In the end, he wouldn't.'[67] The Prime Minister backed off partly because of a residual sense of obligation to the other man and a continuing dependency on his talents. Even Powell acknowledged that 'it wasn't obvious who would fill his shoes.'[68] Most of all, Blair was actuated by fear of the havoc that Brown could wreak in insurrectionist exile on the backbenches.

'I know that sacking Gordon Brown was discussed, but each time it was discussed they realised that it would be Armageddon in the Labour Party,' says Robert Harris, who was intermittently close to Blair as well as being a very good friend of Mandelson. 'At the last moment, he always swerved away.'[69]

It was hard to cut down Brown's power precisely because he had acquired so much of it. The Chancellor's approval ratings were hugely positive. He was receiving a largely adulatory press. Blair would often excuse his hesitancy about striking by saying that it would have been 'impossible to explain' to the Labour Party why he was moving such a successful Chancellor.[70]

The spring of 2001, after Labour had just been re-elected by another landslide and before Blair became overwhelmed by the consequences of 9/11, was his one clear opportunity to deal decisively with Brown. He would subsequently have many reasons to regret that he did not take it.

Yet being confirmed as Chancellor did not satisfy Gordon Brown. He too felt the first term was one of frustrating under-achievement. For all the vast power he had accumulated and all the praise he earned, Brown was nagged by a dissatisfaction even greater than that which gnawed at Blair. From the moment they won that second victory, Brown started to pound at the door of Blair's den with demands for a date for the handover of the premiership. 'Ever since then, it was continuous,' says Barry Cox.[71]

Both men began New Labour's second act in government determined that it would be radically different to the first. Blair thought he now knew what to do with the premiership; Brown expected to seize the crown. The second term would indeed be very different to the first. Yet it would not be for reasons that either Blair or Brown, or anyone else, had envisaged.

2. A Cloudless Day

The noise from above was growing louder and the President was increasingly spooked. George Bush went to the window at Chequers and anxiously scanned the horizon, trying to spot where the aircraft was coming from. It 'sounded like a lawnmower in the sky', perhaps a microlite, and 'it kept getting louder and louder and louder.' The Secret Service detail with the President became jumpy. So did their British counterparts. Accustomed to the protection of the no-fly zone around the White House, Bush became even more agitated when he saw that the plane was now flying over the fields and aimed straight at the Prime Minister's country house.

'How did they get in?' Bush demanded. 'How did they get over the security? How did they get close to the building?'¹ Then the errant aircraft buzzed past and away.

There was one other discordant episode during George Bush's sleep-over at Chequers in July 2001. Tony Blair, hoping to keep things relaxed with his American visitor, had his older children join them for an informal dinner. Euan was there with his close schoolfriend, James Dove. The teenagers raised the subject of the death penalty, which Bush had applied with enthusiasm as Governor of Texas. Cherie liked an argument and joined this one with gusto, challenging the President to justify execution by telling him that it was morally wrong and you couldn't put right a mistake. 'Well, that's not the way it is in America,' shrugged Bush. 'We take the eye-for-an-eye view.'² Bush didn't seem to mind being challenged. His wife Laura was also much more liberal than him. The person who did look uncomfortable was the Prime Minister, who was anxious for this not to turn into the dinner party from hell. Bush's plans for a missile shield also came up. The argumentative Cherie suggested that 'the real danger' was not from a missile strike by Russia but a terrorist attack. That suggestion left Bush bemused.³

Blair was fretful before and during the visit that it should be as smooth as possible. This was only the second time the two leaders had met and they

16

were still at the delicate getting-to-know-you stage of their relationship. It was in the hope that it would deepen the bond between them that the Prime Minister had invited the President and his wife to stop over at Chequers on their way to the G8 Summit in Italy. The American party was surprised to find that the Prime Minister's rural retreat was quite different to Camp David, the President's compound in Maryland where they had first met in February.

'There were not separate cabins, we stayed in their home.' The Bushes ate breakfast at the kitchen table with the Blairs and their youngest son, Leo. 'We felt welcomed. It was a very warm environment for us to be in and we could hear the pitter-patter of feet early in the morning and late at night. The President felt like he was part of the family.'[4] Blair thought he was beginning 'to make a connection' with the Republican.[5] When the Bushes left Chequers, the earlier security scare had faded from memory. No-one gave any more thought to the idea of aircraft crashing into famous buildings.

At lunchtime in Britain on Tuesday, 11 September 2001, the skies were clear and the weather was bright. Tony Blair was in Brighton, a seafront city he had visited many times before to make speeches. He was preparing to deliver his first significant address of the autumn political season, 'a quite tricky speech'[6] which was making him 'pretty tense'.[7] His audience was the assembled trades unionists of the TUC, a body which liked him no more than he cared for them. There was a bit of crackle in the atmosphere: the unions were angry about Blair's plans to increase the use of private operators in the NHS. The Prime Minister planned to give a hard slap to John Edmonds of the GMB. That curmudgeonly old walrus was calling Blair 'a privatisation freak'. Some in the media were trying to build this up as his first trial of strength since Labour's re-election in June. It was not, though, exactly news that he and the unions didn't see the world the same way.

The Prime Minister and his entourage were camped in the usual state of mild chaos in a suite on the seventh floor of the Grand Hotel looking out over the seafront. The suite was divided into a large lounge area and a smaller bedroom which were connected by a short staircase. While his staff sat in the lounge, half paying attention to the television on which Sky News was trailing his speech, Blair worked in the bedroom giving a final polish to the text. As was his habit, he was still fiddling with it right up to deadline. As was also his habit, he was munching on a banana.

For all his rhetoric about creating a modern Britain, Blair never got comfortable with technology. He preferred to write his speeches with a pen in longhand, just as Gladstone might have done. As he scribbled last-minute amendments to the script, they were collected from the bedroom and taken down to the lounge to be typed into the text. Suddenly, at a quarter to two, Sky abruptly switched its coverage to New York, where it was a quarter to nine in the morning.

The lounge television was now broadcasting pictures of a massive gash in the North Tower of the World Trade Center. The wounded citadel of finance was on fire and belching grey smoke. 'Oh my God,' cried Anji Hunter, the personal aide who had known Blair for even longer than his wife. Like people all around Britain and the rest of the world, the Prime Minister's staff and police bodyguards were transfixed by the images coming from Manhattan.

'I was just looking up and saw a plane go into one of the Twin Towers, and just thought, it was some dreadful accident like most people.'[8]

'It wasn't at all clear to us that it was terrorism.'[9]

Working away upstairs, the Prime Minister was not even watching. His Political Secretary, Robert Hill, nipped up the short set of stairs to the bedroom to tell him. 'God,' said Blair. 'That's dreadful.'[10]

The Prime Minister said it quite levelly, in the way that he often responded to news that was slightly astonishing or mildly shocking. After a brief conversation with Alastair Campbell about whether he should refer to the event in front of the TUC, Blair put it out of his mind and asked to be left alone so he could start psyching himself up for his difficult speech. He paced the small bedroom, he patted his hair, he toyed with his tie in the mirror, he twitched at his cuffs, the little rituals he always performed to 'get in the zone' for delivering a major speech.[11] Downstairs, Campbell was on the phone to Adam Boulton, the Political Editor of Sky. The Prime Minister's chief propagandist cracked a characteristically black joke: 'I just knew you guys would set fire to some building in America when you've got an important speech by Tony to cover.'[12]

At just after two in Brighton – just after nine in Manhattan – United Airlines Flight 175, the second plane, plunged into the South Tower. The room instantly sensed, as did anyone else watching that day, that they were no longer looking at a freak crash.

Robert Hill rushed back up the flight of stairs to alert Blair. 'What is it?' he said to his Political Secretary, irritated to have his pre-speech rituals interrupted. 'I said I wanted to be left alone.' 'A second plane,' replied Hill.[13] Now Blair did come down the stairs to look at the atrocious scenes being broadcast from Manhattan. 'Get Alastair back,' he said. Campbell had already gone over to the conference centre. There was a frenzy of phone calls between Brighton and London. Campbell was rung by Tom Kelly, one of his deputies, who was back at Number 10. 'Don't worry, we've seen it,' Campbell told Kelly. Everyone had 'the same thought. One is an accident, two isn't.'[14] One of the Downing Street secretaries, known as the 'Garden Girls' because their room in Number 10 overlooks the back garden, was typing up Blair's speech. She turned to Anji Hunter and asked: 'Is there any point going on with this?'[15]

There was not. After the second plane struck, Blair and his aides rapidly agreed 'that there was no question he had to abandon the speech and get back to London'.[16]

The Cabinet Secretary was lunching at Gran Paradiso, his favourite London restaurant. Sir Richard Wilson heard about the first plane from his driver, Gary. 'I bet that's some amateur,' remarked Sir Richard as he got into the back of his limousine. As they set off back to Number 10, he learnt about the second plane from the car radio. Jeremy Heywood, the Principal Private Secretary, rang as Wilson's car was rounding Parliament Square. 'We've been told that the White House is evacuating,' reported Heywood. 'Should we be evacuating?' 'If you evacuate, where would you evacuate to?' responded Wilson. He had a mental image of the entire staff of Number 10 and the Cabinet Office standing in the street clutching their laptops and mobiles looking lost. 'I think it is a good rule not to evacuate unless you have an idea where you are going to evacuate to,' Wilson drily told Heywood.[17]

Jonathan Powell, the Prime Minister's Chief of Staff, didn't believe the official who ran in to tell him another plane had gone into the towers. 'Don't be silly – they're just repeating pictures of the first plane,' scoffed Powell. 'It really is a second plane,' insisted the official. 'Oh, fuck,' said Powell.[18]

He and Wilson made a conference call to Blair in Brighton. 'This looks bad from here,' they told him. 'You'd better come back.' 'Yes,' Blair replied. 'I'm coming back.' He added: 'Do you know how the Americans are reacting?'[19] No-one did.

After a rapid debate with Campbell, Hill and Hunter, Blair agreed that he could not now possibly deliver the intended speech about public service reform, one of the more minor casualties of that seismic day. At just after 2.30 p.m., the Prime Minister left for the Brighton conference centre. Though the Grand Hotel is right next door, the protection squad insisted that he was driven the short distance between the buildings. At 2.39 p.m. in Brighton, 9.39 a.m. in Washington, American Airlines Flight 77, the third plane, smashed into the west wall of the Pentagon. In the very short time available, Blair and Campbell had been exchanging thoughts about what the Prime Minister should say.[20]

At one minute to three in Brighton, one minute to ten in New York, the global television audience watched the collapse of the shattered South Tower, which engulfed lower Manhattan in a deathly blanket of smoke and debris.

Moments later, Blair delivered his hurriedly prepared lines about the atrocities. 'There have been the most terrible, shocking events in the United States of America in the last hours,' he told the delegates, many of whom were only fuzzily aware of what was unfolding in New York and Washington.

This mass terrorism is the new evil in our world today. It is perpetrated by fanatics who are utterly indifferent to the sanctity of human life and we, the democracies of this world, are going to have to come together to fight it together and eradicate this evil completely from our world. I know that you would want to join with me in offering our deepest sympathy to the American people, and our absolute shock and outrage at what has happened.[21]

These were not words that he had any time to polish. This was pure reflex reaction to the moment on which his premiership would pivot. It was telling that his instinctive response was to reach for biblical language and frame what had just happened as a contest between good and evil.

The delegates rose to applaud, a rare occasion when the TUC gave him a standing ovation. Then Blair rushed off the stage and into his armour-plated Daimler to be sped to Brighton station. The train was 'simply the fastest way to get him back to London'.[22]

While they awaited his return, back at Number 10 there was a frenzy to assemble a crisis meeting of key ministers and officials. Many of the crucial figures were scattered all over the country and beyond. The Home Secretary, David Blunkett, was on a train in the Midlands and first learnt about the attacks from a phone call from one of his sons.[23] Blair's senior adviser on foreign policy, Sir David Manning, was aboard a plane over Staten Island from where he observed the black smoke and at first assumed it had to be coming from a power station.[24] The head of the armed forces, Admiral Sir Michael Boyce, was in Europe.[25] The Commander-in-Chief of the British army, General Sir Mike Jackson, was on an exercise in Canada.[26] Jack Straw was in his room at the Foreign Office holding a meeting about troop deployments in the Balkans with Geoff Hoon, the Defence Secretary. They 'sat transfixed as we saw the first plane go into the Twin Towers and then saw the second one and realised that this was the world's biggest ever terrorist outrage'. Straw said to the others: 'This is going to change the world', which was no less true for being said by so many people that it soon passed into cliché.[27] The Director-General of MI5, Sir Stephen Lander, was at his headquarters in Thames House holding a meeting about 'critical infrastructure protection'.[28]

The instant cause of understandable panic was the fear that if terrorists could strike at the Twin Towers and the Pentagon, then they might have a design to do the same to iconic British landmarks. Buckingham Palace,

Canary Wharf and the House of Commons – the respective citadels of Britain's monarchy, money and democracy – were the obvious targets. 'Was London about to be attacked?' the Cabinet Secretary asked himself. 'My obsession was with protecting London. No-one knew what was happening.'[29]

One of the first calls he made was to Stephen Byers, the Transport Secretary. He ordered an air-exclusion zone over the centre of the capital. His Cabinet career had left Byers progressively more disillusioned about the power of ministers to achieve anything much. So he was pleasantly surprised to find that, on this occasion, his instructions were so swiftly executed that within twenty minutes there were no longer any planes to be seen from his window.[30]

Contingency planning had been exposed as pitifully inadequate during the first term. There was no plan to deal with the fuel protests when they erupted in the autumn of 2000, nor to manage the foot and mouth outbreak in the spring of 2001. As a result of those earlier failures, a Civil Contingencies Unit had been established to handle large-scale disasters. Wilson tried to activate the new unit now, only to discover that its staff were hundreds of miles away on a 'bonding' session in Easingwold in Yorkshire.[31] Also absent were all the officials of the Overseas and Defence Secretariat of the Cabinet Office. They were en route to a meeting at the headquarters of the SAS in Herefordshire and had taken all the keys to their offices with them. The head of MI6, Sir Richard Dearlove, was not in town either. A new telephone system had been installed at the Cabinet Office the previous weekend. To compound the chaos, 'it went down.'[32] Had terrorists or a foreign power planned an attack on Britain, there would rarely have been a better time to strike than on 9/11.

Boarded on a train back from Brighton, Blair's Special Branch protection squad created a makeshift area for the Prime Minister and his aides by sealing off part of a carriage with police 'scene of crime' tape. Blair tried to have phone conversations with colleagues only to be cut off when the train rattled through tunnels, a problem which repeatedly thwarted attempts to have sensible communication with London. Robert Hill passed on what news he could glean from the intermittent reception he was getting from a small radio he was listening to on an earpiece. The Prime Minister was subdued and pensive, spending long stretches of the journey staring out of the window with 'that faraway look in his eyes'[33] that those who knew him well had often seen at times of high stress. 'The full weight of it – the implications of it – were sinking in. He was chewing it over in his mind.'[34] The Prime Minister said to the others: 'This will change everything.' One of his staff concluded: 'Tony Blair intuited within half an hour that this was a historic turning point and

America would be transformed for ever by the experience of such a huge attack on its soil.'[35]

He asked for a pad so he could try to make sense of his thoughts about what had just happened and write down a list of the priority issues to address when he got back to Downing Street. He was increasingly apprehensive about the American response to what he knew they would treat as a military attack. 'How are the Americans reacting?' he again asked, but no-one with him could provide an answer. 'What's happened to Bush?' he fretted and variations like 'Where's Bush?'[36] He wasn't alone in asking that question.

As the hijacked planes converged on New York and Washington, George Bush was on his way to a photo opportunity at an elementary school in Florida. 'It was a cloudless day' and his Chief of Staff, Andy Card, told the President that it was going to be 'an easy day' as well: just talking to the children, parents and teachers. Bush was about to go into a classroom when Karl Rove, one of his most senior advisers, told the President that a small twin-engine prop plane had crashed into one of the towers. To Card and Rove, the President remarked: 'The pilot must have had a heart attack.'[37]

Bush was already in the classroom when his officials learnt that it was not a light aircraft, but a commercial airliner. The photo op proceeded anyway. The TV cameras started to record the Commander-in-Chief reading to the children from *The Pet Goat*.

Card came into the classroom. He answered the inquisitive look on the faces of the reporters in the press pool by mouthing: 'Two planes.'

The cameras were therefore able to capture the moment, though not the words, when his Chief of Staff went up to the President, bent over and whispered into his right ear: 'A second plane hit the second tower. America is under attack.'[38] Then Card deliberately stood back so Bush could not ask any questions while the cameras were trained on him.

At a loss what to do, Bush looked bewildered and frozen, an image that would be repeatedly used to ridicule him, notably in Michael Moore's anti-war film, *Fahrenheit 9/11*. That lampooning would make him the more determined to later prove his machismo, to take the 'eye-for-an-eye' that he had spoken about at Chequers two months earlier.

Shortly afterwards, Bush abandoned the classroom to deliver a rushed and jarring statement. 'Today we've had a national tragedy,' he said in a tone less assured than a local TV newsreader making his first broadcast. 'Terrorism against our nation will not stand.' He would be ordering 'a full-scale investigation to hunt down and to find those folks who committed this act'.[39]

'Folks' was a strangely homely description of terrorists who had just perpetrated a mass murder which would be compared with 'the day of infamy' when the Japanese attacked Pearl Harbor in 1941.

These unconvincing and unnerving words were the last that the world would hear from the President for several long hours as he was rushed to Sarasota airport and bundled aboard Air Force One. The presidential plane took off to circle the skies until it was clearer whether the attacks were over or this was just a beginning. At just after ten o'clock in America came the news that a fourth plane, United Flight 93, inbound to Washington, was not responding to air traffic control. In terror that the White House and the Capitol were the next targets, there was absolute chaos around the American President. While he circled the skies, most of the White House staff were evacuated. The Vice-President and the Secretary of State were locked in the high-security bunker underneath the East Wing. America was left with no visible leadership. The President and his number two were having difficulty communicating with each other, never mind the rest of the world.[40]

At just before five in the afternoon in Britain, the commuter train carrying the Prime Minister pulled into Victoria station. He was hurtled back to Downing Street accompanied by a wail of police outriders. Watching from the doorstep of Number 12, one of his staff was struck by Blair's profile as he strode through the front door of Number 10. 'This was not someone floored by what had just happened. It was someone who had half expected something like this. By the time he got to Downing Street he had analysed the consequences. That was why he was able to respond with such certainty and such strategic sense.'[41] The Cabinet Secretary agrees: 'The moment he was in the building you could see that he regarded this event as of enormous significance.'[42] Wilson checked whether the Prime Minister was content with the protective measures that the Cabinet Secretary had ordered in his absence. 'Sure, sure,' said Blair, a little impatiently. 'Fine.' He went straight into his small den accompanied by Wilson, Campbell and Powell. They were joined by Stephen Lander and John Scarlett, recently appointed as the chairman of the Joint Intelligence Committee, which collates the work of the intelligence agencies and GCHQ. 'Blair comes alive when something exciting and dramatic is going on. The adrenalin was running. He was very focused, very alert.'[43] The Prime Minister addressed the group in the den. 'Who did this?' he demanded. Lander of MI5 spoke: 'This is not my territory particularly,' he said. 'But it's got the whiff of al-Qaeda. I think people will be pointing the finger at al-Qaeda.' Scarlett broadly agreed that was most probable. The intelligence chiefs talked about previous al-Qaeda attacks in Africa and the Middle East, and how they were being harboured by the Taliban regime in Afghanistan. Blair looked fuzzy at the mention of Osama bin Laden's terrorist network. Turning to Lander, he asked: 'Did I know about this?' 'JIC has been reporting about this. It was in the red book,' replied Lander, who knew Blair well enough to be direct with him. 'Perhaps you haven't read them.' Blair shrugged: 'Fair enough.'[44] One of the non-intelligence officials present comments: 'I don't think Blair knew much about al-Qaeda at this point. It was clear to me that he hadn't taken in earlier warnings.'[45]

Jonathan Powell insists that Blair was already 'slightly obsessive' about al-Qaeda before 9/11, but agrees 'we hadn't focused on the Taliban at all.'[46] Powell sent one of the duty clerks out to the Waterstone's bookshop on the corner of Trafalgar Square to buy every book he could find on Afghanistan and al-Qaeda.[47]

Blair would later tell me: 'September 11th was for me a revelation. They killed 3,000, which was a lot. But if they could have killed 30,000, they would have.'[48]

He was again asking: 'What are the Americans doing?' and 'Where's Bush? How will he react?' Lander offered the opinion that there would be massive pressure on the President to retaliate against Afghanistan for harbouring al-Qaeda bases. The Americans might also have their sights on Iran, Iraq and Libya. Blair agreed that there was a big risk that Bush would feel compelled to lash out. He continued to fret about the whereabouts of the invisible President. In the words of one aide: 'We were all thinking: where the fuck are they?'[49]

It was now approaching 5.30 p.m. Blair went down to the basement to chair a meeting of COBRA, the viperish acronymn for Cabinet Office Briefing Room A, Downing Street's cheaper version of the White House situation room. Some sixty people were crowded into the windowless basement room. Ministers and officials had rushed there, invited or not, of their own accord. 'Some Cabinet ministers just turned up.'[50] People stood against the walls.

'This is really big,' Blair told the meeting, rather redundantly. 'This is going to have a huge impact on America.'

Various Cabinet members reported on the action they were taking to protect Britain. Geoff Hoon worried some in the room with a 'gung-ho' declaration that the armed forces were ready for action. Gordon Brown was typically anxious about the impact on the economy, fretting that the evacuation of Canary Wharf and the closure of the Stock Exchange would send out a 'bad signal'. Jack Straw told them that he had just come off the phone with Colin Powell, the US Secretary of State. The Americans were already certain that the atrocities were the work of al-Qaeda.[51]

One of the military reported that they had two fighter planes up patrolling the skies over London. 'I'm worried,' said the Cabinet Secretary to the Prime Minister. 'If we do get an aircraft flying towards London, who takes the decision to shoot it down?' Blair frowned and suggested that it wouldn't be him. 'He clearly didn't want to be thinking about that.'[52] Hoon seemed to some colleagues also reluctant to be given the responsibility for giving the order to shoot down a passenger jet. 'It ended up that the poor bloody fighter pilot would have to take the decision.'[53]

Only later were proper rules of engagement agreed and it fell to Hoon to decide whether or not to shoot down a plane during a scare seven months afterwards.[54]

According to many present, there was an air of barely suppressed terror in the basement room. 'There was the most intense anxiety that the attacks could continue and it would lead to a meltdown across the world.'[55]

The meetings inside Number 10 were interrupted to allow the Prime Minister to make a statement for the six o'clock news. As was ever the case with Blair, he was a master at camouflaging his own anxieties in order to present a face of calm and control to the public. 'It is hard even to contemplate the utter carnage and terror which has engulfed so many innocent people,' he said. 'As for those that carried out these attacks, there are no adequate words of condemnation.' He located some words of condemnation nevertheless. 'Their barbarism will stand as their shame for all eternity.' After listing the security measures that were being taken in Britain, he returned to his central theme, one which would now dominate the rest of his second term:

This is not a battle between the United States of America and terrorism, but between the free and democratic world and terrorism. We, therefore, here in Britain stand shoulder to shoulder with our American friends in this hour of tragedy, and we, like them, will not rest until this evil is driven from our world.[56]

Across the world, leaders expressed their solidarity with the United States. But Blair stood out in crucial respects. One was his clarity and conviction. 'As with all his best statements, he had written it himself.'[57] Another was the way in which he went much further than simply offering sympathy with the United States. He was already embracing America's crisis as his crisis. When he showed the statement to his staff beforehand, there was 'a question over the shoulder-to-shoulder remark'. Campbell was worried that it might be seen as too 'poodling' to America. Blair rejected that advice. 'He was very clear that he wanted to send an unambiguous message because that was the way to make sure that his voice was heard in the White House.' One thing Blair already understood about Bush was the premium the President put on loyalty. 'Blair thought any quiver of equivocation would be misinterpreted. That was his consistent stance throughout.'[58]

This would make him an instant hero in the United States; not least because he gave much more eloquent voice to the shock and horror of this moment, and offered far more reassurance that it could be overcome, than America's own leader who was still on his zig-zagging aerial tour. Bush had just delivered up another stumbling statement to the cameras, this time from an air force base in Louisiana.

Blair was becoming more anxious about how the wounded Prometheus might react. Again he was asking: 'What will the Americans do?'

The consequences of 9/11 would entwine the fates of Blair and Bush, defining a presidency and a premiership which were both utterly changed by this event. What people usually forgot, if they had ever known it, was that they did not start off at all close.

Much of the world believed that George Bush stole the 2000 American election from Al Gore, the Democratic Vice-President. That belief ran especially deep and angry in the Labour Party. The Prime Minister's personal pollster, Stan Greenberg, worked for the Gore campaign and there was no-one in the Labour Party who was not rooting for the Democrat. Blair tried to assist Gore's chances by inviting him to make a status-boosting visit to Number 10 during the campaign. 'The expectation had been that Al Gore would win.'[59] Blair was looking forward to working with Gore, hoping it would be a continuation of his relationship with Bill Clinton but without all the embarrassing bits. When the British ambassador in Washington, Christopher Meyer, sent a cautionary note that Bush should 'not be under-estimated' and might win the election 'this was very unwelcome news in Number 10.'[60] They were stunned when the Supreme Court of the United States, with the assistance of the notorious hanging chads in Florida, tipped the White House to the Republican from Texas.

'Our hearts sank when the result was finally ratified,' says Cherie.[61] Blair 'just could not imagine that Al Gore was not going to be elected which is why it was such a shock'.[62] Soon after, Greenberg came to visit the Prime Minister in the Blairs' flat above Downing Street. 'Stan, if you had done your job, I wouldn't have to deal with this problem,' complained Blair. The problem being 'how to build a relationship' with this very right-wing President.[63]

Blair was worried about Bush's lack of experience in international affairs. The worst crisis he had ever faced as Governor of Texas was comforting families who had lost their homes in a flood. 'No-one needs to tell me what to believe,' Bush had said on the campaign trail. 'But I do need somebody to tell me where Kosovo is.'[64] The Kosovo conflict had been Blair's most significant moment on the world stage in his first term and the new President couldn't even find it on a map. There was more apprehension when Colin Powell, the new Secretary of State, only referred to Britain once in his confirmation hearings before the Senate. Meyer had done his best to cultivate relationships with the Bush team. Karl Rove, Bush's senior political strategist, sent both encouragement and a warning via Meyer: 'You're going to start with a blank sheet of paper. By your works shall ye be known.'[65]

The new President was acutely aware that there was no love for him in Britain's Labour government. Blair and Clinton had their combustions, but they were soulmates of the Third Way. On the campaign trail, Bush expressed contempt for the internationalist, centrist politics which were exemplified by both Clinton and Blair. During the Lewinsky Affair, Blair flew to Washington and stood by the scandal-stained Clinton when no-one else, Hillary included, would. 'Blair was a Friend of Bill, a FOB as they used to say,' says William Cohen, a member of Clinton's Cabinet. 'Anyone who had dealt with President Clinton, the Bush administration was wary of.'[66]

Before Bush's election, he and Blair had never met nor even spoken to one another. On a host of issues, Bush looked like trouble. While Blair was becoming increasingly possessed by the need to take action on climate change, Bush didn't look like he'd be convinced that there was a threat from global warming until the Great Lakes dried up. One of his most senior officials says:

When President Bush came to office, he was sceptical that Tony Blair would embrace him. Prime Minister Blair was seen as very close to Bill Clinton and they shared a party base. And so the President was concerned that they might have a professional relationship, but it would be very hard to have a personal relationship.[67]

Bush might have been even more wary had he known where Blair was when they had their first phone conversation. He was at Warwick University to see Bill Clinton deliver a valedictory speech.

That first call was not much of an icebreaker. On one account 'it was the standard stuff about the special relationship and the importance of working together. They didn't really get into substance at all.'[68] On another account: 'It basically consisted of Bush talking about various places in Scotland where he'd got pissed when he was young and asking Tony whether he knew them and Tony not really knowing what to say.'[69]

After Bush's inauguration, the race to be the first European leader to get to the White House was won by Jacques Chirac, the President of France.

Though this did not turn out to be a reliable indicator of the future pattern of relationships, Blair was highly annoyed at the time.

Many voices, including those of the American Stan Greenberg, were telling him that 'the Bush White House is pretty black and white. They wanted people to know that they didn't like shades of grey.' You were either his loyal ally or you were nothing to him. Precisely because he feared being regarded as hostile, Blair tried extra hard and 'decided that a close embrace' was imperative for both his and Britain's interests.[70] One of the people urging that course on him was, paradoxically, Bill Clinton. At the end of his presidency he came to Chequers for a farewell stay. Clinton counselled Blair on how he should approach Bush. 'Hug him close' and 'make him your friend.' Confirming that he had offered this advice, Clinton later explained to me: 'I told Tony to get close to Bush because that was the way to have influence with him.'[71]

This was advice for which Blair had open ears. It had been an orthodoxy of British foreign policy since the Suez Crisis of 1956, when Anthony Eden's premiership was broken by President Eisenhower's opposition to the Anglo-French invasion of the canal, that there should never be a rupture in what the British liked to regard as the 'Special Relationship'. Though he saw himself as a moderniser, Blair was an absolute traditionalist in this respect. Giving a toast at a White House dinner in 1998 when Clinton was President, the Prime Minister quoted the biblical remarks of Harry Hopkins, FDR's envoy to Churchill, at a wartime dinner: 'Whither thou goest I will go, and whither thou lodgest I will lodge. Thy people shall be my people, and thy God my God.'[72]

Even Robin Cook marked Bush's inauguration in January 2001 by declaring that the 'uniquely warm relationship' between Britain and America would 'renew and deepen', prose so purple that it suggested an alternative career for the then Foreign Secretary as an author of romantic fiction.

Blair also saw a domestic imperative to get close to the new President. Always anxious to protect his right flank, he told the Cabinet that it was important to show that a Labour government could work as well with a Republican President as it had with a Democrat.[73]

In January 2001, I wrote a column predicting that the Bush presidency would 'test to destruction' Blair's conceit of Britain and himself as 'the bridge' between Europe and America. 'The effort of spanning a conservative, unilateralist America and a social democrat, collectivist Europe will stretch even Tony Blair's legendary ability to straddle the mutually incompatible. The Atlantic will be a bridge too far.'[74] The next time I saw him, Blair spent most of the conversation trying to convince me that this was utterly mistaken. It made the role he saw for himself, as the bridge across the Atlantic, all the more essential.[75] He told Jack Straw that 'regardless of whether we agreed or disagreed with particular administration policies, it was crucial that we stayed close to the United States wherever possible.'[76] The alliance with America was 'fundamental', believed Blair.[77]

Before Meyer took up his position in Washington, he went into Number 10 for a briefing with Jonathan Powell. As they sat in one of the grand rooms on the first floor, Powell said, in the typically blokeish way of Blair's Downing Street: 'Basically, Christopher, what we want you to do is get up the arse of the White House and stay there.'[78]

The frost in the relationship began to thaw in early 2001 when an American spy plane was shot down over China. Blair had been anxious about how little communication there was from the new White House. The silence was suddenly broken when the Americans asked Number 10 for advice on how to handle the regime in Beijing, who were screaming foul about the spy plane incident. The rationale for this seemed to be that the British, with their long history in Hong Kong, might have extra insight into the working of Chinese minds. China experts from the Foreign Office were rushed over to Downing Street to furnish Blair with useful advice for Bush.[79]

There was still a lot of nervousness about the relationship in February when Blair crossed the Atlantic for his first face-to-face encounter with the new President. After landing at Andrews Air Force Base, the Prime Minister, his wife and officials were flown down to Camp David in a couple of helicopters from the presidential air armada. At the end of the forty-five-minute journey, they began to descend on to the pad at Camp David. They looked out of the window to see George and Laura Bush waiting to greet them. Cherie groaned: 'I don't expect they are looking forward to this any more than we are.' Her husband looked pained, but said nothing. Christopher Meyer, whose stomach was already knotted with nerves about how this meeting was going to work out, watched this from his nearby seat and thought to himself: 'Jesus Christ, this is going to be a disaster.'[80]

Unknown to the British party, Cherie was not far wrong: Bush was also nervous before his first encounter with Blair. 'He was sceptical that Tony Blair would embrace him. He was concerned that it would be very hard to have a personal relationship,' says his Chief of Staff.

He was nervous about meeting Tony Blair and finding out whether or not there would be a dialogue of trust or one of scepticism. When they first met, I had the same feeling from Tony Blair, that he was nervous about the relationship he would have with George W. Bush, this Texan former Governor, who had replaced Tony Blair's friend in the White House.[81]

The Americans found Cherie 'stand-offish', though things warmed up when Laura was around.[82]

The two leaders and their entourages sat down to lunch in Laurel, the big log cabin in the centre of the rustic compound which has the President's office. As waiters poured iced tea, Bush and Blair sat facing each other across the table. 'Welcome to Camp David, Tony. May I call you Tony? It's great to have you here,' opened Bush. Blair, not missing a beat, replied: 'Well, it's great to be here, George. May I call you George? What shall we talk about?'

The British ambassador began to relax. 'You sort of knew in the first fifteen to thirty seconds that the chemistry was going to be OK.'[83]

Bush very quickly said: 'Look, I'm not Bill Clinton, but I like you and we're gonna work together.'[84]

He went on to 'pepper Blair with questions' about international issues and other world leaders, flattering the British guest with interest in his views.[85]

After lunch, the two men went out for a walk in the woods designed to fake some intimacy for the cameras. Blair was so anxious to get this relationship right that he flapped to his aides about what he should wear. Seeing Bush in his presidential bomber jacket and casual slacks, Blair changed into a pair of crotch-clutching corduroys so tight that he could not get his hands into them when he attempted a casual swagger. They were much mocked. The Prime Minister could at least be relieved that the American seemed to want to hug him almost as tightly as his trousers.

In the evening, the Blairs, the Bushes and their staff relaxed in the Camp David cinema. They watched *Meet the Parents,* a comedy which features a desperate-to-be-liked Ben Stiller as a prospective son-in-law trying to get friendly with Robert de Niro, a hard-faced, right-wing CIA man. No-one there seems to have spotted the potential lurking metaphor.

Though many expressed surprise that Blair could so effortlessly switch from buddydom with Clinton to a best pals act with Bush, it made sense that both men try to get along. Both were politicians governed more by their intuition and their instincts than by ideology. They had other things in common. Both were impatient of formality and ceremony, both believed in God, both were talented mimics, both tended to be bored with detail, both came over as easy-going and affable, and in both cases that concealed streaks of ruthlessness and cunning. Both were believers in the power of their personal charm to induce others to co-operate with them. Cold calculation of their interests gave them another incentive to make the relationship work. For tactical reasons at home and strategic ones on the international scene, Blair wanted to get close to the American. Bush was in desperate need of a friend in Europe. He would say to Blair: 'I know they call me the toxic Texan.'[86]

At the closing news conference, the President remarked: 'He really put the charm offensive on me.'[87] For all the bonhomie, the British thought: 'Beneath it you got a real sense that if he didn't get his way he would be, to quote himself, a tough son of a bitch.'[88]

This became known as 'the Colgate Summit' because the President uttered one of his famously goofy Bushisms at the closing news conference. Asked what the two leaders had found in common, he struggled to articulate an answer and fell back on his trademark flippancy: 'We both use Colgate toothpaste.' To cover his own bemusement, Blair lightly responded: 'They are going to wonder how you know that, George.'[89] Bush's National Security Adviser, Condoleezza Rice, 'wondered what the Prime Minister could possibly be thinking, but at least he laughed'.[90] The banal explanation was that Colgate was the brand provided in all the log cabins at Camp David. A couple of nights in Maryland and one sleep-over at Chequers had brought the two men closer by the autumn of 2001, but it could hardly be said that they knew each other intimately as they faced the seismic event that was 9/11. When he declared his solidarity with Bush, Blair was not standing 'shoulder to shoulder' with a leader he knew at all well. He was aligning himself with a man whom he had not yet fully fathomed.

By late on the evening of 9/11, the Prime Minister had spoken to other key leaders: Jacques Chirac, Vladimir Putin and Gerhard Schröder. What he had not done was what he most wanted to do. He had still not spoken to Bush, now back on board Air Force One and headed for another air base, this time in deepest Nebraska. Blair, not yet grasping the degree of chaos and panic on the other side of the Atlantic, was increasingly baffled that Bush had not returned to Washington to show that he was in charge. 'There's something not right,' he said.[91] Not only could they not get the Prime Minister in touch with the President, but Number 10 was finding it impossible to communicate with anyone in Washington while the White House was still in lock-down.

Blair was not to know that the Americans feared a threat to Air Force One. His Secret Service told the President that it was not safe for him to return to the White House, now largely evacuated and useless. This lack of communication aggravated Blair's anxieties about how the Americans would react to the atrocities. He knew that Bush would face immense pressure to retaliate. He worried that a wounded, angry and frightened America might be panicked into an extreme and unilateral response. One reason he used the formulation 'shoulder to shoulder' was to send a message to America and its President that they were not alone.[92]

What impressed those working closely with him was that Blair was so quick to grasp that 9/11 was a hinge moment of history. In the words of David Manning:

He was very quick to understand that something very profound had changed, this wasn't going to be an isolated act. 9/11 was going to change the way we looked at security policy, foreign policy and was going to have a very, very significant impact on how the Americans viewed the world too. His sense was that it was extremely important for the international community to come together behind the United States and convey this sense of solidarity.[93]

Alastair Campbell found Blair 'worried about the advice Bush would be getting'.[94] The Prime Minister was scared that the Americans would not be 'thinking straight', says Christopher Meyer: 'Blair's real concern was that there would be a knee-jerk reaction by the Americans in retribution for the attacks and that they would go thundering off to Afghanistan and nuke the shite out of the place.'[95]

That was why he was so agitated about speaking to Bush say his senior staff. 'He wanted to get in and influence Bush's thinking so that Bush responded in the right way and not the wrong way.'[96] A Cabinet minister agrees that he was desperate to 'stop them doing something silly . . . stop them being crazy.'[97]

This was a fear with foundation. When Bush finally overruled his Secret Service and ordered Air Force One to return to Washington, he arrived breathing fire. 'I want you all to understand that we are at war,' he told a crisis meeting in the White House bunker. Donald Rumsfeld, the Defense Secretary, pointed out that international law only allowed the use of force to prevent future attacks and not for retribution. 'No,' yelled Bush. 'I don't care what the international lawyers say, we are going to kick some ass.'[98]

Bush's intentions remained Blair's main preoccupation when he woke early the next morning to be briefed about events overnight. He learnt that the President had got back to the White House to deliver an address from the Oval Office. It was regarded as a poor performance even by Bush's own speech-writing team, one of whom despaired that it was 'a doughy pudding of stale metaphors'.[99] The one thing clearly telegraphed was an intent to move against the Taliban regime. Bush declared: 'We will make no distinction between the terrorists who committed these acts and those who harbour them.'[100]

There had been no further attacks in America and none in Britain or elsewhere in the world. Yet nerves were still stretched taut and would remain so for many days after 9/11. 'We didn't know what was going to happen next.' One morning soon afterwards, the whole of Downing Street jumped when they heard the growl of a plane coming in the direction of Number 10. 'It scared the shit out of everybody.'[101] This turned out to be a Second World War bomber flying down the Mall as part of a commemorative fly-past. The night of 9/11, the lights burnt round the clock at the Foreign Office, Cabinet Office, MI5 and MI6 as they prepared 'a mountain of paper' for Blair about al-Qaeda and likely American responses.[102] Satellite photography of Afghanistan was included in the pack, showing the two types of al-Qaeda camps, those where they did 'religious indoctrination' and those where they did 'the terrorist boy scout training stuff'.[103] Dearlove, Lander and their experts then gave Blair a detailed oral briefing. 'Blair punched questions at them and they gave really on-the-ball answers. He was operating at a high-octane level.'[104] Blair was using his lawyer's skill for absorbing and mastering a brief. 'Blair was on the ball, unflustered. He was very quick to get the main point,' says one of the intelligence chiefs.[105] Foggy about the whole subject less than twenty-four hours before, he was soon rattling off references to 'OBL' as if he was now the world's most renowned authority on bin Laden. He told the meeting: 'We're going to have to do Afghanistan.'[106]

At half past twelve, seven thirty in the morning in Washington, the call from the President finally came through. Blair was pleased to learn that he was the first foreign leader to speak to Bush. The President told the Prime Minister that he was not treating this as an act of terrorism. 'All right,' he said. 'We are at war.'

Blair expressed his outrage about the atrocities and offered his sympathy about the deaths. 'We stand with you.' He was building up empathy between them before he tried to press his advice about what should be done.

Blair told Bush, not entirely truthfully, that he himself had 'no concerns' that America might react wildly. He then revealed that he did have precisely such concerns by arguing against instant retaliation.

Bush appeared to be reassuringly calm, replying that he was not going to order a knee-jerk response and 'just pound sand'.[107] He was not going to make Bill Clinton's mistake when he ineffectually fired cruise missiles into Afghanistan and hit only an abandoned terrorist training camp.

On the American side, it was regarded as 'a very comforting' and 'a very important conversation' that established Blair as the most staunch of allies.[108] On the British side, there was a feeling that the bond between the two was strengthened.[109]

Powell wrote up 'a top-speed note of the phone call'.[110] When Wilson suggested to the Prime Minister that he should follow up with a written message to Bush, he was surprised and impressed to learn that Blair had already drafted a memo designed to 'steer Bush, keep him on the rails. The worry was that the Americans would do something stupidly rapidly.'[111] In the note, Blair argued for a measured response, focused on al-Qaeda and the Taliban. The regime in Afghanistan should be given an ultimatum to give up bin Laden and shut down the terrorist training camps. If they failed to comply, only then should they be attacked. Even at this early stage, he was arguing for the publication of a dossier about al-Qaeda and Afghanistan to make the case against them to world opinion. He also grabbed the opportunity to argue for re-energising the Middle East peace process with the suggestion that this would help to sustain Arab support for action against terrorism. When he saw it, the British ambassador in Washington thought the note a 'first-rate piece of work'.[112] It delineated many of the themes which would dominate the years ahead: the imperative for conflict not to be defined as a clash of civilisations between Islam and the West, the need to maintain public support, and Blair's emphasis on creating and sustaining an international coalition behind action.

It was already bothering him that the American President did not seem much interested in that. Bush and his advisers regarded the Middle East peace process as a marginal concern in their current crisis. He was also cool towards Blair's idea that an emergency summit of the G8 should be called so that they could present a united face against terrorism. Bush was already talking about this being a long conflict. 9/11 seized the American with the sense of purpose that his presidency had hitherto lacked. Now, as he said to Blair and many others, he felt he had a 'mission for a presidency'.[113] It was a mission to which Blair was already binding himself tight. In doing so, he entirely changed the trajectory of both his premiership and New Labour.

The next day, Blair received a briefing at Number 10 from his military commanders. Admiral Sir Michael Boyce, the Chief of the Defence Staff, came with the latest intelligence about American intentions which he had managed to glean from conversations with General Dick Myers, his counterpart in the United States. Boyce reported that the Americans had started 'gearing up for a response almost instantly'. Their first target was still not decided on. 'Our worry was that their initial reaction would be to whack Iraq.' That was a prospect that did not at all appeal to the British military, nor, at this stage, to Blair himself.[114]

Massive grey concrete slabs were hurriedly erected around Parliament like a bodyguard of tombstones and cohorts of armed police were mobilised to protect the building when MPs were recalled for an emergency session on Friday, 14 September. The vast majority of MPs murmured in agreement with Blair when he condemned the atrocities and, echoing Bush, warned that there would be no toleration of countries that harboured terrorists. 'We have been warned,' he said. 'Terrorism has taken on a new and frightening aspect. The people perpetrating it wear the ultimate badge of the fanatic: they are prepared to commit suicide in pursuit of their beliefs.' It also featured another consistent theme of the years ahead, and reflected a worry about community relations in Britain, when he said: 'So-called Islamic fundamentalists . . . do not speak or act for the vast majority of decent law-abiding Muslims throughout the world.' In answer to those already expressing alarm about what the Americans might do, he made a point of praising the United States for its restrained response to these 'hideous and foul' attacks.

'They did not lash out. They did not strike first and think afterwards,' he said, not voicing his own fear that this was precisely what the United States might have done – and might yet do.[115]

Bush was still struggling to give America the leadership that a terrified and scarred nation yearned for. 'Where are you Mr President? New York has a right to know,' bellowed one of the city's tabloids about his failure to appear in Manhattan after forty-eight hours had passed since the atrocities.[116]

Blair's apprehensions were exacerbated when the two men had another phone conversation that day. Though Bush thanked him for the memo, and claimed that it 'mirrored' his own thinking, Blair put down the phone worried that he was not yet wielding the influence he hoped for.

His officials found him troubled afterwards. 'Tony wanted to get to Bush straight away,' says Jonathan Powell.[117] Alastair Campbell observes that he was frustrated by 'having stilted phone calls, not knowing who was listening in'[118]. His most senior civil servant agrees: 'He was very angsty. He wanted to get there.'[119]

Blair said to them: 'I need to see him in a room and look in his eyes.'

3. Shoulder to Shoulder

As the Boeing 747 crossed the Atlantic, Tony Blair was sitting in his favoured seat, right up at the front in A1 in first class. A copy of the Koran lay on the table in front of him. He had been interested in the Muslim holy book before 9/11, taking it with him on his August holiday in the Lake District and the south of France that year. When he revealed his summer reading to Alastair Campbell and Philip Gould, his intimates thought this an illustration of his eccentricities, remarking to each other: 'How very Tony that is . . . only Tony would read the Koran on holiday.' Now it seemed 'eerily prescient'.[1] In the days since 9/11, those around him kept hearing Blair quote passages from the Koran, especially those about martyrdom guaranteeing a place in heaven. That was the belief they were up against, he warned.

They got to Manhattan in the early afternoon of Thursday, 20 September. There was a service at St Thomas's, the vast, high-vaulted, neo-Gothic Episcopalian church on Fifth Avenue, not far from the still smoking ruins of the annihilated towers. The church was absolutely packed for the service for the known victims of the attacks and those that were delicately called 'missing'. Tony Blair sat in the front row with Cherie, Kofi Annan, Bill Clinton and his daughter, Chelsea. Sir Christopher Meyer read a message from the Queen, its most beautiful line being the final one: 'Grief is the price we pay for love.' The poignant phrase was later chiselled into the stonework of the church.

Blair read from Thornton Wilder's *The Bridge of San Luis Rey*. He also brought some words of his own. 'After the terrible events of last week, there is still shock and disbelief. There is anger, there is fear, but there is also, throughout the world, a profound sense of solidarity, there is courage, there is a surging of the human spirit.'[2]

After the service, he offered some further words of solidarity, comparing the atrocities to Hitler's Blitz on London: 'As you stood by us in those days, we stand side by side with you now,' he told America.[3] This was not entirely accurate history: the United States joined the Second World War after the

Blitz. The sentiment was appreciated all the same. Every leader in the world of any significance was saying similar things in the days after the attacks. The French proclaimed that 'we are all American.'[4] Vladimir Putin of Russia, believing that signing up to a 'war against terror' would legitimise his brutal campaign against the rebels in Chechnya, was declaring his solidarity. Even the leaders of Iran expressed sympathy and horror. More importantly, they made secret offers of practical assistance in dealing with the Taliban regime in Afghanistan.[5]

There was nevertheless a unique quality to Blair's response to 9/11. This was in part simply because his public performances were so masterly. The *Washington Post* opined that he and Rudolph Giuliani, the Mayor of New York, were the two political figures 'who broke through the world's stunned disbelief'.[6]

There were other distinctions that proved critical in sending him down the road to war in Afghanistan and then in Iraq. From the start, he treated this as much more than a terrible attack on a close ally. He viewed it as a defining event in world history which delineated a new threat. 'The world now knows the full evil and capability of international terrorism which menaces the whole of the democratic world. To commit acts of this nature requires a fanaticism and wickedness that is beyond our normal contemplation,' he said in one of the welter of speeches and statements he made in the days after the attacks.[7] He emphasised it as a direct attack on Britain because of the high number of British casualties. At a news conference he gave just before he flew to New York, he called it 'the worst terrorist atrocity since the war perpetrated against British citizens'.[8] He went further than any other leader in making Bush's 'war on terror' his war, telling MPs: 'Murder of British people in New York is no different in nature from their murder in the heart of Britain itself. We have not just an interest but an obligation to bring those responsible to account.'[9] He amplified these themes talking to journalists on the plane across the Atlantic. He also added a new argument about weapons of mass destruction which was going to be very important for the future.

What has been brought home to people is that this form of terrorism knows no boundaries . . . it knows no limits except those limits that are imposed on them by lack of technical capability. If these people could, then they almost certainly would get access to chemical, biological or nuclear capability. We have no option but to act.[10]

When Tony Blair crossed the Atlantic to see George Bush for the first time since the atrocities, he did not go simply as a sympathetic friend seeking to help an ally in its moment of high distress. He went as a man willing and eager to be a fully fledged partner in what he conceived to be a global struggle with a diabolical new menace.

The unconditionality of this support for America began to stir some dissent in Britain. On the Sunday before his visit, Clare Short, the International Development Secretary, came on to my Radio 4 programme, *The Westminster Hour*, to deliver the opinion that 'strident action' risked 'inflaming' the situation and that high civilian casualties in Afghanistan would be 'unbearable'.[11] Blair was furious with her for giving an interview which provoked the first rash of headlines about splits in his government over the response to 9/11. He wrote her an angry note, saying he was also cross because it sent the wrong signal to the Taliban about the seriousness of their intent. If the regime in Kabul thought the Western response was divided, they would be less likely to respond to the ultimatum to yield up bin Laden.[12]

Very early on, by talking about standing 'shoulder to shoulder', Blair wrote Bush an emotional blank cheque. He was signing up to a global campaign of unspecified duration. His ambassador in Washington came to believe: 'Tony Blair put himself in his own box. Immediately after 9/11, he gave this tremendous, unconditional support for America and having set that as his standard, he never felt he could subsequently fall below it.'[13]

By the time they got to New York airport for the flight to Washington, Blair's party was running two hours late. The traffic was terrible, the usual gridlock in Manhattan made even more hellish since the atrocities and now compounded by slashing rain. Heightened security at the airport led to further delay, adding to the agitation of the Prime Minister that he was going to get to the White House too late to have a proper conversation with George Bush before the President addressed Congress that night. 'Tony was in a complete strop, flapping around the plane,' recalls his Chief of Staff, Jonathan Powell. 'Bush was about to make the speech of his life and we were two hours late.'[14] To cap it all, as the plane stood on the tarmac waiting for clearance to fly to Washington, the British ambassador started to have a screaming fit in the first class cabin because Powell had just told Sir Christopher Meyer that he had been bumped out of a seat at the dinner with Bush to make room for Alastair Campbell. Meyer threatened to resign there and then, bawling at Powell: 'If you do that, you'll fucking well cut me off at my fucking knees for the rest of my fucking time in Washington! Is that what you fucking want?'[15] That spat was eventually resolved by the quiet diplomacy of David Manning, who asked Condi Rice to arrange an extra place at the table.[16]

The public face of Blair's visit to New York and Washington was to express Britain's solidarity with America. The private business was focused on trying to ensure the American response to 9/11 would not sacrifice international goodwill by being wildly disproportionate. During the first Gulf War, Margaret Thatcher told George Bush senior: 'This is not a time to wobble, George.' On the flight over, Jonathan Powell joked that Blair was going to see the younger Bush with the message: 'This *is* a time to wobble.'[17] By that he meant Blair hoped to be a calming influence. The mood in America was fearful and vengeful as its leaders warned the country to brace itself for further attacks. Even the liberal *New Yorker* published a cartoon which had one citizen of Manhattan saying to another: 'I agree we have to avoid overkill, but not at the risk of underkill.'

Blair picked up some useful information about Bush's mood from Jacques Chirac, with whom the Prime Minister breakfasted at the Elysée Palace before flying to America. Chirac, who had recently seen Bush, reported that he was 'calm and measured' and more impressive than the Frenchman expected. The British were relieved that Bush was not being 'the cartoon caricature of Bush, the gunfighter reaching immediately for his six-shooter'.[18]

Once Blair's plane touched down at Andrews Air Force Base, a convoy of black Lincolns took the Prime Minister and his party into Washington. They were already getting intelligence that key figures in the administration wanted to seize on 9/11 as an opportunity to deal once and for all with Saddam Hussein. There was more to this than the British yet knew. Within twenty-four hours of the atrocities, Donald Rumsfeld, the US Defense Secretary, and Paul Wolfowitz, his number two, argued to go after Iraq immediately and pressed the case again at a weekend conclave at Camp David.[19] Colin Powell, the Secretary of State, was the strongest voice against. He won the argument then. Not because Bush was against an attack on Iraq, but because he concluded that America would expect his immediate focus to be on al-Qaeda.

Blair got to the White House too late to have the one-to-one meeting with Bush originally planned for that evening. As their entourages were ushered into the Blue Room for pre-dinner drinks, Bush took Blair to one side. They spoke by the window that looks out on the South Lawn with a view of the Washington Monument. Here was the opportunity that Blair wanted to look into the other man's eyes. When he again stressed the necessity for a measured response with international support, what Bush said to him sounded reassuring. 'The job in hand is al-Qaeda and the Taliban,' said the President before adding, almost as a throwaway remark: 'Iraq we keep for another day.'[20]

Blair took this to be pleasing evidence that his strategy of engagement with the White House was proving effective. It may have encouraged him to exaggerate his assessment of his influence. In truth, he was one voice among many who persuaded Bush that he needed to deal first with Afghanistan. Bush gave Blair the broad outline of what he intended to say in his speech to the Joint Session of Congress later in the evening. This was merely a courtesy, not a consultation. The highlights of the speech had already been briefed to the White House press corps.[21]

It was much the same – briefing, not consulting – at the dinner that followed. Bush dominated the conversation as he told the British how they planned to attack the terrorist sanctuaries in Afghanistan and the quasi-medieval Taliban regime in Kabul – 'a bunch of nuts', said Bush.[22] As they ate their way through scallops and veal, Bush said he would issue an ultimatum to the Taliban to surrender bin Laden and his most senior co-conspirators, but the American President was already assuming that he wouldn't get an answer from the regime in Kabul that satisfied him. Bush also began to scope out a 'war on terror' which would go much wider than Afghanistan. 'We've got to make sure that al-Qaeda doesn't have any safe haven in the world,' he remarked. He wasn't going to tolerate any regime that let 'terrorists do their dirty deeds from their territory'. Blair wanted to stress the importance of carrying international opinion with them. Bush responded that he was happy to have allies on board, but they were going to do this come what may. He was clearly relishing the prospect of flattening the regime, telling the dinner that 'bombers will be coming from every direction.'[23]

Blair got nervous on behalf of his host, who was about to make the most important speech of his life. 'Don't you want to go off and rehearse?' he asked the President. With a calm that struck others listening as either impressive or disturbing, Bush replied: 'No, I've done that already. I know what I'm going to say.'[24] Jonathan Powell thought: 'It was like he'd had a nerve bypass.'[25]

When it was time for Bush to travel over to Capitol Hill, he flattered Blair by asking the Prime Minister to accompany him in the presidential limousine. Once the cavalcade arrived, Bush went in the direction of the podium and Blair was guided to a seat in the 'heroes' gallery' next to Laura Bush. He had the ego-engorging satisfaction of being the only foreign leader there that day.

Bush delivered up an aggressive speech, declaring: 'Our war on terror begins with al-Qaeda, but it does not end there.' Watched by 80 million Americans, he threw down a gauntlet to the rest of the world: 'Every nation, in every region, now has a decision to make. Either you are with us or you are with the terrorists.'[26]

This would cause a shudder in many foreign capitals. Trailblazer was the Secret Service codename for the President and apprehension that he was a trigger-happy gunslinger was already being aroused by his cowboyish talk of 'whuppin' terrorism, 'smokin' out' the killers, taking bin Laden 'dead or alive' and having 'his head on a platter'. He also showed verbal clumsiness about the sensibilities of Muslim countries when he spoke of 'a crusade'. Unlike his British visitor, Bush had not read the Koran.

Before his domestic audience, though, the American President was hitting all the right buttons. The performance created an intensely patriotic fervour which won the roaring approval of Senators and Congressmen on both sides of the aisle. It completed a recovery in the eyes of his country from the anxieties aroused by the ineptitude of his stumbling performance in the immediate aftermath of 9/11. In the wake of the speech to Congress, Bush's approval ratings surged higher than those enjoyed by Franklin D. Roosevelt after Pearl Harbor.[27] The speech was rewarded with thirty-one standing ovations, each one accompanied by a flutter of bangs as the audience rose and its seats flipped back. One of those ovations was for Tony Blair when Bush privileged him with a reference.

'I'm so honoured the British Prime Minister has crossed an ocean to show his unity of purpose with America,' said Bush, glancing up to Blair in the gallery. In Texan vernacular, he added: 'Thank you for comin', friend.'[28]

Blair adopted a mien of modesty at the rapturous applause. But it was bound to be head-swelling, noted Sir Stephen Wall, a senior diplomat who worked at Number 10. 'He was seduced, as most British Prime Ministers are, by the relationship. The red carpet is laid out, the national anthems are played in the middle of Congress, all that stuff is very seductive.'[29] The Prime Minister and his entourage left Washington 'euphoric' about their reception.[30]

Not so much Campbell, who worried 'that some would use it to do the whole "Bush's poodle" thing'[31] that was beginning to run in parts of the Labour Party and the British media. He had even asked Meyer whether it would be possible for Blair to go to the dinner but skip Bush's speech. 'Do we really have to stay? Couldn't he slip away before the speech?' he wondered of Meyer beforehand. 'Yes, he has to stay, Alastair. No, he can't slip away,' responded the ambassador. 'This is going to be a huge occasion. To be invited to sit in the gallery with the President's wife is a signal honour. They won't understand, it will not go down at all well if he says no. It's a moment in history.'[32] Blair liked moments in history and he did not anyway see himself as a poodle. He preferred to think he was a guide dog.

He had prepared for his encounter with Bush by lunching with Silvio Berlusconi in London on the Sunday and dining with Gerhard Schröder in Berlin on the Wednesday as well as breakfasting with Jacques Chirac at the Elysée Palace on the Thursday. The idea was to collect intelligence about the positions of the European leaders which would enhance his value to Bush as an ally.

He'd also been working the phones, talking to the President of China and the President of Iran, the first time that a British Prime Minister had held a conversation with the leader of the regime in Tehran since the overthrow of the Shah more than twenty years ago. Bush was astonished when Blair told him about that call.

Just as Bush felt he had found 'a mission' for his presidency, so Blair believed that he had located an international calling for his premiership. 'He saw it as a moment of destiny,' says his friend Michael Levy. 'Almost instantly, it became the focus of his energy.'[33] Terrorism capable of causing death on a previously unimaginable scale was the new and most mortal threat facing not just the West, but all of what he liked to call 'the civilised world'. In his view, one shaped by his religious belief, it was a Manichaean struggle between good and evil. The military response was inevitably going to be spearheaded by the Americans. It was essential that they sustained international sympathy and did not become isolated. Blair believed he could be instrumental in ensuring both. Among other things, that demanded that Britain make a substantial military commitment to accompany its leader's rhetoric.

General Sir Mike Jackson, the Commander-in-Chief of the British army, began 'force generation' for Afghanistan in 'quite short order' after 9/11.[34] Admiral Boyce started to redeploy elements of the Royal Navy towards the Indian Ocean. He told Blair 'not to worry' that this would look prematurely aggressive because 'no-one would know.'[35] Blair's favourite man in uniform was his first Chief of the Defence Staff, General Sir Charles Guthrie, a foxy and smooth operator who always came with a can-do attitude. He'd been a reassuring ally and mentor in the first term when Blair ordered British forces into action three times: against Slobodan Milosevic in Kosovo, in Sierra Leone to restore democratic government, and in punitive action against Saddam Hussein in Operation Desert Fox. Blair did not gel so well with Guthrie's successor, Admiral Sir Michael Boyce. He was a submariner, from the silent service. Boyce was a careful and precise man who always identified the hazards of military action. At a meeting with the Prime Minister on 27 September, Boyce outlined some of the difficulties of a campaign in Afghanistan. Air power was not sufficient for the task. 'There's not a lot to hit,' pointed out Boyce. 'There's mud huts and people living in caves.' They had to have 'boots on the ground'. The Taliban were not going to be 'friendly foes'. They had a record of giving their opponents 'a hairshirt': skinning alive captured enemy combatants.[36]

Cool with Boyce, Blair was developing a warmer relationship with Sir Richard Dearlove of MI6 and John Scarlett of the JIC. In the view of one senior spook, Blair was turning into 'an intelligence groupie'.[37] Members of the War Cabinet watched him 'being seduced by the confidence with which they would assert things. MI6 did some really good work. He became very reliant on the intelligence services during this period.'³⁸ This was a development which would have huge significance for the future.

Blair was about to send British forces into military action for the fourth time in his premiership. Silvio Berlusconi, the Italian Prime Minister, privately told him that he was supportive of military action 'provided not too many people die'. Blair's response revealed how he'd been battle-hardened by previous conflicts. He shrugged to Berlusconi that there was 'no such thing as a painless war'.³⁹

He was energised in the weeks after 9/11 because Blair was always happiest when he was 'on a big stage trying to achieve grand things'.⁴⁰ With his tremendous powers of persuasion, his experience of office and his range of international contacts, he believed he had a unique value to both Washington and the rest of the world. He also thought that 9/11 was evidence of a talent for prophecy. 'You know, I saw this coming,' he would say.⁴¹ He meant that he had foreseen that a radically altered foreign policy was required in the interdependent world of the twenty-first century where boundaries had been melted by globalisation. Before 9/11, Blair was already reaching for a different philosophy of international relations from the traditional one that had held since 1945, namely that states did not interfere in each other's internal affairs. He first tried to formulate a theory in justification of liberal interventionism two years earlier, in April 1999, during the NATO action in Kosovo. In a speech delivered in Chicago at the height of that conflict, Blair tried to give intellectual underpinning to his interventionist instincts by formulating what he called 'the doctrine of the international community'. He argued the case for military action against sovereign states when they threatened their own citizens, their neighbours or the rest of the world.⁴² In the changed world after 9/11 and in order to build support for action against the Taliban, he now amplified that doctrine, the most consistent belief of his premiership.

His most impassioned statement about interventionism was the speech he gave to the truncated party conference in Brighton at the beginning of October, three weeks after the atrocities. Blair usually agonised about his conference speeches, engaging his staff in endless discussions about themes, phrases and content and was rarely entirely satisfied even when he had won his usual standing ovation. This time was different. 'That speech wrote itself,' he told me. 'I knew what I had to say.'⁴³

The final text was not substantially different to a first draft that he had written one evening the previous week. It was his most definitive statement of the case for moral imperialism when confronted by global terror.

First, he further hardened the commitment to fighting alongside the Americans. 'We were with you at the first. We will be with you at the last,' he declared. While this was the sort of oratorical flourish which Blair loved, it was also writing another large blank cheque to George Bush before the British Prime Minister knew exactly where 'the last' might take him.

There was then the importance of drawing a distinction between terrorists like the IRA, with whom he had negotiated for peace in Northern Ireland, and those like al-Qaeda, with whom he said there could be no bargaining. 'There is no possible compromise with such people,' he said. 'Just a choice: defeat it or be defeated by it.'

This presented al-Qaeda as a more lethal foe than they actually were. While unquestionably ambitious to inflict as much death as they could, bin Laden's murderous network did not represent an existential menace to Britain on a par with the Nazis in the Second World War or the Soviet Union during the Cold War.

He issued a direct threat to the regime in Afghanistan. 'I say to the Taliban: surrender the terrorists or surrender power.'[44] He put stress, in a way his American ally never did, on the need to reconcile Islam with the West. It had by now become quite well known that he travelled with a copy of the Koran nestling alongside his Bible in his luggage. It was not so well known that he read three different versions of the Koran in the quest to find passages that could be used against Islamist extremism.[45]

The main aim of the speech was to develop his thesis about international affairs in such a way that his current actions were located and legitimised in a grander moral design for the world.

'This is a moment to seize. The kaleidoscope has been shaken. The pieces are in flux. Soon they will settle again. Before they do, let us re-order the world around us.'[46]

He contrasted Kosovo, where military intervention stopped an attempt at 'ethnic cleansing', with the absence of international action in Rwanda, where a million people were slaughtered in the mid-1990s. The speech dwelt on Africa, 'a scar on the conscience of the world'.

That was sincerely meant. Ever since the British intervention in Sierra Leone, Blair was preoccupied with the state of Africa. As so often with him, high ideals were married with low politics. There were already voices in his party, and beyond it, protesting against saddling up to join George Bush's Afghan posse. To one member of his Cabinet, Blair's conference speech was also 'a piece of triangulation'. He knew he was going to war so he wanted to project himself as 'a generous and caring person on Africa.

It doesn't mean there wasn't sincerity in it, but he was positioning himself.'[47] Blair was hoping to ease apprehension about Bush by placing the campaign against the Taliban in the context of a grander cause of global renewal.

'The starving, the wretched, the dispossessed, the ignorant, they are our causes too,' he proclaimed in a passage designed to link his moral imperialism with traditional Labour values and concerns. He roped together climate change, the Middle East peace process and free trade into his theme of 'the moral power of the world acting as a community'.

The speech then soared off into passages that might have been accompanied to the tune of 'the whole world in his hands'. He took up as his cause 'those living in want and squalor from the deserts of northern Africa to the slums of Gaza to the mountain ranges of Afghanistan'.[48]

One half-awed, half-apprehensive member of the Cabinet to whom I spoke afterwards described it as 'the inaugural speech of the President of the World'.[49] Colleagues regarded it as a stunning piece of oratory, but the moral fervour of the speech also fed a worm of concern that Tony Blair was beginning to exhibit a messianic tendency.

This had always been present in his character. It was made manifest during the Kosovo conflict, when he went much further than other Western leaders in his zeal to defeat the Serbian dictatorship. But the messianic Blair was largely concealed in the first term behind the cautious, popularity-hoarding dimension of his personality. It was in his second term that the conviction-driven Blair would be thrust to the foreground, transforming how the world looked on him and how he looked on the world.

The speech enjoyed adulatory reception in the hall and in the next day's press. He was laurelled in admiring headlines from both left and right. The *Daily Telegraph*'s leader hailed it as 'Blair's finest hour'.[50]

The speech had a sweeping panorama and was a most eloquent expression of his personal credo. It was visionary, idealistic, inspiring, tremendously well delivered and pumped with moral uplift. It was also unanchored from much realism about his capacity to deliver the utopian world that he described. In the quieter, domestic passages, he conceded that many of the basics of British public services were still deeply unsatisfactory after four years of Labour government. 'Parts of the railways,' he admitted, were 'a disaster'. There was a disjunction between his admission that they couldn't get the trains to run on time at home and his vaulting claim that they could heal the world of conflict, poverty and disease.

I could not resist mocking the more overblown passages, writing in the *Observer*: 'Missionary Tony will cleanse the planet of disease, poverty and conflict. The sun will never set on the Holy British Empire. The tough and tender third way will rule from Kinshasa to Kabul.'[51]

Looking back at it now, the speech is the most ambitious attempt by any politician of that time to visualise building a better world order from the ruins of the Twin Towers. But it also reads as the quintessential example of Blair's weakness for oratorical over-reach, to promise much more than he could conceivably deliver. 'I thought at the time that it was a bit high-flown,' says Sir Christopher Meyer. 'You read it now, it is sheer hubris. It is bonkers.'[52] The slums of Gaza are still the site of endless conflict. British soldiers still fight the Taliban in Afghanistan. The deserts of Africa are still stained by genocide. He left office having got nowhere close to realising the dream world that he presented as within reach in the autumn of 2001.

At the end of the party conference week, Blair flew to Pakistan to lobby its leadership to break with the Taliban. The trip was made against the advice of those responsible for his security and in the face of protests from Cherie, who had become highly strung about her husband's personal safety. Having failed to argue him out of the trip, she turned on Campbell. 'Do you want to be a martyr or what?' she cried, her bottom lip trembling with rage.[53]

They flew to Islamabad in an elderly RAF VC-10, an aircraft despised by Blair and his staff for the antiquity of its communications equipment and the embarrassingly old vintage of the plane compared with those employed by other leaders. Even in good aircraft, Blair was frightened of flying. Few knew about this fear except those closest to him who had watched him battle the phobia. 'He hated flying, but he had taught himself to live with it.'[54] Downing Street frequently toyed with ordering a better aircraft for the dedicated use of the Prime Minister, only to be stymied by a combination of penny-pinching by Gordon Brown and his own fear that the media would ridicule him for desiring to possess a 'Blair Force One'.

As the old plane rattled towards the capital of Pakistan, he had with him Campbell, Hunter, Powell and Tom Kelly, along with two of the intelligence chiefs, Scarlett of the JIC and Dearlove of MI6. The fear was that terrorists might use surface-to-air missiles to bring down the VC-10. Some on board kept their spirits up by cracking black jokes about being hit by a stinger. The pilot implemented evasive manoeuvres, throwing the plane into a steep, twisting and sickening dive on the approach to the airport. 'That was probably the scariest journey into a major capital we ever did. It was a corkscrew descent followed by a journey through a city on the edge.'[55]

As was often his habit, the Prime Minister was sitting up in the cockpit, which afforded the best view, with Anji Hunter next to him for company.

Blair was usually quite sanguine about physical danger, but he suddenly became 'very morbid' as the plane corkscrewed towards the tarmac. 'Tony started talking about his own death, something I'd never heard him do before,' one of those on the trip told me later.[56]

Safely conveyed to his meeting with the President of Pakistan, Blair delivered the message: 'You've got to choose which side you are on.' He was pleased to extract from Pervez Musharraf an assurance that Pakistan was abandoning its support for the Taliban and offering intelligence to assist against al-Qaeda. The British believed it 'corralled Musharraf in the right place', which gave Blair the feeling that this hazardous trip was worthwhile.[57] The most important pressure on Pakistan was from the Americans, who mixed menaces with promises of dollars to induce the General to be co-operative. Pakistan proved to be a highly unreliable ally and its short term co-operation a tactical ruse to appease the United States. It secretly helped North Korea with its nuclear programme. Two months after Blair's visit, Musharraf released two Pakistani scientists who had been detained for providing bin Laden with information about making weapons of mass destruction.

Blair flew on to India and then back to Britain, where he landed at lunchtime on Sunday, 7 October. He was in the car on his way back from RAF Northolt when the Downing Street switchboard put through a call from George Bush. Tony Blair might make himself sound like the man in charge of Western policy, but he was about to get a reminder that the shots were called from the White House. The American President told him that the first air strikes against al-Qaeda camps and Taliban forces in Afghanistan were commencing that evening.

'None of the leaders involved in this action want war,' Blair declared as the first bombers were reaching their targets. 'None of our nations want it. We are peaceful people . . . We only do it if the cause is just, but this cause is just.' The Taliban had it coming: 'They were given the choice of siding with justice or siding with terror and they chose to side with terror.'[58]

At their dinner at the White House, Bush had told Blair that bombers would come from all directions. Now they came, B-1, B-52 and Stealth bombers, supplemented by cruise missiles fired from a naval task force. Some of the missile salvos were launched from *Triumph* and *Trafalgar*, two British nuclear submarines which Admiral Boyce had secretly moved into position. The British contribution was not essential to the military effort, but a symbolic act to show that this was not an entirely American campaign.

Shortly after the bombs and the missiles came the first insertion of ground troops in the form of American Special Forces and their British counterparts.

Within forty-eight hours, Blair was again travelling the globe as the coalition's chief advocate to the world. Not everyone was impressed. Even the saintly Nelson Mandela jibed that Blair was turning himself into 'America's Foreign Secretary'. The Americans were happy for him to take on this role. The Secretary of State, Colin Powell, was preoccupied trying to cover his own back from his enemies inside the administration.[59] George Bush 'felt pinned to Washington'[60] and anyway had little time and even less inclination to trot the globe nurturing allies. It was 'a really trying and stressing time for the United States', says Condi Rice, noting that 9/11 was followed by an alarming spate of anthrax attacks. Blair's willingness to take on the role 'was a multiplier effect for the United States that at that point had a lot to do'.[61]

The opportunity presented itself, and was grabbed with relish by Blair, to be the roving ambassador for the campaign against the Taliban. According to Bush's Chief of Staff:

It was very important because Prime Minister Blair could move more nimbly than the President. When the President of the United States travels he has a very large footprint, and expectations are frequently beyond what can be realised. Whereas the Prime Minister could travel with a relatively small footprint, deliver very important messages and help to find allies that otherwise might not be found.[62]

Blair was not only willing, he was eager to effectively become an Ambassador at Large for Bush. 'Tony is in his element. He loves this stuff,' one of his senior aides told me during this period.[63] 'Blair was at the height of his powers. He had great domestic capital and great international capital,' comments David Manning. 'The role went with his natural activism and suited Bush at the time.'[64] It made him feel pivotal to historic events on a stage much greater than Britain. During a parliamentary debate that autumn, Blair didn't mind at all when a Conservative MP inadvertently referred to him as 'the President'. He was transcending being the electorally successful leader of a European power to become a globe-girdling statesman.

In the eight weeks after 9/11, a period which covered the build-up and the execution of the military campaign in Afghanistan, Blair took thirty-one flights for fifty-four meetings with other leaders.[65] He travelled nearly 50,000 miles, a double circumnavigation of the globe, on coalition-building and intelligence-gathering tours. He called on Berlin, Paris, Brussels, Geneva, Moscow, Islamabad, Delhi, Geneva, Muscat, Cairo, Damascus, Riyadh, Amman and Jerusalem. It was a commitment to the cause that was not displayed by any other ally of the United States.

It was not a role without risk and Blair would candidly confess in private that it meant 'getting his hands dirty' by shaking them with some of the grislier leaders of the unfree world. A tour of the Middle East in late October and early November reverberated to the sound of Arab leaders slapping him in the face. His first call was on Damascus, where Bashar al-Assad, the young new leader of Syria's police state, seemed to offer the prospect of a more constructive relationship with the West than his father. Their private talks went tolerably well, but at the joint news conference afterwards Assad played to the Arab gallery, giving Blair 'a total banjaxing' by lambasting the war in Afghanistan and condoning terrorist attacks on Israel. The look on Blair's face showed that he was already translating it into the headlines he would get back home.

As soon as he escaped that ordeal, he turned to Tom Kelly. 'Don't bullshit me,' he said. 'How bad is it?' 'Bad,' nodded Kelly.[66] The headlines were indeed terrible, speaking of his 'disaster in Damascus'. Afterwards, Blair tried to laugh it off, saying: 'It could have been worse, he could have taken out a gun and shot me.'[67]

Other legs of that tour were mildly more productive. While secretively supportive of the toppling of the Taliban, neither the Crown Prince of Saudi Arabia nor the King of Jordan would publicly support the military action for fear of the reaction on the Arab street. Blair pointedly told the Saudis that George Bush also had 'his street'. They should not think that they were the only ones with public opinion to satisfy.[68] He came away empty-handed when he tried to persuade the Prime Minister of Israel, Ariel Sharon, that this was the moment to advance the peace process. The leaders of the Gulf States, worried that a prolonged conflict would inflame their own populations, urged Blair to tell Bush to hurry up and get the campaign over before Ramadan.[69] Some of the Arab press expressed grudging admiration that he was prepared to engage with their grievances and take hostile questions, not something their own undemocratic leaders ever did.

The slights he was prepared to bear and the miles he was ready to travel enhanced his value to the White House. He was lionised in America. Enormously popular there,[70] he became one of those rare British Prime Ministers – Churchill and Thatcher were others – whom Americans recognise almost as instantly as their own President. The conservative *Wall Street Journal*, which a few months earlier had been describing Britain as a Third World country, now saluted Blair as 'America's chief foreign ambassador'. The *New York Post*, Rupert Murdoch's noisy tabloid, commended his 'bull-dog spirit'. In the American media, his oratorical skills were elevated to the same pedestal as John F. Kennedy and Ronald Reagan. In the British media, he was variously compared with Churchill, Gladstone and Palmerston. These analogies, even when they were intended to be cautionary or jeering, further burnished his status.

As he travelled the globe sustaining the 68-nation alliance against the Taliban, he looked like the staunchest of allies in the eyes of the United States and seemed a moderating influence on Washington to everyone else. Even some of his most vituperative critics at home regarded this period as a high point of his premiership. 'I think this was Tony's best moment,' says Clare Short, who could never be confused with a member of his fan club. 'Tony bestrode the world stage, started getting on aeroplanes, going around the world, trying to hold everyone together with America, have a sensible strategy towards Afghanistan. At that stage, he was doing absolutely the right thing. And I was proud of him.'[71]

It bred an uneasy mixture of respect and resentment among his counterparts in the European Union. European leaders – many more of them than Blair had originally intended – came for a dinner at Number 10 on 4 November. There was already an atmosphere about the way in which Blair had appointed himself as America's voice abroad. Jacques Chirac then launched into a vigorous denunciation of the conduct of the military campaign. Waving his fork as he delivered a mordant warning, the French President predicted: 'A mosque will be bombed during Ramadan.'[72]

The Afghan campaign was being run by a War Cabinet which met daily early in the morning. 'Blair would come down from his flat looking tousled having just had his shower while the rest of us had been up for hours,' noted one envious member of the War Cabinet.[73] The Prime Minister would typically open by turning to Admiral Boyce and asking: 'What are we achieving?' He was visibly frustrated by Boyce's frank replies that it was hard to interpret the impact of the bombing and missile strikes. His 'impatience with the military' was palpable, as was his lack of chemistry with the cautious Boyce.[74] There had been three successful operations by Special Forces, but by their nature they could not be boasted about. The Admiral was badgered by an impatient Campbell: 'We want to show that we're doing something.' Boyce in turn found it hard to conceal his distaste for Campbell's obsession with how the campaign could be sold to the media and thought it 'dangerous' that all else was regarded as subordinate to Downing Street's craving 'for headline success'.[75] Blair also vented some of his irritability on the Defence Secretary. Geoff Hoon remarks: 'Tony was always more concerned about how it looked here rather than how it was going there.'[76] The media was inevitably reporting the victims of the military attacks, refugees flooding out of Kabul and anti-American riots in Pakistan. The Americans started talking about 'running out of targets'. Their use of cluster and daisy cutter bombs, which inflicted large civilian casualties, were alienating public opinion. The world was reacting in a fairly predictable way to the spectacle of the planet's most powerful military machine unleashing so many munitions on one of the poorest countries on the face of the earth.

For ground forces, the Americans were relying on the Northern Alliance, a loose coalition of Afghan tribal chieftains who were united in their hatred of the Taliban but not a whole lot else. Colin Powell would joke that 'they may be in the north, but they are not an alliance.'[77]

By early November, Blair and many of his team were fearful that the campaign was stuck.[78] The apparent lack of progress in defeating the Taliban was accompanied by the flaking away of domestic support for the war. He did not share these fears with his Cabinet, who were only intermittently given progress reports and were never invited to debate strategy, setting a pattern for the future. Decisions were increasingly not taken in the War Cabinet either. The military 'did not like Gordon Brown's presence there. When you're fighting a war, you don't want the bean counter sitting in the corner telling you what you can't spend,' said one senior military figure.[79] Blair was anyway averse to discussion, saying: 'You cannot have a campaign run by committee.'[80]

The key debates took place in cabals convened by the Prime Minister in his den. When Boyce briefed on the progress of the campaign, it left the Prime Minister increasingly apprehensive. 'The military command sounded alarmist about how badly things were going.'[81] As was also totally characteristic, Number 10 displaced its own anxieties by lashing out at media criticism of the conduct of the campaign. Downing Street berated broadcasters for giving too much airtime to 'Spin Laden' as some in Number 10 took to calling him.

The real revelation of the Afghan campaign was about the Americans. Though this was not yet apparent in public, to some on the inside it was becoming clear that the Bush administration was riven with internal conflict. The Pentagon under Donald Rumsfeld and the State Department under Colin Powell were simply not communicating. Boyce found that the Pentagon relied on him to supply information to them about the thinking at the State Department and vice versa. Even more astonishingly, Boyce knew more about US military plans than did America's most senior general, Dick Myers. Rumsfeld entirely bypassed Myers and the rest of the Joint Chiefs of Staff. The US Defense Secretary instead gave orders direct to Tommy Franks, the General running the Afghan campaign. 'The highest part of the American military command were entirely cut out.'[82] This was an early warning, if Blair cared to heed it, of the perils of being too enthusiastic about tying himself to the dysfunctional Bush administration.

On 8 November, the Prime Minister made a quick dash across the Atlantic for a six-hour visit to Washington to try to convince Bush to display more sensitivity towards international opinion and make more effort to win over the Muslim world. A repeated Blair refrain was that the West had to be more vigorous about making its case, an implicit concession that bin Laden, who had become a poster boy terrorist for demonstrators in some parts of the Islamic world, was winning the propaganda battle in Muslim countries. There was also 'a worry about how the Northern Alliance would behave when they occupied Kabul. Would there be a tremendous bloodbath?'[83]

At their joint news conference afterwards, Bush trowelled on the praise for his visitor, saying that America had 'no better friend in the world than Great Britain' and he'd 'got no better person I would like to talk to than Tony Blair'.

The air campaign had begun exactly a month before. Bush shrugged off questions about the apparent lack of progress by saying: 'This is a long struggle and a new kind of war', which Blair echoed by adding: 'This is not a conventional conflict.'[84] In private, Blair was rebuffed when he attempted to interest the President in putting more effort into the Middle East peace process. There was also a clear and public retort to Blair's multilateralism when Donald Rumsfeld declared: 'The coalition must not determine the mission.' Here was another warning of how little the Bush administration cared for the notion of 'the world community' advanced by Blair in his conference speech.

These differences did not erupt any more publicly at this stage because suddenly the campaign scored a sequence of rapid successes. As David Manning puts it: 'There was a worry: "My God is this ever going to move" and then it all moves very quickly.'[85] When the fall of the Taliban regime finally happened, it was swift. The Northern Alliance advanced with the support of the US air force directed by Special Forces teams on the ground. On 9 November, the key objective of Mazar-i-Sharif was captured. The major city in the west, Herat, was taken without a fight. On the 13th, Kabul fell and with it Mohamed Omar's diabolical regime. The next day, Blair boasted to MPs of the 'total collapse' of the Taliban and hailed 'the liberation' of Afghanistan from 'one of the most brutal and oppressive regimes in the world'.[86]

Never had regime change appeared to be so easy. Television images of US missiles and bombs flashing in the night sky over Kabul were deceptive about how the campaign was won. In reality, the unpopular Taliban mostly scarpered from their trenches before the bombs fell. Large bribes supplied by the CIA to local warlords also melted resistance. The war was basically won with 'suitcases of money and buying the Northern Alliance. There was very little standing fighting,' says Admiral Boyce. 'The Taliban faded and disappeared with surprising speed.'[87] Most of them vanished from their front-line positions and fled Kabul and Kandahar without putting up any resistance. The aim of closing down al-Qaeda training camps was easily achieved. The rapidity of this victory seemed to confound all the dire warnings beforehand about Afghanistan being a notorious graveyard for foreign armies.

Bush privately told Blair that he thought Osama bin Laden was dead, but could not say so in public in case he should pop up.[88] Pop up he soon did, issuing bragging and taunting video tapes through al-Jazeera. The principal obsession of the Americans evaded the Special Forces and bunker busters that scoured and blasted the mountains of Tora Bora.

That failure only slightly diluted the triumphalist assessment of the campaign in the White House. One hawk wrote that 'with less than a month to prepare, American troops and aircraft had charged into this country, overthrown its government, destroyed its terrorist bases, and hunted down their enemies, while losing only fifteen of their own to enemy action.'[89]

Bush's approval ratings surged again. He did not have much to say about the future of Afghanistan, which made a striking contrast with his British partner. Blair bought into the argument that the West helped to create the monster of al-Qaeda by allowing Afghanistan to become a failed state in the years after the Soviet Union retreated from its disastrous attempt to occupy the country. 'This time,' he promised, 'we will not walk away.'[90]

In the opening week of the New Year, he was the first foreign leader to make the hazardous journey to Kabul. Though it was now two months since the Taliban retreat, the capital was still like 'a war zone'.[91] Cherie, who decided to risk being 'a martyr' with her husband, joined the trip. They crossed the Khyber Pass aboard a Hercules fitted with counter-measures against missile attack from fighters on the ground. Conditions on board were primitive. The loo was a bucket. As they entered Afghan airspace, all the aircraft lights were turned off. After a corkscrew descent on Bagram air base, the Hercules landed in total darkness. A red carpet was laid out on the tarmac. It served more than an honorific purpose. The airport had been sown with landmines and not all of them were yet cleared. 'Stay on the carpet,' they were all warned as they got off. 'Don't deviate to left or right.'[92]

As Alastair Campbell got off the plane, his big black briefcase burst open, sending all his papers, including secret documents, fluttering over the runway. Campbell and Manning scrambled to retrieve them in the dark without getting themselves blown up.[93]

The Afghan national army band then struck up a welcome. Blair was taken to a former Soviet barracks, in which all the windows had been blown out, for his talks with Hamid Karzai, the interim leader who would become the Afghan President. Trying not to shiver in a temperature of minus ten, the Prime Minister pledged that the West would not betray Afghanistan again. He promised Karzai that the allies were 'in this for the long term'.[94]

Was this a promise that Blair was in a position to keep? George Bush took an utterly divergent view. Much had been changed by 9/11, but one thing that had not was the Republican President's visceral aversion to any sort of commitment to 'nation-building'. The British embassy in Washington warned Blair that he should not even use the phrase, so allergic were the Americans to it.[95]

At a meeting of his National Security Council on the very day that the Taliban fled Kabul, the President declared: 'The US forces will not stay. We don't do police work.'[96]

This disastrous doctrine had a very influential advocate in Donald Rumsfeld. The British were beginning to recognise that he was 'a consummate bureaucratic warrior who knew how to ruthlessly cut other people out of decisions'.[97] Rumsfeld took the view that the mission should be confined to the installation of a US-friendly regime and the hunting of al-Qaeda. One senior British officer characterises the attitude: 'The posse has arrived. We're into Kabul. End of story.'[98]

David Manning was having constant conversations with Condi Rice about how to stabilise the 'very tenuous new regime' in Afghanistan and who was going to contribute to an international force.[99] Blair was forced to spend some of his precious political capital with Bush persuading the American President to overrule his Defense Secretary. Even then, Rumsfeld succeeded in keeping the American deployment to a minimum. The Pentagon was neither interested in making a serious commitment to secure Afghanistan nor in taking action against the heroin trade. Michael Boyce 'stitched together' a NATO peacekeeping force almost from scratch using his personal relationships with other military commanders in Europe and the English-speaking world.[100] The British 'volunteered' to provide the command of the force in the belief that 'you get political clout by having one of your nationals as commander.'[101] For all Boyce's efforts, even he regarded the force as 'not enough' to do the job properly.[102]

The NATO forces lingered there without well-conceived political or military goals. The Taliban regrouped to eventually become so resurgent that America and Britain were forced to commit many more troops later.

In November 2001, though, the Americans were hubristically celebrating what they took to be a swift and famous victory. The White House focus was already swivelling from the mountains of Afghanistan to the deserts of Iraq. As for Tony Blair, he now needed to pay urgent attention to his battles on the home front.

4. The TB-GBs

'Well,' said Cherie. 'I think you should sack him.'[1] She had many times before urged her husband to fire Gordon Brown. She would do so many times again.

Tony Blair was careful to whom he confided the full torture of being umbilically bound to the Chancellor. He feared that it might destroy the Government if the ugly truth came out. So he usually tried to conceal, even from his senior staff, just how toxic the relationship was turning. He would bottle up all his frustration and fury about the other man's impossible behaviour and then pour it out to Cherie when he went up to the flat in the evening. That helps to explain why her hostility to the next-door neighbour was so intense. Barry Cox, a close and non-political friend of the Blairs, explains: 'She bore the brunt of the consequences for Tony of the confrontations with Brown. She reacted personally to what she regarded as Gordon's very bad behaviour and she took deep mortal offence at it. She was not as calm and measured as Tony. She got very angry. She felt betrayed.'[2]

Cox was with them on holiday in the summer of 2001 when he, Tony and Cherie had 'a long conversation' about 'how difficult Brown had turned'. Blair, having not done it after the election, was now asking: 'Should I sack him?'[3]

In the salad days of the Government, when there was some residual trust, respect and even affection between them, Blair often described his relationship with Brown as 'like a marriage'.[4] That, in many ways, it was. There has been no more creative, destructive, talented and turbulent pairing in high British politics. Despite all the difficulties between them, no Prime Minister and Chancellor were twinned together for so long since the Napoleonic Wars. The longevity of the partnership was the more extraordinary because it was so tempestuous. They were the rock on which New Labour was built and the rock on which it so often threatened to break apart. When they were working together, their complementary skills created a synergy which made the Government pretty much unstoppable. When they were at war with each other, it terrified and divided the Cabinet, horrified and bewildered their party, astounded civil servants, transfixed the media and poisoned the Government into paralysis.

As characters, they were a contrast. Blair rose to the top through his charm, communication skills and creative dexterity; Brown by his brain, organisational ability and steamrolling persistence. Blair was much the more emotionally intelligent, which gave him the advantage in connecting with the public and colleagues. Brown was more ruthlessly focused on executing his domestic policy ambitions, an attribute which he frequently used to thwart his nominally superior next-door neighbour. Blair was basically comfortable in his skin; Brown was not at ease with himself, let alone other people.

There was a deep well of fury in Brown which expressed itself in a beetle-browed glower and volcanic eruptions of temper. 'That's none of your concern,' he growled at Cabinet colleagues who dared to offer opinions about the economy, while believing he had the right to interfere in their departments. Battered by one of Brown's pummellings, Geoff Hoon groaned to a friend: 'Why can't he behave like a human being?'[5] After being subject to Brown's bullying about the funding of the Olympics, Tessa Jowell, one of the more placid-natured members of the Cabinet, was provoked into shouting back: 'Don't you ever fucking speak to me like that again.'[6]

Brown was a forceful speaker, but not a great debater. The diplomat and senior official Sir Stephen Wall noted that he did not engage in argument: 'Gordon's technique is to hammer away at the same point in a bulldozing way.'[7] A very senior civil servant agrees that 'He finds argument very difficult. His answer is to thump out bullet points until he has ground you down.'[8] Paul Boateng, Chief Treasury Secretary, once burst into tears with a colleague because of the relentless briefing against him by Brown's acolytes.[9] Alan Milburn's partner, Ruth, a psychiatrist, was once heard referring to Brown as 'a psychopath'.[10]

Blair was not a bully. His friend Charlie Falconer rightly says it was not his style to 'take on other politicians in a very macho way'.[11] There were occasions when he raised his voice and quite a lot when he used Anglo-Saxon language. 'Holy Joe has a dirty mouth,' observes Clare Short.[12] But it was not his way to try to shout other people into submission. His manners were usually impeccable. 'One of Tony's fantastic qualities is that he is always polite with people in almost all circumstances. I've never seen him be rude to somebody,' says Jack Straw. 'If he was frigged off with you, there'd be a certain coolness or you'd read about it in the newspapers.'[13] Bruce Grocott was Blair's Parliamentary Private Secretary for seven years. 'In all that time, we only had one serious set to. Within about an hour, he apologised to me, which I thought was very big of him.'[14]

John Prescott was a man who got up angry and went to bed even more furious. On Prescott's account, Blair was superb at massaging his volatile deputy. Prescott would often storm into Number 10 intent on a fight. After the application of the Blair schmooze, he would find himself saying: 'Christ, Tony, I came in here disagreeing with you – and now we're in agreement.' As Prescott says, it was 'a good trick' to be so 'brilliant at persuading people'.[15]

Blair was a manipulator. 'He believes he can persuade anyone of anything,' remarks Peter Hyman, who was a member of his senior staff for six years.[16] 'Persuasive charm is one of his great weapons,' notes Margaret Jay, a member of the Cabinet. 'He does have to the absolute nth degree the advocate's ability to persuade you of the argument he's thinking about this morning.'[17]

The character differences between Blair and Brown were reflected in their working methods. The Chancellor sweated the midnight oil; the Prime Minister was more likely to be flying by the seat of his pants. Blair was a political glider, riding the thermals of public opinion to soar across the landscape. Brown was the saturnine obelisk glowering over it. 'They were almost the exact opposite of each other in terms of personality types so they complemented each other,' observes Andrew Turnbull, who was Permanent Secretary at the Treasury with Brown before becoming Cabinet Secretary with Blair. 'They were a very powerful duo.'[18]

Brown won his first political campaign in his early twenties when he defeated the establishment of Edinburgh University by getting himself elected rector; Blair spent his time at Oxford acting, playing in a rock group, enjoying a string of attractive girlfriends, finding God and having nothing to do with politics. Blair, the mildly rebellious public school boy, was attracted more to religion and philosophy. Brown, the industrious state school swot, was very young when he published his first socialist tract. Though Brown was only two years older, they seemed to come from different decades. The son of the Manse was shaped by the serious but socially repressed fifties while Blair was much more a child of the trendy but self-indulgent sixties. Blair was most comfortable wearing jeans; Brown was never seen in a pair. Blair was innately optimistic while Brown was more of a miserabilist. Even as a student, Brown behaved as if he were old for his years. Blair managed to sustain an aura of youthfulness about him even as he advanced into middle age.[19]

Blair put in the hours as Prime Minister, but he would, if he possibly could, get up to the flat by the early evening to relax with Cherie, his children and guitar. As an explanation for Brown's obsessive behaviour during the first term, Blair would suggest: 'Gordon's problem is that he hasn't got a family.'[20] The workaholic Brown would rise very early and work late into the night, habits which continued even after his marriage to Sarah Macaulay, a former public relations executive.

Blair was a brilliant communicator. Brown's genius was for carving out dividing lines with opponents that exposed their vulnerability. Blair would often say that Brown was the smartest electoral tactician that he had ever met, though Brown was typically more grudging about offering reciprocating compliments to Blair.

'Tony was the weaker negotiator,' says a very senior civil servant who worked closely with both men. 'If you want to put someone in a room with other EU leaders, give me Gordon any day. Gordon is stronger because he doesn't care whether people hate him and Tony does.'[21]

Blair was an intuitive and sometimes impetuous decision-maker, governed more by his instincts than by evidence. 'Brown was the exact opposite of Blair,' says Richard Wilson. 'He had a capacious brain and an impressive intellect. He did do detail. He really does read Annexe E.'[22] Brown wrestled with problems in a generally more considered, but also more agonised way. 'He likes to know what all the options are,' remarks Murray Elder, a friend since childhood.[23] Brown would brood and brood, within his own head or among his tight circle of trusties, and then suddenly launch his conclusion on to his colleagues. They thought he was late to share decisions with them because he was uncollegiate and cussed. Sometimes it was that; sometimes it was simply because he took a long time to make up his mind.

At their best, Brown's technical mastery allied with Blair's potent powers of persuasion made them a dazzling combination. The barrister son of a lawyer, Blair was the advocate: most effective when addressing the sceptical jury of public opinion. The son of a Church of Scotland minister, Brown was the preacher: most impressive when rousing a crowd of believers. Brown liked to preach to the choir; Blair to reach out to the unconverted.

Blair could understand why people were Tories. His father had been one. Brown could not. Conservatives aroused in him a Caledonian red mist. Blair's lack of tribalism, his fluid and protean qualities, allowed him to reach parts of the electorate that Brown struggled to understand or impress. This combination of personality and talents made them one of the most formidable partnerships in British electoral history. For the purpose of winning and retaining power, the coupling proved stunningly successful by delivering three election victories in a row. As a way of running a government, the results were much more ambiguous.

The root of the evil in their relationship was the arrangement they came to over the leadership in 1994, a deal which programmed a permanent power struggle into the DNA of the Government and led to years of recriminatory accusations of broken promises. Believing that he was an Esau, robbed of his birthright by Jacob, a smoother, younger brother, Brown never forgave Blair for taking the leadership and displaced much of his fury on to Peter Mandelson. The third musketeer later reflected: 'Within the New Labour family there has been a fissure from the word go. The reason is Gordon thought he should have succeeded John Smith, and he has never fully reconciled himself to not doing so. A very deep breach was opened up.'[24]

The events of the traumatic days after John Smith's fatal heart attack became accreted with many myths. The biggest legend was that the bargaining took place on 31 May 1994 at Granita, a now defunct restaurant in Islington. The meeting there was actually the culmination of a series of highly charged encounters, at least ten in all. Brown initially and naively expected his younger partner to defer to him. Blair had to withstand the older man's fury and then manage his bitter feelings. One negotiation took place on the evening of John Smith's funeral in the Edinburgh home of Nick Ryden, a friend of Blair since their schooldays at Fettes. When they turned up, Ryden could see how bad things were between them. 'Don't kill each other. You've both got a lot to offer the country' was his parting advice before he took himself off to the pub.[25] Their arguing was interrupted at one point when Brown disappeared to use the lavatory. When time passed and he didn't come back, Blair assumed that the other man had stormed off in one of his rages. Then he heard the phone ringing and a familiar Scottish voice growling into Ryden's answering machine. Brown was calling on his mobile from the lavatory. The door handle had come off, imprisoning him in the loo. Blair picked up the phone: 'I'll let you out, Gordon, but only if you give me certain assurances about the leadership.'[26]

It was some time before they met at Granita that Brown realised that he would lose a contest with Blair. After a Scottish leader who was preceded by a Welsh one, there was an overwhelming feeling in the Labour Party that it needed a leader with a feel for the centre ground and telegenic appeal to Middle England in order to win power after four election defeats. As Mandelson famously suggested in an interview with me at the time, Blair was the one who would 'play best at the box office, who will not simply appeal to the traditional supporters and customers of the Labour Party, but who will bring in those extra, additional voters that we need to win convincingly.'[27]

That was seen as rank treachery by Brown, to whom Mandelson had originally been closer than he was to Blair. This rupture generated a hatred between Brown and Mandelson which was the more intense because it had been preceded by love. From it flowed fourteen years of venomous feuding. One witness who heard Mandelson's end of a hysterical telephone conversation with Brown in 1994 recalls him screaming: 'I love you, but I'll break you! If you do that, I can destroy you!'[28] Michael Wills, who was one of the few people who managed to be a friend of Brown while remaining on reasonable terms with Mandelson, reckoned they were 'like scorpions in a bottle; only one of them will crawl out alive'.[29]

Mandelson made the rational choice when he backed the more promising candidate. Blair was always going to win. As Jack Straw puts it: 'In May 1994, the stars were saying to everybody that Blair is the leader.'[30] He was more popular in opinion polls, enjoyed much greater support in the media, had a more impressive spread of endorsements from Labour MPs and senior colleagues, and was way ahead among party members.[31]

That ought to have given Blair the strong hand in his negotiations with Brown. Yet he played it weakly. Before he left for Granita, Blair stood in the kitchen of his home in Islington discussing with Cherie and Mandelson how he should tackle Brown. Cherie was always worried that her husband would concede too much, telling him before an earlier meeting: 'If you agree with Gordon that you're going to do this for one term only, don't come back home.'[32] Mandelson believed Brown had to be accommodated for the sake of their project. Blair concurred, says Philip Gould, because 'Tony was nervous about dividing the modernisers.'[33] He left for the restaurant saying: 'I've got to give him something.'[34]

Blair ended up giving so much to Brown that the latter was encouraged to believe that they had effectively agreed a dual premiership. There were several reasons for Blair's timidity at this crucial moment. He had just leap-frogged over Brown, but Blair was the junior partner for most of the decade beforehand. The two first met when they came into Parliament together in Labour's nadir year of 1983 and shared a windowless room dominated by towering heaps of Brown's papers and books. Neil Kinnock, under whose patronage they both rose, regarded them as 'soulmates'.[35] The Newcastle MP Nick Brown correctly identified them as 'the two outstanding personalities of the 1983 intake'.[36] The politically more experienced Scotsman was regarded, not least by himself, as the future Labour leader and Blair was looked on as his impressive but junior brother. 'There was no question which of the virtually inseparable couple was the senior partner,' says Kinnock's deputy, Roy Hattersley.[37] For most of that time, Brown was psychologically dominant. 'You have to remember that for many years Blair was number two to Brown,' says Barry Cox. 'Tony was always talking about Brown as

the great thinker, the great political strategist, and he always assumed that
he would be number 2 to Brown.'[38]

Only in the two years before Smith's unexpected death did Blair achieve
equal status with Brown. So even at the point when he moved ahead, he
approached the other man with a mixture of admiration, dependency and
fear. He worried that he would not succeed in making the Labour Party
electable without the other man's intellectual firepower. 'I love Gordon,' he
told Brown's younger brother, Andrew. 'He's the best mind the Labour Party
has ever had.'[39] There was also some brotherly guilt. Even after the 1997
victory which made him a landslide Prime Minister, Blair remained 'very
defensive and sensitive' about how he had become leader. He even felt it
necessary to explain himself to one of his Cabinet Secretaries. To Sir Richard
Wilson, Blair said: 'He had his chance when Neil Kinnock stood down.
Gordon should have gone for the leadership then. Why shouldn't I have
stood when John Smith died?'[40]

While Brown exhibited an intellectual superiority which often awed Blair,
the Scotsman was internally riven with self-doubt. Charlie Falconer would
tell Blair that Brown was 'not as intellectually confident as he likes to
appear'.[41] Cherie, a woman who came top of almost every exam she took,
was not intimidated by the Scotsman's brain. Her husband was. Blair had
a mild inferiority complex which persisted into government. He would say:
'Gordon has a much more developed political philosophy than me.'[42]

Blair's view, according to Nick Ryden, was that 'a deal had to be done to
put them on a firm footing.'[43] Barry Cox agrees: 'Why did he give so much
power to Brown? He needed a partner. He'd never run anything. He thought
he couldn't do it on his own. It seemed a perfectly sensible deal at the time.'[44]

On the account of the negotiations that Brown gave to his friends, it
was Blair who volunteered the idea that he wouldn't serve as Labour leader
for more than a decade.[45] Blair always denied that he said anything quite
so explicit, but it is entirely plausible that he floated the notion that he
would hand over after ten years, not least because that would have seemed
a very distant prospect to him at that time. As someone close to both of
them once put it to me: 'Tony is a great one for saying what he thinks the
other person wants to hear. Gordon is a great one for only hearing what
he wants to hear.'[46]

The restaurant encounter lasted barely more than an hour; the consequences of the deal would remain undigested for more than a decade. Many
of Blair's friends later concluded that he committed a cardinal error which
compromised his premiership from the beginning. 'I think that the greatest
mistake that has been made in politics in my lifetime was the deal struck

between Blair and Brown that culminated in the Granita agreement,' argues Robert Harris.

In the end, it ruined Blair's premiership. It ruined it politically and it ruined it for him personally. It was an act of supreme folly to allow Brown to get away without having to fight a leadership election. He almost certainly would have come third. He would have been beaten by John Prescott.

Blair would have been 'master in his own house from day one'. By doing the deal, he allowed 'Brown to put his heel on his throat'.[47]

Charles Clarke agrees that it would have been much better had Brown run and been beaten by Blair. 'Tony would have defeated Gordon overwhelmingly. That would have meant that Tony did not owe him a debt.'[48] Frank Field reflects: 'It shows Tony's inherent weakness, which only really became apparent later.'[49] It was 'a massive mistake', says Philip Gould. 'There should have been a contest. Gordon should have stood against Tony. The alternative to a contest was an arrangement. That encumbered Tony with responsibilities to another member of the Cabinet which were not consistent with good Government. Gordon was encumbered with a sense of entitlement which was bad for his personality. It brought out the worst in both of them.'[50]

The deal did not assuage Brown's dark wrath that he was denied the crown. It helped to feed the grievance which corrupted their friendship. He convinced himself that he was somehow cheated out of the leadership. From it came the toxic myth of the 'stab in the back' which was assiduously spread by the Chancellor's lieutenants.[51] Even great supporters of Brown such as Ed Balls came to agree that the deal was a great mistake. 'Tony gave away far too much and Gordon wanted to believe it too much,' says one of Brown's closest allies at that time and to this day. 'The history of the rest of their relationship is Tony trying to claw it back and Gordon trying to hang on to it.'[52]

When New Labour came to power, it was a commonplace cliché to describe Blair as 'presidential'. It was more accurate to see the Government as a dual monarchy. Power was carved into two hemispheres. 'There were Tony's subjects and there were Gordon's subjects,' says Andrew Turnbull. 'Tony did foreign affairs, Northern Ireland and education. Gordon did the economy, overseas development and welfare.' They sparred for control over health and Europe. 'No-one ever really looked after transport. It was a very low priority in the first term.'[53]

Blair allowed more latitude to Brown than any previous Prime Minister conceded to a Chancellor. Cabinet ministers saw 'Gordon roam throughout the Whitehall forest'.[54] In the eyes of Derek Scott, his own economic adviser,

Blair surrendered 'an unprecedented amount of prime ministerial authority to the Chancellor that went well beyond the normal and inevitably central position played by the Treasury in all administrations . . . it soon became known throughout Whitehall that . . . the Chancellor could defy the Prime Minister with impunity.'[55]

Blair was repeatedly warned that this undermined his authority and capped his ambitions. In response, he would say: 'You've just got to get on with your Chancellor. If you look at governments which fall apart, it is because the Prime Minister and Chancellor fall out. Whatever happens, I've got to get on with my Chancellor.'[56]

That made Blair frightened of confrontations with Brown. General Sir Charles Guthrie, the Chief of the Defence Staff, discovered 'to his horror' that Brown wanted to take a large bite out of the defence budget after everyone thought it was all agreed. The General went to Number 10 to protest: 'This is putting me in an extremely difficult position.' The Prime Minister said he agreed with the complaint, but felt unable to take on Brown. 'Will you go and argue with him about it?' asked Blair. Guthrie was astounded. 'Surely you should tell him,' said the soldier. 'This is politics. I don't think I should be doing it. You should tell him what you want because you agree with us.' 'It's very difficult,' responded Blair. 'You know, I don't think I can do it.' 'Well,' said the amazed Guthrie. 'It does seem very wrong that I have got to do it.' The defence budget was eventually saved, but only after Guthrie had a blazing row with Brown and made it clear to Blair that he was on the brink of resignation.[57]

In their early years in power, Blair remained deferential to Brown on many issues. 'For all his faults, Gordon is crucial to me,' he would say. Colleagues and civil servants were astonished by the vast amounts of time he devoted to managing the other man. 'He mediates, he negotiates, he defuses, he cajoles, he rails, he shouts, he hugs, he flatters,' one Cabinet minister explained.[58]

On those quite rare occasions when Brown didn't get his own way, he could not bear it. Frank Field saw 'The Chancellor almost physically exploding with rage and the Prime Minister would behave as though this was an adolescent child who he was kindly dealing with with untold patience.'[59] Officials were astonished that Blair 'spent more time and effort managing the relationship with his Chancellor than on any other issue'.[60] He felt obliged to keep Brown supporters in ministerial jobs even when they were clearly inadequate for fear of 'a war with GB'.[61] Blair so often conceded to Brown in the first term that Roy Jenkins was prompted to write him notes telling him 'not to be so frightened of your Chancellor'.[62]

Blair at first didn't want to listen to Cherie, Campbell, Powell and friends like Charlie Falconer when they warned him that Brown's propagandists were spinning to the media to undermine him and Cabinet colleagues. 'Even as the shit was pouring out of the Treasury, Tony persistently refused to believe that it was coming from Gordon.'[63] A member of the Cabinet notes: 'There is a bit of Tony that always likes to see the good in people whether it is Bush or Brown or Berlusconi. He was in denial about how awful Gordon was because he'd have to do something about it.'[64] Frank Field, whose ministerial career was one of the many casualties on this battlefield, is another who believes that Blair made a fatal mistake. 'There has been this disgraceful behaviour from day one of Blair's leadership. When you're up against a Chancellor that wants to shoehorn you out every day of every year, you are in an enfeebled position.'[65]

One consequence of having a twin-peaks Government was to make all other ministers look small. On this Blair and Brown were agreed: the Cabinet was not a forum for making decisions. Sir Robin Butler, the first Cabinet Secretary to Blair, 'had the impression that they took into Government the habits of Opposition. And the habits of Opposition had been that the New Labour centre, the revolutionary cell within the Labour Party, fixed what the line was going to be. And they continued to do that in Government.'

He noted:

From the start, the proceedings were very informal. Tony Blair wasn't interested in setting an agenda and working through the items. Even I as Cabinet Secretary didn't know what was going to be the business taken that day. And certainly Cabinet ministers were not encouraged to raise issues themselves. If anybody raised an issue, then that was not welcome.[66]

One long-standing and senior member of the Cabinet, Geoff Hoon, thought: 'Tony was paranoid about differences being expressed and exposed around the Cabinet table.'[67] It was also temperament. When Blair played football at Chequers with his staff, he was 'a bit of a lone striker. He was not a great passer. He used to zip down the wing and then almost invariably shoot rather than pass the ball or cross it.'[68]

Brown was even more of a political ball-hogger than Blair. The Chancellor did not treat the Cabinet as his equals. He viewed other ministers as rivals to be crushed, nonentities to be disdained or satraps to be controlled. 'Brown exerted a very strong grip,' comments Andrew Turnbull. 'He had been given a mandate to be the dominant figure on domestic policy. He did not allow any member of the Cabinet to make a public policy commitment without reference to him.'[69] Believing that he could always prevail over ministers – and indeed the Prime Minister – if he had them one-on-one, Brown thought his power would be more easily challenged if he allowed it to be scrutinised by the Cabinet as a collective.

Sir Robin Butler was astonished when he learnt that the Prime Minister and Chancellor had agreed to give control over interest rates to the Bank of England without consulting any of their colleagues. 'Surely the Cabinet should take this decision,' Butler protested to Blair. 'Oh no,' responded the Prime Minister. 'That's not the way we do things. They will agree. The Cabinet won't dissent from it.' Butler tried to marshal a new argument against pre-empting Cabinet discussion. 'I think people outside will expect that a decision of this importance should be endorsed by the Cabinet.' Blair finally offered a sop to the Cabinet Secretary by saying: 'We'll telephone round to them.'[70] Robin Cook and John Prescott were rung in advance, but the rest of the Cabinet were taken completely by surprise. On many other issues, Butler would ask Blair: 'Won't the Cabinet want to discuss this?' to be told that, even if they did, they weren't going to get the opportunity.

Butler's successor fared no better in trying to persuade Blair to restore collective responsibility. 'This ought to go to Cabinet,' Sir Richard Wilson routinely protested to the Prime Minister. 'Why?' 'Because you need collective agreement. You'll leave yourself vulnerable if you don't have it,' argued Wilson. Blair stared at him: 'No, I won't.'[71]

Cabinet meetings were ridiculously brief to begin with and only became a little longer because commentators started to remark on their embarrassing brevity. 'Nothing was being decided,' says Clare Short. 'It was a way of using up the time and pretending we were doing Cabinet government.'[72] On the account of Jack Straw:

We used to discuss a lot of things in Tony's Cabinet, but often they were discussing how we present policies. It was a lot to do with discussing the effects of decisions after in practice they'd been taken. It didn't mean that Tony was a one-man band, but it did mean that the decision-making tended to take place in bilaterals and in Tony's so-called den.[73]

Cabinet was merely 'an opportunity to put down a marker or express a view', agrees Estelle Morris. 'I never saw it as a place where decisions were made.'[74] Paradoxically, this marginalisation of the Cabinet worked to the advantage of the Chancellor more than the Prime Minister. Most of the Cabinet greatly preferred Blair both as a person and as a leader. As a close ally put it to me in the summer of 2001: 'If Tony went and was replaced by Gordon, the Cabinet would be divided between those who feared they would be shot that night and those who knew they would be shot that night.'[75] By failing to use the Cabinet, he did not deploy it as the counter-weight to his mighty rival that it could have been. That was a further reason why Gordon Brown became the most powerful Chancellor there has ever been in British history.

Civil servants witnessed the already tempestuous relationship 'get much more difficult'[76] the moment they were re-elected for a second term. Blair was restless to do more with his premiership, which meant confronting Brown in areas that the Chancellor regarded as his sovereign territory. Brown was obsessed with becoming Prime Minister, which meant getting rid of Blair.

A theme of Blair's private conversation during this period was that he did not want to be remembered as another Harold Wilson who won four elections out of five and talked a lot about modernising Britain but wound up with a lacklustre historical reputation.[77] He wanted his second term to be bigger and bolder than his first. 'In the first term, he was, if you want to be cruel, Mr Focus Group and Mr Spin,' observes Clare Short. 'By the second term, he was thinking: "What's my place in history?" He started to take more control of policy direction. It was a different Tony Blair second time around, more confident, more determined to be in control and to find his legacy.'[78]

The serious opposition was not the Conservatives, who had just gone down to their second landslide defeat and seemed suicidally determined to be out of contention for years to come. To replace William Hague as leader, the Tories passed over the boisterous weight of Kenneth Clarke and the born-again moderniser Michael Portillo to select Iain Duncan Smith, a former army captain who had never been a minister. The Conservatives were so riven with infighting that they made the inhabitants of Sicily look like rank amateurs at feuding. The Tories could not find a voice – literally so in the case of their leader. At Prime Minister's Questions, his nerves were betrayed by the rasping choke that came out of his mouth – 'the croak of doom', one cruel Tory called it.[79] As things went from bad to worse for the Conservatives, it was joked that IDS stood for 'In Deep Shit'.

The real Leader of the Opposition to Blair was his next-door neighbour. Brown was equally fixated with his place in history. 'Gordon was intent on not just being another Chancellor or another Cabinet colleague,' says his ally, the MP and owner of the *New Statesman*, Geoffrey Robinson. 'He was intent on showing that he was the man to succeed. Gordon was expecting an easy, agreed transition.'[80] To Brown and the Brownites, it was 'an article of faith that there was a promise by Blair to hand over'.[81] When a date did not materialise, it became Brown's repeated and angry complaint to Blair that 'he was welshing on the deal.'[82] The Chancellor was driven more demented after 9/11, when Blair's evident relish for his role on the world stage indicated to him and his intimates that 'Tony wasn't planning to go anywhere.'[83]

On the account of one of his circle, Brown was 'in a state of perpetual anger'.[84] There were regular episodes of throwing things at walls, the floor and occasionally other people. He would sit in Cabinet scribbling furiously rather than make contributions. Brown was fixated by his coverage in the press. The Chancellor once called his friend Alistair Darling at six o'clock in the morning on Boxing Day. 'Have you seen today's *Telegraph*?' Brown growled down the line. 'No,' replied Darling, confident that no-one else would have seen it either. Brown 'then went on to complain about something on page 422 or something like that'.[85]

He came into a meeting and hurled a pile of newspapers on the floor, yelling: 'Look at these fucking papers!' Philip Gould picked them up, glanced at the headlines and said gently: 'These are yesterday's papers, Gordon.'[86]

A senior Cabinet minister observed to me at the time that if Blair went on to do a third term: 'It will be too late for Gordon or most of the rest of us.'[87] This was both plausible and hateful to Brown: he might be denied the crown or not get it until Labour's time in power was drawing to a close. Andrew Turnbull observed that Brown was eaten 'with a sense of grievance' and crazed by the question: 'When is it my turn?'[88]

From the moment they won the 2001 election, Brown began to pound Blair with demands for a date. On the account of a Cabinet minister and close friend of Blair: 'All their confrontations between 2001 and 2006 are about Gordon saying: "Why haven't you fucking gone?"'[89] One of the few people the Prime Minister fully confided in was Barry Cox, who could be trusted because he was a very old friend who was not part of the Westminster world. Cox is a reliable and compelling witness. 'It became truly difficult after the 2001 election,' he says.

In the summer of 2001, we had a long conversation, Cherie, Tony and I, about how difficult Brown had turned and what he was doing and the behaviour, the petulant way he was demanding that Tony resign and let him take over. Ever since then, it was continuous. He wanted to be Prime Minister. He wanted to be Prime Minister now. There was nothing else. It was running since 2001.[90]

There were only two ways to resolve this impasse, but Brown wasn't going to resign and Blair ever hesitated over sacking him. The senior Number 10 official, Sir Stephen Wall, thought it always unlikely: 'The prospect of Gordon Brown as a king over the water on the backbenches with a team around him capable of making mischief was too much to contemplate.'[91]

'Tony feared what Brown would unleash – what he would do to the party,' says Michael Levy.[92] Alan Milburn agrees: 'The most telling factor of all was that Tony really thought Gordon would burn the house down.'[93]

Blair's attitude to Brown was also conditioned by mournfulness about the withering of the relationship. 'Gordon is the only friend I have ever lost,' he once lamented.[94] 'Even when it was really bad, Tony was never black and white about Gordon,' says Alastair Campbell.[95] According to Barry Cox:

He used to take the line: 'Look, political ambition is legitimate for major public figures. It's entirely legitimate for Gordon to want to be Prime Minister.' He would try to be understanding about it and lay it off. Many other people would not have tolerated what Gordon Brown was doing. His anger and irritation with Brown was always matched by this generosity towards him, this understanding of why he behaved like he did.[96]

There were still occasional moments of warmth. According to one person on the Brown side who often witnessed meetings or listened in to phone calls, 'there were times when it was strangely intimate – like a husband and wife on the phone.'[97]

Even during the rockiest stretches of the marriage, Blair tried to conceal how bad things were. 'Tony was very discreet about keeping it away from the staff. He didn't do it in front of the children,' says the Number 10 official Steve Morris. 'When everyone around him was really angry about something Gordon had done, Tony was nearly always the calmest. It was that strategy of magnanimity that kept the relationship on the road for so long.'[98]

The price was to leave Brown with his powerbase, where he ran what was both a government within a government and an Opposition within a government. Officials watched the Treasury become 'an enormous empire',[99] an octopus with tentacles which gripped every other department. Crucially, Brown won an early second-term battle to keep control of the Public Service Agreements, which placed every spending minister under the thumb of the Chancellor by making them subject to detailed targets written in the Treasury. Under Brown, the Treasury not only interfered in the spending decisions of other departments, but second-guessed policy development as well. Clare Short's international development budget doubled under his patronage. She had reason to be grateful to Brown, but even then chafed under his control. 'The Treasury was extending its remit through the targets going right into the heart of all departments.' The 'enormous control of lots and lots of detail' gave it 'all the power, day-to-day power'.[100]

Brown reinvented the role of the Treasury. By contracting out monetary policy to the Bank of England, 'he created a lot of spare time', which freed

him to pursue his policy and personal ambitions.[101] Subjects that excited
him – such as welfare reform, employment and poverty – received enormous
attention. Ministers in areas which did not engage him, such as financial
regulation, barely saw him. Ruth Kelly, a young and able junior minister put
in charge of the City, was labelled a Brownite by the media simply because
she worked at the Treasury. In fact, the City minister had one ten-minute
interview with Brown a fortnight after her appointment and then did not
have another one-to-one conversation with him for two years.[102] Sir John
Gieve, a senior official at the Treasury, observes that it was remade in its
master's image. 'The Treasury was extremely powerful in some spheres'
where Brown was 'very engaged and clear in his own mind what he wanted
to do'. It was 'a non-player' in areas that didn't interest him.[103]

The Treasury was historically the referee of spending by other departments. Brown's introduction of tax credits, which came to cost the
equivalent of 4p to 5p on the standard rate of income tax, turned him into
'the largest spending department in Whitehall'.[104] This meant that there was
no-one to invigilate his spending, which was notorious for its waste and
incompetence in the administration of tax credits. The Chancellor traditionally took charge of the macro-economy while the Chief Treasury Secretary
conducted the detailed spending negotiations. 'Public spending was done
completely differently with Gordon Brown as Chancellor,' observes one
senior mandarin. 'Gordon drained the post of Chief Secretary of any function and took over spending.'[105] This further augmented his power over the
rest of the Cabinet.

Chancellors often have difficult relationships with their colleagues, but
the fear and loathing for Brown was unusually sharp because of his secretive
decision-making and bone-crunching style of negotiation. There were
'humdinger' rows with David Blunkett, a short-tempered and stubborn man
himself. On his own account, Blunkett was so infuriated on one occasion
that it came to 'near fisticuffs' when he grabbed the Chief Treasury Secretary
by the lapels.[106]

Brown's explanation to himself for his unpopularity with colleagues was
to blame his role rather than his personality. 'There are tough decisions you've
got to make,' he told me. 'You've got to tell people no. You've got to show
that you can control public expenditure. That requires tough leadership.'[107]

Brown had 'a very cynical view of mankind and his colleagues', thought
Andrew Turnbull, and was 'Stalinist in his ruthlessness' in the way he dealt
with the Cabinet. He would not allow them 'any serious discussion about
priorities' and operated on the principle that 'they will get what I decide.'[108]
He was also compulsive about stealing the glory for any Government

achievements. Civil servants like John Gieve observed him 'pull announcements into the Budget rather than letting other ministers announce them'.[109]

The Budget and the autumn Pre-Budget Report were the big, biennial opportunities for Brown to shape the direction of New Labour, define its message in his terms and remind everyone why he was such a dominant figure. He used his spending announcements in November 2001 to assert his overlordship of the domestic scene. As usual, the spending ministers had been given little or no advance notice of his intentions. 'The Treasury had two tricks,' noted Estelle Morris, the Education Secretary. 'One was announcing things very late. The other was telling you one day that you've got the money and three days later telling you the conditions which come with the money.'[110] When someone called Brown 'a colossus' in the hearing of Alastair Campbell, he pulled a face: 'Yeah, an out-of-control colossus.'[111] One member of the Cabinet protested that Blair had allowed Brown to become 'rampant'.[112]

Alan Milburn, the Health Secretary, boiled over when Brown, with no consultation beforehand, announced his own review of the NHS[113] and made critical remarks about the health service's performance. Milburn complained to Blair that Brown 'saw it as his right to trample on everyone else's territory'. Blair, who had so often been trampled on himself, sympathised.[114]

Brown's own officials were shocked by how contemptuously he treated the Prime Minister. Sir Steve Robson was a senior Treasury civil servant who rated Brown as 'a far-sighted, thoughtful guy'. Even this admirer relates that 'There were times when Gordon would take an opposing view simply to bugger up Blair. Arguments would go on and on and on.'[115]

This had a paralysing effect on Whitehall. 'I had Permanent Secretaries wanting decisions and we couldn't give them because Blair and Brown were in a row,' says Richard Wilson. 'Issues stacked up like aircraft over Heathrow.'[116]

Money is power in Whitehall. So is information. Brown exploited the Treasury's control of both to dominate the rest of the Cabinet and outmanoeuvre his titular senior in Number 10. One tactic was simply to refuse to tell Blair what would be in Budgets. Stephen Wall had been an official under Margaret Thatcher and John Major, both of whom had difficult relationships with Chancellors. Yet he 'could not recall a time when there was such a relationship of non-communication between a Prime Minister and a Chancellor. Number 10 had the greatest difficulties until quite soon before the Budget statement getting the Treasury to cough up the details of what the Chancellor had in mind. It was a constant battle.'[117] When Brown was refusing to divulge his plans, Blair was reduced, and in front of witnesses, to pleading: 'Give us a hint, Gordon.'[118]

A senior aide to the Prime Minister once confided: 'We are lucky if he tells us what will be in the Budget forty-eight hours beforehand.'[119] Sometimes he did not even give that much notice. On one occasion, notorious in Whitehall, Brown would not let Blair see the Budget until six o'clock in the evening on the day before, by which time it was already at the printers.[120] When Brown was proving particularly obstructive before another Budget, Blair asked John Prescott to join them for a meeting. The Deputy Prime Minister told the Chancellor that he was being utterly unreasonable. 'For Christ's sake, Gordon, he's the fucking Prime Minister – you've got to tell him what's in the Budget,' said Prescott.[121] It did no good.

On the account of Geoffrey Robinson, Brown starved Number 10 of information because he 'thought it would get leaked everywhere and it probably would have done'.[122] Yet Brown and his team leaked when it suited them. Blair and his advisers resorted to scouring the newspapers for stories planted by the Treasury to find out what was going on across the road. Andrew Turnbull, the Treasury's most senior mandarin and later Cabinet Secretary, is in no doubt that Brown 'used the denial of information as an instrument of power'.[123] Gus O'Donnell took over as Permanent Secretary at the Treasury in 2002. He felt highly uncomfortable and tried to encourage Brown to be less difficult about Budgets – to little effect.[124]

There was a code in Whitehall for outbreaks between the neighbours of Downing Street. They became known as 'the TB-GBs'.[125] The power struggle was exacerbated by clashing perspectives. Blair wanted to fight wars. Brown gave every impression that he hated giving money to the armed forces. Blair believed that public anxiety about crime had to be acknowledged and addressed. Brown thought Labour could never own law and order as an issue and 'the more you talk about crime the more you build up the problem.'[126] Blair wanted to concentrate spending on health and education rather than Brown's redistributionist and complex system of tax credits. The Prime Minister sat in the Commons watching the Chancellor deliver one Budget speech and was astonished to hear Brown announce extra billions for his pet tax credits when he had denied money for Blair's priorities on the grounds that they couldn't be afforded. Blair turned to Alistair Darling and whispered: 'He told me there was no money.'[127] Brown's 'stealth taxes' often seemed as much intended to sneak them past his next-door neighbour as to mask them from the public. The Chancellor's predilection for over-inflating how much he was truly spending was not just designed to win himself good headlines. It was also about gulling the Prime Minister.

In the view of Sir Stephen Wall, Brown's behaviour was 'outrageous and fundamentally disloyal. But ultimately the Prime Minister has only one sanction and that sanction is dismissal. If the Prime Minister isn't prepared to exercise that sanction, the Chancellor has the whiphand.'[128]

By early 2002, Blair was psyching himself up to have a showdown only for a personal tragedy to intervene when Gordon and Sarah Brown lost their baby daughter, Jennifer. Grieving Chancellor and sympathetic Prime Minister were warm to each other at the funeral, reminding Blair 'of the days when they had been genuinely close'.[129] But their rivalry still cast a shadow even at the funeral of a baby. Blair was astounded to see that Brown had invited a lot of journalists to the funeral, among them Paul Dacre, the editor of the *Daily Mail*, the newspaper unmatched in the virulence of its attacks on the Prime Minister.

The relationship descended to a worse place when the Browns returned from mourning their lost child to Downing Street. The Blairs lived in the flat above Number 11. They would leave little Leo's pram parked outside the flat door, where it was visible to the Browns. 'Tony and Cherie are so cruel to me,' Brown complained to friends. He was genuinely convinced that they were using the pram to deliberately remind him that the Blairs had what was tragically taken from him and Sarah. They were perhaps insensitive, but outside Brown's paranoid imagination there is no evidence that they meant to be malevolent. He nursed this grievance for years. Brown would continue to rage about the Blairs' 'cruel treatment' of him and his wife, bringing it up with one minister a full five years later.[130]

This unstable diarchy had two warring courts. 'There was a real atmosphere of lack of trust,' says Sir Stephen Wall. 'You would hear that for people in the Treasury even to have contact with Downing Street was regarded as a kind of kiss of death for their careers.'[131]

In the words of Sir Richard Wilson: 'Number 10 was obsessed with Gordon Brown. They talked about Gordon Brown more than anything else.'[132] The Treasury was reciprocally fixated with Number 10. 'There was a sense of righteousness' in the Brown camp, says one of his inner circle. 'We genuinely believed that Gordon would be a better Prime Minister.'[133]

His civil servants noted that Brown 'relied on a small cell' of advisers.[134] By far the most influential was Ed Balls, a graduate of Oxford and a Kennedy Scholar at Harvard who was effectively the Treasury's chief executive. Though little known to the public at this stage, he was hugely powerful behind the scenes. Balls was only in his twenties when he played a critical role in the rewriting of Labour's entire economic policy, and was instrumental in persuading Brown of the case for Bank of England independence. He had struggled to conquer a childhood stammer, from which perhaps flowed his determination to present a relentlessly assertive face to the world. Balls was more capable of being decisive than his boss or anyone else around the Chancellor and often made decisions for Brown. Observing them interacting, some in Brown's inner circle occasionally even wondered who was truly the master and who the servant. 'Ed's control over Gordon is the most extraordinary thing I've witnessed,' says another close Brown aide of many years. 'He had this ability to bend Gordon to his will.'[135] As much as Brown, if not more so, Balls regarded politics as a perpetual trial of strength and conducted relations with Number 10 in that belligerent spirit. Says another member of Brown's team: 'Ed's whole analysis was that it was a war, a raw battle for power.'[136]

Jonathan Powell, who barely exchanged a civil word with Brown for all the time they were in government together, thought Balls was 'a perfectly nice bloke' when he worked for the *Financial Times*, but turned 'very unpleasant' in the employment of Brown. 'Gordon had a very strong field of gravity. People became infected by his paranoia.'[137]

Many of the battles were conducted through off-the-record briefings to the media, much of that masterminded by Balls. Ed Miliband, another aide to Brown but a gentler soul than his namesake, told friends that 'Ed's attitude is that it's like a coup – you get control of the television stations and newspapers first.'[138]

Charlie Whelan, Brown's first spin doctor, was forced to resign in the first term when he and his *ad hominem* methods became over-exposed. He was still a presence in the background and an influence. 'Charlie set the bar. You prove your loyalty by your brutality. There's a part of Gordon that likes that.'[139]

One of his successors was Ian Austin, a former regional press officer for the Labour Party. One Number 10 official who knew Austin then as a decent bloke and saw his transformation into an aggressive Brown soldier concluded: 'Working for Gordon did something to people.'[140] A later recruit to the propaganda operation was Damian McBride, who ultimately became Brown's most notorious spinner. A Cambridge graduate, he was a career civil servant at HM Customs & Excise before he turned into a notably brutal partisan for the Chancellor. 'The people around Brown were pretty ruthless,' noted a senior mandarin.[141]

Any Cabinet minister who crossed the Chancellor or who was regarded as a potential threat was in peril of being attacked by Brown's hit squad. In the words of one of Blair's most senior aides: 'Gordon had this King Herod strategy of killing off at birth anyone who might be a rival for the succession.'[142]

They would also turn on their own. Michael Wills, the Labour MP for Swindon, was a long-standing friend and ally of Brown. He nevertheless became the target of press attacks when he fell out with Ed Balls. It was Balls who was viewed with most suspicion inside Number 10. 'He was regarded as the chief stormtrooper of the Brownite shock troops,' says a member of the Cabinet.[143] Jonathan Powell believed that Balls 'egged on' Brown to attack Blair because of his frustration that his own ambitions were impeded. Balls, an undoubtedly clever man, rarely deigned to mask his view that Blair was an intellectual lightweight. 'Tony would be speaking at a meeting and Ed would sit behind Gordon whispering in his ear. He had complete contempt for Tony. He would just lay into Tony at meetings.'[144]

In the words of one of the Chancellor's inner circle, 'Ed was always trying to bring our day closer.'[145] On the account of another, Brown's relentless demands for Blair to give a handover date were partly driven by Balls, who would 'guilt trip' Brown about his failure to force out their rival. 'Why are you being so weak?' Balls would taunt Brown. 'Gordon would be cowed and feel he was letting us down by not fighting harder to get it.'[146]

It was during this long period of nursing his grievances and tending his wrath that the dark sides of Brown's character became entrenched: the bunker mentality, the faction boss methods of operating, the brutal conduct towards colleagues. The struggle for supremacy also brought out the worst in the Prime Minister's entourage and the cynically manipulative side of Blair's personality. He tried to contain Brown by employing psychological games. The stick was to rattle the Chancellor by encouraging other ministers and the media to believe that rivals were being built up to challenge Brown's status as the heir apparent. The carrot was to string him along with quasi-promises about handover dates. As early as 1999, on a believable account from the Chancellor's side, Blair had told Brown he would only want to fight two elections.[147] He made constant suggestions to that effect to try to induce Brown to be less difficult. In February 2002, Blair was accompanied on a tour of west Africa by Clare Short. Despite their many and often manifest differences, they got on in a funny sort of way. During a meal on the plane, Blair indicated that he still regarded Brown as his natural successor and would be more likely to hand over early if only the Chancellor would be more co-operative. Blair was determined to get Britain into the European single currency at this stage. Looking around the plane to ensure that they weren't being overheard and speaking as if confiding 'a big secret', Blair suggested that Brown's assistance in fulfilling his euro ambition would hasten the transition.

As she got up to go back to her seat, Short asked if he wanted her to convey this message to Brown. 'I do, I do,' said Blair. On her return to Britain, she did just that over a lunch with Brown at the Treasury. 'You're not the only one,' said Brown. 'Two other people have brought me this message from Tony.' He went on: 'You can't arrange politics like this. And, anyway, he doesn't keep his word.'[148]

There was some creative product of the struggle. Matthew Taylor was one Number 10 official who believed that 'the policy outcome was often improved' by the ferocity of the arguments between the two sides.[149] The overall effect, though, was debilitating. Neil Kinnock, watching the rift between the two men who had been his protégés, regretted that 'the grand opera of the personal relationship succeeded in obscuring achievements and preoccupying the energies and imaginations of far too many people, including people in government who inevitably started to move towards alignment with one side or the other.'[150]

Some members of the Cabinet took sides; others just tried to keep their heads down. As Stephen Wall puts it: 'Ministers would think to themselves: either I please Tony or I please Gordon, what is the safe thing to do? The safe thing is to do nothing.'[151]

The same was true of civil servants. 'All the Permanent Secretaries were like the fourteen-year-old children of parents who are divorcing. They were all trying to work out whose side they should be on.'[152]

At the beginning, neither would probably have achieved alone what they did together. They were more than the sum of their parts. Two great political talents then squandered a lot in the struggle for supremacy. By the end, they were less than the sum of their parts. They could not kill each other, but the war between Blair and Brown did maim their project and wound their Government. Neither achieved as much as he might have done; nor did New Labour as a whole because so much time, talent and energy was consumed by the perpetual struggle.

In the run-up to the Budget in the spring of 2002, there were the usual games beforehand and vital elements of the package were not divulged to Blair until just before it went to the printers. When Brown sat down to the cheers of Labour MPs, Blair nevertheless thumped him on the back in a show of congratulation. After the restraint of the first term, the spending taps were being turned on to pour unprecedentedly large sums into the public services. The NHS was awarded annual increases of 7.4 per cent above inflation over five years. Famine was followed by feast. Even Derek Wanless, the banker whom Brown had commissioned to write a report to roll the ground, concluded that these huge sums were at the extreme limit of what could be sensibly managed. A few voices cautioned that this would not be sustainable in the longer term should the economy ever turn down.

But Brown confidently proclaimed in that Budget, as he did so often, that he had abolished 'Tory boom and bust'.

This big surge in spending on the NHS was partly funded by an increase in national insurance contributions. Brown had put up taxes before, but furtively, as if raising money for the public realm was shameful. This time he did it openly, which marked a break with their earlier taboo about arguing for explicit tax increases to fund services. Both Chancellor and Prime Minister were very nervous of public reaction. Blair even fretted: 'This could cost me the next election.'[153] To their huge relief, post-Budget polls indicated that the voters overwhelmingly approved of raising tax to improve the NHS, a very rare instance of a tax hike being popular. At the first Prime Minister's Questions after that Budget, not a single Conservative MP stood up to attack the national insurance increase. The Conservatives were put on the intellectual defensive and felt compelled to sign up to Labour's spending plans, a significant shift in the terms of trade between left and right.

Several European social democratic governments were thrown out of office in 2001 and 2002. Blair was convinced that this was because 'they had not modernised enough.'[154] For New Labour to avoid the same fate, the extra resources pouring into public services had to be accompanied by radical reform to bring them up to the promised 'world class' standard. 'It is reform or bust!' he cried in one typically hyperbolic speech.[155] One of the most Blairite members of the Cabinet put it this way: 'We have this huge majority. The Tories are nowhere. If we don't transform public services, there is no excuse for us.'[156]

Geoff Mulgan, the head of the Number 10 Strategy Unit, saw Blair 'impatient with the pace of reform'.[157] This was partly frustration with himself for not making a bolder, quicker start. 'The first few years were rather wasted,' says Sally Morgan, and it was only now that Blair acquired 'a clarity about the level of reform that was needed'.[158] Sir Michael Barber was in charge of a Delivery Unit tasked with driving through change.

The Prime Minister increasingly came to realise that you couldn't improve public services to the level that he and the public wanted simply by driving them from the centre through bureaucratic fiat. They could only be improved by offering choice to the users of the service and diversity among the providers. That's why he got into choice because then the patient or the parent is driving the service and it becomes self-sustaining.[159]

Blair explained himself to me that autumn: 'We will not maintain public services and the welfare state unless we radically recast them. Every great radical Labour government was in its time a change-maker, wasn't a preserver of the status quo.' The days of 'monolithic, one-size-fits-all services' were over. 'There's no way that you can have a 1948 national health service able to provide the quality of service that people want in today's world.'

If they failed to reform, 'people will say: "You've put all this money in, it hasn't delivered the change we wanted, so we'll go for the Tories", who will take the money out and chuck it into the private sector.'[160]

The choice and diversity agenda for public services put Blair on a collision course with a significant section of his party and with his Chancellor. 'The running sore was public sector reform,' says the Number 10 official Tom Kelly. 'Education, health, pensions, you name it. On any kind of reform, the first issue was: how do we square Gordon?'[161] The battleground in 2002 was the NHS. For Blair, what mattered most was what it delivered. For Brown, the health service was defined more by the people who worked in it. 'Deep in Gordon's psyche is the saving of his eyesight and deep gratitude to the NHS for that,' says Andrew Turnbull. 'He was much more committed to the NHS as an institution. Tony was more consumer-focused.'[162]

Brown's Budget speech pointedly did not mention the creation of new 'foundation hospitals' which Blair and his ally Alan Milburn saw as 'the battering ram' for reform of the health service.[163] Milburn, like many of the New Labourites, spent his early political career far to the left of where he ended up. He was brought up by a single mum on a council estate in a north-eastern mining town. It became his passionate preoccupation that Labour had for years let down the people it was supposed to be most dedicated to helping. Someone from his background, he would often say, could no longer hope to reach the Cabinet. His flashy suits and a swaggering hairstyle could make him seem less thoughtful than he was. For too long, Milburn believed, the benefits of choice had been enjoyed only by the middle classes. Public services expected the less affluent to simply put up with what they were given. He made the case in left-wing terms, arguing that 'in Britain we have allowed choice over schools or health provision to be the exclusive preserve of those who can pay directly.' The answer was to break with the 'overly centralised, paternalistic' model and allow 'choice and diversity of provision', as was the case in social democrat Scandinavia.[164]

The idea was to give much more autonomy to hospitals. 'If you're going to genuinely get what is needed, which is local public services to improve their performances, then they've got to own responsibility.'[165] They would also diversify the providers of services by extending the use of the voluntary sector and private companies. The theory was that freedom would encourage innovation, extend patient choice and pump up performance. Milburn envisaged the best hospitals being treated more like universities and enjoying a similar degree of control over their finances.

This aroused the implacable opposition of the much more statist Gordon Brown. The Chancellor attacked on all fronts. Elite hospitals threatened to create a 'two-tier' health service, he argued. He was not against the use of private capital, having been the progenitor of the Private Finance Initiative, but he had a traditional Treasury objection that giving hospitals financial autonomy would weaken the Chancellor's control over spending. What if a foundation hospital went bust? The Government would end up picking up the pieces. This was the weakest brick in Milburn's proposals so Brown kept smashing away at it. 'Gordon just dug his heels in,' says the Permanent Secretary at the Treasury, Andrew Turnbull.[166]

There was a temperamental aspect to this clash. 'Gordon is intrinsically more cautious,' observed a member of the Cabinet. 'Tony is more swashbuckling and flamboyant.'[167]

Brown also saw this battle as a means to make himself more popular within the Labour Party at Blair's expense. The Chancellor's opposition to the NHS reforms, says one of his own inner circle, 'allowed him to play to a constituency'.[168]

It was also a raw issue of control. 'Gordon wasn't necessarily against reform. He was against any reform proposed by Tony. It was about authorship as much as anything,' later reflected one senior New Labour figure.[169] Brown did not offer much by way of an alternative vision or theory of reform. He just knew what he didn't like. What he didn't like was anything coming from Blair. 'Gordon thought Tony was shallow,' observes one of the Treasury ministers of the time. 'By definition, any idea coming from Tony had to be reckless and unworkable because it was Tony's idea.'[170] Brown would tell his friends that 'Tony doesn't think more than an inch deep.'[171]

At a reception at Number 11 that summer, the Chancellor called his guests' attention to the portraits of Gladstone and Disraeli that they passed on their way up to the state room on the first floor. Such was the iron certainty of Gladstone, 'it was said that people left him thinking they had just been listening to the wisest person on earth.' Such was the dazzling charm of Disraeli, 'people left him thinking they were the wisest man on earth.'[172] With Brown, even the jokes were not to be taken lightly. He was implanting the notion that he was the deep and principled Gladstone and the smiler who lived next door was the shallow and convictionless Disraeli.

That July, the Chancellor presented a three-year spending settlement which he boasted was the most sustained investment in public services 'in a generation' and which Blair hailed as yet another 'defining moment'.

Behind the scenes, their struggle over the health service intensified. The battle stirred together a potent brew of personal antagonism, political ambition, ideological difference and technical argument. Both sides saw this as a high-stakes struggle for how the Government would address parallel reforms in education, housing and transport. Brown's aggression was spurred on by Ed Balls. In the words of one of the Chancellor's aides: 'Ed said ad nauseam to Gordon that he could not afford to lose this battle.'[173] On the account of members of the Brown camp, they took 'inflammatory actions to ramp it up', even going so far as to supply rebel Labour backbenchers with information which could be used to damage the Prime Minister and his flagship reform.[174]

Alan Milburn fought back. He was a 'take-no-prisoners type' – just like Brown himself.[175] The Health Secretary bragged to friends that he was adopting a 'flying fuck strategy' towards the Chancellor, as in 'I don't give a flying fuck what he thinks.'[176]

Though Blair urged him not to do battle with Brown in front of colleagues, the Health Secretary took on the Chancellor at Cabinet. Milburn said: 'If it is good enough to devolve power over the economy to the Bank of England, it is surely good enough to devolve power to independent hospitals.' Brown growled back, unable to see Alastair Campbell sitting behind him giving the thumbs up to Milburn. This was not because Campbell was interested in the policy, but because he enjoyed seeing one of the Cabinet sticking it to the Chancellor.[177] That summer Milburn placed an inflammatory piece in *The Times* which framed the conflict as a struggle between radical 'transformers' and reactionary 'consolidators'. Milburn was positioning himself as the leader of the bold 'transformers' and casting Brown as the backward 'consolidator'.

Brown was infuriated to be portrayed as a dinosaur. He raged to his circle: 'Fucking Mandelson is behind this!'[178] His deadly enemy was out of the Cabinet and it was almost universally assumed that he could never return. Yet to Brown 'Peter's hand was seen behind everything.' The Chancellor viewed Milburn 'as a puppet on Peter Mandelson's strings'.[179] This perception was not accurate, but it was highly illustrative of Brown's state of mind.

For months, he was in and out of Number 10 or yelling down the phone complaining that Mandelson was plotting and demanding a gag on Milburn. When Blair refused, Brown escalated the conflict. In September, on the eve of the Labour conference, the Chancellor produced a fifty-page document tearing into foundation hospitals and had it copied to the entire Cabinet. In the context of the Blair Government, this was an extraordinarily belligerent act. Though it had been common in previous Cabinets for papers to be circulated, it was virtually unheard of in this one. Brown was notorious in the civil service for not wanting to commit himself to paper. So Number 10 assumed that the document could only have been produced with the intent to leak it to the press in order to discredit the health reforms, damage the Prime Minister and destroy the Health Secretary.[180] Blair told his officials to ring round departmental private offices and order them not to show the paper to their ministers. Some Cabinet members had already got Brown's document. They were instructed to pretend that they had never received it. The battle between Blair and Brown had reached the surreal stage where the Prime Minister was secretly ordering the shredding of a document produced by his Chancellor.[181]

By the party conference, this battle was noisily unrestrained. In his speech on the Monday, Brown spoke of a historic rebuilding of the welfare state based on traditional Labour values. Ed Balls was explicit in briefings to journalists about the Treasury's dissent from the direction being pursued by the Prime Minister. In his riposte on the Tuesday, Blair told his party why radical reform was imperative. 'At our best when at our boldest' was the striking line from his speech.[182] One of Blair's aides confidently told me afterwards: 'We've dealt with all that Gordon bollocks that he's the lord of the domestic agenda.'[183] This turned out to be something of a feint. It was often the case with Blair that he sounded the bugle of advance most loudly when he was trying to cover a retreat. By now, not least because of the aggressive spin and counter-spin from the two sides, the row was all over the press. Blair was alarmed by that and increasingly diverted by the looming confrontation with Saddam Hussein. Milburn's position was undermined because the argument came to a head a fortnight after the collapse of Railtrack. This bolstered Brown's contention that the state would always end up bailing out nominally autonomous institutions that went broke. What would happen if a hospital went bust? 'Milburn hadn't got an answer,' says Andrew Turnbull. The Cabinet Secretary was brought in to draft a 'peace treaty'. Being a former Treasury man, Turnbull believed Brown to be 'intellectually right' about not allowing hospitals control of their borrowing.[184]

The Sunday after the conference, Milburn got a call from Blair. 'Oh God, this is out of control,' groaned the Prime Minister. 'We're going to have to reach a compromise.' The Health Secretary was angry: 'You must be fucking joking.' He knew he would look humiliated at the hands of Brown. Blair insisted they had to make concessions. 'Fine,' said Milburn. 'But understand you'll not get the full benefit of the reforms.'

The warring parties were brought together in Blair's den a few days later. John Prescott, a natural ally of Gordon Brown in this sort of argument, was slumped in an armchair, his belly cascading over his trousers. Blair, looking tense, sat in an upright chair. Brown and Milburn sat beside each other on the sofa, radiating mutual contempt.

'I know what this is fucking all about,' said Milburn who was convinced that Brown was politicking to hurt a rival and curry favour on the left. 'You know what it is fucking all about.'

Brown barked back: 'You shouldn't have fucking done what you did in the summer.'[185]

A compromise was eventually reached. Blair and Milburn won on the principle that the best performing hospitals should be given much more independence to manage their own affairs. Brown was not obstructive about the plan for a steady increase in the number of NHS operations being delivered by the private sector. But the Prime Minister caved in to his Chancellor on the crucial question of the central control of budgets.

'Alan was annihilated,' in the view of one sympathetic member of the Cabinet.[186] 'Gordon just dug his heels in and won,' observes Turnbull.[187]

Blair soon came to believe that this retreat was a mistake. He told Milburn so. 'Within a matter of months, it was a compromise that Tony regretted.'[188] The Prime Minister would kick himself for his weakness in front of Peter Mandelson, who says: 'He regretted not standing by Alan Milburn in seeing through those reforms. He shouldn't have retreated, he shouldn't have stepped back in the way that he felt forced to do.'[189] The message, damaging for the Prime Minister, was that colleagues could not rely on him to stand steady under fire in a hot battle with the Chancellor. For Blair's closest allies this was a much too typical example of him flinching in a power struggle with Brown.

Cherie continued to be a nagging voice in her husband's ear telling him to sack his mighty and predatory Chancellor. By now, though, even she was beginning to see that it was advice that he was never likely to follow.

'Her anger was an anger which knew it wasn't going to be satisfied,' says Barry Cox. 'She knew it wasn't going to happen.'[190]

Even as the umbilical cord between him and Gordon Brown throttled his premiership, Tony Blair did not feel psychologically or politically strong enough to sever it.

Moreover, he was increasingly preoccupied by the relationship with a different GB, one who was even more powerful than Gordon Brown.

5. Oath of Allegiance

'Look,' Tony Blair told his agitated Cabinet, 'I do want to assure you that the management has not lost its marbles.'

At the meeting around the coffin-shaped table in Number 10 on Thursday, 7 March 2002, there was a sudden eruption from his senior colleagues which caught the Prime Minister by surprise. It was not so much an outburst of dissent as a spasm of anxiety. Many ministers, and not just those Blair found habitually difficult, wanted to put down markers of their concern that they were being pulled towards a war in Iraq. David Blunkett, usually a reliable ally to the Prime Minister, went over the top first. The Home Secretary worried that a conflict would inflame tensions between Muslims and non-Muslims in Britain.

Robin Cook then went into action. He used some strong language about Saddam, calling the Iraqi tyrant 'a shit' and 'the only psychopath actually in government'. This was designed to get Cook a hearing for the point he really wanted to make. 'We cannot afford to be the only European Government supporting an American military venture,' said the Leader of the House.[1]

The Prime Minister grew restless. His chair was the only one with arms. He gripped them. It was an unusual and uncomfortable experience for a Cabinet discussion to run away from him. He tried to close them down 'but other people piled in'.[2]

Emboldened by this surprise outbreak of debate, several ministers voiced concerns about both the drift to war and the Israel–Palestine conflict. There was solid support for the Prime Minister only from Geoff Hoon, the Defence Secretary, and Charles Clarke, the party Chairman. Blunkett returned to the fray, demanding: 'What has changed that suddenly gives us the legal right to take military action that we didn't have a few months ago?'

Patricia Hewitt, the Trade and Industry Secretary, another minister who could usually be counted as a loyalist, wondered aloud why Blair was hugging so close to Bush when the Americans had just shafted Britain over steel tariffs. 'We are in danger of being seen close to President Bush, but without any influence over President Bush.'

The discussion lasted nearly an hour, a long debate in a Blair Cabinet. 'A momentous event,' Cook happily recorded in his diary. 'For the first time I can recall in five years, Tony was out on a limb.' Blair answered them with a passionate restatement of his conviction about Britain's strategic interests. 'I tell you that we must stand close to America. If we don't, we will lose our influence to shape what they do.' Then he sent the Cabinet away with the reassurance that nothing had been decided. 'We are not going to rush in.'[3]

Unknown to nearly everyone around the table, he had already commissioned an 'Iraq Options' paper from the Overseas and Defence Secretariat of the Cabinet Office. He received the paper just a day after that Cabinet meeting. The document outlined the military options 'for achieving regime change', the final one being 'a full-scale ground campaign'.[4]

Few of the Cabinet were on the distribution list for this paper. They were excluded from the crucial conclaves about Iraq and they knew it. But like anyone sentient, they could hear the drums of war being beaten in Washington.

George Bush served notice to the world, and did so in language that didn't need an expert codebreaker to decipher it, when he delivered the State of the Union address at the end of January. He now conceived and projected himself as a 'War President'. 'What we have found in Afghanistan confirms that, far from ending there, our war against terror is only beginning,' he told Congress.

He was further emboldened by the apparent ease of the Afghan campaign and his stratospheric popularity with the American public. In the immediate aftermath of the toppling of the Taliban, and despite the continuing failure to locate Osama bin Laden, Bush's approval ratings surged to over 80 per cent.

Having told Americans that 'our nation is at war', Bush went on to name North Korea, Iran and Iraq as America's most mortal enemies. In early drafts of the speech, they were described as an 'Axis of Hatred'. That became intensified to an 'Axis of Evil', the sort of biblical language that he liked and an echo of Ronald Reagan's condemnation of the Soviet Union as an 'Evil Empire'.[5]

'States like these, and their terrorist allies, constitute an axis of evil, arming to threaten the peace of the world. By seeking weapons of mass destruction, these regimes pose a grave and growing danger. They could provide these arms to terrorists, giving them the means to match their hatred,' declared Bush.

'I will not wait on events, while dangers gather. I will not stand by, as peril draws closer and closer. The United States of America will not permit the world's most dangerous regimes to threaten us with the world's most destructive weapons.'[6]

The blow to America's sense of security caused by 9/11 created a culture in which war seemed like a logical way to prevent further attacks. In the words of Jack Goldsmith, an official at the Department of Defense:

Fear of another attack permeated the administration. Everyone felt it. It led to the doctrine of pre-emption, which has many guises, but basically means that you can't wait for the usual amounts of information before acting on the threat because it may be too late. They were really scared. They were afraid of what they didn't know.[7]

Bush claimed the right to take pre-emptive military action against any country which the United States deemed to be a threat. 'It was that speech which made us all sit up and pay attention,' says Andrew Turnbull.[8] Before then, according to Michael Boyce, 'we were only getting hints that Iraq was in America's sights.'[9] It also made stark the price of sticking close to America. To stay in tandem with Bush, Blair would be asked to commit Britain to indefinite conflict in any theatre where the Americans might consider themselves to be menaced.

The bellicosity of Bush in the State of the Union was widely applauded in his own country, but the speech rang fire alarms in capitals around the world. The with-us-or-against-us test set by the President potentially placed in the column of America's enemies any country that merely differed with the United States about the appropriate policy response to terrorism. Chris Patten, the Tory European Commissioner, scorned Bush as 'simplistic'. The Foreign Minister of France shuddered that America had become the 'hyperpuissance'. The Foreign Minister of Germany complained that European countries were being treated as 'satellites'. Much of Europe saw America as a swaggering behemoth. Much of America dismissed Europe as an axis of appeasers. As the continents drifted further apart, Tony Blair would have to become ever more gymnastic to straddle the widening chasm.

He already knew that Bush was intent on going after Saddam, but he was taken aback that the American President should telegraph his intentions so obviously.

Well before 9/11, it was no secret that the Bush administration was deeply hostile to Saddam Hussein. 'He tried to kill my Dad,' the President had been heard to say in reference to a plot by Iraqi agents to assassinate George Bush senior on a visit to Kuwait. Dick Cheney, the Vice-President, had been party to the first George's decision not to drive on to Baghdad after the liberation of Kuwait in the first Gulf War. Regret about what they came to regard as an act of weakness fired their zeal.

'They wanted to do Saddam,' notes Sir Christopher Meyer, the British ambassador in Washington. 'Paul Wolfowitz was particularly obsessed. He'd been brewing this for ten years. They thought it had been a mistake in 1991 not to march on to Baghdad and topple Saddam.'[10]

Regime change in Iraq had been a public aim of American policy since October 1998, when Bill Clinton was in the White House. Congress voted for the Iraq Liberation Act, which explicitly gave US support to attempts to remove Saddam. Under Clinton, though, this indicated 'no intent of going in' because they did not see him 'as posing an imminent threat'.[11] Action was confined to trying to enforce the UN resolutions which declared limits on Saddam's military capability and demanded that he give up all attempts to equip himself with biological, chemical or nuclear weapons, the weapons of mass destruction short-handed as WMD.

Saddam repeatedly tested the allies' willingness to contain his regime. In December 1998, Clinton launched 'Operation Desert Fox', four days of punitive air strikes against targets suspected of being used in a continuing WMD programme. This was the first occasion in his premiership when Blair ordered British forces into military action. It was also the first time when he had a difference with the White House about how it should be conducted. Not then the hardened warrior he was to become, he argued with Clinton to postpone the bombing until after Ramadan. After a night thinking about it, he rang up Clinton's Defense Secretary, William Cohen, to say: 'We don't think it is necessarily prudent, but we're with you.' Cohen concluded that Blair 'was going to be with the United States, come hell or high water, he was going to be there'.[12] That pattern of behaviour was set very early on.

Desert Fox was a failure. The dictator shrugged off the four days of bombings. The inspectors left Iraq. The sanctions imposed by the UN hurt the Iraqi people more than they did the regime. Saddam achieved a sort of victory.

This was a sign of the chronic weakness of the West in the eyes of 'the Vulcans' who had become increasingly influential in foreign policy thinking in the Republican Party. They saw American interests and security being best served by a more muscular and unilateralist approach to the world, unencumbered by the anxieties of allies, unconstrained by the opinion of the UN and unrestrained to use the might of American power against her enemies. Gulliver would tear free of the bonds imposed by these Lilliputians at the UN and in Europe.

Among a significant sub-set of them known as 'the neo-cons' this was married to an idealistic belief that America had a moral imperative to try to remake the world, especially the Middle East. For too long, the US had prized 'stability' in the region over 'democracy'. That had meant allying themselves with tyrannies (as they once had with Iraq) or seeking to contain rogue states (as they had with Iraq since the Gulf War). The neo-cons argued that America had a mission to spread democracy and by force of arms where necessary. This would have the happy by-product, so they thought, of creating pro-Western governments in a region where so much of the world's oil reserves were concentrated.

The revolution they proposed had a name: 'The Project for the New American Century'. Several of the leading 'revolutionaries' now occupied key positions in the Bush administration. Their aims were crudely, but not inaccurately, summarised by one of their adherents:

If the United States overthrew Saddam Hussein next, it could create a reliable American ally in the potential super-power of the Arab world. With American troops so close, the Iranian people would be emboldened to rise against the mullahs. And as Iran and Iraq built moderate, representative pro-Western regimes, the pressure on the Saudis and other Arab states to liberalize and modernize would intensify.

It was a version of the domino theory. Once the dominos had fallen in the Middle East, so dreamed the neo-cons, the entire region would be under the sway of an even more hegemonic United States. 'An American-led overthrow of Saddam Hussein . . . would put America more wholly in charge of the region than any power since the Ottomans, or maybe the Romans.'[13]

Iraq had come up at the Colgate Summit before 9/11. 'If he hadn't raised it, I would have done,' Blair would say defiantly.[14] But Iraq had not been the predominant topic of that conversation; they'd spent more time talking about national missile defence.[15]

9/11 changed everything. For the neo-cons, 9/11 was both demonstration of the correctness of their diagnosis of the world and opportunity to apply their military remedy. 'The other idea was that the war would pay for itself because we'd have the oil fields.'[16] By November, the Pentagon had secret instructions to update its plans for a war on Saddam.

When Condoleezza Rice called a meeting in spring 2002 with several US senators to discuss diplomatic initiatives concerning Iraq, Bush poked his head in the room and said: 'Fuck Saddam. We're taking him out.'[17]

The debate in the White House was already evolving into one about invasion dates: spring or autumn 2003?

Knowing of this in the early months of 2002, Blair was trying to soften up his much more sceptical public opinion by cranking up the rhetoric about Iraq. 'That there is a threat from Saddam Hussein and the weapons of mass destruction that he has acquired is not in doubt at all,' he declared at a news conference after a Number 10 meeting with Vice-President Cheney.[18]

At the same time, Blair was telling the public, as he had his Cabinet, that 'no decisions have yet been taken' about how Saddam would be dealt with. He knew differently. The White House, with Cheney one of the greatest zealots for the enterprise, was rolling the pitch for war and Blair was already giving a strong indication to Bush that Britain wanted to be part of it.

One of his key linkmen with the White House was David Manning, the Prime Minister's senior adviser on foreign affairs, who had a good relationship with Condi Rice, the President's National Security Adviser. In mid-March, Manning flew to Washington for a frank face-to-face with Rice. He found that 'Condi's enthusiasm for regime change is undimmed' though she was now more appreciative of the difficulties of carrying international opinion behind the idea. He reported back to Blair:

We spent a long time at dinner on Iraq. It is clear that Bush is grateful for your support and has registered that you are getting flak. I said that you would not budge in your support for regime change but you had to manage a press, a Parliament and a public opinion that was very different than anything in the States. And you would not budge either in your insistence that, if we pursued regime change, it must be very carefully done and produce the right result. Failure was not an option.[19]

Manning was grey-haired, cerebral, softly spoken, self-effacing, bespectacled and much more cautious about this enterprise than his master. He made a contrast with the brasher, more thrusting figure of Sir Christopher Meyer, the ambassador in Washington who had a penchant for wearing red socks and vivid braces. They were both picking up the same intelligence about American intentions and relaying the message to the White House that Blair was an enthusiast for removing Saddam. A few days after Manning's encounter with Rice, Meyer met Paul Wolfowitz, the neo-con number two to Donald Rumsfeld. On Blair's behalf, Meyer stuck to the script:

We backed regime change, but the plan had to be clever and failure was not an option. It would be a tough sell for us domestically, and probably tougher elsewhere in Europe. The US could go it alone if it wanted to. But if it wanted to act with partners, there had to be a strategy for building support for military action against Saddam. I then went through the need to wrong-foot Saddam on the [weapons] inspectors and the UNSCRs [UN Security Council Resolutions] and the critical importance of the MEPP [Middle East Peace Process] as an integral part of the anti-Saddam strategy. If all this could be accomplished skilfully, we were fairly confident that a number of countries would come on board.[20]

Several striking things ring out from these memos, which were never intended to see the light of day for years to come, if ever. Blair made a general commitment to regime change, and told Bush so, a full year before the war started. His concern was not whether military action was the appropriate way to deal with Saddam. His central worry was that it be executed properly. 'Failure is not an option' is the phrase which leaps out from both memos. He hoped to lever some concessions out of Bush in return for British support, notably about putting more energy into the Middle East peace process. He was also concerned about how to handle domestic opposition. About the merit of having a war, he raised no objection at all.

Even some of his closest allies struggled to fathom exactly why Tony Blair committed himself to joining the invasion of Iraq. It became a caricature of his premiership, as pervasive as it was inaccurate, that he was 'Bush's poodle'. The truth about Tony Blair is that he was an enthusiastic accomplice in the project to remove Saddam from very early on. Because of the scale of the opposition to war, he had to advance crabwise, but he was always moving in that direction. He had his anxieties and reservations during the months that led up to the invasion, but at each turn he subordinated any apprehension to his desire to make Britain part of this enterprise. He would often feel the need to mask that objective to manage public opinion, but he never fundamentally wavered from it.

He did believe, at least at this stage, that Saddam was a menace with ambitions to acquire nuclear weaponry who couldn't be adequately contained by the sanctions regime and had successfully corrupted the oil-for-food programme run by the UN. David Manning found Blair worrying 'that Saddam – who had, after all, used chemical weapons – would increasingly break out of the containment box'.[21]

Blair was disturbed about Saddam back in 1998, within a year of taking office, when George Bush was still a little-known Governor of Texas. Blair confided his fears about the Iraqi dictator to Paddy Ashdown, who recorded him saying: 'I have now seen some of the stuff on this. It really is pretty scary. He is very close to some appalling weapons of mass destruction. I don't understand why the French and others don't understand this. We cannot let him get away with it.'[22]

Blair singled out Saddam for condemnation in his important speech on liberal interventionism in Chicago in 1999. He was increasingly influenced by the argument that the greatest menace to peace and security in the foreseeable future was not 'two big countries' going to war, but rogue states conniving to equip terrorist associates with chemical, biological and possibly even nuclear weaponry. 'The two coming together is the security threat of the twenty-first century,' he told me. 'We've got to root them out because they are incredibly dangerous, because they know no limits to the destruction they will cause.'[23]

He was heavily influenced by one of his advisers on foreign affairs, the diplomat Robert Cooper, who contended that there would be circumstances in which 'we need to revert to the rougher methods of an earlier era – force, pre-emptive attack, deception, whatever is necessary to deal with those who still live in the 19th century world of every state for itself.'[24]

Blair thought he could make a successful marriage of his liberal internationalism with Bush's aggressive pre-emption to implement a new doctrine of justifiable intervention which would make the world a better place and a less threatening one. General Mike Jackson, who commanded British forces in all of Blair's wars, notes how success in earlier conflicts influenced Blair's thinking about Iraq: 'It's easier, having done it once, to do it again.'[25]

Blair was also animated by sheer terror of an atrocity on British soil. He told me once: 'What changed for me post-9/11 was that you no longer wait for the thing to happen. You go out actively and try to stop it.'[26]

If a nuclear, biological or chemical attack on Britain occurred on his watch, he feared 'they'll be booing me in the streets in a decade that I was the appeaser. I was the Stanley Baldwin who did nothing.'[27] One instant product of this fear was new anti-terrorist laws, more draconian than measures passed anywhere else in the democratic world, which would put him on a collision course with liberal opinion and the judiciary.

Before 9/11, MI5 were principally focused on Irish republican terrorism. Sir Stephen Lander, the head of the security service, warned him: 'We're not talking about the IRA who wanted to go off and have a Guinness after they'd let off their bombs.'[28] Suicide bombers were a threat of a different order. About Islamist fundamentalism 'there wasn't a huge amount of intelligence,' says a senior adviser at the Home Office. 'There was complete ignorance about what we faced. We had no clue what might happen next. It was all the Rumsfeldian stuff about unknown unknowns. The more the security service delved into it, the more worrying it became.'[29]

A lot of extra funding was released to MI5 and MI6. 'Until 9/11, Blair had not been very interested in the intelligence agencies. It wasn't one of his priorities,' noted the Cabinet Secretary. 'After 9/11, they got what they wanted.'[30] A team at the Ministry of Defence compiled a secret dossier of every outrage that might be conceivably perpetrated by dedicated suicide killers. According to one of the committee's members: 'They dreamt up such lunatic scenarios that the JIC suppressed the document.'[31]

Blair would tell visitors to Number 10: 'If you could see some of the stuff that is put in front of me, the hairs would stand up on the back of your neck.'[32]

While it looked improbable that terrorists would manage to obtain a thermonuclear device, there was horror that they might get their hands on the 'poor man's nuclear bomb', a 'dirty bomb' which uses conventional explosive to spread radioactive fallout. He had been 'alarmed' by evidence that the Taliban and al-Qaeda had made 'primitive efforts' to construct a dirty bomb.[33]

'A bomb in central London – we're saying goodbye to a thousand years of British history,' Sir Stephen Lander said to Sir Richard Wilson. 'Oh God,' shuddered Wilson. 'Don't say that.'[34]

Blair became 'very disturbed' when he was briefed about the effects of a dirty bomb exploded in the middle of the capital.[35]

To amplify his nightmares, most of Britain's contingency planning to deal with a massive attack was a relic of the Cold War. 'The only planning was based on a war with the Soviet Union,' says Ken Livingstone, the Mayor of London.[36] David Blunkett and the Home Office were feverishly working from scratch to put in place measures to cope with a 9/11-style atrocity. According to Huw Evans, one of the Home Secretary's senior advisers: 'We were not remotely prepared for a large-scale incident on British soil.'[37]

Blair feared that he would be condemned, both by his contemporaries and by history, if such a horror occurred on his watch. 'I for one do not want it on my conscience that we knew of the threat, saw it coming and did nothing,' he said that autumn.[38] He later explained:

If all this evidence was there and something did happen and nothing had been done, what then would people have said? If you're the American President, and you lost 3,000 people in the attack on the World Trade Center, what are you expected to do? Sit there and just wait for the next one?[39]

Saddam Hussein, whom neither MI6 nor anyone else in the Government believed could be linked with 9/11, was not the most clear and present danger. Jack Straw argued with Blair that North Korea and Iran were more advanced in their nuclear ambitions, which would indeed turn out to be the case. But America's crosshairs were on Saddam. 'They had his zip code.' Blair bought into the idea that defanging the Iraqi dictator would send a strong deterrent message to other rogue regimes.

Blair's ambassador in Washington says: 'He was the neo-cons' neo-con. He was more neo-con than the Americans. This was not the poodle being pulled by the leash. This was a true believer in the threat of Saddam who had instinctive and immediate sympathy for what George Bush was planning to do.'[40]

He was also fired by a genuine revulsion at Saddam. 'Tony thought Saddam was an atrocious dictator, the Pol Pot of the Middle East,' says Sally Morgan, one of his most senior aides.[41] He could never fathom why so many on the left could not see a moral imperative to act against such a tyrant when opportunity presented itself. When protestors against war massed opposite Downing Street, he would react by asking: 'Why aren't they out there demonstrating against the junta in Burma? Where are the protests against North Korea?'[42]

An associated argument in his head was the belief that such regimes would be encouraged if Saddam was not made to pay for his repeated violations of UN resolutions. This meshed with his fears about America under Bush. To Cabinet allies like Tessa Jowell: 'He always said that you couldn't let America do something as major as this on its own.'[43] He knew that the President loathed most of the European leadership and despised the UN. Blair was frightened that Bush would entirely surrender to his unilateralist impulses and step outside the international order altogether. This played to Blair's conceit of himself as the one leader uniquely equipped to bridge the Atlantic. Bush liked to call himself 'The Decider'. Blair saw himself as 'The Explainer' – interpreting the world to Bush and speaking for Bush to the world.

'The thing that really turned him on about power was the opportunity to be on the world stage and to tackle situations and problems which had defeated everyone else,' notes Richard Wilson.[44]

There was another element of vanity. Blair was in thrall to the idea of the strong leader. He had recently consumed biographies of Winston Churchill, Oliver Cromwell, Charles de Gaulle and David Lloyd George.[45]

Layered with that was a conviction that it was strategically imperative to stay in lock step with America. Blair declared to the Commons, in one of his many bursts of passion on the issue, that the Special Relationship was 'an article of faith with me'. Yet he was also often reminded that Britons used the phrase 'Special Relationship' a lot more than you ever heard it in Washington. For all his talk about standing 'shoulder to shoulder', Britain's military capability didn't even come up to America's kneecaps. In private conversation, Blair would often refer to the staggering statistic that America was as militarily powerful as the next nine nations put together.[46] The US did not need allies in order to act. So what influence Britain did possess had to be maximised by staying close to the White House. Fatalism and hubris were both in the mix.

To all of which was added personal history. Leaders often have a defining success in their past which they seek to replicate in the future, whether or not the example is a good guide to action. The major conflict of his first term was Kosovo. He made himself very exposed during that war by issuing unambiguous demands that the West deal with Slobodan Milosevic while Bill Clinton talked in weaselling equivocations. 'He felt he was out on a limb and there was Clinton some way back sawing away.'[47] When that conflict seemed to be going horribly wrong, some wondered whether it might even cost him the premiership. 'It is shit or bust,' he would respond.[48] When the Serbs were thrown out of Kosovo, Blair's lonely stand during the conflict appeared absolutely vindicated and it increased his belief in the beneficient application of force against dictators. 'He felt that his determination, his sense of mission on that occasion had been vindicated,' notes the senior diplomat Sir Jeremy Greenstock. 'He had been the one who sustained the determination of the allies to see it through to the end. I think that increased his confidence as an international statesman that his judgement was good.'[49] Christopher Meyer agrees:

If I'd been Prime Minister and come out of that testing time, worrying time, and realised that I had been right and we had won, I would have thought: 'Hey, I can do this foreign policy stuff, I can do it.' It was his coming of age. You have to conclude that it must have been a huge boost to his self-confidence that he could handle a major international crisis and that he was right.[50]

The apotheosis was when he went to a refugee camp in Kosovo and was greeted as a saviour by people rushing up to him and crying: 'Tonee! Tonee!' One of his Cabinet thinks that was the moment he 'got some iron in his belly' and conceived of himself as a 'heroic' actor on the international stage.[51] 'Without Tony Blair, the likelihood is that we wouldn't have had that campaign,' says William Cohen, US Defense Secretary at the time. Blair was instrumental in dragging Clinton to a position where he didn't want to go.[52] In the eyes of Paddy Ashdown, it was 'one of the most remarkable achievements of any British Prime Minister in recent years'[53] to persuade an American President to commit to a position that many in his own administration vehemently opposed. The difficulties he had in doing that reinforced Blair's conviction that it was imperative to stay close to America; his eventual success magnified his belief that he could be a uniquely persuasive voice in the White House.

Idealism mixed with realpolitik, terror stirred with vanity, this was the cocktail of impulses that drew Tony Blair down the road to war.

*

In the first week of April, the Prime Minister flew to Texas for a crucial encounter with Bush at the President's ranch in Crawford. The *Sun* blared the approved Downing Street interpretation: 'Yet again Britain is punching above its weight – we may be a small country, but we are highly influential.'[54] The *International Herald Tribune*, in its more sober way, echoed that thought: 'A trans-Atlantic deal is possible and Blair is perhaps the only one who can persuade both [Europe and America] to sign on.'[55]

Blair's Foreign Secretary was far from convinced. Jack Straw didn't think the Prime Minister should be making the trip to Texas, fearing that he would be sucked even closer to Bush. Straw wrote him a letter just before he left. He warned: 'The rewards from your visit to Crawford will be few. The risks are high, both for you and the Government.' There was 'no majority' in the Labour Party for 'any military action against Iraq'. He cautioned Blair to beware 'potential elephant traps' and warned that 'regime change per se is no justification for military action.'[56] Manning and Meyer were both briefing the Prime Minister about the battle for the President's ear between the opposing factions in the American Government. Manning was gnawed by anxieties about the American planning. 'How difficult was this operation going to be? What would it be like on the ground? What would happen on the morning after? All these issues needed to be thrashed out. I didn't see evidence at that stage that these things had been thoroughly rehearsed and thought through.'[57]

The hawks were led by Dick Cheney, the most dominant Vice-President for decades. Lined up with Cheney was the erratic but also powerful Donald Rumsfeld. In the other corner was Colin Powell, the Secretary of State, a charismatic figure, popular and respected at home and abroad. Unlike any other senior figure in the administration, Powell had seen combat in the Vietnam War and was Chairman of the Joint Chiefs during the Gulf War. Cautious and internationally minded, Powell was not an enthusiast for war. If there was to be one, he was certain that the US needed allies. That made the position of Britain critical. Without British support for this enterprise, it was highly unlikely that America would find any other meaningful support. Bush was gravitating towards the hawkish pole, but he was still willing to listen to Powell's argument that they needed a coalition. 'Bush didn't want to do it on his own,' says Meyer.[58] William Cohen agrees: 'It was very helpful to have the British with us, it gave some credibility to the notion that we were not solo practitioners here.'[59] Blair's support after 9/11 had 'meant an enormous amount', according to Condi Rice. His willingness to be their global ambassador during the Afghan campaign 'was very important' and gave him more credit in the bank.[60] He had become 'the foreign leader with the greatest respect because Americans value someone who is an instinctive ally,' says Stan Greenberg.[61] The senior Democrat George Mitchell notes that he was 'extremely popular across the entire political spectrum'.[62] That gave Blair additional leverage if he chose to use it. That is precisely what the Prime Minister did not do.

As soon as they landed in Texas, Blair and his party were helicoptered to Bush's Prairie Chapel ranch. The British press boosterishly reported that Blair was being extended the 'ultimate honour' of a two-night stay.[63] Putin of Russia and Crown Prince Abdullah of Saudi Arabia got just the one night. Blair brought Cherie, his daughter Kathryn, and Cherie's mother, Gale, who was there to help care for Leo. On the Saturday night, they joined Bush and some of the President's personal friends for a dinner of pecan-smoked beef tenderloin and pineapple upside-down cake to the accompaniment of country music.

Once everyone was seated, Bush rose to toast his British guest. But Blair had gone missing. 'Where's the Prime Minister?' Laura Bush whispered to the British ambassador. 'He's gone to adjust his dress,' replied Meyer. Blair had arrived at the dinner to note with alarm that he was the only one wearing jeans rather than the 'smart casual' that was the style at Crawford. 'I have to change,' he told Cherie and dashed back to the guest house. He hadn't returned yet. 'Bushie, you'll have to sit down,' Laura said to her husband. When a breathless Prime Minister reappeared, Bush rose again to propose the toast.[64]

President and Prime Minister had several discussions that fateful weekend. Sometimes advisers were in attendance, but David Manning reports that 'a lot of the time there was no-one present other than the two of them', not even a note-taker.[65] 'There was quite a long time when Tony was alone with George. To this day, you can't be sure exactly what they said to each other,' says Christopher Meyer. 'But I am sure that this is where Blair said: "Whatever you decide to do, George, I'm with you."'[66]

This was his golden opportunity to impress his concerns upon Bush and get guarantees that they would be addressed. These were not to do with the morality of war: Blair had made up his mind about that. They were to do with the practicality of action, the need to sustain international support and the absolute necessity of having a proper plan for Iraq after Saddam had been toppled. This was his chance and he did not take it.

Blair was not at his brightest that weekend. Just before he flew out, the Queen Mother died and he had been wrangling with Gordon Brown over the Budget, always an emotionally draining experience. He went without sleep for twenty-three hours in advance of the talks and was visibly fatigued with jetlag.

Bush then exhausted him further by insisting that they go out for a run together, an activity at which the President was fitter than the Prime Minister. Blair groaned afterwards that he hadn't run so far since school.[67]

There was a more fundamental problem, which was about Blair's personality and how it interacted with that of Bush. Sally Morgan, one of his closest aides for many years, says: 'Tony found personal confrontation painfully difficult.'[68] Charles Guthrie agrees: 'He doesn't like to have a row.'[69] Blair rarely did confrontational and never with Bush. 'He operates by charming engagement, getting under people's defences,' says David Manning.[70]

At Crawford, Cherie pestered her husband to argue with Bush about American opposition to the International Criminal Court. 'Don't fuss woman,' he brushed her off. 'I've got important things to do.'[71] A very senior official adds another dimension: 'Remember Blair liked to be liked and Bush was the most powerful man in the world.'[72]

The Prime Minister went to Texas fearful that he would be dumped by Bush if he showed a scintilla of hesitation. To his confidant Michael Levy, Blair explained why he felt compelled to take this approach to Bush. 'You're either with him or against him. That's how he divides people. It is very black and white with Bush.'[73] According to Jonathan Powell, Blair believed 'he'd got to say he was with them to get Bush to listen to him.'[74] Tom Kelly, another of the officials in Texas, says: 'He didn't want to be seen as weak or vacillating. He did not want Bush to think he was backing away because that would lose Bush's trust, Bush would begin to doubt him and he'd lose the relationship.'[75] The result was that there was no proper expression of Britain's terms and conditions at Crawford.

'He never said to Bush, as Mrs Thatcher would have done, that this is not going to happen unless a, b and c happens,' says Meyer. 'He never said: "I can't do this unless we have absolute clarity about what is going to happen."'[76]

This failure to be clear on the details was also of a piece with Blair's personality. It was always Blair's belief, says Peter Mandelson, that 'the best way of persuading people was to look them in the eye, one on one. That was very much his style.'[77] According to Kelly: 'He put the weight on the emotional level of the meeting, the "looking into each other's eyes", not the analytical level. The analytical stuff could be left to David Manning. The emotional chemistry was his part.'[78]

Bush was a politician of some skill. This was rarely noticed by most people in Europe and wholly forgotten later when Bush became such a discredited figure. Yet it was true. Blair was once asked by a colleague: 'What do you see in Bush?' Blair responded: 'He's got charm and peasant cunning.'[79] This was a potent combination when allied with the most powerful office in the world. 'I think Bush genuinely liked Blair,' says Meyer. 'But he used Blair.'[80]

'Bush was a very artful politician,' agrees another senior official. 'Blair thought he was running the relationship, but he was being run.'[81] At Crawford and subsequently, Bush out-Blaired Blair. The Prime Minister thought he could ride the tiger; he ended up inside its stomach.

Among the other treats laid on for Blair at Crawford was an invitation to sit in on a CIA briefing and a drive in Bush's pick-up around the 1,600-acre ranch. The two men were alone for several hours. 'It sent Jonathan [Powell] and David [Manning] mad' because they could not be sure what Blair was signing up to in the absence of any advisers or officials. That was made worse by his reluctance to properly debrief them afterwards. 'He'd drive the foreign policy people nuts because he wouldn't give them a read-out.'[82] When asked by Manning and Powell what he had said to Bush, Blair would shrug: 'You know, I can't really remember.'[83] It was 'partly because he wanted to keep it tight and partly because he just couldn't be bothered'.[84]

From what they did manage to glean was composed a Cabinet Office summary of what was supposed to have been agreed in Texas: 'When the Prime Minister discussed Iraq with President Bush at Crawford in April he said that the UK would support military action to bring about regime change, provided that certain conditions were met: efforts had been made to construct a coalition/shape public opinion, the Israel–Palestine crisis was quiescent, and the options for action to eliminate Iraq's WMD through the UN weapons inspectors had been exhausted.'[85]

Some of the most senior officials at Crawford believe that the note makes Blair sound stronger than he actually was. 'I doubt the conditions were that forcefully expressed,' says David Manning. 'I doubt he even mentioned the UN at Crawford. I don't remember the UN coming up at Crawford. Even if the UN did come up, I doubt there was that much discussion. I don't think Blair was a huge enthusiast for the UN at this stage.'[86]

Sir Christopher Meyer agrees: 'The conditions were supposed to be laid out at Crawford by Tony Blair, but I don't think they ever were.'[87] The caveats were not all that substantial anyway. The Cabinet Office minute does not record him demanding that there should be adequate post-war planning in Iraq, nor that Britain should have influence in shaping it. It is not even mentioned, though it was already a big concern to the British. The conditions that Blair attached to his support for a war were essentially points about presentation. Blair did not demand full engagement by the Americans in the Middle East peace process as a condition of his support, merely that there was 'quiescence' in the conflict. Violence was at that point escalating after the Israeli Prime Minister, Ariel Sharon, ordered tanks into the West Bank in response to suicide bombings by Palestinians. Blair's top condition was that the Americans helped to mould public and international opinion in support of military action, a concern always much greater for him than it ever was for Bush.

Blair's weak qualifications on British support did not make an impact on the Americans, making it even more credible that he never really laid them down. 'I don't remember any quote conditions that were outlined at that meeting,' says Andrew Card, Bush's Chief of Staff.[88] Neither did Colin Powell: 'It was always a given that Blair would back us militarily, should it come to war in Iraq, so far as I was concerned. Right from the start. He didn't attach any conditions to that support. Or none that I recall anyway.'[89]

Richard Armitage, Powell's deputy at the State Department, later explained to the British ambassador the problem with 'your so-called conditions'. 'We've taken your support and buried your conditions.'[90]

At their joint news conference at the end of the Crawford Summit, President and Prime Minister stood together in a flag-decked school gymnasium. While Blair looked tired and uncomfortable, Bush was joshing, in control and more explicit than ever that he was dedicated to toppling Saddam Hussein. 'History has called us into action,' he declared, even making a joke of his lack of finesse. 'Maybe I should be a little less direct and a little more nuanced and say we support regime change.'[91] The media noted that Blair looked awkward at this point. Yet he was really no less explicit himself the next day when he visited the Texas A and M university to deliver a speech at George Bush senior's Presidential Library. This was a highly significant speech, but it was 'never properly reported at the time'.[92] A logistical foul-up by Number 10 meant that it was missed by most of the media travelling with Blair. This speech both endorsed the doctrine of pre-emptive action and effectively announced that Blair was backing regime change. He even paid tribute to himself as a regime-changer.

'I have been involved as British Prime Minister in three conflicts involving regime change. Milosevic. The Taliban. And Sierra Leone.' Milosevic had, in fact, fallen some time after the conclusion of the Kosovo conflict, though that defeat certainly weakened the Serbian dictator.

'Britain is immensely proud of the part our forces have played and with the results, but I can honestly say the people most pleased have been the people living under the regimes in question. Never forget: they are the true victims.

'We must be prepared to act where terrorism or weapons of mass destruction threaten us,' he contended. 'If necessary, the action should be military and again, if necessary and justified, it should involve regime change.'

He had shown the speech to Bush before he delivered it and the American was especially delighted with this paragraph: 'If the world makes the right choices now, at this time of destiny, we will get there. And Britain will be at America's side in doing it.'[93]

On other occasions, when he felt it necessary to make tactical retreats so that war did not look inevitable, Blair would stick to his more opaque lines that 'all the options are open' and 'no decisions have been made.' The truth was that he had sworn his oath of allegiance to Bush.

There were British officers seconded to the CENTCOM American military headquarters based at Tampa in Florida. In the early part of the year, the British were not allowed into the room where invasion plans were being drawn up because Admiral Boyce and other senior officers wanted to concentrate on Afghanistan. The American generals were told by their British counterparts: 'We were not up for it.' Shortly after Blair's commitment at Crawford, the British were admitted to 'the inner cell' at CENTCOM.[94] Mike Jackson, the head of the army, began to 'do a lot of planning, looking at what sort of force it might be in size, in shape, what will be the logistics . . . thinking about how we would generate the force' in the Easter of 2002. He says: 'Our assumption throughout was that if America decided to commit military forces to depose Saddam Hussein it was almost inevitable that British forces would be involved.'[95]

The Cabinet did not see any of this, but they could smell what was in the air. When Blair returned from Crawford, there was another outburst of apprehension around the table. Patricia Hewitt spoke up for the need to get UN support if it was not to be seen as 'unilateralist action'. Blair gave them another passionate declaration of his credo: 'I do believe in this country's relations with the US.' Yes, the UN was important but 'we should not tie ourselves down to doing nothing unless the UN authorised it.' When the question of whether a war would be legal was raised, Blair dismissed that as a problem that could be parked until much later. 'The time to debate the legal base for our action should be when we take that action.'[96]

In the weeks following the Crawford Summit, there was no evidence that Blair had reshaped Bush's approach to the world. The President heaped opprobrium on Yasser Arafat and the Palestinians but refused to apply any meaningful pressure on Ariel Sharon. Neither Blair nor Colin Powell could persuade Bush to lean on the Israelis to halt their military operations on the West Bank. Far from developing the UN route, it was the aggressive unilateralists in the administration who were growing more ascendant. Bush's speech at the US military academy at West Point in June suggested that he was now wholly in their camp.

Richard Haas, a senior State Department official, was in no doubt that by the summer of 2002 'the fuse had been lit, the United States, with Britain in tow, had set forth a set of demands which made war, if not inevitable, highly likely.'[97]

Blair's unswerving, uncritical dedication to the White House was alarming even some Americans. His own pollster, Stan Greenberg, was 'puzzled' by 'the very, very close relationship' between Blair and Bush.[98] Bill Clinton was getting worried. Though Clinton once advised Blair to stick close to Bush, he now feared Blair was taking that advice to extreme lengths. Clinton had a chance to voice his concern when he came over to Britain in early June for a 'progressive governance' conference held at a hotel in Buckinghamshire. At one closed session, the former President began to speak very negatively about the course being pursued by his successor in the White House. Blair shifted uncomfortably in his seat. He tried to catch Clinton's eye. When he did, the two men left the room for ten minutes. On their return, Clinton said no more about Bush in front of the others. Alone with the Prime Minister, he could be frank. Clinton was staying at Chequers. He used the opportunity to warn Blair: 'You're being used by Bush.' Blair told his old friend not to worry: 'I can handle it. I can handle Bush.'[99]

Some of the Prime Minister's most senior advisers and diplomats were not convinced. They increasingly feared that Blair had given away too much. From the Washington embassy, Christopher Meyer began to pepper Number 10 with calls and notes cautioning that the Americans thought they had Britain in their pocket. In the first week of July, Meyer wrote to Manning with the warning: 'We risk being taken for granted in Washington.' The White House now had 'an almost automatic assumption' that Britain was content to be sucked along 'in the American slipstream'. Meyer urged that Blair have a 'plain-speaking conversation' with Bush to nail down Britain's conditions.[100]

Towards the end of July, Blair did write a letter to Bush 'really making the case for going the international route' to deal with Saddam. Diplomats and officials who often despaired of Blair's weak negotiating with Bush when they were face to face thought he was better when he put his concerns in writing. 'Blair's crisp little notes were good pieces of work. Well written. Short sentences. He tended to be much more robust with Bush in his notes than he was in person.'[101]

Yet again, though, Blair had emphasised his 'yes' at the expense of the 'buts'. The July note began: 'You know George, whatever you decide to do, I'm with you.'

When Meyer learnt of it, he rang Manning in horror. 'It's a brilliant note except for this bloody opening sentence: "Whatever you do, I'm with you",'

THE END OF THE PARTY

the ambassador expostulated. 'Why in God's name has he said that again? He's handed Bush carte blanche.'

Manning sighed down the phone: 'We tried to stop him. We told him so, but he wouldn't listen. That's what he thinks.'[102]

The key British players gathered for a highly secret conclave at Number 10 on 23 July. John Scarlett summarised the latest intelligence assessment about Saddam. The Iraqi dictator was 'worried and expected an attack', but his regime was 'tough and based on extreme fear'. In Scarlett's assessment 'the only way to overthrow it [the regime] was likely to be by massive military action.'[103]

That was precisely what the Americans were intent on, according to a Cabinet Office briefing paper prepared for this meeting. That document was suffused with a fatalism that war was coming. It reported that 'US military planning unambiguously takes as its objective the removal of Saddam Hussein's regime' and that 'US . . . planning for action against Iraq is proceeding apace.'[104]

Admiral Boyce shared the intelligence he was getting from the British officers at CENTCOM. Boyce told the meeting that the Americans were 'coming on strong' for an invasion.

Geoff Hoon said that American forces already in the region were engaging in 'spikes of activity' to put pressure on Saddam. Sir Richard Dearlove, the head of MI6, gave a startling report on what he had learnt from a recent visit to Washington. 'Military action is now seen as inevitable,' said 'C'. 'Bush wanted to remove Saddam', which would be 'justified by the conjunction of terrorism and WMD', even though no-one had produced any evidence of a link between Saddam and 9/11. The intelligence and facts were being 'fixed' around the policy, the head of MI6 was minuted to have said after talking to his counterparts in the CIA. As for the concerns Blair presented to Bush at the Crawford Summit, and in phone conversations and memos since, Dearlove reported that there was 'no patience with the UN route, and no enthusiasm for publishing material on the Iraqi regime's record'.

'C' added ominously: 'There was little discussion in Washington of the aftermath after military action.'

Jack Straw agreed that it seemed 'clear that Bush had made up his mind' to go to war. 'But the case is thin,' warned the Foreign Secretary. 'Saddam is not threatening his neighbours, and his WMD capability is less than that of Libya, North Korea or Iran. The desire for regime change is not a legal base for military action.' The Foreign Secretary was 'discreetly' working up the idea of getting the United Nations to present an ultimatum to Saddam, but the White House was highly resistant.

This made it devastatingly obvious that Blair had sold himself too cheap at the Crawford Summit. For fear that he would alienate Bush by being too robust with the President, Blair underplayed his hand. He had sworn up to war without getting anything bankable in return and in the process undercut the saner voices around Bush.

The Prime Minister told that July meeting at Number 10 that the 'two key issues' were whether the Americans' 'military plan worked' and whether they could put together 'the political strategy to give the military plan the space to work'. Even so, the secret official note of this meeting, composed by Manning's deputy, Matthew Rycroft, records Blair saying: 'We should work on the assumption that the UK would take part in any military action.' Blair was confident that if he could get 'the political context right, people would support regime change'.[105]

Many months before the quest for a UN resolution and the elaborate games over weapons inspections, Tony Blair was already committed to following George Bush. The mission he now set himself was to persuade Britain to follow him.

6. Tell Me No Secrets

'I think I'm going to have to do it,' Tony Blair confided to Barry Cox. The Prime Minister and his old friend were having a long conversation about war in Iraq while on holiday together in the south of France in August 2002.

'Well, it's running away from you, the argument is running away from you,' cautioned Cox. 'The public, the party and the papers are clearly getting opposed to any intervention in Iraq.'

Blair nodded: 'Yes, I know that.'[1] Then he outlined his masterplan. Convinced as ever of his powers of persuasion, he still thought he could influence George Bush not to act unilaterally but to use the UN as the instrument to confront Saddam. As for the mounting opposition at home, he had a solution to that problem too. The result would be a dossier, conceived in a panic, drafted in a frenzy, published with hyperbole and resulting in the most calamitous consequences for his premiership.

Many of those close to him noted that Blair had stiffened over the summer. Alastair Campbell found 'TB a lot steelier than when he went on holiday. Clear that getting Saddam was the right thing to do.'[2] His new Cabinet Secretary, Sir Andrew Turnbull, took up the post in September and 'by the time I arrived it was clear that he'd made up his mind that if the Americans went to war, he would definitely be with them and his task was to create support for war.'[3]

To Cox, 'he certainly gave every appearance of having made the decision by the summer of 2002.'[4] Sir Stephen Wall, a senior adviser on foreign affairs, concluded that 'Tony Blair made his mind up in the middle of 2002 that he was going to go to war. He conducted the whole of the subsequent Cabinet meetings very skilfully, but on the basis that he was driving the policy and the others were acquiescing.'[5] Iain Duncan Smith, who was leading the Conservatives in support of confronting Saddam, went to Number 10 for a private briefing in September. Blair began the meeting by thanking the Tory leader for sending flowers to Cherie after her miscarriage. When they'd finished discussing Iraq, Duncan Smith came away with no doubt about Blair's intent. 'He'd decided this was a successful formula. He'd done Kosovo.

He'd done Afghanistan. It was what he believed in. He was of the mindset that good social democrats should not tolerate despotic foreign countries if they didn't have to. He wanted to do Saddam.'[6]

Admiral Michael Boyce 'started to put meat on the bones' of the planning for war.[7] But Blair asked the Chief of the Defence Staff 'to keep your thoughts to yourself' for fear that it would show too much of his hand.

While the Prime Minister was becoming more hawkish, his country was moving in the opposite direction. Opinion polls suggested that more and more voters were opposed to military action. The nerve endings of Labour MPs and Cabinet ministers were electric with anxiety about any rumour of war. When colleagues urged that there should be a recall of Parliament, Blair was initially resistant, not least because it would mean having to reconvene the Cabinet as well.[8] Neil Kinnock, the impeccably loyal former Labour leader and Blair's first political patron, expresses the mood in the party:

There was profound disagreement with and deep resentment against Tony Blair's association with George Bush. There was bafflement and anger about the nature of the relationship, and also about the fact that the loyalty and support appeared to be going in one direction. In raw terms, it was what the hell is a Labour Prime Minister doing in such proximity to, above all people, George Bush?[9]

Blair now had two imperatives: to move Bush into a more international- ist position and to persuade Britain to embrace the view that Saddam was a menace who had to be confronted. He had to sell war to the British and diplomacy to the Americans.

David Manning had crossed the Atlantic at the end of July to impress upon Condi Rice how essential it was for Blair that they went down the UN route. He told her plainly: 'We need this.'[10] The next morning, the National Secur- ity Adviser took Manning into the Oval Office so that he could deliver the plea direct to Bush. During August, Jack Straw made a dash across the Atlantic for a clandestine meeting with Colin Powell.[11] Both the US Secretary of State and his British counterpart were privately alarmed that their leaders were building an unstoppable momentum towards an invasion. The Cabinet Secretary 'knew the Foreign Secretary had doubts about it. Jack Straw and Colin Powell were going back and forth saying: "Oh Christ, what have our bosses got us into."'[12]

Both men feared their respective leaders were being much too blasé about the potential consequences of toppling Saddam, what Powell called the 'you broke it, you own it' problem that would confront them afterwards. Straw did not expect to be made Foreign Secretary in 2001 and had struggled to find a powerful voice. Though a highly experienced politician of considerable guile, he was frustrated by how much of foreign policy was being personally driven by Blair and his impulse at all times to cleave to Bush. 'Jack was under no illusions,' says his adviser Ed Owen. 'He knew that the crucial decisions are taken by the principals. That's the true fact, I'm afraid.'[13]

One senior Cabinet minister told me that autumn: 'I am not at all happy about this march to war and, whatever he says in public, neither is Jack.'[14]

Powell was becoming increasingly isolated and beleaguered as the hawks captured control of the President. 'What's going on?' Straw asked Powell during one phone conversation. 'I was hoping you could tell me what's going on,' replied Powell.[15]

Straw's August trip, made at Powell's suggestion, was 'very hush-hush'.[16] It was even concealed from the Washington embassy for a time. The Foreign Secretary, taking just one official with him, flew across by Concorde and was then helicoptered from JFK airport to Long Island, where Powell was vacationing with friends at a waterfront house in the Hamptons.[17]

The two men were effectively plotting against their leaders. Powell and Straw had tried to push Blair to be firmer with Bush about both using the UN to deal with Iraq and the Israel–Palestine crisis. They were repeatedly disappointed. Powell felt let down by the Prime Minister, whom he thought should be his natural ally against Dick Cheney, the Vice-President and hawk-in-chief. It was Powell's lament that 'Blair would express his concerns, but he would never lie down on the railroad tracks. Jack and I would get him all pumped up about an issue. And he'd be ready to say "Look here, George." But as soon as he saw the President he would lose all his steam.'[18]

Downing Street became reciprocally disillusioned with Powell. 'The difficulty was that Colin Powell didn't really have the traction on Bush that it would have been good to see a Secretary of State having,' notes Sir Michael Jay, the Permanent Secretary at the Foreign Office.[19] Tony Blair and his senior team were disdainful. 'Colin Powell would urge Jack Straw to urge us to make Powell's arguments to the White House. That's the wrong way round. That's not how it should be,' says Jonathan Powell.[20]

At the cloak-and-dagger meeting on Long Island, Powell briefed Straw about the arguments that had been raging between him and Cheney as they warred for Bush's ear at a series of meetings over August. He warned Straw that the Vice-President and the other hawks were 'hell-bent' on an invasion and had no intention of seeking sanction from the United Nations. Straw came with the message that 'the UN route was an essential prerequisite for British involvement', a stance designed to 'strengthen Powell's hand' in his own battles at the White House.[21]

The hawks now over-reached themselves. In late August, Cheney delivered a speech which radiated intent to invade Iraq come what may. He dripped contempt on the idea that the UN offered any solution to the disarmament of Saddam.

'A return of inspectors would provide no assurance whatsoever of his compliance with UN resolutions,' pronounced Cheney, taking his internal battles with Powell out into public. 'On the contrary, there is great danger that it would provide false comfort that Saddam was somehow "back in his box".' Making war sound inevitable, he pronounced that if US forces went into Iraq the streets of Baghdad and Basra would 'erupt in joy in the same way as the throngs in Kabul greeted the Americans'.[22]

This speech ignited cries of protest from around the world and howls of frustration within Downing Street. Blair would sigh in exasperation: 'The Americans are our closest allies and our most difficult friends.'[23] Cheney's clumsy intervention undermined Blair's propaganda strategy, which relied on depicting Saddam as the aggressor. Cheney was making it sound like it was the allies who were spoiling for a fight because the Bush administration wanted to work off a personal grudge. Even Bush, who could be more sensitive to international opinion than he often appeared, registered the global backlash against his Vice-President.

On 8 September, Blair flew in to the presidential retreat at Camp David. This would be a critical meeting decisive to the fate of Iraq. 'The heart of the administration' was waiting for him: Bush, Cheney and Rice.[24] As they talked, thousands of tons of American military hardware were already being dispatched to the Gulf. The service and intelligence personnel accompanying the Prime Minister were briefed on the status of the American invasion planning.[25]

Blair pressed vigorously, much harder than he had at Crawford, for using the United Nations as the instrument to confront Saddam with an ultimatum. Sitting in Bush's study in the big cabin, Blair said that he had to have this to show his party and voters back home that he had tried the UN. Condi Rice says the President listened because 'he knew that Tony Blair never asked for something unless it was absolutely necessary.'[26]

Blair argued that it would make a big difference, politically and legally, if Iraq refused a demand to readmit the inspectors. They would be able to say they had given Saddam 'a last chance'. Cheney always insisted on coming to these meetings 'because he was afraid Bush would give too much to Tony'.[27] The Vice-President sat there in ominous silence. 'He didn't say a word.'[28]

Bush, though, was now much more receptive to the case for using the UN. Influential Republican figures were speaking out, notably James Baker and Brent Scowcroft, respectively Secretary of State and National Security Adviser when Bush's father was President, and Henry Kissinger, the high priest of realpolitik.[29] Public opinion in the US was currently cooling about war. Other allies, such as the Australians and the Spaniards, were also sending the message that they could only support action if America went the UN route.[30] Blair was pushing at an opening door. Sir Christopher Meyer, one of those present at the discussion, says: 'I don't think Bush needed much persuading in the end.'[31] To Blair's great relief, the President swallowed his distaste for the UN and overruled his Vice-President. 'That was the only defeat Cheney suffered at the hands of the other camp.'[32]

The price Blair paid in return was to make his strongest commitment yet to joining an invasion. Bush remarked that it was very likely that they would end up going to war whatever happened at the UN. 'I'm with you,' Blair responded more emphatically than ever. He was ready to do 'whatever it takes'.[33] Afterwards, Bush walked into a nearby conference room where the leaders' entourages were waiting. Bush declared: 'Your man has got cojones.'[34] 'That's balls,' Meyer translated for those who didn't know their Spanish.[35] The President later joked that he would remember this as 'the cojones meeting'.[36]

With this presidential testimonial to the size of his testicles, Blair came away from Camp David believing he had secured a significant victory. Visibly stressed on the way out to America, he was so 'pumped up' on the flight back that he would not go to sleep; nor would he stop talking so no-one else got any rest either.[37]

On 11 September, a year to the day since the atrocities in New York and Washington, the White House faxed over to Number 10 a draft of the speech George Bush was planning to deliver to the United Nations the next day. The speech was searched with increasing palpitations for any mention of a new resolution being sought. There was none. 'We got in a bit of a state,' recalls Jonathan Powell.[38] David Manning rang Condi Rice to find out what was going on. 'What's the news? What's the news?' repeatedly demanded a frantic Blair. Rice rang back late that night to say: 'It will be in. I hope you're pleased.'[39] When Manning reported this to Blair the next morning, it relieved but did not entirely end the Prime Minister's anxiety. He and his senior aides clustered around the television to watch Bush at the UN, a President of unilateralist instinct addressing an institution most of his administration disdained.

The speech went on and still there was no reference to a resolution. They could not know why: the wrong draft of Bush's speech had been typed into the autocue, an earlier draft omitting anything about a resolution.

Realising that something was awry, Bush attempted to ad-lib it back in: 'We will work with the UN Security Council for the necessary resolutions.'[40] This caused some further confusion, because he was supposed to say 'resolution', singular, not 'resolutions', plural.

Blair, though, could sigh with relief. A fierce counter-attack by Cheney had been repulsed. Bush was going to act through the UN. For Robin Cook, Blair's severest critic in the Cabinet, this was the one occasion when there was solid evidence that the Prime Minister had influenced the White House.[41]

The unilateralist hawks in Washington had their beaks temporarily blunted. The Prime Minister could now focus his attention on dealing with his doves at home.

On Tuesday, 3 September, shortly before his trip to Camp David, he called a news conference in Sedgefield to ratchet up his case that confronting Saddam was 'the right thing to do', an early appearance of the phrase relentlessly repeated in the years to come. He announced that the government would imminently reveal why Iraq was 'a real and unique threat to the security of the region and the rest of the world'. This dossier would be published 'within weeks' and it would be based on intelligence.[42]

The idea of a dossier, designed to condition opinion in favour of action against Saddam, had been knocking around Number 10 for several months. The starting point, according to Campbell, was that Blair was 'impressed by the work the intelligence services did, and the way they did it. He was seeing a lot of intelligence which increased his basic concerns about Saddam. It is very hard for a Prime Minister to just push that aside and say it does not matter or it is all likely to be wrong.'[43] One dossier had already been published, to very little contention, laying out the sins of the Taliban and the crimes of al-Qaeda in the run-up to the campaign in Afghanistan. That set the precedent for using intelligence material to sell war.

The initial plan was to publish a dossier about Saddam in March, but Blair drew back then because the material was weak, the Americans were not enthusiastic and it would 'ramp up' controversy about Blair's intentions at a time when he was 'trying to calm it down'.[44]

Now his imperatives were reversed. The private polling and focus groups done for him by his soothsayers of public opinion gave the same message as the published polls. A big majority of the country were against war. As Stan Greenberg, who did that polling for him, says: 'He knew the public was not with him on going into Iraq. He was convinced that he had to stand with the United States and knew he had to bring the country with him if he was going to persuade the Labour Party and the Commons to support him.'[45]

Blair and Campbell believed that 'secret intelligence' had a magical, hypnotising power that might convince sceptical voters and Labour MPs of the case for acting against Saddam. One very senior official notes: 'They always had a hankering to use intelligence going back to Kosovo. They thought it was one of the best ways of convincing people that things were true.'[46]

After declaring his intention to publish the dossier, the Prime Minister conferred with his aides in the garden at Myrobella, his Victorian villa in the constituency. He explained what they needed to Campbell and Tom Kelly, one of the Director of Communications' lieutenants. The West had tolerated Saddam's existence for many years and other rogue states were arguably more threatening. So the dossier had to answer two questions: 'Why Iraq? Why now?'[47]

The true answer was well put by Jack Straw in one of his many confidential notes to Blair. 'If 11 September had not happened, it is doubtful that the US would now be considering military action against Iraq,' wrote Straw some months previously. 'Objectively, the threat from Iraq has not worsened as a result of 11 September.' What had really changed was American 'tolerance' for Saddam 'the world having witnessed . . . just what evil people can these days perpetrate'.[48]

In international law that wasn't a foundation for launching war. An amalgam of impulses was driving Blair, but he ended up resting his case almost exclusively on the claim that Saddam possessed and was threatening to acquire more weapons of mass destruction. This was partly because the Americans wound up in a similar place. It was one of the few points around which there was some consensus in the divided and dysfunctional administration. As Paul Wolfowitz subsequently admitted: 'The Bush administration focused on alleged weapons of mass destruction as the primary justification for toppling Saddam Hussein by force because it was politically convenient . . . because it was the one reason everyone could agree on.'[49]

For Blair, it was also the only *casus belli* that might provide legal, diplomatic and political cover. The Attorney-General, Peter Goldsmith, was clear with Blair that regime change – toppling Saddam on the basis that it was a good thing to rid the world of a very nasty dictator – was not a legal basis for war. Jack Straw further warned him that 'regime change per se is no justification for military action'.[50] While the Americans thought Saddam's violations of previous UN resolutions gave them enough legal cause, Goldsmith told Blair he couldn't advise the same. In the end, Blair's case became a mix of the moral case, the violations case and the menace case. In his public rhetoric he would shift the emphasis from one leg of the argument to another, depending on the exigencies of the moment, but for most of the time he placed the greatest weight on the alleged threat posed by Saddam.

On 5 September and again on the 9th, Alastair Campbell chaired meetings with John Scarlett and other intelligence officials. Campbell's chairmanship of these conclaves, the second being a full gathering of the Joint Intelligence Committee, was hugely revealing about the hierarchy of power within Downing Street. Campbell, the director of spin, sat in a superior seat to Scarlett, the intelligence chief. This was the quintessential example of how pre-eminent propagandists had become in New Labour and how willingly many senior officials deferred to them. Previous generations of intelligence chiefs would have been utterly contemptuous and incredulous if it were suggested that they should be at the beck and call of a spin doctor, however grandiosely he was titled. Campbell was a former tabloid journalist with no experience whatsoever of intelligence and how to handle the dry, contingent and often speculative material that was generated by agents and analysts. Yet it was Campbell who pronounced that the current draft of the dossier was not good enough, e-mailing Jonathan Powell that it needed a 'substantial rewrite . . . as per TB's discussion'.[51] The spinner told the spooks what was expected of them. 'It had to be revelatory and we needed to show that it was new.'[52]

The trouble was that there was very little fresh and revelatory intelligence about Saddam. Clausewitz, the great Prussian military strategist, identified the problem over a century earlier: 'Much of the intelligence that we receive in war is contradictory, even more of it is plain wrong, and most of it is fairly dubious.'[53] For all the developments in intelligence gathering since the nineteenth century, it remained a foggy science in the twenty-first, especially when agents were attempting to penetrate a country as closed and controlled as Iraq.

The JIC's secret assessment in March admitted that intelligence was 'sporadic and patchy. Iraq is well practised in the art of deception, such as concealment and exaggeration.'[54]

Stalinist in both its brutality and control, Saddam's regime was an intelligence black hole. Iraq was 'such a difficult country to penetrate' that the 'intelligence base' was 'fragile', says Robin Butler, the independent peer and former Cabinet Secretary who chaired the inquiry which Blair was later forced to set up.

'The intelligence community warned the Prime Minister that, though they concluded that Saddam Hussein had weapons of mass destruction and was trying to develop more, their intelligence base for this conclusion was very weak. That was explicitly explained to the politicians, but it wasn't the impression that the public had.'[55]

Another confidential assessment by the Cabinet Office's Overseas and Defence Secretariat was also bluntly candid that 'our intelligence is poor.' The paper noted this was a problem because they would need 'incontrovertible proof' to convince the world of the need for military action.[56]

In fact, the intelligence was worse than poor: much of it was seriously misleading or totally false. One source relied on was an agent with the suggestive codename 'Curveball'. This source's material was passed on from the BND, the German intelligence service. They refused to let SIS talk to him.[57] Had they done so they might have discovered just how unreliable he was. The Germans had shared with the CIA their suspicions that 'Curveball' was a mentally unstable drunk and a fabricator.[58]

The subsequent inquiry into the use of intelligence revealed that the sources relied on by MI6 were 'few' and there was 'serious doubt' about 'a high proportion' of them. 'Untried agents' were given 'more credence' than normal because of 'the scarcity of sources and the urgent requirement for intelligence'. One main source was often 'passing on gossip'. A second, who had provided a lot of material on chemical and biological weapons, was untrustworthy. The reports of a third were so discredited that they were officially withdrawn by SIS. Only two MI6 sources were judged to be 'reliable' and these were the two whose 'reports were less worrying' about Saddam's capabilities.[59]

When the material was presented to the Joint Intelligence Committee, Sir Stephen Lander, the head of MI5, made some 'snippy comments' about how thin it seemed. But neither he nor anyone else on the JIC really probed its quality, not knowing how useless it truly was and not thinking it was their job to second-guess Sir Richard Dearlove and MI6.[60] Reflecting later, some senior members of the intelligence committee concluded: 'We let the PM down.'[61]

The urge to make 'poor intelligence', which was in fact worse than poor, look like 'incontrovertible proof' lay at the heart of everything that was rotten about the dossier. It was even mooted that one of Campbell's family practice of spin doctors should take direct charge of the exercise. John Williams, the Director of Public and Press Affairs at the Foreign Office, put himself up for the job. Williams, like Campbell, was a former Political Editor of the *Daily Mirror*. He offered to take full-time responsibility for writing the dossier.

That raised a protest from John Scarlett. The chairman of the JIC argued that he should have titular charge of the operation. Blair and Campbell saw that it would suit them better to let Scarlett have 'ownership'. The dossier would appear more authentic if it could be presented as the work of intelligence officials rather than spin doctors. Blair wanted to be able to present it as coming from 'an objective source' because, in his own words, 'it was important to make sure that no-one could question the intelligence that was in it as coming from the genuine intelligence agencies.'[62] Campbell happily noted that his 'mate' Scarlett and 'the SIS guys' were anyway being 'really helpful'.[63] Scarlett and Dearlove were not politicians, but they had not got to such senior positions in the intelligence bureaucracy without possessing acute political radar. 'They are a service,' notes another member of the JIC. 'They'd made their careers by building their organisations into organisations that are needed by government and deliver what government wants.'[64] As well as more specific pressures to deliver, there was a general psychological one. The intelligence agencies had been delivering all these warnings to Blair over many years; they and even more so their cousins in America were facing enormous criticism over the failure to anticipate 9/11; none of them wanted to be accused of underestimating dangers ever again; now they were expected to produce the goods so the politicians could make the case to the public for doing something about it. On top of that, Blair was a powerful, charming and charismatic Prime Minister with their careers in his hands.

'They never reined him in,' observes one very senior member of the diplomatic corps. 'Dearlove and Scarlett find themselves sitting on the sofa next to Tony in his den, day after day. I think they became intoxicated by their proximity to power.'[65]

A senior figure in intelligence also saw that 'they enjoyed being intimate with this Prime Minister who is taking them very seriously.'[66] Iain Duncan Smith, who led the Tories into enthusiastic support for the war, believes: 'They crossed the line.'[67]

A very senior Whitehall official agrees: 'There was a breakdown in process. The more hot and urgent a situation is, the more important it is that there is a cool body of people assessing the evidence in a rational way. That didn't happen.'[68]

Elements of the intelligence services would later brief that they had always been unhappy about the way in which the dossier was put together and only co-operated through gritted teeth. Yet to Number 10 staff 'they did not give the impression of being dragged along kicking and screaming.'[69] Senior civil servants and diplomats observed plenty of enthusiasm for the exercise on the JIC and at the top of SIS. 'Dearlove, Scarlett and all their guys were really gung-ho for war. They believed there were WMD. They wanted the war.' One influential figure was the SIS bureau chief in Washington, who was very committed to 'doing Saddam'.[70]

The careful Butler inquiry would later suggest that Scarlett was too vulnerable to pressure. That report concluded that they saw 'a strong case' for the chairman of the JIC to be 'someone with experience of dealing with ministers in a very senior role, and who is demonstrably beyond influence, and thus probably in his last post'.[71] In fact, Blair would later reward Scarlett for his services with a knighthood and promote him to head of MI6.

When all the flaws in the dossier were later exposed, Scarlett would take the bigger hit. Yet some very senior figures in Whitehall concluded that this was unjust. 'John has taken more of the flak reputationally. That's unfair. Richard [Dearlove] was more responsible for distorting the process.'[72] In the months after 9/11, Dearlove and Blair had been thrown together as no head of MI6 and Prime Minister had been before.

'They bonded as a result of 9/11. They became very close friends,' remarks another senior mandarin who was friends with the head of MI6.[73]

Sally Morgan, one of the Prime Minister's closest aides, thought the seduction flowed both ways. 'Tony was beguiled by rich people, by military people and by intelligence people. He loved these smooth, urbane, Oxbridge types. There was also running through it a lot of smug British "we're better at this stuff than the Americans".'[74]

One senior civil servant says: 'Whether Richard recruited Blair or Blair recruited Richard, it is hard to say.'[75]

Dearlove was not as he seemed. 'He looks like a clumsy bear. But Richard is really a pirate, he's a buccaneer.' During the frenzied construction of the dossier, the head of MI6 personally delivered to the Prime Minister 'hot' items of intelligence. 'I think he must regret that: taking intelligence direct to the Prime Minister.'[76]

'It was not just Blair's fault,' says one member of the JIC. 'Everyone forgot that intelligence is not fact.'[77]

Over the summer, the weak March text of the dossier was redrafted to depict Saddam as a much graver threat. On 10 September, Scarlett circulated the latest version, including for the first time a claim that the Iraqi dictator had the ability to deploy weapons of mass destruction within forty-five minutes. This was sourced to a 'senior Iraqi officer via a trusted Iraqi agent of MI6'.

The consumers in Number 10 were still not satisfied.

Every senior spin doctor in Downing Street, none of whom had any experience of handling delicate intelligence material and none of whom had a clue about its quality, was invited to throw in their opinions. Phil Bassett, a former industrial relations correspondent who was now a political adviser, e-mailed Campbell that 'it needs to be written more in officialese, lots of it is too journalistic as it now stands . . . reading like *STimes* [*Sunday Times*] at its worst. Crucially, though, it's intelligence-lite.'[78] Godric Smith, a career civil servant with no intelligence experience whatsoever, complained: 'I think there's material here we can work with but it is a bit of a muddle and needs a lot more clarity in the guts of it in terms of what is new/old.'[79]

Tom Kelly, a former BBC journalist, wrote to Campbell suggesting that the dossier was not strong enough on a nuclear threat. 'The weakness, obviously, is our inability to say he could pull the nuclear trigger anytime soon.'[80] Reflecting later, Kelly agrees: 'It got totally ridiculous, the number of people weighing in.'[81]

Campbell liked to joke that things were always done in such a panicked rush inside Number 10 that it should be renamed 'lastminute.com'.

There was a lot of the last minute about the way the dossier was pulled together. 'It was a very tense time,' says Robert Hill, another Blair aide. 'Everyone was working under huge pressure.'[82] The 11th, two days after Campbell had taken the chair at the JIC, was a crucial day in the process. One of the intelligence officials issued a frantic appeal to his colleagues for yet more material as if they might find something that had slipped to the bottom of the filing cabinet: 'This is therefore a last! call for any items of intelligence that agencies think can and should be included.'[83]

In the view of Tom Kelly, it was:

a fundamental mistake to start talking up the dossier with the media before it was completed. That created an expectation that the dossier was going to be a defining moment, that this was going to be a biggy. It created a public expectation that then fed back into the system and fuelled the feeling that we had to come up with the goods.[84]

Pressure was directly applied to Scarlett to think about stripping the dossier of qualifications about the intelligence. Desmond Bowen, the head of the Cabinet Office's Overseas and Defence Secretariat, and one of the cast of the meetings chaired by Campbell, sent an e-mail direct to Scarlett, copying in Campbell, Powell and Manning. The message read:

In looking at the WMD sections, you will clearly want to be as firm and authoritative as you can be. You will clearly need to judge the extent to which you need to hedge your judgements with, for example, 'it is almost certain' and similar caveats.

I appreciate that this can increase the authenticity of the document in terms of it being a proper assessment, but that needs to be weighed against the use that will be made by the opponents of action who will add up the judgements on which we do not have absolute clarity.[85]

An early draft said that Iraq 'would not be able to produce a nuclear weapon' while sanctions remained effective. Even if sanctions were lifted, it would take 'at least five years'. The final document contained the much more blood-chilling line: 'Iraq could produce a nuclear weapon in between one and two years.'

There was internal dissent from some intelligence officials and Iraq experts. One dissenter was Brian Jones, the most senior expert on chemical weapons at the Defence Intelligence Staff. He complained to his superior that the dossier was exaggerating the threat only to be told that there was 'one secret piece of information that could not be shared with him' because it was too hot.[86]

Other intelligence officials complained about 'iffy drafting', protested that elements of the dossier were 'likely to mislead' and exchanged exasperated e-mails that no-one would heed their pleas to moderate its language. One official mocked the claim that Saddam had scientists capable of producing a nuclear weapon. 'Dr Frankenstein, I presume?'[87]

These protests were ignored. By this stage of his premiership, Blair was very impatient of dissent. According to Andrew Turnbull, Blair was 'less and less interested in hearing contrary opinions. He didn't like having people throw grit into the machine.'[88]

In the frenzied September days leading up to the dossier's publication, it was intensively reworked, each edit hardening up the claims within it. Among Blair's staff, the two greatest influences on the shaping of the dossier were Alastair Campbell and Jonathan Powell. Campbell 'never gave the impression that he was enthusiastic' for war in Iraq to other senior staff at Number 10.[89] But he swallowed his apprehensions and threw himself into the dossier with typical obsessiveness because he was 'captivated by it as a project'.[90]

Powell had first been recruited to Blair's team while he was a diplomat at the embassy in Washington. Curly-headed, fast-talking and clever, he was a fervent Atlanticist and the aide who most embraced Blair's belief in pre-emptive intervention and the conviction that they had to stick with the United States no matter what. He was the one 'true believer, the only one who was really gung-ho' next to the Prime Minister.[91]

Previous generations of politicians had learnt to handle intelligence material with scepticism. Geoffrey Howe, a Conservative Foreign Secretary, observed: 'In my early days, I was naive enough to get excited about intelligence reports. Many look, at first sight, to be important and significant and then when we check them they are not even straws in the wind. They are cornflakes in the wind.'

Another Foreign Secretary, Douglas Hurd, remarked: 'There is nothing particularly truthful about a report simply because it is a secret one.'[92]

'Intelligence is not an exact science,' notes Charles Guthrie, whose long military career included being commandant of the intelligence corps. 'You tend subconsciously or consciously to select the intelligence which suits you.'[93]

Which is precisely what Blair did. He was never going to be minded to probe the intelligence with any hard questions about its reliability because he wanted to believe the worst about Saddam. He had already arrived at a conclusion about Iraq and was working backwards from there to try to make a case for confronting its dictator. His senior aide, Sir Stephen Wall, says: 'He didn't ask a lot of crucial questions about the extent of Saddam's nuclear capacity, for example. Partly because he didn't want to ask the questions.'[94]

That was compounded by a failure by all the institutions of the British state which are supposed to ensure quality control. The two big departments – the Ministry of Defence and the Foreign Office – were almost entirely excluded from this process. The Defence Secretary, Geoff Hoon, did not even see the dossier until very shortly before publication.[95] The Cabinet Secretary was 'invisible'.[96] Turnbull, mindful of how previous holders of his post had been damaged by embroilments with security matters, did a deal with Blair which handed over that part of his responsibilities to a new security co-ordinator. Most of the Cabinet were beguiled by what they were shown when they were sent in small groups for private briefings by Dearlove and Scarlett. The way the intelligence was presented, 'there was nothing speculative about it,' says Tessa Jowell.[97]

The intelligence services were not coolly and disinterestedly sifting through their thin material and then making their best estimate of Iraq's capabilities and intentions. They were scrambling under intense pressure to come up with material to support a pre-cooked conclusion that Saddam was a growing menace.

Under the weight of pressure to deliver what the Prime Minister wanted, the integrity of the system was disastrously compromised. Boundaries were trampled, lines of responsibility blurred, objectivity lost in the frantic drive to make a case against Saddam.

One of the frighteners in the dossier was the assertion that Iraq had tried to get the raw material for a nuclear weapon by buying uranium from Niger in Africa. The CIA didn't believe this claim, which originated with documents that were later exposed as forgeries.[98] That didn't stop the bogus claim going into the dossier. Nor did it deter George Bush from repeating it the following January in his State of the Union address.

On 17 September, Saddam Hussein blinked in the face of the growing threat from America and declared that Iraq would allow the UN weapons inspectors to return without any preconditions. One of the motives for publishing a dossier – to put pressure on Saddam by mobilising international opinion around the issue of WMD – was now gone. That still left another reason: Blair's desperate need to rally his own MPs and British public opinion to his point of view. So Saddam's retreat did not end the process. Rather, the redrafting of the dossier went on at an even more frenetic pace.

Paradoxically, given what would later happen, the fear in Number 10 at this stage was not that they would be accused of fabricating a case for war. Their worry was that the media would see the dossier as 'a rather damp squib'.[99]

That was underlined when the pro-war Tory leader was called in to be given a confidential briefing by John Scarlett. Iain Duncan Smith expected to be presented with a 'bang, wallop' case. He was surprised when he read through the draft presented to him. 'There's no great, big smoking gun here, is there?' Duncan Smith said to Scarlett. 'No, I suppose not. That's not the nature of intelligence,' said the chairman of JIC, who protested that he nevertheless thought that 'some of it is compelling.'[100]

Powell was also underwhelmed by the latest drafts, not finding in them a sufficiently strong footing for military action. On 17 September, he pinged off an e-mail to Scarlett with his concerns:

First the document does nothing to demonstrate a threat, let alone an imminent threat from Saddam. It shows he has the means but it does not demonstrate that he has the motive to attack his neighbours let alone the west. We will need to make it clear in launching the document that we do not claim that we have evidence that he is an imminent threat. The case we are making is that he had continued to develop WMD since 1998, and is in breach of UN resolutions. The international community has to enforce those resolutions if the UN is to be taken seriously.[101]

The next draft was produced forty-eight hours later, and the wording had been considerably altered, the changes taking the text in a direction designed to suggest that Saddam was more of a menace. The most striking inflation during the process was about Saddam's ability to use WMD. An early text said: 'Iraq has probably dispersed its special weapons, including its CBW [chemical and biological weapons]. Intelligence also indicates that chemical and biological munitions could be with military units and ready for firing within 20 to 45 minutes.'

The qualifications 'indicates' and 'could be' had gone by the time the dossier was published. They were transformed into the much harder claim: 'Iraqi military are able to deploy these weapons within 45 minutes of a decision to do so.'[102]

Dr David Kelly, the Ministry of Defence's top expert on weapons of mass destruction and an inspector who had been on tours to Iraq on more than thirty occasions, found that claim 'risible'. Though a supporter of action against Saddam, he dissented from the dossier. To a close friend, he 'just laughed' about the impossibility of arming and firing a WMD warhead within forty-five minutes.[103]

Some in MI6 were queasy about the exercise. They knew they had very little that was solid or new to say about Iraq. They were also mindful that their sister agency MI5 had been damaged in the past by being sucked into political controversy. 'C' did send a 'rigorous response' to a memo sent to Scarlett by Campbell trying to further beef up the alleged threat from Iraqi nuclear ambitions. On Dearlove's later account, MI6 insisted that it should 'stick to original intelligence'.[104] Sir Richard otherwise took the view that he could live with the dossier and what the politicians did with it was not his responsibility. Scarlett's professional conscience was satisfied because he did not accept every linguistic alteration pressed on him. But in its final drafting stages Campbell nevertheless sought and secured no fewer than fourteen changes to the wording of the dossier, each one toughening its language.[105]

They were obsessed with how it would play in the media. Five days before its release, Powell asked Campbell: 'Alastair – what will be the headline in the Standard on day of publication?' He added prosaically: 'It needs checking for typos.'[106]

When the final draft was submitted it had the title: 'Iraq's Programme of Weapons of Mass Destruction: The Assessment of the British Government'. On his account, it was Scarlett's own pen that went through the word 'programme' before it was finally published on 24 September.[107] It had a much more certain ring when entitled 'Iraq's Weapons of Mass Destruction: The Assessment of the British Government'.

To add to the drama of the dossier's publication, Parliament was recalled. On the eve of the recall, the Cabinet convened on Monday, 23 September, the first time it had met in more than eight weeks. Blair had already corralled the big beasts behind him in advance of the meeting. Gordon Brown made a brief intervention which stressed the importance of the United Nations and declared the threat of WMD to be 'the best argument'. Afterwards, Alastair Campbell went up to him and said: 'Thanks for that intervention.' Jack Straw, currently believing that he had successfully impaled Blair on the commitment to work through the UN, did not air any of his private anxieties. Blair ignored a suggestion from Patricia Hewitt that the Attorney-General should come to Cabinet to explain the legal position on war.[108]

Only Robin Cook and Clare Short were openly critical about the prospect of military action. It became a prevalent myth that the Cabinet never talked about Iraq in the run-up to the war. In fact, it was a topic at more than twenty of their meetings in 2002 and early 2003.[109] There was plenty of quantity about their discussions; the real flaw was the lack of quality. Much of the time at most of those meetings was dominated by updates on the latest situation from Blair, punctuated with occasional outbursts of anxiety from worried ministers, which were then parried by expressions of support from the loyalists. What the Cabinet never had was a deep debate about the diplomatic and military options with all the facts in front of them.[110] Papers were prepared for Cabinet, but Blair declined to circulate them to his ministers.[111] There never was an agreed Cabinet strategy; they were sucked along in Blair's slipstream. The general view of the Cabinet was: 'We'll hang on to Tony's ankles and he'll hang on to Bush's and we might get through this without blowing the world apart.'[112] On this occasion in late September 2002, ministers eagerly saluted the Prime Minister for securing Bush's agreement to use the UN. Cook was keeping a diary for later publication. In it he lamented that this Cabinet was 'a grim meeting. Much of the two hours was taken up with a succession of loyalty oaths for Tony's line.'[113] He did not record in his diary that even the dissident Cook gushed to Blair: 'Tony, you've played a blinder.' Sycophancy from that source was too much for John Reid, the pugnaciously loyal Northern Ireland Secretary. He acidly remarked that he wanted to join everyone else's admiration for the Prime Minister, but 'the one thing I'm not going to say is that you played a blinder. It would be especially inappropriate when I am sitting next to David [Blunkett].' Nearly everyone, except Cook, chortled at the joke. John Prescott came in at the end. 'We must all stick together behind Tony,' he lectured them and no-one was to breathe a word of their discussions to the press.[114]

The doubters around his own top table made it even more important to Blair that he sounded evangelically certain when he presented the fifty-page dossier to the House of Commons the next day.

The document bore his signature on the chilling foreword: 'I am in no doubt that the threat is serious and current, that he has made progress on weapons of mass destruction, and that he has to be stopped.'

He highlighted the claim that 'the document discloses that his military planning allows for some of the WMD to be ready within forty five minutes of an order to use them.'[115]

The false claim that Iraq could use WMD within forty-five minutes of receiving an order from Saddam was seen as such a potent persuader that it was repeated no fewer than four times in the dossier.

Blair did not reveal to MPs that intelligence officials, WMD experts and even his own staff had privately expressed the view that the material did not show that Saddam was any sort of imminent threat.

Laying the dossier before the Commons, he declared: 'His weapons of mass destruction programme is active, detailed and growing. The policy of containment is not working. The weapons of mass destruction programme is not shut down, it is up and running.' He amplified: 'That means biological, chemical, nuclear weapons capability.'

He presented Saddam as 'a current and serious threat' even though he had been minuted just a week before by his Chief of Staff that they had 'nothing to demonstrate a threat, let alone an imminent threat from Saddam'.

Blair drew attention to the claim that Iraq would 'only be a year or two' away from having nukes 'if Saddam were able to purchase fissile material illegally'. When he declared his 'passionate' belief in the alliance with the United States as 'fundamental' to Britain there was a throaty roar of approval from Conservative MPs.[116] On his own benches behind him, there was a lot of silence. The number of rebels was, though, contained to fifty-six.

The dossier did have some effect in shaping public opinion and minimising dissent. Clare Short reckons it helped to feed a feeling in Labour's ranks that 'Tony must know something we don't.'[117] Jack Straw regards the dossier as 'very, very important in terms of making the argument'.[118] An opponent of war, the former Cabinet minister Frank Dobson believes: 'A few were convinced and more were looking for a reason to be convinced.'[119]

Those deeply sceptical about the case for military action remained unimpressed. Robin Cook was 'surprised there was so little new material in it' and saw 'no new evidence . . . of a dramatic increase in threat requiring urgent invasion'.[120]

Media reaction depended on who was doing the reacting. Newspapers who wanted to be chilled by the dossier turned it into apocalyptic headlines.

The *Times* pleased Number 10 by shivering its readers with the thought that 'Saddam could have nuclear bomb in year'.[121] Its Murdoch-owned tabloid sister, the *Sun*, curdled the blood by shouting: 'He's got them. Let's get him.'[122]

Much of the media got excited by the claim that Saddam could deploy WMD within forty-five minutes, that being one of the apparently genuinely new pieces of information. Journalists got the impression that this meant Saddam could launch WMD on ballistic missiles with sufficient range to hit Cyprus. '45 minutes to attack' was how the *Evening Standard* alarmed Londoners.[123]

The Defence Secretary understood that these were not ballistic missiles. 'I asked. I knew.'[124] Yet no-one corrected this false presentation of the alleged threat. It was only when Scarlett was questioned nearly a year later at the Hutton Inquiry that it emerged that this was only meant to refer to the use of WMD as a battlefield weapon. In other words, Iraq was only equipped to use them if invaded, not to rain WMD down on its neighbours. Even that claim would anyway prove to be false.

The intelligence chiefs had succumbed to the frenzied and insidious pressure from the Prime Minister and his senior staff to deliver the goods. The propagandist Campbell supervised the spinning of thin, dated and flaky material to make the threat look real, new and urgent. The lawyer Blair then further buried all the caveats and uncertainties to present the dossier with his trademark evangelical certainty. Then pro-war elements of the media inflated the claims into the scariest headlines they could contrive.

Within a year of publication, it became apparent that the majority of the claims in the dossier, especially the most frightening ones, were distortions, exaggerations or downright false. The source of the infamously wrong claim that WMD could be launched in forty-five minutes was exposed as an Iraqi brigadier in Baghdad who did 'not know very much about it': a single, uncorroborated source who was passing on hearsay from another single, uncorroborated source.[125] That claim became so infamous that it was even satirised in an episode of *Dr Who*.

Far from bristling with WMD, prior to the war Iraq 'did not have significant – if any – stocks of chemical or biological weapons in a state fit for deployment, or developed plans for using them', concluded the later inquiry.[126] Opinion about Tony Blair then divided into two schools of thought. One very popular view was that the Prime Minister had lied his way into the war. As countless banners, placards, T-shirts and web posts had it, he was the 'Bliar'. Even some who were originally supporters of the war came to the conclusion that they were manipulated by a mendacious Prime Minister.

Another view, held by the minority who still defended him, was that spin was a legitimate response to an aggressive media and Blair had done no more than any leader does when fighting for a cause.[127]

Blair did not take Britain into war on a lie in the sense that he knew all along that Saddam had no weapons of mass destruction and hoped no-one would hold him to account for that afterwards. He genuinely believed that the Iraqi dictator was intent on possessing the most horrific weapons and the Prime Minister was sincerely seized by a fear of the consequences of rogue states combining with terrorist actors.

It should also be added that he was far from alone in that belief. All of the world's leading intelligence agencies, including the French and Russians, believed that Saddam had at least some WMD and a capability to manufacture more.

Sir Michael Boyce, the Chief of the Defence Staff, asked to see the CXs, the raw intelligence material. He came away certain that Saddam had WMD. 'If the head of MI6 tells you this is good stuff, you take it at face value.'[128]

Blair's culpability was in vastly exaggerating the accuracy and potency of unreliable and often bogus intelligence by calling it 'extensive and detailed' when that was the opposite of the truth. 'More weight was put on it than the intelligence was strong enough to bear' is the careful conclusion of Robin Butler, who, being a mandarin, is constitutionally incapable of directly calling Blair mendacious. 'The interpretation was stretched to the limit.'[129]

And beyond it. Blair was a sincere deceiver. He told the truth about what he believed; he lied about the strength of the evidence for that belief.

It was unprecedented for intelligence to be used for propaganda and the discrediting of the dossier did damage without parallel. This episode corroded the credibility of the intelligence services. More than any other single document published in the last fifty years, it shredded public trust in politicians in general and Number 10 in particular. When its claims were exposed as false, a train of events was set in motion which would escalate into the greatest crisis of Tony Blair's premiership.

'I've lost my love of popularity for its own sake,' the Prime Minister told his party conference when he addressed them in the faded baroque of Blackpool's Winter Gardens on the first day of October.[130] That was fortunate since his popularity was decaying anyway.

A third of the emergency resolutions tabled were about Iraq and they were almost unanimously hostile to war. Yet the conference did not prove quite as turbulent as the media predicted and Number 10 feared. Gordon Brown, who complained to ministers close to him that he was being 'excluded' by Blair and felt 'weakened and marginalised',[131] delivered an unthreatening speech. There was not an eruption of protest when Blair told the conference that 'sometimes in dealing with a dictator, the only chance of peace is readiness for war.'[132] Some doubters and dissenters were temporarily muted by the argument that the best way to avoid war was to threaten Saddam with enough force to make him buckle. A motion opposed to war in any circumstances was defeated. In a warning shot to Blair, the conference passed a motion which said that there would have to be explicit sanction from the United Nations for any military action.

Blair was also bolstered by a guest appearance in Blackpool by Bill Clinton. His star quality had the Labour conference swooning in their seats. 'I feel like I've just been made love to,' one male minister sighed as the conference ovated for the former President.[133] Clinton masked his own reservations about where Blair was headed and praised the Prime Minister as the only leader capable of bridging the divide between America and the rest of the world. 'If he weren't there to do this, I doubt if anyone else could.'[134]

Clinton was saying something entirely different in private. His side of the Atlantic, Democrats were bewildered. The former President asked Campbell: 'Why is Blair helping Bush so much?'[135]

Blair was not just marching his own country down the road to invasion. Blair put a high-minded tone on the drive to war in ways that Bush never could and his support helped Bush to answer the criticism that it was a rash unilateral adventure. That thrilled the American neo-cons while disturbing their opponents.[136]

George Mitchell, the former Democratic Senator who was a peace envoy in both Northern Ireland and the Middle East, thought it 'pretty obvious what President Bush got out of the relationship with Prime Minister Blair: a world figure who is articulate, who better explained Bush's policies in the Middle East than he or anybody in his administration was able to do'.[137]

William Cohen, a Republican who served in the Clinton Cabinet, agrees: 'The strength of his conviction bolstered President Bush because of Blair's enormous popularity here. That gave great credibility to the President's advocacy and sure made it more difficult for people to raise their hand and question the wisdom of it.'[138]

That October, and by thumping majorities, Congress gave Bush the broad authorisation to declare a war as and when he saw fit.

7. Trouble and Strife

Nearly two years had passed since Peter Mandelson's second ejection from the Cabinet, but he remained one of the most famous faces in Britain. He took one of the anonymous back entrances into Number 10 that winter's day so his arrival would be invisible to the media mob camped on Downing Street. Once he had slipped inside the Georgian house, he went up to the flat, where he found Tony and Cherie in a desperately bad way. They needed the old svengali's counsel about the worst personal crisis to engulf them since they moved into Number 10.

Mandelson was a veteran of the inferno: he had twice been engulfed by scandal during the first term. 'It's a personal tragedy for Peter,' the Prime Minister remarked to another party leader after the second sacking. 'But he's finished now.'[1]

As it turned out, Peter Mandelson was not quite finished and neither was Blair's reliance on him in a crisis. The Prime Minister needed Mandelson again. Mandelson needed to be needed.

In December 2002, the Blairs were being consumed by 'Cheriegate', the appellation that the media were giving to the affair of the Prime Minister, his wife and a con man.

The root of it, as so often with New Labour, was money. Both of the Blairs liked money, a preoccupation that could be traced back to the insecurities of their childhoods. Tony's family was never destitute, but they were forced to fall back on the generosity of friends during his adolescence when his father was debilitated by a stroke.

Cherie lost her father in a different way. Tony Booth was an actor, a drunk and a philanderer. He became such a mess that on one occasion he set himself alight while in an alcoholic haze. Cherie was largely cared for by her grandparents during the first two years of her life and then deserted by her father. She was scarred by 'my sense of abandonment'.[2] As a scholarship girl from a poor background, she was acutely conscious at secondary school that she came from 'the wrong side of the tracks'.[3] She was a clever woman with many achievements to her credit, but one still haunted by those childhood insecurities.

The more vicious press painted Cherie as entirely money-grubbing. That was a caricature of a complex woman who did a lot of unpaid work for charities, which was largely unsung in the media but appreciated by those whom she helped. The media gorged on an incident in Australia when she was invited to take some free gifts from a shop and helped herself to a lot. The press duly chortled over the spectacle of the Prime Minister's wife on a 'supermarket sweep'.

At conference time, Cherie would return from tours of the exhibition halls laden with bags of the promotional gifts that are given out by the exhibitors. These freebies were never exotic: pens, mouse mats, T-shirts, soft toys, sweets. They were hardly valuable. Yet piles of the bags would litter the Blairs' conference hotel suite, much to the amusement of his aides. One female member of the Prime Minister's court jokingly referred to Cherie as 'a kleptomaniac'.[4]

There was another media feast about her love of money in 2004, when she took a substantial fee for taking part in a fund-raising roadshow for the Children's Cancer Institute of Australia. Even Cherie could see that 'proved disastrous from a PR point of view'.[5]

The Blairs' attitude towards money sparked friction with officialdom. Cherie took the view that she had to spend a lot on her clothing and hair-dressing because she was under constant scrutiny as the Prime Minister's wife.[6] On her reckoning, she ought to have a budget and the taxpayer should reimburse some of the cost. 'These were not small sums,' says one senior official.[7]. It fell to Sir Richard Wilson, the Cabinet Secretary, to tell her that this couldn't be done. She also repeatedly clashed with Sir Richard about how much the Blairs could spend on furnishings at Number 10. That was the cause of many 'icy conversations'.[8]

She 'resented it madly' when Sir Richard vetoed billing the taxpayer for clothes and hairdressing.[9] The Cabinet Secretary found it painfully awkward that he had to repeatedly reject expenses claims by the Prime Minister's wife. 'She didn't like him saying no. Tony didn't like him saying no.'[10] Wilson tried to devolve the responsibility on to other officials, but that didn't work. 'It always comes back to me again,' he would groan to fellow officials.[11]

One day, Sir Richard was taking a group of visitors around Number 10. Cherie materialised. 'Who are these people, Sir Richard?' she demanded. The Cabinet Secretary explained that they were from his village in Bucking-hamshire.

Cherie glinted: 'I hope they've noticed the state of the carpet, Sir Richard.' She turned to the group: 'Look at the state of the carpet! Ask Sir Richard about the state of the carpet!'[12]

Her view was that the spouses of foreign leaders, ambassadors' wives and the Queen's ladies-in-waiting were given financial assistance to help them dress well for official duties. But she got no further with this argument when Sir Richard was succeeded as Cabinet Secretary by Sir Andrew Turnbull.

Another of Cherie's frustrations was that she was never allowed to enjoy the sort of high-profile and quasi-official role taken by her friend Hillary Clinton. Barry Cox, close friend of the Blairs, says: 'She hated being told by the Number 10 machine what she should and shouldn't do.'[13] Officials were happiest if she was rarely seen and never heard. Fiona Millar, Alastair Campbell's partner, took over managing Cherie's public profile. This superficially cosy arrangement was a mistake because it made the internal workings of Number 10 less professional and more soap-operatic. 'Relationships are so complicated when you've got two couples working that closely together,' observes Jonathan Powell. 'Your parallelogram goes wonky.'[14] Campbell himself now acknowledges that 'when the personal and the political collide it is not a healthy place to be.'[15] Fiona sought to prevent Cherie from writing a book about the previous first ladies of Downing Street for fear that she'd be accused of taking advantage of her position.

The book writing was an attempt by Cherie to deal with the feelings of loss of identity and privacy that were the result of her position. She lamented that 'a political wife . . . is disenfranchised' because 'you cannot afford to express any separate views' or 'be seen to have any power'.[16]

She was understandably upset when even her most personal and harrowing experiences were subordinated to the obsession with the media which consumed her husband and Campbell. In August 2002, she suffered a miscarriage. Before he had even seen his distraught wife, Blair phoned up with Campbell also on the line for a conference call so they could discuss how they would handle the media. 'I couldn't believe it,' she complained. 'There I was, bleeding, and they were talking about what was going to be the line to the press.'[17]

She never formed a comfortable bond with any of the female aides closest to her husband. Her relationship with Anji Hunter was 'diabolical' and 'disastrous'.[18] The flirtatious Hunter first met Blair when they were rebellious teenagers at school in Scotland. It was often rumoured, but always denied by both of them, that they had been lovers in their youth. One of Hunter's roles was to give emotional succour to Blair when he was down. This was hard for Cherie: the constant and intimate presence of a woman who had known her husband for longer than his wife. 'She'd go up to the flat and find Anji on the sofa talking to Tony and it made her mad.'[19] There was a colossal row between the Prime Minister and his wife in his den when he kept Hunter on at Downing Street after the 2001 election. When Hunter changed her mind about staying and left later in the year, Cherie walked around with a huge smile on her face.[20]

Sally Morgan returned to Number 10 to assume the role of Blair's most influential female aide. She was a much more self-effacing figure than either Hunter or Campbell and yet Morgan outlasted both of them. After a stint as a primary school teacher, she had worked for the Labour Party since her mid-twenties. She was utterly loyal, tough in a matter-of-fact way, highly astute and fiercely protective of Blair and his image. Her relations with Cherie were also complicated by the damage done by the money issue. 'We all hated the freebies and all that,' says Morgan. 'When we tried to raise it with Tony, he just didn't want to do anything about it. He didn't want the row, the confrontations with Cherie.'[21]

Truth be told, he was interested in money himself. 'He was just a bit better at concealing it,' observes a senior official.[22]

Both the Blairs liked to spend. 'Their children had designer clothing. Not just any old designer clothing, the top-of-the-line stuff.'[23] They both enjoyed expensive travel to exotic climes and Michelin-starred food. They looked enviously at those who could effortlessly afford the finest things in life.

Blair made a revealing aside during a Davos summit where the wealthy, the famous and the powerful annually cluster in the Swiss Alps. Blair found himself seated between Bono, the stupendously loaded rock star, and Bill Gates, the billionaire computer software magnate. Contemplating his neighbours, Blair groaned out loud that he had chosen 'the wrong career'.

This was not the first time, and nor would it be the last, that the super-rich provoked him into expressions of awe and jealousy. In private conversation, the Prime Minister would often wistfully dwell on the wealth of his university contemporaries.[24] Sometimes he would even express this in public, telling one interviewer: 'It's amazing how many of my friends I was in school and university with, they ended up so rich. There's a mate of mine I ran into the other day – we used to run discos together and things – now he's worth millions.'[25] He sometimes seemed to dream of another life in which he was a stonkingly rich actor, rock star or entrepreneur.

The Prime Minister was very affluent compared with most of those whom he ruled. Moreover, he could look forward to making huge sums in his post-prime ministerial life from bank boards, the international lecture circuit and memoir-writing. In retirement, he would join the lower leagues of the super-rich himself.[26] As Prime Minister, he felt impecunious when in the company of the billionocracy. I once asked one of his intimates what lay at the root of the Blairs' blind spot over money. 'They spend too much time in the company of very rich people,' she replied bluntly.[27]

Their desire to live the life of the super-rich was most obviously expressed in their choice of grand holidays, which invariably generated mockery in the press, especially if there was a flavour of the freebie about them. Paddy Ashdown, in many other respects an admirer, was scornful of Blair's penchant for 'surrounding himself with human bling'.[28]

Sir Cliff Richard was wholesome enough as a holiday host. The Bee Gees were harmless. Silvio Berlusconi was not.

Blair's aides often wished that they could persuade him to take holidays which were more like those of the average voter. The Prime Minister, usually so well attuned to Middle Britain, was defiant about his holidays. 'We, as his advisers, would much rather that he'd taken holidays at Center Parcs,' says Matthew Taylor. 'But you can understand. He worked incredibly hard, he needed a proper break, if you do a job like that, if you're under that sort of pressure, aren't you entitled to have a holiday somewhere where you're not constantly besieged by people stopping you and arguing with you?'[29]

His sojourns with the rich and sometimes infamous did not make Blair happier. He would return from breaks in wealthy men's villas to moan to his intimates about how it made him feel poor. Here he was, someone with all the responsibilities of leading a G8 nation, and yet he had little money compared with these billionaire businessmen and rock stars. The aides who were exposed to this whingeing had a declining tolerance for it, not least because they, like most people, had to pay in full for their holidays. Braver members of his staff like Sally Morgan would respond to these outbursts of self-pity by reminding the Prime Minister that he was better off than most Britons and had gone into politics for public service, not to get rich enough to buy Caribbean hideaways, Tuscan villas and super-yachts.[30]

The New Labour period coincided with and helped to fashion an era in which the super-rich increased in both their visibility and influence. The billionocracy rarely had any great allegiance to either ideology or country. A new class of big money held many politicians in their thrall, not least those leading New Labour.

Blair was given a first warning about dangerous entanglements with wealthy men during the Ecclestone Affair early in his first term. He ought never to have exposed himself again to the charge that donations could be traded for favours.[31] That red flag went unheeded and he continued to be reckless with his reputation when it came to fund-raising. In February

2002, there was another sleaze eruption when it was revealed that Blair had written a letter to the Prime Minister of Romania in support of a bid by LNM to take over the Romanian state steel company. LNM was owned by Lakshmi Mittal, who had given £125,000 to Labour for the 2001 campaign and would donate greater sums for the 2005 campaign. Small change to that billionaire created an enormous stink for the Government. Blair subsequently insisted that he did not know that the tycoon was a donor even though they had mingled at a party organised by his fund-raiser.

There were respects in which this saga was worse than the Ecclestone Affair. At least when the Formula One boss got his exemption from a ban on tobacco advertising, he could muster an argument that it might jeopardise the jobs of British workers in a high-tech industry. Lakshmi Mittal was not British. Nor was his business. Contrary to Downing Street's initial protestations, the company was registered in a tax haven in the Dutch Antilles and barely a thousandth of its workforce was employed in the UK.

The accusation of opponents and the press that favours had been bought by a steel tycoon would not have had such traction had they not seemed to fit a pattern of behaviour established from Ecclestone onwards.

Part of the problem was psychological: Blair was brilliant at persuading himself that he was a man of sparkling integrity whatever the evidence to the contrary. The nobility of his ends, as he saw them, blinded him to how others might see his means as squalid.

Challenged about the Mittal donation at Prime Minister's Questions, he blustered away that it was all 'garbagegate'.[32]

He railed at the Tories that he would take no criticism from them when two of their number had gone to jail.[33] What a falling off that was from the ideal he had once expressed to 'restore faith in public life'. He was now reduced to defending his Government on the basis that at least none of its members had yet been sent to prison.

Downing Street was so repetitively hit by sleaze stories that Godric Smith, one of the Number 10 spokesmen, would wearily sigh that it was 'groundhog day' when another one burst into the headlines. Even Peter Mandelson acknowledged that the Government was damaged by 'the appearance that has been created of an overly cosy relationship with business'.[34]

Very soon after the furore over the Mittal money, it emerged that the Prime Minister had embraced a pornographer. Four months before the election, Labour took a donation of £100,000 from Richard Desmond, who presided over a fortune generated in part from magazine and television pornography. The donation was made within days of the then Trade and Industry Secretary, Stephen Byers, giving the go-ahead for Desmond's Northern & Shell group to take over *Express* newspapers.[35] This ignited a blazing row within the Labour Party and another hail of accusations of impropriety from the rest of the press. Blair squirmed when he was asked how he reconciled his professed Christian convictions with taking money from a merchant of porn. The Vicar of St Albion had been caught with *Horny Housewives*, *Big Ones* and *Very Best of Mega Boobs* sliding out of the pages of his Bible. An even worse taste was left in the mouth by the way in which this behaviour was defended. 'We have acted with integrity,' insisted John Reid, the Northern Ireland Secretary. 'If you are asking if we are going to sit in moral judgement on those who wish to contribute to the Labour Party, then the answer to that is no.'[36]

Tony Blair once claimed that his Government would be pureness exemplified. Here was one of his Cabinet loyalists apparently arguing that there were no ethical boundaries which Labour would not cross to get money.

Labour spent the donation on buying campaign adverts in Desmond's papers. In fact, Labour paid £120,000 to his company, more than the size of his donation. They didn't just look very seedy; they looked extremely stupid as well.

Philip Gould, his interpreter of public opinion, reported to the Prime Minister that the country was 'in a pessimistic mood' and viewed its Government with 'distrust and cynicism'.[37] Alastair Campbell, who by now had developed an almost indiscriminate loathing for his former trade, blamed journalists. Number 10's *über*-propagandist sometimes had a good case when he said that the Government was 'more spinned against than spinning'. His myopia was not seeing how the presentational culture he had been so instrumental in creating had encouraged the press to put the most negative construction on government.

While Campbell was at the throat of journalists, Blair had as often been at the knees of the panjandrums of the media. Editors, proprietors and leading commentators were regular guests for drinks, lunches and dinners at Number 10 and Chequers. One tabloid editor, Piers Morgan of the *Mirror*, recorded his astonishment that 'I had 22 lunches, 6 dinners, 6 interviews, 24 further one-to-one chats over tea and biscuits, and numerous phone calls with him.'[38]

That didn't stop Morgan turning on the Government over the Afghan and Iraq wars. Relations with Morgan were soured by the *Mirror*'s resentment at Downing Street's closeness to the *Sun*. He was especially aggravated that Blair and Campbell gave so many scoops to his rival.

Blair had lavished attention on Paul Dacre, the editor of the *Daily Mail*, who had initially declared himself to be 'enthralled by this man [Blair]' in the apparent belief that 'he was going to devote his Government to restoring the family.'[39]

The *Mail* turned viciously on what its editor regarded as 'anti-family' policies such as equalising the age of consent for gay sex. By the second term, the *Mail* had entirely reverted to right-wing type as Labour's most vitriolic press enemy. Blair expressed private regret – 'I feel ashamed,' he confided[40] – that he had once tried to court Dacre. Animated by the editor's intense personal dislike of the Prime Minister, the *Mail* portrayed Blair as the most despicable character ever to inhabit Number 10 and unflatteringly contrasted him with Gordon Brown, whom Dacre saw as a more 'moral' man. Cherie was flayed in his pages as an avaricious witch addicted to crackpot 'New Age' therapies.

The *Daily Mail* spearheaded the attack when the tabloids demanded to know whether Leo had received the MMR vaccine. There was some history of autism on Cherie's side of the family. Alarmist claims that the vaccine could cause autism, claims spread by the *Mail* above all else, generated a public panic which the Government had to spend large sums of taxpayers' money trying to calm. The health ministers would have been greatly assisted by confirmation that the Prime Minister and his wife had followed the advice of his own Government and given the MMR vaccine to their youngest child. Parents might not necessarily have followed the Blairs' example, but they were less likely to trust the Government's advice when the country's leader was furtive about his own child.[41] The Blairs did, in fact, get Leo vaccinated. But Cherie had become so bloody-minded about the press that she would not let Number 10 confirm that this was so.[42]

Much of the press was now turning on the Government. One paradoxical reason for that was the weakness of the Conservatives. Campbell had a point when he complained that much of the media saw it as their task 'to stand up and try to do the job the Opposition was failing to do'.[43]

The Government was pincered. It was attacked from the right because it was Labour and from the left because of the alliance with Bush. Rupert Murdoch's *Sun* and *Times* were the only daily papers which offered consistent support. Cynicism about spin deepened when it was revealed that Jo Moore, a spin doctor to Stephen Byers, had sent an e-mail on 9/11 suggesting: 'It is now a very good day to get out anything that we want to bury.'[44] This was a suggestion revolting even by the debauched standards of some of the spin merchants. Moore was regarded by her fellow practitioners as a tough and able member of their profession. She wrote that memo not because she was bad at her job, but because she was too good at it. It required a terrifying dedication to spinnery to be able to watch the Twin Towers burn and conclude that it was a glorious opportunity to manipulate the news flow.

Once the awful e-mail was exposed, Moore discussed her position with her boss. She, Byers and Campbell rapidly agreed that she would have to go. Moore had 'her bags packed' when the Prime Minister intervened.[45] In public, Blair condemned her behaviour as 'horrible, wrong and very stupid'.[46] Privately, it was he who insisted that she should stay in the Government's employment. Blair did not want to give her scalp to the media and even less did he want to hand it to the civil servants who had leaked the e-mail. 'If they get her, every special adviser will be vulnerable to leaking by the civil service,' Blair told Byers, overruling the minister. 'It will be open season. We have to protect them.'[47]

Blair's intervention only served to prolong the furore over Moore, who was eventually forced to quit four months later. During a further uproar about spin, Sir Richard Mottram, Permanent Secretary and Knight Commander of the British Empire, howled to a fellow civil servant: 'We're all fucked. I'm fucked. You're fucked. The whole department's fucked. It's been the biggest cock-up ever and we're all completely fucked.'[48] It was Byers who ended up in that condition. He made a reasonable start as Transport Secretary by trying to tackle years of neglect of the railways, but ceased to be able to function as a minister when his truthfulness became the central focus of media interest. Byers was no more or less mendacious than the average politician, but it got to the point where he could not utter a sentence without it being pored over for evidence of deceit. The Opposition and sections of the press dismembered his character by serially branding him a liar, a label especially favoured by the tabloids because it was a close rhyme with Byers. In mid-May, I concluded a column with the observation that he looked doomed because 'he is rendered incapable of even selling good news.'[49]

On 28 May, Byers quit. 'I'm going to pack it in,' he told Blair. He felt he had become 'a liability to the Government and a liability to him'. Blair said his resignation statement should be made from Downing Street, 'so you are still seen as a friend.'[50]

Soon afterwards, the right-wing press scored another hit on the Government. Campbell was driven to fury by articles in the *Spectator* and the *Mail on Sunday* accusing Number 10 of trying to enhance the Prime Minister's role at the official mourning for the Queen Mother.[51] He lodged a protest with the Press Complaints Commission and became utterly obsessive about trying to extract an apology. The Cabinet Secretary would hear his ancient fax machine at home churning out 'endless stuff' from Campbell about this affair. When it became obvious that this was a battle Number 10 could not win, Sir Richard finally told Campbell: 'You've got to know when to stop.'[52] In June, Campbell withdrew the complaint, a hateful capitulation to the right-wing press which drove his pathological feelings towards the media to a new and dangerous intensity.

A series of sleaze stories; a press with a taste for scalps and a nose for New Labour mendacity; the paranoia about the media and a particular hatred for the *Mail* newspapers; and the Blairs' appetite for money: this was the combustible cocktail that set the scene for Cheriegate.

The final ingredient was their attitude towards property, a subject on which Cherie was especially insecure. They enjoyed the use of Number 10, a rather splendid town house in the centre of London. They also had Chequers, the lovely prime ministerial retreat in the Chilterns. Yet this did not satisfy them. 'It's living over the office,' Blair would say of Number 10. He preferred Chequers, to which he escaped most weekends. 'There are plenty of phones here, but they just don't seem to ring so much,' he once told me. But he never forgot, he said, that he was 'only the tenant'.[53]

Cherie was always unhappy that they had no house to call their own apart from the three-bedroom Victorian villa in Sedgefield. Shortly before the 2001 election, when all the polls were correctly forecasting Labour would win by a landslide, Cherie fretted to friends about where she and Tony would live if the voters turfed them out of Number 10.

She was angry that they were missing out on the long boom in house prices during her husband's time in office. They sold their home in Richmond Crescent in Islington when they moved into Downing Street. They could have kept their stake in the London property market by renting it out, but that was kiboshed by Alastair Campbell. He remembered how the Tory Chancellor, Norman Lamont, was embarrassed when a 'Miss Whiplash' was found to be renting the basement of his home.[54]

Campbell's thinking was rational, but Cherie was cross. The Blairs sold the house for £650,000 in July 1997. Five years later, it was worth over £1 million, a source of constant irritation to Cherie. She saw her chance to get a piece of the property action when their eldest son, Euan, went to university at Bristol in the autumn of 2002. Cherie set her sights on buying two flats in the city. Her husband was never keen on the idea of buying one flat, never mind two, for fear of how it might be used against them by the press. Cherie went ahead regardless.

To help with the purchase, she turned to a friend. This was Carole Caplin, a former topless model who had reinvented herself as a styling guru. The unlikely relationship between the highly intelligent barrister and the former model went back as far as 1990, when the two met at a gym. When her husband became leader, the ferocity of the scrutiny 'was a big shock for Cherie'. She'd not previously 'cared about make-up and hair and now suddenly she was being judged on these things'.[55] Margaret Jay thought Cherie was 'quite scared' when they first moved into Number 10.[56] Charlie Falconer, a friend of Tony for decades, saw that 'Cherie found it difficult to start with. She was having to make her way in a world in which she'd got no experience.'[57] In her early period in the public spotlight, Cherie was desperately unconfident, a vulnerability which the merciless harridans of the British press were quick to identify, exploit and intensify by mocking her hairstyles and dress sense. At joint appearances with the Prescotts, she would exhibit her nerves by grabbing Pauline Prescott's hand for moral support.

Caplin became an ever more influential prop for Cherie. She helped her to dress more stylishly and develop a more confident public persona. The advice extended to diet and exercise. The two became extremely close, though it was not a straightforward friendship given that it involved Carole taking a fee from Cherie.

Tony didn't mind having Carole around since she seemed to have a calming influence on his wife and boosted her confidence in a way he couldn't.[58] Others were taken aback by the ubiquity of Caplin's presence in Downing Street. 'She started fluttering around Number 10 as if she owned the place,' complained John Prescott.[59]

Alastair Campbell thought Caplin would land them in trouble almost from the day she appeared on the scene. He reacted to her visits by exploding: 'What's that bloody woman doing here?'[60] He claimed to fear that she would kiss-and-tell about the home life of Number 10. As it turned out, it was not Caplin but Campbell who rushed a diary into print the moment that the Blairs left Downing Street. Cherie responded to Campbell's complaints by retorting that she wasn't going to have him or anyone else choose her friends for her. The frustration that Blair would never grasp this nettle extended to all his aides. 'Tony was always at his most irrational whenever it was anything to do with the family,' says Sally Morgan. 'He had this guilt thing about Cherie. He felt guilty that he had stopped her career even though she obviously loved being the Prime Minister's wife.'[61]

For the flat purchases, Caplin involved her Australian lover, Peter Foster, a convicted con man by whom she was pregnant. Foster was already publicly notorious in Britain yet this seems to have escaped Cherie. 'There seemed little harm in it,' she thought, the first of a series of terrible misjudgements.[62] By the last weekend of November, some journalists were starting to join the dots from Foster to Caplin to the Blairs.

'Cherie's style guru has fallen for a fraudster,' cackled the front page of the *Daily Mail* on Saturday, 28 November.[63] That afternoon, its Sunday sister paper sent a list of twenty-two questions about Foster's involvement with Cherie and the flats to the Downing Street press office. The Blairs were at Chequers when the questions were faxed on to them.

'I told you not to buy any bloody flats,' the Prime Minister swore at his wife. She protested that she had never met Foster, though she did confess to having exchanged e-mails with him. Without bothering to look at those e-mails – technology and details were ever his weak spots – Blair answered the *Mail on Sunday*'s questions, mainly with negatives. On Cherie's account, it was her husband who then told Campbell 'in very firm terms' that there had been no contact with Foster whatsoever.[64] On Campbell's account: 'Tony is usually very good at saying: "facts, facts, facts", but we did not get to the facts on this quickly enough, and that led the press office inadvertently to mislead the press.'[65]

They were racing towards one of the most searing episodes in the life of the inner Blair court.

Alastair Campbell had stepped back from giving daily briefings to lobby correspondents, delegating the task to two civil servants, Tom Kelly and Godric Smith. They faithfully repeated the Blairs' line about the flats and gave emphatic, on-the-record statements denying any involvement with Foster. That line collapsed within three days when the *Daily Mail* came into possession of the e-mails between Foster and Cherie, which included one message in which Cherie gushed her thanks to the fraudster for helping to negotiate the flat purchases: 'You are a star.'[66]

Relations within the inner court went 'into meltdown' on the Wednesday evening when they learnt that the *Daily Mail* would be splashing the e-mails the next morning. 'What you got was a coming together of a lot of the underlying problems between Tony, Cherie, Alastair and Fiona, amplified by the whole Carole Caplin thing and a press frenzy,' says a member of the senior staff. 'It is what happens when people are around each other for too long. It was a torrid time, a horrid time.'[67]

By now, says Jonathan Powell, the relationship between the Blairs and the Campbells had 'gone septic'.[68] Campbell and his partner were 'in a state of nuclear outrage', according to a friend and minister with a ringside seat for this affair. 'Fiona loathes Alastair working at Number 10. The Foster stuff gives Fiona a way of saying "these [the Blairs] are the ghastly people we're working for, you've got to get out." Alastair hates Cherie because she's given Fiona that ammunition.'[69]

When he learnt about the *Mail*'s next splash about Cherie, Campbell was incandescently angry, righteously vindicated in his previous warnings and 'determined that if anyone went down for this, it wasn't going to be Alastair Campbell'.[70]

When the Blairs got back from the theatre, Campbell demanded that

Cherie show him and his staff all her e-mail contacts with Foster. Campbell, Jonathan Powell, Tom Kelly and Godric Smith stood around a cringing Cherie's computer while her husband paced in the background. 'It was awful,' says one present at the scene. 'It did look like a Gestapo interrogation.'[71]

The next day, Fiona Millar turned on the Prime Minister's wife: 'Everyone in the press office hates you. They've told lies on your behalf and none of them ever wants to work for you again.'[72] Tom Kelly, for one, was actually feeling sorry for Cherie. 'She was embarrassed and chastened.'[73]

The media and the public had been misled and Downing Street would have to admit so, a reverse the more humiliating for them because the defeat was at the hands of the *Mail* papers that the Blairs loathed so much. Cherie was forced to issue a statement admitting that Foster was involved in the purchase of the flats and taking the blame on herself for the misleading statements put out by Number 10.

A second weekend in a row was consumed by Cheriegate. Blair shut himself in his study at Chequers on Saturday dealing with Iraq. He and his wife barely spoke. The *News of the World* came in with a series of questions for Number 10 about claims that Cherie had known about Foster's past, that Carole had tried to do deals on clothes, and 'wacky stuff about them having mudbaths and showers together'.[74]

Newspapers that Sunday were packed with stories and commentaries pouring opprobrium on Cherie. Campbell had given detailed briefings to selected Sunday journalists heaping all the blame on Cherie, an exercise designed to exculpate himself, Millar and the Number 10 press operation. Never before had the inner court turned so viciously on itself. The Prime Minister's most intimate aide was now spinning against the Prime Minister's wife.

'Cherie is now outraged that Alastair and Fiona won't protect her,' observed one of the Blairs' oldest friends. 'Tony is caught in the middle.'[75]

One person's crisis can turn into another man's opportunity. With Blair and his wife estranged from Campbell and Millar, here was a chance for Peter Mandelson to remind the Blairs that they still had a friend in need. He landed at Heathrow from New York on Sunday morning. As he waited by the baggage carousel, he picked up on his mobile a desperate message from Blair. Mandelson went straight to Number 10, where he spent most of that day and the next up in the flat trying to calm them down and grip the crisis.

'The Prime Minister felt that something very serious was engulfing him,' says Mandelson. 'Cherie was being demonised. She was being pursued, persecuted as if she were a Minister or elected official in her own right.' The story had now made 'the fateful jump' from 'hostile newspapers on to television and radio'.[76]

Blair watched with horror as this media feeding frenzy devoured his wife. 'Tony was beside himself,' says Sally Morgan.[77] Angry as he was with his wife, he also felt spasms of guilt. 'He knew she was trying to make money to make sure they were all right.'[78] He railed to his aides about 'the media scum'. He did not often lose it. Over this, he did. He had one of his 'meltdown moments', raging: 'What do they want me to do? Sack my wife?'[79]

Things turned even blacker on Monday, when Foster's solicitors issued a statement saying that Cherie had contacted them about his appeal against deportation. Campbell confronted the Prime Minister's wife while she was having her hair done. 'That's it,' he snarled, arms folded, glowering at her via the mirror. 'One more time, Cherie, did you at any point have anything to do with the immigration case?'

'I've told you, no,' she said. 'You're determined to humiliate me, aren't you? I know you've been briefing against me.'

'I don't need to. You do it all on your own.'

The hairdresser, André, intervened. 'Don't you talk to Cherie like that!'

'You mind your own business,' said Campbell. 'Remember you're just a fucking hairdresser.'

'Apologise,' demanded Cherie.

'I don't think so,' he snorted. 'Don't forget you brought all of this on yourself.'[80]

Campbell disputes her claim that he swore at the hairdresser.[81]

He would have been angrier still had he known what Cherie planned to do next. After hosting a Christmas party for Barnardo's and presiding over the switching on of the tree on Downing Street, she slipped out of the building via the rear car park for a clandestine rendezvous with Carole Caplin at the hairdresser's flat.[82]

By Tuesday, the Conservatives were calling for an inquiry and the *Daily Mail* was sending questions to Number 10 saying that Cherie had been trying to nobble a judge.[83]

Blair was yet angrier and all for going on the attack against the media himself. Mandelson persuaded him that the only realistic hope of finding closure was for his wife to speak. Cherie was scheduled to present the Partners in Excellence awards at the Atrium in Millbank. She could be sure of a friendly audience from the organisation of which she was a patron. The location was conveniently in the same building as much of the Westminster media. This was an opportunity they could use to try to win some sympathy for Cherie. Charlie Falconer – 'a calming influence'[84] – came in to Number 10 to help write the speech for her and because she wanted someone she trusted to protect her interests from Campbell. Mandelson was still on hand, though he couldn't help reminding them of his summary ejection from the Cabinet two years earlier, remarking that none of them had been there for him, 'when I was thrown out of the top floor window'.[85] After Cherie read through the script written for her, she worried that she might crack up in front of the cameras. Mandelson advised that she would keep her composure by picking out friendly people in the audience and looking in their eyes. She glanced at Campbell and said: 'I certainly don't want to look at him.'[86] Most of her words were written by other hands, but Cherie proved to be effective at conveying the impression that the emotions in it were authentically her own. Some of her husband's and father's thespian talent was on display when she performed at Millbank. 'I am not Superwoman,' she declared in a tearful mea culpa live to the television cameras. She sought public empathy, especially from other women. 'The reality of my daily life is that I'm juggling a lot of balls in the air. And some of them get dropped.'[87] The line about 'juggling balls' was, ironically, scripted by Fiona Millar.[88]

Most of the rest of this feminine appeal was concocted by men: Campbell, Mandelson and Falconer. She defiantly defended her friendship with Caplin, whom she was still seeing and would continue to see, but she admitted that it was an error to allow Foster, 'someone I barely knew, to get involved with my personal affairs'.[89]

Her husband, who was at his weekly audience with the Queen, missed the performance. 'How did it go?' he asked when he got back from the Palace. 'Turn on the television,' said Campbell. 'They are running it over and over again.'[90] The heat began to fade, though the story would continue to flare up in the headlines for a while, not least because of Foster, who made a series of spectacular claims, the most audacious of which was that Tony was the father of Carole's baby.[91] When Cheriegate was still generating headlines for a third weekend, it ignited another ferocious row within the inner court, this one between Blair and Campbell. The propagandist raged at the Prime Minister: 'You're married to a woman who is determined to protect and help a woman who is in love with a con man, so you are linked to a con man.'

Blair shouted back: 'I am not linked to a con man! You think Cherie has done something monstrous and I don't!'[92]

Her husband was right. Cherie was not monstrous. She had not committed a crime, but an idiotic mistake. It was an amazing lapse to permit a known con man to insinuate himself into the lives of the Blairs. When they were then caught out by the press, they committed the habitual offence of trying to cover up rather than coming clean. That made things ten times worse.

Both the Blairs felt guilty about it afterwards. She because she had badly let down her husband at a time of intense pressure over Iraq. He because he felt he had been so consumed by Iraq that he had neglected her.[93]

Their relationship was healed amidst mutual expressions of remorse. Caplin remained a presence in Number 10 despite it all. Cherie even let *Marie Claire* magazine photograph Caplin doing her make-up on the marital bed.

Other relationships were never the same after this psychodrama which tore apart the heart of Number 10. Fiona Millar left a few months later and repeatedly and ferociously rowed with her partner when he would not quit too. Cherie never trusted Campbell again. He and Blair started to drift apart to the point where the Prime Minister dangerously lost control of Campbell during the Kelly Affair six months later.

The inner court was now fractured and just at the moment when Tony Blair was facing the most pivotal decision of his premiership.

8. Naked in the Middle of the Room

The pleasant, upmarket seaside resort of Le Touquet was the venue for an Anglo-French summit in the first week of February 2003. Tony Blair, America's greatest ally in Europe, was head to head with Jacques Chirac, the most vigorous critic of Washington's drive to war. Among officials on both sides, there was high anxiety that their differences would erupt into a public slanging match.

Chirac was mercurial, proud, wily, sometimes avuncular, sometimes bombastic and prone to delivering overbearing lectures to fellow leaders. Entering his eighth decade, he was anxious to rescue the reputation of his scandal-splattered presidency and win a place in history which would compare with the founder of his party, Charles de Gaulle. An American invasion of Iraq was wildly unpopular in Gaullist France. Chirac's opposition was helping to restore his stature with his people.

Chirac's relationship with Blair was a complicated and combustible mix of fascination, irritation and rivalry. The French President was at first intrigued by Blair. The elected monarch of France then bridled at Blair's competition to be the pre-eminent European politician of the day, a position that Chirac regarded as his of right.

In private, Blair was 'a wonderful mimic' of other leaders and would entertain friends with take-offs of the French President. 'Whenever you saw him he'd give you a version of Chirac and Prodi and the others.'[1]

There was an ugly clash between Blair and Chirac at a European Council a few months earlier. 'I've never been spoken to by anybody like that,' the Frenchman yelled at Blair. 'You have been very badly brought up.' He'd also told him that if he went to war in Iraq 'you won't be able to look Leo in the face in twenty years' time.'[2]

Relations between the two had now sunk into 'deep distrust'.[3] Blair was alarmed that the Frenchman seemed to want to put himself at the head of an anti-American bloc. 'Tony had a visceral feeling against this Chirac bipolar view of the world,' says Alastair Campbell. 'He was very worried about the potential for Europe to go that way.'⁴ A senior Foreign Office official recalls it being 'quite widely thought' at Downing Street, as a result of 'snippets of conversation' picked up from within the Elysée Palace, that Chirac was deliberately setting out to exploit the divisions over Iraq to try to destroy Blair.⁵ Iraq 'lit a fuse in Chirac's mind' because he felt he'd a 'special relationship with Iraq over the years'.⁶

The two men made a reasonable effort to disguise the antagonism when they performed in public at Le Touquet. Chirac spoke of 'a very warm feeling' between the two and Blair of 'a tremendous spirit of friendship'.⁷ That mask of amity was ripped off the moment they sat down for a private lunch. Chirac launched into the patronising lecture mode that so irked Blair. 'We don't need any more wars,' declared the French President. War was 'a nasty thing'. He'd been a young soldier in Algeria during France's bloody struggle in its former colony. 'I know what war is like.' Unlike, he implied, his British guest. 'If you go into Iraq you will not be welcomed,' Chirac continued. He predicted 'a civil war'. Majority rule by the Shia will not be 'the same thing as democracy'. Blair absorbed this lecture more than he argued back. He knew that by now Chirac was beyond persuading. As they left the lunch, Blair turned to his senior adviser, Sir Stephen Wall. Rolling his eyes, the Prime Minister sighed: 'Poor old Jacques, he just doesn't get it, does he?'⁸

As it would turn out, Wall later concluded, Chirac had 'got it' about what might happen in Iraq 'rather better than we did'.⁹

Europe was dividing into two hostile camps about Iraq, a split which left Blair's position increasingly exposed. Initially, his diplomatic strategy appeared to reap great rewards. After eight weeks of wrangling at the United Nations building in New York, on 8 November the Security Council passed Resolution 1441 by a unanimous vote of its fifteen members. Even Syria, whose leader had publicly humiliated Blair twelve months earlier, voted for the resolution which declared Saddam guilty of violating earlier resolutions and in breach of his obligations to disarm. The Iraqi dictator was warned that failure to take this last chance to comply would result in 'serious consequences'.¹⁰

Blair was euphoric.¹¹ On the face of it, this was a success for his approach. 'The first five minutes after its passage looked like a mighty triumph,' says Christopher Meyer.¹² If Saddam failed to comply, the international community was now signed up to dealing with the Iraqi tyrant. If Saddam capitulated, he would be weakened, perhaps so fatally that he would be overthrown from within, and it would be much harder for the Americans to justify an invasion.

War planning nevertheless went on apace. America's senior military came over to the British command centre at Northwood to reveal more detail about their invasion plan. Admiral Michael Boyce in turn briefed Blair and lobbied to be allowed to start making serious preparations for conflict. Blair wouldn't let him. Boyce was told by Blair 'to keep my thoughts to myself' for fear that if 'anything about that breaks loose people will get wind of it'.[13] This meant a delay in ordering up all the essentials for conflict such as ammunition, kit, spares, making tanks ready for desert warfare, 'everything you can think of for a war' and an inventory that took weeks to put together. Boyce was not even allowed to give warning of the requirements to the Chief of Defence Logistics.

Blair was afraid that evidence of war planning would make a conflict look inevitable and expose him to the charge that he was lying when he said he still sought a peaceful outcome. A side of Blair continued to hope for that. He was confronted with opposition and demonstrations on a scale he had never before experienced. He was also uncertain that the Americans knew what they were doing. His ideal result, so he would frequently say in private conversation, was the removal of Saddam without the necessity for conflict. In a phone call to Bush, Blair said: 'If Saddam complies, you do realise we will have to take "yes" for an answer?' 'I do,' replied Bush.[14] The British got the impression that Bush would be content with a different route to regime change. 'Cheney wanted a war,' reckoned David Manning, 'but I think Bush would have quite liked that.'[15] Condi Rice told Christopher Meyer that the 'implosion of Saddam's regime' was their preferred outcome.[16] Egypt and Saudi Arabia were encouraged to convey the message to the Iraqi dictator and elements of his regime that America and Britain would be content to see Saddam step down and go into exile with his family.[17]

If this invitation was ever delivered, it did not get a positive response from Saddam. His reign of terror over Iraq had lasted for more than two decades despite his defeat in the first Gulf War and his earlier catastrophic six-year conflict with Iran. The butcher of Baghdad had not survived for so long without possessing both nerve and guile.

This helps to explain one of the great mysteries at the heart of the Iraq conflict: why did Saddam behave as if he had WMD when he hadn't? One plausible explanation is that he wanted the world to believe that he still had an arsenal to deter the Americans, to frighten his neighbours and to keep his population prostrate with fear. In the words of one British official: 'He was like a man who kept a "Beware of the Dog" sign on his front gate, but who had secretly shot and buried the dog.'[18]

The alternative thesis, as expounded by Geoff Hoon, is that 'his generals didn't dare tell Saddam that they no longer had the stuff.'[19] Though Iraq did not have the weapons, Saddam continued to behave in a manner that suggested that they were there somewhere. He responded to the UN resolution in the way that any averagely crafty dictator might do. He did not fully defy the UN and he did not wholly comply either.

On 7 December, the Iraqis produced a 12,200-page dossier which claimed to account for what had happened to Saddam's banned weaponry. This took a while to absorb at Number 10. 'It was all in Arabic so we had to get it translated first.'[20] Once they had, it was grasped that Saddam's 'completely inept' response in this obfuscatory document was going to be a diplomatic disaster.[21] Sally Morgan saw this moment as 'the beginning of the realisation that things were going to be extremely difficult'.[22] Heavy criticism of Iraq from the UN inspectors was topped by total condemnation from the Bush administration, which immediately cranked up the pressure on Saddam to give the inspectors access to his scientists and any site of their choosing. Bush told the Spanish Prime Minister that Saddam's 'joke' declaration proved beyond doubt that he was 'a liar' who had 'no intention of disarming'.[23]

Saddam's manoeuvres tore apart the superficial unity at the UN. The price paid for unanimity over Resolution 1441 was ambiguity. It did not determine how long Saddam should be given to comply. Nor did it define what exactly the 'serious consequences' would be if he didn't. France and Russia viewed the resolution as a brake on America; America regarded the resolution as a trigger for war.

Colin Powell and Jack Straw were still desperately trying to avoid a conflict. 'Colin and I see it as our job to stop the war,' Straw told the British ambassador in Washington.[24] The Foreign Secretary turned bookie and publicly gave odds. It was still '60 to 40 against' conflict,[25] he said early in the New Year, a declaration which even his own Permanent Secretary regarded as heroically optimistic. Michael Jay believes the 'momentum was pretty much unstoppable towards the end of 2002, early 2003'.[26]

At lunchtime on Saturday, 11 January, HMS *Ark Royal* set sail from Portsmouth bound for the Gulf. Straw's odds were wishful thinking, inspired more by what he hoped would be the outcome than by the reality. Events were running away from him and Colin Powell. They were reduced to moaning to each other about their failure. 'By the end, Jack and Colin were like two men in a bar crying into their beer,' says one Foreign Office official very familiar with their exchanges.[27]

Powell, trying to preserve some sway in the White House, joined the war party in mid-January at a meeting with Bush in the Oval Office. The encounter was brief – just twelve minutes long – and critical. 'I think I have to do this,' the President said to his Secretary of State. 'I want you with me.'[28] Powell was still wracked with doubt about the enterprise. But he was never going to resign. According to Richard Armitage, his number two, Powell would always be 'the good soldier'.[29] The last of the American doves had joined the hawks.

The differences between Washington and Paris grew irreconcilable when Dominique de Villepin, the Foreign Minister of France, ambushed Powell at a meeting of the Security Council, talked of an American 'adventure' and described war as a 'dead end'.[30]

If that was intended to restrain Washington, it had the opposite effect. This made it even harder for an infuriated Powell to be a voice of caution within the administration. The hawks felt further vindicated when the UN's team of inspectors presented its first report on 27 January. Criticism of the lack of Iraqi co-operation was seized on by the White House. At the end of January, George Bush was driven down Pennsylvania Avenue to deliver his third State of the Union address. 'The dictator of Iraq is not disarming. To the contrary, he is deceiving,' declared the President, beating the drum louder still. 'If war is forced upon us, we will fight with the full force and might of the United States military – and we will prevail.'[31]

From the British embassy in Washington, Christopher Meyer accurately reported to Number 10 that Bush had taken such an uncompromisingly bellicose position that he had left himself no wriggle room. Short of Saddam fleeing or being toppled, the President had made it impossible for America to back down from an invasion. Meyer also warned that the Pentagon's military timetable could not be synchronised with the laborious process of inspections. Barring a miracle, they were heading for 'a train crash' at the UN. On top of which, the Saudis, Egyptians and Jordanians were telling the Americans: 'If you are going to do it, do it quickly.'[32]

There was additional pressure on Blair from the British military. Admiral Boyce and General Mike Jackson told him that the armed forces would not be combat-ready without clear orders to create supply chains and plan for battle. Towards the end of January, Geoff Hoon announced to the Commons that Britain was now committing a quarter of the army and a third of the air force. The Defence Secretary had to concede to MPs that many of the troops still lacked equipment even as basic as desert kit.[33] That was a consequence of Blair's refusal to let Boyce order up supplies earlier.

George Bush acted in the confidence that he had the votes in Congress and the backing of most Americans, many of whom believed, albeit wrongly, that Saddam was connected to 9/11. There were isolated American voices condemning the idea of a 'dumb war'. One opponent was the author of that phrase, a man called Barack Obama. But he was merely an obscure State Senator from Illinois, barely a household name in his own household. The great majority of America's politicians were behind war.

For Blair, the political alignments were entirely different. In January, public opinion in Britain was hotly hostile to war with less than a third of voters backing action.[34] It was widely conjectured that Blair might not survive in Number 10. Sally Morgan warned him that this could be 'the end of you'.[35] He thought so too. 'This could cost me my job,' Blair confided to Barry Cox and other close friends.[36]

The Prime Minister had driven into the yellow box without a clear exit. He urgently needed a way out. The answer he reached for was getting a second resolution from the United Nations which explicitly authorised military action. Sally Morgan and David Manning were most vehement within Number 10 in arguing that this was absolutely critical. Morgan believed it was essential if there was to be any hope of carrying the Labour Party and public opinion. She said to him directly: 'If we don't have a second resolution and this goes wrong, we are stuffed.'[37] When Blair assessed the balance of opinion within the Cabinet, he reckoned that without a second resolution he could only 'just about get to a majority . . . it was pretty much "future on the line" time.'[38] A second resolution was vital to Blair to make the removal of Saddam look legitimate in the eyes of the world, vital to carry British public opinion with him, and vital to manage his Cabinet and party. Securing one became the absolute priority of his policy.

At the end of January, he crossed the Atlantic to see Bush. He spent the flight over with Manning working on the arguments he could deploy to make the case for a pause for further diplomacy.[39]

This was Blair's toughest meeting to date at the White House. David Manning took a note for the British side as Blair argued for pushing back the invasion. He was confronted by a united front of Bush, Cheney, Rice, Rumsfeld and Powell, all of whom set their faces against that. Tens of thousands of US troops were mobilising, in transit or already deployed on the borders of Iraq. The largest naval armada assembled since 1945 was already stationed in the Arabian Gulf, the decks of the warships bristling with weaponry with a potency that no other state on earth could come close to matching. The planners at the Pentagon argued that they needed to invade in March to be sure of getting to Baghdad before the onset of Iraq's broiling summer. Colin Powell privately regarded this as not conclusive, telling Manning that 'they could always fight at night.'[40] But the argument for war without delay had carried the day in Washington. Blair's case for a pause was rebuffed and he did not anyway push it very hard. In his note of the meeting, David Manning recorded that 'the start date for the military campaign was now pencilled in for 10 March.'[41]

Bush gave an insight into his state of mind when he mused to Blair about painting an American spy plane in UN colours and sending it over Iraq to provoke conflict. The President was insouciant about what might face the allies after the war, saying that the Americans didn't expect an eruption of ethnic and religious sectarian fighting in Iraq once Saddam was gone. Blair asked about planning for the aftermath but did not probe further when Condi Rice responded that 'a great deal of work is now in hand.' As Manning later put it: 'He accepted their assurances.'[42] Blair was so focused on the politics and the diplomacy of going towards war that he was fatally distracted from thinking about what would happen afterwards.

He encountered more resistance from the Americans when the Prime Minister argued for seeking the second UN resolution he now desperately required. None of the Americans embraced that idea. Blair's desire to go back to the UN complicated a stance that they wanted to keep simple. They correctly suspected that there was not enough support in the Security Council and it would be better not to attempt it than to try and fail. In the course of three hours of talks, Blair eventually had to plead: 'I need this.' He told Bush that another push at the UN was essential to secure his position in Britain and would give them an 'insurance policy' and 'international cover' if 'anything went wrong with the military campaign'. Bush then seemed to relent, saying: 'If that's what you need, we will go flat-out to try to help you get it.' But he warned that if they failed 'military action would follow anyway.'[43] Richard Haas, a senior official at the State Department, remarks: 'The administration went along with it to help Tony Blair. He was clearly politically out on a limb.' Bush himself didn't 'see the necessity of a second resolution'.[44]

The President's lack of relish for pursuing another resolution communicated itself at the joint news conference afterwards when he talked about it with no enthusiasm. 'I don't think they saw it as anything like as important as we did,' says Sir Michael Jay, the Permanent Secretary at the Foreign Office.[45] Bush was more interested in the countdown to conflict, declaring that time was running out for Saddam and he was talking 'weeks rather than months'.[46]

David Manning, witness to the entire encounter at the White House, came to regret that Blair had not pushed his case vigorously enough: 'I don't think he impressed upon them enough the political problems and the costs if there wasn't a second resolution.'[47]

It was becoming starkly obvious that Blair 'didn't really have any control', says Sir Jeremy Greenstock. 'He'd handcuffed himself to this wagon and he didn't have any braking influence to slow them down when he felt that they should have slowed down.'[48]

Jack Straw, the optimist of a month before, was now a pessimist, believing that 'unless we can get the Iraqis to back off, the die is cast.'[49]

On 5 February, Colin Powell addressed the UN to make the case that Iraq was in 'material breach' of Resolution 1441. The Secretary of State presented photographs, documents and audio tapes designed to establish Saddam's guilt in the court of world opinion. As a suggestive prop, the Director of the CIA, George Tenet, was sat behind him as Powell laid out 'evidence' of Iraq's failure to disarm. Powell warned the General Assembly that 'this body places itself in danger of irrelevance if it allows Iraq to continue to defy its will without responding effectively or immediately.'[50] Both the White House and Number 10 hoped that Powell's presentation would be a dramatic 'Adlai Stevenson moment'. It aimed for the same electrifying effect achieved by Stevenson in the 1960s when he went to the UN during the Cuban missile crisis to reveal the evidence against the Soviet Union.

Powell failed to pull that off. One reason was because so much of 'the evidence' supplied by the CIA turned out to be what the diplomat Sir Christopher Meyer undiplomatically calls 'bollocks'.[51] The Secretary of State also called the UN's attention 'to the fine paper that the United Kingdom distributed yesterday, which describes in exquisite detail Iraqi deception activities'.[52] This was not the dossier published the previous September, but a piece of propaganda confected by the Campbell spin machine. It was exquisite only in its shabbiness. The 'fine paper' was cobbled together by a few of Campbell's gofers. 'Given haphazardly to a few journalists on the basis that it would be a good story for the next day . . . it really damaged the overall impression that people had about government information on Iraq,' says Ed Owen, another of New Labour's senior spin doctors.[53] 'It was the Alastair operation at its worst,' observed one member of the Cabinet.[54] Blair, apparently unwittingly in this case, represented it to MPs as 'further intelligence'.[55] In fact, much of it was made up of unattributed quotes from a twelve-year-old Ph.D. thesis written by a student in California which had been cut and pasted off the internet and then embellished with stronger language. The British intelligence services were livid at the suggestion that this 'dodgy dossier' had their imprimatur. Even Campbell regarded it as a 'bad own goal'.[56] Jack Straw would later publicly describe it as 'a complete Horlicks'. He rightly feared that 'it undermined our overall credibility.'[57] In private, the Foreign Secretary's language was stronger. He was 'furious, absolutely furious' about this 'fuck-up'.[58]

There was a carnival atmosphere in Edinburgh's Caledonian hotel on the evening of St Valentine's Day. The downstairs bar heaved with rugby fans becoming enjoyably beered in anticipation of the Scotland–Ireland game on Saturday. The mood was much less relaxed in the presidential suite upstairs, where the Prime Minister was holed up working on the speech he would deliver to his party's spring conference the next day. Nick Ryden, lifelong friend and godfather to Leo, dropped in with his wife for a drink. They were shocked by the state of the Prime Minister.

'It was a real contrast between the Tony Blair we'd known and the Tony Blair sitting in front of us in the presidential suite. The contrast was quite staggering. He looked drawn. He wasn't sleeping. He hadn't been eating properly. There was no-one looking after him. There was no energy about him.'[59]

Others had noticed that Blair appeared wrecked. The official line was that he had a bad bout of the flu which he couldn't shake off. The reason he couldn't beat off the flu was because he was so utterly shattered by anxiety over Iraq. 'He wasn't sleeping,' says Sally Morgan. 'He looked terrible.'[60] Heavy applications of make-up concealer turned his face the colour of terracotta for public performances, but it couldn't entirely mask the crow's feet splayed under his darkened eyes, the hollowing of his cheeks and the deepening frown lines carved in his brow. The strain was engraved over a man whose biggest marketing feature was once a light and cheesy grin. Many others who saw him at close quarters were worried about the toll on his health taken by long days and sleepless nights.

His drained, red-eyed appearance shocked one of the party leaders present when he briefly flew out to Belfast in early March. 'The first morning was a shambles. He just wasn't up to speed, he wasn't focused. Jonathan Powell had his head down, frantically writing notes. Blair was completely worn out.'[61]

A Cabinet member noted: 'He lost weight and became quite gaunt. You could see that he was under great strain. He was throwing all his authority at it and desperately trying to hold the thing together.'[62] On Saturday, 15 February, Alastair Campbell and Sally Morgan joined him in Scotland. Neither originally planned to make the trip to the spring conference. Morgan decided to fly north when Blair rang her the night before 'sounding desperate'.[63] Campbell got a similar call. Neither thought they dare leave him on his own. He confessed to them that he had again slept badly. They mordantly joked that it might be his last speech as party leader.[64] The speech needed to be a compelling answer to his opponents, who were planning to take to the streets for anti-war protests the like of which the world had never seen before. Millions were going to take part in some 600 mass demonstrations around the world, the largest global peace protest ever staged.

'Even I am a bit worried about this one,' Blair declared to his aides about the size of the marches which were planned for London and major cities across Britain.[65] A million people, men, women and children, young, middle-aged and old, marched through the capital that Saturday. They massed in Hyde Park, where they were addressed by Tony Benn, the veteran old general of the left; Charles Kennedy, who had found a cause for his leadership of the Liberal Democrats; and celebrity warriors against war such as Harold Pinter and Bianca Jagger. From Edinburgh to Cardiff, protestors were marching with banners and T-shirts emblazoned with 'NOT IN MY NAME'.

'Getting rid of murderous dictators used to be a left-wing cause!' Blair would rail within the walls of Number 10.[66] He was taken aback to learn from aides and ministers that many of their friends, and even family members, were on the march against him. His personal pollster, Stan Greenberg, had become 'very much involved in the anti-war effort in the US.'[67]

Accustomed to being popular, the Prime Minister was both staggered and bewildered by the scale and passion of the opposition he had aroused. One of his senior aides notes: 'He's not a table thumper, he doesn't throw things, he doesn't kick things. It's more: "Why can't they see my point of view?"'[68]

Blair's mode in his first term was to be a big-tent politician who tried to corral everyone behind him with his easy charm and chameleon politics. That had made him an unprecedentedly popular Prime Minister. The maestro of sweet consensus was transformed by Iraq into a leader who bitterly divided his country. The cautious calibrator of the odds had become a risk-taker ready to 'bet the farm', as one of his Cabinet allies put it.[69] The pop star premier of the first term became the conviction-driven lone warrior of the second term.

Helicopters clattered overhead and armed police surrounded the building when Blair arrived from Edinburgh at the Clyde Auditorium in Glasgow. Music from Atomic Kitten, a curious choice, boomed from the sound system as delegates to the conference came into the hall. They were largely silent when Blair spoke. 'I ask the marchers to understand this: I do not seek unpopularity as a badge of honour. But sometimes it is the price of leadership. And the cost of conviction,' he declared.

'The moral case against war has a moral answer,' he went on, namely that the absence of war would also lead to death and suffering, not least of the Iraqi people themselves. A million were marching in London but 'that is still less than the number who died in the wars that he started', Blair argued. 'Ridding the world of Saddam would be an act of humanity. It is leaving him there that is inhumane.'[70]

This speech was his most eloquent riposte to the claim that all the moral arguments belonged to opponents of war. In retrospect, when it became evident that WMD were a false prospectus for the invasion, it became a consensus view among his allies that 'he should have emphasised more the regime change justification'[71] and 'emphasised the humanitarian case more'.[72] Some of the Cabinet, though, were 'uneasy' that weekend to find that they were being asked to suddenly shift the argument from WMD to regime change. They questioned why.[73] What they were not to know was that MI6 had already secretly withdrawn as unreliable some of the claims in the September dossier.[74]

Some found Blair a more impressive politician for the conviction that was now on fervent display. The right-wing polemicist and future Conservative MP Michael Gove wrote a piece for *The Times* swooningly entitled: 'I can't fight my feelings anymore: I love Tony.'[75] Others were roused to equally passionate hate. Philip Gould, his personal pollster, later lamented to others in the inner circle that 'Iraq bent Tony out of shape.'[76]

Another way of dealing with the fierce opposition to war was to confront it head on by making his case on television before hostile audiences. His team dubbed this 'the masochism strategy'. One televised bruising was filmed in the Foreign Office Map Room. Under the gaze of portraits of Wellington and Nelson, Blair was attacked from all sides. 'How many innocent victims are you going to kill?' one woman challenged him. 'Don't do it.' This encounter ended badly when the Prime Minister was slow handclapped by some of the audience.[77]

'Who the fuck fixed that up?' he steamed to his staff afterwards. 'Thanks very much guys.'[78] None of his aides wanted to 'own up'.[79] On another occasion, he took up an invitation from the Political Editor of ITN, Nick Robinson, to argue his case with six sceptical members of the public. When the cameras finished recording, Blair took the six into the Cabinet Room and carried on debating with them for a further half-hour, much to the agitation of those responsible for his schedule. From the campaign to ditch Clause Four with which he had begun his leadership of his party through two election victories, he had grown accustomed to winning arguments. Such was Blair's faith in his own magic, he seemed to believe that he could win round the country through the sheer power of his persuasion.

A slim consolation was that other European leaders who had allied with the Americans were even more embattled. In a phone conversation, José María Aznar remarked that only 4 per cent of Spaniards supported war. 'Crikey,' replied Blair. 'That's even less than the number who think Elvis Presley is still alive.'[80]

He faced another rough ride at the hands of an almost uniformly hostile television audience in Newcastle assembled by *Newsnight*. To one woman, who said she couldn't support a war which didn't have the sanction of the UN, he revealingly replied: 'But with a second resolution?'[81]

As February grew older, securing that second resolution was becoming ever more essential and ever more difficult. As the Foreign Secretary's senior aide notes: 'Getting a second resolution was crucial in terms of getting a proper political consensus behind military action. That's why they invested so much effort in it.'[82] Manning was becoming 'more and more pessimistic' that it could be achieved.[83]

America and Britain were opposed by the other three permanent members of the Security Council. Russia, China and France supported the weapons inspectors' request for more time and resources to do their job, especially after Hans Blix's team destroyed some seventy missiles. 'These are not toothpicks,' declared the lugubrious Swede who headed the inspectors. The split at the UN was widened by his second and third reports. Blix would never give the cut-and-dried assessments that America and Britain so desperately wanted from him. His commentaries on the inspections process resembled the end-of-match analysis of his fellow Swede, Sven-Göran Eriksson, the England football manager: 'The first half, Saddam was good. The second half, he was not so good. We look forward to the next match.' Blix was trying to be judicious, but the effect of his ambiguities was that the rival powers could interpret his reports to suit their own prejudices. 'The trouble with Blix is that he doesn't want to be blamed for starting a war' was Blair's exasperated explanation to himself and his aides.[84] It had not occurred to him or anyone with influence over events that the WMD might simply not be there at all. To the Americans and the British, the failure to locate WMD was proof that the duplicitous Saddam was up to his old tricks of concealment.

'Saddam Hussein had been given specific responsibilities, and it did not appear that he had the interest or the will to do that which the world demanded,' says George Bush's Chief of Staff. 'The clock was running out. When the clock runs out, what is the consequence? The consequence would be war.'[85]

The clock was also running out on Tony Blair's diplomacy. One of his fatal assumptions during this period was his belief that he could win round other major European leaders through his gift for persuasion. 'Tony thought the force of his own personality would bring people along and find a way through,' says David Manning.[86] Blair had always believed that he could conquer the world with charm. He invested huge faith in his ability to talk his way out of trouble, round problems, through dilemmas and into alliances. He did indeed have a talent for it which he had been exploiting since he was a teenager, but now he hit the limits of his ability. Paddy Ashdown observes: 'One of Blair's failings is to over-estimate the power of his charm. It is an exceedingly powerful weapon in his hands, but it is not as powerful as he thinks it is.'[87]

Two of Blair's key relationships in Europe were in tatters. He was bitterly though unreasonably angry with Gerhard Schröder, the Chancellor of Germany. He should have known that the Germans would not be allies for the use of force in Iraq. During the Kosovo conflict, Schröder explained to Blair why his country could not engage in military intervention. The British 'like fighting', he told Blair, but Germany had become 'essentially pacifist'.[88] Schröder had turned round his domestic fortunes by opposing a war. Having narrowly won re-election in September, he would have destroyed himself if he did a volte-face now. 'Germany doesn't matter,' Jonathan Powell would sniff about Europe's richest country. 'It hasn't got a veto.'[89]

France did possess a veto on the Security Council. For a long time, Blair told himself and tried to convince others that Jacques Chirac would ultimately fall into line. 'The French always do this – they'll come round in the end,' he would say.[90] From the moment that Chirac ordered a French aircraft carrier to stop steaming towards Iraq and reverse course in mid-January, it should have been clear that this time France was not going to come round.

As well as being a blow to Blair's conceit of himself as a great persuader, the clear opposition to war from other major European leaders gave encouragement and ammunition to opposition in Britain. In a Commons vote on 26 February, 122 Labour MPs defied the party whip and voted for an amendment declaring: 'The case for military action is as yet unproven.' They were joined by 52 Liberal Democrats and 13 Conservatives. It was the largest revolt by its own MPs against a government since 1886. Many more only hung back from joining the rebellion on the basis that there would be a second UN resolution, a hope which Blair already privately knew was looking forlorn. One of the most Blairite members of the Cabinet gasped to me: 'This could cost Tony everything.'[91]

Donald Rumsfeld sneered that France and Germany were 'the old Europe', calling in aid the support for the Americans among 'the new Europe', the former Warsaw Pact countries who were largely behind the US.[92] Blair could not afford to be so casually derisive of this fracture through the heart of Europe. His entire strategy had been predicated on keeping America and Europe together with himself as 'the bridge' between them. His bridge was now being sawn away at both ends of the Atlantic.

The opposing gangs of New York lined up to do battle at the UN building in Manhattan. Allied with France and Germany were Russia, China and Syria. The British and the Americans could count only on Spain and Bulgaria.

The balance of the vote on the Security Council was held by Angola, Cameroon, Chile, Guinea, Mexico and Pakistan. They were dubbed the 'Swing Six'. Even some of his closest friends wondered how Blair had got himself into a position where his destiny might be decided in the presidential palace in Yaounde.

Britain's ambassador at the UN, Sir Jeremy Greenstock, lobbied furiously among the Six to try to secure a second resolution. For a while the Americans 'tried quite hard' to help, but Greenstock 'didn't believe that their heart was in it because they were doing it for us rather than their own reasons'.[93] Manning became 'increasingly doubtful that the Americans are putting enough effort in'.[94] Blair threw himself at the attempt to get a second resolu- tion 'like a man possessed, like a mad man, he was desperate for it.'[95] He was working on it 'to the bitter end', fearing that 'the UN might be going the way of the League of Nations'. But he had by now 'internalised the view that if it didn't work then he would join military action, however difficult that was'.[96]

Valerie Amos, the Foreign Officer minister, was sent off on a tour of the three African states bearing handwritten notes for their leaders from the Prime Minister. At Number 10, 'we were convinced that the Americans could shift the Mexicans and the Chileans – and they couldn't.'[97] David Manning flew out to Mexico and Chile – 'the last throw' – to personally lobby Presi- dent Fox and President Lagos.[98] It was 'deeply discussed' within Downing Street whether Blair himself should make the long flight to Santiago to personally lobby Lagos, but he drew back when his aides feared that he would come back humiliatingly empty-handed. That would be an 'overt failure and wasn't worth risking'.[99]

France and Germany countered with an alternative resolution of their own, one which advocated strengthening Blix's team and extending the inspection period to 120 days. On 5 March, they joined with Russia to make a public declaration that they would 'not let a proposed resolution pass that would authorise the use of force'.[100]

This was 'a very significant diplomatic defeat both for the United States and the United Kingdom' in the view of Britain's most senior ambassador.[101] America could not even get on board Chile and Mexico, countries in their own backyard. Britain entirely failed with France and Germany. It was now clear to Jeremy Greenstock at the UN that France, Germany and Russia were 'becoming more and more obsessed about stopping the superpower taking unilateral action'.[102]

The Bush White House was being confirmed in its prejudice, expressed by the arch-hawk Richard Perle, that the UN was nothing but a 'looming chatterbox on the River Hudson'.[103] The British could now see that 'the

Americans were not bothered' about getting a second resolution. 'They'd come to a view long before that the legal case for war had been made.'[104] With the trigger date for an invasion very close, Bush declined to make any further serious effort. The American military juggernaut was revving up for an invasion to a timetable determined in the White House and the Pentagon. Bush dismissed calls to give the process any more time as 'like a re-run of a bad movie and I'm not interested in watching it'.

The Cabinet Secretary says: 'Blair really thought he'd get the second resolution.'[105] This failure would haunt the rest of his premiership. He would ever after be accused of leading Britain into an illegal war. The atmosphere in Number 10 was bleak. Jonathan Powell: 'When we couldn't get the second resolution, Tony thought, we all thought: "Oh fuck, what are we going to do now?"'[106]

Blair and everyone around him were 'exhausted' and 'distressed'.[107] Jack Straw came round to Number 10 to issue his starkest warning yet to Blair. The Prime Minister was told by his Foreign Secretary: 'If you go without a second resolution, the only regime change that will be taking place is in this room.'[108] This was not said in a threatening tone; more one of despairing concern. The next day, Campbell was wobbly. Was it, he asked Blair, 'really worth sacrificing everything' for this?[109] More than once, Sally Morgan said directly to Blair: 'This could be the end of you.'

'I know, it may be,' he responded. 'I've got to do what I've got to do. It's the right thing to do. We have to see it through.'[110]

After a deadlocked meeting of the Security Council on 7 March, in the words of Straw, 'we were just drawn down inevitably towards war.'[111]

All the tortuous and febrile activity over a second resolution proved to be merely a speed hump on the road to conflict. Every aspect of Blair's strategy – in terms of the Americans, the Europeans, the UN, the British public and the Labour Party – appeared to lie in ruins. He was now confronted with the hideous choice that he had spent months trying to avoid: either break with the Americans or follow them into Iraq without the express endorsement of the UN and in the face of the opposition of much of his country and party.

Watching with great concern for an old ally's plight was the former American President, Bill Clinton. He later remarked to me: 'Tony was caught naked in the middle of the room.'[112]

9. With You to the End

'I'm going to call him,' George Bush said to his Chief of Staff and his National Security adviser. 'I'm going to tell Tony that he doesn't have to do this.'[1] On the afternoon of Sunday, 9 March, the secure line at Chequers started to ring. Bush and Blair were about to have one of their most significant and revealing conversations.

The White House was suddenly waking up to the scale of the jeopardy facing its British ally. They'd been getting warnings for weeks. 'This is really difficult stuff,' Jack Straw told several members of the administration in an attempt to get them to 'understand the risk the Prime Minister is taking here'.[2] David Manning was so apprehensive about the peril facing Blair that he phoned Condi Rice the day before the Bush call to warn her that the Prime Minister was 'prepared to go down' over Iraq.[3]

The Americans didn't want that. On Sunday morning in Washington, Bush discussed what to do about it with Rice and Andrew Card. 'We didn't want to put Britain in an awkward position,' says Card. 'Would we want the British troops to be there? Yes. Did we need the British troops to be there? We needed them in the context of the world, but we didn't necessarily need them in the context of the military victory.'[4]

Rice agrees that Bush 'didn't want to put at risk' such a loyal brother in arms.[5] To lose a crucial ally at this juncture – the start date for war was less than two weeks away – would be a very bad development for the White House.

When Blair picked up the phone to Bush, the President told him: 'My last choice is to have your Government go down. We don't want that to happen under any circumstances. Tony, I really mean that.'

'It's difficult here,' Blair acknowledged. 'But I'm with you.'[6]

Bush said he understood the 'burden' on Blair and persisted with his offer of an escape route. 'Perhaps there's some other way Britain can be involved.' The British troops could stay on the Kuwaiti side of the border and participate after the invasion by helping with policing and reconstruction.

Blair did not thank Bush for his offer, say he would consider it and consult colleagues. He instantly turned down the opt-out.

'No, I told you that I'm with you and I'm going to be with you.'[7]

Blair later explained the conversation like this: 'He wanted regime change in Baghdad, not in London.'[8]

That Bush offer was one of several junctures when Blair had both reason and opportunity to disengage British forces from the invasion or at least make their participation conditional. At the Crawford Summit in 2002 he could have reserved his position until it was clearer whether the Americans had properly planned for the invasion and the aftermath. Another opportunity presented itself in the New Year of 2003 when he could have joined France and Germany in arguing for the inspections to be given more time. In early 2003, by which time it was already clear that some of the intelligence on Iraq was unsound, he could have rethought his strategy. Many in the intelligence services were by then getting cold feet. Eliza Manningham-Buller, who succeeded Stephen Lander as head of MI5, shared her predecessor's fear that a war would make Britain more vulnerable to attack because it would radicalise young Muslims and recruit them to terrorism.[9] In February, John Scarlett's JIC sent a warning, circulated not just to Blair but also to Brown, Blunkett and Straw, that 'al-Qaeda and associated groups represent by far the greatest threat to western interests, and that threat would be heightened by military action in Iraq.'[10]

A further opportunity to exit was provided when it became clear there would be no second UN resolution to sanction war. Now, in March 2003, Bush himself offered an escape route only for Blair to turn him down.

As expressed to his Foreign Secretary:

Tony's view was that it was a kind of cop-out because we were willing the end and could have ended up in the worst of all worlds. We would look really stupid if, having led people up to the top of the hill on the basis that there was this danger, we then said: 'No thanks, we're not going to take part in this.'[11]

Blair believed it would be fatal to his authority to back down now, according to David Manning:

He felt his own credibility was on the line. You couldn't just be a fairweather friend and change your mind when things got tough. It's also important that he did believe Saddam was a very evil man and somebody needed to do something about it. And it wasn't satisfactory to leave the dirty work to someone else.[12]

The senior British officers, Michael Boyce and Mike Jackson, were strongly of the opinion that 'either we were in or we weren't up for it: you couldn't go in for half measures.'[13] Boyce and Jackson were very apprehensive of the way the US military operated. They had no appetite for following them into Iraq as peacekeepers 'to try and make everything lovely after the Americans had trashed the joint'.[14]

A senior diplomat thinks the Bush offer was one of the psychological games that leaders play. 'It was another of those little tests that leaders give each other,' believes Jeremy Greenstock. '"Are you going to be with me 100 per cent?" You go on asking as it gets more difficult.'[15]

A more cynical view was taken by a very senior civil servant who observed Blair at close quarters over many years. 'Blair saw this as the big throw of his career. They would go into Iraq. They would have a glorious victory. People would shower them with petals. That would strengthen his hand in Europe as the bridge over the Atlantic and strengthen his hand at home over Brown.'[16]

José María Aznar and Silvio Berlusconi, the right-wing Prime Ministers of Spain and Italy, gave the war their support, but did not provide any troops. Blair regarded that as morally cowardly. 'He felt strongly that it was the right thing to do,' says Sally Morgan. 'He has a view that Britain has a role in the world and that we are a serious player. Britain should intervene and shouldn't be people who stand by and let others do it.'[17]

That was certainly part of the reason, but it was fused with another. His bottom line was that he was never going to break with the Americans even when the Americans themselves were suggesting that he could. Jeremy Greenstock understood from his conversations with Blair that 'he clearly believed that there is no ally of the United Kingdom more important to stick with on hard security issues than the United States.'[18] General Mike Jackson agrees that it boiled down to Blair's view of the 'huge strategic importance of the relationship between the UK and US'.[19]

In the view of the Cabinet Secretary, it was simply too late to back out:

Our forces were literally bobbing up and down on the ocean or sitting in the desert. We had said we would do certain things. We would do the south. We were doing certain intelligence operations. It was already complicated by the Turks saying the US couldn't have land access through their territory. If we'd pulled back, the Special Relationship would have been dead for a hundred years.[20]

Many in the Prime Minister's inner circle were desperately disappointed that he hadn't seized on Bush's offer. Sally Morgan never had moral qualms about the war, but was terrified about the consequences of doing it without explicit sanction from the UN. She chose nevertheless to 'click into loyal servant mode'.[21] Peter Mandelson, still advising from the wings, was highly queasy. Stephen Wall was against and came to regard the war as illegal.²² Andrew Adonis, the head of the policy unit, was opposed. David Manning repeatedly told Blair that he didn't have to do it. Alastair Campbell never seemed completely convinced. Campbell says: 'My big worry was his political position vis-à-vis what would be an unpopular war alongside a very right-wing American President. I was worried how it might affect his survival.'²³ His partner, Fiona Millar, was passionately opposed. So was Sarah Helm, the partner of Jonathan Powell, who liked to joke that she would divorce him had they been married. The Chief of Staff, the son of an Air Vice-Marshal, was the only true believer around the Prime Minister.²⁴ 'Jonathan was the most gung-ho. He was more gung-ho than Tony.'²⁵ The vast majority of the Prime Minister's most senior aides did not share his conviction that this was the right course.

To the last, Jack Straw, whose wife and children were all opponents of the war, was still trying to persuade Blair that they could back out. Though he never showed his doubts in public, the Foreign Secretary bombarded the Prime Minister with 'a whole series of minutes to set out various alternatives'.²⁶ He later said: 'You owe a Prime Minister, if you're Foreign Secretary, the best advice you can give.'²⁷

Two members of the Cabinet were known to be deeply unhappy. One was Robin Cook, sacked as Foreign Secretary in 2001 and shifted into the job of Leader of the House. Clever, spiky and self-regarding, an easier man to respect than to like, Cook did not have warm relations with many of his senior colleagues. But he found them being unusually solicitous towards him when he indicated that he would probably resign. He privately joked that his colleagues had 'put me on suicide watch'.²⁸

Clare Short, the International Development Secretary, had also been voicing her dissent in Cabinet. Both Cook and Short were hawkish supporters of the conflict against Slobodan Milosevic to save the Muslims of Kosovo. That had been conducted without a UN resolution.²⁹ Their positions were not without moral ambiguity and political contradiction either. Both were vehemently opposed to military action in Iraq and believed, for slightly different reasons, that it would result in catastrophe. Neither had yet broken cover. Clare Short now did just that.

On 9 March, I arrived as usual at the BBC's studios on Millbank, just down the road from Parliament, to present *The Westminster Hour*, my Sunday evening political programme for Radio 4. There was a telephone message from Short waiting for me. When I called her back, she had just finished serving Sunday lunch to her mother in Birmingham. I established from the conversation that Short appeared ready to say that she would resign from the Cabinet if Blair took Britain to war. She used a striking word about the Prime Minister's behaviour: 'reckless'. The challenge for me was to make sure that we had this on the record before her passion cooled or her nerve failed. John Evans, the programme's ever efficient editor, arranged for a car to whisk her to the BBC studios at Pebble Mill so that we could record the interview quickly.

We sat down and the line went up at 5 p.m. I hoped she would repeat to a million listeners what she had said to me in the phone call. I couldn't be sure. Politicians often flinch in front of the microphone.

She sounded hesitant and cagey at first. Then, deploying as a prompt the word she had used in our earlier phone conversation, I asked her whether she considered Blair to be acting recklessly. The dam broke. The dissent that had been building within her for months cascaded into the microphone.

'The whole atmosphere of the current situation is deeply reckless,' she declared, a slight quaver in her voice. 'Reckless for the world, reckless for the undermining of the UN in this disorderly world, reckless with our Government, reckless with his own future, position and place in history. It's extraordinarily reckless.' By the end of the interview, I had her on the record saying that it would be 'indefensible' to take action without a UN mandate. In the event of war, she would resign: 'Absolutely, there's no question about that.'[30]

She later described it to me as 'my last throw. All I've got left is to say I'm going to resign so I'd better say it in public.'[31]

The interview sent a deep shockwave through the Government. When the programme was broadcast after the 10 p.m. news that night, one Cabinet minister was so enraged by her behaviour that he hurled his radio against the wall. The next morning, she was driving her car on the way to the bank machine when her mobile rang. It was Blair, exploding with a fury that took her aback. 'You never told me. You didn't say you were going to resign,' he lambasted her. 'I'm sorry,' responded Short, contending it should have been clear enough from what she had been saying in Cabinet. She offered: 'I'll resign now.' 'No,' Blair replied. 'I don't want you to do that. I'll talk to you tomorrow.' He was 'angrier than I've ever known him, because he doesn't usually do angry'.[32]

The interview was the splash in all of Monday morning's newspapers, which speculated even more intensely about Blair's chances of survival. It was a 'stunning attack' in the view of the *Mirror*,[33] which 'dealt a body blow to Tony Blair' in the assessment of *The Times*.[34] Tony Blair was left 'facing the opening of floodgates to a catastrophic rebellion', according to the *Guardian*.[35]

There was a widespread expectation that he had no option but to fire Short. She had publicly accused the Prime Minister of being 'reckless' – a word she used six times. That was as flagrant a breach of the conventions of Cabinet loyalty as there can be. Moreover, she unleashed this shot into his exposed flank at a moment of maximum vulnerability. So it was a demonstration of how imperilled Blair now felt that he did not feel strong enough to fire her despite the risk of looking even weaker. 'I don't want to make a martyr of her,' he explained to colleagues.[36]

This did initially make him look feeble, but it was also a display of Blair's tactical guile when in a corner. The resignation of both Short and Cook would be more threatening than losing just the one of them.

Within forty-eight hours of her appearance on *The Westminster Hour* came two more interventions, one from Washington, another from Paris, which further squeezed the vice in which Blair had placed himself. Geoff Hoon had made a call to his American counterpart during which he warned Donald Rumsfeld that Britain would not be able to commit its forces if the parliamentary vote went against the Government. The same message was conveyed to Colin Powell from Jack Straw.[37]

Expecting these exchanges to remain private, there was horror in London when Rumsfeld blithely declared in public that it wasn't a problem if the British couldn't join the invasion. 'There are workarounds,' he shrugged to a news conference.[38]

'It took everybody aback,' says David Manning. Commitments had been made, very difficult commitments for which Blair was 'already taking a lot of flak'. Rumsfeld's unhelpful intervention was 'a pretty odd way of acknowledging that'.[39]

Wedded to his strategy of invasion-lite, Rumsfeld thought he could do the job with fewer US troops than there had been in the first Gulf War. He and the head of US forces, Tommy Franks, reckoned that allies, even their British ones, were more of a nuisance than an assistance. So naturally enough he didn't regard British participation as essential for anything but diplomatic reasons. And diplomacy was of no interest anyway to old Rummy.

The British military regarded his claim that the Americans could do it on their own as 'bollocks' because 'when we actually hit the button the British were absolutely integrated into the plan.' The American forces were already thinned out. The US 4th Infantry Division, which was supposed to be at the cutting edge, was 'nowhere' because the Turks had denied land access. British withdrawal 'would have unstitched the American battle plan'. Britain was contributing about a third of the armour. The British were also an essential feature of the airpower plan.[40]

Blair 'went bonkers' when he was told about Rumsfeld's remarks. 'He couldn't believe how the US kept fucking things up.'[41]

The Prime Minister was risking everything trying to persuade his party and the British people of the value of the Atlantic alliance and the imperative to tackle Saddam. Here was the US Defense Secretary casually saying that they could easily do without the British.

Looked at another way, this presented Blair with one final opportunity to extract himself from the war. Manning, Morgan and Straw made further attempts to persuade Blair to pull back. He was having none of it, dismissing them almost without bothering to argue the case. 'This is really dangerous,' Morgan warned him.

'You don't have to do this, you really don't have to do this,' Manning argued.

'No, David, I really do have to do this,' responded Blair.[42]

Any hope of getting a second resolution at the UN evaporated altogether when Jacques Chirac gave an interview in which he declared that France would wield its veto at the Security Council against the British and the Americans. 'Whatever the circumstances,' said the French President, 'France will vote "Non" because we believe, tonight, that there are no grounds to wage war.'[43]

Chirac's 'Non' destroyed what remained of the already tiny chances of getting agreement at the UN. There was no incentive for the Swing Six to expose themselves by supporting another resolution if the French, probably joined by the Chinese and the Russians, were going to wield the veto.

Blair professed outrage, saying in front of a journalist: 'This is just a foolish thing to do at this moment in the world's history.'[44] At a packed meeting with Labour MPs, he came alive when the subject of the French came up. 'It is a wrecking tactic, done with absolute calculation,' he told them, claiming that 'until a couple of days ago I thought I had a majority.'[45]

Chirac's intervention was a crisis in which Blair spotted a glimmer of opportunity. He now showed the low cunning in his character. Sir Stephen Wall witnessed Blair and Campbell in a Number 10 corridor discussing how they could cast Chirac as the bad guy.[46] On the 11th, and again on the 13th and the 19th of that month, Blair had phone conversations with Rupert Murdoch.[47] The day after the first of those calls, the *Sun*, always eager for any excuse to froth up Francophobia, ridiculed Chirac as 'Le French Worm' and a 'cheap tart who puts price before principle, money before honour'.[48]

As Number 10 orchestrated the campaign to blame Chirac, the French were infuriated. Their ambassador in London, Gerard Errara, complained in person to Number 10 and was met with the response: 'But it's working like magic!'[49]

Francophobia also served to solidify the Cabinet when it met on Thursday. When Blair bade them a good morning, some of the ministers chorused back, in the manner of a primary school French class: 'Bonjour, Prime Minister.' David Blunkett prompted further mirth by suggesting: 'We can all agree that Chirac has been completely reckless', enjoying himself by poking Clare Short in the eye as well. When she made a remark about 'megaphone diplomacy', Charles Clarke jeered across the Cabinet table: 'Like on the radio.'[50]

Gordon Brown had often stayed opaquely mute during earlier Cabinet discussions about Iraq. The Chancellor now made a significant intervention. He declared to the others that 'we pin the blame on France for its isolated refusal to agree in the Security Council.'[51] Afterwards, some of the Blairite ministers muttered darkly that the Prime Minister's position must really be imperilled if the Chancellor was now calculating that it was time to sound loyal.[52]

Of all the people around the Cabinet table, Gordon Brown posed the greatest menace to Tony Blair. The Chancellor's opposition to war would either have stopped it or forced Blair to resign and quite possibly could have achieved both. Brown had not advertised any dissent, but neither had he been conspicuously supportive. 'He was nowhere to be seen for most of the time,' says Sally Morgan. 'He was very nervous about it.'[53] The cautious Chancellor felt impaled on a dilemma. There was a temptation to strike at Blair's moment of extreme vulnerability and some of his camp were urging him to do just that. One of his allies in the Cabinet, Clare Short, thought he was 'willing to wound but afraid to strike. Gordon was always worried that if he really struck, the Labour Party might divide in the way that it has historically done and that would weaken his time when he came to power. His fear was the divided party.'[54]

Greatly though he lusted for the premiership, that craving was always tempered by his terror of inheriting a wrecked government. He would additionally face the ferocious hostility of the pro-war Murdoch press and other newspapers if he struck down their hero, Blair.[55]

On Friday, 14 March, Sir Jeremy Greenstock rang from the UN to definitively report the death of any hope of a second resolution. He and his American counterpart now switched their efforts to thwarting France and Russia from introducing an anti-war resolution. If that got majority support, they would be in the terrible position of having to use their vetoes to block it.[56]

The following morning, the Prime Minister went through the connecting door between Numbers 10 and 11 for an important encounter with his Chancellor. As was often his habit on a weekend when he was not performing in public, Blair was wearing an open-necked blue shirt and chinos. His Chancellor was more formally dressed in a dark suit as they sat in a gloomy reception room. The meeting began with Hilary Armstrong, the Chief Whip, reading out the latest assessment of how many Labour MPs would vote against the Government. For all the pressure already applied by the whips, the rebel numbers were still terrifyingly large. 'They haven't seen the abyss yet,' remarked Sally Morgan, trying to be more optimistic. 'When they've seen it, they will come back from it.'[57]

Gordon Brown sat in one of the gilded, judge-like thrones in the room. Within Number 10 he had been mocked over the preceding weeks for doing his 'McCavity the cat' trick of disappearing in a crisis. They also feared that he was deliberately distancing himself so that he could seize the crown if it all went wrong.[58] Brown became 'angry and frustrated' when he read press reports that he was being half-hearted in support of Blair. The Chancellor told his inner circle this was Blair's fault for cutting him out of all the decision-making.[59] Brown's main argument with Blair was that he was under-estimating Britain's influence over the Americans. 'You've got to get them to go the extra mile at the UN,' he contended.[60]

From his gilded seat, Brown said to Blair: 'What people ask me is, why can't we delay it? Why do we have to do it now?'

Blair was impatient with the question: 'Time, time and more time.' With the second resolution dead, they would 'go back to 1441' as their justification for war.

Brown responded: 'We'll have to produce better language than that if we're going to persuade people to believe us.'

The room was frozen. As one witness to this exchange says: 'Everybody realised that Gordon Brown was still at that stage the one person who could have stopped it.'[61]

The Chancellor persisted: 'Why do we have to go now?'

'It can't wait,' replied Blair with the exasperation of someone who had been through this argument with so many people so many times before.

Brown seemed to be working himself up to have another go. 'You could see how close he was to saying: "This is wrong."'[62] But he didn't. He too had made his decision.

When it came down to it, Brown did not have a fundamental disagreement in principle about Iraq. He agreed that there had to be a response to Saddam to sustain the credibility of the international order. He believed that the intelligence showed there was a genuine threat. In the words of one of his closest aides: 'He was totally coloured by his fervent Atlanticism. His overriding position was that we can't afford to be seen as anti-American.'[63]

Members of the Cabinet noted that 'suddenly Gordon and Tony are together again and Gordon is very engaged on Iraq, which he hadn't been.'

Blair was boosted by having Brown securely onside. 'Tony feels better when he's got Gordon with him. Despite their differences, when he was in these crunches, he liked Gordon there.'[64] And Brown liked to be there. According to one of his aides: 'Gordon was childishly excited when Tony asked him to come on board and help with the strategy.'[65] Clare Short was not alone in gaining the strong impression that it was Brown as much as Blair who 'cooked up' the plan to blame Chirac.[66]

On Sunday, Blair flew out to the Azores for a final council of war with Bush. On Monday, Brown gave an unequivocal statement of public support and threw himself into the effort to win over Labour MPs. 'In the final days, Gordon was absolutely core,' says Sally Morgan.[67]

On 17 March, the Cabinet, meeting unusually on a Monday afternoon, filed into Number 10 to take their places around the coffin-shaped table. Right on the cusp of the conflict, they were finally going to consider whether or not it was actually legal.

An invasion had been secretly discussed for a year now, but for all that time Blair tried to prevent discussion about its legality swimming around Whitehall. Once the Attorney-General warned him that there was no justification in international law for pre-emptive regime change, he told Peter Goldsmith not to produce a legal opinion too early. So it was not until 7 March that the Attorney formally presented Number 10 with a thirteen-page assessment. The Attorney-General concluded that a 'reasonable case' could be made for going to war, but that there was not a legal consensus about this. There certainly was not: the majority of experts in international law took the contrary view.[68] The Attorney's document listed six reasons why it could be argued that a war in current circumstances was a breach of international law.[69]

In Goldsmith's view, a court 'might well conclude' that a second resolution was required to sanction military action. Blair, with his habitually cavalier attitude towards conventions and rules, never seemed troubled by the legality question except in so much as it presented a political obstacle. During the Afghan conflict, the Attorney came to the War Cabinet to explain a legal point about the rules of engagement. 'Oh, for God's sake,' erupted Blair. 'We're not going to be told what to do by lawyers.'[70] He never showed much respect for lawyers even though, perhaps because, he was a lawyer himself. In the high court of his own mind, he had already delivered a verdict that satisfied him.

Goldsmith's equivocal document on the legality of invading Iraq was very much a problem for those to whom international law mattered. It was far too fence-sitting for the senior military officers. Sir Michael Boyce 'made the running on this'.[71] 'More than once', he pressed Number 10 that he needed a much clearer statement from the law officer. 'People doing the fighting and their families need to be sure,' he told Blair. 'All I want is a one-liner saying it is legal.'[72] The same view was taken by Sir Mike Jackson, the head of the army, a blunt-speaking soldier's soldier who was well regarded in Number 10. He'd got so worried he'd done 'my own homework' by pulling the relevant UN resolutions off the internet. General Jackson led the multinational ground force in the Kosovo conflict. The Serbian dictator, Slobodan Milosevic, was now indicted for war crimes and imprisoned at The Hague. General Jackson declared: 'Having played my part in getting Milosevic into his cell in the Hague, I've no wish to be his next-door neighbour there.'[73] Michael Jay, the Permanent Secretary at the Foreign Office, was another voice pressing for unambiguous legal sanction.[74]

On the 14th, Goldsmith produced a second, much shorter statement, shorn of his earlier hesitations and caveats of just a week before. This paper consisted of only 337 words about an issue as complex and contentious as the legality of invading Iraq. This new, short paper unequivocally declared war to be legal. That was 'good enough'[75] for Jackson and for Boyce, who was happy that he had got 'top cover' from the Attorney.[76]

Though it never was tested in court, it would ever be intensely controversial. The country's most senior law lord, Lord Bingham, was the most eminent authority to subsequently declare that the war was 'a serious violation of international law' because it took place without proper sanction from the UN.[77] The Foreign Office's lawyers at the time were unhappy. One of them, a deputy legal adviser, Elizabeth Wilmshurst, resigned in protest. Goldsmith's one-page summary was also the cause of many subsequent allegations – denied by all involved – that the Attorney-General had been pressured by Blair. Just the day before he produced the second document, he had a meeting with Sally Morgan and Charlie Falconer. Peter Hennessy, highly distinguished historian of post-war British politics, would later savage Peter Goldsmith as the most 'pliable' Attorney-General in memory.[78] Goldsmith always maintained it was his 'genuinely held independent view'.[79] Charlie Falconer insists: 'We did not lean on him. He wanted to see us to say that he'd decided it was lawful.'[80] The Cabinet Secretary, Andrew Turnbull, suggests: 'It was very obvious to him [the Attorney] at this stage what the consequences were if he came out and said there is no legal case for war.'[81]

When the Cabinet sat down on the 17th, someone was missing. Just before the meeting, Robin Cook told Blair that he was going to resign; Blair then prevailed on him not to come to Cabinet, thwarting Cook's intention to make one last plea to his colleagues not to 'jump over the precipice'.[82]

Campbell escorted him out of the building the rear way in case Cook should be tempted to rush out front and make a dramatic declaration to the TV cameras on Downing Street. Cook had, in fact, already decided against 'doing a Heseltine'. As a parting shot to Campbell, he said: 'I hope it doesn't end horribly for you all.'[83]

Campbell returned to the Cabinet Room to take his usual seat on a chair against the wall. Goldsmith was being introduced when Clare Short flustered in late. Piquantly, the Attorney, the man declaring the war legal, had taken the seat of Cook, the man who had just resigned in protest that it was unlawful folly. Short asked what had happened to her fellow dissenter. 'He's gone,' said Sally Morgan from her seat against the wall. 'Oh my God!' cried Short.[84]

Blair invited the Attorney to start reading out his judgement. Some ministers pointed out that this was time-wasting: they all had a copy in front of them. They could read the few paragraphs that declared that Saddam's failure to comply with Resolution 1441 gave sufficient authority for a war.

Three days before, Goldsmith's Legal Secretary had written to the Prime Minister's Private Secretary asking for Blair's view. The next day, the Private Secretary responded that 'it is indeed the Prime Minister's unequivocal view that Iraq is in further material breach of its obligations' to comply with resolution 1441.[85]

The declaration that the war was legal therefore depended on a tautology. The Attorney-General could tell the Cabinet that the war was legal because the Prime Minister had told the Attorney-General that the war was legal.

Cook was missed on that fateful morning in the Cabinet Room. His forensic mind would have questioned the legal advice. He might have asked whether it represented a consensus among international lawyers, which it did not. The absent Cook might also have inquired whether this was really the sum total of the Attorney's advice. Few of the Cabinet had read the earlier, much more qualified thirteen-page document.

Clare Short did try to start a debate. 'Why is it so late?' she asked Goldsmith. Did that mean he'd had doubts? She was rumbled into silence.[86] The Cabinet did not want to probe the Attorney with questions because they had made up their minds to be loyal. 'People just wanted comfort,' comments Alan Milburn.[87] Ministers troubled by the war's legality had been squared off in advance. Only two members of the Cabinet, Alistair Darling and Patricia Hewitt, both lawyers themselves, had bothered to question Goldsmith about his opinion before the Cabinet.[88]

'They were looking for their brief to say it was all right,' remarks the Cabinet Secretary. 'If my brief says this is all right, thank God for that. They were looking for reassurance rather than absolute legal advice.'[89] Even Short could sense that 'the Cabinet was impatient with me. They didn't want such a discussion.'⁹⁰ Whatever credibility she had with her colleagues had been destroyed by the 'reckless' interview. Short then spent a sleepless night wrestling her conscience to the ground. In the morning, she announced that she would not be resigning, after all. Both Brown and Blair, who had been phoning her two or three times a day, worked to keep her in the tent.⁹¹ Blair played to her vanity by saying she would be needed for the post-war reconstruction of Iraq. She wrote a pitiful letter to Labour MPs trying to explain why she now supported the war. This turned her into a discredited figure – 'depleted Claranium' – held in contempt by loyalists and rebels alike.

Many of the Cabinet were convinced because they wanted to be convinced. One reason was political self-preservation. Jack Straw, whose resignation would almost certainly have stopped British participation in the war, wrote yet another of his 'personal minutes' urging Blair to think again only the night before. But the Foreign Secretary did not articulate his grave doubts in Cabinet and followed Blair 'with a heavy heart'.⁹² John Prescott, who could also have stopped it, stuck with Blair from gut loyalty to the leader. He revelled in publicly squashing dissident Labour MPs and saw his role as sturdily defending the leader as his hero, Ernie Bevin, had buttressed Clem Attlee. 'Whatever happens, I'll be there all the way,' he told Sally Morgan.⁹³ Some ministers simply invested their faith in the Prime Minister's superior wisdom on foreign affairs. Had he not, they talked themselves into thinking, been proved right before? 'I just have to assume that Tony knows what he's doing,' said one.⁹⁴

In the view of a senior mandarin: 'Blair was in the strongest position of a Prime Minister ever. The checks and balances didn't work.'⁹⁵

The Cabinet did not want to make them work anyway. The fall of Blair would threaten to bring many of them tumbling down too. David Blunkett was previously a vocal sceptic about military action. When they first entered government, he would have found it 'unthinkable and unbelievable' that he would find himself voting to join a very right-wing President in a war against Iraq.⁹⁶ Now Blunkett was doing just that. 'Tony had put his premiership on the line, and those who were very close to him would go down with him.'⁹⁷ Even Cook, the sole resignee, co-ordinated his departure with Number 10 and pledged that he would not make it a personal issue with Blair because 'I do not want to be part of a process that sees Gordon become Prime Minister on the back of this.'⁹⁸

The demise of Blair would mean the succession of Brown, an outcome more terrifying than war to Blunkett, Hewitt, Hoon, Reid and several others in the Cabinet. So they went round the table expressing support for the

Prime Minister, a loyalty ritual designed to bind them to the decision, to dip their hands in the blood.[99] Through the sheer force of his position, his personality and conviction, Tony Blair had driven his Cabinet to a place where few if any of them would have individually gone. Only a couple of junior ministers resigned along with Cook.[100]

Two days of great theatre began in the House of Commons. Previous conflicts had been started without a vote or on the basis of 'take note' motions. Some in Number 10, knowing how difficult it was going to be in the Commons, wanted to avoid a vote if they could possibly get away with it.

They were delusional. This conflict was already hugely contentious. To have proceeded into it in the absence of both explicit sanction from the UN and the House of Commons would be 'a disaster', Jack Straw argued with Blair. The Foreign Secretary's argument was one of both principle and pragmatism. They needed the sanction of the Commons to get 'full and effective legitimacy' for the war. If MPs were denied a proper vote, he contended: 'People will go berserk.'[101]

Straw had deliberately boxed in Blair by making public commitments that there would be a formal Commons vote, as had Robin Cook, before he resigned as Leader of the House. 'Jack effectively bounced us into it,' said one Cabinet colleague.[102] On this point, at least, the Foreign Secretary prevailed.

On Monday lunchtime, Blair phoned Bush to tell him: 'I think I can win. But I don't want the Tories to be able to say "without us, you would have lost".'[103]

He wished Bush luck with the televised address he was making that night in which the President delivered a final ultimatum by inviting the Iraqi dictator to flee: 'Saddam and his sons must leave Iraq within forty-eight hours. Their refusal to do so will result in military conflict commenced at a time of our choosing.'[104]

Blair's problem was his own party. He could win in the Commons with Tory votes, but his moral authority as Prime Minister would be fatally compromised if he could not secure the support of a majority of Labour MPs. He believed 'he'd have to go if he hadn't got a majority of the party', says Sally Morgan.[105] The Chief Whip, Hilary Armstrong, agrees: 'We knew that he would resign. We knew it was high stakes.'[106] Jack Straw feared that the entire Government would be 'in a completely impossible position if we'd plainly lost the confidence of our own side. The Cabinet would have had to resign if a majority of Labour MPs voted against us.'[107]

That weekend Blair sat down with his three oldest children and explained to them that he might no longer be Prime Minister by the end of the week.

He said later: 'In the end, if you lose your premiership, well, you lose it', but it was better to 'lose it [for] something you believe in'.[108] He always had a taste for self-dramatisation, but in this case he was utterly serious. 'He'd have resigned if he lost,' says his faithful constituency agent, John Burton.[109] His old friend Barry Cox agrees: 'Certainly he said: "This could cost me my job." He knew it, he absolutely knew it. He was still prepared to do it.'[110] 'He was putting his political life on the line,' says David Manning. 'If he fell in the process, he would have gone down thinking: "Well, I went down but I tried to do the right thing."'[111] The Shadow Cabinet discussed what the Tories would do if the Prime Minister fell. 'There was a clear sense that Blair could go,' says Iain Duncan Smith, though he was also conscious that 'he played it up to increase pressure on Labour MPs.'[112] Sir Andrew Turnbull, the Cabinet Secretary, wasn't so convinced that it would come to that, but he nevertheless took the precaution of checking the procedures for handling a sudden prime ministerial resignation.[113]

Gordon Brown joined the 'ferocious work' to win the vote. Once Brown had committed himself, Blair could not fairly question his Chancellor's loyalty on this occasion. He and his people became 'part of the team'. Even Sally Morgan, inveterately mistrustful of the next-door neighbour, noted how 'they worked very closely together refining the arguments' and ran the operation 'almost like an election campaign'.[114] Douglas Alexander and Pat McFadden, a Brown acolyte and a Blair aide who would normally be highly suspicious of each other, worked in tandem writing briefings for Labour MPs. The Chief Whip 'gave him [Brown] a list of people he could work on'.[115] Brown put pressure on those of his supporters who were sceptical about war.[116] The whips ran an intense operation to beg, borrow and bully votes from Labour MPs. Frank Dobson had been twice promised by Blair that he would become British High Commissioner in South Africa. He was warned by Number 10: 'If you don't vote with the Government, you can forget about South Africa.'[117] Cherie threw herself into the fray. On some civil liberties issues, she fiercely disagreed with her husband. But she was implacably his supporter on Iraq. When they had dinner with Robert Harris – the novelist was an opponent of the war – there was a *Fawlty Towers* moment' when the topic of Iraq came up. 'Don't mention the war in front of Cherie,' Blair cautioned the author.[118] She called up some women Labour MPs to cajole them into the Government lobby.

The stakes were vertiginous in Parliament. An institution that had often been treated as an irrelevance during the New Labour years was suddenly again a place of supreme importance and electric theatre. 'It was extremely tense, extremely fraught,' remembers Ed Owen.[119] The cockpit of British democracy was more packed than it had been at any time since Labour's victory in 1997. There were two outstanding performers. Cook delivered a fine resignation speech, which earned him a convention-breaking standing ovation from anti-war MPs. He declared that 'history will be astonished' at the 'miscalculations' that led to conflict. 'I cannot support a war that has neither international agreement nor domestic support.' The claims about WMD were merely 'suggestive'.[120] That speech reads even better today because we now know that he was even more right than he then knew about the absence of a WMD threat. On the day, the impact of his speech and resignation was partly neutralised by the volte-face of Clare Short. She had booked a slot to make a resignation speech immediately after Cook, but now cancelled it.[121] Blair made a human shield of Short. When she came into the Commons for the debate, she was told to move up the frontbench to sit by the Prime Minister so that he could display his prisoner of war to other waverers.

Blair made two speeches on the climactic day, one a private address to Labour MPs and then another in the Chamber. He quietly dropped some of the assertions made in the September dossier. There was no mention of the 45-minute claim which he now knew to be unreliable. He nevertheless painted Saddam as a growing menace. 'Our fault has not been impatience. Our patience should have been exhausted weeks, months and years ago,' he declaimed.

'The only persuasive power to which he responds is 250,000 allied troops on his doorstep. To retreat now would be to put at hazard all that we hold dearest. If we do act, we should do so with a clear conscience and a strong heart,' he went on.[122]

Many years later, Cherie would say that invading Iraq 'was one of those 51/49 questions', but her husband was 'very good at then convincing everyone else that it was a 70/30 decision all along'.[123] Turning on the opponents of war he implied that they were making the same mistake as appeasers of Hitler in the 1930s, a line he insisted on including against the advice of Peter Hyman and others on the speech-writing team, who feared it would 'wind up' Labour MPs.[124]

Blair was always at his most effective in a tight spot. 'He's hopeless when you give him a wide-open goal and a roaring crowd,' remarks Paddy Ashdown. 'He doesn't know which goal to shoot at. But put his back against the wall, fighting for his life, and he's absolutely magnificent.'[125]

That speech had to be 'extraordinary' in the view of David Blunkett because 'he wasn't just winning MPs, he was addressing the nation.'[126]

Stan Greenberg, soothsayer of public opinion and an opponent of the war, 'watched in some awe as he set out the case to the country and moved the numbers until the country was supportive of going into Iraq at the time they went in'.[127] A young Tory MP called David Cameron was so wowed by Blair's 'masterful' speech that he circulated it to his constituents.[128]

The *Daily Mail*, which was sceptical about the war and loathed Blair with a greater intensity than any other newspaper, lauded the performance as:

the speech of a lifetime from Tony Blair, one of those rare Parliamentary performances that can change hearts, minds and votes. If last night's backbench revolt was not nearly the meltdown predicted by some, the credit lies with a Prime Minister at the peak of his powers, willing to lay his future on the line for a cause in which he passionately believes.[129]

From the anti-war *Mirror*: 'We do not question his belief in the rightness of what he is doing.'[130]

The anti-war *Independent* called it 'the most persuasive case yet made by the man who has emerged as the most formidable persuader for war on either side of the Atlantic'.[131]

The *Daily Telegraph* reckoned he had the best cards and played the hand 'brilliantly, giving the country a rare reminder of what a first class parliamentary performer he is'.[132]

For the equally pro-war *Sun*: 'With passion in his voice and fire in his belly, Tony Blair has won his place in history alongside Winston Churchill and Margaret Thatcher.'[133]

He had never before, and he would never again, get such universally glowing press notices over Iraq. At the climax of his speech, Blair rhetorically conflated everything that had happened since 9/11. 'We will confront the tyrannies and dictatorships and terrorists who put our way of life at risk. To show at the moment of decision that we have the courage to do the right thing.'[134]

Though some of the factual content of the speech would turn out to be either suspect or false, the emotional power and rhetorical force of the performance was of a very high octane. It was regarded as his parliamentary career best even by some who thought the decision was the worst of his premiership.

After his speech, Blair sat in his office behind the Speaker's chair doing frantic, last-minute lobbying of Labour MPs. 'By the end, we were just pouring alcohol into them.'[135] Jack Straw, disguising his own doubts, wound up the debate. As 10 p.m. grew nearer, whips dashed round the corridors and lobbies telling the wobblers that they risked bringing down the leader who had delivered them two landslides. They even tried to terrify Labour MPs with the thought that if Blair went, he would take the entire Cabinet with him and there would be a general election, a threat which was the whips' 'most devastating weapon',[136] though not an entirely credible one. As the tellers clutched papers bearing the result, Hilary Armstrong, the Chief Whip, came into the Chamber, crouched by the Prime Minister and whispered to him that the revolt had just been contained. 'So it's ok,' he sighed with relief.[137]

The number of Labour MPs who voted against the war was 139, a record revolt in modern times. But to his 'deep relief'[138] he had carried enough of them to claim the support of the majority of his party and Number 10 somehow managed to spin that as a resounding victory.

An exhausted but relieved Tony Blair returned to Number 10 that night with Parliament's sanction for war. He made 'a euphoric phone call' to Bush.[139]

Admiral Boyce picked up the phone to his opposite number in America to tell General Myers: 'The vote is yes.'[140] Forty thousand British troops, airmen and sailors were now committed in the seas of the Arabian Gulf and in the deserts 3,000 miles away. An allied force of some 300,000 in all waited for the final order to invade. Blair's destiny and the fate of his Government were now irrevocably entwined with what George Bush had planned for Iraq. Tony Blair had taken epic responsibility for a war over which he would very soon discover he had virtually no control.

10. Squandered Victory

At just after midnight on Thursday, 20 March, Tony Blair answered the phone in the flat above Downing Street. There was a mild, familiar voice on the other end of the line. 'It's begun,' said David Manning, who was calling from his office downstairs in Number 10. Manning had just spoken to a faintly apologetic Condi Rice, who informed him that there was 'a little change' in their plans: American military action was already underway ahead of the previously agreed timetable. US intelligence had informed the President that Saddam and his sons were located at a farm near Baghdad. The Americans wanted to try 'to decapitate the regime there and then'. Manning agreed: 'You have to take the shot.' Not that the Americans needed or waited on British agreement. Cruise missiles were already flying. Special Forces were in. Stealth bombers were airborne. The full 'shock and awe' designed to batter the regime into rapid submission would follow.

The starting gun was fired a day earlier than Bush, who'd spoken to the Prime Minister less than fifteen hours before, had led Blair to believe. But the Prime Minister took the news calmly. It was hardly 'a huge surprise'.[1]

The next morning, Blair convened a meeting of the War Cabinet at eight and then chaired the Cabinet at ten. Cabinet was even briefer than usual. There was just long enough for Blair to tell his ministers two things. One they already knew: the war had begun. The other most of them didn't: the Americans had gone early to try to assassinate Saddam.

At 4 p.m. in London, Bush called. He thanked Blair for being understanding about the last-minute change of plan. 'I kind of think,' Blair mused to the President, 'that the decisions taken in the next few weeks will determine the rest of the world for years to come.'[2] They would certainly determine much of the rest of his premiership.

Once the conflict was underway, Blair and Bush did not have so much to do. Blair's first day of the war was occupied with preparing the broadcast to the nation he was going to deliver that night. His team gathered on the sofas in the den to help him work on the text.

'How should I start?' asked Blair. Alastair Campbell was in a mocking mood. 'What about "My fellow Americans . . ."?' he suggested.

Blair didn't find that funny. 'What about the end?' he asked impatiently. 'I want to end with "God bless you."'

A cacophony of voices protested that this was not a good idea. 'Don't be absurd,' said Sally Morgan. 'That's awfully American, Prime Minister,' sniffed one of the civil servants. 'We don't want any God stuff,' said someone else. Blair looked around the room: 'You are the most godless lot I have ever known.' Peter Hyman, who was Jewish, interjected: 'Count me out. I'm not godless.'

'That's a different God,' said someone.

'Oh no,' responded Blair. 'It's the same God.'[3]

When the text was finished, he went up to the White Drawing Room on the first floor of Number 10 to record the broadcast.

'Tonight British servicemen are engaged from air, land and sea,' he said, borrowing phrasing used by Winston Churchill in May 1940. 'Their mission: to remove Saddam Hussein from power, and disarm Iraq of its weapons of mass destruction.' Looking lined and faintly red-eyed, he read the address from autocue, though by now he knew all his arguments by heart.

The threat to Britain today is not that of my father's generation. War between the big powers is unlikely. But this new world faces a new threat: disorder and chaos born either of brutal states like Iraq, armed with weapons of mass destruction, or of extreme terrorist groups. Both hate our way of life, our freedom, our democracy. My fear, deeply held, based in part on the intelligence that I see, is that these threats come together and deliver catastrophe to our country and the world.

He told the Iraqi people that they were not the enemy. The allies were coming to liberate them from their 'barbarous rulers'. He returned to 'the courage and determination' of 'our troops' on whom 'the fate of many nations rests'. He ended with a non-religious 'Thank you'.[4] The 'godless lot' had got their way.

That night Royal Marines and echelons of the Special Boat Service launched an aerial and amphibious assault on 'Red Beach' at the head of the Gulf, where the al-Faw peninsula met the Shatt al-Arab waterway. Royal Navy submarines contributed to the 'shock and awe' by launching cruise missiles at Baghdad. RAF Harriers and Tornados flew bombing missions.[5]

Following the campaigns in Sierra Leone, Kosovo and Afghanistan, this was Blair's fourth war. He had sent British forces to fight and die in more theatres than any other Prime Minister since Churchill, whose wartime rhetoric he consciously strained to echo in that address to the nation.

That he should find himself with such a record was a surprise most of all perhaps to himself. His friend Barry Cox once said to him: 'I never thought you were going to be a warrior Prime Minister.' Blair replied: 'Neither did I.'[6]

As a rebellious teenager at school, he loathed the period of compulsory service in the Fettes cadet force and quit as soon as he could. 'We hated the cadets,' says one of his schoolfriends. 'We ended up painting old people's homes instead.'[7] One of his teachers at the school remembers a Remembrance Day service during which the young Blair engaged him in a passionate argument in favour of pacifism.[8] The most remarked upon role of his school acting career was as Captain Stanhope, the whisky-soaked, disillusioned officer in *Journey's End*, R. C. Sheriff's classic play about the First World War. 'That play had a real effect on me,' he remarked on the eve of the invasion of Iraq. 'You have to isolate yourself when people are dying from what you have yourself decided to do. You have to put barriers in your mind.'[9]

There was little trace left of the teenage pacifist. One of the first briefings Blair received when he became Prime Minister was from the Chief of the Defence Staff about Britain's nuclear deterrent. The neophyte Prime Minister's 'eyes opened' and he went 'rather quiet' as Charles Guthrie laid out the responsibility for the awesome power of the nuclear arsenal.[10] Blair was a nervous warrior at the beginning of the Kosovo conflict in 1999. He insisted on being briefed about every bombing run, fretted about hitting hospitals, and wanted to count each British plane out and back. By the end of that conflict he sometimes sounded more cold-blooded about the costs of war, saying of civilian casualties: 'Mistakes will happen from time to time.'[11] That conflict hardened him. It also swelled an admiration for the military, whom he thought of as more can-do types than most of the civil servants who worked for him.

This thickening of the skin continued during the Afghan campaign. 'You toughen,' he told me.[12] While it would be too facile to say that he enjoyed war, it is true that conflict injected an adrenalin rush that he didn't get from the humdrumities of politics as usual. 'War is life and death,' he reflected. 'In international crises, the defining moments loom very large and very clear and very inescapable. With the domestic agenda, it's more of a process.'[13] It was clear which he found more energising. Shortly after the conventional war in Iraq, he told another interviewer that he had experienced 'fantastic highs and fantastic lows'.[14]

He was still capable of being pricked by its casualties. Fourteen British service personnel were killed in the first forty-eight hours of the Iraq conflict. All died in helicopter crashes. 'God, it is awful, this war business,' Blair remarked to Campbell, who acidly replied: 'Yes, that's why it is usually best to avoid it.'[15] Against the wishes of Michael Boyce and contrary to the advice of civil servants, Blair insisted on writing personal letters of condolence to the families of all the British casualties. 'It troubled his conscience that people died because of his orders,' noted one senior officer.[16] In writing these letters of consolation, he was hoping to find some for himself and perhaps seeking a form of absolution.

The Iraq conflict was officially being managed by a War Cabinet, but Blair didn't have much more time for that institution than he had for the normal Cabinet. As ever was the case with him, the critical decisions were made at unminuted conclaves in his den. They met after breakfast each morning. The cast list was the intelligence chiefs, Dearlove and Scarlett; Hoon and Straw, the only two members of the Cabinet in regular attendance; and Admiral Boyce or, in his absence, General Jackson. They were joined by Alastair Campbell, David Manning, Sally Morgan and Jonathan Powell. It soon became apparent to the cannier members of the War Cabinet that all the important decisions had already been made before they met later in the morning. Gordon Brown often didn't bother to turn up.[17]

By 22 March, leading American units were penetrating 150 miles into Iraq. In a call that day to Blair, Bush said that Tommy Franks and his commanders were upbeat. 'No WMD has been shot at us, and we are looking and we'll find the stuff.'

Thousands of Iraqi soldiers were just abandoning their uniforms and going home. 'Yes, they are just melting away,' said Blair.

'Just melting away,' agreed Bush.[18]

By 25 March, British forces were shelling targets in their primary objective, the southern city of Basra.

The consensus of the military predictions about the war was that it would take a month 'if doing well' and eight weeks 'if more difficult'.[19] But there were gloomier forecasts that it could be much longer and uglier than that. The biggest fear among the generals was of protracted fighting in urban areas. On the account of Geoff Hoon, 'Saddam adopted a completely different strategy to the one we expected. His strategy was to hunker down in the cities. We were getting lots of pictures of tanks hidden up street corners. He thought it was going to be like Stalingrad.'[20]

Some in Number 10 feared that it could turn out that way, says David Manning: 'We were also worried that Saddam would set fire to the oilfields. That they might smash the dams and flood the place. We were particularly worried about Baghdad. We thought that might be very difficult. Yes, a sort of Stalingrad.'[21]

As Blair scanned the maps in his den, he began to grow anxious about the rate of progress. Some elements of the media were already questioning why the war wasn't yet won. Blair began to pester Admiral Boyce and General Jackson with the same question. 'After about day four, there was a huge impatience. Tony Blair was getting worried that he wasn't getting headlines that it was already done.'[22] Reluctant, as military men usually are, to offer a hostage to fortune, Boyce was loath to guess how long it would take, but suggested that it could be a fortnight before Basra was in their hands. The Americans were getting impatient with the British 'because we hadn't bulldozed in there and flattened everything in sight'.[23] Ten days into the conflict, Blair fretted to the War Cabinet that we are 'getting bogged down' and wondered whether they had underestimated the forces against them.[24] The pace of the American advance appeared to be growing sluggish and the British had yet to secure their key targets in the south, prompting a lot of commentary from the first battalion of armchair generals in the press that the allies were running into difficulties. Apprehension was compounded by a series of friendly-fire incidents in which British personnel were killed by their American allies. In early April, I was having a conversation with a Cabinet minister in the back of his limousine. 'Look, there's a Union Jack,' he remarked as we were driven around Parliament Square. 'Don't tell the Americans – they'll bomb it.'[25]

Something else was beginning to prey on the British commanders' minds. The battle plan anticipated an Iraqi counter-attack using WMD. Yet as each trigger point was passed, there was no sign of any response.[26] 'Why isn't this happening?' Michael Boyce asked the generals. No-one had an answer. Boyce 'wanted to find something. WMD was the whole rationale for the invasion. The more days that went by without any, the more troubled I became.'[27]

Blair was struggling to get agreement with Bush about what should happen in Iraq after the war. As he flew to Washington at the end of March, he wrote a twelve-page note urging his ally to work at repairing relations with France, Germany and Russia, and trying to convince Bush that the UN should have a central role in post-war reconstruction. Blair believed UN engagement was both a desirable thing in itself and highly useful as a means of reuniting the international community. When they met at Camp David, Bush indicated that he had read the note, but said nothing that guaranteed that he would act on its advice. Blair was also pushing with frustratingly little success on the Middle East peace process. Bush had been persuaded to talk about publishing a 'road map', but the White House was not displaying any enthusiasm for driving along it.

By 2 April, US forces were slaughtering Republican Guard units on the outskirts of Baghdad. Saddam's command and control was so totally shattered that his army was fighting as ineffectively as a headless corpse. The tanks he had parked in cities proved to be death traps as they were targeted by allied aircraft.[28] Forty-eight hours later, the Americans seized Baghdad airport. 'The Iraqi army was evaporating,' noted Britain's most senior military officer.[29] But the Defence Secretary was becoming apprehensive that some of 'the enemy weren't conventional soldiers' and they were unexpectedly 'attacking from the rear as we advanced'.[30]

This made it even more imperative to get the White House to focus on what they might face after the conventional war. Blair had another chance on 7 April when Bush flew across the Atlantic for a meeting at Hillsborough Castle in Northern Ireland. Downing Street chose Hillsborough as the location for two reasons. It might give a boost to the peace process in Northern Ireland. It might also convince Bush to see the merit of being as dedicated to resolving the Israel–Palestine conflict as Blair was to peace in Ulster.[31] For reasons of personal conviction, international diplomacy and political expediency, Blair wanted to balance the war in Iraq with a major push on the Middle East peace process. He raised it at almost every meeting he had with Bush.[32] Blair pressed so often on this issue that conversations would begin with Bush saying: 'I know what you're going to say, Tony.'[33] His persistence could not be faulted; it was his effectiveness that was moot.

At Hillsborough, Blair took Bush for a long evening walk through the castle's gardens. With the defeat of Saddam now apparently in hand, he pressed for a move on the Middle East. For once, the Prime Minister seemed to score a success. Blair and Bush returned from the walk with the President agreed that he would engage on both the UN and the Palestinian question. At the closing news conference, Bush commended Blair's dedication in Northern Ireland and went so far as to declare: 'I'm willing to spend the same amount of energy in the Middle East.'[34]

Blair was 'buoyant' and 'full of himself' on his flight back across the Irish Sea to London. He thought he'd secured a major breakthrough on the Middle East as well as overcoming Bush's reluctance to involve the UN in post-war Iraq.[35] But there was a problem, the same problem which dogged the totality of his relationship with Bush and repeatedly made Blair delusional about how much influence he was truly exerting. The American President would make these promises to Blair, even repeat them for public consumption as he did at Hillsborough. Like Don Giovanni, Bush may even have been sincere at the time. But once he was back in Washington and in the company of Cheney, Rumsfeld and the rest of the Vulcans, he would forget or neglect the promises to his British friend. Blair's personal envoy in the Middle East concludes: 'Tony always kidded himself that he had got from Bush more than he was really getting.'[36]

For the moment, Blair was on an upswing, his mood further lifted that same day when he received news that British forces were entering Basra. On 9 April, Baghdad fell to the American army. Saddam's regime turned out to be as hollow as the broken legs on the twenty-foot bronze statue of the tyrant which was torn down to provide an iconic image of the fall of his hateful regime.

Relief and triumph flooded through Number 10. The war was won in less than a month and with deceptive ease. 'The manoeuvre war was the United States army at its best,' comments General Jackson. 'It's what they do so well. It was a quite extraordinary achievement in three weeks in a country the size of Iraq.'[37]

There was not the feared humanitarian disaster. No chemical or biological weapons were unleashed against either the allied troops or Israel, Kuwait and Saudi Arabia. Sir Richard Dearlove told the Prime Minister that the intelligence services were 'very confident' that they would soon uncover Saddam's stash of WMD.[38] The fallen dictator was on the run; his army was surrendering or deserting; Iraq was in coalition hands. They could laugh in the faces of the doom-mongers who had predicted that the battle for Baghdad would be a replay of Stalingrad.

'There's a feeling of elation. There was a lot of surprise that it was so easy,' says a senior staffer in Number 10 during those heady days. There was particular amazement that the Republican Guard, Saddam's supposed shock troops, had 'apparently melted away'.[39]

Opinion polls indicated that the national mood flipped patriotically once British forces went into action, as Blair always gambled that it would. At the outset of the war, the polls indicated a slim majority in support of the conflict. In the final week, as it became apparent that the allies were enjoying a swift victory, backing for the war rose to nearly two thirds of voters.

There was hubristic chatter that Blair could expect 'a Baghdad bounce'. Some of the Prime Minister's closest allies privately conjectured that he might now feel so emboldened that he would finally steel himself to move against Gordon Brown. Some of the Chancellor's circle feared he might do just that.[40]

Those with a deeper comprehension of conflict were much more sceptical about the rosy view that Iraq was guaranteed a happy ending. 'Everybody knew the coalition was going to win the initial battle, but then what?' remarks General Charles Guthrie. 'Conflict is easy compared with conflict resolution, which usually goes on far, far longer than the conflict itself and is much more expensive.'[41]

Admiral Boyce made himself very unpopular at the Pentagon when he told them: 'This is not going to be the liberation of Paris in 1944. You may get half an hour with roses in your gun barrels. After that, it is going to be misery. We won't be greeted as liberators.'[42]

It was not a message they wanted to hear; the shutters came down. The swiftness of the conventional war created a dangerous complacency. 'It contributed to misunderstanding the aftermath. That's true. It gave people an exaggerated sense of how easy this was going to be,' acknowledges David Manning.[43]

The very rapidity of the advance on Baghdad caught everyone by surprise. 'The march happened faster than people thought,' says Andrew Card. 'The tip of the spear made it all the way to Baghdad and there were no fronts along the way to establish order behind.'[44]

Something else was gnawing away at Admiral Boyce: they'd still not come across any WMD. 'Where is it?' he asked Sir Richard Dearlove. The head of MI6 replied confidently: 'Don't worry, it will be there. We'll find it.'[45]

Blair was careful to strike a sober and untriumphalist tone in public, aware as he was that the war remained hotly contentious, not least within his own party. On 14 April, seven days after British troops entered Basra, he went to the Commons to tell MPs: 'There is upon us a heavy responsibility to make the peace worth the war.'[46]

Even as he said this, the victory was being squandered. The euphoria of liberation was swiftly followed by an orgy of disorder. Within days of the fall of Baghdad, looting erupted across the Iraqi capital. Hospitals and schools were ransacked; shops and offices were stripped bare. Some of this was the uncoiling of the spring after decades of Saddam's savage repression; some was rooted in the desperation of people trying to look after their families in a shattered country; some was sheer criminality. In a symbolically shocking example of the mayhem, even Iraq's National Museum was pillaged as looters trashed and stole thousands of antiquities dating from the dawn of civilisation in Mesopotamia.[47] American troops failed to intervene.

Blair became 'very exercised' about the anarchy breaking out in Baghdad. 'For Christ's sake, get on to Condi,' he said to David Manning, who rang Rice to feed in a suggestion to the White House that they should mobilise troops to guard the hospitals.[48]

Supplies of fresh water began to run out. Power blackouts became frequent. Fuel grew scarce. The borders were not sealed, lacunae which permitted foreign fighters to enter the country to wage jihad against the allied troops.

'I think that's when the moment was lost,' says Richard Haas, who was watching with mounting apprehension from the US State Department. 'When you first win a battlefield victory there's several weeks where you have a degree of momentum and an aura of invincibility. That's when you've got to lock it down, you've got to get it right. We didn't have enough troops, it went bad so quickly and it created a vacuum.'[49]

Sir Mike Jackson, who was in overall command of the British forces, had a useful doctrine which he called 'the rule of a hundred days'. That was the timescale in which an occupying army had to establish law and order as well as deliver basic services if it was to win the respect of the local population.[50] In that critical first one hundred days, the spoils of victory were thrown away. The mayhem legitimised the idea that the allies had brought chaos rather than freedom and a better life, and it destroyed the mystique of the potency of American military might. Jack Straw would later agree that there was 'a three-month window of opportunity to get the country right' between April and July. 'The sense of optimism and gratitude towards the coalition forces was not capitalised on. It was a tragically lost opportunity.'[51]

The rapidity of the disintegration was only gradually appreciated in London. One reason for this myopia was because British forces were not in central or northern Iraq. In their sector 'certainly initially, the very Shia population in the south were very pleased to see us.'[52] Blair thought it most important to establish Basra as 'an exemplar' for the rest of Iraq. He failed to grasp early on that his war was bound to be judged by what happened not just in the sector under British control, but by the state of Iraq as a whole.

It was 'accepted that the immediate aftermath of the war was going to be confused, messy and a bit tricky', according to Ed Owen, the senior adviser to Jack Straw. 'It took a few months to come to a proper realisation of how badly prepared we were.'[53]

On the other side of the Atlantic, there was simply blithe indifference to the mayhem that had broken out in Baghdad. 'Stuff happens,' shrugged Donald Rumsfeld in a notorious display of his criminal insouciance. 'Freedom is untidy.'[54]

Rumsfeld conceived 'Operation Iraqi Freedom', as it was now designated, along similar lines to the earlier campaign in Afghanistan. His doctrine of invasion-lite envisaged going in fast and getting out quick. The Pentagon's own manual said that pacifying a nation the size of Iraq required 500,000 troops. Rumsfeld believed it could be done with 130,000. Tommy Franks was under orders to rapidly draw down the forces in Iraq. 'Shock and awe' was a stunningly successful strategy for toppling Saddam, but no-one had thought through the sequel. 'It was an assumption on the American side that the best-case scenario would happen without any insurance for anything worse,' lamented one senior British diplomat.[55] The 'intellectually bankrupt' Rumsfeld simply did not grasp that 'you needed enough boots on the ground to secure order', says a British general.[56] In the very hierarchical US military structure, none of his commanders were prepared to challenge their reckless and ignorant boss. Regime change was not the same as nation-building. Rumsfeld had little interest in that. Fatally, he was not prepared to let anyone else do it either.

The British foolishly relied on the assumption that Colin Powell and his State Department would be supervising the post-war reconstruction. At a private dinner of foreign ministers at the UN in February, Powell reassured Jack Straw and others present that 'America had a good record in rebuilding Germany and Japan after the Second World War and they were going to draw on that experience.'[57] The State Department showed the British 'very extensive and detailed plans' which brought together 'lots of expertise about what should be done'.[58]

The problem was that the British were talking to the wrong Americans. In the Pentagon, the State Department was derided as 'the Department of Nice'. Powell's department was frozen out and its planning cast aside as Rumsfeld seized control of the running of post-war Iraq even though the Pentagon did not have a properly conceived idea of what to do. It was indicative of Rumsfeld's indifference to planning for the aftermath that he had only now brought a three-star American general out of retirement to run the operation. When Jay Garner tried to get to grips with the challenge he complained that he had been given 'the impossible task' of planning the reconstruction of an entire country from a standing start.[59] The British general seconded to the Pentagon unit found that they were 'still moving the chairs in' just six weeks before the invasion.[60] In the eyes of another senior officer, Garner was 'an old man dragged out of retirement. He was completely beyond it.'[61]

In mid-April, Jack Straw made an eye-opening visit to Garner and his Office for Reconstruction and Humanitarian Aid (ORHA). 'Is this it?' boggled Straw when he was taken to see Garner's headquarters. The Foreign Secretary was staggered to find that the retired US general was trying to run a war-shattered country of more than 20 million people with a staff no more than two dozen strong located in a small suite of rooms on the other side of the border in Kuwait. The Pentagon was not allowing the man now supposed to be in charge of Iraq into the country on the grounds that it was still not safe. Straw was also 'very concerned indeed about the lack of proper planning' for the embryonic provisional authority that would take over Iraq. He reported back to Blair that neither Garner nor his operation was up to the task.[62]

The White House did not want to know. On May Day 2003, Bush was flown out to land on the deck of the USS *Abraham Lincoln*, an aircraft carrier cruising in the Persian Gulf hundreds of miles away from the unfolding reality in Iraq. This stunt was conceived to give him triumphalist footage for his re-election campaign. Under a massive banner reading 'Mission Accomplished' he told the 5,000 crew, and the millions more watching on the TV news, that it was time to celebrate: 'We do not know the final day of victory, but we have seen the turning of the tide.'[63]

If the tide was turning in any direction, it was for the worse. Wanting eyes and ears in Iraq that he could trust, Blair turned to John Sawers, a diplomat who had been his senior adviser on foreign affairs during the first term and was now the British ambassador in Egypt. Sawers arrived in Baghdad on 7 May. He sent his first chilling report back to Downing Street four days later. Entitled 'Iraq: What's Going Wrong?', it could barely have been more alarming. 'The problems are worst in the capital and it is the one place we can't afford to get it wrong,' Sawers reported. 'The clock is ticking.'

He went on: 'Garner's outfit, ORHA, is an unbelievable mess. No leadership, no strategy, no co-ordination, no structure and inaccessible to ordinary Iraqis ... Garner and his top team of sixty-year-old retired generals are well-meaning but out of their depth.' Untreated sewage was pouring into the Tigris. Uncollected garbage was piling up. There was no television service, depriving the allies of any means of getting their messages to Iraqis. Crime was endemic. Money was spent re-equipping ministries so they could resume work only for the buildings to be instantly looted again. Sawers was also very disturbed by what he was learning about the tactics of the American troops, who alternated between being trigger-happy and lethargic. The US 3rd Infantry Division was exhausted by the fight to Baghdad. 'Frankly, the 3rd Inf. Div. need to go home now, and be garlanded as victors.'[64] Sawers suggested the redeployment of British troops to the capital to assist with security and the training of the Iraqi police. British commanders on the ground were willing. They were overruled by London, which did not want to risk exposing British soldiers to the hazardous conditions in Baghdad.

Even Rumsfeld could see that things were not as 'wonderful' as he had proclaimed. His solution made them even worse. The US Defense Secretary put in another American over Garner's head. This was Paul Bremer, a man with absolutely no experience of running a country, let alone one in the Middle East. This actually commended him to Rumsfeld. Bremer arrived in Baghdad on 12 May to effectively become the emperor of Iraq wielding near absolute power. 'I am the law,' he snapped at one British diplomat who found the American viceroy 'allergic to any suggestion, from any quarter, that he should change a decision once he had made it'.[65] Bremer took less than a week to issue the first of a series of catastrophic orders. His first was to ban the four top tiers of Saddam's Ba'ath party from working in the government. Garner protested: 'Hell, you won't be able to run anything if you go this deep.' The CIA station chief warned him: 'You will put 50,000 people on the street, underground and mad at Americans.'[66]

Under Saddam's long dictatorship, membership of the Ba'ath was compulsory for virtually anyone employed by the Government. While taking out the most senior members of Saddam's regime was both inevitable and desirable, it was total folly to purge the middle-ranking administrators when there was no-one to take their places. The chaos intensified.

Bremer persisted with his year zero approach to Iraq. He hadn't been in Iraq a fortnight before he made another fatal executive decision. He ordered the disbandment of the entire Iraqi army, putting over 200,000 discontented soldiers on the streets with no employment. This fed recruits to the insurgency and deprived the country of any indigenous security structure. British post-war planning imagined that Saddam's army would be reformed, retrained and reconstituted, not that it would be abolished at the stroke of a pen.[67] 'To have kept the army would have helped hugely with the security situation,' thought a 'very uncomfortable' General Jackson.[68] To the chaos created by sacking the middle ranks of administrators was now added the menace of sending on to the street thousands of resentful and unemployed Iraqi young men who had military training and access to arms. Bremer then used his 'extraordinary power' to 'tear up' all the plans to introduce local democracy in Iraq.[69]

Key members of the Bush administration, such as Condi Rice, would much later accept that Bremer's purge of the administration and abolition of the army were 'more severe than was wise'.[70] Yet they did nothing to stop it at the time and some elements of the White House actively encouraged it. Blair was 'worried' and 'debated and discussed' what to do with his officials.[71] Rice remembers hearing British 'concerns' that it 'might be going too far' but they did not make any difference.[72] In so much as the British raised any protests, they were clearly too feeble to have any impact. Blair, who always had a weakness for men who were talented at sounding strong, even told his aides that he thought Bremer was 'impressive'.[73] In the Foreign Office it was being grasped that the right-wing Republicans who had seized control 'didn't want their mission undermined by British interference'.[74] As General Jackson regretfully noted, the British were merely 'a bit part player' in the civil administration set up by the Americans.[75] Blair had taken responsibility for events in Iraq without ensuring that he had any meaningful power to shape them.

There would be a colossal price, paid in many bloody instalments in the ensuing years, for the failure to plan properly for the aftermath. Tens of thousands of Iraqi people would pay for that tragic error with their lives. So too would many British and American service personnel. The political price, and an ever steepening one, would be paid by Blair.

In the build-up to the invasion, Peter Mandelson, one of his closest confidants, frequently asked Blair whether he was really confident there was a post-war plan. 'Look, you know, I can't do everything,' Blair shrugged off the question. 'That's chiefly America's responsibility, not ours.'[76]

Even as loyal a friend as Mandelson would later observe: 'I'm afraid that, as we now see, wasn't good enough. Obviously more attention should have been paid to what we would do once Saddam had been toppled.'[77]

Michael Levy, Blair's friend and his Middle East envoy, was another sceptic about the post-war planning. 'What's going to happen on the day after?' he asked Blair. 'It will be taken care of,' the Prime Minister reassured him.[78]

Blair received repeated warnings from people he trusted. David Manning, his senior adviser on foreign affairs, cautioned as early as March 2002, in a memo written after a visit to Washington, that the Americans 'underestimate the difficulties'. Manning said later: 'It's hard to know exactly what happened over the post-war planning. I remember the PM raising this many months before the war began. He was very exercised about it and we had been told that a lot of work was being done. It isn't a question I find easy to answer. I'm not sure we had as much visibility of it as we thought we had.'[79]

At the end of July 2002, Sir Richard Dearlove, the head of MI6, reported directly to the Prime Minister at a meeting at Number 10 that the Americans were giving little thought to the aftermath. In November 2002, a multi-departmental team from Britain flew to Washington to talk to the Americans. The British team had to go and see the State Department and the Department of Defense separately because they were not talking to each other. That was a further warning 'that there was no agreed American plan for what happened once you got rid of Saddam', says the British ambassador. 'There were several people – not just me in Washington – saying to Downing Street that they are at sixes and sevens.'[80]

The former Labour leader, Neil Kinnock, agonised over whether or not to support the war. He made three visits to Blair before the invasion to share his concerns. Kinnock told Blair that he agreed that it would be a good thing to remove such a monstrous tyrant as Saddam, but he needed convincing that the Americans had a coherent plan for the aftermath. 'I said to Tony: "Are you certain that the Americans have made comprehensive, effective preparation for the conditions in Iraq after the war?"' Public opposition to the war from Kinnock would have been dangerous, so Blair told him what he wanted to hear. 'He said to me that he was sure that was the case. That was a good enough reassurance.'[81] It turned out to be a false one.

Some voices had also tried to caution Blair about the high risk of sectarian conflict breaking out between the Shias and Sunnis once Saddam was toppled. For one briefing at Number 10, Jack Straw took with him Dr Michael Williams, a Foreign Office official with great expertise on the Middle East. Williams gave a detailed account of the ethnic and religious tensions within Iraq and why the allies might not be terribly popular as occupiers. Blair casually brushed him aside: 'That's all history, Mike. This is about the future.'[82]

In early March, just before the invasion, Iain Duncan Smith went out to visit the British troops in Kuwait. On his return, the Tory leader talked to Blair in the Prime Minister's office in the Commons. The British commanders had told him they had not been given any instructions about the aftermath. 'There appears to be no clear plan. What is the plan?' Duncan Smith asked Blair. 'Don't worry,' replied the Prime Minister. 'That's all in hand.' The Tory leader came away with 'the impression that he really wasn't interested in that. He'd just left it to the Americans.'[83]

Blair devoted nothing like as much attention to post-war planning – or the lack of it – as he should have done. One crucial reason was that his time and energy were so absorbed by the politics of the war. His fixation in the run-up to the invasion was with securing UN sanction and parliamentary and public support for the war. 'The focus was on doing the deed and not coping with the consequences,' noted one member of the Cabinet.[84] Thinking about the day after went by default.

As Iraq began the descent into violent chaos, it also became starkly apparent just how little traction London truly had on Washington. On Sally Morgan's account, Number 10 began to realise that they were only 'a tiny player in terms of the aftermath' and 'we were nowhere in terms of influencing decisions.'[85] Jack Straw sustained a good relationship with Colin Powell, but it didn't count for much because the Secretary of State was an increasingly isolated figure in the administration and his department was frozen out. Powell relied on the British to send him reports about what was happening on the ground because the Pentagon would not tell him.

Cabinet ministers saw that it was 'absolutely clear that we weren't able to influence Dick Cheney and Donald Rumsfeld who effectively ran the aftermath'.[86]

The British never managed to work out how to have meaningful contact with the Vice-President.[87] He and his notional counterpart, John Prescott, had nothing in common except their girth. Trying to get Geoff Hoon and

Donald Rumsfeld alongside each other 'was like trying to get pandas to mate. It was very slow. It took an awful long time. It was never clear whether it had been consummated or not.'[88] They rarely spoke to each other and when they did senior British officers thought that the American treated Hoon 'with contempt'.[89]

That placed 'a very high premium' on Blair's relationship with Bush.[90] The President was catastrophically incurious about the consequences of his war and the Prime Minister was never robust enough to force his ally to face up to what was happening. The abolition of the army and the administrative purge were discussed by Blair and Bush but never conclusively. 'I don't think anybody knew what the right view was,' says Andrew Card, who was a witness to most of their transatlantic phone conversations and video conferences.[91] As a result, the calamitous Bremer was left unchecked.

The gloomy prediction from Chirac that Blair had dismissed at Le Touquet was now beginning to come horribly true. Iraq became trapped in a bloody vortex of sectarian strife and insurgency.

'I just felt it was slipping away from us from the beginning. There was no security force controlling the streets, there was no police force to speak of, and the vacuum that we left enabled the violent people to come out of the woodwork and exert an influence,' says Sir Jeremy Greenstock. 'When they saw they could not be stopped, they kept going. They multiplied men, materials and motivation and became unstoppable.'[92]

Blair routinely demanded of his officials: 'Why aren't the Americans gripping this?' But he failed to do much gripping himself. Sir Hilary Synnott, a scholarly man who had been High Commissioner in Pakistan, was prevailed upon to delay his impending retirement to become Britain's representative in southern Iraq. He recalls being sent to Basra with instructions covering just 'half a side of A4' and the general advice to 'play things by ear'. He found the army 'incandescent about the inadequacies of the civilian operation' in the four provinces under British stewardship and withering about the 'pathetic' Foreign Office.[93] Blair put relentless public emphasis on the importance and urgency of making progress in Iraq. But in the eyes of his own representative in Basra, the Prime Minister seemed 'little interested in the processes within Government by which this might be brought about'.[94]

In the months after the war, as during the months leading up to it, Blair was fatally and doubly distracted. What leverage he had with the Americans he was trying to use to win their agreement to give the UN a role in postwar Iraq. He had some modest success on 22 May, when the Security Council gave its unanimous support to a resolution to that effect.[95] Yet there was a profound reluctance among other powers to help America and Britain with reconstruction. Chris Patten, the European Commissioner, tartly summarised the attitude of France and Germany as: 'You broke it, you fix it.'[96]

The other distraction was the growing furore around the weapons of mass destruction which had been Blair's principal justification for the war. Where on earth were they? The question was raised in the most mocking fashion by Vladimir Putin when Blair travelled to Moscow at the end of April. He was hoping to heal some of the wounds to international relations that had been caused by the war. They were still too raw for that. When the two men had a caviar and cold meats dinner, Putin angrily turned on Blair, accusing him of making Britain an accomplice in an American bid for global domination. The rawness and vehemence of the attack stunned both Blair and the British officials.[97] The Russian President was scarcely less abrasive in public when he openly scorned his visitor in his opening statement at their joint news conference.

'Where is Saddam? Where are those arsenals of weapons of mass destruction, if they indeed were in existence?' Putin publicly ridiculed a stony-faced Blair. 'Perhaps Saddam is still hiding somewhere underground in a bunker, sitting on cases containing weapons of mass destruction, and is preparing for blowing the whole thing up.'[98]

As the days went by, Blair became 'more and more concerned' that nothing was being found.[99] Specialist teams of British and American forces were on the hunt for the WMD from the moment that Baghdad fell. Blair was 'obsessed' with the search, sending David Manning out to Baghdad to talk to the MI6 officers there and demanding a weekly written report on their progress and sometimes daily updates as well. He became 'increasingly agitated' when they kept coming up blank.[100]

There were no WMD and Iraq was sliding into murderous mayhem. The catastrophic lack of planning for the aftermath of war was already losing the peace. This was a terrible failure that would stalk him for the remainder of his premiership.

11. Broken Dream, Cabinet Nightmare

'Do you think this increases the risk to me?' Tony Blair asked the head of MI5 during the Afghan campaign.

'Yes,' responded Sir Stephen Lander. 'Of course.'

'Mmm,' reflected Blair. 'That's what I thought.'[1]

Whenever the Prime Minister travelled in his armour-plated Daimler limousine, codenamed Pegasus, he was now accompanied by a security detail greatly augmented since 9/11. Police outriders sped ahead to dismount and stop the traffic, as yeomen of the guard would press back the peasantry to clear the way for a medieval royal progress. I travelled with this cavalcade on occasion, sometimes with Blair in his limousine, sometimes with his aides in one of the people carriers. As we hurtled past the stationary and frustrated traffic on our way to an airport, one of Blair's senior aides sighed: 'I can't help feeling that every time we do this we lose a thousand votes.'[2]

It was very different to the days when Clement Attlee could be driven around in a 14 h.p. Humber with his wife, Vi, as the chauffeur. The convoy of vehicles which accompanied Blair on his outings from Number 10 became reminiscent of an American President's motorcade.

His fiftieth birthday in early May was marked by admiring media coverage, often illustrated with pictures of Blair in heroic statesman mode, presidentially striding into destiny. Admirers and critics alike were agreed that he dominated the scene like no Prime Minister since Margaret Thatcher at her zenith.

Yet he did not feel that he was fully commander-in-chief. Gordon Brown was still running a rival government from his mighty powerbase at the Treasury, where he was determined to frustrate one of the Prime Minister's greatest ambitions. The defining collision between them in 2003 was over Europe. Blair was the most instinctively pro-European Prime Minister since Ted Heath. Unlike Heath or any other Prime Minister since, he could speak good French. He was so fluent he could even get the Assemblée Nationale to laugh when he cracked a joke in French. By contrast, Brown spoke only

Scottish and approached Europe with disdain shading into contempt. He became notorious in Brussels for removing his translation headphones while other finance ministers were speaking. He travelled there either to deliver lectures on the superiority of Anglo-Saxon capitalism or to stage rows to court the favour of Paul Dacre, Rupert Murdoch and the Europhobic press. Steve Morris, an official who accompanied the Prime Minister at most European meetings, 'heard Tony defend Gordon to foreign leaders dozens of times. Cherie would be rolling her eyes in the background and officials would be coughing into their sleeves.'[3]

He felt compelled to do this even though Brown used a Eurosceptical posture as one of his dividing lines against Blair. On the eve of the monthly meetings of finance ministers 'stories appear in the British media of a Euro-sceptic kind saying the Chancellor is going off to Brussels to knock together the heads of those ghastly Europeans', noted Sir Stephen Wall, the senior adviser on the EU at Number 10. 'Pretty often the story had no basis in fact and very often Gordon didn't go to Brussels at all.' What it did do was undermine the Prime Minister's efforts 'to build a constructive relationship with our European partners'.[4]

With Blair's approval ratings enjoying a surge in the immediate aftermath of the war, there was a renewed burst of speculation that he would finally make the big push to fulfil his ambition to take Britain into the single currency. That would mean overcoming both the native Euroscepticism of much of the British public and the resistance of his rival across the road. The pro-Europeans among his allies regretted that he had not seized the moment in the first term. 'He should have had the referendum right at the beginning. He should have, very early on, held a referendum on the principle, not on the timing,' believes Peter Mandelson. 'If he had the argument when he was strong enough to do so he would have been much better off. He could and should have done that. It was a mistake not to do so.'[5]

Blair salved the disappointment of Mandelson and other pro-European friends by issuing many private assurances and dropping frequent public suggestions that he would make the leap in the second. From the moment of his re-election in 2001, Blair tried to roll out a road to a referendum on euro entry. He told that year's party conference that 'we should have the courage of our argument' about joining.[6]

'We all thought it was going to be the big battle of the second term,' says Peter Hyman. 'Tony thought it would strengthen our hand in Europe and that's indisputably the case: we would have been a stronger player in Europe if we'd been part of the euro. Politically, it was a big prize.'[7] That aide and another, Steve Morris, prepared a detailed battle plan on how media and public opinion might be won round to the idea for Blair to read during his summer holidays in the Lake District and France in 2002. Morris agrees: 'TB felt this was one of the big things for the second term. There were lots of discussions about how you'd handle the party, the media, how you'd handle Gordon.'[8]

Blair saw it as a historic mission to drain Europhobia from the British body politic, telling me that autumn: 'Our psychology towards Europe has got to change.'[9]

Philip Gould and Stan Greenberg, Number 10's pollsters, were researching strategies to win round Eurosceptical voters. 'He was determined to have Britain go into the single currency and our constant planning was to be ready for a referendum,' says Greenberg.[10]

Euro notes and coins were now in circulation. There was a vaguely hopeful assumption that Brits would come back from holidays across the Channel more comfortable with the idea of having the euro as their own currency.

Blair regularly told his inner circle that he was absolutely dedicated to realising this ambition. Geoff Mulgan, the director of the strategy unit, was in 'absolutely no doubt that he wanted Britain to join the euro; he saw this as the big test of Britain's European commitment.'[11] Peter Mandelson saw Blair 'gearing up to do it'.[12] The more passionate about Europe was his audience, the more fervent were the Prime Minister's declarations of intent to join the euro. He indicated he would do it to other EU leaders.[13] Even when he was hugely distracted by the war, he had Europe in his sights. During a discussion with aides and ministers shortly before Christmas 2002, he surprised them by saying: 'You know, this is more important than Iraq.'[14]

Joining was central to his vision of a modern, outward-looking Britain. He made a growing number of speeches on Europe and the language in them became increasingly bold in advertising his intentions. To his party conference in 2002, he declared it to be 'our destiny to lead in Europe'.[15] He added to expectations that he was going for it in an impassioned speech two months later in which he contended that Britain should stop being 'a straggler' forever 'hanging back' from Europe and decide to 'participate fully'.[16] That was a riposte to Gordon Brown. Just the day before, the Chancellor used his Pre-Budget Report to boast about Britain's superior economic performance compared with France and Germany. Brown did further deliberate damage to the case for the euro by saying that the British economy was currently more aligned with that of America.[17]

Though he understood that the economics of the euro mattered, Blair was most animated by it as an issue of power. To Paddy Ashdown, he said:

'You can't be inside the wheel-house of Europe if you're outside it financially. You have to be in there.'[18] He feared repeating Britain's past mistake of always being late to join every big European project and paying a high cost in influence. To me, he described Britain's history of grudging engagement with its continent as a 'tragedy' of missed opportunities.[19]

While some thought that the Iraq war made the project impossible, Blair took the opposite view that it was more imperative to use euro entry to rebuild his credibility on the Continent.

The missing, crucial ingredient was the consent of Gordon Brown. 'What about Gordon?' asked Jonathan Powell. How would they succeed with this grand project against powerful opposition from the Chancellor? 'Leave Gordon to me' was Blair's regular refrain. 'I can square Gordon.'[20] Colin Marshall, the Chairman of Britain in Europe, and Simon Buckby, the pro-euro group's Campaign Director, visited Blair in Number 10 towards the end of 2002. Marshall raised the problem of Brown's opposition. 'It's really political,' responded Blair. 'I can fix Gordon.'[21]

Such was the mistrust of the Chancellor within Number 10, Blair believed that Brown was only being difficult for the bloody-minded sake of it or because he was using it as a chip on the table in their poker game about the succession. 'He wants something, he always wants something,' Blair told his aides and allies in Cabinet.[22] There were those in Downing Street who even believed that Brown was only thwarting them on the euro so that he could claim the glory of doing it himself when he became Prime Minister.

This was a fatal misreading of the Chancellor. 'They never understood that Gordon was not going to fix it for entry,' says one of his closest advisers.[23] Brown was just about paying lip-service to the official position that the Government had an open mind about euro entry, but he gave every impression that he had absolutely no intention of allowing it. Adamantine opposition was entirely explicable from where he sat. Past enthusiasm for Europe had left him scarred. As Shadow Chancellor, he was a passionate advocate of British membership of the Exchange Rate Mechanism, which made him feel foolish when the pound crashed out of the ERM on Black Wednesday in 1992. That cataclysm ruined the Major Government; it also changed Brown. 'Never, never forget how badly burned Gordon was by the ERM,' a confidant once told me.[24]

He was proud of the monetary and fiscal framework that he had established since 1997. It was Brown's repeated boast during this period that Britain, unlike Germany and some other European states, had avoided recession. More fundamentally, Brown believed that the whole concept of trading and currency blocks like the EU was being rendered irrelevant and anachronistic by the globalised economy.[25] Most crucially of all, if joining the euro turned out to be the disaster he feared, it would ruin his reputation as Chancellor and wreck the inheritance for his premiership.

Blair thought he could square Brown; Brown had already encircled Blair. The Chancellor seized control of the decision in their first term by subjecting entry to five economic 'tests' over which he set himself up as judge and jury.[26] He torpedoed every attempt by Number 10 to build a more positive public attitude by brutally squelching pro-European ministers whenever they tried to make the case. 'There were endless attempts to get a campaign going,' recalls Steve Morris.[27] 'Every time they tried to do so, they got clobbered by Gordon Brown for stepping out of line,' says Stephen Wall. 'Gordon argued on economic grounds that we weren't ready for the debate. But I always felt that he'd actually made up his mind that it wasn't going to happen.'[28]

The Prime Minister only belatedly grasped what a strategic mistake he committed when he allowed his ambition to be put in a box to which the Chancellor held the only key. Blair tried to regain some initiative by pre-emptively declaring, much to the anger of Brown, that they would make a decision by the summer of 2003.

Legend had it that Ed Balls, the Chancellor's 'second brain', composed the 'five tests' on a scrap of paper while riding in the back of a New York taxi. Even if it was a myth, the story illustrated a fundamental truth. The tests were sufficiently elastic that pro-Europeans could argue that they were close to being met and Eurosceptics could interpret them to argue the opposite.

Brown made an elaborate show of making his assessment look scientific. He assigned no fewer than twenty-five Treasury officials to work full-time on the project with additional input from selected outside experts. The result was eighteen separate technical studies. The cost of this exercise approached £5 million.[29]

The thousands of figures being crunched at the Treasury were designed to add up to just two letters: No. To ensure that it had credibility, Brown was careful to officially vest ownership of the process in the Treasury officials led by the Permanent Secretary, Gus O'Donnell. The Chancellor wanted the assessment to be so apparently disinterested, supposedly authoritative and emphatically negative that no-one, especially not the Prime Minister, could argue with the conclusion. There was an echo here of the tactics employed by Blair over the Iraq dossier.

Brown did not really need to lean on his officials because he could be confident they would come to the conclusion that he wanted. The Treasury was institutionally Eurosceptic. O'Donnell, who was John Major's Press Secretary on Black Wednesday, was just as sceptical as his political master.[30]

More hostile still was Ed Balls who was giving political supervision to the assessment.

Blair repeatedly tried to find out what was being cooked up in Brown's secret laboratory. The Cabinet Secretary was amused: 'It was like a child in the back of the car: are we nearly there yet?'[31] The Prime Minister was stonewalled at every turn by Brown, who would reply that they hadn't yet finished 'the technical work'. Whenever the Prime Minister tried to have a conversation about it, the Chancellor simply refused.

They had often had noisy rows. There was now 'a frozen, angry silence', which was more ominous.[32] Blair kept 'psyching himself up' to have it out with Brown, but the other man would not engage.[33] Weeks would now pass when the two men barely spoke. 'It is like a marriage that has gone very badly wrong,'[34] I was told during this period by someone who had known both men intimately since the 1980s. The Cabinet, marginalised yet again, not once debated what was supposed to be this great issue of Britain's destiny. According to one minister speaking at the time: 'It is like an awful family secret that no-one dares talk about.'[35]

Blair asked Jeremy Heywood, his Principal Private Secretary and the Number 10 official with the best connections at the Treasury, to shape the timing and the verdict of the assessment. Heywood met Balls and O'Donnell to try to persuade them that a bald negative would make things extremely difficult for the Prime Minister. At the very least, Number 10 needed a 'not yet' to leave open the possibility of returning to the issue later in the parliament. Heywood met a wall of resistance.[36] Even once the assessment was complete, which was by Christmas 2002, the Treasury remained highly secretive.

A very large hint about their intentions was dropped by Balls that December. He delivered a lecture, and ensured that it got press attention, in which he pointedly rehearsed examples in British history of governments making economically disastrous decisions to satisfy political ambitions.[37]

The Chancellor and his lieutenant Balls would scoff about what they saw as Blair's 'misty waffle' about Britain's destiny, a quest they regarded as vaingloriously dangerous.[38] 'Gordon regarded that with contempt,' noted the Cabinet Secretary.[39] Ed Balls would be openly contemptuous to the Prime Minister's face about Blair's 'ethereal' longings to join the euro. The Chancellor had often got his own way by exploiting the Prime Minister's hazy grasp of economics. Brown and Balls believed they could educate Blair out of his enthusiasm – or, at any rate, baffle him with the data. A series of six seminars, beginning in January 2003, was arranged at Number 10. Blair agreed to attend them only reluctantly and was visibly irritable about what he increasingly regarded as a charade. He wearily sighed about having to listen to 'the man in the white coat' – the nickname he gave to David Ramsden, the Treasury official who led the presentations.[40]

Blair hated these seminars because they were full of highly technical detail that he found irksome. He was also angered 'that all the arguments were couched in a way that put the worst possible light on entry'.[41] Jonathan Powell could now 'see where this story was going to end. They outmanoeuvred us during these presentations.'[42] Blair complained that the seminars entirely missed the big picture: Britain's long-term relationship with the rest of its continent. 'This is a very half-empty assessment,' he complained.[43]

The scene was set for an extraordinary confrontation between Prime Minister and Chancellor, the most dangerous yet of their turbulent partnership. On the suggestive date of April Fool's Day, the Treasury team went to present its final verdict at Number 10. Waiting there were Blair, Heywood, Powell and Wall. The Treasury side consisted of Brown, Balls, O'Donnell, Jon Cunliffe, the head of international finance, and Ramsden. 'The man in the white coat' made a final presentation. Blair sat rolling his eyes as the Treasury boffin treated them to a fifty-page slide show of more graphs and data. Then came the punchline that 'a decision to join now would not be in the national economic interest' because a 'clear and unambiguous' case for entry could not be made.

At this point, Blair erupted. He had already realised that it was unlikely that he would be politically strong enough to risk a referendum on the euro in the near future, especially when he lacked the support of his Chancellor. He was forewarned that the Treasury was going to be negative. But he was stunned that the Treasury's rejection of euro membership was so emphatic. To him, this felt like a typical Brown ambush, made no more acceptable because it had been dressed up as a technical exercise.

'Fine,' snapped Blair. 'But I don't accept it. I don't agree.' Brown growled back: 'You'll have to accept it.' Blair argued: 'It's not just about the economics. It is political. We have to look at the big picture politically.' Brown riposted: 'That's precisely what we shouldn't do.'[44]

The meeting broke up rancorously. Brown and Balls crossed the road back to the Treasury, where they decided on a highly inflammatory act. They told Gus O'Donnell, the Permanent Secretary, to formally submit the assessment regardless of the Prime Minister's wishes. A messenger walked over two copies, one for Number 10 and one for the Cabinet Secretary, with a note: 'The Chancellor hereby formally submits the assessment.'[45]

A further meeting, this time at Number 11, was held that afternoon. It was nasty, brutish and short. Blair said he would not accept that he had received the final assessment. Brown was at his most steamrollering. 'This is the Treasury assessment,' he barked, presenting it as a fait accompli. Balls contemptuously insisted that the only thing left for debate was when it was presented. Blair could like it or lump it.

The two men confronted each other again the next day. The Chancellor remained implacable that this was the last word. He was not going to change a single sentence. Again, the Prime Minister argued that the hardness of the conclusion was not supported by the other evidence and the language had to be softened to allow for the possibility of euro entry later in the parliament. Brown was not budging. Not only was his decision final, he was going to announce his verdict in the Budget next week.

'I'm not having that,' came back Blair, the temperature in the room racing towards boiling point. He was not going to allow the announcement to be made in the middle of the Iraq war, and without any Cabinet debate. Brown repeated that he was going to announce his verdict next week. In utter exasperation, Blair lost it with his Chancellor. This had happened many times before, but it was a rarity for him to get this angry in front of witnesses. 'If you are not going to give me what I want, then you will have to consider your position,' said Blair. Brown responded: 'I'll do just that.' The Chancellor banged out of the room, his team trailing after him.[46]

Back at the Treasury, Brown had a council of war with Balls, Spencer Livermore, Sue Nye and his other closest advisers. 'Everyone was uncertain what had just happened. Had he resigned? Had he been sacked?'[47] They concluded that they would have to wait and see what Blair did. The two men had reached a very perilous place and people on both sides knew it. For Brown to quit would have been the end of his Chancellorship and quite probably his hopes of becoming Prime Minister. There was a matching jeopardy confronting Blair. Beginning to face an increasing backlash over the war as he was, it would be a major risk to lose his Chancellor over the unpopular cause of the euro. Both men contemplated the abyss overnight. Then they drew back for fear of mutually assured destruction. At a meeting the next day, they had sufficiently calmed down to agree that Balls and Heywood should try to work out some language that would at least mask their differences. They spent most of the night haggling and 'Jeremy came back with about four rather minor changes, poor guy.'[48] It was now starkly apparent to Jonathan Powell that they had been 'boxed in' by Brown.[49]

Blair won a small tactical victory over Brown by prevailing about when the announcement should be made. He also successfully insisted that senior ministers should be consulted, an exercise he hoped would force more concessions from the Chancellor. Instead of having an open discussion in Cabinet, which would have nakedly exposed the differences between Prime Minister and Chancellor, ministers were called in individually to discuss the assessment with Blair and Brown. The pro-euro Charles Clarke had 'a lively argument' with the Chancellor.[50] Another pro-European Cabinet member, Alan Milburn, told colleagues the exercise was a farce. He was given just ten minutes to discuss an assessment which was 1,982 pages long.[51] The Cabinet did not provide Blair with a counter-force against Brown, not least because several crucial figures agreed with the Chancellor. David Blunkett was against a referendum on the euro. So was Jack Straw. John Prescott was also sceptical. That powerfully aligned the Home Secretary, Foreign Secretary and the Deputy Prime Minister with the Chancellor. The Prime Minister was 'very isolated right at the top of his Government'.[52] Jonathan Powell reflected later: 'One of the strange things is that Tony never thought about building coalitions in his Cabinet.'[53] This demonstrated a major strategic failure of Blair's premiership. One of the reasons he was thwarted in his European ambitions was that he had surrounded himself with sceptics in the most senior positions in the Cabinet.

In late May, Peter Mandelson let slip a few incautious remarks at a lunch with female journalists. He said Blair had been 'outmanoeuvred' over the single currency because the 'obsessive' Brown thought politics '24 hours a day, seven days a week'.[54] Mandelson hit a very raw nerve and came under venomous attack from all sides. Brown sent out Ed Balls and Damian McBride to brief against his old foe, who was labelled 'poison'; Blair authorised his officials to dismiss his old friend as a mere 'backbencher, no more'. Mandelson's real crime was to have spoken too close to the truth.[55]

The euro verdict was to be announced in the House of Commons on 9 June. Though the meat of the issue was now settled, and against the Prime Minister, there was one final power struggle between Blair and Brown over which of them should make the statement. The Cabinet Secretary notes: 'Blair realised that he couldn't get the verdict he wanted so it then became all about the language of how close we were to entry.'[56]

This dispute was no less ferocious just because it was only about presentation. The Prime Minister did not trust his Chancellor with the statement and vice-versa. Brown was now at his most aggressively assertive. Balls sent a message to Number 10 via Heywood that 'if the Prime Minister wants to make the statement, he can find himself a new Chancellor.'[57] Blair blinked.

Brown made the statement. At a news conference afterwards, their body language screamed fury at each other. As a sop to the Prime Minister, some of the language rejecting the euro was softened. To maintain the fiction that Britain was still serious about entry, a series of studies were commissioned about how to make Britain more compatible with the euro-zone. Number 10 tried to camouflage Blair's retreat by declaring that there would be a new push to make the case for the single currency with a 'euro road show' in the autumn. This was far from the first time they'd pledged themselves to that sort of exercise. Only the serially gullible were taken in. 'What about the road shows?' Wall asked Powell, who 'looked at me as if I was an idiot'.

'Forget that,' Powell laughed bitterly. 'It's not going to happen.'[58]

Euro entry was killed by Brown and with it one of Blair's great ambitions for his premiership. Britain was not going to enter the single currency while he was at Number 10 or at any foreseeable time afterwards. His pro-European allies in the Cabinet 'gave up after that'.[59] Peter Hyman quit Number 10 soon afterwards and Stephen Wall, realising 'that was the end', left a year later.[60]

'All the fizz went out of it,' says a senior civil servant. 'Iraq became all-consuming and the euro just faded away from that point.'[61]

Gordon Brown was not the only reason for this failure. It was also the result of an inability to soften the Euroscepticism of public opinion and the phobia of much of the press; the apparently superior performance of the British economy at this time; the distraction and the consequences of the Iraq war; and the disintegration of Blair's relations with key European leaders because of the conflict. The consensus view among economists in the years that followed was that Brown did Britain a favour by vetoing euro entry because interest rates in the euro-zone were inappropriate for the British economy. 'It would have been a complete and utter disaster had we joined,' says Blair's own Cabinet Secretary of the time. 'To this day, I'd say Gordon Brown was absolutely right.'[62] That argument looked slightly less persuasive when sterling plunged against both the euro and the dollar during the financial crisis of 2008–9.

One side of Blair's brain reconciled himself to this latest defeat at the hands of Brown as probably a sensible outcome in the circumstances. The other side of him knew that he had failed one of the big challenges that he had set for his premiership. It was convenient for him, but not altogether wrong, to blame the death of his dream on the Chancellor. More than ever, Blair now looked on Brown as a deadly rival dedicated to sabotaging his premiership.

On the morning of Thursday, 12 June, ministers started to troop up and down Downing Street, where they were greeted by cheery inquiries about their political health from the ghouls of the media. The very British ritual of the reshuffle was underway. The theory goes that the reshuffle is the ultimate expression of a Prime Minister's power of career life and death over his colleagues. In the case of Tony Blair, it would as often turn out to be a demonstration of his weaknesses.

Sally Morgan, a presence by his side at many reshuffles, says he found it 'painfully difficult' to sack people. 'Hated it, absolutely hated it.'[63] He would complain: 'It's like drilling teeth.' On one occasion, a minister came into his office under the misapprehension that she was about to be promoted, which made it more difficult for him to tell her that she was being relieved of her job. She burst into tears. 'It made me feel like Stalin,' he groaned afterwards.[64]

Blair was 'a very poor personnel manager' in the view of Neil Kinnock. 'He didn't like demoting or displacing people. Really hated it.'[65] For a period, he experimented with giving advance warning to ministers facing the chop in the hope that this might let them down gently. He abandoned that practice because, as he told Jack Straw, 'they go out and brief and fight back.'[66] Peter Mandelson thought Blair was 'not actually a very good butcher as a Prime Minister' even though he twice slit Mandelson's own throat.[67] Blair's dislike of being disliked and his aversion to personal confrontation were a big part of the problem. 'He never liked grasping the personal nettle,' noted one of his Cabinet Secretaries.[68]

During one reshuffle, Blair spent half an hour telling Keith Vaz that he was doing a wonderful job as Minister for Europe. Vaz left the study smiling only to be stopped on the way out by Jonathan Powell, who had to break it to him that he was being sacked.[69]

Blair's weakness also expressed itself in his habit of making promises that he didn't keep, with the result that colleagues came to think of him as dishonest. Geoff Hoon emerged from Number 10 during one reshuffle believing that he still had a seat in the Cabinet.[70] Only afterwards did Hoon discover that he had been stripped of his Cabinet rank. 'I never thought to ask,' Hoon ruefully told friends later. 'I should have asked. Knowing Tony as well as I do, I should have asked.'[71]

Charles Clarke reckons 'a multitude of individuals felt let down by Tony. They didn't know why they left government. They didn't know why they were never in government. He always got it very, very badly wrong.'[72]

In the reshuffle in the summer of 2003, Blair settled some small scores with his Chancellor by refusing to give promotions for Brown's abler acolytes, Douglas Alexander and Yvette Cooper, wife of Ed Balls. He finally sacked Nick Brown from the Cabinet, something he had wanted to do for a long time. But he left the Chancellor and his powerbase at the Treasury largely untouched.

A prevaricator about dealing with foes, Blair was paradoxically at his most icily decisive with his friends. Asked what was the greatest quality that a politician could possess, François Mitterrand answered: 'Indifference.' It was often his closest allies and loyalist supporters who felt the chilliest side of Blair. 'Tony was as hard as nails when it came to his survival,' says Michael Levy. 'Look what he did to Peter, someone who loved him, sacking him twice. Tony's interests always came first.'⁷³

By the summer of 2003, he was becoming persuaded that he would have to move against a senior minister with whom he'd had a relationship since his early twenties. Derry Irvine gave Blair his first job in legal chambers and introduced him to Cherie. He'd been both mentor and matchmaker. The Lord Chancellor regarded himself as fireproof. Moreover, the Prime Minister encouraged him to think that he was invulnerable. 'Tony had given reassurances to Derry that he would remain as Lord Chancellor so long as he remained Prime Minister,' says a Cabinet minister who would know.⁷⁴ Blair said that to try to bolster Irvine when he was depressed after the arrest of his son in the United States. It was a characteristically kindly gesture by Blair to make that promise, as it was also rather typical that he ended up breaking it.

He tolerated the embarrassments generated by the Lord Chancellor in the first term, with his expensive taste in wallpaper and fondness for comparing himself with Cardinal Wolsey. That was a price the then novice Prime Minister was willing to pay to have Irvine's counsel and experience. He was much less indulgent in the second term, when 'Tony became a more confident Prime Minister'⁷⁵ and Irvine caused further furores by taking a large pay rise and a big boost to his pension. Irvine never properly adjusted to the change in their relationship. He was no longer the pupil master and the Prime Minister was no longer a trainee barrister. Yet the Lord Chancellor would still address the Prime Minister as 'Blair' or 'young Blair', sometimes in front of an audience. 'Why don't we have a drink? Get us a drink, Blair,' he demanded on one occasion at Chequers to the astonishment of other dinner guests.

Another problem was not of Irvine's making. He had remained a liberal on crime and judicial issues while his former pupil inexorably moved in a more authoritarian direction. There was consternation in Number 10 when Irvine took to the airwaves to say that there were too many people in prison and courts should consider alternatives to jail for first-time burglars. His proudest legislative achievement was the Human Rights Act, which judges were now using to thwart the Government's attempts to trample on their independence. He stood up for the rights of the judiciary when David Blunkett, with Blair's encouragement, was increasingly at war with the bench.

It wasn't the progressive side of Irvine that finally did for him; it was the reactionary aspect. He stood in the way of reforming the position of Lord

Chancellor. Among constitutional reformers it had long been thought inde-fensible for one peer to wear three hats: as the senior judge who appoints all the other judges; as the presiding officer of the House of Lords; and the highest-paid member of the Cabinet. Andrew Adonis, the head of the policy unit, had taken this up as a reforming cause, as had Pat McFadden, another key Blair aide. They had an enthusiastic ally in the Cabinet Secretary, who agreed that the position of Lord Chancellor 'was riddled with conflicts of interest'.[76]

Blair's zeal for constitutional reform was never great in his first term and was indistinguishable from zero by his second. His indifference and anti-democratic instincts helped stymie attempts to complete reform of the Lords. 'Totally unenthusiastic' is how one senior member of the policy unit of the time describes his attitude to constitutional reform.[77] He developed a great reverence for a couple of ancient British institutions: the armed forces and the monarchy. He couldn't really care less about the House of Lords other than using peerages as a reward for friends and supporters.

There was a brief interruption in that lack of interest in the summer of 2003. Looking to soften liberal and left hostility after the Iraq war and casting around for alternative legacies following his defeat on the euro, Blair was suddenly desperate for a big, progressive reform to prove that there was life left in his premiership. Adonis and Turnbull persuaded the Prime Minis-ter that reforming the Lord Chancellorship was 'a desirable piece of constitutional modernisation' which would make a splash.[78]

Irvine was massively resistant. He was still a believer in the triple-hatted role and was infuriated when he learnt from rumours in the press – a very New Labour way of doing business – that the Lord Chancellorship was being considered for abolition. In the seven days before the reshuffle, the old pupil master went round to Number 10 three times to confront his former trainee in the Prime Minister's den. Irvine angrily, and with some justice, demanded to know 'how a decision of this magnitude could be made without prior consultation with me' or anyone else affected. At the third angry meeting, forty-eight hours before the reshuffle, he handed Blair a two-page note complaining that the Prime Minister was being 'high-handed and insensitive' and that 'I personally am being cast aside' for 'no proven benefit'. The result, he forecast with some prescience, would be a 'botched job'.[79]

Many of his staff wondered whether the Prime Minister would really summon the steel to fire his former pupil master, an act of quasi-patricide. 'Tony was psyching himself up to do it for weeks,' says Sally Morgan.[80] 'He found it immensely difficult' to sack Irvine, noted the Cabinet Secretary. 'It was classic *Henry IV Part One*: "I know thee not old man."'[81]

Not until the very morning of the reshuffle did Hal Blair at last brace himself for the final confrontation with Falstaff Irvine. He asked the Lord Chancellor to stay behind after Cabinet and come into the den. Irvine was astounded, bewildered, bitter and furious, bellowing: 'You can't do this, Blair.' He was more angry when told that he would be replaced by Charlie Falconer, the Prime Minister's old flatmate. 'You are putting in another peer,' he raged.[82]

Blair was 'very shaken afterwards'.[83] Irvine 'was very hurt. He's never recovered from it.'[84] He and Blair did not speak again.[85]

While Blair was giving the push to Derry Irvine, Alan Milburn was about to jump. The Health Secretary was under intense pressure from his partner to spend more time with their family on Teesside, but that didn't entirely explain his shock resignation from the Cabinet. It was harder to argue with his partner's demands that he leave Government when Milburn felt relentlessly undermined by Gordon Brown and dispirited by the lack of support from Tony Blair. When they tried to talk him out of it, he told the Prime Minister's aides that 'Tony doesn't back his people. In the end, he always caves in to Gordon.'

Around the Prime Minister, this was felt to be 'a big blow', robbing Blair of a foul-weather ally and one of the few members of the Cabinet truly committed to a radical agenda for the public services.[86] Over at the Treasury, there was undisguised celebration at the departure of an arch-enemy.

It was Milburn's sudden departure that did most to throw all the reshuffle planning into chaos. After a frenzied discussion about who should move into his job, Blair settled for the loyalist John Reid. As he went over to Number 10 after lunch, it dawned on Reid what he was about to be offered. He muttered: 'Oh fuck, it's Health.'

The Westminster political correspondents were by now scenting that another Blair reshuffle was going awry. As long hours passed before Number 10 made any formal announcements, journalists feverishly exchanged speculations about the fate of Irvine and what really lay behind Milburn's sudden departure. David Blunkett groaned: 'The media have presented the reshuffle as a fiasco, but how could they not?'[87]

The Cabinet Secretary subsequently lamented: 'On the day, it was a complete mess-up.'[88] The judiciary reacted angrily to the removal of the Lord Chancellor for fear that they were losing their advocate in Cabinet. To Number 10's surprise, peers were not pleased to be given the right to elect their own chairman or chairwoman. 'We completely misjudged the House of Lords. They didn't want a Betty Boothroyd telling them when to shut up.'[89] Objections were raised to the Scottish Reid taking responsibility for the health service in England when he would not be in charge of the NHS in devolved Scotland. Number 10 announced that it was abolishing the 1,400-year-old position of Lord Chancellor without taking account of the problem that the title was embedded in about 5,000 sections of legislation which would have to be rewritten. So the title stayed even if the job description did change.

Under the cool consideration of a longer perspective, the separation of the powers of the Lord Chancellorship was right. It was also a good reform to transform the Law Lords into a new supreme court, which finally opened in their new quarters the other side of Parliament Square in the autumn of 2009. There was further merit in creating a commission to make senior judicial appointments. These were long overdue and desirable modernisations of one of the most antiquated elements of the British constitution. But few gave the Government any credit for that at the time. The merits of the changes were drowned out by the chaos which surrounded their announcement and the accusations of cronyism that accompanied the replacement of Blair's old pupil master by his old flatmate.

Headlines threw buckets of scorn at his management skills and asked whether the Prime Minister was losing his grip. Gordon Brown looked ever more predatory.

Tony Blair did have a consolation. It came from across the Atlantic. On 25 June, the House of Representatives voted to award him the most prestigious civilian honour that America can bestow, the Congressional Gold Medal, 'in recognition of his outstanding and enduring contributions to maintaining the security of all freedom-loving nations' and his 'steadfast stand against evil'.[90] In America, at least, they still loved him.

12. A Body in the Woods

In Basra Palace, one of Saddam Hussein's old pleasure domes, the Prime Minister addressed British troops. 'When people look back on this time, I honestly believe they will see this as one of the finest moments of our century. And you did it,' he declared on his first visit to Iraq since the invasion.[1]

He chatted with the soldiers on the palace verandah and enjoyed autographing their khaki kit during a six-hour tour designed to present both them and himself as war heroes. His image handlers were especially pleased by a visit to a primary school rebuilt by British troops. The cameras were there to capture the moment when a young Shia boy kissed Blair on the cheek.

Many of the media representatives travelling with him were not being so co-operative in this project to boost the Prime Minister. In the heart of the palace, under the gaze of a tacky fresco of a maiden, reporters mobbed Alastair Campbell.[2] They wanted to question the scowling Director of Communications about a major accusation against the Government which had just been levelled on the BBC.

At seven minutes past six in London that morning, Andrew Gilligan, the defence correspondent of the *Today* programme, laid the gravest allegation yet about the way in which Blair sold the war. 'What we've been told by one of the senior officials in charge of drawing up that dossier was that, actually the Government probably, erm, knew that the 45-minute figure was wrong, even before it decided to put it in,' said Gilligan. Extraordinarily, his editor allowed him to make this dynamite charge not from a vetted script in the studio. The reporter spoke down an ISDN line from his home in Greenwich in an unscripted conversation with the presenter, John Humphrys. Gilligan, a nocturnal type, had been up all night and his lack of sleep was evident from his thick voice as he went on: 'Downing Street, our source says, ordered a week before publication, ordered it to be sexed up.'[3]

Only a very small audience was listening to Gilligan's first, stuttering broadcast, but many more would hear his central claim as he repeated it in eighteen further broadcasts that day. It was given additional amplification in many other reports on the BBC's huge range of output and by the rest of the media.

The allegation that intelligence was twisted to sell the war applied an electric shock to Number 10's most sensitive nerve. The day before, they'd been horrified when the ineffable Donald Rumsfeld casually declared that WMD were probably not going to be found and Saddam might never have had any on the eve of the invasion. The growing and grisly chaos in Iraq intensified the potency of the accusation that Blair duped his nation into war. Robin Cook and other opponents of the war rampaged on the airwaves. MPs from all parties pressed for an inquiry. Alastair Campbell was responding in his habitual way, which was to become ever more belligerent towards the media. A sense of siege and an atmosphere of panic combined with self-righteousness inside Number 10. This was a cloud of combustible gases waiting to be ignited. Gilligan struck the spark. Blair reacted angrily as he always did when his integrity was impeached. 'It wounded his sense of himself,' remarks one of his staff.[4] As was also typical of Blair, he kept his temper within modulated parameters. The next day, speaking at a news conference in Poland, he dismissed the allegations as 'completely absurd' and put it down to 'people who have opposed this action throughout . . . now trying to find a fresh reason for saying why it wasn't the right thing to do'.[5] The story continued to chase Blair around Europe when he arrived at the Evian Summit later in the week. 'It just wasn't going away.'[6] Again insisting that the dossier was approved by the intelligence services, Blair evinced no sign of wanting to escalate this into a battle to the death with the BBC.

It was Alastair Campbell who decided to do that. In Gilligan's original broadcast, the reporter did not accuse anyone at Number 10 by name. It was in an article for that weekend's *Mail on Sunday* that he pointed the finger. The paper gave the piece a giant headline and published it with an unflattering picture of Campbell looking sinisterly thuggish.[7] It was this, according to Blair's later testimony to the Hutton Inquiry, that fanned a routine blaze between Number 10 and the media into an all-consuming firestorm. On Blair's account, a 'small item' became a vast controversy because that article 'really put booster rockets on it'.[8] This was one of the most extraordinary aspects of the affair. Number 10 responded with categorical denials but relative calm when the Prime Minister's integrity was challenged by the charge that Blair knowingly inserted false intelligence into the dossier. It was only when Campbell became the issue that it exploded into what Blair would describe as 'a raging storm'.[9]

In the six years since they moved into Number 10, Campbell had become one of the most powerful non-elected officials ever to operate from that building. The Prime Minister did not just lean on his ability to craft a phrase and project a headline. Campbell's loyalty, drive and commitment were also greatly prized by his friend. Jonathan Powell sometimes called him 'Tony's extra battery'.[10] There was only one person in Government that Campbell acknowledged as his senior and witnesses to his relationship with Tony Blair occasionally found it difficult to remember who was supposed to be the master and who the servant. He was more famous than most of the Cabinet and so influential that even the eclipsed ministers accepted this as the natural order of New Labour. In Opposition and in the first term, Campbell was both an asset and a liability. In the negative column, his fixation with the daily firefight with the media amplified Blair's own weakness for chasing short-term headlines at the expense of pursuing long-term goals. Campbell had little direct influence on legislation. He fiercely disagreed with Blair's approach to education, but his opposition made no difference. The effect he had was on the overall shape of the Governnment's style and priorities. His huge emphasis on presentation subordinated and crowded out those in Number 10 more concerned with policy. He was an obsessive, a tendency which got worse as time went on, in his battles with the media. The truth was too often a casualty of those venomous struggles. Routinely portrayed in the press as a mendacious bully, for many critics he was emblematic of a lot of what had gone wrong with the Government.

In the positive column, Campbell greatly helped the first-term Blair, an inexperienced and often insecure Prime Minister, to project himself as a commanding leader. It was to Campbell that Blair turned when he needed to fashion an instant and appropriate response to the death of Diana in the first summer of his premiership. When NATO was losing the propaganda war over Kosovo, Campbell deployed to Brussels and turned it around.[11] Campbell was there for the highs and the lows of the tortuous negotiations over Northern Ireland. He was a robust champion of Blair in the gruelling struggles with Brown. He had modernised the hapless communications operation at Number 10 inherited from John Major and turned it into an outfit much better equipped to handle a 24/7 media and the most challenging press in the world.

By the second term, the positives were much more outweighed by the negatives. Campbell had become unstable. His mood swings and negativity were infecting the whole of Number 10. 'Alastair was on the edge,' thought Sally Morgan. 'He was depressed and irrational.'[12] He had always been candid, not least with Blair, about his mental illness. In its darkest furlong, he ended up in hospital after a drink-fuelled psychotic breakdown. The diaries written by Campbell during his time in Downing Street often make him sound like a man on the cusp of another episode. Night after night, he would write up his highs, increasingly rare, and his lows, increasingly frequent. After nine years in one of the most stressed and visible jobs in politics, he was burnt out. When Blair asked if he was clinically depressed, Campbell replied yes.[13] He had turned into a hater not just of the media, but of almost everything. When Peter Mandelson asked him whether he liked anyone, Campbell replied that the only people he really liked were his partner and their children.

To his diaries, he repeatedly groaned about 'swimming through shit' and waking up every morning feeling depressed or even suicidal.[14] He would come home from waging his ferocious battles with the media to fierce rows with Fiona about his refusal to listen to her and quit. Yet the power was a drug that he could not kick.

His pathological animosity towards nearly all of the press and most of the broadcasters was a rising concern to Blair. To his friend Barry Cox, Blair would sigh: 'The trouble with Alastair is that he hates the media.'[15] Yet Blair was reluctant to let him go. Whenever Campbell talked about quitting, Blair pressed him to stay. According to Campbell: 'I had been trying to get out for a while, but Tony was adamant that I couldn't leave until we were through this.'[16] Says a close observer of the relationship: 'Tony knew he was out of control, but there was a real bond between them and Tony was scared of what life would be like without Alastair.'[17] Sally Morgan believed 'Alastair was desperate to get out at this point, but Tony never liked losing people.'[18] Campbell's character was rarely distinguished by moderation in anything. If he were religious, Blair joked, Campbell would have ended up as an Islamic fundamentalist.[19] When he drank, he drank himself into a breakdown. When he stopped drinking, he became a teetotal fitness fanatic. When he took up running, he decided to run the London Marathon and fulfilled his goal of doing it in less than four hours. When he did battle with the BBC, he turned it into a total conflagration between the Government and the nation's biggest broadcaster, the like of which had not been seen for decades.

He was fuelled by genuine indignation, an unrestrained hatred for the media, a particular detestation for Gilligan, and a desperation about his own life. 'It was grim for me and also for TB with huge stuff about trust,' he told his diary. 'It was definitely time to get out.'[20] He was right about that. But his pride fired a craving to score a definitive victory over the media in the hope that this would provide the means to depart on a high. 'He was already looking for an exit. Alastair wanted a scalp,' says one of his closest colleagues at this time.[21]

For months, Campbell had been bombarding the BBC with complaints about its reporting of the war and the aftermath. 'He did it sometimes to intimidate,' confirms another member of the communications team. 'That created a mindset at the BBC to ignore anything Alastair said and to aggressively push back.'[22]

BBC executives, wearily accustomed to these barrages from Downing Street, had a dismissive attitude towards the latest fusillade of furious letters about the Gilligan broadcast. 'It's all drivel,' scoffed the editor of *Today*, Kevin Marsh, to a BBC colleague. 'The man is flapping in the wind.'[23]

Downing Street also came to suspect that elements of the intelligence services fed information to the BBC, which encouraged it to stand firm. John Humphrys, introducing Gilligan on the fateful morning, referred on air to the September dossier being 'cobbled together at the last minute'.[24] In Number 10, it was believed that MI6 was endeavouring to dump all the blame for the dossier on them. Sally Morgan asked the others scornfully: 'Since when did the intelligence services ever support a Labour government?'[25] Humphrys had been briefed at a private lunch by Sir Richard Dearlove, the head of MI6. Whether he intended to or not, Dearlove seems to have left the presenter with the impression that the threat had been exaggerated.[26] A witness statement prepared by Marsh and BBC lawyers for the Hutton Inquiry said that a 'senior intelligence source' had suggested that 'hard evidence of WMD in Iraq would never be found.'[27]

That explained an outburst by John Reid that 'rogue elements'[28] in the intelligence services were stirring things up. This, in turn, further aggravated the spooks. The senior management of the BBC, misjudging the seriousness of what was developing, failed to anticipate where it would lead and did not inquire rigorously into the defensibility of Gilligan's allegations. The reporter was more correct than not in the thrust of the nineteen broadcasts he made on 29 May and that was more than could be said of the dossier that he was criticising. But, as the reporter and his editor would later concede, his reporting was flawed.[29] He was already watering down the allegation about forty-five minutes on the day that he broke the story, calling it 'questionable' rather than knowingly false in later broadcasts.

That allegation was the one Campbell seized on. 'I felt I was being royally set up for a fall,' he told his diary. 'The Sundays arrived, ghastly, full of absolute shit about me.'[30] That fear made him even more obsessed with discrediting the BBC, not least because he wanted a favourable verdict from an inquiry into the use of intelligence which was now being conducted by the select committee on Foreign Affairs.

Campbell insisted, despite the misgivings of Blair, that he would appear before the MPs. 'Tony was so exhausted that he wasn't managing it properly so Alastair was allowed to charge around in this manic way,' says Sally

Morgan.[31] As he marched in to testify in a modern committee room in Portcullis House, Campbell was self-aware enough to realise that he was on a hair trigger. As he sat before the MPs, he had hidden in his hand a paperclip. He had bent it so that he could stick a sharp point into his palm if he feared he was about to go over the edge. After a calm start, he built up to a tirade against the repeated 'lie' of the BBC. 'I will keep banging on, that correspondence file will get thicker and they better issue an apology pretty quick.'[32] Blood squirted out of his palm, splattering the papers in front of him. Colleagues at Number 10 looked on with apprehension. He was breaking the first rule of spin doctoring: don't make yourself the story.

Two days later, he took his son, keen like him on sport, to watch the tennis at Wimbledon. In the middle of the match, Campbell's mobile rang. It was one of his staff reporting that Richard Sambrook, the BBC's Head of News and the executive handling his complaints, had just responded to Campbell's latest letter with another rejection accompanied by the accusation that he was pursuing 'a personal vendetta'. He left Wimbledon early, red mist rising as he listened on his car radio to the BBC's treatment of the story on the six o'clock news. He made an impulsive decision to go to the ITV building in Gray's Inn Road from where the *Channel 4 News* would be broadcast at 7 p.m. 'It's a real mistake,' Jonathan Powell warned Campbell. 'Don't do it.'[33] He did it anyway. Jon Snow, the programme's presenter, got a surprise guest. Four minutes into the show, his producer spoke down Snow's earpiece: 'Alastair Campbell has entered the building.'[34] This was a stunner even to a veteran presenter like Snow. 'What you have to remember is that, in those days, interviews with Alastair Campbell were very rare.'[35]

Moments later, Campbell was in the studio, giving an unprecedented live interview, jabbing his finger in fury, thumping the desk, railing that the BBC had to 'just accept for once they have got it wrong'.[36]

Snow was taken aback by the vehemence of the performance: 'I thought to myself: this man is not long for this world.'[37]

Fiona Millar rang Sally Morgan in horror. 'I've just turned on *Channel 4 News* and he's on there shouting.'[38]

His partner was 'livid'.[39] Even his own staff, who tended to be highly loyal, watched aghast as he displayed an indiscipline that he would never tolerate in anyone else. 'I was horrified. Alastair was out of control,' says another member of the communications team.[40]

Blair agreed. Campbell's manic campaign was fuelling the furore over the elusive WMD and the dossier. An endless war with the BBC would simply make the Government more enemies when it had quite enough of them already. 'Alastair was really angry with the BBC, but Tony had a more considered view,' says Barry Cox, who made his own living as a television executive. 'Tony knew, whatever the problem, you couldn't behave like Campbell was behaving at that point.'[41]

In the middle of 'the raging storm', the Prime Minister even had BBC executives around to Number 10 for a lunch which was entirely convivial. In Blair's view, it was 'not really very sensible for the Government' to be in a 'continuing dispute with the BBC . . . the main broadcasting outlet'.[42]

More than once, Blair told Campbell to 'leave it', but to no avail. His most powerful aide had lost control of himself and the Prime Minister had lost control of his most powerful aide. 'That was the almost inevitable consequence of the space that Tony had given him,' says Cox.[43]

On 3 July, Geoff Hoon rang Number 10 with intriguing news: a Government scientist had come forward to volunteer to his superiors that he had met Gilligan the week before the *Today* broadcast. To this development, Blair initially reacted with caution, telling Jonathan Powell that they should 'keep the information to ourselves' for now.[44] They tried to keep it secret from Campbell because 'Tony had lost confidence in Alastair's objectivity and didn't trust him.' It was Geoff Hoon, who thought Campbell ought to know, who informed him.[45]

The revelation made Campbell explosive with excitement. He knew the scientist, Dr David Kelly, was a WMD expert, but initially mistook him to be much more junior than he actually was. Kelly had not been directly involved in the drafting of the dossier. His account of his meeting with Gilligan did not appear to tally with the reporter's claims. Campbell was euphoric with a 'gotcha' moment. If they exposed Kelly as the BBC reporter's source, so a gleeful Campbell told Hoon, 'it would fuck Gilligan.'[46]

For the next few days, Number 10 was almost wholly consumed by the question of how to handle Kelly. That weekend there were triangular telephone conversations between Blair, at Chequers, and Campbell and Hoon. The trio intensively discussed how they might best exploit this development. Campbell told his diary that the Defence Secretary shared his desire 'to get it out that the source had broken cover',[47] though Hoon says he wanted to privately tell the BBC Governors that they had a name.[48] Blair was now more aggressive about winning the battle with the BBC, not least because he was made frantic by reports from MI6 that the search for WMD in Iraq was still coming up empty-handed.

The Prime Minister got temporarily cold feet when Sir David Omand, the security co-ordinator at the Cabinet Office, warned him that they would have to tread carefully because they had a duty of care towards the civil servant. When Blair returned from the Chilterns to London, he was looking for official cover so that no-one could later accuse him of not playing it by the book. On Monday, 7 July, he presided over a 'running meeting' in his study, a meeting that 'gets smaller and bigger and bigger and smaller'[49] as a remarkable gallery of characters surged in and out of his den. The fluctuating cast included Sir David Manning, Sir Kevin Tebbit, the Permanent Secretary at the Ministry of Defence, Sir David Omand and John Scarlett. Jack Straw dropped in to discuss whether they should produce Kelly for one of the parliamentary committees looking into the war. Blair pressed the officials to find out whether Kelly would back the Government's story on the dossier or not.[50]

Scarlett emerged from the den to dictate a note that the scientist should be subject to a 'proper security-style interview'.[51]

Blair remained leery at this stage about exposing Kelly in public. He still hoped that a compromise might be struck with the BBC. That morning, he rang Gavyn Davies, the Chairman of the BBC. Ignoring the advice of the civil servants not to do so, Blair revealed to Davies that someone had come forward whom they suspected to be Gilligan's source. The BBC was still not budging. The more aggressive Downing Street became, the more the corporation treated the Government's complaints as an assault on its integrity. Greg Dyke, the Director-General, interpreted it as another manifestation of the 'systematic bullying' and 'war of attrition' that Campbell waged on the BBC.[52] Dyke and Blair had known each other for years. When they were first introduced, Dyke jokingly groaned: 'Not another bloody Labour lawyer.' But Dyke was a Labour man. So was Davies. He was married to Sue Nye, Gordon Brown's most long-standing personal aide. The more paranoid element in Blair's entourage even detected the Chancellor's hidden hand. There was no evidence for that, though Brown did display evident relish for Blair's discomfort. The Chancellor cracked jokes in the Commons that a document on health 'has not been sexed up'.[53]

Both Chairman and Director-General of the BBC donated to Labour in the past, which had made their appointments highly controversial. This introduced a flavour of the family feud to the battle which made it even more inflamed. In his phone conversation with Blair, Davies said the BBC was standing by Gilligan and would be neither retracting the story nor apologising for it.

'The whole thing spiralled out of control. The tragedy was that neither side could find a way of finessing this and finding a solution,' observes the Cabinet Secretary, Andrew Turnbull.[54] It was 'almost a constitutional crisis', reflects Peter Mandelson.[55]

The possessed Campbell was not interested in a compromise anyway. He wanted 'a clear win' over the BBC, 'not a messy draw'.[56] At around six o'clock that evening, Godric Smith came into Campbell's office to find him on the speakerphone to Hoon. Campbell was in the middle of suggesting to the Defence Secretary that news that the source had come forward should be leaked to a friendly journalist that evening.[57] An alarmed Smith discussed this with Tom Kelly. Both cautioned Campbell that a crude leak would be a bad idea because it would be much too obvious that it had come from Number 10.[58]

On Tuesday, 8 July, another meeting assembled in the Prime Minister's study. Of the four sessions in the space of two days devoted to Kelly, this was the critical one. It put Tony Blair at the heart of a devious strategy which would lead to David Kelly being outed less than forty-eight hours later. This meeting was the 'decisive' one[59] which set in train the events that turned a nasty affair into a tragic one. Jonathan Powell was among those who were 'surprised it had not already become public' who Kelly was.[60] David Manning also thought it 'almost inevitable that his name would become known'.[61]

Blair now sanctioned a 'naming strategy' which would indeed make Kelly's exposure inevitable. The strategy guaranteed that the scientist's identity got out while making it hard to prove that Downing Street had done the deed itself. It was at this crucial meeting that the 'policy decision' was taken that the Ministry of Defence would issue a statement revealing that one of its officials had admitted speaking to Gilligan. Blair further authorised the department to release biographical details about Kelly, making it more likely that he could be identified.[62]

Though the statement would go out in the name of the MoD, it was actually composed in Number 10 by Godric Smith. Huddled around the Number 10 spokesman's computer screen at various points that day were Campbell, Powell, Tom Kelly and Sir Kevin Tebbit. The statement was finished at around 2.30 p.m., shown to Blair and then Powell told Sir Kevin to take it over to his department.[63] The statement went out to the media at a quarter to six that evening. The MoD also made a very untypically generous offer to the media: it would confirm the identity of the person to any journalist who managed to guess it correctly.

That was red meat for the many reporters ravenous to unmask the mystery source at the heart of the consuming battle between the Government and the BBC. The strength of the clues scattered into the media meant that competent journalists who knew their subject area could get there very quickly.

Richard Norton-Taylor, a specialist in defence and intelligence for the *Guardian*, knew from the MoD that the mystery man had been a UN weapons inspector in Iraq. This reporter fed the clues 'Britain' and 'Unscom' into an internet search engine. Up popped Kelly.[64] Michael Evans, Defence

Editor of *The Times*, was allowed to put twenty-one names to the MoD in order to be told that it was Kelly.[65] The *Financial Times* got the name too. Kelly was outed the next morning.[66]

The atmosphere inside Number 10 is captured by an e-mail to Jonathan Powell from Tom Kelly which reads: 'This is now a game of chicken with the Beeb.'[67]

Geoff Hoon would later tell friends that there was nothing in his political career that he regretted more than this affair. He suffered enduring remorse that he had not argued more strongly with Blair and Campbell when he discussed Kelly with them the weekend before the scientist was exposed. Three years later, Hoon was stripped of his Cabinet rank. Furious, he came close to resigning. Before he changed his mind about quitting, he planned to make a resignation speech fully exposing the process by which Kelly was outed and the extent of Blair's complicity in it. Hoon told friends that he could reveal things so devastating to Blair's reputation that 'Tony could not have remained as Prime Minister.'[68]

David Kelly was now exposed to the world, dragging the shy and introverted scientist out of the shadows and into the furnace heat of a battle between politicians and the media. The Permanent Secretary, Sir Kevin Tebbit, tried to give the scientist some protection. He argued that they should let Kelly appear before a closed session of the Intelligence and Security Committee, but spare him a televised grilling by the Foreign Affairs Select Committee 'to show some regard for the man himself. He has come forward voluntarily; he is not used to being thrust into the public eye, and is not on trial.'[69] Hoon overruled his most senior official because 'presentationally, it would be difficult to defend.'[70]

On 15 July, Kelly was thrust in front of the Foreign Affairs committee for an interrogation which was as long as it was clumsy. The scientist was clearly troubled to find himself caught in the middle of a titanic clash between forces much mightier than himself. The undistinguished and blundering committee managed to grasp the wrong end of several sticks. The Labour MP Andrew Mackinlay dismissed the scientist as a 'fall-guy' and 'chaff'. Evidently disconcerted, Kelly claimed he could not believe that he was Gilligan's 'main source', though he was. He was further thrown when David Chidgey, a Lib Dem MP who had been secretly briefed by Gilligan, asked whether Kelly was the source of a report by Susan Watts, *Newsnight*'s science editor. Kelly denied it, a lie which would increasingly prey on his mind in the days to come.[71]

Campbell, who had been doubtful about letting Kelly go before the committee, regarded the scientist's appearance as 'a disaster'.[72] It only muddied the waters and brought him no closer to winning his battle with the BBC. The exposure of Kelly did not have the result he craved. It did not 'fuck Gilligan'. Even Campbell was becoming exhausted by this destructive struggle which was only adding to the Government's many troubles. He concluded: 'This was something which we were going to have to sort of put behind us and forget.'[73]

On 17 July, Tony Blair crossed the Atlantic, his mind now on a much grander stage than the bitter battle with the BBC and the cynical outing of David Kelly. The Prime Minister was to address a joint session of the House of Representatives and the Senate, a rare accolade bestowed on only three of his predecessors, Winston Churchill, Clement Attlee and Margaret Thatcher. His star might be dimmed in his own country, but in America he still shone bright.

Acutely conscious of the scale of the honour and the size of the occasion, he was both thrilled and fretful. He spent more time on the 32-minute address to Congress than he would even on a party conference speech. On the flight over in a Boeing 777, he took his habitual place in seat A1 up in the first-class cabin. 'He always liked to sit there.'[74] He sat refining his speech as they crossed the Atlantic and displayed his nerves by constantly fussing about what suit and tie he should wear.[75]

As the Prime Minister worried about his clothing, an even more anxious man was hiding at his home in Oxfordshire, sliding into despair under the scorching pressure from the media, MPs and his superiors which menaced every aspect of his life. In David Kelly's briefcase lay an unopened letter from the MoD containing an official reprimand.

A lengthy cavalcade of Lincoln limousines whisked the Prime Minister, his wife and their party from Andrews Air Force Base to Capitol Hill. They were allowed to take several guests so his wife had invited along two of her half-sisters who lived in America. Cherie was excited by the great occasion. 'After all the negativity, it made my heart sing.'[76]

In Oxfordshire, the wife of David Kelly was increasingly troubled: 'He looked dejected. He had a broken heart. He had shrunk into himself. He could not put two sentences together. He could not talk at all.'[77]

Tony Blair had not opened his mouth when he received his first standing ovation from the assembled Senators and Congressmen, who rose to applaud him the moment he appeared on the podium. The Prime Minister immediately had his audience charmed with a typically deft Blair joke. He remarked that one of the Senators had just been reminding him that the British burnt down Washington in 1812. 'I know it's kinda late,' he quipped. 'But sorry.' His audience was rapturous.

After a sandwich lunch, at just past three o'clock in Oxfordshire, Dr David Kelly left his house telling his wife he was going for a walk. He bumped into a neighbour. 'Hello, Ruth,' he said. 'Oh hello, David. How are things?' 'Not too bad,' he said.[78] He had in his pockets his mobile phone, a small bottle of mineral water, a packet of thirty powerful painkillers and an old knife.

Before Congress, Blair offered his audience mutual therapy about Iraq. He told them what both he and they most wanted to believe: history would judge them well, even if their contemporaries did not.

Talking about it later, he would say that he regarded his speech to Congress that day as one of the highlights of his premiership.[79] In the most impressive section of the address, he elegantly affirmed his conviction in the transatlantic alliance while also reasserting his belief in multilateralism. The speech contained a strong message to the unilateralists around Bush who had made working with the Americans such agony and left Iraq in such a bloody mess.

'The world's security cannot be protected without the world's heart being won. America must listen as well as lead,' he told Congress, an unusually blunt message from him and one that he should have delivered much earlier.[80]

Donald Rumsfeld, one of the people at whom that was directed, gave a painful smile. Also watching in some agony was the Shadow Chancellor and future Tory leader Michael Howard, who had been invited to join the audience and now had to endure the misery of being forced to rise to join each of the nineteen standing ovations that Congress bestowed on Tony Blair. That hugely amused the Prime Minister's party.[81]

To a final massive ovation, Blair left the podium 'very excited' by his rapturous reception.[82] He then had a news conference with George Bush and a celebratory dinner at the White House. Noting how Bush's staff deferred to him as 'Mr President', Blair joked to his aides: 'Why can't you be like them?'[83]

Dr David Kelly had clambered through some brambles to get to a secluded glade. He used the mineral water to swallow down twenty-nine of the painkillers, sat on the ground, took off his wristwatch and slit his left wrist.

His tragedy was over; for the Prime Minister, it had only just begun.

Tony Blair was still on a post-ovation high as the 777 took off from Andrews Air Force Base on a fourteen-hour flight to Tokyo. Pleased with his speech, pleased with its fabulous reception, pleased with himself, he settled into A1, had a couple of drinks and chatted and laughed with Cherie about what a wonderful day it had been. The applause of Congress still tingling in his ears, he and his wife had settled down to sleep when Godric Smith came through the curtains into the first-class cabin. He was carrying a satellite phone. It was Number 10: David Kelly had gone missing.[84] Blair's ears began to ring with a sound which wasn't applause.

As the 777 continued its progress round the rim of the world, a few hours later the sun could be seen setting over the Bering Strait. The plane was jolted by severe turbulence. There was another call from Downing Street for the Prime Minister. As he handed the phone back to Smith, Blair slumped into his seat. From sitting upright, he just crashed. He spoke to his wife: 'David Kelly is dead.' She had 'never seen Tony so distraught'.[85] To David Manning, who was also in the cabin, he looked 'shocked, upset and very disturbed'.[86]

He grasped at once that the Government was going to be accused of driving the scientist to suicide by allowing him to be exposed. Spin kills. That would be the charge. He saw that so quickly not least because he had presided over the 'naming strategy' meeting which had made his exposure inevitable. For the remainder of the flight, Blair made a string of calls on the satellite phone. One was to Alastair Campbell. He and Sally Morgan had left the Prime Minister's party in Washington to fly back to London. As they were queuing to get off the plane at Heathrow, Campbell got a text. His face went white. 'Fuck,' he groaned to Morgan. 'I don't believe it. Kelly's dead.'[87] Campbell, now in a very bad way, told Blair on the phone that he couldn't handle it any more. He 'felt the juggernaut coming my way'. He told Blair 'he wanted out.'[88] Blair placed other important calls to Jonathan Powell and to his old friend and new Lord Chancellor, Charlie Falconer. They rapidly agreed that it would not be enough simply to say that the death should be left to the police and the coroner. They would have to announce a judicial inquiry as the best hope of containing the fall-out. Blair believed he had no option but to surrender himself to a judge. By doing so, he accepted that his moral authority in the eyes of the public was so threadbare there was nowhere else to go. 'If he hadn't held the inquiry, for ever after Tony would have been accused of murdering David Kelly.'[89]

The Cabinet Secretary had taken that Friday off to play in the annual golf tournament between Whitehall and Westminster at the RAC course. His mobile rang with news that Kelly was dead as Sir Andrew Turnbull was about to play the thirteenth hole. 'Like everyone, I was shocked rigid.'[90] Turnbull's mobile then didn't stop ringing. He was soon in receipt of a message sent from over the Pacific by the frantic Prime Minister: 'By the time I get off the plane, I have to be able to say what we are going to do about it.'

As Turnbull urgently consulted with other senior officials, the Cabinet Secretary was interrupted by one of the golf club's staff. 'You can't use your mobile here,' he said. 'Believe me, it's very important,' replied Britain's most senior civil servant. 'I don't care,' said the jobsworth. 'What's more – tuck your shirt in.'[91]

Falconer rang Thomas Bingham, the senior Law Lord, to get some ideas about who would be a suitable judge to preside over the inquiry. He told Bingham that their 'over-riding concern was to get someone with credibility'. The name that emerged was Brian Hutton, a septuagenarian Law Lord on the point of retirement with an impeccable reputation for being immune to political pressure. Falconer rang Blair in the Far East to say that Hutton sounded like a reasonable bet.[92] A former Chief Justice in Northern Ireland, Lord Hutton was no radical. He had a reputation as a conservative and cautious judge. He could be relied on to interpret his mandate narrowly and investigate only the death of Dr Kelly, not the wider controversies about the war. He could also be expected to be sympathetic to arguments about the need to protect national security.

The undercarriage of the 777 was already down, preparing to land in Tokyo, when Godric Smith emerged from the first-class cabin to brief the accompanying media. He told them of the Prime Minister's 'distress' and briefly sketched the plan to hold a judicial inquiry. When the plane landed, the journalists were kept from Blair. Looking gaunt and unshaven, he was rushed straight to his hotel late that Friday night. 'It was an absolute low spot for him.'[93]

The Prime Minister 'barely slept'. His wife had 'never seen him so badly affected by anything'.[94] He called friends. Michael Levy found: 'He was in a state of absolute depression. He was questioning himself.'[95] While he sat awake in his hotel suite in Tokyo, in Number 10 the mood was 'grim, really grim'.[96] There was feverish activity to make it possible to announce the full details of the inquiry as soon as possible, in the hope of pre-empting what they knew would be one of the most threatening episodes of Blair's premiership. 'We all knew this looked very, very bad.'[97]

Within days, Geoff Hoon went to see the Kelly family, who could be highly dangerous to the Government if they started to point accusatory fingers. Hoon told a hugely relieved Blair that Janice Kelly did not blame him personally for her husband's death.[98] On his return to Britain, Blair invited the doctor's widow and daughter Rachel for an unpublicised meeting with him and Cherie at Chequers. Blair expressed his personal apologies and that was sincerely meant. Death often weighed on his mind and the more so as his premiership went on. But he was also making a calculated effort to improve his odds of surviving this affair. The Kelly family had the capacity to inflict huge, potentially lethal, damage on him if they were to publicly accuse the Prime Minister of killing the doctor. He needed them kept quiet.

A grim and drawn Prime Minister delivered a formal statement on the Saturday morning in Tokyo in which he declared himself to be 'profoundly sad' about the death of the scientist, 'a fine public servant'.

He signalled his hope that the announcement of the inquiry would close down media questions about the role he and other key figures at Number 10 had played in the events leading up to the scientist's death.

'We shall set aside speculation, claims and counter-claims and allow the due process to take its proper course. In the meantime, all of us, politicians, media alike, should show some restraint and respect. That is all I am going to say.'[99]

Though his entourage tried to keep him insulated from the journalists accompanying them on the trip, it was unavoidable that he would have to take questions when he appeared at a joint news conference with the Prime Minister of Japan. It was there that Blair was ambushed with one of the questions he most dreaded. 'Have you got blood on your hands, Prime Minister?' demanded Jonathan Oliver of the *Mail on Sunday*. 'Are you going to resign?'[100]

In normal circumstances, Blair was smoothly accomplished at shrugging off the slings and arrows of reporters. On this occasion, with the nonplussed Japanese Prime Minister standing beside him, he struggled to locate a response. He stood there in staring silence for several seconds until Japanese officials stepped in to end the news conference. Looking utterly defeated, he just walked away. When Sally Morgan talked to him on the phone 'he was in a pretty bad state.'[101]

On Sunday, the tour reached South Korea. The Blairs attended mass at Seoul's Roman Catholic cathedral. As they went in to say their prayers, they were confronted by a couple of local anti-war protestors who waved a banner bearing a picture of the dead man and asking: 'Who killed David Kelly?'[102] There was no escaping his ghost.

By Tuesday, 22 July, they had flown on to another leg of this Far Eastern tour: China. A photo opportunity was arranged in a hot Beijing warehouse which was exhibiting an installation of terracotta figurines by Antony Gormley. The Prime Minister squatted alone amidst the six-inch soldiers. Then Cherie appeared and embraced him from behind. Out of the earshot of the photographers, she tried to ease her husband's torment. She whispered: 'You are a good man.'[103] At Tsinghua University, the students asked him about Kelly's death. They then hit him with a request for a song. Cherie stepped in to sing a Beatles number, 'When I'm Sixty-Four'. Her haggard husband almost looked that old. He was an entirely different man to the bouncy Prime Minister who had bounded aboard his plane when it left Washington. Even to his loyal wife, 'Tony seemed to age ten years and the stress was written on his face, however much he tried to keep up appearances.'[104]

That stress was multiplied by Campbell, who was 'going to pieces' back in London.[105] Philip Gould went round to see Campbell at his north London home and found him 'ashen, totally ashen. He felt enormous remorse.'[106] In highly charged telephone conversations over that weekend, the Prime Minister tried to calm down Campbell and persuade him not to quit immediately. That would make them both look guilty. But he had also finally reached a conclusion about Campbell. After a suitable interval, he would have to go.[107]

By now the press back at home was in a frenzy about the extent of the Prime Minister's personal culpability in the events that led to Dr Kelly's death, though none of them knew then that Blair had presided over the decisive meeting which authorised the 'naming strategy'. Long-standing foes in the right-wing press lacerated him.

More devastating for Number 10 was the magisterial savaging handed down by Hugo Young from his judge's seat in the *Guardian*. The doyen of liberal columnists had previously admired Blair. In condemnation of the Kelly Affair, Young charged the Government with being 'willing to abandon all sense of proportion' and use 'every available particle of state power' in order 'to score political points against its critics'. Blair, he said in another column shortly afterwards, should quit.[108] Blair was sufficiently wounded by that to respond with a long and impassioned handwritten letter to Young trying to persuade him that he was not too tainted and spent to carry on as Prime Minister.[109]

The Far Eastern tour approached its next destination. As his 777 descended towards Hong Kong, the Prime Minister came through the curtains shielding him in first class and walked back to where the reporters on board were sitting. Paul Eastham, the deputy political editor of the *Daily Mail*, got in his face, demanding: 'Why did you authorise the naming of David Kelly?' Blair responded: 'That is completely untrue.' He was then asked: 'Did you authorise anyone in Downing Street or in the Ministry of Defence to release David Kelly's name?' 'Emphatically not,' said Blair. 'Nobody was authorised to name David Kelly. I believe we have acted properly throughout.'[110] And yet it was true, emphatically so, that Blair presided over the 8 July meeting at Number 10 which authorised the naming process.[111]

An approaching typhoon provided a convenient excuse for Blair to return home early the following day. High winds and heavy rain lashed the plane as it rumbled down the runway. Alarms suddenly sounded in the cockpit and lights flashed: ABORT, ABORT, ABORT. 'I'm going to try again,' said the pilot. This time the 777 achieved takeoff, made a steep ascent over a churning China Sea, banked and headed for London.[112] The Blairs remained cocooned in their first-class cabin all the way home.

On 11 August, Lord Hutton called his inquiry to order in a cramped court room at the back of the Royal Courts of Justice on the Strand. The twenty-four days of testifying and cross-examination over that long hot summer were a peculiarly British affair. Some American and French journalists marvelled that the Prime Minister had placed his own integrity on trial. Neither George Bush nor Jacques Chirac, they observed, would subject themselves to such a public ordeal.[113] Others wondered at the shabbiness of the dirty carpet, nasty chairs and cheap bookcases.

The first of seventy-four witnesses who would give 10,000 pages of evidence was Martin Howard, the deputy chief of Defence Intelligence. Powerful figures who normally remain in the shadows, such as him, John Scarlett and Sir Kevin Tebbit, were briefly thrust into the spotlight before returning to the dark. Sir Richard Dearlove remained a man of mystery, giving his evidence incognito through a voice link from an undisclosed location.

The Kelly family gave moving accounts of the last hours of his life and their distress at his death. Their QC, Jeremy Gompertz, described the scientist as a victim of a 'cynical abuse of power'.

All other business at Number 10 was virtually frozen as Blair and his aides took extensive advice from lawyers. Alastair Campbell was compelled to produce fragments of his diary. He was made uncomfortable when questioned about what he had planned when he wrote that he was going to 'fuck Gilligan'. Even as the documents published on the inquiry's website revealed the number of changes he had successfully introduced into the language of the dossier, he made the claim: 'I had no input, output or influence upon them [the Joint Intelligence Committee] at any stage in the process.' He even claimed about his diary: 'It is not intended for publication.'[114] It was published, for an advance of £1 million, a month after Tony Blair left office.

Tom Kelly had to account for why he had speculated to a journalist, in what he thought was an off-the-record conversation, that the scientist was a 'Walter Mitty' fantasist.

The slew of internal Number 10 documents made available exposed the frantic way the dossier was thrown together. The manipulation of the text was revealed by the publication of the torrent of e-mail traffic that pinged between spin doctors and intelligence officials the previous September. For a while afterwards, some people inside Downing Street stopped communicating anything sensitive by e-mail and resorted to Post-it notes for fear of later exposure.[115]

A pitiless light was shone on Blair's way of making decisions at unminuted and often haphazard meetings with small groups in his den. The inner wiring of his Government was laid bare. A blowtorch was taken to New Labour, burning off any remaining mystique about how it operated.

On top of that, 'there was the psychological pressure of the media coverage over many months.'[116]

Much of the press coverage was shriekingly partisan. Papers and commentators who had opposed the war or had other reasons for disliking the Government amplified every revelation that was damaging to Number 10. For them it 'laid bare the tangled web that politicians weave when first they practise to deceive'.[117]

The *Daily Mail* buried its usual hatred for the BBC because it loathed Blair more and used the inquiry to prosecute its editor's case that this was a uniquely corrupt and mendacious government. Papers that supported the war and were still sympathetic to the Prime Minister savaged the BBC, none more energetically than the *Sun*.

The Government looked bad. But as the proceedings wound on, it should have also become apparent to the BBC's senior executives that things were not going to conclude well for them. They had been warned. Before Hutton started sitting, there was an internal BBC exercise to test the corporation's defences. Greg Dyke was interrogated before an audience of his senior colleagues. Dyke's inquisitor at this private BBC session was the right-wing journalist Andrew Neil, one of the BBC's more robust interrogators. Neil tore Dyke to shreds. 'My heart sank,' says one BBC executive who witnessed this. 'I knew then we were in big trouble.'[118]

Dyke was badly roughed up in front of Hutton.

Andrew Gilligan's broad contention that the dossier was 'sexed up' was correct, but Hutton was not interested in that and the reporter had to withdraw the specific allegation that the Government knew at the time of publication that the 45-minute claim was false. Gilligan had a torrid time in front of Hutton, who displayed signs of distaste for the media and naivety about the civil servants and politicians. One senior Whitehall figure noted that the judge was 'politically innocent'.[119] He was about to encounter a witness who was anything but.

'Good morning, Prime Minister,' said the judge.

'Good morning, my lord,' responded Tony Blair, giving Lord Hutton a little smile. It was the Prime Minister's turn to appear in Court 73 on Thursday,

28 August. He arrived at the Royal Courts of Justice looking glossy with a healthy tan acquired at Sir Cliff Richard's villa in Barbados. Blair had come out as someone who needed reading glasses. These he clutched in his hand when he sat down in the witness box. He gave a hint of nerves by twiddling with the glasses and taking them off and putting them on during the first five minutes of his examination. Then he swiftly and visibly relaxed. 'Never forget that Tony is a lawyer,' his aides would often remark.[120] He had a great capacity to master a brief and a well-honed ability to argue any case, however dodgy. Earlier in the month, he had overtaken Clement Attlee's record. This was now the longest ever period of continuous Labour rule. The ranks of gold-plated QCs in the court would have to be very good indeed to land a knock-out on a politician who had ducked and weaved his way through many searching interrogations on television and radio and in Parliament over the past six years and four months. Being a lawyer himself, he was also well-trained at dealing with his kind. He came over as reasonable and rational, presenting himself as a man only ever concerned to do his sincere best in a difficult situation.

For those who knew how to read him, Blair became twitchy only once during his testimony. This was when he was questioned about the outing of the scientist. That was dangerous territory for the Prime Minister – the 'smoking gun' of the affair for him – and he knew it. He started to wave his hands about, his sentences became tangled and his accent more estuarial. 'Whenever he goes "y'know, y'know" he's uncomfortable.'[121]

He led the court on a winding diversion about his 'quandary' about what to do about Kelly. He was never pinned down about his role sanctioning the outing. The QCs moved on. Blair relaxed. He left the witness box looking comfortable with his performance.

The day after Blair gave evidence, Number 10 announced that Alastair Campbell was resigning. 'He is a strong character who can make enemies. But those who know him best like him best,' said the Prime Minister's rather ambiguous formal farewell to the man who had been his closest aide for six years in government and three years of Opposition before that.[122]

The truth was that Campbell had not wanted to resign now. He hoped to stay at Number 10 at least until Hutton reported, believing the judge might yet provide the vindication he yearned for. 'You could tell by the way he went that he wasn't someone wanting to leave the stage,' thought other Number 10 staff.[123] But Blair had determined that Campbell had outlived his usefulness. Public trust in the Government had collapsed and Campbell was the figure most associated with the spin that was so corrosive to its reputation.

Relations between Campbell and his partner and the Prime Minister and his wife never properly recovered from the savage internal battles over Cherie-gate.[124] His reckless battle with the BBC had kept Iraq, the dossier, spin and Blair's integrity in the headlines for month after searing month.

'In the end Tony had to chop him off,' says Barry Cox. 'It had gone too far. He did get rid of Alastair.'[125]

The inquiry wound on until mid-October. There was some alarm in Number 10 when Sir Kevin Tebbit, the Permanent Secretary at the Ministry of Defence, gave late evidence directly pointing to Blair's deep involvement in the outing of David Kelly by revealing that the Prime Minister had chaired the 'decisive' meeting at which the 'naming strategy' was agreed. It was hard to reconcile that with Blair's denial on the plane: 'I did not authorise the leaking of the name of David Kelly.' Yet Lord Hutton did not seem to read any significance into Tebbit's testimony and it did not attract the airtime and headlines it would have got back during the long, hot August. Media interest in the affair was flagging and much of the press was now more focused on the latest travails of Iain Duncan Smith and the Tories. Tony Blair always was a lucky Prime Minister.

He was not on the list of the witnesses recalled for further examination. Blair voiced an increasing confidence to his aides that Hutton was going to be 'all right for us'.[126]

A Law Lord and some of the most expensive QCs in Britain had not proved a match for him.

13. Dinner for Three

The Labour Party gathered in Bournemouth in September 2003 for a familiar ritual. The pattern of the opening days of the annual conference was so well-established by now that it was almost as traditional as the Changing of the Guard at Buckingham Palace. For more than a decade of their double act, Blair followed Brown as surely as Tuesday followed Monday. Two men, two speeches, two visions of how Labour should govern, two ideas of who should be governing. Some of it was about content, as much was about style, and a lot was about ambition. Gordon Brown always performed just before lunch on the Monday. He would thunder out a speech crafted to project his power, align himself with the traditional passions of the party and wink his dissent with New Labour by suggesting that he was the champion of True Labour. As Sunder Katwala, the General Secretary of the Fabian Society, puts it: 'He was always the person who could rouse the Labour crowd with the Labour argument.'[1] Every year it was the same, the only difference being how subtle or crude the Chancellor was about prosecuting the rivalry. 'Gordon always positions himself five degrees to Tony's left,' complained people around the Prime Minister.[2] This was the obvious place for Brown to put himself in order to create some differentiation between the two. As his allies liked to point out, there was not really any space to Blair's right.[3]

On the Tuesday afternoon, the Prime Minister would respond with a reassertion of his pre-eminence in the Government, a display of his superior talent for talking to the country, and a restatement of his commitment to the New Labour approach. Brown would hurl down the gauntlet; Blair would dash it back. In some ways, this annual battle of the two speeches was a benefit. The competition pumped up both men to give a maximum performance.

There was extra edge to the ritual that autumn. Blair looked more vulnerable than at any previous time in his premiership. On the eve of the conference, he admitted to me that he had taken a 'battering' from 'an onslaught' which had left him 'knocked about' in the months since the war.[4]

Polling suggested that half the public wanted him to resign.[5] Sixty per cent of his own party members said he was wrong to go to war and approaching half of them wanted him to quit immediately or at the next election.[6] In quick succession, he had lost Alan Milburn, one of his closest allies in the Cabinet, and Alastair Campbell from Number 10. He had been defeated on the euro after the April Fool ambush by his Chancellor and then made a botch of the summer reshuffle. He was forced to appease his party by agreeing to legislate a ban on hunting – which he had never wanted to outlaw. He toyed with bringing Peter Mandelson back into the Cabinet, but he was too weak to overcome the resistance to that idea from John Prescott, Jack Straw and, of course, Gordon Brown. He settled for giving Mandelson a more prominent position in the 'kitchen Cabinet' at Number 10. The furore over the death of David Kelly and the relentlessly grim news from Iraq were taking a huge toll on his standing. Labour was hammered by the Lib Dems in the Brent East by-election, the first by-election lost since he became leader, ripping another tear in the suit of invincibility that had once armoured him against his internal critics. Public support for the war was crashing, as was voter trust in the Prime Minister. Few now believed him when he insisted that people should 'just wait and see' before they concluded there never were any WMD.[7] The findings of Philip Gould's focus groups were bleak. 'It had been a bad year.'[8]

Matthew Taylor, a new recruit to Number 10 from the Institute of Public Policy Research, came up with the idea of launching 'the big conversation' – one attempt of many to try to reconnect Blair with voters. His agenda for public services was encountering mounting resistance with a series of parliamentary rebellions against the health reforms.

The Chancellor watched all this and felt both emboldened and desperate. Desperate because he feared he would inherit a wrecked Government if he did not force out Blair. That was his 'nightmare scenario'.[9] Emboldened because his rival was now looking weak, Brown saw himself as a strengthening figure in comparison with a shrinking Prime Minister.

On the Monday in Bournemouth, Brown implicitly attacked Blair for dividing the party over Iraq and public service reform. He presented himself as the unifying prince in waiting, the man 'never losing sight of Labour's vision' who was ready and able to save the party and its 'soul'. He pulled all the stops in his oratorical organ in a speech in which he deliberately never once used the phrase 'New Labour'. It was 'an alternative personal election manifesto', noted an admiring *Daily Mirror*. 'The Chancellor will never be the orator that Mr Blair has trained himself to be . . . but only Mr Brown hits the real Labour G-spot.'[10]

He also delivered a barely coded call to arms. His speech ended by giving a parodying twist to Blair's 'at our best when at our boldest' phrase of the year before.

Brown punchlined his speech: 'This Labour Party, best when we're united – best when we are Labour.'[11] He had for years received help with speeches from Bob Shrum, an American political consultant. The line was invented at a speech-writing session in Shrum's office in Washington during Brown's pre-conference trip to a meeting of the World Bank. He 'angsted and agonised to the last minute' about whether to use it.[12] In his camp 'everyone was absurdly excited' when he went for it, thinking: 'Aren't we terribly clever?'[13]

One unfactional member of the Cabinet was sitting in the audience with delegates from his constituency party. 'They may not be the most sophisticated people in the world, but they instantly knew what Gordon was doing. They didn't need the press to interpret it for them. And they were angry.'[14]

Others were delighted to see Brown unfurling a standard for disgruntled trades unionists and disaffected party activists to rally around.

Unusually, Blair missed Brown's conference speech because he was away attending the funeral of Gareth Williams, the Leader of the Lords who had died very suddenly. Though Blair feigned insouciance about the attack when he returned to the conference, he was 'absolutely furious' when he was told about Brown's unmasked lunge.[15]

Alastair Campbell had been replaced by David Hill, an older figure and a calmer one, who had a reputation among journalists for being decent and straight. Hill had two central aims: to kill the Government's reputation for spin by 'instilling a different style' and to repair relations between the communication operations at the Treasury and Number 10. Brown's open thrust at Blair made it impossible for Hill to sustain a pretence of amity between the two men. 'It was too deliberate to deny. To stories about things that were going on between them behind the scenes, you could say, "I know nothing about that." You couldn't say that about this speech because everyone had sat in the hall and watched it happen.'[16]

In a furious battle of spin and counter-spin, the Blairites sent out the message that Brown had made a strategic blunder by trying to position himself as the leader of the left. But the main answer would have to come from Blair himself the next day.

At midnight on the Monday night – 'it happened every year, you could set your watch by it' – he gathered his advisers around him in his hotel suite to complain about the latest draft of his speech. 'This is rubbish,' he said, going through the text. 'This doesn't work. This has not got enough argument. I need a better joke here. The middle bit is boring.'[17]

He sent them off to find new facts, sharper applause lines and more amusing punchlines. Peter Hyman, his principal speechwriter, has an abiding memory of 'the Prime Minister sitting there in the early hours of the morning in his loosely tied bathrobe, with his hair dishevelled, his glasses perched on the end of his nose, a half-eaten banana somewhere on the table in front of him, surrounded by hundreds of little bits of paper that he's ripped off previous drafts, and he's trying to join them together and he knows how they join together, but no-one else does.' Only after 'hours and hours' of this did he finally go to bed at three in the morning the night before the conference speech. It was crazy and yet somehow it nearly always worked.[18]

After about three hours' sleep, Blair got up at six to finish putting the speech together. Sally Morgan suggested that he needed to 'tickle the tummy' of his party to win back their affections. 'Have I ever been any good at that?' he asked smiling in reply. 'Well, I could start with: "Comrades, speaking as a socialist . . ."'[19]

The message he delivered that afternoon was essentially defiant. 'I would make the same decision on Iraq again today,' he declared. He sounded a note of equal implacability about public service reform, deriding the temptation to retreat into 'a left-wing comfort zone' and declaring: 'Forward or back. I can only go one way. I've not got a reverse gear.'[20] Some around him were apprehensive about including that phrase on the grounds that Blair had reversed in the past and would no doubt need to do so in the future. 'Tony, are you really sure that you are never going to need a reverse gear?' asked Peter Mandelson. Blair insisted on delivering the line nevertheless. It would be used to taunt him when, as was inevitable, he did find subsequent need to retreat.

Where Brown had semaphored his dissent from the choice and diversity agenda and emphasised 'equity', Blair answered him by declaring that the 'demand of the twenty-first century consumer' was for 'excellence'. Blair had torn out of his speech any reference at all to Brown, the first time that had ever happened.

The Chancellor was warned by his aides that the cameras would be trained on him during Blair's speech in the hope of catching Brown with a sulky face. He tried to look interested, but he was too poor an actor to sustain the pretence for the full fifty minutes. The newspapers got the picture they wanted: an occluded Brown with frozen hands while the rest of the Cabinet applauded. By the close of the week, the general verdict was that Brown over-reached on the Monday and Blair did an effective job of putting his Chancellor in his place on the Tuesday. One neutral member of the Cabinet observed that 'Gordon has made himself look disloyal, opportunistic and isolated.'[21]

In the Brown camp, they fumed: 'We put up with three days of being told that using the word Labour was using a dirty word.'[22] In Blair's court, every move made by Brown was seen as an attempt 'to destabilise Tony out of his job'.[23] At all levels, personal and political, tactical and strategic, the two men were now in collision. 'Gordon won't let me do anything' was Blair's regular refrain to his intimates as he felt relentlessly sabotaged by guerrilla attacks on the reform legislation by the Chancellor's allies on the backbenches.[24]

An opportunity for Blair to take some petty revenge presented itself on Guy Fawkes' night. As Prime Minister, he had the right to make three nominations to ex officio seats on the Labour Party's National Executive Committee. In the past, he had done this in consultation with Brown; not now, not any more. Blair had little time for the NEC, a once powerful body which had been emasculated during his time in office, but appointments to it could be symbolic. On 5 November, Blair proposed seats for Hazel Blears, one of his most avid supporters, and Ian McCartney, the party Chairman and a close ally of John Prescott. For the third seat, he nominated not the Chancellor, but one of Brown's junior acolytes, Douglas Alexander.

It was spun to the press on Brown's behalf that he had been insultingly treated and ambushed while on paternity leave in Scotland after the birth of his son John. Blair scoffed to his aides that this was typical of Brown's petulant tantrums about trivial status issues.[25] On the account of one of Brown's own senior staff, 'Gordon was not remotely bothered really about the NEC. It was seized upon to make Tony look unreasonable. The desire to be strong is a determining factor in Gordon's personality. And yet at times he was very willing to play the victim. This gave him the opportunity to play the victim.'[26]

The next day, the Chancellor gave a television interview in which he publicly attacked Blair for excluding him from the NEC and baldly declared that he expected to be in charge of the next election campaign.[27] Headlines screamed about a new low in their relationship. It had become so dysfunctional that the inconsequential was taking on an importance that seemed ludicrous to rational observers. It was also self-destructive. The Tories had just knifed Iain Duncan Smith and replaced him with Michael Howard, who was elected unopposed. For once, the Conservatives were presenting a united face. Labour planned an onslaught on the new Tory leader as 'Mr Poll Tax', a throwback to the past, a creature from the Thatcherite lagoon. This was wrecked by the eruption between Blair and Brown.

That night, the two men were due for dinner with John Prescott. The Deputy Prime Minister had appointed himself to the role of peacemaker. Prescott would not be most people's ideal of a marriage guidance counsellor, but he liked to see himself as the mediator between the warring couple of Downing Street. 'I was ideally suited to it. I am instinctively the trade unionist looking for agreement.'[28] At various times when their relationship was bad, he brought them together to try to get the two men to thrash out their differences, meetings which Prescott put in his schedule as 'Bed and Breakfast', his cipher for Blair and Brown.[29] Prescott was anxious, and was far from alone in the Cabinet in being so, that the TB-GBs were becoming so toxic that they were on the brink of a final and catastrophic implosion. Prescott was often nagged by the fear that there was not much of a personal legacy to show for his years in government. He would be Deputy Prime Minister for longer than Herbert Morrison, Willie Whitelaw, Michael Heseltine or any other politician, Labour or Tory, who had held the position. But historians would struggle to locate many notable achievements from his time in power. He had helped to save the Channel Tunnel rail link in the first term, but was otherwise a failure as transport supremo. In the second term, Blair allowed his deputy to pursue his hobby horse of elected regional assemblies. They were disparaged as 'JP's toy' in Number 10. Blair correctly anticipated that they would get nowhere.

Looking for his place in history, Prescott dedicated himself to being the man whom people might credit with saving the poisoned political marriage at the top of the Government.

That November evening, the three men met at the Deputy Prime Minister's grace-and-favour apartment in Admiralty House with its splendid views of the Mall and Trafalgar Square. Prescott typically liked to serve his guests with steak and kidney pudding.

Brown arrived in a foul temper. When they sat down for dinner, the Chancellor complained that his seat wasn't high enough. Prescott went off to find another. 'Do you want a different chair as well, Tony?' he asked. 'No, it's all right,' responded Blair sardonically. 'Gordon has always looked down on me.'[30]

On Brown's subsequent account to his camp, Blair admitted that he was in a deep hole. 'I won't turn it around before the election,' he said. If Brown was co-operative and helped to 'get me through the next six months', Blair pledged he would hand over the premiership in the summer of next year. 'Naive as always about Tony, Gordon believed him,' says one of Brown's closest confidants.[31] He left the dinner more certain than before that he had a promise of a handover.

The morning after the Prescott dinner, Brown called Spencer Livermore, Sue Nye and the two Eds together for a meeting at the Treasury. 'Tony has said he is going to go,' he told them excitedly. 'We should start preparing.'

'Are you sure?' asked Nye. 'We've been here before,' remarked Balls, unconvinced. Livermore and Miliband also expressed scepticism.

'It's going to happen,' Brown assured them. 'He said it in terms. Prescott was there. Prescott won't let him break the promise this time.'[32]

Blair gave a rather different account of the dinner to his friends, suggesting that he'd implored Brown to be more co-operative by saying: 'I'm happy to give you your place in the sun, but you've got to accept that I am Prime Minister.' He suggested he'd done a half-deal making a handover conditional on Brown's good behaviour.[33]

Their memoirs, assuming they are even prepared to acknowledge how poisoned the relationship became, will not agree on what happened. But at this crucial meeting there was indeed a witness. Prescott believed he heard a definite promise from Blair to hand over Number 10 in 2004.[34] Without going so far as to call Blair a liar, Prescott alludes to this in his memoir when he says, 'Tony's technique was to persuade him [Gordon]to back him on certain matters . . . and in return Tony would come out with the same old promise. He was definitely going in, er, six months, perhaps a year, certainly before the election. When it never happened, Gordon was furious – and the whole cycle began again.'[35]

'I have no doubt that Tony was most to blame. He broke his agreement with Gordon, not once but several times. However, in Tony's defence, most of his promises were ambiguous and on condition anyway.'[36]

The condition was always that Brown should support rather than sabotage Blair on policy. The two big divisions at the time of that dinner were over the health reforms and student tuition fees. There had been constant rebellion by Labour MPs against foundation hospitals even in the watered-down form which emerged from the compromise of a year before. This guerrilla warfare was encouraged by Brown's now open dissent with Blair's approach to public services. 'We risk giving the impression that the only kind of reform that is valuable is a form of privatisation,' he declared earlier that year in an 11,000-word speech, part academic treatise about the vices and virtues of the market, part full-frontal assault on Blair's idea that choice, competition and diversity would work in delivering better health and education. The 'consumer can't be sovereign' in public services, so Brown argued, because they did not have sufficient information to make sensible choices.[37]

One product of the Prescott dinner was Brown's reluctant agreement to try to stem the opposition to the health legislation. Even then, it was tight. In the vote on 19 November, the Government majority fell to the anorexic margin of seventeen, the lowest of their time in power so far. Embarrassingly, in order to pass legislation which only applied to the NHS in England they had to rely on the votes of Labour MPs with seats in Wales and Scotland.

The legislation on tuition fees was formally launched in the Queen's Speech at the end of November, but there had already been many months of struggle leading up to the moment when Her Majesty announced the Higher Education Bill from the throne.

Blair became convinced that one of his legacy projects should be putting the financing of universities on a more sustainable footing. He was vigorously lobbied by the Russell Group of top universities, who contended they needed to be able to increase their income so that they would not fall behind the rest of the world. Blair was always very receptive to arguments of this sort about backing British institutions that could be 'global champions' and he was very swayed by their case that something had to be done to keep them internationally competitive.[38] His old mentor, Roy Jenkins, the Chancellor of Oxford University, was another voice urging him in this direction. Especially influential was Andrew Adonis, a former member of the SDP whom Blair had put in as Head of the Policy Unit to pursue a more radical agenda for public services in his second term. Blair was persuaded that the way to sort out university finances was to charge students 'top-up fees' of up to £3,000 a year.

In their first term, Brown largely accepted that education fell into the Blair hemisphere. But this was about money, which the Chancellor regarded as his domain.

Brown's opposition to top-up fees was both personal and political. He feared that they would deter children from poorer backgrounds from attending university. He worried that there would be a backlash among the middle classes as well. He did not see, as Blair did, any need for urgency in dealing with the issue. As a student at Edinburgh, he had first made his name fighting the university establishment and didn't have a high opinion of many dons. 'They'll only spend the money eating swan' was how his friend Alistair Darling liked to mock the universities pleading for more income.[39]

Sir Andrew Turnbull, the Cabinet Secretary, noted: 'Gordon never thought well of the grander universities. He had a view that you shouldn't give these people lots more money until they'd reformed themselves.'[40] He unleashed a visceral attack on Oxford University three years earlier for refusing a place to Laura Spence, a state school pupil.[41] Blair, by contrast, was 'pretty contemptuous of class politics'.[42]

Brown argued: 'There's got to be an alternative.' 'All right,' replied Blair. 'What alternative?'[43] Brown didn't have one. He wanted a review, similar to the Wanless exercise that he used to pave the way for raising tax to produce more funds for the NHS. Change should wait until after the next election. After all the difficulties with the health legislation, he contended they should not risk another confrontation with a large slice of the Labour Party. 'Gordon was not articulating an alternative agenda – he was in blocking mode.'[44]

Blair was not having that. 'I've never understood this "you do one thing or you do another" argument,' he told me. 'You do what is right.'[45] He was already stalked by the fear that time was running out on him to leave lasting domestic reforms. He saw Brown's opposition as driven by posturing and positioning, not by any real conviction that the fees were wrong. Treasury civil servants tended to agree with the Prime Minister. 'It seemed a sensible reform,' says one of Brown's most senior officials. 'Gordon was digging in against it and it wasn't clear why apart from the fact that it was Tony's idea. From a Treasury point of view, it was quite hard to see why we were opposing this.'[46]

The first Cabinet minister caught in the middle of their argument was Estelle Morris, the Education Secretary. She was under intense pressure from Number 10 to swallow her own concerns about top-up fees and countervailing pressure from the Treasury to resist. In the words of Morris, there was deadlock.

'It froze, nothing happened. During those long months when I had on my desk lots of options as to the way forward and I had my own views, I thought I can't resolve this until they resolve it between them.'[47]

Suddenly, in the last week of October 2002, Morris quit the Cabinet. She was engulfed in a controversy about A-level standards and was fraying under media intrusion into her private life. In a refreshing and uniquely candid admission, she said she did not feel up to being a Cabinet minister.

While expressing public disappointment, Blair was privately glad of the opportunity to replace her with a more robustly constructed minister who also happened to have a well-developed and reciprocated dislike for Gordon Brown. To take on the Chancellor, Blair gave education to a formidable bruiser of his own, Charles Clarke. Built like a bull elephant and sometimes displaying the temperament of one, Clarke had a thick skin grown as a senior aide to Neil Kinnock during the battles of the eighties. The son of a distinguished civil servant, he had read mathematics at Cambridge. Unlike Morris, he was not a man troubled by many anxieties about his own abilities. Unlike many members of the Cabinet, he did not feel intellectually or politically intimidated by Brown.

Clarke was initially attracted by the alternative idea of a graduate tax. On arrival at the department, he ordered papers on various schemes from his civil servants. Within eight weeks, he concluded a graduate tax would not work and came round to top-up fees as the best way of dealing with university finances.[48]

Provocatively, Brown wrote a letter to the Cabinet arguing that fees would reduce the number of less affluent students going to university. This was reminiscent of his pre-emptive attack on Milburn and foundation hospitals. Charles Clarke remembers: 'What he'd do is he'd go along, go along, go along and when it came to the point he'd then blast out a very, very full and very, very technically correct document at enormous length, which he wouldn't have shared with any of us at any point before.'[49]

This time, though, he would lose. Clarke intensively lobbied his colleagues and Blair squared off Prescott.

In mid-January 2003, Prescott refereed the bout when Brown and Clarke slugged it out at a Cabinet committee meeting. For once, the Chancellor was floored in an internal battle. Not having any alternative to propose himself, he could not prevail in his opposition to fees. He was left arguing for the status quo which no-one else thought sustainable. Civil servants believed it was a seminal moment.[50] 'It was the first time that he had been comprehensively defeated in an area of domestic policy,' says Turnbull. 'When he couldn't win, it became a question of trying to corral it.'[51]

Charles Clarke was more amused than frightened by Brown when the Chancellor launched a final fusillade of objections on the very day that the White Paper, already back from the printers, was going to be unveiled to MPs. 'I had a 25-page letter from Gordon coming through our fax machine the morning I was making the statement to the House with a whole string of changes which he thought were necessary at this very last minute.'[52]

Clarke ignored them. The White Paper was published on 22 January 2003. It unveiled the plan to allow universities to charge tuition fees of up to £3,000 a year from 2006. The current upfront annual fee of £1,100 was abolished. Graduates would repay loans at a rate of 9 per cent of any income earned over £15,000 a year.

This detonated an explosion of protest from students and ignited opposition amongst many Labour MPs. There were a lot of former teachers and lecturers in the party. The Chief Whip, Hilary Armstrong, warned Blair that education stirred high emotions because 'it goes to their guts rather than their intellect.'[53] One of the rebels' arguments was that they were being more faithful to Labour's manifesto commitments than the Government. Just before the 2001 election, the then Education Secretary, David Blunkett, pre-empted debate by categorically ruling out the introduction of top-up fees. Stupidly, given that his mind was already moving in that direction, Blair allowed the manifesto to include a pledge that 'we will not introduce top-up

fees and will legislate to prevent them.'⁵⁴ It was one of the best examples of
Blair failing to think strategically about his second term and then paying a
price during it. The Government tried to shimmy around the manifesto
pledge by saying that the fees would not be paid until after the next election
so technically they were sort of not breaking the promise. That sounded like
sophistry. At a time when Blair already had a very bad reputation for 'trust',
the accusation that he was breaking a manifesto promise was one of the
most potent arguments in the arsenal of his opponents.

No fewer than 160 Labour MPs signed a motion opposing the policy,
more than enough to defeat Blair. Some of the parliamentary rebels belonged
to the same cohort who voted against the Iraq war. Others had been loyally
supportive then, but were no longer prepared to be so now. Some wanted
to punish the Prime Minister for dragooning them into supporting a war
that had gone so badly wrong. Others had developed a visceral loathing
which was either ideological or personal or both and craved to eject him
from Number 10.

Revolt was now in Labour's bloodstream, another legacy of the war.
Among those most prominent in the rebellion were some well-known
acolytes of the Chancellor, including George Mudie and Nick Brown, no
relation to the Chancellor but so close to him that he might well have been.
The former Chief Whip was now whipping a revolt. One Blair loyalist noted
acerbically that it was 'the first time I'd ever known Nick Brown take an
interest in education'.⁵⁵ This left Number 10 convinced that the Chancellor
himself was 'absolutely dominant in terms of organising the opposition' to
the Prime Minister, a remarkable state of affairs.⁵⁶

Charles Clarke was his combative and bullish self in making the argument. A more emollient approach was taken by his deputy, the Universities
Minister, Alan Johnson. A former postman who had not enjoyed the benefit
of a higher education, he was an effective frontman for a difficult cause. It
was hard to suggest that a man brought up by his sister in a council flat was
an enemy of the less advantaged. He made a persuasive advocate of the
argument that it was reasonable to expect well-off graduates to make a
bigger financial contribution to the cost of their education. They were a
soft-cop, hard-cop routine. Johnson liked to joke: 'It's a charm offensive. I
do the charm and Charles does the offensive.'⁵⁷

The scale of the Labour revolt forced the Government to concede a lot
to appease the concerns of the rebels. The very poorest students were
exempted from the fees. There was a guarantee that they could not be
increased above £3,000 until 2010. There were also promises of reviews
into the impact on less affluent families.

This made some wonder whether it was worth all the turmoil. The issue gave a cause to Charles Kennedy and his Liberal Democrats. Fees would cost Labour both votes and seats at the next election. Against that, there was no question that the issue of university financing had to be addressed. It was an equitable solution to ask graduates, who could generally look forward to earning more than other citizens, to pay when the alternative was for them to be subsidised by poorer taxpayers who had not enjoyed the benefit of higher education. The Conservatives later came to regret and ditch Michael Howard's opportunistic stand against fees. They embraced them. That made it very likely that this was a Blair reform which would endure.

In the last week of January 2004, his survival was put to an especially severe test. The crucial vote on tuition fees was set for Tuesday, 27 January. The next day, Lord Hutton was scheduled to finally announce his verdict. Into forty-eight frenzied hours were compressed the two great issues of Blair's second term: the war in Iraq and the battle for public service reform. He had staked his personal authority on both. A damning verdict from Hutton or a defeat on fees could be a fatal blow.

Blair was in one of his 'taxi driver' moods about the Labour rebels. If the Labour Party did not have the will and discipline to support him on this, he said to his aides, they were not worth leading any more.[58] He was telling people that he would rather resign as Prime Minister than accept defeat over top-up fees. Some of his senior staff took this seriously enough to be nervous that he might well quit.

At the Monday morning strategy meeting at Number 10, Jonathan Powell asked where they were in terms of voting numbers. Sally Morgan replied that they couldn't be sure because they didn't know whether the Chancellor would instruct his supporters to vote for or against. Other members of the senior staff listening to this exchange were flabbergasted. Says Sir Stephen Wall: 'I remember thinking: This is a very, very extraordinary situation when the Prime Minister does not know whether he can carry a crucial piece of legislation because he doesn't know whether his Chancellor of the Exchequer is going to support the Government or not.'[59]

It was indeed an extraordinary situation that the Chancellor was threatening to torpedo the Prime Minister's legislative flagship. There were two schools of opinion within Number 10 about the Chancellor. 'There were those who thought Gordon wanted to seize the opportunity to cause Tony to fall. Then there was a more sophisticated camp who took the view that Gordon was not seeking to use one single event to bring down Tony because that risked toppling the whole edifice. What he was doing was death by, maybe not a thousand cuts, but a dozen cuts. That camp saw this as another one of those.'[60]

Shortly before the vote, Brown called his most trusted advisers together for a breakfast at the Treasury. The Eds Balls and Miliband, Sue Nye and Spencer Livermore debated with him whether 'we push this all the way or do we back off?'[61] Brown concluded that they should back off, partly because 'the destabilisation of Blair had already been effective' and partly for fear of the consequences of bringing the roof in.[62] At Number 10, they believed that 'Gordon became scared at the last minute that he'd be known as the person who defeated it.'[63] That would arouse the anger of powerful forces, not least Rupert Murdoch's newspapers.

He also had the promise from Blair of a handover in the summer of 2004, though Brown remained suspicious that 'Tony will never go.' In the weeks since the Prescott dinner, he repeatedly asked Blair: 'Why aren't we discussing how we are going to do this?' Blair responded: 'I've said what I've said. You know where I am. You've got to work with me.'[64]

Passing the loyalty test set by Blair was an additional incentive for Brown to call off the dogs. He started to lean on his supporters to reverse their opposition to the fees. Shortly before the vote, he called George Mudie and Nick Brown over to his flat in Great Peter Street to try to persuade them to end their rebellion. He argued 'for all the usual complicated Gordon reasons' that they should now support the Government.[65] One of those arguments was that he would not be able to impose discipline on the Labour Party as Prime Minister if his people had led a major revolt.

Brown's camp made a highly contentious claim that he had talked round forty potential rebels and so made the crucial difference. That persuaded *The Times* that 'The Chancellor has shown that he is the only man who can save the Prime Minister in his hour of need.'[66] That interpretation – portraying a drowning Blair clutching a lifeline from Brown – was hateful to the Prime Minister and his people. As Stephen Wall puts it, they had got to 'a stage where people inside Number 10 felt they couldn't govern with Gordon Brown, but they couldn't govern without him either'.[67]

He failed to persuade Mudie to end his rebellion, but he did get Nick Brown to switch sides, an important signal to the Chancellor's supporters on the backbenches about what they were expected to do.

The vote was still 'genuinely knife edge'[68] and the atmosphere inside Number 10 'febrile'.[69] At lunchtime on Tuesday, the Chief Whip told Blair she feared that they were still in high peril of defeat.[70] Blair was not someone 'who usually shows agitation, but he was like a cat on a hot tin roof in the last few hours'.[71]

Potential rebels were brought to him in his office at the Commons as the clock ticked down to the vote. Clarke was forced to make further last-minute concessions from the dispatch box. 'Hell's bells, it couldn't have been closer,' observed one Cabinet minister.[72] A member of Blair's senior staff thought 'a few votes the other way would have spelled the end of his premiership.'[73]

MPs voted at seven that evening. There were whoops from the Opposition benches and gasps from the Labour side when the tellers for each side marched up to the Mace, faced the Speaker and revealed that the Government had won only by the narrowest margin and would have lost if the Opposition had got its full numbers in. 'The ayes to the right: 316!' cried one teller. 'The noes to the left: 311!' cried the other teller. A Prime Minister elected by a landslide had been reduced to a majority that could be counted on one hand. Brown stuck up five fingers and thrust them into Blair's face.

The Prime Minister shrugged. A win was a win, after all. He left his seat on the frontbench, slipped behind the Speaker's chair, walked into the ministerial corridor and turned into his Commons office for a victory drink. A few hours earlier, he had learnt something else which put him in a mood to celebrate.

14. Too Good to be True

Tony Blair came into the Cabinet Room and asked: 'What's the verdict?' While he had been in the Commons frantically lobbying Labour MPs over tuition fees, his senior aides were poring over the Hutton report, a task to which they had devoted themselves from the minute it was delivered to Number 10 at midday. The Prime Minister was greeted with a set of grim faces, those of David Hill, Tom Kelly, Sally Morgan, Jonathan Powell and Godric Smith. Blair frowned, sensing that there was something not quite right about their reaction. 'We had a joke with him. When he came in, we all looked down. He got wind of it quite quickly.'[1] The aides started to break into smiles. 'It's very positive for us,' said Powell. 'It's almost too good to be true.'[2]

The death of David Kelly had hung like a shroud over Blair for six months. 'There was a sense that we couldn't do anything else until we had got past Hutton.'[3]

The 740-page report was delivered to Number 10 by secure courier at noon on Tuesday, 27 January, allowing Downing Street twenty-four hours to prepare its lines before the judge's verdict was made public. Once they'd got the report, the aides separated into groups and spread out around the government buildings in Downing Street. Some of the team sat at the conference table in David Hill's office at Number 12. Others went to the Cabinet Room or the private office adjacent to the Prime Minister's den. Each aide was armed with two highlighter pens: a yellow pen to score findings that were favourable to the Government, a pink one to mark passages that were hostile.

As they scoured the report, the team in Hill's office started to look at each other 'in complete disbelief'.[4] Their copies were soon covered in lots of positive yellow and almost no negative pink. The verdict from Hutton was more favourable than they had imagined even in their most wildly optimistic moments.

The teams gathered together in the Cabinet Room at three that afternoon to share their findings. There was a brief palpitation when Jonathan Powell produced his copy of the report to reveal that it was glowing with negative pink. That little panic subsided when the others realised that the Chief of Staff had muddled his colours. 'That was typical of Jonathan,' remarks another member of the team. 'Jonathan has a big brain, but he was never much good with practical things like that.'[5]

Hutton pronounced Number 10 innocent of manipulating or falsifying the intelligence. The judge was unsympathetic to Kelly, criticised the scientist for talking to journalists and suggested that he deserved no protection once he had been exposed. There was only the mildest criticism, which was directed at the Ministry of Defence rather than Number 10, for the way in which Kelly was handled by his superiors. There was 'euphoria' in Number 10. 'If he'd come down on the other side, God knows what would have happened.'[6]

In this, his last case, the judge had exculpated the politicians, the civil servants, the spin merchants and the spooks. Lord Hutton discharged Tony Blair, Geoff Hoon and Alastair Campbell without a stain on their characters. He crucified the BBC. At every twist and turn of the Kelly Affair, Hutton heaped opprobrium on the corporation's journalism, its editors, its executives and its governors.

'Two things saved Tony Blair's bacon,' believed Sir Andrew Turnbull, the Cabinet Secretary. 'One was the absolutely magnificent performance by David Omand, the security co-ordinator, who realised that you had to create an account of what happened that was coherent. The other was the retention of Jonathan Sumption as our QC. He did a wonderful job for us both by demolishing the BBC and presenting a case why it was entirely reasonable to reveal the name of David Kelly.'[7]

There was disbelief of a different kind the next day when the judge appeared at the Royal Courts of Justice to unveil his verdict to the public. A leak to that morning's *Sun* gave forewarning of what was in store.[8] Yet there was still astonishment as Hutton read out his conclusions in his Ulster baritone. As the judge drily returned his pro-Government findings, some of the journalists in the court room shook their heads in disbelief. There were sniggers at the judge's observation that 'the desire of the Prime Minister to have a dossier which was as strong as possible . . . may have subconsciously influenced Mr Scarlett.'[9] By the end, some in the court were snorting with open derision that his scant six pages of conclusions seemed so unrelated to much of the evidence.

Alan Milburn was one of the Blair loyalists primed to swarm on to the airwaves to proclaim a victory for the Prime Minister. But they hardly needed to bother, says David Hill. 'There was no need to spin Hutton. It spoke for itself.'[10]

The BBC had also been given twenty-four hours' advance notice, but its leaders were paralysed with bewilderment at the savagery of the judge's verdict against the corporation for its lack of editorial controls and stubborn refusal to acknowledge error. Expecting a balanced assessment criticising both them and the Government, the BBC had no contingency plan for dealing with such a one-sided result. While the BBC's own news bulletins reported the judge's flagellation of their journalism, the corporation fielded no-one to defend its reputation. Hours went by and its senior ranks of highly paid executives remained entirely mute. Britain's largest media organisation had lost its voice. Not until *Newsnight* was on the air did anyone of stature appear for the defence of the BBC and that was Sir Christopher Bland, a former chairman of the corporation.

Floundering also was the Leader of the Opposition. In the build-up to the publication of the report, Michael Howard made a defining issue of Blair's integrity. At successive bouts of Prime Minister's Questions, the Tory leader raised the stakes by suggesting that Hutton would prove his opponent to be mendacious. 'He has . . . effectively accused me of telling lies,' said Blair.[11] Howard thought Hutton would supply him with a sword. He was the one skewered by it. On the afternoon of publication, the Tory leader drowned to the sound of Labour MPs hissing and jeering as Blair flipped it into a question of his opponent's character. 'What you should understand is that being nasty is not the same as being effective,' he crushed Howard. 'Opportunism is not the same as leadership.'[12] It was Blair's best day in the Commons for a considerable time.

What it did not provide was the catharsis that he was looking for. Jonathan Powell was right about it being 'too good to be true', a line that Blair repeated to allies like Stephen Byers when they discussed how it should be presented. 'He meant that it would be very hard to make it look credible to the public.'[13] The verdict was so disappointing for the Tories, so generous to the Government and so excruciating for the BBC that it was soon joked that its ghost writer must have been Alastair Campbell. Many press commentators, and not just those who had always been hostile to the war, expressed incredulity that the judge could ignore so much of the evidence that had been revealed during the inquiry. 'No amount of judicial laundering' could remove the 'stains on their character', wrote the historian and journalist Sir Max Hastings.[14] Matthew d'Ancona, a pro-war commentator not unsympathetic to Blair, observed: 'Hutton's verdict invited scorn upon the very notion that such inquiries are any more trustworthy than the politicians who commission them.'[15]

Alastair Campbell went on a vengeful rampage. 'Alastair couldn't control himself.'[16] Blair did not attempt to stop him. The former spin king was almost certainly beyond restraint anyway.[17] He called his own news conference that afternoon at the headquarters of the Foreign Press Association in St James's, where he angrily demanded that 'heads roll' at the BBC. 'If the Government had faced the level of criticism that Lord Hutton has directed at the BBC, there would clearly have been resignations by now, several resignations at several levels,' fulminated Campbell.[18]

He was rapidly granted his wish for rolling heads. The BBC's Chairman, Gavyn Davies, volunteered his neck to the governors in the hope that this would save anyone else at the corporation from resignation. Within twenty-four hours, the governors also sent the protesting Director-General, Greg Dyke, to join the Chairman on the chopping block. This unprecedented double decapitation plunged the BBC into the most severe crisis of its existence.

While this slaked the vindictive Campbell's thirst for scalps, it was of no benefit to the Government. Scenes of BBC staff mobbing a tearful Dyke at TV Centre made it seem as if the defenestrated D-G was the hero of the hour. Many gagged at the spectacle of Blair's former propagandist issuing decrees on media ethics. The resignations, which looked like they had been bullied out of the prostrate BBC by the marauding Campbell, moved public feeling against the Government. One astute minister noted: 'The sight of us walking away from this entirely unscathed offends people's sense of fair play. It could even make some hate us more.'[19] Tessa Jowell, the Culture Secretary, pointed out to Blair that people didn't just look at the BBC as a news organisation. Campbell's angry campaign against the corporation risked alienating the large constituencies that loved *The Archers*, tuned in for *EastEnders* or admired the BBC for its nature documentaries, costume dramas and many other areas of output.[20] Blair eventually prevailed upon his former spinmeister to shut up, but not before more damage had been done.

Opinion polls published in Hutton's wake indicated that most of the public thought the report was a whitewash and that the judge was wrong to clear Downing Street of 'sexing up' the dossier.[21] Voters still invested far more trust in the BBC than they did in the Government. The number who thought Blair had lied about exposing Kelly was barely changed by the report.[22]

Blair yearned for the Hutton verdict to give him closure on Iraq and produce a springboard for recovery. In that hope Number 10 was confounded: 'It didn't give us the fresh lease of life we were looking for.'[23] The judge might have pronounced him innocent of all charges, but the Prime Minister was still in the dock in the eyes of the jury of public opinion.

Within weeks of the verdict of one inquiry, he was compelled to concede to pressure for another. It was no longer possible to sustain the line that WMD would be found in Iraq. In January, the American head of the search team, David Kay, admitted defeat. While they had found some evidence that Saddam had ambitions to possess WMD, Kay conceded that an intense quest to find stockpiles of deadly weapons had turned up nothing. 'I don't think they exist,' he admitted to a Congressional hearing. 'We were almost all wrong.'[24]

This was bad for Bush, but it was worse for Blair, who had based his case for war so heavily on the claim that Saddam menaced the world. On 2 February, the White House was forced to announce a commission to review US intelligence. Two days later, Blair was compelled to set up the Butler Inquiry into his use of intelligence.

The public might have been more forgiving that the war was sold on a false prospectus if there were compensating signs that Iraq was moving towards the better and more peaceful future that Blair had promised. The reverse was the case. In July 2003, Jack Straw flew out to Baghdad and was taken aback by 'the primitive security' around the British embassy and other key buildings when it was clear that Iraq was increasingly violent.[25] The first big warning came in mid-August, when the United Nations headquarters in Iraq, based at a hotel on Canal Street in Baghdad, was devastated by a colossal truck bomb. Twenty-three people died, among them the UN's chief envoy to Iraq. Straw later realised that this 'really marked the time when authority started to be difficult to exercise and you got the beginnings of the terrorism and the sectarian violence'.[26] Ten days later, terrorists demonstrated their growing capacity to wreak death on a large scale when they bombed the Iman Ali mosque in Najaf, killing eighty-three people. The UN relocated to another hotel in Baghdad. In mid-September, the new HQ was targeted by a massive car bomb. Kofi Annan, the UN Secretary-General, ordered the withdrawal of his 600 staff. With the UN bombed out of Iraq, all the energy expended by Blair trying to internationalise the reconstruction effort was rendered futile. America and Britain would now have to cope with the consequences of their invasion alone.

British generals grew alarmed that their American counterparts seemed ill-trained to deal with this form of conflict. 'They are less comfortable with the messier part of conflict where it's not manoeuvre war,' noted General Mike Jackson, 'where there is no clear enemy visible in the conventional sense.'[27]

Blair had hoped that British-controlled Basra might be 'an exemplar' to both the Americans and the Iraqis.[28] They were still feeling self-congratulatory about the calmer situation in the south, but in the British sector there were also signs of deterioration. On 24 June, six Royal Military Police were murdered by a mob at an Iraqi police station near Basra. On 23 August, another three red berets were killed when their taxi was ambushed in the centre of the city. British troops came under attack from protestors rioting over fuel and electricity shortages.

Since talking to Washington seemed to be having so little traction, an increasingly agitated Blair tried to get himself 'a direct voice on the ground'.[29] Sir Jeremy Greenstock, the former ambassador to the UN, resisted taking on the job until he was personally cajoled by the Prime Minister to become the most senior British figure in Iraq from September 2003. Greenstock was a supporter of the war, though a sceptic about the way in which they had got into it. His first encounter with the reality in Iraq was when he arrived at the 'pretty chaotic' headquarters of Paul Bremer, the American viceroy. Based at the Republican Palace of Saddam in the centre of Baghdad, Greenstock found the place to be a 'dusty marbled mess of military and civilians and plywood and wires and vehicles'. He got 'an immediate feeling that we were an island in the middle of a stormy sea'.[30] Bremer had all the power. Blair urged his official to 'get close', but the American wasn't interested and Greenstock 'was not valued by Bremer in the way he should have been'.[31] The American occupied a smart office at one end of the building and underlined the subordinate status of his British colleague by putting Greenstock in a less smart office at the other end. The two men did not get on.[32] Bremer was an intense ideologue with no feel for the country he was running; Greenstock was a pragmatic diplomat who spoke Arabic. The American emperor did not share the British representative's belief that they were equals. The most crucial difference between them was that Greenstock did not agree with Bremer's upbeat assessment of Iraq. Greenstock saw that 1,200 civilians were 'hopelessly inadequate' to the task of trying to run a country of 25 million people and yet found that the Americans weren't willing to give Iraqis 'responsibility to run their own country'. He knew his observations did not make him popular with the Americans, who became suspicious and scornful of 'those mealy-mouthed Brits sitting in a corner saying all is going to hell in a handcart.'[33]

Greenstock sent urgent messages to London warning that security was rapidly deteriorating and sectarian conflict intensifying. 'Things don't add up,' he reported to his masters back in Britain. 'You haven't got on the ground what is necessary to control the situation that we're responsible for.'[34] Greenstock's reports began to 'stir real fear in Tony'.[35] There was more blood-drenched evidence that he was right in October when the headquarters of the Red Cross in Baghdad was attacked.

This descent made it even more imperative for Blair to convince Bush to engage with what was happening. Downing Street thought technology might help provide an answer. The two leaders started regular communication by video telephone so that they could see as well as hear each other. These video conferences commonly took place on a Tuesday, lasted for up to an hour, and were fortnightly, sometimes weekly, events.[36] Yet they would only have real value if Blair was prepared to be robust with Bush about the failure of US policy in Iraq. 'Did he ever really read the riot act?' says one British diplomat who saw many of their encounters and read transcripts of their conversations. 'I never saw it, I never heard of it, I never saw a record of it.'[37] Andrew Card and Condi Rice did not witness one serious argument between the two leaders.[38] 'I just don't think Blair is capable of being confrontational in that way,' says David Manning.[39] Others present at either these video conferences or their direct meetings agree. 'Tony's view was that if he was antagonistic to Bush, Bush simply wouldn't listen at all,' says Sally Morgan.[40]

Even when Bush seemed committed to action it rarely materialised. The British were gradually grasping that the Commander-in-Chief was not truly a chief in command of his own administration. 'It was very hard to influence Bush because Bush couldn't actually influence his own administration,' says Jonathan Powell. 'Rumsfeld and others were running rings around him.' They tried having video conferences involving 'their generals and our generals on the ground' talking to Blair and Bush simultaneously. 'Even doing that we couldn't get into the nitty gritty of the decision-making.'[41]

When Greenstock made a trip back from Iraq to give a direct report to Blair in his study, the envoy was the bearer of bleak news about the escalating violence. He was worried that London was 'too focused on their role in Basra'. He warned Blair: 'This whole thing will be won or lost in the centre. If Baghdad and the central authority isn't strong, you can wish goodbye to Basra as well.'

'Come on,' responded Blair. 'Let's get the police properly trained by the end of the year.' Greenstock pointed out that it took three years to train a police force. 'What on earth are the Americans up to in the field of the media in Iraq?' demanded Blair, ever more agitated that the allies were losing the propaganda battle against the extremists. 'They don't seem to have a media operation going.' Greenstock believed it was clear 'what has to be done'. The top priority was to 'put enough resources into the security situation'. Blair responded positively to the envoy's suggestion that he should write up a detailed note about the six most critical items. Greenstock accompanied his memorandum with a plea to Blair 'to get President Bush to understand that more has to be put into this'.[42]

In the second half of November, there was a chance for Blair to do that in the flesh. On the 19th, the American President arrived in Britain on a three-day State visit, an idea originally conceived many months previously when Downing Street expected a very different outcome in Iraq. Bush's political strategist, Karl Rove, was already planning their re-election campaign. He was entirely frank about the advantages of capturing pictures of Bush with the Queen and with Blair, a popular figure with centrist voters in America. Robin Cook, speaking for a considerable segment of the Labour Party, asked why the Prime Minister should be 'offering up Buckingham Palace as the mother of all photo-ops for President Bush'.[43]

Bush was now wildly unpopular with much of Britain and the association was becoming increasingly toxic for Blair. Every time they were pictured together, groaned Sally Morgan, 'it's 100,000 votes lost.'[44]

On arrival in Britain, the President declared: 'America is fortunate to call this country our closest friend in the world.' But he was not entirely unaware that he was the man that millions of Britons loved to hate. In the one speech of the trip, he compared himself with the illusionist David Blaine. 'The last noted American to visit London stayed in a glass box dangling over the Thames. A few might have been happy to provide similar arrangements for me.'[45]

More than a few. Some in Number 10 agreed with Cook and thought they could have 'done without this visit'. They feared that Bush was only really interested in boosting his image at home, while his physical proximity to Blair would incite fresh accusations of poodleism. Sally Morgan had fruitlessly lobbied to 'stop it altogether.'[46] Blair wouldn't hear of any curtailment, according to David Hill: 'There were constant arguments inside Number 10 about this, but there was never a time when Tony was prepared by one jot to put distance between himself and Bush.'[47]

The Americans were nightmarishly paranoid about security, even trying to demand the reinforcement of the walls of Buckingham Palace and the closure of the M4 to create a security corridor into London from Heathrow. 'They wanted to close down half of Britain.'[48]

Though it was supposed to celebrate the friendship of Britain and the United States, the premium was put on limiting the potential for disaster. The pomp was constricted by the security and the ceremony constrained by the visitor's unpopularity. Bush was moved round in a steel bubble of distant ceremonial. There was not even the traditional carriage procession down the Mall with the Queen for fear that it would attract protestors. His keynote speech was delivered to an audience of Whitehall grandees and foreign policy dons at the Banqueting House rather than to Parliament, where some MPs might have made rude noises. The speech was, as even some of his sternest critics acknowledged, more subtle, fluent and multidimensional than many anticipated. Bush tried to challenge the belief that he was a blind unilateralist. 'Freedom is a beautiful thing,' he said, trying to emphasise the better half of the neo-con doctrine by arguing that it was 'pessimism and condescension' to say the Middle East was not ready for democracy.[49] He claimed inspiration from the internationalist idealism of Woodrow Wilson, the last of his predecessors to bed and board at Buckingham Palace.

On the second day, both the speechifying and the pageantry were drowned out by a horrible noise off. Blair was in the middle of chairing Cabinet when he was passed an urgent note. Bush was in Westminster Abbey paying his respects to the Tomb of the Unknown Warrior when the bad news was communicated to him. Two massive car bombs had been exploded in Istanbul outside the British consulate and the headquarters of the HSBC bank. The death toll was thirty-one, among them the British Consul-General. Al-Qaeda had again demonstrated its murderous talent for grabbing the world's attention. In public responses to this attack, Blair and Bush uttered the now familiar vows to defeat 'the fanatics of terror'. There must be, declared the Prime Minister, 'no holding back, no compromise, no hesitation in confronting this menace'. He was forced to acknowledge that 'there may be some who think that Britain, the United States and our allies have somehow brought this upon ourselves.'[50] This was indeed a growing view. 'The whirlwind is being reaped,' argued the *Guardian*.[51] *Time* magazine speculated that Britons were 'now al-Qaeda's favourite target'.[52]

Two hundred thousand demonstrators marched across Westminster Bridge, booed, jeered and whistled as they passed Downing Street and rallied around Trafalgar Square that afternoon. The crowd roared its approval as a five-metre papier mâché effigy of Bush was pulled down in mimicry of the toppling of the statues of Saddam seven months earlier.

When Blair and Bush posed on the doorstep of Number 10, the American President laid his hand on the shoulder of the Prime Minister. Bush was very adept at power gestures which sent subliminal messages about who was in charge of a relationship. David Hill, Blair's communications chief, was once surprised to be grabbed in a neck lock by the President: an apparently playful but also domineering gesture.[53] When Blair and Bush turned to go inside Number 10, Bush placed his hand in the small of Blair's back to usher him through the famous black door as if the American owned the place and the Prime Minister was his guest. Consciously or not, he made Blair look small even when they were in the Prime Minister's home. Their 150 minutes of talks also had the damaging effect of casting the host as the petitioner. Blair had equated the long-term shared strategic interests between Britain and America with giving unswerving support for one particular, right-wing administration. The tighter he hugged, the less he seemed to be getting in influence. Bush gave nothing on the US trade tariffs which were a sharp point of dispute between the governments. Some of his advisers urged the Prime Minister to say: 'Get your tanks off my lawn.' As ever, says Stephen Wall, Blair's preference was 'to duck and weave rather than have a confrontation'.[54] Nor did the discussions yield any fresh strategy to retrieve the situation in Iraq. They were also supposed to have talked about the fate of British citizens and residents held at the American base at Guantanamo Bay in Cuba. Camp X-Ray became globally notorious from the moment it was set up during the Afghan campaign. Some of those caged at Gitmo were truly very dangerous men; some might be a threat, but there was no hard evidence against them; some should never have been caged at all. The use of this legal black hole to detain prisoners without charge on an indefinite basis undermined the allies' claims that they were champions of human rights and the rule of law. Many regarded the camp as a monstrosity. The most senior legal figures in Blair's Government were appalled. Peter Goldsmith, the Attorney-General, regarded Camp X-Ray as 'an outrage'.[55] Charlie Falconer, the Lord Chancellor and one of the Prime Minister's oldest friends, thought the prison camp was 'very damaging'.[56] Falconer and Goldsmith repeatedly urged Blair to press Bush to close it down. They were wasting their breath. Blair contemptuously shrugged aside their objections to Camp X-Ray. 'If you want to fight terrorism, you've got to be serious about it,' he dismissed his lawyer friends.[57] Blair would only ever describe the camp as 'an anomaly'. He did not dissent at their joint news conference when Bush scorned the prisoners' right to rights by dismissing them as 'illegals picked off of a battlefield'.[58]

The Government briefed that it was lobbying the Americans to release the British detainees at Guantanamo. The Foreign Office 'constantly raised' the issue with the Americans.[59] Yet Blair himself would not apply any pressure, which left the White House with the understandable impression that he was not seriously interested in the prisoners. The Prime Minister was told that they almost certainly couldn't be tried under British law.[60] Charles Kennedy and Sir Menzies Campbell, the leader and foreign affairs spokesman of the Liberal Democrats, raised the question of the prisoners at a private half-hour meeting with the President during the State visit. Bush told them: 'If you want these people back from Guantanamo, send us the plane tickets.'[61] The problem was not his unwillingness to let them go; the problem was that Blair wouldn't press for their release.

On the final day of Bush's visit, the American cavalcade descended on Sedgefield. Marine One, accompanied by a decoy duplicate of the presidential helicopter and three Apache gunships, thundered towards Trimdon. 'We could hear the helicopters long before we could see them,' says one awed member of Blair's staff. 'It was *Apocalypse Now*.'[62]

The American Valkyries swooped down on the field behind Blair's house. They descended in such a blast of wind that the soldiers ringing the field swayed like trees in a hurricane. One trooper was blown clean off his feet. Myrobella was a modest three-bedroom home among humble mining terraces. The President's Secret Service detail registered the difference in scale between the Prime Minister's constituency home and Bush's 1,600-acre ranch in Texas. Looking at Myrobella, one of the Secret Service men said to another: 'We're not going to lose him in here.'[63]

In a bizarre scene, Blair and Bush ate fish, chips and mushy peas in the snug of the village pub talking global politics with John Burton and a selection of well-behaved local Labour activists supping at their pints. The teetotal Bush sipped a non-alcoholic lager. Anti-war protestors were contained behind rings of steel barriers well out of earshot of the President.

Air Force One then took the American tourist home. One US commentator noted: 'Everything President George Bush did in London reinforced the idea that this was a trip made not so much to thank the British people for their friendship, but to send a message to the voters back home that he was at ease as a world leader.'[64]

That was confirmed by the broad smile on the face of Karl Rove. He had the video footage he wanted of Bush with the Prime Minister and the Queen. What benefit it served Tony Blair or Britain was much harder to discern.

Soon after breakfast on Sunday, 14 December, the phone rang at Chequers. It was Jonathan Powell on the line with breaking news from Iraq. We've got him, the Chief of Staff told 'a very pleased' Prime Minister.[65] They had finally captured Saddam Hussein, who was run literally to earth. American forces found him lurking in a rudimentary hideout in a 'spider hole' dug beneath the farm of his former cook, ten miles south of the former dictator's home town of Tikrit. 'He was caught like a rat,' rejoiced the American Major-General in charge of the operation.[66] He revealed that Saddam was captured with a pistol he did not use, a couple of Kalashnikov assault rifles and a stash of three quarters of a million dollars in $100 notes.

The allies had been so desperate to capture 'High Value Target Number One' that the Americans put a bounty on his head of $25 million. Many Iraqis celebrated this as the final release from his vicious dictatorship. Blair was cheered but sensibly wary of looking too euphoric. He left Chequers for Number 10, changed out of Sunday casuals and went out into Downing

Street to deliver some consciously ungloating remarks expressing the hope that the lifting of Saddam's 'shadow' would open the way to the reconstruction of Iraq.[67]

That lack of triumphalism was well-judged. The strutting dictator who had ruled millions by fear emerged from his hole in the ground with a long, grey beard and looking haggard and mangy, a tyrant turned into a tramp. To the surprise of intelligence officials, Saddam did not have any communication equipment in his bolt-hole, not even a mobile phone. That wrecked their theory that he was the spider at the centre of a secret web which was co-ordinating resistance to the allies. It shattered the belief that getting him was the key to reducing the violence. 'Although his capture was a major news event, our abiding concern by this stage was how could we put out the fires that had been unleashed,' says one of Blair's officials.[68] George Bush made a special televised address in which he celebrated Saddam's capture: 'A hopeful day has arrived.'[69] Moments later, a bomb blast shook the centre of Baghdad and was followed by a series of increasingly bold drive-by shootings, explosions and suicide attacks.[70]

When Blair went out to Iraq in early January, he did not visit Baghdad, which was now judged too unsafe after an assassination attempt on Paul Bremer. The Prime Minister's visit was confined to British-controlled Basra. The public relations dimension of the visit was a speech to British soldiers and marines at their base outside the city in which he repeated his constant assertion that 'in years to come' people 'will look back on what you have done and give thanks and recognise that they owe you a tremendous debt of gratitude'.[71]

The more crucial element of the visit was supposed to be the opportunity to get a first-hand assessment of the facts on the ground from Bremer, the American potentate responsible for the calamitous decisions to disband the Iraqi army and to purge the Government of its administrators.[72] Blair and Bremer chatted over a cup of tea in the British commander's quarters at the airport. There was a long discussion about the negotiations over a new constitution and elections. Only then did Blair ask: 'What's your opinion of the security situation?' Bremer gave an optimistic account. Most of the soldiers of the disbanded army were farmers 'happy to be home alive with their children'. Jeremy Greenstock flew down from Baghdad with Bremer. On the account of both of them, the American viceroy faced no serious probing from the Prime Minister. At the conclusion, they shook hands, with Bremer remarking: 'Failure is not an option.' 'I agree completely,' said a smiling Blair, who left the American with the impression that the Prime Minister was 'sympathetic' and 'relaxed'.[73]

Greenstock was frustrated that Blair had not asked the hard questions about the state of Iraq. 'He didn't want to confront the full horror of it all.'[74]

In the New Year, the prescient British envoy warned London that another 50,000 to 100,000 allied troops were required if Iraq was not to tip over the abyss. The message was not welcome.

Blair's attitude towards Iraq in 2003 and 2004 travelled through the spectrum of emotions from triumph, complacency, anxiety, denial, panic and terror before he reached despair. At this stage, he was still in denial. Some of his colleagues were already travelling to despair. During Foreign Office questions in the Commons, Jack Straw whispered to one of his junior ministers: 'I long for Iraq to go away. Every morning I get up and it is still there.'[75]

It had become the defining issue of Blair's premiership. Europe, public services, everything that once seemed so important were subordinated by war and terror in both his own mind and the view of his shrinking band of friends and growing army of enemies. In a speech in his constituency in early March, he acknowledged that 'a large part of the public want to move on.' He had read the results of Philip Gould's focus groups saying that voters wanted the Government to concentrate on the economy, health, education and crime, the things it had been elected to sort out. Blair could not move on. 'It remains my fervent view that the nature of the global threat we face is real and existential and it is the task of leadership to expose it and fight it, whatever the political cost,' he contended. 'Sit in my seat. What would you have done?' he asked his critics. This marked how altered he had been by the Iraq experience. He was saying: you may not trust me any more, but I am still right. Once the master of the politics of persuasion, he was retreating into the politics of assertion. This was accompanied by rhetorical inflation of the nature of the menace. He spoke of a 'mortal threat' from 'devilish' fanatics 'prepared to bring about Armageddon'.[76] His main speech-writer these days often appeared to be the Book of Revelations.

Just a week later, al-Qaeda committed mass murder on a vast scale in Spain, when terrorists exploded ten bombs on commuter trains during rush hour at the Atocha, El Pozo and Santa Eugenia stations in Madrid. More than 200 people were slaughtered, and another 1,500 injured, in the worst atrocity since 9/11. For Blair, this was the latest proof of the deadliness of 'the new menace of our time' posed by those 'hellbent on doing evil' through 'terrorism waged without limit'. In the immediate aftermath of the outrages in Madrid, he warned that 'we must be prepared for them to strike whenever and however they can.'[77] This was giving voice to his worst inner fear. As one of his intimates put it: 'You can never over-estimate how anxious Tony feels about something horrendous happening on his watch.'[78] He told his country that Britain should 'never be afraid to be at the front of this new war'.[79]

Many Britons were afraid. And they blamed him for putting their families on that front line. To a growing body of opinion, the Madrid atrocity was further evidence that the war in Iraq served only to intensify the threat and make targets of European countries that supported the invasion. 'This is the story of how a sophisticated democracy has been misled by one misguided messianic figure,' read one typical hostile commentary. 'Mr Blair by his words and actions has identified this country as the one which al-Qaeda – after America – most wants to attack.'[80] Polling suggested that three quarters of British voters now thought that the war had made an attack on Britain more likely.[81]

At the dramatic election four days after the bombings, Spain's centre-right Popular Party, which had been ahead in the polls until the attack, was swept out of power. It was the first time that a single terrorist act had a direct effect on the outcome of an election in a Western country. The anti-war Socialist Party came to power, announcing that Spain would be ending all its commitments to Iraq. 'Mr Blair and Mr Bush must do some reflection,' said the new Spanish Prime Minister, José Luis Zapatero. 'You can't organise a war with lies.'[82] This was a shock to Number 10: it was unusually blunt for one European leader to publicly brand another as mendacious.

On 24 March, Blair flew out to Madrid for the state funeral of the victims and forty-five minutes of talks with the new Prime Minister. Blair spent nearly all of that time trying to persuade Zapatero not to withdraw the 1,300 Spanish troops in Iraq until security could be handed over to the UN. He failed. The military importance of those troops was not great; it was the symbolism that counted. Blair now looked yet more isolated in his continuing alliance with Bush.

From a funeral for victims of atrocity, Blair flew across the Mediterranean for a remarkable visit to a regime with a notorious history of sponsoring terrorism. When he landed in Tripoli, it was the first time a British Prime Minister had visited the capital of Libya during the long, eccentric and murderous dictatorship of Colonel Muammar Gaddafi. The previous December, the Colonel declared that he was abandoning his WMD programme in the hope that this would end three decades of isolation. Sir Richard Dearlove and MI6 officers played a critical role in persuading Gaddafi's regime to give up on chemical and nuclear weapons. For Blair, this capitulation by one of the world's rogue states, identified by Bush as a member of the 'Axis of Evil', was one result of the war in Iraq that he could hail as a success. It was

nevertheless risky and controversial to visit a tyrant once condemned by
Ronald Reagan as the 'mad dog' of the Arab world. Margaret Thatcher had
allowed Reagan to send US planes from British soil to bomb Libya in retaliation for its role in terrorism.

Gaddafi had armed the IRA and sponsored an alphabet soup of other
murderous groups. A Libyan spy was the only person ever convicted for the
bombing of Pan Am flight 103 over Lockerbie in 1988.[83] Jack Straw and
the Foreign Office took considerable care to prepare the ground with the
relatives of the Lockerbie victims. Officials also talked to those campaigning
to bring to justice the killer of Yvonne Fletcher, the policewoman who had
been shot from within the Libyan embassy twenty years previously. 'It is
strange, given the history, to come here and do this,' Blair acknowledged
during the trip. 'But the world is changing and we have to do everything we
can to tackle the security threat.' That included grasping 'the hand of partnership' when it was offered by regimes ready to change their ways.[84]

It was a consistent characteristic of Blair that he would try to do business
with any foreign leader of just about any complexion who showed some
indication of wanting to reciprocate. This led him to Libya and the most
remarkable international encounter of his premiership.

A darkened Mercedes drove him out to the southern outskirts of Tripoli,
where Gaddafi was waiting in his tented mini-city in a grove of eucalyptus
trees. 'Are you exhausted?' asked Gaddafi. 'You do age quickly in this job,'
responded Blair. Camels grunted in the background. Blair had been warned
that Gaddafi would probably offer him camel milk. He was told not to touch
the stuff, which was notorious for causing flatulence. That was why Gaddafi
would offer it.

Dressed in an ankle-length maroon robe, with a matching velvet cap,
Gaddafi lounged back in his seat. He displayed the sole of his foot – a highly
insulting gesture in the Muslim world – at Blair. This was designed to play
to the Arab street when they saw the encounter on television. The Prime
Minister pretended that he hadn't noticed what the dictator was up to. Over
lunch, he talked about New Labour's version of the 'Third Way'. Gaddafi
delved into his robe and produced a copy of his *Third Universal Theory*. He
then offered some suggestions on how to run a totalitarian state. When Tony
Blair used to talk about 'Big Tent' politics, he never imagined that it would
encompass sharing fish couscous in a Bedouin marquee with Colonel Gaddafi.
He found the entire experience surreal, but worth it.

He did not have any illusions about Gaddafi. The Colonel wanted to come
out of the cold because his wrecked economy was screaming for relief from
sanctions. He had long been an enemy of al-Qaeda, who had previously tried

to kill him. One valuable product of the visit was Libyan agreement to provide intelligence on al-Qaeda.[85]

Back at the British embassy, Blair hailed the moment as an example of how his foreign policy of force and engagement was winning the most unexpected allies for the 'fight against al-Qaeda extremism and terrorism'. Michael Howard sought to make political capital by attacking the handshake in the desert. That backfired on the Tory leader when the trip was endorsed by Sir John Major, who agreed with Blair that it 'was the right thing to do' to bring Libya in from the cold.[86]

This was a coup for Britain and a desperately needed filip for Blair. Libya's admission that it had pursued WMD demonstrated that the threat of rogue states developing frightening arsenals was not just a figment of his imagination. It also sent a message to the White House that diplomatic engagement could sometimes be a successful alternative to war. To other states in the neighbourhood, it dangled before them the potential rewards for engaging with the West. To Britain as a whole, it reasserted Blair's belief that his country and its Prime Minister could play a pivotal role in global affairs.

He and his officials in Number 10 were still trying to convince themselves that even in Iraq 'lots of things were going OK.'[87] An interim constitution was agreed in March. This guaranteed to Iraqis democratic rights, freedom of religion and freedom from torture. It also reserved a quarter of seats in the Iraqi parliament for women, which was an advance towards equality between the genders greater than had ever been achieved in either the US Congress or the House of Commons. The trouble was that they were trying to build an enlightened democracy on foundations that were violently unstable because of the calamitous errors made in the year since the toppling of Saddam. Sentient members of Bush's own administration like Richard Haas could see that 'things weren't working, but policy never caught up with the reality.'[88]

At the end of March, a convoy of 4x4s carrying American security contractors was ambushed as they drove through the centre of Fallujah. Gunmen sprang out to rake one vehicle with AK-47s. It was then set alight. The corpses were still smouldering when a frenzied mob dragged them from the car and hacked at them with shovels. The grisly ritual was still not quite over. The blackened bodies were tied to the back of cars and dragged around the streets. Two of the corpses were then hung from their feet from a green metal pontoon bridge over the Euphrates.[89] TV cameras were there to record horrifying images which were soon playing on Arab satellite channels. Edited versions were shown on British and American television. It was no longer possible for either the White House or Downing Street to deny the brutal ferocity of the insurgency.

America's fierce response, unleashed without consulting the British and against the protests of the Iraqi Governing Council, was a bloody offensive as US marines assaulted the towns of Fallujah and Najaf. That was the 'key point' when Downing Street finally woke up to 'the full horror of the insurgency'.[90] Jack Straw had no choice but to publicly acknowledge that the 'lid has come off the pressure cooker'.[91]

This was the bloody backdrop to Blair's mid-April visit to the United States. He came away empty-handed from a meeting with Kofi Annan in New York. The Secretary-General was not to be persuaded that the UN should re-engage in Iraq. Blair's visit to the White House the next day was an opportunity to express the high alarm of the British about the perils of fighting on two fronts against both the insurgency and the Shia militias.[92] The British were also horrified by the Americans' use of white phosphorus bombs in the offensive on Fallujah, partly for fear of retaliation against their own soldiers in Basra.[93] That tension was masked when Bush and Blair came out for the cameras to utter their now familiar expressions of mutual regard. 'The American people know that we have no more valuable friend than Prime Minister Tony Blair,' declared Bush as they stood next to each other in the Rose Garden. 'As we like to say in Crawford, he's a stand-up kind of guy. He shows backbone and courage and strong leadership.' Blair reciprocated by declaring that the 'friends and allies' would carry on 'standing side by side'.[94]

Throughout it all, Blair insisted that unswerving public unity with the Americans was the way to maximise his private influence over the President. Sucking up to Bush was how he got suction on the White House. A mounting number of sceptics, including members of his own Cabinet, asked for evidence of this fabled influence. To visitors to Number 10, the Prime Minister's usual response was to claim that he had been instrumental in persuading the White House to issue the vaunted 'road map' to peace in the Israel–Palestine conflict.[95] So it was a sharp humiliation when Bush rolled up that map in the very week that Blair was his guest in Washington. The previous day, the Israeli Prime Minister, Ariel Sharon, was at the White House. He came to America with his unilateral and aggressive plan to build a 'Security Fence' which would effectively annexe a big chunk of Palestinian land on the West Bank. Though this was also accompanied by a promise to withdraw some forces from Palestinian territory, the Sharon plan suggested that the Israelis never had any intention of withdrawing to their 1967 borders, the basis on which the Middle East peace process was founded. The White House endorsed the Sharon plan. That left Blair trapped when he stood side by side with Bush in the Rose Garden. He felt compelled to swallow his own forebodings and voice public support for the Israeli plan rather than open a transparent breach with the American President. Cabinet members watched and winced. For all Bush's clichés about his British ally being 'a stand-up kind of guy', Blair was being publicly knee-capped. Even some of his most loyal allies privately groaned that the Prime Minister appeared incapable of indicating that Britain might have a foreign policy in any way independent of that set in the White House.[96] Soon afterwards, fifty-two former British diplomats wrote an open letter denouncing the Government's policy towards the Middle East as hopelessly subservient to the Americans.[97]

By that spring, Blair's strategy of hugging close to Bush looked increasingly bankrupt even to some of the Prime Minister's best friends. While he tried to maintain a public face of confidence about Iraq, he could no longer deny to himself that it was being engulfed by mayhem and death. He 'felt quite powerless', says Sally Morgan. 'He didn't know what to do about it.'[98]

Sir Jeremy Greenstock came to Number 10 at the end of his service in Iraq to give a final briefing to the Prime Minister. Greenstock knew that his 'very gloomy assessment' had made him highly unpopular with some in the building who would be 'happy to see the back of that kind of pessimism'. Some at Number 10 tried to keep him away. They feared the impact on Blair's crumpling morale of a candid account of what was happening to Iraq. As they sat in Blair's den, Greenstock warned the Prime Minster that the situation now looked 'unbelievably bad' and was going to get more desperate in the months to come. 'What can we do?' despaired Blair. 'We have told them again and again what we think is necessary. If it doesn't happen, what can we do?' Greenstock was left with the image of the Prime Minister 'tearing his hair' over Iraq and 'throwing his hands in the air'.[99]

15. The Long Dark Tunnel

The wall of the staircase which sweeps up from the ground floor of Number 10 to the first is lined with portraits and pictures of all its previous occupants, the still famous and the long-forgotten men and one woman who have ruled Britain from Downing Street. They are in chronological order. At the bottom of the stair is Sir Robert Walpole, the first and longest-serving Prime Minister. At the top, a hanging space waited for Tony Blair. When he was in a mordant mood, he would draw the attention of a visitor to the spot. He would say: 'That's where they put you when you're done.'[1]

By the spring of 2004, he felt done. The amazing run that began with his election to the leadership in 1994 and swept him through two landslide victories was definitively over. His morale was collapsing, his health was deteriorating, his unpopularity was spiralling, and many of the ambitions of a badly wounded leader seemed to have crumbled to dust. He had hit the rock bottom of his premiership.

Consummate actor that he was, Blair was skilful at concealing the severity of the descent from the public and the media. He was also adept at masking it from the great majority of his colleagues and officials. 'He managed to disguise it from most people,' says his Cabinet Secretary. 'It wasn't visible to me. I only believed in The Wobble when it became clear afterwards that there had been one.'[2]

Only those closest to him could see the interior collapse of the Prime Minister. There had been few days since 9/11 when he had not been living on his nerves. He found it difficult to sleep. When it eventually came, rest often did not last long. He would wake with a start in the middle of the night to find sweat trickling down the back of his neck.[3]

His hair was dramatically thinner and what remained of it was much greyer than it had been in May 1997. There was a yellow tone to his skin. 'You look young. Why do you look so much younger than me?' he remarked to a junior minister of a similar age. The other man responded: 'Because I'm not Prime Minister.'[4]

The make-up that was slapped on him for public appearances did not entirely camouflage the stress and exhaustion that were etched into his face. Those who saw him when he was not wearing pancake were often shocked by how he looked.

Nights were also broken by Leo, now aged nearly four. Leo would be disturbed by the ring of the phone in the flat, or just wake up anyway, and then refuse to go back to sleep. Blair had 'a day from hell' when he came back from a European Council late one night to find that Leo was with Cherie in their bed. The Prime Minister ended up trying, and failing, to get his own rest in Leo's little bed in the nursery.[5] During a short break in Bermuda at Easter, another holidaymaker thought Leo was the Prime Minister's grandson. That commentary on how old he was looking made Blair sigh: 'I obviously need to get to the gym.'

He had tried to deal with the stress by taking up a fitness regime about which he had become quite fanatical. He would work out at Number 10 and use the running machine in the gym in the police guardhouse at Chequers. The result was to make him look thinner and more haggard. He would complain of exhaustion to close friends, groaning: 'I'm so tired.'[6]

His heart condition was worrying both him and Cherie. In October 2003, he had a scare while spending the weekend at Chequers. His chest was gripped with pain and on Sunday evening he was rushed to Hammersmith hospital in London to be given emergency treatment and placed under supervision for five hours. An irregular heartbeat was diagnosed. He and his aides were frightened that this intimation of his mortality would weaken his political authority. That Sunday night, David Hill arranged to rush the Government's chief medical officer, Sir Liam Donaldson, to an interview for *The Westminster Hour* in order to deliver reassurances that the condition was neither life-threatening nor incapacitating.[7] That did not entirely succeed in smothering speculation about the Prime Minister's health. There was more reason to be anxious than the media knew. Blair cut down on coffee, but perversely refused to take the pills that were prescribed for his condition. His heart would suddenly and scarily start to race, most alarmingly when he was performing at news conferences and in the Commons. 'I had the feeling that he was only operating at sixty to seventy per cent or so of his capacity,' thought one of his intimates.[8] He confided to one of his most trusted aides that he even 'spaced out' several times in the middle of Prime Minister's Questions.[9]

There was a further toll on his family. Blair was 'utterly aware of the fickle nature of people's adulation and people's hatred', says his friend Charlie Falconer. He tried to insulate himself and his children by 'preserving an ordinary family life'.[10] Leo was too young to be aware of what was happening to his father. Not so Euan, Nicky and Kathryn. The Blairs' children had to make a difficult adjustment. Their dad had been a hugely popular leader in his early years and they had largely enjoyed the celebrity that went with that. Now the children had a father who was widely loathed for the war, not least by their own age group.

An emotional trauma with one of the children came as a terrible shock to both the Blairs. As one of his aides says: 'He's a decent human being. He's a very good dad. It shook him very deeply.'[11]

Blair got some comfort from another member of the New Labour inner circle who had been through something similar. That confidant says: 'It profoundly affects your confidence and your sense of self-worth.'[12]

The Prime Minister rang the editors of national newspapers to ask them not to report the story. Cherie also made calls to editors with whom she was on friendly terms. Sir Christopher Meyer, in his new role as Chairman of the Press Complaints Commission, successfully urged restraint on the media. In the absence of any published account of the episode, some of the speculation in the media and Westminster villages ran wild. There was even a fantastic rumour that the incident involved the fraudster Foster's dodgy dieting pills.

Blair was increasingly doubtful that he could achieve more with the premiership. The Northern Ireland peace process, to which he had devoted commendably vast amounts of time and energy, was at an impasse. Iraq was so dire that Tessa Jowell, one of his closest Cabinet allies, publicly called it 'a shroud over the Government'.[13] Public service reform was still proving frustratingly intractable. A senior politician who saw a lot of him observed: 'He's not very happy. I'm not convinced he gets to the end of many weeks and thinks he has really achieved something.'[14]

A threatening band of Labour MPs appeared to be in permanent revolt. 'No Prime Minister can survive long-term with a deadweight of sixty or seventy rebels out to get him by any means possible,' noted a member of the Cabinet. 'If thirty more have a genuine concern about an issue, that's a hundred against you from the start.'[15]

Then there were the endless guerrilla attacks orchestrated by the impatient Gordon Brown. 'It's just constant psychological warfare from Gordon,' one of Blair's most senior aides told me at this time. 'He will not give up until he has got Tony out.'[16] Cherie was livid about the 'constant attrition' from Brown 'rattling the keys above his head'.[17]

Blair's ambition to take Britain into the euro had been murdered by Brown. Worse, he was so politically weakened by the Easter of 2004 that he suddenly capitulated to the Eurosceptics by agreeing to a referendum on the new constitution proposed for the European Union. Blair originally set his face against a referendum, believing that the battle would be both a massive distraction and extremely hard to win. He repeatedly argued that the constitution should be dealt with, like previous treaties under both Tory and Labour governments, by Parliament. But he was 'never comfortable with the argument. The politician in him knew it sounded shifty and evasive.'[18] Against him was building a clamour for a plebiscite from the Conservatives and the Europe-hating press. 'A thousand years of British sovereignty are about to be buried by Undertaker Blair,' shouted the *Sun* in a campaign personally authorised by Rupert Murdoch. 'Britain demands the right to a referendum before our country goes six feet under.'[19] The *Daily Mail* bellowed as loudly. Michael Howard seized on the issue as an opportunity to win support among the tabloids, cast himself as the voice of the people and used the issue as a populist stick with which to beat the Government. The Liberal Democrats also supported the idea of putting the constitution to a national vote, though from a position positive to the treaty. That meant that a referendum could be forced on the Government in the House of Lords by a combination of Tory and Lib Dem peers.

The negotiations with other leaders at European Councils became 'incredibly fierce. They were real blood-against-the-wall events.'[20] Jack Straw was no admirer of the constitution, which he regarded as far too federalist and 'full of all kinds of crap'. The Foreign Secretary referred to the negotiations as 'a fucking fandango'.[21] He started badgering Blair to lance the controversy by commiting to a referendum.

'Jack is devious, but he is straightforwardly devious,' notes a colleague who sat with him in Cabinet.[22] The previous autumn, Straw went to Chequers to argue with Blair that they would need to promise a referendum to get them through the Euro-elections in June 2004 and the next general election. As was Straw's habit, he peppered Blair with personal minutes arguing the case. By the spring, he had important allies in John Prescott and John Reid while Gordon Brown was courting the Eurosceptic press.[23]

Already groaning under the pressure of Iraq, Blair caved in. He knew it was going to look humiliating, saying to one close colleague: 'I'm going to have to eat shit for a few days.'[24]

The retreat forced upon the Prime Minister was made to look even worse when it was pre-announced in the Europhobic *Sun* and *The Times*.[25] That also aroused the indignation of the many Cabinet members who had never been consulted. Nor had Blair discussed this flip-flop with any of his fellow leaders in Europe on whom it increased pressure to hold difficult referendums in their own countries. For Jacques Chirac, with whom he had previously struck a pact that neither of them would hold a plebiscite, this was another example of Blair being perfidious. Chirac was now compelled to promise a referendum to the French, the result of which would eventually wreck the constitution.[26]

As ever with Blair, he was the master of disguising private weakness with the strength of public performance. He put a brave face on this defeat at the hands of his Foreign Secretary and the forces of Europhobia. He presented his panicked retreat as a bold offensive, crying to MPs: 'Let the issue be put and let the battle be joined!'[27]

His closest allies, especially the pro-Europeans among them, saw this for the reverse it was. 'The Tony Blair I knew pre-Iraq would never have done this. He would never have conceded to a referendum. It's a sign of him being defensive and weakened,' one of them told me that week.[28]

As things turned out, battle never was joined because French voters rejected the constitution in their plebiscite and the Dutch then did the same. This subsequently presented the Government with an excuse to wriggle off the referendum hook. Blair was not to know this in the spring of 2004, so his retreat on a referendum was emboldening to his enemies and alarming for his friends. 'We were all absolutely furious.'[29] The day before the statement to Parliament, Charles Clarke bearded Blair at Number 10 and told him he was making a monumental error. Alan Milburn and Stephen Byers, his two most reliable cheerleaders outside the Cabinet, despaired. No-one was angrier than Peter Mandelson, who told Blair he had made the single worst decision of his premiership. 'Tony regrets this already,' Mandelson let it be known that weekend. 'But, then again, that is typical Tony.'[30]

Graphic pictures of American soldiers abusing Iraqi prisoners first began to surface in the US media on 28 April. They were broadcast on network television the next day and then carried around the world.[31] In one of the most shocking photos, a female American soldier, Lynndie England, was shown with a cigarette dangling from her mouth giving a thumbs-up sign while pointing at the genitals of a naked and hooded young Iraqi who has been ordered to masturbate. In another, a prisoner was put on a box and wired up. In a third, naked prisoners were piled in a human pyramid. The abuse was committed at the Abu Ghraib prison, one of Saddam's torture chambers near Baghdad, which added to the ghastly symbolism. The iconic image of Iraq was no longer the toppling of the tyrant's statue. It was a female American soldier holding an Iraqi detainee on a leash. Soon afterwards, the *Mirror* published pictures purporting to show British troops committing abuses.

When these were exposed as a fraud, the paper's editor, Piers Morgan, was forced to resign. Damage was already done and, in any case, there was nothing fake about the terrible evidence of abuse at Abu Ghraib.

After many months of ignoring warnings from Amnesty International and others who had gathered allegations about torture and killings, Tony Blair was forced to respond. He called himself 'appalled' and declared: 'Nobody underestimates how wrong this is or how wrong this will seem to be.'[32]

His brother in arms, George Bush, claimed to feel 'deep disgust', though it was only forty-eight hours after the torture story went televisual on 60 Minutes that he got round to expressing his revulsion. 'I do not like it one little bit,' said the President. 'That's not the way we do things.'[33]

In fact, it was the way things were done and they were done with the effective authorisation of the President. Prisoner abuse, along with much more brutal forms of degradation and illegal imprisonment, became a semi-official American policy after 9/11. The Red Cross unequivocally concluded that there was systematic torture.[34]

Torture was green-lighted by Bush in February 2002 when he signed a memorandum declaring that the Geneva Convention on the treatment of prisoners of war did not apply to members of al-Qaeda and the Taliban.[35] The Office of Legal Counsel reinterpreted the legal definition so as to sanction US intelligence and army personnel to use some forms of torture, of which water-boarding – simulated drowning – became the most notorious. Senior figures in the administration gave the go-ahead for the CIA's plans to use what was euphemistically called 'enhanced interrogation'.[36]

From this flowed the outrages in the cells of Abu Ghraib and the cages of Guantanamo, at the Bagram air base in Afghanistan, and CIA 'black sites' in Europe and around the world. From that sprang 'extraordinary rendition', the Orwellian term for state-licensed kidnap. Why America turned to the dark side was briskly explained by Joseph Cofer Black, a head of the CIA Counter Terrorist Center. 'There was a world before 9/11 and there was a world after 9/11,' he told a Congressional hearing. 'After 9/11, the gloves came off.'[37]

The 'War on Terror' became such an absolutist mission for both George Bush and Tony Blair that the noble cause of protecting liberal democracies from murderous extremists became the justification for using the most repulsive means. This was explicitly so in the case of the Bush administration, which barely attempted to be secretive about it. Dick Cheney declared that these were necessary evils in the 'tough, mean, dirty, nasty business' of 'keeping the country safe'.[38]

The American and British intelligence agencies were so enmeshed with each other that it was impossible to believe that no-one in London knew what was being perpetrated in the name of the alliance. After years of denials, it was finally officially admitted in 2009 that Britain was involved in at least one case of rendition.[39] Following allegations that MI5 agents were complicit in torture, a police investigation was announced.

One very senior member of the Cabinet subsequently admitted to me that they had got 'fragments' of information about the ghost prisons and dark operations being run by the CIA.[40]

Yet Blair never once raised his voice in protest. The use of torture wrecked the allies' reputation for respecting human rights and following the rule of law with a crippling effect on their claims to moral authority. By torturing prisoners, some of whom were implicated in horrendous terrorist crimes, the United States also made it impossible to bring them to justice so they were left in the indefinite limbo of the Guantanamo camp.

General Charles Guthrie was one of those appalled. Guthrie was no-one's idea of a bleeding-heart liberal. He served with the SAS and was commandant of the Intelligence Corps before he became Chief of the Defence Staff. As he put it, torture was immoral, illegal, ineffective, cruel and counter-productive. 'Western use of torture to counter terror has been a propaganda coup for al-Qaeda and a recruiting sergeant for its global jihad. Our hypocrisy has radicalised our enemies and corroded the power we base on our proclaimed values.'

Blair's favourite general delivered a resounding verdict: 'We have condoned with our silence the torture committed by others.'[41]

This was arguably the largest personal moral failure of Tony Blair's premiership.

The full extent of the barbarity was not yet publicly revealed in 2004. But the pictures from Abu Ghraib were quite appalling enough to add to the crisis of Tony Blair's premiership that spring. Already facing relentless accusations that he was mendacious about the WMD, these revelations ate into the moral case for the war. The head of the Foreign Office, Michael Jay, regarded it as hugely damaging.

'You have to conduct foreign policy in accordance with the values you espouse. If you don't do that, you lose an enormous amount of moral authority.'[42]

The British commanders in Iraq feared the 'psychological effect'. In the words of General Mike Jackson, it was 'very damaging to the coalition position and cause. Not only is it unlawful to do these things, besides immoral, it's operationally stupid because you are hurting your position.'[43] In the view of Sir Jeremy Greenstock, this marked the point where the allies 'had no hope remaining of winning the hearts and minds of the Iraqi people. We lost them during that period.'[44]

Tony Blair only ever discussed when he might quit with those very closest to him and his mind was in regular flux on the subject. To his friend Barry Cox, he had quite often expressed the view that 'ten years is long enough for anyone.'[45] On other occasions, he had been heard to say: 'Two terms is all you get these days.'[46] Two years earlier, in 2002, he had flirted with the idea of announcing that he wouldn't run for a third term. Campbell, Mandelson, Morgan and Powell, all his closest advisers, thought that was a terrible idea. Cherie told her husband that it was 'mad'. They do not seem to have found it that hard to talk him out of it.

There were other times when he indicated an ambition to beat the modern record of eleven and three quarter years that Margaret Thatcher clocked up in Downing Street.[47] His ideas about how long he wanted to be in Number 10 changed with the political climate of the moment, the state of his relationship with Gordon Brown and his fluctuating morale. That had never been in a deeper pit than in the spring of 2004.

'He got down because of the aftermath of Iraq,' says Peter Mandelson. 'There was a temporary lapse of morale, spirit, heart. He was prepared at that moment to walk away from it all.'[48] Philip Gould agrees that it was 'Iraq – the enormity of it weighed him down.'[49] Tessa Jowell, a Cabinet minister very close to Blair, says: 'He was very low, he was very lonely and he was very tired.'[50] 'It wasn't a spasm,' believes another ally, Stephen Byers. 'He was wobbling for a while.'[51] David Blunkett felt Blair 'was really down and needed lifting . . . when things are going badly you sometimes go into a black hole'.[52] Peter Hain agrees that it 'was a period of tremendous darkness for him'.[53] Alan Milburn reckons: 'He'd lost confidence, the Government had lost direction, he looked very vulnerable.'[54] A senior member of the Cabinet who had known Blair for years says:

This was a very bleak part of Tony's premiership. The war had changed the whole atmosphere of British politics. The north London liberal middle class where he came from was turning viciously against him over Iraq. He was utterly miserable and the neighbour was saying: 'When the fuck are you going?'[55]

Cherie was consumed by anxiety that they would find themselves out on the street if her husband suddenly quit. With his agreement, she secretly arranged the purchase of a £3.6 million house in Connaught Square. 'A mortgage the size of Mount Snowdon' was guaranteed against his future earnings in retirement.[56]

'It was all coming in on him at once,' comments David Hill.[57] In the words of Sally Morgan: 'Iraq was a quicksand swallowing him up. The atrocities. Those terrible photos. And he started losing people who had supported him throughout. He was stuck in this long, dark tunnel and could see no way out of it.'[58]

The Cabinet Secretary saw it eating away at the Prime Minister: 'The justification for the war didn't stand up. In terms of making Iraq a more decent place to live, was it? No, it was in a worse place.'[59]

The Chancellor and his circle took a more clinical and cynical view of Blair's desperate condition. 'He was talking about resigning because he didn't think he could win the next election.'[60] Blair previously believed that he had a special connection with the public. Iraq 'seemed to take him down step by step', says his pollster Stan Greenberg. 'He knew that when weapons of mass destruction weren't found there would be a broken bond of trust that would be very hard to rebuild. That bothered him more than anything.' This was 'a good part of the reason why there were doubts whether he would run again for that third term'.[61]

The Tories were advancing on Labour in the polls and Blair's personal ratings dropped to the lowest of his premiership. Those of Brown sparkled in comparison. The Chancellor consolidated his position with a 2004 Budget that increased spending on health and promised a further £8.5 billion over four years for education. 'Gordon was at his peak,' comments Philip Gould.[62] Brown also found more money for pensioners. This was what the average Labour MP had come into politics to do rather than fight a disastrous war in the Middle East alongside a very right-wing President. A typical poll had more than a quarter of Labour supporters saying they might switch their vote because of the war.[63] Polling indicated that Labour would have a much bigger majority at the next election if Blair was replaced with Brown.[64]

Cabinet colleagues had rarely seen Brown so cheerful. 'Gordon has got such a spring in his step, he's so whistle-while-you-work,' noted one minister. 'Something about the succession must have been said.'[65] John Prescott knew that something had been said. In the early spring, Blair rang up his deputy and confirmed: 'I'm going in June.'[66]

The Chancellor's camp grew in confidence that they were about to take over. Ed Miliband returned from a sabbatical at Harvard in the expectation of becoming the head of the Number 10 Policy Unit in a Brown premiership. He and Ed Balls planned a new government. Blair encouraged allies like Philip Gould to 'reach out to the other side'.[67] Gould and Spencer Livermore for the Brown team 'spent a lot of time together' on transition planning.[68]

Aides and allies of the Chancellor cancelled their holidays in anticipation of an imminent take-over.

The full story was not detected by the media, but hints began to bubble to the surface. In an interview in May, Prescott remarked that 'plates appear to be moving.'[69] This was interpreted as being a reference to tectonic plates. In fact, Prescott later explained, he was using a phrase from his seafaring days. 'Plates move' in stormy seas. The remark was also aimed at Jack Straw, who was very obviously shifting towards Brown.[70] There was some more media excitement when it was reported that Prescott had discussed the succession with Brown in the back of Prescott's official Jaguar in the car park of the Loch Fyne Oyster Bar in Argyll.

Brown had, in fact, already made a colossal miscalculation two months earlier. He just didn't know it yet. At a meeting between Prime Minister and Chancellor in March, Blair floated the idea that he should pre-announce his resignation. He told Brown that he wanted to make an Easter announcement that he would quit Number 10 that autumn. Expecting Brown to be pleased with this suggestion, Blair was surprised to find that the other man was aghast. 'Don't do that,' Brown responded. 'It would be crazy.' Brown said he feared that Blair would make himself 'a lame duck'. The Labour Party would be in 'turmoil', it would cause 'instability' and damage the party's chances in the elections in June.[71] Though he dressed up his objection as a concern for Blair and the Government, Brown was mainly worried that he was being set a trap. He was always obsessed with the idea of securing the crown without a contest.[72] He feared that the Blairites would resist his succession and rivals might have time to establish themselves as competitors for the throne if there was a six-month interval between Blair's announcement of his departure and actually going. 'Gordon thought it would give challengers the time to build themselves up,' says one of his confidants. 'He wanted to do it by a backroom deal.'[73] The Chancellor was being characteristically over-paranoid and over-calculating. He was self-defeatingly so. Had he been smarter, he would have agreed and got Blair absolutely committed to making the announcement. Brown was untainted by the war and the dominant figure of the Cabinet. It is hard to conceive that anyone would have stood a chance against him in a contest in 2004. He could have been Prime Minister that autumn. After his conversation with Blair, Brown returned to the Treasury to tell his circle that he had spurned Blair's suggestion. Douglas Alexander, the two Eds, Spencer Livermore and Sue Nye all reacted with incredulity. 'Why on earth have you done that?' they asked. 'We all said that he had made a mistake.'[74] The two Eds were especially angry with their master for 'not taking the bird in the hand'.[75]

Over the road, in Number 10, Sally Morgan was hatching a quiet conspiracy to stop the Prime Minister from resigning. She would check his appointments diary. If she saw that he was due to meet a friendly face, she would ring the visitor beforehand to encourage him to pump oxygen back into the morale of the Prime Minister. She also invited allies in the Cabinet to drop by to cheer him up, call him at weekends and in the evening, and have him to lunches and dinners so that he felt less isolated.

In late April, Tessa Jowell came to Blair's study to offer her shoulder to him. 'You're going to get through this,' she told him. 'I'm fine, darling. Don't worry about me. I'm fine,' he responded, unconvincingly. Jowell told him: 'Never think you're alone. We're here for you.'[76]

Philip Gould observes: 'He goes to women a lot at these moments: he finds it easier.'[77] It was 'women who were best at reassuring and bolstering him', agrees Jonathan Powell, because Blair felt he could be more emotionally open with them.[78]

Other callers who worked to persuade him to stay were Hilary Armstrong, David Blunkett, Stephen Byers, Charles Clarke, Charlie Falconer, Alan Milburn and John Reid, who were all recruited to the campaign to make Blair feel loved. 'Our job is to sustain him until the safety of summer,' Blunkett told colleagues.[79] Patricia Hewitt, not so personally close to Blair, but no enthusiast for a Brown premiership, wrote a note urging him to stay. Peter Mandelson was an influential voice. 'Don't be so daft,' Mandelson told Blair when they discussed resignation. 'Come on. Buck up. Buck up. Think of what you have to do. Think of what you've got to achieve. You're the best politician in this country by a mile. So just get on top of this.'[80]

Staff at Number 10 noted that Mandelson and Morgan suddenly started to involve themselves intensely in a plan to speed up 'Iraqisation', the handing over of control to Iraqis. 'They were trying to show Tony that there was a way out.'[81]

Cherie was the most crucial actor in the campaign to stop her husband resigning. She had her moments of doubt about whether they could endure the pressures of power, and she worried about his health and the children. But Cherie enjoyed being the chatelaine of Number 10 and didn't want her husband to quit while he was behind. She detested the thought of surrendering the keys to Gordon Brown.

On the evening of Tuesday, 11 May, the Blairs had dinner with Michael Levy, old friend, fund-raiser and Middle East envoy, and Levy's wife, Gilda. Jonathan Powell rang Levy beforehand with a warning that the Prime Minister was near resignation. 'This is very important, Michael,' said Powell. 'He really needs a lift.'[82] The foursome sat down in a small private dining room at Wiltons in Jermyn Street. With paintings of hunting scenes on the walls, the restaurant was a traditional haunt of old-school Tories. Levy came to the dinner with both a warning and an encouragement. The warning was that donors to the party were picking up rumours that Blair might not be around for much longer. That was making it hard for Levy to prise open their cheque books. 'You have to make a decision, Tony,' Levy told him.

The encouragement came in the form of praise for all Blair had achieved and all he could yet achieve as Prime Minister. Levy, ever the salesman, laid on his best patter to sell Blair to Blair. 'Now is not the time to give up,' said Levy, flattering Blair with the argument that he was the only person who could win Labour a third term.

It seemed to have the desired effect. The next morning, Cherie waited until her husband was in the shower and out of earshot. Then she rang Levy. He had Cherie's thanks: 'Tony came home much happier last night.' A little later, she sent the peer some flowers.[83]

Cherie was 'by miles' the most significant influence in convincing her husband not to quit, according to Charlie Falconer.[84] David Blunkett agrees she was 'really crucial in persuading Tony not to step down'.[85] She argued with him that to go now 'would be read by history as a tacit admission of failure',[86] as indeed it would have been. 'For her, it was beyond the pale to surrender to the next-door neighbour.'[87]

Some close to him always bet that Blair would manage to talk himself out of resigning. 'The nature of the man is that he's an optimist. I never believed that he would resign in the end,' says David Hill. 'He pulled himself round. He argued himself round that there were still things for him to do.'[88] A member of the Cabinet noted: 'He got a new lease of life around June.'[89]

Blair's morale was decisively rallying by the time he flew out to Turkey in the early summer. Preparing for a news conference with the Turkish Prime Minister in Ankara, Tom Kelly warned him that the main issue in the media was whether the allies were going to make a sudden retreat from Iraq. Blair declared that there would be 'no cutting and running or ducking out', he was 'for staying the course and getting the job done'.[90] There was a subliminal message about his own future which was detectable by the few who knew how close he had come to quitting. When he returned to Downing Street, the Prime Minister was greeted by one of his senior aides, Pat McFadden. The aide said knowingly: 'I particularly liked the line about not "cutting and running".' 'That was Tom's phrase,' said Blair, smiling. 'I liked it too.'[91]

16. On and On

Tony Blair celebrated the end of a lacklustre G8 Summit on Sea Island off the coast of Georgia by challenging his aides to a game of beach football. Nigel Sheinwald, who had taken over as his chief adviser on foreign affairs, put his bulky frame in goal. Tom Kelly, who had neglected to bring any sports clothing, played in his suit. The Prime Minister, who always travelled with his gym kit, hogged the ball. 'He was a completely selfish player.'[1] They noted the buoyancy of his mood despite impending elections back home which looked dire for Labour.

He was still out of the country when the country returned its verdict on him. Blair had travelled on to Washington for the funeral of Ronald Reagan as Britons went to the polls for the local and Euro-elections on 10 June. The results were phoned through to the Prime Minister at the British embassy in the American capital. Labour lost over 450 council seats, slumping into third place behind the Liberal Democrats. The Euro-elections were even worse. Labour's share crashed to a terrible 23 per cent. Blair was not exactly cheerful when he got the news, but neither did he react despondently. 'They're bad, but they're not that bad,' he told those travelling with him.[2]

One bright spot was Ken Livingstone, who was re-elected as Mayor of London having this time stood as the Labour candidate. In a popular first term, he had confounded the fears of Labour's high command by boldly and successfully introducing congestion charging and proving unexpectedly Blairite in his friendliness towards business and property developers. Four years earlier, Blair denounced Livingstone as 'an absolute disaster' and strained every sinew to try to stop him becoming Mayor.[3] This time a 'really enthusiastic' Blair was on the phone to congratulate Livingstone the moment it was announced that he had held London.[4]

The other comfort was the performance of the Tories. Michael Howard's Conservatives fell short of the psychologically crucial 40 per cent threshold in the locals[5] and scored a paltry 27 per cent in the elections for the European Parliament, a dismal result for the principal Opposition party at a time when the Government was so unpopular. 'We seized on that very quickly,' says David Hill.[6] The Tories lost a big chunk of the anti-European vote to the withdrawalist UK Independence Party led by Robert Kilroy-Silk.[7] It was an irony to savour. Tony Blair was thrown a lifeline by Livingstone, once his *bête rouge*, and Kilroy-Silk, the tangerine-skinned Europhobe.

In the wake of the results, Cabinet loyalists flooded the airwaves to play up the disappointment for the Tories and play down Labour's pummelling at the hands of the voters. 'They were crap elections, but there was a brilliant operation afterwards. We had our people on every media outlet.'[8] The exercise successfully smothered attempts by some of the Chancellor's supporters to stir up discontent against the Prime Minister.

The agitation was anyway half-hearted because Gordon Brown was working on the assumption that he would soon be moving into Number 10. 'Gordon trusted him to hand over,' says one of Brown's closest allies. 'Against all previous experience, he still trusted him.'[9]

To help save the elections from being a total catastrophe for Labour, Brown and his team had put a lot of effort into the campaign. They were disconsolate and mutually recriminatory when the outcome weakened Howard and therefore strengthened Blair. To Brown's face, Ed Balls said: 'You've been a mug.'[10]

On 12 July, he unveiled his Comprehensive Spending Review, setting out three years of spending on health, education and the other public services. The spending taps were turned up to maximum on the twin assumptions that economic growth would continue into the indefinite future and he would soon reap the political benefits as Prime Minister. His team were now intensively planning the crowning of their king. The media choreography of the take-over was all gridded out. Brown's senior aides had even allocated to themselves the offices in Number 10 they intended to occupy.

One warning that they had got ahead of themselves appeared on the very morning of Brown's big spending statement. 'Blair's shock blow for Brown' was the headline to a story by the Political Editor of the *Sun*, Trevor Kavanagh. 'Tony Blair has vowed to be Prime Minister for five more years in a crushing blow to Gordon Brown.'[11]

Blair was now almost completely resolved not to leave Number 10, his morale further buoyed by advice from Philip Gould that Labour could win another three-figure majority at the next general election.[12] What Blair had yet to summon up was the courage to tell Brown that his promise of a handover was not worth the paper it was not written on.

There were several reasons why Blair felt stronger by July. One was a victory in Europe over his old adversaries, Jacques Chirac and Gerhard

Schröder. Blair thwarted their attempt to impose Guy Verhofstadt, the arch-federalist Prime Minister of Belgium, as the next President of the European Commission. Britain successfully manoeuvred to get the job for José Manuel Barroso, the Portuguese premier, whose Atlanticist, freemarket, non-federalist tilt was much more aligned with Blair's preferences.

There was also some positive news about Iraq. The United Nations Security Council passed a resolution sanctifying the plan to appoint an interim Iraqi government and giving an international mandate for American, British and allied military forces to remain there until January 2006.[13] Blair was with Bush at the NATO summit in Istanbul when civilian power was formally handed over to the acting Prime Minister, Ayad Allawi. Condi Rice scribbled a note to the President: 'Iraq is sovereign.' Bush showed the note to Blair and scrawled across it: 'Let Freedom Reign!'[14] This was one of the many false dawns in Iraq, but it gave Blair further encouragement to remain at Number 10.

Before he got to the safety of the summer recess, the next potential booby trap was in mid-July, when the Butler committee unveiled the findings of its inquiry into the use of intelligence in the run-up to the war. Butler was far more critical than Hutton. When he presented his conclusions at a news conference, the former Cabinet Secretary expected journalists to ask whether he thought the Prime Minister should resign. He pre-agreed with the committee that he would reply: 'That question is not for us, but for Parliament and the people.'[15] To Butler's amazement, the question was never put. The report did provide ample and compelling evidence about the inflation of the flaky intelligence, but it pulled its punches by clearing Blair of 'deliberate distortion or of culpable negligence'.[16] The media herd had anyway come to one of its unconscious, collective decisions that it was now bored with trying to nail Blair on Iraq.

The following night, Thursday, 15 July, Labour lost the Leicester South by-election to the Liberal Democrats on a massive swing.[17] But that blow was softened because Liam Byrne just clung on for the Government at the by-election in Birmingham Hodge Hill. Only later did Byrne discover how much had been at stake when he was told by an ally of the Prime Minister: 'If you hadn't won, Tony might have had to go.'[18] The Tories came third in both contests. Blair retired to Chequers that weekend feeling that he had survived the worst that could be thrown at him. Brown grew increasingly agitated that nothing was being said about the handover.

'All conversation stopped,' says an aide at the centre of Brown's circle. 'It all went suspiciously silent. Tony couldn't bring himself to tell Gordon directly. He couldn't explain what he was doing.'[19]

Brown came round to Number 10 to try to get an answer. 'Gordon was just losing it. He was behaving like a belligerent teenager. Just standing in the office shouting: "When are you going to fucking go?"'[20]

Members of the Chancellor's entourage tried to take things into their own hands. Ed Miliband was always regarded as the least thuggish of the Chancellor's crew, but the iron had now entered his soul. He stormed in to see Sally Morgan. 'Why are you still sitting here? Why haven't you packed up to go?' demanded Miliband. 'There's a deal and he's got to go. There's a deal. Prescott was the witness to it.' Morgan claimed to have never heard of any such deal: 'I don't accept what you're saying is true.' She went into the den to tell Blair: 'You're not going to believe this. I've had Ed Miliband round telling me to pack up.' Blair contacted Prescott, who 'went mad' because he didn't want to be dragged into it. Miliband phoned Morgan soon afterwards. 'How dare you tell people?' he shouted down the phone. 'That was supposed to be a private conversation.'[21]

According to David Hill: 'It happened quite regularly. You'd have numbers of Brown people coming round to Number 10 saying: "You shouldn't be here any longer."'[22]

Brown's camp were becoming demented in anticipation of what they saw as an incipient betrayal. No-one was more maddened than the Chancellor, who had been readier to believe the promises of a handover than the more sceptical Ed Balls and the rest of his entourage. Blair could not bring himself to tell Brown directly. So the media had the conversation for them.

July the 18th was the beginning of the tenth anniversary week of Blair's leadership of the Labour Party. On that day, the *Observer* splashed: 'Blair: no deal with Brown on No 10'. My story and the commentary inside were based on extensive conversations at the highest levels within Number 10, where I had been given the emphatic impression that Blair had totally recovered from the psychological pit of the spring and was now fixed on fighting another election and serving a full third term.[23]

It was widely conjectured among lobby correspondents that the principal source for this exclusive was Tony Blair himself. The Treasury took that as read. Brown vented his fury with his confidants. 'Newspapers were hurled around the office and trampled on.'[24] A boiling Brown then demanded an explanation from Blair. 'I was asked a question,' replied Blair, mock innocently. 'I answered it.' Brown shouted back: 'Are you fucking going or not?' He did not get a straight answer from the other man.[25]

John Prescott got the two of them together for one of his marriage counselling dinners at Admiralty House. 'Give me a date,' demanded Brown. Blair finally admitted to his change of mind. He couldn't go now, he contended, because it would look like he had been defeated by Iraq. 'I need more time,' he told Brown. 'I can't be bounced.'[26] The dinner ended badly.

The night sky over the Sardinian coast lit up with a massive display of fireworks laid on for the Blairs' entertainment by Silvio Berlusconi.

Their Italian host kept the best for the end. The spectacle climaxed with 'VIVA TONY!' sparkling across the sky. Cherie was amused. Her husband was mortified.

They'd made polite excuses on all the previous occasions when the Italian Prime Minister issued invitations to stay at the billionaire's Villa Certosa. Blair's officials, fearful of the bad publicity and the political controversy of associating too closely with the Italian, were alarmed when the Prime Minister decided he would stay with Berlusconi in August 2004. Sir Stephen Wall and others argued that it was 'best to sup with a long spoon'. Having politely listened to their objections, Blair responded: 'I think you should leave the politics to me.'[27] Berlusconi was a rare ally over Iraq and could deliver votes in support of a British bid for the Olympics.

Blair began to have second thoughts when he set eyes on the Italian waiting to greet them aboard his colossal yacht. 'Oh my God,' he muttered to Cherie as they walked across the gangplank. 'The office is going to have a fit.'[28] Berlusconi was dressed in an extraordinary white outfit. Around his head was a piratical multi-coloured bandana. With his ability to instantly spot a presentational disaster in the making, Blair could already visualise the embarrassing pictures and mocking commentary this was going to generate in the British press.

As the boat cruised out of the harbour, the Prime Minister reminded his Italian host that there would be photographers about and gently suggested he might like to change. 'You're right, Tony,' said Berlusconi. 'I should change.' He excused himself and disappeared below. Blair was relieved. Moments later, Berlusconi reappeared looking exactly the same – except that the bandana had been exchanged for a fresh, white one to match the rest of his outfit.[29]

The association with Berlusconi, one of the few pro-war leaders still in power, was an illustration of how far Blair's politics were bent out of shape by Iraq and its aftermath. The continuing friendship with Bush was the most vivid example of all. In August 2004, the Democrats nominated Senator John Kerry as their candidate to take on Bush in the November presidential elections. The Labour Party, in common with the vast majority of Britons, was rooting for Kerry. He was the candidate of their sister party and promised to be a much more productive partner on global issues such as climate change and the Middle East peace process. One very pro-American member of the Cabinet declared that if Bush was defeated: 'I will do cartwheels down the street.'[30]

There was one exception: Tony Blair. He did nothing to help Kerry and forbade colleagues from doing so either. When Bush's poll ratings dipped in the closing weeks of the contest, Labour MPs became excited by the prospect of seeing the back of the Texan. The exception again was Tony Blair. 'Whenever Bush weakens in the polls, they start mucking about,' he would say privately. The 'they' being Iran, Syria and North Korea. Were Bush to lose, 'the bad guys' would be encouraged to come out 'from under their rocks'.[31]

Blair maintained an ambivalent public face about the presidential race, which encouraged pundits to speculate about his real preference. The truth was that he wanted Bush to win – an extraordinary position for a Labour Prime Minister to have got to. The pro-war leaders of Spain and Poland had already lost office. If the architect of the invasion was thrown out of the White House, it would be a vote of no confidence in the war by the country that led it and a vote of no confidence in Blair's judgement in joining it. He feared that the ejection of Bush would be seen as a rejection of himself.[32]

On the night of the American election, he went to bed with exit polls indicating a victory for Kerry. Everyone in the Labour Party was happy. Except Blair. He was roused at 5.30 the next morning to be told that Bush had won a second term. Everyone in the Labour Party was depressed. Except Blair.

The Prime Minister's summer break that year was long even by his standards. The fireworks with Berlusconi came at the end of a twenty-six-day absence from Britain which had begun with a fortnight at Sir Cliff Richard's villa in Barbados, taken in a visit to Athens to see the Olympic Games and also included a stay at a Tuscan palace belonging to the wealthy Strozzis.

Blair returned home on 25 August with any residual thoughts of surrendering power to Gordon Brown burnt away by prolonged proximity to Cherie and the restorative effects of several weeks in the sun. His Cabinet Secretary noted that Blair possessed 'these fantastic powers of recuperation. He loves lying in the sun – that's how he recharges himself. He's like a solar battery.'[33]

He bounced back from holiday with what he regarded as a secret killer plan, to be unveiled in stages, which would deal with the Chancellor. He was encouraged by all the important people around him. Jonathan Powell was as adamant as ever that Brown had to be cut down. So was Sally Morgan.

Matthew Taylor began his time in Number 10 in a more conciliatory spirit, believing that there was fault on both sides and things might be done to make the relationship less dysfunctional. The others regarded Taylor as naive. After his attempts to reach out to the Treasury were repeatedly rebuffed, Taylor too became a Number 10 hardliner on Brown. When David Hill, a temperamentally unfactional personality, became communications chief, he endeavoured to create 'a better relationship with Gordon, but he was not interested in people who could bridge things'.[34] Peter Mandelson's views about Brown were so well known he hardly needed to repeat them.

One of Blair's thoughts was to bring Mandelson back into the Cabinet. That encountered too much resistance from John Prescott, Jack Straw and others to make it feasible. Mandelson instead became Britain's new European Commissioner. It was a glittering consolation prize, but also a form of exile. He left for Brussels sharing everyone else's belief that he would never again have a role in the front rank of British politics.

Seeking someone else to strengthen his arm against Brown, Blair turned to Alan Milburn. They shared the same ideas about the future direction for New Labour and Milburn exceeded Blair in hostility towards the Chancellor. Initially, the former Health Secretary played hard to get, turning down a first offer in July. He was still scarred by Blair's failure to support him in the battles over the NHS with Brown. His friends were telling him that he would suffer the same fate if he came back. Blair persisted, even ringing up Ruth, Milburn's partner, to lobby her.

On 8 September, four of the core Blairites – Stephen Byers, Tessa Jowell, John Reid and Milburn himself – gathered to discuss what to do. They met first at Reid's home near Smith Square and then convened in Byers's room in Portcullis House. Byers told his friend it would be a mistake for Milburn to put himself back on the bloody chess board between Prime Minister and Chancellor. Whatever Blair promised now, Milburn would end up being sacrificed again. It was a consistent feature of the Blair years that his best supporters did not trust him not to leave them twisting in the wind. If Milburn was going to return, the quartet agreed, it would have to be on tough terms. 'We all knew how weak Tony could be and how badly Gordon would behave,' said one present at the discussion. 'Alan had to be made bombproof from Gordon.'[35] They drew up a list of demands about powers and job titles for Milburn to present to the Prime Minister. Rather to their surprise, nearly all of them were met. Blair released a statement announcing that Milburn would direct the work of the Number 10 strategy and policy units as well as being in charge of the election campaign and getting a seat on the National Executive Committee.

This was a triple whammy to the Chancellor. It displaced one of his people, Douglas Alexander, from the campaign co-ordinator role. Even more woundingly to Brown, who had chaired Labour's election news conferences in both 1997 and 2001, it deprived him of his status as the chief election strategist. On top of that, it was obviously designed to freeze him out of discussion about the next manifesto.

Brown's circle had found him 'very depressed, very inactive' since the summer, when he realised that Blair was not going to hand over in 2004.[36] The return of Milburn re-energised him, at least with fury. Within the Brown camp, 'Milburn assumed the Mandelson status of number one hate-figure.'[37] The appointment was 'like poking the angry bull in the eye with a sharp stick. Brown was completely outraged,' observed the Cabinet Secretary.[38]

This was Blair's most nakedly aggressive act against Brown since 1997. The Chancellor and his court took it to be 'a declaration of war'.[39]. They interpreted the recall of Milburn as meaning that Blair wanted to campaign solo at the next election, unencumbered by any obligations to Brown, so that he could claim the next victory as a totally personal mandate. They were correct: that was exactly the intention. Blair told one Cabinet colleague: 'I am sick of government by perpetual negotiation with Gordon.'[40] Philip Gould observed to a friend: 'Tony wants to win on his own next time.'[41]

The Cabinet Secretary saw the strategy: 'All the people in Number 10 – particularly Jonathan Powell, Sally Morgan, Matthew Taylor and John Birt – were telling him to go it alone: get to the point where you are powerful enough to sack Brown or powerful enough to dictate the terms on which he can stay. This is what they all pushed him to do. That is what he wanted to do.'[42]

The build-up to the Labour conference in Brighton was feverish with speculation about their relationship and what it meant for the Government's prospects. Labour had slipped just behind the Tories in the opinion polls. Reports from Hartlepool suggested that Labour would win the imminent by-election triggered by Peter Mandelson's departure to Brussels, but the majority was going to be savagely slashed in this very safe seat.[43]

Iraq cast a dark shadow. Ken Bigley, a 62-year-old engineer, was one of more than 140 foreigners who had been taken hostage. His terrorist captors released a harrowing video tape of their British hostage pleading for the Prime Minister to save him. In a pre-conference interview for the *Observer* at Chequers, Blair complained about the terrorists' ability to 'manipulate the modern media to gain enormous publicity for themselves', betraying his anxiety that they were making a hostage of his conference too. In sharp contrast to his optimistic assertions of just a year before, he talked about

Iraq being convulsed with 'terror and chaos' and likened the conflict to the darkest days of the Second World War. This was a telling insight into his state of mind.

'There is disillusion and disappointment. That's politics,' he said, acknowledging his unpopularity while not surrendering to it. 'What you've got to do is not buckle under it, but go out and make your case.'

He attempted to reassure people that he wasn't becoming as mad as a Thatcher. He wasn't going to 'get into this on and on and on business'. Asked what arrangement he had come to with Brown, he baldly denied there had ever been one: 'You don't do deals about jobs like this.'[44]

That same weekend, there was ample evidence that a deal was precisely what Brown thought he once had. A glossy, full-dress profile of the Chancellor was published in the *Guardian*'s Saturday magazine. He posed in a manner that projected him as a leader in waiting for whom the waiting was almost over. Brown gave a rare glimpse of the personal, saying that he was so devastated by the death of his daughter in 2002 that he couldn't bear to listen to music for a year. He shut down when asked whether he felt betrayed by Blair over the leadership. Brown refused to answer the question, calling it 'not helpful'. [45] In other words, the answer was yes.

When he addressed the conference on Monday, Brown presented himself as the man who wanted to heal and unify. He implied that Blair's agenda for public service reform was divisive and aligned himself with the Prime Minister's critics by declaring: 'There are values beyond those of contracts, markets and exchange.'[46]

The next day, Blair riposted that choice for all citizens regardless of wealth was 'precisely what the modern Labour Party should stand for'. The speech was the flattest and least oratorically extravagant conference performance of his premiership. For the first time he openly acknowledged that 'the problem of trust' flowed from 'the decisions I have taken' over Iraq. Some in his team urged him to make a show of contrition to give disaffected Labour supporters 'a way home'. He was good as a Prime Minister at offering apologies for things which were not his fault and about which he could do nothing, such as the slave trade or the Irish potato famine. His stubborn streak rarely allowed him to admit to his own mistakes. There was a half-sorry.

'The problem is I can apologise for the information that turned out to be wrong,' he said. 'But I can't, sincerely at least, apologise for removing Saddam. The world is a better place with Saddam in prison not in power.'[47]

As he delivered the speech, the conference centre was besieged by protestors. Those howling about the war competed to generate more decibels than several thousand baying huntsmen and their hounds, who massed to protest about the outlawing of blood sports.

It was the potential for an uprising inside that made Blair's team most apprehensive. A mass protest by the delegates, in the form of a walk-out during his speech or a demonstration from the floor, would have been very damaging to his authority. His team pre-prepared ripostes for the heckling about Iraq that they expected to interrupt the speech.[48] There were some scattered shouts of 'You've got blood on your hands' which momentarily froze his performance. But Labour's instinctive tribal loyalty kicked in for the leader. 'Every year, as you come up to conference, he's going to be killed. Then, you get to conference and they are kneeling wanting to touch the hem of the gown,' remarks one of Blair's friends in the Cabinet.[49] They did not actually kneel. They did give him his usual long standing ovation.

Blair referred to Brown in his speech as 'a personal friend for twenty years and the best Chancellor this country has ever had'.[50] That was warm, laudatory and entirely deceptive.

On the penultimate day of the conference, Wednesday, 29 September, the two men had another confrontation. At 3 p.m., Brown went to see Blair in his suite at the Metropole Hotel. Brown continued to rage about the recall of Milburn – 'that fucker', as the Chancellor called him.[51] Blair countered that he had every right 'to bring my people in'. It was down to Brown, said Blair, to show that he was serious about repairing their relationship. 'You've got to stop working against me and start working with me,' he said, as he had said many times since 2001.[52]

Then and ever after those closest to Blair say Brown might have had the premiership earlier if he had been less obstructive. 'Gordon was always his own worst enemy. He would have become Prime Minister much sooner if he'd only worked with Tony.'[53]

To Brown and his camp, the opposite was obvious: Blair would never voluntarily surrender the premiership. The demand that Brown should 'work with me' was simply another way of stringing him out.[54]

Both men afterwards told their respective intimates that it was 'a very bad' or 'an absolutely awful' conversation.[55]

After the Chancellor's stormy exit, Blair called in his most senior aides to tell them what he had just concealed from Brown.

'Sorry about this,' he smiled to Sally Morgan and Jonathan Powell as they sat down in the hotel suite. 'I've got three things to tell you. First, I'm going to say that I will fight the next election and serve a full term, but I will not fight a fourth election.' Before they'd fully absorbed that, he went on:

'Second, I'm going into hospital tomorrow.' While they tried to process that, he added: 'And I've bought a house.'[56] Morgan burst out laughing. Powell was not sure what to think.

None of this sensational information had he revealed to 'his personal friend for twenty years and the best Chancellor this country has ever had'. In fact, Blair had discussed his plan with hardly anyone at all. He'd talked about it with Cherie in Barbados and with his friend Barry Cox. They'd turned over the idea during a walk through the countryside around Chequers in late August. 'He discussed with me whether he should say it or not. He was pretty well decided that he should say it and, in so far as I had any influence, I agreed with him.'[57] No previous premier in British history had pre-announced his departure in this fashion. That very novelty was one reason the stroke attracted Blair, who always liked to be a game-changer.

The germ of the idea came from José María Aznar, who served two full terms as Prime Minister of Spain and then handed over to a successor just before the next election. That example appealed to Blair, though it was not an encouraging precedent for Labour: Aznar's party lost the subsequent election.

Another strand of Blair's reasoning was that the pre-announcement of his departure would forestall plots against him. 'There's no point them coming after me if I've already said I'm going,' he would explain.[58] Why try to stab Caesar if he's already said he will hang up his toga?

Added to that was the belief that he had to clarify his intentions; otherwise the next election would be 'completely impossible'. Unless he ended the uncertainty, the campaign 'was going to turn into a nightmare', with questions about his intentions dominating 'to the exclusion of everything else'.[59]

One of his closest associates also reported: 'He thinks it is very difficult to stand at the next election while in your head saying: "Well, I'm only here for two years."'[60]

This was married with Blair's belief that he needed to snuff out the Tory slogan: 'Vote Blair, Get Brown'. Blair believed that Brown would not be an electorally appealing leader. The only way to secure Labour's future chances was either to have someone else at the head of the party or to create a very short gap between Brown taking over and an election.

Brown was also on his mind in another respect. By publicly setting an end-date on his premiership, even if it was one in the distant future, he thought it might somehow make it easier to control his rival at the Treasury. According to Barry Cox: 'He wanted to give Brown something, some sense that he was just not going to go on and on and on.' Blair thought 'it might calm Brown down' and 'stop the trouble'.[61] If Blair truly believed that, he was utterly deluded.

The final decision to execute the plan was made under the pressure of events. David Hill discovered on the Wednesday of the conference that Andy Grice, the resourceful Political Editor of the *Independent*, was on to the Blairs' secret purchase of the £3.6 million house in Connaught Square. That revelation would bring attention to The Wobble earlier in the year. When the world also learnt that he was going into hospital the combination would 'make him look vulnerable'.[62]

It was Cherie who had arranged the operation. Anxious about her husband's reluctance to get proper treatment for the atrial flutter in his heart, she took things into her own hands. Without telling him, she had rung up the surgeon and booked the operation for that Friday.[63]

When he had sprung his triple whammy on his senior aides, Sally Morgan thought that Blair's announcement plan was 'the right thing to do' on the grounds that it might counter the accusation that he was turning into a Thatcher-like 'obsessive leader' and deflect attention from the house and the operation.[64] Jonathan Powell had always been against setting a public end date on his premiership because 'he'd reduce his power.' But the Chief of Staff found it harder to resist in these circumstances.[65]

At the end of the conference at lunchtime on Thursday, Blair and his team were driven along a 'weird route' through the backstreets of Brighton on their way back to London. They continued to discuss the logistics of making the announcement.[66]

Back in Number 10, on Thursday afternoon Blair shared the plan with more of the team. 'Sorry about this,' he smiled to this larger group. 'I've got three things to tell you . . .' and he dropped the triple bombshell on them. No-one argued. They could all see that 'his mind was made up.'[67]

There was very little time to break the news to the Cabinet and senior officials, who had been kept entirely in the dark. Stunningly, Blair had not even bothered to discuss it with the Cabinet Secretary, who was out of town at the civil service college at Sunningdale. Sir Andrew Turnbull's mobile began to ring as he was in the middle of addressing all of the Permanent Secretaries. 'He can wait,' thought Sir Andrew and decided to ignore the Prime Minister's call until he had finished his speech. When he rang back, the Cabinet Secretary was flabbergasted to hear the Prime Minister say: 'I've got three things to tell you . . .' and then list the heart operation, the house and not standing for a fourth term. Turnbull was even more astounded to discover that he was only hearing it two hours before Blair intended to go public.[68]

That evening, he and his fellow mandarins had a dinner at which virtually the only topic of conversation was what this would mean for the orderly running of government. Most of the civil servants concluded that Blair's plan would boomerang on him by undermining his authority. 'It was obvious that he wouldn't go into a fourth term so he had to find some way of exiting,' Turnbull reflected later. 'But I thought it was a bit unrealistic to think he could do a full third term. These things don't work like that. The economist in me thought: if you announce you are going to devalue the currency in three and a half years, the devaluation happens now.' [69]

David Blunkett was 'astonished' when Blair told him.[70] Tessa Jowell was 'hopping mad'.[71] Peter Hain, the Leader of the House, was among the many Cabinet members both gobsmacked by the decision and angry that there had been no consultation. 'We were all pretty astounded. It was a shock to the system of government and to all party members. Everybody was taken aback. A lot of his closest colleagues thought it was a terrible mistake.'[72]

Even Peter Mandelson 'wasn't given a lot of warning'. He was in the minority of Blair's close allies who thought it the right move.[73]

'Why didn't you talk to me?' asked a horrified Stephen Byers. 'I didn't want to get talked out of it,' replied Blair.[74] Neil Kinnock warned Blair: 'What you're doing is giving up control of your own future.' Briskly, Blair responded: 'It had to be done,' speaking with 'a certainty that he'd done the right thing'.[75] Alan Milburn exploded: 'You're fucking mad.' Later explaining why, Milburn said: 'It was a very foolish and indeed mad thing to do. You never pronounce your own demise.'[76]

He and many other allies feared that Blair would become a self-lamed duck. But their protests and warnings were to no avail; it was too late. David Hill and Tom Kelly briefed the Political Editors of the national papers, taking 'a slightly sadistic pleasure in telling them the news' one hit after another.[77] Even the veterans of political surprises in the Westminster lobby were stunned. Hill's partner, Hilary Coffman, another member of the Number 10 team, talked to Blair's consultant so that they could provide the media with every detail of the operation and pre-empt any suggestions that anything was being hidden from the public.[78] When Coffman offered to brief Blair about the operation 'Tony squirmed. He didn't want to know.'[79]

Hill called in Adam Boulton, Andrew Marr and Nick Robinson, the Political Editors of Sky, the BBC and ITN. He told them, with masterful understatement, that he had 'something important to tell you'. They stayed only for so long as it took them to pick their jaws off the floor. 'They wanted to get away and report it.'[80]

TV crews were then brought into Number 10 from 7 p.m. to record interviews with the Prime Minister for the ten o'clock bulletins. 'If I am elected, I will serve a full term. I do not want to serve a fourth term – I don't think the British people would want a Prime Minister to go on that long,' he said. 'I'm not going on and on for ever.'[81]

That was supposed to suggest that he was not going to repeat Margaret Thatcher's fatal mistake of thinking she could. Yet he was actually announcing an audacious ambition to remain in power for even longer than her. Three full terms would beat her record by giving him at least twelve years in power. In his first *coup de théâtre* as Labour leader in 1994, he sprang upon an unsuspecting party his plan to rewrite its constitution. Ten years later, he was redrafting the British constitution.

He was either conning himself or trying to fool everyone else if he really thought this was going to appease Gordon Brown. 'I don't think it rules out Gordon in any shape or form,' Blair insisted in the interviews that night. 'He will be younger than many Prime Ministers have been if he took over at the end of a third term.'[82]

This offered absolutely zero consolation to Brown. It was always his nightmare that he would get the premiership too late to make a success of it. There was no appeal to being a brief epilogue to a long Blair era. He feared sharing the fate of other premiers who have followed long-serving and dominant occupants of Number 10. Brown did not want to be Roseberry to Blair's Gladstone or Chamberlain to Blair's Baldwin or Callaghan to Blair's Wilson.

Blair's astounding gambit could very well mean that Brown wouldn't even achieve that meagre distinction if Labour lasted three terms and then lost power. Only one party under universal suffrage had ever won four continuous terms.[83]

Blair had not given a scintilla of a hint of his grand plan to Brown when they met at the Metropole the day before. Nor did he subsequently phone Brown, supposedly his 'close personal friend of twenty years', to warn him about what he was going to do. He also knew that Brown was flying across the Atlantic that day to a meeting of the IMF in Washington.

As they sat in the den that afternoon, Jonathan Powell teased Blair: 'Don't you have to phone Gordon?' 'No,' responded Blair. 'You tell Gordon.'[84] They scanned the room looking for someone else to do the deed. Everyone laughed except the official on whom their gaze alighted. It fell to Ivan Rogers, the Prime Minister's Principal Private Secretary, to ring James Bowler, the Chancellor's PPS, who was with his master in Washington. 'I've got three interesting pieces of news, and you'll have to think carefully how you're going to relay this to your boss,' said Rogers to Bowler. 'Good luck.'[85]

Brown duly detonated. It was 'an African coup' raged one of his camp. Ed Balls later told friends that this was not him, 'but it was an accurate summary of what we all felt'.[86] Once he had calmed down a little, Brown put a sardonic face on his fury, saying to his circle: 'Perhaps I should announce how long I intend to remain as Chancellor.'[87] Beneath their angry complaints, he and his circle despaired about 'a fait accompli' which had caught them entirely by surprise.[88] 'Gordon's lot were stunned,' says a senior official at the Treasury.[89] Paradoxically, while many civil servants and most of Blair's supporters thought he had committed a grave error, the Chancellor and his acolytes at first feared it was a masterstroke. 'Everyone was quite stunned,' confirms one of Brown's intimates. 'We thought: "Fuck, he's outmanoeuvred us. He's not going anywhere. He's here for another election." Then we started asking ourselves: is Gordon viable for another three to four years?'[90]

On 1 October, Blair went into hospital for the operation on his heart. He was 'quite scared' about it.[91] The surgeon asked him: 'Would you like me to explain the procedure to you?' Blair, never interested in procedural details and squeamish about surgery, told the surgeon to just get on with it: 'You do your job and I'll do mine.'[92]

The procedure was a success. His staff thought he was 'visibly better and more energetic' afterwards.[93]

On 5 October, Brown returned from his foreign tour for a confrontation with Blair in the den. That morning's *Guardian* had a story saying Blair wanted Brown to chair Labour's election news conferences – an attempt to offer a bit of an olive branch. Brown threw it aside with contempt. If Blair wanted to fight the election on his own, so be it. He would arrange his own independent tour of the country.

He furiously asked why Blair had concealed his intentions when they had met in Brighton the day before the announcement. 'I told you that before,' replied Blair, which he really had not.[94] They started yelling at each other. It was a 'foul and ugly conversation'.[95]

For the ten years since their partnership first became poisoned by Brown's thwarted ambition, Blair had attempted to contain the other man by stringing him along about a handover. That strategy of accommodation and appeasement had reached the end of its life. So had the power-sharing deal they had agreed a decade before. The Granita agreement was already tattered. Now it was shredded.

In a curious sort of way, both men talked afterwards as if they were liberated. Brown no longer had to pretend that he felt any loyalty or trust towards Blair. Blair believed he could now unchain himself from the incubus at the Treasury and slip the surly bonds of Brown.

17. Another One Bites the Dust

'Hi, Euan,' said Tony Blair, glad to hear from his son. The Prime Minister was in jeans, casual shirt and bare feet, relaxing with a beer in a suite at the Caledonian Hotel in Edinburgh. His eldest was ringing from university for Dad's help with a history essay. Blair told his son that he'd phone back later with more thoughts; he had to change and leave for a dinner. As he was driven through Edinburgh in his Daimler, there was another call, this time on the car phone. SWITCH, the Number 10 switchboard, connected the Prime Minister to a frantic Home Secretary.

'I understand, David, I understand,' said Blair, verbally mopping the other man's brow. 'I don't think you've done anything wrong.' There followed another long burst of self-justification from the Home Secretary. 'Don't worry,' replied the Prime Minister. 'I believe you, I believe you, David.' Blair put the phone back in its cradle and frowned.[1]

The extraordinary misadventures of his Home Secretary came to a head at the end of 2004. It was both a shock and a blow. Blair prized David Blunkett as one of the heaviest hitters and shrewdest players in his senior team. 'Canny operator, David,' he had often been heard to say. When Blunkett took over as Home Secretary in 2001, he boasted: 'I will make Jack Straw look liberal.' His was a tough voice on crime and terrorism that shared Blair's disdain for 'the liberati'. Blunkett's personal odyssey from leader of the socialist republic of Sheffield in the eighties to hard man of the Home Office was an essential metaphor for how Labour changed under Blair. Anti-social behaviour orders might be scorned in the chambers of liberal lawyers, but not among those on the rough end of disorder on crime-ridden council estates. 'It's the vulnerable who always suffer from crime,' argued Blair. 'Crime is very much a working-class issue.'[2]

Underneath the calculated populism of Blunkett, there were some liberal aspects to his regime. He presided over the removal of laws discriminating against gay men and lesbians, relaxed the policing of cannabis, reformed the law on domestic violence and opened new legal routes for economic migrants. But the tender side of his record was out-shouted by the tough. He presented no fewer than six new pieces of legislation, including one – to introduce identity cards – which split the Cabinet, in that autumn's Queen's Speech. This was the latest instalment of an annual slew of Home Office legislation which was generally characterised by authoritarianism. He shared Blair's obsession with guarding Labour's right flank from the Tories. The complaints of judicial and liberal opinion sounded soft to a man who had had it rough.

Sightless since birth, at the age of just four Blunkett was packed off to a boarding school for the blind where his teachers thought the limit of his ambition ought to be training as a piano tuner. He lost his father to a horrible industrial accident at twelve and grew up in bread-and-dripping poverty when his mother was denied compensation. It was testimony to his talent and tenacity that he had risen to such heights. Along the way, he developed a taste for some of the finer things in life. He was always especially delighted if a vintage Burgundy was ordered with dinner. Yet he still managed to retain one of the more authentically working-class voices among the middle-class metropolitans of New Labour.

This made it the more bewildering to his party and the more comic for satirists when it was revealed that he had been having an affair with Kimberly Fortier, the American publisher of the Tory *Spectator* magazine and the wife of the managing director of the fashion glossy *Vogue*. Of their first encounter in a restaurant, Petronella Wyatt wrote: 'Mr Blunkett and I ate Dover sole. Ms Fortier ate Mr Blunkett.'[3] Even Blunkett could see the peculiarity of this dangerous liaison between the socialist from Yorkshire and the socialite from New York. They had a child: 'the little lad', Blunkett called William when appealing for public sympathy. By November 2004, it was public knowledge that Mrs Quinn, as she was now called, was pregnant again.

Blair had known about the affair almost from its inception, some three years before. He was never terribly judgemental about the affairs of his ministers. One senior aide notes: 'He was surrounded by many couples who weren't married or who were on second or third relationships.'[4]

The media maelstrom around Blunkett grew fiercer when he and his former lover became locked in an increasingly sulphurous paternity battle over the boy. This was a world first: a politician trying to prove that he *was* the father of an illegitimate child. For day after day, the press served up drooling accounts of the consuming love of a powerful but lonely man for the voracious Kimberly.[5]

This typified the evolution of politics and its relationship with the media in the New Labour era. In an age when ideological differences were de-emphasised, more attention was paid to the character of politicians than their convictions. That induced the media to dwell more heavily on the soap operatics. The Blunkett saga had every ingredient of a lurid TV drama: class, money, power, adultery, blind love and blind hate. It was later turned into both a piece of television and a stage play.[6] There was also the added spice of treachery. Blunkett had assiduously courted the editors of the right-wing press. He found that this was no protection when they decided his life was their story.

It was a fatal blurring of the personal and the political that would do for the Home Secretary. The saga developed a career-threatening dimension on 28 November, when the *Sunday Telegraph* splashed with accusations fed to the paper by 'friends' of his former mistress that he had provided her with first-class rail travel at the taxpayers' expense and used his Government chauffeur to ferry her to Derbyshire for weekend trysts. Most dangerously, the Home Office was charged with arranging the 'fast-tracking' of a visa for the boy's Filipina nanny so that she could stay in Britain indefinitely.[7]

That Sunday, Blunkett hotly denied the charge and was in an exceptionally wrought-up state when he rang his Permanent Secretary, Sir John Gieve. 'Are you really sure you want to set up an inquiry?' asked Sir John, worrying where it might lead. 'We must have it,' responded Blunkett. 'We must announce it by Monday morning.' Gieve assumed that Blunkett had to be absolutely sure of his ground.[8]

He seemed bullish that he could endure 'the shitstorm' that the press labelled 'Nannygate'. The following day, Blair put the protective arm of Number 10 around his Home Secretary. 'I have absolutely every confidence in him,' the Prime Minister declared, loudly pre-judging the result of the inquiry. 'He has been, is, will continue to be, a first-class Home Secretary.'[9]

Gieve discussed the inquiry with the Cabinet Secretary, Sir Andrew Turnbull. They decided to put it into the hands of Sir Alan Budd, an old friend of Gieve and a former chief economist at the Treasury who had become Provost of Queen's College, Oxford. Sir Alan had no background as 'a forensic investigator'. He was chosen because he was 'a completely unimpeachable guy'.[10]

When the allegations first surfaced, his senior colleagues stood solidly behind the Home Secretary. 'David hated half the Cabinet and they hated him,' said one of his aides.[11] Even so, convention demands that Cabinet ministers behave like a loyal band of brothers in the eyes of the public and keep hidden their real feelings about each other. Support for Blunkett began to crumble when it was revealed that he had trampled over that convention by scorning a variety of his colleagues in conversation with a biographer,

Stephen Pollard. It was sensationally reckless of Blunkett to have committed to Pollard's recorder the view that Tony Blair 'tolerated more from Gordon than he ought to', Jack Straw bequeathed him 'a giant mess', Charles Clarke had 'taken the foot off the accelerator', Patricia Hewitt didn't 'think strategically' and Tessa Jowell was 'weak'.[12] That was a very poor reward for all the support Jowell had given him over the years. Stupidly, Blunkett had kicked his colleagues when he was down.

'Blunkett had got into this pattern of behaving unreasonably,' remarks the Cabinet Secretary.[13] The Home Secretary's senior aide, Huw Evans, knew the foul side of his temper, but even he was 'shocked' by the extent to which he had ripped into Cabinet colleagues. 'It annoyed his friends and empowered his enemies. Prescott saw the opportunity to brief against him.'[14] The egotistical, bad-tempered and cavalier side of Blunkett was exposed just at the moment when he most needed support. He had to phone round grovelling apologies to all the aggrieved Cabinet members he had abused. 'He'd pissed them all off just at the moment when he needed their help.'[15]

He'd also supplied the Tories with ammunition. Blair was taunted at Prime Minister's Questions by Michael Howard, who hurled Blunkett's caustic remarks about the Cabinet across the dispatch box – and chucked over a copy of the book as well.

On 9 December, the Prime Minister visited Sheffield to open a sixth-form college and display continuing solidarity with the city's most famous MP. Blunkett, knowing how easily Number 10 could have cancelled the visit, was grateful. He felt that the Prime Minister 'could see the deterioration in my physical and emotional health. He knew that we were on a knife edge.'[16]

The Home Secretary turned up at a Christmas reception for Labour MPs. He handed out songsheets with the words of the Sinatra number 'Pick Yourself Up, Dust Yourself Off'. Then he launched into a lusty rendition of the song. Next to the line 'start all over again . . .', one cruel Cabinet colleague scribbled '. . . in Sheffield' and held it up to general sniggering.[17]

On the afternoon of 14 December, Sir Alan Budd came to see Blunkett in his ministerial suite at the Home Office. Even in the immigration service, which was not renowned for its efficient filing, Sir Alan had managed to unearth evidence. His investigations turned up a fax and some e-mail traffic. They showed that, contrary to the vehement denials issued by the Home Office, Blunkett's Private Office had communicated with the Immigration and Nationality Directorate about expediting the nanny's visa. 'Sorted . . . no special favours, only what they would normally do – but a bit quicker', read an e-mail to Blunkett's Private Office from the office of the IND's Director-General. Budd's later report revealed that the nanny got the visa in fifty-two days, 120 days faster than the average time for processing applications from domestic workers.[18]

'Budd managed to trace the e-mails and he did produce the smoking gun,' comments the Cabinet Secretary. 'Blunkett's story fell apart.'[19]

Huw Evans had been manfully defending his boss throughout the storm. As soon as he knew what Budd had discovered, this most loyal of aides already had 'a gut instinct' that it was all over.[20]

At 2.30 p.m. on the afternoon of the 15th, the two of them went over to Number 10 to see Tony Blair. David Hill, Tom Kelly, Sally Morgan and Jonathan Powell joined the meeting in the den. Reflecting on it later, the Cabinet Secretary thought that what Blunkett should have done was send the nanny to her constituency MP for help with the visa.[21] Blunkett's critical offence was to display unhinged judgement, so often the fatal flaw in leading New Labour figures.

Everyone in the den knew they had a hugely difficult election ahead of them in less than six months. They could not have a Home Secretary whose credibility was shot. It was apparent to most in the room that the Prime Minister had already arrived at the conclusion that he had to go.[22] Blair's 'judgement was that David would be ripped to pieces if he tried to carry on, but if he went now there would be a way for him to come back.'[23]

Blair and Blunkett sat opposite each other on the sofas. The conversation was made slightly more awkward because Blunkett's blindness meant he couldn't read the body language of the Prime Minister and his team. Blair asked Blunkett whether he thought he could retrieve the situation: 'Can you go on?' Blunkett threw the question back at the Prime Minister: 'Can you see a way of handling it?'[24]

Blair was by now a veteran of losing Cabinet ministers. That didn't mean he liked doing it. 'Tony hated these things, hated telling people they had to go. It was Tony's style to want people to come to the conclusion themselves.'[25] Blair 'did his usual lawyer thing', asking Blunkett a series of questions and taking notes.[26]

When Blunkett was too upset to answer, Evans did so for him. 'Tony was pushing it, pushing it, so David had to confront the reality of it.'[27]

Blunkett broke down and couldn't continue. 'He was shrinking into his suit.'[28] The Prime Minister turned to Evans: 'What do you think?' Rather than reply directly to the Prime Minister, Evans put his arm round Blunkett and spoke to his weeping boss: 'You know what I think. You haven't got any choice. I think you have to resign.'[29]

No-one in the room argued. Everyone except Blair and Blunkett then left the den. Blunkett choked up again, saying how sorry he was. 'Not as sorry as I am,' replied Blair. 'I was relying on you.'[30] As he often did in these situations, he tried to soften the blow by suggesting that he'd find a way of getting him back into the Cabinet soon after the election. That did not stop Blunkett, both a highly remarkable and deeply flawed public figure, from descending into an emotionally wretched state – 'a very, very bad place' – for many months afterwards.[31] He was the first Home Secretary to resign since Reggie Maudling more than thirty years previously. Blair had lost both a committed supporter and a Cabinet heavyweight crucial to his electoral strategy.

The fall of Blunkett came six years on from the first resignation of Peter Mandelson. It was the latest example of the Curse of the Blairites. There seemed to be a jinx on those ministers in whom Blair invested the greatest expectations.

All four of the key 'delivery' ministers that he appointed in June 2001 had crashed and burned. Stephen Byers resigned as Transport Secretary in May 2002.[32] Estelle Morris quit as Education Secretary that autumn.[33] Alan Milburn jumped ship from Health in June 2003.[34] On the eve of Christmas 2004, Blunkett, the last of this gang of four, was gone too.

Excluding Blair himself and Brown, just four of the original Cabinet of 1997 were still standing.[35] This high casualty rate in pivotal positions was one reason why New Labour struggled to shape and sustain a consistent strategy towards the public services. Another important factor was Blair's fidgety habit of moving ministers around before they ever mastered their departments. 'He moved people far too quickly,' observes one senior mandarin. 'Experience was not a valued quality.'[36] The endless musical chairs meant that the average tenure of ministers fell to less than eighteen months, an insufficient time to grip policy areas, implement decisions and establish authority over civil servants. John Reid, who was moved around so often that he barely had time to hang up his coat, held seven different positions in eight years.[37] Charles Clarke thinks Blair's 'biggest failure as Prime Minister was that he didn't use people well. He didn't think properly about his personnel policy.'[38]

Mario Cuomo, the American politician, once said that politicians 'campaign in poetry, but govern in prose'. Blair was unmatched at the theatre of politics from his instant reaction to the death of Diana to his faultless response immediately after 9/11. Confronted with big moments like these, he was superb at rising to the occasion.

He was much less accomplished when it came to the grinding prose of day-to-day administration. He was an acrobat politician not an engineer politician.

'His eyes rather glazed over' when Sir Robin Butler, his first Cabinet

Secretary, tried to talk to him about the mechanics of governing. 'He said it was the job of people like me to run the machine.'[39]

'The truth was that a lot of government bored him,' agrees Sir Richard Wilson, his second Cabinet Secretary. 'If you used the word "management", he'd look at his shoes. I found that the only way to get his attention was to say: "What Margaret Thatcher would have done . . ."'[40]

As a lawyer, Blair came from a background in which the emphasis was on individual skill rather than managing a team. 'He thinks about his own performance,' noted Charles Clarke. 'He doesn't think well enough about how organisations operate.'[41] On top of which, he had never been a departmental minister.

Blair's reluctance to engage in personal confrontation also weakened his ability to make his writ run through Whitehall. 'It's part of the attractiveness of Blair that when you meet him you think he's agreed with you,' says Frank Field. 'But everyone then has a different view of what the Prime Minister has agreed. While that's a wonderful technique for keeping people together, it ain't the best technique if you want to be an effective, radical Prime Minister.'[42]

His style was not to be 'fussed about the hierarchy', whether it was within Number 10 or Whitehall as a whole. Peter Hyman says Blair thought he could 'just get people to do whatever was on his mind at any given time'.[43] Alan Milburn 'gradually realised that it suited Tony not to have clear lines of accountability because he was a magpie – he liked to pick one thing from here and another from there'.[44]

Big organisations, in which hierarchies do matter, cannot be successfully run like that. He suffered from the illusion that he just had to click his fingers and action ought to follow. Butler observed that

the attitude of Tony Blair and New Labour was that it was their job to have the concept. They would define the New Jerusalem. It was the civil service's job to get there. So if one failed to achieve everything that the Government wanted, this was somehow the fault of the technicians, the civil service. Of course, it's not as simple as that. Objectives require resources, organisations, discussions about capacity.[45]

Even after several years in office, Blair had not learnt. His third Cabinet Secretary, Sir Andrew Turnbull, says: 'Tony thought that if you said to someone "reduce crime" or "improve the health service", they would just go away and do it.'[46]

It was wrong to say that he never did detail. 'He could do detail if he decided to do the detail,' says Jonathan Powell. 'Like the barrister he is, he'd get into it. He had to be interested in it.'[47] Richard Wilson saw that he 'got into a frenzy' when a subject fired his imagination or was causing a furore in the media. For a time, 'he got very active on juvenile crime', calling together summits on the subject in the COBRA emergency room.[48]

What Blair lacked was a sustained interest in the mechanics of delivery. 'He latched on to issues,' observes Sir Stephen Wall. 'But he didn't have a really determined follow-through.'[49] Margaret Jay coined a phrase for the boredom in Blair's eyes when he was forced to listen to the 'nitty gritty' of policy. She called it 'the garden look'. His 'gaze would shift' and look longingly through the window and out into the back garden of Number 10.[50] Philip Gould once challenged Blair to his face to admit that he found foreign affairs much more energising than domestic policy.[51]

Sir Michael Barber, the head of the Delivery Unit, agrees: 'It's true to say that Tony Blair was much more interested in the vision and the strategy and the direction than he was in the details of delivery. If you're not going to get involved in the details and structures of implementation, what you need is a machine that will do that for you.'[52]

In his first term, he was 'almost wholly uninterested in civil service structures and the machineries which turn a policy idea into reality in schools and hospitals on the ground', observes Geoff Mulgan.[53]

'Early on, Tony was in awe of the civil service,' says Sally Morgan. 'There was a nervousness about taking on the establishment. We let them bully us.' He was frustrated in his attempt to open up senior Whitehall positions to outside competition in order to bring in talented managers. 'When he tried to appoint a Permanent Secretary from the outside, Tony was given a bloody hard time by all the others.'[54]

Awe turned into angst. When Sir Richard Wilson became Cabinet Secretary, he found the Prime Minister seething with frustration about his inability to master Whitehall. 'I feel like I'm sitting in a Rolls-Royce and I can't find the key,' Blair complained to Wilson. 'Well,' the mandarin replied smoothly, 'what you shouldn't try to do is get out and push it yourself. You need a chauffeur.'

Seeing himself as that person, Wilson responded by sending a series of carefully crafted minutes suggesting how the Prime Minister might get more performance out of the Cabinet and Whitehall. He never received any evidence that Blair bothered to read them. 'I certainly never received a reply.'[55]

Wilson argued that using the Cabinet and its committees in the traditional manner was 'the way to get action from the Whitehall machine'. Jonathan Powell warned the Cabinet Secretary that he would never get anywhere with this argument because 'Tony equates committees with nothing happening.'[56]

Blair preferred to deal with ministers one-to-one at stock-taking sessions. Estelle Morris believed these were quite rigorous, saying it was like being subject to the equivalent of 'your own personal Ofsted inspection in the Cabinet Room'.[57] Some officials were sceptical. 'Blair's meetings were usually dreadful because he was not remotely interested in government.'[58]

By the second term, Blair 'had become much more interested in the underlying wiring of the system'.[59] He felt underpowered, especially in comparison to the mighty machine that Gordon Brown had at the Treasury and the large bureaucracies run by departmental ministers. Sir Michael Barber believed that Number 10 was 'not at all as strong as much of the commentary would have you believe'.[60]

Blair concluded that the answer was to meld Number 10 and the Cabinet Office into a version of the White House: an Office of the Prime Minister in all but name. He invited Richard Wilson to sit with him in the flat above Downing Street, where Blair tempted the civil servant with the idea that he would become the supremo of this new powerhouse at the centre. Wilson refused. This traditionalist saw it as his job to try to sustain the old checks and balances of Cabinet government. He told colleagues: 'I am not going to have Blair moving into presidential mode and finally dismantle all collective responsibility.'[61]

Wilson grew more anxious about Blair's trampling over conventions that were sacred to the mandarin. The Prime Minister and his team became 'very fed up' with what they saw as the Cabinet Secretary's 'nit-picking'.[62]

Blair got together a group of the Permanent Secretaries and told them that he wanted them to stop being 'classic administrators' and turn into 'social entrepreneurs'. He exhorted them: 'I want you to be people who achieve change.' Geoff Mulgan was present and thought 'half of them got what he was on about. The other half were completely baffled.'[63] As the Government became frustrated by its inability to deliver the results it had promised, 'the Prime Minister and others started to blame the civil service and a tension built up,' says Peter Mandelson.[64] The civil service became, in turn, alienated from its political masters. Towards the end of his time as Cabinet Secretary, Wilson was openly withering of Blair's weaknesses.

'The trouble is that you have no-one around you who has got any experience of managing anything,' the Cabinet Secretary said to the Prime Minister's face and in front of witnesses.

'What do you mean? There's me,' responded Blair, slightly stunned. 'I've managed the Labour Party.'

'You didn't manage the Labour Party, you led it,' came back Wilson. 'There's a big difference.' Blair needed to learn that there was more to delivering change than throwing out orders to officials.

This was uncharacteristically unsmooth of the Cabinet Secretary. 'He was very cross by now,' says Jonathan Powell. 'He was near the end of his time and didn't care any more.'[65]

Wilson was made to pay for his *lèse majesté*.

An ugly scene ensued at Cabinet in March 2002. The Cabinet Secretary was sitting, as usual, next to the Prime Minister. Seemingly from nowhere, John Reid launched into an angry tirade against Whitehall. He declared that he had 'never been able to trust my officials' when he was at Transport. Other ministers weighed in to roast the civil service. 'We all enjoyed ourselves.'[66] It culminated in a prolonged and scathing contribution from David Blunkett about the incompetence of civil servants at the Home Office, where Wilson had previously been Permanent Secretary. They were still operating, said Blunkett, as if they were 'back in the nineteenth century'. Wilson was promoting a Civil Service Bill to protect officials from being misused by ministers. Blunkett dripped with sarcasm: 'What we need is a Bill to protect ministers from civil servants.'[67]

For Wilson, forced to sit there taking the official minute as his profession was savaged, this was the most searing experience of his long civil service career. 'I was shocked. It was humiliating for me. It was a very bad moment for me. I had no right of reply.'[68] He thought about speaking out, but feared that he might say something 'too violent' and the scene would become even nastier.

When this ritual humiliation was complete, Blair summed up. He did not defend the civil service; nor did he offer the Cabinet Secretary an opportunity to defend the honour of his profession. The Prime Minister made light of it. 'Well, I'm sure Sir Richard will record that the Home Secretary is thoroughly satisfied with the performance of his civil servants.' Everyone cracked up. Everyone except a bleak-looking Sir Richard.[69]

By the end of his time, Wilson was so frozen out of Blair's inner counsels that he had to resort to sneaking peeks at the Prime Minister's diary to try to find out when important meetings were happening. He would then pop into Blair's den uninvited and ask: 'Can I be helpful?'

The candidates to succeed Wilson were told to write a manifesto on how they would modernise Whitehall. The winner was Sir Andrew Turnbull, the Permanent Secretary at the Treasury, who broadly agreed with the critique that civil servants should be more focused on delivery. He inherited a mess. To try to get round Wilson's resistance to a presidential system, Blair created 'a parallel organisation' of special units working at Number 10 and the Cabinet Office. These included the Office of Public Service Reform, the Delivery Unit, the Strategic Communications Unit and the Future Strategy Unit. As Turnbull puts it: 'There were dozens of these units. It was like the

Bird and Fortune sketch. The Social Exclusion Unit was for those who hadn't got a job in any of the other units.'[70]

Blair never had an 'entirely satisfactory relationship' with any of his Cabinet Secretaries, says Peter Mandelson.[71] Powell later concluded that 'we were lousy' at civil servant appointments.[72] Blair's relations with Butler, Wilson and Turnbull were 'pretty awful' in the view of another senior civil servant.[73] There were differences of both temperament and age. When Gus O'Donnell succeeded to the job in 2005, Blair remarked to him: 'You're the first person I've had who I feel is of the same generation as me.'[74]

The proliferation of units at Number 10 was supposed to focus the civil service on delivering change, strengthen the Prime Minister's command and challenge the domination of the Treasury. With the partial exception of the Delivery Unit, they did not fulfil these goals because they tripped over each other and muddled the lines of authority. Charles Clarke and other Cabinet ministers complained that there were 'a thousand people' claiming to speak for the wishes of Number 10.[75] Michael Barber agrees it looked 'a bit chaotic and confusing' to the rest of the machine. 'There could be several bits of Number 10 or the Cabinet Office intervening in a department at a given moment.'[76]

The relationship between the higher mandarinate and the politicians soured as they developed a mutually disdainful view. Clarke believed that the entire research wing of the Home Office, which cost as much to run as the University of East Anglia, could be abolished and no-one would notice. He regarded the lack of civil service reform as 'one of our greatest failures', as did senior Number 10 staff.[77]

One Permanent Secretary whose department was publicly notorious for its incompetence had to be secretly paid off to the tune of around £1 million to get rid of him.[78] Towards the end of Blair's time in power, the Prime Minister's Chief of Staff came to the conclusion that their mistake was 'not to be brutal enough'. Says Jonathan Powell: 'We should have got their attention by making civil servants responsible and accountable and sacked some people.'[79]

Peter Mandelson laid more of the blame on the politicians, lamenting that it was 'a mistake not to embrace the civil service'.[80]

As the relationship got worse, some officials leaked material damaging to ministers. Beverley Hughes, praised by Blair as 'first class' and a minister who seemed destined for Cabinet rank, was forced to resign in the spring of 2004. The Shadow Home Secretary, David Davis, destroyed her by dribbling out a series of damaging e-mails from dissident immigration officials and disgruntled diplomats, orchestrating their release to cause maximum impact in the news bulletins. Her fatal error was to deny that she was aware of fraudulent visa applications from Bulgaria and Romania when leaked correspondence from a fellow minister showed that he had written to her about precisely that.

In the dictionary of New Labour speak, there was no more well-used word than 'strategy'. This was not a Government satisfied with publishing a plan for the railways. It had to be a 'Ten-Year Strategic Rail Plan'. In fact, the Government published two such ten-year plans in the space of just eighteen months. Commuters would have been happier had the trains been as snazzy and appeared with the regularity of the plans. In the case of rail, the constant use of the word strategy only underlined the absence of one.

Transport was a cinderella department because Brown only looked to it for revenues and Blair was not interested at all. Britain's railways were crying out for the long-term strategic thinking that equipped Germany, France, Italy and Spain with superb high-speed networks. The first eight years were instead expended trying to make workable the hopeless privatised structure inherited from the Tories.[81] Blair had a fatalistic attitude towards sorting out the railways, once telling a Cabinet colleague: 'There's nothing that can be done about them.'[82]

He was much more preoccupied by immigration, which regularly exploded into the headlines throughout the second term. New Labour was torn between liberal opinion and the authoritarian instincts of the tabloids and many voters, for whom they could never crack down hard enough. Blair had a weakness for thinking that the answer to any controversy was to pass a law. 'The trouble with Tony was that he thought that legislation was the solution to every problem,' reflects one minister.[83] What was actually needed was not more law but reform of the appallingly inadequate immigration bureaucracy that was overwhelmed by a backlog of applications.

The numbers of asylum-seekers peaked in the last three months of 2002 amidst a massive tabloid clamour. In February 2003, without first bothering to consult the Home Office, Blair made a pledge to halve the numbers in six months.[84] The target was hit and the numbers dropped to 7,000 by the first quarter of 2005, the biggest fall of any country in the EU. Even so, it took until the first half of 2006 before Britain was finally managing to deport more failed asylum-seekers than were entering the country.[85]

As asylum-seekers dropped down the agenda, general immigration was pushed up it. The large influx of workers from Poland and other entrants into the EU was a surge which the Government failed to anticipate. Labour's broad policy towards immigration was liberal, but it rarely had the courage to boldly make the case that bringing in young, skilled and motivated workers was beneficial for the economy. It was also vulnerable to the charge that the country's borders were laxly controlled. In an interview with me early in 2005, Blair made an admission, which was widely seized on, that he did not know, even roughly, how many people were illegally in Britain.[86] The Government moved to a new points system under which the more skilled and desired applicants from outside the EU would be more likely to be allowed entry.

The Government was by now pumping unprecedented increases in funding into the key public services. The NHS was employing many more nurses and doctors. New hospitals and medical facilities were appearing across the country. In April 2005, hospitals were given greater incentives to control costs and deliver more care. Money would in future follow patients, who were to gain wider choice about where they received their treatment. Both waiting lists and waiting times fell dramatically. In 2000, more than 250,000 patients waited more than six months for an operation in England. John Reid, who had succeeded Alan Milburn as Health Secretary, now felt confident enough to promise that they would have that figure down to zero by the end of 2005.[87]

So it was not true to say that all the money was wasted. What was moot was whether all the additional resources were efficiently spent. Productivity in the NHS fell. Much of the extra health spending was absorbed by higher wages. Milburn and Reid, the two supposed hard men of health, proved to be a soft touch for the doctors. GPs and consultants were given remarkably generous new contracts which allowed them to earn more for less work.

There were some groups of public sector workers that New Labour was prepared to take on in the struggle for reform. The firefighters foolishly provoked Government interest in their unmodernised practices when they took brief industrial action in the winter of 2002. There were other workers for the state whom the Government recoiled from confronting. The police were over-ripe for reform, but that was a casualty of 9/11 and Blair's shyness of the battle. He told colleagues: 'We don't want to be seen at war with the police.'[88] About 15,000 extra police officers were recruited, which took their numbers to record levels and they were supplemented by new community support officers. Overall levels of crime fell, not least because of sustained prosperity. Increases in some high-profile violent offences, especially gun and knife crime, and the propensity of the media to highlight them, kept the public mood on edge.[89]

Blair rightly saw that state education was failing many pupils and moved towards devolving budgets to individual schools and encouraging specialisation and excellence. The school building stock, which had been neglected for a generation by parties of both stripes, was renovated.

'Now you can't move in this country without finding refurbished or entirely new schools, the same with hospitals, the same with police stations,' notes Sir Michael Barber.[90]

After incremental improvements in standards, by the end of the second term progress was hitting a plateau. Blair set more radical reform of schools as one of the pre-eminent goals of the third term.[91]

Progress was sporadic and patchy in part because New Labour did not have a fully thought-through model for how public services should be reformed for the twenty-first century. The creation of foundation hospitals and City Academies was a tentative shift away from top-down command and control towards a more decentralised system. It had a long way to go before the health service and schools were truly accountable and responsive to their users.

Even when the Government had achievements to its name, the public was made cynical by spin. Voters were also left unengaged by the technocratic language of reform. No-one was emotionally stirred by phrases like 'purchase–provider splits'.

Towards the end of the second term, two senior figures at Number 10 reflected thoughtfully on New Labour's flaws as a project for government. Peter Hyman spent six years in Downing Street before leaving to teach in an inner-city school. He lamented that New Labour emphasised 'momentum, conflict and novelty' when 'empowerment, partnership and consistency' were required to get product on the ground. He now realised that 'real delivery is about the grind, not the grand.'[92]

Geoff Mulgan regretted that they had been too scared 'of taking on major public professions' and too cautious about reform that might arouse opposition from powerful interests such as 'the London media, the super rich, big business and the City'. As a result, New Labour had turned out to be 'mainly a way of winning elections rather than a transformative government project'.[93]

They say that no man is a hero to his valet. No Prime Minister is a hero to his former advisers. Yet there was force in both critiques. Towards the end of the second term, Blair himself acknowledged to me that he had not been sufficiently 'radical' or 'fundamental' in reform. 'I would have liked to push further and quicker.'[94] He would do better, he promised both interviewers and himself, if he got a third term.

In preparation for it, he instructed the ministers in the key public service departments to draw up five-year plans. This was his latest attempt to set a Blairite agenda for domestic policy and wrest control away from Gordon Brown.[95]

The five-year plans were kept almost entirely hidden from the Treasury before publication for fear that Brown would try to unpick them. Brown believed that his spending reviews were the real Five Year Plans.[96] Prime Minister and Chancellor were now effectively running two rival governments that barely spoke to each other. 'The Treasury were much better at critiquing the ideas that we put forward than they were at sharing ideas that they were developing,' regrets Matthew Taylor. 'One of the dysfunctional aspects of the hostility at the end of the second term around the Five Year Plans was that too much policy development was taking place in Number 10 and the Treasury that was being hidden away from the other side. You wouldn't know what they intended until the day before it was published and they felt the same way about us.'[97]

On the account of Sally Morgan, by now Blair 'had absolutely had it with Gordon. He was organising rebellions in the PLP. There was the constant briefing of the press. It was open warfare.'[98]

Number 10's most secret plan was to cut the Treasury back down to size after the election. Worked up by John Birt, the former Director-General of the BBC who had joined Blair as an adviser, the plan envisaged a 'new Chancellor' after the election who would have a 'lack of personal investment in previous policies' and be good at 'teamwork', none of which described Gordon Brown.[99]

'I'm taking no more crap from across the road,' the Prime Minister would routinely declare to his inner circle. He swore to them that he would finally be master of his Government in the third term.

'I don't believe you'll ever do it,' said Alan Milburn. Jonathan Powell expressed similar scepticism. Sally Morgan agreed: 'It's a complete waste of time. You won't do it.'

'I'm going to do it. I will do it,' responded Blair. 'I will.'[100]

18. The Ugly Campaign

In the first week of the New Year, Tony Blair and Gordon Brown made television appearances on the same day at the same time to speak about the same catastrophe that was transfixing the world. This was not, though, positive synchronicity between the two most powerful men in the Government. They were literally and metaphorically hundreds of miles apart. One spoke in London; one in Edinburgh.

More than 200,000 people lay dead, the victims of the tsunami that inundated swathes of Asia on Boxing Day. Multitudes were in desperate need of aid. Tony Blair smarted from criticism that he had not returned early from his Christmas break in Egypt. That absence was unflatteringly contrasted with other leaders and the early-years Blair who would offer 'emotional leadership' at the drop of a tear on any subject from the death of Diana to the imprisonment of a fictional character in *Coronation Street*. 'He thought his Princess Di phase was over,' explains Sally Morgan. 'The public had had enough of that.'[1]

Gordon Brown saw an opportunity and decided he could use a speech long scheduled for 6 January to present himself as the man leading the British response. Blair then hurriedly called a news conference at Number 10 timed for exactly the moment when Brown started to speak.

Rolling news channels split-screen the rival performances. Interactive viewers could mute Blair and turn up Brown or vice-versa. No longer was there even a vestigial pretence that their rivalry was merely the confection of over-excited journalists or the product of over-aggressive briefing by their entourages. This was their competition for glory and control at its most naked and unedifying. There was no difference of philosophy or policy. When it came to the tsunami and aid issues more generally, there was nothing of substance over which they disagreed. This was a monstrous clash of egos. It looked grotesque to be conducting that fight over the corpses of the tsunami victims.

'By then, it was just total war,' says Morgan. 'Things had broken down completely.'² Geoffrey Robinson agrees it was 'the nadir of the competitiveness between the two of them'.³ Gwynneth Dunwoody, a redoubtable Old Labour select committee chairwoman, spoke for many of her colleagues when she told the pair of them to 'grow up'.⁴

A few days later, more of the poison in the relationship seeped into public view when the *Sunday Telegraph*⁵ began to serialise Robert Peston's biography of Brown, the latest salvo in the long war of the books which had begun early in the first term with another Brown biography, by Paul Routledge. Peston was extensively briefed by Ed Balls and other senior Brownites. The book had a dynamite quote: 'Brown routinely says to Blair, "There is nothing that you could ever say to me now that I could ever believe."'⁶

The Tories gleefully stuck that on their campaign propaganda. Brown had indeed repeatedly accused Blair of lying to him, as Blair had repeatedly accused Brown of sabotaging him. The only oddity about the quote was that it did not contain an expletive.

The Prime Minister summoned some of his closest confidants to meet him at Number 10. Pat McFadden, Philip Gould, David Hill, Alan Milburn and Sally Morgan gathered in the flat above Downing Street, where they were witness to an extraordinary spectacle. Blair did not often lose it in front of large numbers of people, but on this occasion 'Tony was in as angry a mood as is possible.'⁷

He fulminated at length about how Brown had undermined him for years and raged against the other man for imperilling Labour's election chances. Then he declared to the startled group: 'That's it. I'm taking no more of this shit. Let's smoke him out. Let's have a leadership contest.'⁸

Blair presented them with an extraordinary plan to stage a contest between him and Brown in order to settle once and for all which of them was the master. At that moment, Blair seemed serious. He even asked them to go away and look into the rules for a contest. It never, of course, happened. 'None of us really thought he meant it,' says one in the room. 'These were rantings born of utter frustration.'⁹

With just a few months to go before the general election, the headlines were screaming about the split at the top of the Government, and even then the media didn't know the tenth of it.

There was both bewilderment and anger among Labour MPs, who had been given years of lectures about discipline from Blair and Brown only for their election prospects to be endangered by the fratricidal struggle between the men at the top. Prime Minister and Chancellor faced the fury of their MPs when they made a joint appearance before the Parliamentary Labour Party. Dale Campbell-Savours demanded that Brown disavow the remark about Blair: 'We can't go into the election with that on the record.' Barry Sheerman, a select committee chairman and mainstream MP, warned them that if they carried on in this fashion: 'You won't be forgiven.' Prime Minister and Chancellor were 'given a bollocking the like of which I have never previously witnessed', one senior backbencher recorded in his diary.

'I hear what you say,' said Blair, glancing at Brown, who sat in silence just three feet away from him. 'We all have, and we will act on it.'[10]

The rivalry often rendered the Government dysfunctional and frequently generated headlines, but it had not prevented them from winning two landslide victories. There was even a case to be made that the TB-GBs gave the impression that all the big political debates took place within the Government, which helped to cast the Tories as irrelevant. Now, though, the vicious competition threatened Labour at a time when its prospects seemed fragile.

The general election was gridded for 5 May. Few bookies, commentators or pollsters fancied the chances of the Tories. Even a damaged Tony Blair enjoyed approval ratings which easily bettered those of Michael Howard. His Tory colleague Ann Widdecombe memorably remarked that there was 'something of the night' about the vampiric Tory leader. Howard said: 'I didn't come into politics to be liked.' Good job, because he wasn't.

That didn't stop New Labour being neurotic about the election. They were riddled with anxiety in 1997 and 2001 when heading for landslide wins. So they were scared when not a single published poll in January put Labour above 40 per cent. One poll placed them as low as 34 per cent. All put Labour ahead of the Tories, but often only by a slender margin.[11] This was frightening to a party accustomed to going into general elections with handsome advantages over its opponents. Blair's personal ratings had plummeted, especially for trust. The Iraq war did not just discredit him with a segment of the electorate; it also undermined the credibility of claims he made about anything else: 63 per cent of voters thought the Government was not 'honest and trustworthy'.[12]

Like nineteenth-century physicians, Labour's strategists prescribed a purge to try to release the bad blood the public felt for the Government. The voters might get over their anger if they were allowed to vent it at the Prime Minister. So they reprised the 'masochism strategy' that was employed in the run-up to the Iraq war. Blair was sent out to be ritually flogged on television. In one encounter recorded for Channel 5, Neil from West Sussex was seen demanding: 'How do you sleep at night, Mr Blair?' Marion, a hospital worker from Brighton, demanded of the Prime Minister: 'Would you wipe somebody's backside for £5 an hour?' Maria from Essex became so animated about provision for children with special needs that she leapt out of her seat at him shouting that he was 'talking rubbish'.[13]

While Blair was beaten like a punchbag, Brown sulked in his dressing room. He continued with his policy of total non co-operation. When the Conservatives published a report claiming to be able to identify £35 billion of savings from government waste, Labour needed to have an answer. Brown could have done the maths in a moment, but he simply refused to produce a response. When he deigned to come to election strategy meetings, he would sit in saturnine silence broken only by flashes of stinging criticism, usually for any idea that emanated from Alan Milburn. Matthew Taylor, seeing a grim analogy from football, dubbed the strategy group 'the Group of Death'.[14]

Brown's team set out to destroy Milburn. Quentin Tarantino had recently released his slaughter movie *Kill Bill*. Brown's character assassination squad launched an operation dubbed 'Kill Mil'. 'Gordon had to destroy Alan. He had done it before when Alan was in the Cabinet. Gordon thought: if Alan is the face of the campaign and it goes well, then he'll be a threat. So we must kill him.'[15] Milburn became wearily resigned to waking up most days to see another attack on the campaign, usually in the right-wing papers that Brown favoured as muck-spreaders against colleagues. Milburn said to friends: 'It's not pleasant having a bucket of shit flung over you, but this was inevitable from the day I walked into the job. The rod attracts the lightning.'[16] The Brownites openly scorned Labour's election slogan, 'Forward, Not Back', when it was unveiled in early February. Poetry it certainly wasn't, being about as inspirational as 'Open Other End' or 'This Way Up'.

Cabinet ministers sympathised. 'Alan is being very badly treated,' one remarked at the time. Milburn created a professional campaign organisation for Labour which had not existed six months before. 'He gets no credit for that.'[17]

Senior staff on the campaign agree: 'He did a very good job. He played a pretty crucial role.'[18] In the eyes of Cabinet colleagues, Brown's behaviour was 'absolutely selfish and destructive, Gordon at his very worst'.[19]

In February, the Chancellor left Britain for a tour of Africa and China, attracting the accusation inside Number 10 that he was now in 'a global sulk'.[20] Spencer Livermore, the only one of his aides that Brown would allow to go to campaign meetings, faced 'a barrage of abuse about Gordon's behaviour' from Alastair Campbell, Philip Gould and Sally Morgan.[21]

Huw Evans joined the campaign in the middle of March to take charge of the 'story grid': the schedule of events for the campaign. He found all the work done – except for one huge hole in the middle. 'There was no involvement from Gordon and no contribution from his team. They'd done the

work, but they were withholding it all.'²² 'The problem was this was assy-
metric warfare,' says Jonathan Powell. 'There was nothing we could do. We
couldn't fight back against him without damaging Labour's chances.'²³

Philip Gould gave a presentation to the Cabinet at which he worried
many ministers by saying that the key voters were the 'Labour doubtfuls'.
If enough of them refused to vote, or switched to the Lib Dems or protest
parties, then the Government could be in trouble.²⁴ Blair, more popular than
his party in 1997 and 2001, was now regarded as a liability by many Labour
candidates. At the last two elections, his face smiled out of nearly every
campaign leaflet; at this election, many candidates airbrushed him off their
literature.

Milburn could see what was coming next, telling colleagues: 'It's all been
about setting the stage for Gordon to race on to the scene as the saviour on
a white charger.'²⁵ He was right, according to one of Brown's aides: 'Obviously, we made the most of riding to the rescue.'²⁶

That Brown did when he presented the Budget in mid-March. It was not
a lavish giveaway, but he unashamedly targeted segments of the electorate
by raising the threshold on stamp duty for first-time buyers and giving
pensioners free bus travel and a discount on their council tax bills.

There were two main sources of economic growth in the second term.
One engine was the large increase in public spending in part financed by a
rise in government debt. The other was the low cost of borrowing, which
fuelled a consumer boom on the back of rising house prices. A small number
of voices suggested this was not ultimately sustainable, but they went
unheeded. Brown used the occasion of his Budget to boast that he was
presiding over 'the longest period of sustained growth since records began
in 1701'.²⁷ It was a reminder to the country and his party that the strong
performance of the economy was the bedrock of support for New Labour.
Even a Blairite foe like Stephen Byers acknowledged that, in terms of tactics,
'Gordon played a blinder.'²⁸

The economy was the Government's strongest suit in all the polling, and
the Chancellor's ratings bettered those of the war-tainted Prime Minister. A
typical poll found that 49 per cent of respondents thought Brown was doing
a better job as Chancellor than Blair was as Prime Minister. Just 19 per cent
thought the opposite.²⁹

It would not be possible to maximise the advantage on the economy so
long as Brown was in exile from the campaign.

'The gung-ho "fuck Gordon" position, most strongly held by Peter
[Mandelson], wasn't possible,' argues one of the inner circle who was now
desperate to engineer a reconciliation.³⁰

The impasse between Blair and Brown was of mounting anxiety to every-one else who had a stake in Labour winning. Philip Gould talked it over with Alastair Campbell, a presence again having returned to help with the election campaign. Whatever they thought about Brown's behaviour, their first loyalty was to the Labour tribe. Both were being kept awake at night by the fear that the publicly visible estrangement between Blair and Brown was jeopardising an election which was now less than six weeks away. Gould explains: 'To go into the election campaign at such a dangerous time with the two main protagonists at each other's throats was a huge risk. It could have cost us a lot of seats. Alastair was more nervous than me that we might lose our majority.'[31]

Campbell was alarmed: 'We couldn't build an argument about the econ-omy when the backdrop was all TB-GB. Unless it was sorted, it was going to be a disaster. Even though Howard and the Tories were pretty useless, I worried that, if this was not sorted, it was possible we could lose.'[32]

They both repeatedly said to Blair: 'You've got to work with Gordon.' Campbell took Spencer Livermore aside after a meeting. 'What does Gordon want?' Campbell asked Brown's senior aide. 'Does he want Alan hung from a lamp post?' Livermore replied: 'Gordon just wants to be asked back by Tony.'[33]

Neither man wanted to make the first move. Forced into each other's company to unveil a poster claiming that the Tories planned '£35 billion in cuts', they made a poor job of either defending the claim or looking as though they were on speaking terms.

Blair was now panicked by the opinion polls and weakened in his resolve to try to win without owing anything to Brown. 'He'd never done an election campaign without Gordon absolutely centrally involved,' notes Sally Morgan.[34] Always a pragmatist when it came to the electoral crunch, the Prime Minister knew it would be insane to enter the campaign openly at war with his Chancellor.[35] 'Maybe we could have won without him,' says Jonathan Powell. 'We could have left him sulking in the tent, but it wasn't worth the risk of losing.'[36]

After weeks in which they barely exchanged a sentence, the two men were thrown together at the conference of the Scottish Labour Party. When Blair returned to London, he sighed: 'It was such a relief to speak to Gordon again.'[37]

On Tuesday, 29 March, Campbell went up to Scotland to see Brown at the Chancellor's home in Fife. There were years of mutual suspicion in their relationship but also a wary respect for each other as strong personalities with a total commitment to the Labour cause. Campbell visited Brown with a warning and an offer. The warning was that carrying on like this was putting at risk both Labour's chances of retaining a majority and his own hopes of the premiership. The offer was that Blair was now ready for a rapprochement. Campbell returned from Scotland with the outlines of what became known in Whitehall as 'the peace treaty of North Queensferry'.[38]

Prime Minister and Chancellor talked soon afterwards. Both had a huge incentive to bury their differences to get them through the campaign. Blair would be an enfeebled Prime Minister if Labour's majority was devastated and perhaps not Prime Minister at all if things went really badly. As for Brown, it would not serve him and his ambitions if Labour suffered a major reverse. And what if Blair managed to pull off a decent third victory without him? Then Number 10 would have Brown exactly where they wanted him. An aggressive start to Tory campaigning was a reminder to them and every-one else at the apex of Labour that their enemy was supposed to be the Conservatives not each other. 'An election campaign concentrates the mind wonderfully,' noted Bruce Grocott, Blair's former PPS, who was on the campaign team.[39]

Brown demanded a high price for ending his strategic sulk. He wanted full consultation about the content of the manifesto, policy-making in the third term and future Cabinet reshuffles. In effect, he was seeking Granita II.

Blair did not give Brown all he asked for, but he did concede most of it. Brown was restored to his role as campaign supremo, shafting Milburn. He also wanted an absolute guarantee that he would not be moved from the Treasury after the election and he wanted that promise made publicly so that Blair couldn't wriggle out of it.

The Prime Minister paid that price on 6 April, when he made a statement describing Brown as 'the most successful Chancellor in a hundred years. We would be crazy to put that at risk.'[40]

The next day they did a photo opportunity together to unveil two posters. One had giant pictures of Blair and Howard with the question: 'Who do you want to run the country?' The other had mugshots of Brown and Oliver Letwin, the Shadow Chancellor, with the slogan: 'Who do you want to run the economy?' That made it near impossible for Blair to fire Brown after the election.

Blair could not live with Brown, but yet again he found he could not live without him either.

The ultra-Blairites despaired that the Prime Minister had once again caved in to the Chancellor. The secret plan to reduce the power of the Treasury after the election was a non-starter once Blair effectively guaranteed that Brown would be staying there. The Cabinet Secretary was correct to regard the Birt plan 'as now no more than an interesting intellectual exercise'.[41]

John Reid and other Blairite ministers were furious. They believed Labour was going to win anyway and Brown had been allowed to project himself as the hero striding in at the eleventh hour to save the campaign. Reflecting on it later, one senior Blairite asks: 'Did Tony ever once stand up to Gordon on anything important?'[42] In their view, he had buckled yet again in the face of the Chancellor's outrageous behaviour. Alan Milburn was humiliated. Just as his friends had warned, and he had feared, he'd been sacrificed by Blair when it came to the crunch with Brown. 'Alan was very good at keeping up appearances and being very active,' says one of the campaign team. 'But in the laws of the jungle – who's up and who's down – it was very bruising for him.'[43] Philip Gould and Alastair Campbell were ragged as 'appeasers'. Gould would later sometimes have doubts about whether they had done the right thing.[44]

Blair was not going to fulfil his ambition to win on his own and escape from the chains that bound him to Brown. As a result of the latest tortured deal, Government would continue to be double-headed into the third term.

Yet there was something inevitable about it. For all the hideous aspects of the Blair–Brown relationship, one of its underlying strengths was that they never allowed it to become so evil between them that they went over the brink. They agreed on one thing at least: it was better to fight in government than to be impotent in Opposition. They were often on the edge; they always pulled back just before they went over it.

The Chancellor's people – Douglas Alexander, Ed Balls, Ed Miliband and Spencer Livermore – moved into campaign headquarters with central roles. The realists around Blair, such as David Hill, were not that surprised at the turn of events. 'There was a sense that it had to happen. It was inevitable. Realpolitik prevailed.'[45]

It boosted spirits at Labour headquarters when Brown finally returned from his moody exile and brought the New Labour family back together again. 'It helped lift morale to have everyone working together,' says Huw Evans.[46]

Watching Brown and Blair discuss election tactics with each other, one close associate of the Chancellor was impressed by their ability to suppress all the bitterness of the past eight years and 'get it together again. You'd hear them talking and it was a bit like the good days.'[47]

From Blair's side of the fence, one of his senior aides noted: 'Something seemed to happen. They switched back to how they'd once been. Some of that old spark was rekindled.'[48]

But it was merely a truce, and an uneasy one. The divide was physically manifest at Labour's campaign headquarters in Victoria Street. Campbell,

Milburn and the Blairites sat on one side of the war room; Brown's team on the other.

Another of the Chancellor's prices was co-star status with the Prime Minister in the campaign. The Cabinet Secretary watched these developments with the wry detachment of the professionally impartial civil servant: 'To start with it is Blair alone, then you go to the other extreme – you have a campaign in which they get double-billing.'[49]

The two men were brought together in the Prime Minister's room at the Commons to film a party political broadcast shot by Anthony Minghella, the Oscar-winning movie maker whose canon included *The English Patient*, a film about a doomed relationship. Aides on both sides were highly nervous about what might transpire given the poison still seething just below the surface. Expertly edited by a man of Minghella's skill, to the casual viewer the broadcast successfully presented his co-stars as two long-standing friends reflecting on their achievements and setting out their shared vision for the future. Philip Gould's focus groups responded positively.[50] The sharp eye noticed that Blair seemed fairly relaxed but Brown, never anything like as accomplished as a thespian, looked twisted with tension.

'It's all about working as a team,' Brown was recorded saying to the Prime Minister he wanted rid of. 'It's a partnership that has worked,' said Blair of the Chancellor he had planned to sack.[51]

Before the filming began, Minghella did a warm-up exercise with his subjects to get them into the mood for some acting. The director gave each of them a notepad on which they were to write down the greatest achievement of the other man. On his notepad, Blair's looping handwriting paid tribute to Brown for: 'A strong economy'.

On his notepad, Brown wrote in his cramped script: 'A strong economy'. The Chancellor could think of no achievement that he wished to credit to Blair so he wrote down a tribute to himself instead.[52]

After the ritual call on Buckingham Palace to ask the Queen formally for her permission, at just after noon on Tuesday, 5 April, Tony Blair launched his third campaign as leader. Standing outside Number 10, he did not mention Iraq, placing the stress on 'hard-won economic stability' and 'investment in our public services', the Government's two strongest cards. 'It is a big choice. It is a big decision. The British people are the boss and they are the ones who will make it.'[53]

During equally ritual exchanges the next day at the final Prime Minister's Questions, Michael Howard jeeringly invited Labour MPs to raise their hands if they had put Tony Blair's face on their election addresses. A dozen or so suckers on the Labour benches fell into the Tory leader's trap by putting their hands up.

This set the tone for a nasty and brutish campaign. In 1997 against John Major and in 2001 against William Hague, Blair was a young, charismatic and popular leader cruising to landslide victories against opponents who were weak, unpopular and widely ridiculed. They were not so much contests as coronations. His third election was an assault course. He entered the 2005 campaign as a battered and distrusted leader often most reviled on the left among those who ought to be Labour's natural supporters. The Tories had a lot of money to spend on mail shots and target constituencies. For his chief strategist, Howard imported Lynton Crosby who had run four ruthlessly successful campaigns for Australia's right-wing party. After a slick start that worried Labour, the heavy emphasis the Tories put on immigration made them look opportunistic, monomaniac and unattractive to centrist and floating voters. In a well-timed speech in Dover, Blair charged his opponents with seeking 'to exploit people's fears' and skilfully punctured Howard's posturing on the issue. 'The Tory party have gone from being a One Nation party to being a one-issue party.'[54] The leadership of Howard exemplified the Tories' struggle to find fresh personalities and winning strategies. Fifteen years after they had ditched Margaret Thatcher, the Conservatives were going into a fourth election still led by one of her protégés.

Blair's principal opponent was not really the Tory leader with his widely satirised slogan: 'Are You Thinking What We're Thinking?' The person whom Blair was running against was himself. To secure the sort of majority he required to give himself a fresh start and to contain Gordon Brown, he needed to answer the intense anger aroused by the Iraq war and the corrosive distrust towards him personally.

Labour's election War Book, its campaign bible, put it this way: 'TB must connect with the electorate . . . and make it clear that he has not abandoned them.'[55]

Connecting with voters was his strength in the past. He was the first premier to understand the 24/7 media age. Those who worked with him said he was often ahead of the aides paid to plan events in thinking about presentational details. He became supremely accomplished at making himself comfortable and conversational in the nation's living rooms. Blair's response to celebrity culture was to turn himself into the first celebrity Prime Minister. In pursuit of popularity, and to show himself attuned to mass culture, Blair had gone where no Prime Minister had gone before. He recorded dialogue for an episode of *The Simpsons* and was a regular on the soft sofas of daytime TV, where he would adopt a Mockney accent that they hadn't taught him at Fettes.

One of his early campaign appearances was with Richard and Judy, who extracted an admission that he never sent flowers to Cherie. He also agreed to do a turn for Ant and Dec's *Saturday Night Takeaway*. The appeal of this fixture was that it had a massive audience. The Blair team calculated that it would give them access to 8 million viewers who would rarely watch any news or current affairs programmes.[56]

'Little Ant and Dec', pint-sized versions of the show's hosts who specialised in faux-naif interviews with the famous, showed up at Number 10 wearing little black suits and oiled hair. The crew set up in one of the drawing rooms. It was obvious the moment the cameras turned over that this was a lunge too far downmarket. 'My Dad says you're mad' was a typical line of interrogation from one of the ten-year-old inquisitors. 'Are you mad?' They went on to ask a startled Blair: 'If you make an ugly smell do people pretend not to notice it because you are Prime Minister?'[57]

To make the encounter even more surreal it was witnessed in all its toe-curling horror by the editor of the *New Yorker*, who had come to do a deep piece about Blair for the readers of that liberal and cerebral organ. 'It's always a battle, isn't it, between the modern world in which people expect their leaders to be more accessible and the dignity of the office?' Blair tried to explain. 'And you've got to be careful that you don't compromise the one in the attempt to enter into the other.'[58] Quite. It is impossible to imagine any earlier Prime Minister abasing himself like this.

At the end of an hour of torture at the hands of the diminutive duo, Little Ant and Little Dec presented a 'gobsmacked' Prime Minister with some souvenir tat from the show and a pair of Union Jack panties for Cherie. 'I don't believe this,' gasped Blair. He looked at his aides with murder in his eyes. 'How much of this will they use?' 'About half,' replied David Hill, to which Blair said: 'I can think of some things to cut out.'[59]

The cheesiest campaign interview for a newspaper was with the *Sun*. After the formal sit-down with Blair, the paper's Political Editor, Trevor Kavanagh, and its editor, Rebekah Wade, went out into the back garden of Number 10 to watch the Blairs having their pictures taken. Cherie joked with the photographer that her husband should show them his 'fit body' and suggested he was up for it 'five times a night'.[60] Wade's face lit up: 'That's your story, Trevor.' Kavanagh 'looked like a man in shock'.[61]

On Wednesday, 13 April, Labour launched its manifesto at the Mermaid Theatre in the City of London. 'I have said I will serve a full term,' Blair declared under questioning. 'That's what people are electing if they elect this Government. When I say a full third term, that's exactly what I mean.'[62] Brown looked as though he was passing a gallstone. They were flanked by five other Cabinet ministers, each brandishing their copies of *Britain Forward, Not Back*, a 112-page booklet reminiscent of Chairman Mao's *Little Red Book* in style – if obviously not in content. The economic sections were written by Brown. The rest was principally authored by Matthew Taylor. It was more policy-rich and better argued than the manifestos of 1997 and 2001. Blair had finally grasped what a mistake it was to run on bland manifestos which did not provide enough of a mandate for reform. It was his regular private refrain that 'the third term will be what my second term was supposed to have been' before it was diverted by 9/11, Afghanistan and Iraq.[63] This manifesto was designed to be the springboard. It promised to get to 'maximum waits of 18 weeks in the NHS' and to have opened 3,500 children's centres for the under-fives: pledges that would have once been regarded as crazily unrealistic. Blair was right to say it was 'far more ambitious' than eight years earlier.[64]

On page 30 of the Labour manifesto there was the offer of a guaranteed place in sixth form, college or training for every sixteen- to nineteen-year-old. On page 30 of the rival Tory manifesto there was a blank space because that was the back cover of a Conservative prospectus that had already run out of things to say. Michael Howard offered a list of things to hate rather than a blueprint for government.

Charles Kennedy got into a terrible muddle trying to explain his party's plans for a local income tax. The Lib Dem leader admitted he could not win and the Tories did not behave as if they had any expectation of becoming the Government. Labour continued to fret that it could nevertheless lose its majority.

Blair reluctantly agreed to continue with the masochism strategy. One woman in a television audience complained about the lack of NHS dentistry and opened her mouth in front of a wincing Prime Minister to expose the empty gums from which she had extracted her rotten teeth. He looked like his teeth were being pulled without benefit of anaesthetic when he appeared on a special edition of *Question Time*, chaired by David Dimbleby. All three leaders appeared on the programme, but separately, Blair having ruled out a leaders' debate. Charles Kennedy went first and received a fairly easy half-hour. Then came Michael Howard, who experienced a rougher ride. One questioner asked him how it felt to be less trusted than the Prime Minister he was calling a liar. As Blair headed into the ring, he groaned: 'God, this is going to be grim.'[65] By the time he was in the hot seat the temperature in the studio had become sauna-like and the audience was boiling over. During a sustained bombardment about Iraq, he was told that he should resign. He was then badly thrown by a woman with a question about how Government targets had actually made it harder to book an appointment with a GP. 'I'm absolutely astonished,' Blair floundered. 'That's news to me.'[66] Under the tropical heat of the TV lights, he broke into a Nixonian sweat. He was booed. He was jeered. The audience was near riotous by the end. Blair looked numbed. It was 'the low spot'.[67]

Jonathan Dimbleby – it is part of Britain's unwritten constitution that hereditary Dimblebys must host election programmes – was in the chair when Blair faced another battering on ITV's *Ask the Leader*. One striking moment illustrated how he had changed. During the Ecclestone Affair in his first autumn at Number 10, he asked people to believe that he was 'a pretty straight kind of guy'. The Blair of eight years later would no longer make an appeal like that. 'I'm not going to stand here and beg for my own character. People can make up their minds whether they trust me or not.'[68]

Brown, who was always averse to going into any environment which he could not completely control, did not subject himself to any close encounters with the voters. While the Prime Minister took all the heat and the hits, the Chancellor magisterially floated above the fray. This was cunning and cowardly in equal measure.

Iraq, the worst territory for Labour, dominated the final stretch of the campaign. For the first time, in an interview with the *Observer*, Blair acknowledged: 'There is a question about the judgement of the decision.' He now simply asked people to appreciate the dilemma that faced him at the time: 'Whichever way it went, it was not going to be easy.'[69] Controversy about the legality of the war was reignited when extracts of the Attorney-General's advice were leaked to the *Mail on Sunday* and *Channel 4 News*, which finally compelled the Government to publish Goldsmith's document in full after two years of trying to keep it secret.[70] It swamped Labour's launch of its business manifesto at the headquarters of Bloomberg the next morning. Brown made a key intervention. Asked if he would have gone to war the same way as Blair, there was a dramatic pause before he simply said: 'Yes.' The answer received a smattering of applause from the businessmen in the audience. 'I not only trust Tony Blair, but I respect Tony Blair for the way he went about that decision,' the Chancellor declared.[71] Blair looked relieved, but it was also a painful reminder of his dependency on the other man.

Michael Howard directly accused the Prime Minister of lying his way into Iraq. 'He's told lies to win elections,' sniped the Tory leader. 'On the one thing where he's taken a stand in the eight years he's been Prime Minister, which was taking us to war, he didn't even tell the truth about that.'[72] The Conservatives put up posters with the slogan: 'If he's prepared to lie to take us to war, he's prepared to lie to win an election.'

Even some senior Tories thought this was counter-productively aggressive.[73] It also looked hypocritical coming from a party that enthusiastically supported the war. Charles Kennedy observed that criticism from the Tories was 'laughable' when 'they were the principal cheer-leaders for George Bush and Tony Blair.'[74]

The Tory assault on Blair did little for Michael Howard's reputation, but Iraq certainly had an effect. One post-election analysis found that a quarter of defecting traditional Labour voters cited the war as the reason.[75] The 'heavy onslaught on Iraq' ate into Blair's already low morale.[76] Even after so many toughening years at the top, his skin was pierced by attacks on his personal integrity. 'He hates it if people question his character or whether he's been honest,' says Sally Morgan.[77]

In the last week of the campaign, he groaned to me: 'A very, very direct character attack, day after day after day – who knows what the impact is? The question is whether some of the mud sticks. The honest answer is, I don't know.' He feared that it might so depress the Labour vote that it could cost him his majority or even let the Tories 'get in by the back door'.[78]

The electoral sorcerer knew that his powers were fading. In conversation, he did not deny that there was a section of the electorate who did not want to vote Labour because they simply hated him. 'They've got to make up their minds whether that is enough for them to reject the whole Government.'[79] The maestro who once invited people to vote Labour because of him and in spite of the party now asked people to vote Labour because of the party and in spite of him.

'It was an ugly election,' says Matthew Taylor.[80] Blair usually relished campaigning because he thought it was something at which he excelled. He hated this campaign. When he joined Peter Hain at a campaign rally in south Wales, the minister could see 'he was clearly not enjoying it; it was a pretty unpleasant experience for Tony.'[81] 'It was an awful campaign,' says Alan Milburn. 'We were playing a very defensive game and counting the days for it to be over.'[82]

The campaign was not just psychologically painful for Blair; he was also in physical agony because of an injury incurred in the gym. He was suffering from a slipped disc, which he couldn't get treated without alerting journalists. It was masked from the media at the cost of Blair spending the campaign in severe physical distress, made worse because he refused to take painkillers.

'If you offered Tony a pill he reacted as if you were trying to get him to take heroin,' says one of his staff.[83] He was persuaded to dose himself up with Nurofen to get through the campaign. In its last week, he also went down with a heavy cold.

'I think you've got be pretty abnormal not to be affected if somebody's calling you a liar repeatedly and in a very aggressive way,' says Sally Morgan. 'He was also in pain, which didn't help. The combination of having a bad back and being called a liar doesn't make you feel great.'[84]

Cherie came into campaign headquarters forty-eight hours before polling day and berated Philip Gould for giving her husband too much bad news about how things were looking. 'I'm just trying to tell him the truth,' protested Gould. 'Well, you shouldn't be,' said Cherie. 'It's depressing him.'[85]

There was a rising panic about Labour voters expressing disenchantment by switching to the Lib Dems or staying at home in high numbers. Alastair Campbell tried one of his old tricks by leaking an internal memo which detailed Labour's anxieties about the election. He planted it with the *Sunday Times*. The idea was to scare Labour supporters to the polling stations with the thought that they might accidentally let in Howard. This attempt at 'reverse spin' backfired when the *Sunday Times* gave the story the headline: 'Campbell: we're home and dry', precisely the opposite of what he had intended.[86] Tricks from the New Labour playbook no longer worked as they once did.

Most of the press gave a grudging vote for Labour. The *Sun*, having played a game of tease about its intentions, released red smoke over Wapping. Since they also had the support of the *Mirror*, the two biggest-selling red-top tabloids were both voting Labour. The black tops, the *Express* and the *Mail*, backed the Tories. 'Give Blair a bloody nose,' yelled the *Mail*, a headline which acknowledged that the Tories weren't going to win.[87] Most of the qualities, including the *Financial Times* for a third election in a row, supported Labour.

That gave the party a solid advantage in the press, but editorial endorsements were much more qualified than they had been in 1997 and 2001. Many papers wrote of Blair as damaged goods and the lesser of two evils. Reflecting the mood of the general public, there was no yearning for the return of a Tory government, but no enthusiasm for Labour either.

In the final stretch of the campaign, Blair was 'absolutely exhausted' and 'very, very jumpy'.[88] The last two days were 'ghastly' and 'totally Iraq-dominated'.[89] With forty-eight hours to go, much of the media coverage was focused on the young widow of a soldier killed in Basra who personally blamed the Prime Minister for his death. When David Blunkett talked to the Prime Minister, he found Blair worried 'that it was slipping away' and fearing 'he may have lost us an overall majority' because of the war.[90]

Blair's desire to win with a convincing majority was not just driven by a hope that an emphatic victory would smash Michael Howard's style of

Conservatism and draw a line under Iraq. He was as much concerned, if not more, to win a victory that would make him safe from backbench revolt and the predatory Brown.

May the 2nd was a sunny Bank Holiday Monday. The two men began a campaign day together in south London, where they unveiled a poster warning: 'If one in ten Labour voters don't vote, the Tories win.' Blair slipped off his tie to look more relaxed than he felt. Brown kept his tie round his neck. Visiting the Kent marginal of Gillingham, they exchanged compliments. Blair hailed Brown as 'my friend, our Chancellor, a fantastic asset for our country'. Brown urged voters to 'put Tony Blair in Downing Street on Friday'.[91]

Blair strolled over to an ice-cream van to buy a couple of 99s. ''Ere, Gordon!' he said, calling on the other man to get his cornet. Watching the pictures on television, Jonathan Powell wanted to 'throw up'.[92] Others who knew the true state of the relationship laughed.

'You lick my ice cream and I'll lick your ice cream,' chuckled Andrew Turnbull. 'I don't think Blair was much of an ice cream person and Brown certainly wasn't.'[93] Cherie hated to see Brown given co-star status. Her constant refrain was: 'Can't Tony do more things on his own?'[94]

Off camera, the big chill was again descending between the two men. 'In the last week of the campaign, the shutters came down again,' says one of the leading Brownites in election headquarters. 'All conversation stopped.'[95]

Both men were now looking beyond the election. 'It always went cold when Tony was about to become Prime Minister again and Gordon wasn't,' says Philip Gould.[96] They both saw the future – and it hurt. Blair would be manacled to a Chancellor he didn't want and Brown would be back with a Prime Minister he craved to replace.

The view around Blair was that 100 was the benchmark figure for a Labour majority that would permit him to stay for a full third term.[97] A majority of less than fifty would make it very difficult for him to withstand pressure to quit Number 10 much earlier. Majorities in between were a grey area in which anything might happen.

There was the traditional frantic hurtle around the country on the last day which saw Blair and his wife campaign in London, the Midlands, the north-east of England and the west of Scotland. Cherie was insistent that 'she wanted the last day to be her and Tony together.' And no Brown.[98] On the morning of 5 May, the Blairs and their children walked to their local polling station in Sedgefield and then spent the rest of the day at Myrobella. Most of the core of the old gang was there: Alastair Campbell, Sally Morgan and Jonathan

Powell. They were joined by Bruce Grocott, the Labour Chief Whip in the Lords, who'd spent the campaign with Blair. Powell hoped they would use the day to plan a third-term government. But the usual combination of nerves and not wanting to tempt fate meant that this did not happen. Nor could they be sure whether Cabinet ministers in more marginal seats – such as Charles Clarke and Ruth Kelly – were going to hold on.[99] Instead of studying the proposed ministerial changes, a 'gloomy' Blair kept 'pacing around', refusing to believe Grocott's reassurances that it would turn out all right.[100] He obsessed over a list of marginal Labour seats. 'Election night was very tense,' says Sally Morgan, whom Blair 'compelled to make endless phone calls which produced very little information because nobody really knew'.[101]

As it grew darker, the house began to fill with friends and local activists. The gang sat with Blair around the kitchen table. There was soon alarm shading into terror that the election had gone horribly wrong. Morgan was getting word from the counts around the country texted to her mobile phone. Around eight in the evening, she was receiving alarming reports that Labour was staring at defeat in a sweep of key marginals. 'We would have lost our majority. That's how it looked relatively early in the evening.'[102]

There was especially panicking news coming from university seats, where opposition to student tuition fees was costing support, and crucial constituencies in southern England. 'What is it?' Blair demanded. He could 'smell the anxiety' on Morgan. She pretended that nothing was wrong, but the angst on her face gave her away. 'It looks like we've got a few problems,' she said and shared the bleak outlook with the rest of them. Campbell slumped on the table, head in hands, groaning: 'We've lost, we've lost. It's all over.' Blair abruptly picked up his glass of wine, left the kitchen and walked into the garden. The others hurried out to be with him. In the words of one of those who stood shivering with him in the chilly night air: 'It was a pretty grim hour or so.'[103]

Blair started to flagellate himself. 'It's all my fault, it's all my fault,' he muttered repeatedly. He had become a liability because of Iraq. 'I should have resigned.'[104]

On the eve of the invasion of Iraq, he had declared himself prepared to pay the cost of conviction. Neither he nor most of his Government had foreseen that the toll was going to be so steep.

PART TWO

The Price of Ambition
Third Term
2005–2010

19. Sore Winners

By 10 p.m., everyone at Myrobella was clustered around the television set. The moment the polling stations closed, the BBC and ITV released the results of their joint exit poll, which predicted that Labour had 3 per cent more of the vote than the Tories. It also forecast, with an impressive accuracy for which exit polls were not always renowned, that this would translate into a Labour majority of sixty-six seats. Blair remained highly agitated. There were rumours whirling around party headquarters that the exit poll was wrong.[1] Another wind of fear blew through Sedgefield. 'I can't bear it,' said Blair and demanded that the TV be switched off.

There was a further surge of panic around half past midnight when a Tory victory was declared in the south London seat of Putney. 'The first results that came in from London and the south-east were not good. If it had been at that level across the country, if it had been uniform, we would have been in serious trouble.'[2] Another fright occurred when Estelle Morris was wrongly thought to have lost her seat in the west Midlands. Bob Marshall-Andrews, the serially dissident Labour MP for Medway, popped up on TV to incorrectly declare that he had lost his seat. There were cheers at Labour campaign HQ. When he blamed Blair, they booed.[3]

At half past one, a still nervy Prime Minister left Myrobella for his own count in Sedgefield. He was now reasonably confident that Labour had a majority, but unsure of what size. He feared that he would be 'in real trouble' if the majority fell below fifty.[4]

Blair looked utterly shattered when he joined the other candidates on the stage at quarter past two in the morning to hear his constituency result. 'I know Iraq has been a divisive issue, but I hope now we can unite again and look to the future,' he said in flat response. 'It seems as if it is clear that the British people wanted the return of a Labour government with a reduced majority. We have to respond to that sensibly.'[5] His personal majority went up, though the share of the Labour vote decreased. He sounded so deflated it was as if he was the vanquished not the victor.

'He was totally exhausted,' explains one of those with him that night. 'He was still in pain from his back and he was worried that Keys would kick off.'[6]

Reg Keys, whose son had been killed serving with the Royal Military Police in Iraq, stood in Sedgefield as an anti-war, anti-Blair candidate. When it was his turn to speak at the count, the TV cameras captured the frozen features of Blair and Cherie standing behind Keys as he denounced the Prime Minister and demanded that 'he say sorry to the families of the bereaved'.[7]

Cherie looked as though she was close to tears, though they may have been tears of anger when Keys condemned her husband for not visiting wounded soldiers in hospital. Blair had, in fact, made unpublicised visits to some of the wounded and was an assiduous writer of notes to the bereaved.

Blair and his retinue departed to Teeside airport for the flight south. This was a very different plane journey to the one in 1997 when he and Cherie exchanged gasps of amazement as Tory seat after seat tumbled to his landslide. This time Labour was counting its casualties. The most vivid demonstration of the Iraq effect was Oona King's loss of Bethnal Green in London's East End to George Galloway's anti-war Respect Party.

Low clouds of anxiety encased Blair. He remained sunk in pensive silence for much of the plane journey, deadening the atmosphere for those who were in a mood to celebrate. Alan Milburn, who had hitched a ride to London with his partner and children, tried to cheer up the Prime Minister. 'For God's sake, we've won,' said Milburn, trying to shake the other man out of it. 'Three terms. That's fucking awesome.'[8] Yet Milburn had made his own contribution to Blair's depression. He had already told him that he did not want to serve in government again. Once they touched down in London, his Jag whisked the Prime Minister to Labour's victory party at the National Portrait Gallery, overlooking Trafalgar Square. His arrival there at shortly after five in the morning was heralded by yet another blast of 'Beautiful Day', the U2 anthem that Labour had taken as its campaign theme tune. There was some chanting of 'Four more years!'

Yet few there were feeling terribly uplifted that night despite the historic achievement of winning three elections in a row. The Blairites worried that the big reduction in the majority meant their leader's days were now foreshortened. Others could not suppress the feeling that, with a strong economy and record sums going into public services, they would have won another landslide but for the war.

Blair made a few brief remarks to the party. 'There are good comrades who have fallen,' he said, an exceptional use of the c-word from him. 'First time, third term. Let's make the most of it.'[9]

Many previous Prime Ministers would have relished a majority of sixty-six. It was, from one perspective, a remarkable comeback for Blair, who had taken his country into a highly unpopular war with a terrible aftermath and come close to resigning a year earlier. He had inflicted a third successive defeat on the Tories, once the hegemonic party of British politics. Michael Howard announced he would be quitting as Tory leader. There was now something of the goodnight about him. He was the fourth Tory leader to be seen off by New Labour. Blair was indisputably one of the greatest election winners in British history and his party's most electorally successful leader by a long way.

Yet it was also evident from the result that the electoral sorcerer had lost his magic. He knew that his personal authority, which rested so heavily on his ability to win votes, was damaged by the result. His original coalition was fragmented by voter disaffection and pincered from left and right. The haemorrhaging of the Labour vote and the loss of forty-seven seats made it feel like a severe retreat and a very reluctant endorsement after the two back-to-back landslides of 1997 and 2001. Worse still for Labour morale, the Tories had won a larger share of the vote in England and Labour only just clung on by its fingertips in many seats which had now become super-marginals. Only 9.5 million people voted Labour in 2005, 4 million fewer than in 1997.

'We didn't win the 2005 election because people loved us, we won the 2005 election because people were willing to tolerate us and they didn't really fancy the look of the Tory party,' comments Matthew Taylor. 'So we had a hell of a job to do to reconnect with people.'[10]

Under no other system but first-past-the-post would Labour have got anywhere near a parliamentary majority. It had won the election with just 35.2 per cent of the vote, barely more than Neil Kinnock achieved when he went down to defeat in 1992. It was the lowest share for a party winning a majority of parliamentary seats since the 1832 Reform Act. Factoring in the low turn-out, barely one in five of those eligible to vote put a cross beside the name of a Labour candidate.[11] Rarely had Britain returned a government with such a palpable lack of enthusiasm. It was a victory that tasted like defeat.

That was reflected back at Blair in the next morning's headlines. He was the only Prime Minister of modern times other than Margaret Thatcher to win three consecutive terms. Yet the press concentrated on Labour's losses.

'You did give him a bloody nose!' gloated the *Daily Mail*.[12] 'Blair limps back', declared *The Times*.[13] The *Guardian* saw it as a blow to Blair's ambitions to stay at Number 10 for another four years with the interpretation:

'Time is running out'.[14] That was encouraging for Brown and his camp, who 'wanted the spotlight to be on Tony winning by the skin of his teeth'.[15] The press coverage further blackened Blair's mood and amplified his disappointment that he had not won the victory that he hoped for.[16] The next morning, he was asking miserably: 'We did win, didn't we?'[17]

Speaking to the cameras in Downing Street he struck a note of humility rather than celebration: 'I have listened and I have learnt. And I think I have a very clear idea of what the British people now expect from this government for a third term.'[18]

It was a downcast address from a Prime Minister who had just been elected for a third time.

'He didn't look like a newly elected Prime Minister full of the joys of spring. There was no spark,' thought his friend Stephen Byers.[19] 'He was in a very bad place,' according to one of his intimates.[20] Some of his circle tried to gee him up. 'It's a very good result,' Philip Gould endeavoured to encourage Blair. 'If anyone had told us back in 1997 that we were going to win three terms, we would have said they were mad.'[21]

If anything, though, Blair's mood became more occluded in the days immediately after the election. 'It was inevitable that he felt a sense of personal rejection. It took him a bit of time to come out of it, to come to terms with it,' says David Hill. 'After two landslides, he had to psychologically retune himself to the fact that the electorate had changed their view of him.'[22]

The shrinkage of the majority meant tougher battles ahead with his parliamentary party to get through the domestic reforms he had set his sights on as his legacy. 'He thought it weakened him politically in the party,' says Jonathan Powell. 'He was worried about rebellions.'[23] It had been hard enough to get the health and university reforms through the previous Parliament with a majority of more than 160. It would now only require thirty-five of the rebellious or the irreconcilable to combine against him and threaten defeat. Sally Morgan agrees that 'he was worried that it would be harder to do the next stages of reform and was going to affect the ability to govern. He also thought Gordon would come and get him.'[24]

It did not help that some of his allies refused to serve alongside him. Milburn wouldn't come back. 'After everything that had happened, Alan didn't trust Tony to stick up for him.' Stephen Byers also said no.[25] 'The Friends of the Man know the game is almost up,' one senior MP recorded in his diary.[26]

There was a widespread feeling that Labour would not have lost so many seats had Blair given way to Gordon Brown, an idea that was aggressively pumped around the party's bloodstream by the Chancellor's supporters. It became common currency in the media. The *Daily Mail* and the *Guardian* rarely agreed on much, but it was a shared theme of their commentators that Labour owed its salvation to the Chancellor.

Blair thought that a third win would strengthen his hand against Brown and the big beasts of the Cabinet. He found the opposite when he embarked on a reshuffle on Friday morning. He was defied by bolshy ministers at almost every turn. The first showdown was with John Prescott. He had no more managed to make sense of his departmental empire in the second term than he had in the first. Blair wanted to take away communities and local government from Prescott and hand them over to a returning David Blunkett. Prescott blew up into a terrific rage. In the face of his deputy's resistance, Blair backed down. Blunkett was instead resurrected as Work and Pensions Secretary in place of Alan Johnson. He shifted to the DTI, which was rebranded as the Department for Productivity, Energy and Industry, a title rather redolent of the corporatist seventies. As satirists were quick to spot, it could also be turned into the acronym 'PENIS'. A few days later, Johnson protested to Blair that the department was becoming a laughing stock.[27] So the nameplates were all changed back, encouraging the media to treat this as another chaotic Blair reshuffle. Ruth Kelly, a relatively junior member of the Cabinet, dug her heels in when Blair tried to move her out of Education. Peter Hain was aggrieved to be made Northern Ireland Secretary when he had been hoping for something grander. Blair tried to sweeten the posting by remarking: 'You get a castle, you know.'[28] Other ministers refused to move or briefed the press about their disappointment with what they'd been offered.

With hindsight, many at Number 10 felt it would have been better had Blair postponed the reshuffle until he was feeling physically and mentally stronger. 'He was still in incredible pain and he had just gone through the most awful experience,' says Jonathan Powell.[29]

Jack Straw was now regarded with considerable suspicion inside Downing Street, having been sliding into Brown's camp in the eighteen months before the election. Blair toyed with moving Straw from the Foreign Office and replacing him with Charles Clarke. But that was too fidgety even for Blair. Clarke had been Home Secretary for just six months and it made sense to keep Straw where he was for the moment, when there was the Gleneagles Summit and tricky European business immediately ahead.

As always, the most tempestuous and protracted negotiations were with his Chancellor. 'He's gone off to form his Cabinet again,' Brown sourly remarked to Philip Gould. 'Do you know what is in it?'

Brown too was in a post-electoral depression.[30] He believed that he would have won a much better victory for Labour and was maddened by the thought of having to carry on waiting for the premiership. He retreated to his private flat in Great Peter Street with Ed Balls, Spencer Livermore and Sue Nye to wait for Blair to call. 'Tony took a long time to ring Gordon to confirm him as Chancellor.'[31] That further blackened his mood. 'Gordon was genuinely hurt. He had rescued the election. He had surgically attached himself to Tony. He'd said he'd have done the same thing on Iraq. He expected more co-operation.'[32]

When Blair did finally call, he made an astonishing remark that he had only been playing games before the election. 'I'm sorry about all that Alan stuff. I was just messing about. I never meant it to get that serious, Gordon.'[33]

The two men had a running, vicious row over Friday and into the weekend. Blair tried to push a diluted version of the plan to reduce the powers of the Treasury. Brown simply said no; Blair was not strong enough to insist. 'It would never work unless he moved Gordon,' observed the Cabinet Secretary. 'Given the way the campaign had been conducted with them getting double-billing, I never believed for a moment that Blair would be in a position to dictate terms to Brown.'[34] So it proved. Even Jonathan Powell realised that 'after the ice cream, it was impossible.'[35]

Blair wanted to give the job of Chief Treasury Secretary to John Hutton, a former flatmate of Milburn and very Blairite. Brown vetoed Hutton and a series of other candidates proposed by Blair until they eventually compromised on Des Browne.

The Chancellor demanded instant ministerial jobs for Ed Balls and Ed Miliband, who had just been elected as MPs. Blair refused, arguing that it 'wouldn't be good for them'.[36] Brown fought back when the Prime Minister attempted to fire some of the Chancellor's less impressive ministerial acolytes. 'Isn't it at last time to sack Dawn Primarolo?' Blair wearily asked. Brown wasn't having that. 'We fired Dawn Primarolo about ten times,' says Jonathan Powell. 'And every time Gordon insisted we put her back.'[37]

Brown angrily protected his clan. 'It was a case of you take one, you take all,' remarks one of his inner circle.[38]

Brown 'genuinely thought it was going to be a dual premiership' in which Blair would share power for a year or two before ceding Number 10.[39] Most of the Brownites had never taken the idea that Blair would serve a full third term seriously. As it became clear that Blair was not interested in having any conversation about a transition, Brown began to rage about another betrayal.[40]

The Chancellor's team gave aggressive briefings to political journalists that Blair had broken a pre-election promise to consult him about Cabinet appointments. They set about actively trying to undermine the reshuffle.

Blair was going to make Andrew Adonis, the head of his policy unit, a member of the Lords so that he could insert him as the Minister of State at Education in order to drive through the reforms planned for the third term. When Brown got wind of this, his team briefed the press in order to whip up opposition among the many Labour MPs who regarded Adonis with suspicion. The *Observer* reported that Brown was 'fiercely resisting the appointment amid signs that Downing Street was backing down. "Gordon will never let this happen," said one well-placed source.'[41] Adonis had to settle for the lesser rank of Parliamentary Under Secretary. He went on to be a highly effective minister and one whom Brown himself eventually promoted to the Cabinet. Rarely did the infighting about positions have much to do with the quality of the individuals in question. It was all about who wielded the power and was seen to do so. The impression that Brown had a veto over appointments was sapping of Blair's authority. So was the general air of acrimony around the reshuffle. Blair seemed weaker. Brown looked more menacing than ever.

There had not been a true peace between the two men during the election campaign. There had only been an absence of war. The armistice was now over.

'Your time is up,' warned a typical headline that weekend over stories that a growing number of backbenchers were urging the Prime Minister to resign sooner rather than later.[42] Robin Cook was the most prominent of a string of Labour MPs, not all of them predictable names, who went public with demands for Blair to give a date for his departure. They were cheered on by the right-wing press who were pleased to see Labour behaving as if it had lost as well as by some in the left-wing press who wanted Blair out. Cook suggested that Labour should have a new leader by the autumn.[43]

Blair's private response was bitter: 'I have not just gone through four weeks of hell to bugger off in a few months' time.'[44]

His staff noted with distress how the demands for his head from within his own party 'skewed the public perception of a phenomenal third victory and instead of it being described as amazing it was a bit of a crisis'.[45]

Phil Collins joined Number 10 as Blair's principal speech-writer immediately after the election. He found 'a subdued atmosphere. There was a palpable sense of time being short – of there being a deadline.'[46] In the immediate aftermath of the election, there was even some fear that he might be vulnerable to an immediate coup attempt. Anxious not to be caught by surprise while out of the country, Blair cancelled a planned trip to attend the commemorations of VE Day in Moscow, annoying the Russians, who had to make do with John Prescott.

He had gone into the 2005 election campaign believing that he might fulfil his plan to serve a full third term, or something very close to it, and beat Margaret Thatcher to become the longest continuously serving Prime Minister since Lord Liverpool in the early nineteenth century.[47] He was not yet talking to his senior staff about recalibrating his preferred timescale. 'We'll see how the size of the majority works out,' he would say to them, and more darkly: 'We'll see how Gordon behaves.'[48]

Jonathan Powell was on the maximalist end of the spectrum, believing that Blair should be aiming to be around at least until 2008. 'If you promised to do that, you should do it,' Powell argued.[49]

Sally Morgan believes: 'In his head, he thought it was three years rather than two', but she was already doubtful that 'he'd get further than halfway through the parliament'.[50] Matthew Taylor also thought it more realistic to plan for two.[51] Neil Kinnock agreed, telling friends: 'Gordon will go mad if Tony makes him wait three years.'[52]

On Wednesday, 11 May, both men appeared before a meeting of the Parliamentary Labour Party. Blair appealed to the MPs not to 'act like this was a defeat, not a victory'. There was applause and desk-banging from the loyalist majority in the room. Calls for his departure came from some MPs. To his face, Glenda Jackson, the MP for Hampstead and Highgate, declared: 'I was not up against the Tories, I was not up against the Liberal Democrats, I was fighting you. I was told on the doorstep time and again that they cannot vote for me while Tony Blair remains as leader.'

He won a laugh at the expense of Roy Hattersley, the former deputy Labour leader, who had become one of his fiercest critics. 'I was very loyal throughout three defeats,' remarked Blair. 'All I would ask is a bit of loyalty throughout our three victories.' He promised that there would be a 'stable and orderly' transition to a new leader and he would ensure that the party had 'time and space' to elect someone in his place.[53]

This was his first concession that he would not be able to remain as Prime Minister right to the end of the third term. Just as many allies feared when he made his announcement the previous autumn, his authority was being chipped away. 'The moment he had made that statement in 2004 the crack was in the dyke,' says Neil Kinnock.[54] In the words of Alan Milburn, 'the dynamic of demise' had been set by Blair's announcement that he would not fight another election. 'The clock starts ticking. From the start of the third term, the only question that people are asking is: "When are you going?"'[55]

As Blair addressed the MPs, a brooding Brown sat alongside him, staring at the ceiling, rubbing his face and gazing at his watch.

The post-election depression was somewhat lifted at the end of May when the French rejected the European constitution and were then followed by the Dutch. That provided the chance to escape from the commitment to hold a referendum that looked completely unwinnable. Blair was then boosted by a rapturous reception when he visited the European Parliament in June. 'It was a brilliant day. He was like a film star signing autographs for people.'[56] In a compelling speech to the Parliament, Blair challenged the EU to listen to 'the trumpets around the city walls'.[57] The Chancellor was meantime raked with criticism by stinging reports about the maladministration of his tax credits.[58]

In the early summer, Gordon Brown came round to Number 10 for a conversation which managed to remain civil. 'What is the plan?' the Chancellor asked the Prime Minister. Blair handed him a document setting out Number 10's schedule for how they should time and sell their third-term legislative agenda.

Brown didn't bother looking at it and demanded: 'Yes, but what is the plan?'

Blair smiled impishly and succumbed to the temptation to wind up the other man. 'Oh, you mean: when am I planning to go?'

'No,' protested Brown, shaking his head as if Blair's departure was the last thing on his mind. 'No, no, no.'[59]

20. Rules of the Game

Waiting to greet the Prime Minister at Singapore airport was Sebastian Coe, the gold medallist who was leading the British bid for the Olympics.

'I just need a quiet word,' said Coe and they went into a little room at the terminal.

'I've got some good news and some bad news,' announced Coe. Blair said he'd like the good news first. 'We could win this,' replied Coe. Blair smiled: 'You can be honest with me.' 'No,' responded Coe. 'I really think we can actually win this.' Blair then asked: 'What's the bad news?' Now Coe smiled: 'It's down to you.'[1]

Blair started out a sceptic about launching a British bid to host the 2012 Games. Everyone was burnt by New Labour's previous entanglements with expensive glamour projects: the fiascos of the Millennium Dome and Wembley Stadium. Those planning a London bid were frustrated that 'we couldn't get a decision out of them.'[2]

Two women were instrumental in converting the Prime Minister. One was his wife, who had a lifelong love of athletics. The other was the Culture Secretary, Tessa Jowell. 'Just tell me how you answer this question,' Jowell challenged the Prime Minister when they debated whether to back a bid. 'We're the fourth-biggest economy in the world, we're a nation which loves sport and London is one of the world's great cities. And we don't dare bid for the Olympics?' He looked at her: 'I see what you mean.'[3]

Jowell's enthusiasm was in defiance of the Permanent Secretary and other senior officials at her department, who were against the Games on the grounds of the risk and the cost. There were also many doubters in the Cabinet when the bid came before ministers in May 2003. David Blunkett was 'very sceptical' and John Reid was 'dead against it', but they didn't say so aloud because they were allies of Blair and Jowell. 'Those were the days when the Blairites could organise eight votes in the Cabinet.'[4]

Gordon Brown feared a repeat of those earlier expensive debacles, but he didn't attempt to veto the Games. He was afraid that Number 10 would spin against him and cast the Chancellor as the killjoy who stopped Britain from hosting the Games.[5] The Treasury signed off on the bid without subjecting the costings to forensic examination. Everyone assumed that this was a race that Britain was entering for show without any expectation of winning. Ken Livingstone, the Mayor of London, thought at the beginning that 'it was a very long shot.'[6] Blair did not really focus on the Olympic bid until the summer of 2004, when Cherie persuaded him to go to the Athens Games. It was after that, Coe believed, that they finally had the Prime Minister fully engaged. When the evaluation team from the International Olympic Committee made its visit to London, Blair spent quite a lot of time with them, the better to convince the IOC that the bid had the full-blooded support of the Government. He also locked in backing from the Tories and Lib Dems.

Coe, a Tory peer as well as a celebrated Olympian, was chosen as chairman of the London bid. Livingstone was also giving energetic support. The Tory lord and Labour Mayor were enthusiasts for different reasons. For Coe, winning the bid would be a glorious addition to his sporting achievements. For Livingstone, who had no interest in sport at all, the Olympics was a means of 'getting billions for London' out of Government for transport and regeneration in east London.[7] The zeal of both men helped to fuel Blair's enthusiasm. By spring 2005, the Prime Minister had entirely conquered his earlier hesitation. 'He got religion about the Olympics,' says Blair's communications chief, David Hill. 'By the end, he really wanted it.'[8]

The competition would be settled at a meeting of the International Olympic Committee in Singapore in the first week of July 2005. There were all sorts of reasons why Blair should not fly out. He was hosting the G8 at Gleneagles in the same week. If he went and Britain was beaten, as seemed the most likely outcome, he would look like a loser. Paris were the favourites. That raised the threat of being worsted by his old rival, Jacques Chirac.

There were similar debates throughout his premiership and it was Blair's habitual response to throw caution to the winds. 'He is one of the most instinctive politicians I have ever known,' a senior civil servant remarked. 'He just hurls himself at things.'[9] Blair resolved the arguments between his aides by declaring that he would fly to Singapore, a decision that was even more emphatic once it was known that Chirac was planning to go to the Far East.

After being greeted by Coe, Blair and his party were driven to the Raffles Hotel, where the Prime Minister immediately switched into campaign mode. Coe's 'incredibly professional'[10] team lined up IOC delegates outside Blair's suite to come in at ten- to fifteen-minute intervals. 'He just did it, hour after hour.'[11] In the whirl of lobbying, there was the occasional mix-up. A Czech skater and a Norwegian skier turned up in the wrong order. Blair tried to impress the Czech with his admiration for Norway. Realising the mistake, one of the team in the room dropped a loud hint: 'What's the weather like at this time of the year in Czechoslovakia?'[12]

In the forty-eight hours Blair spent in Singapore, he held more than thirty face-to-face meetings with IOC delegates selected by Coe's team for schmoozing by the Prime Minister because they were regarded as especially influential or potential swing voters. In the admiring estimation of Tessa Jowell, who was out in Singapore with Blair, 'he's pure rock star in circumstances like these.'[13] This was Blair doing what he did best: charming, persuading, never bullying, subtly working on the delegates that Coe identified as crucial. Ken Livingstone thought: 'Blair's lobbying was absolutely essential. He was on top form. What I found impressive was that he was willing to be part of the team. How many world leaders would say: "What do you want me to do?" and then go and do it?'[14] Cherie – 'absolutely brilliant' in Singapore in the estimation of Blair's staff[15] – arrived on the Monday and was deployed as another ambassador for the bid. One reason Blair 'threw himself into it in such a frenzy' was that he felt 'guilty' that he had to leave before the vote in order to get back for the G8.[16]

Officials in the rival French team became increasingly nervous that Jacques Chirac was only deigning to arrive two days after Blair. The French became more worried when they spotted that delegates were still streaming out of Blair's suite as they were taking themselves to bed. When he did turn up, Chirac 'blundered in conveying an air of utter self-importance'.[17] He grandly decided that lobbying delegates was beneath him. According to a French official, he 'did not want to be seen grubbing for votes, and wanted to appear more presidential than Blair'.[18] That was a massive miscalculation. So was the impression of French hauteur created by Chirac's dismissive attitude towards other European nations. The week before, he declared that British cuisine was 'the worst after Finland's'. That didn't win France any friends among the Finns.[19]

The presentation on behalf of Paris was dominated by middle-aged men in suits. Much better designed to appeal to this multi-national jury was a London bid which projected Britain's capital as a young, vibrant, multicultural and multi-ethnic city. Alain Danet, a French member of the IOC, later conceded that the British 'message was so much more seductive than the image France portrayed'.[20]

In a speech recorded by Blair which was played to IOC members just before the vote, he hailed London as 'a global platform for the Olympic message to young people. Not just for the seventeen days of the competition, but for the years leading up to the Games and beyond.'[21]

By the time the delegates watched this pre-recorded speech, he was already fast asleep on-board his 777, flying back to Britain for the G8. London had moved from outsiders to serious contenders. 'You may just have made the difference,' Coe told Blair shortly before he left. But the Prime Minister and his party returned to Britain still thinking they hadn't won it.[22]

Early on the morning of Wednesday, 6 July, the 777 landed in Scotland. The venue of the G8 was the Gleneagles Hotel, an elite golf resort set in 850 acres of gorgeous Highland scenery. The stunning views were not the main reason it was chosen for the summit. It was also regarded as a location that could be well guarded from both terrorists and protestors.

With the result of the IOC vote anticipated at lunchtime, a vast crowd gathered in Trafalgar Square in front of a huge screen relaying pictures from the ceremony in the Far East. Many other Britons were watching and listening on TVs and radios. Most of the Prime Minister's party at Gleneagles were clustered around David Hill, who had a portable radio with him. He was shouting out the results of the preliminary rounds: 'New York's down! Moscow's down! Madrid's down!'[23] That put London into the final with Paris.

Blair was displaying his idiosyncratic aversion to listening to the radio or watching television when something important was at stake. He and Jonathan Powell remained apart from the others. They stood in the main conference room with the doors open looking out on to the gardens.

At ten to one in Britain, ten to eight in Singapore, the President of the IOC, Jacques Rogge, appeared on the podium to announce the result. 'The Games of the thirtieth Olympiad in 2012 are awarded to the city of . . .' Rogge paused to squeeze maximum dramatic effect from the announcement. '. . . London!' The crowd in Trafalgar Square went wild, as did Coe's team in the Far East. Powell's mobile rang with a call from SWITCH, the legendary phone operators at Number 10.

'I think this will be the news we didn't want to hear,' said the Chief of Staff. 'We've won!' yelled the excited switchboard operator.[24] Blair punched the air and gripped Powell's arm. They did not embrace. 'We didn't do hugs,' says Powell.[25]

Blair danced out into the garden and started to jig around on the lawn, leaving Powell thinking: 'For Christ's sake, what if the cameras see him?'[26]

It was a very close victory over Paris, by a margin of just four votes, which made Blair's personal intervention look even more crucial. Jowell believed 'we wouldn't have won if he hadn't come out to Singapore.'[27] Coe, Livingstone and many neutral observers agreed.[28] So did the French. The Mayor of Paris, Bertrand Delanoe, paid a bitter compliment to his rivals by complaining that his team was outmanoeuvred. 'We should have gone to war, like the British did.'[29]

Once the initial triumphalism wore off, this victory would look more tarnished. The original costings of the British bid were hopelessly unrealistic. Jowell had to deny that the figures were dreamed up on the back of an envelope when no-one expected Britain to win. The bid ignored the findings of a confidential 250-page expert report, drawn up by her department and the Number 10 strategy unit, that the Games would not produce significant economic gains nor inspire more people to play sport.[30] There were endless rows between Jowell and the Treasury about funding. This author was among those sceptics who long argued that the five-ring circus was a fabulously expensive folly whose legacy threatened to be like that of previous Games: unused facilities and huge debts.[31]

But the doubters were drowned out by the joy of the many enthusiasts on the day that the bid was won. For many Britons, it was a glorious 6th of July. There was 'a terrific sense of elation' recalls one senior civil servant at Gleneagles.[32] For Tony Blair, it was an important tonic. 'Those two days showed him at his best. He had put an enormous amount of personal energy into it and I think it made the difference,' says Sally Morgan. 'It was a crowning moment.'[33] After his battering during the election campaign and his depression with the result, this victory boosted both his self-confidence and his public standing. He punted with his personal prestige in Singapore and the gamble was handsomely rewarded.

The next morning he woke up early and in good spirits. The press was fantastic, much the best Blair had received in years. The *Sun* celebrated 'Our heroes'. At the top of its list, the currant bun put Tony Blair, 'who made a huge impact'.[34] Even his enemies at the *Daily Mail* gave him 'full credit'.[35] The *Daily Telegraph* commented: 'It would be churlish not to acknowledge that Mr Blair has the qualities of a great statesman.'[36]

The Prime Minister's mood was further lifted by the weather at Gleneagles. Thursday, 7 July was a bright, sunny day in Scotland. After breakfast, he went for a stroll around the hotel gardens accompanied by George Bush, who offered his congratulations on the success of the London bid. The summit would formally open in a couple of hours and there were still big obstacles to agreement. The British had set ambitious goals for the G8 to make progress on both climate change and financial relief for Africa. Blair set the bar high 'despite a very clear recognition that they were going to be very unpopular issues with the Americans,' says Sir Michael Jay, the Permanent Secretary at the Foreign Office.[37]

As Blair and Bush walked and talked in the secure Perthshire countryside,

London's tubes and buses were heaving with rush hour travellers, some of them nursing hangovers from the Olympic celebrations. At Luton railway station, four young men intoxicated with fanaticism joined the commuters bound for the capital.

At a quarter to nine in the morning, Blair and Bush came in from the gardens. By now, the quartet of suicide bombers was in the capital. The Prime Minister headed for a reception room at the front of the hotel for a pre-summit bilateral with the President of China.

Five minutes later, there were simultaneous explosions on three underground trains on the Northern line. London had joined New York, Bali, Istanbul and Madrid as the target for indiscriminate slaughter.

Jonathan Powell, David Hill and Tom Kelly, upstairs in a first-floor hotel room, were alerted by the rolling news on Sky. Almost immediately, Number 10 was on the line to confirm that there had been explosions. The cause of them was unknown. 'There was real confusion. It was maybe gas, maybe terrorist.'[38]

As things became a little clearer, Kelly dashed downstairs and broke into the Prime Minister's meeting to hand him a note saying it looked like terrorism. The Chinese President readily agreed when Blair told him he had to cut the meeting short. The Prime Minister came out looking grim. 'It was always in the back of his mind, in the back of everyone's mind, that something like this was going to happen.'[39]

After a brief debate with Powell and his press advisers, Blair decided they had too little information to make an immediate broadcast to the nation. That might simply cause a panic.[40] George Bush emerged from his suite to find out what was going on. He then retreated back into his rooms for a video conference call with security officials in America, where he asked whether there were any indications of an imminent attack on commuters in the United States.[41]

A little less than an hour later, another bomb exploded, this time on the number 30 bus as it was making its way around Tavistock Square. This was a deadlier attack than had ever been managed by the IRA even at the height of the Provos' bombing campaign of the 1970s. Londoners had not lost their lives to bombs in such numbers since the Second World War.

Blair proceeded with the official opening of the summit, greeting the other leaders as they came into the conference room, twenty minutes of the stilted formalities of an international talkfest contrasting with the bloody mayhem on and below the streets of London.

The leaders had just started to discuss the global economy when Blair received confirmation that it was definitely a major terrorist attack in the style of al-Qaeda.[42] In real time and without benefit of much advice, the eight leaders had to decide what to do in an emergency. The meeting descended into mild chaos as the leaders piled in with contradictory advice for Blair. The ineffable Silvio Berlusconi declared that the Prime Minister should immediately fly south and 'all of us should go with you' in a display of solidarity. That would have been a security nightmare: bringing every leader of the G8 to a capital in which the police were already stretched to maximum capacity coping with terrorist atrocities and unsure whether there were more to come. George Bush made a sensible intervention to that effect, saying: 'You go, Tony. We'll stay here.' Jacques Chirac, for once in tune with the instincts of the American President, agreed that it would be both dangerous and silly for them all to decamp to London. One senior official present thought that Blair, Bush and Chirac stood out as the three leaders who knew 'instinctively' how to respond.[43]

The Cabinet had just started meeting in London under the chairmanship of John Prescott when it got news of the explosions. The meeting was hastily abandoned. Charles Clarke, the Home Secretary, and other relevant ministers hurried down to the basement and along the tunnel into COBRA. The windowless room was soon fully occupied by all the key players except Blair himself. Along with Clarke and Prescott there was Patricia Hewitt, the Health Secretary, and the Transport Secretary, Alistair Darling. Ian Blair, the Commissioner of the Metropolitan Police, came over from Scotland Yard and they were also joined by Eliza Manningham-Buller and Sir John Scarlett, the heads of MI5 and MI6.

Details about the exact scale of the atrocities and the casualty numbers were still very foggy, not least because three of the explosions were underground. 'There was massive uncertainty about what had actually happened,' Clarke later reflected.[44] Their first fear was that it might not just be London, but many other British cities too, which was under attack. With relief, they received a report from the London fire brigade that there seemed to be no evidence that it was a chemical or biological attack. But they would not be able to begin a rescue until atmospheric samples were analysed to be absolutely sure. Off-duty nurses and doctors were already coming in to hospitals to help with the casualties. There was a brief squabble between the ministers about whether they should call an immediate news conference. Prescott won the argument by saying they didn't have enough answers to the inevitable questions. 'We don't even know whether it is over yet,' he pointed out.[45]

Blair was then connected to COBRA by conference call. Clarke told him that they were now pretty certain that there had been several explosions and that it was a concerted terrorist attack. 'We can handle it,' he told the Prime Minister. If Blair didn't want to abandon the G8, he did not need to. But it was his advice, said the Home Secretary, that the Prime Minister should come back to London.[46] This chimed with Blair's own instinct always to be seen taking personal charge of a crisis.

Up in Gleneagles, he appeared before the cameras at midday. He was flanked, in a show of unity, by the presidents and prime ministers, supplemented by more heads of state and government from the 'plus 5' who had been invited to the summit. As usual, Blair placed most emphasis on the will to defeat terrorism. His consistent theme since 9/11 was echoed again on what became known as 7/7.

Our determination to defend our values and our way of life is greater than their determination to cause death and destruction to innocent people in a desire to impose extremism on the world. Whatever they do, it is our determination that they will never succeed in destroying what we hold dear in this country and in other civilised nations throughout the world.[47]

Jack Straw was 'told to get in a helicopter' to go to Scotland.[48] Michael Jay took the chair – 'Help!' he messaged other officials – in the interregnum between Straw's arrival and Blair's departure. Though the Prime Minister hated travelling by helicopter, speed was of the essence and so was security. He used two choppers to get him back to London, one from Gleneagles to Dundee airport. From RAF Northolt he was then choppered to the Chelsea barracks as the fastest practicable way to get him into central London.[49] By mid-afternoon, he was back in Downing Street for a reconvened COBRA. In the eyes of his Chief of Staff: 'He was always good in a crisis. When there was no crisis, he could be fuzzy and all over the place. In a crisis, he gets steely and gets things under control rather than floundering around.'[50]

The meeting discussed how the emergency services were coping with the bombings and what contingency arrangements were in hand to deal with the further attacks that they feared. As the day progressed, the death toll became clearer. The four bombers had killed fifty-two people as well as themselves. Some 700 people were injured, many of them very seriously. The emergency response was generally magnificent and vindication of the contingency planning done since 9/11. They had practised 'every conceivable war game', says Ken Livingstone, including ones which envisaged multiple attacks on transport coinciding with the Prime Minister being away, the Mayor of London killed and Scotland Yard demolished. 'The response was designed so it would work even in a decapitation scenario.'[51]

When COBRA broke up, Blair delivered another statement, his third of the day, this one outside Number 10. He declared that 'we will not be divided and our resolve will hold firm.' There would be 'the most intensive action to make sure we bring those responsible to justice'.[52] He did not know yet that those responsible had blown themselves up too.

In the late afternoon he called in at the operations centre at Scotland Yard, a visit without much practical purpose, but it did allow him to thank the police and be seen thanking them by the television cameras. After a debate with his aides, it was decided that he should not visit any of the locations of the atrocities on the grounds that this 'would give the terrorists the pictures they wanted'.[53]

Then he flew back up to Gleneagles, tired and by now very hungry, to deliver his fourth statement of the day. Against a background of flags flying at half-mast, he declared that the summit would go on. 'Here the world's leaders are striving to combat world poverty and save and improve life. The perpetrators of today's attacks are intent on destroying human life.'[54]

It was never established how strongly the G8 summit featured in the minds of the bombers when they planned the attacks. Paradoxically, this atrocity helped to make a success of Gleneagles by creating an aura of gravity and injecting a sense of urgency. There were serious fears within Number 10 beforehand that the summit might fall laughably below the expectations Blair had raised for it. 'We could crash and burn and very publicly,' Sir Nigel Sheinwald, his foreign affairs adviser, had warned the Prime Minister.[55] The Americans were difficult throughout the pre-summit process. Their regular refrain was: 'Don't think we owe you just because of Iraq.'[56] During a business dinner between the British and US pre-summit negotiating teams two weeks before Gleneagles, 'the American sherpas were just blocking everything.'[57] Michael Jay made an appeal to the Americans which was untypically passionate for a senior mandarin. 'Think of your children! What will your children think if you don't do this?' the head of the diplomatic corps proclaimed, flourishing a text on financial assistance for Africa so vigorously that he waved the document too close to a candle and it went up in flames. The head of the American delegation sardonically remarked: 'Pity it wasn't the climate change text as well.'[58]

The Make Poverty History campaign pushed the G8 leaders to make commitments on aid and write off debt for Africa. The terror attacks amplified the pressure on the leaders to display a united front. 'They were all frightened that they were going to be accused of failure,' noted one official.[59] Jacques Chirac was 'unbelievably gentlemanly' despite his loss of the Olympics. Not so Gerhard Schröder, who still hated Blair because of Iraq. When Blair returned to Gleneagles, his officials briefed him that they still hadn't secured the aid agreement. Blair went down to the hotel bar where Schröder was drinking with Vladimir Putin. 'Tony got him up against the wall and twisted his arm.'[60]

The debts of the world's fifteen poorest nations were entirely wiped out, saving them an annual interest bill of around $1.5 billion. Gordon Brown had worked very productively on that for weeks. 'You see how good he can be,' Blair remarked to one of his aides.[61] In the estimation of one senior official who closely observed both of them: 'Gordon and Tony were a brilliant double-act. Gordon got everyone lined up into position for the summit and then Tony finished it off. Tony really pushed Bush over the line.'[62] This showed what could be achieved when Brown's technical skills and Blair's advocacy were combined in the same cause, though it didn't stop some unseemly spinning by their rival entourages about which of them most deserved the credit. The British also tried to set up mechanisms to ensure that the G8 lived up to its commitments to double aid. That was less successful. While Britain made good on its pledges, others did not. What it is fair to say is that this G8 had much more meaningful product than most summits.

That extraordinary seventy-two hours, from the euphoria of the Olympic victory on the Wednesday to the atrocities in London on the Thursday to the signing ceremony at Gleneagles on the Friday, encapsulated many of the features of Blair's premiership. He displayed his lobbying skills at their most charming in Singapore, he cunningly corralled reluctant foreign leaders into signing up to the pledges at Gleneagles, and he then deployed his oratorical talents at their most unifying in the wake of the London bombings. He always looked and sounded impressive in a crisis. 'It reminded everyone that he was fantastically good at being Prime Minister,' says Phil Collins. 'The rumblings against him disappeared for a while. There was a feeling that he'd bought himself some more time.'[63]

The national mood in the immediate wake of 7/7 was as Blair hoped it would be. Few Londoners were scared off the streets, though sales of bicycles surged as people became nervous of the tube. There was a lot of tabloid talk about London displaying a defiant 'Blitz spirit'.

This wasn't likely to last and it didn't. Three of the killers were from Leeds and Dewsbury in Yorkshire. The fourth was from Aylesbury in Buckinghamshire. There was widespread horror at the discovery that these were not foreign terrorists, but Britain's first home-grown suicide bombers. Blair had, as usual, framed the conflict as one between barbarity and civilisation. Yet it was his 'civilised society' of Britain that produced four young men prepared to kill themselves in order to commit mass murder.

It also undermined an element of his case for the conflicts in Afghanistan and Iraq. Those wars had not, it seemed to many, made Britain any safer from Islamist extremism. It had, many thought, rendered Britain less secure. The truth was that al-Qaeda had been committing atrocities long before the toppling of the Taliban and the invasion of Iraq, but emotion was more powerful than chronology for many of Blair's critics.

Exactly a fortnight after 7/7, the menace of suicide bombing returned to the capital. Four more bombers attempted to replicate the first atrocity. Though this attack was foiled, the attempt to repeat the earlier devastation greatly increased apprehension about terrorism. The streets of the city howled with police sirens. Ugly concrete blocks were hastily erected outside prominent public buildings. On the 22nd, anti-terror officers put five bullets into the head of Jean Charles de Menezes, an innocent Brazilian electrician, at Stockwell tube station. The Metropolitan Police outraged civil liberties groups and Labour MPs when it was slow to confess to its mistake and prevaricated over an apology. For Blair's critics, vocal once again, Jean Charles de Menezes joined the fifty-two innocents killed on 7/7 as casualties of his misconceived war on terror.

His characteristic response was to propose another slew of anti-terror law, which predictably courted even more opposition. After 21/7, Blair shifted into demotic gear. This was a response to the tabloids who were running noisy campaigns depicting Britain as a lawless haven for extremists and its capital as 'Londonistan'. It was also an attempt to control the public mood. 'I can sense that people are getting angry,' he explained. 'I have to respond.'[64] As one of his advisers puts it: 'He did feel instinctively that things needed to be done. He also feared that the media and the Opposition were about to turn on the Government and say "it's all your fault." He wanted to forestall that.'[65]

In early August, at a hurriedly arranged news conference at Number 10 held just before he left Britain for his summer holiday, Blair declared: 'Let no-one be in any doubt, the rules of the game are changing.'[66] He listed a 'twelve point' anti-terror plan of varying practicality and effectiveness. The Home Secretary would that day be publishing 'new grounds for deportation and exclusion' of those implicated in inciting extremism. After suggestions that preachers of hate might even be tried using fourteenth-century treason laws, Omar Bakri Mohammed fled to the Lebanon. No-one was entirely sure how the Prime Minister actually intended to deal with the rest. Both the abruptness and the content of the statement caught Charles Clarke and the Home Office by surprise.[67] The Labour chairman of the Home Affairs select committee, John Denham, remarked that many of the proposals were 'half-baked'.[68] That was generous: some of them weren't even quarter-baked.

While the Home Office tried to work out which could be implemented and which would have to be quietly abandoned, the Prime Minister took off for a holiday in Barbados at Sir Cliff Richard's Sugar Hills mansion.

When Charles Clarke first met a young Tony Blair when they were both party activists in Hackney, the future Prime Minister struck the future Home Secretary as a 'classic liberal Labour lawyer'.[69] He came across the same way to Jack Straw.[70]

In his first term, Blair introduced the Human Rights Act and legislated for freedom of information. This had been used to embarrass him by compelling the Government to publish details of things such as his dinner guests at Chequers. There was chortling at the revelation that these included Michael Winner and Joan Collins. 'Remind me, whose idea was that?' Blair would remark sourly about freedom of information. Privately he would sometimes even describe it as his worst mistake as Prime Minister.[71] As for the Human Rights Act, he routinely railed against the restraints it placed on dealing with terror suspects.

Already drifting in an authoritarian direction in his first term, in his second and third he accelerated along that trajectory. His Cabinet Secretary, Andrew Turnbull, is in no doubt: 'He got more authoritarian from 9/11 onwards.'[72]

Matthew Taylor agrees: 'I don't think there's any question that over Tony Blair's time in office he became more authoritarian.'[73] Phil Collins found that 'Tony was getting really hardcore' by the third term.[74]

MI5 briefed him that there could be 500 or more Islamist terrorists waiting to strike.[75] When Blair inquired why they couldn't be rounded up, he was exasperated to be told that there was not sufficient evidence to do so under the law as it stood. He would regularly explode with frustration that the law didn't allow him to simply throw out foreign nationals suspected of terrorism. 'This is ridiculous!' he would erupt. 'The public will never understand why we can't get rid of them.'[76]

He was absolutely right that there was a very serious threat. In February 2003, MI5 detected an al-Qaeda plot to fire ground-to-air missiles on airliners as they took off from Heathrow. This was far from incredible: such an attack had already taken place in Kenya. In a spectacular bungle, light tanks were deployed to Heathrow. There were bitter recriminations within Whitehall about the failure to catch those terrorists who were tipped off that their conspiracy was blown.

In March 2004, another plot was exposed, its potential targets ranging from the huge Bluewater shopping centre in Kent to the Ministry of Sound nightclub in London. Five men were later jailed for life.

A great deal more money was poured into both MI5 and the anti-terror units of the police. The intelligence-led approach to the threat was success-ful. At least twenty separate plots to commit atrocities in Britain were detected and prevented by the intelligence services and the police during Blair's premiership.[77] Given the scale of the threat, and the murderous deter-mination of this form of terrorism, it could be considered near miraculous that, between 2001 and 2009, the only plot to succeed was 7/7.

Much less convincing was the case for the increasingly draconian, highly contentious and often ineffective legislation introduced by the Government. A lot of it wasn't even wanted by those hunting the terrorists, and all of it sucked power to the state and its agents at the expense of the individual.

Britain became the most watched society on the planet. It had a fifth of the earth's CCTV cameras covering less than one hundredth of the world's population. The number of organisations permitted to legally use invasive surveillance grew from nine in 2000 when the legislation was first passed to nearly 800 by 2009. Use of the powers was no longer confined to the investigation of serious crimes. Councils were even using them to spy on dog owners who didn't clean up after their pets and to see if people were lying about where they lived for school catchment areas.

The Government struggled to make headway with its arguments to intro-duce ID cards. In the meantime, it built the largest DNA database in the world, far larger than its American equivalent. The data of 4 million people had been captured by 2009. They included both children and many people innocent of any crime.[78]

At the party conference that autumn, Walter Wolfgang, an 82-year-old lifelong Labour member, was grabbed by stewards and ejected for having the temerity to mildly heckle the Foreign Secretary's speech. Both Jack Straw and Tony Blair had to offer him apologies.

'Blair's police state' became a regular refrain of his opponents, especially when surveillance and anti-terror powers were abused and deployed against protestors who had nothing to do with terrorism. Britain was not 'a police state'. The very fact that people were free to say it was proved that it wasn't. What was true was that no British government since 1945 had taken so many powers to monitor and intrude into its citizens' lives.

A continual problem was what to do with foreign terror suspects against whom there was not enough evidence for a trial and who could not be deported back to countries where they would be at risk of torture. The first large piece of anti-terrorism legislation was rushed on to the statute book in the wake of 9/11 in October 2001. Key planks of it were then overthrown by the Law Lords in December 2004. The judges ruled that the Government breached the European Convention on Human Rights by jailing nine foreign suspects in Belmarsh high-security prison, where they had been held without trial since 2001.

Blair responded by expressing 'mounting impatience with judges for constantly telling him what he couldn't do and never saying what he could do'. The Prime Minister would regularly steam to officials: 'Here I am trying to protect the country and they won't let me lock up or deport these people.'[79]

Blair was contemptuous of the Law Lords' ruling. In the words of his Home Secretary: 'Tony got very frustrated by the way that lawyers simply looked at the letter of the law rather than at the overall national position for which he bore responsibility. Over time, he became less sympathetic to the lawyerist arguments.'[80]

Matthew Taylor agrees: 'Tony was consistently confronted with the fact that the criminal justice system wasn't working and it wasn't addressing the really difficult issues. Over time that just made him feel: "Actually, I've just got to do whatever needs to be done."'[81]

The Law Lords' ruling led to the introduction of 'control orders' which created a form of house arrest. Terror suspects were restricted in where they could go and whom they could meet. This neither satisfied Blair, especially when suspects subsequently absconded, nor his critics among civil libertarians, who pointed out that it undermined the presumption of innocence and the right to a fair trial.

The Prime Minister's wife was one of those concerned about the direction in which he was headed. In a speech that summer, Cherie said: 'It is all too easy for us to respond to terror in a way which undermines our most deeply held values and convictions and which cheapens our right to call ourselves a civilised nation.'[82]

That argument had no traction on her husband. He returned from his August holiday determined to overrule the doubts of the Home Office and the opposition of the many who thought he had become completely cavalier about the principles of justice. The Queen's Speech of 2005 produced yet more legislation of an authoritarian flavour. Blair had always been obsessed with crime as an influence on voters' allegiances. He 'got into a funk' about anti-social behaviour and binge drinking which was 'led by the politics of it'.[83] He also became frustrated by what he saw as the liberalism of the Sentencing Guidance Council.

'Why can't we get a grip on them?' he complained to his aides. Matthew Taylor had to point out that the Government had invented the Council. 'Oh, bloody hell,' groaned Blair.

More than 3,600 new criminal offences were put on the statute book during New Labour's time in office and the prison population reached record levels. As a satirical joke, Phil Collins wrote a memo proposing that everyone should start life in prison and have to work their way out. Blair quipped: 'That's a great idea.'[84]

The central proposal of the latest anti-terror legislation was to permit the detention of suspects without trial for up to ninety days, a huge increase on the existing fourteen-day limit, which was already one of the longest in the democratic world. The Prime Minister claimed the support of the police, but the only senior officer to really argue the case for it was his namesake, Sir Ian Blair, the commissioner of the Metropolitan Police, and he later finessed his position.

Ninety days had not been asked for by the intelligence services. They were, in fact, privately against detention without trial for such a long period. The head of MI5, Eliza Manningham-Buller, was the opposite of a hand-wringing liberal. A robust, commonsense, 'no bullshitting'[85] intelligence veteran, she was her father's daughter and his soubriquet was 'Bullying Manner'. She saw the ninety-day legislation as counter-productive, fearing that it would make it harder to gather intelligence from within an alienated Muslim community. Her opposition would remain secret until she retired from the service.

Charles Clarke and his Permanent Secretary, John Gieve, were sceptical, not least because they were very doubtful from the start that it could be got through Parliament.[86] Both the Attorney-General, Peter Goldsmith, and the Lord Chancellor, Charlie Falconer, were opposed to ninety-day detention. The Chief Whip, Hilary Armstrong, warned Number 10 that she simply didn't have the numbers to get it through the Commons. 'We knew we were going to get hammered.'[87] Blair's senior staff 'never thought we were going to win'.[88]

Brinkmanship was becoming a more pronounced streak in Blair's character. He ignored the fears of the head of MI5, the opposition of the Lord Chancellor, the apprehensions of his whips' office and the concerns of the Home Office. He pulled the rug from underneath Clarke's attempts to find a compromise with the Opposition parties and swept aside suggestions from his own aides that they should settle for sixty or forty-five days.

The moment of truth came on Wednesday, 9 November, and it was clear by now that Blair had over-reached. The whips nevertheless made a frenzied effort to get as many Labour MPs as they could into the 'yes' lobby even if it meant calling senior ministers back from abroad. The day before the vote, Gordon Brown was on his way to the airport to fly to Israel. The Chief Whip called him with a warning that he might have to return. From Heathrow, the Chancellor rang up his Tory opposite number, George Osborne. Brown wanted a 'pairing arrangement'. When MPs from opposing parties are 'paired', both agree not to vote, thus cancelling each other out.

Osborne was in Pizza Express having dinner with David Cameron when Brown called. 'George, it's Gordon. Just confirming that we're paired.' The Shadow Chancellor responded that he had already twice told Brown's office that he couldn't be paired for this vote. That set Brown off. He raged down the phone: 'I've never heard anything more ridiculous in the twenty-two years I've been in Parliament!'[89] Brown flew on to Israel. Within minutes of landing, he was told he would have to come back. He fumed to his team that the Government could not carry on like this.[90] His return would make no difference anyway.

Blair arrived in the Commons for Prime Minister's Questions at noon on the day of the vote already aware that he was heading for the first major parliamentary defeat of his premiership. He defiantly told MPs: 'Sometimes it is better to lose and do the right thing than to win and do the wrong thing.'[91]

That exemplified how office changed him. The pre-Iraq Tony Blair never believed there was anything to be said in favour of losing. Losing was for losers. Here he was deliberately courting defeat.

The Government lost by 323 votes to 290. A total of 49 Labour MPs voted with the Opposition. A compromise of twenty-eight days, a deal that Blair could have embraced much earlier and emerged looking like a winner, was passed. At twenty-eight days Britain would still have the longest period of detention without charge in the Western world.[92]

When the tellers read out the results, Blair gave a theatrical shake of his head. 'They'll live to regret this,' he muttered.[93]

In terms of political positioning, Blair calculated that he was in the correct place. He believed he was outflanking the Tories by making himself look tougher on terror. No-one would be able to point the finger in his direction and say he hadn't done all he could to stop terrorism. Opinion polls suggested the public were much readier than MPs or judges to support detention for ninety days. Blair later condemned Parliament for being 'deeply irresponsible', speaking less like a Prime Minister operating in the environment of a parliamentary system of government and more as an American President might scorn an obstructive Congress.[94] He had regularly detached himself from his party. He was now seeking definition from his opposition to Parliament. Aides noted the growing inflexibility in his attitude, one of 'there's nothing you can do to me because I'm not standing for another election so I'm going to do what I think is the right thing to do.'[95]

Yet he was too insouciant about the high political cost of losing his first parliamentary vote, especially when he had ignored the advice of so many senior colleagues and deliberately hurled himself at defeat. He'd long since abandoned the Third Way. Now there was only My Way.

'Tony is becoming wilful and impetuous,' Jack Straw worried to a senior colleague.[96]

The defeat undermined his authority and lessened respect for his judgement among both Labour MPs and senior ministers. The rebellious on the backbenches had bitten the Prime Minister and relished the taste of his blood. Gordon Brown fretted to his intimates about inheriting a party in which discipline had entirely collapsed.[97] To Cabinet colleagues, the ninety-day defeat underlined the hazards of being led by a Prime Minister who would not be fighting another election. He could afford to be careless of risk; they could not.

Tony Blair once regarded winning as everything. Now he was acting like a man with nothing to lose.

21. Back to School

'This is going to be interesting,' mused Tony Blair as he sat in the den preparing for his first encounter with a new opponent at Prime Minister's Questions. He was now a veteran of this form of parliamentary mouth-to-mouth combat. During his final bout with the outgoing Michael Howard the week before, Blair taunted the Tories by reminding them that he had seen off four Conservative leaders. Blair mastered them all: the defeated John Major, the ridiculed William Hague, the hapless Iain Duncan Smith and the unpopular Howard. The first was Tory leader for six years; the second for four years; the third for two years, one month and sixteen days. Blair jeered at the exiting Howard: 'The right honourable and learned gentleman has lasted just two years and one month.'[1]

Since they could not beat Blair, the Tories finally decided to copy him. At thirty-nine, David Cameron was two years younger than Blair when he became Labour leader. Cameron won the Conservative leadership on the basis that he would be their Blair: a fresh and youthful moderniser to take them back to power after many years in the wilderness of Opposition.

The Prime Minister left Number 10 for the Commons accompanied by the voluminous, burgundy folder of briefing notes on any subject that might conceivably come up at PMQs. Placed inside the folder was a piece of paper with a patronising welcome, a pre-prepared put down to squelch his new opponent. Yet when they faced off at noon, Blair did not use the stinger. It was Cameron who pierced Blair. In an accomplished debut, the neophyte Tory leader made an audacious slash at the long-serving Prime Minister. He was 'stuck in the past, and I want to talk about the future', said Cameron. 'He was the future once.'[2] The Tory benches cheered the jibe while some Labour MPs winced in sympathy with their leader.

Blair reacted with a slight lift of his eyebrows and a mild smile, the practised professional of the art of parliamentary jousting appreciating the artistry of a younger thruster, even if the sally was at his expense. Talking to his staff afterwards, he wryly shrugged off the barb: 'As I'd expected,

Cameron is going to be a contender.'[3] By this stage of his premiership Blair was 'much more sanguine' about this sort of thing.[4]

Not so Gordon Brown. He was sitting next to the Prime Minister on the frontbench and grew increasingly aerated. He shouted and gesticulated in evident frustration that Blair was not going for the kill. Brown's agitation became so great that it almost propelled him off the green leather bench and up to the dispatch box. His body language screamed: let me at him then.

The many quarrels between the two men were now supplemented by a clashing view about how to engage with Cameron. Blair and Brown differed in their assessment of what the new Tory leader represented as they disagreed about how he should be dealt with.

Blair was intrigued by this new opponent. On the way to the Tory leadership, Cameron survived a media maelstrom of questions about his youthful drug habits. I was the first to pose this question during an interview with Cameron at that year's Tory conference in Blackpool. The grandly named Baronial Hall – in reality, a function room in the Winter Gardens – was packed to overflowing with Tory activists wanting to see their party's coming man. 'Did you use any drugs at Oxford?' I asked. Amidst nervous laughter from the audience, he answered by not answering: 'I had a normal university life.' I pressed: 'So that's a yes then?' 'There were things I did as a student that I don't think I should talk about now that I am a politician.' I suggested: 'I can take that as a "yes".' He did not argue.[5]

There was a media furore over the following days as other journalists took up the question.[6] Blair was privately impressed that Cameron successfully held to his line that he wouldn't talk about his life before politics.[7]

The Prime Minister could not help but see some of his younger self in Cameron, another presentationally adept, rhetorically fluent, only partformed public school charmer, a pragmatic moderniser who had risen rapidly and without much trace to seize the leadership of his party from under the noses of older colleagues who thought they were much better qualified to do the job.

Blair's private claim had been: 'I could sort out the Tory party in five minutes.'[8] What he meant was that he would make the Conservatives sound moderate, look modern and move them to the centre ground, where British elections are won and lost. Cameron followed this Blair-approved prescription. In an interview with me shortly after he became leader, Cameron said: 'What I want to do with the Conservative Party is get it into the mainstream of British politics, broadly appeal as a party.'[9] That was precisely the approach described in almost identical language that Blair took when he refashioned the Labour Party as New Labour. In his early years as leader,

Blair enjoyed a eulogising media because he could do a few headers on the football pitch. Cameron got rave reviews for being capable of riding a bike and smiling at the same time. The media was enjoying the novelty of reporting a Tory leader with a whiff of hope and a dusting of charisma. In further echoes of Blair circa 1994–7, Cameron said: 'I'm not a deeply ideological person. I'm a practical person and pragmatic.'[10] His blueprint for renewing the Tories was a Blairprint. He adopted the New Labour mantra of 'social justice and economic efficiency' as his own. At a dinner with journalists from the *Daily Telegraph* during that year's Tory conference, Cameron even declared: 'I am the heir to Blair.'[11]

The Cameron generation of Tories were mesmerised by Blair. He had dominated the formative years of their political lives and subjected their party to a hat-trick of defeats. They regarded the Prime Minister with much more respect and awe than did many in the Labour Party. Cameron's claim to be the son of Blair might be arguable, but it paid homage to the Prime Minister.

To Gordon Brown, Cameron was not a compliment; he was a threat. Refusing to accept that the Conservatives were changing, the Chancellor wanted to define him as a 'new gloss on the same old Tories'. To visitors to Number 11, he would pour contempt on Cameron as a fake, a lightweight, 'a namby pamby' and 'a libertarian'.[12] One who witnessed the private debates between Blair and Brown says: 'Gordon's view was that you've got to crush this little Lord Fauntleroy from day one and Tony wouldn't do it.'[13] A close friend of Brown says: 'Gordon could only be more contemptuous of Cameron if he were a lawyer.'[14] The lawyer Blair disagreed. 'We would just leave ourselves open to ridicule if we launched an over-the-top attack,' he argued. 'Some massive personal attack' on Cameron wouldn't work. There was 'no point denying' that he represented some sort of change.[15] Blair could not anyway attack Cameron for being an Old Etonian when he was a product of Fettes, the Eton of Scotland. 'Who cares if Cameron is an Old Etonian?' he remarked to one Cabinet colleague. 'It doesn't matter if he comes over as classless.'[16]

Blair recognised that the advent of Cameron was an important development in their opponents. 'You've got to accept that they are trying to make big changes.'[17]

Speaking to me at Chequers shortly after Cameron became leader, Blair contended that Labour should be celebrating the fact that 'the Conservative Party is trying to reinvent itself in order to become a party of government again. Put the flags out. This is a great moment for us.' It confirmed that 'progressive politics is in the ascendant. When you read what the Tories are trying to do, it is the most enormous compliment to what we have achieved in the past eight years.'[18]

Brown's proposed line of attack reminded Blair of how the Tories had tried and failed to demonise him when he was Leader of the Opposition.

There were deeper, more psychological impulses at work in this argument between them. It was natural for Blair to be flattered when he was imitated by the Tories. He would like to leave Number 10 with the thought that his final and most comprehensive victory over the Conservatives was to force them to emulate him. It was equally natural that Brown did not want it to be true that the Tories were finally grasping what they needed to do to become competitive for power. A more appealing and centrist Tory party was going to be harder to beat. Extra edge was given to their argument by Cameron's early honeymoon. Within days of his election as leader, the Tories vaulted into their first, albeit narrow, opinion poll lead over Labour for years.[19]

That wasn't Blair's problem: he was not going to fight another general election. It was Brown's. He had once before been denied the crown by a younger, smoother public school rival. He was gnawed by the fear that it might happen yet again if he was kept waiting for the premiership any longer.

The Tory leader's jibe – 'the future once' – had increasing resonance. When Blair said he wouldn't fight any more elections, he calculated that he'd gain a kind of counter-intuitive authority. Colleagues would not see the point of plotting against him when they knew he was going anyway.[20] That was a misreading of the chemistry of politics. Just as most of his allies feared, he had weakened himself by putting a sell-by date on his premiership. It was a source of instability that every minister, civil servant, Labour MP, journalist and other actor of influence now knew that the Prime Minister's days were numbered. 'We know he is going,' one minister complained that autumn. 'The problem is we don't know when he is going.'[21]

It was another source of destabilisation that the media interpreted almost every act of government in terms of how it might affect the timing of Blair's departure. In the immediate aftermath of the election, many put his end date at 2006. In the resurgence that followed, the clock was put back to 2008. As the public mood turned sour again, the assumed end date crept forward in the collective consciousness. One loyalist minister feared: 'It's beginning to dribble away from Tony.'[22] Gordon Brown and his allies saw it the same way. As one of the Chancellor's inner circle puts it: 'From the 2005 election onwards, there is a general sense that power is draining away from Blair to Gordon. The tide is flowing our way.'[23]

To fight that tide, Blair tried to prove that he was not a diminishing Prime

Minister who was merely working out his notice. He returned from his holiday that summer to fire off a long memo to his staff telling them 'the next six months are vital.' They had grown accustomed to receiving such instructions. One senior aide jokingly groaned: 'It would be more of a surprise if he came back from holiday and sent us a memo saying the next six months aren't that important.'[24]

The Cabinet was increasingly torn between trying to serve their present master and positioning themselves for their next. Ministers who had grappled with the Chancellor in the past were becoming blackly humorous about their prospects under a Brown regime. There was little loathing lost between Gordon Brown and John Reid. Reid drily commented that if Brown took over: 'I confidently expect to become chairman of the catering committee.'[25]

John Prescott argued with Blair that he should snuff out the end-less speculation by announcing a departure date. 'They'll salami-slice me,' Blair replied. 'If I say I'm going in two years, they'll say make it one year.'[26]

Blair still believed that he might achieve his ambition of serving a full third term, but did not spell that out in public for fear that it would make his Chancellor 'explode'.[27] He could dangle the possibility of an earlier handover in front of the Chancellor as a potential reward for being co-operative. To Neil Kinnock, Blair said: 'I've told Gordon I'll be his campaign manager when the time comes.'[28]

In the run-up to that year's party conference, Cabinet ministers closely associated with Blair were publicly warm about Brown in an effort to convince him that he could relax because they would not try to impede his way to Number 10. David Miliband and Tessa Jowell spoke of a Brown premiership as if it were a foregone conclusion. Even Charles Clarke, whose relations with the Chancellor were always extremely pungent, described a Brown succession as 'very likely' and predicted that he would be 'a very good Prime Minister'.[29]

Clarke was, in fact, viscerally antagonistic to the idea of Brown becoming Prime Minister. Miliband was highly wary. Jowell wanted Blair to carry on for as long as possible. All were among the many sceptics in the Cabinet that Brown had the temperament required to be a successful Prime Minister.

There was a state of armed truce between the two camps at the party conference in Brighton. Brown's speech superficially lauded his rival. 'I believe Tony Blair deserves huge credit not just for winning three elections, but for leading the Labour Party for more than a decade,' said the Chancellor. By pointedly reminding everyone how long Blair had been in the job, this pat on the head was also a shove in the back.

Brown offered to give Labour back its 'moral compass' and dwelt heavily on the need to restore 'trust'.[30] Everyone understood that he was arguing that only a change of leadership could restore the trust lost by Blair. That passage so infuriated the Prime Minister that some of his aides suggested that he should insert a line into his speech the next day saying that he had changed his mind and would be running for a fourth term after all. It would be worth it, they joked, 'just to see the look on Brown's face'.[31]

Brown concluded his speech by announcing that they had 'to begin to plan ahead' and declared that he would tour all the regions of Britain to 'listen, hear and learn' and discuss 'economic, social and constitutional changes',[32] with the clear implication that he expected Blair to have his bags packed by the time he had completed this twelve-month regal progress. His camp were determined that they would have Blair out of Number 10 by the next year.[33]

On the afternoon after Brown's speech, David Hill told journalists what they could expect to hear from Blair the next day. Hill briefed that it would be a speech showing that the Prime Minister had 'plenty of work' to do 'for a couple of years or more'.[34] Brown reacted violently to that and interpreted the briefing as a malevolent attempt to reduce the press coverage of his own speech. His people went into attack mode. Damian McBride denigrated Hill to reporters. He was also heard nakedly 'slagging off Tony'. McBride operated incautiously. He was venting spleen against Blair so aggressively to some journalists at the conference hotel bar that he did not notice that one of the Number 10 staff was in the group.[35]

Cherie enjoyed tweaking Brown's tail. Asked when the Blairs would be leaving Number 10, she cried: 'Darling, we are a long, long way from that!'[36]

Her husband opened his speech with the declaration: 'I stand before you as the first leader in the Labour Party's history to win three full consecutive terms in office.' The 'full' was deliberately emphasised. He talked rather mistily about 'the patient courage of the change-maker'. He was more crisp about the imperative to drive on reform of public services. Blair often used the process of writing speeches to 'find out what he thought'.[37] This speech contained his clearest rebuttal of the idea that choice was antipathetic to social democracy. 'The twenty-first century's expectations in public services are a world away from those of 1945. People demand quality, choice, high standards.' He went on: 'Choice is what wealthy people have exercised for centuries' and they should celebrate and grasp the chance to extend it to the less affluent. 'Some of the poorest families in the poorest parts of Britain' were benefiting from specialist schools and City academies. 'The greatest injustice I know is when good education is the preserve of the privileged. If there's one thing that motivates me it is to redeem the pledge I made to give the chance of a first-class education not only for Britain's elite but for all Britain's children.' The most revealing line was his admission: 'Every time I've ever introduced a reform in government, I wish, in retrospect, I had gone further.'[38] The unspoken thought was that he would have gone further had he not been thwarted by his obstructive Chancellor.

Immediately after the conference, a sequence of controversies suggested that discipline in the Government was breaking down. The most incendiary erupted around the proposal to ban smoking in public places. John Reid, a reformed smoker, had put forward a partial ban when he was Health Secretary. He argued that working-class folk, like his mother, should not be denied their pleasures. Patricia Hewitt, who had succeeded him at Health, wanted to strengthen the policy into a total ban. Blair did not regard this as 'any great point of principle' or part of his 'core agenda' so it did not much register on his radar.[39] It was one of those disputes within Cabinet that he was content to leave to his deputy to resolve. Whatever his faults, John Prescott had a talent for forcing colleagues to stay in a room until they compromised. But Prescott was away when the domestic affairs sub-committee of the Cabinet met on Monday, 24 October. Jack Straw took his place in the chair. The Foreign Secretary was just off a plane from America and confessed to the committee: 'I'm not well briefed on this issue.'[40]

Reid and Hewitt clashed fiercely. Straw took Reid's side. Tessa Jowell, whose department had responsibility for pubs and clubs, aligned herself with Hewitt. Blow-by-blow accounts of the battle were extensively briefed to the press by the warring ministers. There was an irony here. For years, many Labour MPs and much of the media attacked Blair for imposing a stifling conformity on his Cabinet. When the 'control freak' relaxed his grip, leaving ministers to sort out their differences between themselves, they spun against each other and generated headlines about the Government whirling into chaos. Some in Number 10 also put this anarchic spasm down to ministers being more likely to take a 'sod it attitude' when they knew he was going.[41]

Reid ultimately lost and Hewitt won. A total ban on smoking in enclosed public spaces became law after a free vote in the Commons produced a majority of 200 in favour. The ban was introduced in July 2007 to much less opposition than had been feared. At no cost whatsoever to the taxpayer, the ban was one of the single most effective measures passed by New Labour to improve public health.

This storm in an ashtray split three of the core Blairites: Hewitt, Jowell and Reid. That breakdown in discipline was shortly followed by the downfall of an ally. David Blunkett had spent just six months on the backbenches between his resignation from the Home Office and his restoration to the top table as Secretary of State for Work and Pensions. That was a sign of the Prime Minister's esteem and affection. Blair told Blunkett that he hoped a resumption of ministerial responsibilities would help him to shake off depression and 'sort out his head'.[42] It was a risk to use ministerial office as a form of psychological therapy for a damaged friend.

Salacious, and often untrue, stories about Blunkett's private life continued to dog him. It was an exclusive in the upper end of the press that tripped him up at the end of October. The *Independent on Sunday* revealed that he had breached the Ministerial Code by not seeking the advice of the Advisory Committee on Business Appointments before becoming a director of a DNA testing firm while he was out of office.[43] The Cabinet Secretary confirmed, and Blunkett accepted, that he had breached the code.[44] He was forced to quit, making him, after Peter Mandelson, the second double resignee from Blair's Cabinets.

The legislative flagship of this parliamentary session was Blair's latest attempt to reform Britain's schools. There were useful improvements in the first term in Blunkett's happier and more productive days as Education Secretary. These achievements were mainly concentrated in primary schools, where standards of literacy and numeracy rose. The biggest leaps in attainment were in the areas of highest poverty. By the second term, experience of office was evolving Blair's thinking. He saw that it was impossible for ministers and civil servants sitting in Whitehall to try to improve thousands of individual schools by centrally imposed diktat. He proclaimed the 'post-comprehensive era' and made incremental progress towards giving good schools more autonomy over their budgets and scope to innovate. The physical fabric of schools, neglected for a quarter of a century before New Labour came to power, was renovated. Shiny new facilities replaced the decaying buildings inherited from the Tories. Class sizes came down. There were 32,000 more teachers than when Labour came to power. Those teachers were better rewarded, which led to improvement in the calibre of entrants into the profession. The amount of money spent per pupil doubled between 1997 and 2008. GCSE and A level scores rose, though they were subject to accusations of grade inflation.

For all these improvements, there were wild variations in performance. While Britain had some excellent state schools, many of its children were appallingly let down. Approaching half of eleven-year-olds still left primary school without an adequate grasp of the 3Rs. Less than half of secondary school pupils secured five good GCSEs if Maths and English were included. Thirty thousand teenagers left school every year without any qualifications to their names.[45]

That was why so few working-class children were getting to university, with a freezing effect on social mobility. The culprit was not so much bias in university admissions. Not enough working-class children were doing A levels. Much of Britain was still waiting for the 'world class' schools that Blair had again declared to be a soaring ambition of his premiership in his party conference speech.

'He had a vision of a completely transformed education system that would be so good that people who had the wealth to choose the private system would still choose the public system because it was good enough for their children,' says Sir Michael Barber, the head of the Delivery Unit.[46] The hope was that Britain would eventually emulate Europe, where state schools were sufficiently attractive to the affluent that only a tiny minority of parents educated their children privately.[47] That vision was a long way from being realised. The numbers paying to escape state education actually rose. Under Labour, a record proportion of children were now in private schools and not all of them for reasons of parental snobbery. In London, a rich city served poorly by state education, approaching a fifth of children were educated privately.[48]

Blair was an admirer of faith schools and the independent sector and what they achieved for their pupils. Had he not become a Labour MP, it is almost certain that he would have done the same as his friend Charlie Falconer and sent his children to private schools. Euan and Nicky, his two oldest sons, went to the London Oratory, a selective state school where the masters wore gowns. One of Euan's friends described it as 'a state school trying to pretend to be a private school'. Blair's boys received private tuition for their A levels and university entrance by masters at Westminster public school.

Blair believed local education authorities were at the heart of the problem with state education because their default position was to defend the perfor-mance of their schools, however poor, rather than champion achievement. If he had not faced too much resistance to try, 'he'd have got rid of local education authorities altogether.'[49]

Blair envisaged a new world in which schools were largely autonomous units, competing to show that they could offer the best. By this late phase of his premiership, Blair had fully bought into the idea that enduring improvement in the public sector could not be achieved by 'bureaucratic fiat' from the centre and they had to create 'self-sustaining incentives'.[50] Blair 'fastened on to that model' in the hope that 'competition and choice will drive continuous improvement.'[51]

He looked to social democratic Sweden in which local authority schools competed with state-funded but independent schools run by charities and other non-profit-making organisations. There was other international evidence that this worked. He could also point to the American charter schools and the Dutch education system. Blair's desire to pursue excellence through diversity and choice put him on a collision course with the many in the Labour Party still wedded to uniformity even when it also meant mediocrity.

On 25 October, the reform plan was unveiled in a White Paper entitled 'Higher Standards, Better Schools for All: More Choice for Parents and Pupils'. Publication had been postponed until October to avoid galvanising opposition at the party conference, where the teaching unions were strongly represented among the delegates. The word 'choice' was in itself inflammatory for the many in the Labour Party attached to an egalitarian vision of education.

The foreword to the White Paper, which appeared to promise the introduction of a version of the Swedish system, bore Blair's signature and was largely written by Andrew Adonis, the former Head of the Policy Unit whom he had made an Education Minister to drive the reforms. Adonis was an example of the social mobility that Labour often talked about. His father was a Greek Cypriot waiter; his mother abandoned him when he was very young. He was brought up in a north London care home. He had risen a long way from those roots. Intense, hard-working, courteous and soft-spoken, Adonis looked like the Oxford academic that he had been. He was an evangelist for city academies as a means to provide more ladders of advancement. The legislation also envisaged creating 'trust schools'. Ben Wegg-Prosser, who became a senior member of the Number 10 staff in the third term, says the idea was that trust schools would enjoy similar freedoms 'without all the palaver of creating academies'.[52] The problem was that Adonis was virtually the only person at the Department of Education who was a true believer. The other ministers and their officials feared that anarchy would result from liberating schools.

The foreword to the White Paper talked a good game: 'The local authority must move from being a provider of education to its local commissioner and the champion of parent choice.'[53] The rest of the White Paper was written by Ruth Kelly, the Education Secretary, and reflected her department's wariness of radical reform. Local authorities would continue to control most of the funding and teachers' pay would still be set centrally. The 'trust schools' would remain under the overall direction of councillors. The White Paper was a diluted version of Blair's original vision, but even that was too much for many in his party. Kelly cautioned him that Labour MPs and the teaching unions would become 'riled up' if he wasn't careful with his rhetoric.[54] He ignored her. Blair 'had a glint in his eye' on the day of the launch and used language that 'sent Labour MPs bananas'.[55] He was frustrated that he had been forced to retreat. As was typical of him, he dealt with this disappointment by rhetorically compensating and presenting an evolution as a sensational revolution. 'They spun it terribly,' says the former Education Secretary, Estelle Morris, who was provoked into publicly opposing the reforms not so much because of this legislation but because it 'gave the clear signal to me where they wanted to go next'.[56]

Huw Evans, a member of Blair's senior staff, agrees: 'The launch went horribly wrong. It made it seem to backbenchers that this was another huge new reform which was too much for them.'[57] It aroused their suspicions that the Prime Minister was driven by what they saw as a reckless frenzy to burnish his legacy. The effect was to turn this into a virility test of Blair's authority.

His opponents had support in the Cabinet. The Treasury was 'very very sceptical both in ideological terms and cost terms, because academies are expensive to build'.[58] Gordon Brown also complained to Blair that the legislation was divisive. 'Why are you trying to destroy the Labour Party?' he shouted at the Prime Minister.[59] But the Chancellor was relatively restrained compared with the guerrilla campaigns he ran against foundation hospitals and university tuition fees in the second term. He did not do anything to support the schools reforms, but he did not actively sabotage them either. Like an alligator, Brown lay low and quietly in the water, waiting to snap, but keeping his jaws closed for the moment.

The big obstacle was John Prescott. He viewed education through the distorting prism of his own childhood. 'It ran very deep with him.'[60] When he was at primary school, classmates who passed the 11-plus went to the smart grammar school in the leafy suburbs of Chester. Those who failed the 11-plus, as John did, went to a secondary modern in Ellesmere Port on the muddy mouth of the Mersey. 'I felt stigmatised,' he wrote. 'The chip on my shoulder got bigger.'[61]

Prescott had surpassed many people with much more impressive academic qualifications to become Deputy Prime Minister of the United Kingdom. Yet the chip still sizzled on his shoulder. That early rejection was one of the sources of his deep and lifelong neurosis about his status. It had left him with a burning detestation of selection in education.

When Blair argued with Prescott, he tried to persuade his deputy that the purpose was not to return to the 11-plus. The point was to increase the quality of education available to children. That didn't convince Prescott, who feared that academies would become grammar schools with a different badge, favouring the children of the affluent.[62] 'If you set up a school and it becomes a good school, the great danger is that everyone wants to go there,' contended Prescott.[63] This was crazy logic. Yet it was a view representative of the many in the Labour Party who could only ever see choice as a friend to the affluent middle classes and an enemy of the less well-off. It was revealing that some Labour MPs denounced middle-class parents for trying to get their children into decent schools as if it were a crime for parents to want a good education for their children and as if that was not also the ambition of working-class parents. The truth about British education was that there were already multiple tiers of schools, state and private, in a system which allocated places on the basis of where someone lived, what mortgage they could afford and what religion they practised or pretended to. Yet the cry went up from the Labour benches that the reforms would create two tiers of schools as iniquitous as the old split between grammars and secondary moderns.

Shortly before Christmas, Ruth Kelly made a presentation to the Cabinet. A sullen Prescott sat through it grunting his unconcealed dissent before loudly complaining that it would lead to first- and second-class schools. He then gave an interview to a Conservative newspaper conducted by Susan Crosland, widow of a former Labour Cabinet minister. Prescott gave encouragement to rebellious Labour MPs by declaring that there was 'a great danger' that city academies would become grammar schools by a different name. The old seaman had fired a torpedo straight into the hull of the Prime Minister's flagship.[64] Shortly afterwards, more than ninety rebel Labour MPs put their names to an 'alternative White Paper'.

In the New Year, another dangerous opponent, Neil Kinnock, unfurled his banner. The former Labour leader was also shaped by bitter memories of the 11-plus and how the selection exam branded generations of children as failures. Kinnock's opposition was the more potent because until now he had been impeccable in his public loyalty to Blair. 'I had to speak up,' says Kinnock. He thought 'the multiplication of types of schools was a false objective that was bound to come to grief.'[65] Within Number 10, they saw that 'Neil was a big problem. He legitimised the rebellion.'[66] Blair had three meetings with the former Labour leader to try to talk him round. When they got nowhere, Kinnock eventually said: 'I'm wasting my bloody time and yours. Let's talk about something else.'[67]

Kinnock chaired a meeting at the Commons in mid-January at which Blair's reforms were denounced. Alastair Campbell and Fiona Millar were an eye-catching and headline-generating presence sitting on the front row.

Though Campbell once described earlier schools reform as the end of the 'bog-standard comprehensive', he was viscerally opposed to the entire choice and diversity agenda.

Blair was rightly impatient with their view that parents should be compelled to use the local state school whether it was decent or rotten. 'It's true that if you create more good schools, then people will want to go to them, and it's also true that the middle class will fight very hard to get into the best schools,' he argued.

Middle-class folk will always find their way through the system. That is just the way it is. That's life. It cannot be a reason for not creating more good schools. I'm more concerned about people living in an area where there isn't a school that offers them anything other than a three in ten chance that they can get five good GCSEs, never mind getting into university. It's not on.[68]

He had the arguments, but not the numbers. 'We're losing it badly,' said one of his senior aides in the New Year. 'We're not going to win this.'[69] They had 'misread the opposition that was going to come his way', says Wegg-Prosser. 'In the end, it was daily battle stations.'[70] Blair had to announce further retreats from his original ambition, says Phil Collins, because it was 'hell's own task to get it through even in diluted form'.[71]

He was thwarted in his intention to introduce mechanisms to speed up the closure of bad schools and the expansion of good ones. He had wanted local education authorities to be stopped from setting up any further schools so that all new ones would be established by independent providers. He gave way on that, too. A strict admissions code was conceded in order to appease the fears about the extension of selection. 'Tony just cut his losses in the end,' remarked one disappointed ally.[72] This was Blair's last battle on public service reform. Stymied in his original ambition to free all schools, he would devote the remainder of his premiership to rush-building the elite city academies, a programme almost single-handedly driven by the evangelical Adonis. By February, Prescott was sufficiently satisfied that the legislation was neutered that he made a speech in support. The more radical spirits at Number 10 concluded that Blair ended up 'kidding himself' about what finally emerged and the legislation was so compromised that it was 'not really worth putting on the statute book'.[73]

Blair had believed that saying he would fight no more elections would 'liberate' him to be more boldly reforming in the third term than he was during the first and second terms.[74] The fatal flaw in this calculation was its assumption that his party would let him be as radical as he wanted to be. The 'almighty struggle' over this legislation 'brought it home' that Labour

MPs were not going to let him do just as he pleased.[75] His tragedy was that by the time he finally arrived at clarity on what needed to be done in education and other public services he was drained of the political capital to achieve the vision.

The size of the rebellion left him riskily dependent on Tory support. When the Bill was published in late February, David Cameron and his education spokesman, David Willetts, declared that they would vote for it because they agreed with the thrust and could use it to go further when they were in government.[76] 'I'm saying to the Prime Minister: if you want these education reforms, you can have them. Be as bold as you like, because you've got my backing,' said Cameron, who praised city academies as 'a very good idea'.[77]

This was tactically astute. It made Blair look like a leader who needed Tory help to prevail over the jurassic types in his own party. Cameron also calculated, correctly, that his support would make Labour MPs more suspicious of the legislation and more inclined to damage the Prime Minister by rebelling.[78]

MPs voted on the crucial second reading on 15 March 2006. The result was a superficially resounding victory. The Bill was passed by 458 votes to 115. Conservative support guaranteed its safe passage. The problem for Blair was that he had only won because of Tory votes. A total of fifty-two Labour MPs voted against and a further twenty-five abstained. On a later vote on timetabling of the legislation, the Tories swung into opposition and the Government won by only the alarmingly thin margin of ten.

No leader can expect to last for long if he is dependent on the unreliable support of the principal Opposition party. To some of his colleagues, Blair's position was becoming reminiscent of David Lloyd George's towards the end of his time at Number 10. Tony Blair was turning into a Prime Minister without a party.

22. The Hollowed Crown

At a quarter to seven on the night of the crucial education votes in the Commons, a key Labour functionary was at a television studio in north London being dusted with powder. Jack Dromey, the Deputy General Secretary of the Transport and General Workers Union and Treasurer of the Labour Party, was an angry man that evening. Ninety minutes earlier, he released a statement announcing that he was setting up an inquiry into 'the securing of loans in secret by the Labour Party'.[1] Now he was going on television to explain why. Just as Tony Blair was negotiating one minefield in Parliament, Dromey detonated the 'cash-for-coronets' affair by lobbing dynamite directly at the door of Number 10. On *Channel 4 News* and later that evening on *Newsnight*, the party Treasurer made several extremely damaging accusations about the way in which Labour financed its 2005 election campaign. Elected officials such as himself were 'kept in the dark' about a secret funding operation. He went on: 'We have once and for all to end any notion that there is cash for favours in our political culture.' He pointed the finger at the Prime Minister. 'Number 10 must have known about the loans.'[2]

This struck a spark which led to a police inquiry that culminated in Tony Blair gaining the unenviable distinction of being the first sitting Prime Minister to be interrogated in the course of an investigation into criminal corruption.

The origin of the affair was his desperate attempt to scrabble together money to fund the last campaign. Labour was 'broke' in the run-up to the 2005 election.[3] Blair was 'in a state of panic' about the lack of funds and 'seized by the fear' that they would be 'fatally outgunned'[4] by the Tories, who were able to direct large sums at target seats thanks to the long pockets of Michael Ashcroft, the billionaire Tory peer from Belize.

Blair turned to Michael Levy, his fund-raiser for more than a decade. Levy was an East End boy made good. He escaped an impoverished childhood in Hackney, trained as an accountant and then became a millionaire pop impresario whose creations included Alvin Stardust. When Blair became leader, Levy spotted another star in the making and hitched himself to it. Blair grew fond of Levy, shared his passions for tennis and religion, and was wowed by the way in which he raised huge sums for Jewish Care, turning it into one of Britain's most successful charities. Those prodigious fund-raising talents were exploited for New Labour.

Both men agreed that the party needed to reduce its dependence on money from the trades unions. The union contribution fell from two thirds of funding when Blair became Labour leader to less than a quarter at the lowest point. Levy liked to boast that he had entirely changed the rules of the game.[5] So he had. But not by raising money from a mass membership party. It was from rich individual donors that Levy harvested some £100 million between 1995 and 2005. Labour now aped the Tories by relying on plutocrats. That made both the main parties unhealthily dependent on a cash stream from a small number of very wealthy men.

The ebullient Levy was permanently tanned with immaculately coiffed grey hair. A natty dresser, he stood five foot six in stack-heeled shoes. Baron Levy of Mill Hill, as he had become in Blair's first honours list, operated from Chase House, his hacienda-style mansion in Totteridge in north London. His genius as a fund-raiser was to understand the craving for status and recognition among men like himself who had risen from poor backgrounds. Levy denied the legend that he baited potential donors with an invitation to play tennis at the mansion with a hint that Tony might drop by for a set or two.[6] What he did do was throw dinner parties at which he mingled members of the Government, VIPs and celebrities with wealthy men whose cheque books he wanted to prise open. The guests clustered for drinks on the pristine white fitted carpets. They gawped at the nouveau riche gold-leaf decorating the mansion. They might envy the huge lawn, the tennis court and two swimming pools, indoor and outdoor. Once they were seated at the glass and marble dinner table, the star guest would appear: the Prime Minister. Blair told friends that he 'loathed and despised the business of raising money' but swallowed his distaste because 'it needed to be done.'[7]

Donations were not discussed at the table. It was not that crude. Levy waited until later to snare rich men by gripping them with his firm double-clasp handshake. Then he would pat, hug, wink, flatter and charm before going for the squeeze: 'You look like you could afford a million.' He revelled in his image as friend and tennis partner of the Prime Minister and in his role as a Middle East envoy. In an odd way, he even derived pleasure from being known as 'Lord Cashpoint', embracing the soubriquet as a compliment to the way he treated 'fund-raising as an art'.[8]

Even this world-class schmoozer was struggling to raise funds in the run-up to the 2005 election. Blair's magic had faded. Rich men were fearful of the media attention attracted by big donations. 'Fund-raising was getting very difficult,' says Levy. 'People didn't want to pay. They didn't want to be beaten up by the media any more.'[9] Disaffection with the Government had caused party membership to shrivel to less than 200,000. Blair didn't want to appeal to the trades unions, who were alienated from him anyway. Gripped by panic, he decided to break a last taboo about fund-raising.

He had cleaned up elements of party funding during the first term by legislating to ban secret donations and ones from abroad. It was no longer lawful, as it was under the Tories, for parties to trouser enormous sums and keep the source of the cash indefinitely concealed from the public. The Elections and Referendums Act 2000 compelled declarations of donations over £5,000. But the law left a loophole. Cash that came in as a loan could be kept hidden. Here was a mechanism for securing extra funds at a time when rich men had become averse to publicity because of earlier money scandals of the New Labour era. Thus did previous sleaze eruptions lead to the most volcanic of all.

Labour had previously forsworn copying the Conservative practice of taking money in hidden loans. Blair's fear of being financially out-gunned during the 2005 campaign was amplified when Levy warned him that the Tories were raising 'a fortune in loans, at least £25 million.' Levy argued that it was 'nuts' to let their opponents have this advantage and the law should be changed to ban undisclosed loans.[10] On his account, it was Blair, against the fund-raiser's advice, who made the 'ill-considered, panic-stricken'[11] decision that Labour should start taking loans as well. Levy did not like it on the grounds that 'loans, unlike gifts, had to be paid back.'[12] That wasn't true, though, if a sugar daddy was later persuaded to change a loan into a donation. This was not illegal, but it hardly met the 'purer than pure' test that Blair once set for his Government. It was a blatant violation of the spirit of disclosure in the rules on funding that New Labour had itself enacted. Loans had the potential to be more perverting than straightforward donations because they left the party in debt. Any lender disappointed that the money was not reciprocated with an honour or favours could demand his or her money back.

Levy was becoming disillusioned and estranged from Blair, who had bruised his ego by going behind his back to approach Ronnie Cohen, another multi-millionaire, to do some fund-raising. He nevertheless set about collecting loans before and after the election. The curry meal king, Sir Gulam Noon, agreed to lend £250,000. David Sainsbury, the grocery lord and Science

Minister, added a further £2 million in loans on top of a £2 million donation. The stockbroker Barry Townsley lent £1 million to Labour in addition
to the £2 million he spent sponsoring a city academy. Other loans were
raised from the property developers Sir David Garrard and Andrew Rosen-
feld. Garrard pledged a £2 million loan; £1.5 million was raised in a loan
from Chai Patel who founded the Priory group of clinics.[13] Blair 'knew about
every single one'.[14]

Violating the spirit of transparency by taking clandestine loans showed
how far Blair had left behind his promise of ten years before that he would
re-establish 'the bond of trust between the British people and the Government' and be 'tough on sleaze and tough on the causes of sleaze'.[15]

The first 'cash for peerages' headline appeared in the *Independent on
Sunday* in October 2005.[16] It then emerged that Blair had nominated for
peerages Garrard, Noon, Townsley and Patel, who had between them made
loans to Labour of £4.7 million.[17] The loans had not been disclosed to the
House of Lords Appointments Commission, the body set up by Blair to
scrutinise peerages after earlier scandals. The loans were hidden from
Labour's own fund-raising committee and concealed from Ian McCartney,
the party Chairman, who signed the nomination forms for the four peerages
in his hospital bed while recovering from a heart bypass operation.[18]

The four peerages were blocked by the commission or withdrawn. Early
in the New Year, an undercover reporter from the *Sunday Times* recorded
Des Smith, a headteacher from Essex, claiming that for a donation of £10
million to a city academy 'you could go to the House of Lords'. He resigned
as a Government adviser the next day and was arrested in April.[19] The police
abandoned interest in the shattered model head when they grasped that
Smith was making a cynical observation rather than a criminal one. The
focus concentrated on the loans and peerages.

The story rumbled for months, but it only became a full-blown crisis
once Jack Dromey publicly pointed the finger at Number 10. He felt he had
been lied to over the previous forty-eight hours about the sums involved.
A news conference at Downing Street the morning after his intervention
was one of the most squirming of Blair's premiership. He was compelled
to admit for the first time that he had not told the scrutiny committee about
the loans to Labour from his nominees for the peerages.[20] Downing Street
was ultimately forced to confess that a total of £14 million was raised in
hidden loans from a dozen wealthy men. An MP of the Scottish National
Party, Angus MacNeil, lodged a speculative complaint with the Metropolitan Police. The Commissioner, Sir Ian Blair, was fighting for his own
professional life over the de Menezes shooting. There was widespread

surprise when he ordered an investigation by Scotland Yard's Specialist Crimes Unit. From March, John Yates, a Deputy Assistant Commissioner who dealt with highly sensitive inquiries, was on the case at the head of a team of eight detectives.

A toxic cloud hung over Number 10 for the remainder of Blair's time in office. Then and ever after he believed that this chain of events was deliberately triggered by Gordon Brown. To a senior aide, Blair said: 'This didn't happen by accident.'[21] Dromey was married to Harriet Harman. Sacked from the Cabinet in the first term, Harman was back in Government as a minister at the Department of Constitutional Affairs. Her boss, Charlie Falconer, was one of the Prime Minister's closest friends. He reported to Blair that Harman was being 'immensely disloyal'. She had directly said to Falconer that Blair should quit and be replaced by Brown.[22] That was not the only reason why Blair saw Dromey's intervention as an act of naked aggression by the Chancellor.

His relationship with Brown was at a new nadir. 'The rows were constant,' says one Cabinet minister. 'Absolutely stupendous rows.'[23] Staff on both sides of the divide 'felt like children of a dysfunctional marriage where mum and dad are too busy arguing to ever talk to the kids. We're sitting there on the bottom of the stairs, saying "Could we have a decision please?" and the crockery is being thrown around.'[24]

One combustion was about the size of Britain's contribution to the European Union. This had to be renegotiated because of the enlargement of the EU. Brown 'was always very difficult' over Europe. 'It was like negotiating with an extra member state.'[25] Shortly before the European Council in December 2005, the Prime Minister's entire negotiating strategy was leaked to the *Daily Telegraph*, which published it under the headline 'Blair ready to surrender EU rebate'.[26] It was widely believed inside Number 10 that this was an attempt by Brown to sabotage the negotiation, undermine Blair and curry favour with the Europhobic press.

The negotiations in Brussels were 'tortuous and arduous'.[27] They were injected with additional venom because of Jacques Chirac's bitter feelings towards Blair. These talks occurred during Britain's turn in the chair of the Council, so it was for Blair to announce the budget package when the intense bargaining was finally concluded late on the second night. At around 10.30 p.m., Blair sat with his team of officials from Number 10 and the Foreign Office preparing the statement that he was scheduled to deliver an hour later. 'Like a bolt from the blue' they were told that Chirac had already started his own news conference, claiming credit for the deal and presenting it as a victory for the French.[28] Blair sighed: 'He really is a cunt, isn't he?'

Then, with a slightly apologetic glance at the female officials in the room, he put his hand over his mouth.

The British concession on the rebate amounted to about £1 billion each year. That was a reasonable bargain. There was bound to be some price to pay for the enlargement which had always been one of Britain's pre-eminent foreign policy goals. Brown's camp aggressively briefed that Blair had given away too much, which encouraged more hostile headlines about 'surrender'.[29]

In February, Labour lost the Dunfermline and West Fife by-election to the Liberal Democrats even though the third party was leaderless at the time in the wake of the chaotic defenestration of Charles Kennedy. Blairites and Brownites offered competing interpretations of the loss in the seat where the Chancellor kept his Scottish home. Proof of how unpopular Blair was, said Brownites. Evidence that Brown could not win in his own living room, said Blairites. The Prime Minister then had to throw a protective arm around Tessa Jowell, who was caught in a sleaze eruption. She separated from her husband, David Mills, when he was charged with taking a bribe from Silvio Berlusconi.

Alastair Campbell and Philip Gould tried to cast themselves as peace-makers. They cajoled Blair and Brown to agree to talks about repairing their relationship and working towards a handover of power. Jonathan Powell refused to have anything to do with it, predicting that it was futile.[30] Campbell and Gould began to sense that he was right when Ed Balls was brazenly rude to the Prime Minister. More shocking in its way was the behaviour of Ed Miliband. Blairites had regarded him as the most reasonable member of Brown's court. At Number 10, the other Ed was known as the 'representative from Planet Fuck'. To the Prime Minister's face, and more than once, Miliband demanded: 'What is to be gained by you staying on for another six months?'[31] Blair turned on Campbell and Gould for embroiling him in an exercise he found hateful. The talks were fruitless when all trust between the two principals was incinerated. They collapsed.

Bust-ups in the den were now routine. Brown would thunder round to Number 10, the door on Blair's study would close and yelling at dispatch box levels began almost immediately. 'The noise was so loud you could hear the screaming and shouting from the other side of the door,' says one member of the Cabinet.[32]

Shortly after breakfast, officials and advisers held an 8.30 a.m. planning meeting in the Cabinet Room. It was not unusual for these meetings to take place to the background noise of high-decibel swearing coming from the nearby den. Blair and Brown were rowing so violently that sometimes the words were audible to the staff in the Cabinet Room. 'The shouting was so loud you could hear it. Everyone would be pretending to focus on what we were discussing and the entire room would be earwigging the conversation next door.'³³

The most epic struggle between Prime Minister and Chancellor of this period was about pensions. Blair had commissioned a report into pension reform by the former Director-General of the CBI, Adair Turner. That was an intrusion into territory which Brown regarded as his exclusive fiefdom. He was even more maddened by the appointment of John Hutton as Work and Pensions Secretary. Hutton was the first occupant of the job to strike out independently of the Chancellor. He agreed with Blair in favouring Turner's recommendation to restore the link with earnings which would make the basic pension more generous. This ran counter to the entire means-tested approach to pensions pursued by Brown since he became Chancellor. He tried to kill Turner's proposals by declaring them unaffordable. There were months of ferocious argument and corrosive leaking to the press. On one occasion, Hutton came to Number 10 for a meeting and was left sitting outside the den for ninety minutes while the Prime Minister and Chancellor rowed with each other.³⁴

An especially venomous confrontation over pensions took place in the den on the morning before Dromey intervened on the peerages. On Blair's account to his friends, this fight climaxed with Brown making a direct threat. On a mild version of what took place, Brown left the den issuing the parting shot: 'You haven't heard the last about these peerages.'³⁵ Cabinet ministers and other politicians and advisers very close to Blair say that Brown was more directly menacing than that. Brown said: 'I'll get you over the peer-ages.'³⁶ Afterwards Sally Morgan was told by Blair: 'For the first time, I'm scared. He's going to bring me down.'³⁷ Blair was so stunned and disturbed by Brown's behaviour that he called in the Cabinet Secretary, Sir Gus O'Donnell. He asked O'Donnell, who was very shocked by what Brown had said, to make an official note of Brown's threat.³⁸ Blair told O'Donnell that he was afraid that 'Gordon is going to do something very unconstitutional.'³⁹

Dromey absolutely denies that he was an actor in a Brown plot to knife Blair. 'It is utterly preposterous. I did what was right not what I was being encouraged to do by anyone else for political reasons. I had no discussion with Gordon Brown about this at all.' That claim, he says, was a product of 'this extraordinarily dysfunctional relationship. They and their courtiers saw shadows.'⁴⁰

Blair remained utterly convinced that Brown had stabbed him in the front. To one close friend in the Cabinet, Blair called it 'the single most treacherous act ever committed by Gordon'.⁴¹ According to another member of the Cabinet: 'Tony absolutely believes that Gordon did that. This was one of a whole variety of threats that Gordon issued.'[42] Blair told his non-political friend Barry Cox that Brown was behind it. 'He believes that that was a put-up between Harman, Dromey and Brown. He did say specifically that this was a set-up. That was the time that he began to believe that Brown was behaving truly badly. Cherie would say the scales took a long time to fall from his eyes,' recounts Cox. 'He did begin to believe the worst of Gordon Brown.'[43]

The 'cash-for-coronets' affair sharpened the questions about how long Blair could survive. They pursued him across the Pacific during a trip to Indonesia, Australia and New Zealand in late March. This was, in the words of David Hill, 'the craziest foreign tour of them all'.[44] The Conservative John Howard in Australia and Labour's Helen Clarke in New Zealand were also long-serving leaders. They were as one in believing that Blair made a terrible error when he pre-announced the end of his premiership. When Clarke and Howard talked it over, 'John and I agreed that we would never make the mistake of announcing when we were going in advance.'[45]

In an interview for Australian television, Blair remarked: 'It was an unusual thing for me to say, but people kept asking me the question so I decided to answer it. Maybe it was a mistake.'[46]

David Hill vainly tried to explain that the interviewer interrupted before Blair could make clear that he meant his mistake was to believe that it would end speculation about his departure date.[47] It set off another press frenzy about just that.

Though he didn't want to admit it publicly, Blair now realised that his friends were right: it had been a strategic blunder to pre-announce his departure. Neil Kinnock was 'certain that Tony regrets having said it'.[48] He had weakened his authority over colleagues and fed speculation about how much longer he could last without doing anything to contain Gordon Brown.

The two men were forced into each other's company in the first week of April when they shared a car journey to the launch of Labour's campaign for the local elections. As they sat in the back of the limo, Blair attempted to engage Brown in conversation. Brown responded by taking out some papers and burying himself in them. He refused to reply to every overture until Blair eventually gave up trying to make conversation. The journey passed in bitter silence.[49]

The media had fallen into a compulsive habit of labelling troubled times for the Government as 'Blair's worst week'. This became a weary joke within Number 10. 'It's the worst week since the last worst week,' they would shrug. Amidst the fierce competition for that accolade, the last week of

April 2006 was a strong contender. The Government found itself 'in the eye of three storms at once'.[50] The first blew up over health. On Monday, 24 April, Patricia Hewitt faced a hostile reception when the Health Secretary tried to defend the Government's record in a speech to UNISON, the largest of the public sector unions. Hewitt was a less swaggering figure than her two self-consciously macho predecessors at the department, Alan Milburn and John Reid. She was also arguably braver than either of them in tackling some of the structural problems of the NHS. Large sums had been poured into health, but many hospitals were still finishing the financial year in deficit, at which point they had to be bailed out. Hewitt set about ending the persistent deficit problem. This generated a rash of predictions, for the most part alarmist, that it would lead to swingeing job losses. On top of that, the clumsy launch of reforms to primary care trusts were electrifying the nerve endings of this natural Labour constituency. Despite the large numbers of extra staff recruited to the NHS, the unions and professional groups rarely struck a note which was anything but sour towards the Government.

Hewitt's successor at Health, Alan Johnson, would later thank her for his inheritance, a rare example of comradeliness between colleagues. He would enjoy the political benefit of the record public satisfaction ratings that the NHS eventually received. At the time, Hewitt was an unpopular figure trying to implement contentious reforms to an organisation which had long ago fallen out of love with its political masters. Her presentational style grated. In Cabinet, she would talk about 'the silly doctors'.[51] Though born in Australia, she could come over in public as the worst sort of condescending upper-middle-class Englishwoman. Audiences felt as if they were being addressed by a teacher who thought she was talking to a class of especially slow five-year-olds. She was a New Labour case of the substance being better than the style.

Two days after Hewitt's mugging at the UNISON conference, she was mauled even more severely when she addressed the Royal College of Nurses in Bournemouth. The RCN had just published an inflammatory survey suggesting that 13,000 nursing posts might be lost. This was not the best environment for Hewitt to claim that the health service had never been in better shape.[52] The 2,000 nurses in the audience refused to clap a word as the Health Secretary, croaky with flu, spoke. The mood of the angels then turned really evil. They booed and jeered. As Hewitt came off stage, Blair rang her to sympathise.

An even greater tempest was brewing at the Home Office. This was the most severely dysfunctional and serially incompetent department in Whitehall throughout the Labour years. Its latest horrendous bungle concerned foreign citizens who were in British jails. Having served their sentences, they were supposed to be considered for deportation. On Tuesday, 25 April, Charles Clarke called a news conference at which he was obliged to admit that 1,023 foreign convicts had been released without being considered for deportation. He was never able to give a coherent explanation for why this debacle happened because his officials could not supply one. The real reason was discovered many months later, though it was never revealed publicly. I later learnt from a Home Office minister that the files relating to these prisoners were eventually found by accident piled up and languishing un-noticed on the desk of a civil servant who had long since moved on from the Home Office.[53]

The failure was emblematic of one of the Government's persistent flaws. It was mad for writing new laws, but bad at ensuring that existing legislation was applied effectively. Clarke was first warned about the foreign prisoners in July 2005. When the controversy broke publicly, he responded in typically bullish fashion. Hoping to get on the front foot and demonstrate he was in charge of the situation, he declared that things had gone 'horribly wrong' in his department, but 'very, very few' foreign prisoners had slipped through the system since he found out about it.[54] That very night it was revealed that he was wrong: 288 foreign criminals had been freed since he was alerted. Worse, it would emerge that a small number had gone on to commit further serious offences, including crimes of violence and sexual attacks.[55] The morning after his *Newsnight* performance, Clarke was on the airwaves again, saying that Blair had turned down his offer to resign.[56]

In the Commons at noon, the Tories seized on this as evidence of an enfeebled Prime Minister presiding over a ramshackle Government. David Cameron lacerated him: 'When a Prime Minister cannot even deport danger-ous criminals in our jails, aren't the public entitled to say enough is enough?'[57] New Labour had always sold itself as professional. 'What matters is what works' was one of Blair's favourite mantras. His Government was not deliv-ering even the most basic levels of competence.

After the foreign prisoners fiasco, a 'Securing Your Streets' campaign, which was planned to be the centrepiece of Labour's local elections effort, had to be 'completely pulled'.[58]

The third blow of triple whammy Wednesday was delivered by that morn-ing's *Mirror*. John Prescott's infidelity had caught up with him. The day before, Number 10 learnt that the *Mirror* had discovered Prescott's affair with his Diary Secretary, Tracey Temple. The Deputy Prime Minister slipped into Number 10 accompanied by his aide, Alan Schofield. Waiting for them in the Prime Minister's den were Blair and David Hill. Prescott was shocked to have been found out and most anxious about the reaction of his wife, Pauline. Blair was cold. 'Go away and manage it,' he told them.[59]

Given what the *Mirror* already had, their only hope was to try to do some sort of deal with the paper's editor, Richard Wallace. In a bargain typical of its kind, Prescott gave a confessional interview to the *Mirror*. 'Prezza: My affair'[60] was the front page of the Labour-supporting red top the next morning. Many more pages inside were lavished on the story in grisly detail. Readers were treated to gruesome images of a Christmas party at which Prescott cavorted with Temple like a mastodon on heat.

There was more savaging of the 67-year-old Deputy Prime Minister when the *Mail on Sunday* bought up Temple's 'diary' of the affair for a rumoured £250,000 in a deal brokered by Max Clifford, purveyor of sleaze stories to the tabloids. The squalid details included accounts of how they had sex in Prescott's official residences and in his ministerial office while civil servants were outside. 'Anyone could have walked in,' said Temple. One encounter took place minutes after the Iraq war memorial service at St Paul's. On another occasion, Prescott and his mistress had sex in a Southampton hotel while Pauline waited downstairs to meet him for dinner. Prescott underlined an old rule: the less a politician resembled George Clooney, the more likely he was to confuse himself with a sex god. The paper said he 'exploits his power for his sexual gratification'.[61] His old soubriquet of 'Two Jags' was updated to 'Two Shags'. According to Temple's account, power was not always a reliable aphrodisiac. Prescott often had difficulties performing. Humiliated, he went to ground at his Gothic pile in Hull. Prescott had endured mockery for years and yet still managed to retain significant influence within Labour. Now he became a figure of national ridicule stripped of any moral authority he might have once wielded in the party. Serious questions were raised about the propriety of him remaining in office. It was pointed out that a senior officer in the army or police who had sex with a junior in his office on the taxpayers' time would be fired.

On one thing the Prime Minister could agree with the Chancellor: neither wanted an immediate election for the deputy leadership so both tolerated Prescott's survival.[62] The downside of allowing him to continue as Deputy Prime Minister was that it made the Government seem simultaneously arrogant, shameless, incompetent, sleazy and ridiculous. Within Number 10, the survival of this 'absurd figure with no job'[63] was viewed as the most damaging event of that spring 'in terms of the overall credibility of the Government'.[64]

Philip Gould was warning that the local elections were going to be dire even before the mauling of Hewitt, the storm around Clarke and the disgrace of Prescott. The Prime Minister took himself off to bed early on the night of Thursday, 4 May. He woke up to learn that Labour had won just 26 per cent of the national vote. That left them in third place behind the Lib Dems on 27 per cent. The Conservatives, reinvigorated under David Cameron, hit a psychologically important mark by winning 40 per cent. It was their best performance since the original Tory 'Black Wednesday' in 1992. For Blair, this was another downward lurch in his position. Inside Number 10, 'it felt precarious and panicky'[65] and they feared there was 'a pretty high chance' that Gordon Brown would finally go for the Prime Minister.[66]

Brown had disappeared during the final days of the election campaign by taking himself off to Africa. Though he had often proclaimed the continent to be one of his great causes, this was, in fact, his first visit to Africa. The friendly journalists he took with him portrayed Brown as unusually relaxed. He was even seen out of a suit and wearing chinos. They depicted him as a confident man growing into the role of Prime Minister presumptive. It drew a contrast to his advantage with the besieged incumbent back in Britain.

Blair had given private indications to Brown that he now planned to leave Number 10 in the summer of 2007. That did nothing to reassure the Chancellor. Brown was not going to take Blair's word for it 'after so many previous broken promises'.[67] He was probably wise not to. Others heard Blair suggesting he fully intended to stay at least until 2008.[68]

Brown feared that Blair's true intention was to squat in Number 10 for as long as it took to deny his chance to the Chancellor. Ed Balls and Nick Brown, the most belligerent voices around the Chancellor, believed that they had to use brute force. 'Blair doesn't want anyone to succeed him,' the impatient Balls would angrily complain to other members of the Chancellor's court.[69] He argued to Brown that he had to say in unambiguous terms that the transition should begin at once. A more cautious view was taken by Douglas Alexander, Ed Miliband and Sue Nye, who feared that an assassination attempt would leave everyone drenched with blood.

Brown was, as ever, torn. His seething fury that Blair would not give way to him was tempered by his habitual fear of the consequences if he was too obvious about trying to oust Blair. The day after the elections, the Chancellor appeared on Radio Four's *Today* in the programme's prime interview slot immediately after the eight o'clock news. The elections had been a 'warning shot for the Government', he said. That was a fairly mild interpretation of Labour's worst defeat in more than two decades. 'We have to renew ourselves,' he went on. 'It must start now.'[70] That was more naked. It did not take the skills of GCHQ to decode that as meaning Blair should go. But it was not the direct and explicit challenge to the Prime Minister that Brown's hawks wanted and Number 10 feared.[71] The sense around Blair was that Brown had 'pulled back'.[72]

Andrew Smith, a former Cabinet minister close to Brown, led calls for Blair to set a date for his departure.[73] But the Brownites could not press hard without a clearer lead from the man they were trying to get into Number 10. The Chancellor took the aggression up a few notches in subsequent days. His most menacing remark was to make a direct comparison between Blair's position and that of Margaret Thatcher, who had been ejected from Number 10 by her own party in 1990.

'Remember when Mrs Thatcher left,' he told a breakfast television programme on Tuesday of the following week. 'It was unstable, it was disorderly and it was undignified.'[74]

The defenestration of Thatcher had often come up when Brown and Blair argued behind closed doors. 'You'll end up like Thatcher,' Brown routinely told Blair. Blair did indeed shudder about that fate, telling confidants: 'I don't want to leave like her' and 'I don't intend to be dragged out by my fingernails.'[75] So when Brown waved Thatcher's blood-stained, tear-smeared shroud, he turned a private warning to Blair into a very public threat. For the first time, he was visibly putting himself at the head of those wanting to tear down the Prime Minister.

This first attempt at a coup failed. The Brownites were not sufficiently well-organised, and their leader was too hesitant about going for the jugular, to make a success of it. Blair had also seen it coming. In an attempt to pre-empt them by seizing the initiative, he announced a Cabinet reshuffle the day after the May elections. He could not move against Brown: Blair's position was far too fragile to even think about that. He did strike against some Cabinet ministers who were sliding into Brown's camp. Jack Straw gave a thumbs-up as he walked up Downing Street only to emerge from his reshuffle interview having been sacked from the Foreign Office and demoted to Leader of the House, the same manoeuvre Blair executed on Robin Cook after the 2001 election. Straw angrily asked Blair why he had not at least given him advance warning.[76]

Even more furious was Geoff Hoon, removed as Leader of the House after just a year in the job, and deprived of his Cabinet rank and salary. Hoon left his reshuffle interview thinking that he was going to be Secretary of State for Europe. Only afterwards, in a phone call from Ruth Turner at Number 10, did he discover he had been demoted to a Minister of State with only visiting rights to Cabinet. He was so angry that he wrote out a resignation statement.[77] He planned to make a speech with revelations about the Kelly Affair that he told friends could trigger the instant downfall of the

Prime Minister. Hoon thought better of quitting, but he was now thoroughly disaffected. He told his friends that he was now going to 'make an application to become a Brownite'.[78]

Brown could not resist boasting about his new allies. 'Gordon would torment Tony by telling him which ministers had defected,' says a Cabinet member very close to Blair. 'He'd tell him about all the double-dealing Jack was doing. He'd tell him about Geoff too.'[79]

Blair was making new enemies. He also disappointed his friends. Many of his senior staff pressed the Prime Minister to promote David Miliband to the Foreign Office.[80] Miliband was not a wholly true Blairite, being some degrees to the left of the Prime Minister. He was loyal, he could work with colleagues, he had bright ideas about how to renew the Government, and he needed to be built up if he was going to be a serious potential rival for the leadership to Brown. After some prevarication by Blair, he denied Miliband such rapid advancement. 'The argument was that David was too young and it would damage him to promote him too early,' says Jonathan Powell. 'Gordon would come and kill him.'[81] Miliband was instead moved to Environment and Blair astonished Westminster by handing the Foreign Office to Margaret Beckett. She arrived at the audience with the Prime Minister apprehensive that he might be about to clear her out to make way for fresher faces. When he told her that she was getting one of the big offices of state, she conveyed her shock with one word: 'Fuck.'[82]

The big casualty of the reshuffle was Charles Clarke, who was almost alone in thinking that he could soldier on at the Home Office after the furore over foreign prisoners. Blair, the reluctant butcher, did not want to lose this solid ally altogether. He even told Clarke that, before his troubles, he was planning to move him to the Foreign Office in order to build up him and John Reid as competitors to Brown.[83] Blair offered Clarke a move to Defence. Clarke turned that down and other offers from Blair. Stubbornly believing he should stay at the Home Office, and that he could convince Blair to change his mind, he went round to Number 10 the night before the announcement of the reshuffle and demanded to see the Prime Minister. Blair came down from the flat above wearing jeans and a T-shirt. Clarke again argued that he should be kept on as Home Secretary. 'No, Charles,' responded a chilly Blair who reckoned he had been generous to offer him alternative positions. 'My mind is made up. That's it.'[84] Clarke was replaced at the Home Office by Reid, who infuriated his predecessors and many of his civil servants by promptly declaring that the department was 'not fit for purpose'.[85]

The reshuffle was intended by Blair to be 'the launch pad for his final glorious period'[86] but it did not succeed in bolstering his authority or increasing his longevity. Frank Dobson reached for a briny cliché and decried it as 'rearranging the deckchairs on the Titanic'.[87] The Blairites felt increasingly isolated. Stephen Byers and Alan Milburn travelled on a train together to watch Newcastle play Chelsea. They morbidly joked that if the train crashed there would be no Blairites left.[88] The Prime Minister was not as friendless as that, but his position was weakening. At a meeting of the parliamentary party on 8 May, Labour MPs demanded a timetable for his departure. He did not feel strong enough to reassert his right to serve a full third term. He had to promise them that he would give a successor 'ample time', which surrendered ground while fuelling a new bout of speculation about how long was ample.

This reshuffle was seen by many ministers as his last shot. Another disappointed member of the Cabinet was Peter Hain, who thought he was on a promise of promotion from the Northern Ireland Office. Like many such Blair promises, it didn't prove to be bankable. At their interview, Blair tried to soften the other man's disappointment with the usual patter about not wanting to move a vital minister at a critical period. 'I'll make it up to you next time,' said Blair. Hain responded sardonically: 'But there won't be a next time, Tony. Everyone knows this is your last reshuffle.'[89]

At ten o'clock on the morning of 12 July, Michael Levy, peer of the Labour realm, Middle East envoy for the Prime Minister, and the party's principal fund-raiser, presented himself with his lawyer at Colindale police station in north London. By 10.30, he had been arrested and booked. Levy was walked down the police station's dirty magnolia corridors and seated in an interview room where forty-eight hours of interrogation began. 'Cash-for-coronets' thus moved into an entirely new category of affair which now menaced Number 10 even more directly. 'No-one thought it would come to this and no-one knows where it is going,' groaned one of Blair's closest confidants.[90]

Levy told the police that he had supported recommendations for peerages, but it was ultimately the Prime Minister and his inner circle who decided who got honoured. He denied being any part of a cash-for-peerages deal.

Levy never tried to pretend that the thought of honours didn't come into the equation, later writing: 'The reality was that very few of the businessmen who gave large-scale donations to any of the parties did so without at least the vague hope that they might get some honour in return.'[91]

The hope didn't have to be that vague. It was a squalid but open secret of British politics for years that offering a big sum to a party massively advanced a rich man's chances of being cloaked in ermine and acquiring a seat on the claret-coloured benches in the Lords. It was true under the Tories as it was under Labour. Analysis showed that large donors to the Labour Party were 1,657 times more likely to receive an honour than a non-donor and 6,969 times more likely to receive a peerage.[92] The bargain did not need to be made explicit, which was what Yates of the Yard would need to prove to get a successful prosecution under The Honours (Prevention of Abuse) Act of 1925. That Act was passed after David Lloyd George made the sale of honours so brazen that there was even a price list. The Act did not legislate against the nudges and winks which were more often the British way of corruption. Only one person – Maundy Gregory, Lloyd George's bagman – had ever been jailed under the 1925 Act.

For month after month, the coronets affair nevertheless produced a torrent of bad headlines for the Government. Many of the lenders expressed their bitter dismay as their reputations were trashed in the media. They turned on Downing Street. Sir Gulam Noon, a prominent philanthropist who had openly supported Labour for more than a decade, said: 'I would have given them the money, but they wanted to do the loan.'[93]

Sir David Garrard complained: 'I bailed the Labour Party out and now I am in the worst position I have ever been in my life.'

The police believed they had uncovered a key piece of evidence when they got hold of a diary kept by Sir Christopher Evans, the biotech entrepreneur and Labour donor. An entry referred to him and Levy discussing a 'K or a P', meaning a knighthood or a peerage. But this was still not enough to prove a crime: discussing honours was not illegal unless explicitly linked to the exchange of money.[94]

Yates steadily worked his way towards the one person who had indisputably known about the hidden loans and made the honours recommendations. In December, Blair himself was interviewed for two hours, one of the least attractive firsts of his premiership. At the dispatch box, David Cameron mockingly invited the Prime Minister 'to speak for the benefit of the recording'. Some newspapers mocked up pictures of Blair in handcuffs. Jonathan Powell was questioned twice under caution. 'Is Daddy going to prison?' one of his daughters asked his wife before bursting into tears. Powell says: 'It absorbed a huge amount of time and emotional energy which made it difficult to do other things.'[95] For David Hill, 'cash-for-honours was the most difficult, unpleasant and debilitating thing during my time at Downing Street. You couldn't get into arguments with the police. You couldn't say where the leaks had come from. You were stuck in totally defensive mode.'[96] In January, Levy was arrested again, this time on suspicion of perverting the course of justice. He let it be known that he feared being 'hung out to dry' by Downing Street.[97]

On Friday, 19 January, Ruth Turner, the Director of Government Relations at Number 10, was arrested during a dawn raid on her flat. That was the 'single darkest moment' at Downing Street.[98] The only consolation was that it attracted accusations that the police were becoming increasingly theatrical, heavy-handed and desperate. When the investigation was over, Sarah Helm, a journalist and Powell's wife, attacked that arrest as 'Gestapo tactics'.[99] Number 10 itself was 'shocked, really shocked. It looked like part of a pattern to terrorise people.'[100]

Blair would sit in his den and explode about the police tactics: 'This is fucking ridiculous!' He felt 'outraged' but also paralysed 'because things were out of his control: he did not know what was going to happen next.' He told his staff: 'We can't attack the police because we will not win in the court of public opinion.'[101]

To most people, Blair adopted a mien of injured innocence and insouciant confidence about the outcome. When Sir Gus O'Donnell had to tell the Prime Minister that the police wanted to interrogate him for a second time, Blair responded: 'The rotters!'[102] As the headlines grew ever blacker, the Cabinet Secretary felt obliged to warn Scotland Yard about the size of the stakes. They were told: 'You need to realise this is a very big thing and think very, very carefully.' Were the detectives to treat Blair as a suspect by interviewing him under caution, they would force his resignation as Prime Minister.[103]

The impact of the debilitating affair was not ultimately legal. Sixteen months after the investigation began, the Crown Prosecution Service concluded, to the chagrin of Yates, that it could not bring any charges against anyone. The impact was political. In the assessment of Blair's own Cabinet, 'it cast a very damaging shadow over the end of his premiership.'[104] It completed a transformation from the first term's Teflon Tony, the Prime Minister to whom nothing really stuck, to the Toxic Tony, whom the voters saw as presiding over a sleazy regime. Polls indicated that a majority believed peerages had been traded for cash and he had dishonoured his promise to clean up public life.[105]

Blair paid a huge price for his folly in raising campaign funds through loans and not disclosing them to the Lords Appointments Commission. The consequences corroded his reputation, humiliated his chief fund-raiser and several of his senior staff by making criminal suspects of them during the investigation, and trashed the reputations of rich admirers, who would demand their loans back and never want to help the party again. The Labour Party came close to bankruptcy.[106] Blair had taken money from plutocrats in pursuit of his goal of ending Labour's financial reliance on union money. As rich men abandoned the party, Labour ended up almost entirely dependent on the unions. It was massively weakening of Tony Blair for crucial months when he was under siege from Gordon Brown. The Chancellor's acolytes unremittingly briefed that only a change of Prime Minister could reinvest the Government with integrity and purpose. The police investigation ate away at Blair's position throughout his remaining time at Number 10. Not only was his premiership stained by 'cash-for-coronets': the affair played a large part in bringing it to an end long before he had served the full third term he had once promised himself.

23. Bad Vibrations

The helicopter flew fast and extremely low: hugging the ground, hopping power lines and yawing this way and that as the pilot executed continuous evasive manoeuvres. The speeding Chinook was loaded with chaff to be fired if the faintest flash of light from the ground suggested an incoming surface-to-air missile. By May 2006, it was more hazardous than ever to fly into the fortified Green Zone in the centre of Baghdad. Even for those who enjoyed this form of travel, the ride was hair-raising. For Tony Blair, phobic about flying, it was his worst nightmare. Staff who accompanied him saw 'how he had to psyche himself up. He would grip the seat. You'd see his knuckles go white.'[1]

Blair wanted to go to Baghdad to be the first Western leader to endorse the newly installed Iraqi Prime Minister and his optimistically named 'National Unity Government'. At a news conference with Nouri al-Maliki, Blair talked about 'a new beginning'.[2] In some respects, there was evidence of that. Iraqis defied the threat of bombs and shootings by insurgents and sectarian killers to turn out in their millions to approve a new constitution the previous October.[3] There was another impressively high turn-out, larger than was usual in elections in either America or Britain, when 12 million Iraqis took part in the national elections in December.

What these displays of democracy did not produce was a stable government or a peaceful country. The violence escalated to a higher pitch. The hundredth casualty among British service personnel occurred at the end of January, when a remote-detonated roadside bomb, the insurgents' weapon of choice, blew up a convoy. On 22 February, al-Qaeda terrorists disguised themselves as police to bomb the al-Askari mosque in Samara, a ninth-century shrine and one of the most revered Shia sites in Iraq. The collapse of its famous golden dome marked another savage lurch into civil war. By nightfall that day, more than a hundred Sunni mosques had been attacked by vengeful Shia mobs.

The conditions in the capital during Blair's visit underlined how distant

Iraq was from being the peaceful oasis of democracy in the heart of the Middle East that he and Bush had promised would be the outcome of the invasion. Even the Green Zone was no longer regarded as entirely safe for the Prime Minister. On previous visits, he was able to go out in the streets. On this occasion, he was confined inside for fear of assassination. There was even anxiety that extremists might have infiltrated the Iraqi presidential guard of honour which was presented for his inspection. The honour guard were all given a full body search before they were allowed anywhere near Blair.

The main topic of his talks with the new Government was the handover to Iraqi forces which was scheduled to begin in July and a timetable for drawing down the number of British troops in the south. The Iraqi police and army were still not ready 'to take over security fully', said their new Prime Minister. 'We will start in the provinces and do them in turn.'[4]

In the immediate aftermath of the invasion, the British were self-congratulatory about their handling of the four southern provinces and thought it made a flattering contrast with the disastrous engagements by the Americans in the rest of Iraq. By the summer of 2006, Basra was less secure than at any time since the toppling of Saddam. The threats had grown more lethal, not least because of Iranian aid to Shia fighters, who were using mines and rockets with increasing sophistication and deadliness. At the beginning of the month of Blair's visit, five British service personnel were killed when their Lynx helicopter was shot down by a surface-to-air missile. The casualties included Flight Lieutenant Sarah-Jayne Mulvihill, the first British servicewoman to die in action in Iraq.

Moqtada Sadr, a radical Shia cleric, stood at the head of the Mehdi army, a paramilitary force which was conducting increasingly aggressive attacks on British forces. By the end of the month, a state of emergency was declared in Basra. The level of British forces had been cut from 46,000 at the time of the invasion in spring 2003 to just 8,000 by 2006. That was woefully short of the numbers required to cope with an increasingly disaffected Shia population and the rising threat from militias and criminal gangs. Operation Sinbad, in the autumn of 2006, was the last serious British effort to impose order and authority in Basra. Blair craved an exit from Iraq which he could hail as a success, but he was not prepared to provide the means that might have achieved that outcome. Major General Richard Shirreff was the last British commander to make an attempt to try to break the power of the Mehdi army and the other paramilitary groups. His requests for a surge of military support were turned down by London. Despite the mounting British casualties, no reinforcements were sent. Sending more troops clashed with Blair's political imperative to try to give a sense of progress in Iraq, illusory though that was.

By 2006, the Chiefs of Staff despaired of Iraq as unwinnable. 'The intensity of the sectarian violence between Sunni and Shia was not forecast,' says General Sir Mike Jackson. 'Nobody forecast it would be as dire as it turned out to be.'⁵ In August, he was succeeded as head of the army by General Sir Richard Dannatt, who promptly warned that the army was 'running hot' and could 'break' if it was not soon withdrawn. Rather than look to create a liberal democracy as 'an exemplar for the region' they should settle for 'a lower ambition' and 'get ourselves out sometime soon because our presence exacerbates the security problems'.⁶ When Dannatt went boldly public with these views, Blair was 'furious', but felt too weak to risk sacking a serving general who openly challenged his political masters.⁷

Britain's 'main effort' changed focus to Afghanistan, a switch prompted by a mixture of fatalism about Iraq and fright that Afghanistan was also spiralling into chaos. Just as in Iraq, there had been a woeful lack of postwar planning in Afghanistan. After the toppling of Mullah Omar's diabolical regime in 2001, there were elections and some other dividends. Millions of girls could now go to school. But Hamid Karzai's government was tenuous and the international presence far too slight to cope with the scale of the security challenge. Drug traffickers continued to ply their trade and warlords to control large swathes of the country. Though the whole of NATO made a commitment to Afghanistan, many of its European members were not willing to send personnel in meaningful numbers. The Germans took responsibility for training a new Afghan police force. Berlin sent a grand total of seventeen officers to carry out the task. The Taliban were given the space to become resurgent. As Iraq looked increasingly hopeless, Blair became agitated that Afghanistan was sliding away as well.⁸ His concern meshed with the feeling of General Dannatt and other senior officers who lobbied for more concentration on Afghanistan. Jonathan Powell says: 'The army wanted to have a nice, straightforward fight against the Taliban that they thought they could win.'⁹

At the end of January 2006, John Reid, the Defence Secretary, announced a significant amplification of the size of the British force. 'We cannot risk Afghanistan again becoming a sanctuary for terrorists,' he declared to MPs. He also made the point that 90 per cent of the heroin that went into 'the veins of the young people' of Britain came from Afghanistan. An extra 3,700 troops were added to the 2,000 already committed. More than half of them were mobilised to the southern province of Helmand. The Defence Secretary offered MPs the reassurance that he was deploying 'this potent force to protect and deter'. Their mission was to guard 'provincial reconstruction teams'. They were not intended 'to wage war; that is not our aim,' Reid said cheerfully: 'We would be perfectly happy if they returned without firing a shot.'[10] As it turned out, millions of rounds were fired in the first year of the deployment alone. Within months of Reid's statement, the mission was changing drastically as the Taliban responded with unanticipated ferocity. As early as that September, General David Richards, the British commander of the NATO forces, was warning: 'We need to realise that we could actually fail here.'[11] On a daily basis, the fighting became much more intense than in Iraq. The British army was drawn into the most protracted ground combat conducted by them since 1945, but without clear political and strategic goals that pointed to an eventual exit. That autumn, fourteen British servicemen were killed when their Nimrod crashed in Afghanistan, the largest loss of life in a single military incident since the Falkands War. A devastating official report subsequently blamed the Ministry of Defence for sacrificing essential safety for the sake of saving money.[12] The lack of adequate equipment in Afghanistan, and the needless casualties that resulted, became a growing issue of political controversy and shame. To the horror of senior officers, Gordon Brown chose this period to put a squeeze on defence expenditure. 'The Chancellor became really unpleasant'[13] towards the armed forces' budgets in 2006, the very year that the Prime Minister was committing more troops to Afghanistan and security was deteriorating in southern Iraq.

The dysfunctional relationship and clashing priorities of Blair and Brown meant that they did not ensure that military commitments were backed with the necessary resources. As a result, soldiers were put in harm's way without adequate protection or support.

Soon after his trip to Baghdad, Blair flew to America, where support for the Iraq war was also collapsing. George Bush's approval ratings, once higher than those of FDR after Pearl Harbor, were plunging. They would not reach bottom until he was as unpopular as Richard Nixon when he was forced to resign over Watergate. The disintegration of support for Bush was accelerated by his utterly inept response to Hurricane Katrina and the inundation of New Orleans. The White House wondered in advance of Blair's visit whether the Prime Minister might now like to be formally presented with the Congressional Gold Medal that he was awarded in the deceptively euphoric aftermath of the fall of Saddam. Number 10 had then viewed the medal as a stupendous accolade; three years later, it was too toxic to touch. There was horror among the Prime Minister's officials at the thought of TV pictures of Bush hanging a medal around the neck of Blair.[14] Every time the

White House raised the subject of the medal, Jonathan Powell 'just played the Americans along', telling them the timing was not quite right. Washington did not try to press the medal with great vigour. 'The antennae of their people were pretty acute. They knew it was a problem for us.'[15]

The air was heavy with failure when the two leaders held a joint news conference in the White House Rose Garden. A third-term Prime Minister with draining authority stood next to a second-term President in steep decline. They sought comfort by clinging to each other. 'Don't count him out,' Bush said of Blair. 'I want him to be here as long as I'm President.'[16] American newspapers which had previously lauded Blair for his eloquence now found him 'dismayed and tongue-tied'.[17]

Both men felt compelled to do some penance for the mistakes made in Iraq. Bush conceded there were 'setbacks and missteps'. That was a wild underestimate of the catastrophic failures in Iraq, but a greater acknowledgement of error than before. Blair publicly admitted for the first time that it had been a mistake to abolish the Iraqi army and purge the administrators. Yet both men were still fundamentally unapologetic about the enterprise. Blair declared: 'For all the hardships and challenges in the past few years, I shall always think that it was a cause worth fighting for.'[18]

He clung to his theory of interventionism despite the practical experiences of Afghanistan and Iraq. The next day at Georgetown University, he delivered a speech drafted from scratch on the flight across the Atlantic. It was a defiant attempt to re-argue the case for intervention in which he cited the killings in Darfur as well as Milosevic's ethnic cleansing in Kosovo and the oppression of Saddam and the Taliban. Yet even Blair had to acknowledge that this idealistic cause was massively compromised by the experience of Iraq. He conceded, in a companion speech of this period, that the war was widely seen as the 'wreckage' of his world view. So it was. Many of the American neo-cons were recanting, as were some British interventionists. They had lost their religion in the bloody sands of Iraq. Blair regretted that 'a doctrine of benign inactivity' had become 'the majority view of a large part of Western opinion'.

He nevertheless remade the argument that 'liberating oppressed people in distant lands' was 'not just an abstract moral duty but essential for our security'.[19] The interventionist doctrine had never had a more passionate advocate than Tony Blair. He still clung to the high vision that brought his premiership low. He was both the best advocate of the case and its worst for he had been party to so many of the terrible mistakes in Iraq. One of the many tragedies of that war was that it discredited the very cause that he championed.

An insistent critique of his doctrine was that its application was highly partial and often hypocritical. Britain and America toppled tyrannies in Afghanistan and Iraq, but they tolerated and connived with dictatorships in Pakistan and Saudi Arabia. When the vast majority of the Labour Party and many others beyond its ranks looked at the Middle East, the Palestinians numbered among the 'oppressed people' about whom Blair spoke. That summer, the Israel–Palestine conflict erupted more violently than at any time during his premiership. Hezbollah, the extreme Islamist group who were resourced by the Syrians and Iranians, had been repeatedly firing rockets into Israel and organising suicide bombings. On 12 July, Hezbollah crossed over the border from Lebanon to kidnap two Israeli soldiers and kill eight others. The next day, the Israelis sent troops into Lebanon on a retaliatory expedition.

The chances of arresting an escalation were even lower than usual in this combustible region. The recent elections to the Palestinian parliament were a defeat for Fatah and a victory for the uncompromising militants of Hamas, a party which did not accept Israel's right to exist. The result was an absolute shock to both London and Washington.[20] The Israelis were led by an untested and insecure Prime Minister. Ehud Olmert had taken over less than four months earlier after Ariel Sharon was struck down by a massive stroke.

Omert was anxious to prove his mettle to both Israel's voters and its enemies. He blundered into an atrociously planned onslaught. The Israelis unleashed large-scale air, artillery and ground attacks on targets in Lebanon. Most of the world agreed with Jacques Chirac that this response was totally disproportionate. At a meeting of the UN Security Council on 14 July, America and Britain stood alone in opposing a call for an immediate ceasefire. Their line was that the provocateurs were Hezbollah not Israel. There was some traction in Blair's argument that the crisis needed a serious, widely backed UN resolution rather than politically expedient gestures and soundbites. But the refusal to call for a ceasefire was an invitation to Tel Aviv to ramp up the offensive. Once again Blair cast himself as the White House's faithful echo when he contended that it was fruitless to demand a ceasefire from the Israelis without the disarmament of the militias in Lebanon.

The next day, the Prime Minister flew to Russia for the G8 Summit in St Petersburg. At the opening plenary, he approached Bush, already seated at the conference table and chewing on a bread roll.

'Yo, Blair!' drawled the Texan. 'How are you doin'?'

The Prime Minister was neither fazed nor offended by this salutation. He was very familiar with the quirks of Bush and his frat boy habit of addressing friends by surname. What neither knew was that their conversation was not private. The microphone in front of Bush was live and picking up the entire exchange.

Bush thanked Blair for a recent birthday gift of a Burberry sweater. 'Awfully thoughtful,' smirked Bush. 'Know you picked it out yourself.' 'Oh, absolutely,' Blair bantered back.

The Prime Minister then suggested himself as a peace-making envoy in the Lebanon crisis. 'I am perfectly happy to try and see what the lie of the land is, but you need that done quickly because otherwise it will spiral.' Bush blanked him: 'I think Condi is going to go pretty soon.'

Blair, incoherently stammering, responded: 'That's, that's, that's all that matters. But if you . . . you see it will take some time to get that together.'

'Yeah, yeah,' said Bush through a mouthful of bread roll.

Blair tried again: 'Well, it's only if, I mean, you know, if she needs the ground prepared as it were. Because obviously if she goes out, she's got to succeed, whereas I can go out and just talk.'

Bush acted as if he had heard none of that. The President opined that the solution to the crisis was to get the Russians 'to get Syria to get Hezbollah to stop doing this shit and it's over'.

After a few more exchanges, Blair squinted at the microphone. 'Is this . . .?' he asked and gave it a tap.[21]

When he asked his aides, they confirmed what he feared: the entire exchange had been overheard. 'He didn't know whether to laugh or cry.'[22] There was nothing his media managers could do to limit the damage.[23]

The 'Yo, Blair!' was mercilessly mocked by the British press, among whom it was taken as confirmatory evidence that he was Bush's poodle. Yet it was Bush's 'No, Blair' when he vetoed a trip by the Prime Minister that was truly more revealing and humiliating. It was demeaning for Blair to be caught asking Bush's permission to go to the Middle East. He was supposed to be the leader of a sovereign nation. This made him sound like a presidential underling asking for the boss's permission to travel – which he did not get because the President was sending one of his other employees instead. Blair was cast as a supplicant and a spurned one.

'I just cringed with embarrassment,' said one of his closest allies in the Cabinet.[24]

The only fragment of consolation was that the live microphone also illustrated what Blair had been struggling with during all the years of trying to handle the White House. Bush was recorded complaining about the flying time from Washington to St Petersburg. He remarked to the Chinese President that it was all right for him 'because this is your neighbourhood'. Bush expressed amazement when he was told that it actually took eight hours to fly from Beijing to St Petersburg.

The communiqué cobbled together at the end of the summit did nothing to defuse the conflict in Lebanon. The Israelis, encouraged by the G8's fail-ure to call for a ceasefire, intensified their military strikes. Beirut was repeatedly bombed. Large numbers of Israeli troops crossed the border. The blitz took hundreds of lives, among them thirty-seven children in a single attack. This onslaught was subsequently seen in Israel itself as a totally misconceived response that failed in its objective of crushing Hezbollah while alienating world opinion.

Blair stuck to the position, for which Bush was the only other advocate, that nothing would be achieved by calling for the Israelis to stop. On 18 July, appearing in the Commons before hostile MPs, Blair defended the G8's failure to call for an immediate cessation of the attacks and placed nearly all the blame on Hezbollah for 'acts of extremism that were designed to provoke the very response that followed'.[25]

Downing Street was privately agitated about the death toll being inflicted on civilians. Nigel Sheinwald, Blair's foreign affairs adviser, had a number of conversations with the Israeli Government, including Olmert himself, to press Britain's concerns.[26] Publicly, though, Blair sounded callously indiffer-ent to the casualties because he would not condemn the Israeli attacks. He would not give an inch to the growing number of critics who saw him putting Britain slavishly in tow behind the Americans yet again. 'If I call for a cease-fire, I play myself out of the game with the Israelis,' he argued with Justin Forsyth and other dissenting aides.[27] 'All of us were telling him he was wrong – substantially as well as tactically.'[28] He was also not prepared to put any daylight between himself and the White House. 'It was Bush again really,' says Sally Morgan. 'He would not break with Bush.'[29]

To several confidants, it appeared to go even deeper than that: Blair agreed with the Bush policy of green-lighting the Israelis to try to destroy Hezbol-lah, despite the damage done to Lebanon and the low chances of achieving the objective.[30] 'Bush had persuaded Tony that it could be done very quickly,' says Michael Levy, another ally who protested to Blair that he was taking the wrong position.[31]

Blair saw this crisis through the distorting lens of the struggle with Islamist fundamentalism. He had started to speak of an 'arc of extremism', an echo of Bush's old 'axis of evil'.[32] He viewed the Lebanon conflict simplistically as another front in the struggle against the Taliban in Afghanistan, al-Qaeda in Iraq and the regime in Iran. From his hardened perspective, a ceasefire would reward terrorist aggression; it would make Britain and America look weak in the eyes of Syria, Iran and the Iraqi insurgents; and it would do nothing to resolve the underlying sources of the conflict. 'He just fitted it into his jigsaw, his great scheme of things,' observed one of his staff. 'He took this view that you can't give way anywhere.'[33]

By late July, international condemnation of Israel had reached an even more intense pitch. Kofi Annan, the UN Secretary-General, condemned the 'excessive use of force' to inflict 'collective punishment' as a violation of the Geneva Convention.[34] Blair's posture put him in a more belligerently pro-Israeli position than the Tories. William Hague, the Shadow Foreign Secretary, condemned the Olmert Government's attacks as 'disproportionate' and damaging to 'the Israeli cause in the long term'.[35] Labour MPs, already upset, were further aghast to sit in the Commons and hear the Conservatives condemn the death and suffering in Lebanon in stronger terms than their own Prime Minister. Chris Mullin, a former Foreign Office minister and erstwhile admirer of Blair, spoke for the great majority of his colleagues when he called it 'shameful that we can find nothing stronger than the word "regret" to describe the slaughter and misery and mayhem that Israel has unleashed on a fragile country like Lebanon'.[36] Keith Hill, whose job as PPS to the Prime Minister was to read the mood of Labour MPs, saw that 'his refusal to come out with a condemnation of Israel hyped up a lot of people, angered MPs across the board.'[37]

Yet Blair remained defiant in his growing isolation: 'Some people will want me to go further in condemning Israel, say if I don't condemn Israel it means I don't really care about Lebanon. All of that means absolutely nothing but words.'[38] For a man who had made his career from words, this was remarkably cavalier about their effect. Everyone close to him begged Blair to at least recalibrate his language and nuance his position. 'The party could not understand why he would not use a set of words,' says Matthew Taylor. 'What possible harm was there in using a set of words?'[39]

Sally Morgan no longer had an official position at Number 10, but she remained close. She repeatedly rang Blair to warn that he was haemorrhaging support among Labour MPs. She told him directly: 'This will do for you.'[40] Phil Collins, a very loyal member of his staff, observed later: 'He didn't think it through. It was a massive error. Those political antennae that usually worked so well – he just turned them off.'[41]

On Thursday, 27 July, the Cabinet convened for their last meeting before the summer break. David Miliband, who had never before at Cabinet criticised Blair, warned that the refusal to call for a ceasefire was causing swelling uproar in Labour's ranks.[42] That weekend, Jack Straw, having failed in private attempts to shift Blair, went public with his opposition. In a statement to Muslim leaders in his Blackburn constituency, Straw said that 'ten times as many' Lebanese civilians had been killed or injured as Israelis and warned that 'disproportionate action only escalates an already dangerous situation'.⁴³ Number 10 was bombarded with letters and phone calls from angry Labour MPs, many of them mainstream ministers and backbenchers who had no previous history of animosity towards Blair. Tessa Jowell, one of his most loyal supporters in the Cabinet, privately implored him to adjust his stance.⁴⁴ She told Ken Livingstone: 'There's no-one – not even me – who agrees with Tony about this.'⁴⁵

His lonely position aligned him with a view in Washington that even suggested that the mounting casualties in Lebanon were something to celebrate. Condi Rice went so far as to claim that the bloodshed represented the 'birth pangs of a new Middle East'. The neo-cons were now trying to find a virtue in what they called the 'creative chaos' unleashed by the invasion of Iraq.⁴⁶ It was certainly chaos; it was harder to see what was creative about the indiscriminate slaughter of civilians.

Blair became more isolated at home and abroad than he had been on Iraq. He stuck to his deeply unpopular position not oblivious to the fury, but in spite of it. The Lebanon crisis delineated the arc of his premiership. A leader who loved to be loved in his first term had morphed into a leader who didn't seem to care whether he was hated. He almost relished being stubbornly defiant of opinion internationally and in his own party. It had got to the point, says Matthew Taylor, where 'you could convince him to do something' not by saying it would be popular, but 'by saying it's a really unpopular thing to do. He'd be more likely to do it.'⁴⁷

At the end of July, he was back in America. During a news conference with George Bush, neither man made any call for restraint by the Israelis.⁴⁸ From Washington, Blair flew west for a long-scheduled trip to California. The idea was to highlight climate change and hi tech. He was also keen to spend time with Arnold Schwarzenegger, the action movie actor turned state governor, whom he found an intriguing figure. He was joined on the six-hour flight to the west coast by Sir David Manning, who had become the British ambassador in Washington. Manning joined the trip in the hope that he could get Blair to grasp that he was committing a terrible error over Lebanon. They sat together in the first-class cabin along with two of the Prime Minister's aides, Justin Forsyth and Liz Lloyd. In his soft voice, Manning spoke bluntly to the Prime Minister. 'This is crazy – it's undermining everything you want to achieve in the Middle East.' The Israelis had invaded the Lebanon three times before and each time it was 'a complete disaster'. Manning argued: 'For us to condone it is a great mistake.' Blair responded that Hezbollah started it: 'You can't expect the Israelis to sit there and keep taking it.' If he joined the condemnation: 'I'll lose my leverage.' 'What leverage?' asked an exasperated Manning. 'We can't send any troops.' All they were achieving was the alienation of the Arab world.[49] Here was his most senior ambassador and a foreign policy adviser he hugely respected telling the Prime Minister that he was wrong. As Manning battered away, Blair became 'chilly' and 'resistant' to hearing any more.[50]

On the last weekend in July, it was reported that an Israeli strike in Quana had killed more than fifty people, many of them children. As the death toll rose over 1,000, even the Americans got cold feet. They started to work with the French, not the British, to frame a UN resolution, which was passed on Friday, 11 August.[51] It called for a cessation of hostilities by both Hezbollah and Israel. On the same day, a letter of protest against Blair's stance was delivered, in his absence, to Number 10. The letter was signed by a hundred Labour MPs. Downing Street shrugged it off. Sticks and stones could hurt his bones, letters could surely never hurt him.

The UN resolution came far too late for those already dead and maimed in Lebanon. It was also far too late for Tony Blair to repair the grave damage he had done to his already fragile position. Later, reflecting with friends, he came to see how badly he had misjudged the Lebanon crisis and was 'rueful that he brought about the end of himself by what he did that summer'.[52] He looked wilfully and pointlessly isolated when he refused to call for a ceasefire. He seemed insensitive when he would not condemn the killing of innocents in Lebanon. He had once again bound himself to a hugely unpopular position taken by George Bush for no obvious purpose or gain other than of cleaving to the White House. The Lebanon crisis reinflamed the unhealed wounds of Iraq. Frank Dobson, a member of Blair's Cabinet in the first term, had become one of the most vocal agitators for his departure. Dobson is in no doubt what finally shattered Blair's hold on power: 'It was Lebanon that did it. There were only three countries in the world against a ceasefire. Israel was one. The United States was another. And we were the third. People were nauseated.'[53] Peter Hain, a member of the Cabinet, remarks: 'Loyal colleagues who'd never voted against the Government – many of them would have described themselves as Blairites – were expressing an unease that I'd never seen before.'[54] Huw Evans, a senior member of the Number 10 staff, agrees that 'Lebanon was the last straw' for the party.[55] Sally Morgan concurs that it was then 'that he lost mainstream Labour MPs, the core people'.[56]

On 8 August, Tony Blair left for his delayed holiday in the West Indies having been briefed that a major event was about to happen in Britain. The following evening, there were raids and arrests at addresses in London, Birmingham and High Wycombe. Soon afterwards, it was announced that the police and intelligence services had foiled an audacious terrorist plot to use chemical bombs, secreted in items such as shampoo and medicine bottles, to blow up at least seven airliners flying to North America from British airports. John Reid thrust himself in front of the cameras to take charge of the response. He had replaced Charles Clarke as Home Secretary in the spring reshuffle. Reid's pugnacity, authoritarianism, proficiency and loyalty all commended themselves to Blair. So did the idea that he could be a potential challenger to Gordon Brown for Number 10. Reid was more complicated than he looked and liked to suggest that he was more sensitive too. He had a doctorate. He was married to a film-maker. He liked to weave into his speeches quotations from Bertolt Brecht and Eduard Bernstein. He took it as an affront, or at least pretended to, when he was routinely described as an 'attack dog'. His political teeth were certainly sharp. John Prescott was nominally in charge of the Government while Blair was on his summer sojourn in Barbados. Prescott was elbowed aside by Reid, who made himself the face of the Government. The airline terror plot was an opportunity to maximise his image as the tough guy of the Cabinet and demonstrate that he could grip a crisis. The plot was big: twenty-four suspects were arrested. According to the authorities, if the conspiracy had succeeded it would have resulted in mass murder on a greater scale than 9/11.[57]

Airports and airlines rushed to stiffen security and implement much tighter restrictions on hand luggage. There were chaotic scenes at Heathrow and other airports which didn't have the staff or equipment to cope with the new measures. Tens of thousands of travellers suffered long delays, often stretching into many days. Some families lost their holidays altogether. While the airports overflowed with delayed and distressed families, the press published pictures of the Prime Minister tanning himself in the West Indies on a loaned 'luxury yacht' called *Good Vibrations*. The 'luxury yacht' was, in truth, a relatively modest catamaran. Blair was in daily contact with Reid. He was content that the Home Secretary was on top of things and pleased to give this ally the opportunity to build his profile as a potential leader.[58] In his early premiership, Blair would probably have come back to Britain, if only for presentational reasons. In his late period, he could no longer be bothered with what he now dismissed as gesture politics. His return would have had little practical use. But perceptions always matter in politics, as the past master of image once understood. 'Crisis? Yacht Crisis?' mocked the *Daily Mail*.[59] While thousands of his fellow citizens were contemplating ruined or truncated holidays, Blair was pictured in floral swimming shorts improving his tan. This was the last thing any adviser would recommend to a Prime Minister already accused of being out of touch.

*

Before his departure for the Caribbean, his closest allies had counselled him that he would have to come back from holiday with a strategy to manage the rising clamour from Labour MPs for clarity about how long he intended to go on as Prime Minister. Blair remained hugely reluctant to say any more about this in public on the grounds that talking about it would just lead to 'another Hiroshima of speculation'.[60] His silence only made his critics more voluble. The issue grew hotter after the defeats in the May elections and the arrest of Lord Levy, and was now even more sensitive because of his isolation over the Lebanon crisis. There was a major debate with his aides at Chequers in April and another in July. Jonathan Powell was the leader of the diehards. The Chief of Staff believed that Blair should still be planning to remain at Number 10 at least until 2008.[61] Phil Collins took his side. So did David Hill, mainly on the grounds that the media would try to drag him forward from whatever deadline he set.[62] That chimed with Blair's own feelings. 'Whatever date I give, my enemies will come back and demand a date six months earlier,' he told his aides.[63] Collins observes: 'He was always reluctant to give the date. That was the only thing he had left.'[64]

Matthew Taylor was the most persistent advocate within Number 10 for a precise timetable. He argued that Blair would squash the endless speculation, silence his enemies and snuff out Brownite plots if he was publicly clear that he would leave in the summer of 2007. 'Matthew was always for clarity'[65] and 'very keen on naming a date'.[66] Ruth Turner tended to agree because she was 'getting it in the neck from Labour MPs and the Cabinet all the time – he's got to tell us, he's got to give a date.'[67] There was a strong dimension of Blair, the side of him that was anxious to avoid the fate of Margaret Thatcher, that wanted to leave Number 10 with dignity. That was in contention with the other side of Blair, who meant it when he said he wanted to serve a full third term and hated the idea of handing the crown to Brown under duress. He would talk 'in almost mystical terms' about how 'he had made a contract with the British people to serve a full term.'[68] Whatever view they took, there was near universal agreement among his senior staff that Blair had to be more precise about his intentions. Even the ultras like Ben Wegg-Prosser could now sense that 'it was going to be difficult to get beyond 2007.'[69] The current vagueness offered no fixed point for his allies to rally around while providing ammunition for the Brownites and other Labour MPs who were saying that the uncertainty damaged the Government.

As the pressure mounted, some of Blair's closest confidants were increasingly worried that it would all end badly for their friend in Number 10. One of them mournfully remarked to me that summer: 'Prime Ministers never get their departures right, do they?'[70]

What no-one else knew was that John Prescott had presented Blair with a stark ultimatum. The two of them met alone in July shortly before Blair went abroad. Prescott was a very weakened figure, but he still retained one weapon, the threat of revelation, that he could use on Blair. The deputy had long been telling Blair he had to announce his departure date. Prescott also believed that it was only fair to give Brown two years as Prime Minister to establish himself before a general election. When they met that July, Prescott told Blair that he must make a public declaration that he would leave by the summer of 2007. He said Blair had to make that announcement in his speech on the Tuesday of that autumn's party conference. If he didn't deliver, Prescott threatened, he would announce his own resignation in his speech on the Thursday and reveal that he was quitting because Blair had broken the promises to Brown witnessed by Prescott. 'I will make it clear that you are to blame,' Prescott menaced the Prime Minister.

Blair protested that this was unnecessary. He had already given assurances to both Brown and Prescott that he was secretly planning to leave in 2007 anyway. But this time his deputy was not willing to be smoothed into submission. Prescott responded that private promises like that weren't good enough any more. 'Gordon doesn't believe you. And I don't fucking believe you.'[71]

24. A Very Brownite Coup

'What's the line then, Phil?' asked Tony Blair as lunch was served by the RAF stewards who wait at table at Chequers. Philip Webster, the Political Editor of *The Times*, and his colleague Peter Riddell had just conducted the first post-holiday interview with the Prime Minister. He'd invited the journalists to eat with him afterwards. Webster replied: 'It's Blair defies the Labour Party.' 'Right,' said Blair and flicked his eyes to his aides.[1]

Jonathan Powell looked pleased. David Hill frowned with concern. They'd prepared for the interview by trying to find verbal formulations that did not concede any ground to Blair's enemies while not sounding so stubborn that it would inflame further opposition. But the issue of when Blair would go was now too hot to be nuanced. 'What we were trying for was a delicate balancing act,' Hill subsequently lamented. 'It turned into a "Here I stand."'[2]

Blair returned from the West Indies in an uncompromising state of mind, which was nearly always his mood when he'd had prolonged exposure to Cherie and her adamantine opposition to giving an inch to Gordon Brown. That expressed itself in the interview which he gave holding a mug with the legend: 'You're the man who's in charge.' Blair told his party to 'stop obsessing' about his departure date and drop the 'absurd' speculation. 'I've said I am not going to go on and on and on, and said I'll leave ample time for my successor,' he added without offering any definition of what 'ample time' might mean. 'People have to accept that as a reasonable proposition and let me get on with the job.'[3]

After the men from *The Times* left, Alastair Campbell, Philip Gould and Sally Morgan arrived at Chequers. These three long-standing confidants came with a single message: he would be in serious trouble unless he named a date for his departure at the party conference. They decided they had to go together to make him listen. 'Are you sure?' asked Blair as they sat in the sun-dappled garden. He was still highly reluctant to accept that he had less than a year left in power. 'Are you sure it will strengthen me rather than weaken me?' They pressed their advice only to later learn what he had said in the interview. 'We all went spare.'[4]

That evening, the Prime Minister threw a 'back-to-work party' at Chequers for Downing Street staff to mark the beginning of the new political season. He and his senior aides were by now increasingly anxious that the interview 'had gone wrong'.[5] Hill confirmed that *The Times* would splash with the headline: 'Blair defies his party over departure date'.[6] The Press Secretary began a frantic ring-round of political editors to try to spin down the idea that an unyielding Blair was challenging his critics to come and get him. Ruth Turner and Ben Wegg-Prosser also made 'endless calls' to journalists and Labour MPs.[7] It was too late. The headline in the *Independent* was 'Blair risks party's wrath by refusing to reveal his exit strategy'.[8] The *Daily Telegraph* went further: 'Labour at war as Blair refuses to name date'.[9] Scanning the front pages, David Hill sighed to colleagues: 'I'm afraid that didn't work.'[10] Keith Hill, Blair's PPS, regarded the interview as 'a tactical balls-up' and 'a provocation' to Labour MPs.[11] Some of Brown's supporters instantly ramped up the pressure. 'The debilitating uncertainty over the leadership can't go on,' declared Andrew Smith, a former Cabinet minister and hardcore Brownite.[12] Don Touhig, another Brownite MP, accused Blair of 'bleeding the Labour Party at its heart' by clinging on to power.[13] Members of the Cabinet could sense that 'feeling in the party was building up quite explosively. There was uncertainty over the departure timetable and you could feel it around you,' says Peter Hain. The 'unwisely judged' interview 'had given the impression that he would go on forever. The boil had to be lanced.'[14]

Estelle Morris thought it inevitable that they would get to 'a point where a set of things happened that put the tensions within the Government out into the public domain. That is what happened in the autumn of 2006. A number of things happened which literally lifted the lid and it was all there waiting to come out.'[15]

'There is shelf time for everybody,' says Geoffrey Robinson, long-time adherent of Gordon Brown. It was 'entirely misconceived' for Blair to think that he could 'go on and on'.[16]

The *Times* interview appeared on Friday, 1 September. The following day, the Blairs left for the traditional annual weekend with the Queen at Balmoral. Gordon Brown was at his home in Fife. He was infuriated by the interview, interpreting it as meaning that Blair had no intention of leaving. Yet the public response from the heart of the Chancellor's camp was deceptively muted. Ed Balls wrote a piece for the *Observer* dismissing the idea that they needed a debate about how to renew the party as 'internal navel-gazing' and demanding a 'stable and orderly transition' to a new leader.[17] This was

Brownite code for saying that Blair should hand over to his Chancellor without argument. From the pages of the *Sunday Times*, Alan Milburn fired back that Blair was 'right to resist pressure' for a timetable and 'a new leader is not a political panacea.' He concluded: 'Forget the date. It's the debate that matters.'[18] Debate was the Blairite code for saying that Brown would face rivals for the succession.

The Chancellor was convulsed by rage when he saw Milburn's article. Brown interrupted Blair's Balmoral visit by ringing the Prime Minister on Sunday morning. The Chancellor's fury was titanically demented even by his standards. 'You put fucking Milburn up to it,' Brown raged down the phone. 'This is factionalism! This is Trotskyism! It's fucking Trotskyism!' Blair was nonplussed. He had not even seen the article. After the call, he then read it and phoned Milburn to say it was excellent. They laughed about Brown's hysterical reaction.[19]

There were people in both camps scared that the struggle was about to spiral out of control. Charlie Falconer, close friend of the Prime Minister, got in touch with Alistair Darling, ally of the Chancellor, to suggest that there should be peace talks before the party became polarised from top to bottom over the leadership question. Darling put the idea to Brown, but the Chancellor dismissed it out of hand. He would settle for nothing less than an irrevocable, inescapable public promise from Blair to step down.[20]

Brown agonised about how far to push it. Though he craved the crown, 'Gordon is absolutely gripped by the idea that if there is not an agreed transition and there is a bloody bust up, it will be the end for the party and the Government,' says one of the hawks in his camp, who were furious with Brown when he did not strike in the spring. Brown was also 'very worried' that Rupert Murdoch's titles, the *Sun* and *The Times*, would be 'very hostile to Gordon making a direct personal attack on Tony'.[21] The hawks feared that he would yet again pass up the opportunity to strike. Chief among them was Ed Balls, who for years had lambasted Brown for being timid and tried to 'guilt trip' him into action. 'Why are you being so weak?' Balls had repeatedly challenged Brown behind closed doors. 'Why aren't you forcing him out?' As another member of his inner circle puts it:

Ed was vehement that Gordon had been too weak for too long. There is no question that Ed thought Gordon had acted insufficiently strongly in the spring and felt he had to take things into his own hands. The coup was not run by Gordon. It was run by Ed. Gordon was almost horrified when he realised how far it had gone.[22]

It was important to Balls and fellow conspirators to try to keep Brownite fingerprints off the plot. Ian Austin, Brown's former press spokesman, was now MP for Dudley North in the Midlands. He had been cultivating relationships with two Labour MPs known as Blairites who had become disaffected with the Prime Minister. One of them was Sion Simon, the MP for Birmingham Erdington. Simon had savagely satirised Brown in the past and voted for many of Blair's most contentious policies, including the Iraq war, student top-up fees and anti-terror laws. This made Simon an ideal assassin. He could not be dismissed by Number 10 as one of the usual Brownite suspects. Simon was 'a clean skin'. Another was Chris Bryant, the MP for the Rhondda, a former vicar whose main claim to fame was posing in his underpants on a gay dating internet site. Bryant, like Simon, was a formerly ardent Blairite who failed to secure advancement from Blair. Their first outing on behalf of Brown was at the end of August, when they attacked the Blairite Stephen Byers for having the temerity to suggest that the Chancellor might need to respond to discontent about inheritance tax.[23]

Simon became an MP in 2001. That Friday and into the weekend he began a ring-round to gather support among his intake to Parliament for sending a letter to Blair with a demand for his departure. Rumour of this letter plot reached Ben Wegg-Prosser, who had been close to Simon for years. When he phoned the MP, Wegg-Prosser was stunned to learn that this former ally had decisively moved into the 'Blair must go' camp.

'We warned you he couldn't carry on like this, but you wouldn't listen,' Simon told Wegg-Prosser. 'New Labour is about more than one man. The game's up. He's got to go.'

Wegg-Prosser then asked the big question: 'Do you think Gordon is prepared to stick the knife in this time?' Simon's reply was ominous: 'In the past, I've always assumed he wouldn't. Now I think he might.'[24] On Saturday morning, Blair had a conference call from Balmoral with his senior aides. Wegg-Prosser reported his 'chilling' conversation with Simon. There was 'a collective gulp' at this development, but 'there was nothing we could do.'[25] Blair and his team still didn't know quite what they were dealing with. 'Tony took a bit of convincing that it was serious,' says Jonathan Powell. 'We'd been so used to being attacked and not retaliating that we didn't take action.'[26]

By Sunday, Simon had the letter primed. He met Tom Watson, MP for West Bromwich East. Watson was a junior Defence Minister, acolyte of the Chancellor and fixer. He had helped Simon and Austin get their seats in Parliament. Burly and a former engineering union official, he had been an enforcer for Brown as the Treasury whip. Watson was the archetypal Brownite soldier. Simon and Watson met, with six other people believed to be fellow plotters, at the Bilash Tandoori in Wolverhampton on Sunday night. On the menu was chicken vindaloo, diced lamb in yoghurt and skewering the Prime Minister.[27] The mood was 'very angry with Blair'.[28]

They needed a signal from their master to put the plot into motion. Gordon Brown had just had a second son, Fraser. It was the perfect excuse to maintain an invisible public profile up in Scotland at his clifftop home in North Queensferry. On Monday, he received a visitor there. It was Watson, hot from his curry dinner with other conspirators, who went up to Scotland and booked himself into the St Andrew's Bay Golf Resort and Spa, a luxury hotel just forty-five miles from Brown's home.[29]

When his visit to Brown became public knowledge the following weekend, it was claimed that this was purely a social call so that Watson and his wife, Siobhan, could deliver a present for the Browns' baby boy. Westminster was asked to suspend its disbelief and accept that they 'watched *Postman Pat* on a DVD and played with their babies'.[30]

'Everyone laughed at that,' says Wegg-Prosser. 'If I was the acolyte of a politician and I was planning a coup to bring down his greatest rival, I think I would mention it.'[31]

Even some veteran Brownites raise their eyebrows at the idea that the letter was never mentioned. George Mudie says: 'The big question is whether Gordon gave him the nod.'[32] It is hard to see how that question can be sensibly answered entirely in the negative. Brown had nothing in common with Watson except politics.

There is a question about what Brown thought he was giving the nod to: the full-blown coup which was about to be triggered by his lieutenants or just another of his guerrilla campaigns of destabilisation against Blair. One person at the heart of Brown's inner circle believes: 'He would have given the plotters the green light to cause trouble.'[33]

By Monday morning, Keith Hill, Blair's Parliamentary Private Secretary and his eyes and ears among backbenchers, was alert to the existence of the Simon letter. He'd been tipped off by 'a secret squirrel', an MP friendly to the Prime Minister whom the plotters were trying to recruit.[34] Hill rushed into the Number 10 office shared by Matthew Taylor and Ruth Turner and broke the news. Alarm turned into total fright when they heard that there also appeared to be 'go now' letters circulating among the 1997 and 2005 intakes. According to the intelligence gathered by Hill, these letters would be delivered over the next forty-eight hours in 'a rolling programme of confrontation'. If Blair didn't capitulate, then a delegation of MPs and ministers would follow. Hill's informant told him that Jack Straw stood at the head of a faction of alienated and opportunistic Cabinet ministers who were poised to tell Blair to go.[35] This sounded plausible to them. Straw was now clearly in Brown's camp and had publicly predicted in July that 'Tony will go well before the next election.'[36]

Shortly before noon, Hill received a call from Chris Bryant, who said the plotters had sent their letter to Number 10 by fax that morning and were worried that it had not arrived because they had received no response. They appear to have sent it to the wrong fax machine. Even in moments of high drama, there is always room for some farce. Bryant now emailed the letter to Hill.[37]

Number 10 was stunned by the brutality of the letter. It offered one pat on the back – 'we believe that you have been an exceptional Labour Prime Minister' – before the stab in the front. 'Sadly it is clear to us – as it is to almost the entire party and the entire country – that without an urgent change in the leadership of the party it becomes less likely that we will win the next election. That is the brutal truth. It gives us no pleasure to say it. But it has to be said. And understood. We therefore ask you to stand aside.'[38]

Keith Hill was shocked by the signatories who were 'for the most part, absolutely mainstream figures, solid citizens, respectable people that would be taken seriously by other people in the Parliamentary Labour Party. It seemed to me that the rebellion was at the heart of the PLP.' When he talked to the Prime Minister, Hill had a grave message: 'These are serious names. It's a terrific threat.' Blair sounded fatalistic: 'If they want me to go, I'll go.'[39]

The Prime Minister was out of London on a two-day tour of the north of England designed to show his commitment to core Labour issues. Now he was in a fight for his premiership. Among the aides with Blair, there was 'an immediate sense of deep crisis. Shit. This is it.'[40]

His senior staff back at Number 10 gathered in Taylor's office for a conference call with the Prime Minister. This was clearly the beginning of a putsch, but its true shape and scale were still foggy to them. The one possible bright side was that the letter appeared to have been signed by just seventeen Labour MPs. Only one of them was a Government minister. His name: Tom Watson.

That signature put some Brownite dabs on the operation. Rumours began to reach Number 10 that Ed Balls had been 'spotted around the House of Commons' having booked himself out of the Treasury so that he could machinate without civil servants listening in.[41] The involvement of Ian Austin and Nick Brown was also assumed. Some in Number 10 later concluded that 'Ed and Nick decided they were going to precipitate this by forcing the indecisive Gordon into decisive action.'[42] It fitted with 'a pattern of behaviour over thirteen years'.[43] Blair himself was 'absolutely totally convinced that they were all over it. If Gordon wasn't pulling the strings, he knew about it. He could have stopped it. He didn't.'[44]

Towards the end of the day, Jonathan Powell finally got hold of Watson on the phone and demanded to know whether it was true that he had signed the letter. Watson confirmed that he had. 'Are you going to resign from the Government?' asked Powell. 'No,' replied Watson to Powell's amazement. 'Are you sacking me?'[45]

By Monday evening, there was a consensus among Blair's closest advisers that he was in mortal danger. Calls to the Cabinet established that most of them were solid, but it was hard to read the mood of Labour MPs who were still in their constituencies for the summer recess. Up in Yorkshire, the Prime Minister oscillated between fury, defiance and resignation. That evening, he had dinner in his hotel with David Hill, Jo Gibbons, Phil Collins and Hilary Coffman, the small entourage who were accompanying him on the regional tour. There was a long silence before anyone spoke. Then Blair sighed: 'If they don't want me any more, then I'll have to go.'[46] Later, to other allies, he said: 'I'm not going to beg for the job.'[47] When he spoke on the phone to Philip Gould, he was 'very pensive' and sounded like he felt 'that it could all be up'.[48] Some of his allies, who had warned him for years what Brown was capable of, could not restrain themselves from saying: 'We told you so.'[49]

Blair and his entourage felt 'cut off and a long way from the action' in York. He was 'desperate to get back to London'. After a short debate, it was concluded that he couldn't abandon his regional tour because 'it would look like a panic.'[50]

Back at Number 10, his senior staff were scrambling together a plan to try to save him. They concluded that he would have to make a strategic retreat by clearly signalling that he would not try to stay on beyond the summer of 2007. Blair did not want to say this himself. The compromise was to put up David Miliband to say it for him. The Environment Secretary was reliable, he was well-liked, he represented the younger generation and a statement from him would be taken as bearing the imprimatur of Downing Street. Matthew Taylor rang Miliband on Monday evening. 'We're on the skids,' Taylor told Miliband, who readily agreed to help.[51] Blair was absent from the dinner with his staff for long periods to make several lengthy calls to Peter Mandelson and other close allies.[52] After consulting them, he accepted the plan. Just before midnight, Wegg-Prosser rang Miliband to confirm that he was booked on the next morning's *Today* programme.

The Environment Secretary delivered the formula: 'The conventional wisdom is that the Prime Minister sees himself carrying on for about another twelve months. It seems to me that the conventional wisdom is reasonable.'[53]

Blair's aides rang round Labour MPs and contacted journalists to ensure it was understood that the Prime Minister was in agreement with this. By now, though, message management was escaping their control. News of the plot was getting out. Tuesday's *Guardian* splashed with an exclusive from its well-connected and respected Political Editor, Patrick Wintour, who had learnt about the Simon letter calling for Blair to go.[54]

Kevin Maguire, the Political Editor of the *Mirror* and a long-standing Brown sympathiser, secured another scoop. He had been leaked a memo written by Wegg-Prosser five months previously which described how Blair should choreograph the last chapter of his premiership. 'As TB enters his final phase, he needs to be focusing way beyond the finishing line. He needs to go with the crowd wanting more. He should be the star who won't even play that last encore.' Maguire reported this as evidence that Blair was consumed by hubris and ego. Labour MPs, he wrote, 'will be stunned to learn from the memo that the main thing on the PM's mind is the PM himself'. He mocked Wegg-Prosser's suggestion that Blair should go on *Songs of Praise* as evidence that he wanted 'a celestial choir' to hymn 'the most drawn-out exit in British political history'.[55] Blair hated the leak of the memo, which he had never previously seen, 'because it made him look mad'.[56]

The senior staff at Number 10 gathered in Matthew Taylor's office at eight that morning to assess the state of play. They feared that more than half the backbenches, and an unknown number of ministers, were involved. That would be lethal. 'We knew that one letter was on its way,' says Taylor. 'If there was going to be two or three letters calling for him to go, and an ever-growing number of MPs, then, you know, it felt like that was it. The Labour Party, almost by default, was going to get rid of him.'[57]

Jonathan Powell agrees that it looked frightening because 'the momentum appeared to be full pelt against us.'[58] It didn't look like Blair was going to fulfil the farewell tour plan as 'the star' who goes 'with the crowds wanting more'. The band was knocking hell out of each other, the stage was on fire, and the lead vocalist was being strangled from behind by the Scottish bass guitarist.

'This is a fucking coup!' one of Blair's closest aides raged to me that night. 'This is a coup attempt organised by one man for the benefit of one man. Brown is behind it all.'[59]

Blair was also deprived of key allies in the Cabinet who were abroad. Tessa Jowell ran up a £999 mobile phone bill ringing London from China. Sitting on the edge of a pavement in Shanghai, she told Blair: 'You're not going anywhere.' He put a larky face on his predicament: 'Of course I'm not, darling.'[60] But his allies could sense that he felt very vulnerable. He sounded 'in a pretty worried mood' to Sally Morgan.[61] Charlie Falconer told him to stand firm: 'This is all froth.' Blair replied to his old flatmate: 'You don't understand the Labour Party like I do. This has got to be managed.'[62]

He arrived back in Number 10 that evening and was briefed by his aides that they were having some success with the attempt to mount a fightback. A rival, loyalist letter was published with sixty signatures from backbench Labour MPs and eventually attracted the backing of 115.[63] This letter took the line that Blair should be given until 2007. It was organised, at the urging of Matthew Taylor, by the MP Karen Buck, a plausible figure with mainstream backbenchers. She warned her colleagues not to turn an 'orderly transition into a crisis of regicide'.[64] Keith Hill was encouraged when he found 'high levels of antipathy towards Simon and Bryant among colleagues who didn't like them as people'.[65] Tony Wright, an independent-minded Labour select committee chairman, rallied to Blair's defence. He warned the plotters that they:

were taking self-indulgence to the point of self-destruction. People are living in a kind of fantasy land. What do they think is going to happen the day after Tony Blair has gone? The problems are going to be the same, the solutions are going to be the same, and nothing much is going to happen to the opinion polls.[66]

Over at the Treasury, the Chancellor convened a council of war with the two Eds, Sue Nye and Spencer Livermore. Brown asked apprehensively: 'Where are we going with this?' Balls argued: 'We have to push this. Blair is never going to go. He has to be pushed. You mustn't be weak. You've been weak for too long.' Brown was still wary: 'I'm not going to go somewhere when I can't see where it will end.' Balls was aggressive: 'It never goes anywhere, because you're never willing to do anything.'[67]

Wednesday morning's press reported this as the final showdown for Blair. At a quarter to eight that morning, Prime Minister and Chancellor had a face-to-face confrontation in Number 10. Blair 'just knew it was Gordon behind it. It was all Gordon's people.'[68] The two-hour encounter was one of the rawest of the many vicious struggles over the years. Blair expressed fury about the coup and Brown's failure to condemn it. He had already told him he was going next summer. Why was that not good enough? It was not good enough, responded Brown, because Blair had broken so many promises before. When Blair directly accused him of being behind the plot, Brown denied it. But he also made it clear he would not lift a finger to stop it unless a list of demands was met. He wanted a public declaration by Blair that he would hand over power. He sought to be effective co-premier in the interim. He wanted a gag put on Byers and Milburn. 'I don't control them,' said Blair. 'I can't stop them speaking.'

Brown added a further demand: a guarantee that Blair would arrange 'a clear run' by preventing anyone else from the Cabinet competing for the leadership. Blair protested that he couldn't stop other people standing and this sort of behaviour made a contest more likely. Angrily, Brown asked: 'Who do you think is better than me? Do you think there is anyone who is better than me?' John Reid was 'far too right-wing'. Alan Johnson was 'a lightweight'. David Miliband was much too young. Was Blair saying, Brown demanded, that any of them was better qualified to become Prime Minister? This face-off came to an end without resolving anything. Talking about it afterwards to close allies, Blair described this confrontation with Brown as 'ghastly' and 'terrible' and told them that 'he kept shouting at me that I'd ruined his life.'

Though the Chancellor denied any involvement in the coup, the confidence and belligerence with which he behaved suggested to Blair that Brown knew that further attacks were planned. On both sides of the divide, it is agreed that 'Gordon said something that was interpreted as a threat.'[69]

Brown returned to the Treasury and gathered his inner circle in his private lounge area, known as 'the sofa room'. Spencer Livermore, Ed Miliband and Sue Nye discussed what had passed between him and Blair. Ed Balls then came in looking excited. In his hand was a resignation letter he had drafted for Tom Watson. Brown asked: 'What is this? What are you doing?' Balls responded: 'Why would I not be doing this? It's the obvious thing to do.' Ed Miliband was taken aback. 'Where's this going?' he asked, unconvinced that it would end well. 'What is your next move?' He turned to Brown: 'We have to be very careful.'

Brown was, as ever, torn between his craving to bring down Blair and his fear of the consequences of being seen with the dagger in his hand. He said he needed time to think. Balls replied bluntly: 'It's too late. It's all in place. It's all going to happen.'[70]

Tom Watson quit the Government at 11.12 that morning. The resignation letter said: 'It is with the greatest sadness that I have to say that your remaining in office is no longer in the interests of the party and the country.' Within minutes, Doug Henderson, a veteran Brown camp follower, was on TV from the garden of his constituency home to demand Blair's departure, another indicator to Number 10 that it was all being masterminded from the Treasury. Blair responded at two minutes to noon with a letter of his own which said he had been 'intending to dismiss' Watson anyway. 'To sign a round-robin letter which was then leaked to the press was disloyal, discourteous and wrong.'[71] Watson was followed by the staggered resignations over the day of seven Parliamentary Private Secretaries. In the early afternoon, the plotters were confidently briefing: 'Tony is going to be told it is moving time. He's got hours left.'[72]

In the middle of the day, Blair went into the Cabinet Room for a meeting with the parliamentary committee on anti-Semitism, who were surprised that their engagement had not been cancelled at this moment of high crisis for his premiership. One of the delegation was Iain Duncan Smith. When he was toppled as Tory leader, Blair sent him a handwritten note of commiseration: 'Why do our parties do these things to us?' When Blair looked up and noticed that Duncan Smith was coming into the Cabinet Room, he gave a weak smile: 'I suppose you're laughing, Iain.' 'No,' the former Tory leader replied. 'I know only too well what can go on.' Blair just nodded.[73]

A more cheering visitor to Number 10 was Frank Field, who came round to plead with Blair not to quit. 'You can't go yet. You can't leave us without an alternative,' protested Field. 'You can't let Mrs Rochester out of the attic.' Blair, who had listened to this without saying a word, roared with uncontrolled laughter at Field's description of Brown as Mrs Rochester.[74]

Ben Wegg-Prosser asked the Prime Minister how they should be briefing the press. 'People need to understand exactly what these people are doing,' responded Blair. 'It's blackmail isn't it?' said his aide. 'Yes,' replied Blair. Wegg-Prosser took that as a green light to start telling selected journalists that this was not a spontaneous uprising by backbenchers but an attempt by Brown to blackmail Blair out of office. Phil Collins enthusiastically joined the briefing operation.[75]

Blair went for a walk in the garden. When he came back in, he had essentially decided to semi-capitulate. This took aback some of the Brownites. 'What surprised me was how Tony panicked,' says George Mudie. 'There was no weight to the revolt.'[76] Keith Hill believes 'we'd beaten the buggers pretty comprehensively' by Wednesday.[77] Blair still had the support of a majority of the Cabinet. Only one of the threatened letters had materialised. Just eight unknown members of the Government had resigned. Tom Watson was a junior minister. The PPSs were of even slighter rank. They amounted to one Brownite and seven dwarves. Why did that seem so menacing that Blair felt compelled to cave in?

First, because Brown had led Blair to fear that they merely represented the first of 'wave after wave of attacks'.[78] Brown had implied as much during their earlier conversation, saying that the trouble would not stop until Blair publicly declared a resignation date.[79]

Jacqui Smith, the Chief Whip and a close ally of the Prime Minister, told him that it looked 'extremely well-orchestrated' and that she could no longer be confident that he commanded the support of the majority of Labour MPs. She later wondered if her advice had been too pessimistic.[80] The general atmosphere inside Number 10 was 'a bit hysterical'.[81] Blair 'was frightened of what was coming next and he didn't think he was giving that much in the end'.[82]

The prospect of being overwhelmed by mutiny scratched on his fear of going the same way as Margaret Thatcher. 'I don't want to be another Thatcher,' he had frequently said. How he went was in the end more important to him than exactly when. He would rather depart with dignity than fight in the last ditch.

At lunchtime, Number 10 rang the Treasury to say the Prime Minister wanted to see the Chancellor again. Brown arrived at 2 p.m. for a ninety-minute meeting which was still sulphurous but not quite as shouty as the earlier encounter. Brown arrived in a less confidently aggressive mood than in the morning. Over lunchtime, his camp started to worry that the mood was turning against them.[83] The full extent of their involvement in the coup remained masked, but Wegg-Prosser's briefing about Brown's blackmail was encouraging journalists to ask questions. Only a minority of the Cabinet favoured Brown and the Blairites among them were threatening terrible vengeance on him if it was taken any further. Many Labour MPs, even ones highly critical of Blair, could not see the point of tearing him down for the sake of a few months. John Prescott, who believed all this was unnecessary because of his July ultimatum to Blair, was furious about what he called 'the corporals' coup'. He warned Brown not to push it.[84] Peter Hain was in his Neath constituency in the early part of the week. He rang Brown to warn him that the mood of his activists was switching from disaffection with Blair to fury with the plotters. 'You must be very careful, Gordon,' he cautioned. 'It's turning completely against you.'[85]

Middle-ground Labour MPs were beginning to rally to Blair now it was clear that he would be gone by 2007. As Matthew Taylor puts it: 'Most Labour MPs wanted clarification about Tony's intentions, but they did not want a bloody coup to take place immediately.'[86]

Senior Conservatives were watching with wry amusement, not least William Hague: 'There was a moment when the tanks were nosing out of the barracks, the troops were about to take to the streets in the coup and then they went back in. Gordon's boys were called off at the last minute.'[87]

When previously explaining his hesitancy about striking to his inner circle, Brown would often cite Michael Heseltine as an example of 'he who wields the dagger doesn't inherit the throne.'[88] Brown did not want to be caught with his hand on the knife.

That afternoon, Blair and Brown went into the back garden of Number 10 and sat in the wicker chairs on the patio. Blair told Brown that he still wasn't going to buckle to the other man's demand for a Christmas handover.

'I'm not prepared to be bundled out.' One of his arguments was that he wanted to stay on until May to try to bring the Northern Ireland peace process to a resolution. What he was prepared to concede was a public statement that he would leave Number 10 by the next summer. This was a considerable shift in Blair's position since the *Times* interview of less than a week before. Blair refused to give Brown a promise that he would endorse his succession and work to prevent anyone else standing. From his perspective, he had conceded quite enough for one day.

Brown decided that he had pushed things as far as he dared. At that meeting, and in subsequent phone calls that evening and early the next morning, they got down to the business of discussing the content and timing of the statements that they would make.[89]

Brown had been trying to stay entirely invisible to the media throughout the coup. He slipped out of Number 10 via a back entrance and into his limousine. He was surprised by photographers, who captured him with a shark-like grin on his face, as if he had just swallowed the Prime Minister whole and was now digesting what remained of his rival. The pictures would be on front pages of the papers the next day, depicting him as an assassin relishing a kill. He later claimed he was talking to Sue Nye about Fraser, deploying his baby son as his alibi once again. In truth, Brown had come out of the latest meeting with Blair in a foul mood and the grin on his face was a back-firing attempt to cover it up. 'Gordon saw the photographers, thought: "I must not look grumpy", and put on a smile.'[90]

He had finally got what he had agitated, bullied, plotted, dreamed and schemed to secure for so long. The messy coup orchestrated by Ed Balls had finally forced Blair to give a public leaving date. Yet Brown still wasn't content. He had to contemplate waiting nearly another year for the succession that he had yearned after for more than a decade.

On Thursday, Tony Blair used a visit to a north London school to announce that he would serve not a full term, but about half of one, a dramatic truncation of his original ambition. A group called School Students Against War were waiting for him. 'Tony! Tony! Tony!' they shouted. 'Out! Out! Out!' He took along with him the Education Secretary, Alan Johnson. 'You've got to have a friend,' the Prime Minister said lightly. 'At least I've got one.'

He gave a masterclass in how to put a graceful face on humiliation. 'The first thing I would like to do is apologise on behalf of the Labour Party for the last week,' he said. 'It has not been our finest hour, to be frank.'

Then he made the statement that he had long resisted. 'I would have preferred to do this in my own way,' he said, but he was now confirming that the next party conference would be his last as Prime Minister. In a strong indication that this meant he intended to go the next summer, he said the forthcoming TUC would also be his last speech to the trades unions – 'probably to the relief of both of us'. He then delivered a rebuke to the plotters. 'It's the country that matters, and we can't treat the public as bystanders in a subject as important as who is their Prime Minister.'[91] He was not going to 'set a precise date now' for his departure. Blair was hanging on to one of the remaining cards in his hand.

The deftness with which Blair dealt with his enforced retreat made a striking contrast with the clunking and opaque statement that Gordon Brown delivered from a Glasgow sports centre an hour earlier. He gave an account of his conversations with Blair the day before which was risibly distant from the truth. 'I said to him, it is for him to make the decision.' Brown then went on to make the even more incredible claim: 'I said also to him that I will support him in the decision he takes.'[92]

Some of the plotters continued to agitate. Chris Bryant declared that it would be better for Blair to be gone 'sooner rather than later'.[93] But the pressure now eased on Blair as the coup rebounded on Brown. He was hurt by the picture that made him look like the grinning assassin. Cherie exchanged e-mails with the Blairs' friend Barry Cox. She confided that they had been frightened at the beginning, but 'Gordon was much more damaged by the end of the week.'[94] The Chancellor was panicked by the fingers pointing at him. He frantically rang round Cabinet ministers and other leading party figures to try to convince them that he had nothing to do with the plot. Some pretended to take his word for it. 'I believe you, Gordon,' said Philip Gould, but he warned that others did not. John Prescott scorned Brown's protestations of innocence. 'Tom Watson is one of your people. They're all your fucking people,' Prescott said to Brown. 'There's not a fucking one who is not your people.'[95]

Though a semblance of unity was now being projected in public, the two men had only come to a half-deal on Wednesday afternoon. Brown was still not satisfied with the terms of surrender that he had extracted from Blair. On Friday, the Chancellor opened another bout of arm-wrestling for the crown. He was again pressing for a public endorsement from Blair at the forthcoming party conference, which he coupled with renewed demands that Stephen Byers, Alan Milburn and other prominent Blairites should be silenced. Blair refused. Even if his supporters were biddable, which they were not, he was in no mood to make any further concessions.

Foes of the Chancellor started to take revenge. Frank Field said his behaviour had raised 'serious questions' about his fitness to be Prime Minister.[96]

Alan Milburn issued a barely coded attack on Brown for 'strong-arm, boss-style, plot-filled politics'.[97] He and other allies would have gone even further in suggesting that Brown was unfit to be Prime Minister if Blair had not restrained them.[98] Nick Robinson, the Political Editor of the BBC, reported the view of an unnamed Cabinet minister that Brown would be 'an effing disaster' as Prime Minster.[99] This was, in fact, John Hutton, the Work and Pensions Secretary.

Brown was on the defensive by the weekend and forced to issue a series of implausible denials. 'There is no truth in the suggestion that there was an attempted coup,' he said torturing the truth. 'The situation was sad, regrettable and has caused us a great deal of grief.'[100]

The former Home Secretary, Charles Clarke, detonated with a denunciation of Brown for his 'absolutely stupid behaviour' and the 'complete madness' of the putsch, which he could have stopped 'with a click of his fingers'.[101]

Brown was a 'deluded control freak', 'totally, totally uncollegiate' in the way he sought 'to control everything'. He 'lacks confidence' and didn't have 'the bottle' to be Prime Minister. Most piercingly, Clarke said Brown had 'psychological' issues, echoing the old charge that Brown suffered from 'psychological flaws'.[102]

This was a brutally direct onslaught on one colleague by another which spelt out in public many of the behavioural and character traits of Brown that ministers had privately complained about for years. The Chancellor affected to have a thick skin, saying that: 'I'm not going to hold it against him.'[103]

Brown rang up Clarke that weekend, but not to shout at him. In a tone more of sorrow than anger, Brown asked Clarke to desist on the grounds that 'it will make it more difficult to bring you back.'[104] At the same time, his attack dogs were unleashed to brief the press that the former Home Secretary was a 'bloated suicide bomber'.[105]

Number 10 hadn't put Clarke up to it, but Downing Street spokesmen were conspicuously reluctant to criticise him. The longer Blair dwelt on the events of that week, the more angry the Prime Minister became as he concluded that the Chancellor had knifed him. Blair was 'very hurt' by the coup, says Nick Ryden, who had been a friend since they were teenagers.[106] 'It is dire for Tony,' sighed someone who had been close to him for more than a decade.[107] He became increasingly vituperative about Brown. 'After all this, he's brought it forward by a few months,' Blair said to one aide.[108]

Following considerable debate within Number 10 about whether it was safe to leave Britain, that weekend he flew out to Jerusalem. He was in a suite at the King David Hotel on Saturday night when his staff brought him news of Watson's visit to Brown on the eve of the coup. 'Cherie was right all along,' Blair remarked bitterly to one civil servant with him.[109] Michael Levy was also present. 'That's when I really saw him lose it about Brown. Tony got angrier and angrier. He kept saying he'd never realised how duplicitous Gordon was – and what a "liar".'[110]

Many of Blair's staff and friends wanted to 'kill the bastard' that weekend by exposing all of Brown's dreadful behaviour over the years.[111] Blair would not sanction it. He told Wegg-Prosser to cease his briefing operation and phoned allies to tell them 'not to go for Brown'.[112] He might have liked to take his revenge, but his position was too fragile to risk another eruption of open warfare. As ever, he preferred to hide the animosity between them both for his own sake and for that of the party.

In the immediate aftermath of the coup, no-one at the top of Government quite knew what they should say, even behind closed doors. The Prime Minister had just been putsched by his Chancellor. Yet at the next meeting of the Cabinet they carried on with business as usual. One official present says: 'They acted as if nothing had happened.'[113]

There was not much evidence that the coup would do Labour any good. The party's poll ratings were at a nineteen-year low, a deficit to the Tories which had helped fuel the rebels. But the polls also suggested that replacing Blair with Brown would make scant difference. Blair's approval rating was still the best of any party leader among his own supporters.[114] According to one poll just before the coup, Labour support would be only one point higher with Brown as leader; according to another poll on the eve of the party conference, Labour's position was going to be worse if Brown took over.[115] The divisions exposed and feelings of treachery aroused during that week in September injected toxin into Labour's bloodstream as well as giving credence to David Cameron's claim that the Government was 'in meltdown'.

The Labour conference met in Manchester at the end of September. Nervous delegates were not sure whether they would be witnesses to an outbreak of civil war. The poison between the camps was still suppurating through the bandages. The rival gangs circled each other in the conference hotel lobbies, bars and restaurants, just as they had for year after year, but with more edge than ever. One of Blair's closest and most veteran aides described Brown as 'unstoppable but unelectable'.[116] The breakdown of relations was so total that the two men gave interviews and made their speeches without having any idea what the other man would say.

Gordon Brown was Prime Minister-presumptive. But the events of September inflicted serious damage on him. Polls cast him very unfavourably against David Cameron, especially when voters were asked who would be most likely to stab colleagues in the back.[117] Martin Kettle, the astute commentator of the *Guardian*, noted: 'When Labour delegates cheer the Chancellor, as they will, there will also be a voice in their heads reminding them that the public sees Brown as arrogant, dishonest, selfish, treacherous and unpleasant.'[118]

Brown's speech to the conference on the Monday was regarded by one member of his team 'as the most important and difficult in ten years'.[119] He sweated over it for days, devoting himself to little else during a pre-conference trip to the Far East. He would either seal his dominant position or make himself vulnerable to a competitor for the succession. What emerged was a typical Brown speech in which he pounded out points like a machine gun and pummelled his audience into clapping. He got his loudest applause when he declared that he 'would relish the opportunity to take on David Cameron'.[120] He name-checked thirteen Cabinet colleagues in an attempt to show that he was not the bullying Stalinist of Whitehall legend. Peter Mandelson interpreted that with a typically double-edged compliment to his old enemy. He saw a man with 'all sorts of flaws and shortcomings' who was nevertheless 'coming to terms with the need to change to a more collaborative and unifying style'.[121]

The Chancellor embalmed the victim of his putsch with praise. Brown said of Blair: 'It has been a privilege for me to work with and for the most successful ever Labour leader and Labour Prime Minister.'[122]

The hypocrisy of this was too much for the stomach of one listener. Cherie chose to snub the Chancellor's speech by declining to sit in the conference hall. She was instead making a tour of the stands in the exhibition area. Hearing a broadcast of Brown's claim to have been privileged to work with her husband, she could not stop herself blurting: 'Well, that's a lie!' The outburst was overheard by a journalist from the financial news agency, Bloomberg. By the time Brown was enjoying his ovation, the conference was already beginning to buzz with rumour that Cherie had called him a liar.

David Hill went through the motions of trying to deny it, suggesting that she might have said something like 'I need to get by'. It is as likely that she said: 'I've just swallowed a fly.'

The team working on Blair's speech for the following day wrestled with how they could deal with Cherie's remark. His main speech-writer, Phil Collins, had brought with him a large compendium of jokes from which he extracted a Les Dawson gag about wives and next-door neighbours. This was then customised for the speech in a brainstorming session with Alastair Campbell and David Bradshaw, another of the communications team. It was not in the text handed out to the press beforehand. Only at the last moment did Blair finally decide that he would begin the speech with the crack.[123] Having thanked his children and wife for their support over the years, he said: 'I mean, at least I don't have to worry about her running off with the bloke next door.'[124]

Over the years, it was his speech-writers' lament that Blair was bad at delivering jokes prepared for him. There was no cause for complaint this time. The crack brought the house down. 'It released all the tension,' says David Hill.[125] It also effectively confirmed the loathing the Prime Minister's wife felt for his Chancellor and implicitly suggested that Blair did not disagree with her assessment of Brown.

His speech was formally quite lavish in its compliments to the other man. 'I know New Labour would never have happened, and three election victories would never have been secured, without Gordon Brown. He is a remarkable man, a remarkable servant to this country.'[126]

What he did not do was endorse the other man as his successor. Blair was keeping back one of the high-value cards left in his hand. Nor was he any more precise about exactly when he would leave Number 10.

'This is a changed country,' he declared and listed some of the positive ways in which it had been transformed. His central intention was to impress on everyone what had been achieved since 1997, drum home how much the party owed to him, suggest he would be a very hard act to follow and leave them wondering what they were going to do without him. It was a success at all those levels. The speech was a virtuoso display of his gifts for apparently effortless eloquence and conversational charm. There were the customary 'y'knows', 'I means', choked-up pauses and clever applause lines. As he meant it to be, the performance was an intense 56-minute reminder of why he had been such a formidable leader. It demonstrated his talent for delivering meticulously prepared speeches full of deft switches from the light to the serious in a way that was good-humoured, strong on argument and rich with policy. Even one of his assassins, Sion Simon, hailed it as 'a great speech' from 'the greatest Prime Minister we have ever had'.[127]

One of the most striking aspects of the speech was that Labour's most electorally triumphant leader was still, after all these years, having to explain himself to his party. 'They say I hate the party, and its traditions. I don't. I love this party. There's only one tradition I hated: losing. I don't want to be the Labour leader who won three successive elections. I want to be the *first* Labour leader to win three successive elections.' Counselling them to stick to the centre ground and 'get after' the Tories, he declared that 'a fourth-term election victory' was 'the only legacy that has ever mattered to me'.[128]

He had managed to avoid the fate of most Prime Ministers, which is brutal and abrupt ejection from Number 10. Even when he finally reached the end of the road, he contrived a classically Blairish Third Way compromise. He quit in slow motion. He resigned by instalments. 'You're the future now,' he told the conference. Yet there would be another nine months before his final exit.

'You can't go on for ever,' he said in Manchester as if he were reconciled to what had happened. The truth was that he had been forced to leave earlier than he intended. Though some in his camp claimed later that he always planned to leave in the summer of 2007 anyway, those very closest to him say that his true ambition was to remain at Number 10 at least until 2008.[129] He was serious in his original ambition to serve most of a full third term, but he was denied it by a combination of his own tactical and strategic mistakes combined with the inevitable disaffection towards any leader who has been dominant for so long. That depressed support in the opinion polls which then fed back into the mood among Labour MPs. The Brownites had exploited, but were not solely responsible for unleashing, the furies. 'Two years of pent-up anger with Tony suddenly erupted,' said one Cabinet minister.[130] The easy dominance of Blair's early years had left many in his party ill-equipped to cope with being behind in the polls. It was notable that those Labour MPs who had known the truly miserable years of Opposition before 1997 were steadier than those elected then and later. His brand of political stardust had reached its sell-by date. Though it was an unprecedented achievement to secure a third term for Labour, it was a sullen victory won with an exceptionally low proportion of the vote. Public trust and party support for him bled away with every returning bodybag from Iraq and Afghanistan. His handling of the Lebanon crisis was the last straw for some Labour MPs and a perfect excuse for others who wanted to be rid of him. He was again swirled in corrosive allegations of sleaze. The prospect of the Prime Minister being interviewed by the police over 'cash-for-coronets' added to the *fin-de-siècle* aura around his premiership. He had pushed his party as far as it was willing to go on public service reform and was now effectively operating without a parliamentary majority for his ambitions. At the dark heart of the coup was the long struggle with Gordon Brown. 'Gordon wouldn't take him on trust when he said he was planning to go in 2007,' said one of the Prime Minister's friends.[131] Even some of Blair's allies would admit that he had too often made promises to Brown that weren't worth the paper they were not written on. He had become so weakened that in the end Brown overcame his natural caution and went for a clumsy kill.

That did not efface Blair's achievements. At the end of his speech, with the audience on its feet, he left the stage while a stirring video montage reminded them of some of the highlights of his years: the landslide of 1997, the Good Friday Agreement, the spending on public services, and a third election victory in 2005. He came back out, like a rock star milking his encores, to work the crowd to the sound of rhythmic applause.

Yet the same hands had also clapped with approval when he said it was 'right to let go'. The voters did not force Tony Blair into early retirement from Number 10. He was not driven out by the tormenters he complained about in the media, many of whom were rapturous about his speech. 'Phew! What a superb performance,' gasped the *Mirror*.[132] The speech 'set a new and very high standard for his successor', thought *The Times*.[133] 'A vintage performance from the greatest actor-politician of our time,' said the *Daily Mail*.[134] 'Has Labour gone stark staring mad?' wondered the *Sun*. 'It is hard to reach any other conclusion after seeing the party stand and cheer the most successful leader they've ever had – the man they've forced out of office.'[135]

It was not the media nor the Tories nor the voters who did for him. Tony Blair's premiership was brought to a premature termination by his own party.

Many of them, if not most, were relieved that he was leaving. What was slightly ominous for Labour was that the Conservatives were even gladder to see the back of the man who had beaten the Tories three times in a row. David Cameron and George Osborne watched Blair's final conference speech on television. They were awestruck. Cameron remarked soon afterwards: 'I must be one of the few people left in the country who still thinks Tony Blair is a brilliant politician.'[136] Osborne texted a friend: 'Thank God he's going.'[137]

25. Miracle Worker

At seven o'clock on the Friday morning, Jonathan Powell returned to the Prime Minister's suite at the Fairmont Hotel in St Andrews. Powell stood at the bedroom window looking out at the golf course and the grey-green North Sea. An unshaven Tony Blair sat limply on the sofa in his pyjamas. Their latest attempt to broker agreement between Northern Ireland's quarrelsome politicians was foundering. Both men had barely slept. In the remaining months left to him at Number 10, Blair craved above all else to achieve the goal to which he had dedicated so much of his premiership. Yet these talks in Scotland in October 2006 seemed stuck up another dead end. Gloom shrouded the Prime Minister. 'It's hopeless, isn't it?' he groaned from the sofa. He began to take out his frustration on Powell by blaming his Chief of Staff for not properly preparing. 'Don't be so stupid,' Powell responded sharply. 'We have to remain patient.'[1]

From the beginning to the end, Powell was Blair's closest collaborator in the peace process. Oftentimes, the roles were reversed. Powell would be the one in despair; Blair would be the optimist insisting they'd find a way through. Powell 'lost count of the number of times I came back from exhausting all-night sessions with Gerry Adams or David Trimble to tell him it was all over, and Tony would refuse to give up, saying I had to get back in touch with them and start again.'[2]

This time was unusual because both men were feeling simultaneously hopeless. 'The situation was grave,' Powell confided to his diary. 'Both sides had pulled well back from their opening positions and were now too far apart to allow us to close the gap.'[3] Down that gap threatened to tumble all their hopes of finally securing a settlement.

Soon afterwards, Peter Hain, the Northern Ireland Secretary, arrived at the hotel suite. By now Blair had slipped on a tracksuit, but was still barefoot, unshaven and hadn't touched breakfast. He was rallying. Hain was impressed to find him working on a new idea to save the talks from collapse.[4]

*

Tony Blair dedicated himself to this goal for longer and more intensively than any other challenge of his premiership. Even during the build-up to and aftermath of the Iraq war, there was rarely a day when he was not engaged with the peace process.[5] Richard Haas, a US envoy to Northern Ireland, found Blair 'extraordinarily hands on when you think of all the things a Prime Minister has on his plate – at times, his own action officer: literally thinking of what he would say, writing the speeches, writing the memos'.[6] That dedication to a cause that often seemed so hopeless was the best evidence against the charge that he was only a skilful opportunist. Northern Ireland was the seat of the longest political conflict in Europe and the longest war, on and off, in world history. This bloody tribal struggle had defied every previous attempt at resolution. There were no votes in it. There was only prestige to be lost from failure.

Ancestry was one factor that drove him. Blair was more Irish than he ever appeared. Ireland was 'in my blood' he once explained to an Irish audience.[7] His father's adoptive parents, with their colourful background in music hall, always attracted most media attention, but the other branch of his family tree grew in Irish soil. Blair's mother, Hazel, was from Ballyshannon. Her father was a member of the Orange Order, named after King William of Orange whose crushing of Catholics at the Battle of the Boyne in July 1690 was celebrated by marching Orangemen every summer. Blair's maternal grandmother was a Protestant from Donegal. Most of his childhood summer holidays were spent in Ireland until the Troubles took hold. 'It was there in the seas off the Irish coast that I learnt to swim, there that my father took me to my first pub, a remote little house in the country, for a Guinness, a taste I've never forgotten and which is always a pleasure to repeat.'[8]

On her deathbed, his grandmother said to him: 'Promise me, Tony, you will never marry a Catholic.'[9] He did marry a Catholic, his children were brought up as Catholics and he was a closet Catholic. This was not something he mentioned when he was with Unionists, to whom he emphasised the Orange in his ancestry. To John Taylor, a Unionist MP, Blair once joked: 'John, you've got six children. What are you? Are you a Catholic?'[10]

To such an ecumenical politician as Blair, a man who regarded Christians, Muslims and Jews as equally 'Abraham's children',[11] there was no sense to a conflict rooted in religion. Blair would often say: 'I simply want to stop people killing each other.'[12] The Donegal connection helped him forge a bond with his Irish counterpart, Bertie Ahern, who was 'often struck that we know much more about the English than they do about us, but that wasn't true of Tony'.[13] Ahern had militantly Republican ancestry, but he too was of a new generation, unburdened by historical baggage and keen to resolve the conflict. Their close and generally trusting relationship was a key to success.

The challenge of Northern Ireland also appealed to Blair's conceit of himself as a politician with special gifts. 'He liked throwing himself at that sort of challenge,' observed his Cabinet Secretary, Sir Richard Wilson. 'He thought he had the unique abilities to resolve problems that had defeated his predecessors.'[14] Mo Mowlam, his first Northern Ireland Secretary, talked about Blair having 'a Jesus complex'.[15] A danger in his personality in other contexts, notably Iraq, this was an advantage in making peace in Ireland. Self-belief and natural optimism drove him on long after more pessimistic types would have given up.

Blair took instant advantage of the landslide victory in 1997 to 'kick things forward'. In the words of Sir John Holmes, a senior official who provided expertise developed working on Northern Ireland with John Major: 'He saw a real opportunity by moving fast to get everybody caught up in the whirl, not let them think too hard about what was happening and get some momentum in the process.'[16]

Within two weeks of becoming Prime Minister, Blair made the first of what would be many flights to Belfast to make a speech, with a great deal of input from Holmes, which reinvigorated the stalled process inherited from Major. The speech was 'well-balanced, thoughtful and it established a sense of urgency', in the expert view of George Mitchell, the former American senator who was guiding the process.[17] Blair reassured the Unionists that he was not going to give away Northern Ireland by declaring: 'My agenda is not a united Ireland . . . I believe in the United Kingdom. I value the Union.'[18] In an unscripted addition which appalled some of his officials, he stood amidst a group of primary school children and declared that he didn't think a united Ireland would happen in their lifetimes. This helped to reassure the Unionists, whose leader, David Trimble, was impressed because it 'not just re-energised the process, but set out what we would now call a road map'.[19] To the Republicans, Blair declared that 'the settlement train was leaving' and he wanted them aboard.[20] Martin McGuinness says they took this as an encouraging sign that Blair:

recognised that there wasn't going to be a solution unless Irish Republicans were part of that. He was challenging the Thatcher mentality that the enemy was the Republicans, the enemy was the IRA, that they had to be defeated at all costs. It was his willingness to do that that made an impression on me.[21]

Blair's facility for getting people to like him was also at work. Gerry Adams found him 'the opposite of the stuffy, arms-length attitude of the Tories. He was personable and informal, easy to talk to . . . an engaging personality. I dared to hope that there was a chance that we could actually do business with him.'[22]

The Good Friday Agreement signed during Holy Week in 1998 was a high point of his first term. When those talks teetered on the brink of collapse, Blair gambled with his reputation by dashing across the Irish Sea to hurl himself into the negotiations. George Mitchell calls it 'a courageous, critical and decisive' intervention. He negotiated 'paragraph by paragraph, sentence by sentence, word by word. He was personally and directly involved in the critical negotiation. On this I am absolutely certain: without the direct intervention of Tony Blair there would not have been an agreement.'[23] Martin McGuinness agrees 'that if the Taoiseach and the British Prime Minister had not come to Castle Buildings we'd probably still be sitting there. That was of critical importance.'[24] From the other side of the divide, David Trimble concurs that Blair 'made the difference'.[25]

That agreement secured a historic compromise between Unionism and Nationalism. For the first time, Unionists accepted that they shared Northern Ireland with another tradition that deserved equality of respect, conceded to the principle of power-sharing in Northern Ireland and accepted a cross-border dimension. For the first time, Nationalists explicitly acknowledged that the status of Northern Ireland could not be changed without the consent of the majority of its population. The Irish Government removed the territorial claim to Northern Ireland from the Republic's constitution.

The Good Friday Agreement enjoyed a further crucial advantage over all previous attempts. It had a popular mandate. More than 90 per cent of voters in the Republic ratified it in the cross-border referendum. In the north, it won the support of 96 per cent of Nationalists. Unionists approved by the narrower margin of 53 per cent following another decisive intervention by Blair, when he threw himself into the campaign to secure endorsement.[26] Trimble believes Blair 'probably turned the campaign round and enabled us to get a narrow majority of Unionists'.[27]

The Agreement was a triumph, but a necessarily imperfect one which still left chasms of mistrust between the two communities. Blair and Powell initially and wrongly thought that their main challenge was simply to get it implemented. Only after a while did they grasp that what they actually faced was 'an endurance test'.[28] It left unclear the extent to which the IRA would be required to disarm before its political twin, Sinn Féin, could become part of a devolved government. In the words of Powell: 'There was deliberate constructive ambiguity about decommissioning which came back to haunt us as it became destructive ambiguity.'[29] The refusal of the IRA to unequivocally declare an end to its 'war' was not just an affront to the Unionists. All the constitutional parties had reason to object while Sinn Féin sat at the table with a private army at its back. 'Guns and government' bedevilled the negotiations for years. The Unionists were resistant to allowing Republicans into government so long as they had their guns. Republicans were reluctant to surrender their arsenal before the Unionists demonstrated a sincere intent to share power.

In mid-August 1998, a splinter terrorist group, the Real IRA, killed twenty-nine people and injured hundreds more with a massive bomb in the market town of Omagh. The leadership of Sinn Féin condemned that atrocity, but resisted taking the next step. Republican theology would not let them be seen to surrender. Gerry Adams argued: 'Historically the IRA has never decommissioned weapons and it is not going to start now.'[30]

Adams and Martin McGuinness were the principal negotiators for Sinn Féin throughout the many tortuous years of the process. Both had joined the IRA as young men. Adams first grew his beard when on the run from arrest during internment in the 1970s. He represented Belfast, the ideological centre of Republicanism. McGuinness came from Derry, its emotional heart. He was a former Chief of Staff of the IRA who commanded its Derry Brigade during some of the bloodiest years of the Troubles that had claimed 3,326 lives and maimed many more.[31]

Adams and McGuinness made a first and highly symbolic public visit to Number 10 at Christmas 1997. What was at first a momentous shift – the Prime Minister shaking hands and talking over the table with Sinn Féin when the IRA had tried to murder both of his immediate predecessors – rapidly became part of the scene. Yet the full scale of the encounters would have shocked and repelled a lot of opinion had it been known at the time. Their many subsequent visits to Downing Street and to Chequers were largely kept hidden from public view. Paddy Ashdown and his wife drove up to Chequers one weekend and had to wait for a while at the police checkpoint because the car in front of them was being 'searched minutely'. It turned out to be Gerry Adams arriving for a meeting with Blair. The Ashdowns went in to see Cherie, who was feeding baby Leo. The Prime Minister suddenly appeared. 'I must show him to Gerry Adams!' he said and grabbed his son to do just that.[32]

During a big negotiation at Number 10 in May 1999, Adams and McGuinness managed to slip out of the building and into the back garden, the same garden over which the IRA fired mortars in an attempt to kill John Major. Jonathan Powell looked out of the window and was horrified to witness the

Sinn Féin leaders playing with the Blairs' children. Adams and McGuinness were trying to ride Nicky Blair's skateboard down the path through the Downing Street rose garden. At a time when the IRA still retained the arms which had caused so many deaths, a picture of this remarkable scene would have caused widespread outrage. 'Oh fuck,' Powell whispered to himself. He ran out into the garden to get them back inside before anyone noticed.[33]

The Chief of Staff spent more face-time negotiating with Sinn Féin than anyone else. Many clandestine encounters took place at the Clonard monastery in west Belfast. Powell would turn up clutching his official briefcase embossed with the royal crest to parley about the intentions of the IRA, an organisation which had blown up the Queen's cousin and put his elder brother, Charles, on its death list when he worked for Margaret Thatcher. MI5 grew very apprehensive that the Prime Minister's Chief of Staff was endangering himself by becoming 'over-exposed'.[34]

Powell trusted McGuinness more than Adams.[35] The former IRA capo was a paradox: a dedicated Catholic with an unblemished family life. In the assessment of one senior intelligence official: 'McGuinness hated lying.'[36] Adams was a more conventional politician. During one heated negotiation in the Sinn Féin centre on the Falls Road, Adams leaned across the table towards Powell and said: 'The thing I like about you, Jonathan, is that you always blush when you lie.' Another official present, Bill Jeffrey of the Northern Ireland Office, quipped back: 'Unlike you, Gerry.' They all laughed.[37]

The Sinn Féin leaders had a hostile relationship with Peter Mandelson when he was Northern Ireland Secretary. 'When Gerry Adams and Martin McGuinness entered the room, you were expected to stand up,' says Mandelson. 'They were senior military, they were top brass. Apart from being leaders of Sinn Féin, they were leaders of the military council. And they knew you knew it. I did not address them as if they were leaders of the military council, so that fiction was maintained. They were lordly, this pair. They are bloody hard people. There was very, very tough psychological game-playing, a lot of unspoken intimidation.'[38] Peter Hain found them 'professionally probably the best negotiators I have come across'.[39]

British ministers and officials would look into the clear, ice blue eyes of McGuinness and the bearded face of Adams and try to gauge their sincerity. 'We were very worried the Republicans could go back to violence,' says Powell.[40] That fear was understandable. Violent splits had been a regular feature of the history of republicanism since 1921. John Reid, Mandelson's successor as Northern Ireland Secretary, observes: 'Any time the Republican movement has tried to reach an accommodation with the British Government before, there has been a split and they've ended up killing each other.'[41] The

Sinn Féin leaders would amplify that fear by stressing that they were risking their own lives. Explaining why the IRA would not agree to start decommissioning in 1999, Powell was told by McGuinness that 'There was a real threat that someone would give a gun to some impressionable seventeen-year-old and get them to shoot Adams or him.'[42] Tom Kelly, a Protestant from Northern Ireland who was heavily involved throughout the process, accepts that they might have 'put more pressure on the Shinners to deliver decommissioning earlier, but you could never be quite sure how far you could push Adams and McGuinness without pushing them over the edge'.[43] Blair and Powell 'wanted to make peace once, rather than many times'.[44]

While this goal was right, it also handed a negotiating lever to Adams and McGuinness not available to parties which did not have gunmen in the shadows. They exploited it. Mandelson complained that they would present 'the Sinn Féin shopping list' of demands and intimate that if they didn't get what they wanted 'then power would pass back to the bad men'.[45]

This caused serious division between Mandelson and Blair. 'Tony used to say "the process is the policy". If it stops, you will roll back into disaster and God alone knows what.' Mandelson thought Blair was too willing to concede 'sweeties' to Sinn Féin and 'dangle carrots' before them which were 'calculated to push the Unionists off the other end of the table'.[46] David Trimble agrees that Blair was 'nervous' about 'bringing pressure to bear on Republicans', which made it appear that they were 'driving the agenda'. Concessions to Sinn Féin 'wore out the patience of Unionist voters'.[47]

Blair had deployed his talent for winning friends to forge a vital relationship with Trimble. They were very different people: the smooth and supple Blair was the temperamental opposite of the prickly and proud Trimble, a man who could erupt in red-faced rages. Yet Blair admired Trimble for his bravery and Trimble was fascinated by Blair. In the view of one sympathetic biographer: 'At some level, Trimble hero-worshipped Blair and was loath to say no to a politician still at the height of his powers.'[48] The connection was instrumental in inducing the Unionist to make the courageous decision to sign up to the Good Friday Agreement. Trimble made that leap conscious that he could be next in the long line of moderate Unionists to be destroyed when they tried to compromise. Despite his eventual fate, he would still call it 'the high point' of his political life.[49]

The power-sharing executive was finally set up at midnight on 30 November 1999, but was suspended after just seventy-two days over the issue of 'guns and government'. John de Chastelain, the Canadian general who was head of the body monitoring the process, reported that there had been no progress on IRA decommissioning. In early May 2000, the IRA did finally agree to open its arms dumps to inspection by the Independent International Commission on Decommissioning. The executive came back to life at the end of the month only to founder again later on the same issue.

Trimble was intermittently First Minister when the devolved executive was functioning. He was feted internationally when he won the Nobel Peace Prize jointly with John Hume, the constitutional nationalist who had been a brave pathfinder for peace. The international accolades were not enough to bolster Trimble's crumbling position with his own community. The Good Friday Agreement was a victory for the Unionists on what mattered most to them: the guarantee of their place in the United Kingdom. Yet many of them saw themselves losing more than they were gaining. IRA prisoners were released two years after the agreement. 'It was an extremely distasteful business. Nobody wanted to do this,' says John Holmes. 'But it was clear to all of us that if we didn't do this then there wouldn't be a deal.'[50] The Royal Ulster Constabulary was being transformed into the Police Service of Northern Ireland. The police, heavily dominated by Protestants and with a history of brutality towards Catholics, needed reform to reconcile them with the Nationalist community. But Unionists recoiled at the conjunction of their police force, many of whom had lost their lives fighting terrorism, being 'destroyed' while killers went free and the IRA was still not disarmed. Trimble felt it was the absence of early decommissioning, changes to the police that 'failed to acknowledge the service and sacrifice that had gone before' and the agreement to 'unconditional prisoner release' that 'caused the disenchantment' and 'the eclipse' of him and his party.[51] His position became increasingly precarious as he clung on by his fingertips from one cliffhanging meeting of his party's ruling council to another.

Unionist disenchantment was fed on both by his internal opponents and by Ian Paisley's Democratic Unionists, who had boycotted the Good Friday Agreement. The general election in May 2001 squeezed the moderates in Northern Ireland. David Trimble won six seats to Ian Paisley's five, but half of Trimble's MPs 'were at odds with me on policy'.[52] The constitutional nationalists of the SDLP, who rightly felt taken for granted because they did not have arms to lay down, were overtaken by Sinn Féin. Six days of talks at Weston Park that July broke up without agreement. When Adams and McGuinness were pressed to produce more movement on decommissioning, they came back with the familiar refrain that if the Republicans were pushed too fast it would 'lead to the emergence of a new IRA which would do nothing to solve the historical problem'.[53]

In late August 2001, Powell wrote a note to Blair arguing that it was time to call Sinn Féin's bluff. It had been a violent summer in north Belfast and the IRA was clearly encouraging the trouble. Three alleged senior IRA members were arrested in Colombia that summer and accused of collaborating with FARC, a vicious terrorist organisation fuelled by the cocaine trade. In pursuit of the prize of peace, the British Government had adopted a Nelsonian blind eye and pretended not to see many things which would be normally intolerable to a democratic government. They could not indefinitely ignore continuing criminal and paramilitary activity.

9/11 added further pressure to lay down arms, one of the few instances of those atrocities having a benign effect. The mass murder in New York and Washington made the IRA's brand of terrorism seem obsolete. They could not compete when al-Qaeda was prepared to use suicide bombers to kill people in their thousands. Those Americans who had been romantically indulgent of violent republicanism became intolerant of any form of terrorism. In October 2001, the IRA finally conducted its first act of decommissioning. The international monitors reported that they witnessed the destruction of arms, ammunition and explosives. In the view of Republicans, this was a major concession and a historic step. But it came too late, and the disarmament was not visible enough, to satisfy distrusting Unionists. They felt vindicated in their suspicions when there was a break-in at the headquarters of Special Branch in Belfast in March 2002. A large number of police officers were forced to move home for fear that their addresses were compromised. Those and other lower-profile episodes suggested that the IRA might be relatively quiescent, but it had not gone away. This was one of several acts which Number 10 interpreted as 'the Provos doing things to reassure supporters that they hadn't gone soft'.[54] That October, the police raided Republican addresses in Belfast and stormed into Sinn Féin's offices at Stormont. It was declared that they had found evidence of an IRA 'spy ring' which was collecting information to target police officers and soldiers.[55]

In the wake of the 'spy ring' affair, the pressure on Trimble from his own side became even more intense. The devolved government was suspended in October 2002 and would not function again for more than four years. After many years trying to climb ladders to agreement, the peace process was slithering back down the snake.

This forced Blair into a major reappraisal of how he had been trying to progress. 'It looked as though the institutions we had worked so hard to create in Northern Ireland were falling, irreparably, apart,' observes Powell.

We had struggled for four years to implement the Good Friday Agreement, by giving a few concessions to one side and then a few to the other in the hope that we could build trust between the sides over time. But time had worked against us: the peace process had become badly discredited and morally undermined. It no longer seemed to be based on principle. Now we had to restore its credibility and force the Republicans into a choice between the ballot box and the Armalite.[56]

Tom Kelly commissioned regular private polling in Northern Ireland. It showed the Unionist community becoming 'more and more aggravated'.[57] Kelly wrote a first draft of a tough speech which was then refined by Blair and Powell on a flight back from Moscow. 'There was a good deal of agonising' that the newly robust tone towards Republicans might drive them out of the process altogether. 'Will they just walk away from it?' Blair worried to his aides.[58] Powell and Kelly 'ganged up' on the Prime Minister to convince him he had to deliver an ultimatum.[59] The speech was made on 17 October 2002 at the Harbour Commissioner's Office beside the Belfast docks. He declared that there now had to be a commitment to 'exclusively peaceful means, real, total and permanent'. He went on: 'The crunch is the crunch. There is no parallel track left. The fork in the road has finally come. We cannot carry on with the IRA half in, half out of this process. Not just because it isn't right any more. It won't work any more.' There would be no more 'inch by inch negotiation'. What was now required was 'acts of completion' to prove Republican commitment to democratic politics and a 'complete end' to paramilitarism, spying, punishment beatings and weapons-buying.[60]

This new approach was occasionally called the 'big bang', an unfortunate label in the context of Northern Ireland. Blair was 'very twitchy' about the reaction.[61] When a response came from Gerry Adams, it was extraordinary: the Sinn Féin leader asked Jonathan Powell to help him draft a reply. Eagerly taking up this unexpected invitation, Powell's draft included the following:

The IRA is never going to disband in response to ultimatums from the British Government or David Trimble. But I do believe the logic of the peace process puts all of us in a different place. So if you ask me do I envisage a future without the IRA? The answer is obvious. The answer is yes.

To the amazement of Blair, Kelly and Powell – the only people who knew that Number 10 was drafting speeches for Sinn Féin – Adams delivered the crucial passages with barely a word altered. He included the vital line about the disappearance of the IRA.[62] Soon afterwards, Martin McGuinness, who joined the IRA at nineteen, declared: 'My war is over.'[63]

That was progress, but far from enough to dissolve the impasse over 'guns and government'. The IRA refused to move towards full decommissioning until the Assembly and Executive were restored; the Unionists required decommissioning before they would go back into government. Neither side wanted to jump first for fear that the other was not sincere about reciprocating. This was the obstacle time after time. Talks at Hillsborough Castle in March 2003 again snagged on the IRA's refusal to unequivocally declare that its weapons would be destroyed and the Unionists' unwillingness to share power without that pledge.

Even the usually inexhaustible Powell was sometimes driven to despair 'that perhaps Northern Ireland was insoluble after all . . . every time we made a breakthrough we faced a new crisis immediately, and maybe the only thing we could do was manage the problem, keep talking so that people didn't go back to killing each other.'[64] Through all the many sudden crises and dashed hopes, Blair demonstrated an astonishing persistence and a stubborn conviction that they would get there in the end. 'Tony kept going when most of us were ready to give up.'[65] Another of Blair's officials marvelled at how much time and energy he would devote, even when it seemed utterly fruitless, to coaxing and cajoling the recalcitrant parties. 'These people are very, very high maintenance. All ringing up constantly, all demanding meetings constantly, all slagging each other off.'[66]

At the end of May 2003, Blair invited Adams and McGuinness to a secret lunch at Chequers. They were still maintaining that the IRA should be left to gradually 'fade away', an idea that would never satisfy Unionists. Blair proposed that he should meet the IRA leadership. Certain as ever of his powers of persuasion, he believed he only had to get in the same room as the IRA high command to convince them that a much bigger and more definitive act of disarmament was required. He made this remarkable offer 'repeatedly' over the years.[67] The Sinn Féin leaders always fobbed him off by saying the time was not quite right. Some will suggest that they declined because a meeting with the high command of the IRA would have brought Blair face to face with the same Adams and McGuinness. Mandelson regarded it as 'a fiction' that they were not talking to the IRA when they negotiated with Sinn Féin. 'Of course we knew,' Powell later accepted.[68] When they used to say they couldn't agree to something without consulting the Army Council, Mo Mowlam would say to the Sinn Féin leaders: 'Why don't you go out and look in the mirror and come back again.'[69] One senior British official comments: 'If they didn't represent the IRA in some way, what's the point of talking to them because the whole process had to be an end to violence.'[70]

When elections were held for the Assembly on 26 November 2003, the failure to make political progress polarised the voting and left the centre ground scorched. Ian Paisley's DUP, which had said from the start that

Republicans could not be trusted, greatly gained at the expense of Trimble's UUP. The constitutional nationalists of the SDLP lost further ground to Sinn Féin, who seemed to have more power to lever concessions from London than their more moderate competitors for Catholic votes. That election marked the final eclipse of the moderates who had made brave compromises for peace and the ascendancy of the extremes who had so often wrecked it.

It put an end to Blair's original strategy to 'build out from the centre'.[71] Powell lamented: 'All our hopes . . . were dashed.'[72] They now faced what looked like an utterly impossible challenge: reconciling such implacable enemies as Sinn Féin and Ian Paisley. The DUP leader's instant reaction to his victory was to declare: 'I'm not talking to Sinn Féin. I think I'm entitled to ignore terrorists.'[73] Blair initially responded to this blow by refusing to come to terms with it and clinging to the hope, shared by none of his officials, that Trimble might somehow make a comeback. 'There was guilt' about what had happened to Trimble. 'He felt he'd let David down.'[74] The triumph of Paisley appeared disastrous. Dr No had been the ranting voice of Protestant supremacy for decades. 'No surrender' and 'Not an inch' were his war cries. His forty-year career was founded on the politics of division and destruction during which he successfully set out to obliterate any moderate Unionist politician who attempted an accommodation and denounced compromise as a selling out of Ulster to 'fiendish republican scum'.[75]

Paisley was a bigot who had made a career out of denouncing the Catholic Church as 'the Whore of Babylon, the mother of abominations'.[76] He would not shake the hand of the Irish Prime Minister nor that of Cherie because she was a Catholic. His party had marched in protest against the Good Friday Agreement. 'Tony didn't trust Paisley and he didn't like Paisley,' says Tom Kelly.[77] According to Jonathan Powell, 'he was convinced that Paisley would never do a deal.'[78] Blair lamented that it would be another ten years before there was a Unionist leadership ready to settle.[79]

This gloom was pierced by a few shafts of hope. The people of Northern Ireland were enjoying the diminution of violence and the growing prosperity that accompanied the absence of terrorism. No party wanted to be blamed for wrecking that. Sinn Féin emitted signals that it could be open to a deal even with the Reverend. Paisley and his deputy, Peter Robinson, might have been unyielding in their public rhetoric. Yet they began to move into a slightly more flexible position once they were the dominant Unionist players. In February 2004, a DUP delegation came to Downing Street. They surprised Blair and his officials with their professionalism and sophistication when Robinson gave a PowerPoint presentation of their negotiating position in the state dining room.[80] He declared that they would be prepared to share power if Republicans met what the DUP called the 'Blair necessities': the end of criminality and paramilitarism spelt out in the Belfast Harbour speech.

In the summer of 2004, the Euro-elections confirmed the ascendancy of the DUP and Sinn Féin. In September, talks were convened at Leeds Castle, a picturesque Norman fortress in Kent. Proceedings began with some amateur theatrics. Adams and McGuinness turned up brandishing a five-foot bugging device which they said had been uncovered at a Sinn Féin office in the Falls Road. They made a show of presenting the 1980s-vintage bug to Blair as 'an offering to the mighty god of British intelligence'.[81] Everyone knew it was a stunt. McGuinness was 'smirking like a schoolboy' while Adams was 'desperately trying to keep a straight face' and Powell could 'barely control his giggles'.[82] Once they had plonked the ancient bug in front of him and departed, Blair joked to his aides: 'I thought we could do better than that!'[83]

It was much more important that Adams was declaring 'we want to do business with Ian Paisley' and the DUP leader didn't reject the idea out of hand. Blair and Powell became encouraged by what seemed to be a personality change in Paisley, now in his seventy-eighth year. He came very near to death in August and looked emaciated when he arrived at Leeds Castle, having travelled there by ferry and car because he was still too ill to fly. His brush with mortality seemed to be altering how he saw the purpose of his life. Powell began to believe that 'Paisley wanted to be remembered not as Dr No but as Dr Yes.'[84] Kelly was also 'convinced at Leeds Castle that the Doc was up for it. The question was whether he would survive for long enough to do it and could he bring his party with him.'[85]

Nigel Dodds, a leading member of Paisley's party, had been the target of an assassination attempt by the IRA on his way to visit his terminally ill son in hospital. His police bodyguard was shot. It was going to be hugely difficult to persuade a Unionist with that history to strike a bargain with Sinn Féin. Paisley still refused to sit down and negotiate with the Republicans face to face. After such a long wait for decommissioning, the DUP wanted tangible proof that IRA weapons were being destroyed, not least to convince their own supporters that they were not being played for dupes. At root, this was about symbolism. Even if they did completely disarm, the IRA could always re-equip. Decommissioning was not really a guarantee that they would never return to terrorism. But it was a symbolism that hugely mattered to both sides. Paisley demanded that a Protestant clergyman be allowed to observe decommissioning with the unrestricted ability to take video or photos: what became known as a 'Kodak Moment'.

Blair was visibly frustrated and tired when he held a closing news conference at Leeds Castle on Saturday lunchtime with Bertie Ahern. The two Prime Ministers had to admit that the three days of talks had not reached a resolution; the 'moment of decision' he had spoken of at the start had still not been achieved.[86]

Shortly afterwards, the chances seemed to recede even further. Paisley came under pressure from fundamentalists in his party, to which he responded by telling a rally in his constituency: 'The IRA needs to be humiliated. And they need to wear their sackcloth and ashes – openly.'[87] That had a predictably inflammatory effect on the other side. The IRA definitively rejected the idea of a 'Kodak Moment'.

Four days before Christmas, Jonathan Powell landed at Belfast airport for another clandestine rendezvous with Adams and McGuinness at Clonard monastery. He was met by Jonathan Phillips, the Political Director and later Permanent Secretary at the Northern Ireland Office. The civil servant had a grim look on his face. Once their car had left the airport, Phillips asked the driver to pull over. On a grass verge on the side of the road, he told Powell that he had just received stunning news from the police. The headquarters of the Northern Bank had been raided and more than £26 million stolen from vaults which were full of Christmas takings from the city's stores. 'The dogs on the street know that the IRA carried out the crime,' said Phillips.[88]

Powell went ahead with his meeting with Adams and McGuinness, but he could not say that he knew about the robbery because it had not yet been officially announced. He returned to London feeling 'completely conned' and seized by fear that the raid, the largest ever bank robbery in the history of the United Kingdom, left 'the whole process in deep shit'.[89]

Tony Blair was aboard a Hercules flying across the Middle East when news of the robbery reached the Prime Minister. 'It looks like a Provo job,' reported Tom Kelly. A shocked and dejected Blair replied: 'If it is, we're not going to get the Unionists back.'[90] The most positive gloss put on the robbery by security sources was that the IRA was trying to finance a 'retirement fund' in advance of winding up. Others reckoned they 'just couldn't help themselves'.[91] Throughout the process, Blair and his team repeatedly asked themselves whether the Republicans were genuinely on the road to peace or playing games. 'For all of us, there was a chill down the spine.'[92]

The Prime Minister of Ireland also felt betrayed. 'This was an IRA job,' said Bertie Ahern in a fierce public denunciation of Sinn Féin, whom he accused of having prior knowledge of the bank heist. 'This was a job that would have been known to the political leadership. What kind of idiots are people taking us for?'[93] The Independent Monitoring Commission, the official assessors of terrorist activity, declared that the bank robbery was one of a 'series of crimes' by the IRA.[94] Far from winding up, it looked like they were trying to establish themselves as the largest criminal organisation in Europe. Adams responded by attacking both the IMC and Ahern and challenging them to send the police to arrest him if they had any proof he knew about it.[95] One typical commentary pronounced the Good Friday Agreement as good as dead. 'We are back to square one in terms of building a peace deal.'[96]

Fury about the continuing criminality of the IRA intensified further after the brutal murder of Robert McCartney, a Catholic father of two, in a bar near the Belfast law courts on 30 January 2005. The leadership of the IRA did not order the murder, but did organise the cover-up. There were seventy-two witnesses to the killing but every one was intimidated into silence.[97] The crime scene was wiped clean before the police arrived. The murdered man's bereaved fiancée and five sisters were not prepared to let his death become another killing which was briefly mourned and then swiftly forgotten. The McCartneys – articulate, determined and charismatic – launched a hugely effective campaign demanding justice. It put a spotlight on the violence and intimidation of Catholic working-class communities by those who claimed to be their champions. Blair reached out to Nationalists by showing that the British state was prepared to acknowledge its past sins when he gave a comprehensive apology to the 'Guildford Four' and 'Maguire Seven' for their false convictions in the 1970s.[98] The IRA then made an extraordinary offer to shoot the killers of Robert McCartney, a suggestion which only confirmed their gangsterism.

The united condemnation of London, Dublin and Washington, combined with the huge public sympathy for the McCartney family's campaign, put Adams and McGuinness in a corner. When the Sinn Féin leaders were smuggled into Number 10 for a clandestine meeting on 23 February, Adams looked 'shell-shocked' and 'physically shrunken'.[99] The IRA initially sounded belligerent. It made a statement with a whiff of Semtex when it declared that the IRA 'would not remain quiescent'.[100] The Governments were 'unnerved' by the fear that they had 'lost the Provos'.[101] But they didn't buckle in the face of this shrill attempt to shiver everyone's spines. The Republicans were, in truth, deeply rattled by the backlash from both international opinion and within their own community.

The McCartneys hit Sinn Féin where it hurt when they embarked on a media-saturated tour of the United States in mid-March. George Bush welcomed the sisters to the White House on St Patrick's Day. Gerry Adams, previously treated as a celebrity in Washington, had the door shut in his face for the first time in more than a decade. The President announced that he believed Sinn Féin was no longer 'a reliable partner for peace'.[102] Senator Edward Kennedy, a veteran friend of Irish Republicanism, cold-shouldered Adams.[103] Pete King, a New York Congressman who was a personal friend of the Sinn Féin leader and his closest ally on Capitol Hill, declared: 'The time has come for the IRA to disband.'[104] In April, Adams attempted to recover ground by making an 'appeal' to the IRA to 'fully embrace and accept' democratic means. In the May general election, reaction against IRA criminality worked to the benefit of the SDLP at the expense of Sinn Féin. Paisley further consolidated his grip on Unionism when Trimble lost his seat in the Commons and his party was defeated in every other seat but one.

The McCartney murder and the Northern Bank robbery, two shocking events which initially seemed so bleak for the peace process, had the ultimate effect of jolting it forward. The 7/7 bombings in London added further pressure. Republicans finally had to make the choice, spelt out by Blair at Belfast Harbour three years before, between ballot box and bullet.

On 25 July, Number 10 waited to receive the text of an IRA response to the 'appeal' to disarm for good. As always, there was a series of intricate and secretly choreographed moves to get to this point. An IRA declaration that the 'armed struggle' was over would be reciprocated with an amnesty for IRA men on the run and the dismantling of army watchtowers. Number 10 awaited delivery of the text with apprehension. The IRA was notorious for making statements which were so obfuscatory that they left room for multiple interpretations which did not build confidence in the other actors. The Sinn Féin leaders were warned that they had 'only one chance at this, the language has to be clear.' When the text arrived, Blair and Powell handed it to Tom Kelly, who had the best nose for Unionist opinion, and waited for him to react. He only needed to read it once. 'Bingo,' he said. 'We're in business.'[105]

On the 28th, a DVD was released by the IRA declaring the end of the nine-decade-long struggle to create a united Ireland through force of arms. With an Irish flag in the background, the statement was delivered by Seana Walsh, a former Maze prisoner who was a cellmate of Bobby Sands. 'The leadership of Óglaigh na hÉireann has formally ordered an end to the armed campaign,' he said. That was the key phrase that so many had longed to hear from the IRA. The statement continued: 'All IRA units have been ordered to dump arms. All volunteers have been instructed to assist the development of purely political and democratic programmes through exclusively peaceful means. Volunteers must not engage in any other activities whatsoever.'[106]

TV news channels marked the moment with archive footage reminding viewers of the many casualties of that 'armed struggle': the mass murders at the cenotaph in Enniskillen, in the pubs of Birmingham, at the bandstand in Regent's Park, at the Grand Hotel in Brighton and so many other locations. Blair welcomed 'a step of unparalleled magnitude'. He was careful to acknowledge that people were going to be sceptical after so many 'false dawns and dashed hopes', but he hoped: 'This may be the day when finally . . . peace replaced war, politics replaces terror on the island of Ireland.'[107]

On 26 September, General de Chastelain announced that all IRA weapons had been put beyond use. Two clergymen, a Protestant minister and a Catholic priest, were the witnesses.[108] The Provisional IRA was once one of the world's most merciless killing machines. It took 1,700 lives in Northern Ireland, Britain, the Republic and Europe in its twenty-six years of existence. A terrorist organisation which invented the car bomb and still regarded itself as undefeated in the field had finally gone into liquidation.

The absence of war was not a guarantee of a stable peace. There was still the epic challenge of convincing Ian Paisley's Unionists to share a government with the Republicans. Many of the DUP were viscerally hostile. They first demanded a period of 'decontamination' before they would engage in serious talks and then said they would put the issue out to 'consultation' of their members. It was still inconceivable to many that old Dr No would really be capable of saying yes to power-sharing with Republicans. Here a critical mellowing role was played by Blair's gift for cultivating relationships. He gradually forged a bond with the Unionist founded in their shared interest in religion. They were very different faiths: the Presbyterianism of Paisley and the closet Catholicism of Blair. Yet Blair made it work. On one occasion, he rang the Unionist from the King David Hotel in Jerusalem and described to an appreciative Paisley the biblical view over the Mount of Olives. The Unionist leader would visit Number 10 bearing religious texts for Leo. Staff were at first surprised and then grew accustomed to the sound of warm laughter coming from the Prime Minister's den when the two men were having a tête-à-tête. 'They seduced each other.'[109] Reflecting on his illness the previous summer, Paisley told Blair that he'd had 'a near meeting with my Maker' which had altered his perspective.[110] The Prime Minister was further encouraged when the other man told him, and more than once, that he did not want to be remembered as 'just an old man determined to say no'.[111] He seemed increasingly attracted by the idea of being the leader who presided over a definitive end to the Troubles. 'Did we play on that?' says Tom Kelly. 'Of course.'[112]

On 6 April 2006, Blair visited the Navan Centre in County Armagh, the ancient capital of the High Kings of Ulster. It was eight years since the Good

Friday Agreement. Much had been achieved since. The IRA had declared itself out of business. Northern Ireland was enjoying the blossoming of normal civic life. Where once troops were on the streets, now the police patrolled as they would in the rest of the UK. Splendid new buildings, dockside developments and restaurants were flourishing in Belfast. Locals went to see the Buena Vista Social Club and the Royal Shakespeare Company.[113]

The worst year of the Troubles saw the murder of almost 500 people. The annual killing rate had now fallen to single figures. Though at a lower intensity than at any time since the 1960s, there was always the risk of a slide back into bombings and mass murders if politics could not be made to work.

The Prime Minister and his Chief of Staff could not yet be certain whether what they now faced was 'the final ascent or just another false summit'.[114] Blair used the speech at Navan to reflect on the long climb so far. 'What has happened is an object lesson in conflict resolution. The problem is that the Good Friday Agreement can provide procedures, mechanisms and laws. What it can't do is enforce a belief in the other's good faith.'[115] He challenged the DUP and Sinn Féin to come to terms and employed the pressure of the deadline to force the pace. The leaders of the parties were set a November end date for agreeing to the reformation of a power-sharing executive. If they didn't come to a deal 'we call time on this and seek another way to go.'[116] That would mean prolonged direct rule from London with the implied threat to the Unionists of ever closer involvement by Dublin. Further psychological pressure was applied by Peter Hain, the fifth Northern Ireland Secretary under Blair. The first, Mo Mowlam, deployed her vibrant, gutsy and impetuous personality to win over the Nationalist community. 'She was like a personal whirlwind,' observed one who saw the 'huge infusion of energy' she brought to the task.[117] To Nationalists, she cut an attractively different figure to her male and often patrician predecessors who had come over as colonial viceroys. She melted Catholic suspicion towards the British Government with her frank and warm style. The price of her success with Nationalists was that it provoked an allergic reaction to her among Unionists. Her successor, Peter Mandelson, kept the Unionists on board and persuaded them to make the first leaps into government. John Reid, an unusual hybrid of Catholic, Celtic-supporting, working-class Unionist, presided over the first act of IRA decommissioning. He was followed by Paul Murphy, who helped keep the process breathing through some of its most perilous and least rewarding years. He also gained the unique distinction of 'being the first Secretary of State who didn't offend either side'.[118]

Peter Hain's contrasting contribution was to unite all the Northern Ireland

politicians in hostility towards him. He energetically set about turning Northern Ireland into the People's Republic of Peter Hain. He announced the
abolition of grammar schools, the introduction of water rates and other
measures that were unpopular in Northern Ireland, especially with Paisley's
party. As an additional goad, he threatened to cut off the salaries and
expenses of the Assembly members, who were still being paid even though
it had been suspended since 2002. 'The stark choice we presented them with
was go into power or we close you down.'[119] It was a cunning form of
blackmail.

The deadline for agreement was very tight when the parties were brought
together for three days of talks at a golfing hotel at St Andrews in October
2006. The location was chosen rather whimsically because Powell felt Scotland was physically and spiritually closer to Northern Ireland. On the eve
of these talks, the Independent Monitoring Commission produced a report
which was positive about the cessation of IRA activity.[120] This gave credibility to Gerry Adams's claim that the Republicans were delivering 'big time'
on their commitments.[121] Ian Paisley was continuing his evolution from
demagogic dinosaur to man of peace. On the eve of the St Andrews talks,
he met with Archbishop Sean Brady, the head of the Catholic Church in
Ireland. The Paisley of earlier times had denounced the Pope as 'the Anti-
Christ'.[122]

They arrived on the east coast of Scotland to be greeted by lashing rain,
biting wind and fog so thick you couldn't see the sea. 'This is Ballymena
weather,' joked Paisley, who lost his hat to the wind.[123] To make the scene
more surreal, the hard man of Unionism and former terrorists negotiated
amidst tartan-clad American golfers.

'We have been almost ten years working on this, myself and the Taoiseach,'
said Blair a little wearily at an opening news conference with Ahern. 'Now
is the time to get the business done.'[124] The mood soon soured when they
got down to hard talking. Proximity didn't seem to bring the two sides
together. It drove them further apart. The big trust issue now was policing.
Once the IRA declared its 'war' over, the Unionist focus concentrated on
the Republicans' willingness to endorse the Police Service of Northern Ireland
as a sign that they were committed to the rule of law. As was so often the
case over the many years of negotiating, mistrust between the two sides was
manifested as an argument about sequencing. The Unionists demanded that
Sinn Féin commit to the police before they were let into government. The
Republicans wanted the government set up and policing and justice devolved
to the Assembly before they would endorse the police service. Paisley still

427

would not talk directly to Sinn Féin. His delegation, worried that the old man was being charmed into softness, wouldn't let him hold one-to-one talks with Blair. The DUP demanded that Sinn Féin hold an Ard Fheis – party meeting – to endorse the police. Adams scornfully wondered whether Paisley could even pronounce Ard Fheis. By the Friday morning, when Blair sat in his hotel suite groaning to Powell that it was 'hopeless', his pessimism seemed well-founded. These talks, like so many before them, were descending into the excruciatingly familiar exchanges of recrimination. Later that day, the British and Irish governments circulated a 5,000-word document setting out an intricate set of moves designed to build confidence between the two sides with a new target of creating an executive on 26 March 2007. Peter Hain hyped this as 'an astonishing breakthrough'.[125] Yet there was not truly a real deal between the parties.

In an attempt to make it look as though they had made solid progress, Tom Kelly ran off to the press centre and changed the backdrop for the final news conference from 'St Andrews Talks' to 'St Andrews Agreement'.[126] This was a ruse into which the media bought. Once they had the leaders lined up in front of the banner, Tony Blair prevented any discussion, which might have exposed the absence of a solid agreement, by getting up to make a short speech to Paisley and his wife congratulating them on their golden wedding anniversary. Wags joked that his wedding day was the last time the Reverend had ever said 'yes' to anything. Blair presented the Paisleys with a leather photo album. Bertie Ahern had come with a much better gift: a bowl made of wood from a walnut tree at the site of the Battle of the Boyne. When Blair learnt about Ahern's superior present the night before, he complained to Powell: 'We have to get something better than a photo album!' Blair then said to Ahern: 'Bertie, I wonder, should we give them the bowl from both of us?' Ahern laughed that it was 'a nice try'.[127]

It was probably more persuasive on Paisley that the best token came from the Prime Minister of the Republic. Paisley clasped the hand of Ahern, the first time the Unionist had ever shaken the hand of an Irish Taoiseach. Paisley called it a 'great day for peace' and 'a great day for all Ireland'. Gerry Adams got to his feet and led the applause for Paisley and his wife. Blair and his team took this as proof that the DUP leader had finally crossed 'the psychological barrier' of accepting that he would become First Minister in tandem with a Sinn Féin deputy.[128] It was certainly a remarkable spectacle that no-one ever expected to see.

Yet as soon as the two sides departed Scotland, they were again bitterly quarrelling about sequencing and the wording of the loyalty oath to the police. By the Christmas of 2006, the long and winding road was at another

impasse. Blair's premiership had only months left. He had just been interviewed by the police over 'cash-for-coronets'. Pressure from within the Labour
Party for him to quit Number 10 interlocked with a growing media view
that there was little remaining purpose to his premiership. He was ridiculed
when the press discovered that he was spending a week of the Christmas
and New Year break at the Florida villa of Robin Gibb. Commentators
hooted that the Bee Gees' 'Stayin' Alive' was an appropriate soundtrack for
his dwindling premiership. The media were wrong. Blair spent virtually all
of that holiday trying to sweat the peace process to a resolution. In Florida,
he got up at five in the morning because of the time difference to call the
principals. Only on Christmas Day and Boxing Day did he not work the
phone. He made more than a dozen long calls on New Year's Day, most of
them to Paisley. He did not tell the Reverend that he was ringing from a
room where John F. Kennedy had sex with Marilyn Monroe. The phone
talks were conducted to the background sound of Cherie complaining that
it was ruining their break and threatening divorce.[129] Blair eventually decided
to leave his family to enjoy Miami's winter sunshine and flew back to Britain early to try to fix the latest crisis.

After constant back and forth, a big hurdle was cleared at the end of January 2007. A secret IRA Army Convention and then a public Ard Fheis gave
a mandate to Adams and McGuinness to support the police. This was a major
overturning of historic republican theology. It was made easier because, thanks
to earlier reforms, a third of police officers were now Catholic. In early March,
there were elections for a new Assembly. The DUP and Sinn Féin were
confirmed as the two largest parties at Stormont. The DUP won 36 of the
108 seats in the Assembly. Sinn Féin secured 28. The UUP took 18, the SDLP
16 and the non-sectarian Alliance party 7.

This was the moment of truth. Polling suggested that a good majority of
the people of Northern Ireland wanted the restoration of devolved government, including most of Paisley's voters. He was increasingly seduced by the
prospect of being First Minister. Gordon Brown met him, Adams and
McGuinness to talk about an economic package for Northern Ireland which
was desired by both sides. To the amusement of the others, Paisley walked
out of the meeting at one point loudly declaring that he had to take a call
from President Bush. This artful stroke of his ego had been set up by Blair.[130]

The more resistant members of his party wanted another delay in the
timetable. Sinn Féin was induced to agree in return for Paisley appearing
with Adams in a staged reconciliation photograph to demonstrate that the
DUP was serious about power-sharing. Tony Blair was in Berlin, listening
to Simon Rattle conduct a performance of Beethoven's Fifth, when Tom

Kelly took a call from a senior official at the Northern Ireland office. Robert Hannigan reported: 'We've got a problem with the table.' It was a classic Northern Ireland quarrel about symbols. The Unionists and the Republicans had agreed on the photo only to fall out about how they would pose for it. The DUP demanded an adversarial seating plan. They wanted Paisley to sit opposite Adams in order to prove to Unionists that he wasn't selling out to their enemies. Sinn Féin wanted the table arranged so that Adams and Paisley sat next to each other like partners. They needed to demonstrate to their supporters that power-sharing was going to be for real. This squabble over seating brilliantly encapsulated what Blair and those who worked with him had been up against for a decade. The conundrum was eventually resolved by the ingenuity of Robert Hannigan. He proposed making the table diamond-shaped and sitting the two men at the apex.[131] Paisley and Adams would then be both next to each other and opposite each other, adversaries and partners at the same time.

On Monday, 26 March 2007, the two men sat for the historic photograph and pledged that power-sharing between their parties would begin on 8 May. It was a spectacle that no-one familiar with the history of Northern Ireland thought they would ever see. The two parties came to remarkably quick agreement about which ministries they would take in the new government. 'This is going to be all right, you know,' Peter Hain said to the Prime Minister. Blair gave Hain a 'quizzical, somewhat sceptical' look.[132] After so many previous crises and collapses, seeing would be believing.

There was something repellent about the eventual outcome of the peace process: the power was going to be carved up and the glory enjoyed by the two parties who had most fed the hatreds that fuelled the Troubles. They got to enjoy the rewards of the efforts and sacrifice of moderates who had dedicated themselves to peace for far longer than the extremes. Yet it was probably inevitable, if regrettable, that the peace could only be made secure through a deal between the polarities. This was not the route to a settlement that Blair originally intended to take, but he had got to the destination in the end.

Many others played vital roles, but the single most important factor in achieving this prize was the dedication displayed by Tony Blair. Though David Trimble paid for his courageous contribution with the loss of his seat in the Commons, he was still prepared to praise the Prime Minister. 'You could say that eventually something would have happened. It wouldn't have happened at this time without Tony Blair.'[133] Martin McGuinness sees him as 'The first British Prime Minister to make a seriously positive contribution to the resolution of all the injustices and conflict and violence and death that existed here for far too long.'[134] Peter Hain is right to say that no previous Prime Minister gave Northern Ireland such 'laser-like focus' and 'continuous attention' to keep 'the show on the road'.[135] Bertie Ahern was another impressed that 'in spite of all the different pressures on him . . . he kept at it, bringing the full force of the Prime Minister's office. The peace process just would not have happened without him.'[136] John Major laid some foundations, but his party had too much historical baggage and he had too little authority to progress further. Gordon Brown had neither the personal skills nor the empathy for Ireland that were required. Blair sustained the process through all the cycles of breakthrough, deadlock and setback. He pressed on when most leaders would have given up. One of the senior civil servants at the Northern Ireland office observed that he'd 'seen the Prime Minister almost literally pick up the parties and carry them over a line they didn't want to cross'.[137] Powell recalls: 'He was constantly ordering me to make impossible things happen'[138] and eventually the impossible did.

Blair drew on the full hand of his skills: his persevering optimism, his capacity for forging relationships with a wide variety of enormously tricky characters, his deviousness in negotiation when it was called for, his courage in taking risks, his inspirational talent with words, his capacity to immerse himself in detail when he wanted to, his ability to read moods, situations and other politicians, his energy and his creativity. This was a win for both his style and his substance. It was a victory for political ingenuity, persuasion and persistence over decades of hatred and violence.

On Tuesday, 8 May 2007, a remarkable ceremony took place in the Palladian grandeur of the parliament building at Stormont. On the flight over to Belfast the night before, Blair turned to his staff and asked: 'This is going to happen, isn't it?'[139] They were still pinching themselves the next day when Ian Paisley came forward to be sworn in as the First Minister of Northern Ireland. He read out the oath in his familiar booming bass, taking his time, milking the moment by pausing between words as if he expected them to be chiselled in marble. Then it was the turn of Martin McGuinness to be sworn in as Deputy First Minister, including the oath to uphold law and order. McGuinness had been a commander in a terrorist organisation which killed nearly half of the dead of the Troubles. Paisley's DUP and Free Presbyterian Church did not directly kill anyone, but for decades he unleashed incendiary bombast. The former IRA leader and the former Dr No were now going to sit together at the pinnacle of the new government, these two warriors and their communities brought to a better place by the peace process. They were watched from the gallery by Blair and Ahern, the two Prime Ministers whose productive and trusting relationship was so important. With them was the former Taoiseach Albert Reynolds, who had begun the process with John Major. Also gazing down from the gallery was Jonathan Powell, the most important British contributor to the success after Blair. Powell later recorded that 'I felt dizzy and slightly faint, as if I had just finished pushing a very large boulder uphill. If anyone had ever asked me in May 1997 whether I ever expected to see Ian Paisley and Martin McGuinness sharing power in Stormont I would have thought they were mad.'[140]

Sitting just a few feet away from the two Prime Ministers were a group of middle-aged, greying men, some of whom looked thin and frail. Only after the ceremony did Blair and Powell discover that these men were the high command of the IRA who had between them served more than fifty years in jail and were always 'an invisible presence at the negotiating table during all our talks'.[141] They too had come to witness this last, momentous act of the peace process.

The Assembly elected a Speaker and an entire cross-party ministerial team without a single cry of dissent. The two Prime Ministers then took tea with the new, improbable partnership. Paisley laughed to Blair: 'You're a young man of fifty-four going out of office and I'm an old man of eighty-one coming in.' A decade before, Blair would never have dreamt that he would feel better about losing power because Paisley was gaining it.

The four walked together into the Great Hall, where they made speeches from its marble steps. Paisley began by saying: 'I would have been totally disbelieving' if anyone had told him that 'I would be standing here today to take this office.' His oratorical power, so often before a divisive and destructive force, now spoke of reconciliation and healing. He quoted Solomon from the Old Testament: 'To everything there is a season . . . A time to kill and a time to heal. A time to break down and a time to build up . . . A time to love and a time to hate. A time of war and a time of peace.'[142]

Martin McGuinness quoted Seamus Heaney and the poet's counsel not to talk too much of Others. They must all, he said, 'get to a place through Otherness'.[143]

It was nine long years since Blair rushed to Northern Ireland to save the Good Friday Agreement. At that time he said: 'Now is not the time for sound-bites' before promptly delivering one of his most famous: 'I feel the hand of history on our shoulders.' In his speech in the marble hall, he echoed that phrase by declaring: 'Look back and we see centuries marked by conflict, hardship, even hatred among the people of these islands. Look forward and we see the chance to shake off those heavy chains of history.'[144]

The praise Blair offered to the contribution of Ahern was reciprocated when the Irish premier lauded his partner's determination to stick with a process that never 'promised quick or easy rewards. He has been a true friend of peace and a true friend of Ireland.'[145]

Paisley and McGuinness, the arch-demagogue of Unionism and the former Republican gunman, this oddest of political couplings, began governing together. To general amazement, they seemed to establish a real rapport and were dubbed 'the Chuckle Brothers'. Powell received a surprise call from a civil servant in Northern Ireland. Such calls had previously been a thing of dread because they were to report an atrocity, the outbreak of rioting or, at best, the breakdown of talks. On this occasion, the civil servant was calling to report that First Minister Paisley was rather tired that day because he had been up late the night before Scottish-Irish dancing with Martin McGuinness.[146]

There was a question mark for the longer term about the ultimate sustainability of power-sharing built on political blocs still largely defined by religion and history. For the moment, the executive ran with a remarkable smoothness and continued to do so after Paisley's retirement. In March 2009, cross-community revulsion greeted a spasm of the terrorist past when a police officer and two soldiers were murdered. The leadership of the DUP and Sinn Féin joined voices in condemnation. The terrorists were 'traitors to the island of Ireland', declared McGuinness.[147]

The British had an Irish problem – or perhaps it is fairer to say that Ireland had a British problem – since the Earl of Pembroke landed at a rocky headland near Waterford in 1170. A settlement of peace and justice had eluded kings and prime ministers ever since. The problem defeated William Gladstone and beat David Lloyd George. A resolution to the gruesome and apparently eternal cycle of sectarian violence that broke out in the 1960s was beyond Harold Wilson, Ted Heath, Jim Callaghan, Margaret Thatcher and John Major. Peace in Northern Ireland was Tony Blair's crowning claim to have achieved something of enduring and historical greatness with his premiership.

26. The Long Goodbye

'The next election will be a flyweight versus a heavyweight,' Tony Blair jabbed at David Cameron during the debate on the Queen's Speech on 15 November 2006. 'However much he may dance around the ring, at some point he will come within the reach of a big clunking fist and, you know what, he will be out on his feet, carried out of the ring.'[1]

Gordon Brown, taking himself to be that big clunking fist, beamed with pleasure and thumped the Prime Minister's shoulder with gratitude. He had finally got the craved endorsement – or had he? In so much as this was a commendation, it was a double-edged one. Brown's brutalist style was among the reasons that Cabinet colleagues feared his succession both for their own sakes and because rule by clunking fist might repel voters. The Tories, who wanted to present Brown as a psychotic thug, regarded it as a gift. One senior member of their frontbench commented: 'We've spent a lot of time trying to come up with an analogy that would capture and maximise Gordon Brown's unattractiveness to women and his authoritarianism. The Prime Minister, with his usual brilliance, has now done it for us.'[2] 'That will stick,' one of his aides remarked to Blair afterwards. The Prime Minister smiled.[3]

Blair was a mess of ambivalence about the prospect of handing over to Brown. 'It's obviously going to be terrible,' he sighed to one of his closest friends in the Cabinet around Christmas. To the same minister, Blair remarked a few weeks later: 'Maybe he'll change.'[4]

There were three potential challengers. One was Alan Johnson, the Education Secretary. The former postman was an engaging personality with a biography that offered a potent contrast with the Old Etonian David Cameron. On the negative side, he had no known philosophy and little reputation for developing original policy. He told *Desert Island Discs* that he didn't feel up to the job, which was refreshingly modest but not good for his credibility. He made a poor speech to the party conference that suggested that he was not a serious contender.

David Miliband also gave a lacklustre speech in Manchester which failed to seize the opportunity to promote himself to the party activists, trades unionists and MPs who would elect the next leader. The Environment Secretary was young and unfactional and fizzed with bright ideas. He also had a sharper appreciation of the scale of the challenge of renewal than the many in Labour's ranks who foolishly assumed it would be sufficient to segue from Blair to Brown. Miliband saw that Labour would have to 'defy political gravity' in order to win a fourth term and presciently forecast on *Question Time*: 'I predict that when I come back on this programme in six months' time or a year, people will be saying: "Wouldn't it be great to have that Tony Blair back because we can't stand that Gordon Brown."'[5] Members of the Cabinet urged him to run, as did many of Blair's staff. Yet Miliband was scared of the Brown machine and apprehensive about becoming Prime Minister after just two years in the Cabinet. He told friends that the thought of assuming responsibility for Iraq brought him out in 'night sweats'.[6] Blair told him 'to think about it' but 'didn't want to press him'.[7] According to one Number 10 official: 'Tony's attitude towards David was that he's got to show that he's up for it.'[8]

The third potential challenger was John Reid. The Home Secretary did deliver an effective speech to the conference, but he was a Marmite politician: people either loved him or hated him. He could do the maths of the electoral college and was privately sceptical that he could make a meaningful contest of it with Brown, never mind beat him.[9]

Media speculation about potential competitors ebbed and flowed. This mightily wound up Brown without actually producing a challenger to the big clunking fist. Reid fiddled with his gumshield. Miliband hesitated to enter the ring. Johnson threw in the towel before he had even tried on the gloves.

Many things pointed to Brown's inevitability: his heft, his experience, his record, his superior organisation, his pre-eminence over the rest of the Cabinet, the sense in Labour's ranks that his long wait deserved its reward. That made him the overwhelming favourite. Yet there were compelling arguments for a contest. After a decade in power, the Government needed a serious examination of its achievements, its failings and its post-Blair direction. A contest would be an opportunity to test Brown for flaws rather than wait for his weaknesses to be exposed once he was at Number 10. It was at least arguable that Labour needed to move on from both Blair and Brown by finding a fresher figure to take on David Cameron. Polling in the first quarter of the year put Labour about ten points behind the Tories. More ominously, polls often indicated that the Conservative lead would increase when Labour was led by Brown.[10] 'We never got a grip on the fact that we needed to move on from the Tony–Gordon generation to a new generation,' says one Cabinet minister.[11]

Philip Gould sent a stream of memos to Brown arguing that a contest was 'essential for your own sake'. He was going to be an unelected Prime Minister. 'Without a contest, you will have no legitimacy.'[12] Brown told me and other interviewers: 'I would welcome a contest.'[13] This was the opposite of the truth. He contemplated having a contest with a fringe left-winger whom he could crush and even then wasn't keen on the idea.[14] His paranoia about rivals and his sense of entitlement meant that he wanted to leave nothing to chance. He wanted not a contest but a coronation. Nor was Blair ever really going to fight a handover to Brown. There remained the vestiges of what one Cabinet minister called 'a complicated love'.[15] Shortly after the September coup, Matthew Taylor predicted – to Blair's face – that 'you're going to end up backing him, because that is what you always do.'[16] Jonathan Powell thinks Blair 'still felt some guilt' about taking the leadership in 1994. 'Tony thought Gordon was the biggest figure in the party. He never saw anyone who was a rival to that stature.'[17] Even during some of their worst episodes, says one of Brown's court, 'they could still pick up the phone to talk political tactics and it would be like two brothers having a chat.'[18] Philip Gould agrees: 'Tony could not cure himself of his ambivalence towards Gordon. He had this view of the younger brother to the older brother. Gordon was still a politician of substance. Tony knew the situation, but he couldn't rid himself of that feeling.'[19] 'Rightly or wrongly, Tony always felt it was going to be Gordon,' says Alastair Campbell.[20] Phil Collins 'never thought he was serious' about finding an alternative to Brown. 'He tried to persuade himself that Gordon could change and that Gordon would be OK. There was this blood brother connection. They were still umbilically joined. At some level, he was sorry for Gordon and felt guilt that he usurped his position all those years ago.'[21]

Blair held back from endorsing Brown not because he thought it ever likely that there would be a supportable alternative, but because this was one of his remaining psychological pressure points on the other man.[22] Blair's objective during his final months in office was to try to prevent a deviation away from New Labour. He wanted to 'cement things in place'[23] and get Brown to 'sign up for New Labour policies'.[24] Blair initiated a policy review, entitled 'Pathways to the Future', which was supposed to map a course for the next decade. This exercise could have had a valuable purpose for a Government which needed renewal after ten years in office, but it foundered on the hostility between Numbers 10 and 11. Brown was affronted and suspicious. 'Gordon's lot didn't want to have anything to do with it.'[25] He saw Blair's review as an attempt to bind his hands as Prime Minister and further delay his succession. When I asked him in an on-the-record interview whether Blair had 'hung around too long and damaged you in the process', he tellingly replied: 'Yes, well, that, you have, you have to establish.'[26] In private, it was Brown's routine complaint: 'We shouldn't have a handover in the fucking summer.'[27]

From Blair's side of the divide, he nominated Pat McFadden as the minister who would oversee the policy review process. Brown provocatively proposed Ed Balls, the figure regarded with most fear and loathing at Number 10. Things improved only a little when he was replaced by Ed Miliband. The Brownites regarded it as 'ridiculous that McFadden and Miliband were supposed to write the manifesto for the next ten years'.[28] There was little incentive for Cabinet ministers to engage with the exercise when Brown was so obviously hostile to it.

There was some policy product from Blair's final chapter, more than is often the case when Prime Ministers are in the departure lounge. He prevailed on pensions reform, perhaps his most significant victory over Brown on an issue of finance in their entire time in office. A long-term commitment was made to a new generation of nuclear power stations. The Government introduced climate change legislation, bolder than anything else in the world, which enshrined in the statute book targets for reducing emissions. This might endure beyond Blair, but he could not be sure of it. There was no guarantee that decisions that cast so far ahead would survive future events or changes of government. They were symptoms of Blair's yearning to burnish his legacy and his reluctance to come to terms with the fall of the curtain. He would sigh wistfully that, far from being tired and ready to leave, he'd never felt fitter and more equipped to do the job.[29]

Brown was right that it was fundamentally deluded for Blair to think he could lock the steering wheel of Government for the next decade. This also fed Brown's fear that Blair would somehow even now contrive to find an excuse not to leave. The Brownites were very struck by the Wegg-Prosser strategy memo which read: 'He needs to go with the crowd wanting more. He should be the star who won't even play that last encore.'[30] Ed Balls told other members of their inner circle that Blair didn't really believe that he'd done his last party conference. 'He's hoping people will cry: "Don't go" so he can say: "All right, I'll stay."'[31]

Brown announced that, as Prime Minister, he would modernise the Trident nuclear deterrent. This was widely interpreted as him sucking up to the right-wing press and getting in early with his disappointment of left-wing supporters. His main motivation was to pre-empt Blair so that his rival could not use the future of Trident as an excuse to delay his departure.[32] There was a rebellion by eighty-eight Labour MPs in the Commons vote on Trident in March 2007, but the Government won an overwhelming majority thanks to Conservative support.

Though it looked less and less likely that there would be a rival for the succession, Brown remained in a persistently foul temper. That spring, there was a meeting of the Cabinet sub-committee on energy to hear Peter Hain, wearing his Welsh Secretary hat, make the case for financing a Severn Barrage. 'The meeting was all civil and nice' until Brown turned up twenty minutes late 'stomping in like Harry Enfield's stroppy teenager'.[33] An official leapt out of a chair to make room for the glowering Chancellor. He slammed down a file, started to scribble furiously on some papers, and joined the discussion only to growl at Blair and Hain: 'It costs seven billion. Do you have seven billion?' A pained expression crept over the Prime Minister's face.[34]

Brown and his entourage often spoke of Blair with contempt. Yet they were simultaneously and neurotically desperate for him to anoint Brown as his successor. 'The pursuit of the Blair endorsement became all-consuming' for Brown because 'he didn't want a factionalised party, he didn't want a challenge and he thought he needed the Murdoch press.'[35]

In March, the Chancellor suddenly told Number 10 that he wanted to join the Prime Minister for the launch of the conclusions of the first policy review. This was on the subject of public service reform – the issue on which they had so repeatedly clashed. Brown was now nervous that he'd damaged his reputation with his opposition to Blair's reforms. Even among some in his own camp, it was now viewed as 'a strategic mistake which made him look anti-reform'.[36] When the two men appeared together, Brown suddenly started speaking fluent Blairite. The Chancellor hailed the idea of 'greater choice, greater competition and greater local accountability'.[37] This was a somersault from his previous position that choice and diversity were not the way to reform public services.

Staff at Number 10 'had hysterics watching that on television'.[38] To them, it made his previous sabotage of health and education reform look even more cynical. Whether it was a change of conviction or mere expediency remained to be seen. It did help to reconcile Blair to being succeeded by Brown.

The launch was at a city academy in Hackney in east London. That also represented a significant break for Brown, who had previously refused all invitations to visit an academy. The Treasury was resistant the previous November when Blair announced a final push on academies, doubling to 400 the target for the number to be built by 2010. In another volte-face,

Brown embraced that target as his own and let it be known that he would keep Andrew Adonis, the ultra-Blairite proselytiser for academies, in his ministerial post. One senior aide to Brown observes: 'Gordon had to give all sorts of pledges to Tony. Despite the weakness of his position, Tony found one last turn of the screw.'[39]

It was only as they travelled together to this event that Brown disclosed to Blair the secret income tax cut he had planned for the Budget forty-eight hours later. On this occasion, Blair was pleased with a Brown Budget surprise. He had been arguing with the Chancellor that he needed to display New Labour credentials.[40]

As it would turn out, both Blair and Brown were wrong about this Budget. Brown was about to commit a major error, though few grasped just how massive until a year later. His eleventh Budget was delivered on Wednesday, 21 March. There was little room for fiscal manoeuvre because of his past decisions to open the spending taps. Yet he needed a flourish for a Budget that was both his final performance as Chancellor and the overture for his premiership. He was especially anxious to demonstrate to Middle Britain – or, at any rate, to the newspapers that claimed to be its representatives – that he could be just as New Labour as Tony Blair.

The previous autumn, Brown started to toy with the idea of abolishing the 10p income tax band to finance a cut to the basic rate. Spencer Livermore, his most senior adviser on tax policy, successfully argued him out of it on the grounds that this would create a lot of losers among the less affluent. Ed Balls was also opposed. Brown dropped the idea of announcing it in his Pre-Budget Report. In the New Year, he returned to the idea. There was a big pre-Budget meeting with officials in February – 'the sort of set-piece meeting that Gordon always hated'.[41] The officials again cautioned that abolishing the 10p band would create many losers. Livermore maintained his opposition. Balls, a much more powerful figure at the court of Brown, now flipped in support.[42]

When he presented the Budget, Brown saved the 2p cut in the headline rate to the end for a theatrical climax. He won cheers from Labour MPs and rave reviews in some of the press. 'The powerhouse Chancellor's bold 2p cut was as sensational as it was audacious,' trilled the left-wing *Daily Mirror*.[43] 'He can hold his head justifiably high,' gushed the right-wing *Daily Mail*. 'His stewardship of the nation's finances has been remarkable.'[44] The *Mail*'s political commentator, Peter Oborne, hailed 'a great Chancellor' whose 'political dominance and intellectual mastery' made him the equal of David Lloyd George and William Gladstone. Oborne predicted that 'historians will look back at the Brown years and marvel.'[45]

For one day's good notices, Brown committed a blunder that would later bite him savagely. The change didn't come in for a year and only a small minority fully foresaw the consequences of abolishing the 10p band. One of the few was Frank Field. The MP for Birkenhead combined a serious intellect with an impish sense of mischief. This veteran antagonist of Brown tabled a series of parliamentary questions about how many millions of the less well-off would lose out, questions which the Treasury refused to answer. On the last day of the Commons debate on the 2007 Budget, Brown barked at Field: 'I want to see you.' They met in the Chancellor's room at the Commons. When Field arrived, Brown was hovering outside in deep conversation with Ed Balls. They went inside to find Hazel Blears sitting there, picking at a bowl of nuts as she waited for an audience with Brown about what job she might expect in his Cabinet. Brown ushered Field into an adjacent box room cluttered with chaotic piles of files. 'I'm moving,' the Prime Minister-elect excused the mess. 'I know you are,' smiled Field. Brown rounded on Field for putting down an amendment demanding a compensation package for poorer workers. 'There will be no losers,' he insisted. If that was really the case, responded Field sarcastically, the Government ought to be able to support his amendment. Brown demanded: 'Are you going to push your amendment?' 'Yes,' replied Field. 'Unless you make some concessions.' Brown grew angry: 'I'm not going to do that.' 'I'll move my amendment then,' retorted Field. He stood up to leave. Brown thrust his face into the other man's and yelled: 'You've always been against me!'[46]

Field got nowhere. The Conservatives voted for the abolition of the 10p rate. Only the Lib Dems, a handful of Labour MPs, and a single Tory supported Field's lonely stand. Brown had primed a bomb which would detonate under his premiership a year later.

For the moment, the deceptive tax theatrics of the Budget assisted his inexorable campaign to stitch up the succession. A few voices continued to resist the juggernaut – one of the sharpest belonging to Peter Mandelson. The day after the Budget, Mandelson made a jibing intervention that made it clear he was far from reconciled to a Brown premiership. 'I don't know whether this is going to come as a disappointment to him, but he can't actually fire me,' said the European Commissioner in the course of a thinly cloaked attack. 'Like it or not, he will have to accept me as a commissioner until November 2009.' To deny Brown the pleasure of refusing to nominate him for a second term, Mandelson said he would not seek one.[47]

His was an isolated and exiled voice of dissent. It required the signatures of forty-four Labour MPs to nominate a candidate for the leadership. Stephen Byers, the Blairite former Cabinet minister, was gathering names in a notebook. By Easter, he had thirty-eight backers for John Reid and twenty-four behind Miliband. He could not persuade many Reid supporters to switch behind Miliband or vice-versa. Byers found: 'There was a belief that Gordon was going to win anyway so why have a divisive election and there was a worry that if you backed the losing candidate Gordon's people would do for you.'[48] Many Labour MPs feared they would be signing a career suicide note if they provoked Brown's wrath by backing a challenger. In the words of one Cabinet minister: 'It is impossible to overestimate the scale of the terror there was of the Gordon machine.'[49] A backer of John Reid found that 'the Brownites were very good at getting up the idea that Number 10 was Gordon's right.'[50]

It was also true that many Labour MPs sincerely thought Brown deserved to become Prime Minister. Peter Hain encapsulates their view: 'He was Tony Blair's natural successor. There was nobody else with his stature, his grasp and his strategic vision.'[51]

The sceptics about Brown lacked a standard to rally around in the absence of a declared challenger. Nor was there any encouragement from the top of the Government. At least eight members of Cabinet harboured grave doubts about Brown becoming Prime Minister, but not one put his or her head above the parapet. 'As a group, we were pathetic,' laments one Blairite member of that Cabinet. 'We will be caned for this by history.'[52] Reflecting on it two years later when the Brown premiership unravelled, one of Blair's closest allies sighed: 'The reason that we are where we are is in large part Tony's fault because there was no succession plan.'[53] Blair could almost certainly have created a challenge to Brown had he given it any encouragement. 'Ultimately, it was down to Tony,' says one of his most senior staff. 'If he'd got John Reid and David Miliband and some others together for dinner and said: "I want there to be a challenger", there would have been one.'[54]

Soon after the Budget, Blair sat on the back patio at Number 10 with Phil Collins. 'They've worked it out, haven't they?' said Blair despondently. 'Yes, they have,' responded Collins. 'The country, they don't like Gordon, do they?' sighed Blair. Yet Collins found it fruitless trying to engage Blair with the idea of creating a contest. 'Tony, if he had wanted to, could have said to David Miliband: "This is your moment and I'll back you." He didn't want to hear about it, he didn't want to talk about it.'[55] To Michael Levy, he said on several occasions: 'Gordon can't beat Cameron.'[56] Among his own staff, there were those who felt Blair had let down both his party and the country:

Some will say that Tony behaved disgracefully. He knew that Gordon was incapable of communicating with the public, incapable of handling anything which he had not had months to prepare for and incapable of making a swift decision. Tony knew better than anyone that Gordon was bonkers and would be a disastrous Prime Minister and yet he was prepared to let the Labour Party and the British people live with the consequences.[57]

Jonathan Powell 'wouldn't use those words', but believes that Blair's handling of the succession 'will be a bigger criticism of Tony than the Iraq war'.[58]

At the end of April, Miliband formally announced that he would not be a challenger with an article in the *Observer* in which he declared: 'I will vote for Gordon Brown . . . No-one is better qualified to lead.'[59] Miliband was not really sure whether he was doing the right thing, fearing that his generation of younger Labour politicians might grow old and grey in Opposition if their worst fears about Brown were realised. Miliband backed out partly because he feared that the character assassins in the Brown spin machine would make a contest dirtily personal. There had already been some media nastiness about his adopted son which 'unnerved him'.[60] He was worried that the party would split whether he won or lost. He was uncertain that he was ready. Most of all, he simply did not think he could win. By that weekend, Nick Brown had already secured for his namesake and master the declared support of more than 200 Labour MPs, well over half the parliamentary party. John Reid then formally took himself out of contention.

After all those years during which Brown thirsted for the prize and was tormented by the thought that it would be snatched from him again, the long-distance runner looked over his shoulder to find there was no-one there after all.

On Tuesday, 1 May 2007, the tenth anniversary of the election that brought New Labour to power, Tony Blair finally gave an endorsement of sorts. 'Within the next few weeks, I won't be Prime Minister,' he said at a Labour rally in Edinburgh. 'In all probability, a Scot will become Prime Minister . . . someone who, as I've always said, will make a great Prime Minister for Britain.'[61]

Forty-eight hours later, Labour was given a tremendous kick in the ballots. There had been some Brownite agitation for Blair to quit before the spring elections, but they had not pressed hard because it suited Brown to let Blair take the hit. Labour lost more than 500 council seats and eight local authorities in England. The most seismic result was in Scotland, where the Scottish National Party made enough gains in the Edinburgh Parliament to put it just ahead of Labour. Alex Salmond became the First Minister at the head of a minority government.

The Cabinet met on Thursday, 10 May. Blair briefly outlined his plan to go to his constituency later in the day and confirmed that he would finally announce a timetable for his departure – a joke intended for the benefit of Gordon Brown. Blair claimed he did not want 'a big song and dance' made out of it.[62] Yet he managed to squeeze every ounce of media attention. He flew 250 miles from London to Trimdon, creating a reverse echo of the journey he took in the small hours of the morning in May 1997 when he first became Prime Minister. The speech he delivered in the Labour club in his constituency was a classic Blair synthesis. It was simultaneously defiant and apologetic, aggrandising and self-deprecating, rueful and proud, authentic and manipulative as he defended his record while acknowledging that many were disappointed by it.

Twenty-four hours later, Brown formally announced his candidacy at an event that instantly confirmed that he would never be a master thespian. It looked bad on television because of the primitive presentational error of allowing his face to be obscured by the autocue so that he appeared to be addressing the nation through frosted glass. Brown tried to flip his handicaps into virtues. 'I have never believed presentation should be a substitute for policy,' he declared in an obvious attempt to seek definition from a contrast with the man he would soon replace. 'I do not believe politics is about celebrity.' He talked about the 'new challenges' for a 'new government' as if temporarily forgetting that he had been Chancellor for a decade. He claimed his guide was his 'moral compass'. He pledged to run a 'humble' government that sought 'consensus' and would 'give power away'.[63] With no competition, he was running against his own reputation. Humility, consensuality and sharing power had never been the hallmarks of his treatment of colleagues.

On 17 May, his team announced that they had secured nominations from 313 Labour MPs. This made it mathematically impossible for any challenger to get on the ballot. Even his fiercest foes – Milburn and Byers – felt compelled to nominate him and kiss the ring. He would be the first person to become Prime Minister without any competition since Winston Churchill was succeeded by Anthony Eden more than half a century previously.

Tony Blair's last six weeks as Prime Minister touched on all the main points of his decade. In mid-May, he flew to Washington for a valedictory with George Bush. At their last shoulder-to-shoulder news conference in the Rose Garden, Bush was asked whether Blair's association with the unpopular President had contributed to his demise. 'Could be,' replied Bush, untypically pensive. 'Am I to blame for his leaving? I don't know.' They exchanged parting expressions of mutual admiration. Blair described his host as 'unyielding and unflinching'. Bush flattered back that his guest was 'a courageous man' and 'a clear strategic thinker' who 'can see beyond the horizon'.[64] When they first met at Camp David six years before, neither had seen far enough over the horizon to this day when their special relationship would end blighted by the war that one willed and the other joined. Blair, who had wanted to be the transatlantic bridge, now had to admit: 'In any part of Europe today, if you want to get the easiest round of applause, then get up and attack America.' Bush chipped in that anyone who attacked him would receive a 'standing ovation'.[65]

Blair still didn't pick up the Congressional medal first awarded nearly four years earlier in the deceptively euphoric aftermath of the invasion. It was eventually hung around his neck at an awkward and furtively brief ceremony at the White House just before Bush departed in January 2009. It had also been awarded to Dick Cheney, Donald Rumsfeld and Tommy Franks, the men who went to war with too few troops, and to Paul Bremer, the viceroy in Baghdad who made catastrophic errors in the first year of occupation.

In the immediate aftermath of 9/11, Blair won himself a privileged place with Bush as well as heroic status with both the American public and political classes. He never maximised the influence this ought to have given him. Bush by and large took Britain for granted and the way in which Blair behaved consistently gave the President grounds for thinking he could do so. In return for helping to remove the Taliban in Afganistan and Saddam in Iraq, Blair hoped that Bush would commit to resolving the Israel–Palestine conflict. Blair could not be faulted for his persistence. Whenever they met, Bush would say, almost with a groan: 'I know what you're going to say.'[66] But it didn't yield results. George Mitchell, Middle Eastern peace envoy under Bill Clinton and Barack Obama, concluded there was no 'tangible change in US policy' as a result of Blair's interventions.

On at least half a dozen occasions, the Prime Minister says it is time to do something on the Middle East, President Bush says I agree, then they go their separate ways, and six months or a year later the same process is repeated. There was not the sustained, persevering effort that is necessary.[67]

To the end, Blair refused to hear criticism of Bush even at the most private conclaves of his inner circle. 'If anyone attacked George Bush in a meeting, Tony would slap them down immediately,' says one of his senior staff. 'I never heard him express a whiff of criticism of Bush.'[68] 'He'd been a disaster, but Tony couldn't admit it to himself.'[69]

Shortly after the final call on Bush, Blair landed in Iraq, scene of the great calamity of their alliance. Iraq consumed his second term and cast its baleful shadow into the third. 'Iraq turned his hair grey,' says Tessa Jowell. 'He will live with Iraq for the rest of his life. He will keep on revisiting it to ask whether he made the right decision.'[70] He did not join the war for ignoble reasons, but the peace was lost because of grievous errors for which he bore a share of the guilt. Even Blair now accepted that the bloody mayhem in the years since the invasion was a 'disaster'.[71] The Americans finally committed the troops necessary for 'the surge' led by General David Petraeus which would eventually master the insurgency. The British, once so self-congratulatory about their performance, were heading for a humiliating denouement in southern Iraq. The army was too stretched and Blair too politically weak to attempt a surge against the rampant militias. In his conference swansong, Blair publicly set his face against any 'craven act of surrender' in Iraq.[72] This rhetoric was hollow. In February 2007, the Prime Minister announced a further cut in British forces in Basra to 5,500 with the justification that 'increasingly our role will be support and training'.[73] But it was obvious that the Iraqi army was not yet up to the task of securing order. At the end of his time at the head of the British army, General Richard Dannatt candidly regretted that the 'early switch' to Afghanistan meant that 'we failed to maintain the force levels required' in Basra, which 'sowed the seeds' for 'the rise of the militias supported so cynically by the Iranians in the south'.[74] The undermanned British force left in Iraq concentrated on protecting itself. The troops retreated to the base at the airport, surrendering Basra to the mercy of the militias and criminal gangs, a betrayal of the promises once made by Blair. The Americans complained that the British had 'lost the south'. The militias were finally dealt with only after Blair left office. In March 2008 the Americans and the Iraqis launched Operation 'Charge of the Knights', which routed the Mehdi army and imposed the Baghdad Government's authority on the city. The British could claim credit for training two divisions of the Iraqi army, but it was an otherwise ignoble finale.

The conflict was enormously expensive in both blood and treasure. It claimed the lives of 179 British military personnel and left more than 800 seriously wounded and disabled by the time the last of them finally withdrew altogether in May 2009. The cost approached £10 billion. More than 4,000 American troops were killed. There had been anything between 100,000 and 650,000 Iraqi deaths – the precise number is not known. Rather than water the flowering of democracy in the Middle East, as Blair, Bush and the neo-cons had once imagined, the war emboldened and strengthened Iran, the power that most menaced Western interests.

On his final visit to the denuded British force in Basra, Blair thanked them for performing 'absolutely brilliantly'. Even as he spoke, a mortar blast shook the ceiling.

In late May, further foreign travel took him to a part of Africa where his liberal interventionism was a success. In Sierra Leone, where democracy had been rescued with British military help from the murderous thugs of the RUF,[75] he was greeted as a hero.

Blair timed his departure so that he could attend one last G8 Summit at Heiligendamm in Germany in early June. The main product, for which Blair deserved some of the credit, was a declaration that negotiations on a new climate change treaty should have as their start point the goal to halve global emissions by 2050. Climate change animated him during the final years of his premiership. It was progress to persuade Bush to put his signature on such an ambition. But it was more of an aspiration, and an undetailed one at that, than a commitment. Serious progress was going to have to wait on a change of President.

The final item of foreign business was a difficult European Council at the end of June which agreed a new treaty in the wake of the rejection of the constitution. Blair was better at selling Britain and its pro-reform agenda to Europe than he was at selling Europe and the European ideal to Britain. Liberalisation and enlargement, two big goals of British foreign policy, were achieved during his premiership. The failure to join the euro turned out to be less weakening of his position in the EU than Blair originally feared and the malignant isolation of Britain during the Tory years was ended. At home, he consistently stuck his neck out for a pro-European position of positive engagement whether it was giving early admittance to workers from Poland and elsewhere in eastern Europe or backing the Amsterdam, Nice and constitutional treaties. As Steve Morris, one of his European advisers, puts it: 'It was a massive vote loser, but he did it because he thought it was the right thing to do.'[76] What he did not succeed in doing was draining Europhobia from the body politic. Britain's ambivalent relationship with its continent remained unresolved.

Straight from the European Council, he was flown to Rome for an audience with Pope Benedict XVI. This visit to the Vatican prompted a burst of speculation in the media that Blair was planning to become a Catholic. The President of Poland asked if the stories were true. Blair deflected him by replying: 'You're not having that in the Constitution as well.'[77]

Throughout his time in office, Blair masked both his denominational allegiance and the true level of his convictions. His religion was 'a huge part in Tony Blair's life', says Peter Hyman, an aide who was a practising Jew, and influenced him in ways which 'people consistently underestimated'. Hyman once offered to get Blair some modern novels to read on holiday. 'No, thanks,' replied the Prime Minister. 'It's Cherie who likes that sort of thing.' He instead asked the Number 10 library to order him a book on twelfth-century Christianity. 'His main reading matter was religious books of various kinds.'[78] No Prime Minister since William Gladstone read the Bible more regularly.

On the night before one conference speech, Blair waited until the non-believers on his staff had left the room before asking Hyman to find a quote from Proverbs. 'I want to end the speech with it.' Hyman was pleased with himself the next morning when he presented the quote. Blair responded: 'You've done pretty well, but I am sure there are more poetic versions than this. Have you looked at the King James bible?'[79]

Once he had left Number 10, he set up the Tony Blair Faith Foundation and voiced regret that religious conviction was seen as 'a personal eccentricity' in 'an age of aggressive secularism'. He argued that 'people should be proud of their Christianity and able to express it as they wish.'[80] He went even further in a speech to a 'prayer breakfast' in America, a country where talking about God is not only much easier for politicians than in Britain but almost compulsory. He declared that faith should be restored 'to its rightful place, as the guide to our world and its future'.[81]

In office, though, he ignored the Bible's injunction that the believer should not hide his light under a bushel. He almost never discussed religion with his staff nor even with colleagues who were also practising Christians.[82] His faith was an enigma to them, never mind the voters. This concealment was partly for fear of exposing himself to more satirists after Private Eye's 'Vicar of St Albion' lampooned him as a preachy hypocrite. He later admitted that he avoided talking about his religious views because he feared voters would think of him as 'a nutter' who made decisions after a 'commune with the man upstairs'.[83]

Thanks to laws passed by his Government, his period in office saw an unholy boom in lap-dancing clubs, an explosion in internet gambling and twenty-four-hour licensing of bars and pubs. His most senior aides were virtually all non-believers. The atheist Campbell famously stopped an interviewer from asking Blair about religion by interrupting: 'We don't do God.'[84] According to Tim Allan: 'That was as much Tony's view. He did not want to make religion a big part of his public persona.'[85]

In the build-up to the war in Iraq, both David Frost and Jeremy Paxman tried to get a rise out of him by asking whether he prayed with George Bush. Blair reacted as if the question was ludicrous, though it was perfectly reasonable to ask, given that both he and Bush were professed Christians.

The devout Anglican Frank Field thinks that 'part of his strength' was to understand that 'the Church of England survived because it realises how much religion the English will take, which is not very much.'[86]

His religion, like much else about Blair, was contradictory. He had a 'big tent' view, believing that Christians, Jews and Muslims were all essentially children of the same God. He often told me about the latest inter-faith book that he had read on holiday or was keeping by his bedside.[87] He was anti-fundamentalist. To his credit, he did not seek to serve his political interests when making Church appointments. In 2002, he chose Rowan Williams as Archbishop of Canterbury even though the Welsh cleric had described the war in Afghanistan as 'morally tainted' and was volubly opposed to the invasion of Iraq.

To Matthew d'Ancona, the only journalist to get Blair to talk at length and on the record about his faith before he became Prime Minister and closed down on the subject, he described himself as an 'ecumenical Christian' with 'deep respect for other faiths'.[88] His friend Barry Cox found Blair 'fascinated by other religions and, kind of characteristically, he spotted common links in all of them which made him think they could all work together'.[89]

Yet it was only six months after his departure from Number 10 that he finally came out as a Roman Catholic, a more dogmatic faith than Anglicanism. He told a Catholic conference in Italy that it felt like 'coming home'.[90]

During his time at Number 10, he repeatedly denied any intent to leave the Church of England, but he was a quasi-Catholic for many years. He regularly went to Mass at St Joan of Arc in Islington in the 1990s and continued to do so as Prime Minister until he was asked to desist by Cardinal Basil Hume. Blair wrote back agreeing to stop, but protesting: 'I wonder what Jesus would have made of it.'[91] He attended Mass at Westminster Cathedral, prompting more protests, this time from the then Archbishop of Canterbury, George Carey. Blair replied to Carey with reassurances that he was not about 'to defect'.[92]

A variety of priests, including Father Michael Seed, from Westminster Cathedral, who had prepared other Anglican politicians for conversion, paid backdoor visits to Number 10 and to Chequers. When at the country retreat, Blair attended services at the Catholic Church of the Immaculate Heart of Mary at nearby Great Missenden. On a visit to the Vatican on the eve of the Iraq war, he took Catholic communion at a Mass in the Pope's private chapel presided over by John Paul II. This was never publicised at the time. After Blair had said his final thanks to the pontiff, the frail Pope cried: 'God Bless England!'[93]

Britain had never had a Catholic Prime Minister. Jonathan Powell says Blair did not convert while in office not so much for fear of a negative reaction from the public or the potential impact on the Northern Ireland negotiations: he held back primarily because of the 'constitutional complications'.[94] One of these was that the Prime Minister appointed Anglican bishops.

He became a Catholic even though he disagreed with or openly flouted many of that Church's doctrines. Cherie used contraception and Tony was certainly not a virgin on his wedding day. He voted the liberal line in the Commons on abortion. He also did so when his Government equalised the age of consent, legalised gay marriage and permitted adoption by gays. He evidently did not believe in papal infallibility since he ignored the opposition of John Paul II to the Iraq war.

It is the certainties and rituals of Catholicism, as well as the influence of Cherie, that seemed to attract him. What he got from religion was not so much a set of precise beliefs or even a firm guide to moral behaviour: Blair found in religion a motivator and a consolation.

His friend Charlie Falconer believes faith gave Blair 'his strong sense of good and evil.'[95] John Burton, his constituency agent, thinks that 'Christian fervour' was the best explanation for the Warrior Blair. The many military interventions were 'Tony living out his faith' in the belief that it was 'all part of the Christian battle; good should triumph over evil'.[96] His aide Robert Hill, himself an evangelical Christian, agrees that faith shaped Blair's conviction that the Iraq war was 'a crusade for good'.[97] When it went bad, Blair told the journalist Peter Stothard: 'I will answer to my Maker for the people who died.'[98] It was never entirely clear whether he anticipated a more forgiving verdict from the Almighty than from his contemporaries. It was from his religion that he got 'the sense that there is meaning to the world and his part in it', says Geoff Mulgan. Blair was 'an extraordinarily resilient person . . . I suspect his resilience comes from his faith.'[99]

On 12 June, Blair delivered another valedictory speech, this one about the media. 'The media as a collective absolutely loathed him by this stage' and 'he couldn't be bothered to try to charm them any more.'[100] Compared with some Prime Ministers, Blair did not have that much to complain about. He enjoyed the support of the majority of the press at all three of his elections, enthusiastically in 1997, more lukewarmly in 2001 and very grudgingly in 2005. He used the broadcast media with much more intensity than previous Prime Ministers to conduct a continuous conversation with the electorate. As the shrewd Steve Richards of the *Independent* put it:

In terms of communication, he was a revolutionary. Blair chose to be our round-the-clock guide, responding within seconds to every event, from the death of Princess Diana to the imprisonment of Deirdre Barlow in *Coronation Street*. He was a rolling commentator on his leadership and an eternal advocate.[101]

His ubiquity and skill set a standard which Gordon Brown and other successors would find very difficult to match.

As he matured as Prime Minister, Blair acquired a more composed attitude, but he never entirely shook the habit of chasing headlines, with especially terrible consequences over the Iraq dossier and the death of Dr David Kelly. The phrase that leapt out of his speech was 'feral beast' and came in a passage attacking the media for 'just tearing people and reputations to bits'. He complained that it sapped 'the country's confidence and self-belief' and claimed that 'it reduces our capacity to take the right decisions' by which he was reflecting at least somewhat on himself.[102]

There was power in his critique, but he was the person least well placed to make many of the criticisms. It was also disingenuous to focus on the *Independent*, the quality paper with the lowest circulation, and say nothing about the *Daily Mail*, the paper that he and Cherie most loathed. The speech was most interesting for its confessional aspect. He admitted that he and his staff had been 'complicit' by giving 'inordinate attention to courting, assuaging and persuading the media'. He correctly identified many of the faults of the modern media: its craving for novelty, its hunger for sensation, its tendency to trivialise. Yet New Labour had encouraged those bad appetites by pandering to them and running government as if it were a twenty-four-hour newsroom. Blair had fed 'the feral beast'. It was too late now to complain that he felt bitten by it.

'A new dawn has broken – has it not?'[103] So he had said on the May morning when he first brought New Labour to power. In the following decade, Blair dominated the British political landscape like few other leaders. Labour was ahead of the Tories, often by intimidatingly big margins, throughout the first term and into the second. It did not lose a single by-election for his first six years. Even from 2003, when the consequences of the Iraq war began to consume his premiership and devour his popularity, his mastery continued. It was a supremacy challenged only by Gordon Brown.

History will always recall Blair as a winner. The electoral magician dispelled Labour's historic hex. He took a party that had lost four elections in a row and turned it into a serial victory machine. He achieved what no leader of his party had done before and won not just two full terms for

Labour, itself a record, but three. His accumulated parliamentary majorities[104] were greater even than those of Margaret Thatcher, the other hat-tricker of modern times. A decade in Downing Street was rare. Just eight previous Prime Ministers in three centuries had occupied Number 10 for a double-digit stretch.[105]

One positive dimension of the Blair era was its social liberalism. There was progress on female equality, gay rights and race. The police were made subject to race relations legislation. There were black faces around the Cabinet table for the first time, more female ones than ever before and gay ministers no longer had to pretend that they weren't. As well as the age of consent being equalised and civil partnerships introduced, the ban on gays in the armed forces was ended. Matthew Parris, the Conservative commentator for *The Times* who was a savage critic of nearly everything else about Blair, acknowledged that 'Britain is a nicer place than when he entered Downing Street. Something tolerant, something amiable, something humorous, some lightness of spirit in his own nature has marked his premiership and left its mark on British life.'[106]

These shifts in the culture of Britain were accompanied by changes in its centre of political gravity. Despite his personal lack of enthusiasm for constitutional reform, he left behind permanent new democratic institutions in Belfast, Cardiff, Edinburgh and London. That was not matched by a reinvigoration of democracy in a deeper sense, a lacuna that was manifest in declining turn-outs at elections. He disappointed those who had been prepared to believe his early rhetoric about a new politics. His controlling and centralising impulses made the British state even more top-heavy. Distrust of government reached record highs by the end of his time, not least owing to the sleaze eruptions that punctuated his premiership from beginning to end. His instinctive authoritarianism and the lack of enthusiasm of nearly all his senior colleagues stopped him embracing electoral reform, the prerequisite for the permanent realignment of British politics that he had once seen as a goal for his premiership. The historic split between the labourist and liberal traditions of the British left was not healed. That kept the door open for a return of the Conservatives on a minority of the vote once they got themselves under sensible leadership.

He was a lucky Prime Minister. Few of his predecessors at Number 10 had the good fortune to preside over a decade of continuous growth. That cushioned him when the public admiration of the early years soured into disillusion and hostility. Doubly fortunate, he left Number 10 just before that unprecedented run of prosperity came to an end. The growth dividend was spent on generous investment in health and education which reversed years of neglect of the public realm. State-funded childcare was introduced alongside the minimum wage. There was considerable redistribution, mainly the work of his Chancellor, from the affluent to the poor. Tax and benefit changes since 1997 broadly raised the incomes of the poorest fifth of society by 12 per cent and reduced them for the richest tenth by about 5 per cent.[107] This was not enough to entirely counteract the global forces which were stretching inequalities and the super-rich continued to pull away from everyone else. That was compounded by New Labour's fear of ever confronting the power centres in the City, big business or the media. He left Britain wealthier and more diverse, but not much happier than he found it.

While he was always ready to take on his own party, Blair's default position when dealing with powerful external forces was to accommodate rather than challenge them. This flowed from his temperamental aversion to confrontation. He was weak when dealing with strong men, a flaw which was most apparent in the two most important relationships of his premiership. A less deferential attitude towards George Bush could have shaped a better outcome in Iraq. A more assertive approach to Gordon Brown would not have tolerated a Chancellor who so brazenly sabotaged some of the Prime Minister's key ambitions.

Blair's actorly gifts for communication and reinvention combined with his deft ability to escape from tight corners were crucial elements of his remarkable resilience. It was an achievement extraordinary in itself to last ten years at Number 10 under the voracious scrutiny of a 24/7 media. It was even more of a feat when he had led his party into a hugely unpopular war on a prospectus that turned out to be false. He was repeatedly pronounced doomed and as routinely he somehow managed to shimmy to safety. From the death of Diana to 9/11 to 7/7, he always had an acute instinct for emotional leadership.

After his departure, he wistfully remarked: 'I began hoping to please all of the people all of the time; and ended wondering if I was pleasing any of the people any of the time.'[108] Polling in fact suggested that to the end he bested any rival at matching the mood of the electorate.[109] He left office with very high ratings among Labour supporters, 89 per cent of whom rated him as a good Prime Minister overall. The same was said by 61 per cent of all voters. A majority of voters still thought of him as 'likeable'.[110] That was an outstanding result after ten years at the top.

The downside of his charm, panache and opportunism was that Blair leaned too heavily on those talents and made his party over-dependent on skills which were highly peculiar to him. He based success on the politics of personality. He was only intermittently engaged with the politics of ideas.

One of the few occasions when he was totally confounded in the House of Commons was when a Labour MP asked him to 'briefly outline his political philosophy'. In so much as Blairism was an ideology, it was one subject to constant revision. He did not have a coherently worked-out agenda before he became Prime Minister, he delayed developing and articulating one in the first term because he was obsessed with winning the second term, and then he became diverted by terrorism and Iraq. He did not have a theory for public service reform until the end of his first term, struggled against the opposition of Brown during the second, and was too drained of political capital by the third to fulfil all his goals. He never had sufficient interest in the politics of organisation. That showed in his inability to fully master Whitehall and the neglect of his withering party. By all accounts from his staff, he was both a pleasant boss and a poor personnel manager. In common with many charismatics, he was often inept at harnessing the talents of others. Appointments to the senior civil service and the Cabinet were frequently misjudged. Crucially, he had no strategy for the succession other than to hope, against all his own experience to the contrary, that Gordon Brown might become a changed man once he was Prime Minister.

On Thursday, 21 June, Tony Blair chaired his final Cabinet. They'd had a whip-round, enforced on rather reluctant ministers by Gus O'Donnell, to buy some farewell gifts for him and John Prescott: a painting of Chequers for the outgoing Prime Minister and one of Admiralty House for his deputy. Brown led the formal tributes: 'Whatever we achieve in the future will be because we stand on your shoulders.'[111]

Their relations were relatively untroubled in the final days of transition. 'I give 90 per cent of the credit to Tony for the smoothness of the handover,' says one senior civil servant at the heart of it. 'Tony behaved incredibly well. He was very good to Gordon, even helping him with preparing for things like PMQs.'[112] He wrote a series of notes urging his successor not to forget aspirational voters.[113] He also offered to take difficult decisions before he left, like ordering a proper prime ministerial aircraft, but Brown turned that down.[114] There remained an underlying tension between them about the extent to which Brown would present his premiership as a sequel or a break. Blair worried that Brown would repeat what he saw as Al Gore's error when he distanced himself from Bill Clinton in the 2000 American presidential election.[115] It would be revealed only once Brown moved into Number 10 that he had not resolved in his own mind how to reconcile being both a continuation of the last decade and a change from it.

Severe doubts about Brown persisted in Number 10. Some feared that he and his acolytes were arrogantly unconscious of the level of performance required to be a successful Prime Minister. 'They thought it was going to be easy,' comments David Hill. 'Their attitude was: "If Tony can do it, they'll be able to do it."'[116]

Jonathan Powell was even more strongly sceptical and was often heard to say: 'Gordon has not got his head around how many decisions a Prime Minister has to make every day.'[117]

Powell derived a certain amount of sadistic pleasure from torturing Blair for not finding an alternative to Brown. 'Will he be the worst Prime Minister in half a century – or a century?' Powell taunted Blair, who would curl up in his chair and not say much in response.[118]

Blair's own doubts were profound. He emerged from one long meeting with Brown in despair: 'Gordon hasn't worked out that you can't fix the country like you can fix the Labour Party. He has no plan. He doesn't know what he's going to do.'[119] It was too late now.

On Sunday, 24 June, the two men flew up to Manchester for the formal coronation. Harriet Harman narrowly won the deputy leadership. After the transfer of preferences from less popular candidates, she beat Alan Johnson by a margin of 50.4 per cent to 49.6 per cent. Jon Cruddas, who had run on a ticket advocating a break with Blairism, performed very well. Hazel Blears, the most avowedly Blairite candidate, came last.

His last weeks were the longest goodbye in British political history: tears and cheers from his local party in Sedgefield, a last twosome with George Bush at the White House, a final summit with European leaders the week before, a visit to the *Blue Peter* studio. As a leaving present, Labour MPs bought him a guitar. There was something about this drawn-out goodbye of the ageing rocker on a farewell global tour who doesn't really want to leave the stage at all. Philip Gould found Blair 'sad and reflective' in his final weeks in power. 'He believed he was leaving too early and he was right about that. He had got clarity about what he wanted to do; he was at the peak of his powers. One of the tragedies is that you don't crack it until the end.'[120] To his staff, he usually put a light face on it. After a last visit to Jacques Chirac, a broken figure by this stage, Blair had his entourage 'in stitches' on the way home as he joked about how they'd have to prise his hand off the door knocker of Number 10.[121] He was anxious that his life would be empty, a fear expressed in a desperation for a busy retirement. He took the poisoned chalice of being a Middle East envoy. Jonathan Powell was horrified when he later discovered that Blair accepted no fewer than 500 engagements around the world for the year after his premiership.[122] On his last full day in office, he was still talking to his aides about what the Government would be doing in coming months. Powell murmured to Justin Forsyth: 'I don't think he knows he's going.'[123] That night, he padded around Number 10 in bare feet, shorts and T-shirt saying farewells and offering thanks to the staff.

At just before eight on the morning of Wednesday, 27 June, Gordon Brown walked through the connecting door between Number 11 and Number 10 to transact some last business with the man he would that day finally replace. Brown had with him a list of the ministerial appointments he planned to make. He did not require Blair's approval, but he felt the need for the other man's acquiescence. Brown did not want anything – especially not noises of dissent from Blair – to ruin his arrival. In earlier discussions, Blair tried to save his friend Charlie Falconer from the sack. He continued to make the case with Brown that he should not fire Tessa Jowell, another minister very close to Blair.[124] Some of Blair's worst fears about his successor – especially the anxiety that Brown would pack the Cabinet with factional acolytes – appeared dispelled. Seeing that some of his allies were protected, and some given dramatic promotions, Blair offered little criticism of the list.

Given the depths to which their relationship plunged in the year before, the transition was remarkably free of public rancour. They had a mutual interest in trying to make the day presentationally immaculate. Brown desired a smooth entrance; Blair wanted his exit 'to be good-tempered and positive'.[125]

He went into the den to prepare for his final Prime Minister's Questions. It was Blair's boast, and the brag was just about accurate, that he never had three bad PMQs in a row. His swansong was always likely to be an easy ride. Yet he was 'very nervous' as he rehearsed his lines that morning.[126] He was obsessed 'with getting the tone right' and 'scared about getting it wrong'.[127] He had put on his 'lucky brogues'– a pair of Church's handmade leather shoes which he had worn for every PMQs of his premiership. At noon that day he stood at the dispatch box for his 318th performance. It was stylish, graceful and humorous. By the end, he even had his opponents on their feet to applaud.

He gave the usual weekly announcement of his engagements and added a poignant twist. 'I will have no further meetings today. Or any other day.' MPs chortled.

In that half-hour were encapsulated both the highs and lows of his premiership. The session began with a sombre recital of the latest deaths among British service personnel in Iraq and a last blast of self-justification about their sacrifice. 'I know there are those who think that they face these dangers in vain. I do not, and I never will.'[128]

The ancient walrus Ian Paisley then led several tributes to his successful pursuit of peace in Northern Ireland. 'Could I say that I fully understand the exasperation that you felt many a day when I visited your office!'

On the back of a helpful question about jobs, Blair launched into a prepared joke about receiving his P45. Another, more spontaneous opportunity to display his humour was offered by Nicholas Winterton. This foghorn of the Tory backbenches erupted into a denunciation of the European Union. Blair laughed: 'First of all, I like the honourable gentleman. As for his good wishes, I would say to him: Au revoir, auf Wiedersehen, arrivederci.' Winterton joined the merriment. The ability to lightly disarm opponents was always one of Blair's gifts. Earlier in the year, he made an appearance on the *Catherine Tate Show* in which he gave a talented rendition of the comedienne's catchphrase: 'Am I bovvered?' He'd been looking for an excuse to deploy it from the dispatch box. The opportunity was offered by Richard Younger Ross, an eccentric Lib Dem MP, who tried to engage him with a byzantine question about the relationship between church and state. Blair paused for a moment and then, to roars of amusement, simply said: 'I am really not bothered about that one.'

At the end, and over time, he delivered a short speech which closed not only his premiership, but also his twenty-four-year parliamentary career for he had announced that he was also quitting as MP for Sedgefield. He 'never pretended to be a House of Commons man' but 'I can pay the House the greatest compliment I can by saying that, from first to last, I never stopped fearing it. That tingling apprehension that I felt at three minutes to twelve today, I felt as much ten years ago, and every bit as acute.' Then he paid a wider compliment to the profession he shared with them all. Politics had 'harsh contentions' but it was an arena in which 'people stand tall'. He went on: 'If it is, on occasions, the place of low skulduggery, it is more often the place for the pursuit of noble causes.'

To the last, Blair was brilliant at bringing an audience on his side by flattering it.

'I wish everyone, friend or foe, well.' There was a tremor in his voice. 'And that is that.' His throat cracked. 'The end.'[129] Labour MPs rose to reward him with a standing ovation. David Cameron, who had praised Blair for 'considerable achievements that will endure', motioned his side to join the tribute and the Tories stood too. The packed public galleries rose to applaud as well.

Gordon Brown thwacked him on the back, once to say well done, and then again as if to be sure that Blair really was leaving. He was departing at least a year earlier than he had originally intended, but the manner of his departure successfully masked any bitterness about that. Lauded by his opponents, clapped out of the chamber, celebrated as a leader above party, he choreographed for himself a very elegant exit.

He returned to Number 10 and addressed the Downing Street staff in the Pillared Room on the first floor. He thanked everyone for 'going the final mile with me'. His audience could see that he 'had to stop himself crying'.[130] Many others were in tears as applauding staff lined up either side of him and Cherie. It is traditional for outgoing Prime Ministers to be clapped out. Though he had said he didn't want this, they ignored him.[131] Then he and his wife emerged through the door to pose on Downing Street for one last time. He ruffled his son Leo's hair for the family's final photograph outside the famous door. Cherie, fearsome in magenta, could not resist firing a parting shot at the media. 'Goodbye,' she shouted over her shoulder as they got into the car. 'I don't think we'll miss you!'

Not for the first time, she was voicing what her husband thought. 'You can't resist it, can you?' he said to his wife as the door of the Jaguar was closed. 'For God's sake, you're supposed to be dignified, you're supposed to be gracious.' There were some moments of stony silence as they rounded Parliament Square. Then, as the car turned into the Mall, he shrugged, took his wife's hand and grinned.[132]

The Jaguar drove on to Buckingham Palace and Tony Blair finally relinquished power after ten years and fifty-five days in Downing Street.

The moment he left, officials back at Number 10 began to move furniture around to prepare for Gordon Brown. Blair's Chief of Staff and the rest of his people were meanwhile 'scuttling out through the basement so that we didn't spoil Gordon's triumphant entrance'.[133]

27. A Short Honeymoon

After thirteen years of waiting for the crown, Gordon Brown had become king without a contest. He was still biting his nails. On the day that he finally ascended to the premiership, he nervously started phoning around his confidants at just before six in the morning, which was slightly later than had been feared by those long accustomed to his voice jolting them awake before sunrise. One of the first calls was to Spencer Livermore, the senior aide who worked intensively with Brown on the short speech he would make outside Number 10. They had been at it for days and Brown was not yet satisfied. Down the phone, he rehearsed his performance once again.

He had chosen to memorise it for fear of repeating the embarrassment when he launched his candidacy with his face obscured by an autocue screen.[1] He continued to worry over it when his team met for a cooked breakfast at Number 11 after Brown's final conversation about his first Cabinet with the outgoing Prime Minister. Then, for one last time, he was kept waiting for the premiership as Tony Blair milked his last moments.

One hundred and ten minutes after Blair's final ride to the palace, the armour-plated Jaguar nosed back through the Downing Street gates now carrying Gordon and Sarah Brown. On the May morning in 1997 when New Labour made its triumphant entrance, the sun shone brilliantly from a sky untroubled by clouds. Blair processed up to Number 10 to the cheers of hand-picked Labour activists waving Union flags. When Brown made the same journey, there was an absence of rapture. A grey sky gloomed overhead. The loudspeakers were wrapped in bin bags to protect them from threatened rain. The only people to greet him were the media corralled behind the steel barriers on the opposite side of the street. It was almost as if his team had reviewed video of Blair's exultant arrival a decade ago and decided to do the exact opposite.

Brown emerged from Pegasus and then paused to pat his jacket pocket like a man wondering where he has left his house keys. In a becomingly courtly gesture, he walked round the Jag to open the car door for his wife.

He approached the microphone and tapped at it, apparently less than confident that it would be switched on. Then, at 2.52 p.m., he made his first
statement to the nation as Prime Minister.

There was a whiff of the pulpit when he pledged to be 'strong in purpose,
steadfast in will, resolute in action'. He fell back for inspiration on his childhood in Kirkcaldy by recalling his school motto: 'I will try my utmost.'[2]

Though a self-declared enemy of the politics of celebrity and image, Brown
was not entirely without vanity. He had his teeth fixed before he became
Prime Minister and could be highly sensitive to how he was portrayed by
cartoonists. 'Why do you draw me so fat?' he complained to Martin Rowson
of the *Guardian*. He made the identical protest to Dave Brown, who
cartooned for the *Independent*.[3]

His most audacious aim that day was to reinvent himself as the agent of
a fresh start. 'This will be a new government with new priorities,' said the
man who had run at least half the government for a decade. 'I have heard
the need for change. Change in our NHS, change in our schools, change
with affordable housing, change to build trust in government, change to
protect and extend the British way of our life. This change cannot be met
by the old politics.' His brief statement contained no fewer than eight references to 'change', which climaxed with the declaration: 'And now let the
work of change begin.'[4] His pollsters were telling him that 'change' was the
most popular word with their focus groups.[5]

In this respect, there was a similarity with Blair's arrival ten years before.
Brown wanted to represent himself as a new dawn and his very lack of
showmanship was supposed to be an element of the contrast.

He and his wife turned to walk into Number 10 only to find that the
door remained stubbornly shut, as if Cherie had superglued the locks. The
famous black door opens only from the inside. The officials watching on
the TV monitor inside the lobby were assuming that the new Prime Minister would want to enjoy his moment for longer than he actually did. They
missed their cue to open the door.[6] For want of a better idea, the Browns
were forced to linger on the doorstep for a while longer. He fixed a rictus
on his face and awkwardly waved to the cameras. Then the door finally
opened and he was inside at last. Soon afterwards, it began to drizzle.

As the door closed behind them, the Browns were ritually clapped in by
the Number 10 staff. 'Everyone in the building was trying to be friendly,'
says one civil servant. 'But the atmosphere was odd. It was a bit like the
barbarians entering the city because everyone knew Brown and his people
had been working against not just Blair, but everyone in the house.'[7] After
taking some congratulatory calls from foreign leaders – the first was with

George Bush – the new Prime Minister made some brief, pleasant remarks to the people who would be looking after him. In the Pillared Room on the first floor where they had listened to Blair's farewell a few hours earlier, Brown said: 'I know you're all sad that Tony has gone. One of the reasons I'm glad to be here is that you looked after Tony so well.' He invited them to call him 'Gordon' and offered one of his little prepared jokes: 'It's not every day that you meet the Queen at 1.30 p.m., become the Prime Minister at 2 p.m., speak to the President at 3 p.m., and get told by Sarah to put the kids to bed at 7 p.m.'[8]

No previous Prime Minister of modern times moved into Number 10 better qualified or prepared for the role – on paper at least. He had more than a decade to think about what he wanted to do with the premiership, nearly a year's notice that there would be a vacancy, and six weeks of formal transition to plan his arrival. Sir Gus O'Donnell had organised a series of briefings by senior civil servants, defence chiefs, intelligence chiefs and public service professionals.[9] Some of that time was well spent. The choreography of his first twenty-four hours was pretty immaculate. The new Cabinet was announced on Thursday without a visible ripple of dissent. Margaret Beckett's tears when she was sacked as Foreign Secretary were shed in private and prominent Blairites like John Reid had already announced that they were going. It looked like a generous and inclusive gesture to award the Foreign Office to David Miliband, giving the promotion to his predecessor's protégé that Blair himself had not. Jacqui Smith was an even more Blairite minister destined for a big leap up the ladder. With 'a twinkle in his eye', Brown said to her: 'I think this might be a bit of a shock.' He then told a 'very surprised' Smith where he was putting her, an appointment which generated positive headlines about the first female Home Secretary.[10]

After the shambles of some Blair reshuffles, Brown's first looked unusually well-organised.

The slickness of the presentation on the day disguised the long period beforehand which Brown spent brooding over his first Cabinet. Weeks before he moved into Number 10, in his room at the Treasury a board was set up with all the ministerial slots to be filled. Brown also had a piece of paper with a sketch of the Cabinet table. 'He was careful to use a pencil so he could erase names.'[11] He agonised most over who to make Chancellor. His original intent was to reward Ed Balls and make absolute their control over Government by putting his closest ally in charge of the Treasury. So great was Brown's reputation for being tyrannical that even Balls made jokes about it. 'What is the difference between Gordon Brown and Stalin?' Balls asked in a speech at the Fabian Society's summer party. 'One is a ruthless and determined dictator who brooks no opposition. And the other was the leader of the Soviet Union.'

It was Balls's ambitions that fell victim to Brown's reputation. One day not long before Brown moved into Number 10, an aide came into his room at the Treasury to find Brown at his Cabinet diagram 'furiously rubbing out the name of Balls as Chancellor'.[12] He had been thwarted by the objections of other Cabinet ministers, the loathing for Balls by many of the Blairites, and the fear of looking authoritarian and cronyistic.[13]

The Exchequer went instead to Alistair Darling, another long-term ally but a less intimate one and a less factional personality. Darling was an unostentatious Edinburgh lawyer with a decent heart who had almost made a Cabinet career out of cultivating his anonymity. His reputation was built on keeping himself and whichever department he was running out of the headlines. A wittier man than he usually appeared on the media, in his early weeks at the Treasury it was Darling's private joke that he was 'trying to find out where Gordon has hidden all the money'.[14] He would soon discover that there was nothing down the back of the Treasury's sofa: the money had all been spent.

An unacknowledged, but hugely important, influence on the creation of Brown's first Government was focus groups and opinion polls. Deborah Mattinson, the managing director of Opinion Leader Research, was his personal pollster. Before the handover, she did weeks of research to identify Brown's positives and negatives in the eyes of the voters. On the plus side, her work told Brown that voters thought of him as a large and serious figure. 'Our whole political positioning was around strength,' says one of Brown's strategists.[15] On the minus side, voters suspected him of being scheming, bullying and to the left of Blair and themselves. One thing he felt he had to address was 'the concern that he was slightly Old Labour'. Brown's early days were a 'very systematic' attempt to address 'the concerns the public had about him when he came into office'.[16]

The emphasis was on changes of style rather than content. He made a show of giving Alastair Campbell's old office at Number 12 back to the Chief Whip, a gesture supposed to illustrate his claim that he would put substance before spin and value Parliament rather than media manipulation. Within months, the room was re-colonised by Brown's own spin doctors. Knowing that he was regarded, not least by Cabinet colleagues, as secretive, cliqueish and vengeful, Brown reached out to supporters of his predecessor. John Hutton, the author of a prediction that Brown would be 'a fucking awful Prime Minister', was not sacked but made Business Secretary. James Purnell, who was in his teens when he first worked for Tony Blair, was

promoted into the Cabinet as Culture Secretary. While publicly inclusive of
the Blairites, privately Brown remained intensely suspicious. When Tessa
Jowell was summoned to see him, she assumed that she was getting the sack.
'That's it. I'm out,' she told a friend. Brown regarded her warily when they
met at Number 10. 'You were very loyal to Tony,' he said in an accusatory
tone. 'How do I know you will be loyal to me?' Jowell responded that she
would be loyal to him because he was now the Prime Minister. 'It's your
fault,' growled Brown, still gnawed by resentment that he had to wait so
long. 'You persuaded Tony to stay when he'd promised me he was going.'
He left Jowell in charge of the Olympics, but she lost the rank of Secretary
of State. Brown struggled as badly as Blair when it came to being direct with
colleagues about sackings and demotions. Rather than straightforwardly
tell Jowell that she was no longer a full member of the Cabinet, he tried to
blame his officials for capping the numbers. 'They won't let me' was his
excuse for reducing her to visiting rights.[17]

The desire to seem magnanimous to old enemies did not stretch to a
reconciliation with Peter Mandelson, who was 'still in the outer darkness
from a Gordon perspective'.[18] Nor did it extend to bringing back to the
Cabinet either Alan Milburn or Charles Clarke. The former Home Secretary
was made offers that he could refuse. One untempting suggestion was to go
to Iraq to sort out the Port Authority in Basra. Brown then followed up with
a bizarre offer to send Clarke as a special envoy to the Caribbean during
the winter months, a posting that might have been good for a suntan, but
not for a political reputation.[19]

Once the new Cabinet was announced, early on Thursday afternoon its
members began to arrive at Number 10, walking up Downing Street mostly
in twos, like the animals boarding the Ark. Brown, enthroned at last in the
chair with the arms, cracked a faintly menacing joke: 'It's very interesting
to look across at the Chancellor and to think I'm no longer the man who
says "no". I'm looking forward to my first battles with him.'[20] How they all
laughed, carefully.

He wanted the world to see him as the acme of congeniality and collegi-
ality, telling me: 'I think it's important to show that the executive is
accountable to Parliament and equally I think it's important that the Cabinet and the role of individual ministers is properly respected.'[21] At meetings
of the Cabinet early in his reign, he made a point of inviting every minister
to make a contribution in order to strike a contrast with both the brevity
of their meetings under his predecessor and his own reputation as a man
intolerant of debate. At their second meeting on Friday, the Cabinet ran on
for two hours, a length unheard of when Blair occupied the top chair. There

was a 'huge discussion' about constitutional reform by the end of which Ministers were 'getting a little tired'.[22] Jack Straw, who was now Justice Secretary, joked that 'younger members of the Cabinet will not realise that this is not how it was.' He contended in an interview that Cabinet 'is now more collegial'.[23] Harriet Harman, who had become Leader of the House, also found that 'Cabinets take much longer because everybody has their say on just about every issue.'[24] Peter Hain was struck that 'Cabinet meetings suddenly involved a lot of listening by the Prime Minister, which was not always Tony's biggest forte. And Gordon would scribble things down in his inimitable way if something particularly struck him.'[25] The Big Clunking Fist presented himself as The Huge Listening Ear.

Their discussions were longer, but this was a veneer on Brown's controlling temper and compulsion to micro-manage. He remained cliqueish. Ed Miliband was given charge of the Cabinet Office and manifesto preparations. Douglas Alexander combined the roles of International Development Secretary and election campaign co-ordinator. Ed Balls's consolation prize for not getting the Treasury was a magnified empire called the Department for Children, Schools and Families. His wife, Yvette Cooper, got visiting rights to the Cabinet as Housing Minister and would soon after be promoted to full membership. This was the first Cabinet in British history to contain two brothers plus a husband and wife. Straw gained the chairmanship of key Cabinet committees and was delighted if people regarded him as the Deputy Prime Minister, though he was privately discontented that Brown wouldn't give him the actual title. Geoff Hoon was made Chief Whip, but correctly suspected that he was 'cover'. Giving the job immediately to Nick Brown, who was his namesake's true enforcer, would be seen as too factional.[26] The Newcastle MP became deputy head of a whips' office packed with acolytes of the Prime Minister, including some of the key plotters in the coup against Tony Blair.

Only two ministers other than Brown had been in the Cabinet continuously since 1997.[27] During an awkward encounter with George Bush at Camp David at the end of July, Brown boasted: 'Six of my Cabinet are under forty.' 'Are they?' responded Bush sarcastically. 'You must be feeling damned old then.'[28] It was a top table with a paucity of big reputations. The stifling dominance of Blair and Brown for the past decade had made it hard for other figures to grow in stature. The Cabinets of Major, Thatcher, Callaghan, Wilson, Heath, Douglas-Home, Macmillan, Eden and Attlee all contained figures with large reputations and power bases independent of the Prime Minister. Even Tony Blair's Cabinets had some personalities of sufficient stature and character to argue with him and even thwart the Prime Minister. There was no-one with the weight to challenge Brown in this Cabinet. There was no David Blunkett,

Charles Clarke, Alan Milburn, John Prescott or John Reid. When it was Blair and Brown, New Labour was a bipolar government. Now it was just Gordon, a unipolar regime. Brown had the potential to be one of the most hegemonic Prime Ministers of all time providing he knew how to use that domination wisely and well. It gave him all the power and no alibis.

His version of Big Tent politics was not truly evidence that the old control freak was being reborn as a new pluralist. He was following a blueprint provided by Blair's Operation Hoover during New Labour's early years in office[29] and more recently by Nicolas Sarkozy when he became President of France. It was not a good indicator of the character of his premiership, but it was a preliminary tactical success. He wanted a Tory scalp as a pre-emptive strike against David Cameron and got a surprising one when Quentin Davies, the Conservative MP for Grantham and Stamford, defected to Labour. A farmer who once lost a lot of his sheep, he was used to being greeted by Labour MPs with cries of 'Baaaa!' Now they welcomed him to their benches as their newest colleague and the first Labour MP ever to be called Quentin. Brown seduced other Opposition MPs alienated from their leadership by recruiting them as advisers. This created the impression that Tory MPs were so dispirited by their own party's prospects that they'd rather cosy up to Gordon in his Big Kilt. It was a gimmicky but effective ruse which looked generous to opponents, destabilised the Conservatives, and surrendered nothing in terms of real power.

To some on the left, this was disturbing early evidence that Brown would not be so different to Blair. Jon Cruddas, the strong contender in the deputy leadership campaign who turned down a job in Government, later complained:

The trouble is that the tent was only half-filled and wasn't complemented by some of the more radical elements we could have brought in to cement a coalition of interest that should be the modern Labour Party. We've tilted only one way and that is to the right.[30]

Paddy Ashdown once predicted that a Blair handover to Brown would be 'Camelot converted into Gormenghast. Owls will hoot as you go up Downing Street.'[31] Brown nevertheless offered him the job of Northern Ireland Secretary. Ashdown turned it down, but the manoeuvre successfully spread confusion among the Liberal Democrats.

Brown felt he needed to show he was friendly to business. Digby Jones, the ebullient former Director-General of the CBI, was induced to give up his other jobs to become Trade Minister. When he made the invitation, Brown asked: 'Do you want to phone your wife?' Jones laughed: 'No, I want to phone my bank manager.' Brown was desperate enough to get him on board that Lord Jones, as he became, successfully resisted several attempts by Brown to get him to agree to join the Labour Party.[32] The outside recruits became known as GOATS – the acronym for 'Government of All the Talents'. Another of these non-party animals was Professor Sir Ara Darzi. The renowned surgeon became a Health Minister in the Lords, where he would prove his worth to fellow peers by saving the life of one of them. Brown wanted protection from the accusation that he was unfriendly to the armed forces. He fixed on Sir Alan West, the former First Sea Lord. For 'a whole raft of reasons' West initially said no. Brown was relentless in pursuit of the admiral, even getting Sarah to invite West's wife round to Downing Street. Brown argued with him: 'I really do believe that you can do something for the nation.' Bombarded with such appeals to his sense of patriotic duty, West found it 'impossible not to accept' the job of Security Minister.[33] Another recruit, this time to the Foreign Office, was Sir Mark Malloch-Brown, a former Deputy Secretary-General of the UN and fierce critic of George Bush, who declared soon after his appointment that Britain and America were no longer 'joined at the hip'. The Prime Minister 'knew remarkably little about Mark Malloch-Brown before he appointed him', says a Number 10 official.[34] The point was to signal that the long nightmare of Iraq and the relationship with Bush were drawing to a close.

Many of these GOATS would have short lives. Digby Jones quit after just sixteen months and subsequently complained that being a junior minister was 'one of the most dehumanising and depersonalising experiences a human being can have', because Government was designed to squeeze them dry of 'personality, drive and initiative'. He further claimed that half the civil service could be sacked and no-one would notice the difference.[35] He and the other GOATS served their presentational purpose in the early days. By recruiting people of all parties and no party, Brown presented himself as a presidential figure creating something akin to a national government.

This avoided making a strategic choice about the Government's direction. The fundamental questions facing Labour after Blair were how to renew their policies, refresh their communications and reconnect with voters. How you answered depended on your analysis of the root causes of Labour's unpopularity. Those in the party who only ever tolerated New Labour as a necessary evil to win power now wanted a swing leftwards to recover the party's standing among traditional supporters. The primary challenge from a Blairite perspective was to remain centrist and appealing to aspirational voters. The shrewdest thinkers saw that the Government needed to locate ways of attracting both constituencies in order to rebuild the coalition which put them into power in 1997.

Gordon Brown's answer to these strategic questions was opaque in the months before his coronation as Prime Minister. In the absence of a challenge, he had not been under serious pressure to reveal a plan. Civil servants were surprised to find that the man who had come from the Treasury with a reputation as a grand strategist arrived at Number 10 apparently without one. 'They had a three-week plan up to the summer recess. Beyond that, you looked at the pad and it was blank.'[36] There was a conflict of expectations about his premiership. Among left-wing Labour MPs like Frank Cook, 'everybody felt that we were destined for a period of more traditional Labour.'[37] A Blairite Cabinet minister like Hazel Blears could equally believe that there would be 'a significant change of tone' but not 'a massive change of policy direction'.[38] Brown had been Chancellor for a decade and yet even his Cabinet were unsure what he would make of the top job. In the words of Peter Hain: 'None of us really knew what sort of Prime Minister he would be.'[39]

Gordon Brown retired to bed on the second night of his premiership with the transfer of power having gone as smoothly as he could have hoped. As he slept, in the early hours of Friday morning two car bombs were discovered, one outside a popular West End nightspot in the Haymarket and the other in nearby Cockspur Street. The new Home Secretary, less than twenty-four hours into the job, was woken up to be told that she had her first terrorist incident on her hands.[40] Over at Number 10, Brown's officials decided to leave the Prime Minister in his bed. The plot having been foiled, they saw little point in disturbing the new boss. He got up at around five thirty that morning, turned on the radio in the flat and rapidly learnt from the news about the night's events. Brown stomped downstairs in a dark temper and demanded: 'Why wasn't I told?'[41] For those on the staff who were only just getting to know the new Prime Minister, this was their first experience of Gordon Brown in a bad mood. It was also an early warning of his neuroticism about always being in control.

Brown got himself in front of the cameras as soon as possible after breakfast on Friday. He interrupted a trip to a pre-school centre in north London – his first official engagement as Prime Minister – to warn that there was a 'serious and continuous threat' and urge the public 'to be vigilant at all times'.[42] At a meeting in the Cabinet Room with the Prime Minister and Jacqui Smith, Brown's new Security Minister, Alan West, found him calm but also nervous. 'He didn't know what was going to happen next.' West counselled against 'mad knee-jerk reactions' and tried to reassure Brown that he could 'rely very heavily on the agencies'. He was impressed that the new Prime Minister 'listened to advice and was willing to let people get on with things'.[43] COBRA was convened under Smith's chairmanship and the

Cabinet meeting that day was extended so that the Home Secretary could brief ministers about the level of the threat.

On Saturday, a blazing Jeep was driven at high speed at the main terminal building of Glasgow Airport. This attempt to explode a car bomb was also thwarted. Early that evening, COBRA was convened again – this time Brown decided he wanted to take the chair. It was agreed that the threat level should be raised to 'critical'. Alan West was mildly amused that 'he does have a passion for COBRA. It's not some magic place. It's just a room really.'[44]

COBRA does weave a certain spell on the media. It conveys the impression that the Prime Minister is gripping a crisis. Addressing the public, Brown reached for a Churchillian tone: 'We will not yield, we will not be intimidated', and used Blairish language about 'an act of evil'.[45]

In comparison with 7/7, these were relatively minor incidents which mercifully took no innocent lives. The episode nevertheless sent a shiver of fear down the spine of Government. In the words of Jacqui Smith: 'It did involve multiple attacks, and thank goodness nobody was injured, but you don't know that at the time that you're dealing with it.'[46]

Blair was famously adept at finding the right language and putting himself visibly in charge during a crisis. Brown was especially anxious that he should not look poor in comparison. As one senior aide puts it: 'There was always Tony's voice in Gordon's ear: "If you want to be successful, you've got to be like me."'[47]

To his satisfaction, it was the almost universal verdict of the media that his solid performance during this early emergency redounded to his credit.

Behind the scenes, the new Prime Minister was living hand to mouth. 'He came in with a weak team,' says one long-serving official.[48] 'They were under-prepared and arrogant,' remarks a very senior civil servant.[49] Another experienced official thought 'they were grievously under-manned.'[50] There had been an almost total purge of the political staff at Number 10, which deprived the building of a lot of experience. Only two political aides, Justyn Forsyth and Geoff Norris, survived the handover to be present at both the clapping out of Blair and the clapping in of Brown. Brown had brought with him to Number 10 some of the small coterie that he relied on at the Treasury. Spencer Livermore, an adviser for nine years, became the Director of Political Strategy at Number 10. In one of those lists beloved of newspapers, he was named that summer as the seventh most powerful gay man in Britain.[51]

The chief propagandist was Damian McBride, the former civil servant who had become Brown's most infamous spinner. McBride was a graduate of Cambridge who could brief intelligently about policy. But Brown mostly valued this spin doctor for his apparent talent for understanding the appetites of the tabloids and how best to feed them to keep those beasts content. One of McBride's fatal flaws was a very reckless streak. His spinning against other members of the Government could be as brazen as it was vicious. He often left a trail by using e-mails and texts. He also sent rashly rude messages to journalists who displeased his master. He liked a drink. Those who knew McBride would never confuse him with a teetotaller.

His friends called him 'Mad Dog' and his foes 'McPoison', a soubriquet invented by Peter Mandelson. McBride did not then enjoy the public notoriety that he was to later acquire, but his reputation in Whitehall and among the Cabinet preceded him into Number 10. At the Treasury, Gus O'Donnell had insisted that McBride cease to be a civil servant and become a political adviser because he had gone so far over the line into partisanship. O'Donnell was very against McBride coming to Number 10. The Cabinet Secretary tried to warn Brown that it would be a bad idea because of his spin doctor's brutal briefings and the fear and loathing he aroused among ministers. 'You need to build bridges,' argued O'Donnell to Brown. The Cabinet Secretary's protests were ignored by the Prime Minister, who saw McBride's aggression as a sign of his loyalty.[52]

Shriti Vadera was an investment banker before joining Brown at the Treasury. She was so devoted to him that she would fly to Scotland at weekends and take a hotel room near his home in Queensferry to be instantly on hand if he needed her. He valued her passionate commitment to tackling global poverty, her toughness and her intellect. She had a steely brain and a sharp tongue, which made her too abrasively demanding for some civil servants, who nicknamed her 'Shriti the Shriek'. To admirers, she was 'a brilliant ideas person for Gordon'.[53] Given the lack of ideas people at Number 10, Brown might have been better served had he brought her into Downing Street. She was instead given a ministerial job at International Development. With Vadera and Sarah Brown, Sue Nye was the third woman of influence in an otherwise masculine gang. Nye had known him longest of all. The veteran and intensely loyal Political Secretary had years of experience of managing his diary and his moods. 'Sue looks after him, but she doesn't look after politics,' observes one Number 10 official. 'She's not a political fixer. She's not a Sally Morgan.'[54]

That was one of several significant gaps in essential personnel. It was not visibly apparent to the voters nor noted by the media at the time, but Brown's Number 10 had major structural flaws from the start. He arrived without a Chief of Staff. Tom Scholar, Brown's former Private Secretary at the Treasury, 'pitched up as Chief of Staff after they'd settled in'.[55] Scholar was a highly able and personable civil servant, but this was not a role which he really wanted nor one to which he was suited. The Cabinet Secretary told other officials that he was strongly against the appointment 'because Tom is not cut out for it.'[56] Gavin Kelly, the Deputy Chief of Staff, 'had no experience of dealing with Gordon'.[57] Brown did not have a proper speech-writer. Nor did he have an experienced Director of Communications with a strategic grasp of handling the media and tested experience of dealing with the huge demands on Number 10 from broadcasters. McBride's speciality was doing backstairs deals on stories with a small clientele of writing journalists. Brown lacked a strong body of close advisers to fill the roles which had been performed for Blair by the likes of Jonathan Powell. 'The core group was too small.'[58] As early as July, in the Cabinet 'there was a feeling this doesn't work. When you wanted decisions made, who did you go to? Who did you speak to? It wasn't at all clear.'[59] There was a dissonance in the early weeks between the glowing media that Brown was enjoying and the chaotic reality behind the scenes.

He had for years relied on a trio of younger allies who reflected back to him dimensions of his own personality. Ed Miliband, son of the Marxist thinker Ralph and younger brother of David, most expressed the academic element of Brown. Douglas Alexander was, like Brown, the son of a Church of Scotland minister and mirrored his high-minded self. Ed Balls remained, as he had been for years, the single most powerful confidant. Of the troika, Balls was the one who shared and amplified the side of Brown that saw politics as a perpetual trial of strength. In the words of one Brown aide: 'Ed's instinct was always to be brutally tribal.'[60]

This triad, his praetorian guard during the long march to Downing Street, was now dispersed around Whitehall. While Miliband was trying to make sense of the Cabinet Office, Balls and Alexander had departments to run. Brown felt naked without his old coterie and was soon summoning them back to his side. Alexander spent at least a third of his time at Number 10 and more of it answering calls and e-mails from the Prime Minister. The same was even truer of Balls. Witnesses report that half of his ministerial meetings at the Department for Children would be interrupted by an official poking his head round the door to say to Balls: 'Number 10 wants you to ring urgently.'[61] The Chief Whip was 'amazed how often I'd go to meetings at Number 10 and find Ed there'.[62]

Balls had taken primary responsibility during the handover for the organisation of Brown's Number 10. Several observers, both political aides to the Prime Minister and neutral civil servants, came to the conclusion that he left Brown exposed. One official believes: 'Ed picked a deliberately weak team to ensure his own continuing influence as the most powerful voice in

Gordon's ear.'[63] A long-standing Brown aide agrees: 'Ed's objective was always to prevent any rival powerful figure emerging.'[64]

These unsound foundations were initially masked because Brown's early weeks were cosmetically successful.

One costless, symbolic announcement was to scrap the plan to try to re-create Las Vegas in Britain. At Prime Minister's Questions, Brown announced that there would be no super-casino. In typical style, he had only told the relevant minister, James Purnell, earlier that morning. The abandonment of the super-casino was popular, says Jack Straw, with 'a lot of us' in the Cabinet who felt 'uneasy about the super-casino' because it was 'too big, too in-your-face for many people'.[65] Another early move was to retighten the law on cannabis. These acts, a combination of the moralistic and the populist, won cheers from commentators of both left and right. A flurry of policy reviews was announced on everything from citizenship to binge drinking to internet porn. None of this resolved the question about the Government's strategic direction, but it did answer Brown's need for immediate hits in the headlines.

Matthew Taylor, who had become Chief Executive of the Royal Society of Arts after serving as a senior strategist to Tony Blair, thought:

the early period was extremely impressive. He reassured people that he wasn't going to throw out the New Labour centrist politics, but he also suggested to people that they were going to get something which they had lost with Tony: a leader that they could trust, a leader who was going to be more answerable, a leader who was less about spin and more about substance.[66]

That was rather deceptive: Brown had always been as much of a spinner as his predecessor, if not more of one. 'All the polling' from Deborah Mattinson told Brown that the way to beat David Cameron was by playing 'strength versus inexperience'.[67] So he got his greatest boost that summer from appearing to respond in a masterful fashion as one emergency was succeeded by another. The terrorist incidents were followed by the flooding of large parts of Britain. On Tuesday, 24 July, Brown again convened COBRA. The COBRA compulsion 'started for genuine reasons', says one civil servant. 'They then very quickly learnt that they could get an easy headline on the Sky news banner from "PM chairs COBRA."'[68] Hilary Benn, the Environment Secretary, and his officials outlined their departmental response before the discussion quickly turned to media handling. 'I must do another clip,' said Brown before leaving the basement to address the TV cameras.

'I have just come from a meeting of the emergency committee, COBRA, where we have heard first hand of the heroic efforts of the emergency services, our armed forces and communities who are battling the flood waters,' he declared.[69]

One dismayed civil servant concluded:

That's all he cared about – doing a clip for TV every two hours. I'd always bought the line that Gordon was the great strategist, the thinker, and Tony was the one obsessed with the media. The scales fell from my eyes. With Gordon, it was all about the headlines.[70]

Most of the practical leadership and real work to cope with the floods came from the Environment Agency and senior police officers on the ground, working with the fire service and the army. But the constant convening of COBRA projected the image that the Prime Minister was in charge.

After some adverse comment that he was slow to visit the flood zones, Brown got travelling. On a visit to an inundated area in the west of England:

he came straight in on the helicopter, shook a few hands in front of the cameras and then got the hell out again. That had all the character of a press stunt. But nobody in the media wanted to have a bad word to say about Gordon Brown in that period and he got away with it. If Tony Blair had done that, he would have been crucified.[71]

Still enjoying the benefit of a media honeymoon, Brown was hailed as a demi-god for striding around in wellies. 'The coverage was absolutely fantastic, amazing. But Gordon was never happy. He was stomping around Number 10. He seemed in a permanently foul mood. People were asking: "If he's like this when things are going well, what's he going to be like when things are going badly?"'[72] He was obsessive about his image in the media. 'There was an incredible barrage of phone calls from Downing Street,' recalls an official at the Department of the Environment. 'They would be ringing up to complain about something on page 17 of the *Guardian*. You'd then look at it and the headline would be something like "Gordon Brown walks on water".'[73]

The situation in Gloucestershire became critical when they nearly lost a power station to the floods and the army had to be called in to distribute water to 300,000 people. Number 10 insisted that Brown should visit the scene even when the authorities sent a clear message that they had too much on their hands to cope with receiving the Prime Minister. Officials were taken aback by the Brown team's desperation to divert any criticism of the response to the floods. 'There was a day of blaming Severn Water,' says one official. 'They briefed against the water companies, they briefed against the Environment Agency, they briefed against Gold Command. It was all about shifting the blame. Anyone must get the blame except Gordon.'[74]

On one of his visits to Gloucestershire, Brown learnt that there was a grave danger of conditions becoming insanitary. The chairman of the civil contingencies unit back in London got a phone call from the Prime Minister directly ordering him to rush 900 Portaloos to Tewkesbury.[75] Brown became 'very, very hands on', thought one Number 10 official.[76] This was commendable, but it was also seeding what would grow into a huge problem in the future. In the words of one of his closest aides: 'You could see the early signs of Gordon trying to micro-manage everything.'[77] That included the media operation. He would suddenly turn up in the Number 10 press office, point to the headline running on the BBC or Sky twenty-four-hour news and bark an order: 'That headline has got to be changed.'[78]

In the early hours of the morning, the night-time security shift at Number 10 was alerted to an intruder on the ground floor. Someone was trying to break into the Prime Minister's office. They arrived on the scene to find that it was Gordon Brown. He had come down from the flat before sunrise to start work and made the frustrating discovery that he couldn't get through the locked door.

His nocturnal habits were already legendary among those who knew him well. Murray Elder, one of Brown's closest friends, was used to being 'got out of my bed by an early-morning phone call' and was accustomed to finding e-mails from Brown timed at six o'clock in the morning.[79] Others reported calls and in-boxes filling up with long messages at even smaller hours. The habit of ringing up at all times of day and night sometimes exhausted the patience of even his most devoted followers. Ed Miliband became so worn down by the demands for twenty-four-hour attention that he once took Brown's mobile when the boss wasn't looking and erased his number from the phone's memory.[80]

The Prime Minister's flat at Downing Street, home now to two young boys, was 'like a giant creche'.[81] Brown was genuinely indifferent to the trappings of power, though he and Sarah soon fell for Chequers. So did Fraser and John, who loved its fantastic swimming pool.[82]

Brown began his time at Number 10 by using the same office as his predecessor, the small study by the Cabinet Room where they had had some of their most explosive confrontations. Tony's den became Gordon's lair. Soon after Brown's arrival, a large plasma television was fixed to the wall. The new Prime Minister would tell visitors that he had it installed so that he could watch football, but it was as likely, if not more so, to be tuned to the twenty-four-hour news.[83] Blair, for all his rhetoric about modernising Britain, was phobic about technology. He never mastered e-mail or text messaging as Prime Minister and wrote his speeches in longhand using a fountain pen and then had them typed up by secretaries. Brown's way of speech-writing was to thump his thoughts into the keyboard of a computer using two fingers and block capitals because of his poor eyesight.[84] A new computer was installed in the study for this purpose with the font set to a very big size to help him read the text. A kick to the head on the rugby pitch had left Brown blind in his left eye since he was sixteen. His right eye was only saved by experimental and painful surgery. He spent almost a year in complete darkness and underwent five operations which might have resulted in total loss of sight. That ordeal, which he once described as 'living torture', was a terrible blow to a teenager who loved sport and was a voracious reader. This dark trauma profoundly shaped his character. One of his intimates once told me: 'You can't understand Gordon unless you understand his fear that he could go blind.'[85] Some elements of his behaviour – appearing to not recognise or to rudely blank people, the awkward scrunching of his face when reading a speech and his generally unrelaxed public appearance – were partly explained by his lack of peripheral vision and his need to look to the side in order to focus. 'You're always so nervous around Gordon,' says one of his colleagues. 'You always think he's going to fall over something because his sight is so poor.'[86] Sympathetic members of his staff thought his volcanic temper was rooted in his frustration with his disability.

When he was not at the computer, Brown's instrument of choice was a thick black marker pen to get the necessary contrast because of his sight. One senior member of the Cabinet who tried to read Brown's handwriting found it 'indecipherable – like ancient Hittite'.[87] The Prime Minister's hands were routinely covered in black ink. When one of the Browns' little boys made an appearance smeared with felt tip, the nanny laughed: 'Aaah, Gordon II.'[88]

After long-haul trips abroad, his staff would quietly note the amount of debris left behind by the Prime Minister. 'There'll be KitKat wrappers and banana skins. It's like a child has been sitting in the seat.'[89]

Personal messiness did not cramp his desire to impose an absolute order on the Government. If Blair was a control freak, Brown was the control freak's control freak. An edict was issued that no motion could go on the parliamentary order paper without the personal approval of the Prime Minister.[90] It was further decreed that even minor departmental press releases could not be issued without the authorisation of Number 10. From the beginning, he involved himself in issues that should have been beneath his attention. Digby Jones, the new Trade Minister, had an early spat with departmental officials about the brand of chauffered car he could have. He rejected the cars on the official list because none were made in Britain. Jones wanted to fly the flag with a baby Jag, a demand that the civil servants resisted. At his insistence, this dispute went all the way up to Number 10. Jones knew his problem had reached the very top when he saw Brown at a drinks reception. The Prime Minister asked: 'Have you got your Jag yet?'[91] Jones was grateful that his little problem had got Brown's attention, but this was a disturbing portent. A junior minister's travel arrangements ought not to have been commanding the Prime Minister's time.

After the bombs and the floods, the Government was unsure what might hit it. Hazel Blears sums up the mood: 'I think we were all waiting for the plague of locusts to come down next.'[92] What came next was not locusts, but it was a plague. There was an episode of foot and mouth, the disease that broke out with such virulence in 2001 that it forced the postponement of the election. Brown had just arrived in Dorset for a summer holiday with Sarah and his sons. He turned around within an hour. According to Murray Elder, Brown was 'absolutely instinctive' in rushing back to London 'simply because the right place to be was back in charge'.[93] He returned in a black mood which got worse. Furious with what he saw as the ineptness of the Department of the Environment, he routinely barked out the cliché: 'Heads must roll.' One civil servant observed: 'It was a blame culture. The default response to any problem was that someone must have fucked up.'[94]

COBRA was again convened. In early August, Number 10 proudly announced that the Prime Minister had chaired five meetings of the emergency committee in four days.[95] Civil servants once more got the impression that this was less for practical reasons than presentational purposes. 'It was not a war room, it was a newsroom.'[96] The foot-and-mouth outbreak was ultimately traced back to a government laboratory, but 'Gordon's people went out hammer and tongs to blame a private laboratory' and then bogusly spun it to the media as a 'bioterrorism threat'.[97]

Gordon Brown's early weeks in Number 10 were seen as a baptism by fire, flood and pestilence. From these potential nightmares, with the help of his spinners and the media, he fashioned a honeymoon. When he first became Prime Minister, observes Jacqui Smith, 'some people did have a question mark about how will he respond to events.' That question 'was answered pretty resoundingly' – or so at least it appeared.[98]

The summer emergencies came in sizes which were perfectly proportioned for a new leader anxious to prove his competence in a crisis. As Frank Field puts it: 'Mother luck was with Gordon in those early days. If you are going to have foot and mouth, it's really rather nice if it is twelve animals. And if you are going to have a terrorist attack, that an ambulance crew happens to notice that there's a car misbehaving itself.'[99]

The foot-and-mouth outbreak was limited in scope and duration. There was some criticism of the Government for not spending enough on flood defences, to which Brown's characteristic response was to promise a review. It was David Cameron who received the most negative press for leaving his own drowned constituency rather than abort a trip to Rwanda. The terrorist attacks were frightening, but the only fatality was one of the would-be bombers.

They fitted into the script for Brown's early premiership recommended by his pollsters: the strong national leader, robust in a crisis and elevated above petty party politics. Jon Cruddas observes: 'The brilliant thing that Gordon Brown managed to forge in those first few months was to almost transcend normal political divides to become the sort of "father of the nation".'[100] Even opponents like Vince Cable, the deputy leader of the Lib Dems, acknowledge: 'He got off to a very good start.'[101] A senior Tory feared that Brown was being 'scarily effective'.[102] The press was almost universally glowing. Labour was steadily rising in the opinion polls at the expense of both the Lib Dems and the Tories. Gordon Brown's personal ratings waxed positive. Peter Hain recalls:

people being very sceptical about Gordon as Prime Minister and that worrying concern just turned absolutely on its head. Within a few months of his premiership, the same people were saying: 'Well, I was wrong about Gordon. He's very impressive.' This was somebody who had surprised them by his capacity for leadership.[103]

The honeymoon put a temporary disguise on the weaknesses at Number 10, reinforced Brown's compulsion to control, and deflected him from addressing the strategic choices facing Labour. Reflecting on that period, one of Brown's aides later concluded that there was 'a false confidence because of those early crises'.[104] A senior civil servant thought: 'It was surreal being inside the Brown Bounce when we knew about the chaos behind the scenes.'[105] Another official observes: 'Even in that period, you got the sense that he was chasing it. He was constantly stressing over the media.'[106]

To the outside world, Gordon Brown was making an assured start to his premiership, surprising even some of his fiercest critics with the superficial aplomb with which he settled into the role. Within his own world, the Prime Minister was already beginning to suffer from the structural flaws and personnel gaps at Downing Street. Working in Number 10 one day that August, he found the building deserted. Douglas Alexander received a frantic cry for help. 'There's no-one here!' complained Brown. 'I've no staff!'[107]

28. Run on the Rock

Gordon Brown looked out on the bow-tied ranks of money-changers and declared: 'A new world order has been created.'[1] The oligarchs of high finance were by now accustomed to being hosed with praise whenever he addressed them. In his very first speech in the Square Mile as Chancellor in 1997, he proclaimed: 'The City has demonstrated the best qualities of our country, what I describe as the British genius.'[2] In 2004, he said: 'I want us to do more to encourage the risk-takers.'[3] The following year, he genuflected again to the gods of finance when he paid homage to their 'unique innovative skills, . . . courage and steadfastness' and offered his personal thanks 'for the outstanding, the invaluable contribution you make to the prosperity of Brit-ain'.[4] After a decade of showering the City with plaudits, Brown surpassed himself in June 2007 when he made his last Mansion House speech as Chancellor just a week before moving into Number 10. He told them that Britain was 'a new world leader' thanks to 'your efforts, ingenuity and creativity'. Everyone should follow the City's 'great example' and emulate this 'high value-added, talent-driven industry'. Brown congratulated himself for presiding over a light-touch system of regulation and asked them to applaud him for 'resisting pressure' for a crackdown. Moving to his perora-tion, he smothered them with more unction. 'Britain needs more of the vigour, ingenuity and aspiration that you already demonstrate.' He extolled the City for inventing 'the most modern instruments of finance' – the very instruments that would soon afterwards bring the entire Western banking system to the edge of destruction. Because of their 'remarkable achievements' the nation had the privilege to live in 'an era that history will record as the beginning of a new Golden Age'.[5] They reciprocated by giving him a standing ovation.

As he spoke, the air was already beginning to rush out of the financial bubble celebrated by Brown. The financiers' 'ingenuity' had created a peril-ously unstable edifice and their avaricious 'aspiration' ultimately wrecked swathes of their own industry and the rest of the economy. Events were in train that would lead to the first run on a British bank for more than a

century, then the Great Crash of the following year, culminating in the severest economic crisis since the 1930s. Brown would soon re-christen the bubble
as the 'Age of Irresponsibility'⁶ and hope that no-one remembered that he
once lauded it as a 'Golden Age'.

He was not alone in taking the supposed masters of the financial universe
at their own vaulting estimation. A generation of political leaders, in Britain
and much of the rest of the world, fell under the thrall of high finance. The
pre-crash David Cameron was just as mesmerised by what he trumpeted as
'the victory of capitalism, privatisation and liberalisation' and claimed the
credit for 'critical Conservative decisions' in favour of 'low regulation'.⁷ As
late as September 2007, when the bubble was already beginning to burst,
the Tory leader asserted that 'our hugely sophisticated financial markets
match funds with ideas better than ever before' and contended that 'the
world economy is more stable than for a generation.'⁸

Right-leaning politicians eulogised unfettered markets from ideological
belief; left-leaning politicians were schooled to think that obeisance to finance
was the price that had to be paid for power. The instinct to be seen as friendly
to profit was encoded in the genes of New Labour. As James Purnell says:
'It was a founding principle of New Labour that we were going to be pro-
business.'⁹ Blair and Brown both believed that power could not be won and
held unless they purged the party of past associations with economic failure
and hostility to wealth creation. Because Old Labour had been seen as 'anti-
success', says the Blairite MP, Sally Keeble, 'we almost had to overdo it to
make the point that we supported the City and weren't going to cap people's
aspirations to get very rich.'¹⁰ Tony Blair opened a meeting with one group
of bankers by saying: 'I've taken the view all my time in office that I should
leave you people to get on with making money for yourselves.' After a pause,
he added: 'And the country.'¹¹ Peter Mandelson made a speech in California
to computer executives in which he declared that New Labour was 'intensely
relaxed about people getting filthy rich', though he was subsequently keen
to point out that he said: 'as long as they pay their taxes.'¹² Mandelson, like
Blair, was fond of money and the company of the monied.

Brown was not so personally awed by riches. He disdained most City
people, though he did mix with Democrat-supporting Wall Street bankers
on his summer holidays in Cape Cod. 'Gordon doesn't like wealth,' says a
minister who got to know him well.¹³ His relationship with the City was
scratchy for the first five years and then he had 'a sort of Damascene conversion' to championing Britain as the global capital of finance.¹⁴ He recruited
Sir James Sassoon, an investment banker, to be his emissary to the City. In
Brown's eagerness to be associated with banks, he presided over the opening

of Lehman Brothers' new headquarters at Canary Wharf in 2004. The following year, he did the honours for HBOS when it unveiled a new headquarters in Edinburgh. HBOS went bust in 2008. So did Lehmans.

Brown's weakness was one of the intellect. He became beguiled by the notion that globalisation had created a new economic paradigm in which growth might be perpetual. He revered Alan Greenspan, the Chairman of the US Federal Reserve between 1987 and 2006, and the father of the bubble. Greenspan built an awesome reputation on the back of the apparent skill with which he guided the world through a sequence of financial shocks from the 1987 crash via the 1998 collapse of Long Term Capital Management to 9/11. Dr Greenspan's patent medicine was to slash interest rates and flood cash into the markets. This softened those crises at the price of storing up even greater trouble for the future. Having survived such seismic events, markets thought of themselves as invincible. This fool's paradise encouraged reckless behaviour by investors and speculators. The markets assumed there would never be a day of reckoning because Greenspan would always come to the rescue with an infusion of cheap money. The role of the central banker should be to shut the bar whenever the party threatens to get too raucous. Greenspan led the revellers to believe that there was an endless supply of drink and no threat of a hangover at the end of it.

Brown cultivated an alliance with Greenspan to enhance his own economic legitimacy. In conversation with Andrew Gowers, the editor of the *Financial Times*, 'Gordon Brown could not get half-way through a sentence without mentioning Alan Greenspan and what a great intellectual influence he was.'[15] It was on Brown's recommendation that Greenspan received an honorary knighthood. It was on Brown's instruction that a plaque was put up in the Treasury to celebrate Greenspan. It was at Brown's invitation that Greenspan gave the annual Adam Smith lecture in the Kirkcaldy church where Brown's father had been the minister.[16] 'He is a brilliant guy,' Brown would say of the American, the highest commendation in his lexicon.[17]

Early in his premiership, he hosted a Sunday dinner at Chequers for guests who included Lord Evelyn de Rothschild, Dame Marjorie Scardino of Pearson, Sir Terry Leahy of Tesco and Stephen Green of HSBC. Greenspan was the guest of honour. The first tremors of the great quake were already being felt in July 2007. Yet visitors to Number 10 that summer found Brown boasting about how often the two men talked and extolling Greenspan's new book, *The Age of Turbulence*.[18] That title barely did justice to what was about to unfold. The former Chairman of the Fed was the author of the Greenspan Doctrine. This held that it was too difficult for central bankers to identify what was a bubble and what was not so it was futile to try to prevent the inflation of asset prices. According to this theory, it was better to let bubbles burst and then mop up afterwards. The world was about to receive a scorching tutorial in the terrible risks of this doctrine.

Britain's GDP increased by a third in the decade after 1997.[19] The growth of the boom years came from a mixture of genuine economic advance, expansion of the public sector and synthetic gains from a self-fuelling bubble of rising debts and house prices which could not be sustainable for ever. Brown was more the beneficiary of luck than he knew. That luck was a long period of non-inflationary growth and cheap money from Asia that fuelled prosperity in a lot of the industrialised world.

Brown became seduced by his own propaganda that the long boom derived from his brilliant stewardship of the economy. A decade of continuous expansion fooled him into thinking, and carried many others along with the illusion, that he had somehow transcended the laws of economics. It was his routine boast that he had discovered the nirvana of permanent growth, low inflation and high employment. Central to the New Labour proposition was the claim that it had avoided the financial calamities that swamped every previous Labour government and the wild swings of the economy under the Conservatives. One phrase came to define his Chancellorship. 'No return to Tory boom and bust!'[20] was Brown's brag for a decade whenever he delivered a Budget, a financial statement or a conference speech. It was not a conscious fiction. The Conservatives would later taunt him with it, but even his opponents bought into the claim. The economic policy adopted by David Cameron and George Osborne when they took charge of the Tory party promised to 'share the proceeds of growth'. The Conservatives too swallowed the assumption. 'We will not return to the old boom and bust!'[21] Brown cried yet again when he delivered his eleventh and final Budget shortly before becoming Prime Minister. It became easier to say and harder to argue with as the boom bubbled on. He was so addicted to this mantra that he used it more than one hundred times in the House of Commons between 1997 and 2007.[22]

This belief that growth was never-ending also encouraged Brown to run larger government deficits to finance spending on public services and benefits. The prudence of early New Labour was long cast aside by the time the economic weather began to darken. There were two separate surges in public spending. The first phase took spending from a near post-war low of 36.3 per cent of GDP in 1999–2000 to 41.3 per cent by 2005–6. This was what New Labour had been elected to do to improve public services and social justice. Spending then remained at roughly that level until 2007–8. It was the next leg up that was the mistake which stored up big problems for the future. The second surge, timed to coincide with Brown's premiership, saw spending rise above 43 per cent of GDP in 2008–9 and head upwards to a planned 48.1 per cent in 2010–11.²³ This was a dramatic surge in both a historical and an international context. In the assessment of one senior Treasury official who had been in charge of public spending, the national finances were 'up shit creek' by the time the crisis broke because surpluses were not banked during the good years.²⁴ The Governor of the Bank of England subsequently said: 'We entered this crisis with levels of public borrowing which were too high and that made it more difficult.'²⁵ Brown was especially sensitive to criticism that the national finances were becoming dicey. At a breakfast at Number 11 with senior journalists from the *Financial Times*, he embarrassed those present by exploding in an angry tirade because the paper had challenged his figures. As his visitors left, he grabbed the *FT*'s editor and hauled him into his study, where Gowers was subjected to a further twenty minutes of Brown's fury. He fulminated: 'What do I have to do to get your respect?'²⁶

Much of the growth during the New Labour years was generated by the City of London. 'There's almost nothing in the world to rival it,' said Peter Mandelson. 'Of course, you have to support it. You want to advance it and you want it to grow.'²⁷ By contrast, manufacturers felt that they were treated as a poor and neglected relation. 'We were not seen to be part of the future,' says Paul Everitt, Chief Executive of the Society of Motor Manufacturers and Traders.²⁸ At its peak, the financial sector was expanding four times as fast as the rest of the economy, had a larger share of the economy than in any other major country, and was providing a substantial and growing proportion of tax revenues. New Labour's relationship with the City was accurately called 'a pact with the devil'.²⁹ The Faustian bargain was explicable because the devil had such apparently seductive tunes. Easy credit kept house prices escalating, shop tills ringing and consumers content. The feel-good factor helped to persuade the country to vote Labour three times in a row. Brown saw the City as a cash cow which produced revenues to be spent on health, education, poverty and other Labour priorities. The financial alchemists running banks and hedge funds in the Square Mile, Canary Wharf and Mayfair were celebrated. Less strictly regulated than rivals in New York and Frankfurt, and in an ideal time zone, London became an offshore financial centre for the rest of the world and a pioneer in the invention and dealing of complex instruments. By 2007 there were 550 international banks in Britain and 170 global securities houses. It was the location of approaching half of over-the-counter derivative trades and home to more than two thirds of the global secondary bond market. Brown liked to boast that London was 'the capital market place of the world'.³⁰

There were a few sages who cautioned the bankers and politicians that they were courting catastrophe. Warren Buffett, the great American investor who had seen markets rise and fall since the 1929 Crash, warned that they were trading in 'weapons of mass financial destruction'. Vince Cable, a former Chief Economist for Shell and the lead Treasury spokesman for the Liberal Democrats, was a lonely British voice forecasting disaster. Buffett was ignored; Cable was derided as 'Dr Doom'. Only a select minority in politics, the media, academia and the markets pointed to the risks being run. Most were captured by the 'Mutually Assured Delusion' that fuelled the bubble built on leverage of debt.[31] In so much as the Conservatives raised any objection, they argued that there should be 'even less need for regulation'.[32] As George Osborne subsequently admitted: 'The British political classes were somewhat bedazzled by the enormous success of Britain's financial services internationally.'[33]

Bankers, regulators, central banks, finance ministers, economists and leaders were all guilty of failing to see that the entire edifice was structurally unsound. Who killed the economy? It was like Agatha Christie's *Murder on the Orient Express*. They all did it.[34] The central culpability of the politicians was to allow the environment in which it could occur. The financiers were the reckless and intoxicated drivers who smashed the economy; the politicians failed to set speed limits or administer the breathalyser.

The political elite treated the City of London as if it were a City of Gold. There was a disinclination to ask searching questions about ballooning debt, financial instruments so opaque that they were often incomprehensible even to those trading them, and gargantuan bonuses that incentivised madness. Bonus payments nearly tripled between 2001 and 2008 to reach £16 billion. The Governor of the Bank of England later characterised the bonus culture in the City as 'a reward for gamblers'.[35] Yet there was no attempt to restrain the casino when the tables were busy. The City was cosseted and its excesses encouraged. 'The hedge fund guys had a lot of fun under Labour,' says one observer who monitored them closely. 'They had more fun than they had under the Tories.'[36]

During the 1997 election campaign, Labour ran a funny party political broadcast in which Stephen Fry and Hugh Laurie played tycoons revelling because the Conservatives allowed them to use offshore havens to avoid paying tax. Yet Labour went on to be so indulgent of rich foreign residents that it effectively turned Britain into the world's most popular tax haven among millionaires and billionaires. The treatment of private equity firms and some hedge funds allowed them to enjoy much lower tax rates than poorer citizens. Even those enjoying the prodigious rewards occasionally wondered why. Nicholas Ferguson, the Chairman of SVG Capital, asked how it could be right that some in his industry were allowed to get away with paying 'less tax than a cleaning lady'.[37]

Brown was personally austere. When a colleague once suggested that he should buy a national lottery ticket, he recoiled with horror: 'What would people say if I won?'[38] He wore his 'moral compass' on his sleeve and liked to advertise the 'Presbyterian conscience' that he claimed to have inherited from his minister father. Yet it was the preacher's son who presided over a brittle age of avarice, vulgarity and rapacity. The era was epitomised by the diamond-encrusted skull manufactured by Damien Hirst. This grotesque was a classic sign of a bubble about to burst. The jewelled death's head sold for $100 million to a consortium of investors, who included Hirst himself, at the end of August 2007. It was the symbolic artefact of an age which had lost both its aesthetic and its moral bearings. Homeowners measured their self-worth by the value of their houses, boasting of how much they had made as if this was a personal achievement rather than the simple good luck of surfing a property boom. Brown himself talked about a 'bubble' as early as 2005, but he did not act to control it. He chose to ignore the explosive growth of the balance sheets of British banks. Moderately sized when New Labour came to power, a decade later Britain's banks dwarfed the rest of the economy. Their accumulated liabilities grew larger than the entire economic output of Britain. No other major country had such disproportionately enormous banks. This made it even more imperative that Britain had a robust system of regulation.

One of Brown's first significant acts as Chancellor in 1997 was to take regulation of the financial sector away from the Bank of England and transfer responsibility to a new Financial Services Authority. In his habitually pre-emptory way, Brown sprang this as a rude surprise on the Bank's Governor, Eddie George. He was so stunned and angry that he almost resigned.[39] 'Eddie felt terrible because he thought he'd walked into a trap set by Brown,' says a very senior Treasury official who was close to the Governor. 'Eddie felt he'd let down everyone at the Bank. He thought he was looking at the dismemberment of the Bank.'[40] Tony Blair helped to draw back the Governor from resignation by taking up some of his concerns, but he did so in a half-hearted way. As Derek Scott, Blair's economic adviser, puts it: 'Ultimately, Gordon Brown had his way.'[41] Blair fought Brown over other turf, but 'he accepted that the Chancellor was king on economic policy and he was very happy to let him lead on that,' says Sir John Gieve, a senior Treasury official.[42] Blair was content to let Brown have that crown because there seemed to be no need to question the stewardship of the economy when growth was good and the money rolled in.

The new architecture of regulation created by Brown was called 'the tripartite system' because it split responsibility between the Treasury, the Bank of England and the FSA. Once this triangular arrangement was established, Blair paid it no further attention. More remarkably, neither did Brown. 'As dysfunctional as he is, Gordon has a very keen sense of what he can deal with and those things he isn't comfortable with,' observes a Treasury mandarin.[43] Brown displayed a lack of interest in his own creation from early on. He left Alistair Darling, then the Chief Treasury Secretary, and Sir Steve Robson, a senior civil servant, to take through Parliament the legislation creating the FSA.[44] From long and close observation of Brown, Robson says: 'I don't think he was terribly interested in the regulation of financial services really.'[45]

There were 'long and tortuous negotiations over the Financial Services Authority' which resulted in a Memorandum of Understanding. This was supposed to delineate who was responsible for what in the tripartite arrangement known to Whitehall as 'T3'. This left a fatal flaw which was concealed during the bubble and exposed only once it burst. The Bank of England Act 1998 left the Governor with 'no formal powers' to intervene to save banks.[46] A senior official at the heart of those negotiations later concluded: 'What was never really resolved was who would be the lender of last resort, what was the Bank of England's role in a crisis, and who had the final say.'[47]

Brown's priorities inevitably shaped the behaviour of the civil servants at the Treasury. Officials focused on child poverty, international development, welfare reform – 'Gordon's pet causes'. They took little interest in financial regulation because their political master did not.[48] After a decade of prosperity, there was barely any institutional memory within the Treasury about how to deal with an unbenign economic environment. Few of the officials had experience of coping with a crash or responding to a recession. Rachel Lomax, who was the Permanent Secretary at the Department of Trade and Industry before she became a member of the Monetary Policy Committee, went to the Treasury to give a talk in 2007. She asked the senior civil servants present: 'Put up your hands if you were here before 1997.' Not a single hand was raised.[49]

Brown had no desire and felt little necessity to pay attention to financial regulation. One of his City ministers, Ruth Kelly, did not have a one-to-one conversation with Brown for two years after her arrival at the Treasury.[50] Kitty Ussher, another City minister, had a brief interview with Brown when she took up her post. The one-sided conversation consisted of him instructing her to keep the City sweet.[51] Ed Balls, Brown's 'second brain' and City minister from May 2006 to June 2007, bragged that Britain had developed a system of 'increasingly light touch and risk-based regulation' so superior to its international competitors that it had 'made London a magnet for international business'.[52]

Self-congratulation at the Treasury was accompanied by wilting interest in financial regulation at the Bank of England once its authority over banks was deliberately diluted by Brown. Threadneedle Street was the traditional sentinel of the soundness of banks. After losing powers to the FSA, the Bank focused on monetary policy. This was especially the case after Mervyn King became Governor in 2003 because that was his speciality. The Bank's lodestar of economic stability was the control of inflation, at which King excelled, to the neglect of other potential threats. 'The leadership of the Bank of England was really much more interested in monetary policy issues and interest rate issues than it was in financial-stability issues,' observes Sir Steve Robson. 'The stability wing of the Bank did wither . . . the resources did drain away from that area.'[53] Sir John Gieve, who became the Deputy Governor with responsibility for financial-stability in January 2006, agrees that his remit 'did take second place to monetary policy'.[54]

Complacency at the Treasury and indifference at the Bank were compounded by the flaws in the third pillar of the house built by Brown. The Financial Services Authority concentrated on consumer issues rather than invigilating systemic risks. In the words of the FSA's Chief Executive from July 2007, Hector Sants: 'The prevailing climate was that the market does know best . . . that was the mood of society and politicians. The FSA just wasn't a forward-looking organisation in respect of business model risk.'[55] The FSA took a box-ticking approach. There had already been some warning that it was ticking the wrong boxes. The regulator was heavily criticised over the collapse in 2000 of Equitable Life, Britain's oldest insurer. Yet in so much as the Government took an interest in the FSA, it was to push for weaker rather than stronger scrutiny of financial institutions. Adair Turner, who became chairman of the regulator in 2008, observed that 'All the pressure on the FSA was not to say: "Why aren't you looking more closely at these business models?", but to say: "Why are you being so heavy and intrusive? Can't you make your regulation a bit more light touch?"'[56] Mervyn King later noted that any regulator who told bankers to stop being reckless during the bubble years 'would have been seen to be arguing against success'.[57]

A design fault of the tripartite system was that it operated 'on auto-pilot in the good years'.[58] The principals – the Chancellor, the Governor of the Bank of England and the head of the Financial Services Authority – 'never met' according to one senior Treasury official.[59] Another mandarin agrees: 'Gordon just wasn't interested. He didn't want to do it.'[60] The monthly meeting of the standing committee was attended by the deputies. Sir Andrew Large, the Deputy Governor of the Bank from 2002 to early 2006, came the closest to foreseeing how the asset price bubble could one day explode. 'Andrew was the Jeremiah of these meetings,' recalls one participant. 'No-one wanted to believe it. They'd bought into the Greenspan consensus that somehow the good times would keep rolling.'[61]

Officials at the Treasury and the Bank met each other much less frequently than they had before 1997.[62] There was little communication between the Treasury and the FSA. The regulator did flag as many as thirty warnings about individual banks and yet on Brown's own account they were never discussed with the Treasury.[63] The three corners of the triangle would come together only in a crisis. This meant that it would take a crisis to expose the flaws in the design. By that time it would be too late.

To make things even more dangerous, nearly everyone in charge was looking in the wrong direction. The Bank of England 'placed all its emphasis' on threats from terrorism after 9/11 and even more so after 7/7.[64] 'War games' were conducted to test the robustness of the financial system in the event of massive terrorist attacks. The avian flu scare prompted further war gaming about the consequences of a pandemic. This missed the much more potent threat to the economy lurking in reckless gambling by the banks themselves. The authorities were doing horizon planning, but their binoculars were not scanning the right horizon. According to one official at the top of the Treasury's finance directorate, there was 'an unwillingness to stress-test extreme scenarios' involving banks.[65] Only one war game of a financial crisis took place within the Bank of England in 2004–5.[66] One participant says that 'no-one acted on any of the suggestions that came out of it.'[67]

Another war game at the Treasury raised serious questions about the structure created by Brown. It revealed that 'thinking was relatively undeveloped as to how the resolution of an insolvent firm with systemic repercussions would be handled and by whom.' The deficiencies were regarded as so troubling that a plan was drawn up with target dates for remedial action. This plan was submitted to ministers, but never acted upon. Rather than fix the flaws, 'work on improving the existing arrangement was not judged by the Treasury to be a priority in a benign economic environment.'[68] A war game conducted at the FSA's headquarters in late 2006 concluded that the deposit guarantee scheme was not adequate to prevent bank runs, a gaping deficiency which would be a critical element of the crisis that broke nine months later. Yet nothing was done to remedy a flaw even when it had been identified.

Gordon Brown subsequently claimed that he supervised a 'huge simulation exercise' in 2006 to test what would happen in the event of a major institution 'running into problems' in either America or Britain.[69] It was true that there was a video conference that year involving Brown and Hank Paulson, the US Treasury Secretary, along with officials and regulators from both sides of the Atlantic. But one participant recalls 'we spent an awful lot of time introducing people to each other' and others involved agree.[70] Sir John Gieve lobbied for more war gaming. So did some Treasury officials. Brown got Paulson to agree to another exercise, but 'it never happened because it was very complicated to arrange and the Americans did not want it.'[71] Paulson, the former Chief Executive of Goldman Sachs, reluctantly became US Treasury Secretary in 2006 for an unpopular, lame-duck President. His comprehension of financial regulation was far from complete – he later admitted: 'I knew a lot about regulation, but not nearly as much as I needed to know, and I knew very little about regulatory powers and authorities.'[72] It was a rather sensible idea to stress-test what might happen in the event of a global banking crisis, but it was quietly forgotten.

Westminster goes on a long holiday in August, as do many journalists, with the result that the month has long been known as 'the silly season' in the belief that nothing of significance ever happens. This is a myth. The First World War broke out in August, Saddam Hussein invaded Kuwait and the Second World War began three days after the end of the wicked month. The initial tremors of the financial quake were felt in early August 2007. The first bubble to burst was the American market in sub-prime mortgages. In the greedy pursuit of higher returns, US banks had lent far too much to poor borrowers who would never have the means to repay them. These 'liar loans' were sliced and diced, churned with other loans to disguise them as better assets than they were and turned into tradable packages which were exported all over the world. 'Securitisation' was the jargon, but there was nothing secure about it. It fuelled the creation of a vast $6.5 trillion market in mortgage securities which was played by banks around the globe.[73] Though the instruments were complex, the root cause of the credit crunch was simple. Banks had lent money they didn't really have to people who could never pay it back. By the summer of 2007, interest rates were rising, American property prices were slumping and the bottom had fallen out of the sub-prime bonanza. To magnify the crisis, the conversion of dodgy mortgages into exotic instruments meant that no-one could be certain who was holding the bad stuff and how much of it. Banks, pension funds and investment houses were waking up to their exposure to liabilities that they could only guess at and holding toxic contracts they didn't understand. HSBC, the British-based global bank, caused a shock early in the year when it announced a staggering write down on its sub-prime loan book of more than $10 billion. Share prices of major banks tumbled over the summer. By early August, three German banks were close to collapse because of sub-prime. The boulder that caused an avalanche began to roll on Thursday, 9 August, the day that changed the world. BNP Paribas, the largest bank in France, revealed that it was exposed to huge losses. What really spooked the markets was that no-one, including the bank itself, could say precisely how huge. John Eatwell – a Labour peer and President of Queens' College, Cambridge – was one of the select minority of economists who had foreseen the potential for disaster. He observes that 'nobody expected the collapse of the sub-prime market in the United States to have the knock-on effect into the rest of the securitised market with a total collapse of confidence in all those markets.'[74] Almost overnight, banks lost trust in each other. They became hugely reluctant to lend between themselves and would only do so at punishingly high levels of interest. Credit markets seized up.

Alistair Darling was on holiday in Majorca with his wife and children. The Chancellor was not really alert to the severity of the crisis until he picked up a copy of the *Financial Times* in the supermarket and read its reports of extraordinary measures by the European Central Bank.[75] He rang his officials that morning.[76] They confirmed that Jean-Claude Trichet, the Frenchman who headed the ECB, was pumping unprecedented billions of euros into the money markets to try to alleviate the credit crunch. Ben Bernanke, the successor to Greenspan at the US Federal Reserve, followed suit by injecting billions of dollars of liquidity to forestall a chain reaction of banking collapses. The Bank of England, however, was staying aloof. Mervyn King, who had led the Bank for the past four years, was a former professor at the London School of Economics and the first Governor with a largely academic CV. John Eatwell, a contemporary at Cambridge, describes King as 'a thinker and rather cerebral for a central banker. He's just not a down and dirty markets man.'[77] An alpha mind in his specialist subject of controlling inflation, King was a novice when faced with a crisis in the money markets. Colleagues noted that he had long been 'intensely suspicious of the City side of banks'.[78] The chairman of a large retail bank contrasts him with his predecessor: 'Mervyn is not a deal-maker like Eddie George was. Eddie loved a bargaining session in a smoke-filled room. That's not Mervyn's forte.'[79]

He was also intellectually stubborn. One Treasury mandarin observed that 'it was not very easy to change his mind.'[80] A very senior official of the Bank itself goes further and describes the Governor as 'rigid and doctrinaire'.[81] There had been some forewarning of the attitude he was likely to take towards banks that got into trouble. According to a colleague at the Bank: 'In war game meetings, Mervyn used to say there was no point as he would never bail anyone out.'[82]

The academic Governor was a rigid adherent to the theory of 'moral hazard'. King took the view that banks in difficulties should not be rescued from their mistakes, but punished as a warning to others. 'He was a hawk on moral hazard,' says his deputy, Sir John Gieve.[83] From his desk overlooking the fine courtyard of the Bank building in Threadneedle Street, King took an important decision about the August crisis. Alone among the major central bankers, he refused to pump cash into the inter-bank market. Even when he later relented a little, he released much smaller amounts of liquidity than the American and European central banks and demanded a punitive rate of interest. The City protested. The Treasury pressed. Number 10 was agitated. King dug in. Brown and Darling were frustrated by his inflexibility, but feared the consequences of overruling the Governor. 'It took all of us some time to see how serious this financial crisis was,' says Gieve. 'We were slow off the mark.'[84] King was encouraged to maintain his stubborn position because the Governor wrongly believed that no British bank was at imminent risk.

Eyes blinking behind spectacles, King looked owlish. That didn't mean he was entirely wise. 'He hadn't grasped the full extent of the crisis that was unfolding,' says Sir Steve Robson. 'He put a good deal more emphasis on what he saw as the concerns of moral hazard – if you rescued people it would encourage other people to behave badly – than he did on the need to deal with a threat to financial stability. The contrast between the speed with which the European Central Bank responded to the crisis and the speed with which the Bank of England responded doesn't cover the Bank in great glory.'[85]

World stock markets hurtled downwards with shares in banks leading the plunge. On Friday, 10 August, the FTSE 100 suffered its biggest drop in more than four years. The first response from Gordon Brown was to argue that his superb stewardship of the economy had insulated Britain from the worst of previous crises and could be relied on to do so again. He genuinely, if wrongly, believed this: the British economy was more resilient than most during the emerging-markets crisis of 1997–8 and after the bursting of the dotcom bubble. 'Gordon was taken by surprise by the speed with which the credit crunch unravelled,' observes Irwin Stelzer, an American economist who was close to Brown. 'He also had a big stake in persuading himself that he had immunised the British economy from this disease that he figured was coming from across the ocean.'[86] Brown either didn't see or didn't want to see why a crash in the financial sector would be peculiarly challenging for

Britain because he had allowed banks to become such a large part of the economy. On Saturday, 11 August, he optimistically declared that Britain was in 'as good a shape as it could be to weather the storm'.[87]

Whether or not this was at all correct, it certainly was not true of some of its banks. The storm would expose their unsound foundations. The first revelation was that Northern Rock was built on sand. The unstable Rock was by now far removed from its origins in the regional friendly societies of the north-east of England. The parable of the Rock was, in some ways, similar to the story of Labour. Both party and former building society had grown out of the self-help and co-operative ethic of what was called 'the respectable' working class in the nineteenth century. Both bank and party had been transformed by global capitalism into unrecognisably different creatures.

Northern Rock was no longer a mortgage bank at all by any normal definition. It had been turned into a vehicle for highly leveraged financial engineering designed to implement a ferocious expansionary strategy. The author was the Chief Executive, Adam Applegarth, who was the second-youngest boss of a FTSE 100 company. Aged just thirty-eight, and without any banking qualifications, Applegarth was charismatic, a driven marketing man, brazenly confident and animated by a thirst for glory. He dominated Matt Ridley, the gentleman amateur who chaired the company, and the rest of a board which was unwilling to restrain Applegarth or was incapable of doing so as he made a dash for growth by seizing a big portion of the British mortgage market.

His pioneer product was the 'Together' loan, which allowed young customers to borrow six times their annual income rather than the much safer multiple of three. The bank also lent up to 125 per cent of the value of a property. These loans came to represent nearly a third of its book. The traditional mortgage bank drew its money from a stable base of customer deposits. To finance these extraordinary deals, the Rock borrowed in the wholesale market, where banks make short-term loans to each other. This phenomenally risky business model left the bank acutely vulnerable in the event that credit suddenly became more expensive. 'We were all fascinated by Northern Rock and how it was expanding so fast,' says the chairman of a rival mortgage bank. 'It was destroying our market.'[88] When Applegarth's big gamble appeared to be paying off, City analysts lauded the Rock's Chief Executive as he gobbled up market share from the old mortgage giants such as the Halifax and Nationwide. Funds piled in to fill their boots with the bank's shares. By early 2007, it had grown from a small regional operator to the fifth-largest mortgage lender in Britain. Other banks succumbed to the temptation to imitate. The prudent old disciplines of lending were thrown aside. It became easy for borrowers to get a mortgage on high multiples of salary, adding further fuel to the property boom. Personal debt in Britain swelled to a size larger than anywhere else in western Europe.

The Abbey was owned by Santander, a Spanish bank which wasn't allowed to behave the same way because it was subject to stricter Spanish banking law. 'We were being murdered on the mortgage side by Northern Rock,' recalls one of Santander's board members. The irritability of the Santander board was tempered by their conviction that 'Northern Rock was going to end in tears.'[89]

By the summer of 2007, Applegarth depended on the inter-bank market for some 70 per cent of his funding just at the moment when that market was freezing up. The credit crunch bit most immediately and deeply on Northern Rock. Unable to raise fresh financing as loans fell due, the bank was a matter of weeks away from insolvency. The Financial Services Authority finally became alive to the crisis at the Rock on 10 August. A further four days passed – a sign of a serious lack of communication between the T3 – before the Bank and the Treasury were alerted. Warning lights at last began to flash in Threadneedle Street, where the Rock's problems were regarded as 'alarming because it showed how fragile even the safest bit of banking actually is'.[90] Darling was back from holiday. He was briefed by John Kingman, his Second Permanent Secretary, and Clive Maxwell, the Director of Financial Services. Darling's officials told him that it looked bad, but should not be a cause for immediate panic because the Rock ought to have enough cash to survive into September. The traditional solution in this situation was to forestall a public panic by getting a larger and healthier institution to take over a troubled bank and keep the rescue secret until it was a done deal. The Treasury was initially optimistic that there was enough time to mount such a rescue. But Kingman became disturbed when he opened talks with the chief executives of other banks and found them apprehensive about 'contagion risk'. One official realised: 'These were conversations they were only willing to have out of politeness. They didn't think they could sell it to their boards.'[91] The two likeliest white knights – ironic candidates as saviours in the light of later events – were the Royal Bank of Scotland and Lloyds TSB.[92] RBS pulled out because Sir Fred Goodwin, its Chief Executive, wanted to conserve cash for what would prove to be a ruinous acquisition of the Dutch bank ABN Amro. Lloyds TSB was ready to buy the Rock, but after looking at the books said it would only do so if the rescue was underwritten with a £30 billion two-year loan from the Bank of England so that Lloyds could rebuild the Rock without putting itself at risk. Hector Sants, the Chief

Executive of the FSA, thought this was a reasonable proposition. Mervyn King, with his stern view about moral hazard, did not believe the Bank of England should be financing take-over deals. The Governor continued to set his face against helping a feckless bank because he believed 'it was better in the long term for them to fail.'[93]

That should have left the deciding vote with the Treasury. On the evening of Sunday, 9 September, Darling had a conference call with King and Sir Callum McCarthy, the Chairman of the FSA. The Governor was still refusing to co-operate. The Chancellor did not feel confident enough in either the deal or himself to take the advice of those officials telling him to overrule King.[94]

This was the first major test of Brown's tripartite arrangement and it cracked under the stress. The authorities failed to spot the risks being run at the Rock. They were then slow to see the potential for disaster. Even once they did they couldn't agree on a rescue. It exposed the ambiguities about who was supposed to be in charge during a banking crisis. 'I got the sense that the Treasury didn't know what their role was,' says the chairman of a large retail bank. 'In the old arrangement, everyone knew what their job was and it was the Chancellor who had the final say. Under the tripartite arrangement, everyone was confused about what everyone's powers were.'[95]

It was a failure of both institutions and people. The structural weaknesses were exacerbated by repeated 'personality clashes' between the most important players.[96] Mervyn King had a mutually suspicious relationship with Gordon Brown. 'Mervyn got up Gordon's nose,' says one senior Treasury official. Brown was hugely infuriated by King's previous criticism of Government policy, especially the level of debt. 'Gordon is a very sensitive man and that really wound him up.'[97] Brown retaliated by withholding confirmation that King would be reappointed as Governor for a second term. King 'scarcely saw him' for the first year that Brown was Prime Minister.[98] Alistair Darling was an inexperienced Chancellor, less than two months into the job and still finding his depth, working for a Prime Minister who thought he knew everything there was to know about how to run the Treasury. Darling was also at a psychological disadvantage in dealing with King, a veteran of Threadneedle Street whose financial expertise was regarded as far superior to that of the new Chancellor. 'Alistair did not stand up to Mervyn over Northern Rock. Gordon and Ed Balls would have told Mervyn what to do,' says a Treasury official.[99] A member of the Monetary Policy Committee, who also knew how Whitehall worked, thought the new Chancellor 'was initially in awe of Mervyn'. When the Governor was obstructive over the rescue, 'Alistair started to get pissed off with Mervyn. After the Northern Rock fiasco, he started to stand up to Mervyn a bit.'[100] On the account of Sir Steve Robson, the Governor even went so far as to suggest he would resign if Darling tried to compel him to put the Bank's money behind a rescue of Northern Rock.[101] The assessment of one expert witness with very senior experience in both the banking and Treasury world is scathing: 'The tripartite arrangement couldn't cope with the pressure. As soon as a crisis broke, the whole thing blew apart.'[102]

To justify his resistance to the rescue, King additionally argued that European law prevented the sort of covert action that had saved troubled banks in the past. This was debatable. The Germans swiftly and smoothly moved to save their three endangered banks without worrying about that. Yet King had his way. On Tuesday, 11 September, Sir John Gieve, the Bank's Deputy Governor, rang Applegarth to say there was no deal to rescue the Rock.

As markets continued to plummet, and rumours about the Rock rattled around the City, King's reputation took a hammering. The next day, MPs on the Treasury select committee received a letter from the Governor formally expounding his unbending view about rescuing feckless financiers. 'The provision of large liquidity penalises those financial institutions that sat out the dance, encourages herd behaviour and increases the intensity of future crises.'[103]

In theory, this was correct. In practice, even 'Unswerving Mervyn' was beginning to bend under the weight of this crisis and the pressure of so much criticism. By the time that letter was delivered, he was already beginning to 'somersault'.[104] On the evening of the 13th, King told a secret session of the Bank's Court, its governing body, that he was going to give an emergency loan to the Rock using the Bank's facility to be a lender of last resort.[105] Darling, sceptical that this would remain secret for long, successfully argued that they should bring forward the announcement to the next morning.[106] Even that wasn't soon enough. The emergency loan leaked that very night. Robert Peston, the Business Editor of the BBC and biographer of Brown, had the scoop which generated huge media headlines that the Rock was shattering. This turned a hidden drama into a public crisis. Some in Whitehall suspected that the journalist's source was within the bank or acting for it and hoped to calm the speculation which was destroying the share price. Some in the Treasury and the banking world believe that the leak came from Number 10 in a misguided effort to suggest that Gordon Brown was on top of the crisis.[107] Whoever was responsible, the result of this leak was calamitous for both the Rock and the Government.

On the morning of Friday, 14 September, long queues began to form at branches of the Northern Rock. Depositors were rushing to extract their money. The lines grew longer when these anxious savers were joined by others who found they could not make withdrawals online because the bank's website was overwhelmed by the volume of customers trying to access their accounts.

The media called it a panic, but the behaviour of these depositors was perfectly rational. Told that their bank was running out of cash, it made absolute sense to retrieve their savings before all the money was gone. The Government guarantee plan for depositors only promised a full refund of the first £2,000 of lost savings, 90 per cent of the next £33,000, and nothing at all above that.

Northern Rock was now in a double vice. It could not raise fresh funds on the wholesale market and money was gushing out in withdrawals by terrified depositors. Britain had its first bank run in more than a century and that appalling event was being broadcast to the world by television pictures of the customers clamouring to escape the Rock. 'It was stunning to see these lines of people waiting to get their money out,' says Irwin Stelzer. 'There were two reactions in America. One was: "My God, they've got a bank run." The other was: "Look how nice and orderly the Brits are when they queue up."'[108] In the context of the greater banking collapses that followed later, this came to seem less globally significant. In September 2007, the run on the Rock seized both Number 10 and the Treasury with terror that it would be catastrophic for the Government's reputation and Britain's global standing as a safe home for investment. Cabinet ministers were flabbergasted by the 'huge great queues'.[109] Officials saw that 'it was a searing experience' for Brown and Darling.[110] The Prime Minister made 'anxious' phone calls to colleagues.[111] One recipient of a call was his former adviser at the Treasury, Shriti Vadera. 'What are people saying about Northern Rock?' he asked. The International Development Minister replied: 'I'm in Addis Ababa. They're not saying anything about Northern Rock here.' 'Right,' said Brown. 'We'll have to do something about that.'[112] Soon afterwards, he moved her to the Business Department.

Neither Brown nor any of the other key actors had yet got on top of events. Confronted with the first bank run since the nineteenth century, the authorities continued to flounder. Darling was trying to follow events from abroad. He was at a summit of European finance ministers in Portugal as the Rock went critical. Christine Lagarde, the Finance Minister of France, observed Darling dash in and out of the meeting to make calls to London. Eventually he did not return at all.[113] The obvious move was to stem the flow of withdrawals by announcing a more solid government guarantee for depositors. According to the chairman of a retail bank, they spent Friday 'fiddling around with the legal position' rather than acting swiftly. 'They should have guaranteed deposits quicker, on the Friday rather than the Monday evening.'[114]

That weekend a 'really worried' Chancellor discussed guaranteeing the deposits with the Prime Minister.[115] Brown hesitated. He refused to sign off on a guarantee until the Treasury gave him a clearer idea about the extent of the Government's exposure.[116]

A decision was going to be forced upon the procrastinating Prime Minister. The torrent of withdrawals from the Rock continued on Monday: £2 billion flowed out in the space of just four days. 'This showed that the general public could lose confidence quite quickly and that has obviously coloured everything that's been done since, here and abroad,' comments Sir John Gieve.[117] On the stock market, there was frenzied dumping of not only shares in the Rock, but those of several other institutions now rumoured to be at risk. The Treasury's senior officials became 'hugely concerned about the ramifications for other institutions, potentially much larger ones'.[118] At Number 10, Brown also became highly alarmed that it could 'spread to other institutions'.[119] By lunchtime, the Government was seized by the fear that it was about to face runs on several other banks, including 'the big ones'.[120]

After a frantic discussion between Brown and Darling, that afternoon the Chancellor called an emergency news conference at the Treasury at which he announced that the Government was going to 'guarantee all the existing deposits in the Northern Rock during the current instability in the financial markets'.[121] As soon as this was clear, the queues at the Rock began to disappear. The Rock was rescued, but in such a clumping fashion that it did not inspire any confidence in the authorities. John Gieve later lamented that their footwork was so leaden that it was 'more John Sergeant than Fred Astaire. We did not need two days of queues in the streets.'[122]

The flawed and sloppy regulator failed to see the crisis coming. Mervyn King was inflexible and off the pace when the crisis broke. Alistair Darling lacked the experience and clout to take a grip. Gordon Brown dithered. In the aftermath, they all blamed each other. One senior Treasury official at the heart of the crisis comments: 'We thought it was the end of the world. People were saying that was it for Britain's international reputation.'[123]

Less fortunate than the depositors were the shareholders. Shares valued at more than £12 just seven months earlier when the City was still in love with Applegarth crashed below 50p. The bank, once the pride of Newcastle, was dubbed 'Northern Crock'. The Chief Executive left three months later, though his disgrace was sweetened by being allowed to leap clear of the wreckage with a pension pot worth £2.6 million and the proceeds from the fabulous salary and bonuses he had enjoyed in his days of glory. Nearly all the discredited board went too. The Government was left holding the corpse of a bank which no-one wanted to buy, along with a large and rising exposure for the taxpayer.

The 'Golden Age' trumpeted by Brown less than three months earlier was turning to dust. The wreck of the Rock was the first dramatic manifestation of the bursting of the financial bubble of Chancellor Brown. Yet its paradoxical consequence was to inflate a temporary political bubble for Prime Minister Brown. He feared, and the Tories hoped, that the run on the Rock would prove to be a fatal blow to his reputation for economic stewardship. Opinion polls indicated the reverse. A poll in mid-September had well over half of voters trusting Brown and Darling on the economy while less than a fifth reposed faith in their Tory rivals.[124]

George Bernard Shaw once said: 'My reputation grows with every failure.' The same was true of Gordon Brown. In the immediate aftermath of the crisis, the run on the Rock encouraged voters to flee to Brown. They threw themselves into his arms in the belief that he was the helmsman best qualified to steer Britain through a financial storm. 'With the way Gordon's star really shot high,' Cabinet ministers began to think, 'it was now possible to win an election and win big under Gordon.'[125]

There was growing speculation that Britain was heading for the polls.

29. The Election That Never Was

The idea of an autumn general election was first put into the Prime Minister's head at the end of July. The Cabinet were summoned to Chequers just before the summer break to be given what one Minister recalls as 'a rather saccharine presentation' by Deborah Mattinson, Brown's personal pollster.[1] Once the Cabinet departed, the Prime Minister's closest advisers joined him in the downstairs sitting room overlooking the country house's handsome grounds.

'It looks strong,' remarked Spencer Livermore. The private polling shown to the Cabinet put Labour eight points ahead of the Tories and suggested that Brown was seen as a superior leader to David Cameron. Douglas Alexander and Sue Nye agreed that results were good. Livermore went on: 'You should think about going early.' Brown was pensive. 'You mean April?' he said, thinking his aide was suggesting an election in the early spring of next year. 'No,' said Livermore. 'I mean the autumn.' Brown, Alexander and Nye all laughed at the audacity of the idea.[2]

Brown had originally told his team that he ideally wanted to call an election in the early summer of 2008: somewhere around the anniversary of his arrival in Number 10. Alexander, who was in charge of planning campaign strategy, and Ed Miliband, who was supervising manifesto preparation, were working to that timetable. Brown's calculation was that he would need twelve months to establish himself as Prime Minister, heal the wounds of Iraq and restore trust in the Government. He'd deflected calls for an immediate election by correctly pointing out that there hadn't been one when John Major took over from Margaret Thatcher. He told me in an interview: 'I think people want to give their leaders a chance, and they want to give them the opportunity to show what they can do.'[3]

Speculation about an election was nevertheless encouraged by Labour's growing advantage in the opinion polls. In the last six months of Blair, Labour was behind the Tories in all but one poll. Since Brown moved in, Labour was ahead in every single poll. By the second half of July, the Government was hitting or breaking through the psychologically important mark of 40 per cent for the first time in two years.[4]

The shine was coming off David Cameron. The Conservatives came third in the Sedgefield by-election triggered when Tony Blair stood down as an MP to spend more time with his money. The poor Tory performance in such a safe Labour seat was not terribly surprising. The bigger blow to Cameron was another wooden spoon in the by-election in the west London seat of Ealing Southall. The Tory leader invested himself heavily in that contest by making five campaign visits only for his candidate to come third.

The right-wing press turned on him for visiting Rwanda when the summer floods hit his constituency. 'Where's the Rt Hon member for washed-out Witney?' bellowed the *Daily Mail*.[5] During his trip to Africa, a rattled Cameron was overheard telling his adviser Steve Hilton: 'I should have stayed at fucking home.'[6]

Brown had 'gone round the Cabinet table' at the Chequers meeting, but 'most people were still sceptical' about an early election.[7] At this stage, Livermore was alone among the Prime Minister's inner circle in pushing hard for the autumn. On the aide's return from his August holiday, he wrote a memo listing the pros and cons. Among the arguments favouring going early, he prophetically listed the potential for the 10p tax issue to blow up next April. Livermore's memo warned: 'We will inevitably face this question at conference. If you don't want to do it, we will have to rule it out before conference because we don't want it to dominate conference.'[8] Brown passed a copy of the note to his allies in the Cabinet. Ed Balls was cool, as was Ed Miliband. Douglas Alexander was growing warmer, telling the Prime Minister: 'You must look at this seriously.' But it was not properly discussed by Brown and his team during August, partly because of the distraction of Northern Rock and partly because 'Gordon didn't want to think about it because it was such a risk.'[9] Brown later told his circle that one of his great regrets was 'those lost weeks'.[10]

It was only in the first week of September that he dug out and re-read the Livermore memo. He discussed with Alexander, Balls and Miliband how they were going to deal with the subject when the trio, assumed to be privy to Brown's innermost thoughts, were asked about an early election in pre-conference interviews. They were sanctioned 'to keep it running'. Not because Brown had decided on an autumn election – he was still far from persuaded – but 'as a means of toying with the Conservatives. It was tactics not strategy.'[11]

Michael Gove and other members of Cameron's inner circle were aware that 'He saw it as a way of destabilising the Conservative Party and a way, essentially, of making political mischief.'¹² A minister very close to Brown agrees: 'It started as a tease, then Gordon let it all get out of hand.'¹³

As a short-term tactic, it worked. The Conservatives did get panicky. David Cameron was increasingly convinced that his opponent would make an early dash for the country because 'I can't see how it gets better for him.'¹⁴ He truncated his August holiday and Oliver Letwin, the Tory policy chief, cancelled his altogether to rush together the bones of a Conservative manifesto.¹⁵

Brown executed another stunt to destabilise the Tories in mid-September. Back in 1989, when Margaret Thatcher was Prime Minister and Gordon Brown was a young MP, he published a 182-page attack on her premiership, entitled *Where There is Greed: Margaret Thatcher and the Betrayal of Britain's Future*. Eighteen years on, he invited her for tea and posed on the doorstep of Number 10 with the woman he once excoriated. The Conservatives muttered that the Thatcher visit took advantage of an old lady suffering from senile dementia, but they dared not openly complain. Brown hailed the Iron Lady as 'a conviction politician' and asserted that he was cast from the same steely mould.¹⁶

He also continued his practice of calling COBRA, convening two meetings of the emergency committee in the space of forty-eight hours when there was a suspected case of foot and mouth at one farm in Surrey.

By the week before the Labour conference, he was intensely preoccupied with the idea of an early election but no closer to taking a decision. Gamble successfully and he would have his own personal contract with the country, the lack of which he felt quite acutely. Until he won an election in his own right, he would remain in the shadow of Tony Blair, the victor in three. 'Gordon wants his own mandate,' one Cabinet minister told me after a conversation with Brown.¹⁷ Gamble wrongly and history would remember him as the fool who waited more than a decade to become Prime Minister and then chucked away a perfectly healthy majority after just three months in Number 10. If he lost, he would be the shortest serving premier since George Canning in the early nineteenth century. And Canning had the excuse that he died.

Divided in his own mind, Brown found that the Cabinet was utterly split when they discussed it again shortly before the Labour conference. 'Some people were putting forward the argument as a new Prime Minister he should seek a mandate,' says Harriet Harman. 'But then others were reminding us that if you have an election late on in the year it gets darker earlier and then fewer people vote.'¹⁸

Jacqui Smith, not only the Home Secretary but a former Chief Whip, was prominent in the camp arguing for an early election. Her West Midlands seat of Redditch was one of the marginals being targeted by the Tories with 'the Ashcroft money' – campaign funds from the Conservative peer. The longer they delayed, Smith feared, the more they would be out-spent by the Conservatives.[19] Nick Brown was confident that they would win and told his friend in Number 10 that it 'would be better to have his own mandate'.[20] Jack Dromey, the party Treasurer, reassured Brown that, though money was tight, they could scramble together enough funds from the unions and other donors for a campaign.[21]

Jack Straw, the most senior member of the Cabinet, was 'always sceptical about an early election'.[22] Straw told Brown that it was not worth the risk: 'You only get an extra two years.'[23] Also hostile were the Health Secretary, Alan Johnson, and the Chancellor, Alistair Darling.[24] The Chief Whip, Geoff Hoon, argued that an election would be 'a disaster' and held to the view that 'the Labour vote would have haemorrhaged.'[25] They formed an axis which became known as 'the greybeards'.

There was another group who didn't want to decide until they had clearer answers to crucial questions. At the pre-conference Cabinet, some ministers asked whether there was any polling from marginal seats. Peter Hain became alarmed when he realised that they were rushing towards an election without solid evidence.

When I was asked, by senior people very close to Gordon, what my view was, I asked two questions. I said: 'What are the polls in the marginal seats?' and I asked another question: 'What is the polling in London and the south?' Because my political antennae told me that it didn't feel very good.

The answer left him apprehensive. 'They didn't know. So those pressing for an early election, talking it up to journalists at the party conference, did not have an answer to those two crucial questions. That worried me.'[26]

Some veteran associates of Brown reflected his innate caution back to him. Murray Elder, the Labour peer, actually had a grey beard. Elder had known Brown since they were at nursery school together. 'I didn't see any merit in an early election,' he says and he told the Prime Minister so. 'It seemed to me there are some long-term rules in politics: that if you want to win an election, you ought to be ahead in the polls for really quite a long time and two months doesn't constitute a really long time.'[27]

Brown's inner circle could not make up his mind for him because they were divided and in flux. Spencer Livermore, the hottest advocate, argued with Brown that he should announce an election in his speech to the party conference. Douglas Alexander was growing more bullish. So was Bob

Shrum, the American political consultant who had been close to Brown for years. Ed Miliband remained unconvinced. Ed Balls was beginning to change his mind, a shift which was reflected in the spin put out by Damian McBride. Sue Nye was 'in a frenzy' about how she would organise a leader's campaign tour at such short notice.[28]

Brown pored over any sign, tea leaf or entrail that might indicate the mood of the voters. In the week before the Labour conference, he became hypnotised by local council by-elections, something normally well below the radar of a Prime Minister. Those who talked to him on the eve of the conference found that he could rattle off the details of council results all over the country. He knew precisely, to decimal points of percentages, how Labour had gained at the expense of the Tories in Birmingham and the Lib Dems in Nuneaton. 'The Lib Dems lost two seats during their conference week,' he happily noted. He read great significance into a Labour victory at the expense of the Conservatives in Worcester, the city which produced the iconic electoral figure of Worcester Woman. 'A 17 per cent swing!' the Prime Minister triumphantly observed.[29]

He commissioned Deborah Mattinson and Stan Greenberg, the American pollster who previously worked for Tony Blair, to do detailed polling in the marginal constituencies which determine election outcomes. The raw results from the fieldwork came in on Saturday, 22 September. The refined data was ready to be presented to Brown by Sunday, the opening day of the conference in Bournemouth. He gathered his inner team at the Highcliff Hotel, overlooking the Dorset resort's sandy beach. They sat in a suite which had been turned into the Prime Minister's office for the conference week. Alexander, Livermore, Miliband and Shrum were with him in the room as Stan Greenberg gave the presentation in his New York drawl. He confused some present by 'using American terminology'. But his headline conclusion was clear enough: Labour would win an autumn election with a probable majority of between thirty-five and forty-five. Brown was taken aback. This was not what he had been anticipating. The press, applying crude extrapolations to their poll results, was suggesting that Labour could do much better than that. 'Gordon had been reading newspapers saying he'd get a three-figure majority,' says one present in the room.[30] Brown grumpily wrapped up the meeting by telling the pollsters to go away and 'do more work'.[31]

The hot house of the conference became feverish with speculation. Sunder Katwala, the General Secretary of the Fabian Society, recalls: 'At a conference, everyone's in an unreal bubble, everyone's talking to everyone else and it was the only thing that anybody was talking about. And suddenly, by Wednesday, I thought: "My God, they're actually going to go for this."'[32]

Journalists who spoke to members of the Prime Minister's entourage were encouraged to believe that an autumn election was for real. John Kampfner, the editor of the *New Statesman*, reports:

There was a lot of nudge, nudge, wink, wink. We all asked questions in code and we got answers in code. Such as: 'Will it be safe to go off on our half-term holiday at the end of October?' 'Ooh, I'm not sure, especially if you are going abroad. Better stay closer to home.' Those sorts of conversations were being had all the time.[33]

Members of the Cabinet were led to believe that they had most of the media, including the right-wing newspapers, on side. Peter Hain recalls: 'I remember editors of national newspapers, including the *Telegraph* and News International [*The Times* and the *Sun*], all of them contemptuous of David Cameron and eulogising Gordon's strength and his capacity as a Prime Minister and really praising him to the roof tops.'[34]

The press became increasingly convinced that it was on. 'Election fever rages as Brown's lead grows,' reported *The Times*.[35] The *Mirror* cried: 'Go for it Gordon'.[36] Michael Portillo, the former Conservative Cabinet minister, admitted that the prospect was 'frightening the Tories'.[37] The electioneering atmosphere was heightened further by the abundant evidence that Labour was road-testing campaign propaganda. Saatchi & Saatchi, who had just been awarded the Labour account, unveiled a new slogan: 'Not flash – just Gordon'. It was personally approved by the Prime Minister.

Jack Straw argues: 'It's hard to see, in retrospect, how that much specula-tion could have been avoided given the fact that there was active consideration being given.'[38]

Gordon Brown opened his speech to the conference with a jab at humour. 'People say to me: "Would you recommend this job to anyone else?" I say: "Not yet."'[39]

He continued with the projection of himself as a 'father of the nation'. 'Tested again and again,' he said of the summer terror plots, floods and outbreaks of animal diseases. 'The resilience of the British people has been powerful proof of the character of our country.'[40] What he hoped to suggest was that his handling of them was powerful proof of why he should remain as Prime Minister. He disdained to make a single direct reference to the Conservatives or their leader. David Cameron was as much an unperson in the speech as Tony Blair, who was privately wounded and annoyed that he rated just one reference. Yet sentence after sentence had a partisan purpose designed to leave the Conservatives naked before the electorate by appro-priating their clothes. Brown spoke against a blue backdrop on which the word 'Labour' was nowhere to be seen. He used tropes such as 'our island story' and pressed right-wing buttons about bringing back matron and encouraging have-a-go heroes. For lengthy passages, the speech was an echo chamber of sound-bites which had been pre-tested on sample voters. 'It was very focus-grouped,' says one of Brown's team. 'There was no over-arching narrative.'⁴¹ In the most shameless section, he implied that immigrants were the main cause of drug dealing and gun crime. They would be 'thrown out'. For that excursion into Tebbitry, he was rewarded with the endorsement of the retired Tory polecat. In an ugly phrase that would come back to haunt Brown, he talked of 'British jobs for British workers'.⁴² This was a slogan of the BNP and a promise that he could not keep unless Britain left the European Union. 'That made me wince,' says Jon Cruddas, a Labour MP battling with the BNP in his Dagenham constituency, because it sounded like 'a dog whistle to the far right'.⁴³

The speech was neither a programme for government nor the exposition of a coherent ideology. It was a let-down to the more cerebral members of the speech-writing team like Ed Miliband. Their attempts to craft something more inspirational were overwhelmed by Brown's insistence on lumping in long laundry lists of initiatives.

The speech was nevertheless rewarded with a prolonged standing ovation from a Labour Party currently happy to worship the man who had put them back ahead in the polls. The overall media conclusion was that Brown was a leader in command of his party and ruthlessly preparing the ground for an election.

'Brown's winning ways will take some beating,' swooned the *Daily Telegraph*. 'Everything points to a snap poll.' It quoted Hilaire Belloc. 'The stocks are sold, the press is squared, the middle class is quite prepared.'⁴⁴

Rupert Murdoch, though, did not think there should be an early election and was using his biggest-selling daily organ to try to prevent one. 'Not his finest hour' was the verdict of the *Sun*, which attacked Brown for dismissing the calls for a referendum on the EU treaty.⁴⁵ Brown's anger about that was as nothing compared with his reaction on Wednesday evening, when he learnt of the coverage in *The Times*. Danny Finkelstein, the paper's Comment Editor, a former speech-writer to John Major and a keen student of American politics, had been struck by the familiarity of many phrases in Brown's speech. Finkelstein confirmed his suspicions by Googling any line that sounded like a speech-writer's phrase.⁴⁶ Brown said: 'Sometimes people say I am too serious.'⁴⁷ That was awfully similar to a sentence used by Al Gore in 2000 when he accepted the Democratic nomination: 'I know that sometimes people say I'm too serious.' Brown: 'This is my pledge to the British people: I will not let you down.' Gore: 'I pledge to you tonight: I will never let you down.'[48] Finkelstein identified several examples of phrases recycled from speeches by Gore and Bill Clinton, both former clients of Bob Shrum, adviser and speech-writer for Brown. When Finkelstein posted it on his blog that afternoon, the deputy editor of The Times, Ben Preston, thought it would make 'a great splash' for the next morning's paper.[49]

When Brown learnt that The Times planned to lead its front page with how he had rehashed American phrases, he was 'incandescent'.[50] From his suite at the Highcliff, he rang complaining to Preston and Robert Thomson, the editor of The Times. 'It's a Tory plot,' he raged, trying to bludgeon them into pulling the story. 'This won't be forgotten.' He was maddest of all with his own team. Brown went berserk with Bob Shrum, whose long friendship did not protect the American from a ferocious blast of Brown's temper. 'How could you do this to me, Bob?' Brown screamed at a shaking Shrum. 'How could you fucking do this to me?' Then the Prime Minister started yelling at the other aides present: 'Just get out! Just get out of the fucking room!' Sue Nye became so alarmed that she felt compelled to come into the room to protect the unfortunate Shrum.[51]

Most of the media chose to ignore the Times story, but Brown continued to rage about it in private for days afterwards. 'It totally threw Gordon off,' says one of his inner circle. 'When he should have been thinking about the election, he was boiling about this.'[52]

This angry face of Brown was masked from the public. On the Wednesday of the conference, his handlers put him in a format designed to show a relaxed and humorous dimension to the Prime Minister. He sat in an easy chair on the conference stage alongside the journalist and broadcaster Mariella Frostrup, who hosted a question-and-answer session. Always wary and often paranoid about live events, the Prime Minister felt comfortable with this interlocutor, who had previously interviewed him at a literary festival.

Before the event, Frostrup was led through the corridors of the conference centre to a 'back room in the depths of the building behind the big hall'. Waiting to perform, she and Brown 'were just left there for about two hours'. As they separately made notes in preparation for the event, she was most 'struck by what a lonely job it is'.[53]

On stage, Brown dealt easily with the soft questions from delegates and got them laughing with anecdotes about the old days of the health service when a trolley would come round the wards to serve drinks. 'You could have Guinness, you could have beer,' he amused them. 'Free beer for all the workers.'

Then Frostrup popped the big question. 'It's been a very successful three months. It's been a very successful conference. And I wondered if, in the intimate atmosphere of the conference centre here, you wanted to illuminate me on whether you felt it would be a good time for an election?'

The friendly interviewer relaxed Brown into dropping his guard. 'Charming as you are, Mariella, I think the first person that I would have to talk to is the Queen.'[54]

With that unwise tease, which publicly confirmed for the first time that he was thinking about an early election, the Prime Minister himself openly joined in the game. That lunchtime, the fever was further intensified by Ed Balls, when he was asked on the radio whether it might not be risky to go to the country early. The Children's Secretary revealingly replied: 'It's a very interesting question as to where the gamble really lies.'[55] Balls 'kicked himself' the moment the interview was over.[56] He was now converted to the idea, but he had not meant to go that far in public. The Sunday after the conference, Balls had a long and influential discussion with Brown. 'It is your decision, but I would go for it,' said Balls. 'What you can't do is make a half-decision.' One reason to go for it, he argued, was that it was unlikely the media 'will give us such an easy ride at any other time'.[57]

By the end of the week in Bournemouth, ministers felt it 'building to a frenzy'.[58] Ed Miliband began trawling 'frantically' among Cabinet ministers for ideas to put in the manifesto.[59] Most Labour MPs were convinced that it was on. Jon Cruddas – whose partner, Anna Healey, was principal aide to Harriet Harman – was typical: 'I remember going away that weekend, talking to my agent and preparing the ground, as every MP in the land was doing. There was no doubt that it looked like a no-brainer that we were heading for an election.'[60] Frank Field had been sceptical, but 'by the end I believed that he was going to have an election. I even wrote my election address; fortunately, I didn't put a date on it.'[61] The published polls the weekend after the conference gave Labour a lead of between six and eleven points. Some of the Cabinet openly talked about a dash to the country. 'We could turn a majority of 60 with two and a half years to run into a majority of 100 with five years to run,' said John Denham of the 'exciting' poll results in the press.[62]

Staff in the Number 10 Policy Unit were working flat-out, 'all writing chapters for the manifesto. We really thought it was going to happen.'[63] Campaign grids were drafted. The unions were 'kicking in money'.[64] Brown ordered several crucial events to be brought forward to create a springboard. The most significant was to instruct Alistair Darling to advance the date of the Pre-Budget Report and the comprehensive spending review in order to splice them together so that election sweeteners could be scattered before the voters. The weekend between the Labour and Tory conferences, Darling told Andy Burnham, the Chief Treasury Secretary, to hurry up settlement of the spending negotiations with ministers so that they could be announced in ten days' time. 'It was all systems go,' says one member of the Cabinet.[65] Discreet inquiries were made of Buckingham Palace to ensure that the Queen would be in London if Brown needed to ask for a dissolution of Parliament.

The Tories trudged up to Blackpool for their conference looking as defeated as the faded Lancashire resort. 'Cameron meltdown as public urge early vote' was the *Observer* splash on a poll giving Labour a seven-point advantage over the Tories. Better still for Brown, he was trouncing his Tory opponent on all the key qualities that people look for in a Prime Minister. More than two thirds of voters expected Labour to win an election.[66]

The Lib Dems were also in a miserable state. Sir Menzies Campbell's qualities counted for little with a press which had largely made up its brutal mind that he should be in a retirement home. Senior Conservatives that I spoke to during this period trembled before the prospect of a fourth defeat. One member of the Tory frontbench said: 'David Cameron may no longer be leader of the Conservative Party by Christmas.'[67] Cameron told a friend: 'My political career could be over before I'm forty-two.'[68]

Brown's calculation when he stoked election speculation was that it would divide the Tories and they would fall apart under pressure in Blackpool. Given the Conservatives' long history of committing suicide in public, it is easy to see why Brown gambled on the Tories imploding. Yet it turned out to be a serious miscalculation to assume that Cameron and his party would not fight back. The threat of an imminent election galvanised the Tory leadership, rallied their activists and muzzled dissent. David Davis, who was Cameron's rival for the leadership two years earlier, cancelled all his appearances at fringe events to deny the media any opportunity to interpret anything he said as divisive.[69]

The centre of attention on the first day of the Tory conference was George Osborne, the Shadow Chancellor. The issue he targeted was inheritance tax. More people had been sucked into its net over the past decade, largely as a result of the boom in property prices. Even so, barely more than a twentieth of Britons were wealthy enough to be touched by inheritance tax.[70] It had nevertheless become a hot-button issue among the middle classes, not least owing to noisy press campaigns against 'the death tax'. Osborne unveiled a crowd-pleasing promise to exempt all but millionaires from inheritance tax. He said he would finance his pledge by introducing a new levy on wealthy foreigners living in Britain – the 'non-doms'. This artfully made his promise seem a cost-free gift to British citizens at the expense of rich foreigners.

Douglas Alexander and Spencer Livermore watched Osborne's speech on a television at Labour's headquarters in Victoria Street. 'That's it,' said Livermore. 'We can't have an election.' Alexander looked glum: 'Do you think?' The next morning's press largely cheered Osborne for proclaiming 'Death to Death Taxes'. Deborah Mattinson was running focus groups in key southern marginals – places like Croydon, Watford and Slough – to test voter reaction to the Tory conference. She was soon reporting a 'definite mood swing' to the Conservatives. Osborne's inheritance tax pledge 'was like a laser to the heart of the swing voter in marginal seats'.[71]

Brown had received and rejected advice to do something about inheritance tax in his last Budget the previous March.[72] Alistair Darling had no plans to tackle it in his financial package that October.[73] After Osborne's speech, Brown told Darling to quickly rustle up a Labour version of an inheritance tax cut. The Chancellor was resistant. Darling protested that there was not time for the Treasury to do proper costings. Shaky maths was precisely the grounds on which Labour was attacking Osborne. Brown overruled Darling. He told the Chancellor they had to be able to neutralise the Tory promise before an election.[74] The Treasury began to scrabble together its own scheme.

Campaign planning continued to gather pace. Billboard sites for advertising were hurriedly booked. Battersea Heliport in south London was asked to find 100 landing and take-off slots for campaign tours. By the end of the week, Labour had committed itself to £1.2 million of campaign spending.[75] As one Cabinet minister puts it: 'It had gone way beyond "on your marks".'[76]

In the middle of the Conservative conference week, the Prime Minister made a sudden appearance in Iraq. The concept was to upstage and diminish David Cameron by projecting Brown as an international statesman while his petty opponents fought among themselves. But the Tories did not fall apart in Blackpool. And Brown did not look statesmanlike in Iraq. He came over as crudely opportunistic when he promised that 'by Christmas, 1,000 of our troops can be brought back.'[77] This announcement was leaked to the BBC on Monday night in time for its main ten o'clock bulletin in an attempt to steal some of the thunder of the Tories' inheritance tax promise. It swiftly emerged that half of the troop withdrawals had been previously announced and about a quarter of the troops were already home. This reawakened memories of Brown's vice of double-counting and triple-announcing. His fly-in, fly-out visits to Baghdad and Basra did not look like the 'new politics' he promised when he arrived at Number 10. It came over as the brazen exploitation of British troops for electioneering. Sir John Major, in a rare and therefore more salient intervention by the former Conservative Prime Minister, attacked Brown for the 'pretty unattractive . . . cynicism' of using the troops for partisan purposes.[78] The headlines were almost universally critical.

This also supplied David Cameron with the opportunity to present himself as a contrast to the machinating Prime Minister. On his conference's climactic day, the Tory leader delivered his sixty-seven-minute speech without an autocue. He spent the previous day committing his text to memory, a trick he mastered at Eton. 'It might be a bit messy, but it will be me,' he declared before achieving a near-faultless delivery as he strode the stage of the Winter Gardens. This feat – 'Look, Mum, no notes' – was a stylistic triumph. It was a high form of spin for Cameron, the former PR man for a TV company, to project himself as unspun. Yet even Labour people acknowledged the success of the performance. He presented himself as nerveless and bluffed that the Conservatives were much more confident than they truly felt. 'You go ahead and call that election,' Cameron goaded Brown. 'Let the people pass judgement.'[79]

By dithering over the decision, Brown had already trapped himself in a crucial respect. The earliest possible election date was now 1 November, a wintry Thursday for a British election. Bob Shrum argued with Brown that this wasn't decisive. Shrum was accustomed to the American practice of holding presidential and congressional elections in November. Those with more experience of fighting British elections could see a problem, a very big one. The clocks would have gone back, bringing nightfall earlier. 'Getting your vote out is crucial,' argued Hazel Blears, who did not like the prospect 'of knocking on doors in November with dark nights closing in'.[80] It was also dawning on the Brown team that the contest would be on a dated electoral register. Even if they won, their mandate would not seem so refreshed if the turn-out was low and accompanied by claims that many people had been disenfranchised.

At the end of the Tory conference week, there were three more published polls to digest. In one, Labour's lead was cut from eleven points to four.[81] In another, a ten-point lead shrivelled to just three.[82] In a third, the Tories had closed an eight-point gap since the start of the conference season to get neck and neck with Labour.[83]

The 'crunch meeting'[84] took place at Number 10 on Friday, 5 October. Early that morning, in a phone conversation with a close Cabinet ally, Brown was 'still going for it' but sounded anxious about what he was going to hear from his pollsters.[85] The inner court gathered in a ground floor room on the right-hand side of Number 10 with a view of Downing Street through its bow-fronted window. Ed Balls was the only absentee. Stan Greenberg put his laptop down on the table and fired it up. Sue Nye then brought in the Prime Minister. Brown sat opposite the pollster, who positioned the laptop between them so that the Prime Minister could squint into the screen. Everyone else stood about, shifting nervously. Alexander and Livermore, who had already been shown the polling, looked grim. Greenberg presented a gloomy analysis of fieldwork from 150 key marginal seats. Labour had lost ground to the Tories whose promise on inheritance tax appeared to be responsible for much of the dramatic swing to them, especially in marginal seats in the Midlands and the South. The 'balance of risk' was that Labour would achieve 'a small win'. Looking across at Brown, Greenberg said: 'I can't guarantee what your majority will be.' They were in the territory of a parliamentary majority in the teens. If the campaign didn't go well, it could be worse: a hung Parliament. 'It was awful, a depression settled on the room,' says one present.[86] Brown looked at the pollster: 'So we can't do it?' Greenberg responded: 'It looks very difficult now.'

Livermore made the case that they had gone too far to pull back now: 'If we don't do it, the only people who will be celebrating are Tory Central Office.' Shrum disagreed: 'That's the very worst reason to do it.' Miliband said it confirmed his view that an election would be a mistake. Alexander shifted towards the antis.[87]

Brown walked out saying he was late for a meeting on Burma. Once he was gone, they had a franker debate. They could say in his absence what they could not say in his presence: that pulling out would be devastating to his reputation. But to nearly all in the room it was already obvious that 'Gordon had gone cold on the whole idea.'[88]

The Prime Minister looked into the suddenly icy water and became scared of a risky plunge. One member of the Cabinet very close to Brown says: 'Gordon had never been that firmly persuaded. So it didn't take much to push him off.'[89] If he pressed ahead now, it would be against his cautious instincts, against the advice of the most seasoned operators in the Cabinet, against the pleas not to send them into battle from some Labour MPs in marginal seats, and against the counsel of his opinion pollsters.

The inner circle reconvened that afternoon, this time in Brown's office. He asked each of them in turn – Alexander, Balls, Livermore, Miliband, McBride and Nye – what they thought. No-one expressed a clear view. No-one wanted responsibility for the decision. 'So we are not going to do it then?' asked Brown morosely. Everyone avoided his gaze.[90]

Less than a fortnight since the triumphalist Labour conference and his ill-judged tease about seeing the Queen, he was going to have to retreat. He asked Balls to walk with him in the garden to discuss how they might limit the damage.[91]

Most of the Cabinet were in a state of ignorance about what was happening inside Number 10. The majority of ministers assumed that they were heading for an election having heard nothing to the contrary from Downing Street. That Friday evening, I spoke to several senior members of the Cabinet, all of whom believed that Brown was now so far down the runway that it was too late to abort take-off. One senior minister said: 'You know I was always against this, I told you that at the party conference and I haven't changed my view, but Gordon has let it go so far that I can't see how he can back off now.'[92] Another senior minister who always regarded an early election as crazy believed it was too late to retreat because 'it would look like we were running scared.'[93] Labour MPs likewise assumed that 'it was a lock-down decision, there was no getting out of it, there was no rewind button to hit, we were off, the election was about to be called.'[94]

Senior Lib Dems and Conservatives thought so too.[95] David Cameron briefed staff at Tory party headquarters that Friday and told them the date would be 8 November.[96]

By breakfast-time on Saturday, Brown had absolutely concluded that he would not risk it. The next question was how to announce his climb-down to the world. In the middle of the morning, Damian McBride rang Barney Jones, the editor of the *Andrew Marr Show*, to fix an interview with the Prime Minister. Brown had got into a habit of doing pre-recorded interviews with Marr because Brown thought it was more controllable than a live interview. Jones warned McBride that it was perilous to record this interview on Saturday afternoon and expect its contents to remain secret until the next morning. 'If he is going to say what I think he is going to say, the idea that this will hold till Sunday is for the birds,' the BBC editor presciently protested to McBride. 'This is bad for us and bad for you.'[97] McBride rejected that advice and insisted that Brown would only do it as a pre-record. Jones and Marr were told by Number 10 that they were to share the Prime Minister's announcement with no-one else, not even colleagues at the BBC. To a member of the Number 10 communications team, this showed that Brown 'fundamentally didn't understand the media. He thinks it is about dividing and ruling with journalists as it is with everyone else. There was never a shift in the mindset from being a Chancellor who wants to be Prime Minister to being Prime Minister.'[98]

It was delusional to think that news of such magnitude could be managed like this in a 24/7 media environment. By Saturday morning, senior members of the Cabinet were in the loop and word of the cancellation of the election was reaching any political journalist with decent contacts. One troubled member of the Cabinet observed to me that morning: 'The big, precious thing Gordon had – his reputation for solidity – that will be eroded.'[99] 'We're going to take a terrible hit for this,' correctly predicted one of Brown's

Cabinet allies.[100] 'So much for Gordon, the great strategist,' sighed a third member of the Cabinet.[101]

The Tories got wind of it by Saturday lunchtime.[102] As Jones and his crew tried to slip in and out of Number 10 that afternoon to record the interview, rival broadcasters already had the scoop. Adam Boulton, the Political Editor of Sky, stood outside Downing Street venting his fury that a statement of such importance had been exclusively handed to the BBC and describing the retreat from an election as an abject humiliation. By mid-afternoon, the airwaves were already shrieking with the scorn of Opposition MPs and derision from some Labour ones as well. John McDonnell, the Labour MP for Hayes and Harlington, laid into the 'inexperienced testosterone-fuelled young men in Brown's team' who had 'presented the Tories with an open goal'.[103]

This was kind to the Prime Minister for it laid the blame on his courtiers rather than the king himself. That court started to devour itself as members of the inner circle attempted to dump culpability for the farrago on each other. To try to distance Brown and Balls from the debacle, Damian McBride spent Saturday afternoon on the phone to journalists of Sunday newspapers. He was spinning all the blame on to Douglas Alexander, Spencer Livermore and Ed Miliband. Several reporters were successfully persuaded that they were at fault for pushing Brown towards an election and then getting last-minute cold feet. As McBride rubbished other members of the Prime Minister's inner circle to reporters, he was caught in the act by Livermore who yelled at the spin doctor: 'What the fuck are you doing?' McBride retorted that he was obeying orders from Balls: 'I've been told to by Ed.' The two aides screamed at each other in front of civil servants until Sue Nye dragged them out of the room.[104]

Many relationships in the Brown court were permanently poisoned by this calamitous episode. Alexander and Miliband would never again trust Balls and McBride. An utterly disenchanted Livermore, who was least skilful in deflecting blame for a debacle that had many authors, left Number 10 six months later.

The fratricidal spinning and the interview fiasco added tactical foolishness to strategic stupidity. Gordon Brown was supposed to be the great chess player of British politics, the man who always thought a dozen moves ahead. The legend was exploded that weekend when the supposed grandmaster checkmated himself.

The fatal error was procrastination. Even Brown, never a man happy to confess to error, would later acknowledge 'maybe I should have done it earlier.'[105] He left the decision ten days too late. The time to decide was when he spoke on the Monday of the Labour conference. Had he ruled out an election at that point, he would have done so from a commanding position in the polls and presented himself as a statesmanlike leader rising above the temptation to make an opportunistic dash to the country. That was a context in which it would have been hard for his opponents or the media to accuse him of cowardice.

Had he chosen to announce an election in his conference speech, he could have dramatically changed the political dynamic. The Conservatives would have been thrown off balance. Their inheritance tax promise would have been less of a bombshell, submerged as it would have been in the wider election story. It would have looked less like a clever stroke and more like an act of desperation.

To this day, there is no agreement in Labour's ranks about whether an early election would have been a triumph or a disaster. The result of an election that never happened is unknowable. What we do know is that Labour was ahead in the polls in the autumn of 2007 and then fell behind, and for most of the time very badly behind, for the following two years. Had he gambled and won, Brown would have enjoyed a personal mandate along with up to five years to get through the oncoming economic downturn. What we also know is that many senior Tories feared they were about to go down to a fourth defeat. Michael Gove 'thought at the time that he had a very good chance of pulling it off. Labour had a strong chance of doing well and securing another mandate.'[106] One member of the Shadow Cabinet likened Brown's hesitation to Dunkirk, when Hitler delayed sending in his Panzers and gave the British army the chance to escape over the English Channel to fight another day.[107] Vince Cable of the Lib Dems believes: 'He should have gone for the election. He may have lost some seats, but he would have come back with real legitimacy and authority.'[108]

His closest allies saw the election debacle as the moment when it all began to unravel for the Prime Minister. 'The sense of it being on and it being off was a watershed looking back at it,' says Nick Brown. 'Because I think people felt that if there wasn't going to be an election, the speculation should have been damped down earlier than it was.'[109] Cabinet ministers agree that it was a terrible self-inflicted wound. In the words of Peter Hain: 'The mistake was to allow this particular train to leave the station in the first place when you weren't clear about the destination and that was a fiasco which did the Government a lot of damage.'[110]

The press on the Sunday and Monday after his retreat savagely questioned the Prime Minister's judgement and temperament. Iron Gordon was rechristened Bottler Brown. It wrecked the image of a commanding and straightforward leader that had been successfully cultivated during the first ninety days of his premiership. At his party conference, he was marketed with the slogan 'The Strength to Succeed', offering his character as the issue on which he asked to be judged. Of the many ironies about The Election That Never Was, one was that he had planned to fight it on his decisiveness and competence. Now he looked incompetent and indecisive. Brown had not really changed. For good and bad, he was still the man he had always been. It was perceptions of him that were utterly transformed. Overnight, his positives were flipped into negatives. It was like one of those sci-fi movies in which a mad scientist throws a switch and all the polarities are reversed. The strong Gordon who had fathered the nation through the summer crises flipped into the chicken Gordon who didn't dare face the country. The Prime Minister who presented himself as a spin-free break with the artifices of his predecessor was now seen as a manipulator obsessed with pursuing narrow partisan advantage. The self-described conviction politician was exposed as a furtively calculating politician. Worse, a calculator who miscalculated. The opportunity to have a new relationship with the electorate and start afresh was squandered. A year's work was undone in fourteen fatal days. The character question about Brown was revived. There was a reawakening of the Cabinet's misgivings about his temperament. His credibility was diminished in the eyes of the media. His Tory opponents were invigorated.

David Cameron was gifted a second honeymoon with journalists who again became respectfully interested in the Tory leader. Having won the game of election bluff, Cameron was positioned to scorn Brown for a 'humiliating retreat' and pretend that the Tories had always been confident about facing the country. 'I am disappointed,' he claimed. 'I wanted an election from the moment he walked into Downing Street because I don't believe he has a mandate and I want to take our arguments to the British people.'[111] Alex Salmond mocked Brown in Scots as 'the big feartie from Fife'.[112] On Monday morning, Jack Straw conceded the obvious: 'The opinion polls are one of the factors that we take into account. It would be ridiculous to suggest otherwise, and I don't think anybody is doing that.'[113]

One person did try to pretend otherwise: Gordon Brown. He made a painful position even more excruciating for himself by insisting that the retreat had nothing to do with the polls. Everyone found this incredible and would have been even more derisive had they known just how much secret polling he had commissioned in the weeks leading up to the debacle. At noon on Monday, he faced political journalists at a Number 10 news conference. Ruefully, he said: 'I think your weekend has been better than mine.'[114]

This did not win him their sympathy. Many of the journalists, just like the Labour Party, had been marched up the hill and down again by the

Grand Old Duke of Fife. His honeymoon with the media was definitively over. Reporters dropped any deference as they taunted Brown to admit that he had run away from the country because of the turn in the polls. They were mocking to his face when he claimed that he was so keen to 'deliver my vision' that he would have called off the election even if his pollsters had told him he would have won with a majority of 100. This untruth was so transparent that he set himself up for further laceration when he faced David Cameron in the Commons two days later. The Tory leader jeered: 'He's the first Prime Minister in history to flunk an election cos he thought he was going to win it!'[115]

The Tories fell about laughing. On the benches behind Brown, there was a funereal silence and matching faces.

The following day, Alistair Darling rose to deliver a pre-election financial package when there was no longer an election. On the Saturday that Brown called it off, the two men agreed that they should pull the inheritance tax cut hastily cobbled together in imitation of the Tories. In the words of a Treasury minister: 'We were told to slam everything into reverse.'[116] Only they couldn't. A dismayed Darling was told by his officials that it was too late: the Pre-Budget Report was already at the printers.[117] The Chancellor's wife would later confide to friends: 'It was not Alistair's PBR.' This was true: it had been dictated to the Chancellor by the Prime Minister. Before he moved into Number 10, Brown joked that he did not intend to emulate William Gladstone, who combined being both Prime Minister and Chancellor. It was becoming painfully apparent to Darling that this was precisely what Brown wanted to do. 'Alistair was practically camping in Number 10 in the days leading up to the PBR,' says a member of the Cabinet. 'Alistair was not at all happy.'[118]

When he addressed MPs, Darling made the announcement on inheritance tax with not a drop of conviction. The most he would subsequently say in defence of it was that it had 'some merit'[119] – damning with the faintest of praise what was supposed to be the centrepiece of his first big occasion as Chancellor. Sitting beside him in the Commons, the true author had a glint in his eye, but it was swiftly apparent that Brown had again been too tactical for his own good. Rather than trump his opponents with this manoeuvre, it looked as though Labour was lamely playing catch-up. Responding for the Conservatives, George Osborne largely ignored Darling and went straight for Brown. 'He talks about setting out his vision of the country, but he has to wait for us to tell him what it is,' the Shadow Chancellor mocked a glowering Prime Minister. 'We all know this report was brought forward so it could be the starting gun for the campaign – before you took the pistol and fired it into your foot.'[120]

It was not just the imitation inheritance tax cut that came under fire. The CBI and the trades unions were in rare unity when they condemned a bizarre new regime for capital gains tax which gave privileged treatment to wealthy partners in private equity funds and rewarded short-term speculators in antiques and fine wines while hitting ordinary workers in share ownership schemes and genuine entrepreneurs who had built up businesses over many years. The Government was soon in retreat.

Both the mini-Budget and the accompanying spending review were all too obviously cobbled together on the back of a (now redundant) campaign leaflet. Irwin Stelzer, a man of the right, observes: 'It let the Tories have the initiative. Gordon was the King of the Hill on tax policy and suddenly he's playing "me too" catch-up. That was a very bad policy decision and a bad political decision.'[121]

While the Conservatives claimed to be winning the battle of ideas, Labour MPs were uneasy that their Government was crudely apeing the other side. 'It looked like it was solely about political positioning and it looked like we were playing fast and loose with the electorate,' says Jon Cruddas. 'That was crystallised by the look in Gordon Brown's eye which signalled that it was all an exercise in smoke and mirrors.'[122]

The *Daily Telegraph*, which just a week before praised Brown as 'formidable', scorned a 'theme-free statement' that gave 'the overwhelming impression' that 'this Government is coming perilously close to running on empty.'[123]

Darling, who received a highly negative press for his first important outing as Chancellor, became angry with Brown for forcing him to do it, cross with himself for not standing up to the Prime Minister and determined to be stronger in future. The PBR was both a significant political error which reduced confidence in the Government's decision-making and a financial misjudgement which left them behind the curve of events. Expensive games were played with inheritance tax rather than taking measures to prepare for the oncoming economic storm already being signalled by the markets. Six months later, Darling acknowledged to me: 'If you were able to wind the clock back and do things differently, of course you would have done things differently. If I knew then what I know now, some things would be different.'[124]

After the debacle of the phantom election, what the Government most needed was to be calm, solid and purposeful. This episode instead made it look frantic, hollow and rudderless. Gordon Brown, the master of events just a month before, had now put himself at the mercy of them.

30. It Eats My Soul

Alistair Darling was at his home in Edinburgh on the morning of Saturday, 10 November, when the phone rang. His Private Secretary broke it to him that Her Majesty's Revenue and Customs had somehow lost two computer discs containing the confidential personal and banking information of more than 20 million people.

The Chancellor swore to himself. Darling instantly grasped that this was 'really very, very bad'[1] for a Government still reeling from the double debacles of the phantom election and the Pre-Budget Report.

The poor unfortunate with the unenviable task of briefing the Prime Minister was Gavin Kelly, the Deputy Chief of Staff at Number 10. Gordon Brown was so enraged that he leapt across the room. Grabbing a startled Kelly by the lapels of his jacket, Brown snarled: 'They're out to get me!'[2]

The timing of the data disc disaster, coming so soon after those other reverses, suggested to him a conspiracy against his premiership.[3] There was absolutely no evidence for that outside his paranoid imagination. He always had something of a victim mentality. Some friends believed it derived from failing to get the leadership in 1994 and others traced it further back to the long and agonising weeks in his youth when he was imprisoned in a hospital bed brooding on the injustices of life after the rugby accident which left him with only one functioning eye.

His horror about the discs was understandable. Discussing with allies how he planned to fight back from the October disasters and regain the respect of the country, Brown had told them that the key was to deliver a period of 'good government'.[4] Now what had happened? The personal information of nearly half the population had gone missing.

For ten days after the Prime Minister and Chancellor were alerted, they kept it secret from the public, first in the hope that a frantic search by HMRC and the police would turn up the discs and then to buy time to give the banks a chance to implement security measures. No-one ever did discover what happened to the lost discs. For all anyone knew, they might still be lost in the mail, being used by an unobservant official as a drinks coaster or in the hands of a criminal gang.

Finally, on Tuesday, 20 November, Darling publicly admitted to the loss in a statement to incredulous MPs. When a government is in trouble, the House of Commons often generates farmyard noises: exaggerated groans, stagey shouts, pantomime jeers. Much of this is synthetic sound and fury. Only a few days earlier, the latest bungle at the Home Office was exposed when it was revealed that 5,000 illegal immigrants had been cleared to work in security. One illegal was employed on the front desk at the Home Office. Even more astonishingly, another was given a job guarding the Prime Minister's car. Yet MPs were by now so inured to examples of administrative incompetence that there was no significant clamour for the resignation of the Home Secretary.

The lost discs were of a special category of calamity. The entire child benefit database had been placed on two unencrypted discs which a junior official then popped into a courier's envelope. The package was neither recorded nor registered. Genuine gasps of amazement greeted Darling when he admitted that Revenue and Customs had perpetrated the 'huge, massive, unforgivable mistake' of losing the confidential data of more than 9 million adults and 15 million children. 'It includes child benefit numbers, national insurance numbers and, where relevant, bank and building society account details,' said a visibly shaken Darling as Brown sat slumped behind him, face like thunder.[5] Haunted by the run on the Northern Rock, the Chancellor pleaded with those affected not to stampede to banks to close their accounts. This blunder was at the same time childish in its simplicity and gigantic in its scale. Every voter could instantly grasp what had been done wrong and how it might impact on millions of them. Sir Paul Gray, the Chairman of HMRC, took some of the heat off the Chancellor when he accepted responsibility for the scandal and resigned. Yet such a fundamental breach of faith between state and citizen was bound to reflect on the Government. Opposition MPs were quick to point accusing fingers at Brown's decision as Chancellor to order staff reductions after creating a monster department by merging Customs and Excise with the Inland Revenue. The press of all political complexions was lacerating. 'Mind-blowing incompetence', shrieked the *Daily Mail*.[6] '25 million victims', screamed the *Mirror*.[7]

Senior Cabinet members had no doubt that it was 'a serious debacle'.[8] Neither the Prime Minister nor the Chancellor was personally culpable for the loss of the discs, but it hurt the reputations of both. For the Chancellor, it came on top of continuing trouble at Northern Rock. Darling, whose pre-Treasury reputation was as a dull but safe minister, appeared to have become a magnet for trouble.

As for the Prime Minister, it accelerated the change in his media image from Capability Brown into Calamity Brown. To shudders inside Number 10, Steve Bell of the *Guardian* started to draw Brown in the grey underpants that the cartoonist had first used to exemplify the haplessness of John Major.

Some of the many enemies that Brown had made over the years began to break cover. Two days after the revelation of the discs disaster, five former Chiefs of the Defence Staff launched a co-ordinated attack on him for under-funding the armed forces and treating them with 'contempt' when men and women were being killed and maimed in Iraq and Afghanistan.[9] The Conservatives were enjoyably astonished to find that a poll deficit to Labour of ten points had flipped into a Tory lead of ten points in just eight weeks. 'I keep pinching myself to make sure I am not dreaming,' chuckled one senior Tory.[10]

Troubles were hitting the Government 'one after another after another'. Jack Straw 'got a sense that Gordon thought: "What else is going to come through the window?"'[11]

On the last weekend of November, the Prime Minister was flying back from a summit of the Commonwealth Heads of Government in Uganda. As his plane cruised above Africa, he sat in the first-class cabin, his usual black marker pen in hand, working on the speech he was going to deliver to the CBI on Monday. His officials briefed the accompanying media that it would scotch suggestions that Brown was a reincarnation of Major and his Government was lurching from blunder to scandal. Yet even before his plane touched down in Britain, the Prime Minister was aware of another torrent of trouble. On Saturday night he was alerted to an exclusive in the *Mail on Sunday* about David Abrahams, a Newcastle property developer.[12] This maverick figure was simultaneously ubiquitous and mysterious, a strange hybrid of Zelig and Walter Mitty. Abrahams had given Labour in excess of £630,000 over four years and was the party's third-most generous donor since Gordon Brown became leader. Abrahams had often used intermediaries to channel large sums to the party. His conduits included such unlikely high rollers as a Tyneside jobbing builder who drove a battered transit van and lived in an ex-council house. Other proxies were a secretary in Gateshead and a Tory-voting lollipop lady. Transparency was supposed to be the founding principle of the laws on party funding enacted by Labour. Concealment of a donor's identity was banned in Section 54 of the 2000 Act, while Section 56 requires parties to take all reasonable steps to establish the bona fides of their donors.[13] Abrahams threatened to sue anyone who linked his masked donations with a controversial planning application for a business park in prime land off the A1. He said: 'Any suggestion that I have made donations in exchange for favours is false and malicious.'[14] He also contended that he wasn't aware that he was at risk of breaking the law by using intermediaries. 'Mistakes were made, of course, and no-one is denying that,' he later wrote. 'I donated money to the Labour Party through intermediaries because of a desire for anonymity, not secrecy.'[15]

His 'anonymity' was now blown as the exposure of these donations dominated the front pages and news bulletins. The Electoral Commission launched inquiries into potential breaches of the law. It also became apparent that the millionaire was not always shy of the limelight. Abrahams was a well-known figure in Labour circles in the north-east and had once entertained ambitions to be a parliamentary candidate. He had met Gordon Brown and enjoyed a front-row seat for Tony Blair's farewell in Sedgefield earlier in the year.

Labour had hoped that it had heard the last of donations scandals with Blair's departure, only for another one to erupt less than six months into Brown's premiership. Some of Blair's friends derived bitter satisfaction from the spectacle of Brown, the self-styled possessor of a 'moral compass' who advertised himself as so ethically superior to his predecessor, floundering in the mire. The early rhetoric of Brown's premiership came back to bite him. By claiming to be a sweeping new broom who would clean up and restore trust in politics, he had issued an invitation to the media to take any transgression and turn it into an enormous scandal that proved he hadn't kept the promise. 'It's a nightmare,' said one of Brown's closest ministerial allies. 'People are very edgy because they don't know what else is going to come out.'[16] Brown called a news conference at Number 10 with the principal aim of establishing his own innocence and casting the blame on to colleagues. 'I knew nothing of these donations,' he declared. 'I had no knowledge until Saturday night, neither did I have any knowledge of this practice.'[17] It was true that Brown was hyper-sensitive on the whole issue of donations. The party's fund-raisers complained that they were finding it more difficult to attract money because the Prime Minister was reluctant to make himself available to potential donors or to entertain them at Number 10 and Chequers.[18] In his desperation not to be tainted by the Abrahams Affair, Brown overruled party officials by insisting that all the money be returned immediately. He told reporters that these things 'were going on for some time'.[19] In other words: blame Blair.

Harriet Harman was a recipient – an unknowing and innocent one, she said – of an Abrahams donation to her deputy leadership campaign. Her partner, Jack Dromey, was the party Treasurer who did not know the source of the money for the second scandal in a row, even when some of the cash was banked by the campaign team of his wife. It took seven attempts by reporters at the Number 10 news conference to get the Prime Minister to say that he still had confidence in Harman. She reacted by letting it be known that she would not go down without a fight. Dromey angrily claimed that there had been 'complete concealment' and described the use of conduits as 'absolutely wrong'.[20] Her camp then revealed that the idea of getting a donation from one of Abrahams's intermediaries had come from within Brown's campaign team. The murk got even thicker when it emerged that Jon Mendelsohn, Brown's own election fund-raiser, had discovered the hidden payments after taking up his job in September and discussed his concerns about it with the party's General Secretary.[21]

Brown was frantic to put as much distance between himself and the donations as he possibly could. In an endeavour to make himself sound the most outraged of all, he declared: 'What happened over these donations that had not been lawfully declared is completely unacceptable.'[22]

By making that pronouncement, Brown was covering his own back at the price of making a nonsense of his own internal inquiry. That statement also ensured that an investigation would have to be conducted by the police and left the party's General Secretary to swing in the wind. Peter Watt resigned. On his later account, Brown had promised to 'look after' Watt when the General Secretary took the fall only then to betray him twenty-four hours later at the news conference. 'There was huge pressure for someone to take the rap. I knew that elected politicians were going to dive for cover. There was no way Gordon or Harriet were going to stand by me. They made a choice that I was expendable,' said Watt. 'Publicly, Gordon talks about values and his moral compass, but actually the way he conducts himself behind the scenes is anything but that – it's brutal.'[23]

The Metropolitan Police launched another long investigation into Labour donations. In a further echo of the Blair years, yet again it did not result in any prosecutions. Peter Hain was forced to resign as Work and Pensions Secretary in January – the first Cabinet casualty of Brown's premiership – when the late declaration of £100,000 in donations to his failed deputy leadership campaign was referred to the police. No charges followed. Hain was later cleared by Parliament of any 'intention to deceive', but rebuked for a 'serious and substantial' breach of the rules.[24]

The damage of the Abrahams Affair was done in the court of public opinion. Jack Straw described it as 'mind-blowing'. Alan Johnson called it 'a lousy and very depressing week for the party'.[25] Once again, Labour looked as though it had an appallingly casual attitude towards laws passed by its own Government. Voters were left with the impression that the whole business of party fund-raising was by definition sleazy.

Gordon Brown's morale sank lower. He privately groaned: 'For this to happen to me, it eats my soul.'[26] Number 10 lived on shredded nerves. 'It was one damn thing after another,' says one senior aide. 'We just didn't know what was going to hit us next.'[27] Visitors to Downing Street found the staff in 'shellshock' and asking: 'How can this have happened to us? We're still the same people who were very popular two months ago and now we're besieged.'[28]

It accelerated the profound psychological descent of Brown since the election debacle. One of his most senior and longest serving aides says: 'He closed in on himself. He went to ground. He was a lonely figure.'[29] His inner demons gnawed at him with the fear that perhaps he was not up to being Prime Minister. 'It's my fault, it's all my fault,' he self-flagellated in front of some intimates.[30] He was consumed with remorse and guilt for the mistakes he made over the phantom election. The fit of paranoia with Gavin Kelly over the data discs was just one of many manifestations of his raging moods. He became even more temperamental about his coverage in the media, obsessively monitoring the press headlines and the prominence he was getting in television news bulletins. If his speeches and initiatives were ignored or got less coverage than David Cameron, he would 'lash out' at those around him.[31]

A dark pall descended on the whole building. An official noted that 'he surrounded himself with people who amplified his weaknesses rather than compensated for them. There was no camaraderie. It was a quite depressive, introverted, dysfunctional coterie.'[32] Long-standing members of his inner circle had endured Brown's temper for years and accepted the tantrums as part of the price of working for a complex man they admired. One veteran of his court says: 'Over the years, I've had all sorts of things thrown at me – newspapers, pens, Coke cans.'[33] This sort of behaviour was a shock to staff at Number 10 who had been accustomed to the courteous manners of Tony Blair and John Major. 'Gordon's mood was absolutely black the whole time. He was in a permanent state of rage,' observes one civil servant. 'Staff were afraid of him because he was always shouting at people, being unpleasant, constantly blaming people for things going wrong. He never had a nice word to say to anybody.'[34] Another official agrees: 'He was astonishingly rude to people.'[35] Civil servants were shocked by his habit of abruptly getting up and leaving meetings when officials were in the middle of speaking. He became notorious within the building for shouting at the duty clerks, bawling at the superbly professional staff who manned the Number 10 switchboard and blowing up at the affectionately regarded 'Garden Girls', so called because the room from which they provide Downing Street's secretarial services over-looks the garden. When one of the secretaries was not typing fast enough for an angrily impatient Prime Minister, he turfed the stunned garden girl out of her chair and took over the keyboard himself.[36] Word of these incidents reached the alarmed ears of the Cabinet Secretary, Sir Gus O'Donnell, who was becoming increasingly anxious about the Prime Minister's behaviour.[37] The Cabinet Secretary was so concerned about the garden girl episode that he made his own inquiries into it.[38]

Though the worst excesses of the Prime Minister's temper were kept hidden, it was inevitable that some accounts began to filter out across White-hall and then into the media, which reported stories about mobile phones being hurled in fury and the furniture being kicked.

One civil servant who applied for a position at Number 10 was asked at the interview whether he could cope with 'extreme verbal abuse' and violence done to objects. The civil servant was so scared by the description of what it could be like to work for the Prime Minister that he withdrew his application.[39]

Wednesday was an especially hazardous day to be working in close prox-imity to the Prime Minister. He was getting pulped at the dispatch box by David Cameron with a regularity which Labour MPs found excruciating to watch.

'For ten years, you plotted and schemed to have this job – and for what?' the Leader of the Opposition ridiculed him during one typical encounter that autumn. 'No conviction, just calculation; no vision, just vacuum. How long are we going to have to wait before the past makes way for the future?'

Brown responded by complaining that the Tory leader had once promised 'an end to the Punch and Judy show'.[40] So Cameron had. But it sounded painfully lame for Brown to protest about being punched too hard. He became increasingly obsessive about preparing for these clashes. The prep team would meet at Number 10 on Tuesday evening for a preliminary discus-sion about what might come up at PMQs and how he should handle it. They then reconvened on Wednesday morning. In rehearsals, Ed Miliband played the part of David Cameron. This was not a role to which he was ideally suited because Miliband was not temperamentally equipped to be brutal with his boss.[41] Geoff Hoon, the Chief Whip, was another regular member of the prep team for PMQs. One Wednesday morning, having had an early engagement that day, Hoon arrived at Number 10 at breakfast-time. Enter-ing the prep room, he expected to have a long wait for the others only to find that Gordon Brown was already there, sitting alone, scribbling notes with his black marker pen, worrying away about how he was going to handle that day's high noon with Cameron.[42]

Brown had been 'ferociously hard-working' since childhood, says his friend Murray Elder.[43] The eternal scholarship boy responded to adversity by thinking that he would find the answer to his problems by labouring even harder. He went to bed later and got up earlier, working even more fiercely in the belief that this was the way to get on top of things. He did not grasp that what he most needed to do was to learn to delegate and to prioritise. Sarah Brown despaired that her husband could not be persuaded to stop. 'I used to believe Gordon when he said he wasn't a workaholic,' Sarah sighed over a lunch with one friend. 'I don't now.'[44]

Members of the Cabinet began to worry that 'he is going to make himself ill if he carries on like this.'[45] Jacqui Smith told him to his face that it was a mistake not to have a summer holiday and 'he ought to back off and have a bit of a rest.'[46]

Brown found being Prime Minister much harder than either he or his acolytes had imagined. It is a short walk from Number 11 to Number 10, but a giant leap for one man. 'There was a belief that as soon as Tony went everything would be fine', which 'led to there not being as much preparation as could have been done and not enough recognition of the sheer challenge of being Prime Minister'.[47] The Brown team had been adept at destabilising guerrilla warfare against Blair. When they were the insurgents, they could pick the issues where they wanted a fight and ignore others. This left them underequipped for the very different demands of being responsible for an entire government and having to battle on many fronts at once.

As Chancellor, Brown had often been able to do his Macavity trick of disappearing in a crisis. As Prime Minister, he could no longer play the mysterious cat. There is no hiding place at Number 10. Jack Straw, a Cabinet colleague broadly sympathetic to Brown at this stage, thought that he was still 'feeling his way into the job' as he discovered that it was 'very different' to and 'much more multi-faceted' than being Chancellor.[48] He was on a steep learning curve. But since experience was supposed to be the reason he got the job, inexperience was not an alibi Brown could ever use. He sounded surprised to make the discovery that 'hundreds of things pass your desk every week'.[49] He did not excel at multi-tasking. His preference and his forte were to concentrate on one big thing at a time. He had largely been able to do that at the Treasury, where he could focus on the four or five major events of a Chancellor's year. Prime Ministers can get hit by four or five major events in a month, even a week. 'As Prime Minister, you are bombarded with things, everything happens in real time,' says one Downing

Street official who closely observed both Blair and Brown.[50] Jack Straw agrees: 'As Prime Minister, you have crises coming out of a clear blue sky to a degree you don't as Chancellor.'[51] Jon Cruddas, who worked at Number 10 before he became an MP, believes Brown underestimated 'the sheer velocity of decision-making' required of a Prime Minister.[52]

Torrential volumes of business flow through Downing Street, much of it demanding instant attention. Civil servants at the Treasury had adapted to and covered for Brown's chaotic and intermittently intense way of making decisions. Officials at Number 10 and the Cabinet Office were at a loss how to deal with his working habits. Confronted with difficult decisions, one senior civil servant found: 'He just delays and delays, thinking he will get a better set of options later. But quite often the options just get worse.'[53]

This was exacerbated because Brown was so power-hugging. Geoff Hoon summarises it well: 'One of the great ironies of Tony and Gordon is that both of them didn't have any time for ministers. The difference is that Tony broadly let you get on with it. He wasn't much interested unless something went wrong. In contrast, Gordon wants to interfere in everything. He's temperamentally incapable of delegating responsibility. So he drives himself demented.'[54]

That autumn, one of Brown's officials told me: 'You can get nothing agreed unless you can get thirty seconds in front of Gordon.'[55] Even a Prime Minister as fanatically workaholic as Brown had only so many thirty seconds in his day. He could not hope to rule successfully by micro-managing every last detail of government. 'There's no number of hours you can work to solve the problems that come on a Prime Minister's desk,' notes Irwin Stelzer. 'Getting into the office at five o'clock in the morning ain't going to do it. There was a floundering.'[56]

His chronic aversion to delegating was deadly when combined with being slow to make decisions himself. 'Gordon is cautious by nature,' says Alistair Darling.[57] In the words of Harriet Harman: 'Gordon likes to think his way round all the problems.'[58] Murray Elder agrees: 'He wants a lot of information before he makes decisions and he wants to know every angle.'[59] As a result, he had a tendency to analyse to the point of paralysis.

'Gordon is somebody who is cautious in his decision-making,' concurs Jack Straw. 'Tony was a much more instinctive decision-maker. With Tony you had the reverse problem that you'd find there was a decision and then he had to think of the arguments in favour of it.'[60]

Civil servants noted the contrast in prime ministerial style and put it this way to the veteran Whitehall watcher Sue Cameron:

When John Major was in Number 10 and there was a big decision to be taken, he would order papers and he would read through them, often quite late into the night. The next morning, he'd make a decision. When Blair was in Number 10, he'd tell his civil servants to read the papers and give him a shortlist of options and in the morning he'd make a decision. With Gordon, he sends for the papers, he reads them late into the night and then the next morning he sends for more papers.[61]

That was compounded by the serious flaws in the structure and staffing of Number 10. No-one around Brown had enough of his trust or sufficient clout to force him to make decisions or to take them for him. 'It was a set-up that reinforced Gordon's weaknesses.'[62]

People were also too scared to give him advice. 'His nearest and dearest all seemed to be physically intimidated by him,' says one civil servant who observed him with Spencer Livermore, Ed Miliband and Damian McBride. 'They were very tense around him. They were very reluctant to tell him when he was wrong. None of his people liked to contradict him.'[63]

One of his closest allies in the Cabinet believes that Brown had 'got into bad habits' in his final years at the Treasury.[64] Murray Elder agrees that 'one of the difficulties was that on so many subjects people would behave in the same way as they had done when he was Chancellor and just walk in and speak to him. Actually, you need more structure than that.'[65] One of Brown's most loyal supporters in the Cabinet described the state of Number 10 as 'chaos'.[66] Nor was he good at masking it from opponents, who could tell that he was 'just overwhelmed by the pressures of being Prime Minister'.[67]

Even the basic housekeeping wasn't being done. Letters from important people, including MPs, went unanswered. An aide to one senior minister lamented that when they called Number 10 'no-one answers the phone.'[68] There were cases of foreign embassies not being told whether a visiting leader was going to be granted a meeting with the Prime Minister and dates being muddled up.[69] The French Prime Minister offered to come over for the opening of the splendid new Eurotunnel station at St Pancras in November. The Foreign Office was excited, but could not get Brown interested and there was a gratuitous snub to the 'very offended' French.[70]

Routine decisions took weeks to process. Cabinet ministers and their senior officials began to speak with extraordinary vehemence about what one called 'the sheer dysfunctionality' of Number 10.[71] They did not know the half of it. On the account of one civil servant: 'However chaotic it looked from the outside, it was a billion times worse inside.'[72]

The building was in a state of near anarchy. 'Gordon was wandering around Number 10, talking to people, e-mailing people, getting lots of little bits of advice from different people. What he wasn't getting was that advice synthesised by somebody whose responsibility was to think strategically.'[73]

What most shocked those who had admired him as Chancellor was his failure to convey any clear sense of purpose for his Government. His first Queen's Speech was widely regarded, on both right and left, as a damp squib. John Kampfner, the editor of the *New Statesman*, lamented: 'There is no sense at all that Gordon Brown knows the extent to which he really wishes to change Britain and if so where.'[74] One senior civil servant confided: 'At least with Blair, I always knew what the story was. With Brown, I don't. I don't know where we stand.'[75]

It was always a Blairite critique of Brown that he was a poor communicator. In his first phase at Number 10, his leaden style appealed to some as a refreshing change from the flashy thespianism of Tony Blair. As time went on, it became increasingly evident that Brown lacked the range of presentational skills required to be a successful modern leader. He seemed incapable of telling the electorate a persuasive story.

That was linked to his propensity to freeze when confronted with a dilemma. Labour's refusal to make good on the manifesto promise of a referendum on the European treaty was exciting the predictable animosity of the phobic press. The *Sun* and the *Daily Mail*, who scared Brown even more than they had Blair before him, were especially vitriolic. Brown's response was not to take on the argument, but to hope that it would go away if he kept his head down for long enough. Jim Murphy, the able Europe Minister, was instructed to take the legislation ratifying the treaty through Parliament by making the proceedings as tedious as possible. David Miliband attempted to take on the opponents with a speech in favour of the EU only for Brown to order the Foreign Secretary to delete the most positive passages. Number 10 then briefed the phobic press that it had cut off the knees of the Foreign Secretary. This was the sort of gratuitous aggression that poisoned Brown's relations with colleagues.

The Portuguese laid on a grand signing ceremony in Lisbon in December. Brown agonised over whether he should attend. His presence would give the phobic press further ammunition, but to stay away would offend European allies. He resolved his dilemma by trying to split the difference. He did fly to Lisbon, but timed his arrival late so that he missed the ceremony and the celebratory leaders' lunch. This only succeeded in infuriating everybody. His European peer group were annoyed, while he attracted the scorn of both pro-Europeans and anti-Europeans in Britain.

During his long agitation to take over at Number 10, Brown privately attacked Blair and Mandelson for practising 'triangulation', the political tactic pioneered by Bill Clinton of trying to be popular by occupying a position equidistant between your party's position and that of its opponents. It was a recipe, he used to argue, for being pushed ever rightwards and meant that Labour could never build a long-term consensus around its true values.[76] Yet Brown now habitually practised the politics of splitting the difference and did it with such lack of finesse that he made himself popular with no-one.

He made a similar error a few months later when confronted with a dilemma about the Olympics. In the build-up to the Beijing Games, the famous torch was making its way around the world to the accompaniment of protests against China's atrocious record on human rights. The torch was bodyguarded by a phalanx of Chinese security men in tracksuits. This created an especially delicate situation for the British Government because London was the host of the subsequent Olympics. Confusing signals came out of Number 10 about whether Brown planned to attend the games in Beijing or boycott them. When the torch reached London, the question was whether it should be allowed up Downing Street for a photo opportunity. Advised that a refusal would cause ructions with the Chinese, Brown let it come to his front door. The mistake was to permit the shell-suited squad of Chinese heavies through the gates as well. He stood by the torch, but not touching it, surrounded on his own street by the Chinese goons. Says one of the ministers involved on the day: 'It was total disaster.'[77]

These presentational pratfalls were the symptoms of something more profound. The Government lacked a coherent programme and a compelling narrative. One member of the Cabinet lamented: 'The dots aren't being joined up.'[78] Others feared that the problem was even more fundamental: there were no dots to join. 'He hasn't got a plan,' Tony Blair sighed to one of his staff shortly before he handed over the premiership.[79] The absence of a plan was becoming stark. One of Brown's senior aides later confessed: 'We had a strategy for the transition, but not a strategy for government.'[80] Another long-time associate and admirer was driven to the sad conclusion that 'maybe Gordon used up all his ideas when he was at the Treasury.'[81]

It became a constant theme of conversations with Cabinet ministers of all varieties – Brownite, Blairite and neither – that the Government was adrift. This failure to establish a clear sense of direction made them more vulnerable to both opponents and bolts from the blue. 'What disappointed me and I think disappointed a lot of people was that when he'd actually got to the top there wasn't a great deal of steam left,' comments Vince Cable, the Deputy Leader of the Lib Dems. 'He seemed to have run out of ideas, seemed to have run out of big projects and that by itself makes you at the mercy of events.'[82] Cable had known Brown for longer than most of the Prime Minister's colleagues in the Cabinet. He was a fellow Labour council-lor in Glasgow in the 1970s and a contributor to *The Red Papers for Scotland*, the first political tract that Brown published as a young man. Brown regarded Cable with more respect than most opponents. So he felt it particularly sharply when the Lib Dem produced the most piercing jibe about the tragic decay of his premiership.

Standing in as leader of his party – the Lib Dems were in the throes of yet another leadership contest – Cable rose at Prime Minister's Questions: 'The House has noted the Prime Minister's remarkable transformation in the last few weeks from Stalin to Mr Bean.'[83] The rest was lost in howls of laughter. Members of the Cabinet, lined up along the frontbench beside Brown, struggled not to join the merriment. Hazel Blears found it 'a pretty good joke'.[84] Jack Straw says: 'It was a good moment for Vince Cable, it was a very good line.' The Justice Secretary only managed to suppress guffaws because 'I've got used to not showing my emotions at Prime Minister's Ques-tions.'[85] Several members of the Cabinet came up to the Lib Dem afterwards. They did not upbraid him for being so rude at the expense of their leader, but told him 'they'd rather enjoyed the joke.'[86]

Vince Cable was the temporary head of a party which had gone through three leaders in less than two years. It was a new nadir when Gordon Brown could be tormented by the mockery of a Lib Dem.

At the end of the year, the Prime Minister retreated to his home in Fife to nurse his wounds in the company of some of his oldest friends. His summer honeymoon now seemed to belong to a long-gone era. It had turned into an awful autumn and then a wicked winter. He was stripped of the aura of invincibility which secured him an uncontested coronation and then cloaked him for the early weeks in Number 10. The multiple accidents and errors which began with the election debacle reminded people that this was a rusty government presided over by a flawed man who had been at the centre of power for more than a decade. Labour's position was now as troubled, if not more so, as it was in the last days of Tony Blair. Gordon Brown was a wounded and often ridiculed Prime Minister.

Hogmanay is an important night for most Scots, but there was little air of celebration at the Prime Minister's home in North Queensferry. Brown was not up at midnight to see in the New Year. He took himself off to bed at ten.[87]

31. The Penny Drops

Whenever the Prime Minister was anxious, one of the first people to get a call was his namesake and veteran of the long march to Number 10, Nick Brown. The Deputy Chief Whip was on holiday in Cuba on Sunday, 17 February, when the phone rang.

'We're going to nationalise Northern Rock,' the Prime Minister confided to this old ally, a Newcastle MP with a keen constituency interest in the fate of the stricken Geordie bank. His friend in Havana saw the funny side. 'Gordon, I'm in Cuba,' laughed Nick Brown. 'Here, all the banks are nationalised.' The Prime Minister growled down the line: 'It's only temporary.'[1]

Gordon Brown had never envisaged himself as a political cousin of Fidel Castro. Apprehensive of any act which might be interpreted as a lurch leftwards, he spent months searching for an alternative to nationalising the wrecked mortgage bank. 'The fear was that this would be tantamount to Gordon Brown hitting the rewind button to circa 1983.'[2]

The Rock caused many weeks of fright within Government after it was bailed out with an emergency loan from the Bank of England the previous autumn.[3] Despite the Government guarantees to depositors, savers continued to flee the bank whenever it made alarming headlines. In November 2007, there was another run on the Rock, this time a 'silent run' when customers stampeded to remove their money via the internet.[4] At a withdrawal rate of £200 million a day, the bank would have no money by the end of the year. The share price whipsawed violently as hedge funds bought in and out with a view to making a quick killing. Trading was suspended three times. On one especially nerve-jangling day, Alistair Darling came into his office in the morning to be greeted by a deputation of senior civil servants. 'How bad is it?' asked the Chancellor. 'Pretty bad,' responded John Kingman. 'We're not standing on the window ledge, but we're keeping the window open just in case.'[5] By year's end, the Treasury's exposure was escalating towards £50 billion and the Rock had become a deadweight on the Government. Senior figures at the Bank of England were growing 'pretty cranky' and began to brief that 'there was a kind of paralysis at the Government level in handling this crisis.'[6] John McFall, the Labour chairman of the Treasury select committee, concluded that 'a number of weeks were wasted' in a futile search for a private sector rescue when it was already clear 'there wasn't a deal on the table.'[7] The vacillating Tories never produced a plausible solution, but that didn't stop them flaying the Government for failing to bring the saga to a conclusion. The Lib Dems and some Labour MPs said the Government should just get on and nationalise it. It was not just on the left that public ownership was seen as the clean solution to the most ignominious episode in modern British banking history. Sir Gus O'Donnell, the Cabinet Secretary who had previously been Permanent Secretary at the Treasury, shared the view that they should go for public ownership.[8] Even such an unrevolutionary organ as the *Economist*, where they worshipped Adam Smith not Karl Marx, advocated nationalisation.

Both Prime Minister and Chancellor remained 'very nervous about nationalisation'.[9] They were fearful of the n-word because of its associations with the 1970s and for fear of the response from the right-wing press. Brown's friend Paul Dacre, the editor of the *Daily Mail*, ran a leader in January declaring: 'The dramatic step of nationalisation would be the day when Labour's hard-won reputation for economic competence is finally lost.'[10] Cabinet colleagues noted that Brown didn't want people 'saying it's Old Labour going for nationalisation'.[11]

As a result, Alistair Darling 'moved heaven and earth to try and find a buyer'.[12] John Kingman, the Treasury's Second Permanent Secretary, headed the effort to secure a private sector buyer who would take the sinking Rock off their hands. Tension between the Prime Minister and Chancellor increased as Brown constantly went round Darling and directly badgered Kingman for progress reports.[13]

The most flamboyant bidder was Sir Richard Branson, a man who could rarely see a spotlight without wanting to be at the centre of it. He presented himself as the Rock's bearded saviour and won 'preferred bidder' status even though he did not have a banking licence and his operation, Virgin Money, was small in comparison with the bank he sought to acquire. The Government's negotiating position was compromised by the knowledge in the markets that ministers were frantic to avoid public ownership. 'That was obvious to potential bidders, which gave them an incentive to play endless negotiating games,' says one senior Treasury official.[14] Pressing on Brown and Darling from another direction was the political imperative to be able to present a deal as reasonable for the taxpayer. Howls of outrage greeted the Chancellor when he presented MPs with a scheme to use government bonds to pay off the bank's debts. Vince Cable of the Lib Dems led the criticism that this had the potential to leave any profits with a new owner while saddling the taxpayer with all the risk.

The aversion to nationalisation was eventually outweighed by fright at the idea of doing a deal which might hand a windfall to Branson of billions of pounds. That would set them up for a terrible hammering from both the Opposition parties and Labour MPs. 'The conditions got worse and worse and worse,' Darling later reflected. 'You just couldn't sell a bank at that time. The people who were interested were offering to take it off our hands at a fraction of what it was worth.'[15]

He told Brown: 'There's no way I can stand up in the House of Commons and justify selling the bank to a private sector buyer in these conditions.' Darling feared he would be 'lynched'.[16]

By mid-February, they finally concluded that nationalisation – the course they had been least keen on – was their only realistic option. The Chancellor phoned the news to a disgruntled Branson.[17] He and Brown then spent that Sunday lunchtime discussing how the Chancellor would present it at a hurriedly arranged news conference that afternoon. Brown pressed for Darling to emphasise that it would not be like the nationalisations of old. The Chancellor told the reporters summoned to the Treasury that the Government would be an 'arm's length' owner, not interfering in the day-to-day management, with a view to returning it to the private sector as soon as possible.[18]

It had taken five tortuous months to get there. For a long time afterwards, Treasury officials at the heart of the process were still shuddering over 'the horror of Northern Rock'.[19] It presented the Government with one of those nasty political dilemmas where the choice is between the unpalatable and the unappetising. Letting the damaged bank go bankrupt would have cost the taxpayer an estimated £7 billion.[20] That would also have been a major blow in Labour's north-eastern heartland. In fragile financial markets, there was no private buyer willing to make rapid repayment of the loans from the taxpayer. All the bidders wanted the Treasury to underwrite them for a long time, allowing a new owner to profit from any upside while the taxpayer bore the risk of the downside. This left nationalisation as the lesser of evils.

For both political reasons and to protect the Government against any legal action by shareholders, they felt they had to exhaust the search for a private sector rescue before they went for public ownership.[21] But the time it took to get there was taken as confirmatory evidence that Brown's Government was characterised by dither.

At least the nationalisation, when it was finally decided upon, was quick.

In the week after Darling's announcement, and with the co-operation of the Opposition, the legislation taking the bank into public ownership was sped through the Commons. When it passed its final stages late on the night of Thursday, 21 February, some old comrades on the Labour benches sang a chorus of the 'Red Flag'. They were being ironic: they knew the Government had not acted out of a sudden conversion to command economy socialism, but because there was simply no alternative.[22]

The failure to find a private sector buyer rang alarm bells deep within the Government. It was this saga that began to open their eyes to the precariousness of the entire banking system. In April, Brown summoned the chiefs of the major banks to a breakfast at Number 10. The bankers were insistent that the problem was market liquidity not their balance sheets. 'But what about your losses?' asked the Prime Minister. 'What about capital?' Afterwards, he expressed his frustration to Yvette Cooper and Shriti Vadera. 'Why are the bank executives not admitting their losses?' Vadera, who knew the City, responded: 'They don't want to admit it, because they'll be fired.'[23]

Northern Rock had a reasonably 'good book' of mortgages, 2 million customers and a large presence in the high street. In normal times, it ought to have been an attractive purchase for one of the other banks, especially when the Government was on bended knee to find a buyer. When no other big institution was prepared to make an offer for it, even on terms whose generosity reflected the Government's desperation not to nationalise, Alistair Darling and his senior civil servants concluded that this had to be because the finances of the other banks were in a much worse state than they were publicly admitting. In the words of one of those officials: 'When none of them would buy Northern Rock, our view of the world changed. It was then that we began to realise that things must be very bad indeed.'[24] Darling began to fear that the Rock was 'the tip of a very nasty iceberg'.[25]

The Chancellor came into the Treasury one Monday morning to tell his officials that he had been in his local supermarket in Edinburgh at the weekend and overheard two elderly shoppers talking about the 'sub-prime crisis'. That was one of many signs that the credit crunch was beginning to bite on real voters. Mortgages became much harder to come by and the terms demanded were much stricter than during the bubble years. Property prices began to fall at the fastest rate since the crash of the early 1990s.[26] Repossession rates were rising, retail sales were falling, consumer confidence was slumping and increasing numbers of businesses issued profit warnings.

There was another distress signal from the world's unstable financial system in mid-March. Bear Stearns, America's fifth-largest bank, collapsed into the arms of JP Morgan for the fire sale price of $2 a share. Mervyn King was becoming so anxious that he was getting over his earlier preoccupation with moral hazard. The Governor was 'very badly scarred by his late reaction to Northern Rock'.[27] He set up a new 'special liquidity scheme' to allow British banks to swap mortgage-backed securities for Treasury bonds.

Darling presented what he called a 'stability Budget'. The dull title endeavoured to make a virtue of the fact that it was a do-little Budget because his room for manoeuvre was cramped by lack of money and the mistakes made the previous autumn. He dutifully rehearsed Brown's line that 'Britain is better placed than other economies to withstand the slowdown in the global economy.'[28] Darling lowered the Treasury's previous forecasts for growth, though the Government's claims for the outlook were still far too optimistic in the view of many analysts who could see the storm clouds massing on the horizon.

There had been a mild recovery in Labour's opinion poll rating before the Budget. Afterwards, the trend reversed and the Tories began to stretch their advantage. John McFall explains: 'There was nothing that shone out of the Budget for people.'[29] The fault did not lie with any particular measure announced by Darling. It was the overall impact of a gloomy Budget which concentrated voters' minds on the deteriorating state of the economy and crystallised fears about their livelihoods. 'Labour's vote went over the cliff.'[30]

Further tension was twisted into the relationship between Numbers 10 and 11 as Brown's acolytes blamed Darling for being undynamic and downbeat. Brown was especially furious when increases to car tax attracted a bad press. The Prime Minister raged to his aides that the Chancellor hadn't warned him, an exquisitely ironic complaint when for years he had concealed the contents of Budgets from Tony Blair. 'It was a very bad patch with Darling.'[31] Brown complained that Darling was failing to establish himself as a strong figure in the City or the country. There was some truth in this, but whose fault was it when he was constantly second-guessed by his next-door neighbour? There was a growing rumble from within Number 10 that the Government needed a bold and aggressive Chancellor who would take the fight to the Tories. The corridors of Whitehall began to whisper with suggestions that he would be replaced at the Treasury by Ed Balls, Brown's first choice.

Yet it was not Darling's first Budget that posed the most significant risk to the Government in the spring of 2008. The truly explosive danger lay in Brown's final Budget the year before, the one in which he abolished the 10p income tax band to finance a headline-chasing cut in the basic rate from 22p to 20p. That finale to his Chancellorship was designed to impress Labour

MPs with his cleverness and prove to the right-wing press that he could be as friendly to Middle Britain as Tony Blair. Brown had done this at the cost of planting a time bomb under his own premiership which was now about to detonate.

He had been dismissive of the red flags raised by those who spotted that this tax change was going to hit many of the less well-off when they had to start paying tax at 20 rather than 10 per cent. When Alistair Darling first arrived at the Treasury, his officials briefed the new Chancellor about the consequences of the tax change and gave him the same warnings they had delivered to Brown before he scrapped the 10p band.[32] As Darling later revealed to me: 'I became Chancellor and you "open the books", if you like, and you say: "Look, what are the problems we're facing?" I knew this was a problem.'[33]

More than 5 million people would be potentially worse off when the 10p band disappeared at the beginning of the new tax year on 6 April. Darling raised the issue with Brown in the months beforehand, but the Prime Minister pushed him away. The difficulties were minor, Brown argued, and they could be fixed by tweaking tax credits to compensate the losers. So the chance to defuse this bomb was not taken in the March Budget. Alistair Darling never tried to pretend that some people would not lose out, though the Chancellor could not publicly call it a mistake, because it was his next-door neighbour's mistake. Gordon Brown, in the words of one senior member of the Cabinet, remained 'in denial'.[34]

At his worst, Brown's decision-making process was almost endless prevarication followed by almost absolute inflexibility. That was to be his undoing over the 10p tax rate. The vast majority of Labour MPs voted for the tax change the previous year, but by the spring of 2008 they were suddenly alert to what it meant for many of their least affluent constituents. By late March, with days to go before the change began to eat into the pay packets of low earners and payments to poorer pensioners, backbenchers were in a highly agitated state. They were waking up to the fact that an already unpopular Government was about to take money out of the pockets of millions of the less well-off.

On Monday, 31 March, the mood among Labour MPs was restless when they crowded into committee room 14 at the Commons to hear the Prime Minister. Nia Griffith, the Labour MP for Llanelli and a backbencher regarded as a loyalist, told him that it was going to hit the less well-off in her constituency. Eric Martlew, the MP for Carlisle, added that he'd had complaints about the tax change at his weekend surgery. Other MPs, who were having similar experiences, murmured agreement.[35]

Brown entirely failed to read the mood of the meeting. 'That's wrong,' he insisted. 'No-one is going to lose out.' This was met with a rumble of disbelief and some cries of dissent from Labour MPs. According to one very Brownite MP present: 'There was a stunned realisation: "this man doesn't know what he is talking about." It was like a light came on in everyone's head: "this man isn't living in the real world."'[36]

Brown was shocked and bewildered by the sulphurous response from his MPs. He put up his hands and lamely asked them to write to him with suggestions, a spectacle which some present found pitiful.[37]

A week later, the Labour-dominated Treasury select committee joined the fray by confirming that the abolition of the 10p rate would leave many low-income households worse off. It criticised the Government for failing to address the problem in the most recent Budget.[38] John McFall, the Labour chairman, had grasped many months previously that the 10p tax change was a potential disaster. As the furore intensified, he went to see Brown to try to persuade him he had to shift. 'What were you thinking of Gordon?' asked McFall, telling him something had to be done. 'Listen, John, I'm trying,' responded Brown. 'Don't you think I'm fucking trying?'[39]

Michael Wills, a minister who had been close to Brown for years, also warned him that he was in serious trouble after constituents in Swindon came to him with their payslips to show how they were going to lose out.[40] Nick Brown went so far as to compare the intensity of the feeling among Labour MPs with the revolt against the Iraq War.[41] David Cameron, whose party had originally supported abolition of the band, saw a chance to pose as a friend of the poor. Nick Clegg, the newly elected leader of the Lib Dems, spoke from higher moral ground because his party consistently opposed the abolition of the 10p band. Frank Field, who had been ignored when he tried to alert colleagues to Brown's mistake a year before, claimed the status of the wise seer who had seen this disaster coming.

Despite the warnings of his friends and a growing coalition of dangerous opposition, Brown was still hugely reluctant to budge. The Scottish word 'thrawn', meaning an especially mulish form of stubbornness, might have been invented for him. According to one of his senior aides: 'It was a mixture of not wanting to admit a mistake and genuinely believing he had done the right thing and the Treasury saying there was no money.'[42] Brown had never been permeable to other views once he had made up his mind about something. He found it especially hard to accept that he had got this wrong because it collided so completely with his concept of himself as the friend of the disadvantaged. 'The trouble with Gordon is that he creates his own reality,' sighed one Cabinet colleague.[43] Even as this freight train of trouble bore down on him, he tied himself even more tightly to the railway tracks.

His core belief, central selling point and authenticating value was supposed to be his concern for the poor. This issue raised large questions over both his judgement and his character. 'The emperor has no clothes, the box of secrets is empty,' wept Polly Toynbee of the *Guardian*, previously an enthusiast for Brown. She despaired: 'The 10p tax fiasco is serious: in one iconic error Brown has blown away his most admirable reputation – a ten year record of directing money to the poorest. This does inestimable harm.'[44]

Even Government office holders, including aides to some of his closest allies in the Cabinet, were in open rebellion. When Brown flew out to meet George Bush in the second half of April, the furies pursued the Prime Minister across the Atlantic. Reports reached him that Angela Smith, the parliamentary aide to Yvette Cooper, the Chief Treasury Secretary, was on the edge of resignation. From Washington, the Prime Minister had to make a phone call to persuade her not to quit. That vignette captured the dreadful pass he had come to: forced to interrupt his international schedule to make a pleading phone call back home to forestall the resignation of a Parliamentary Private Secretary.

The trip to the United States was ill-starred in other respects. It was badly scheduled, clashing with the arrival of Pope Benedict XVI, the first Pope to visit the White House in nearly thirty years and a figure who captured the attention of the US media much more than the British Prime Minister. It was apparent that few Americans knew anything about Gordon Brown, except that he was not Tony Blair. 'Who's that man?' asked a photo caption on the popular American website The Drudge Report. CBS felt the necessity to introduce an interview with Brown by telling its viewers: 'He's known as the stern Scotsman who rarely smiles.'[45] During an awkward encounter with Diane Sawyer, the queen of American breakfast television, Brown found himself forced to talk about his predecessor as the only way to get Americans to take much interest in him.[46]

The furore about 10p tax was significant in itself and symbolic of Brown's wider problems. It prompted unflattering comparisons between his tin ear for trouble and clumsy handling of a crisis with his predecessor's sharp antennae and deft touch. Lord Desai, a professor at the LSE and Labour peer, told an interviewer that 'Gordon Brown was put on Earth to remind people how good Tony Blair was' and described Brown's leadership style as 'porridge or maybe haggis' compared with Blair's 'champagne'.[47]

It was entirely predictable that there would be nostalgia for Tony Blair, and forgetfulness that he too had become very unpopular, once Gordon Brown ran into serious difficulty. Yet it was not just his enemies but also his erstwhile admirers who pointed to the Prime Minister's paucity of commu-nications skills. As he became ever more unpopular, it was the routine lament of his friends that the attractive side of him which was sometimes on display in private was never conveyed to the public. To Mariella Frostrup, he was 'much warmer and funnier and nicer than you imagine' as well as a person of 'incredibly noble intentions'.[48] Vince Cable thought the private Brown 'has a nice sense of humour, a pleasant chuckle, which doesn't really come across publicly'.[49]

Gordon Brown was a highly volatile man, more so than his predecessor, who usually kept his emotions tightly disciplined. Some colleagues who found Blair to be chilly or always acting a role even in private thought Brown the warmer and more authentic personality. The private Brown could be thoughtful, clever, funny, engaging and self-deprecating when he was in the right mood and in company that made him comfortable. He was capable of being incredibly solicitous towards colleagues at times of family emergency, illness or bereavement. He was also a man who could be seized by titanic rages, or be consumed by awful self-pity and break down in tears. But put him in front of a camera and he struggled to do human.

In public, he was a constipated performer who found it beyond him to display any emotional range to the voters. Kathy Lette, a friend of Sarah Brown, found 'a Grand Canyonesque chasm between his public and private persona. In private life, he's witty and warm and engaging. He can seem very austere in his public persona and it's a shame.'[50] His fellow Scot Alistair Darling thought it came down to the fact that 'basically he's quite shy.'[51] Others believed that Brown felt 'spooked' by 'following on from one of the most successful political campaigners anywhere in the world'.[52]

Attempts to humanise his public image nearly always came off as comi-cally inauthentic. So did efforts to suggest that he was trendier than he was. When he remarked that 'the Arctic Monkeys really wake you up in the morning'[53] there was widespread mockery of the notion that he leapt out of bed to the sound of the noisy Sheffield band. In a subsequent interview, he could not name a single one of their tracks.[54] As Matthew Taylor observes: 'I'm afraid the great British public tend to think this is all a bit sad.'[55] Another prompt for mockery was his odd pronunciations, especially of English words. 'Born Mouth' was how he rendered the city in Dorset and 'York-shyer' how he referred to the northern county. Some in Number 10's dysfunctional communications operation thought the answer to his poor public image was to put the Prime Minister on more chat shows. One of the maddest ideas to circulate in Number 10 was to book him on *Friday Night with Jonathan Ross*, a disaster that very nearly happened until

Damian McBride intervened to put a stop to it.[56] In a clunking response to rising grocery bills, Brown suggested voters should toast their stale bread and take other money-saving measures. This invited additional derision because the publication of these good housekeeping tips coincided with his attendance at a G8 Summit in Japan where the leaders dined on an eight-course meal which began with caviar and climaxed with a 'fantasy dessert'. When out amongst voters, Brown often performed like an automaton who had been programmed to repeat the same joke and a script from which he never deviated. One minister who accompanied him on a visit to a children's centre watched wincing as Brown moved from room to room 'saying the same things in the same order in each room. It was robotic.'[57] His lack of an ability to speak fluent human or form easy bonds with other people was a serious handicap. Modern politics demands from leaders the ability to make – or at least fake – an emotional connection with voters. Tony Blair had that capacity to excess, which made it even more starkly obvious that Gordon Brown could not do it.

A disadvantage at any time, this deficit was more acute when the country was feeling the economic pinch. In interviews and speeches, Brown banged on monotonously about making 'the right long-term decisions'. The language of a desiccated calculating machine conveyed no sense that he empathised with voters' immediate and everyday struggles to pay their mortgages and grocery bills. He often sounded impatient and irritated with the anxieties of the electorate. David Cameron, the son of a stockbroker married to the daughter of a baronet, lived a life remote from the experiences of most ordinary Britons. Yet he bested Brown when it came to projecting concern for their daily struggles. Cameron responded to voter angst about rising fuel prices by talking about how much it cost to fill up the car; Brown by theorising on the workings of international oil markets. Jon Cruddas accurately observed that Cameron showed more 'emotional literacy' than his own leader. He regretted that Labour MPs 'find it quite difficult to say "What is the story?" and if we can't do it, we shouldn't be thinking that the voters can supply that for us.'[58]

This inability to communicate was calamitously combined with arrogance and indecision in the mismanagement of the 10p tax issue. By late April, the rebellion among Labour MPs was gathering weight and pace. A growing number of backbenchers were voicing support for an amendment to the Finance Bill drawn up by Frank Field to provide compensation for the 5.3 million people estimated to be worse off as a result of the abolition of the 10p rate. The prospect of losing the Budget caused high alarm in both

Downing Street and the Treasury. Darling would have to resign if he was defeated on the Finance Bill.

On Sunday, 20 April, the Chancellor appeared on television. Caught between an irresistibly mutinous Labour Party and an immovably stubborn Prime Minister, Darling was obliged to insist that it would be 'totally irresponsible' to 'unravel or rewrite' the Budget and could only offer the vague promise that he would do something for the losers in the future.[59] Brown still seemed to be in denial. He did not want to rewrite a Budget. He did not want to borrow any more money, a worry that had evaporated when the financial crisis hit later in the year. He did not want to face up to his own mistake. He spent his trip to America railing to his entourage that all the trouble was the work of Field – 'he's always been against me' – and a handful of other MPs. It was also Darling's fault, Brown complained bitterly, for not explaining the situation properly.[60] He met Labour's national executive that weekend. 'No-one will be worse off,' he insisted again to protesting members of the NEC and challenged them to 'send me pay slips' to show otherwise.[61] Number 10 and the whips tried to frighten Labour MPs with the idea that a defeat on the Finance Bill would be so devastating that it would bring down the Government.[62]

Monday morning dawned to feverish predictions that Brown could be out of Number 10 within a week and more accurate suggestions that the issue was doing huge damage to Labour in the campaign for the local elections. Even senior ministers were referring to it privately as 'our poll tax'.[63] Reality finally began to penetrate the Prime Minister. His diary was hastily rearranged so that he could speak to that night's meeting of the parliamentary party. He tried to undo the damage of his disastrous performance three weeks before. 'I get it,' he told them and promised there would be a review before the autumn which would 'lead to action'. 'But,' he came close to begging, 'we can't have a Budget defeated.'[64]

It was too late. Semi-penitence and half promises of action later were not enough to calm the tempest. By Tuesday morning, forty Labour MPs, enough to deprive the Government of its majority, had signed up overnight to Frank Field's amendment demanding the retention of the 10p band until the Government produced compensation measures. Geoff Hoon and Nick Brown warned the Prime Minister that they were heading for a terrible defeat.[65]

Sue Nye phoned Field to organise a meeting in the Prime Minister's suite at the Commons. It contains an imitation version of the Cabinet table. When Field came in, Brown was at the table, hunched in the Prime Minister's chair, looking dishevelled and surrounded by piles of paper with scribbled calculations. 'We could change tax credits,' said Brown. He frantically wrote some numbers with his black marker pen and shoved them across. 'People don't want a tax credit,' replied Field. 'What will be enough for them?' asked Brown desperately.

Jeremy Heywood at Number 10 then invited Field over to try to find a face-saving formula for Brown. Field and Greg Pope, the other principal leader of the revolt, also met Alistair Darling, who 'knew it was a mega balls-up and understood it all perfectly' but was 'never disloyal despite the way Brown treated him'.[66]

With the rebel numbers continuing to mount, the capitulation finally came on Wednesday, 23 April, when Brown sanctioned Darling to announce a compensation package. Field withdrew his amendment after the concessions were rushed out before noon to try to rescue Brown from a humiliation at Prime Minister's Questions. It did not spare him from a brutal assault by David Cameron. 'Isn't it the case that the Labour Party have finally worked out that they have a loser, not a leader? Has the Prime Minister got any idea what a pathetic figure he cuts today?'[67] Brown privately complained that Cameron was a 'public school bully'.[68] The Tory leader was pursuing a deliberate strategy of trying to destroy Brown's character in the eyes of the voters just as Labour had pilloried John Major when they pitilessly ridiculed him as weak in the run-up to the 1997 election. Nick Clegg joined in: 'You used to be a man of principle, but if you can't deliver on poverty, what on earth is the point of this increasingly pointless Prime Minister?'[69]

After this battering, Brown summoned television Political Editors to Number 10 for a series of hastily arranged interviews to try to shore up his authority. 'I don't think I've been pushed about at all,' he insisted to Nick Robinson of the BBC.[70] Yet the facts spoke for themselves. He had only conducted a disorderly retreat when faced with an imminent and catastrophic defeat in the Commons. Just weeks after insisting that nobody would lose out, and forty-eight hours after maintaining that an immediate compensation package was neither necessary nor possible, he had been forced to cave in to the weight of opposition on his backbenches. There was nothing elegant about the retreat. Everyone could hear the squeal of the Prime Minister's wheels and smell the burnt rubber left along Downing Street. The *Daily Mail*, which Brown had worked so hard to cultivate, described his U-turn as 'desperate', 'humiliating' and 'screeching'.[71] The *Times* called it 'The humbling of a Prime Minister'.[72]

The concessions were too piecemeal, grudging and last minute to save Labour from an electoral mauling just a week later. Millions of Labour's natural supporters had found they were out of pocket on the eve of the May elections. The Labour MP Janet Anderson told colleagues that she had been chased down the street by a furious voter.

To compound the damage, the issue ignited great anger among the party's activists, the very people Labour needed to be on the knocker getting out the vote. 'The 10p tax issue was toxic. In my local general committee, people were outraged by it,' says Peter Hain. 'There were people who showed me their payslips. What they said was: "We don't expect this from a Labour Government. This is the sort of thing the Tories do."'[73]

Though the impact was felt only by a minority of voters, it became a catalyst for the wider discontent with the Government and disaffection from the Prime Minister. The 10p issue had turned difficult elections for Labour into dreadful ones. Brown had 'thrown the entire Labour machine' into the contest for London. 'I wanted for nothing,' says Ken Livingstone. 'Agents were brought in from all over Britain.'[74] To no avail. His eight-year reign in the capital was terminated by Boris Johnson as voters preferred the Old Etonian's ebullient inexperience to the Labour machine. In the local elections elsewhere in the country, the Conservatives secured 44 per cent of the vote while Labour on just 24 per cent came third behind the Liberal Democrats. This was Labour's worst performance in a national election in four decades. Brown had not reversed the post-Iraq decline under Blair. He had made it considerably worse. After less than a year at Number 10, he was plumbing depths not visited by Blair even at his lowest. 'The voters are no longer just moaning from the back of the car,' observed one member of the Cabinet. 'They are angrily getting out of the car and walking off elsewhere.'[75] The wilful refusal to concede over 10p tax until it was too late was widely and correctly blamed for the massacre. 'That was the real killer,' says the defeated Livingstone.[76] Nick Brown, close ally of the Prime Minister, agrees that it was 'the single most important factor' in the defeats of that May. 'There was just no escaping it.'[77]

The writing was on the wall for many Labour MPs. Derek Wyatt, the MP for Sittingbourne and Sheppey in Kent, wobbling on a majority of just seventy-nine, helpfully called it a 'John Major moment' and said: 'Gordon has committed spectacular own-goals and the public is punishing him for it.'[78]

There was a devastating disintegration of Brown's standing with the public. Only one in five of voters now thought he was doing a good job. His reputation had collapsed on every front. He was rated worse than David Cameron on every key leadership quality, including competence, decisiveness, fairness, likeability, intelligence, being in touch with ordinary people, trustworthiness and strength.[79]

Brown became consumed by desperation to avoid another humiliation in the looming by-election in Crewe and Nantwich, which had turned into a mini-referendum on the tax issue. On Tuesday, 13 May, Alistair Darling introduced an emergency Budget just ten weeks after his original one. The Chancellor declared that he would spend £2.7 billion, money that the Government previously insisted it could not find, to raise personal tax allowances. The package compensated many, though not all, of the losers while also handing extra money to lots of more affluent taxpayers. This completed the trajectory from total denial to absolute capitulation. The Government was now giving an across-the-board tax cut, but got no credit for it because of the appalling handling of the issue. It utterly failed as a by-election bribe.

New Labour was once the cleverest and slickest electioneering machine in Europe. It fought a crudely misconceived parody of a campaign in Crewe and Nantwich. Labour activists dressed in top hats and tails tried to bash the Conservative candidate as a 'Tory toff'. Edward Timpson's family had made its fortune from the unaristocratic business of repairing shoes. It was Labour which parachuted in a political heiress. Tamsin Dunwoody was the granddaughter of a Labour baroness and the daughter of the late MP Gwyneth. Labour campaigners had apparently not noticed that the Bentley luxury car factory was in the constituency. Quite a lot of voters in Crewe and Nantwich depended on selling 'toff' limousines for their livelihood. By the end of the campaign, it was clear that it was not David Cameron whom voters regarded as out of touch with ordinary people. It was Gordon Brown whom they viewed as detached from reality. Tellingly, his photo did not feature on Labour's campaign material in Crewe while it was plastered all over Tory leaflets. It is always a very bad sign when a party leader is regarded as their greatest propaganda asset by his opponents.

He did not stay up to wait for the votes to be counted. At around two in the morning of Friday, 23 May, the returning officer declared that a Labour majority of 7,078 had been converted into a Conservative one of 7,860 on a high turn-out. This was a better result than the Tories had dared hope for and a worse one than Labour at its most pessimistic had feared. Voters whose families were Labour for generations deserted the party. Crewe and Nantwich was the first time that the Tories had directly taken a seat from Labour at a by-election since Ilford North in 1978. The 18 per cent swing matched those achieved at by-elections by Ted Heath and Margaret Thatcher on their way to Number 10. Voters there, as in the local elections earlier in the month, did not spray their dissent among protest parties. They switched to the Tories, which put momentum behind a growing assumption that the Conservatives would form the next Government.

On Friday morning, Brown ordered an emergency conference call of members of the Cabinet in an attempt to steady nerves. He then gave a round of interviews which had his own staff despairing because they were so poor. Within Number 10 'morale hit the floor.'[80] The questions about his style, character and judgement began to metastasise into questions about whether he should be leader at all.

32. An Enemy in Need

As the Queen and the President of France took their places at the centre of the top table, someone was missing from the state banquet at Windsor Castle. 'Has the Prime Minister got lost?' asked a bemused monarch as she and Princess Anne looked around for him. 'That's Gordon,' Nicolas Sarkozy smirked to his wife, Carla. The Queen remarked: 'He disappeared the wrong way at the crucial moment.'[1] This was in danger of being Gordon Brown's epitaph: the Prime Minister who got lost.

There were unresolved tensions at the heart of his premiership from the moment that he stepped into Number 10. One was within his own character. Gordon Brown was a cross between nervy journalist and nerdy academic. A news obsessive and a lofty visionary uneasily coexisted in the same head. Irwin Stelzer found him an 'extraordinarily intelligent man' who was 'better read than anybody I've ever met'.[2] Kathy Lette thought similarly: 'It's like he's been hooked up intravenously to an encyclopedia.'[3] Alan West was rather awed: 'His depth of knowledge is phenomenal.'[4] A senior member of his staff reported: 'Every morning we get these e-mails from Mount Olympus about fantastically nerdy policy points.'[5] He made self-consciously intellectual speeches which did not wear his learning lightly. In a long discourse 'On Liberty', Brown referenced John Stuart Mill, Milton, Locke, Orwell, Churchill, Bolingbroke, Voltaire, de Tocqueville, Coke, Locke, Macaulay, Himmelfarb, Green, Hobson, Hobhouse and Tawney.[6] It was rare for a modern leader to mention one philosopher or historian in a speech, never mind more than a dozen. 'He wrote it all himself,' said a friend believably.[7] This was Dr Brown, the Prime Minister with a Ph.D. This Brown wanted to read every book, absorb every research paper and talk to every expert about an issue that caught his attention. When he engaged with a subject that animated him, his depth of understanding and mastery of the detail could be hugely impressive.

That April, George Clooney was a guest at Number 10. Just about all the staff found an excuse to be present for the movie star's arrival. The cleaners in their pinnies lined up outside the Cabinet Room 'like a guard of honour'.[8] Brown was oblivious to the aphrodisiacal effect his visitor was having on everyone else. 'Gordon wanted to talk to him about Darfur,' says one of his aides. 'Everyone else wanted to goggle at Clooney.'[9] This was the high-minded Brown, the leader who had global visions.

The other Brown was still the journalist he had been as a young man. He never grew out of many of the compulsions of that profession. One of his senior staff found that 'the first conversation every morning with Gordon was about what was in the newspapers.'[10] He would participate in the 7.30 a.m. 'morning call' when the Number 10 spin doctors discussed media handling. On flights abroad, he would sit in the first-class cabin obsessively asking aides: 'What's the story? What's the story?' During a trip to the Vatican, he badgered his staff so repetitively that one aide eventually groaned to another: 'Prime Minister meets Pope. Why doesn't someone tell him that's the fucking story?'[11] The neurotic journalist in Brown was addicted to headline-chasing through the production of instant and often artificial initiatives. In the space of just five days, he popped up in the *Sun* and on *American Idol* to promise that he would wipe out malaria; signed up to a *Daily Mail* campaign against supermarket plastic bags; told football crowds they should be nicer to referees; and talked about constitutional change and Aids and Britishness. As his difficulties deepened, he became more compulsive. It generated an atmosphere of 'randomness . . . initiatives going off everywhere'.[12] There was a lot of noise, but little signal.

Voters tend to be most impressed by practical promises to enhance their lives delivered over a realistic timescale. New Labour always had a vice for being either frenetically short-term or unbelievably long-term. Brown exemplified that as he swung between announcing five-year plans that were too grandiose to be credible and mayfly initiatives that were here today and forgotten tomorrow.

This handicap was married with the continuing inability to create an orderly regime at Number 10. By the turn of the year, Brown had grasped that it was 'pretty essential' to try to sort it out.[13] He now saw that the small shell of former Treasury apparatchiks whom he had brought with him to Number 10 were not up to the task of running Government. In January, he promoted Jeremy Heywood, the former Principal Private Secretary to Blair, who returned to Downing Street after a stint in the private sector with Morgan Stanley, to the newly created position of Permanent Secretary at Number 10. This cut across the traditional responsibilities of the Cabinet Secretary, but Sir Gus O'Donnell did not resist the innovation. He and Heywood were friends. O'Donnell had once rented out his house to the other man. The Cabinet Secretary was hugely relieved that someone was taking on the challenge of trying to create some order out of the chaos at Number 10.[14] Heywood took over 'running everything that was not political'.[15] A highly able and workaholic official, he had some limited success trying to focus Brown, but his efforts would always be compromised so long as the Prime Minister remained pathologically determined to try to run every bit of Government himself.

Less fortunate was Stephen Carter, a talented recruit from the private sector in his mid-forties who was also imported into Number 10 in the New Year. Carter's impressive résumé included being a former Chief Executive of OFCOM and of the Brunswick PR agency. The Prime Minister was so desperate to get him on board that he rang him on Christmas Eve to offer him the job of Director of Strategy and then rang him again on Boxing Day. They had met just twice, at a wedding and at a party. This was a fragile basis for a relationship, especially with someone like Brown. 'He needed Gordon's trust and that is very hard to win.'[16] Carter came to Number 10 mainly on the recommendation of Sarah Brown, who had heard good things about him from Alan Parker.

The arrival of Carter also meant the departure of Tom Scholar, whom Brown had persuaded to return from a plum posting in Washington as Britain's representative at the World Bank to become his short-lived Chief of Staff. Brown was going to ring Scholar on his wedding day to tell him that he was losing his job. When the Prime Minister was warned that it was Scholar's wedding day, he was still going to ring him.[17]

'Gordon is like a lighthouse,' says one Number 10 official. 'The light is on you at full intensity for a while and then his attention sweeps elsewhere and you are plunged into darkness.'[18] To begin with, Brown was deferentially interested in Carter's advice. The new Director of Strategy was horrified by what he found at Number 10. Three essential policy positions were vacant, the private office was under-resourced, the speech-writing capability was considered inadequate, and there was no serious effort on the web or other digital communications. Within a month, he had given Brown a list of twenty-five key deficiencies that had to be tackled.

Things began to go wrong for Carter when he tried to create order among the political staff. He sent an e-mail to Brown recommending that some of them be removed, not knowing that e-mails to the Prime Minister were automatically copied in to others at Number 10, including some of those that Carter was suggesting for the sack.[19]

He tried to prune the Prime Minister's schedule and curb Brown's impulse to unleash barrages of noisy but ineffective announcements. 'Stephen would badger away at Gordon on presentational things – to take his jacket off, to use more approachable, more human language – things the rest of us had given up on,' says one senior Brown aide.[20] Carter was among those who believed, correctly, that one of the reasons the public were resistant to 'bonding' with Brown was because he lacked a proper 'contract' with voters because he had never been elected in his own right.[21] Carter never succeeded in getting Brown to accept that he had to radically change his style, tone and way of running things. 'It was an impossible job spec,' says one Brown aide sympathetic to Carter. The Director of Strategy grew to dread having to present Brown with polling and focus group research about the low regard the voters had for him.

A senior civil servant thought it was 'ill-fated from the start'.[22] Carter was not what Brown supposed him to be. The Prime Minister was really looking for his own Alastair Campbell. 'Gordon thought he was getting a comms person, but Stephen was a management person.'[23]

He was undermined from the start by the old Brown clique. 'He bumped into Damian McBride, who saw him as a threat,' says another of Brown's aides. 'It was a turf thing.'[24] A senior civil servant saw that 'from the word go, he and Damian were at each other's throats.'[25] There was a stream of stories from within Number 10 which were usually coloured in a way designed to discredit Carter in the eyes of Brown and Labour MPs. At one meeting he was reported to have asked: 'Who is JP?' – a leak designed to show his ignorance of the Labour Party, where everyone knew that JP stood for John Prescott.

'Stephen was a really nice bloke,' comments one civil servant. 'He just didn't know what he was letting himself in for. They made a decision to fuck this guy. By April, it was transparent to everyone in the building that he was dead.'[26] In the eyes of another witness, Carter 'had a bloody awful time'.[27] One member of the Cabinet saw the Carter experience as characteristic of Brown's approach to relationships. 'Gordon falls in love with people, calls them up the whole time at all hours. Then he decides he's disappointed with them and freezes them out.'[28] Carter left Number 10 that autumn with a peerage and was briefly berthed as a minister before leaving Government altogether the year after.

Carter was one of many advisers who tried to furnish Brown with a theme for his premiership. 'There was an endless quest for Gordon's purpose.'[29] For a short while, policies were packaged around the slogan 'On Your Side'. The Prime Minister had another brief enthusiasm for 'The Opportunity Revolution'. For a month or so, 'the flavour of the month' was Lucy Parker, sister of Alan and friend of Sarah Brown. She came up with 'The Talent

Agenda'. Instructions went out that everything had to be branded under that heading. 'Every department was told to shape its policies to "talent". Then overnight it was dropped.'[30]

One very senior civil servant sighs: 'In the Treasury, he did have a strategic narrative, but he never found one as Prime Minister. All sorts of people tried to give him one. Number 10 tried. The Cabinet Office tried. Whatever strategic narratives he's been given, he's never been happy with it.'[31]

A lengthy e-mail dropped into the Prime Minister's inbox that spring with advice on how he might recapture the initiative, fashion a theme for the Government and take on the Tories. 'This is absolutely on the money,' Stephen Carter remarked to Jeremy Heywood, both of whom automatically received copies of Brown's e-mails. 'Who is it from?' 'It's Tony Blair,' explained Heywood.[32] The unravelling of Brown's premiership fulfilled all Blair's worst fears about the man who had levered him out. Yet the former Prime Minister was magnanimously anxious to help.

Part of the explanation for the internal contradictions and cramping caution of Brown was that he could not decide what he wanted to preserve about the Blair decade and what he wanted to repudiate. 'Gordon never resolved in his own mind the tension between continuity and change.'[33] A test case was security and civil liberties. Brown began his premiership with a strong signal that he intended to rebuild bridges with liberal Britain by softening the authoritarianism of his predecessor. In the speech 'On Liberty', he contended that it was the 'animating force' and 'founding value of our country' and declared that all future policies would be subject to a 'liberty test'.[34]

He proposed to MPs 'a new constitutional settlement that entrusts more power to Parliament and the British people'.[35] He talked about introducing a Bill of Rights and also a Civil Service Act to entrench Whitehall's neutrality. His long-time friend and ally Michael Wills worked enthusiastically on the constitutional project, but it was progressively neutered. Some reforms were delivered, such as the formal enshrinement of Parliament's right to a vote before the country went to war. He surrendered the prime ministerial prerogative to appoint bishops, the Poet Laureate and the Astronomer-General, but these were not powers he was interested in wielding anyway. They were more acts of symbolism than of substance.

He told his first Cabinet that policy would in future be made through the machinery of Government and Parliament, not from the sofa in Number 10 and through the media, a promise to return to collective decision-making that pleased the mandarins and won admiring early press notices. That was a pledge not kept either. Civil servants who were initially 'really pleased and very hopeful' about the commitments to 'a return to Cabinet decision-making and an end to sofa Government' were left feeling let down and 'tremendously marginalised'.³⁶ Brown was, at heart, a constitutional conservative, as was Jack Straw, the lead minister. It was two years into his premiership, much too late to do anything substantial, before a constitutional Bill was finally produced. This contained a mishmash of tinkering reforms which were a thin shadow of the original bold plans floated in the first flush of his premiership, when he talked so much about restoring public trust. Introducing an elected House of Lords was kicked into touch, substantial reform to party funding ran into the sands, there was no attempt to revive local government, introduce fixed-term parliaments or lower the voting age. Even the plan to make the Attorney-General independent of government, which had been included in the draft Bill, was dropped. Whitehall was successfully resistant to a Bill of Rights. 'It ran into a vicious attack from hardline officials at the Home Office', who found allies in other departments which were 'very anxious about the Bill of Rights because it fetters executive action and entrenches the protection of the individual against the state'.³⁷ A Cabinet revolt against Straw killed the idea. Brown had opposed ID cards as Chancellor. Now, thinking to project himself as a security Prime Minister, he supported them.

A big choice, and one that might also define how he related to his predecessor, was the balance between preserving civil liberties and taking measures against terrorism. Early on, he sounded keen to fashion a fresh and less divisive approach. 'I think over the next few years, we will have to deal with it in new ways,' he told me in an interview. 'It is not simply a military, intelligence and policing problem, we're going to have to win the battle of hearts and minds.'³⁸ He reached out to the Opposition parties and to Shami Chakrabati, the charismatic and effective head of Liberty. She found him 'incredibly generous with his time', willing to listen, 'charming, polite and thoughtful' and apparently sincere when he talked about getting to a 'consensus' about how to legislate against terror.³⁹ She thought 'we were still talking' when the Government abruptly abandoned the search for consensus and announced legislation to greatly extend the amount of time that terror suspects could be held without charge. One of Brown's motives was to show that he could win a battle which had defeated Blair.⁴⁰ To Labour MPs like Jon Cruddas, it looked like 'an exercise in political positioning' rather than a stance of conviction and was designed to build 'a political hedge fund against future terrorist attacks'.⁴¹

Extending pre-trial detention to forty-two days, less than the ninety days attempted by Blair but still multiples longer than anywhere else in the Western world, aroused the opposition of both Charlie Falconer and Peter

Goldsmith, Justice Secretary and Attorney-General until June 2007. They were joined by a Who's Who of senior figures from the judiciary. An especially significant opponent was the Director of Public Prosecutions, Sir Ken Macdonald. It was hard for the Government to make a case for taking powers that the chief prosecutor declared to be an unnecessary violation of civil liberties. Alan West, whom Brown personally recruited as Security Minister, caused a flurry by going on radio to admit: 'I still need to be fully convinced that we absolutely need more than twenty-eight days and I also need to be convinced what's the best way of doing that.'[42] An hour later, after a meeting with Brown at Number 10, the former admiral did a hard tack and came back into line, saying: 'Maybe I didn't choose my words well.' He covered his climb-down by calling himself 'a simple sailor'.[43] The former Chief of Defence Intelligence was far from simple, but he had been politically naïve. 'The lesson I learnt is that one can't be quite as open as that.'[44]

The crucial vote on the report stage of the legislation came on Wednesday, 11 June, in the wake of the debacle over 10p tax and the rout at Crewe and Nantwich. Brown was frantic to avoid yet another authority-shredding defeat. Amidst feverish horse-trading and arm-twisting, Labour MPs reported that they were offered all manner of sweeteners in return for their votes. A Labour MP who had not been spoken to by Brown for twenty years was treated to a twenty-minute conversation with a Prime Minister desperate for his vote. One Labour MP who was still recovering from surgery was pushed into the division lobby in a wheelchair. Another who was fighting cancer was asked to leave his hospital bed. Even then, the Government only just squeaked a victory and owed it to nine votes from MPs of the Democratic Unionist Party. There was a temporary distraction when David Davis, condemning what he called the chicanery in the Commons, resigned as Shadow Home Secretary to trigger a protest by-election. His gesture was drained of potency when Labour made the smart, albeit cowardly, decision not to put up a candidate.

The Government's debilitatingly narrow win on forty-two days proved to be pointless. Cathy Ashton, Labour's leader in the Lords, warned that the legislation would be shredded by peers and it duly was. A hostile speech by Eliza Manningham-Buller, the former head of MI5, dealt the coup de grâce. It was eventually pulled altogether that autumn under the cover of the financial crisis. As for the grand promises of constitutional renewal, they gathered dust.

On Friday, 27 June, Brown had his first anniversary in Number 10, an event marked not by celebration but by further humiliation. He woke up to the result of the Henley by-election in which Labour finished an awful fifth, beaten not just by the Tories and Lib Dems, but also by the Greens and the BNP. He spent much of the rest of the day trying to persuade Wendy Alexander not to resign as Labour leader in Scotland after she was suspended from the Edinburgh Parliament for twenty-four hours over campaign donations. She quit the next day.

All this deepened the darkness encroaching over his premiership. There were cries of betrayal from the left-wingers who had foolishly imagined that Brown would give them socialism in one country. Liberals found his premiership no less centralising and authoritarian, and in some ways more so, than his predecessor's. That did not mean that there was contentment among the Blairites. They didn't like Brown's backpedalling on public service reform and complained that he was even more useless as a strategist and communicator than they had feared. The Tories were almost Oedipal in their awe for Blair even when he had his back to the wall. They were becoming contemptuously confident against Brown. Critics from across the spectrum were united in saying that his premiership lacked shape, vision and any palpable purpose other than its own survival. The hero of the summer of 2007 descended into the zero of the summer of 2008. He knew that the worst wounds on his premiership had not been inflicted by the Conservatives or the media, but by himself.

That summer, Brown descended into a terrible place, politically, psychologically and physically. 'He looked awful,' says a senior member of his staff. 'People at Number 10 were pinning their hopes on the holiday, but the fear was that he wouldn't have a proper holiday.'[45] A retired senior civil servant came to visit former colleagues at Downing Street. He was spotted by the Prime Minister who, desperate for someone to talk to, dragged him into his office for a chat. 'He looked tired in his bones,' the former mandarin told friends. 'It was that sort of tiredness that a week's sleep won't cure.'[46] A senior politician had a meeting with the Prime Minister shortly before the recess and was shocked by what he saw. 'He looked absolutely terrible. The shoulders were hunched. The flesh was literally dripping off his face. I wanted to give him a hug.'[47]

Some of his friends wondered how long Brown, a proud, clever and sensitive man, could endure being routinely roasted in the media as a semi-autistic, mendacious liability. 'Why are they saying these things about me? Why are they doing this to me?' the Prime Minister beseeched one aide.[48] To a senior Scottish Labour MP, he confided: 'So much has been thrown at me, I can't go any lower.'[49] Sarah Brown told a friend that she was 'very worried' about her husband. A sympathetic Labour peer thought he was 'very crushed'. Brown could sense that even his closest allies were distancing themselves, even Ed Balls. 'It was not exactly what was said, it was what wasn't said. Ed wasn't responding instantly any more when Gordon needed help.'⁵⁰

On another account, Ed Balls, Douglas Alexander and Ed Miliband 'all decided that they were too busy running their departments to spend as much time as they used to with Gordon'.⁵¹

There was an embarrassing scene at the summer barbecue in the back garden of Number 10 for those who worked there. It was customary for the Prime Minister to make a speech to the staff. This required no fancy oratory; just a few words of thanks. When Brown proved reluctant, Jeremy Heywood endeavoured to persuade him. 'It would be really good if you could do it,' the senior official came close to begging the Prime Minister. 'It would mean a lot to people.' Brown shook his head: 'I can't do it. I can't do it.'⁵²

Brown's exhaustion and sense of isolation made his temper even shorter and blacker. Officials became more apprehensive than ever about delivering unwelcome news for fear of the reaction. One aide with bad tidings decided to break it to the boss when they were travelling in the back of the Prime Minister's Daimler. As was customary, the aide took the rear seat behind the driver. Brown sat behind the protection officer. The cream upholstery of the seat back in front of Brown was flecked with black marks. When having a meltdown, the Prime Minister would habitually stab the seat back with his black marker pen. On this occasion, what the aide had to tell the Prime Minister provoked a more scary response than the stabbing of the pen. Face like thunder, Brown reacted by swinging back an arm and clenching his fist. The aide cowered back, fearing that the Prime Minister was about to hit him in the face. Brown crashed his fist into the back of the passenger seat in front of him. The protection officer flinched. This was happening more and more often. The Prime Minister's compulsion to vent his temper by hitting the upholstery became so regular that sitting in front of him was regarded as the worst duty among the protection squad.⁵³

Immunity from Brown's rages was not conferred on officials just because they had been long-time and loyal servants. If anything, he seemed to think he could be more abusive to those who were closest to him. He was probably right: they were the most likely to bury the darker truths about his behaviour. Stewart Wood – a senior adviser on Northern Ireland and foreign affairs and a fellow of Magdalen College, Oxford – had served Brown intelligently and faithfully for years. In advance of the June meeting of the European Council, Wood arranged a lunchtime reception at Number 10 for the ambassadors representing the European Union. Brown joined them only for the coffee. Wood was waiting at the door of the first-floor Pillared Room, where the reception was being held, when Brown came up the stairs. The Prime Minister was in an especially evil mood. When Wood tried to brief him on which of the ambassadors he should speak to, Brown blew up in a staggering rage. 'Why have I got to meet these fucking people?' he yelled at his adviser. 'Why are you making me meet these fucking people? I don't want to meet these fucking people!' Brown roughly shoved his adviser aside. He stormed into the room, leaving behind a shaken and shocked Wood.

Several of Brown's senior staff collectively decided they weren't going to put up with this sort of conduct and told the Prime Minister to his face that he couldn't go on behaving so badly.[54]

Sir Gus O'Donnell became 'very worried' about Brown's treatment of staff at Number 10. If it led to a formal complaint against the Prime Minister that would be both unprecedented and disastrous. The Cabinet Secretary tried to calm down frightened duty clerks, badly treated phone operators and other bruised staff by telling them 'don't take it personally'. O'Donnell eventually felt compelled to directly confront the Prime Minister and gave him a stern 'pep talk' about his conduct towards the staff. 'This is no way to get things done,' he told Brown and warned him that he had to moderate his behaviour.[55] This seemed to have some effect. Brown was more careful in future about whom he made a victim of his temper.

In July, Jeremy Heywood was on his way out of Number 10 for lunch when he was waylaid by Gordon Brown. The Prime Minister asked his Permanent Secretary whom he was seeing. A slightly sheepish Heywood confessed that he was having lunch with Peter Mandelson, the man with whom Brown had conducted an epic feud for more than a decade. To the civil servant's surprise, Brown responded: 'Can I come too?' Heywood politely demurred. Brown then said: 'Can you ask Peter to come and see me after lunch?'

Unknown to the world, and to most of those who worked in Number 10, the Prime Minister had acquired a new and secret adviser whose identity would have been astonishing to everyone at Westminster. Not only was Peter Mandelson back at court, but he had returned to offer counsel and support to Gordon Brown. For fourteen years they had engaged in fratricidal struggle alternated with frozen silences. Their enmity – Mandelson called it an 'uncivil war' – was so deep for so long that it was the unanimous view that the relationship was irretrievably poisoned.[56] Just before Brown became Prime Minister, relations fell to a new nadir after Mandelson's radio interview in which he declared that he would not seek a second term as a European Commissioner in order to deny Brown the pleasure of sacking him. No-one had found it more difficult to reconcile themselves to Brown being premier than Mandelson. He didn't care who knew it. He was a guest at a dinner party in the autumn of 2007 thrown at the Holland Park home of Roland Rudd, a City PR executive. Mandelson did not mask his disdain for Brown in front of other guests, who included David Owen, the former leader of the SDP; Matthew d'Ancona, the editor of the Tory-leaning *Spectator* magazine; and Nick Clegg, the future leader of the Lib Dems, and his wife. 'He was openly slagging off Brown,' says one at the table.[57] Even at the height of Brown's early honeymoon, when just about everyone else was at his feet, Mandelson rained on the emperor's parade at the 2007 conference by publicly expressing scepticism about Brown's speech.

Paradoxically, the first intimations that their past affection might be rekindled came once Brown's premiership ran into serious trouble. In February 2008, Mandelson gave a lecture in Cambridge defending globalisation against its critics.[58] This attracted Brown's attention and agreement. 'He's got it,' Brown remarked to one surprised aide.[59] In March, Brown went to Brussels for a meeting with the man he had for so long regarded as a sworn enemy. Officials doubted that the encounter would last its allocated twenty minutes. After an initially frigid start, the permafrost began to melt. When they discussed the gathering storm in the international economy, Mandelson turned on his charm. 'It's a good thing you're there,' he remarked, saying that Brown had the requisite experience and expertise for this moment. 'The country is going to turn to you.'[60] Officials were amazed when the two men chatted amicably for more than an hour – and about much more than trade – while the British ambassador kicked his heels waiting to get back the use of his office.[61]

That conversation, the longest and friendliest that they had enjoyed in years, initiated a rediscovery of the things that they had once admired in each other. They began to remember that once upon a time, before the great rupture after the death of John Smith, they had been closer to each other than either had been to Tony Blair. Now that Blair was gone from Number 10, the relationship was also no longer complicated by being a three-sided marriage.

The thaw was helped along by go-betweens. Stewart Wood, for a long time the only one of Brown's officials whom the Prime Minister would allow to have contact with Mandelson, invited him to dinner at Wood's London home. Wood's wife was Brazilian, which helped make the occasion warm for Mandelson's partner, Reinaldo. Shriti Vadera was also at the dinner. She and Mandelson, both being sharp, gossipy and internationally minded, enjoyed each other's company. The reconciliation was also aided by a mutual foe when Brown and Mandelson fought on the same side against Nicolas Sarkozy in the world trade negotiations.

This rapprochement was further spurred by mutual desperation. Mandelson's time as Trade Commissioner was winding down to retirement in 2009. With little prospect of a world trade deal, it looked as though his term in Brussels would end on a note of failure. The intellectual challenge and the perks of being a Commissioner had never fully reconciled him to his separation from British politics. His yearning to return was an ache more sharp because there seemed to be no chance of ever satisfying the desire. He told Philip Gould that he woke up every morning with 'an almost physical pain' because of his detachment from Westminster.[62]

At his best, Mandelson had a most acute grasp of political strategy and communication, a talent sorely absent in Brown's Number 10. A flailing and isolated Prime Minister needed those skills. The two men began to have increasingly frequent conversations on the phone in which Brown would seek advice from Mandelson about speeches and float policy ideas with him. One aide who overheard Brown's end of a call recounts: 'Gordon would ask: "What should we do about today's *Sun*?" and "What should I say on tomorrow's *Today* programme?" and "What should we do about this problem?" He was talking to Peter like he used to talk to Ed Balls.'[63]

As far as the outside world knew, they were still enemies. In an interview, Mandelson made remarks which the media interpreted as another attack on Brown for failing to fashion a coherent and consistent message. 'Jumping on passing bandwagons, hobby horses or marginal issues is not the way, in my view, for any government to present itself if it is going to sustain its support in the country.'[64] Journalists, being in ignorance of their gradual and clandestine rapprochement, universally interpreted this as another shot of the uncivil war.

Yet Brown did not take offence to this intervention as once he would have. Mandelson was saying in public what he was already telling Brown in private but more starkly. By the summer, Mandelson was slipping secretly into Number 10 or up to Chequers almost every weekend that he was in Britain.

There were still many edges to this emotionally tangled relationship. Mandelson's first Cabinet career was destroyed by Brown's acolytes when they leaked the Geoffrey Robinson home loan.[65] Mandelson could not resist poking a finger into this deep scar. During one of their tête-à-têtes, he interrupted a discussion about a speech: 'Gordon, we haven't talked about what you let your people do to me.' Brown looked down into his papers and grunted: 'Yes, well, that should never have happened.' After an awkward pause, Brown then said: 'Now, what about the speech?'[66]

Brown occasionally teased Mandelson with the thought that he might one day return to British politics, but the other man supposed that this was just joshing. His assumption that he could never return to the Cabinet liberated him to be increasingly blunt with Brown about the terrible state of his premiership. By July, Labour's poll rating had descended from dire to diabolical. For fear of another petrol tax revolt, the Government committed another panicky U-turn by suspending indefinitely the scheduled 2p rise in fuel duty. Brown could sense the hostility towards him in the Cabinet when he could not even win their confidence about his economic messages. 'Gordon started to think: "If I can't convince them on the economy, that's it."'[67] The media turned feverish with speculation that senior members of the Cabinet were steeling themselves to sack the Prime Minister. David Marshall, the MP for Glasgow East, resigned – officially on the grounds of ill health. This triggered a by-election that Brown was so frantic to avoid that he rang Marshall 'about fifteen times' to plead with him not to quit.[68]

At one meeting that summer, Mandelson issued Brown with a dreadful warning. You are in peril, he said, of going down in history as one of the worst post-war Prime Ministers. 'If you don't change, you are going to lose Number 10. You'll be out by October or November.' This was brutally accurate and franker than anyone else around Brown would dare to be. Yet Brown did not react angrily. He instead responded by nodding sadly and giving the other man a pitiful look. 'I know. I know I'm going to lose it,' the Prime Minister said to the man who had once been his closest ally, then his bitterest enemy and was now his secret confidant. 'Will you help me?'[69]

33. Assassins in the Shadows

'Tis now the very witching time of night,' declaimed David Tennant in the title role of the Royal Shakespeare Company's production of *Hamlet*, 'when church-yards yawn and hell itself breathes out.'[1] Gordon and Sarah Brown were in the audience at the Swan Theatre in Stratford-upon-Avon, but both were having difficulty focusing on the performance when that night's by-election could be so critical to the Prime Minister's fate. With them were Paul Dacre of the *Daily Mail* and his wife. Brown was anxious that he was losing the editor who had recently dictated an editorial which heaped praise on the 'formidable' David Cameron and talked of the Government 'destroying itself'.[2] The theatre party also included Stephen Carter, the Number 10 Director of Strategy, and his wife. When they had seen the last act of the tragedy at Elsinore, Carter turned his mobile phone to show the text on it to Sarah Brown. He asked: 'Do you want to tell him or shall I?'[3]

The text warned that Labour had lost what was supposed to be its third-safest seat in Scotland. A Labour majority of 13,507 in Glasgow East was overturned by the Scottish Nationalists on a swing of 23 per cent. The triumphant SNP candidate, a charisma-free local councillor transformed into a swaggering conqueror for the night, proclaimed: 'This victory is not just a political earthquake, it is off the Richter scale.'[4] It was hard to argue with that.

Under Brown, Labour had lost elections in suburban London, working-class Crewe and Nantwich, leafy Henley and one of the most deprived areas of Glasgow. One former member of the Cabinet grimly observed: 'We have gone from being the One Nation party to being the No Nation party.'[5] If Labour was losing in metropolitan England, southern England, northern England and the west of Scotland, where precisely were they going to be able to win with Brown? Gordon Prentice, the MP for Pendle, became one of the first Labour backbenchers to openly call for the Prime Minister to resign in the Government's 'best interests' on the grounds that he lacked the skill 'to persuade and enthuse' voters.[6] The MP spoke for more than himself.

The day after that terrible defeat, Brown was in Warwick to address party activists, union leaders, MPs and ministers at the party's national policy forum. He dealt with the by-election disaster by pretending that it hadn't happened. He offered his audience a hollow recital of tired phrases and uninspiring statistics with which they were wearily familiar. One member of the Cabinet in the audience groaned to another that the Prime Minister appeared to be 'in total denial'.[7] Brown delivered a second address to the forum later that day. Some of his colleagues expected him to use this occasion, from which reporters were excluded, to talk frankly about their plight and outline a plan for recovery. To the horror of Cabinet ministers present, he instead delivered almost exactly the same speech 'except that it was worse'.[8] Another minister present says: 'He sent them away more depressed than when they arrived.'[9]

The following day, Number 10 was visited by Barack Obama, not yet the Democratic nominee for the White House, but already hugely popular in Europe after his dazzling arrival in the political firmament. Asked about his host's plight, Obama tactfully remarked: 'You're always more popular before you're in charge.'[10] He very obviously hedged his bets by also meeting David Cameron. The effect of the visit was not to sprinkle Brown with some second-hand Obama stardust. It drew an unflattering contrast between the idolising reception for the American and the public alienation from Britain's leader.

'This was absolutely rock bottom,' believed one Cabinet minister. 'None of us thought it could go on.'[11] The Blairites could not resist saying privately that 'we told you so, we warned that he would be a car crash of a Prime Minister.'[12] Even some of Brown's closest allies in the Cabinet feared it was near terminal: 'There's only so long that we can say that we need time to turn things around before people say we've had enough time.'[13] Peter Mandelson, watching from the wings, thought that 'New Labour was close to a nervous breakdown.'[14]

The principal cause of it was the failings of Brown. What to do about him was the subject of 'constant conversations' among members of the Cabinet over June and July.[15] David Miliband, the Foreign Secretary, and his friend the Work and Pensions Secretary, James Purnell, were agreed that the Prime Minister had to be replaced if Labour was to have any chance of recovering. At least a third of the Cabinet took the same view, but these ministers were as yet unsure how his removal could be brought about without destroying the Government.[16] The younger ministers were looking for a lead from older hands. The two key figures were Jack Straw and Geoff Hoon. Straw was the senior member of the Cabinet and had been Brown's campaign manager for the leadership. Hoon was the Chief Whip. It would be very hard for Brown to resist if they headed a delegation of senior ministers telling him that he had to resign. Straw was regularly mentioned in speculative press pieces as the figure to lead 'the men in grey suits'. He became so alarmed by this that he stopped wearing any of his grey suits.[17] The hidden truth was that he was preparing to take action. The Justice Secretary was in constant clandestine communication with those plotting to topple Brown. One of those plotters was Charles Clarke. The former Home Secretary now had ample vindication for his predictions that Brown would turn out to be a dreadful Prime Minister. Shortly before the summer recess, Clarke and Straw had lunch together. As they sat down, Clarke expected the two men to dance around the issue. Clarke was taken by surprise when Straw talked immediately and directly about Brown. The Justice Secretary said in explicit terms that Brown had to go and declared that 'something will be done.' Straw also gave a very strong indication that a coup was in preparation when he talked to Frank Field, another veteran opponent of the Prime Minister who was more or less openly calling for him to quit. The Justice Secretary invited Field to come talk to him. The notional subject of their meeting – the criminal injuries compensation arrangements – was soon abandoned for a discussion about the Prime Minister. Straw spent much of the conversation trying to find out whether Field would back the Justice Secretary for the top job. Field, just like Clarke, left the meeting convinced that Straw was ready to move. Stephen Byers, the Blairite former Cabinet minister who tried to organise a leadership challenge against Brown in 2007, was a very active plotter. In the weeks between the Crewe and Nantwich by-election disaster and the summer recess, Byers had no fewer than six face-to-face meetings with Straw. The last of their discussions took place in Straw's office at the Commons the day before the loss of Glasgow East. Straw indicated that he and Hoon would take action before the party conference. He suggested to Byers that they might also have the support of Alistair Darling, who was 'very pissed off with the way he was being treated by Gordon'. The embryonic plan was to remove Brown at the beginning of September so that they could use the party conference at the end of the month as a showcase for potential successors.[18]

As Straw plotted in the shadows, the first public strike was launched by David Miliband at the end of July. The Foreign Secretary set out his own recovery plan for Labour in a piece for the *Guardian* calling for 'a radical new phase'. It was a manqué manifesto for the leadership. Not once in the course of a 975-word article did he mention the name of the Prime Minister. Presented as a critique of David Cameron, much of it could be read, as it was intended to be read, as an attack on the failings of Gordon Brown. 'I disagreed with Margaret Thatcher, but at least it was clear what she stood for,' wrote Miliband. At a time when Brown was widely mocked for being visionless, dithering and arrogant, the Foreign Secretary added that 'we must be more humble about our shortcomings but more compelling about our achievements.' He went on: 'In government, unless you choose sides, you get found out.'[19] Miliband's move looked highly aggressive, though in some ways he was defensively trying to prevent anyone else from overhauling him as the most likely successor. Having failed to contest Brown for the premiership in 2007, he felt pressure to advertise his readiness to take over. 'He had to settle the cojones question,' said one of his nascent campaign team. 'He's pinned them on now.'[20]

The Prime Minister was incandescent. He saw this as a betrayal when he had given Miliband the promotion to the Foreign Office that he had never got from Blair. There was a hot debate within his court about how he should deal with the threat. Brown was initially sympathetic to the view of some advisers that he should feign being relaxed. 'If we attack Miliband, we'll only give him momentum,' argued one of his aides. Brown responded: 'That's exactly my view.'[21] Ed Balls then convened a conference call with Ian Austin, Damian McBride and Tom Watson. The attack dog view prevailed. 'It was decided to go for him.'[22] Off-the-record briefings to the press were employed to denounce Miliband as 'immature', 'self-serving' and 'disloyal'.[23]

This backfired. Brown looked panicked while Miliband was not deterred. In subsequent appearances before the media that week, the Foreign Secretary confirmed that he was putting his ambitions on the map. On a radio phone-in show, a caller urged him to 'put up a leadership challenge and get that God-awful man Brown out.' Rather than contradict her, Miliband joked: 'That's not one of my stooges, I promise.'[24]

There was some consolation for the Prime Minister. The Foreign Secretary moved unilaterally without consulting any of the other would-be regicides. He had shown a draft of his *Guardian* article to James Purnell, but discussed his plans with hardly anyone else.[25] 'He didn't tell any of us,' says a former Cabinet minister at the heart of the plotting.[26] Miliband in turn complained that colleagues failed to rally to his standard.[27] His timing was poor. He made his move just as Parliament was heading into its summer break. The minds of MPs were already on the beach. If they were going to deal the death blow to their leader, it would not be in August. That gave the Prime Minister the summer holidays to hatch a plan for his survival.

It was Sarah Brown's idea that they should spend the first week of their break in the Suffolk coastal town of Southwold, a favourite among the affluent English middle classes who liked an upmarket bucket-and-spade holiday. Her career had been in public relations, at which she was a more skilled operator than either her husband or anyone else around him. Her personal PR was good: she won an almost universally positive press in her opening twelve months as the first lady of Number 10. She cultivated a much less controversial image than Cherie Blair by deliberately staying on the edge of the limelight. Her public appearances were mainly confined to charitable events. 'She has not made herself a public figure,' remarked Murray Elder, who saw her as 'a tremendous supporter in every conceivable way' for his friend in Number 10. 'Sarah is very shrewd and capable politically.'[28] Mariella Frostrup thought: 'Sarah must be close to the perfect wife. She's clever, kind and supportive.'[29]

Brown deployed his wife as a human shield against the accusation that he did not understand the English middle classes. To one interviewer, he insisted: 'My wife is from Middle England, so I can relate to it.'[30]

The demure public image was the front on a woman with a steely mind who was fiercely protective of her husband and family. She formed a strong, and to some at Number 10 surprising, alliance with Damian McBride and Charlie Whelan based on their mutual interest in defending her husband. Sarah took charge of who came to lunches and dinners at Chequers. She rewarded McBride by telling him he could throw a Chequers lunch with guests of his choice – which he did.[31] Downing Street regarded the Prime Minister's wife as his best and chief propagandist. One member of the Brown communications team even went so far as to describe her as 'Magda Goebbels'.[32]

She designed the sojourn in Southwold, the quintessential English resort, to suggest that the Prime Minister was on the same wavelength as Middle Britain. It was entirely her idea, imposed on her protesting husband. 'I don't even know where it is,' Gordon Brown groaned to one friend before he left for Suffolk. 'He hated every minute of it and couldn't wait to get to Scotland.'[33]

Officials at Number 10 were desperate for the exhausted Prime Minister to get some rest. He was put on a fitness regime to try to improve his health and sleep. They tried to force him to take a proper holiday. 'Systems were put in place to stop him being bothered.'[34] These measures were not terribly successful as Brown defied their efforts to make him rest. A steady stream of his confidants slipped up to Southwold for councils of war with the Prime Minister. One visitor was Shriti Vadera. She stayed overnight for a 'brainstorming session' about what they were going to do about the precariousness of the banks, a discussion which began to incubate the idea of the comprehensive recapitalisation that would follow in the autumn. Vadera shrugged off complaints that she was interfering with the scheme to force the Prime

Minister to take a holiday. She said to friends that 'his form of diversion is an intellectual problem.'[35]

Other holiday visitors were Ed Balls, Damian McBride and Sue Nye, with whom Brown discussed how they were going to save his premiership from its encircling enemies. He was now so besieged that he was contemplating recruiting figures who were among his bitterest foes during the Blair years. This was also a sign, not lost on Balls and other veteran allies, that the Prime Minister's confidence in the support and advice of his old clique was waning. Approaches were made to Alastair Campbell, who modestly told friends that Brown had offered 'any role I wanted'. Campbell did not want to return to Number 10 in a communications capacity and talks about a ministerial role did not lead to one. 'There was an issue about what exactly he would do.'[36]

Brown's thoughts turned to Peter Mandelson. They were in regular phone contact over August, though there was still residual mistrust in the relationship and both were keeping secrets from each other. Brown did not know that Mandelson was spending part of that summer in Corfu, where he would share confidences with George Osborne, the Shadow Chancellor. On Osborne's later account, Mandelson 'dripped pure poison' about the Prime Minister's performance. Even not knowing that, Brown remained highly suspicious of what he saw as Mandelson's 'compulsion for plotting'.[37] He nevertheless discussed with Balls the idea of bringing Mandelson into the Cabinet. Balls was very wary, and Brown not much less so, but the Prime Minister was now so weakened that he was giving serious consideration to resurrecting the Cabinet career of the man who was once his mortal foe.

Alistair Darling also spent that August worrying about his future. The spinning against him from within Number 10 was becoming more nakedly aggressive as the Prime Minister's acolytes sought to displace blame for the Government's travails. One point of friction was Darling's resistance to Brown's idea of relaunching his premiership with an 'economic recovery plan' in September. Darling thought it would look panicky when they'd already been forced to announce one emergency Budget that year. His officials didn't like the idea of pre-empting the autumn financial statement.[38] Another source of tension was Brown cutting out Darling by talking directly to Mervyn King. The Prime Minister was trying to repair his relations with the Governor and create an alliance against the Treasury.[39] Further trouble was caused by Number 10's habitual spinning of headline-chasing economic initiatives without telling the Chancellor. A story about a possible stamp duty 'holiday' to encourage the housing market suddenly appeared on the same morning that an evidently bewildered Darling was interviewed on the *Today* programme. Not knowing whether or not this had been ordered by Brown, the Chancellor was reduced to stuttering incoherence.

Darling was a decent man in a highly difficult position. He was struggling with an economic downturn much worse than the Treasury had anticipated, he was trying to clear up mistakes made by the man who was his boss, and he was working for a Prime Minister who was frantically fighting to save his own job. The Chancellor had suffered months of being second-guessed by the Prime Minister and bad-mouthed to the media by Brown's retinue. Darling, an essentially passive politician, endured this with stoical patience. 'Alistair sucked it up and sucked it up for a very long time.'[40] His wife Maggie, a gregarious and vivacious former journalist, was made of feistier fibre than her husband. She persuaded him to sharpen up his defences by hiring a new chief political adviser. This was Catherine Macleod, the respected former Political Editor of the Glasgow-based *Herald* and a close friend of the Darlings for years. As part of a campaign to buttress his position, they invited influential journalists to dine with the Darlings in Downing Street to cultivate alliances with leading commentators. Hoping to establish Darling as a larger, more independent and more rounded public personality, they agreed to a request to do an in-depth interview for the *Guardian*'s Saturday magazine. The journalist Decca Aitkenhead spent two days over the summer with the Darlings at their remote croft on the Isle of Lewis in the Hebrides. She successfully discovered the deadpan wit and disarmingly frank character cloaked by Darling's buttoned-up and monochrome public persona. With refreshing candour, the Chancellor 'several times' told his interviewer that 'people are pissed off with us'.[41] He also predicted that the coming year would be 'the most difficult 12 months the Labour Party has had in a generation', acknowledged that 'we patently have not been able to get across what we are for' and declared that it was 'absolutely imperative' that Brown communicate a clearer message at the party conference.[42] Darling was equally direct about the state of the economy. His interviewer was 'completely taken aback'[43] when he told her that conditions 'are arguably the worst they've been in 60 years' and went on to forecast that 'it's going to be more profound and long-lasting than people thought.'[44]

The *Guardian* originally planned to publish the interview on the eve of the Labour conference, but then brought it forward to the end of August. Darling's arresting description of the economic outlook was projected on to the front page. The *Daily Telegraph*, which had somehow got sight of the interview, also had the story that Saturday morning and gave it the hostile interpretation that 'many of his comments will be read with dismay in Downing Street.'[45]

If Darling was at fault in his diagnosis, events would prove that he had underestimated the scale of the crisis. He subsequently said to me: 'The only thing I'd change if I had my time over again is that I should have said: "arguably, the worst for a hundred years".'[46] Reaction to the interview from the Cabinet was divided. Some colleagues accused the Chancellor of talking down confidence and handing ammunition to the Tories. Others agreed with Darling that frankness with the voters about the economic outlook was a better strategy than the Panglossian picture painted by the Prime Minister. The most extreme reaction to the interview was inside Number 10, where the Chancellor's cool truthfulness provoked raging fury. Through the paranoid prism of a Prime Minister under siege, it was seen as a premeditated attack and an attempt to sabotage the autumn relaunch. Brown phoned Darling on Saturday morning to tell him to back down. 'This will be over in six months,' insisted the Prime Minister. 'Well,' responded an astonished Darling. 'I'm glad you think so.'[47]

He refused to eat his words, instead repeating them in weekend television interviews in which he insisted he had a duty to be 'straight'.[48] The Prime Minister's attack dogs were then unleashed to savage the Chancellor. Charlie Whelan, Brown's ex-spinner, was informally back on the team. His official job was as Political Director of the Unite union, but Whelan was in regular attendance at Number 10 meetings. Whelan turned up at a book launch party at the Pillars of Hercules pub in Soho. He called together some of the journalists present. Unprompted, he started to 'lay into the Chancellor'. He told them 'this was "a gaffe", "what a terrible thing to say", "proves he doesn't understand", all stuff like this.' One of the journalists in his audience, Nick Cohen of the *Observer*, 'thought it extraordinary that at a moment of national crisis all the Prime Minister can do is send out his henchman to undermine the Chancellor of the Exchequer'.[49] McBride was even busier spreading poison against Darling. 'He told every journalist who had access to a pencil that Alistair's interview was a disaster. There was the most absolutely vicious briefing against him.'[50]

The result was a stream of front-page stories suggesting that Darling faced the sack. 'Darling's job on the line after recession blunder' was the headline in *The Times* over the byline of the paper's Political Editor, Philip Webster.[51] The Chancellor knew where this was coming from. 'A journalist of Phil Webster's calibre doesn't write a front-page splash unless he's got a very good source. We really thought they were coming to get us.'[52] Maggie Darling, a good woman who couldn't stand the bad treatment of her husband, was understandably enraged. She could not contain her fury that the Chancellor was being so brazenly traduced from next door. She blew up to one friend: 'The fucking cunts are trying to stitch up Alistair! The cunts! I can't believe they're such cunts!'[53]

The Chancellor confronted the Prime Minister. 'I don't know who's doing it,' stonewalled Brown. As he always did when his acolytes were attempting to destroy a minister, Brown denied any responsibility. This episode further ratcheted up the tension within the Cabinet. The Darlings had been so close to the Browns that Maggie babysat for John and Fraser. If the Prime Minister allowed this to be perpetrated against a friend as old as his Chancellor, the Cabinet reasoned that none of them were safe.

In the eyes of many ministers, Damian McBride was the principal villain in Number 10 and the ugliest manifestation of the Prime Minister's dark side. Some of that reputation was well-deserved. In the words of another member of the communications team: 'Damian was garrotting ministers left, right and centre.'[54] He was also a poorly cloaked and foolishly reckless assassin who spread a lot of nasty briefing via text and e-mail. That did not mean that the chief propagandist was responsible for every media hit job perpetrated by the Brown machine on members of the Government. The finger was pointed at him when Ruth Kelly's departure from the Cabinet was revealed in chaotic briefings in the early hours of the morning at the party conference. Kelly herself did not hold him responsible.[55] McBride had got himself such a reputation that he now attracted the blame for both what he did and what was perpetrated by other operatives in the Brown spin machine. Several senior members of the Cabinet confronted Brown about the activities of his hit squad. Jacqui Smith told him: 'This isn't doing you any good. It's got to stop.' Brown, as usual, pleaded ignorance: 'I'm not doing it.' Ed Miliband and Douglas Alexander, two of the Prime Minister's closest associates for years, repeatedly gave him the same warning.[56] 'Douglas had spectacular rows with Gordon about McBride.'[57] Both Jeremy Heywood and Gus O'Donnell, the Prime Minister's two most senior officials, urged him to remove McBride.[58]

He survived because he was protected by powerful allies. One of them was the Prime Minister's wife. Sarah Brown bought into McBride's argument that he had protected the Browns' young sons from press intrusion.[59] Brown, who had always retained in his entourage at least one assassin, was the most important reason why he stayed. As another aide put it: 'You prove your loyalty through brutality – there's a part of Gordon that likes that.'[60]

Another target of the hit squad was Ivan Lewis, a junior Health Minister and ally of Alan Johnson, a potential candidate to replace Brown as Prime Minister. Lewis aroused Brown's ire by being noisily critical in a series of interviews and articles. One in *The Times* in May was entitled 'A final warning for Gordon Brown' and another for the *Sunday Times* in August called for higher taxes on the rich and lectured the Prime Minister that 'there must be no more 1op-tax-style mistakes.'[61] For such a public breach of the conventions of loyalty, Brown would have been quite within his rights to either rebuke a junior minister or to fire him. An uglier method was employed to mete out punishment to Lewis and make an example of him designed to terrify anyone else who was thinking of voicing dissent. On Sunday, 7 September, the *News of the World* blared an 'exclusive': 'Txt pest shame of minister' with the subheading 'Lewis is so "sorry" for behaviour'.[62] The front page of the *Mail on Sunday* trumpeted the same story that Lewis had sent a stream of over-familiar phone text messages to a young female civil servant in his private office.[63]

This was damaging to a highly embarrassed Lewis from whom not a peep was heard thereafter. It was hardly helpful to the Government as a whole. Yet there were few Labour MPs who doubted that the story was planted by Number 10, which was privy to a confidential Whitehall report about the civil servant. The hit on Lewis stunned ministers who had regarded themselves as unshockable. One tough-minded minister says: 'The phones were buzzing that weekend. Red hot. It was brutal, it was vicious, it was unnecessary. We all – most of us, anyway – have skeletons in the cupboard which they know about. If Number 10 would do that to him, it would do it to anyone.'[64]

On the same Sunday, a venomous personal attack was launched on David Miliband. The author of it was Derek Simpson, the joint leader of the Unite union, whose political department was run by Charlie Whelan.[65] Nick Cohen of the *Observer* put it neatly: 'As the Don went for all his enemies at once, the Sunday papers looked like the closing scenes of *The Godfather*.'[66]

The new political season opened in early September with the Prime Minister's soldiers stabbing at both the Chancellor and the Foreign Secretary while key Cabinet members debated whether to send the Prime Minister to sleep with the fishes. This was an unpromising environment in which to launch a 'recovery plan' which was massively over-hyped. 'The expectation management was dreadful,' agrees one official.[67] It coincided with the release of grim data detailing the collapsing confidence in the housing market and among consumers. A scheme to give one-off payments to help the poor with their fuel bills had to be abandoned when Brown could not win the agreement of the energy companies. Proposals to boost the housing market received an unenthused reception from the construction industry and estate agents. That was accompanied by a worthy but dull initiative to encourage home insulation. Brown was not going to save his premiership with loft lagging. The relaunch sank without trace.

Rumours reached the Prime Minister that an unknown number of Labour MPs planned to go public with demands for him to quit. The threat of a letter-writing campaign by backbenchers held a particular terror for Brown because it was precisely the same device his acolytes employed two years earlier to force a resignation date out of Tony Blair. Brown loyalists were sent out to gather intelligence about the weight behind the revolt. 'Blair was taken by surprise when MPs moved against him,' says one Cabinet minister close to Brown. 'We did not want to repeat the same mistake.'[68]

Charles Clarke then launched his most direct attack yet when he warned that Labour was sleepwalking towards 'utter destruction'.[69] In subsequent interviews, Clarke expanded on his theme. If Brown did not go of his own volition, 'then I think it would be down principally to the Cabinet to decide what to do. I think many in the Cabinet share the view that we are in great difficulty and are doubtful about our capacity to get out of it, but there is not a view in the Cabinet at the moment that they should go and speak to Gordon.'[70] He accurately represented the angst in the Cabinet.[71] Eight Cabinet ministers contacted by a Sunday newspaper, including Alan Johnson, David Miliband, James Purnell and Jacqui Smith, did not respond when asked whether Brown should lead Labour into the next election, despite a specific instruction by Number 10 that they should reply yes.[72] But it was Clarke's last point that proved to be the crucial one: the Cabinet was not ready to act.

Jack Straw spent his August holiday on the east coast of America in Martha's Vineyard, where he wrestled with what to do. His despair about Brown's leadership was balanced by a fear of the implications of changing Prime Minister without an election twice in the same parliament, something that had not been done since 1945. He and other plotters were also apprehensive that Brown might simply refuse to go and they would then be in a disastrous situation if there was insufficient support among Labour MPs to force him out. 'You only get one shot,' Straw told another member of the Cabinet.[73] He came back from holiday to indicate to other plotters that he and Geoff Hoon had changed their minds about telling Brown that he had to go. Some involved believed that Hoon was 'bought off' with a promise from Brown that he would be nominated as the next European Commissioner. Straw's wife, a former senior civil servant, was thought influential in persuading him to keep his knife sheathed. There was an additional complication that the Justice Secretary fancied the leadership for himself, which made him reluctant to dethrone Brown for the benefit of someone else.[74]

The consensus view in the Cabinet was that Brown had to be 'given the autumn' to show whether or not he could recover.[75]

Some in Labour's ranks were not prepared to wait. In frustration with the paralysed Cabinet, more junior figures tried to precipitate events. On Friday, 12 September, Siobhain McDonagh, the MP for Mitcham and Morden, became the first member of the Government to call for a leadership contest. She was dismissed as a whip when it was revealed that she was among about a dozen MPs to write to party headquarters asking for leadership nomination papers in order to trigger a challenge. Joan Ryan was sacked as a vice-chairwoman of the party when she backed McDonagh. So did Janet Anderson and George Howarth, who were both close to Jack Straw. In the most savage attack on Brown to date, Howarth declared: 'No-one can remember a time since Neville Chamberlain, after Hitler invaded Norway, that anyone was so unpopular. We can't allow that to continue.'[76] They were joined by long-standing critics, including Frank Field, Peter Kilfoyle and Fiona Mactaggart. Barry Gardiner, a Blairite former minister, came out as another Septembrist in a newspaper article that Sunday which charged Brown with 'vacillation, loss of international credibility and timorous political manoeuvres. The tragedy for those of us who nominated the Prime Minister is that since achieving power he appears to have forgotten what it was he once wanted to do with it.'[77] Gisela Stuart, another former minister, joined their insurrection by declaring that Labour had gone from 'things can only get better' in 1997 to 'surely it can't get much worse'.[78] Charlie Falconer, close friend of Tony Blair, was giving them informal legal advice on the procedures for forcing a leadership contest.

David Cairns, the Minister of State for Scotland, was a former priest who had wrestled with his conscience for months about whether he could continue to support the Prime Minister. His name was on a list of ministers drawn up inside Number 10 who it was feared would join calls for Brown to go. On 16 September, his hand was forced by media reports that he was on the brink of resignation. He left the Government declaring that it was no longer possible to maintain the fiction that there was not a debate about Brown's future. He wrote to the Prime Minister that it was time 'to take the bull by the horns and allow a leadership debate to run its course'.[79]

The rebels were a mixed bag of ex-ministers, well-established critics of Brown and former loyalists who despaired of the party's prospects under his leadership.

The dissenting dozen had more support than their numbers suggested. Number 10 knew this from its own information-gathering operations.[80] Key

Cabinet ministers were strikingly reluctant to attack the mutineers. The Chief Whip merely questioned their timing. Geoff Hoon said: 'I simply don't think at this stage it's appropriate.' This was hardly a ringing endorsement of Gordon Brown nor a crushing rebuke to the rebels from the man supposed to be in charge of maintaining party discipline. John Hutton, the Business Secretary, also declined to condemn the revolt. 'I'm not going to criticise any of my colleagues who want Labour to do better,' he said and added: 'I think my colleagues are right to say that the Government needs to do better. For heaven's sake, we are 20 percentage points behind in the opinion polls.'[81]

On Tuesday, 16 September, Brown convened a 'political Cabinet' – called such because the civil servants are excluded from the room so that, in theory, ministers can talk candidly. It soon became clear that the Prime Minister did not want a frank conversation with his colleagues about Labour's plight. Deborah Mattinson was wheeled in to give a polling presentation about the weaknesses of the Tory party. She told them that voters saw David Cameron as likeable and compassionate, but remained unsure what the Tory leader really stood for. Mattinson concluded her presentation by observing that the Conservatives had not yet 'closed the deal' with the electorate so it was still possible for Labour to win. Several ministers listened to this with mounting and undisguised amazement. It was not that they quarrelled with the pollster's obvious account of the potential vulnerabilities of the Tory party. What they found astonishing was that they were being asked to talk about the weaknesses of their opponents rather than address their own epic unpopularity. 'It was terrible,' says one Cabinet minister. 'The unbearable thing about Gordon's Cabinets is the refusal to discuss the truth.'[82] Hazel Blears braved Brown's wrath by pointedly asking for the findings from the focus groups about voters' views of the Government. The Communities Secretary wondered whether it might not be useful to hear about Labour's strengths and weaknesses ahead of the party conference. Several other ministers raised their voices in support of that view. As Brown glowered, Ed Balls came to his defence, saying: 'We know why the electorate do not like us.'[83]

The atmosphere turned dark. Some of the Cabinet were so embarrassed that they could not bring themselves to look at the Prime Minister and stared at their hands, buried their heads in papers, or fiddled with Blackberries. Accounts of this disastrous Cabinet were then partially leaked to some newspapers. The *Evening Standard* was told that the meeting was 'just excruciating'.[84] The *Guardian* heard from one minister that it was 'bizarre and a denial of reality' and from another that it was 'a dreadful misjudgement'.[85] This seriously alarmed Number 10. 'Even someone with a skin as thick as Gordon's was bound to be wounded by that,' says one of his most senior aides. 'If members of the Cabinet were prepared to so openly and shamelessly brief that his performance was dire, it looked as though the game might soon be up.'[86]

A convergence of factors came to his rescue. The backbench insurrection was lacking in numbers, organisation and an agreed outcome. The plotters of autumn 2006 had a precise ambition: to replace Tony Blair with Gordon Brown. The plotters of autumn 2008 were never clear where it all might end. 'People couldn't agree who would replace him,' says one key conspira-tor.[87] It was the wrong plot at the wrong time. By acting just before the Labour conference, a point in the calendar when the party tends to feel the urge to display its unity, they had increased the likelihood that their insur-rection would be smothered. The party machine squashed the attempt to trigger a leadership contest. On the day of the Cairns resignation, the National Executive Committee took the advice of Labour's General Secretary, Ray Collins, that the party was under no legal requirement to issue nomina-tion papers. One leading figure plotting to remove Brown later lamented: 'It was like First World War troops going over the top and getting mowed down by the machine-gun fire.'[88]

The Cabinet was not ready to do the deed. 'We didn't get a decisive lead from the Cabinet,' says Frank Field. 'There was not an agreed view in Cabi-net what the alternative was and in those circumstances it's very hard to dislodge a Prime Minister.'[89] The senior ministers were Hamlet-like in their wavering over wielding the dagger. Jack Straw debated with himself many times afterwards whether he was right not to move against the Prime Minis-ter. Once he had decided against, the Justice Secretary presented himself as the acme of public loyalty, declaring: 'I'm absolutely clear Gordon Brown is the man with the experience and the intellect and the strategy to lead us through these current difficulties.' Straw added: 'Although I understand the frustrations that some of my colleagues feel, I don't think they are correctly directed.'[90] Alistair Darling also issued a loyalty oath, saying he had 'every confidence' in the Prime Minister. Harriet Harman described Brown as 'the best person when there are difficult international economic circumstances'.[91]

The person who did most to throw a lifeline to Brown's premiership was an American. That weekend, the US Treasury Secretary, Hank Paulson, made the fateful decision to allow the collapse of Lehman Brothers. The fall of Lehmans, the first major Wall Street house to go bankrupt because of the credit crunch, triggered the most savage convulsions on the world's financial markets.[92] A calamitous event for the economy, it was politically fortuitous for Gordon Brown. He realised this almost at once, telling one confidant: 'This changes everything.'[93] Even those in the Cabinet who utterly despaired

THE END OF THE PARTY

of him thought it would look unforgivably self-indulgent of the Labour Party to wage a battle over its leadership when the country was facing the most seismic financial crisis in generations.[94] As one of the backbench rebels ruefully concluded: 'Our timing was terrible.'[95]

The Labour conference in Manchester opened with huge pressure on the Prime Minister to perform. Some around him feared that his second speech as the party's leader would also be his last unless he found a way of stabilising his position. 'The speech had to be perfect. We knew that everything would fall apart if it was just another wall of Gordon sound.'[96]

One device was to deploy his wife. Ed Miliband was present at the Democrat convention in Denver in August when Barack Obama was introduced by his wife, Michelle. Brown had claimed to despise Blair for being too schmaltzy and previously sought credit for repudiating 'personality politics' and the 'politics of image'. He was wary of the notion that his wife should be his warm-up woman when it was first suggested.[97] By the time of the conference, his hesitation succumbed to his desperation. His wife did a deft job of raising the curtain for his speech, winning both warm applause from the delegates and sparkling press notices for a poised performance. The implicit suggestion of her remarks was that if she loved him then her husband must be human after all.

There were further borrowings from across the Atlantic in Brown's speech. He plagiarised one of Obama's signature phrases: 'This is not about me but about you.' He also borrowed another quintessentially American technique, the power of the humanising anecdote to make a political point. Brown related how the NHS saved his sight when he was young by giving him care that his parents could not have afforded to pay for. He tried to alchemise his weaknesses as a communicator into a strength. 'I'm not going to try to be something I'm not. And if people say I'm too serious, quite honestly there's a lot to be serious about. I'm serious about doing a serious job for all the people of this country.' He made a personal attack on David Cameron, whom he accused of exploiting his children by 'serving them up for spreads in the papers'. This was rich from a leader who had just leant on his wife as a prop.

There was a lively argument within his team about whether he should confess to his mistakes, especially the debacle over the abolition of the 10p tax band. Gordon Brown never did contrition. He was 'stung' by that furore, he told the conference. 'It really hurt that people felt I was not on the side of people on middle and modest incomes.' Thus he portrayed himself not as the author of the mistake, but as the victim of the way people interpreted him.

This fifty-three-minute speech was generally better constructed and delivered than the conference performance of a year before. Its central assertion was that he was the only person qualified to lead Britain through the crisis engulfing the financial markets. The past seven days were 'the week the world was spun on its axis, and old certainties turned on their heads', declared Brown, a formulation that echoed Blair's 'the kaleidoscope has been shaken' in the wake of 9/11.

The sharpest passage was aimed at puncturing the pretensions of those who wanted his job. 'Everyone knows that I am in favour of apprenticeships, but this is no time for a novice,'[98] he said, delivering the line with a smile of satisfaction. It was inspired by Ed Balls, who had said something similar during a dinner conversation with the editor of the *Sun*, Rebekah Brooks, formerly Wade. 'You should use that,' she said.[99] The crack about novices was Goliath's swipe at both the Davids, Cameron and Miliband. The TV coverage cut away to David Miliband when Brown delivered the slap-down. The Foreign Secretary was obliged to grit his teeth, hail Brown as 'excellent' and claim to believe: 'I think Gordon found his true voice.'[100]

Miliband had a bad week. He did not locate a resonant voice when he made his own speech. He was then embarrassed when he was overheard in a lift excusing his failure to rouse the delegates by saying he couldn't have 'done a Heseltine'.[101] The truth was that his performance came nowhere near hitting the conference G-spot in the way mastered by that Tory performer. The enduring image of the Foreign Secretary's conference week captured him in a ridiculous rather than heroic pose. He allowed himself to be photographed wielding not a shining sword, but a bathetic banana.

Gordon Brown emerged from the conference stronger than he went into it. His exploitation of the financial crisis to assert his credentials as the right leader for the hour stayed the hand of plotters in the Cabinet and snuffed out the backbench revolt. Yet many senior Labour figures regarded it as merely a stay of execution. They departed Manchester unconvinced that he had a plan to lift the Government from the deep pit into which it had sunk. One of the most sceptical was Peter Mandelson. He was publicly loyal during the conference week, and helped with the speech. Yet his support had an ambivalent flavour even so, telling one interviewer: 'I do not think changing the face at the top is the panacea some imagine', not the most resounding endorsement.[102] He privately continued to express despair to colleagues and some journalists about Brown's capacity to turn things around.[103]

On Thursday, 2 October, Mandelson slipped into Number 10 to see the Prime Minister. He had received 'absolutely no intimation whatsoever' of what was to transpire.[104] He assumed that Brown wanted to continue to use him in the strange new role of secret adviser that had developed over the past few months. When they sat down, a light lunch of sandwiches, yoghurt and bananas was laid out before them. Suddenly, 'without any warning', Brown popped the question: he wanted his visitor to return to the Cabinet. Mandelson recalls: 'I choked on my yoghurt.' He had come to the meeting thinking that Brown wanted his advice on the reshuffle not that he was going to be the centrepiece of it. Having established that Brown really meant it and wanted to give him a serious job, he responded that he had to have time to think. 'I need to call a friend,' he said. That friend was Tony Blair. Mandelson slipped out of Number 10 and nipped across London that afternoon to see the former Prime Minister. 'After he'd finished laughing out loud at the irony of the situation', Blair told Mandelson: 'It's a no-brainer. You have to do it.'[105]

This was the wildest plot twist in the stunningly convoluted history of the personal relations between the founding fathers of New Labour. Yet it had a strange kind of logic, almost an inevitability. 'Peter was Gordon's person before he was Tony's person,' reflects one of Mandelson's friends. 'They have a lot in common. Both are loners. They are not family people. They are both very selfish when they want to be. They are both political to their fingertips. They both have a deep Labour heritage. They are both intellectual.'[106]

The small group who founded New Labour had ever been a family. In the good times, they were a band of blood brothers who fashioned one of the most successful political projects. In the bad times, the family resembled a cross between *The Sopranos* and *The Simpsons*. Now, in these bleakest of times, two of the founding fathers were drawn back together to try to rescue their creation from oblivion. Whatever else divided the two men, they had a mutual stake in trying to save from destruction what they had made with Tony Blair.

For Mandelson, his remarkable third coming as a Cabinet minister, one of the most startling comebacks since Lazarus, satisfied his yearning to be back on the frontline of British politics and gave him the opportunity to redeem his reputation. When he sashayed up Downing Street in a blue double-breasted suit and strawberry cashmere sweater, he told reporters it would be 'third time lucky'.[107] For Brown, it created a *coup de théâtre* which stunned both friend and foe when the reshuffle was unveiled on Friday, 3 October. None of the media, all of whom had been working to the dated script that they still hated each other, saw this coming.[108] To Brown's anger, the *Daily Mail* snickered: 'Arise, Lord Sleaze'.[109] Most of the press, though, was dazzled. The *Guardian* saw it as 'one of the most brilliant coups of his career', which 'reminded sceptics that he still retains plenty of political cunning'.[110] 'For a sinking Prime Minister,' opined the *Financial Times*, 'it is a gamble of astonishing audacity.'[111]

Brown suggested that he had recalled Mandelson to draw on the other man's 'immense experience and expertise' at a time of financial crisis, saying 'serious times need serious people'.[112] He privately said: 'I'm trying to use every talent I can lay my hands on.'[113] His primary motive was political. In a stroke, it blunted the knives of the assassins. For most of his career, Mandelson had been a high-maintenance politician, a divisive and turbulent figure. In these strange circumstances, his recall was unifying and calming while also adding heft and celebrity to a generally colourless Cabinet. Blairites could not be part of any move against Brown now that the high priest of Blairism was back. 'He's extended the hand of friendship and we've got to take it and see what can be done,' said one Blairite Cabinet minister.[114]

This dramatic flourish also distracted the media while Brown made other moves to strengthen his grip over the party. Geoff Hoon was replaced as Chief Whip by Nick Brown. As part of the price for his return, Mandelson thought he had extracted a promise from Brown that he would dispose of Damian McBride. McBride was moved to a less prominent role, but he remained at Number 10. With time on his hands, his activities would actually become more dangerous to Brown.

The new Business Secretary was ennobled as Baron Mandelson of Hartlepool and Foy, though he was always more Foy than Hartlepool. There were many predictions that it couldn't last five minutes, that Mandelson was as certain to sting Brown as the scorpion was the frog in Aesop's fable. This proved to be wrong. Cabinet members reported that Mandelson was having a positive effect on both the direction of the Government and the morale of the Prime Minister. James Purnell put it like this: 'It's a bit like people who created a rock band together, had a great success, and then had their ups and downs in their relationship. When they come back together as a band, they suddenly remember what it was that made them so close in the first place.'[115]

Mandelson managed to coexist, albeit with wariness on both sides, alongside Ed Balls. They agreed a mutual non-aggression pact in which they would not spin against each other as they had in the past nor argue in front of others at meetings.[116] He provided Brown with some strategic nous, presentational flair and emotional support. 'I know it sounds strange, but Peter has made Gordon much more relaxed and confident,' said one member of the Cabinet. 'At the same time, Peter can be blunt with Gordon about his faults in a way no-one else can.'[117] Another minister who saw the two men together marvelled at how 'they spoke to each other like brothers.'[118] A third noted that 'they have their own little code' often impenetrable to anyone else, a semaphore which could convey a thousand words of meaning in a look or a phrase.[119] At New Labour's time of gravest crisis, Brown and Mandelson had found something which surpassed even the oceans of poison that had flowed between them. They were drawn back together by their mutual desperation to save the project itself.

34. The Great Escape

Gordon Brown rang Shriti Vadera when he heard the news. 'How serious is this?' 'Oh crap,' responded the former investment banker. 'It is very, very serious.'[1]

Lehman Brothers collapsed into bankruptcy on Monday, 15 September. The 158-year-old investment bank had behaved like a wild teenager in its reckless pursuit of profits, leveraging its books by an astonishing factor of 44, meaning it had forty-four dollars of debt for every dollar of tangible capital. Leverage magnifies profits in booms and multiplies losses in busts. Huge bets on the American property market left the bank on its knees. Up to this point, no major financial institution had been allowed to go bankrupt. Hank Paulson put up $30 billion from the American Government to help rescue Bear Stearns earlier in the year. The US Treasury Secretary also set aside Republican free-market ideology to effectively nationalise Fannie Mae and Freddie Mac, the two mammoth institutions which stood behind more than half of all American mortgages. Merrill Lynch, whose 'raging bull' logo was totemic of the bubble, was about to be folded into the arms of Bank of America. The assumption in London was that Paulson would act to save Lehmans rather than risk triggering a cascade of banking collapses. Gordon Brown 'didn't expect Paulson to let Lehmans go'.[2] Neither did Alistair Darling: 'The feeling was the Americans would step in to save Lehmans. That was my assumption. The weekend before, that's what I understood was going to happen.'[3] At the Bank of England, they shared that mistaken belief, says the Deputy Governor, Sir John Gieve: 'The markets thought and we thought that Paulson would prop them up.'[4]

The first indication that this assumption might be wrong came on Sunday, when Paulson rang Darling. The Chancellor was at his home in Edinburgh and the US Treasury Secretary was calling from the headquarters of the New York Federal Reserve, where he had spent the weekend trying to cajole Wall Street bankers to rescue Lehmans because he didn't want to put up any taxpayers' cash. Dick Fuld, Lehman's intensely aggressive boss, had declined earlier opportunities to sell parts of his crippled bank. Paulson reckoned that Wall Street needed to be taught a lesson. Another bail-out was also politically unattractive. The previous rescues were sparking angry attacks from both the Republican right wing, who saw it as interference with the free market, and the Democratic left, scandalised by giving tax dollars to the rich and reckless of Wall Street. The fierce anti-banker backlash in America was heightened by the presidential election campaign. Paulson rang Darling to seek his assistance with a potential takeover of Lehmans by Barclays. Down the line from New York, the US Treasury Secretary complained that the British authorities were being obstructive by raising a huge number of questions about the viability and safety of the deal. Darling responded that they needed cast iron assurances that bringing the enormous liabilities of Lehmans on to the books of a British bank was not going to endanger the UK's financial system.[5] Paulson remarked to aides: 'He doesn't want to import the American disease.'[6] The two men could not give each other what they wanted. The call ended with Darling still assuming that, when push came to shove, Paulson would retreat and rescue Lehmans. He said later: 'The American purse would have been big enough to do it.'[7] The Chancellor discovered he had misjudged his American counterpart in a later call from New York that Sunday. Barclays was walking away from the deal and Paulson was still not prepared to act. 'Hank told me that basically they were gonna let them go.' The Chancellor was stunned, but felt powerless to protest. 'Both of us were aware of the seriousness of it. But I could no more tell the US Treasury Secretary that he'd got to save a bank than he could tell me that I'd got to save a bank. It is American taxpayers' money he was on about.'[8] Darling immediately rang his officials to tell them to accelerate contingency planning to cope with more British bank failures.[9]

The fall of Lehmans, the largest corporate bankruptcy the world has ever seen, was an incredible shock to the brittle confidence of the financial markets. At the Bank of England, it was seen as a 'disastrous error' after which 'things really fell apart.'[10] Lehmans was the counterparty to some $440 billion of trades with other financial institutions. As John Eatwell puts it: 'A whole series of trades just failed all around the world.'[11] There was blind panic and modern communications transmitted the virus around the globe in an instant. Credit markets went into cardiac arrest. Banks lost all confidence in banks. The amount they charged each other for short-term loans doubled overnight as borrowing rates between them went 'through the roof'.[12] Within forty-eight hours, European banks simply stopped lending dollars to each other. There was massive dumping of shares in any institution that appeared the least bit fragile; there was a crash in the shares of those which looked most exposed. By the end of Monday, the Dow had dived 504 points, its biggest drop since 9/11. Paulson, flipping from one stance to another from day to day, did intervene on Tuesday to spend $85 billion rescuing the giant AIG, which had insured many of the toxic loans held by the banks. The authorities also responded with a temporary ban on short-selling of financial shares and central banks flushed hundreds of billions of dollars of liquidity into markets. This parachute was not strong enough to brake the freefall. The measures were totalling billions, but they were a response to an evaporation of confidence in instruments valued in trillions. The heart of the problem was the $55 trillion of credit derivatives, a market that had been allowed to grow to a monetary value more than twice the size of the combined GDP of America, Japan and the European Union. In the bubble years, bankers convinced themselves that by spreading these instruments everywhere they had derisked the financial system. What they had actually done was ensure that the contagion would infect every financial centre in the world when the greed of the boom turned into the panic of the bust. No-one could be certain which contracts still had value and which were now worthless. More than any other single event, it was the fall of Lehmans that turned a crunch into a meltdown.

At the Bank of England, 'the big question on everyone's lips was "Who's next?"'[13] As the tide goes out, you discover who is swimming naked. British banks had short-term borrowings of an incredible £750 billion which had to be refinanced every fortnight to three months. When global credit markets froze 'that money vanished'.[14] Two of Britain's largest banks – Halifax Bank of Scotland and the Royal Bank of Scotland – were starkly exposed. Darling was warned that the position of HBOS, Britain's biggest mortgage lender, 'was absolutely dire'.[15] Within thirty minutes of the stock market opening on Wednesday, 17 September, its share price was cut in half. The Government really didn't want to be forced to take it over. Fortunately – or so it seemed at the time – there was a white knight on a black horse willing to come to the rescue. Lloyds TSB had been Britain's most conservatively managed bank and was thirsty to make acquisitions. At a drinks reception before a bankers' dinner in St James's on the Monday, Gordon Brown had a conversation with Sir Victor Blank, the Chairman of Lloyds TSB, a respected figure in the City and a long-time Labour sympathiser. Blank was not interested in HBOS to do a favour for the Government. Lloyds had been frustrated for a long time that competition rules prevented it from expanding by buying other banks. As waiters hovered with trays of champagne, the Prime Minister indicated to Blank that the rules would be waived in these exceptional circumstances, a promise which helped the Lloyds Chairman sell the take-over to his board.[16] Darling agreed that the risks of financial contagion 'trumped the competition concerns'.[17] Just forty-eight hours after Blank's conversation with Brown, the deal was announced. The Prime Minister was keen for his personal intervention to be advertised as an example of his leadership in a crisis. 'Brown knew Blank very well and was able to have a laugh and a chat with him,' a Number 10 spinner bragged to the press. 'Would any other leader be able to do that?'[18] This boast would later boomerang horribly on Brown. When Lloyds ate HBOS, a bank loaded with toxic assets, it gulped down a poison pill.

The next British bank on the skids was the Bradford & Bingley which 'was getting into deeper and deeper trouble'.[19] After 'the horror of Northern Rock' both ministers and Treasury officials regarded it as vital to the Government's reputation that 'B&B was done quickly and cleanly'.[20] On Saturday, 27 September, Darling called the leaders of the big banks into the Treasury to try to persuade them to buy B&B. To his alarm, the Chancellor found that none of the banks were biting. 'We all basically said we weren't interested,' says one of the bankers at the table. 'No-one wanted it.'[21] Anxious to avoid outright nationalisation, by Sunday night the Treasury had scrambled together a hybrid solution. It was announced the next day that the Government had taken over the £50 billion mortgage book while the rest of the bank was sold off to Santander, the Spanish bank which already owned Abbey and Alliance & Leicester. Thirty-six hours of high-speed negotiations were smoothed by the involvement of Terry Burns, a former Permanent Secretary at the Treasury, who was a member of the Santander board as the Abbey's Chairman. Some lessons had been learnt from the Northern Rock debacle. The Government had since equipped itself with better legal powers to effect quick rescues.[22] What took five months with the Rock was telescoped into a weekend when it came to the Bradford & Bingley. The Treasury quietly congratulated itself that this rescue was implemented without a panic and no queues of depositors clamouring for their money. Yet they were also becoming daily more troubled that much larger banks were near the edge. In the words of one senior Treasury official: 'Most of our internal discussions asked: "How big is the problem?" and concluded that was anyone's guess.'[23]

The Government had so far responded like firefighters, dashing from blazing bank to bank to hose them down before they set light to another institution. 'We are dealing with the problems one by one,' remained the public line from Gordon Brown.[24] In private, Number 10, the Treasury and the Bank of England, all increasingly terrified by the escalating scale of the crisis, were converging on the view that a much more comprehensive answer was required to shore up confidence before the entire British banking system slid towards collapse. Darling was now 'reaching the conclusion it was the systemic problem we had to deal with' and they couldn't go on 'dealing with this piece by piece'.[25]

In a little-remarked-upon speech nine months earlier, Mervyn King had first suggested that the surest way to restore trust and stabilise the financial system was to recapitalise all the banks by injecting them with public money. Something similar had been done successfully by Sweden during a banking crisis in the early 1990s. The Governor was now minded to force help on them even if it meant effective nationalisation of every British bank. 'Mervyn would have done the lot,' says one senior civil servant. In a 180-degree turn from his earlier inflexibility about moral hazard, 'Mervyn had gone completely to the other extreme.'[26]

Brown and Darling were reluctant to go so far as to nationalise every bank, but they were coming to agreement that they needed 'a generic solution' to recapitalise all the troubled institutions.[27] Brown first started to think about this seriously during his summer holiday when he talked about it in general terms with his closest advisers, principally Ed Balls and Shriti Vadera. 'What was the mechanism became the big question.'[28] By the autumn, it was apparent that the markets could not supply the solution. Only vast sums of public money would do the job.

While increasingly persuaded intellectually that this was the correct course, Brown was highly fearful of the political fall-out. He expected outrage among voters if taxpayers' money was used to save banks from their own follies. 'How do we explain this to people?' was the Prime Minister's repeated question to Balls, Vadera and his new best friend, Peter Mandelson.[29]

Brown would later boast that he was the inspired author of a grand plan that was emulated around the world, as indeed it was. But during the gestation of the bank bail-out he was gripped by this private terror that it would destroy him politically. The financiers were being flayed across the media spectrum and denounced for their reckless greed in speech after speech on party conference platforms that autumn. Brown felt even more exposed because there was scant international cover to help legitimise the idea of bank bail-outs. 'No-one else is doing it,' he worried to his intimates. Neither Nicolas Sarkozy in France nor Angela Merkel in Germany were pumping their taxpayers' money directly into banks. The Americans were not recapitalising in this way either. If Britain acted alone, Brown worried, 'Where is this going to leave us?'[30]

The Prime Minister hoped to bring the Americans round when he flew out to New York in the last week of September. As the plane crossed the Atlantic, Sarah Brown strolled towards the back to chat to the accompanying journalists. As a treat for them, she brought along the Australian super-model Elle Macpherson, who was doing an appearance for charity with the Prime Minister's wife.[31] While the reporters at the rear of the plane were distracted by the celebrity eye-candy, up in the first-class cabin sat the Prime Minister gnawing on his dilemma about the banks. He made a long-scheduled address to the UN General Assembly on Thursday, 25 September. The focus was originally going to be global poverty, but the trip was now dramatically reshaped by the crisis. It was here that Brown first talked of 'the end of the Age of Irresponsibility'.[32] He diverted to Washington for a hurriedly arranged meeting with George Bush on Friday afternoon. The President looked strained. Documents marked 'Top Secret' were scattered on his desk. Brown quickly got to the point and endeavoured to persuade Bush to look at recapitalising American banks. The President responded with a lack of interest. He explained that he had been arm-twisting Congressmen to vote for the different strategy of creating a toxic dump for bad debts: Hank Paulson's $700 billion 'Troubled Asset Recovery Plan'. Brown felt obliged to express support when reporters asked him about TARP. In private, he thought the American scheme was going to be expensive and ineffective.[33] He came away from the White House disappointed and dispirited.

Just before he got on the plane home from Washington, a document was faxed through to the Prime Minister's party. It was from Jeremy Heywood, back in London, who had pulled together the clandestine work on recapitalising banks which had been done at Number 10, the Treasury, the Bank and the FSA.[34] On the flight home, Shriti Vadera and his other advisers gathered round Brown in the first-class cabin. He now knew for certain that going ahead with a bail-out would mean taking a course that the Americans seemed dead set against. 'It felt very lonely.'[35] That magnified the risks that voters would rebel against giving billions to the banks. Yet Brown was beginning to reach the conclusion that he had no choice but to take the gamble. The perils of delay were underlined by the frantic weekend trying to find a buyer for the Bradford & Bingley and the continuing evaporation of credit for institutions, large or small. It was getting perilously close to the point where blue chip businesses might not be able to pay their employees. As they crossed the Atlantic, Brown addressed his advisers: 'I think we're just going to have to do this.'[36]

The next shattering blow to confidence came on Monday, 29 September. Paulson's TARP scheme was rejected by Congress, where representatives railed against writing an enormous blank cheque with American taxpayers' money for a poorly presented scheme of suspect merit to save financial institutions from their own stupidity. Within moments of the no vote, Wall

Street was hurtling downwards, plunging a record 777 points in a day. Though a panicked Congress passed TARP four days later, the damage was done. Fresh spikes of fear convulsed global markets. Lending rates sky-rocketed even higher. Major financial institutions folded on both sides of the Atlantic. Night after night, news bulletins showed frenzied dealers yelling in trading rooms and staff who had lost their jobs in the City carrying boxes of belongings from crashing citadels of finance. In a single week, 734 second-hand Ferraris were put up for sale. The Dow dived below 10,000 for the first time since 2004.

Fear fuelled itself and infected leaders around the world. Frightened governments began to act unilaterally to try to insulate their national banks from the pandemic of panic. Ireland, faced with the collapse of its banks, broke with the rest of the European Union to guarantee all deposits. On Sunday, 5 October, Angela Merkel appeared to follow suit by suggesting she was ordering a unilateral guarantee of 570 billion euros in deposits held in the German banking system. This threatened to endanger the rest of the EU by encouraging investors to suck their money out and transfer it to Germany. At the Treasury, officials spent Sunday 'frantically trying to speak to some-one in Germany' to clarify their intentions. 'There was no-one there. Germany wasn't answering the phone.'[37]

The next day, there was so much carnage on the British stock market that it was dubbed 'Meltdown Monday'. The FTSE 100 suffered its biggest one-day points fall on record when almost £100 billion was wiped off the value of Britain's top hundred companies. A stand-out target for this latest selling frenzy was the Royal Bank of Scotland. That morning, RBS's Chief Executive, Sir Fred Goodwin, was addressing a roomful of investors in the opulent ball-room of London's Landmark Hotel near Marylebone station. In a half-hour presentation, he endeavoured to reassure them that the bank was still sound. One fund manager then raised his hand: 'In the time that you have been speaking, your share price has fallen 35 per cent. What is going on?' Goodwin turned white.[38]

The Chief Executive of RBS was the son of an engineer from the unglamorous Glasgow suburb of Paisley. He gained a reputation for maximising profits through ruthless cost-cutting which earned him the soubriquet 'Fred the Shred'. Founded in 1727, RBS had been the reliable but unexciting old lady of Edinburgh banking until 2000, when Goodwin arrived with an aggressive strategy for expansion. Like so many of his ilk, he took advantage of the over-tolerance of risk and indulgence of excess during the bubble. On both sides of the Atlantic, financiers had successfully lobbied politicians to relax the laws to make banking safer which had been introduced in the wake of the 1929 Wall Street Crash. In the 1980s and '90s, they tore down the firewalls that previously separated high street retail banks, serving the public by looking after savings and making loans, from the much riskier activities of investment banks, which place colossal bets as market speculators. The utility banks behaved more and more like casino banks. Behind the respectable, boring high street exteriors of the retail banks, there were gambling dens at the back. RBS had hugely expanded into derivative trading. During the years of success, Goodwin was feted by the City for transforming a sleepy Scottish institution into the world's fifth-largest bank. RBS expanded its loan books to a size where they were enormous in comparison with the resources of the nation that ultimately had to underwrite them. The bank's assets and liabilities were almost $2 trillion apiece. Its balance sheet was larger than the entire GDP of Britain.

This was one manifestation of the decade of global dominance enjoyed by financiers in New York and London. Not only had they convinced themselves that they were close to being gods, but their huge wealth and deceptive success dazzled politicians, who were beguiled by the myths of unrestrained markets, ever-rising asset prices and endless growth. In the boom years, RBS's behaviour did not arouse the apprehension of Gordon Brown. It attracted his admiration. Goodwin was knighted for 'services to banking' in 2004. Two years later, Brown appointed his fellow Scot to his International Business Advisory Council. The title that Goodwin truly deserved was fool's gold medal in the fiercely contested competition to be the most stupid British banker. He continued to pursue a megalomaniac lust for expansion even once it was evident that the bubble was burst. His most ruinous purchase – paying a vast price for ABN Amro, a Dutch bank loaded with toxic assets – was made in autumn 2007 when the credit crunch was already beginning to bite. The collapse of the derivative markets and the soaring cost of short-term loans in the wake of the Lehmans bankruptcy left RBS 'really hanging over the edge of a cliff'.[39] The bank's chief revealed the precariousness of the position to George Osborne. 'We're on a hair trigger,' he confided in a telephone conversation with the Shadow Chancellor. 'He was having to arrange overnight financing for the Royal Bank of Scotland's positions and it would take only one thing to pull that trigger and he couldn't get the overnight financing.'[40]

This made it even more imperative for the Government to get together a rescue plan. Shriti Vadera, on Brown's behalf, had joined forces with Tom Scholar, who had become Managing Director of International and Finance at the Treasury, to put together a secret and informal committee of City advisers to work up a blueprint for a recapitalisation. They turned to the few bankers not tainted by the crisis who could be expected to offer an impartial opinion. One was Peter Sands, the Chief Executive of Standard Chartered, who hosted a meeting on 2 October at his City headquarters to develop the plan. The next day, Vadera presented their conclusions to the Prime Minister. Brown continued to agonise between the political risks of action and the perils to the financial system of inaction. 'He knew he had a choice,' says Peter Mandelson. 'He could be paralysed in fear in reaction to what was happening or he had to react with boldness, with decisiveness and take a great deal of policy and political risk. He chose the latter.'[41] Brown was also hurried to a decision by the pace of events and rumours about his intentions. The plan was supposed to be secret, but word that the Government was considering this momentous step began to seep out. An infuriated Prime Minister privately blamed this on 'blabbing' by Mervyn King, who had briefed David Cameron and George Osborne that there would have to be a state-financed rescue. He suspected that the tip-off from the Governor had prompted the Tories to announce their conversion to a bail-out in weekend television interviews.[42] On the evening of Sunday, 5 October, Brown, Darling and King met to discuss the recapitalisation plan and 'decided we were definitely going ahead'.[43] Paul Myners, who had just been recruited as the City Minister, agrees that this was when they came to the conclusion 'that something big needed to be done, with an element of shock and awe, with big numbers'.[44] The initially hesitant Brown was now impatient for the bail-out to be put into action as soon as possible. 'When are we going to do this?' Brown badgered Darling and other ministers. 'Which day?'[45] The answer would partly depend on whether the banks were ready to accept that they needed help.

While the Prime Minister worried about the political consequences of giving billions to the banks, the irony was that the bankers were hugely reluctant to take the money. The chairmen and chief executives were coming over to the Treasury for clandestine crisis meetings on a 'weekly or twice-weekly' basis.[46] The Chancellor chaired an important encounter on the evening of Monday, 6 October. All of Britain's seven big banks along with the Nationwide building society were represented round the table in the conference room just outside his Treasury office. Mervyn King and Adair Turner, the head of the FSA, were also present. The mood was grim after the day's record plunge in share prices. Darling began by expressing his irritation that the plan for a bail-out was already becoming public knowledge and urged everyone around the table to keep their discussions secret.

The Treasury, the Bank and the Financial Services Authority had by now done 'a ton of work' on the state of the banks and it told them that RBS and HBOS in particular were perilously close to having 'no cash'.[47] Yet the bankers were reluctant to admit it. One bank chairman explains that this was partly because 'no-one liked talking about their problems in front of their competitors.'[48] Alistair Darling agrees that this was a difficulty with these group meetings: 'When you've got ten people in a room, no-one is going to put their hand up and say: "Excuse me, could we have a private word because we're really in a terrible position."'[49] It was also because they were in collective denial. 'There was no acceptance or recognition on their side that they needed capital,' says a Treasury official present. 'That was the case until a very late stage.'[50] Ego was another explanation for the bankers' refusal to face reality. Accepting that they needed Government support meant acknowledging that these supposed titans of finance had brought their businesses to the edge of collapse. 'They were struggling to keep up with the pace of events – that's the truth of it,' says John Gieve. 'Their line throughout was you should help us with the liquidity because the markets are illiquid, but we have solvent, viable enterprises.' He found them 'reluctant to accept that actually they weren't viable and they were slower to come to the view that they needed recapitalisation on a big scale than we were.'[51] When Sir Fred Goodwin held private talks with ministers that evening, he was still denying that RBS had a problem with capital. The most he was prepared to admit was that his bank might have 'the wrong sort of capital'.[52]

Darling thought he had a way of detecting when one of the bankers wasn't coming clean. Their body language spoke more truthfully than their lips. 'I'm no expert, but you just had to look at people's demeanour. You could generally tell how much trouble someone was in by the extent to which they denied they had a problem.'[53]

The conclave chaired by Darling was followed by a meeting of bank chiefs alone where they argued about what sort of deal to do with the Government. The Chancellor took the opportunity to slip away to Number 11, where he was very late for a reception he had thrown for journalists. When he finally turned up, he joked to a group of reporters: 'All my political career people have been telling me to stop being so left wing, to give up on socialism, to move away from the left, follow the focus groups and embrace the centre. Now they want me to nationalise the bloody banks!' Martin Bright of the *New Statesman* remarked that he seemed strangely calm. 'The panic will come later,' deadpanned the Chancellor.[54] He maintained his forced jollity for a little while and then left his own party after less than an hour to hurry back to the Treasury. The Monday night meeting broke up without agreement on the terms of a bail-out. When Brown was informed of the deadlock, he reacted with angry frustration.[55]

The Chancellor was woken at four the next morning to be driven to RAF Northolt to board a chartered jet to Luxembourg for a meeting of European finance ministers. He landed in pelting rain at just after seven. One of his officials was alarmed by what he was reading on his Blackberry and passed it to the Chancellor. A version of the Monday night meeting with the bankers, the one at which Darling had urged secrecy on everyone, was posted on the blog of the BBC's Robert Peston. He wrote that 'a trio of the biggest banks' was blaming Darling for not presenting 'a fully elaborated rescue plan' and had told him to 'pull his finger out' and come up with the money.[56] This disclosure of the crisis talks at the Treasury intensified the mayhem on the markets. As one banker says: 'Banks are very easy things to destabilise. You only need to start a rumour that someone can't pay and it brings about the very thing you fear. That is why the Peston story was so destructive.'[57] Both Treasury officials and bankers in the room deny responsibility for the leak and insist that the account supplied to the BBC was a distorted version of what occurred. At the time, the Government blamed the banks, but one Treasury official contends: 'Banks would never sit round a table and say "we're fucked".'[58] There was considerable suspicion among some Treasury officials and bankers that the leak came from Number 10 trying to satisfy the Prime Minister's desire to force the pace. 'Gordon's time horizon is extraordinarily short. He's always thinking how do we get ourselves out of a corner and put someone else in a corner,' comments one banker with intimate experience of how the Prime Minister liked to operate.[59] Earlier leaks had forced forward the announcement of the Lloyds TSB take-over of HBOS and revealed the Bradford & Bingley deal before the legal documents had actually been signed. 'They wanted to get the bail-out show on the road,' says a bank chairman. 'All these leaks have the characteristic of someone trying to make things happen faster than they were.'[60]

Whoever was responsible for leaking to Peston, his story had catastrophic consequences. By the time Darling started the Luxembourg meeting with his European counterparts, there was a feeding frenzy of bank shares. His officials called him out to report that the share price of RBS was 'dropping like a stone'.[61] Darling went into an anteroom to make calls back to Britain to try to find out what the hell was going on.[62] When he returned to his European colleagues, they could see that Darling was 'clearly tense'.[63] Christine Lagarde, the Finance Minister of France, read the alarm on the face of her British counterpart.

I remember clearly Alistair standing up, leaving the room, coming back. Being in and out very much. That worried me quite a bit, because the previous recollection that I had of Alistair having to leave the room, and eventually not returning, was at the time when Northern Rock collapsed.[64]

The Chancellor abandoned the Luxembourg meeting to rush back to London. Arriving at the Treasury shortly after three o'clock, he went straight into a crisis conference with all his senior officials and then went to see Brown at Number 10. Darling said that leaks were making things impossible. They needed to 'bring it forward, do it now, announce it on the Wednesday'.[65] The Chancellor had been deeply alarmed by a telephone conversation with Sir Tom McKillop, the Chairman of RBS. 'How long do you think we've got?' asked Darling. The banker responded: 'I think we've got a day.'[66]

The Chancellor told the others that he feared 'the banking system was on the verge of collapse.'[67] Shriti Vadera agreed: 'We have to keep things moving.' They had to get a deal announced before the markets opened the next day. Yet many of the bankers were still insisting that they could ride out the storm. Brown gave the order: 'Whatever they say, plough on.'[68] One senior civil servant, who had previously despaired of Brown's inability to make timely decisions, was impressed. 'He's really good in crises in a subject he understands. He's energised by it.'[69] Mervyn King and Adair Turner of the FSA were called to Number 10 to finalise the details.

The Governor, who was now as petrified as the politicians that major banks were about to fold, had started to make massive covert emergency bridging loans to HBOS and RBS. Only a handful of people were told about these clandestine loans for fear that public knowledge would precipitate multiple bank runs. Even members of the Bank of England's Monetary Policy Committee were kept in the dark. At the peak of the emergency loans, the Governor demanded over £100 billion of bank assets as collateral because he was so scared that these fragile institutions would go bust and be unable to repay. The secret loans were a desperate holding measure to buy a bit more time for these banks; they were not a solution to the crisis of confidence threatening to bring down the financial system. King agreed with Brown and Darling that the only hope of forestalling a collapse was to have a comprehensive recapitalisation plan announced before the markets opened the next day.

That evening the bankers were summoned back to the Treasury. Fifty billion pounds in direct support – an adrenaline shot into the stuttering heart of the banking system – was on offer from the Government. The 'crunch negotiations' were with Lloyds, RBS and HBOS, who 'had nowhere else to go for capital except the Government'.[70] Despite another torrid day, many of the bankers were still stubbornly in denial. 'We still had this problem of how to put capital into a bank which says it doesn't need it,' says one present on the Government side. 'This would only work if they expressed willingness to come in.'[71] In some cases, the leaders of banks simply didn't want to face up to the fact that they had led their institutions to the brink of collapse. As John Gieve notes, 'for the boards and chief executives this was their strategy in tatters.'[72] As a collective, they were also apprehensive that publicly accepting that they needed as much as £50 billion would magnify the panic by revealing what a desperate state they were in. 'There was a lot of resistance to the quantum,' says one senior Treasury official at the centre of this negotiation. 'They thought it would scare people.'[73]

Barclays and Lloyds TSB protested most strongly about the size of the bail-out and argued that the sum should be cut in half. Andy Hornby of HBOS, whose bank was already being swallowed up, was 'completely silent'. HSBC, who were sound enough to genuinely not need support, 'were in it for the ride'.[74] Darling felt the banks had a 'big psychological problem' with accepting state intervention. 'Banks basically don't like governments. They don't want governments to have anything to do with them.' It took them a while before they got to the 'growing realisation that if the Government didn't help, then that was it'.[75] There was an exception. As the evening wore on, Sir Tom McKillop and Sir Fred Goodwin were finally beginning to face up to reality. 'They were not in denial any more,' says a senior official. 'They knew they were in a very difficult position.'[76]

Thrown into the deep end of this crisis was Paul Myners, whom Brown had recruited as City Minister in the reshuffle just four days before. Myners recommended himself because he knew his way round company boardrooms. His CV included the chairmanship of Marks and Spencer, Land Securities Group and the Guardian Media Group. He started his life in an orphanage having never known his parents. Myners was quite a rare thing: a rich man from the City with Labour sympathies that came from conviction not merely expediency. 'He was the right man for the job' in the estimation of John Gieve, 'rather relished it' and played 'a critical role'.[77]

The key, face-to-face negotiations between the Government and individual banks were held across an oak table in Myners's second floor ministerial office. Curries were ordered in from Gandhi's, an Indian restaurant in Kennington, which prompted some of the press to headline it as 'the Balti bail-out'. The curry was scoffed by civil servants. Myners didn't get any and neither did the bankers. 'It is not our job to feed them,' John Kingman told a fellow official and perhaps calculated that empty stomachs would help concentrate the bankers' minds.[78] One bank executive was parked between negotiating sessions in the room where the food had been served. He was marooned there with only the lingering aroma of tandoori for company. When he was eventually let out, 'he didn't look very happy.'[79]

Satisfied that the deal was broadly done, Darling went to bed at shortly before two in the morning. Myners continued to work on the detail through the night along with Nick Macpherson, the Treasury's Permanent Secretary, Kingman, Scholar and other officials.

The next morning, Wednesday, 8 October, Prime Minister and Chancellor met before dawn to sanction the final stages of the deal and discuss how they would present it at the Number 10 news conference early that morning. Shriti Vadera says: 'It was for me the scariest moment because we had no idea who was going to follow, no idea what the markets would think, no idea what the public would think, no idea whether it would boost confidence.'[80] Brown continued to be gripped with apprehension that there would be a violent voter reaction against rescuing the banks. 'People won't understand this,' he said repeatedly before the news conference.[81] He later gave a public hint of his fears when he said: 'We hadn't yet persuaded other countries that it was a necessary thing to do. No-one had talked in these sorts of figures before. It could have been an initiative that went entirely wrong because no other country was prepared to support us.'[82] One minister very close to him reports: 'The morning the bail-out was announced, Gordon was convinced that was it. He really thought it was going to be a political disaster.'[83]

The sums were unprecedented. On top of the £50 billion directly injected into banks to strengthen their balance sheets, it was further revealed that the Government was putting up £250 billion in guarantees of lending in the inter-bank market. The special liquidity scheme, which allowed banks to dispose of mortgages by exchanging them for Bank of England bonds, was doubled in size to £200 billion. This stunning total of £500 billion in support of Britain's paralysed financial system was the biggest and most comprehensive rescue package of its kind by any Western government since 1945. Even then, it would not prove to be enough.

'People saw it was a very good holding statement,' says Paul Myners. 'But taking that to specificity was going to take more time.'[84] Precise terms and conditions had yet to be negotiated, bank by bank. Everyone assumed they would have several months to complete this; no-one yet knew that it would have to be done in less than a week.

In politics, how you place the blame can be as important as how you play the game. Fearful of a public backlash, the Prime Minister was anxious to displace culpability to the other side of the Atlantic and on to the reckless banks. 'It's pretty clear to me that this problem started in America,' he said at Number 10 that morning. 'It started with irresponsible actions and lending by individual institutions.'[85] To his great relief, early reaction to the bail-out from the markets and media seemed to be positive.[86]

At nineteen minutes to noon that day, just as Brown was about to appear in the Commons for Prime Minister's Questions, he took a call from Mervyn King. With the minutes ticking away to the first PMQs since the summer break, Brown needed some good news from the Governor. The previous night, when the Governor had been called over to Number 10 to agree the basic structure of the bail-out, he had been urged by both Brown and Darling to cut interest rates. King was now calling Brown to report that the world's most important central banks had agreed to make the largest co-ordinated cut in rates there had ever been.[87] The move was announced at midday London time, setting up Brown for his best half-hour in the Commons for many months. He gave a patronising welcome to David Cameron's support for the bank rescue plan and then squelched his opponent by reminding the Commons of the inconsistent and contradictory statements the Tory leader had made about the crisis. 'Novice!' gleeful Labour MPs jeered at an unsteady and wounded Cameron.[88] They ecstatically waved their order papers at the end of Questions.

Any sense of triumph did not endure for long. The half-point cut in rates across the world, a move which once would have been regarded as sensationally bold, was now viewed as too little and too late to restore confidence in the ability of central banks or governments to arrest the crash. Fresh waves of selling broke over the markets.

The scale and speed of events appeared to be turning the Prime Minister unusually giddy. Making a speech that evening, he was interrupted when a mobile rang in the audience. Brown joked: 'I don't know if another bank has fallen.'[89]

His rare excursion into black comedy was a mask on his fear that even the huge bail-out plan he had just announced wouldn't avert a total collapse. Shriti Vadera was lying on the sofa in her ministerial suite, trying to catch up on some of the sleep lost during the Tuesday night negotiation, when Sir Fred Goodwin rang. He was now ready to admit that RBS desperately needed capital from the Government and at once. 'You'll be shocked by the number,' Goodwin said to Vadera. 'It's ten billion.' She responded: 'I am shocked. That's quite small. I think you need a lot more than that.'[90]

She reported the conversation to Brown. While trying to sound publicly confident, the Prime Minister privately knew that they were on the brink. A global bank like RBS, with its massive international exposure, was still in peril of going down in the absence of recapitalisation by America and the

Europeans. There was only so much one government could do in a global financial pandemic that required co-ordinated international action. 'We've got to get the others to do this,' he sweated to his close allies. 'If they don't do it very soon, RBS will collapse on us. That will be a disaster.'[91] From then on Brown worked the phones trying to persuade other leaders that they should follow the British lead.

Iceland, whose massively over-extended banks had imploded, was going bust, the first entire country to be bankrupted by the crisis. In response to the Icelanders' refusal to pay back billions of pounds of British savers' money, on Thursday Brown resorted to anti-terrorism powers to freeze Icelandic assets.

World markets were in a death spiral by the end of the week. There was a vertiginous sell-off across the board as investors dumped stocks, commodities and currencies. The markets had no faith in their own ability to stabilise, nor in the capacity of governments to rescue them. The crisis of capitalism so long predicted by communists had arrived even if they were no longer in a position to take advantage of it. Every major index was plunging, day after day. Wall Street suffered the worst week in its history. Stocks on the Dow lost 18 per cent of their value in just five days. General Motors, once the pride of the American car industry, was now worth less than it was in 1929. London and Frankfurt were down 21 per cent on the week. Japan's Nikkei index crashed 24 per cent. 'Black Friday', the name given to 10 October, was too tepid a headline for what was happening. There was no precedent for this combination of a worldwide collapse in asset values, a global run on banks and the freezing up of all credit markets. Dominique Strauss-Kahn, the head of the IMF, warned that the world's financial system was on 'the brink of systemic meltdown'.[92]

Major depositors were now so scared about the state of RBS and some other British banks that they were trying to withdraw – and willing to pay large penalties for early withdrawal – all their money. At the Treasury, an alarmed Paul Myners saw that this 'was happening with more than one bank'.[93]

This was the day, of all days, that Brown was spending out of London on a 'regional tour' along the M4 corridor. He had embarked on it as part of a campaign to explain to voters why he was giving billions to the banks. 'I want you to know that we are doing this for you,' he argued in a podcast[94] hurriedly recorded that morning in which he contended that the bail-out was vital to save jobs and businesses. So it was from a train carriage with imperfect phone reception that he spoke to Angela Merkel, Nicolas Sarkozy and other European leaders to urge them to recapitalise their banks as well.

The British plan, unveiled by Brown and Darling just forty-eight hours earlier, was supposed to have bought the Government three months to resolve the crisis at the most endangered British institutions in an orderly fashion. This was time they no longer had. By the end of Black Friday, says John Gieve, HBOS and RBS had 'run out of money'.[95] Alistair Darling agrees 'they had run out of capital.'[96] Treasury officials confirm that these two massive banks would not be able to open their doors on Monday morning.[97]

This was a stunning development for the bankers and the politicians. If both HBOS and RBS went down, it was thought highly likely that they would tip over Barclays, which would in turn crash Lloyds TSB. The chain reaction could topple the majority, even perhaps all, of the major British banks. Sober experts like John Eatwell 'thought there was a real possibility of a total banking collapse. That is, the banks actually shutting their doors and all the cash machines stopping, which would be a complete disaster.'[98] Alistair Darling believed 'we faced a situation where the banking system right across the world, never mind Britain, could have collapsed.'[99] Paul Myners agrees that they were now 'very close' to 'a series of dominos falling' and 'a systemic collapse of the banking system'.[100] John Gieve concurs that 'we were right at the brink of two of our major banks closing and if those two closed that would have a knock-on effect. You could have got Northern Rock times ten.'[101] Mervyn King was also in no doubt that 'not since the beginning of the First World War has our banking system been so close to collapse.'[102]

That would be a cataclysm without precedent. Cheques would be valueless. Credit cards would be useless. With the cash machines shut down, families would not be able to buy food. 'Literally you wouldn't have any cash. The money would disappear.'[103] Most of those things regarded as the essentials of modern civilised society would cease to function. The public order implications were nightmarish. A hedge fund manager who lives in Sussex later told me that he went to a local farmer that weekend and bought a flock of sheep out of fear that this would be the only way to feed his family.

Most Britons understood that something serious was unfolding, but the awesome gravity of this crisis was concealed from the public precisely because of the sheer terror that would have been ignited had the truth been known. Few outside Government and the banks fully appreciated just how close the country was to an apocalyptic implosion of its entire banking system. Britain teetered on the lip of the abyss.

The bankers were called back into the Treasury on Friday evening for what became known among those involved in the crisis negotiations as 'the long weekend'. In the words of Alistair Darling: 'The deadline that all of us set ourselves was seven o'clock on Monday morning when the markets would open. You couldn't have the markets opening with the deal not done.

That would have been catastrophic.'[104] They had just forty-eight hours to avert apocalypse. They worked 'through the night every night' from the evening of Friday to breakfast-time on Monday. Some at the Treasury found it 'slightly surreal' as 'all these bankers slipped in and wandered around the building, looking lost.'[105] There were so many people crowding into the Treasury that they ran out of chairs. Bankers, lawyers and six-figure consultants ended up sitting on the floor to do their business.

The situation was further complicated because both the Prime Minister and the Chancellor were out of the country for stretches of this pivotal weekend. Darling flew out to Washington for a meeting of the finance ministers of the G7. Tom Scholar went with him while Nick Macpherson and John Kingman stayed back in London 'minding the shop'.[106] The mood at the Washington summit was deeply frightened. 'People were in a state of shock about the scale of what was happening,' says one present. 'Stock markets around the world were falling by 5 per cent a day and looked like they would never stop.'[107] Darling responded with anger and alarm when he was shown the first draft of a statement prepared for the G7. He agreed with Scholar that it was 'a crappy communiqué': three pages of platitudinous waffle which would make the panic worse.[108] Hank Paulson looked a wreck. He was publicly still committed to his contentious TARP scheme, which had only won approval from Congress at the second attempt. Privately, the US Treasury Secretary revealed to Darling that he was preparing to switch tracks and fall in with the idea of recapitalisation. The British were suspicious of Christine Lagarde. They feared the French Finance Minister was under instructions from the Elysée Palace not to agree anything of substance so that Nicolas Sarkozy could claim the glory by announcing a grand plan at the European Council in Brussels the following week.[109]

Darling argued to his G7 counterparts that recapitalising banks with public money – the British approach – was the only solution with a chance of working in these circumstances. He received support from the Japanese. Normally among the most passive attendees at international meetings, the Japanese delegation argued with a rare passion that the rest of the world needed to learn the searing lesson from their country's banking crisis of the 1990s that inflicted a 'lost decade' on Japan. Mervyn King was also at the Washington talks. The Governor took to using a line from another King, Elvis Presley. What they needed, he said, was 'a little less conversation, a little more action'.[110]

They agreed a five-point plan which included a pledge to prevent the collapse of 'systemically important banks' by using taxpayers' money to buy up stakes.[111] The final communiqué lacked precision, but for the first time there was something resembling a plausible global framework for bank recapitalisation.

While the Chancellor was selling that to the finance ministers in America, the Prime Minister was promoting the British plan to his European counterparts at a meeting to which he had not originally been invited. Sarkozy asked Brown to join his summit of the leaders of the euro-zone at the Elysée Palace that weekend. At one point, the French President said: 'You know, Gordon, I should not like you. You are Scottish, we have nothing in common and you are an economist. But somehow, Gordon, I love you.' Just in case Brown got the wrong idea, the Frenchman quickly added: 'But not in a sexual way.'[112]

Also present at the Elysée were José Manuel Barroso, the President of the European Commission; Jean-Claude Trichet, the Chairman of the European Central Bank; Silvio Berlusconi of Italy; and Angela Merkel. The scepticism of the German Chancellor had been a formidable obstacle to a comprehensive solution. At a Paris summit a fortnight before, Merkel declared: 'It's up to each country to clean up its own shit.'[113] She was now shifting her position, not least because her officials were constantly in and out with updates about teetering German banks. To one present at this conclave, it was 'a mad meeting'[114] as Brown and his European counterparts clustered around a tiny table in the Elysée discussing what to do. At 8.30 that evening, Paris time, the French President came out to tell the media that they had broadly embraced recapitalisation schemes along the lines of the British plan.

There was a further vote of confidence in the Sunday edition of the *New York Times*. Paul Krugman, the Nobel Prize-winning economist, wrote in praise of the British plan:

Brown and Darling have defined the character of the worldwide rescue effort, with other wealthy nations playing catch-up. The Brown Government has shown itself willing to think clearly about the financial crisis, and act quickly on its conclusions. This combination of clarity and decisiveness hasn't been matched by any other western government.[115]

I'd first learnt of the Krugman article from the *New York Times* syndication service on the Friday before publication and mentioned it to Brown during a phone conversation with the Prime Minister that afternoon. It became apparent to me soon afterwards that he was so keen for this endorsement to be widely known that he ordered his staff to do a ring-round of commentators. An hour after I'd brought the article to the attention of Brown, one of his aides rang me to ask whether I knew Paul Krugman was writing in praise of the Prime Minister.

Plaudits in the international press hailing Brown as a world saviour were highly flattering. But the cheers were not going to last beyond the weekend if the critical negotiations at the Treasury failed, Monday morning came and Britain's own banks couldn't open their doors.

Darling left Washington on Saturday night on the red-eye to Heathrow and landed back in London at breakfast-time on Sunday. When he arrived at the Treasury, the negotiations with the stricken British bankers had made important progress. The dynamic was changed by the fright they received on Friday. 'When we began to have one-to-one meetings on Saturday, it was pretty clear to all the major banks that needed capital that they would have to do a deal,' says Paul Myners.[116] He and Kingman found that HBOS, Lloyds TSB and RBS were now willing to accept that they had to have immediate help. Barclays, though still preferring to recapitalise from foreign sources rather than the British Government, saw the necessity for urgent action. 'No-one wanted to be naked on Monday morning without a deal in place.'[117]

According to John Gieve, 'essentially the Treasury laid out the terms on which it was prepared to support them and they had to accept it.'[118] Some of the bankers found these terms humiliating: 'We were given a menu and there was no à la carte option.'[119] It was the end of the road for Fred Goodwin. 'Technically speaking, RBS was bust.'[120] In one of the gaps between meetings in Myners' office, someone referred to a 'negotiation'. Goodwin remarked: 'This is not a negotiation; it is a drive-by shooting.'[121] His tone was more fatalistic than furious. 'He said this with a rueful smile.'[122]

That smile was perhaps enhanced by the knowledge that the ruin of his bank would still leave him exceedingly rich. In between negotiating the rescue, and having just four hours' sleep on Friday and Saturday night and none at all on Sunday, Myners was also supervising the terms of the departure of Goodwin and other failed executives. 'Most of the focus on our side was ensuring that Fred Goodwin and Andy Hornby were not going to stay,' says another minister present.[123] Goodwin had smashed his bank, but the RBS board said it had advice from its lawyers that they could not sack him and Myners did not press them to take that route. Goodwin was instead paid off with an extraordinary deal, which would remain secret until it exploded into the headlines several months later, to double his pension pot to more than £16 million. What exactly passed between Myners and the representatives of RBS subsequently became the subject of intense dispute and huge embarrassment for the Government. On Myners' later account, he knew Goodwin's pension was 'a large sum' but the minister suggested that he was the victim of an 'elaborate ruse'. This was denied by Sir Tom

McKillop, as he also argued with the minister's assertion that he was misled into believing that the pension was a 'contractual obligation' and not open for negotiation.[124]

There's no dispute about this: Goodwin, the man who presided over the biggest corporate failure in British history, was allowed to float away on a vast golden parachute. A fellow minister felt 'very sorry for Paul. He'd only been there for three seconds.'[125] Some Labour MPs later concluded he was a political innocent who wasn't adequately protected by officials. George Mudie, a member of the Treasury select committee, argues that 'he should never have gone into that meeting' without 'the usual team of officials for a negotiation of that seriousness'.[126] Myners was a peer, very new to Government, and this gargantuan pension pot might not seem so excessive in the eyes of someone from the City. He was not equipped with the antennae of an elected politician which might have twitched over the potential for the Goodwin deal to ignite voter rage. The fundamental reason that Goodwin got away with it was the very crisis that had been caused by him and his fellow bankers. The financial terms of his exit were a low-order priority that frantic weekend at the Treasury in comparison with the paramount importance of saving the banking system from implosion. 'I wish I'd had more time to ask more questions. But I had no time,' says Myners. 'If we'd had more time, we would have done everything a bit better. This was the most complex and largest corporate finance transaction ever done in Britain: the recapitalisation of four banks, three of them with public money.'[127]

'These were extraordinary days,' says one Treasury official present. 'Goodwin's pension was a side issue compared with negotiating billions of pounds of taxpayers' money for the banks.'[128]

Failure remained a serious possibility into Sunday. Lloyds talked of calling off its takeover of HBOS, a prospect which threatened the whole deal until the two banks came to agreement. Right up until the Sunday evening, some of the bankers were 'still fighting the proposition' that they had to agree to the terms and conditions offered by the Government. Darling eventually said to them: 'You've got a choice. We're going to offer capital and we're going to impose conditions. If you don't like it, there's an alternative, but that's too awful to contemplate.' In a display of brinkmanship untypical of the undemonstrative and cautious Chancellor, he declared: 'I'm staying until midnight and then I'm going to bed. If you haven't done the deal by then, it's too late.'[129]

The bankers were 'more or less signed up' to the broad structure when the Chancellor took himself off to bed, telling officials he had to get some rest when he would be presenting the deal to MPs and on the media the next day.[130] As he slept, the lights continued to burn at the Treasury as the bankers wrangled over details. Sir Victor Blank of Lloyds was arguing with Myners about bonuses in the early hours of the morning.[131] Very late, at four o'clock in the morning, some bankers tried to reopen terms which ministers thought were already agreed.[132] 'That is what these people do,' says Darling.[133] They were getting 'down to percentages', haggling over the precise size of the stake the Government would take in the rescued banks.[134] At five o'clock, with just two hours left before the deadline to announce an agreement in advance of the markets opening, Darling held a stock-taking session in his ground-floor study at Number 11. The Chancellor was joined by Kingman, Myners, Scholar and Vadera, none of whom had had any sleep at all. They were agreed they had a deal they could live with. Now they needed Gordon Brown's sign-off.[135] The Prime Minister had returned from Paris late on the Sunday night and was still asleep in the flat above Downing Street. 'Who's going to wake him up?' asked Darling. Eyes fixed on Shriti Vadera, the person in the room closest to Brown. 'You need to get him up.' She went through the connecting door into Number 10 and sought out the night duty clerk. 'We need the Prime Minister,' she said. 'Can you get Gordon up?' 'No,' the duty clerk laughingly refused. 'You go and get Gordon up.'

Vadera made her way upstairs to the Browns' flat. She had never been in there before and stumbled around in the dark trying to locate the bedroom. Tripping over a child's tricycle, she disturbed Sarah Brown, who assumed one of her sons was up. The Prime Minister's wife shouted out: 'John, go back to bed.' Vadera identified herself: 'Sarah, it's Shriti.' A familiar growl then rumbled from the Browns' bedroom: 'What's going on?'[136]

Soon afterwards, the Prime Minister came down to join the meeting in the Chancellor's study. A purple tie at half mast around his neck, he 'looked like a man who had jumped out of bed and thrown his clothes on in thirty seconds'.[137] Brown asked the multi-billion-pound question: 'Will it work?' When the rest of them sounded positive, he gave his seal of approval. They had just met the deadline. Before the markets opened on Monday, it was announced that the Government was taking stakes in HBOS, Lloyds TSB and RBS in return for a £37 billion injection of capital while Barclays would be recapitalising from private sources. The state was now the majority share-holder of RBS and would own 40 per cent of the new bank created by merging HBOS and Lloyds. Britain's banks opened their doors that morning. The cash machines still worked. As far as most people knew, it was just business as usual.

Brown declared that morning: 'This is the first government to do what a large number of governments are going to do over the next few days.'[138]

This claim to be an international leader proved to be accurate. The next day, Hank Paulson did a dramatic volte-face, put aside his TARP plan and pumped capital into the nine major US banks. Similar bail-outs were unveiled by France, Germany, Italy, Spain and Switzerland. Countries around the globe, from Australia to South Korea, followed suit. All the schemes broadly copied the rescue first announced by Britain. As John Gieve puts it:

It was an occasion when the British machine worked quickly and genuinely led the world. What we did over those two days was set a pattern which was blessed in Washington, blessed in Paris and more or less followed in a matter of days by the US and the rest of Europe.[139]

One very senior civil servant, in many ways a sceptic about Gordon Brown's leadership skills, gives him much of the credit for bold action in this crisis: 'Gordon was prepared to say: "We need to bail them out" despite the political risks. He took the lead and then allowed Alistair to do it.'[140] On the account of Paul Myners: 'Gordon displayed a phenomenal capacity to grasp the issues as he was briefed. Alistair was extraordinarily methodical in the way he worked through the details.'[141] James Purnell, a Blairite member of the Cabinet who was otherwise utterly disillusioned with Brown, credits him and Darling for acting 'faster, more comprehensively, more boldly than anybody else. The financial world was caught in the headlights and Gordon came forward with the right plan which was then broadly followed around the world.'[142] Peter Mandelson, who had previously despaired of Brown's indecisiveness, was an impressed witness. 'He did immediately what others couldn't, wouldn't or didn't have the nerve to do. He was the market leader in taking action which others have followed. Nothing will detract from his place in history in taking that action.'[143]

Only those at the heart of the crisis knew just how close Britain had come to tumbling into the abyss. Whatever else the rescue of that long weekend ultimately failed to do, it did successfully set an example to the world and save the country from the apocalypse of a total banking collapse.

35. Land Without Maps

Gordon Brown turned to Peter Mandelson during one of their regular meetings and inquired: 'Are you happy?' He had never asked that before. Mandelson was stunned into silence. The Business Secretary eventually responded: 'I am happy if you are happy. Are you happy?' 'Yes,' said Brown. 'I am happy.' Mandelson completed the surreal conversation: 'We are one happy family then.' Then they both burst out laughing.[1]

As the banks crashed, Brown bounced. The rescue plan also bailed out his precarious premiership. The floundering, defeated leader of the summer was re-galvanised into a man of action and conviction. Mandelson later observed: 'Along comes this crisis and he feels equipped. He feels confident.'[2] It gave Brown a mission that his premiership had lacked over the previous year. In interviews, he sounded more authoritative and appeared slightly more relaxed. As the Foreign Office Minister, Mark Malloch-Brown, puts it: 'The international crisis stemmed the internal criticism because it so evidently needed someone with his CV in charge during this global economic storm. It came along on cue.'[3] Among Labour MPs like Jon Cruddas, 'There was a sense that he was rising to the challenge, he was ahead of the game. He was the man with the beginnings of a plan.'[4]

He returned to the projection of himself as the right leader in a crisis, the image that had worked well during his first summer in Number 10, but this time he did so on a much grander, global scale. He created a new National Economic Council which was explicitly described as a 'war cabinet' and met in COBRA. He invoked the 'calm, determined British spirit' of the Blitz and the Battle of Britain and implicitly cast himself as the Churchill of this Battle of the Banks when he told the country that 'Britain will lead the way in pulling through.'[5]

Many hands at the Treasury, Bank of England and FSA worked on the rescue, but the bulk of the glory was refracted on to the Prime Minister. Even in the French press he was hailed as a 'magician' who had 'rediscovered' his touch.[6] Mandelson went biblical in his tributes: 'Internationally people say to me, "Your Prime Minister has been transformed. His standing has soared." People really do look to him like some Moses figure who is going to lead them away from this economic mess to the promised land.'[7]

The opinion poll zero of the early autumn had, for now at least, made himself look like a global financial hero. 'The crisis is a chance to be heard again,' said one of his senior aides that autumn. 'People are now willing to listen to him again.'[8] He was clawing back some respect from the voters, a substantial majority of whom thought he had handled the crisis well.[9] More importantly, he won back his self-respect. The hunched and hunted Prime Minister of just a few weeks previously was replaced by a confident, even swaggering figure. 'Gordon got his mojo back,' says one of his senior aides.[10] His brow lifted, his shoulders broadened, his stride lengthened and for a while he became a nicer man to work with. 'I have not seen Gordon so happy for years,' remarked one minister.[11] Those close to him talked of Brown finally finding his purpose as a Prime Minister.

This was paradoxically because he could go back to being Chancellor. Where he palpably struggled to master many of the other demands of modern leadership, this crisis played to his strengths. Stock markets might be plunging and banks tottering, but he was in his comfort zone. Global finance was an arena in which he could deploy deep knowledge, draw on years of experience and exploit the international contacts that he amassed during his decade at the Treasury. Even his bitterest enemies in the Labour Party were prepared to laurel him. Charles Clarke, who just two months earlier had suggested the Cabinet should give him the bullet, declared that Brown had shown 'genuine economic and political leadership at a time when it was both desperately needed and difficult to do'. It had put Labour 'back in the race' for the next election.[12]

On 6 November, there was a further boost from the by-election at Glenrothes, where the headmaster of his old school was the Labour candidate. Brown took the unusual step for a Prime Minister of personally campaigning and his wife made several visits to the constituency that neighboured his own in Fife. Against earlier predictions, Labour held the seat with a reduced but respectable majority.

He displayed a sense of humour, albeit of a very clunking variety, when in the company of other party leaders on Remembrance Sunday. Before the ceremony at the Cenotaph, the trio assembled in a corridor in the Foreign Office. David Cameron was anxious to be clear about the order of precedence. 'So you go first,' he said to the Prime Minister. Turning to Nick Clegg, Cameron added: 'And you follow me.' Brown lugubriously remarked to Clegg: 'You may be following him, but I won't be.'[13]

The upturn in his political fortunes was accompanied by the rewriting of almost every economic axiom he had preached for more than a decade. His 'golden rule', which said borrowing should never rise above 40 per cent of GDP, had long been bent. In late October, Alistair Darling officially announced it was being altogether abandoned.[14] The Chancellor Brown who once extolled 'prudence' was now the Prime Minister Brown who toured the world arguing for a global spending spree financed by massively increased borrowing to sustain the economy. The man who once eviscerated opponents for the 'black holes' in their plans now promoted unfunded tax cuts as the 'fiscal stimulus' that would save the world. The leader who procrastinated for months over nationalising one relatively small northern bank now staked hundreds of billions on saving several of the biggest banks. This Moses was taking the tablet of stone and rewriting all the economic commandments. The man who put Adam Smith on the banknotes was a born-again Keynesian. As the impossible and the incredible became almost overnight the inevitable and the orthodox, there was a stunning inversion of many of the original economic maxims of New Labour. He championed measures that he had once taught his party were economic lunacy and political suicide.

Justifying this dramatic shift in a speech to the CBI in November, he argued that 'leaving behind the orthodoxies of yesterday' was the only way to avoid a repeat of the Great Depression. 'A new approach is needed if we are to get through this unprecedented global financial recession with the least damage to Britain's long-term economic prospects.'[15]

He took a similar message abroad, telling an audience of panjandrums in New York: 'The cost of inaction is greater than the cost of no action.'[16] This speech was funny. It was fluent. He was confident enough to speak without notes. He quoted presidents, economists and the poet Shelley as he developed his theme that extraordinary times demanded extraordinary action. When he took questions from the audience, one of them addressed him as 'Your Excellency'.

The reborn Brown took the breath away, especially of the Conservatives. To their collective bewilderment, he was presiding over the mother of all economic crises and yet closing the opinion poll deficit as voters leant back to Labour. The Tory lead shrank to low single figures, falling to a mere three points in one poll in mid-November. The Conservatives fluttered with anxiety when their lead shrivelled to just a single point in a poll at the end of that month.[17] David Cameron struggled to look relevant as banks crashed and markets convulsed while Brown travelled the world looking decisive and statesmanlike. The Conservatives feared a snap election and started to put together a manifesto.[18] The Tories' youth, inexperience and privileged backgrounds also worked against them during this period. George Osborne, the Shadow Chancellor, was trapped in a poisonous dispute about an encounter with Oleg Deripaska, a Russian metals magnate, during an August holiday at the Corfu villa of Nat Rothschild. Osborne's other dangerous liaison was with Peter Mandelson, also present in the eastern Mediterranean over the summer. A version of their private table talk at a taverna was leaked by Osborne to Martin Ivens of the *Sunday Times*. Osborne claimed plausibly that Mandelson 'dripped pure poison' about Brown.[19] It was the Shadow Chancellor who got served with the strychnine cocktail for crossing the Dark Prince. Rothschild retaliated and Osborne was ensnared in a thicket of accusation and counter-claim with his Oxford contemporary about who said what to whom about a donation to the Tory party from the Russian tycoon.[20] Consorting with a billionaire on his super-yacht jarred with the mood of national austerity. More damage was done by photos of Osborne and Rothschild as undergraduates, including one of Osborne in plus fours at a shoot and another of him in the Brideshead rig of the Bullingdon Club. The Tory responses to the financial crisis were inconsistent and unconvincing. More than half of the public thought that Brown was the right leader to deal with a recession while less than a third favoured Cameron.[21] Voter scepticism about the callowness of the Tory team worried Cameron so much that he would soon recall to the Opposition frontbench the 68-year-old former Chancellor, Ken Clarke.

Striding on and off aeroplanes for international summits, Gordon Brown looked like a man who had finally found his vocation as a leader and a global stage on which to perform. Yet his feet were unsteadily balanced on a very thin tightrope strung over a chasm the bottom of which could not be seen. The financial crunch was now biting deep on the real economy. Unemployment surged. House prices tumbled.[22] Retailers – Woolworths being one sentimentally mourned example – went broke. This was the bleak context for the Pre-Budget Report – in reality, an emergency Budget – which was unveiled on Monday, 24 November. The Prime Minister and Chancellor quarrelled in advance about the extent to which they could afford to spend to avert a depression. The Treasury did not agree that every rule in the fiscal book could be torn up. Officials were increasingly alarmed by the size of the deficit, which they could already see soaring in excess of £100 billion in the coming year. They were also apprehensive about the fragility of the currency as sterling slithered towards parity with the euro. 'Gordon would have gone for a bigger stimulus, but he was resisted by the Treasury,' says John McFall, the Labour chairman of the Treasury select committee. 'They got very frightened about the amount of red ink.'[23] One Treasury official describes the arguments between Prime Minister and Chancellor as 'comical' because of the way roles were reversed. To Brown's demands for more spending, Darling would reply: 'Where is the money coming from?' This was precisely the line Brown used to take as Chancellor when he was rejecting spending demands from Tony Blair.[24] They compromised on a package which was less than Brown wanted but larger than the cautious Treasury regarded as prudent.

There was also a long and ferocious internal argument about the best way to put money in the pockets of voters. Brown, backed by Ed Balls, James Purnell and most of the Number 10 Policy Unit, wanted to make tax credits more generous. Darling, supported by his officials at the Treasury and Jeremy Heywood at Number 10, argued that it would be technically simpler, get quicker results and produce headlines everyone could understand to announce a cut to VAT. That battle was won by the Chancellor.[25] The main measure was a cut in VAT from 17.5 to 15 per cent for the next thirteen months. The cost was £12.5 billion a year. Reaction was mixed. Frank Field scoffed that 'it would be better to throw the money up in the air in Birkenhead market.'[26] Digby Jones, the recently departed Trade Minister, was another sceptic of the value of 'two and a half per cent off five quids' stuff from Marks and Spencer'.[27] It had a 'negligible impact' on a crucial sector like the car industry because dealers were already offering hefty discounts.[28] The presentation was undermined by the accidental publication on a Government website of an internal Treasury discussion paper about a later claw-back by hiking VAT to 18.5 per cent. This fomented the suspicion that the Chancellor's figures were fudged to mask the growth of the deficit. The press was almost unanimous in depicting it as a gamble for which the country would pay later. The *Independent*: 'Brown goes for broke'.[29] The *Guardian*: 'The £21 bn tax gamble'.[30] The *Daily Telegraph*: 'Middle-class tax time bomb'.[31] 'Into the red' was the interpretation of *The Times*,[32] which stressed the explosion in borrowing. George Osborne recovered some of his confidence and hit an exposed nerve when he jibed: 'In the end all Labour Chancellors run out of money and all Labour governments bring this country to the verge of bankruptcy.'[33]

It was certainly true that this was the definitive end of more than a decade of healthy growth, rising incomes and low unemployment built on the property boom, finance, cheap labour from migration and public spending. When headlines interpreted it as the death of New Labour, Mandelson – in his role as the keeper of the Blairite flame – was sent out to argue otherwise. So did Brown when he rang round newspaper editors. There was no denying that it was the last rites for the years of easy prosperity that had underpinned New Labour as an electoral project.

The opinion polls the following weekend indicated that the Conservatives were gaining again. Voters were not as impressed by the VAT cut as they were frightened for their future livelihoods. Brown's personal recovery stalled and then reversed as the recession closed its icy fingers around the heart of the economy. Peer Steinbrück, the Social Democratic Finance Minister of Germany, scorned him for a 'breathtaking' switch from laissez faire capitalism 'all the way to crass Keynesianism' and forecast that Britain would be left with a pile of debt 'that will take a whole generation to work off'.[34] Brown reacted in characteristic fashion. To his staff, 'GB sent out a barrage of e-mails demanding a history of the economic philosophy of the SPD.'[35] Nicolas Sarkozy then disdained the British VAT cut in a television interview. 'That will bring them nothing,' scoffed the French President, adding that the British deficit could 'ruin the country'.[36] The anger this provoked in Downing Street surfaced when Darling next met his French counterpart, Christine Lagarde. 'Why did your President have to comment on my VAT reduction?' he demanded. Lagarde responded with a Gallic shrug: 'We're not convinced that kind of cut is going to work when prices are going down anyway.'[37]

The French later partially imitated the VAT cut and the Germans embarked on a fiscal stimulus which was actually larger than the British one. But at the time these criticisms from abroad made the Tories seem less internationally isolated. They were emboldened to make a definitive issue of the ballooning size of the deficit, unveiling one particularly potent poster depicting a baby saddled with debt for the rest of its life. They flipped their economic policy when David Cameron ditched his previous pledge to match Labour spending levels. The Tory leader rediscovered virtues in Margaret Thatcher, the woman hitherto largely airbrushed from history in his speeches. Cameron and Osborne made themselves champions of fiscal conservatism, opening up the biggest divide on economic policy between the parties for more than a decade. Cameron made the break complete in a speech at the London School of Economics in early December in which he attacked Brown for a 'reckless' policy of 'spend now, forget the future.'[38]

In the Commons the next day, the Leader of the Opposition taunted the Prime Minister about the failure of the bank bail-out to unfreeze credit markets. This provoked Brown into a Freudian slip. 'We not only saved the world . . .' he said and paused for a fatal heartbeat to look down at his notes.[39] He meant to say 'the world's banks'. His attempt to correct this hubristic-sounding slip was drowned by the tidal wave of hoots and jeers from his opponents. The delirious Tories slapped their thighs and threw their order papers in the air. Many Labour MPs openly laughed. David Miliband gagged with the effort of not joining the chortling.

When the Chancellor began his working day at the Treasury, he routinely asked two questions: 'How bad is it today?' and 'Why is this not working?'[40] The bank bail-out had prevented a catastrophic implosion of the entire financial system, but it did not succeed in sustaining lending to home owners and businesses. There were multiple reasons for this. Nearly a third of borrowing by British consumers and companies during the bubble had come from overseas, notably American, banks. They were drastically reducing lending or completely withdrawing it. The British banks – traumatised and still deeply mistrustful of each other – were clinging to whatever capital they had. That hoarding was made worse by the Government's initial line, taken for political reasons, that they did not intend to hold stakes in banks for long. Those banks borrowing from the government had to pay 14 per cent, a very high premium. 'Therefore there was a very powerful incentive built in for the banks not to lend but to conserve their resources to pay back the Government as fast as possible.'[41] During the frantic negotiations over the bail-out, the banks had not been nailed down to guarantees that they would sustain lending. The agreements 'had to be pretty generalised because you were doing this at speed', Darling later argued. 'To enter into a detailed contract wasn't possible. You cannot do all that detail over a weekend.'[42] The banks were being pulled in opposite directions by the authorities. The Bank of England and the Financial Services Authority pressed them to unwind bad risks and rebuild their balance sheets. At the same time, bank executives were summoned to a string of Downing Street 'summits' to exhort them to keep lending. While the Prime Minister made tough noises about the banks for public consumption, the Chancellor and Business Secretary were privately telling bankers they sympathised with their predicament.[43] Peter Mandelson, who was spending a lot of his time with bankers, told fellow ministers that they were like men who had 'just suffered a massive heart attack'.[44] Cabinet ministers admitted that the Government was not speaking to the bankers with 'one voice' and they were being 'asked to do two contradictory things'.[45]

Dramatic measures designed to boost the economy sometimes had an unexpectedly negative effect on consumer confidence. In the space of just eight weeks, the Bank of England slashed the base rate from 5 to just 2 per cent, its lowest level since the Prime Minister was born in the 1950s. The Cabinet were shown polling suggesting that the public became deeply scared about the economy when the Bank made these dramatic reductions. According to one minister at the presentation: 'It made people go: "Oh fuck, this really is serious."'[46]

As the base rate approached zero, that left one unprecedented and uncertain measure. 'Quantitative easing' was the unlovely jargon for what was colloquially known as 'printing money'. When this was first suggested, Brown recoiled in horror. Publicly and privately, he ruled it out.[47] 'Printing money' conjured up the spectre of the hyper-inflation in Robert Mugabe's Zimbabwe and in the Weimar Republic during the rise of Hitler. 'He feared the political fall-out,' according to one minister close to Brown.[48] Yet he was now desperate enough to be secretly contemplating this leap into the unknown. When he left London for his Christmas break in Fife, he took with him holiday reading composed of a large number of papers on quantitative easing.[49] The Treasury was also becoming so alarmed about the economy that it began to seriously consider this extraordinary step 'over the turn of the year'.[50]

Ex-leaders can often tell truths that incumbents dare not. In the New Year of 2009, Tony Blair broke his silence about the crisis. The former Prime Minister, never very economically literate, did not have a prescription for curing the world. What he did offer was a candid observation about the limitations of politicians and their advisers when confronted with such seismic events. 'We live in an era of very low predictability,' observed Blair in a speech in Paris. The 'best and most honest answer' about how the future would unfold was 'we don't know.'[51] The closest that Gordon Brown came to admitting this was in a little-reported speech at the end of the same month at the Davos Summit. 'This is the first financial crisis of the global age,' he said. 'And there is no clear map that has been set out from past experience to deal with it.'[52] To audiences in Britain, he could not publicly admit that he was driving in the dark. His self-projection was as the man with the plan even if the truth was that he was a leader busking it through several different plans which were subject to constant revision.

He had over-sold the October bail-out as the definitive answer to the crisis. He said then that he would not 'come back with another partial proposal and then another partial proposal'.[53] Just three months later, the Government was forced to do exactly that. The announcement of huge losses at two of America's biggest financial institutions triggered a fresh stampede out of shares in British banks on Friday, 16 January. A panic about Barclays saw a quarter of the value of its shares wiped out in just one hour of frenzied trading. That weekend, Alistair Darling, Paul Myners and their senior officials camped out at the Treasury again for another long weekend of negotiations with bank chairmen and chief executives. Left in the arsenal were the last resorts of entirely nationalising the banks or creating a state-owned 'bad bank' to buy up toxic assets. At a high-pressure, five-hour discussion on Sunday night which 'went through a wide range of solutions' the Government settled on a hybrid, multilayered scheme.[54] Gordon Brown touched down at Heathrow at four on Monday morning, having snatched some fitful sleep on a flight back from Jerusalem while Jeremy Heywood worked on how they would present this latest rescue.[55] By five, Brown was back in Downing Street for a meeting with Darling to finalise what would become known as the 'second bail-out'. At nine on Monday, 19 January, Prime Minister and Chancellor appeared at a joint news conference to unveil their latest attempt to put a floor under the banks. The central feature was taxpayer-backed insurance schemes to guarantee new bonds issued by banks and allow them to cap losses on their toxic assets if loans went bad. This approach appealed to the Government because 'it didn't require us to end up owning the assets.'[56] Both Prime Minister and Chancellor looked absolutely shattered. Brown had eye bags on his eye bags. His voice was like gravel as he called them 'comprehensive measures' for 'extraordinary times'. He expressed fury that the full scale of RBS's past recklessness was only now coming to light. Several times, he said: 'I'm angry.'[57]

There was nothing like the political consensus in support of this scheme that there had been behind the October bail-out. Vince Cable thought Darling was 'really rather shamefaced' when the Chancellor appeared in the Commons and had to 'acknowledge he was going to have to help the banks all over again and this time in a much more questionable form'.[58]

The Tories demanded that the Chancellor come clean about the risk. That rather missed the point: the problem was that no-one, including the banks, was sure of the exact extent of the bad loans on their balance sheets. The Government was navigating in darkness. 'We don't really know whether this will work,' one senior member of the Cabinet told me. 'Alistair is just hanging on for dear life.'[59] When this bail-out, the earlier one and further measures were accumulated, the sums committed to supporting the banks rose to the highest in the G7. The full taxpayer exposure to the banks could only be guessed at, but reasonable estimates put the upfront costs at a minimum of £289 billion, more than the £203 billion the financial sector had paid in taxes in the five years before the crunch. The total exposure could be as high as £1.3 trillion, roughly equivalent to the value of the whole British economy for a year.[60]

The timing of the announcement was terrible because it coincided with a sequence of dire economic data. Unemployment hit 1.9 million. Sterling tumbled to a twenty-three-year low against the dollar. It was officially confirmed that this was already the worst recession since the 1980s. Brown's repeated mantra about Britain's resilience was contradicted by the IMF when it predicted that the downturn would be deeper than in the United States, Germany or any other advanced nation.[61] This generated confidence-sapping headlines like 'The deepest recession' on the front page of *The Times*[62] and 'It just gets worse and worse' from the *Independent*.[63]

The markets' initial response to the bail-out was coloured by more horrific news from the financial sector. The banks' losses were turning out to be 'higher than anyone had anticipated' in Government.[64] The Royal Bank of Scotland announced losses of a staggering £28 billion, the largest in British corporate history. Stephen Hester, the bank's new Chief Executive, rang Darling to reassure him that he did not need to be panicked into total bank nationalisation. 'It is just the market trying to find its level,' Hester endeavoured to convince Darling.[65] There seemed to be no knowing how low that level might be. RBS's share price fell by more than two thirds in a day. The once mighty bank, worth £78 billion just eighteen months before, was now valued at less than £5 billion despite the injection of so much state support. It was entirely conceivable that the taxpayer might ultimately make a profit, even a handsome return, when the banks recovered and the Government stakes were sold off in the future. At this moment, many voters were bound to think that Brown and Darling were pouring taxpayers' money into a black hole.

Bankers already competed with paedophiles for the lowest position on the league table of public esteem. There could not have been a worse time for it to emerge that bankers wanted to carry on remunerating themselves as if the crash had never happened. On 5 February, *The Times* revealed that RBS, 70 per cent of which was now owned by the taxpayer, was planning to pay out large sums in bonuses to senior staff and traders.[66] It was then reported that Lloyds, which had also been rescued by the Government, was planning to do the same. So was Barclays, which had tapped the Bank of England for billions of pounds in loans and guarantees.[67] This raised anti-banker rage to an even higher pitch. The Government's response was confused and merely rhetorical. Peter Mandelson exhorted the bankers to 'understand the heat, the anger that many people feel. They certainly don't want to see banking chiefs benefiting from past failure.'[68] Harriet Harman, flavouring her attack with feminism, denounced the City's 'old boys' network' to a Labour conference in Sheffield.[69] This was well received by activists who liked the sound of banker-bashing. It was less popular with other ministers, who interpreted this as Harman positioning herself to run for leader after a general election defeat.[70]

From the autumn, and repeatedly since, Brown had promised that 'excessive and irresponsible risk-taking has got to be punished' and that he would not tolerate 'rewards for failure'.[71] Yet there had been massive rewards for colossal failure. Adam Applegarth, the man who wrecked the Northern Rock, took a £760,000 pay-off and a pension pot of £2.6 million. Andy Hornby, the fallen 'Boy Wonder' of HBOS, was now earning £60,000 a month for consultancy services to the bank he brought to its knees. The non-executive directors of RBS who had not prevented its ruination were still sitting on that bank's board several months later.

The political heat was increased when Barack Obama announced a salary cap and bonus ban at banks bailed out by the American taxpayer and Nicolas Sarkozy, facing mass protests in France, did something similar. The issue split the Cabinet when ministers met on Tuesday, 9 February. Harman led the charge by giving the Cabinet an abridged version of her anti-banker speech in Sheffield the previous Saturday. The City was 'rotten', she declared. They should claw back the bonuses paid to the executives of failed banks. This intervention did not impress all her colleagues. 'Knee-jerk, crudely populist stuff,' one minister sniffed after the meeting.[72] There was a sharp response from John Hutton, Hazel Blears and others in the Cabinet who contended that they couldn't just tear up contracts. It might be superficially popular now, but it would do Labour no good in the longer term to be seen as hostile to business. Harman retorted that it was not anti-business to be anti-banker 'because no-one hates bankers more than businesses'. Peter Mandelson observed to his colleagues that the furore over bonuses was symptomatic of a larger danger. The Government looked as though it was being 'blown this way and that' by the prevailing storms in the media. The meeting broke up without any agreement about what they would actually do.[73]

Brown produced a variety of convoluted verbal formulas, but he did not articulate a robust plan. This paralysis was partly induced by listening to advice from lawyers about the difficulties of unwinding contractual obligations. It was 'a legal nightmare', groans one minister at the centre of the discussions.[74] The bailed-out banks were under the supervision of John Kingman. The Treasury civil servant was in charge of UK Financial Investments, the body set up to manage the Government's stakes in the part-nationalised banks. The bank executives argued with Kingman that they needed to be able to pay bonuses to retain staff who could generate profits in their investment arms to help mop up losses.[75] Added to this was the psychological legacy of New Labour's decade of genuflection to the City, a muscle memory which persisted even once the titans of finance were dethroned. 'There was a big reluctance to lay down the law on salaries and bonuses,' observes Digby

Jones from a pro-business perspective.[76] As a result, Labour MPs saw that the Government put itself 'on the wrong side of that populist wave'.[77]

The disgraced bankers came out of hiding for a three-hour interrogation by the Treasury select committee. It was not so much a show trial as a pantomime. 'We are profoundly and unreservedly sorry at the turn of events,' intoned Lord Stevenson, the former Chairman of HBOS, as if he and the other executives were the unfortunate victims of forces beyond their control rather than the authors of the most spectacular banking failures. As the questioning went on, it became apparent that the bankers were still baffled about what had gone wrong and why. 'I don't think I am particularly personally culpable,' said Andy Hornby, the fallen Chief Executive of HBOS, in a remark he was made to almost instantly regret. 'You're all in bloody denial!' erupted one exasperated MP, Labour's George Mudie.[78] Their performance fed rather than assuaged public anger.

David Cameron saw which way the wind was blowing and decried 'markets without morality and capitalism without a conscience'.[79] This was shameless from the leader of a party which had argued during the boom years for even less regulation. It was Brown's inability to channel public anger and address it that left the space free for the nimble Cameron to pose as the tribune of the people. Voters were overwhelmingly of the view that the Government should stop the bailed-out banks from paying bonuses.[80] Brown's response was to announce yet another review into City remuneration conducted by a City figure. That was an example of his habit of trying to look as if he was doing something while distancing himself from taking action. 'We got behind the story,' laments one member of the Cabinet.[81]

Every drama must have its villain. The iconic example of the rapacity of the disgraced bankers was Sir Fred Goodwin, the fallen boss of RBS. In mid-February, Treasury officials were going through the RBS accounts when they spotted the enormous pension secured by Goodwin under the severance deal thrown together during the crisis weekend the previous October. It came to some £700,000 a year, which he would start to receive at the youthful age of fifty. Political dynamite in any circumstances, this was going to be absolutely incendiary when millions of voters were facing a straitened future after the shrivelling of their pension funds as a result of the collapse in share prices. The officials told Alistair Darling, who in turn alerted Gordon Brown. Both were also warned that there was no keeping this secret for very long: the pension details would be revealed in the RBS annual report due to be published in a few weeks' time.

Looking to defuse this time bomb before it went off, they first hoped to persuade Goodwin to voluntarily surrender at least a portion of his outrageous pension. The task fell to the City Minister, Paul Myners. On Wednesday, 25 February, he telephoned Goodwin to suggest he ought to make 'a gesture of goodwill'.[82] Goodwin later claimed that he had been warned that if he didn't hand back some of the money, 'things would get very nasty indeed.'[83] The pension became publicly notorious that night. It was leaked to Robert Peston, the Business Editor of the BBC, who shared his scoop with viewers of the ten o'clock news. 'No shred of shame,' the cry of the next morning's *Mirror*, was a typical headline.[84] Some thought the leak had 'the grubby hallmark of a Labour dirty tricks operation. As the hapless Sir Fred took his turn in the stocks, the Government's failure to resolve the banking crisis . . . would get lost amid the sound and fury.'[85] Goodwin himself accused the Government of exposing his pension to put him under pressure. If this was a Government leak, the tactic boomeranged. At breakfast-time on Thursday, Darling said that he had only learnt about the Goodwin pension the week before.[86] To widespread incredulity, Number 10 said the same on behalf of the Prime Minister.[87]

Fred the Shred was perfectly cast as a villain. He had walked away from the biggest corporate disaster in British history with an annual pension worth more than many people would earn in a lifetime. Yet the affair could hardly make heroes of ministers who were unwilling or unable to do anything practical to remedy this scandal. The Government was reduced to pleading with Sir Fred to examine his conscience. 'The ball is in his court,' the Chancellor told MPs.[88] Completely predictably, the hard-boiled Goodwin rebuffed the suggestion that he should make any sort of gesture to public anger. As the media and politicians bayed for his blood, he tried to present himself as the injured party. He claimed that the doubling of his pension pot to more than £16 million had been personally approved by Myners.[89] The heat turned on the City Minister and what he had known when the deal was done. Myners said he had not objected because he was led to believe that there was no discretion about the pension. This was an important technical point, but one entirely mystifying to the vast majority of the public, who could not comprehend how Goodwin was being allowed to get away with it. Peter Mandelson escalated the language of outrage about Goodwin in an interview for the *Observer* in early March, when he called the pension 'obscene'.[90] That same Sunday, Harriet Harman declared that 'Sir Fred should not be counting on being £695,000 a year better off, because it's not going to happen. The Prime Minister has said it's not acceptable and therefore it won't be accepted. It might be enforceable in a court of law, but it's not enforceable in the court of public opinion and that's where the Government steps in.'[91] This posturing was mocked by commentators and annoyed Number 10. For it drew attention to the awkward truth that Number 10 had decided to accept what the Prime Minister had called unacceptable.

At a meeting of the National Economic Council, Brown vented his frustration at his ministers. 'Why are the Tories running the agenda? Why aren't we getting our message out?' He directed a blast of temper specifically at Yvette Cooper, the Chief Treasury Secretary, wife of Ed Balls and one of his most loyal allies. 'Why don't people know the message? Why aren't ministers out there?' he raged at her as colleagues and officials cringed in sympathy and embarrassment. 'Every Cabinet minister should be doing regional visits.' Some present thought Cooper was close to tears.[92]

It was only some months later that Goodwin finally agreed to surrender a slice of his pension, leaving him to scrape by on a mere £342,000 a year.[93] In addition, he kept more than £5 million in a tax-free lump sum and a bonus. He also retained his knighthood. Ministers hoped that this was the end of it as a political issue, but it had already done its damage as the exemplification of the Government's impotence when confronted with the bankers' excesses.

Brown had told three stories about the crisis. First, that it was made in America. Second, that Britain was uniquely well placed to endure it. Third, that he had the will and the ideas to see the country through. This narrative, which had served him well the previous autumn, was now losing the benefit of the doubt. There were fewer buyers for his 'made in America' line as commentators and MPs began to interrogate his stewardship of the economy over the past decade. Hearings and media investigations focused attention on his authorship of the failed regulatory structures. He had authorised knighthoods and given places on Government task forces to the bankers, many of them fellow Scots, who were now in disgrace. A particular cause of squirming was the case of Sir James Crosby. He was forced to resign as Deputy Chairman of the FSA, having been appointed to the regulator by Brown, in the wake of allegations by a whistleblower that he ignored warnings of excessive risk-taking during his time in charge of HBOS.

The previous autumn, for sensible economic reasons as well as self-serving political ones, Brown downplayed the likely severity of the recession and spun up his own ability to deal with it. Many of those boasts came back to taunt him. One Downing Street strategist reported the alarming findings the Government was getting from its own samples of the voters' mood. 'What we are hearing from the focus groups is: "Why does nothing appear to be working?" It is the men especially. The men are very angry.'[94]

Number 10 bombarded the rest of Whitehall with daily demands for initiatives that would help Brown to make his argument that he was the man of action and Cameron was the leader of a 'do nothing party'.[95] Some of these schemes were well-purposed and creative acts of policy, some were ill-conceived and ineffectual, and some reflected Brown's vice of making announcements that came to nothing. They generated the headlines – 'Brown acts to help jobless',[96] 'Brown launches rescue package for small firms'[97] – that were desired on the day. But thoughtful Labour MPs became concerned that 'initiative after initiative after initiative . . . comes across as white noise to an electorate that wants a bigger story.'[98] One member of the Cabinet admitted: 'People are confused', not least because the 'complexity of the various schemes' meant there were long lags between the trumpeting and the implementation.[99] 'Real Help Now' was the slogan plastered on Government websites. The help, when real, was rarely now. A 'mortgage protection plan' was announced the previous September with the promise that it would spare vulnerable people from being thrown out of their homes. By May, the scheme had assisted just one family in England.[100]

Some Cabinet colleagues also despaired because 'Gordon wouldn't say no to anyone.' He made promises of financial assistance to just about every union, industry or other lobby group knocking on the door, which 'spread the money too thin' among a confusing myriad of schemes.[101] This further worsened his relationship with Alistair Darling. The Chancellor disliked the National Economic Council because it cut across the Treasury and was a forum which generated more demands for spending that he regarded as unaffordable. Darling complained to colleagues in Cabinet that Brown was not thinking strategically: 'He keeps making these random demands for money.'[102]

Peter Mandelson put his finger on the conundrum. 'High-level meetings and action . . . generate big expectations which, in turn, trigger disappointment and market reaction when immediate results are not produced,' he observed, repeating in public some of the cautions he had been privately giving to Brown about the perils of chasing headlines. 'There is no value in trying to create a frenzy around these issues every day.'[103] His own department was among those guilty of arousing expectations which were not then met. A £10 billion business lending guarantee scheme fell weeks behind schedule.[104]

The car industry, which employed directly or indirectly a million people, was terribly mauled by the recession. At a summit with the major manufacturers, suppliers and retailers in November, Mandelson sounded sympathetic to their pleas for help while declining to be specific about how he would respond. Paul Everitt, the Chief Executive of the Society of Motor Manufacturers and Traders, anxiously approached the Business Secretary at the end of the meeting. 'What's the timetable?' he asked. 'What can I go away and tell our people?' The feline Mandelson responded: 'Well, Paul, I'd be very careful. In my experience, it can be very dangerous to raise expectations.' There then followed a period of 'radio silence' when nothing was heard from Government, which left the industry 'confused as to what exactly was going on'.[105] This was partly because Mandelson was wrangling with Mervyn King about the Bank of England's refusal to extend the same credit to the car industry as it had to the banks. At the end of January, the Business Secretary finally announced a £2.3 billion rescue package, which he said would draw on funds from the European Investment Bank as well as other lending. With a typical anxiety not to be seen reverting to an Old Labour past, Mandelson denied that he was giving a 'blank cheque' to 'a lame duck'. He argued: 'Britain needs an economy with less financial engineering and more real engineering.'[106] Yet the money was dwarfed by the hundreds of billions committed to the banks, leaving those in manufacturing with the impression that Government thought 'the real economy is a second-order problem that somehow will fix itself if the first-order problem can be resolved.'[107] Both the manufacturers and the unions said that no support had been seen several months after the announcement of the aid.[108] The most visibly effective form of help for the industry was the much simpler, relatively low-cost car scrappage scheme, which offered a £2,000 inducement to drivers to swap old cars for new ones. It was introduced by Mandelson in May, and car sales began to recover the same month.

The honeymoon he had enjoyed with his party on his return to the Cabinet soured when he brought forward plans to part-privatise the Royal Mail. This aroused fierce opposition from a significant number of Labour MPs which would later force the Government to retreat. Mandelson sighed to a friend: 'I have returned to my historical role of being hated by everyone.'[109]

Brown, though, was more and more politically and psychologically dependent on the other man. One civil servant described Mandelson as 'Gordon's heroin – every now and again he needs a hit of Peter.'[110]

There was a brief cessation in the party political battle in late February when David Cameron's six-year-old son Ivan, who had suffered from cerebral palsy since birth, died suddenly following an epileptic seizure. Prime Minister's Questions was suspended for the first time since the death of John Smith in 1994. Gordon Brown, whose newborn daughter Jennifer had died seven years previously and whose youngest son had acute cystic fybrosis, led the expressions of sympathy. His voice choked when he told MPs that the death of a child was 'an unbearable sorrow that no parents should ever have to endure'.[111] He achieved an empathy and authenticity in that moment which he struggled to display when talking about the trials and tribulations of voters enduring the recession. He was again making things worse for himself because of his habitual reluctance to ever admit to a mistake. A ritual became established in the Commons which was not to his advantage. Each week, the Tory leader would rise to taunt Brown to concede that he had got something wrong. In a typical exchange, Cameron demanded: 'Will he finally admit: he did not abolish boom and bust?' 'Look,' shouted Brown, 'we can play his game of student politics as long as he wants to!' Cameron came back: 'Only one of us was a student politician and he has never grown out of it!'[112] The Tory leader had hit upon a simple, but effective trap. Brown looked both silly and stubborn when he declined to accept responsibility for any errors during the ten years he was in charge of the economy. During his autumn revival, he had been combative and confident in the Commons. He was again sounding tired, cornered, monotonous and unconvincing.

Away from cameras and microphones, during his long nights of the soul within Number 10, Brown was often tormented by his mistakes. He 'beat himself up'[113] after he made another Freudian slip at the dispatch box and talked about a 'depression' when he had meant to say 'downturn'.[114] After parliamentary performances and speeches, he would anxiously demand reviews from his staff. He came back from an event with the Prince's Trust in a self-flagellating mood, saying to aides: 'I was no good – was I?'[115] He agonised over whether he could have pressed the case for stronger international regulation more robustly during the boom years. 'I heard many mea culpas from Gordon, but in public he just wouldn't do apologies,' says one minister close to him.[116] The most that could be extracted from him was the grudging admission: 'What we didn't see, and nobody saw, was the possibility of complete market failure, that markets seized up across the world.'[117]

Brown looked more isolated when others did own up to error. His erstwhile hero, Alan Greenspan, admitted that he was 'partially wrong' in his economic theories and 'shocked' and 'very distressed' to find that he made 'a mistake' about 'how the world works'.[118] Brown's inner circle tried to persuade him that the apology – or, rather, the absence of one – would remain the story so long as he refused to acknowledge any culpability. Douglas Alexander argued with Brown that they would not be able 'to own the future' until they had accounted for the past.[119] Ed Balls broadly agreed that they would not be able to move on and take the argument to the Conservatives until they had released themselves from this snare.[120] Balls, the co-architect of the regulatory regime, gave an example of what was required when he conceded to one interviewer: 'In retrospect we all underestimated the risks and we were nowhere near tough enough. We need to learn from that and do it better in the future.'[121] Alistair Darling also offered nostra culpas on behalf of the Government. Before a committee of the Lords, he accepted that 'with the benefit of hindsight, lots of things might have been different. We need to tighten up our own regulatory regime.'[122] To a newspaper, he conceded that 'all of us have to have the humility to accept that, over the last few years, things got out of alignment.'[123]

Brown no more did humility than he did apologies. During an aggressive appearance before twenty-one select committee chairmen, in which he variously scorned questions from these senior MPs as 'absurd' or 'ridiculous', he continued to insist that 'it started in America' and refused to concede to a single mistake.[124] 'I found myself squirming as he refused, again and again, to apologise for any failings on his part,' wrote Jackie Ashley of the *Guardian*, once a great admirer. 'This has become embarrassing.'[125]

He began to retreat again into a mental bunker. His staff had to endure his angry tirades against the media for never reporting his speeches or giving him any credit. He leant even more heavily on Peter Mandelson, a constant presence in Number 10 who was now 'intervening everywhere'.[126] Shaun Woodward, the Northern Ireland Secretary, also offered himself as a comforter and emotional prop to the Prime Minister. One evening, around 7 p.m., the Business Secretary came out of Brown's office to find Woodward waiting to go in. Mandelson arched his eyebrow and said: 'Ah, the night shift.'[127]

Brown appealed for help from Alastair Campbell and Philip Gould, the chief propagandist and pollster of his predecessor. They joined the political strategy meetings inside Number 10, which were also attended by Ed Balls, Charlie Whelan and some Downing Street officials. Much of the time at these meetings was wasted looking for scapegoats. Whelan routinely mouthed profanities about Alistair Darling. Brown did not intervene to stop him, even though civil servants were witnesses to the cursing and bad-mouthing of the Chancellor. 'It was all "Darling is such a useless wanker" from Charlie and not just from Charlie,' says one appalled witness. 'It was shocking to hear, especially when officials were present.'[128]

Cabinet discipline was fraying as those with ambitions to lead the party in the future began to position themselves for defeat. There was a steady drizzle of leaks about rows between ministers, notably when Ed Balls and Geoff Hoon went to war with the Miliband brothers over a third runway at Heathrow. Brown opened a Cabinet awayday in Southampton with a ten-minute lecture about leaks. He threatened them: 'If this happens again, there will be an investigation.'[129]

*

The economy was shrinking savagely along with most of the world's. Speaking in March, Mervyn King said: 'I cannot recall any previous experience of such a sudden, severe and synchronised downturn in world output of the kind we have seen in the last three to four months.'[130]

The base rate was cut to 1.5 per cent in early January, the lowest in the Bank of England's 315-year history. Two months later, it was brought down to a new record low of 0.5 per cent. At the same time, the Bank started to increase the quantity of money circulating in the economy. On Thursday, 5 March, Mervyn King began 'quantitative easing'. The £150 billion, later raised to £175 billion and then £200 billion, was a much larger slug than most expected. The money supply was not increased by physically printing banknotes; the Bank created electronic cash, which it used to buy financial assets from banks in the hope of encouraging them to extend more credit to consumers and businesses. Britain was now in uncharted territory. A member of the Monetary Policy Committee, Andrew Sentance, called it 'a step into the unknown'.[131]

In the same week, the FTSE 100 sunk to a six-year low. Labour's poll ratings were also deeply bearish. From the end of January to the beginning of March, all five of the main polling organisations gave double-digit leads to the Conservatives. When Brown bounced after the first bank bail-out, one of the Cabinet described it as an opportunity for the Prime Minister to have a 'second audition' with the voters.[132] He had failed it. Labour MPs slumped into renewed despair about their leader's inability to communicate with the country. By a majority of more than two to one, voters were of the opinion that Labour would do better at the next election led by someone else.[133] Terrible poll ratings, crumbling parliamentary discipline and Cabinet disunity created a feedback loop, each negative fuelling the others. Brown had travelled through his own personal boom to bust. The 'saviour of the world' the previous October had crashed back to earth by March.

He still blamed it all on America. Yet it was to an American that he now looked for salvation.

36. Trillion Dollar Man

'Have you heard from your friends in the White House?' Gordon Brown asked Stewart Wood. Then the Prime Minister turned to Tom Fletcher, his Private Secretary. 'What's happening with the French and the Germans?'[1] He had been pestering them for updates on a daily basis.

As soon as one race for the White House ends, another begins: the contest to be the first European leader to get a foot inside the Oval Office. The competition for the invitation was even hotter than usual because the new President was the most charismatic and popular politician on the planet. When Barack Obama was elected in November, there was a preliminary skirmish to be the first leader to put in his congratulatory phone call. Brown won that only for the Elysée Palace then to brief that Nicolas Sarkozy's phone conversation was twice as long at half an hour. One of Brown's aides scoffed: 'Yes, but fifteen minutes of that was translation.'[2]

Number 10 had excellent contacts among the Democrats in the new administration, but there were anxieties that Obama would regard the British Government as 'part of the Bush baggage because of Iraq'.[3] The rival eyed most warily by Brown was Angela Merkel. Obama chose to speak in Berlin during his election campaign and identified Germany as crucial for rebuilding America's relationships in Europe. Sir Nigel Sheinwald, the British ambassador in Washington, was left in little doubt that his life wouldn't be worth living if the Prime Minister was beaten to the prize.[4] The Foreign Office Minister, Mark Malloch-Brown, accurately observes: 'It would have been a big thumbs-down if this beauty contest had not been won.'[5]

The good news came late, just ten days before the actual trip.[6] It was gilded by a lustrous invitation to address a Joint Session of Congress. Tony Blair had to wait six years and fight a hugely unpopular war in Iraq before that rare accolade was bestowed upon him.[7] One obsession satisfied, another and even greater one immediately consumed the mind of the Prime Minister: what would he say in his important address? 'He thinks speeches are a noble thing,' comments one official who worked with him on this one.[8] A similarity between Brown and his predecessor was that both used the process of speech-writing to try to crystallise their thoughts and marshal their arguments. By the week before his trip to America, he was dragging his confidants in the Cabinet away from their departmental duties to help craft the address to Congress. Late one night, Douglas Alexander received a call. His keen interest in American politics was a resource that Brown wanted to tap. 'What time can you be here in the morning?' Alexander replied that he could get to Downing Street around nine. 'Make it seven then,' responded the Prime Minister and detained the other man at Number 10 all morning brainstorming ideas and phrases for the speech.[9]

He flew out to Washington on 2 March against a background of continuing scares in the financial markets and growing fears that this recession had the frightening potential to slither into a depression. The Dow Jones fell through 7000 points to its lowest level since 1997. The FTSE 100 was down more than 5 per cent to a low not seen in six years.

When they touched down at Andrews Air Force Base, Sue Nye performed her customary valeting service for the Prime Minister: brushing his hair and applying make-up before he got off the plane. He arrived in Washington to a modest fanfare. Brown still lacked the instant recognition in the United States enjoyed by Blair. As if like a ghost determined to spook his successor, he was also in the American capital, to make a speech about global warming.

The advance team was led by Fletcher and Wood. To their alarm, they learnt that the White House planned to limit the leaders' public time together to a brief photo opportunity. There would be no joint news conference in the Rose Garden. Obama's officials were against setting a precedent for giving a twosome to visiting leaders. The Downing Street officials frantically sought to persuade the Americans that this would be 'a disaster' for Brown.[10] As new arrangements were hastily put together, British journalists were left at the gates of the White House, where they shivered in sub-zero temperatures and composed stories about how the Prime Minister had been frozen out.

The White House agreed to stage 'a spray' – a smaller, more informal news conference inside. Brown had been self-consciously stiff when he met with Bush, whom he addressed as 'Mr President', and recoiled from first-name terms. In contrast, he called his host 'Barack' when they sat in blue and yellow antique armchairs before a painting of George Washington. For all his attempts to look at ease, Brown was never adept at the fake bonhomie which is *de rigueur* for these encounters between leaders. 'I don't think I could compete with you at basketball,' he said to the svelte American. 'Maybe tennis.' Obama smiled: 'I hear you got a game.' 'I think you'd still be better,' Brown gratuitously sucked up to the younger man.[11]

The Obama team, not yet properly staffed and with a hazy comprehension of all the protocols, made a hash of the ritual gift exchange which is supposed to betoken mutual esteem. Downing Street agonised thoughtfully for many weeks over what might be an appropriate present for the new President. 'There was an enormous e-mail chain.'[12] They settled on a penholder carved from the oak timbers of the HMS *Gannet*, a ship deployed to suppress the slave trade in the nineteenth century. Wood from its sister vessel, the HMS *Resolute*, was used to make the desk in the Oval Office. In return for that resonant and tasteful token, the White House presented Brown with what smelt like a panic buy: a boxed set of twenty-five American movies. The collection included *Raging Bull*, *The Godfather* and *Gone With the Wind*, all titles which might be loosely metaphorical of Gordon Brown's political career and what the financial crisis had done to it. You could buy a box set of 100 Hollywood classics from Amazon for just $17.99. It was not so much the cheap price tag that was wounding to British pride; it was the evident lack of thought displayed by the Obama team. 'When we'd been so careful, that looked so desperate,' lamented one of Brown's officials. 'It looked like they'd found it in Wal-Mart.'[13] For John and Fraser, the Browns' young sons, Sarah was presented with toy models of Marine One which could be bought in the White House gift shop for less than ten bucks. Brown was 'furious that most of the press were obsessed with "snubs"'.[14]

He consoled himself that the private talks at the White House appeared to be productive. Obama was an instinctive internationalist and relatively multilateralist by the standards of American leaders. Brown's principal aim was to recruit the President as an ally in order to make a success of the G20 Summit in London the following month. There had been an anxious wait before the Americans even made a firm commitment that Obama would attend the G20. Says Mark Malloch-Brown: 'There was a real early problem about American engagement and it was a problem right up until Gordon Brown visited the US.'[15]

Leaders smell vulnerability on each other like sharks scent blood in the water and Labour's dire position in the polls had not gone unnoticed in Washington. It became clear to the British team that the Oval Office was closely monitoring the Prime Minister's political pulse. Rahm Emanuel, the White House Chief of Staff, and David Axelrod, the president's senior political strategist, discussed with their British visitors how they had bounced back the previous autumn and why Brown had since slumped back into the valley of electoral death.[16]

To Brown's relief, Obama treated him as a serious player. The two leaders found that they were ideologically simpatico and broadly on the same wavelength about the crisis. The American President had committed to a big stimulus for his economy. Indeed it made the British one seem slight by comparison. After their private tête-a-tête, they were joined by their teams for a chicken salad lunch. Obama invited Brown to repeat for the edification of the table some of the observations about the economic crisis he'd made during their earlier one-to-one. Brown was duly flattered. When he was so unpopular at home, it was crucial to both his domestic authority and his international credibility that he was not treated as a lame duck by the White House. That mattered much more to him than the crappy gifts.

The speech to Congress the next day was well-received even if it struggled to make the front pages of much of the US press. Brown won early and easy applause when he punched predictable buttons by hailing America's heroes and praising its genius for renewal. He had always been an enthusiast for the United States and took his summer holidays on Cape Cod for many years. That gave a ring of authenticity to his rhetoric when he declared: 'America is not just the indispensable nation but the irrepressible nation.' He won loud approbation when he argued that 'wealth must help more than the wealthy, and riches must enrich not just some of our community, but all of our community.' That line hit the spot with the Democrats, who controlled both houses of Congress. The Republicans sat on their hands when he called for a new global agreement on climate change. He did not repeat the frequent charge he made at home that the origins of the crisis lay in the United States. But he did try to challenge as well as flatter. Neither side of the aisle clapped when he warned that protectionism was 'a race to the bottom' which 'in the end protects no-one'.[17]

They gave him nineteen standing ovations, the same tally clocked up by Blair in 2003. This was important not just for the satisfaction of his ego but also because Brown knew that the media was counting. His eagerness to be seen as Obama's First Friend was an incentive to many journalists to search for any indications to the contrary. Some located them in the rubbishy gifts and the lack of a full-scale news conference at the White House. These were used to fashion raspberry-blowing headlines. One of Brown's aides groaned: 'They were determined to find a snub story and they got it.'[18]

Obama, as savvy about the media as any politician on the planet, quickly grasped that the White House's fumbling had inadvertently hurt his guest. About an hour into Brown's flight back home, one of the comms team brought a satellite phone to the Prime Minister. To his surprise, it was the American President on the line, wanting another word. Apologetic about what had happened, Obama said: 'I want you to know, Gordon, that I've got the pen holder on my desk.'[19] He made a point of saying how much he was looking forward to seeing him again at the G20 in London. Brown 'visibly relaxed' and was put 'in a much better temper than on the way out'.[20] He had champagne opened to celebrate and then took some bottles of the fizz down to the junior staff – the clerks and secretaries – who were sitting in the middle of the plane.[21]

The G20 was previously a junior event in the calendar of international talk-fests: a fixture of such slight significance that anti-capitalism demonstrators couldn't be bothered to turn up to protest at its meetings. A forum for finance ministers and central bankers to debate technical minutiae, their dull discussions and dry communiqués rarely attracted interest beyond the business pages of the newspapers. It was back in the autumn that Brown saw an opportunity to use Britain's chairmanship of the organisation for both personal and global advantage. There were warnings that promoting the G20 might offend the Italians, who held the chair of the traditionally more prestigious G8. Brown didn't care. He hatched a design to invite the heads of government of the twenty countries, a move which would elevate the G20 into the geopolitical equivalent of the Olympics. This was one of his smartest gambits. The twenty together represented countries with more than 80 per cent of the world's output. It made huge sense to bring them together to address the global crisis. In the words of one senior civil servant who worked with him at close quarters: 'Gordon may not be much good with people, but he is a great believer in process.'[22] Relegating the older and narrower G8 and promoting the G20 was also a logical acknowledgement of China's rise to great power status and the increasing importance of other nations such as Brazil, India and South Korea. As ever with Gordon Brown, global vision was twinned with parochial calculation. Hosting the world in London might give him a much needed boost in the eyes of his domestic audience. It would allow him to reprise the role of finance minister to the globe which received such plaudits the previous autumn. This could boost his claim to be the man who saved the world while casting the Tories as petty and marginalised.

Barack Obama's commitment was crucial to the pre-summit diplomacy. Once the American rock star was on the billing, every other leader was gagging to come to the gig. In fact, more leaders clamoured to attend than were on the original guest list. The Spanish, the Dutch and the Ethiopians gatecrashed the party. It was a tribute to Gordon Brown's cunning eye for an opportunity and the thickness of his international contacts book that he manoeuvred a mighty cavalcade of presidents and prime ministers to convene in Britain under his chairmanship.

That left the Prime Minister with a dilemma. Set the bar too low and there would be no pressure on the leaders to come to meaningful agreements. Set the bar too high and it risked being a flop. He chose to aim high – very high indeed. In the build-up to the summit, he raised the stakes by talking up the prospect of a 'grand bargain' being struck in London and the sealing of 'a global new deal'.[23] He further hyped it by repeatedly suggesting in the months before the summit that it had the potential to be a 'new Bretton Woods', as significant as the 1944 conference in New Hampshire which established the post-war financial order.[24] His answer to criticism that he was over-inflating expectations was to quote Michelangelo: 'It is better to aim too high and fall short than to aim too low and succeed.'[25]

Jon Cunliffe, his senior adviser on international finance, took charge of the team of 'sherpas' preparing for the summit. David Miliband and the Foreign Office were marginalised. For weeks, Brown and his inner team devoted themselves to preparing for the summit to the exclusion of most other work in Number 10. Members of the Cabinet quietly moaned that Brown was too busy calling the President of China or the Prime Minister of India to have any time to talk to them.[26]

Harriet Harman decided that she wanted a slice of the action and attempted to give the summit a more feminine flavour. At a meeting of the National Economic Council, Gordon Brown looked at the schedule of events, turned to Peter Mandelson and asked: 'Why are we having this Women's G20, Peter?' Mandelson sighed: 'I have had to say no to Harriet on so many things, I can't say no to her on this.' Brown groaned in sympathy: 'Oh God, I understand how you feel.'[27]

By the end of March, the potential for failure at the summit proper looked high. The mood music was increasingly discordant. The key European leaders were volubly opposed to the Anglo-American view that the world needed another massive round of fiscal stimulus. The Chinese and Russians needled Washington by arguing for a new global reserve currency to replace the dollar. One senior civil servant says: 'Two weeks beforehand, we thought we were in serious trouble. There was no agreement.'[28] Number 10 suddenly went into reverse spin and tried to massage down the expectations inflated by the Prime Minister. Ministers close to him like Mark Malloch-Brown began to fear that they would end up with 'a lot of grinning world leaders with frozen smiles on their faces accompanied by an empty communiqué and this would be a devastating blow to whatever was left of global confidence'.[29]

The week before the world was due in London, Gordon Brown embarked on a sun-chasing tour of the globe. This frantic airborne quest took him to three continents in the space of just five days, a trip of 17,500 miles in all.

It was reminiscent of the globetrotting by Tony Blair in the weeks after 9/11 when he also cast himself as the international co-ordinator in a crisis. Brown's first stop was Strasbourg to deliver a speech to the European Parliament, where he called for world leaders to do 'whatever it takes to create growth and the jobs we need',[30] the formula for arguing there should be further government spending to try to avert a depression. He was given advanced warning that he would have to stay for responses from members of the parliament, but that had not prepared him for what followed his politely received address. A Conservative MEP, the laissez-faire nationalist Daniel Hannan, erupted with a ferociously abusive denunciation of Brown as a 'Brezhnev-era apparatchik'. Hannan's performance was posted on YouTube and linked to by right-wing websites, which made it a brief sensation on the internet. Brown tried to look unbothered in front of the cameras, but he strode out of the parliament in an angry mood.

Ambushed by a Tory in Strasbourg, the Prime Minister was also banjaxed back at home. Mervyn King chose the same day to go public with his opposition to more spending in the next Budget. The Governor declared that 'another significant round of fiscal expansion' was unaffordable because 'we are facing very large deficits.'[31] For some months, Brown had been attempting to improve his relations with the Governor in order 'to get Mervyn on his side against the Treasury'.[32] But the Governor agreed with the Treasury's resistance to splashing any more red ink on the public finances. For the delighted Tories, George Osborne crowed that the Governor had 'cut up the Prime Minister's credit card' and 'leaves Gordon Brown's plans for the G20 in tatters'.[33] Vince Cable called it 'a very British coup d'état when the Governor sent his tanks down the Mall . . . and put the Government under house arrest.'[34] Brown was 'very furious' with the Governor for what allies regarded as 'unforgivable behaviour'.[35] In an attempt to deflect the interest of the media, his team briefed journalists about a supposed plan to reform the monarchy, trying to use the Queen to take attention away from King.

The second leg of the three-continent tour was the United States. As the chartered Boeing 747 cruised across the Atlantic, Brown sat in the first-class cabin, his customary black marker pen in hand, writing his next speech. This was an intellectual lecture delivered at a five-star New York hotel to an audience which included the presidents of Citibank, Nasdaq and Goldman Sachs. Brown began to sound a retreat from injecting more borrowed money into the economy, but insisted that he was already making pre-summit progress when he contended that tax havens were now under pressure to agree to tighter regulation. Before the crisis, he devoted scant attention to tackling these shadowy hidey-holes in palm-fringed islands and snow-capped principalities. During his decade at the Treasury, he had done little to crack down on tax havens. Britain was inextricably linked to eleven of the thirty-seven 'suspect jurisdictions' being targeted by a proposed American law against tax evasion. Brown had blocked the efforts of other members of the EU, notably the Germans, to force banks to be more transparent. This sudden enthusiasm for having a crack at tax havens represented a tremendous volte-face. If he was not a hypocrite, he was certainly a late convert. Most of his New York speech was devoted to his argument that the world needed to reform international institutions such as the IMF and the World Bank.[36] Here Brown was being consistent. He had been saying for many years that it was essential to modernise organisations set up in the aftermath of the Second World War. As long ago as 1998, in the wake of the Asian crisis of that period, he pressed for a more rigorous system of global oversight. Alas for him and for the world, those events were seen not as early warnings. They were shrugged off as hiccups because the boom years then merrily carried on. Now, at last, Brown had a global audience for his argument that the world needed to renew its financial architecture. He was warmly received by his audience at the Plaza Hotel. Again, though, he was dogged by bad news from Britain. An auction of Government gilts that Wednesday failed because the Treasury could not find enough buyers for British debt for the first time since 1995. This underscored Mervyn King's warning of the day before.

On Thursday, Brown's whistlestop tour of the planet landed in Brazil, one of the ascending G20 powers. His talks with President Luiz Lula da Silva went well: they were agreed about the imperative to resist protectionism. Brown regarded this as the most productive meeting of the tour.[37] Yet its public face again seemed strained. The Brazilian leader was a former shoeshine boy from an impoverished background who made his name as a populist trade union leader. He liked to emphasise his credentials as a champion of the working class by waving his left hand with the missing finger lost in a factory accident. At their joint news conference, Brown looked mildly discomfited when Lula blamed the crisis on 'the irrational behaviour of people that are white and blue-eyed' in the rich West and declared that they should pay to clean it up.[38] Brown flew on to Chile, where a news conference in Santiago generated more headlines he did not like. President Michelle Bachelet boasted that her economy was in good shape 'because of our decision during the good times to save money for the bad times'.[39] This echoed the Tory line that Brown 'failed to fix the roof when the sun was shining'. The Prime Minister was moody with journalists who asked him what he was achieving with his globetrotting. He snapped: 'I haven't been going round the world talking to leaders in every country simply to say we are having a communiqué.'[40]

The 747 took off for home on Saturday. Damian McBride walked to the rear of the plane to try to spin the accompanying media, who were also being briefed by Peter Mandelson. When the Business Secretary saw the spin doctor he had dubbed 'McPoison' coming down the aisle, Mandelson jumped into a vacant seat, put up a newspaper and pretended that the other man did not exist.[41]

Gordon Brown sat closeted in the first-class cabin. As most of his entourage and the journalists tried to catch some sleep on the long flight home, the Prime Minister sat awake, hunched over a sheaf of papers, furiously attacking them with his black marker pen.

The three-continent tour had seen serial ambushes and battered expectations. He returned home to a swelling chorus suggesting that the project in which he had invested so much time and hope was teetering on the edge of failure. 'A lot is riding on the London summit,' opined one typical American commentary the day before the leaders started to arrive in Britain. 'Right now, the G20 is on the precipice of irrelevance.'[42] George Soros, the man who made $1 billion by betting against sterling on Black Wednesday, ominously forecast that the summit was a 'make or break event' for world markets.[43]

As with most international meetings, there were months of preparatory negotiation behind the scenes in the lead-up to the climactic burst of highly orchestrated activity of the actual summit. Before a single foreign leader made landfall in Britain, there were tentative deals to increase the financial firepower of the International Monetary Fund and set up 'early-warning systems' to forestall future crises. Even so, 'a lot was still in flux' with just forty-eight hours to go.[44] Many of the leaders barely knew each other; each one had particular interests to champion and domestic audiences to satisfy. The British were very conscious that 'all the leaders showed up needing to have a win that they could take home.'[45] No-one was sure whether Gordon Brown possessed the skill to be a successful ringmaster of the colossal number of international egos descending on London.

At the head of the cavalcade was Barack Obama. He landed in Britain on Tuesday night with an epic entourage which included a security force of 200, six surgeons and a clutch of chefs. Early on Wednesday morning, the black gates at the mouth of Downing Street drew open to admit the President's fortified Cadillac, known as 'The Beast'. Obama, the world's most glamorous politician making his first visit outside North America since his election, was the most valuable ally to Brown. They broadly agreed about the diagnosis and the prescription for the crisis. As they breakfasted in Number 10, Obama sympathised with the challenge facing his host. 'Just Roosevelt and Churchill sitting in a room with a brandy, that's an easy negotiation,' he mused. Getting some two dozen leaders to agree: 'That must be like herding cats.' Brown did not argue.[46]

Obama knew that Brown still felt bruised about the White House's clumsy handling of the Washington visit. The American more than made up for it when the two men held an hour-long news conference at the Foreign Office. Speaking in the gilded grandeur of the Locarno Room, Obama turned on his megawatt smile, exuded easy calm and lavished praise on his host for the 'energy and leadership and initiative' Brown displayed in creating the summit. 'The world owes you an extraordinary debt of gratitude.'[47] A beaming Brown radiated rapture as he was licked all over by the most powerful man in the world.

The Obama–Brown double act was rivalled by a continental tag team with a competing agenda. There were many differences of style, policy and temperament between Angela Merkel, the solid, shrewd and unshowy Christian Democrat who led Germany's coalition government, and Nicolas Sarkozy, the mercurial and flamboyant Gaullist in the Elysée Palace. They nevertheless forged a common front for the summit to demand action to cleanse the murky worlds of tax havens and the shadow banking system. Learning that Brown and Obama were planning a joint appearance, Merkel and Sarkozy flew into London early to stage their own news conference in order to attack the draft communiqué for being too feeble about curbing turbo-capitalism. When he got wind of their pre-emptive attack, Brown rang both Sarkozy and Merkel to try to deter them. He failed.[48] 'France and Germany will speak with a single voice,' declared Sarkozy. They duly did, pouring cold water on the idea of further fiscal stimulus and amplifying their calls for greater regulation of international finance.

Sarkozy made a theatrical threat to walk out. 'This has nothing to do with ego, this has nothing to do with temper tantrums,' he claimed. 'This has to do with whether we're going to be up to the challenges ahead or not.' Merkel pointed out: 'The tendency is not to deal with the roots of the evil. We need to learn something from this crisis.'[49] They were essentially right. The world had been far too indulgent of what the French called *paradis fiscaux*. Tax havens were popular only with banks, corporations and the wealthy who did not want to pay their fair dues to society, and with dictators, terrorists, drugs lords, fraudsters and other criminals who used them to hide and launder their loot. It was reliably estimated that more than $10 trillion of private wealth was concealed in *paradis fiscaux*, the lost tax on which was more than double the world's global aid budget.⁵⁰ After many years of being subjected to arrogant lectures about the superiority of the Anglo-Saxon model of capitalism, this was the great opportunity for the French and the Germans to try to reset the global rules.⁵¹ Their stances were also influenced by domestic politics. Merkel faced elections in the autumn; Sarkozy was becoming unpopular in France.

Brown lightly dismissed the threat that the Frenchman would flounce out and referred to the dinner at Downing Street that evening. 'I'm confident that President Sarkozy will not only be here for the first course, but will still be sitting as we complete our dinner.'⁵² For Gordon Brown, that was a good joke.

This show of insouciance about the Gallic theatrics masked his private nerves. What if Sarkozy pushed things so hard that he had to make good on his threat to storm out? 'It was alarming.'⁵³ Brown also worried that Sarko was feeding the media narrative about a split between the Europeans and the Anglosphere and that would make it more difficult to get agreement among the leaders.⁵⁴

The glamour quotient at the summit was filled by Michelle Obama. The comic relief was provided by Silvio Berlusconi, back in power in Italy at the age of seventy-two. Advancing years had not withered his capacity for acting the clown. The Italian Prime Minister's central ambition was to engineer his way into as many encounters and photo opportunities with Obama as he could contrive. Berlusconi spotted his first chance on Wednesday afternoon when the Queen hosted a reception at Buckingham Palace and the leaders were ushered into the Throne Room for a group photo. The Queen sat in the middle at the front, with the leaders arrayed around her. The ineffable Berlusconi, standing in the back row of the group, became loudly insistent in his attempts to grab the attention of Obama. When the American tried to quieten him, the Italian simply got noisier. 'Mr Obama! Mr Obama!' he cried from the rear. 'Mr Berlusconi!' The Queen turned to locate the source of the noise and sighed when she identified the Italian *enfant terrible*. Her arms raised in frustration, she complained: 'What is it? Why does he have to shout?'⁵⁵ Even the Italian press was unsure whether to laugh or cry over the antics of their septuagenarian clown. One Italian cartoonist depicted the Queen with fingers in her ears and the other leaders looking astounded by Berlusconi.⁵⁶

More noises off came from the large numbers of protestors who descended on the City. A small group of hooded anarchists smashed their way into a branch of the Royal Bank of Scotland. Sir Fred Goodwin was hanged in effigy. Slogans were sprayed: 'Eat the rich'. City dealers mocked the demonstrators by waving £10 notes at them from upstairs windows. There were more than a hundred arrests. One man was killed by a heart attack and his death became a cause célèbre amidst allegations of police brutality. Yet there was also a carnival atmosphere about many of the protests and none of the mass rioting predicted by alarmists.

The Wednesday night dinner at Number 10 was a so-called 'austerity meal' cooked by the celebrity chef Jamie Oliver and some of his apprentices. Nicolas Sarkozy did stay for the Bakewell tart dessert, but the French President gave the British a small scare by arriving late for the Scottish salmon starter. When he finally turned up, Sarkozy found himself seated next to Hu Jintao, the President of China. Sarkozy was very unpopular with the autocratic regime in Beijing for promoting the cause of Tibet. His campaign against tax havens was also a big irritant with the Chinese, who were jealously protective of Hong Kong and Macau. Hu Jintao, a taciturn man even when in a sunny mood, exchanged only a few frosty sentences with his French neighbour.

There was some direct negotiation at the table as the leaders, each wearing translation headphones, chewed their way through a lamb main course. Brown was focused on the leader seated to his right, Dr Hu. His agreement was vital if China's vast foreign currency reserves were to be accessed to refinance the IMF. The Chinese were also expressing resistance on behalf of many of the non-Western economies to their sovereignty being infringed by international regulation. Differences about how far and fast they should go were narrowed over the dinner table. As the leaders talked, the British team of summit 'sherpas' were gathered nearby at Church House under the direction of Jon Cunliffe. The latest intelligence from the dinner was communicated from Number 10 to the Cunliffe team so that they could update the text of the communiqué.[57]

When coffee was served, the leaders moved into a state room, where they were joined by their spouses, who had been having a parallel dinner with Sarah Brown and a selection of celebrities. Silvio Berlusconi, shifting character gear from superannuated clown to aged playboy, quickly alighted upon the supermodel Naomi Campbell. Barack Obama, whose children were Harry Potter fans, bagged an autograph from J. K. Rowling. The sherpas carried on working into the night as the leaders departed for their accommodation in embassies and hotels. Shortly before midnight, Gordon Brown retired to his own bed.

He was up at five on Thursday morning for his first briefing from the Cunliffe team. The report was broadly positive. The Prime Minister was also buoyed by news that Asian markets rose overnight partly in expectation that the G20 would be a success.

As the sun came up over London, the most powerful men and women in the world were on the move. Some clattered across the city by helicopter, others travelled in snaking convoys of polished limousines, each headed towards the Docklands of east London in the shadow of the tottering citadels of finance in the Square Mile and Canary Wharf. The summit venue was the ExCeL centre, a gargantuan windowless tin shed on the Thames. 'What a dump!' groaned one Italian correspondent, surveying the baleful moonscape of concrete, graffiti and unfinished building works in the Docklands dawn.[58] The soulless venue stood on the remains of what was once the world's largest port. The Peruvian Wharf was originally built for unloading shipments of guano. The world's leaders were meeting on a site most famous for bird shit. The setting was about as remote from the Palace of Versailles as it is possible to be.

The huge throng of journalists, 2,000 in all, were penned in the summit yellow zone entirely sealed off from the presidents, prime ministers and potentates cocooned in their VIP area in the summit red zone. As the leaders began arriving, Brown worked the room, trying to ensure that no-one was wriggling out of agreements made at dinner the night before. Obama, placed at the centre of the table, dominated the conversation over breakfast. Sarkozy, who looked frustrated in a seat at the far end, started making and taking an endless number of calls on his mobile. 'He was never off the phone.'[59]

The formal session then began in a windowless oval room with each leader restricted to just four officials. This was not one of those summits where everything is fixed in advance. A lot would depend on what happened around the table. There was a lively if unconstructive contribution from Cristina Fernández de Kirchner, the President of Argentina. Known as the Queen of Botox, she launched into a tirade against Western capitalism. 'You could see Obama sitting there thinking: "I've got four, probably eight more years of this."'[60]

Brown, in the chair, let the Latin Botox Queen expend herself before bringing the leaders back to the formal agenda. He and Obama had been forced to accept that they were not going to get agreement to a new fiscal stimulus in the face of the opposition of France and Germany. Merkel – 'a very impressive negotiator' – was not budging about that.[61] Brown had refocused on persuading the leaders to sign up to other measures that he could present as a plan for recovery and reform. 'Grinding out deals, that is what Gordon likes doing and that is what he does best.'[62] During breaks, they retired to a 'leaders' lounge' fitted out with white and pea green sofas and artificial trees, an attempt to synthesise a bucolic scene inside the metallically cavernous ExCeL centre.

Nicolas Sarkozy located a new target for his anger. This was Mirek Topolánek, the Prime Minister of the Czech Republic. He had just lost a confidence vote in his own country, but he still retained a seat at the G20 because the Czechs currently held the rotating presidency of the European Union. The Czech had dismissed Obama's spending plans as 'the road to hell'. Sarkozy hauled Topolánek aside to accuse him of presuming to speak for the whole of Europe. The two men got into a finger-pointing row. The Czech then gave the other leaders a bizarre explanation for his attack on the Americans: the night before he made the inflammatory remark he had been listening to Meat Loaf's *Bat Out of Hell*.[63]

Mid-morning, the leaders were ushered out for another 'family photo'. As the curtain on their private area was opened, the incorrigible Berlusconi barged his way to the front on his continuing mission to get close to the American President. Obama fell into conversation with Dmitry Medvedev, the President of Russia. Berlusconi inserted himself between them, beamed and gave the thumbs-up, like an over-excited tourist collecting photos of himself with famous people. Someone not so famous was absent from the line-up: Stephen Harper, the Prime Minister of Canada. No-one spotted the gap next to Angela Merkel until Obama asked: 'Where are the Canadians?' Canada resented its designation as a 'tier two' nation in pre-summit briefing by British officials insensitive to Canadian pride, a fragile commodity which was further dented by the time it took for anyone to spot that their Prime Minister was missing. The explanation for his absence turned out to be prosaic: he was in the toilet. A few minutes later, the leaders were back, refixing their rictuses to have the picture retaken. The President of Indonesia had now gone missing. The previously inescapable Berlusconi, having already bagged the snap he came for, had also vanished. After a bit of flapping among the officials, they decided to abandon any further attempt to take the photo.

When the leaders returned to the negotiating table, the British began to swell in confidence that they had agreement within grasp. 'I cannot imagine the G20 happening in that way without Gordon,' says one admiring minister on his team that day. 'He uniquely gets international financial governance. He knows how to chair these meetings. Unlike most leaders, he's prepared to do the negotiating at the table rather than leave it to the sherpas.'[64]

The atmosphere over the roast beef lunch seemed so positive that the British decided to effectively scrap the afternoon 'plenary' and keep the leaders at the dining table to conclude the business.[65] Brown was exploiting his 'skill set' as the person 'who knows the subject better than anybody else around the table'.[66] According to one impressed civil servant in the room: 'Gordon just bulldozed it through. He crashed the gears.'[67] This approach was not without risk. There was still an outstanding disagreement on IMF gold sales. Nor had everyone signed up to the communiqué's wording about fiscal stimulus and tax havens. All of this had to be resolved in the two hours left. 'We were pushing things to the wire,' says one of the British team.[68]

As the clock ticked towards three o'clock, Sarkozy made a final thrust for more aggressive terms about tax havens. 'Sarkozy was fighting until the final minutes to make sure it was something he could live with.'[69] The Chinese pushed back. The two delegations got into a 'wrestling match'.[70] This climactic flare-up meant that the final communiqué was not going to be printed in time for the Prime Minister's closing news conference. If this quarrel turned really ugly, it would wreck the plan to smoothly announce a success before the close of the London markets. As the chairman, Brown could not leave his seat to take aside the French and Chinese to sort out their differences. He turned to the team sitting behind him: Jon Cunliffe, Tom Fletcher, Jeremy Heywood and Shriti Vadera. Brown groaned to them: 'God, this tax thing.' His eye focused on Vadera: 'Can you fix it, Shriti?' She grimaced and responded that the Presidents of France and China were unlikely 'to listen to me'. They would, she suggested, listen to Obama.[71] So it was the American who pulled the two warring Presidents to a corner of the room, their officials and translators scuttling along behind them. Obama suggested that the communiqué should 'take note' of an OECD list which named and shamed rogue offshore tax havens rather than 'endorse' the blacklist. He was essentially proposing an agreement to disagree that allowed both the squabbling leaders to claim a victory. Hu Jintao could save face because China did not belong to the Paris-based OECD. Sarkozy would still be able to brag that he had scored a victory against the *paradis fiscaux*. 'We twisted the language of the communiqué a bit to keep Sarkozy happy.'[72]

The intervention of the American was admired. 'Obama was a class act,' thought one wowed British official.[73] To Mark Malloch-Brown, he 'showed a judgement, a maturity, a sureness of touch in the actual room itself which was remarkable for what was the newest member at the table'.[74] On Peter Mandelson's account:

anyone there could not fail to be struck by President Obama's contribution. A combination of political skill, intellectual sharpness and charm, and an ability to work with our own Prime Minister in such a quick way, given that they had barely known each other or worked together before the G20.[75]

As the leaders formally signed off on the summit communiqué, Obama beckoned over a couple of Brown's officials and asked whether they'd mind if he said a few words before the leaders got up from the table. Of course, they didn't mind. Obama had already been repeatedly flattering about their boss. He self-deprecatingly referred to himself as 'the new kid on the block' and charmed everyone present by saying that the summit had demonstrated their ability to be 'confident in a crisis'. The American then poured yet more praise on the Prime Minister for the skill with which he had chaired their talks. After Obama's classy toast to the host, the rest of the leaders clapped Gordon Brown.

Then Nicolas Sarkozy made his move. The applause had barely died before the diminutive French President was out of his seat and moving for the door. He hurtled out of the VIP suite in the summit red zone and sped in the direction of the yellow zone, where the media waited for the closing statements. In his haste to get there, the French President banged past Michael Ellam and Stewart Wood, two members of the Number 10 team. It took the British officials a moment to work out that Sarko was determined to breach summit protocol by getting in front of the cameras before his host. Once Team Britain comprehended the intentions of the French athlete, the Prime Minister's officials dispatched Brown off at a pant to his news conference. It was too late to catch up. By the time the Prime Minister got to his podium, his French rival was already speaking from his lectern in the next-door room. It was cheeky of the impish French President to try to upstage his host and he was chastised for it even by some of his own press.[76] Yet Sarko's sprint was also a form of compliment to Gordon Brown. The French President arrived in London breathing Gallic threats to walk out. By the end of the summit, Sarkozy wanted to be the first to make a public claim that the G20 was a triumph.

He had not been speaking for long when, just before four, Gordon Brown arrived at his podium. Flanked by flags, he declared: 'This is the day that the world came together to fight back against the global recession, not with words but with a plan for global recovery and reform.'[77] The American networks switched their coverage to him. Obama, more graceful than Sarkozy and happy to let Brown have his moment in the sun, did not begin his news conference until the Prime Minister was finished. Brown's biggest boast was that they had collectively pledged large sums to inject life into the global economy. The resources of the International Monetary Fund would be tripled to $750 billion, a bigger boost than British officials had expected to achieve. Developing nations would be given access to $250 billion of currency reserves. Another $250 billion was promised in credit for trade finance.[78] Gordon Brown, with his eye on the headlines, had wanted to be able to package up the sums to produce a plump, round headline figure of $1 trillion.

On closer inspection, not all the pledges were as solid as he made them sound. They included re-announcements of previous promises and deals that were only half done. Some of the money was not really new and some of it might not be spent. Brown's familiar vices of numerical inflation, double-counting and re-announcing promises had now gone global. From his rival podium, Sarkozy was inevitably proclaiming victory for the French by declaring that 'a page has been turned' on 'Anglo-Saxon' capitalism and 'the madness of this time of total deregulation'.[79]

Obama declared it to be a collective endeavour: 'By any measure, the London summit was historic. It was historic because of the size and the scope of the challenge that we face and because of the timeliness and the magnitude of our response,' said the President. The decisions they had made were 'bolder than any other response to a crisis in living memory', though 'whether they are sufficient, we've got to wait and see.'[80] Angela Merkel was probably closest to the mark with her assessment that they had reached 'a very, very good, almost historic compromise. This time the world does not react as in the thirties. This is a victory for global co-operation.'[81]

Divisions about how to tackle the crisis were not entirely bridged and imbalances in the global economy were not addressed. Brown flirted with hubris when he declared that reformed global regulation of financial markets would 'prevent such a crisis ever happening again'. Ever is a very long time in both politics and economics. He was supposed to have ended boom and bust once before.

He was over-reaching rhetorically when he proclaimed that this was the birth of 'a new world order'. Yet the achievements of the summit were not trivial. The positive post-summit mood music was a boost to confidence. It was important that all the leaders wanted to be seen as part of the solution, even the showboating Sarkozy and the prickly Medvedev. The Russian President accurately observed: 'Twenty or twenty-five years ago one could not even imagine that such different countries with such different economies, such different mentalities and historic traditions, would sit at the table and could agree in such a difficult situation on how to act.'[82]

The agreements did generate some of the 'oxygen of confidence' hoped for by Brown. A rally in global stock markets gave credence to his claims to success. The verdict from George Soros was a thumbs-up: this was 'a turning point' because 'for the first time' the world's leaders had got ahead of the curve of the crisis.[83] By hothousing the leaders at the summit, they were driven to agreements that might not otherwise have happened quickly or even at all. Putting them together also produced some progress on off-agenda issues: the Russians and the Americans started talking about cutting their arsenals of nuclear warheads. The additional resources for the IMF would help rescue fragile emerging-market countries from a slide into even worse slumps. Tax havens were now on notice to clean up their acts or face sanctions by the end of the year. The international regulatory system was at last to be extended to large hedge funds and other elements of the shadow banking system that could pose a systemic risk. The squeals of complaint from the gambling community in the banks suggested that they regarded these measures as a serious threat to their under-regulated world.[84] The leaders failed to set a date for completing world trade talks, but they did at least pay lip-service to not sliding into beggar-my-neighbour protectionism. There was also a commitment from all, including the previously resistant Chinese and Indians, to engage with the climate change talks in Copenhagen.

Vince Cable, so often one of the Prime Minister's most piercing critics, was positive: 'The world is a different place today. I think it's better. This meeting could have failed completely, but it's come to some good positive conclusions.'[85]

There was a healthy probability that the London summit would be seen in years to come as a double watershed. The reckless era of untrammelled finance capitalism, which had broadly begun with the election of Ronald Reagan in 1980, was officially pronounced over by the world's most senior leaders in April 2009. The summit's other claim to historic significance was that it marked a formal recognition of the shift in the balance of economic power between nations. The G8 clique of rich Western states was supplanted in the hierarchy of international summitry by the G20, a bigger, broader and more global governance in which Brazil, China, India and the other rising economies were properly seated at the top table of international decision-making.

It was also a showcase for the positive characteristics of Gordon Brown as a leader. He had been in his element. 'Gordon was born for this moment,' Justin Forsyth observed to a fellow official at Number 10.[86] Sarkozy, despite his differences with Brown, praised him for playing 'a very, very excellent role'. Even David Cameron was privately heard to say that Brown 'looks good' doing global economic summitry.[87]

It cost nearly £20 million, consumed 84,000 hours of police time and devoured weeks of Downing Street's attention and energy. That was all well spent for Gordon Brown. He palpably enjoyed being Chancellor of the World. He looked much more comfortable in that part than he ever did when he was Prime Minister of Britain. Global Chancellor played to his strengths, fed his self-confidence, garnered approving headlines and won the applause of his international peer group. The missing ingredient was making it relevant to voters. At his news conference, Brown was dazzlingly in command of the detail when explaining items like the significance of the Special Drawing Rights of the IMF. What he struggled to communicate clearly was why it mattered to the livelihoods of people in Birmingham, Bristol or Bury. Malloch-Brown thought it 'one of the finest days of his premiership' but laments that his friend in Number 10 could not make a 'fluent connection' with why it was important to Britain and 'struggled to demonstrate why this international stuff mattered back home to the voter'.[88] He sounded like a man who had spent so long thinking in trillions that he had forgotten how to speak in pounds and pence. Philip Gould, veteran reader of the mind of the voter, regretted: 'It did not scratch the conscious- ness of the public.'[89]

It was nevertheless an extremely good two days – probably the most person- ally satisfying forty-eight hours of his premiership – for Gordon Brown. It was a risky coup to persuade such a pageant of leaders to convene in London. Failure would have been his failure; success was his success. His pre-summit shuttling and phone diplomacy equipped him with a comprehensive under- standing of the negotiating positions and bottom lines of his counterparts. By most accounts, he was an effective chairman. One admiring historian remarked: 'His force of character and political capital ensured an unprecedented turnout and successful outcome. Can one honestly imagine Obama, Sarkozy, Merkel or Hu Jintao answering the call from David Cameron?'[90]

The next morning, Brown was rewarded with his most sparkling reviews in the British press for at least six months. 'The London United', proclaimed *The Times* on its front page and headlined its leader comment: 'Summit of Achievement'.[91] 'The fight back starts here', declared the *Daily Telegraph*, which commended 'some sensible measures' to 'rescue the world from depres- sion'.[92] The *Financial Times* believed: 'The world is better for having held this summit. The possibility of dangerous contagion is lower and useful progress has been made across a range of issues.'[93]

The international press was also generally admiring, though it distributed the praise differently. The *Washington Post* hailed the G20 as 'a rare summit of substance' and gave most of the credit to a successful debut on the world stage by Barack Obama.[94] The hero of the day for much of the French press was their President with *Le Monde* claiming victory for the campaign to make 'a world less Anglo-Saxon'.[95] Readers of the Chinese press were under the impression that Dr Hu was the go-to guy at the G20.[96]

Downing Street didn't mind that. Most of the home media had given the Prime Minister at least two cheers for the G20 and some were awarding him the full three huzzahs. As the leaders flew out of London, the protestors dispersed, the world's journalists decamped, and the security was dismantled, Gordon Brown returned to Number 10 on Thursday evening sounding more cheerful than he had for a long time. Over celebratory drinks with his team, he told them: 'We've achieved more on financial reform in ten weeks than I managed in ten years.'[97] But he did not stay with them long to savour the achievements. 'He suddenly looked absolutely shattered. It was as if all the tiredness of the last three months had caught up with him at once.'[98]

On the drive back from the Docklands, he had asked Mark Malloch-Brown to sit in the back of the Daimler with him. The minister effused: 'Gordon, this is a corner turned.' The Prime Minister nodded and then grew pensive: 'You watch. There'll be plenty of stuff domestically ahead.'[99]

37. Chamber of Horrors

'Gents' was the salutation with which Damian McBride began his infamous e-mail to Derek Draper, a former sorcerer's apprentice to Peter Mandelson who had asked the Prime Minister's spinner to supply gossip for a scurrilous website venture. McBride had 'taken the hit' for the Cabinet revolt against Brown's methods the previous autumn and had been 'very down' since he was pushed into a role with a lower profile.[1] During the G20, he was given the relatively trivial duty of briefing the media, on behalf of Sarah Brown, who still held a candle for the spin doctor, about the activities of the leaders' spouses. Now he was 'under-employed' at Downing Street,[2] the devil had made work for an idle spinner. In the e-mails, McBride outlined a plan to attack senior Tories by spreading libellous inventions about them and their families, including one smear that David Cameron suffered from 'an embarrassing illness' and another that the wife of a senior Tory had mental health problems.[3]

The e-mails were acquired by Paul Staines, a right-wing libertarian who blogged under the pseudonym Guido Fawkes. This Fawkes lit the fuse with perfect timing. He detonated this political dirty bomb on the Easter bank holiday weekend. In a stroke, it blew away all the momentum that the G20 had generated for Brown.

The Prime Minister was up in Fife. McBride rang Brown on Saturday morning when reports started to appear that a scandal was brewing. He later said that 'it was as bad as telling my dad. He was just so angry and just so let down that he could barely speak to me.'[4] Yet it was not until that afternoon, when it became clear that they were failing in an attempt to shrug away the e-mails as no more than a juvenile misdemeanour, that McBride's resignation was announced. The Prime Minister was initially resistant to letting him go.[5]

The Tories howled with outrage about the smears while being privately delighted at the damage this did to Brown's claims to be guided by a 'moral compass'. The media went into sanctimonious mode with some newspapers condemning McBride for supplying stories they had themselves run. Then the Prime Minister got out his trademark thick black marker pen to write letters of regret to his spin doctor's intended targets and disavow any knowledge of his activities.

The attempt to create distance from McBride by portraying him as a rogue agent was not credible. McBride had been Brown's chief propagandist for six years. He was also extremely tight with Ed Balls, closer some thought than he was to the Prime Minister. Balls, knowing that he would be spattered by association, raged at his friend: 'I can't believe you have been so fucking stupid.'[6]

The more scrupulous members of Brown's staff had long been horrified by what they saw of McBride at work. His modus operandi was to offer 'trades' to journalists who boosted Brown or killed stories that Number 10 didn't want published.[7] Brown had ignored repeated warnings, from Gus O'Donnell, from Jeremy Heywood, from senior colleagues in the Cabinet, to get rid of him. McBride was not a lone wolf; he was one razor-toothed but sloppy dog in the Brown pack with a licence from the Prime Minister.

The e-mails were an extreme example of the macho and nasty tactics that had been employed on Brown's behalf by members of his cabal for many years. McBride operated in the dark side of Downing Street which was an expression of the dark side of Brown's personality. Ministers had long spoken of a 'good Gordon' – the high-minded man with ambitions to change the world – and a 'bad Brown' who surrounded himself with thuggish acolytes who used the press to carry out punishment beatings and character assassinations of colleagues who crossed or threatened their master. Entirely untrue rumours were spread that James Purnell, the Work and Pensions Secretary, was gay.[8] Alistair Darling had been continually briefed against. They would eat their own: Douglas Alexander was made the scapegoat for the election that never was. The spin-assassins were not ashamed of their reputation; they revelled in it. By eerily exquisite timing, Armando Iannucci was about to release *In the Loop*, a satirical film about spinners based on his television series *The Thick of It*. The leading character was a brutal, foul-mouthed, mendacious, psychopathic spin doctor from hell called Malcolm Tucker. Remarkably, Iannucci was given permission to film inside Downing Street. When Peter Capaldi, the actor who played the part, arrived on set 'all the real Malcolm Tuckers brought their cameras because they were quite excited.'[9] The villain was, to them, a hero.

In the aftermath of the exposure of the e-mails, a long history of dirty tricks came to light. Steve Richards, the highly respected commentator of the *Independent* who was broadly sympathetic to Brown, revealed that a

TV presenter was about to interview a Cabinet minister when McBride texted him with the message: 'Ask him about his drinking problem.'[10]

Ed Miliband, one of the Prime Minister's closest allies in the Cabinet, was put up to defend Brown on *Newsnight*, but he had to concede that the episode was 'incredibly damaging' and did not try to deny that the McBride e-mails had sunk to 'new depths'.[11]

The terrible headlines generated by Smeargate were prolonged by Brown's characteristically constipated attitude towards making a proper public apology. He was in a 'foul, foul mood' for days after he was forced to relinquish McBride.[12] Douglas Alexander told a friend: 'The problem is that Gordon is trying to explain himself to the Reverend Brown.'[13] Peter Mandelson had to plead with Brown 'to use the "s" word'.[14] Only after six days of invisibility did the Prime Minister finally bring himself to say that he was 'sorry about what happened'. Speaking at the Govan shipyard before a Cabinet awayday in Glasgow, he claimed: 'I was horrified, I was shocked and I was very angry indeed.'[15]

Rumours swirled that McBride was still lurking in the background. Peter Mandelson became so anxious that he eventually confronted the Prime Minister. 'Have you exchanged any e-mails with him?' Mandelson demanded to know. Brown swore: 'Absolutely not.'[16]

The McBride Affair was an appetiser before the blow-out feast of scandal that was about to be served up that spring. A High Court judgement the previous year had finally quashed attempts by MPs to prevent exposure of their expenses claims, a conspiracy to keep them hidden in which both Labour and the Tories were complicit. The Commons was forced to agree that it would publish in July, but some were already beginning to leak. The first to be hit was Jacqui Smith, the Home Secretary, when it was revealed in February that she claimed £116,000 in expenses by designating her sister's terrace house in south London as her 'main home' rather than the house in the West Midlands she shared with her husband and children.[17] Outrage was followed by humiliation when it was next revealed that her expense claims had included porn films watched by her husband and an 89p bath plug.[18] Her credibility never recovered. Tony McNulty, the Employment Minister, was exposed for claiming over £60,000 for the house in which his parents lived which was just eight miles from his main home. His ministerial career would soon be over too.[19]

Brown was doubly panicked. He was alarmed by what was going to be uncovered when the Commons published every MP's claim. Even in the heavily censored form planned by the authorities, he knew it would be horribly embarrassing. His pollsters were also warning him that voters would probably vent their anger most intensely at the Government. In an attempt to take the initiative, on Tuesday, 21 April, he finalised a quickly cobbled together proposal to reform parliamentary expenses and recorded a three-minute monologue announcing the package which was then uploaded on to YouTube. Brown was hoping to copy Barack Obama's successful exploitation of on-line communication. He was influenced by David Muir, the Director of Strategy at Downing Street, who had recently hired two of Obama's campaign strategists, Joel Benenson and Peter Brodnitz. They urged Brown to use YouTube as a way of bypassing the mainstream media and showing he was in touch with the digital age.[20] It was not bad advice in principle, but they forgot that the medium can only ever be as good as the messenger and his message. Ridicule greeted Brown's performance on YouTube in which he manically grinned and grimaced like a contestant in a gurning competition. 'Just too horrible to watch,' shuddered the Labour MP Gordon Prentice.[21] The number of hostile posts grew so great that Number 10 was forced to disable its site's comment section.

The YouTube recording was made in a hurry on his return from abroad just before he went into Cabinet. 'It was a complete cock-up,' says one of his senior staff. 'Someone should have checked it and seen that it was no good. No-one did.'[22] This was a further demonstration that Brown nearly always made himself less popular when he strained to be a populist. The YouTube howler was the woeful performance of a man trying to play a part that he did not enjoy and could never master. Only after he had made the disastrous recording announcing his reform plan did Brown go into Cabinet to inform his colleagues.[23] Nor had he bothered to consult senior MPs, nor the Opposition leaders, nor Sir Christopher Kelly, the chairman of the Committee on Standards in Public Life, who was aggravated that Brown was pre-empting an inquiry he had started at the Prime Minister's request. There was instant hostility to Brown's idea that the second-home allowance should be replaced by paying £150 a day to MPs for attending Westminster. MPs objected to 'clocking in'; the media and the public were scandalised by the notion of giving a bonus to politicians for turning up to do jobs for which they were already paid.

One member of the Cabinet was relieved that Brown was so preoccupied with the McBride Affair and the uproar over expenses. In advance of the Budget, Brown had again been leaning on Alistair Darling to spend money that the Treasury did not have. 'Alistair was saying no. Gordon was saying gimme, gimme, gimme.'[24] Relations between the two men had sunk to a new nadir. Brown railed to his inner circle that Darling was incapable of thinking politically and had been captured by cautious officials at the Treasury. The

Chancellor did indeed agree with his officials that the Prime Minister wanted to be reckless with the public finances. During one confrontation over the Budget, Darling said he was not going to give in to Brown's spending demands and be remembered by history as a disastrous Labour Chancellor. 'You're not going to make me Philip Snowden,' Darling said to Brown.[25]

As the Budget approached, Brown was distracted. 'The problems in his own backyard meant that Gordon couldn't interfere as much,' says one pleased Treasury official.[26] Brown nevertheless made two crucial interventions. The previous December, Darling announced a new 45 per cent income tax rate for higher earners. It was Brown who suggested that this should be lifted to 50 per cent for those earning £150,000 or more. Treasury officials cautioned that about two thirds of those in the bracket would probably find a way of avoiding the top rate.[27] Brown was not interested in that argument. He was calculating that it would distract from the horrendous borrowing figures and hoped to snare the Tories into opposing the new top rate so he could cast them as the friends of the rich. Darling did not put up much of a fight. Neither did Peter Mandelson. On his account, he was 'not entirely comfortable, but certainly accepted it and signed up for it. There was no alternative.'[28] Mandelson was lobbying for extra funding for his department and didn't see how he could simultaneously argue for more spending and against any tax rises. Darling and his officials were more resistant, but gave some ground, when Brown also put them under pressure to massage upwards the growth figures.[29]

On Wednesday, 22 April, the Chancellor rose to deliver the Budget. It confirmed that borrowing was rising to a peacetime record and that the recession would very likely be the most severe since the Second World War. Even on the rosy assumptions about future growth read out by the Chancellor, the Government would not balance its books until 2018. His figures suggested that the country faced spending reductions and tax rises for many years ahead, putting the final punctuation mark on the feel-good era. Darling had barely finished before both the numbers and the politics were under attack. The International Monetary Fund, City analysts and the Labour-dominated Treasury select committee all declared the growth projections to be wildly optimistic.[30] The Institute for Fiscal Studies estimated that there was a £45 billion hole in the Budget arithmetic.

The shocking size of the deficit and the substantial tax increases on higher earners produced another rash of headlines and commentaries calling this the last rites for New Labour. The new 50p rate broke the signature pledge, made at three elections in a row, not to touch income tax. They had slyly bent and sometimes flagrantly bust other promises over the years, but the pledge not to touch income tax had been treated as inviolate – until now. Superficially, this polled well. Most voters agreed that the wealthiest ought to take more of the pain of the recession. Yet it was also a symbolic retreat from the original New Labour prospectus. They were back to where they were before Tony Blair successfully won over aspirational voters. Labour was again the party that jacked up income tax. The Blairites, who had kept quiet for several months, broke cover. Stephen Byers predicted that Labour would live to 'regret for many years to come' the betrayal of the tax pledge. He attacked a 'cynical' piece of 'political positioning' which didn't even work because the Tories were not so stupid as to say that they would make a priority of reversing the 50p rate. 'If it was an elephant trap, it was so large and well signposted that even the most myopic old tusker would have little trouble avoiding it.'[31]

Brown bulldozed on with his expenses plan. On the night of the Budget, he invited David Cameron and Nick Clegg to meet him in the Prime Minister's room behind the Speaker's chair. Both the Opposition leaders were resentful and suspicious that Brown was presenting his plan as a fait accompli. Their mood was not improved when Brown opened the meeting in a patronising fashion by reminding the two younger leaders that he'd been in Parliament for much longer than either of them. The discussion became bad-tempered. Brown turned on Cameron. 'It's your fault,' he said, accusing the Tory leader of whipping up public anger by constantly raising expenses at Prime Minister's Questions. Cameron pinked a little and retorted that Brown was to blame for coming up with a scheme designed for partisan advantage. The Tory leader, himself alarmed about exposure of his MPs' expenses, was also struggling to come up with a credible reform package. Cameron arrived at the meeting with his own hastily composed set of proposals on a sheet of A4 paper. Brown dismissed it without even bothering to look at it and met their criticisms of his own plan by repetitively banging out his points. Clegg eventually groaned: 'Please stop saying the same thing over and over again.' They got nowhere near agreement. Voices were raised. Clegg later remarked to a friend: 'It was three rutting males. Thank God the voters couldn't see the three of us.'[32] After forty minutes getting nowhere, the meeting broke up with the Lib Dem leader declaring that his time would be better spent reading a bedtime story to his children. Brown fared little better in winning the support of his own MPs. On Monday, 27 April, he was forced to back away from his widely derided 'clocking on' idea. He had gone from YouTube to U-turn in less than a week.

He had also failed to head off another threat marching on Number 10: the Gurkhas. The year before, the High Court had ruled against the Government for refusing to allow 36,000 of the soldiers to live in Britain. The Nepalese veterans enjoyed widespread sympathy in the media and among the public. Even those most rabidly opposed to immigration wanted to make an exception for these old allies of Britain. They also acquired a charismatic commander for their campaign in the shape of Joanna Lumley, whose father's life had been saved by a Gurkha. The much loved actress did an absolutely fabulous job of presenting their cause. The Home Secretary sniffed trouble ahead when she met Lumley and was exposed to the actress's steely charm. But Jacqui Smith was distracted and weakened by the furore over her expenses. She failed to convince her colleagues that they needed to act.[33] Ministers wrangled inconclusively about the issue when the domestic affairs sub-committee of the Cabinet met under the chairmanship of Jack Straw before Christmas. Alistair Darling was not prepared to loosen the purse strings for the soldiers. 'There is no money,' he routinely told colleagues. John Hutton, the Defence Secretary, did not want to set a precedent, the costs of which would come out of his budget. The MoD took 'a rigid position' and the Treasury was 'extremely stubborn' on the account of one Cabinet minister who was a neutral observer.[34] A properly functioning Number 10 would have spotted and defused the threat from the Gurkha campaign, an emotive cause led by a figurehead adored by the tabloids. Yet Lumley later revealed she had written three letters to Brown and not even received an acknowledgement.[35]

When the issue did finally register on Brown's radar, he was 'exercised about the price tag' and colleagues heard the Prime Minister dismiss the support for the Gurkhas as 'sentimental'.[36] He lacked the emotional intelligence or the media savvy to grasp the importance of sentiment. The heart matters in politics as well as the mind. The cause was taken up by Nick Clegg, who needed popular issues to give definition to his leadership of the Lib Dems. He tabled a motion for debate on Wednesday, 29 April. On the Monday, Jacqui Smith grew anxious. 'I think we are going to lose this,' she worried to Nick Brown. The Chief Whip shook his head: 'I don't think so.'[37] At Prime Minister's Questions on the day of the vote, Brown was stumbling and sagging after an exhausting trip to Afghanistan and Pakistan. Clegg had his day in the sun. 'Can he not see that there is a simple moral principle at stake?' the Lib Dem challenged Brown. 'If someone is prepared to die for this country, surely they deserve to live in this country.'[38] The Prime Minister replied with a mechanical rehearsal of the Government's argument that it could cost £1.4 billion to allow all the Gurkhas to live in Britain, a figure dismissed as a scare by the campaigners. Clegg became encouraged as he noted the poor reception Brown was getting among Labour MPs.

The Government finally rushed out concessions that afternoon, but the decision had been taken so late that many Labour MPs were not aware of the package and the Tories were now committed to voting with the Lib Dems. To make things worse, some loyal Labour MPs were allowed to go home by the whips in their blasé belief that the Government was not at risk of defeat. Watched from the gallery by Joanna Lumley and bemedalled Nepalese veterans, MPs voted at four o'clock that afternoon. A total of twenty-seven Labour MPs backed the Lib Dem motion and a further seventy-seven abstained. It inflicted the first Commons defeat of his premiership on Brown and the first loss for a government on an early-day motion in thirty years.

Phil Woolas, the Immigration Minister, was the battered frontman for decisions made – or not made – way above his pay grade. He had had enough. On the night of the defeat, he quit the Government. Only the direct intervention of Brown persuaded Woolas to withdraw his resignation and not tell anyone about it.[39] The cause of the Gurkhas was a lightning rod for other discontents. 'Lots of people were pissed off about expenses and wanted to let off steam,' believed one Cabinet minister.[40] In an orgy of recrimination, ministers blamed each other and the whips. At an impromptu news conference outside the Commons, David Cameron and Joanna Lumley appeared with Nick Clegg, who celebrated his coup: 'This Government has now lost its moral authority.'[41] With a kukri knife at his throat, Brown agreed to a meeting with Lumley, who emerged from it to declare that he had surrendered to the Gurkhas.

The day after that parliamentary defeat, there were more angry and chaotic scenes during a Commons debate on expenses. Brown got some of his package through, including a measure forcing all MPs to disclose additional incomes. The 'clocking on' proposal, the centrepiece of his original plan, was ditched entirely as the only way to avert a second defeat in forty-eight hours. Tony Wright, the Labour chairman of the public administration committee, sighed: 'It is a rather large understatement to say that we are in a bit of a mess.'[42]

For Brown, April proved the cruellest month. The hero of the G20 Summit at the beginning of the month, he was back to zero by the end of it. Both the media and his MPs detected a common theme to these apparently unrelated debacles. The McBride Affair, the unravelling of the Budget, the YouTube fiasco, and the defeat over the Gurkhas all had one thing in common: Gordon Brown. It revived once more all the questions about his character and judgement that had raged a year before. 'He's had it. He's finished,' cried Bob Marshall-Andrews, the MP for Medway, who had agitated for years for his erstwhile hero Brown to replace Blair. 'All my colleagues think so too. For the first time in my life I've seen them united. They are united in despair.'[43]

A disaffected member of the Cabinet was emboldened to openly mock the Prime Minister. On the night of Saturday, 2 May, Number 10 was alerted to a cheeky attack on the Prime Minister by Hazel Blears, the diminutive, lively, red-haired Communities Secretary who was usually so relentlessly loyal in her public statements that she was known as 'Little Miss Sunshine'. She had put her name to a piece in the next morning's *Observer* accusing her own Government of a 'lamentable failure to get our message across' and putting itself 'on the wrong side of the British sense of fair play' over the Gurkhas. The article also included a piercingly accurate critique of Brown's entire modus operandi. 'All too often we announce new strategies or five-year plans – often with colossal price tags attached – that are received by the public with incredulity at best and, at worst, with hostility.' In case anyone failed to understand where the finger was being pointed, Blears gave a twist to one of Margaret Thatcher's lines. She mocked Brown with the witty crack: 'YouTube if you want to.'[44] The piece was actually written by Paul Richards, her political adviser. Blears had cheerfully signed off on it and told her aide that she particularly liked the YouTube joke at Brown's expense.[45] That night an incandescent Prime Minister blasted his fury down the phone at her. In the words of a Cabinet colleague: 'He gave Hazel the full hair-dryer treatment.'[46] In the early hours of Sunday morning, she issued a retraction. It was too late. The damage was done.

Number 10's panic about expenses was magnified because it was known that a leaked disc containing the details of four years of MPs' claims had been touted around the press for some weeks. The disc found a buyer in the *Daily Telegraph*. 'The truth about the Cabinet's expenses' was the huge headline over the paper's first shot on Friday, 8 May.[47] This focused on Gordon Brown sharing a bill for cleaning with his younger brother, Andrew, an arrangement for which he had a reasonable explanation. Brown responded with fury and mortification. 'He reacted like it was a dagger to his heart,' says a senior civil servant. 'It crashed the whole day.'[48]

The *Telegraph* began to dish out its revelations in daily and devastating instalments. Jack Straw claimed for the full cost of council tax even though he received a 50 per cent discount. He had already repaid the £1,500, happily noticing his mistake shortly after the High Court ruling requiring receipts to be published. The Justice Secretary accompanied the repayment with an oh-silly-me note pleading: 'Accountancy does not appear to be my strongest suit.' Straw was a Fellow of the Royal Society of Statisticians. Andy Burnham, the Culture Secretary, was embarrassed by correspondence with the Fees Office in which he pleaded for them to cough up on his claims to spare him the wrath of his wife: 'I might be in line for a divorce!' The taxpayer had contributed almost £100,000 in mortgage interest payments to Shaun Woodward, the Northern Ireland Secretary and the husband of a Sainsbury heiress who owned seven properties. Hazel Blears, the minister responsible for housing, certainly seemed to know her way round the property expenses game. She was a little whizz at Commons Monopoly. She sped round the board, claiming on three different properties in a single year. It was revealed that ministers had put in claims for everything from pergolas to pot plants. Both the Foreign Secretary, David Miliband, and the Housing Minister, Margaret Beckett, had expensive tastes in topiary.[49]

The public was astounded and then disgusted. Penny-pinching claims for chocolate bars, packets of biscuits, even carrier bags made MPs look pathetically money-grubbing. From Christmas decorations to Remembrance Day wreaths, there seemed to be nothing that tawdry parliamentarians would not stoop to claim. Luxury items – massage chairs, champagne flutes, silk cushions, whirlpool baths, plasma TV screens – suggested the funding of sybaritic lifestyles on the taxpayer. Outrage jostled with hilarity at some of the revelations. John Reid, the former hard man of the Home Office, claimed for a pouffe and a 'black glitter' toilet seat from Homebase.[50] John Prescott, scourge of the bankers' bonuses and self-styled champion of the working man, had mock Tudor beams fitted to the front of his home in Hull at the taxpayers' expense and twice claimed for repairs to a toilet seat.[51] Thus the former Deputy Prime Minister went from two Jags to two shags to two bogs.

MPs had long been resentful that their basic salary of £65,000 a year had been outstripped by many lawyers, GPs, head teachers, council executives and other professionals. Denied improved remuneration by successive Prime Ministers and not daring to make the case to the public that their salaries should be higher, MPs had treated expenses as a clandestine scheme for giving themselves tax-free top-ups. The system was inherently dishonest; the rules were lazily constructed and sloppily policed. Sheer greed then kicked in among the most opportunistic and rapacious of parliamentarians. The most lucrative racket was the practice of 'flipping'. MPs played the property market at the taxpayers' expense by making claims for mortgage interest and refurbishment on one house and then changing the designation of their 'second home' to start claiming on another. Among the most astonishingly brazen was Margaret Moran, the Labour MP for Luton South, who claimed £22,500 to treat dry rot at her partner's seafront property in Hampshire a hundred miles away from her constituency.[52]

The Government's initial response to the scandal was terribly misjudged. It lashed out at the media as if the disgrace was the exposé rather than the scandal that had been exposed. Peter Mandelson went into attack dog mode, accusing the 'Tory-supporting' *Telegraph* of 'spraying machine-gun bullets across the Cabinet'. With ill-placed confidence, Mandelson suggested the paper didn't really 'have evidence of wrong-doing'.[53] While most of the Cabinet skulked away from the cameras, Harriet Harman trotted on to the airwaves. 'I know this looks bad,' she bleated before pleading that it was all 'within the rules' as if the patently rotten rules were an immutable law of physics rather than an invention of MPs themselves. This generated rage-inflaming headlines. 'Ministers: We are NOT sorry'.[54] Margaret Beckett was nearly lynched when she tried to blame 'the system' before a jeering audience on *Question Time*.[55]

The economic crisis already besetting the Government was now compounded by a constitutional convulsion and they fed on each other. The recession made voters even less tolerant of squalid money-grubbing at their expense by politicians. The expenses scandal made it even harder for politicians to justify economic pain to the country at a time when unemployment had topped 2 million. Gordon Brown was in part paying the price for failing to make good on the promises of parliamentary and constitutional reform that he made early in his premiership. The first weekend of the expenses crisis, several ministers and officials e-mailed Brown with suggestions of bold reforms that he could announce in order to seize the initiative.[56] The Prime Minister didn't take them up. He still felt burnt by the YouTube fiasco. He was furious that the *Telegraph* had gone for him personally over expenses. He was fatally distracted that weekend, much of which he spent hunting around to find tax and national insurance records so that he could answer the charges about his cleaning arrangement.[57] On Monday, his response to the public uproar was limited to a few words inserted into a speech about an entirely different subject. It blandly offered an apology 'on behalf of all parties'.[58]

'Paying bills for Tory grandees' was the huge front-page headline in the *Daily Telegraph* on Tuesday, 12 May, following on from revelations the day before about the expenses of the Shadow Cabinet. Sir Michael Spicer, the chairman of the Tory backbench 1922 committee, claimed for the installation of a chandelier at his Worcestershire manor house. Other Tories billed for horse manure for their roses and the maintenance of swimming pools.[59] Sir Peter Viggers, the veteran Conservative MP for Gosport, claimed for an ornamental 'duck house' for his pond.[60] The ducks had not even liked it. At £1,645, this was by no means the most outrageous claim, but the 'duck island' turned into one of the totemic examples of bilking the taxpayer. Another classic was Douglas Hogg, a former Tory Cabinet minister, who claimed for clearing the moat around his thirteenth-century manor house in Lincolnshire.[61]

The *Telegraph* now appeared to be swivelling its guns on the Conservatives. Labour foolishly relaxed. That morning, the Cabinet met for a complacent three-hour session during which they spent little time discussing how they might address the fireball of public fury about the expenses scandal. They were instead treated to a Panglossian presentation by the Prime Minister's pollsters and communication advisers about how they could still come back from the mammoth deficit in the polls to win the next general election.[62]

By contrast, David Cameron was in a series of emergency meetings exclusively devoted to handling the scandal. The revelations about chandeliers, swimming pools and horse manure threatened to undo all his attempts to detoxify the image of his party. There was additional pressure on the Tory leader because some of the worst offenders were fellow Old Etonians. 'It was the moat that did it. That was the turning point,' says one Tory official. 'We knew we had to act fast.'[63]

Cameron called a hastily arranged news conference which would turn this into a defining day of the saga. 'I want to start by saying sorry,' he began, using the word his rival in Number 10 always found so difficult to get out of his mouth. The Tory leader expressed contrition in strong, clear language. 'People are right to be angry that some MPs have taken public money to pay for things that few could afford. You've been let down. Politicians have done things that are unethical and wrong. I don't care if they were within the rules – they were wrong.'[64]

He promised that all future expense claims by Tory MPs would be published on the internet and banned 'flipping'. He made a theatrical show of naming and shaming eight members of the Shadow Cabinet whom he had ordered to reimburse the taxpayer. Michael Gove, the Shadow Schools Secretary, would repay £7,000 in claims for furniture; Alan Duncan, the Shadow Leader of the House, would repay more than £5,000 in gardening costs; George Osborne, the Shadow Chancellor, would repay a £440 bill for a chauffeur company to drive him from Cheshire to London. At the risible end of the scale, Cheryl Gillan, the Shadow Welsh Secretary, would repay £4.47 claimed for dog food. Cameron announced that he was paying back £680 he had claimed for cutting down wisteria at his home in Oxfordshire. 'No more bathplugs. No more barbecues,' he chanted. 'No more patio heaters.'[65]

Conservative MPs were just as mired in the scandal as their Labour counterparts. Cameron had tolerated the expenses racket until it was exposed. He had personally exploited the housing allowances to near maximum, taking in excess of £100,000 from the taxpayer for his mortgage, a much higher figure than the claims made by Brown. Cameron nevertheless had the better of it presentationally. He put himself in a much more decisive posture by displaying a Blair-like agility in a crisis which nimbly leapfrogged the ponderous Brown. The *Daily Telegraph* hailed 'courageous Cameron' for 'a bracing blast of real leadership'.[66] That might be expected from a Tory newspaper. Less predictably, the Labour-leaning *Guardian* thought his 'engaged response' had 'showed some leadership' in contrast with Brown, who was 'slower to do the right thing'.[67] To *The Times*, he 'took command of the situation' while Gordon Brown was 'letting the furore crash on around him'.[68] Influenced by the media, voters concluded that the Tory leader was handling the crisis better than the Prime Minister. More than 60 per cent of voters thought that Brown was the most damaged of the two leaders; just 5 per cent said that of Cameron.[69]

A panicked Brown tried to wrest back the initiative by giving hastily arranged television interviews that evening. Wanting to look as tough as the Tory leader, he had his revenge on Hazel Blears by making an example of her. She was directly ordered by the Prime Minister to make a payment to HM Revenue and Customs to cover the capital gains tax on the sale of a London flat. The Revenue was not making any demand for the money, but Blears 'with a gun to her head' did not feel in a position to resist the pressure from Number 10 to make the payment, and to do it quickly and publicly.[70] Appearing on television that night, she declared that she had heard 'the outrage and anger that the public feel'.[71] It was Blears's own idea to wave on TV a cheque made out for £13,332. The cheque was then walked round to the HMRC headquarters that night. The TV clip, endlessly replayed in news bulletins about the affair, turned into one of the emblematic images of the saga. It did Blears no good at all: most of her constituents in Salford, in common with most other Britons, would never have instant access to a five-figure sum.[72] Her cheque-waving simply seemed to demonstrate that MPs inhabited a different planet to most voters.

A few genuine mistakes, a lot of sly fiddling and some absolutely outrageous scams conflated into a storm of indiscriminate loathing towards all MPs, saints and sinners alike. As Westminster was daily pounded with the revelations, MPs wandered around Parliament like shell-shocked soldiers not knowing which of their number would next step on an expenses mine. The homes and offices of exposed MPs were attacked. Labour's Diane Abbott said voters wanted 'dead MPs hanging from lamp posts'.[73] The crisis of confidence in Parliament was more acute because it brought to a head questions that had bubbled throughout the New Labour years about the emasculation and corruption of the Commons. Even before this scandal erupted, one survey found that only 19 per cent of Britons thought Parliament worked for them.[74] In a desperate attempt to save their skins, there was a shame-faced reversal in the flow of traffic to the Fees Office. Where once MPs jostled to extract money from the cash machine, now they queued to pay it back. By mid-June, they had repaid a total of nearly £500,000 between them.⁷⁵ Rather than assuage public anger, the effect of these repayments was to make the Commons look even more guilty.

Selected heads began to roll. Andrew MacKay, a senior adviser to the Tory leader, and Julie Kirkbride, his wife, who was also an MP, had claimed more than a quarter of a million pounds between them. He had claimed the second-home allowance on their London property that his wife declared to be their main home. He was forced to agree that he would step down as an MP after being shouted down at a public meeting in his constituency. A few days later, his wife announced that she would not stand again either.⁷⁶ Elliot Morley, a former minister who claimed more than £16,000 for a mortgage that had been paid off, announced he would stand down.⁷⁷ David Chaytor, the Labour MP for Bury North who also claimed for a phantom mortgage, was barred by his party from standing at the next election. So was Margaret Moran of dry rot infamy. In a separate scandal, two Labour peers became the first members of the Lords to be suspended in more than 350 years after undercover reporters recorded them offering to change legislation in return for money.⁷⁸

The highest-profile casualty was the Speaker. Michael Martin had never been a distinguished occupant of the chair since his installation in 2000 when Labour MPs preferred him for tribal reasons over alternative candidates of greater calibre. He was already a wounded Speaker after his ignominious role in the Damian Green Affair when he allowed the Metropolitan Police to raid the parliamentary offices of the Conservative immigration spokesman. Behaving like the shop steward he once was, Martin was at the fore of the futile court battle to try to shield MPs from exposure of the corrupted expenses system over which he had presided. He came to personify what the press dubbed the 'Parliament of Shame'. Even then, he might have survived. Out of reverence for the office, MPs had not ejected a Speaker for several centuries, previously tolerating the chair being held by drunks, crooks and total incompetents. Martin sealed his fate by making petulant and undignified outbursts against backbenchers who questioned his handling of the scandal. Westminster had run the gamut of emotions from denial to shock to trauma. Now they needed a blood sacrifice to offer to the angry gods of the electorate. On Monday, 18 May, wrathful MPs from both sides of the aisle gave an unprecedented monstering to the Speaker. To their calls for his resignation, he could only muster an abject and stuttering response. The man who was supposed to represent the authority of the Commons was utterly bereft of it. After being ritually slaughtered in the Chamber that afternoon, he left the chair, crossed Speaker's court and returned to the magnificent grace and favour apartments overlooking the Thames that had been his for nine years. Shortly afterwards, the Prime Minister paid him an unexpected call. The two Scots had known each other for twenty-five years. Brown had thrown a protective arm around Martin even after several members of the Cabinet warned him that the Speaker had become a joke and a liability.[79] Under the rules of Britain's unwritten constitution, the Prime Minister has no authority to sack the Speaker. As they sat together in his apartments, Brown did not explicitly tell the other man to quit. What he did make clear was that the Government could no longer shield him from the no-confidence motion tabled by backbenchers. David Cameron and Nick Clegg had given the nod to their MPs that they could sign it. Brown invited his old friend to reflect overnight on his position. The next day, Cabinet was just coming to a conclusion when one of Brown's officials passed him a note. It told him that the Speaker would resign that afternoon. Michael Martin took just thirty-three seconds to read out a statement which changed centuries of history. He was the first Speaker to be unseated since 1695, when Sir John Trevor was removed for the 'high crime and misdemeanour' of taking bribes.

Another Scot was fearful that he was next in line for decapitation. Within hours, Gordon Brown made a further attempt to get control of the convulsion by calling a news conference at Number 10. He announced fresh proposals to end what he called 'the gentleman's club' of Parliament. Centuries of self-regulation would be terminated by transferring oversight of MPs' pay and expenses to a new statutory independent regulator.

It was also announced that there would be an audit of MPs' expenses going back over four years conducted by Sir Thomas Legg, a retired civil servant. Misgivings about this appointment among some of the Cabinet proved well-founded when Sir Thomas was tougher than Number 10 bargained for. Legg reported in the autumn and told more than 300 MPs to make repayments or produce evidence to back up old claims. Brown himself had to refund £12,415. This both reignited headlines about the scandal and created a furious backlash among MPs when Legg imposed retrospective caps on claims. A 'star chamber' was established to deal with transgressing Labour MPs. This also boomeranged. Ian Gibson, the MP for Norwich North, was barred from standing again and instantly quit his seat, triggering a July by-election at which nearly three quarters of the Labour vote evaporated and the Tories won with a swing similar to that at Crewe and Nantwich.

A visitor who called on the Prime Minister's office in the Commons one day in early June found Brown sitting amidst a sea of copies of ministers' expenses records which he was wading through alone. 'He wanted to clear out all ministers with dodgy expenses because he didn't want to keep them and then find he had to sack them later.'[80] Brown had already publicly put Hazel Blears on ministerial death row by again using her as a whipping girl at his Number 10 news conference. She was far from the only Cabinet minister who had flipped properties and avoided capital gains tax, but the Prime Minister singled out her expenses as 'completely unacceptable' – his harshest condemnation yet.[81] Blears angrily complained to Brown that he had denounced her property dealings when he defended similar transactions made by other ministers. 'Hazel was shafted,' says another member of the Cabinet.[82] Brown also pointedly declined to express confidence in Jacqui Smith, which was an encouragement to the media to pronounce that the Home Secretary's career was circling the plughole.[83]

Both women chose to jump rather than wait to be dumped. On Tuesday, 2 June, just two days before the local and Euro-elections, Smith confirmed that she would be standing down as Home Secretary. The Blairite Bev Hughes and the Brownite Tom Watson announced they too were quitting as ministers. Brown's paranoia about his colleagues intensified when rumours reached Number 10 that Blears had tried to persuade Smith to do a simultaneous resignation 'to bring Gordon down'.[84] Blears felt horribly exposed, scapegoated by Brown over her expenses and had concluded that she was 'definitely for the chop'.[85] One Number 10 official says it had become 'a game of chicken' between her and the Prime Minister.[86]

After an angry confrontation with Brown at Number 10 on Tuesday, Blears quit the Cabinet on Wednesday morning. She wore a brooch that sported the legend 'Rocking the boat', an accessory that thrust two fingers at the Prime Minister. She did not call for him to go, perhaps for fear of how Number 10 might use its information on her expenses against her, but her resignation letter was entirely devoid of any of the traditional expressions of loyalty and esteem for the Prime Minister. Resigning on the eve of the elections was a reputation-wrecking move for which Blears subsequently grovelled apologies to her party. It was also a highly damaging blow to Brown. Two members of the Cabinet had decided on pre-emptive resignation, another savage tear in his tattered authority. At Prime Minister's Questions, David Cameron cried with delight that the Government was 'collapsing before our eyes'.[87] At noon, there came the first revelation of 'the Hotmail Plot', so-called because Labour MPs who wanted Brown out were being asked to add their names to a hotmail account. This threw

Number 10 into a frenzy. Six hours later, in a botched attempt to flush out the plotters, Nick Brown, the Prime Minister's chief enforcer, produced an inaccurate list of the conspirators.

The previous weekend, in a stab at soft-soap populism, the press was told that Gordon Brown had rung up to inquire about the health of Susan Boyle, a *Britain's Got Talent* contestant who had been admitted to the Priory health clinic. The cruel joke now in circulation at Westminster was that Boyle had rung Number 10 to ask after the Prime Minister's health. 'Brown at bay', shouted the *Daily Mail*.[88] 'Brown fights for survival', agreed the *Financial Times*.[89] The *Guardian*, which Alastair Campbell had once mocked as the *Gordian* because of the paper's support for him over Blair, called for Brown to resign in a full-page editorial telling Labour to 'cut him loose'.[90]

He had contributed to this wild febrility by allowing his acolytes to brief many journalists at Westminster that he was going to give the Chancellorship to Ed Balls in place of Alistair Darling. It was also briefed that David Miliband was about to be removed from the Foreign Office.[91] Darling was in 'a terrible state' when he was attacked over his expenses and had to repay nearly £700.[92] Three times at Prime Minister's Questions that week, Brown refused to endorse the Chancellor and spoke of him in the past tense.[93] Asked about his future, Darling gave the apparently feeble response: 'It is up to the Prime Minister . . . at the end of the day, it is his call.'[94] This made it sound as if he were reconciled to being fired. 'We did not want to put Brown in a corner,' explains one of his team.[95] Darling's public passivity was misleading. His stoical loyalty had been stretched to breaking point. He was incandescent that Brown appeared to be using his expenses to try to lever him out. He also had the heavyweight support of Jack Straw and other members of the Cabinet who were trenchantly opposed to Balls getting control of the Treasury and 'encouraged Alistair to fight'.[96] When Prime Minister and Chancellor met in the early evening of Thursday, Brown tried to bully him into agreeing to shift to another job. Darling pushed back, saying that he would rather leave the Government if he could not remain at the Treasury.[97]

Later that evening, Brown moved to his 'war room' at Number 12 to prepare a response to election results which he knew would be diabolical. He had set up this 'war room' after being frustrated that his senior staff were not instantly to hand in the rabbit warren of offices at Number 10 and having been impressed by a visit to the 'war room' of the Mayor of New York, Michael Bloomberg. The room was dominated by a horseshoe-shaped table with places for all his key aides and officials, and a seat reserved for Peter Mandelson to the Prime Minister's right.

That night, a big magnetic board had been set up to organise the reshuffle which Brown was planning to hold after the weekend. When he had talked over what might happen with Ed Balls, they assumed that any coup attempt would probably start on Friday morning after the results of the local elections. As Thursday evening wore on, the Prime Minister became increasingly fearful that a putsch was about to be launched before midnight. He had Peter Mandelson summoned to Number 12 from a dinner. Jeremy Heywood had just got home when he received an urgent call telling him to return to Downing Street. Having sent his driver away for the night, the Permanent Secretary grabbed a taxi.[98]

At just before ten, minutes before the polls closed, Sue Nye came into the room to say that there was a phone call from James Purnell, the Work and Pensions Secretary. This bright young protégé of Tony Blair had always thought Brown would be a disastrous Prime Minister, an expectation that had been amply confirmed by serving in his Government. He also had some specific grievances, one of which was Brown's refusal to support a second phase of welfare reform. Purnell was among the growing number of ministers who did not believe that it was credible for the Government to carry on pretending that there wouldn't have to be future reductions in spending to deal with the deficit. At a recent 'political Cabinet', Purnell had argued that they ought to acknowledge that some programmes would be cut. If they didn't, the voters would think massive tax rises were coming and Labour would be rendered incapable of making any plausible promises at the election. Andy Burnham tried to support Purnell only to be cut off by an angry Brown. After Cabinet, Brown hauled Purnell aside and blasted him for twenty minutes. 'Why are you saying that in Cabinet? You can't say that. We can't make the next election our cuts versus their cuts. Take it from me. I've won elections on this. It's got to be Labour investment versus Tory cuts.'[99]

Purnell found that argument incredible and Brown's behaviour impossible. He had been agonising for weeks about whether to resign. He confided to a few close friends that he simply could not stomach the thought of appearing before television cameras on Friday morning to express his continuing support for a Prime Minister in whom he had lost all confidence. He told friends: 'I could not carry on with the lie.'[100] Shortly after his resignation, he explained:

Over the last six months, I had been thinking: has the elastic stretched beyond where I feel I was being true to myself? I remember doing an interview with Andrew Rawnsley and having to find things to say that were just about true enough . . . I thought: this is too much – too much of a stress.[101]

Not wanting to be seen as a plotter, he had shared his intentions with very few people. Blairites like Tessa Jowell were left 'shocked and very surprised'.[102] One of the few he did confide in was his close friend David Miliband. When they spoke earlier that evening, Miliband tried to talk him out of it. The Foreign Secretary entirely shared Purnell's despair about Brown, but feared the consequences of taking action.[103]

At 9.53 p.m., Purnell e-mailed his resignation to Downing Street and then put in the call. 'James, how are you?' asked Brown, who had yet to see the e-mail. 'I'm resigning,' came Purnell's blunt reply. 'You're doing what?' said Brown. He did not shout or swear. Brown was too stunned for that. 'I'm resigning from the Government,' repeated Purnell. At a loss for words, the Prime Minister said: 'Let Peter talk to you.' He passed over the phone to Mandelson, who regarded Purnell as 'one of my boys'. Mandelson started to argue with him that he was being stupid. 'What do you think you are doing? This is mad, James.' Purnell interrupted: 'It's too late.' 'What do you mean, it's too late?' asked Mandelson.[104] Purnell had already given copies of his resignation letter to the *Guardian*, the *Sun* and *The Times*. His call for Brown 'to stand aside to give our party a fighting chance of winning' would be leading news bulletins from ten that night. 'I quit, now you quit' was the *Sun* headline on display on the TV screens in the 'war room' moments after the call.[105]

Brown knew that his premiership now dangled by the thinnest of threads. If this was the beginning of a well-organised putsch, his premiership could be dead by midnight. Purnell's lead only had to be followed by David Miliband and Alan Johnson, the Health Secretary, who was most widely tipped as the best replacement Prime Minister. If they struck, it would be fatal. These two men held his fate in their hands. 'I thought this could be it,' says one senior official present in the 'war room' that night. 'It could all be over.'[106] Both Brown and Mandelson started to make frantic phone calls to find out whether Purnell was a lone gunman or the first shot in a firing squad. Mandelson phoned Miliband, who extracted a guarantee that he would be kept at the Foreign Office.[107] It was then established from Johnson that he was not going to join Purnell. Brown rang Tony Blair for advice and asked his predecessor to intervene with Blairites to prevent them from resigning. Brown, who had used a coup to push out Blair, had been reduced to pleading for Blair's help to protect him from a coup. The irony was not lost on the other man.[108] Ed Balls arrived in the war room to learn that imminent danger appeared to have passed. 'The opportunity was handed to them on a platter,' says one of Brown's closest Cabinet confidants. 'They did not take it.'[109] By eleven o'clock, Brown could breathe a little easier. He had survived the most dangerous hour of his premiership.

Mandelson, turning himself into Brown's life support machine, made more calls to flush out and bind in suspected doubters. They were desperate to get prominent Blairites on television to make declarations of loyalty. Mandelson reached Tessa Jowell as she was driving her car. 'Would you go on television?' he asked. She hesitated. 'I need to think about what's happened.' She was driving to the London home of Charlie Falconer. When she arrived, the two Blairite friends started arguing about what to do. Falconer planned to add his voice to those calling for Brown's head. 'He's a disaster,' said Tony Blair's old flatmate. He urged Jowell to join them. She wasn't convinced: 'It's no good going on the television and saying the PM must resign. Then what? Won't the Labour Party kill us if we do this?' Their argument was interrupted by another call to Jowell from Mandelson. In his feline way, he took the blame on himself: 'It's my fault. I haven't been strong enough.' It was Brown's bad treatment of colleagues that had provoked Purnell to resign. 'I love James,' said Mandelson. 'I should have done more to stop Gordon's misconduct.' Mandelson promised Jowell that 'Gordon can be different.' He pledged to her, as he did to many others that night, that the Prime Minister had had such a severe fright that he finally understood he had to change the way he ran the Government. She was eventually booked on to Sky at two thirty in the morning.[110] The loyal Jowell would be rewarded with a return to full Cabinet rank.

Around midnight, Mandelson told Brown he should go to bed. The Business Secretary said he and Heywood would stay up to supervise bringing forward the reshuffle from Monday to Friday. The Prime Minister took himself off upstairs to the flat while the man who had been his close friend, then his deadly enemy, and was now his most essential prop carried on working the phones into the early hours.

On Friday morning, Labour contemplated the results of local elections which were utterly catastrophic. All four of its remaining county councils were lost. There were further resignations from the Cabinet. John Hutton quit as Defence Secretary and Geoff Hoon departed too. Both had no faith in the Prime Minister, but neither made a call for him to quit. Caroline Flint noisily resigned a little later with a scathing attack on Brown for running a 'bullying' regime which treated women like 'window-dressing'.[111] Her knife was blunted because she had given a declaration of loyalty to him less than twenty-four hours earlier, which made her seem motivated by pique that she hadn't been promoted to the Cabinet. 'It was resignation by hissy fit,' scoffed one minister.[112]

Brown was fortunate that potential regicides were even more inept, indecisive and ill co-ordinated than the tottering king. John Hutton had made a promise to Brown that 'he would go in a gentle way.'[113] Geoff Hoon was hoping to be nominated as the next European Commissioner.[114] James Purnell 'didn't want to be seen as part of a plot' so had told hardly anyone what he planned.[115] A dozen resignations occurred over seven days. Had all the departing ministers resigned in a choreographed fashion with an agreed candidate to replace him, they would have left his premiership mortally threatened. Had Miliband and Johnson joined them, it would have been terminal. They were restrained not by any admiration for Brown nor because they invested any hope in him. They were paralysed by terror that a change of leader, especially if he had to be dragged out kicking and screaming, would create irresistible pressure for an early general election at which Labour would be massacred.[116] 'Never mind an autumn election, there could have been a July election,' says one pivotal figure in the Cabinet who decided not to make the move.[117] They clung on to Brown for no more noble reason than fear of something worse.

On Friday morning, the Prime Minister again talked to the Chancellor. Darling's hand was now immensely strengthened. Both men knew that Brown could not afford to lose any more ministers. Both men were also aware that the Chancellor knew so many of the Prime Minister's dark secrets that he could deliver a resignation speech that would kill his premiership. Brown buckled and agreed that Darling would stay at the Treasury. James Purnell, by sacrificing his own job, had inadvertently secured both Darling and Miliband in their places. Brown was also forced to elevate Alan Johnson to the Home Office. Where once he crushed rivals, Brown's grip was now so weakened that he had to promote them.

As the threat of a Cabinet coup evaporated, there remained the potential menace of a backbench uprising. Barry Sheerman, a select committee chairman, demanded a secret ballot of Labour MPs on the leadership. Brown's acolytes responded with a clumsy attempt to foment trouble for Sheerman with his constituency party.[118] On Friday afternoon, the Prime Minister broke off from the reshuffle to call a news conference at Number 10. 'I will not waver and I will not walk away,' he said, a declaration designed to warn Labour MPs that they would have to break his fingers before they could prise them off the doorknob of Number 10.[119] Nick Brown brandished 'the rule book' and dared the plotters to come up with a challenger and the signatures of seventy-one Labour MPs, which was the number necessary to trigger a contest.[120] It was a display of the raw power politics at which the Brownites had always excelled.

On Sunday evening, the results of the European elections were declared and they were even more cataclysmic for Labour: Wales lost, Scotland lost and fifth place in the south-east of England behind the Tories, the Lib Dems,

UKIP and the Greens. Labour's share of the vote crashed to 16 per cent, the party's worst result in a national election since the First World War. The British National Party secured two seats in the European Parliament. The election results were 'absolutely dreadful', says Tessa Jowell, and left Labour 'in a very bad place indeed'.[121]

Perversely, this calamity threw another lifeline to Brown by making Labour MPs even more petrified of an early general election. 'The whips were telling us that if he went down, we would all go down with him,' says one Labour MP.[122] The attempt by Charles Clarke, Stephen Byers and others to organise a backbench uprising was fizzling out. When the leading rebels met on Monday afternoon, the number of MPs supporting a putsch had dropped to fifty-four, short of the seventy-one they needed.[123] The crucial handicap was that they did not have a plausible challenger now that all the senior figures were bound into the Cabinet. They required a Labour equivalent of Michael Heseltine to do to Gordon Brown what Heseltine had done to Margaret Thatcher. 'There was never a Heseltine figure – that was always the fatal flaw,' remarks one former Cabinet minister.[124]

Brown survived, though in a horribly mauled condition. At his next encounter with David Cameron in the Commons, the Tory leader crowed: 'Can I first of all say how pleased I am to see the Prime Minister in his place!'[125] The Prime Minister was forced to retain both a Chancellor and a Foreign Secretary he wanted to move. Ed Balls, denied the promotion to the Treasury that he craved, was sore and depressed. Darling held on to his job but at the price of everyone knowing the Prime Minister did not want him there. The reputations of Johnson and Miliband suffered when they were accused of having less spine than a jellyfish.

Only one member of the Cabinet stepped out of the smoking wreckage of electoral calamity and abortive coup as an enhanced figure. That was Baron Mandelson. His position as the effective Deputy Prime Minister was confirmed when he was made Lord President of the Council and additionally garlanded with the baroque title of First Secretary of State. During the time of Brown's maximum peril, it surely crossed Mandelson's serpentine mind that he was presented with a golden opportunity for retribution. He might have terminated Brown's premiership as payback for the way in which Brown allowed his acolytes to destroy Mandelson's first Cabinet career. One Iagoesque hint that Brown should step aside for the good of the party would have been deadly. Yet sometimes in politics there are tastes even sweeter than revenge. It was more satisfying for Mandelson to make a dependent of Brown.

Mandelson had never thought that he could climb to the very top. He was the ultimate courtier who pursued his ambitions through getting close to the Labour leader of the time: first Neil Kinnock, then Tony Blair and now, most remarkably, Gordon Brown. Mandelson was at last enthroned where he had always wanted to sit. He was the leader's indispensable grand vizier, the undisputed right-hand man. He once hoped to occupy this role for Tony Blair when New Labour was at the peak of its powers with many years in office to look forward to. All those titles and all that influence had finally come to him under Gordon Brown just as twilight was falling on their project. That was the tragedy for Peter Mandelson of his late triumph.

He nevertheless pomped in his new status. On Monday evening, Brown faced 300 Labour MPs and peers in committee room 14 at the Commons. Mandelson sat directly behind him, ostentatiously passing down notes of advice to the Prime Minister. Brown admitted that he needed to 'address my weaknesses', a rare concession from such a proud and stubborn man. He promised he could change, casting himself as a bad husband pleading to be allowed back into the marital home. He managed to keep his temper when Charles Clarke and four other MPs told him to his face that he should quit.

The mutineers were met with silence. The insurrection had flopped. The general mood of the meeting was supportive. Geraldine Smith, the MP for Morecambe, a Brown loyalist and previously no fan at all of Mandelson, rose to say that she had seen the Baron batting for the Government and defending the Prime Minister on Sunday television. 'I found myself suddenly falling in love with Peter Mandelson.'[126]

From his perch behind the Prime Minister, Mandelson peered over his spectacles, puckered his lips and blew her a little kiss.

38. No Time to Lose

The crew of the Hercules were making their final checks before take-off. Gordon Brown was at the end of his trip to Camp Bastion, the headquarters for the British army in the lethal Afghan province of Helmand. He had made a private visit to the wounded in the hospital during this August trip. He had paid tribute to 'the courage, the bravery, the professionalism and the patriotism' displayed by the soldiers in a conflict which had killed and maimed so many of their comrades. He had promised them that more helicopters and armoured vehicles were on the way.[1] He had worked hard to dispel the belief, widely held among soldiers, that the Prime Minister neither understood the armed forces nor valued them. As he prepared to board the Hercules, Gordon Brown bade the troops farewell with the words: 'Thank you for all you do.' Then he added: 'Enjoy the rest of the summer.' Many of the aides and officials travelling with him were accustomed to the Prime Minister's verbal malfunctions, but they could not believe that they had just heard him say that to soldiers in harm's way in Afghanistan.

Brown flew back to growing domestic opposition to the conflict and the continuing fallout from another storm with its origins in the 'war on terror'.

On 20 August, a private jet took off from the west of Scotland. It was bound for Tripoli. On board was Saif Gaddafi, favoured son and potential successor of the Colonel-tyrant. He was accompanying Abdelbaset al-Megrahi, the Libyan convicted of placing the bomb on Pan-Am 103 and the only person ever imprisoned for the explosion over Lockerbie in 1988. Suffering from advanced prostate cancer, he had been freed from Greenock prison on compassionate grounds by the Nationalist government in Edinburgh. A hero's welcome awaited him in Tripoli.

Gordon Brown was not entirely oblivious to the potential for the prisoner's release, after serving less than a fortnight in jail for each victim of the Lockerbie atrocity, to ignite a firestorm of outrage. He had discussed the Megrahi case with Gaddafi when the two met at the G8 in Italy in July and had tried to persuade the Colonel to keep it low key.² It had also come up when Peter Mandelson encountered Saif during another summer sojourn at the Rothschild villa in Corfu. A spokesman later insisted that there was only 'a fleeting conversation about the prisoner; Peter was completely unsighted on the subject.'³ As al-Megrahi was flown home, a private 'Dear Muammar' letter from the Prime Minister was delivered to the Libyan dictator by the British ambassador in Tripoli. It asked the Libyans to avoid giving his return a 'high profile' and ensure it was 'a purely private family occasion'.⁴ That plea to spare Britain embarrassment went unheeded. Gaddafi then deepened it by publicly thanking 'my friend Brown' for 'encouraging the Scottish government to take this historic and courageous decision'.⁵ Al-Megrahi was greeted by an exuberant Libyan crowd waving Saltires in a display orchestrated by the regime as part of the build-up to Gaddafi's gaudy celebration of the fortieth anniversary of his seizure of power. Disgust with these scenes swelled the outcry from the many who saw the release as a betrayal of the 270 victims of the atrocity, the majority of them American. Barack Obama expressed himself outraged.

Gordon Brown said nothing at all. He carried on with his holiday in the Lake District and Fife as if nothing unusual was happening. Sarah Brown, in an attempt to force her husband to take a proper rest, had insisted that Number 10 officials could call the Prime Minister only between two and three each afternoon.⁶ Even those who did get through to him did not feel able to press him to take action. 'He has never to this day sorted out the political part of Number 10,' one senior civil servant told me in the immediate aftermath of this affair. 'It was weak to begin with. It's still weak now.'⁷ Key advisers were not to hand as the furore developed. Ed Balls was on a family holiday in California. Jeremy Heywood was sailing in the Mediterranean. The 'unsighted' Peter Mandelson, the man who was supposed to be so good at 'seeing around corners', had not seen round this one. 'We were caught cold. The system failed him. We all failed him,' says one senior official. 'We had no idea about the furtive discussions between the Foreign Office and the Libyans.'⁸

Even when it was evident that this was escalating into a huge controversy, Brown tried to maintain a position that it was solely a matter for the Edinburgh Government, which took the brunt of the initial outrage. Yet he was never going to be able to sustain this defence for his silence. According to Saif, the prisoner had been 'on the table' in all the commercial dealings between Britain and Libya⁹ which followed Tony Blair's ground-breaking visit to Tripoli in 2003.¹⁰ The prisoner transfer agreement under which he was released was in negotiation during Blair's second visit in 2007. That trip, made just before he left Number 10, also sealed lucrative contracts for British energy firms, including one that brought BP back to Libya after an absence of more than thirty years. A week after the release, it emerged that Jack Straw had reluctantly agreed to include al-Megrahi in the prisoner transfer deal at a critical point in BP's negotiations with Gaddafi's regime for a gas and oil deal potentially worth £15 billion.[11] There was not evidence of a crude oil-for-terrorist deal, but there were plenty of indications that commercial interests were entangled with the negotiations leading up to the release. The Justice Secretary subsequently confirmed that trade was 'a very big part' of the talks with the Libyans over the prisoner. 'I'm unapologetic about that . . . Libya was a rogue state. We wanted to bring it back into the fold. And that included trade because trade is an essential part of it.'[12]

This was the realpolitik defence which Brown could have mounted by arguing that al-Megrahi's release was the unsavoury price to be paid for bigger prizes. Bringing Libya out of the cold was not just good for British businesses, but also for the fight against al-Qaeda and nuclear proliferation. Yet even when he returned to Number 10, he issued only a brief and evasive statement, saying merely that he was 'angry and repulsed' by the celebrations in Tripoli.[13] For thirteen days, he sustained a monastic silence about whether it was right or wrong to release the Libyan. He was frozen by fear that, whatever he said, it would infuriate someone: the United States, the Scottish Government, the Labour Party in Scotland, the Lockerbie families, the Libyan dictatorship, or the oil companies. He stayed silent even as his silence became the loudest story about the affair. This failure to adopt a position and defend it was like hanging up a sign outside Number 10 with the invitation: 'Post your conspiracy theories here'. Not to have a view also looked ridiculous when Downing Street was issuing opinions on his behalf on everything from England's victory in the Ashes to the death of Michael Jackson. One of Brown's closest confidants in the Cabinet laments: 'I've no idea why silence was regarded as the best strategy. It was a screw-up.'[14]

A cascade of papers was then released by the Westminster and Scottish governments which revealed that the Libyans had been secretly told by the Foreign Office that Britain did not want al-Megrahi to die in prison. David Cameron accused the Government of 'double dealing' for reassuring Washington that it wanted the Libyan kept in jail while telling Tripoli that it hoped he could die with his family.[15] The outcry finally compelled Brown to speak the next day. He broke his silence during a visit to Birmingham to promote a youth unemployment plan, a launch that was swamped by the affair. He was forced on to his critics' ground when he issued a blanket denial: 'There was no conspiracy, no cover-up, no double dealing, no deal on oil, no attempt to instruct Scottish ministers, no private assurances by me to Colonel Gaddafi.' Only now did he make the case that it was 'in all our interests and Britain's national interest that Libya rejoins the international community'.[16]

There were no sound grounds for saying he had behaved with impropriety. Yet his days of paralysed muteness and miserable equivocation contrived to make him look shifty. He was once again the calculator who miscalculated; the media obsessive who did not understand how to deal with the media. For his many critics, it was further confirmatory evidence of his character flaws. One typical commentary said scornfully: 'The alleged author of a book entitled *Courage* has once again shown his complete lack of this essential element in political leadership.'[17] It was added to the list – which included the phantom election, the 10p tax debacle and the expenses scandal – of examples of his fatal procrastination, his inability to communicate a case and his propensity to try to duck below the parapet only to get hit anyway. In early September, polling suggested that less than a fifth of voters thought he was doing a good job as Prime Minister.[18]

Gordon Brown stomped around Number 10 in a foul temper. 'Why wasn't I told?' he demanded. 'Why wasn't he stopped?'[19] He had again been taken by surprise, this time by the resignation as a parliamentary aide of Eric Joyce, the Labour MP for Falkirk and a former major in the Black Watch. He held the insignificant political rank of PPS to the Defence Secretary, but his decision to tear off his stripes resonated because he was previously characterised by his *über*-loyalty and was unique among Labour MPs in having any recent experience of serving as an army officer. His resignation letter accused the Prime Minister of not making a convincing case for the war in Afghanistan and charged colleagues with using 'behind-the-hand attacks' to smear senior military officers critical of the Government.[20]

The galloping major hit the Government in one of its most tender spots. Eight years since the invasion of Afghanistan to topple the Taliban and chase out al-Qaeda, there was evaporating support for what was once seen as the 'right war' and what Barack Obama still liked to call the 'war of necessity'.[21] The war was being lost. Not so much on the battlefield as in the living rooms of the public at home. There was a rapidly shrinking appetite for an apparently indefinite and increasingly deadly campaign in the heat and dust of Afghanistan. The intervention had been very popular in the wake of 9/11. Now a sceptical public asked what the soldiers were dying for. Surveys indicated that most voters thought British troops should never have been sent. Even bigger majorities wanted the troops home within a year. Most of the public felt that the mission could not succeed.[22] There were echoes of the darkest days of Iraq: confused and shifting aims, mounting casualties and a growing fear of strategic defeat. The *Sun* was running an especially aggressive campaign against the Government under the banner: 'Don't you know there's a bloody war on?' The original all-party consensus behind the intervention was disintegrating. The Liberal Democrats edged towards advocating withdrawal while the Tories repeatedly attacked the Government for not resourcing the war properly. The international coalition was fraying. The Canadians, who had taken the third-most casualties after the Americans and the British, announced they would be pulling out by 2011. The Dutch and the Spanish indicated that they might withdraw even more imminently.

Gordon Brown would never be mistaken for Henry V. He struggled to mount a cogent and eloquent case that the allies had a strategy worthy of the sacrifices being made. In his first two years as Prime Minister, he rarely made speeches explaining the war and when he did so it was with the passion of a man reading out the weather forecast for Kirkcaldy. That lack of commitment suggested that he regarded it as another conflict regretfully inherited from Tony Blair; at best, a grim necessity from which he could not extract himself rather than a cause in which he really believed. At the most recent reshuffle, he had given the job of Defence Secretary to Bob Ainsworth, the fourth holder of the post in just three years and the most mediocre. Brown had persistently given senior officers the impression that he had no feel or care for the armed forces. 'You don't think I understand defence, do you?' Brown had once said to General Charles Guthrie. 'No, I bloody well don't,' replied the General.[23]

Flying visits to the front were not enough to repair the serious damage to the relationship between politicians and the military which was the result of the failure, first in Iraq and now in Afghanistan, to provide resources commensurate with strategic ambitions. Some frustrated commanders had become almost anti-constitutional in the vehemence of their attacks on the Government for asking the armed forces to do too much with too little. This was most explosively so in the case of General Sir Richard Dannatt, who quarrelled very publicly with ministers about soldiers' pay, conditions and equipment, complaining that his political masters had to be dragged 'screaming and kicking' into resourcing the war properly.[24] Shortly before his retirement as head of the army, the rebellious General made a valedictory tour of the battlefield in which he ostentatiously used an American helicopter to draw attention to the lack of British air support. Relations had reached a low in March 2009 when Brown vetoed the military's 'preferred option' to send 2,000 reinforcements. Worried about the cost of the war, he sent just over a third of that number on an initially temporary basis. The Chief of the Defence Staff, Sir Jock Stirrup, usually a much more reticent and cautious character than the head of the army, publicly declared in July that he was taking to Number 10 a shopping list of demands for more equipment. The senior officers did not like having their advice turned down by Brown. He did not like being told what to do by men in uniforms. The mutual hostility was increasingly overt and explicit. Three former Chiefs of the Defence Staff mobilised to attack the conduct of the war when it was debated in the Lords in November. Field Marshal Lord Inge said that the armed forces 'felt that the Prime Minister has never really been on their side and they have not had his support'. General Lord Guthrie accused Brown of 'dithering' over sending reinforcements. 'The Government do not recognise that we are at war,' declared a withering Admiral Lord Boyce, who described ministers' treatment of the men they put in danger as 'wrong and immoral'.[25] The politicisation of elements of the military was one of the unintended consequences of the New Labour era. Dannatt had barely retired as a general before he was recruited to the Tories.

There had been some gains from the NATO intervention in Afghanistan. It was no longer a functioning base for al-Qaeda. Under the Taliban, only a million children were getting an education in a country with a long history of chronic illiteracy and none of them were girls. Now more than 6 million were in school, more than 2 million of them girls. Large tranches of international aid contributed to improvements in health care. Some of the provinces were stable and improving. In an impoverished country which had been ravaged by conflict for three decades, it was a miracle of sorts to have established even the vestiges of democracy.

Yet the strategic failures were also very manifest. None of the differing ambitions for the intervention that had been articulated over the years – from the eradication of the opium trade to the creation of a stable state – had been fulfilled. Many of the current difficulties flowed from the deluded triumphalism of eight years previously when the easy toppling of the Taliban regime had not been followed by a properly resourced commitment to stabilise security and build a civic society.[26] Just as in Iraq, there was scant attention paid to the tough, complex and expensive long-term challenge of conflict resolution and nation-building. Proportional to the population, the number of international troops was a twentieth of those deployed to postconflict Kosovo. The Taliban became resurgent. They and other warlords filled the vacuum left by the thin allied forces and the weak central government. President Hamid Karzai, with his handsome profile, multicoloured Uzbek cape and astrakhan hat, was originally promoted by Western leaders as his country's saviour. He had now become an embarrassing liability.

Corruption and criminality, often linked to the very heart of the Government in Kabul, were endemic. The police were notoriously predatory. Drug traffickers continued to ply their trade. Afghans, fearing that the Western forces would tire of the conflict and abandon them to the mercy of the Taliban, were given no incentive to commit to the building of a stable state. The shortage of NATO troops left generals over-reliant on air power. Large numbers of civilian casualties were inflicted by clumsy air strikes, which many times massacred civilians at wedding parties and killed sleeping villagers. These further damaged the war effort by alienating Afghans.

When the British went into Helmand in 2006 they got a much nastier welcome than either the generals or politicians anticipated. The deployment rapidly migrated from a mission to help reconstruction into an intense all-out battle with the Taliban.[27] Many soldiers fought heroically, but they were over-exposed and under-resourced. As Alan West, the former head of the navy who became Brown's Security Minister, puts it: 'We didn't have our armed forces configured to fight a war in the centre of Asia.'[28] The British had too few vehicles with sufficient protective armour and too little helicopter capacity, both of which deficiencies led to additional casualties. Major-General Andrew Mackay, the commander in Helmand between October 2007 and April 2008, sent a 'ground truth' memorandum to London which listed grave problems with his troops' equipment. He had tanks which could not get into reverse gear without restarting their engines. New Vector armoured vehicles to replace their inadequate predecessors could not be used because 'the wheels kept falling off.'[29]

The culpability did not lie solely with the politicians. Senior officers went into Helmand believing that the British army was a world expert in counter-insurgency operations because of its now dated experiences in Northern Ireland. Sir Jock Stirrup later acknowledged that 'we were a bit too complacent . . . we were a bit too smug.'[30] Constant claims of decisive engagements with the enemy raised public expectations of a successful exit, hopes which were then repeatedly shown to be illusory. Military commanders made regular boasts that they were 'routing' the enemy[31] when they were only temporarily displacing it. The army made intermittent and dangerous sweeps through Taliban-controlled zones, a mad tactic known as 'mowing the lawn'. When the British retired to their Beau Geste-style bases, the Taliban returned, ready to kill again.

The safe transport of a huge hydroelectric turbine through Taliban-held territory to the Kajaki dam in September 2008 was a major feat by the British army. Yet since, a year later, it was still offline, it also seemed a pointless one. The Taliban, roundly defeated whenever drawn on to a conventional battlefield, adapted to lethal asymmetrical warfare. Their most murderous tactic was to blow up patrolling troops with roadside bombs known as improvised explosive devices. IEDs became the principal killer of British soldiers in Helmand. Mullah Omar, their fugitive leader, was still able to terrorise Afghan civilians eight years after he fled Kabul. In the run-up to the presidential elections on 20 August, he ordered his fighters to punish civilians found exercising their democratic rights by slicing off any finger bearing the indelible ink designed to prevent repeat voting. Even the NATO headquarters in Kabul was not safe from Taliban bomb attacks.

Those in charge of the war acknowledged that the military strategy to date had been misconceived. General Stanley McChrystal, the new US and NATO commander, likened Western forces to 'the bull that repeatedly charges a matador's cape – only to tire and eventually be defeated by a much weaker opponent'.[32]

For the British forces in Afghanistan, 2009 was the deadliest year since 2001. Paradoxically, this was because they were finally trying to pursue a more coherent strategy. The British joined the American summer offensive in Helmand designed to clear out the Taliban and then hold territory so that something better could be built for Afghans. Pakistan finally made a push against the Taliban on their side of the border in the Swat Valley and Waziristan. Operation Panther's Claw, the name for the British contribution, was very costly. Between the beginning of May and early September, more than fifty British service personnel lost their lives and sixty-four were seriously injured. The total death toll of British military personnel climbed to over 230, exceeding the number killed in Iraq. For every death, more than four members of the armed forces were being wounded. The number of those seriously maimed, many with loss of limbs and some with permanent brain damage, was also climbing sharply.[33] The perils of the conflict were highlighted when two Chinook helicopters were damaged. Unable to guard them safely until they could be lifted out for repair, the British army resorted to destroying the helicopters, worth £40 million each, rather than take the risk they would fall into enemy hands. The total bill to the taxpayer was approaching £12 billion. This steep cost in blood and treasure, paid in the name of helping Afghanistan to progress towards being a civilised state, was harder to justify when the presidential election was accompanied by massive fraud. The rampant rigging was a tipping point for much of opinion: there seemed nothing noble about sending soldiers to die to protect the tainted re-election of a corrupt regime.

There were still compelling arguments for not abandoning Afghanistan yet again. One was the threat that al-Qaeda would once more use the country as a base. Another risk was of a rampant Taliban destabilising Pakistan and even seizing control in Islamabad to become the world's first Jihadist Government with nuclear weapons. Gordon Brown warned about the former, but left the latter peril unvoiced, when he made a lengthy speech in early September designed to address the mounting opposition. He insisted that the objectives were 'realistic and achievable' without being able to say when they might be realistically achieved. 'People in Britain . . . ask what success in Afghanistan would look like. The answer is that we will have succeeded when our troops are coming home because the Afghans are doing the jobs themselves.'[34] He suggested that British soldiers would be doing less fighting in future and concentrating on the 'mentoring' of Afghan security forces, a policy which was much more risky than he made it sound in that speech. A few weeks later, five British soldiers were shot dead and others critically wounded when a rogue Afghan policeman turned a machine gun on them.[35]

In a further speech on Afghanistan in early November, Brown described the war as a 'conflict of necessity not choice' and said 'we cannot, must not and will not walk away.' Yet in the same speech he warned Karzai, now reinstalled as President, that 'I am not prepared to put the lives of British men and women in harm's way for a government that does not stand up against corruption', implying they would walk away if the Kabul government was not cleaned up.[36] That exposed the dilemma and contradiction at the heart of Western policy. Despite this barrage of speeches, the British public remained unconvinced by his argument that fighting in Afghanistan made the streets of Britain safer from terror. Polling suggested that 60 per cent of voters thought the war either made no difference or heightened the threat.[37]

Trying to convince the public that there was a credible exit strategy, the Prime Minister implied that British troops could be home within two years.[38] That was at some variance with the forecast of General Sir David Richards, a former commander in Helmand who became the new head of the army, that troops would be in Afghanistan for another five years and Britain's engagement would continue 'for many, many years after that'.[39]

Brown finally agreed to send a further 500 troops, but imposed conditions that delayed their departure. The previous Defence Secretary, John Hutton, who had been angry about Brown's earlier veto, remarked that 'it would have been much more helpful had we had the additional troops there six months ago' and went on to warn that undermanning the force threatened to 'screw it up really badly'.[40] The extra troops were a supplement amounting to barely more than a twentieth on the 9,000 already there. These reinforcements were too slight to make the difference between victory and defeat. That really depended on the Americans. London was waiting on Washington to conclude its major reappraisal of strategy in Afghanistan, and Washington was waiting for Barack Obama to make up his mind about surging US forces. Sir Jock Stirrup was frank: 'What we do does rely very heavily on whatever the Americans decide to do.'[41] It was always the case, whether the Prime Minister was Blair or Brown and whether the President was Bush or Obama, that the British forces marched to tunes written in the White House.

The arguments over Afghanistan and the eruption of the Libya affair deflected Brown's efforts to launch an autumn fightback around tentative signs that the worst of the recession was over. The attempt to get back on the front foot was further undermined when the Attorney-General, Patricia Scotland, was fined £5,000 for illegally employing a Tongan housekeeper, a tale with the satirical twist that the Government's chief law officer had broken a law that she herself steered through Parliament. When the peeress shrugged off the clamour for her resignation by comparing the offence to a motoring infraction, the *Daily Mail* bellowed: 'Baroness Shameless'.[42]

During a visit to the United States, Brown's anxiety to get himself photographed with Obama rebounded in headlines that he had been 'snubbed' and initially reduced to a fifteen-minute encounter with the American President in a kitchen at the UN building. The French President and the German Chancellor didn't get quality time with Obama either, but they were not mocked by their press. He had brought this trouble on himself by being over-desperate.[43] This is what happens to leaders who are trapped in a downward spiral. Frantic efforts to contrive status-boosters backfire and then leak out in a way that further corrodes authority. He was then placed in the humiliating position of having to deny to interviewers that his eyesight was failing and that he was using happy pills. His entire party looked like it could use some anti-depressants as each publication of relentlessly bleak opinion polls took another bite out of morale.

Labour met for its last conference before the election to the sound of the Cabinet competing to make the most gloom-laden remarks. Alistair Darling won this contest by comparing his party with a gutless football team that had 'lost the will to live'.[44]

On the Monday in Brighton, the dispirited gathering was briefly roused by Peter Mandelson. The man who was once treated by his party as its pantomime villain was now received and performed like a lovable pantomime dame. His first speech from the conference platform in nine years was a triumph of over-acting: a winking, grimacing, snarling, smirking performance which blended arch attacks on opponents and camp self-deprecation with psychological soul-baring and not a little self-indulgence. Yet it also expressed a passion to take on the Tories which was notably absent from much of the

Cabinet. Telling them that Labour was 'in my blood and in my bones', Mandelson also delivered nearly all of the best lines from the conference. He admitted that they were 'underdogs' and in 'the fight of our lives' before getting roars of delight for the cry: 'If I can come back . . . we can come back!'[45]

Mandelson promised Brown his 'full, undivided loyalty'. That evening, the First Secretary confirmed that he was the most significant block on any further attempt to replace Brown with a new leader who might be more popular. Asked by me if there were any circumstances in which he would tell Brown to go, Mandelson offered an unequivocal 'No'.[46] New Labour was still dominated by the tormented relationship between its founding fathers. Mandelson had shown rational judgement back in 1994 when he switched allegiances from Brown to Blair, the most electorally appealing leadership candidate at the time. He could see the logic of replacing a leader who had become so unpopular, but to throw over Brown a second time would be to brand himself as treacherous in a way he could not bear. The party was still captive to the triangular psychodrama begun all those years before.

The conference gave him a whooping standing ovation, a career first for the man once demonised by activists. Afterwards, Tony Blair exchanged teasing phone texts with him about finally being loved by the Labour Party. Mandelson seemed genuinely touched by a transformation into conference darling which was also a sign of his party's desperation. Labour now relied on the former Prince of Darkness to offer it a glimmer of hope.

Gordon Brown arrived in Brighton still tired after his trip to America and in a state of permanent fury about the media which erupted publicly in bad-tempered performances on television. Worried that he had been thrown off-balance by the interrogations about his eyesight and whether he was using pills, the Prime Minister's team were highly nervous about how he would perform on the platform. On Tuesday morning, he rehearsed his speech using a full-sized replica of the conference podium set up in his hotel suite. There was even more stress than usually surrounded his conference speeches. David Muir and Kirsty McNeill, the principal members of the speech-writing team who had been working on it since August, were rewriting with him up to the wire.[47] 'They were still tearing stuff out and shoving things in as late as Tuesday lunchtime.'[48]

He was again introduced by his wife, whose own profile had undergone a transformation since she first performed as his warm-up woman the year before. Sarah Brown was now a much more visible public presence, though still a carefully uncontroversial one. A Sarah craze on the internet saw her attract more than three quarters of a million followers on Twitter for a bland mix of chatty observations about summits, charity announcements and fragments of family news. She had more than five times as many fans as there were members of the Labour Party. She had her own 'Sarah Brown section' on the Number 10 website, where devotees could follow her through 'pictures, news and blog posts'.[49] Cherie Blair would have been flayed by the press had she done that. Sarah Brown had also become an increasingly assertive presence behind the scenes. She encouraged her husband in his loathing towards journalists, which dismayed those on his staff who thought it was counter-productive to try to do battle with the entire British media. She was even known to upbraid members of the Cabinet for not being supportive enough.[50]

His wife introduced the Prime Minister as if she was talking about a stroppy teenager. 'He's not a saint. He's messy. He's noisy. He gets up at a terrible hour!'[51] This attempt to humanise his eccentricities sounded over-scripted and awfully similar to Michelle Obama when she told Americans that her husband snored, smelt and didn't do his share of the housework. This transatlantic device got much less approving notices than a year earlier. This was not because Sarah Brown's performance was any less professional, but because deploying the Prime Minister's wife to hail him as 'my hero' was a novelty the first time, but looked desperate the second.

When he came on to speak, the most successful paragraphs were at the beginning and absent from the script handed out to journalists, because they were one of the last-minute insertions during the feverish rewriting over lunchtime. He gave a storming list of Labour's achievements, a reminder to his party, and anyone listening from outside, that they had achieved things with power. This brought the conference to its feet. He was also compelling when he repeated his argument that he acted in the financial crisis while the Conservatives 'faced with the economic call of the century . . . called it wrong'.[52] Clever economists, such as Joseph Stiglitz, who featured in a video trailer before the speech, agreed. Labour retained some potentially persuasive narratives to tell the electorate: the banking system would have collapsed and the recession would have been worse but for the action they took; public services had been massively improved; the poor were better off than they had been. History might be kinder to Gordon Brown than the contemporary media and the electorate. It was also true that the New Labour formulation in favour of both enterprise and social justice was still an essentially attractive prospectus. The Conservatives often borrowed from it.

Yet even when he had a story to tell, Brown could not get the voters to listen to him. It was also unwise for politicians to expect voters to reward them for their record, even when they got some things right. Mandelson had made public some of the advice he was tendering in private when he told the conference the day before: 'Do not make the mistake of sitting back and expecting people to be grateful.' Elections, he correctly contended, are won 'on the future, not the past'. This would be 'a change election . . . either we offer it or the British public will turn to others who do.' He was equally right when he said Labour needed 'new reform, new policies and new thinking'.[53]

There was little evidence of that holy trinity in the speeches made to the conference by the Cabinet. In the rare cases where ministers had bright notions, most of them had been stolen by the Prime Minister for his speech. Yet it still lacked a bold, big idea and relied on small-bore announcements designed to attract back target slivers of the electorate. There was no magnetic theme, killer punch, dramatic game-changer or memorable zinger. The performance was sufficient to get him through the conference week, but nothing like enough to change the terms of the struggle with the Tories. The clunkingly populist elements of the speech included one claim that he would put teenage mums in hostels. This echoed his 2007 effort to crudely appeal to the right-wing tabloids. Within hours, the biggest-selling of those papers threw it all back in his face.

At just before ten that evening, at restaurants, drinks receptions and hotel suites around Brighton, the mobiles and Blackberries of ministers began to buzz with the news. With malevolent timing, the *Sun* chose the evening of the big speech to reveal that its front page the next morning would declare that Rupert Murdoch's weathervane tabloid was switching support to the Tories under the headline 'Labour's lost it'.[54] The paper's increasing aggression towards the Government had been signalling this defection for some time. Murdoch never knowingly backed any party that looked like a loser. What Number 10 had not expected was that the attention-seeking tabloid would try to ruin the Prime Minister's speech. Peter Mandelson told News International's Chief Executive, Rebekah Brooks, that the Murdoch empire would look like 'a bunch of chumps, we will not lose any sleep over this'. Some claimed he used a rather stronger word beginning with 'c'. The next day on the conference platform, the Liverpudlian union leader Tony Woodley ripped up a copy of the newspaper to loud cheers.

Whether or not the *Sun* could actually shift significant numbers of votes – academic studies suggested not – the switch was symbolic. The conversion of the tabloid to Tony Blair before the 1997 election was a milestone on New Labour's march to power. Its reversion to the Tories under Gordon Brown was a marker of decline. Domination of the media had been one of New Labour's touchstones during its years of success. 'Gordon has no constituency in the media,' remarked one gloomy ally of the Prime Minister,[55] an observation which, with the partial exception of the *Mirror*, was true.

At 6 p.m. on Remembrance Sunday, Number 10 officials took a call from the *Sun*. It was giving a few hours' warning that the tabloid was about to launch its most vicious attack yet on Brown. Under the headline 'Bloody shameful', the next morning's front page accused him of failing to bow his head after laying his wreath at the Cenotaph.[56] That lapse his staff put down to disorientation due to his poor eyesight.[57] The stinger in the splash was a furious assault on the Prime Minister by Jacqui Janes, the grieving mother of a twenty-year-old soldier who had died of horrific injuries sustained in Afghanistan. She complained that a letter of condolence from Brown was a 'disgraceful, hastily scrawled insult' to her and the sacrifice of her son.[58]

Brown had continued with Blair's practice of sending handwritten notes to the relatives of the dead. His handwriting was bad, as he himself acknowledged, and became more indecipherable when condolence letters were written in spare moments while travelling on trains, in planes and in the back of the car.[59] The messiness of the letter to Mrs Janes was the result not of disrespect but of bad eyesight and tiredness. It was physically laborious for a man without sight in his left eye and a right eye compromised by a damaged retina. It was, though, inexcusably maladroit to send a letter to a grieving mother with her name misspelt and the name of her dead son apparently corrected with a scribble. This was also a consequence of the continuing dysfunctionality of the Number 10 machine. Though his staff knew that the Prime Minister's penmanship was poor, none of them had ever dared suggest that Brown's condolence letters should be checked before they were posted. 'It was difficult. It was very personal. It was sensitive. It was a line we thought we could not cross.'[60]

On Sunday evening, Brown phoned the bereaved mother in an attempt to assuage her wrath. This backfired when she recorded the acrimonious thirteen-minute conversation in which she angrily blamed her son's death on equipment shortages. A transcript of the call provided the *Sun* with more material on Tuesday. At a news conference that day, even hardened Westminster reporters found it painful to watch as Brown fell back on alluding to his own loss of his baby daughter to suggest that he understood bereavement.[61] One sketchwriter present thought: 'It was excruciating. You'd have needed a heart of Kevlar not to sympathise with Gordon Brown yesterday.'[62] There was a backlash against the *Sun*. Most of the rest of the media accused the tabloid of crudely exploiting a mother's grief to spring a nasty ambush on the Prime Minister. The majority of the public sympathised with him.[63]

After this episode, he spent 'two to three times as long' when he wrote letters to the bereaved, and systems were put in place so that they were checked by his staff before they were posted.[64]

In mid-November, Labour won a comfortable victory in the Glasgow North-East by-election triggered when Michael Martin stood down as an MP. This was a rare moment of respite as opinion polls continued to bring relentlessly bleak news for Labour about its national unpopularity. In the polls published in October and November, the Tories enjoyed an average lead of 13 per cent.

Tony Blair had remained entirely silent about his party's plight since he left Number 10. He had made up his mind not to stalk his successor as Margaret Thatcher had haunted John Major. He also wanted to become the first 'President of Europe' – the actual title was President of the European Council – the first permanent leader to chair summits and represent the EU abroad. It was one of the world's worst-kept secrets that he desired the job, an ambition that he first began to harbour when he was Prime Minister. For the previous eighteen months, Jonathan Powell, his former Chief of Staff, had been running a behind-the-scenes lobbying campaign.[65]

Blair's chances initially looked quite promising. Nicolas Sarkozy had told Blair that he had the French President's support. During one discussion with Angela Merkel, the German Chancellor joked to Brown that, though Blair was nominally a member of the socialist group, she would regard his appointment as a victory for Christian Democrats like herself.[66]

David Miliband urged support for Blair on the grounds that the EU needed to be represented by someone with global name recognition whose motorcade could 'stop the traffic' in Beijing, Washington or Moscow.[67] Blair would not campaign openly for the post, for fear of being too visibly rebuffed if he didn't get it. This made him seem aloof. Only belatedly did he make a flurry of personal telephone calls to European leaders, by which time his hopes were already fading. Brown went to the other extreme and waged a campaign which was both loud in public and aggressive in private. 'You need to get real,' he tried to bully other centre-left leaders at a meeting in late October. He urged them to seize 'a unique opportunity' to put a 'strong, progressive politician' in the top job. Brown ended up in a shouting match with Martin Schultz, the anti-Blair leader of the socialist group in the European Parliament.[68] The German media, reflecting opposition to Blair on both left and right in Europe's most powerful country, reported that the chances of the one-time favourite for the presidency had crashed to 'almost zero'.[69]

The horse-trading came to a climax at a summit in Brussels towards the end of November. The dominant centre-right in Europe demanded the job for one of their own members. There was little support among the socialist group, who had not forgotten how Blair had often disdained them when he was Prime Minister. The Iraq war and Britain's exclusion from the euro-zone also stacked up against him. Blair did not get the presidency in part because of those things he did and did not do as Prime Minister. His international fame was more a handicap than an advantage. Sarkozy and Merkel had concluded that they wanted a low-profile fixer in the role, not a globe-trotting character who would rival them on the world stage. There was a traditional Franco-German stitch-up in favour of an obscure candidate from the Low Countries. The presidency was conferred on Herman Van Rompuy, Prime Minister of Belgium for less than a year. Blair's friends briefed the press that the former Prime Minister was unsurprised, relaxed, and very content to go on being a Middle East envoy, running his foundations and making money.[70] This was putting a brave face on the rejection. It couldn't but be wounding to be passed over for an uncharismatic Belgian who would not stop the traffic even in his native Brussels.

The second new prize job created by the Lisbon Treaty was 'High Representative', essentially foreign minister of the EU. This was Miliband's for the taking and Brown sought to persuade him to do it, but the Foreign Secretary decided his future lay in British politics. Mandelson flirted with the idea, but did not persist when the Prime Minister implored him not to put himself up for the job.[71] It would have been almost universally interpreted as Mandelson ratting on a sinking Brown.

The post ended up dropping into the astonished lap of Cathy Ashton. This capable but little known Labour peeress was not Brown's first choice by a long way. She had been sent to Brussels just thirteen months earlier as a stop-gap appointment to eke out the remainder of Mandelson's term as a commissioner when he returned to Britain. The day before her appointment, she would not have stopped the traffic in Basingstoke. Not thinking that she was even a serious candidate, she had been planning to leave Brussels on the 8 p.m. Eurostar when word came that she had better hold on.[72] She had no speech prepared when she appeared alongside Van Rompuy at a news conference to announce their appointments as the EU's two most senior officials.[73]

Many felt that these timid choices were a missed opportunity for Europe to translate its economic strength into global clout. The *Financial Times* groaned that this 'exercise in Euro-minimalism' was 'a colossal failure of ambition'.[74] Nicolas Sarkozy openly gloated that he had got the better of the horse-trading by grabbing key economic portfolios on the Commission for the French and their allies. Mandelson, who didn't rate Ashton, furiously complained to colleagues that Brown had made a hash of the negotiations.[75]

A member of the Cabinet groaned about Van Rompuy and Ashton: 'We have ended up with two garden gnomes.'[76]

As winter grew colder, there were many signs which pointed to the terminal fragmentation of the coalition that had originally brought New Labour to power. The three election victories were built on five pillars. One was the peculiar presentational and positioning skills of Tony Blair. Another was the continuous prosperity which fed a feel-good factor. A third component in their success was the unattractiveness of their opponents for many years after the first Tory defeat in 1997. The fourth was sustained investment in education, health and other popular public services. The fifth was representing themselves as the force of change, modernisation and the future.

Each of those pillars was now badly fractured or entirely collapsed. The claim to be the party of the future was always going to be a challenge to sustain during a second decade in office. For more than a century, no government but one had managed to win more than three consecutive terms in Britain. It was even harder to present themselves as the agents of change and renewal when the Prime Minister was a man often crippled by his caution who had been at the apex of the Government throughout its time in power. Voters and the media were now more minded to notice New Labour's failures than its achievements, and well-schooled in the flaws of its personalities, a familiarity which bred contempt. Cynicism and mistrust towards the Government were more striking because of the contrast with the euphoric salad days in power when it laid claim to idealism and hope. The voter revolt against the political establishment, intensified by the parliamentary expenses scandal, was felt most acutely by Labour because it was in government. When the state is seen as failing or corrupt, it is especially damaging for the party that proclaims the merits of the state. One astute analysis by Peter Kellner, the president of the polling organisation YouGov, observed that 'the over-riding fact about most lost Labour voters is that they have been repelled by the Government, not attracted by the Conservatives.'[77]

The Tories, having knocked themselves out of contention in the first two parliaments after 1997, were able to profit from anti-Labour sentiment. This was not because they had found a prospective Prime Minister who commanded absolute confidence nor because they had a fully coherent prospectus. What they did have in David Cameron was an apparently personable leader well-regarded by most of the public, who turned them back into highly professional, tightly disciplined competitors for power. The Conservatives struggled to mask their expectation that they were on their way back. 'Bye! Bye!' Tory MPs jeered at their Labour opposite numbers when the

Commons met in October. Bono, the rock star cheerleader for Labour in the past, gave a video testimonial at the Tory conference. The followers of political fashion in celebrity, business and elsewhere were very obviously preparing for a change of government. It remained highly moot to what extent progressive Conservatism was genuine and to what extent it was reaction in disguise. Voters trusted Cameron much more than they did the rest of his party. The Tory poll rating, bobbing in the low forties, did not indicate a wave of national enthusiasm for the Conservatives. It was nevertheless enough to win so long as revulsion with Labour put the Tories at a handsome poll advantage.

There was a creditable depth and variety of achievements, from peace in Northern Ireland to the minimum wage to Sure Start to vastly increased spending on education and health, all of which even the Tories commended. Yet Labour now seemed incapable of fashioning its record into an account that the electorate wanted to appreciate nor to weave a narrative about what it would do in the future. The increases in the funding of public services had been on a scale without precedent, and delivered dramatically shorter waiting times for operations and much better-funded schools, but those achievements were now undermined by the voters' suspicion that they had been built out of financial straw. The spending bonanza was coming to an end. The public knew that the scale of the deficit would demand a squeeze whoever won the next election. This effaced the dividing line between 'Labour investment' and 'Tory cuts' which had been so electorally lethal to the Conservatives in 2001 and 2005. Still fighting the last war, and perhaps incapable of fighting any other, Brown had wasted vital months over the summer and autumn by trying to pretend otherwise. He further damaged his credibility in the process. It took a long and concerted effort by Peter Mandelson and Alistair Darling, helped by other senior figures such as Jack Straw, to push Brown into a grudging acceptance that he needed to move to a more defensible position.[78] Even then, Brown barely acknowledged the deficit in his conference speech and could not resist throwing out a confetti of new promises. The Chancellor was 'pretty annoyed. We thought we'd moved Gordon and then the old recidivist started making spending pledges that didn't add up.'[79]

He continued to rest his hopes on economic recovery being firmly established by the time he faced the voters in the spring of 2010. The recession was officially announced to be the longest and deepest since 1945, but it looked as though it would be considerably less painful in some respects than the Tory recessions of the early eighties and the early nineties when unemployment peaked at much higher levels and many more people lost their homes. Brown aspired to take credit for that. Yet he would never again be able to vaunt the uninterrupted prosperity which had underpinned New Labour as a victorious electoral project. Even among those who gave him credit for intervening to soften the recession, it would not be quickly forgotten that he was the long-serving and boastful Chancellor in the years of excess leading up to the collapse. He who had bragged of ending boom and bust had instead presided over the biggest bust since the 1930s. The era of easy money was over for most people. The rapidity with which some bankers went back to paying themselves vast bonuses only made the voters angrier, especially when the Royal Bank of Scotland and Lloyds Group received a further injection of taxpayer subsidy costing between £29 billion and £39 billion.[80]

There were other fundamental reasons for their unpopularity. New Labour was a somewhat artificial construct as broad coalitions for power usually are. The attempt to fashion a big tent which would appeal to voters and interests with opposed aspirations always threatened to end in disappointment among both the traditionalists and the modernisers. The project which had once attracted both working-class and middle-class voters, north and south, male and female, had haemorrhaged support from all points of the demographic and geographic compass. Sustaining that coalition was proving beyond even the supple Blair by the end of his decade. His successor lacked the requisite temperament, communication skills, tactical agility or grand strategy to renew a coalition that was built more than a dozen years ago in a very different economic and political climate.

Gordon Brown was liked even less than Labour. His personal ratings were almost uniformly dire. Opinion polls suggested that less than a third of the electorate were satisfied with his performance as Prime Minister.[81] David Cameron was regarded as the better candidate for Number 10 by large margins which sometimes exceeded more than two to one.[82] Ministers were reduced to hoping that last-minute doubts about the Tories might ultimately trump the voters' aversion to Brown. There was a constant, low-intensity grumble from within Labour's ranks about the inadequacies of the man they had put in Number 10 by acclaim. Yet the party appeared to have neither the energy nor the will, nor the faith in any of the likely replacements, to find a new leader who might save them from defeat – or at least ameliorate what threatened to be a terrible rout. A central characteristic of New Labour had been its absolute appetite for power, the burning conviction that there is nothing to be said for the impotence of Opposition. That hunger had now transmuted into a fatalism that invited the defeat portended in the polls.

All three of the founding fathers of New Labour were watching the crumbling away of their personal and political dreams. Tony Blair maintained his public silence about the Government's plight. He did not want to say or do anything which would attract any blame for election defeat. Behind the scenes, he continued to offer advice to Brown and to despair that it was so rarely taken. Peter Mandelson, while loyal in public, was increasingly asperic and fruity in private conversation about Brown and his failings. He shared Blair's dismay that the third founding father was leading their project towards a potentially cataclysmic defeat.[83]

That anguish was shared across the party, from the Cabinet downwards. At the last conference before the election, they had sung their anthems, 'The Red Flag' and 'Jerusalem', to the elegiac accompaniment of a violin. The melancholy strains of the strings added to the feeling that the light was failing on a project that had once had the world at its feet.

References

PART ONE: THE COST OF CONVICTION

1. Twice Promised Land

1. Interview, Richard Wilson
2. Tony Blair to author at Number 10 news conference with Bill Clinton, 29 May 1997
3. *Servants of the People*, Chapters 20 and 23
4. Interviews, Jack Straw and others
5. Interviews, senior intelligence officers
6. Interview, Peter Hyman
7. *Servants of the People*, Chapter 17
8. Ibid., Chapter 18
9. Ibid., Chapter 6
10. Interview, Neil Kinnock
11. *Servants of the People*, Chapter 12
12. Interview, Barry Cox
13. Interview, Peter Mandelson
14. Interview, Peter Mandelson
15. Interview, Robert Harris
16. Interview, Tim Allan
17. *Servants of the People*, Chapter 4
18. Interview, Stan Greenberg
19. Interview, Charles Kennedy
20. Interview, William Hague
21. Interview, Jack Straw
22. Interview, Jon Cruddas
23. Interview, Matthew Taylor
24. Interview, Paddy Ashdown
25. Interview, Stephen Wall
26. Interview, Alan Milburn
27. *Servants of the People*, Chapter 16
28. Ibid., Chapter 13
29. Ibid., Chapter 8
30. Ibid., Chapter 11
31. Ibid., Chapter 14
32. Interview, Roy Jenkins
33. Interview, Michael Levy
34. Interviews, Charlie Falconer and Peter Hyman
35. Interview, Geoff Mulgan
36. Interview, Sally Morgan
37. Interview, Peter Hyman
38. Interview, Geoff Mulgan
39. Interview, David Blunkett
40. Interview, Peter Hyman
41. Interview, Peter Hyman
42. Interview, David Blunkett
43. Interview, Peter Mandelson
44. Interview, Geoff Mulgan
45. *Servants of the People*, Chapter 19
46. Conversation, Cabinet minister
47. Conversation, Blair aide

48. *Servants of the People*, Chapter 24
49. Interviews, Sally Morgan and others
50. Interview, Tony Blair
51. *Servants of the People*, Chapter 15
52. Interview, Andrew Turnbull
53. Interviews, David Blunkett, Stephen Byers, Alan Milburn and Estelle Morris
54. Interview, Jack Straw
55. Interview, Richard Wilson
56. *Servants of the People*, Chapter 3
57. Ibid., Chapter 9
58. Interview, Jonathan Powell
59. Andrew Rawnsley, 'What Blair really thinks of Brown', *Observer*, 18 January 1998
60. Interview, Brown inner circle
61. Conversation, Blair inner circle
62. Conversations, Cabinet ministers
63. Interview, senior civil servant
64. Conversation, senior Blair aide
65. *Servants of the People*, Chapter 17
66. Interview, Jonathan Powell
67. Interview, Sally Morgan
68. Interview, Jonathan Powell
69. Interview, Robert Harris
70. Interviews, Sally Morgan, Jonathan Powell and others
71. Interview, Barry Cox

2. A Cloudless Day

1. Interview, Andrew Card
2. Interviews, Andrew Card and others; C. Blair, p. 316
3. Interviews, Andrew Card and others; C. Blair, p. 305
4. Interview, Andrew Card
5. Interview, Jonathan Powell
6. Interview, Tom Kelly
7. Interview, Robert Hill
8. Interview, Peter Hyman
9. Interview, Robert Hill
10. Interview, Robert Hill
11. Interview, Robert Hill
12. Boulton, p.116
13. Interview, Robert Hill
14. Interview, Tom Kelly
15. Interview, Blair aide
16. Interview, Alastair Campbell
17. Interview, Richard Wilson
18. Interview, Jonathan Powell
19. Interviews, Jonathan Powell and Richard Wilson
20. Interviews, Alastair Campbell and Robert Hill
21. Tony Blair, remarks to TUC about 9/11, Brighton, 11 September 2001
22. Interview, Robert Hill
23. Interview, David Blunkett
24. Interview, David Manning
25. Interview, Michael Boyce
26. Interview, Mike Jackson
27. Interview, Jack Straw
28. Interview, Stephen Lander
29. Interview, Richard Wilson
30. Interview, Stephen Byers
31. Interview, Richard Wilson
32. Interview, Richard Wilson
33. Interview, Blair aide
34. Interview, Robert Hill
35. Interview, Geoff Mulgan
36. Interviews, Robert Hill and others
37. Interview, Andrew Card
38. Interview, Andrew Card
39. George W. Bush, remarks at

Emma Booker Elementary School, Sarasota, Florida, 11 September 2001

40. 9/11 Commission Report, p. 40
41. Interview, Tom Kelly
42. Interview, Richard Wilson
43. Interview, Richard Wilson
44. Interviews, Stephen Lander, Jonathan Powell, Richard Wilson and others
45. Interview, senior official
46. Interview, Jonathan Powell
47. Interview, Jonathan Powell
48. Interview, Tony Blair
49. Interview, No 10 official
50. Interview, Richard Wilson
51. Interviews, David Blunkett, Stephen Byers, Geoff Hoon, Alan Milburn, Jack Straw, Richard Wilson and others
52. Interview, Richard Wilson
53. Interview, Cabinet minister
54. Interview, Geoff Hoon
55. Interview, Jack Straw
56. Tony Blair, statement in Downing Street, 11 September 2001
57. Interview, Tom Kelly
58. Interview, Tom Kelly
59. Interview, Jack Straw
60. Interview, Christopher Meyer
61. C. Blair, p. 313
62. Interview, Stan Greenberg
63. Interview, Stan Greenberg
64. Riddell (2003), p. 119
65. Interview, Christopher Meyer
66. Interview, William Cohen
67. Interview, Andrew Card
68. A. Campbell, p. 485
69. Interview, Foreign Office official
70. Interview, Stan Greenberg
71. Conversation, Bill Clinton
72. *Guardian*, 5 April 2002
73. Interview, Jack Straw
74. Andrew Rawnsley, 'America or Europe: Tony, the choice is yours', *Observer*, 21 January 2001
75. Conversation, Tony Blair
76. Interview, Jack Straw
77. Interview, Tony Blair
78. Interview, Christopher Meyer
79. Interview, Foreign Office official
80. Interview, Christopher Meyer; C. Blair, p. 314
81. Interview, Andrew Card
82. Interview, Andrew Card
83. Interview, Christopher Meyer
84. Interview, Andrew Card
85. Interview, Christopher Meyer
86. Conversation, Cabinet minister
87. Blair–Bush news conference, Camp David, 24 February 2001
88. A. Campbell, p. 507
89. Blair–Bush news conference, Camp David, 24 February 2001
90. Interview, Condoleezza Rice
91. Interviews, Jonathan Powell and Tom Kelly
92. Interview, Tony Blair
93. Interview, David Manning
94. Interview, Alastair Campbell
95. Interview, Christopher Meyer
96. Interview, Tom Kelly
97. Interview, Clare Short
98. Clarke, p. 24
99. Frum, p. 127
100. George W. Bush, broadcast from Oval Office, Washington, 11 September 2001
101. Interview, Tom Kelly
102. Interview, Richard Wilson
103. Interview, senior intelligence officer
104. Interview, Richard Wilson
105. Interview, Stephen Lander

106. Interviews, Stephen Lander, Jonathan Powell and others
107. Interviews, Andrew Card, Jonathan Powell and Richard Wilson
108. Interview, Andrew Card
109. Interview, Jonathan Powell
110. Interview, Richard Wilson
111. Interview, Richard Wilson
112. Interview, Christopher Meyer
113. Conversation, Cabinet minister
114. Interview, Michael Boyce
115. Hansard, 14 September 2001
116. *Newsday*, 13 September 2001
117. Interview, Jonathan Powell
118. Interview, Alastair Campbell
119. Interview, Richard Wilson

3. Shoulder to Shoulder

1. Interview, Philip Gould
2. Tony Blair, remarks at St Thomas's Church, New York, 20 September 2001
3. Michael White, 'On the brink of war', *Guardian*, 21 September 2001
4. *Le Monde*, 12 September 2001
5. Interviews, senior officials
6. Kampfner, p. 120
7. Tony Blair, news conference, Downing Street, 12 September 2001
8. Tony Blair, news conference, Downing Street, 20 September 2001
9. Hansard, 14 September 2001
10. Tony Blair, briefing to media en route to New York, 20 September 2001
11. *The Westminster Hour*, BBC Radio 4, 16 September 2001
12. Interview, Clare Short; A. Campbell, p. 569
13. Interview, Christopher Meyer
14. Interview, Jonathan Powell
15. Interview, Christopher Meyer
16. Interviews, David Manning and Jonathan Powell
17. Interview, Jonathan Powell
18. Interview, David Manning
19. Woodward (2002), pp. 49, 91
20. Interview, Christopher Meyer
21. Ed Vulliamy, Peter Beaumont, Kamal Ahmed and Jason Burke, 'War on terrorism', *Observer*, 23 September 2001
22. Interviews, Andrew Card, David Manning, Christopher Meyer, Jonathan Powell and others
23. Interviews, Andrew Card, David Manning, Christopher Meyer, Jonathan Powell and others
24. Interviews, Christopher Meyer and Jonathan Powell
25. Interview, Jonathan Powell
26. George W. Bush, address to Joint Session of Congress, Washington, 20 September 2001
27. From a low of 51 per cent in the last Gallup poll taken before 9/11, Bush's approval rating surged to 90 per cent in Gallup's poll of 22 September 2001 and remained above 85 per cent for the rest of the year
28. George W. Bush, address to Joint Session of Congress, Washington, 20 September 2001
29. Interview, Stephen Wall
30. Interview, Christopher Meyer
31. Interview, Alastair Campbell
32. Interview, Christopher Meyer
33. Interview, Michael Levy
34. Interview, Mike Jackson

35. Interview, Michael Boyce
36. Interviews, Michael Boyce and others
37. Interview, member of Joint Intelligence Committee
38. Interview, member of War Cabinet
39. A. Campbell, p. 569
40. Interview, Stan Greenberg
41. Interview, Tom Kelly
42. Tony Blair, speech, 'Doctrine of the International Community', Chicago, 22 April 1999
43. Interview, Tony Blair
44. Tony Blair, conference speech, Brighton, 2 October 2001
45. Conversation, Tony Blair
46. Tony Blair, conference speech, Brighton, 2 October 2001
47. Interview, Clare Short
48. Tony Blair, conference speech, Brighton, 2 October 2001
49. Conversation, Cabinet minister
50. *Daily Telegraph*, 3 October 2001
51. Andrew Rawnsley, 'Missionary Tony and his Holy British Empire', *Observer*, 7 October 2001
52. Interview, Christopher Meyer
53. A. Campbell, p. 576
54. Interview, Tom Kelly
55. Interview, Tom Kelly
56. Conversation, Blair aide
57. Interview, Jonathan Powell
58. Tony Blair, statement on military action in Afghanistan, Downing Street, 7 October 2001
59. Interview, Richard Haas
60. Interview, David Manning
61. Interview, Condoleezza Rice
62. Interview, Andrew Card
63. Conversation, Blair aide
64. Interview, David Manning
65. Riddell (2003), p. 161
66. Interview, Tom Kelly
67. A. Campbell, p. 585
68. Conversation, Cabinet minister
69. Conversations, Cabinet ministers and officials
70. 82 per cent of Americans had a favourable view of Blair according to Gallup in mid-October 2001. Just 7 per cent viewed him negatively
71. Interview, Clare Short
72. Riddell (2003), p. 167
73. Interview, member of War Cabinet
74. Interviews, members of War Cabinet
75. Interview, member of War Cabinet
76. Interview, Geoff Hoon
77. Interview, Jack Straw
78. Interview, David Manning
79. Interview, senior military officer
80. A. Campbell, p. 581
81. Interview, Tom Kelly
82. Interview, Michael Boyce
83. Interview, David Manning
84. Blair–Bush news conference, White House, Washington, 8 November 2001
85. Interview, David Manning
86. Hansard, 14 November 2001
87. Interview, Michael Boyce
88. Private information
89. Frum, p. 194
90. Hansard, 14 November 2001
91. Interview, Tom Kelly
92. Interview, Tom Kelly
93. Interviews, Tom Kelly and David Manning
94. Interviews, Tom Kelly and David Manning

95. Interview, Christopher Meyer
96. Woodward (2002), p. 310
97. Interview, Jonathan Powell
98. Interview, Michael Boyce
99. Interview, David Manning
100. Interview, Michael Boyce
101. Interview, Mike Jackson
102. Interview, Michael Boyce

4. The TB-GBs

1. Interview, Barry Cox
2. Interview, Barry Cox
3. Interview, Barry Cox
4. Conversation, Cabinet minister
5. Conversation, Cabinet minister
6. Conversation, Cabinet minister
7. Interview, Stephen Wall
8. Interview, senior civil servant
9. Interview, Cabinet minister
10. Conversation, media executive
11. Interview, Charlie Falconer
12. Interview, Clare Short
13. Interview, Jack Straw
14. Interview, Bruce Grocott
15. Prescott, p. 311
16. Interview, Peter Hyman
17. Interview, Margaret Jay
18. Interview, Andrew Turnbull
19. J. Campbell, p. 346
20. *Servants of the People*, p. 146
21. Interview, senior civil servant
22. Interview, Richard Wilson
23. Interview, Murray Elder
24. *Today*, BBC Radio 4, 26 September 2006
25. Interview, Nick Ryden
26. Interview, Nick Ryden. He has never forgiven himself for erasing the tape of this priceless moment
27. *The Week in Politics*, Channel 4, 17 May 1994

28. Private interview; Bower, p. 153
29. Macintyre, p. 290
30. Interview, Jack Straw
31. Blair, 47 per cent; Prescott, 15 per cent; Brown, 11 per cent; Beckett, 5 per cent; Cook, 3 per cent; Don't Know, 19 per cent: Gallup for BBC1's *On the Record*, 30 May 1994
32. C. Blair, p. 172
33. Interview, Philip Gould
34. Interview, Derek Draper
35. Interview, Neil Kinnock
36. Interview, Nick Brown
37. Interview, Roy Hattersley
38. Interview, Barry Cox
39. Peston, p. 59
40. Interview, Richard Wilson
41. Interview, Cabinet minister
42. *Servants of the People*, p. 144
43. Interview, Nick Ryden
44. Interview, Barry Cox
45. Interviews, Brown inner circle
46. Conversation, New Labour inner circle
47. Interview, Robert Harris
48. Interview, Charles Clarke
49. Interview, Frank Field
50. Interview, Philip Gould
51. That sense of grievance is most explicitly and comprehensively retailed in Routledge (1997)
52. Interview, Brown inner circle
53. Interview, Andrew Turnbull
54. Interview, Margaret Jay
55. Scott, pp. 20, 24
56. Interview, Paddy Ashdown
57. Interview, Charles Guthrie
58. *Servants of the People*, pp. 144–5
59. Interview, Frank Field
60. Interview, Stephen Wall
61. A. Campbell, p. 312
62. Interview, Roy Jenkins

63. Interview, Cabinet minister
64. Interview, Cabinet minister
65. Interview, Frank Field
66. Interview, Robin Butler
67. Interview, Geoff Hoon
68. Interview, Peter Hyman
69. Interview, Andrew Turnbull
70. Interview, Robin Butler
71. Interview, Richard Wilson
72. Interview, Clare Short
73. Interview, Jack Straw
74. Interview, Estelle Morris
75. Conversation, Blair aide
76. Interview, Andrew Turnbull
77. Conversation, Cabinet minister
78. Interview, Clare Short
79. Conversation, member of Shadow Cabinet
80. Interview, Geoffrey Robinson
81. Interview, Brown aide
82. Interview, Barry Cox
83. Interview, Brown aide
84. Interview, Brown inner circle
85. Interview, Alistair Darling
86. Interview, Blair inner circle
87. Conversation, Cabinet minister
88. Interview, Andrew Turnbull
89. Interview, Cabinet minister
90. Interview, Barry Cox
91. Interview, Stephen Wall
92. Interview, Michael Levy
93. Interview, Alan Milburn
94. Interview, Michael Levy; Levy, p. 212
95. Interview, Alastair Campbell
96. Interview, Barry Cox
97. Interview, Brown aide
98. Interview, Steve Morris
99. Interview, Richard Wilson
100. Interview, Clare Short
101. Interview, Steve Robson
102. Interview, Cabinet minister
103. Interview, John Gieve
104. Interview, Richard Wilson
105. Interview, senior civil servant
106. Interview, David Blunkett
107. Interview, Gordon Brown
108. Interview, Andrew Turnbull; *Financial Times*, 20 March 2007
109. Interview, John Gieve
110. Interview, Estelle Morris
111. Conversation, Cabinet minister
112. Conversation, Cabinet minister
113. By the banker, Sir Derek Wanless
114. Interview, Alan Milburn; A. Campbell, p. 590
115. Interview, Steve Robson
116. Interview, Richard Wilson
117. Interview, Stephen Wall
118. Scott, p. 28
119. Conversation, Blair aide
120. Interviews, Andrew Turnbull and Richard Wilson
121. Conversation, Cabinet minister
122. Interview, Geoffrey Robinson
123. Interview, Andrew Turnbull
124. Interview, senior civil servant
125. Having picked this up, I used the phrase in a column after which it became common currency. Andrew Rawnsley, 'Loneliness of the long-distance premier', *Observer*, 11 November 2001
126. Interview, Peter Hyman
127. Conversation, Cabinet minister
128. Interview, Stephen Wall
129. A. Campbell, p. 602
130. Interviews, Brown inner circle and Cabinet ministers
131. Interview, Stephen Wall
132. Interview, Richard Wilson
133. Interview, Brown inner circle
134. Interview, John Gieve
135. Interview, Brown aide
136. Interview, Brown aide

137. Interview, Jonathan Powell
138. Interview, Brown inner circle
139. Interview, Brown aide
140. Interview, Number 10 official
141. Interview, senior civil servant
142. Interview, senior Blair aide
143. Interview, Cabinet minister
144. Interview, Jonathan Powell
145. Interview, Brown inner circle
146. Interview, Brown inner circle
147. Interview, Brown inner circle
148. Interview, Clare Short
149. Interview, Matthew Taylor
150. Interview, Neil Kinnock
151. Interview, Stephen Wall
152. Interview, senior civil servant
153. Conversations, Blair aides
154. Interview, Tony Blair
155. Tony Blair, speech at Royal Free Hospital, London, 15 July 2001
156. Conversation, Cabinet minister
157. Interview, Geoff Mulgan
158. Interview, Sally Morgan
159. Interview, Michael Barber
160. Interview, Tony Blair
161. Interview, Tom Kelly
162. Interview, Andrew Turnbull
163. Interview, Alan Milburn
164. *The Times*, 7 August 2002
165. Interview, Alan Milburn
166. Interview, Andrew Turnbull
167. Interview, Charles Clarke
168. Interview, Brown aide
169. Interview, Cabinet minister
170. Interview, Treasury minister
171. Conversation, Brown inner circle
172. Gordon Brown, remarks to reception for John Smith Foundation, Number 11, 18 July 2002
173. Interview, Brown aide
174. Interview, Brown aide
175. Interview, Robert Hill
176. Conversation, Cabinet minister
177. Interviews, Cabinet ministers
178. Interview, Brown aide
179. Interview, Brown aide
180. As it turned out, the document wasn't leaked
181. Interviews, Cabinet ministers
182. Tony Blair, speech to Labour conference, Blackpool, 1 October 2002
183. Conversation, Blair aide
184. Interview, Andrew Turnbull
185. Interviews, Cabinet ministers
186. Interview, Cabinet minister
187. Interview, Andrew Turnbull
188. Interview, Alan Milburn
189. Interview, Peter Mandelson
190. Interview, Barry Cox

5. Oath of Allegiance

1. Interviews, Cabinet ministers and officials; Blunkett (2006), p. 359; A. Campbell, pp. 608–9; Cook, pp. 115–16
2. Interview, senior civil servant
3. Interviews, Cabinet ministers and officials; Blunkett (2006), p. 359; A. Campbell, pp. 608–9; Cook, pp. 115–16
4. SECRET. UK EYES ONLY. Iraq: Options Paper. Overseas and Defence Secretariat, Cabinet Office, 8 March 2002. One of several documents originally leaked to the journalist Michael Smith. Read them at www.michaelsmithwriter.com
5. Frum, p. 238
6. George W. Bush, State of the Union address, 30 January 2002

7. 'An Oral History of the Bush White House', *Vanity Fair*, February 2009
8. Interview, Andrew Turnbull
9. Interview, Michael Boyce
10. Interview, Christopher Meyer
11. Interview, William Cohen
12. Interview, William Cohen
13. Frum, pp. 196, 233
14. Interview, Tony Blair
15. Interview, Andrew Card
16. Interview, Christopher Meyer
17. 'An Oral History of the Bush White House', *Vanity Fair*, February 2009
18. Blair–Cheney news conference, Downing Street, 11 March 2002
19. SECRET – STRICTLY PERSONAL. Prime Minister. Your Trip to the US. Memo, Manning to Blair, 14 March 2002
20. CONFIDENTIAL AND PERSONAL. Letter, Meyer to Manning, 18 March 2002
21. Interview, David Manning
22. Ashdown (2002), p. 127
23. Interview, Tony Blair
24. Robert Cooper, *Prospect*, October 2001
25. Interview, Mike Jackson
26. Interview, Tony Blair
27. Interview, Robert Harris
28. Interviews, senior intelligence officers
29. Interview, Huw Evans
30. Interview, Richard Wilson
31. Interview, member of Joint Intelligence Committee
32. Conversation, Cabinet minister
33. Interview, David Manning
34. Interviews, senior officials
35. Interview, Huw Evans
36. Interview, Ken Livingstone
37. Interview, Huw Evans
38. Tony Blair, speech to TUC, 10 September 2002
39. Interview, Tony Blair
40. Interview, Christopher Meyer
41. Interview, Sally Morgan
42. Interview, Tony Blair
43. Interview, Tessa Jowell
44. Interview, Richard Wilson
45. Conversation, Cabinet minister
46. Interview, Charles Clarke
47. Interview, Christopher Meyer
48. Conversation, Cabinet minister
49. Interview, Jeremy Greenstock
50. Interview, Christopher Meyer
51. Interview, Clare Short
52. Interview, William Cohen
53. Interview, Paddy Ashdown
54. *Sun*, 6 April 2002
55. *International Herald Tribune*, 4 April 2002
56. SECRET AND PERSONAL. Crawford/Iraq. Letter, Straw to Blair, 25 March 2002
57. Interview, David Manning
58. Interview, Christopher Meyer
59. Interview, William Cohen
60. Interview, Condoleezza Rice
61. Interview, Stan Greenberg
62. Interview, George Mitchell
63. *The Times*, 6 April 2002
64. Interview, Christopher Meyer
65. Interview, David Manning
66. Interview, Christopher Meyer
67. Conversation, Cabinet minister
68. Interview, Sally Morgan
69. Interview, Charles Guthrie
70. Interview, David Manning
71. C. Blair, p. 320
72. Interview, senior civil servant
73. Interview, Michael Levy
74. Interview, Jonathan Powell

75. Interview, Tom Kelly
76. Interview, Christopher Meyer
77. Interview, Peter Mandelson
78. Interview, Tom Kelly
79. Conversation, Cabinet minister
80. Interview, Christopher Meyer
81. Interview, senior civil servant
82. Interview, Tom Kelly
83. Interviews, David Manning and Jonathan Powell
84. Interview, Jonathan Powell
85. SECRET. UK EYES ONLY. Iraq: Conditions for Military Action, Cabinet Office briefing paper for Number 10 meeting, 23 July 2002
86. Interview, David Manning
87. Interview, Christopher Meyer
88. Interview, Andrew Card
89. Seldon (2007), p. 94
90. Interview, Christopher Meyer
91. Blair–Bush news conference, Crawford, Texas, 6 April 2002
92. Interview, Christopher Meyer
93. Tony Blair, speech at the George Bush Senior Presidential Library, Texas, 7 April 2002
94. Interview, Michael Boyce
95. Interview, Mike Jackson
96. Interviews, Cabinet ministers and officials; Cook, p. 135
97. Interview, Richard Haas
98. Interview, Stan Greenberg
99. Private information
100. Interviews, David Manning and Christopher Meyer; confidential cable, Meyer to Manning, 3 July 2002
101. Interview, Christopher Meyer
102. Interviews, David Manning and Christopher Meyer
103. Interviews, ministers, military officers and officials; SECRET. UK EYES ONLY. Iraq: Prime Minister's meeting, 23 July 2002
104. SECRET. UK EYES ONLY. Iraq: Conditions for Military Action, Cabinet Office briefing paper for Number 10 meeting, 23 July 2002
105. Interviews, Michael Boyce, Geoff Hoon, Jack Straw and others; SECRET. UK EYES ONLY. Iraq: Prime Minister's meeting, 23 July 2002

6. Tell Me No Secrets

1. Interview, Barry Cox
2. Interview, Alastair Campbell; A. Campbell, p. 632
3. Interview, Andrew Turnbull
4. Interview, Barry Cox
5. Interview, Stephen Wall
6. Interview, Iain Duncan Smith
7. Interview, Michael Boyce
8. It is a curiosity of Britain's constitution that the Cabinet usually only meets when Parliament is sitting
9. Interview, Neil Kinnock
10. Interview, David Manning
11. Interviews, Ed Owen and Jack Straw
12. Interview, Andrew Turnbull
13. Interview, Ed Owen
14. Conversation, Cabinet minister
15. Conversation, Foreign Office official
16. Interview, Ed Owen
17. Interview, Jack Straw
18. Seldon (2007), p. 102
19. Interview, Michael Jay
20. Interview, Jonathan Powell

21. Interviews, Ed Owen and others
22. Dick Cheney, speech to the Veterans of Foreign Wars, Tennessee, 26 August 2002
23. Conversation, Cabinet minister
24. Interview, David Manning
25. Interview, Michael Boyce
26. Interview, Condoleezza Rice
27. Interview, Jonathan Powell
28. Interview, Christopher Meyer
29. *Washington Post*, 12 August 2002; *New York Times*, 16 August 2002
30. Interview, Andrew Card
31. Interview, Christopher Meyer
32. Interview, Christopher Meyer
33. Interviews, Andrew Card, Condoleezza Rice, David Manning and Christopher Meyer
34. Interviews, Andrew Card, Tom Kelly, Christopher Meyer and others; Campbell on p. 635 of his diary has Bush saying: 'balls'. 'Cojones' sounds very much more like Bush and is remembered by the others there
35. Interview, Christopher Meyer
36. Interview, Andrew Card; Woodward (2004), p. 178
37. Interviews, Tom Kelly, Sally Morgan and others
38. Interview, Jonathan Powell
39. Interviews, David Manning and Condoleezza Rice
40. George W. Bush, address to United Nations General Assembly, New York, 12 September 2002
41. Cook, p. 205
42. Tony Blair, statement, Sedgefield, 3 September 2002
43. Interview, Alastair Campbell
44. Alastair Campbell, evidence to Hutton Inquiry, 19 August 2003
45. Interview, Stan Greenberg
46. Interview, senior civil servant
47. Interview, Tom Kelly; A. Campbell, p. 633
48. SECRET AND PERSONAL. Letter, Straw to Blair, 25 March 2002
49. Sam Tanenhaus, 'Bush's Brain Trust', *Vanity Fair*, July 2003
50. SECRET AND PERSONAL. Letter, Straw to Blair, 25 March 2002
51. E-mail, Campbell to Powell, 5 September 2002, evidence to Hutton Inquiry
52. A. Campbell, p. 634
53. Clausewitz, Vol. I, Book I, Chapter VI
54. JIC, 15 March 2002, quoted in Report of the Butler Inquiry, HC 898, 14 July 2004
55. Interview, Robin Butler
56. SECRET. UK EYES ONLY. Iraq: Options Paper, ODS, Cabinet Office, 8 March 2002
57. Interviews, Number 10 and intelligence officials
58. Tenet, pp. 568–71
59. Report of the Butler Inquiry, HC 898, 14 July 2004, pp. 151–2
60. Interviews, members of Joint Intelligence Committee
61. Interview, senior intelligence officer
62. Tony Blair, evidence to Hutton Inquiry, 28 August 2003
63. Alastair Campbell, evidence to Foreign Affairs select committee; A. Campbell, p. 636
64. Interview, member of the Joint Intelligence Committee

65. Interview, senior British diplomat
66. Interview, member of the Joint Intelligence Committee
67. Interview, Iain Duncan Smith
68. Interview, senior civil servant
69. Interview, Tom Kelly
70. Interview, senior British diplomat
71. Report of the Butler Inquiry, HC 898, 14 July 2004, p. 159
72. Interview, senior civil servant
73. Interview, senior civil servant
74. Interview, Sally Morgan
75. Interview, senior civil servant
76. Interview, senior civil servant
77. Interview, member of Joint Intelligence Committee
78. E-mail, Bassett to Campbell and Smith, 11 September 2002
79. E-mail, Smith to Campbell, 11 September 2002
80. E-mail, Kelly to Campbell, 19 September 2002
81. Interview, Tom Kelly
82. Interview, Robert Hill
83. E-mail, unidentified intelligence official to colleagues, 11 September 2002
84. Interview, Tom Kelly
85. E-mail, Bowen to Scarlett, 11 September 2002. This is one of several documents finally released on 12 March 2009 under Freedom of Information legislation after years of resistance by the Government
86. Brian Jones, evidence to Public Administration Committee, 19 March 2009
87. E-mails between unnamed intelligence officials, 16 September 2002
88. Interview, Andrew Turnbull
89. Interview, David Manning
90. Interview, Sally Morgan
91. Interview, Sally Morgan
92. Evidence to the Scott Inquiry into arms-to-Iraq, cited by Richard Norton-Taylor, *Guardian*, 28 June 2003
93. Interview, Charles Guthrie
94. Interview, Stephen Wall
95. Interview, Geoff Hoon
96. Interviews, senior civil servants
97. Interview, Tessa Jowell
98. Exposed by the UN's International Atomic Energy Authority; Tenet, pp. 680–721
99. Interview, Ed Owen
100. Interview, Iain Duncan Smith
101. E-mail, Powell to Scarlett, 17 September 2002
102. Report of the Butler Inquiry, HC 898, 14 July 2004, pp. 85–6
103. Tom Mangold, evidence to Hutton Inquiry, 14 September 2003
104. Richard Dearlove, evidence to Hutton Inquiry, 15 September 2003
105. Correspondence released to Hutton Inquiry
106. E-mail, Powell to Campbell and Scarlett, 19 September 2002
107. John Scarlett, evidence to Hutton Inquiry, 23 September 2003
108. Interviews, Cabinet ministers and officials
109. Interviews, Richard Wilson and Andrew Turnbull
110. Interviews, Richard Wilson and Andrew Turnbull
111. Interview, Robin Butler
112. Interview, Clare Short

113. Cook, p. 212
114. Interviews, Cabinet ministers and officials; Blunkett (2006), p. 395; A. Campbell, pp. 639–40; Cook, pp. 212–13
115. 'Iraq's Weapons of Mass Destruction: The Assessment of the British Government', 24 September 2002, p. 4
116. Hansard, 24 September 2002
117. Interview, Clare Short
118. Interview, Jack Straw
119. Interview, Frank Dobson
120. Cook, p. 215
121. *The Times*, 25 September 2008
122. *Sun*, 25 September 2008
123. *Evening Standard*, 24 September 2008
124. Interview, Geoff Hoon
125. Brian Jones, evidence to the Hutton Inquiry; Tom Mangold, *Mail on Sunday*, 20 July 2003
126. Report of the Butler Inquiry, HC 898, 14 July 2004, p. 156
127. Most trenchantly argued in John Lloyd, 'Lies, spin and deceit', *Prospect*, October 2006
128. Interview, Michael Boyce
129. Interview, Robin Butler
130. Tony Blair, speech to Labour conference, Blackpool, 1 October 2002
131. Interview, Clare Short
132. Tony Blair, speech to Labour conference, Blackpool, 1 October 2002
133. Conversation, minister
134. Bill Clinton, speech to Labour conference, Blackpool, 3 October 2002
135. A. Campbell, p. 641
136. Jo Conason, 'Love ya Tony', *Guardian*, 23 April 2003
137. Interview, George Mitchell
138. Interview, William Cohen

7. Trouble and Strife

1. Interview, David Trimble
2. C. Blair, p. 17
3. Ibid., p. 35
4. Interview, Blair aide
5. C Blair, p. 369
6. Ibid., p. 346
7. Interview, senior civil servant
8. Interview, senior civil servant
9. Interview, Blair aide
10. Interview, senior civil servant
11. Interview, senior civil servant
12. Interview, senior civil servant
13. Interview, Barry Cox
14. Interview, Jonathan Powell
15. Interview, Alastair Campbell
16. *More* (US) magazine, 17 February 2009
17. C. Blair, p. 328
18. Interviews, Number 10 officials and aides
19. Interview, Blair aide
20. Interviews, Number 10 officials and aides
21. Interview, Sally Morgan
22. Interview, senior civil servant
23. Interview, Blair aide
24. Conversation, Cabinet minister
25. Ann Applebaum, *Sunday Telegraph*, 18 March 2001
26. In the first year after he left Number 10, it was estimated that he coined £12 million.
27. Conversation, Blair aide
28. Interview, Paddy Ashdown
29. Interview, Matthew Taylor
30. Conversations, Blair aides
31. *Servants of the People*, Chapter 6

32. Hansard, 13 February 2002
33. Jeffrey Archer and Jonathan Aitken
34. *Observer*, 19 May 2002
35. Patrick Wintour, *Guardian*, 13 May 2002
36. Ibid.
37. Interview, Philip Gould
38. P. Morgan, p. x
39. Bill Haggerty, 'Paul Dacre: The Zeal Thing', *British Journalism Review*, 3, 2002, pp. 11–22
40. Conversation, Cabinet minister
41. Interview, Cabinet minister
42. Interviews, Blair aides; C. Blair, p. 308
43. Alastair Campbell, 'It's Time to Bury Spin', *British Journalism Review*, 4, 2002, pp. 15–23
44. *Guardian, Independent*, 10 October 2001
45. Interview, Stephen Byers
46. *Observer*, 21 October 2001
47. Interview, Stephen Byers
48. *Sunday Times*, 24 February 2002
49. Andrew Rawnsley, 'Even when he's right, he'll be wrong', *Observer*, 12 May 2002
50. Interview, Stephen Byers
51. Peter Oborne, 'How Tony Blair tried to muscle in on the mourning', *The Spectator*, 11 April 2002
52. Interview, Richard Wilson
53. Interview, Tony Blair
54. Conversations, Blair aides
55. Interview, Robert Harris
56. Interview, Margaret Jay
57. Interview, Charlie Falconer
58. Interview, Blair friend
59. Prescott, p. 264
60. Interview, Tom Kelly
61. Interview, Sally Morgan
62. C. Blair, p. 334
63. *Daily Mail*, 28 November 2002
64. C. Blair, p. 337
65. Interview, Alastair Campbell
66. *Daily Mail*, 5 December 2002
67. Interview, Number 10 official
68. Interview, Jonathan Powell
69. Interview, Cabinet minister
70. C. Blair, p. 337
71. Interview, Blair aide
72. C. Blair, p. 338
73. Interview, Tom Kelly
74. A. Campbell, p. 650; C. Blair, p. 338
75. Interview, Cabinet minister
76. Interview, Peter Mandelson
77. Interview, Sally Morgan
78. Interview, Blair aide
79. Interview, Blair aide
80. C. Blair, pp. 339–40
81. Interview, Alastair Campbell
82. C. Blair, p. 341
83. Ibid.; Campbell, p. 651
84. Interview, Sally Morgan
85. Interview, Blair inner circle
86. A. Campbell, p. 651
87. Cherie Blair, remarks at Atrium, Millbank, London, 10 December 2002
88. Interviews, Alastair Campbell and Sally Morgan
89. Cherie Blair, remarks at Atrium, Millbank, London, 10 December 2002
90. Conversation, Blair aide
91. C. Blair, p. 345
92. A. Campbell, p. 652
93. Interviews, Blair aides and friends

8. Naked in the Middle of the Room

1. Interview, Barry Cox
2. Interviews, Jack Straw and Stephen Wall
3. Interview, David Manning
4. Interview, Alastair Campbell
5. Interview, Michael Jay
6. Interview, Jeremy Greenstock
7. Blair–Chirac, news conference, Le Touquet, 5 February 2003
8. Interview, Stephen Wall
9. Interview, Stephen Wall
10. UNSCR 1441, 8 November 2002
11. Interviews, David Manning and Sally Morgan
12. Interview, Christopher Meyer
13. Interview, Michael Boyce
14. Interviews, Barry Cox, David Manning and Jonathan Powell
15. Interview, David Manning
16. Interviews, Christopher Meyer and Condoleezza Rice
17. Interview, David Manning
18. Interview, Foreign Office official
19. Interview, Geoff Hoon
20. Interview, Jonathan Powell
21. Interview, David Manning
22. Interview, Sally Morgan
23. Woodward (2004), p. 240
24. Interview, Christopher Meyer
25. *Today*, BBC Radio 4, 1 January 2003
26. Interview, Michael Jay
27. Interview, Foreign Office official
28. Woodward (2006), p. 106
29. Interview, Christopher Meyer
30. Riddell (2003), p. 234
31. George W. Bush, State of the Union address, 28 January 2003
32. Interview, Christopher Meyer
33. Hansard, 20 January 2003
34. 43 per cent against, 30 per cent in favour, ICM for the *Guardian*, 21 January 2003
35. Interview, Sally Morgan
36. Interview, Barry Cox
37. Interview, Sally Morgan
38. A. Campbell, p. 660
39. Interview, David Manning
40. Interview, David Manning
41. Interview, David Manning; Manning's record, 31 January 2003, first published in the *New York Times*, 27 March 2006. The timetable would slip by a fortnight when Turkey refused to allow land access into Iraq from its soil
42. Interview, David Manning
43. Interviews, David Manning and Condoleezza Rice; Manning's record, 31 January 2003; Woodward (2006), pp. 296–7
44. Interview, Richard Haas
45. Interview, Michael Jay
46. Blair–Bush news conference, the White House, Washington, 31 January 2003
47. Interview, David Manning
48. Interview, Jeremy Greenstock
49. Interview, Jack Straw
50. Colin Powell, address to UN, New York, 5 February 2003
51. Interview, Christopher Meyer
52. Colin Powell, address to UN, New York, 5 February 2003
53. Interview, Ed Owen
54. Conversation, Cabinet minister
55. Riddell (2003), p. 242
56. A. Campbell, p. 664
57. Interview, Jack Straw
58. Interview, Ed Owen
59. Interview, Nick Ryden

60. Interview, Sally Morgan
61. Conversation, Privy Counsellor
62. Interview, Clare Short
63. Interview, Sally Morgan
64. Interviews, Alastair Campbell and Sally Morgan
65. Interview, Sally Morgan; A. Campbell, p. 667
66. Interviews, David Manning and Sally Morgan
67. Interview, Stan Greenberg
68. Interview, Peter Hyman
69. Interview, Alan Milburn
70. Tony Blair, speech to Labour spring conference, Glasgow, 15 February 2003
71. Interview, Peter Mandelson
72. Interview, David Manning
73. Interview, Tessa Jowell
74. Interviews, Cabinet ministers and officials
75. Michael Gove, 'I can't fight my feelings anymore: I love Tony', *The Times*, 25 February 2003
76. Conversation, Blair inner circle
77. ITV, 11 March 2003
78. Interviews, Sally Morgan and Tom Kelly; Kampfner, p. 286
79. Interview, Sally Morgan
80. Interview with Trevor Kavanagh, *Sun*, 18 April 2003
81. *Newsnight*, BBC2, 6 February 2003
82. Interview, Ed Owen
83. Interview, David Manning
84. Interviews, Sally Morgan and Jonathan Powell
85. Interview, Andrew Card
86. Interview, David Manning
87. Interview, Paddy Ashdown
88. *Servants of the People*, Chapter 14
89. Interview, Sally Morgan
90. Conversation, Cabinet minister
91. Conversation, Cabinet minister
92. Donald Rumsfeld, news conference, Pentagon, 22 January 2003
93. Interview, Jeremy Greenstock
94. Interview, David Manning
95. Interview, Sally Morgan
96. Interview, David Manning
97. Interview, Jonathan Powell
98. Interview, David Manning
99. Interview, Jeremy Greenstock
100. Chirac–Putin–Schröder Joint Statement, 5 March 2003
101. Interview, Christopher Meyer
102. Interview, Jeremy Greenstock
103. Bryan Burrough et al., 'Path to War', *Vanity Fair*, May 2004. In fact, the UN building is not on the Hudson River, but on the East River
104. Interview, Ed Owen
105. Interview, Andrew Turnbull
106. Interview, Jonathan Powell
107. Interview, Sally Morgan
108. Interviews, Sally Morgan and Jack Straw
109. A. Campbell, pp. 671–2
110. Interview, Sally Morgan
111. Interview, Jack Straw
112. Conversation, Bill Clinton

9. With You to the End

1. Interviews, Andrew Card and Condoleezza Rice
2. Interview, Jack Straw
3. Interview, David Manning
4. Interview, Andrew Card
5. Interview, Condoleezza Rice
6. Interviews, Andrew Card and Condoleezza Rice

7. Interviews, Andrew Card and Condoleezza Rice
8. Interview, Tony Blair
9. Interviews, senior intelligence officers
10. Rogers, p. 302
11. Interview, Jack Straw
12. Interview, David Manning
13. Interview, Jack Straw
14. Interview, Michael Boyce
15. Interview, Jeremy Greenstock
16. Interview, senior civil servant
17. Interview, Sally Morgan
18. Interview, Jeremy Greenstock
19. Interview, Mike Jackson
20. Interview, Andrew Turnbull
21. Interview, Sally Morgan
22. Interview, Stephen Wall
23. Interview, Alastair Campbell
24. Interview, Jonathan Powell
25. Interview, Sally Morgan
26. Interview, Jack Straw
27. Interview, Jack Straw
28. Conversation, Robin Cook
29. *Servants of the People*, Chapter 14
30. *The Westminster Hour*, BBC Radio 4, 9 March 2003
31. Interview, Clare Short
32. Interview, Clare Short
33. 'Rebel MPs should take Short's lead', *Daily Mirror*, 10 March 2003
34. Philip Webster, 'Clare Short ready to resign over Iraq war', *The Times*, 10 March 2003
35. Patrick Wintour, 'Short spearheads rebellion with threat to quit', *Guardian*, 10 March 2003
36. Conversations, Cabinet ministers
37. Interviews, Geoff Hoon and Jack Straw
38. Donald Rumsfeld, news conference, Pentagon, 11 March 2003
39. Interview, David Manning
40. Interviews, Michael Boyce and senior British officers
41. A. Campbell, p. 676
42. Interviews, David Manning, Sally Morgan and Jonathan Powell
43. TF1 reported by the *Guardian*, 11 March 2003
44. Stothard, p. 14
45. Mullin, p. 378
46. Interview, Stephen Wall
47. Cabinet Office response to FoI request by Lord Avebury, 18 July 2007
48. *Sun*, 12 March 2003
49. Conversation, European diplomat
50. Interviews, Cabinet ministers and officials; Blunkett (2006), p. 460
51. Interviews, Cabinet ministers and officials; Cook, pp. 320–21
52. Conversations, Cabinet ministers
53. Interview, Sally Morgan
54. Interview, Clare Short
55. Interviews, Cabinet ministers and Brown inner circle
56. Interview, Jeremy Greenstock
57. Interviews, Hilary Armstrong, Sally Morgan and others; Stothard, p. 53
58. Conversations, Blair aides
59. Interviews, Brown inner circle
60. Interviews, Blair aides and Brown inner circle
61. Interview, Peter Stothard
62. Interview, Peter Stothard
63. Interview, Brown inner circle
64. Interview, Clare Short
65. Interview, Brown aide
66. Interview, Clare Short

67. Interview, Sally Morgan
68. See Sands for the best unpacking of this issue
69. The full document can now be read in, among other places, Sands, pp. 328–42
70. Interview, member of War Cabinet
71. Interview, Andrew Turnbull
72. Interview, Michael Boyce
73. Interview, Mike Jackson
74. Interview, Michael Jay
75. Interview, Mike Jackson
76. Interview, Michael Boyce
77. Lord Bingham, Grotius Lecture, Lincoln's Inn, London, 17 November 2008
78. *Channel 4 News*, 27 April 2005
79. *Observer*, 24 April 2005
80. Interview, Charlie Falconer
81. Interview, Andrew Turnbull
82. Conversation, Robin Cook
83. A. Campbell, p. 680; Cook, p. 325
84. Interviews, Cabinet ministers and officials; A. Campbell, p. 680
85. Cited in Report of the Butler Inquiry, HC 898, 14 July 2004
86. Interviews, Cabinet ministers and officials
87. Interview, Alan Milburn
88. Interview, Sally Morgan
89. Interview, Andrew Turnbull
90. Short, p. 186
91. Interview, Clare Short
92. Interview, Ed Owen
93. Interview, Sally Morgan
94. Conversation, Cabinet minister
95. Interview, senior civil servant
96. Blunkett (2006), p. 463
97. *Guardian*, 26 April 2003
98. A. Campbell, p. 678
99. In February 2009, Jack Straw used veto powers to overrule a decision by the Information Commissioner that the minutes of this Cabinet meeting should be released. The bland minutes would not have actually revealed much except that there was embarrassingly little debate at this meeting
100. Philip Hunt, a member of the Lords, and the Home Office Minister John Denham
101. Interview, Jack Straw
102. Interview, Cabinet minister
103. Woodward (2004), p. 365
104. George W. Bush, address from the Oval Office, Washington, 17 March 2003
105. Interview, Sally Morgan
106. Interview, Hilary Armstrong
107. Interview, Jack Straw
108. Interview with Trevor Kavanagh, *Sun*, 18 April 2003
109. Interview, John Burton
110. Interview, Barry Cox
111. Interview, David Manning
112. Interview, Iain Duncan Smith
113. Interview, Andrew Turnbull
114. Interview, Sally Morgan
115. Interview, Hilary Armstrong
116. Interview, Geoffrey Robinson
117. Interview, Frank Dobson
118. Interview, Robert Harris
119. Interview, Ed Owen
120. Hansard, 17 March 2003
121. Interview, Clare Short; she finally quit on Monday, 12 May 2003
122. Hansard, 18 March 2003
123. Cherie Blair, remarks at Cheltenham Literary Festival, 10 October 2009
124. Interview, Peter Hyman

125. Interview, Paddy Ashdown
126. Interview, David Blunkett
127. Interview, Stan Greenberg
128. *Guardian Unlimited*, 1 April 2003
129. *Daily Mail*, 19 March 2003
130. *Daily Mirror*, 19 March 2003
131. *Independent*, 19 March 2003
132. *Daily Telegraph*, 19 March 2003
133. *Sun*, 19 March 2003
134. Hansard, 18 March 2003
135. Interview, Sally Morgan
136. Mullin, p. 388
137. Interview, Hilary Armstrong
138. Interview, Sally Morgan
139. Interview, Andrew Card
140. Interview, Michael Boyce

10. Squandered Victory

1. Interviews, David Manning and Condoleezza Rice
2. Woodward (2004), p. 399
3. Interviews, Peter Hyman, Sally Morgan, Peter Stothard and others; Stothard, pp. 106–7
4. Tony Blair, televised address from Downing Street, 20 March 2003
5. *Guardian, The Times, Daily Telegraph*, 21 March 2003
6. Interview, Barry Cox
7. Interview, Nick Ryden
8. Interview, Colin Niven
9. Stothard, p. 91
10. Interview, Charles Guthrie
11. *Servants of the People*, Chapter 14
12. Interview, Tony Blair
13. Interview, Tony Blair
14. Trevor Kavanagh, *Sun*, 18 April 2003
15. A. Campbell, p. 683
16. Interview, Michael Boyce
17. Interviews, members of War Cabinet
18. Woodward (2006), p. 154
19. Interview, Michael Boyce
20. Interview, Geoff Hoon
21. Interview, David Manning
22. Interview, senior officer
23. Interview, Michael Boyce
24. Interview, member of the War Cabinet
25. Conversation, Cabinet minister
26. Interviews, Geoff Hoon and Michael Boyce
27. Interview, Michael Boyce
28. Interviews, Geoff Hoon and others
29. Interview, Michael Boyce
30. Interview, Geoff Hoon
31. Interview, Tom Kelly
32. Interview, Andrew Card
33. Interview, David Manning
34. Blair–Bush news conference, Hillsborough, Northern Ireland, 8 April 2003
35. Interview, Tom Kelly
36. Interview, Michael Levy
37. Interview, Mike Jackson
38. Interview, Andrew Turnbull
39. Interview, David Manning
40. Conversations, senior Blair and Brown aides
41. Interview, Charles Guthrie
42. Interview, Michael Boyce
43. Interview, David Manning
44. Interview, Andrew Card
45. Interview, Michael Boyce
46. Hansard, 14 April 2003
47. The museum would not reopen until six years later
48. Interview, David Manning
49. Interview, Richard Haas

50. Interview, Mike Jackson
51. Interview, Jack Straw
52. Interview, David Manning
53. Interview, Ed Owen
54. Donald Rumsfeld, news conference, Washington, 11 April 2003
55. Interview, Jeremy Greenstock
56. Interview, senior British officer
57. Interview, Jack Straw
58. Interview, Clare Short
59. Woodward (2006), pp. 108, 113
60. Interview, Clare Short
61. Interview, senior British officer
62. Interview, Jack Straw
63. George W. Bush, speech on the USS *Abraham Lincoln*, Persian Gulf, 1 May 2003
64. Confidential cable, Sawers to 10 Downing Street, 11 May 2003; Gordon and Trainor (2007), pp. 541–2
65. Synnott, pp. 46, 85
66. Woodward (2006), p. 194
67. Interviews, Michael Boyce and Mike Jackson
68. Interview, Mike Jackson
69. Interview, David Manning
70. Interview, Condoleezza Rice
71. Interview, David Manning
72. Interview, Condoleezza Rice
73. A. Campbell, p. 699
74. Interview, Ed Owen
75. Interview, Mike Jackson
76. Interview, Peter Mandelson
77. Interview, Peter Mandelson
78. Interview, Michael Levy
79. Interview, David Manning
80. Interview, Christopher Meyer
81. Interview, Neil Kinnock
82. Interviews, civil servants
83. Interview, Iain Duncan Smith
84. Interview, Alan Milburn
85. Interview, Sally Morgan
86. Interview, David Blunkett
87. Interview, Michael Jay
88. Interview, Christopher Meyer
89. Interviews, senior British officers
90. Interview, David Manning
91. Interview, Andrew Card
92. Interview, Jeremy Greenstock
93. Synnott, pp. 5, 13
94. Ibid., p. 252
95. UNSCR 1483, 22 May 2003
96. *Observer*, 30 March 2003
97. Interview, David Manning; A. Campbell, pp. 694–5
98. Blair–Putin news conference, Moscow, 29 April 2003
99. Interview, David Manning
100. Interview, Andrew Turnbull

11. Broken Dream, Cabinet Nightmare

1. Interview, member of War Cabinet
2. Conversation, Blair aide
3. Interview, Steve Morris
4. Interview, Stephen Wall
5. Interview, Peter Mandelson
6. Tony Blair, speech to Labour conference, Brighton, 2 October 2001
7. Interview, Peter Hyman
8. Interview, Steve Morris
9. Interview, Tony Blair
10. Interview, Stan Greenberg
11. Interview, Geoff Mulgan
12. Interview, Peter Mandelson
13. Conversations, European diplomats
14. Conversations, minister and Blair aides
15. Tony Blair, speech to Labour

conference, Blackpool, 1 October 2002

16. Tony Blair, speech, Cardiff, 28 November 2002
17. Hansard, 27 November 2002
18. Interview, Paddy Ashdown
19. Interview, Tony Blair
20. Interview, Stephen Wall
21. Conversations, members of Britain in Europe
22. Conversations, Blair aides and Cabinet ministers
23. Interview, Brown inner circle
24. Conversation, Brown inner circle
25. Conversation, Cabinet minister
26. *Servants of the People*, Chapter 5
27. Interview, Steve Morris
28. Interview, Stephen Wall
29. For the best accounts, predominantly from the Treasury's perspective, see Keegan, pp. 320–28, and Peston, pp. 217–46
30. Interview, senior civil servant
31. Interview, Andrew Turnbull
32. Interview, Stephen Wall
33. Conversation, Blair aide
34. Conversation, Blair adviser
35. Conversation, Cabinet minister
36. Interviews, civil servants
37. Ed Balls, Cairncross Lecture, 4 December 2002
38. Conversations, Brown inner circle
39. Interview, Andrew Turnbull
40. Interview, Jonathan Powell
41. Interview, Stephen Wall
42. Interview, Jonathan Powell
43. Interview, Andrew Turnbull
44. Interviews, Brown inner circle, Jonathan Powell, Stephen Wall and others

45. Interviews, Brown inner circle, Andrew Turnbull, Stephen Wall and others
46. Interviews, Jonathan Powell, Andrew Turnbull, Stephen Wall, Number 10 and Treasury officials, Blair and Brown aides; Peston, p. 238. Witnesses from both sides of the Blair–Brown divide agree that this is what happened
47. Interview, Brown aide
48. Interview, Stephen Wall
49. Interview, Jonathan Powell
50. Interview, Charles Clarke
51. Interview, Alan Milburn
52. Interview, Charles Clarke
53. Interview, Jonathan Powell
54. Oonagh Blackman, *Daily Mirror*, 22 May 2003; Andrew Grice, *Independent*, 22 May 2003
55. Andrew Rawnsley, 'Peter Mandelson's cardinal sin', *Observer*, 25 May 2003
56. Interview, Andrew Turnbull
57. Interview, Stephen Wall
58. Interviews, Jonathan Powell and Stephen Wall
59. Conversation, Cabinet minister
60. Interview, Stephen Wall
61. Interview, Andrew Turnbull
62. Interview, Andrew Turnbull
63. Interview, Sally Morgan
64. Conversation, Cabinet minister
65. Interview, Neil Kinnock
66. Interview, Jack Straw
67. Interview, Peter Mandelson
68. Interview, Richard Wilson
69. Interview, Geoff Hoon
70. The reshuffle of 2006
71. Conversation, Cabinet minister
72. Interview, Charles Clarke

73. Interview, Michael Levy
74. Interview, Cabinet minister
75. Interview, Sally Morgan
76. Interview, Andrew Turnbull
77. Conversation, Blair aide
78. Interviews, Andrew Turnbull and others
79. Paper from Irvine to House of Lords select committee on the Constitution, 26 October 2009
80. Interview, Sally Morgan
81. Interview, Andrew Turnbull
82. Interviews, Blair inner circle
83. Interview, Sally Morgan
84. Interview, Andrew Turnbull
85. Interview, Cabinet minister
86. Interview, Sally Morgan
87. Blunkett (2006), p. 512
88. Andrew Turnbull, evidence to House of Lords select committee on the Constitution, 1 July 2009
89. Interview, Andrew Turnbull
90. Congressional Citation, 25 June 2003

12. A Body in the Woods

1. Tony Blair, speech to troops, Basra, 29 May 2003
2. Nicholas Watt in Rogers, p. 42
3. *Today*, BBC Radio 4, 6.07 a.m., 29 May 2003
4. Interview, Tom Kelly
5. Tony Blair, news conference in Poland, 30 May 2003
6. Interview, Tom Kelly
7. *Mail on Sunday*, 1 June 2003
8. Tony Blair, evidence to Hutton Inquiry, 28 August 2003
9. Tony Blair, evidence to Hutton Inquiry, 28 August 2003
10. Interview, Jonathan Powell
11. *Servants of the People*, Chapter 14
12. Interview, Sally Morgan
13. A. Campbell, p. 606
14. Ibid., p. 602
15. Interview, Barry Cox
16. Interview, Alastair Campbell
17. Interview, Number 10 official
18. Interview, Sally Morgan
19. A. Campbell, p. 585
20. Ibid., p. 700
21. Interview, Number 10 official
22. Interview, Number 10 official
23. E-mail, Marsh to Mitchell, 9 June 2003, evidence to Hutton Inquiry
24. *Today*, BBC Radio 4, 29 May 2003
25. Interview, Sally Morgan
26. John Humphrys interview with *Q* magazine, 19 December 2008
27. Kamal Ahmed, *Observer*, 1 February 2004
28. *The Times*, 4 June 2003
29. Andrew Gilligan, evidence to Hutton Inquiry, 12 August 2003
30. A. Campbell, p. 703
31. Interview, Sally Morgan
32. Alastair Campbell, evidence to Foreign Affairs select committee, 25 June 2003
33. Interview, Jonathan Powell
34. Interview, Jon Snow
35. Interview, Jon Snow
36. *Channel 4 News*, 27 June 2003
37. Interview, Jon Snow
38. Interview, Sally Morgan
39. A. Campbell, p. 711
40. Interview, Number 10 official
41. Interview, Barry Cox
42. Tony Blair, evidence to Hutton Inquiry, 28 August 2003
43. Interview, Barry Cox

44. Tony Blair, evidence to Hutton Inquiry, 28 August 2003
45. Interview, Geoff Hoon
46. A. Campbell, p. 713
47. Ibid., p. 714
48. Interview, Geoff Hoon
49. Jonathan Powell, evidence to Hutton Inquiry, 18 August 2003
50. Scarlett's Note headed 'Meeting in Prime Minister's Office', 7 July 2003; Omand's Memo headed 'Meetings in the Prime Minister's study', 21 July 2003
51. Letter, Scarlett to Omand, 7 July 2003, evidence to Hutton Inquiry
52. *Sunday Times*, 1 February 2004
53. Hansard, 7 July 2003
54. Interview, Andrew Turnbull
55. Interview, Peter Mandelson
56. A. Campbell, p. 714
57. Godric Smith, evidence to Hutton Inquiry, 20 August 2003
58. Interview, Tom Kelly
59. Kevin Tebbit, evidence to Hutton Inquiry, 13 October 2003
60. Jonathan Powell, evidence to Hutton Inquiry, 18 August 2003
61. David Manning, evidence to Hutton Inquiry, 18 August 2003
62. Kevin Tebbit, evidence to Hutton Inquiry, 13 October 2003
63. Jonathan Powell and Kevin Tebbit, evidence to Hutton Inquiry
64. Richard Norton-Taylor, evidence to Hutton Inquiry, 21 August 2003
65. Michael Evans, evidence to Hutton Inquiry, 21 August 2003
66. *Financial Times, Guardian, The Times*, 10 July 2003
67. E-mail, Kelly to Powell, 10 July 2003, evidence to Hutton Inquiry
68. Conversation, Cabinet minister
69. Letter, Tebbit to Hoon, 10 July 2003, evidence to Hutton Inquiry
70. Letter, Hoon's Private Secretary to Straw's Private Secretary, 11 July 2003, evidence to Hutton Inquiry
71. David Kelly, evidence to Foreign Affairs committee, 15 July 2003
72. Interview, Alastair Campbell; A. Campbell, p. 720
73. Alastair Campbell, evidence to Hutton Inquiry, 22 September 2003
74. Interview, Tom Kelly
75. Interview, Sally Morgan
76. C. Blair, p. 356
77. Janice Kelly, evidence to Hutton Inquiry, 1 September 2003
78. Ruth Absalom, evidence to Hutton Inquiry, 2 September 2003
79. Interview, Tony Blair
80. Tony Blair, address to Joint Session of Congress, 17 July 2003
81. Conversations, Blair aides
82. Interview, Sally Morgan
83. Interview, Sally Morgan
84. Interviews, David Manning and others
85. C. Blair, p. 357
86. Interview, David Manning
87. Interview, Sally Morgan
88. Interview, Alastair Campbell; C. Blair, p. 357
89. Interview, Cabinet minister
90. Interview, Andrew Turnbull
91. Interview, Andrew Turnbull

92. Interview, Cabinet minister
93. Interview, Andrew Turnbull
94. C. Blair, p. 357
95. Interview, Michael Levy
96. Interview, Tom Kelly
97. Interview, Number 10 official
98. Interview, Geoff Hoon
99. BBC News, 20 July 2003
100. Jonathan Oliver, *Mail on Sunday*, 20 July 2003
101. Interview, Sally Morgan
102. Melissa Kite, *The Times*, 21 July 2003
103. C. Blair, p. 358
104. Ibid., pp. 358–9
105. Ibid., p. 359
106. Interview, Philip Gould
107. Interview, Barry Cox
108. Hugo Young, *Guardian*, 8 July 2003 and 19 July 2003
109. Conversation, Hugo Young
110. Boulton, pp. 127–8
111. Kevin Tebbit, evidence to Hutton Inquiry, 13 October 2003
112. C. Blair, p. 359
113. Conversations, American and French reporters
114. Alastair Campbell, evidence to Hutton Inquiry, 19 August 2003
115. Interview, Steve Morris
116. Interview, David Hill
117. Simon Jenkins, *The Times*, 26 September 2003
118. Interview, BBC executive
119. Interview, senior civil servant
120. Conversations, Blair aides
121. Interview, Number 10 official
122. Tony Blair, statement about Campbell's resignation, Number 10, 29 August 2003
123. Interview, Tom Kelly
124. See Chapter 7
125. Interview, Barry Cox
126. Conversations, Blair aides

13. Dinner for Three

1. Interview, Sunder Katwala
2. Conversation, Blair aide
3. Conversations, Brown aides
4. Interview, Tony Blair
5. MORI for the *Financial Times*, 27 September 2003
6. *Observer*, 28 September 2003
7. Interview, Tony Blair
8. Interview, David Hill
9. Interview, Brown inner circle
10. *Daily Mirror*, 30 September 2003
11. Gordon Brown, speech to Labour conference, Bournemouth, 29 September 2003
12. Interview, Brown aide
13. Interview, Brown aide
14. Conversation, Cabinet minister
15. Interview, Sally Morgan
16. Interview, David Hill
17. Interview, Peter Hyman
18. Interview, Peter Hyman
19. Interview, Sally Morgan
20. Tony Blair, speech to Labour conference, Bournemouth, 30 September 2003
21. Conversation, Cabinet minister
22. Conversation, Brown aide
23. Conversation, Blair aide
24. Conversation, Blair inner circle
25. Interview, Sally Morgan
26. Interview, Brown aide
27. *GMTV*, 6 November 2003
28. Prescott, p. 302
29. Conversation, Cabinet minister
30. Conversation, Cabinet minister
31. Interview, Brown inner circle

32. Interviews, Brown inner circle
33. Interviews, Sally Morgan and others
34. Conversation, Cabinet minister
35. Prescott, p. 308
36. Ibid., p. 310
37. Gordon Brown, speech to the Social Market Foundation, Cass Business School, London, 3 February 2003
38. Interview, Robert Hill
39. Conversation, Cabinet minister
40. Interview, Andrew Turnbull
41. Though in that case he got his facts wrong
42. Interview, Charles Clarke
43. Interview, Sally Morgan
44. Interview, Robert Hill
45. Interview, Tony Blair
46. Interview, senior Treasury official
47. Interview, Estelle Morris
48. Interview, Robert Hill
49. Interview, Charles Clarke
50. Andrew Rawnsley, 'The Chancellor isn't scary any more', Observer, 9 February 2003
51. Interview, Andrew Turnbull
52. Interview, Charles Clarke
53. Interview, Hilary Armstrong
54. 'Ambitions for Britain', Labour manifesto, 16 May 2001
55. Interview, Hilary Armstrong
56. Interview, Sally Morgan
57. Interview, Alan Johnson
58. Interview, David Hill
59. Interview, Stephen Wall
60. Interview, Number 10 official
61. Interview, Brown aide
62. Interview, Brown inner circle
63. Interview, Sally Morgan
64. Interviews, Blair inner circle and Brown inner circle
65. Interview, George Mudie
66. The Times, 29 January 2004
67. Interview, Stephen Wall
68. Interview, David Hill
69. Interview, Geoff Mulgan
70. Interview, Hilary Armstrong
71. Interview, David Hill
72. Blunkett (2006), p. 583
73. Interview, Geoff Mulgan

14. Too Good to be True

1. Interview, David Hill
2. Interviews, Tom Kelly, Sally Morgan, Jonathan Powell and others
3. Interview, David Hill
4. Interview, David Hill
5. Interview, Tom Kelly
6. Interview, David Hill
7. Interview, Andrew Turnbull
8. The source of the leak has never been identified. Campbell denied it was him and Downing Street that it was them
9. Report of the Hutton Inquiry, HC 247, p. 320
10. Interview, David Hill
11. Hansard, 7 January 2004 and 14 January 2004
12. Ibid., 28 January 2004
13. Interview, Stephen Byers
14. Max Hastings, Daily Mail, 29 January 2004
15. Matthew d'Ancona, Sunday Telegraph, 12 December 2004
16. Interview, Tom Kelly
17. Interview, David Hill

18. Alastair Campbell, news conference, FPA, London, 28 January 2004
19. Conversation, Cabinet minister
20. Conversation, Cabinet minister
21. 55 per cent said it was a whitewash; 54 per cent said Number 10 had 'sexed up' the dossier: YouGov for ITV, 1 February 2004
22. Three times as many voters trusted the BBC as trusted the Government; 45 per cent of voters still believed Blair had lied about Kelly's outing, down just three from 48 per cent in a pre-verdict poll: ICM for the *Guardian*, 30 January 2004
23. Interview, David Hill
24. David Kay, evidence to Senate Armed Services committee, 29 January 2004
25. Interview, Jack Straw
26. Interview, Jack Straw
27. Interview, Mike Jackson
28. Interview, David Manning
29. Interview, David Manning
30. Interview, Jeremy Greenstock
31. Interview, David Manning
32. Bremer barely mentions Greenstock in his account of his time in Iraq. Of just four references, two are unfriendly. Greenstock was prevented from publishing his own account by a Foreign Office gag
33. Interview, Jeremy Greenstock
34. Interview, Jeremy Greenstock
35. Interview, Sally Morgan
36. Interviews, Andrew Card and David Hill
37. Interview, Christopher Meyer
38. Interviews, Andrew Card and Condoleezza Rice
39. Interview, David Manning
40. Interview, Sally Morgan
41. Interview, Jonathan Powell
42. Interview, Jeremy Greenstock
43. *Observer*, 16 November 2003
44. Interviews, Tessa Jowell and Sally Morgan
45. George W. Bush, speech at Banqueting House, London, 19 November 2003
46. Interview, Sally Morgan
47. Interview, David Hill
48. Interview, Sally Morgan
49. George W. Bush, speech at Banqueting House, London, 19 November 2003
50. Blair–Bush news conference, Number 10, 20 November 2003
51. *Guardian*, 21 November 2003
52. *Time*, 1 December 2003
53. Interview, David Hill
54. Interview, Stephen Wall
55. Conversation, minister
56. Interview, Charlie Falconer
57. Interview, Cabinet minister
58. Blair–Bush news conference, Number 10, 20 November 2003
59. Interview, Michael Jay
60. Interview, Cabinet minister
61. Interview, Menzies Campbell
62. Interview, David Hill
63. Interview, David Hill
64. Maureen Dowd, *New York Times*, 20 November 2003
65. Interview, Jonathan Powell
66. *USA Today*, 14 December 2002
67. Tony Blair, remarks about capture of Saddam, Number 10, London, 14 December 2003
68. Interview, David Hill

69. George W. Bush, television address, Washington, 14 December 2003
70. Rory McCarthy and Julian Borger, *Guardian*, 18 December 2003 and 20 December 2003
71. Tony Blair, speech to troops in Basra, 4 January 2004
72. See Chapter 10
73. Bremer, pp. 267–70
74. Interview, Jeremy Greenstock
75. Mullin, p. 455
76. Tony Blair, speech in Sedgefield, 5 March 2004
77. Tony Blair, speech to Labour spring conference, Manchester, 13 March 2004
78. Conversation, Blair aide
79. Tony Blair, remarks in Downing Street, 12 March 2004
80. Stephen Glover, *Daily Mail*, 16 March 2004
81. YouGov for Sky News, 16 March 2004
82. Giles Tremlett, *Guardian Weekly*, 18 March 2004
83. His release from jail in August 2009 is discussed in Chapter 38
84. Nicholas Watt, *Guardian*, 26 March 2004
85. Interviews, Government officials; conversation, Cabinet minister
86. Nicholas Watt, *Guardian*, 27 March 2004
87. Interview, Andrew Turnbull
88. Interview, Richard Haas
89. McCarthy, p. 152
90. Interview, Andrew Turnbull
91. *Observer*, 11 April 2004
92. These discussions were so sensitive that officials were later jailed for leaking the minutes
93. Interviews, senior officers
94. Blair–Bush news conference, White House, Washington, 16 April 2004
95. Conversation, Cabinet minister
96. Conversations, Cabinet ministers
97. *Guardian*, 27 April 2004
98. Interview, Sally Morgan
99. Interview, Jeremy Greenstock

15. The Long Dark Tunnel

1. Conversation, Cabinet minister
2. Interview, Andrew Turnbull
3. Interview, Cabinet minister
4. Conversation, minister
5. Interviews, Cabinet minister and Blair aides
6. Interview, Cabinet minister
7. *The Westminster Hour*, BBC Radio 4, 19 October 2003
8. Interview, Blair aide
9. Interview, Sally Morgan
10. Interview, Charlie Falconer
11. Interview, Blair aide
12. Interview, Blair inner circle
13. *The Westminster Hour*, BBC Radio 4, 6 June 2004
14. Conversation, former Cabinet minister
15. Conversation, Cabinet minister
16. Conversation, Blair aide
17. C. Blair, pp. 368, 370
18. Interview, Steve Morris
19. *Sun*, 10 September 2003
20. Interview, Steve Morris
21. Mullin, pp. 461, 464
22. Interview, Frank Dobson
23. Conversations, Cabinet ministers
24. Conversation, Cabinet minister

25. *Sun*, 15 April 2004; *The Times*, 16 April 2004
26. Conversations, European diplomats
27. Hansard, 20 April 2004
28. Conversation, former Cabinet minister
29. Interview, Stephen Byers
30. *Sunday Times*, 25 April 2004
31. *Sixty Minutes*, CBS, 29 April 2004
32. *Guardian*, 1 May 2004
33. *Daily Telegraph*, 1 May 2004
34. *Report on the Treatment of Fourteen 'High Value Detainees' in CIA Custody*, International Committee of the Red Cross, February 2007
35. Report of the Senate Armed Services Committee, 22 April 2009
36. Ibid.; timeline released by the Senate Intelligence Committee, 23 April 2009; Bush administration top secret memos declassified and released by White House, 16 April 2009
37. Testimony to Joint House and Senate Intelligence Committee, September 2002
38. CNN, 4 February 2009, cited in *The New York Review of Books*, 18 April 2009
39. Hansard, 26 February 2009
40. Interview, Cabinet minister
41. *The Times*, 6 February 2009
42. Interview, Michael Jay
43. Interview, Mike Jackson
44. Interview, Jeremy Greenstock
45. Interview, Barry Cox
46. Conversation, Blair aide
47. Conversation, Cabinet minister
48. Interview, Peter Mandelson
49. Interview, Philip Gould
50. Interview, Tessa Jowell
51. Interview, Stephen Byers
52. Interview, David Blunkett
53. Interview, Peter Hain
54. Interview, Alan Milburn
55. Interview, Cabinet minister
56. C. Blair, p. 369
57. Interview, David Hill
58. Interview, Sally Morgan
59. Interview, Andrew Turnbull
60. Interview, Brown inner circle
61. Interview, Stan Greenberg
62. Interview, Philip Gould
63. YouGov for Sky News, 16 March 2004
64. YouGov for the *Sunday Times*, 16 May 2004
65. Conversation, Cabinet minister
66. Conversation, Cabinet minister
67. Interview, Philip Gould
68. Interview, Brown aide
69. Tom Baldwin, *The Times*, 15 May 2004
70. Conversation, Cabinet minister
71. Interviews, Blair and Brown inner circles; Peston, pp. 337–8
72. Interviews, Brown inner circle
73. Interview, Brown aide
74. Interviews, Brown inner circle
75. Interviews, Brown inner circle
76. Interview, Tessa Jowell
77. Interview, Philip Gould
78. Interview, Jonathan Powell
79. Conversation, Cabinet minister
80. Interview, Peter Mandelson
81. Interview, Tom Kelly
82. Interviews, Michael Levy and Jonathan Powell
83. Interview, Michael Levy
84. Interview, Charlie Falconer
85. Interview, David Blunkett
86. C. Blair, p. 370

87. Interview, Michael Levy
88. Interview, David Hill
89. Conversation, Cabinet minister
90. Blair–Erdogan news conference, Ankara, Turkey, 17 May 2004
91. Interview, Tom Kelly

16. On and On

1. Interview, Tom Kelly
2. Interview, Tom Kelly
3. *Servants of the People*, Chapter 18
4. Interview, Ken Livingstone
5. The Tory vote was 37 per cent
6. Interview, David Hill
7. UKIP won 16 per cent of the vote in the European elections
8. Interview, Sally Morgan
9. Interview, Brown inner circle
10. Interview, Brown aide
11. Trevor Kavanagh, *Sun*, 12 July 2004
12. Interview, Philip Gould
13. UNSCR 1546, 8 June 2004
14. Bremer, p. 394
15. Interview, Robin Butler
16. Report of the Butler Inquiry, HC 898, 14 July 2004, p. 152
17. It was 26 per cent
18. Interview, Liam Byrne
19. Interview, Brown inner circle
20. Interview, Sally Morgan
21. Interviews and conversations, Blair aides and Brown inner circle
22. Interview, David Hill
23. Andrew Rawnsley, 'Blair: no deal with Brown on No 10', 'Blair still believes in himself', *Observer* 18 July 2004
24. Interview, Brown aide
25. Interviews and conversations, Cabinet ministers, Blair inner circle and Brown inner circle
26. Interviews and conversations, Cabinet ministers, Blair inner circle and Brown inner circle; Peston, p. 343
27. Interview, Stephen Wall
28. C. Blair, p. 374
29. Interview, Matthew Taylor; C. Blair, p. 374
30. Conversation, Cabinet minister
31. Conversation, Cabinet minister
32. Conversations and interviews, Cabinet ministers
33. Interview, Andrew Turnbull
34. Interview, David Hill
35. Interview, Cabinet minister
36. Interview, Brown aide
37. Interview, Brown aide
38. Interview, Andrew Turnbull
39. Interview, Brown inner circle
40. Conversation, Cabinet minister
41. Conversation, Blair inner circle
42. Interview, Andrew Turnbull
43. Labour did hold the seat, with a much reduced majority. The Tories came fourth behind UKIP
44. Interview, Tony Blair with Andrew Rawnsley and Gaby Hinsliff, *Observer*, 26 September 2004
45. Suzie Mackenzie, *Guardian Weekend*, 25 September 2004
46. Gordon Brown, speech to Labour conference, Brighton, 27 September 2004
47. Tony Blair, speech to Labour conference, Brighton, 28 September 2004
48. Conversations, Blair aides
49. Interview, Cabinet minister

50. Tony Blair, speech to Labour conference, 28 September 2004
51. Interview, Brown aide
52. Interviews, Blair inner circle and Brown inner circle; Peston, p. 347
53. Interview, Cabinet minister
54. Interviews, Brown inner circle
55. Interviews, Blair and Brown inner circles
56. Interviews, Sally Morgan and Jonathan Powell
57. Interview, Barry Cox
58. Conversation, Cabinet minister
59. Interviews, David Hill and others
60. Conversation, Blair aide
61. Interview, Barry Cox
62. Interview, Sally Morgan
63. C. Blair, p. 367
64. Interview, Sally Morgan
65. Interview, Jonathan Powell
66. Interview, David Hill
67. Interviews, David Hill and Tom Kelly
68. Interview, Andrew Turnbull
69. Interview, Andrew Turnbull
70. Interview, David Blunkett
71. Interview, Tessa Jowell
72. Interview, Peter Hain
73. Interview, Peter Mandelson
74. Interview, Stephen Byers
75. Interview, Neil Kinnock
76. Interview, Alan Milburn
77. Interview, Tom Kelly
78. Interview, David Hill
79. Interview, Tom Kelly
80. Interview, David Hill
81. BBC Ten O'Clock News, 30 September 2004
82. Ibid.
83. The Conservatives between 1979 and 1997. The dismal

fourth Tory term under John Major was not an alluring precedent
84. Interviews, Tom Kelly, Sally Morgan and Jonathan Powell
85. Seldon (2007), p. 301
86. Interview, Brown inner circle
87. Interview, Brown inner circle
88. Interview, Brown aide
89. Interview, senior Treasury official
90. Interview, Brown inner circle
91. Interview, Sally Morgan
92. Conversation, Cabinet minister
93. Interview, Sally Morgan
94. Interviews, Blair and Brown inner circle; Peston, p. 349
95. Interview, Sally Morgan

17. Another One Bites the Dust

1. The author was in the car
2. Interview, Tony Blair
3. *Sunday Telegraph*, 26 December 2004
4. Interview, David Hill
5. Another lover turned out to be Simon Hoggart, the parliamentary sketchwriter of the *Guardian* and chairman of Radio 4's *News Quiz*
6. Alistair Beaton, *A Very Social Secretary*, More 4, 10 October 2005
7. *Sunday Telegraph*, 28 November 2004
8. Interviews, senior civil servants
9. Tony Blair, news conference, Number 10, 29 November 2004
10. Interview, Andrew Turnbull
11. Conversation, Cabinet minister's aide

12. Pollard, pp. 29, 269, 241, 28, 27
13. Interview, Andrew Turnbull
14. Interview, Huw Evans
15. Interview, Andrew Turnbull
16. Interview, David Blunkett
17. Interview, Cabinet minister
18. Budd report, 21 December 2004, p. 5
19. Interview, Andrew Turnbull
20. Interview, Huw Evans
21. Interview, Andrew Turnbull
22. Interviews, David Hill, Tom Kelly, Sally Morgan and Jonathan Powell
23. Interview, Huw Evans
24. Interviews, Huw Evans, David Hill and others
25. Interview, David Hill
26. Interview, Huw Evans
27. Interview, David Hill
28. Interview, Tom Kelly
29. Interviews, David Hill, Huw Evans, Sally Morgan and Jonathan Powell
30. Blunkett (2006), p. 736
31. Interview, Huw Evans
32. See Chapter 7
33. See Chapter 13
34. See Chapter 11
35. Beckett, Darling, Prescott and Straw
36. Interview, Andrew Turnbull
37. Hugh Cleary and Richard Reeves, 'The Culture of Churn', Demos paper, 12 June 2009
38. Interview, Charles Clarke
39. Interview, Robin Butler
40. Interview, Richard Wilson
41. Interview, Charles Clarke
42. Interview, Frank Field
43. Interview, Peter Hyman
44. Interview, Alan Milburn
45. Interview, Robin Butler
46. Interview, Andrew Turnbull
47. Interview, Jonathan Powell
48. Interview, Richard Wilson
49. Interview, Stephen Wall
50. Interview, Margaret Jay
51. Interview, Philip Gould
52. Interview, Michael Barber
53. Interview, Geoff Mulgan
54. Interview, Sally Morgan
55. Interview, Richard Wilson
56. Interviews, Jonathan Powell and Richard Wilson
57. Interview, Estelle Morris
58. Interview, senior civil servant
59. Interview, Geoff Mulgan
60. Interview, Michael Barber
61. Interviews, senior civil servants
62. Interviews, senior civil servants
63. Interview, Geoff Mulgan
64. Interview, Peter Mandelson
65. Interview, Jonathan Powell
66. Interview, Stephen Byers
67. Interviews, David Blunkett and others
68. Interview, Richard Wilson
69. Interviews, Stephen Byers, Richard Wilson and others
70. Interview, Andrew Turnbull
71. Interview, Peter Mandelson
72. Interview, Jonathan Powell
73. Interview, senior civil servant
74. Interview, senior civil servant
75. Interview, Charles Clarke
76. Interview, Michael Barber
77. Interviews, Charles Clarke, Sally Morgan and Jonathan Powell
78. Private information
79. Interview, Jonathan Powell
80. Interview, Peter Mandelson
81. Interviews, Cabinet ministers and Blair aides
82. Conversation, Cabinet minister
83. Interview, Cabinet minister

84. Interview, Huw Evans
85. Home Office, Quarterly Asylum Statistics
86. *The Westminster Hour*, BBC Radio 4, 6 February 2005
87. Toynbee and Walker, p. 45
88. Conversation, Cabinet minister
89. Home Office Quarterly Reports; British Crime Survey
90. Interview, Michael Barber
91. See Chapter 21
92. Hyman, pp. 384–5
93. *Prospect*, April 2005
94. Interview, Tony Blair
95. Andrew Rawnsley, 'Whose lead will Labour follow?', *Observer*, 21 March 2004
96. Interview, Brown inner circle
97. Interview, Matthew Taylor
98. Interview, Sally Morgan
99. Marie Woolf, 'The Birt Papers', *Independent on Sunday*, 24 June 2007
100. Interviews, Sally Morgan, Alan Milburn and Jonathan Powell

18. The Ugly Campaign

1. Interview, Sally Morgan
2. Interview, Sally Morgan
3. Interview, Geoffrey Robinson
4. *Observer*, 9 January 2005
5. *Sunday Telegraph*, 16 January 2005
6. Peston, p. 349
7. Interviews, Blair inner circle
8. Interviews, Blair inner circle
9. Interview, Blair inner circle
10. Interviews, Barry Sheerman and others; Mullin, p. 524
11. www.ukpollingreport.co.uk/blog/historical-polls
12. YouGov for the *Daily Telegraph*, 25 March 2005
13. *Observer*, 20 February 2005
14. Interviews, Labour campaign team
15. Interview, former Cabinet minister
16. Conversation, Cabinet minister
17. Conversation, Cabinet minister
18. Interview, Huw Evans
19. Interview, Cabinet minister
20. Conversation, Blair aide
21. Interview, member of campaign team
22. Interview, Huw Evans
23. Interview, Jonathan Powell
24. Conversations, Cabinet ministers
25. Conversation, Cabinet minister
26. Interview, Brown aide
27. Hansard, 16 March 2005
28. Interview, Stephen Byers
29. Blair's asset rating was −10 per cent; Brown's rating was +46 per cent: YouGov for the *Daily Telegraph*, January 2005
30. Interview, Labour strategist
31. Interview, Philip Gould
32. Interview, Alastair Campbell
33. Interview, Brown aide
34. Interview, Sally Morgan
35. Interview, Philip Gould
36. Interview, Jonathan Powell
37. Interview, Philip Gould
38. Interview, Andrew Turnbull
39. Interview, Bruce Grocott
40. BBC News, 6 April 2005
41. Interview, Andrew Turnbull
42. Interview, former Cabinet minister
43. Interview, Huw Evans
44. Interview, Philip Gould
45. Interview, David Hill

46. Interview, Huw Evans
47. Interview, Brown inner circle
48. Interview, David Hill
49. Interview, Andrew Turnbull
50. Interview, Philip Gould
51. Labour PPB, broadcast all channels, 11 April 2005
52. Private information
53. Tony Blair, statement in Downing Street, 5 April 2005
54. Tony Blair, speech, Dover, 22 April 2005
55. Cited in Kavanagh and Butler (2005), p. 57
56. Interview, David Hill
57. *Ant and Dec's Saturday Night Takeaway*, ITV, 2 April 2005
58. David Remnick, 'The Real Mr Blair', *New Yorker*, April 2005
59. Interview, David Hill
60. 'My Tony is fit . . . and up for it', *Sun*, 4 May 2005
61. Interview, David Hill
62. Tony Blair, remarks at manifesto launch, Mermaid Theatre, London, 13 April 2005
63. Conversation, Cabinet minister
64. Interview, Tony Blair
65. Interview, David Hill
66. *Leader's Question Time*, BBC1, 28 April 2005
67. Interview, David Hill
68. *Ask the Leader*, ITV, 2 May 2005
69. Interview, Tony Blair with Andrew Rawnsley and Gaby Hinsliff, *Observer*, 1 May 2005
70. *Mail on Sunday*, 24 April 2005; *Channel 4 News*, 27 April 2005
71. Labour news conference, Bloomberg HQ, London, 28 April 2005
72. *Breakfast With Frost*, BBC1, 24 April 2005
73. Conversations, members of Shadow Cabinet
74. *The World This Weekend*, BBC Radio 4, 24 April 2005
75. By Liam Byrne
76. Interviews, David Hill and Sally Morgan
77. Interview, Sally Morgan
78. Interview, Tony Blair
79. Interview, Tony Blair
80. Interview, Matthew Taylor
81. Interview, Peter Hain
82. Interview, Alan Milburn
83. Conversation, Blair aide
84. Interview, Sally Morgan
85. Interviews, Alan Milburn and others
86. David Cracknell, 'Campbell: We're home and dry', *Sunday Times*, 24 April 2005
87. *Daily Mail*, 5 May 2005
88. Interview, Alan Milburn
89. Interview, Sally Morgan
90. Interview, David Blunkett
91. J. Smith, p. 256
92. Interview, Jonathan Powell
93. Interview, Andrew Turnbull
94. Interview, member of campaign team
95. Interview, Brown inner circle
96. Interview, Philip Gould
97. Interview, David Hill
98. Interview, Brown aide
99. Interview, Jonathan Powell
100. Interview, Bruce Grocott
101. Interview, Sally Morgan
102. Interview, Sally Morgan
103. Interview, Sally Morgan
104. Interviews, Sally Morgan and others

PART TWO: THE PRICE OF AMBITION

19. Sore Winners

1. Interviews, Huw Evans, Philip Gould and Sally Morgan
2. Interview, Sally Morgan
3. Interview, Huw Evans
4. Interview, Sally Morgan
5. Tony Blair, speech at count, Newton Aycliffe Community Centre, Sedgefield, 6 May 2005
6. Conversation, Blair aide
7. Reg Keys, speech at count, Newton Aycliffe Community Centre, Sedgefield, 6 May 2005
8. Interviews, Alan Milburn and others
9. Tony Blair, remarks at National Portrait Gallery, London, 6 May 2005
10. Interview, Matthew Taylor
11. Turnout was 61 per cent. Only 21 per cent of the eligible electorate voted Labour
12. *Daily Mail*, 6 May 2005
13. *The Times*, 6 May 2005
14. *Guardian*, 6 May 2005
15. Interview, Brown aide
16. Interview, David Hill
17. Conversation, Cabinet minister
18. Tony Blair, remarks in Downing Street, 6 May 2005
19. Interview, Stephen Byers
20. Conversation, Blair inner circle
21. Interview, Philip Gould
22. Interview, David Hill
23. Interview, Jonathan Powell
24. Interview, Sally Morgan
25. Interviews, Blair inner circle
26. Mullin, p. 556
27. Interview, Cabinet minister
28. Conversation, Cabinet minister
29. Interview, Jonathan Powell
30. Interview, Brown inner circle
31. Interview, Brown inner circle
32. Interview, Brown inner circle
33. Interviews, Brown inner circle
34. Interview, Andrew Turnbull
35. Interview, Jonathan Powell
36. Interview, Sally Morgan
37. Interview, Jonathan Powell
38. Interview, Brown inner circle
39. Interview, Brown inner circle
40. Interview, Brown inner circle
41. Gaby Hinsliff, 'I won't quit vows Blair as Cabinet rift opens', *Observer*, 8 May 2005
42. *Sunday Telegraph*, 8 May 2005
43. *Observer*, 8 May 2005
44. Conversation, Cabinet minister
45. Interview, Sally Morgan
46. Interview, Phil Collins
47. Interviews, Philip Gould, Jonathan Powell, Andrew Turnbull and others
48. Conversations, Blair aides
49. Interview, Jonathan Powell
50. Interview, Sally Morgan
51. Interview, Matthew Taylor
52. Conversation, senior Labour figure
53. Conversations and interviews, Labour MPs; Michael White and Patrick Wintour, 'Blair appeals in lion's den', *Guardian*, 12 May 2005
54. Interview, Neil Kinnock
55. Interview, Alan Milburn
56. Interview, Phil Collins
57. Tony Blair, speech to the European parliament, 23 June 2005

58. By the Parliamentary Ombudsman and the Citizens' Advice Bureau
59. Conversation, Cabinet minister; interviews, Number 10 officials

20. Rules of the Game

1. Interviews, Tom Kelly and others
2. Interview, Ken Livingstone
3. Interview, Tessa Jowell
4. Interview, Tessa Jowell
5. Interview, Brown inner circle
6. Interview, Ken Livingstone
7. Interview, Ken Livingstone
8. Interview, David Hill
9. Interview, senior civil servant
10. Interview, Tessa Jowell
11. Interview, David Hill
12. Interview, Tom Kelly
13. Interview, Tessa Jowell
14. Interview, Ken Livingstone
15. Interview, Tom Kelly
16. Interviews, David Hill and Tom Kelly
17. Interview, Tessa Jowell
18. French official cited by Duncan Campbell, *Observer*, 10 July 2005
19. *Libération*, 7 July 2005
20. Cited by Duncan Campbell, *Observer*, 10 July 2005
21. Tony Blair, speech to the IOC, Singapore, 6 July 2005
22. Interview, David Hill
23. Interviews, David Hill and Tom Kelly
24. Interview, Jonathan Powell
25. Interview, Jonathan Powell
26. Interview, Jonathan Powell
27. Interview, Tessa Jowell
28. Interview, Ken Livingstone
29. Cited by Duncan Campbell, *Observer*, 10 July 2005
30. Ashling O'Connor, 'Olympics good for a party but not much else', *The Times*, 8 December 2008
31. Andrew Rawnsley, 'We don't need this five-ring circus', *Observer*, 19 January 2003
32. Interview, Michael Jay
33. Interview, Sally Morgan
34. *Sun*, 7 July 2005
35. *Daily Mail*, 7 July 2005
36. *Daily Telegraph*, 7 July 2005
37. Interview, Michael Jay
38. Interview, Michael Jay
39. Interview, David Hill
40. Interview, Tom Kelly
41. Interview, David Hill
42. Interview, Michael Jay
43. Interview, Michael Jay
44. Interview, Charles Clarke
45. Interviews, Cabinet ministers
46. Interviews, Charles Clarke and others
47. Tony Blair, statement on terrorism, Gleneagles, 7 July 2005
48. Interview, Jack Straw
49. Interview, Tom Kelly
50. Interview, Jonathan Powell
51. Interview, Ken Livingstone
52. Tony Blair, statement in Downing Street, 7 July 2005
53. Interview, Tom Kelly
54. Tony Blair, statement on terrorism, Gleneagles, 7 July 2005
55. Conversation, Number 10 official
56. Interview, Foreign Office official
57. Interview, Number 10 official
58. Interviews, Number 10 officials

59. Interview, Number 10 official
60. Interview, Number 10 official
61. Interview, Blair aide
62. Interview, Number 10 official
63. Interview, Phil Collins
64. Conversation, Cabinet minister
65. Interview, Huw Evans
66. Tony Blair, news conference, Downing Street, 8 August 2005
67. Interviews, Home Office officials
68. *Observer*, 14 August 2005
69. Interview, Charles Clarke
70. Interview, Jack Straw
71. Conversations, Blair aides
72. Interview, Andrew Turnbull
73. Interview, Matthew Taylor
74. Interview, Phil Collins
75. Interviews, senior intelligence officers
76. Interview, Phil Collins
77. Private information
78. A judgement by the European Court of Human Rights in May 2009 ordered the Government to remove them
79. Interview, Andrew Turnbull
80. Interview, Charles Clarke
81. Interview, Matthew Taylor
82. *Observer*, 14 August 2005
83. Interview, Phil Collins
84. Interview, Phil Collins
85. Interview, Huw Evans
86. Interviews, Home Office officials
87. Interview, Hilary Armstrong
88. Interview, David Hill
89. Interview, George Osborne
90. Interview, Brown inner circle
91. Hansard, 9 November 2005
92. More than twice the length of the next common law country, Australia's twelve days
93. Conversation, Cabinet minister
94. *Observer*, 13 November 2005
95. Interview, Ben Wegg-Prosser
96. Conversation, Cabinet minister
97. Conversation, Brown inner circle

21. Back to School

1. Hansard, 30 November 2005
2. Hansard, 7 December 2005
3. Interview, David Hill
4. Interview, Huw Evans
5. *Observer* conference interview, Andrew Rawnsley with David Cameron, Winter Gardens, Blackpool, 5 October 2005
6. Andrew Sparrow, 'How a question of drugs engulfed Cameron and hijacked race for the Tory leadership', *Daily Telegraph*, 15 October 2005
7. Conversation, Cabinet minister
8. Conversation, Cabinet minister
9. Interview, David Cameron
10. Interview, David Cameron
11. Andrew Pierce, 'Horror as Cameron brandishes the B-word', *The Times*, 5 October 2005
12. Conversation, Cabinet minister
13. Interview, Number 10 official
14. Conversation, minister
15. Interview, Tony Blair
16. Conversation, Cabinet minister
17. Interview, Tony Blair
18. Interview, Tony Blair
19. Conservative, 37 per cent; Labour, 35 per cent: ICM for the *Sunday Telegraph*, 11 December 2005. Conservative, 37 per cent; Labour, 36 per cent: YouGov for the *Sunday Times*, 11 December 2005

20. Conversation, Cabinet minister
21. Conversation, minister
22. Conversation, Cabinet minister
23. Interview, Brown aide
24. Conversation, Blair aide
25. Conversation, Cabinet minister
26. Conversation, Cabinet minister
27. Conversation, Cabinet minister
28. Conversation, senior Labour figure
29. *New Statesman*, 23 September 2005
30. Gordon Brown, speech to Labour conference, Brighton, 26 September 2005
31. Conversations, Blair inner circle
32. Gordon Brown, speech to Labour conference, Brighton, 26 September 2005
33. Interviews, Brown inner circle
34. Michael White, 'Rift over PM's intention to carry on', *Guardian*, 27 September 2005
35. Interview, Huw Evans
36. BBC News, 27 September 2005
37. Interview, Phil Collins
38. Tony Blair, speech to Labour conference, Brighton, 27 September 2005
39. Interview, Tony Blair
40. Conversations, Cabinet ministers
41. Conversations, Blair aides
42. Conversation, Cabinet minister
43. Francis Elliott, 'Revealed: Blunkett broke rules on job with DNA firm', *Independent on Sunday*, 30 October 2005
44. Blunkett, p. 850
45. Department of Education; Number 10 Strategy Unit
46. Interview, Michael Barber
47. In Switzerland, a country richer than Britain, only 2 per cent of children were privately educated
48. 17 per cent in 2005–6, Independent Schools Council
49. Interview, Estelle Morris
50. Interview, Michael Barber
51. Interview, Matthew Taylor
52. Interview, Ben Wegg-Prosser
53. 'Higher Standards, Better Schools for All: More Choice for Parents and Pupils', White Paper, 25 October 2005
54. Interview, Cabinet minister
55. Interview, Ben Wegg-Prosser
56. Interview, Estelle Morris
57. Interview, Huw Evans
58. Interview, Matthew Taylor
59. Conversation, Brown inner circle
60. Conversation, Cabinet minister
61. Prescott, pp. 23–4
62. Interviews, Cabinet ministers
63. John Prescott interview with Susan Crosland, *Sunday Telegraph*, 18 December 2005
64. Ibid.
65. Interview, Neil Kinnock
66. Interview, Ben Wegg-Prosser
67. Interview, Neil Kinnock
68. Interview, Tony Blair
69. Conversation, Blair aide
70. Interview, Ben Wegg-Prosser
71. Interview, Phil Collins
72. Conversation, former Cabinet minister
73. Interview, Phil Collins
74. Conversation, Cabinet minister
75. Interview, Ben Wegg-Prosser
76. Interview, David Willetts
77. Interview, David Cameron
78. Conversations, Shadow Cabinet

22. The Hollowed Crown

1. David Hencke and Will Woodward, 'Blair plunged into secret loans crisis', *Guardian*, 16 March 2006
2. *Channel 4 News*, 15 March 2006; *Newsnight*, BBC2, 15 March 2006
3. Interview, Labour Party official
4. Interview, Michael Levy; Levy, p. 224
5. Interview, Michael Levy
6. Interview, Michael Levy
7. Interview, Tim Allan
8. Interview, Michael Levy
9. Interview, Michael Levy
10. Interview, Michael Levy
11. Levy, p. 120
12. Ibid., p. 229
13. Francis Elliott and Marie Woolf, 'Cash for peerages', *Independent on Sunday*, 19 March 2006; Jon Ungoed-Thomas, Robert Winnett and Jonathan Calvert, 'What price power?', *Sunday Times*, 19 March 2006; Levy, p. 230
14. Interview, Michael Levy
15. Tony Blair, speech to Labour conference, Blackpool, 1 October 1996
16. Marie Woolf, 'Cash for peerages row as Blair honours top donors', *Independent on Sunday*, 23 October 2005
17. Jon Ungoed-Thomas and Robert Winnett, 'Blair gave "honours for loans"', *Sunday Times*, 12 March 2006
18. Andrew Pierce and Rajeev Syal, 'Two Ministers are questioned as inquiry nears Blair's door', *The Times*, 15 July 2006
19. Rebecca Smithers and David Pallister, 'City academies adviser resigns after cash-for-honours accusation', *Guardian*, 16 January 2006
20. Tony Blair, Number 10 news conference, 16 March 2006
21. Interview, Ben Wegg-Prosser
22. Interview, Cabinet minister
23. Interview, Cabinet minister
24. Interview, Matthew Taylor
25. Interview, Number 10 official
26. *Daily Telegraph*, 30 November 2005
27. Interview, David Hill
28. Interview, Steve Morris
29. David Cracknell and David Smith, 'Brown fury at Blair EU climbdown', *Sunday Times*, 18 December 2005
30. Interview, Jonathan Powell
31. Conversations and interviews, Blair aides
32. Interview, Cabinet minister
33. Interview, Tom Kelly
34. Interview, Cabinet minister
35. Interviews, Cabinet ministers and Blair inner circle
36. Interviews, Cabinet ministers and Blair inner circle
37. Interview, Sally Morgan
38. Interviews, Cabinet ministers and civil servants
39. Interviews, Cabinet ministers and civil servants
40. Interview, Jack Dromey
41. Interview, Cabinet minister
42. Interview, Cabinet minister
43. Interview, Barry Cox
44. Interview, David Hill
45. Conversation, Helen Clarke
46. ABC, 27 March 2006

47. Interview, David Hill
48. Interview, Neil Kinnock
49. Interview, Cabinet minister
50. Interview, David Hill
51. Interview, Cabinet minister
52. Patricia Hewitt, speech to RCN, Bournemouth, 26 April 2006
53. Interview, Home Office Minister
54. *Newsnight*, BBC2, 25 April 2005
55. *Observer*, 30 April 2006
56. *Today*, BBC Radio 4, 26 April 2005
57. Hansard, 26 April 2006
58. Interview, Ben Wegg-Prosser
59. Interview, David Hill
60. *Daily Mirror*, 26 April 2006
61. Simon Walters, 'John Prescott's lover reveals'; Jo Knowsley and Dominic Turnbull, 'We made love in John's office', *Mail on Sunday*, 30 April 2006
62. Conversations and interviews, Blair inner circle and Brown inner circle
63. Interview, Blair aide
64. Interview, Ben Wegg-Prosser
65. Interview, Phil Collins
66. Interview, Ben Wegg-Prosser
67. Interview, Brown inner circle
68. Interviews, Blair inner circle
69. Interviews, Brown inner circle
70. *Today*, BBC Radio 4, 5 May 2006
71. Interviews, Blair inner circle and Brown inner circle
72. Interview, Ben Wegg-Prosser
73. *Observer*, 7 May 2006
74. *GMTV*, 9 May 2006
75. Conversations and interviews, Cabinet ministers and Blair aides
76. Interview, Jack Straw
77. Interview, Geoff Hoon
78. Conversations, Cabinet ministers
79. Interview, Cabinet minister
80. Interviews, Jonathan Powell, Matthew Taylor, Ben Wegg-Prosser and others
81. Interview, Jonathan Powell
82. Conversation, Cabinet minister
83. Interview, Charles Clarke
84. Conversation, Cabinet minister
85. John Reid, evidence to Home Affairs select committee, 23 May 2006
86. Interview, Ben Wegg-Prosser
87. *Observer*, 7 May 2006
88. Conversation, former Cabinet minister
89. Conversation, Cabinet minister
90. Conversation, Blair inner circle
91. Levy, p. 253
92. Chris Philp, *The Price of Dishonour*, Bow Group Report, 22 July 2006
93. Francis Elliott, 'Cash for honours', *Independent on Sunday*, 26 March 2006
94. Vikram Dodd and Patrick Wintour, 'No-one to face charges', *Guardian*, 20 July 2007
95. Interview, Jonathan Powell
96. Interview, David Hill
97. Levy, p. 265
98. Interview, Ben Wegg-Prosser
99. Sarah Helm, 'My family's ordeal', *Observer*, 22 July 2007
100. Interview, Jonathan Powell
101. Interviews, Tom Kelly and Ben Wegg-Prosser
102. Interview, Tessa Jowell
103. Interviews, Jonathan Powell and senior civil servants
104. Interview, Peter Hain
105. 64 per cent thought the Government traded honours for

loans and donations: YouGov for *Daily Telegraph*, 22 December 2006

106. Interview, Jack Dromey

23. Bad Vibrations

1. Interview, Tom Kelly
2. Blair–Maliki news conference, Baghdad, 22 May 2006
3. According to the Iraqi electoral commission, 78 per cent of voters approved the constitution on a turnout of 63 per cent
4. Blair–Maliki news conference, Baghdad, 22 May 2006
5. Interview, Mike Jackson
6. Sarah Sands, 'A very honest general', *Daily Mail*, 13 October 2006
7. Interview, Jonathan Powell
8. Interview, Michael Jay
9. Interview, Jonathan Powell
10. Hansard, 26 January 2006
11. *Independent on Sunday*, 10 September 2006
12. Report of the Haddon-Cave Inquiry, published 28 October 2009
13. Interview, Michael Boyce
14. Interview, Sally Morgan
15. Interview, David Hill
16. Blair–Bush news conference, White House, Washington, 26 May 2006
17. *New York Times*, 27 May 2006
18. Blair–Bush news conference, White House, Washington, 26 May 2006
19. Tony Blair, speeches in London, 21 March 2006, and at George-town University, Washington, 26 May 2006
20. Interview, Michael Jay
21. *The Times*, 18 July 2006
22. Interview, Tom Kelly
23. Interview, David Hill
24. Conversation, Cabinet minister
25. Hansard, 18 July 2006
26. Interviews, Number 10 officials
27. Interviews, Number 10 officials
28. Interview, Number 10 official
29. Interview, Sally Morgan
30. Interviews, Cabinet ministers
31. Interview, Michael Levy
32. Ned Temko, *Observer*, 6 August 2006
33. Interview, Phil Collins
34. BBC News, 19 July 2006
35. Hansard, 20 July 2006
36. Ibid.
37. Interview, Keith Hill
38. *The Rise and Fall of Tony Blair*, Channel 4, 25 June 2007
39. Interview, Matthew Taylor
40. Interview, Sally Morgan
41. Interview, Phil Collins
42. Interviews, Cabinet ministers
43. Patrick Hennessy, 'Straw leads revolt against Blair', *Sunday Telegraph*, 30 July 2006
44. Interview, Tessa Jowell
45. Interview, Ken Livingtone
46. Toby Harnden, 'Middle East crisis: death and despair', *Sunday Telegraph*, 30 July 2006
47. Interview, Matthew Taylor
48. Blair–Bush news conference, Washington, 28 July 2006
49. Interviews, Number 10 and diplomatic officials
50. Interviews, Number 10 and diplomatic officials
51. UNSCR 1701, 11 August 2006

52. Interview, Cabinet minister
53. Interview, Frank Dobson
54. Interview, Peter Hain
55. Interview, Huw Evans
56. Interview, Sally Morgan
57. Three men were convicted for the plot in September 2009
58. Conversation, Cabinet minister
59. *Daily Mail*, 12 August 2006
60. Conversation, Cabinet minister
61. Interview, Jonathan Powell
62. Interview, David Hill
63. Interviews, David Hill, Sally Morgan and others
64. Interview, Phil Collins
65. Interview, David Hill
66. Interview, Ben Wegg-Prosser
67. Interview, Phil Collins
68. Interview, Sally Morgan
69. Interview, Ben Wegg-Prosser
70. Conversation, former Cabinet minister
71. Private information

24. A Very Brownite Coup

1. Interview, Philip Webster
2. Interview, David Hill
3. Philip Webster and Peter Riddell, 'Voice of defiance from country mansion', *The Times*, 1 September 2006
4. Interview, Sally Morgan
5. Interview, Ben Wegg-Prosser
6. Philip Webster and Peter Riddell, *The Times*, 1 September 2006
7. Interview, Ben Wegg-Prosser
8. Andrew Grice, *Independent*, 1 September 2006
9. Graeme Wilson, *Daily Telegraph*, 1 September 2006
10. Interviews, David Hill and Tom Kelly
11. Interview, Keith Hill
12. BBC News, 1 September 2006
13. Interview with ePolitix.com, 30 August 2006
14. Interview, Peter Hain
15. Interview, Estelle Morris
16. Interview, Geoffrey Robinson
17. Ed Balls, 'Labour can handle the power switch', *Observer*, 3 September 2006
18. Alan Milburn, 'After Blair, new Labour must find a new project or perish', *Sunday Times*, 3 September 2006
19. Interviews, Alan Milburn and others
20. Interviews, Cabinet ministers
21. Interview, Brown inner circle
22. Interview, Brown inner circle
23. *Sunday Telegraph*, 20 August 2006
24. Interviews, Ben Wegg-Prosser and others
25. Interview, Ben Wegg-Prosser
26. Interview, Jonathan Powell
27. Jonathan Oliver and Christine Challand, 'Baltigate', *Mail on Sunday*, 17 September 2006
28. Interview, Labour MP
29. Jonathan Oliver and Simon Walters, 'Gordon, the golf hotel plotter', *Mail on Sunday*, 10 September 2006
30. *Guardian*, 11 September 2006
31. Interview, Ben Wegg-Prosser
32. Interview, George Mudie
33. Interview, Brown inner circle
34. Interviews, Keith Hill and Ben Wegg-Prosser
35. Interview, Keith Hill
36. *Observer*, 9 July 2006

37. Interview, Keith Hill
38. *Observer*, 10 September 2006
39. Interview, Keith Hill
40. Interview, Phil Collins
41. Interview, Keith Hill
42. Interview, Keith Hill
43. Interview, Jonathan Powell
44. Interview, Phil Collins
45. Interview, Jonathan Powell
46. Interviews, Phil Collins and David Hill
47. Interview, Ben Wegg-Prosser
48. Interview, Philip Gould
49. Interview, Stephen Byers
50. Interview, Phil Collins
51. Interviews, Matthew Taylor and others
52. Interview, Phil Collins
53. *Today*, BBC Radio 4, 5 September 2006
54. Patrick Wintour, 'New Labour MPs to call on Blair to quit', *Guardian*, 5 September 2006
55. Kevin Maguire and Oonagh Blackman, 'The Blair switch project', *Daily Mirror*, 5 September 2006
56. Interview, Ben Wegg-Prosser
57. Interview, Matthew Taylor
58. Interview, Jonathan Powell
59. Conversation, Blair aide
60. Interview, Tessa Jowell
61. Interview, Sally Morgan
62. Interviews, Cabinet ministers
63. Interview, Keith Hill
64. Patrick Wintour, *Guardian*, 6 September 2006
65. Interview, Keith Hill
66. *Channel 4 News*, 5 September 2006
67. Interviews, Brown inner circle
68. Interview, Sally Morgan
69. Conversations and interviews, Blair inner circle and Brown inner circle
70. Interviews, Brown inner circle
71. Will Woodward and Patrick Wintour, 'Labour in crisis', *Guardian*, 7 September 2006
72. Ibid.
73. Interview, Iain Duncan Smith
74. Interview, Frank Field
75. Interviews, Phil Collins and Ben Wegg-Prosser
76. Interview, George Mudie
77. Interview, Keith Hill
78. Interview, Phil Collins
79. Interviews, Matthew Taylor, Ben Wegg-Prosser and others
80. Interview, Cabinet minister
81. Interview, Jonathan Powell
82. Interview, Phil Collins
83. Interview, Brown inner circle
84. Interviews, Cabinet ministers
85. Interview, Peter Hain
86. Interview, Matthew Taylor
87. Interview, William Hague
88. Interview, Brown inner circle
89. Interviews, Blair inner circle and Brown inner circle
90. Interview, Brown inner circle
91. Tony Blair, remarks outside Quintin Kynaston school, St John's Wood, London, 7 September 2006
92. BBC News, 7 September 2006
93. Will Woodward and Tania Branigan, 'Labour in crisis', *Guardian*, 8 September 2006
94. Interview, Barry Cox
95. Conversation, Cabinet minister
96. *The World at One*, BBC Radio 4, 8 September 2006
97. Alan Milburn's blog, 9 September 2006

98. Interviews, former Cabinet ministers and Blair aides
99. BBC News, 7 September 2006
100. Ian Kirby, 'Interview: Gordon Brown', *News of the World*, 10 September 2006
101. Anne McElvoy, *Evening Standard*, 8 September 2006
102. Rachel Sylvester and Alice Thomson, *Daily Telegraph*, 9 September 2006
103. *Sunday AM*, BBC1, 10 September 2006
104. Interview, Brown inner circle
105. Jonathan Oliver, *Mail on Sunday*, 10 September 2006
106. Interview, Nick Ryden
107. Conversation, Blair inner circle
108. Interview, Phil Collins
109. Interview, Tom Kelly
110. Interview, Michael Levy; Levy, p. 258
111. Interview, Phil Collins
112. Interviews, Ben Wegg-Prosser and others
113. Interview, David Hill
114. ICM for the *Guardian*, Populus for *The Times*, September 2006
115. Labour support dropped from 32 per cent to 31 per cent if Brown replaced Blair: ICM for the *Guardian*, 22 September 2006
116. Conversation, Blair inner circle
117. Brown trailed Cameron by 17 points for the man who looks most able to work with colleagues; by 8 points for honesty; 25 points for being a pleasant personality; and by 23 points for being the man most likely to stab colleagues in the back: ICM for the *Guardian*, 22 September 2006
118. Martin Kettle, *Guardian*, 23 September 2006
119. Interview, Brown inner circle
120. Gordon Brown, speech to Labour conference, Manchester, 25 September 2006
121. *Today*, BBC Radio 4, 26 September 2006
122. Gordon Brown, speech to Labour conference, Manchester, 25 September 2006
123. Interview, Phil Collins
124. Tony Blair, speech to Labour conference, Manchester, 26 September 2006
125. Interview, David Hill
126. Tony Blair, speech to Labour conference, Manchester, 26 September 2006
127. BBC News, 26 September 2006
128. Tony Blair, speech to Labour conference, Manchester, 26 September 2006
129. Interviews, Cabinet ministers and Blair inner circle
130. Conversation, Cabinet minister
131. Conversation, Blair aide
132. *Daily Mirror*, 27 September 2006
133. *The Times*, 27 September 2006
134. *Daily Mail*, 27 September 2006
135. *Sun*, 27 September 2006
136. Conversation, member of Shadow Cabinet
137. Conversation, member of Shadow Cabinet

25. Miracle Worker

1. Interview, Jonathan Powell
2. Powell, p. 4
3. Powell, p. 287
4. Interview, Peter Hain

5. Interview, Tom Kelly
6. Interview, Richard Haas
7. Tony Blair, speech to the Irish parliament, Dublin, 26 November 1998
8. Tony Blair, speech to the Irish parliament, Dublin, 26 November 1998
9. Conversation, Cabinet minister
10. Interview, David Trimble
11. Tony Blair, speech to Labour conference, Brighton, 2 October 2001
12. Conversation, Cabinet minister
13. Ahern, p. 178
14. Interview, Richard Wilson
15. Interview, Mo Mowlam
16. Interview, John Holmes. One of a series of interviews about Northern Ireland conducted by Nicholas Watt, Patrick Wintour and Owen Bowcott, extracts from which were published in the *Guardian*, 13 and 14 March 2007
17. Interview, George Mitchell
18. Tony Blair, speech at the Royal Ulster Agricultural Show, Balmoral near Belfast, 16 May 1997
19. Interview, David Trimble
20. Tony Blair, speech at the Royal Ulster Agricultural Show, Balmoral near Belfast, 16 May 1997
21. Interview, Martin McGuinness. See note 16
22. Adams, pp. 314, 324
23. Interview, George Mitchell
24. Interview, Martin McGuinness. See note 16
25. Interview, David Trimble
26. *Servants of the People*, Chapter 8
27. Interview, David Trimble
28. Interview, Jonathan Powell
29. Interview, Jonathan Powell
30. Powell, pp. 139, 144
31. 3,326 people were killed as a result of The Troubles between 1969 and 1997, Royal Ulster Constabulary Chief Constable's Report, 1999
32. Interview, Paddy Ashdown
33. Interview, Jonathan Powell
34. Interview, senior intelligence officer
35. Interview, Jonathan Powell
36. Interview, senior intelligence officer
37. Interview, Jonathan Powell
38. Interview, Peter Mandelson. See note 16
39. Interview, Peter Hain
40. Interview, Jonathan Powell
41. Interview, John Reid. See note 16
42. Powell, pp. 148–9
43. Interview, Tom Kelly
44. Interview, Jonathan Powell
45. Interview, Peter Mandelson. See note 16
46. Interview, Peter Mandelson. See note 16
47. Interview, David Trimble
48. Godson, p. 426
49. David Trimble, Alcock Memorial Lecture, University of Ulster, 24 April 2007
50. Interview, John Holmes. See note 16
51. David Trimble, Alcock Memorial Lecture, University of Ulster, 24 April 2007
52. *Guardian*, 5 April 2008
53. Powell, p. 167
54. Interview, Tom Kelly
55. The episode is still murky: the

chief spy suspect, Dennis Donaldson, later revealed that he had been a British agent and in 2006 was found shot dead in a remote part of Ireland

56. Powell, p. 210
57. Interview, Tom Kelly
58. Interviews, Tom Kelly and Jonathan Powell
59. Interview, Tom Kelly
60. Tony Blair, speech at the Harbour Commissioners' Office, Belfast, 18 October 2002
61. Interview, Tom Kelly
62. Gerry Adams, speech, Monaghan, 26 October 2002
63. BBC Northern Ireland, 29 October 2002
64. Powell, p. 181
65. Interview, Jonathan Powell
66. Interview, John Holmes. See note 16
67. Interview, Jonathan Powell
68. Powell, p. 24
69. Interviews, Mo Mowlam and Jonathan Powell
70. Interview, senior civil servant. See note 16
71. Powell, p. 17
72. Ibid., p. 236
73. BBC News, 27 November 2003
74. Interview, Tom Kelly
75. Liam Clarke, 'Paisley rewrites his own history', *Sunday Times*, 15 October 2006
76. Moloney, p. 445
77. Interview, Tom Kelly
78. Interview, Jonathan Powell
79. Interviews, Tom Kelly and Jonathan Powell
80. Interview, Tom Kelly
81. Nigel Morris, 'Time is running out, Blair warns at start of crucial talks', *Independent*, 17 September 2004
82. Interview, Tom Kelly
83. Interviews, Tom Kelly and Jonathan Powell
84. Interview, Jonathan Powell
85. Interview, Tom Kelly
86. Henry McDonald, 'Irish talks fail at DUP hurdle', *Observer*, 19 September 2004
87. Ian Paisley, speech to North Antrim DUP Association, 27 November 2004
88. Interview, Jonathan Powell
89. Interview, Jonathan Powell
90. Interview, Tom Kelly
91. David Lister, 'Proceeds could pay IRA "pensions"', *The Times*, 29 December 2004
92. Interview, Tom Kelly
93. *This Week*, RTE, 9 January 2005
94. IMC Report, 10 February 2005
95. David Lister, 'Adams tells Ahern to put up or shut up', *The Times*, 11 February 2005
96. Kevin Toolis, 'Trust Gerry Adams?', *The Times*, 8 January 2005
97. Henry McDonald, 'Fight for justice', *Observer*, 13 February 2005
98. They had been wrongly convicted for the IRA bombings in Woolwich, London, in 1974
99. Powell, pp. 267–9
100. 'IRA offer withdrawn', *An Phoblacht*, 3 February 2005
101. Interview, Tom Kelly
102. David McKittrick, 'McCartney sisters eclipse Adams', *Independent*, 15 March 2005
103. 'Kennedy snub for Sinn Fein', *Daily Mirror*, 14 March 2005

104. Liam Clarke and John Burns, 'US turns its back on Sinn Fein', *Sunday Times*, 13 March 2005
105. Interviews, Tom Kelly and Jonathan Powell
106. BBC News, 28 July 2005
107. Tony Blair, statement, Number 10, 28 July 2005
108. BBC News, 26 September 2005
109. Interview, Jonathan Powell
110. Conversation, Cabinet minister
111. Interview, Jonathan Powell
112. Interview, Tom Kelly
113. David McKittrick, 'An amazing conversion', *Independent*, 10 October 2006
114. Powell, p. 278
115. Tony Blair, speech, Navan Centre, 6 April 2006
116. Tony Blair, speech, Navan Centre, 6 April 2006
117. Interview, George Mitchell
118. Interview, David Trimble
119. Interview, Peter Hain
120. Report of the Independent Monitoring Commission, 4 October 2005
121. BBC News, 13 October 2006
122. *Daily Telegraph*, 10 October 2006
123. BBC News, 11 October 2006
124. David Sharrock, 'Blair hails a pivotal moment', *The Times*, 12 October 2006
125. BBC Radio 5, 15 October 2006
126. Interview, Tom Kelly
127. Interviews, Tom Kelly and Jonathan Powell; Ahern, p. 301
128. Interview, Jonathan Powell
129. Conversation, Cabinet minister
130. Interviews, Tom Kelly and Jonathan Powell
131. Interviews, Tom Kelly and others
132. Interview, Peter Hain
133. Interview, David Trimble
134. Interview, Martin McGuinness. See note 16
135. Interview, Peter Hain
136. Ahern, p. 313
137. Interview, Stephen Wall
138. Powell, p. 3
139. Interview, Tom Kelly
140. Powell, p. 1
141. Ibid., p. 2
142. Ian Paisley, speech, Stormont, 8 May 2007
143. Martin McGuinness, speech, Stormont, 8 May 2007
144. Tony Blair, speech, Stormont, 8 May 2007
145. Bertie Ahern, speech, Stormont, 8 May 2007
146. Powell, p. 308
147. Gordon Rayner, 'United in wave of revulsion', *Daily Telegraph*, 11 March 2009

26. The Long Goodbye

1. Hansard, 15 November 2006
2. Conversation, member of Shadow Cabinet
3. Interview, Tom Kelly
4. Interview, Cabinet minister
5. *Question Time*, BBC1, 8 February 2007
6. Conversation, Cabinet minister
7. Interview, Cabinet minister
8. Interview, Tom Kelly
9. Interviews, Cabinet ministers
10. A Conservative lead of 10 points widened to 15 points under Brown, according to ICM for the *Guardian*, March 2007. Other polls of the period indicated a similar difference

11. Interview, Cabinet minister
12. Interview, Philip Gould
13. Interview, Gordon Brown
14. Interview, Brown inner circle
15. Interview, Cabinet minister
16. Interview, Matthew Taylor
17. Interview, Jonathan Powell
18. Interview, Brown aide
19. Interview, Philip Gould
20. Interview, Alastair Campbell
21. Interview, Phil Collins
22. Interviews, Jonathan Powell and others
23. Interview, Tom Kelly
24. Interview, Jonathan Powell
25. Interview, Ben Wegg-Prosser
26. *The Sunday Edition*, ITV, 29 April 2007
27. Interviews, Blair and Brown aides
28. Interview, Brown inner circle
29. Conversation, Cabinet minister
30. See Chapter 24
31. Interview, Brown inner circle
32. Interview, Brown inner circle
33. Interview, civil servant
34. Interviews, ministers and officials
35. Interview, Brown inner circle
36. Interview, senior Brown aide
37. Gordon Brown, remarks at Mossbourne City Academy, London, 19 March 2007
38. Interview, Jonathan Powell
39. Interview, senior Brown aide
40. Conversations, Cabinet ministers
41. Interview, Brown aide
42. Interviews, Treasury officials
43. *Daily Mirror*, 22 March 2007
44. *Daily Mail*, 22 March 2007
45. Peter Oborne, 'The Brown era', *Daily Mail*, 22 March 2007
46. Private interview
47. Colin Brown, Ben Russell and Stephen Castle, 'Mandelson reveals plan', *Independent*, 23 March 2007
48. Interview, Stephen Byers
49. Interview, Cabinet minister
50. Interview, Hilary Armstrong
51. Interview, Peter Hain
52. Interview, Cabinet minister
53. Interview, Cabinet minister
54. Interview, Blair aide
55. Interview, Phil Collins
56. Interview, Michael Levy
57. Interview, Blair aide
58. Interview, Jonathan Powell
59. *Observer*, 22 April 2007
60. Interview, Cabinet minister
61. Will Woodward, 'PM signals end and backs Brown', *Guardian*, 2 May 2007
62. Interview, Tom Kelly
63. Gordon Brown, speech at the Imagination Gallery, London, 11 May 2007
64. Blair–Bush news conference, 17 May 2007
65. Blair–Bush news conference, 17 May 2007
66. Interview, David Manning
67. Interview, George Mitchell
68. Interview, Ben Wegg-Prosser
69. Interview, Blair aide
70. Interview, Tessa Jowell
71. Hansard, 15 November 2006
72. Tony Blair, speech to Labour conference, Manchester, 27 September 2006
73. Hansard, 21 February 2007
74. General Sir Richard Dannatt, speech to Royal United Services Institute Land Warfare conference, London, 23 June 2009
75. *Servants of the People*, Chapter 10

76. Interview, Steve Morris
77. Seldon (2007), p. 579
78. Interview, Peter Hyman
79. Interview, Peter Hyman
80. Interview with Church of England newspaper, 5 March 2009
81. Tony Blair, speech to US National Prayer Breakfast, Hilton Hotel, Washington, 5 February 2009
82. Interviews, Frank Field, David Hill, Sally Morgan, Stephen Wall and others
83. *The Blair Years*, BBC1, 2 December 2007
84. *Vanity Fair*, June 2003
85. Interview, Tim Allan
86. Interview, Frank Field
87. Conversations, Tony Blair
88. Matthew d'Ancona, *Sunday Telegraph*, 7 April 1996
89. Interview, Barry Cox
90. Tony Blair, speech to Communion and Liberation conference, Rimini, Italy, 27 August 2009
91. Rentoul, p. 352
92. Seldon (2004), p. 521
93. Interview, Stephen Wall
94. Interview, Jonathan Powell
95. Interview, Charlie Falconer
96. Burton, pp. xv, 133, 219
97. Interview, Robert Hill
98. Interview, Peter Stothard
99. Interview, Geoff Mulgan
100. Interview, Number 10 official
101. Steve Richards, 'The media spotlight', *Independent*, 4 September 2009
102. Tony Blair, speech at the Reuters building, Canary Wharf, London, 12 June 2007
103. Tony Blair, speech at the Royal Festival Hall, London, 2 May 1997
104. The majorities were 179, 167, 66
105. Robert Walpole, Henry Pelham, Lord North, William Pitt, Lord Liverpool, William Gladstone, Lord Salisbury and Margaret Thatcher
106. Matthew Parris, 'I'm no fan, but I do love Blair's Britain', *The Times*, 23 December 2006
107. DWP, IFS
108. Tony Blair, speech to Communion and Liberation conference, Rimini, Italy, 27 August 2009
109. ICM for the *Guardian*, 24 May 2007
110. ComRes for the *Independent*, 1 May 2007; ICM for the *Guardian*, 10 May 2007
111. Downing Street briefing, 21 June 2007
112. Interview, senior civil servant
113. Interviews, Cabinet ministers
114. Interview, senior civil servant
115. Conversations, Cabinet ministers
116. Interview, David Hill
117. Interviews, Jonathan Powell and others
118. Interviews, Tom Kelly and others
119. Interview, Phil Collins
120. Interview, Philip Gould
121. Interview, Steve Morris
122. Interview, Jonathan Powell
123. Interview, Blair aide
124. Interviews, Cabinet ministers
125. Interview, David Hill
126. Interview, Jonathan Powell
127. Interview, Tom Kelly
128. Hansard, 27 June 2007

129. Ibid.
130. Interviews, Blair aides
131. Interview, Tom Kelly
132. C. Blair, pp. 2, 404
133. Interview, Jonathan Powell

27. A Short Honeymoon

1. Interviews, Brown aides
2. Gordon Brown, statement in Downing Street, 27 June 2007
3. Patrick Sawer, 'Brown: why do you make me fat?', *Sunday Telegraph*, 25 January 2009
4. Gordon Brown, statement in Downing Street, 27 June 2007
5. Interview, Labour strategist
6. Interviews, Number 10 officials
7. Interview, civil servant
8. Interview, Brown aide
9. Interviews, civil servants
10. Interview, Jacqui Smith
11. Interview, Brown aide
12. Interview, Brown aide
13. Interviews, Cabinet ministers and Brown inner circle
14. Conversation, Cabinet minister
15. Interview, Labour strategist
16. Interview, Matthew Taylor
17. Interviews, Cabinet ministers
18. Interview, Ben Wegg-Prosser
19. Interviews, former Cabinet ministers
20. Interviews, Cabinet ministers
21. Interview, Gordon Brown
22. Interview, Peter Hain
23. Interview, Jack Straw
24. Interview, Harriet Harman
25. Interview, Peter Hain
26. Interview, Geoff Hoon
27. Alistair Darling and Jack Straw
28. Brown–Bush news conference, Camp David, 30 July 2007
29. *Servants of the People*, Chapter 11
30. Interview, Jon Cruddas
31. Interview, Paddy Ashdown
32. Interview, Digby Jones
33. Interview, Alan West
34. Interview, Number 10 official
35. Digby Jones, evidence to Public Administration Committee, 15 January 2009
36. Interview, civil servant
37. Interview, Frank Cook
38. Interview, Hazel Blears
39. Interview, Peter Hain
40. Interview, Jacqui Smith
41. Interviews, Number 10 officials
42. Gordon Brown, remarks at Fawood Children's Centre, London, 29 June 2007
43. Interview, Alan West
44. Interview, Alan West
45. BBC News, 1 July 2007
46. Interview, Jacqui Smith
47. Interview, Brown aide
48. Interview, Number 10 official
49. Interview, senior civil servant
50. Interview, Number 10 official
51. 'The pink list 2007', *Independent*, 6 May 2007
52. Interviews, civil servants
53. Interview, Brown aide
54. Interview, Number 10 official
55. Interview, Number 10 official
56. Interviews, civil servants
57. Interview, Brown aide
58. Interview, senior civil servant
59. Interview, adviser to Cabinet minister
60. Interview, Brown aide
61. Interviews, ministers and officials

62. Interview, Geoff Hoon
63. Interview, Number 10 official
64. Interview, Brown aide
65. Interview, Jack Straw
66. Interview, Matthew Taylor
67. Interview, Labour strategist
68. Interview, civil servant
69. Gordon Brown, remarks at Number 10, 24 July 2007
70. Interview, civil servant
71. Interview, John Kampfner
72. Interview, civil servant
73. Interview, civil servant
74. Interview, civil servant
75. Interview, Brown aide
76. Interview, Number 10 official
77. Interview, Brown aide
78. Interview, Number 10 official
79. Interview, Murray Elder
80. Conversations, Brown inner circle
81. Interview, Kathy Lette
82. Interview, Mariella Frostrup
83. Conversation, Cabinet minister
84. Interviews, Murray Elder and others
85. Conversation, Brown inner circle
86. Interview, Cabinet minister
87. Conversation, Cabinet minister
88. Interview, Brown aide
89. Interview, Brown aide
90. Interview, Labour whip
91. Interview, Digby Jones
92. Interview, Hazel Blears
93. Interview, Murray Elder
94. Interview, Number 10 official
95. www.number10.gov.uk, 7 August 2007
96. Interview, civil servant
97. Interview, civil servant
98. Interview, Jacqui Smith
99. Interview, Frank Field
100. Interview, Jon Cruddas
101. Interview, Vince Cable
102. Conversation, member of Shadow Cabinet
103. Interview, Peter Hain
104. Interview, Brown aide
105. Interview, civil servant
106. Interview, Number 10 official
107. Interview, Brown inner circle

28. Run on the Rock

1. Gordon Brown, speech at Mansion House, London, 20 June 2007
2. Gordon Brown, speech at Mansion House, London, 12 June 1997
3. Gordon Brown, speech at Mansion House, London, 17 June 2004
4. Gordon Brown, speech at Mansion House, London, 22 June 2005
5. Gordon Brown, speech at Mansion House, London, 20 June 2007
6. Gordon Brown, address to the UN General Assembly, New York, 26 September 2008
7. David Cameron, speech, 'The New Global Economy', 22 June 2006
8. David Cameron, speech at London School of Economics, London, 17 September 2007
9. Interview, James Purnell
10. Interview, Sally Keeble
11. Interview, Director of UBS Warburg
12. *Servants of the People*, p. 213; Peter Mandelson, letter to the *Guardian*, 12 January 2008

13. Interview, Cabinet minister
14. Interview, senior Treasury official
15. Interview, Andrew Gowers
16. Adam Smith lecture, Kirkcaldy, 6 February 2005
17. Conversation, Cabinet minister
18. Conversation, Cabinet minister
19. HM Treasury; IMF
20. Gordon Brown, speech to Labour conference, Blackpool, 28 September 1998 and ad nauseam
21. Hansard, 21 March 2007
22. Q2891, Treasury select committee, 19 March 2009
23. HM Treasury
24. Interview, senior Treasury official
25. Mervyn King, evidence to Treasury select committee, 26 February 2009
26. Interview, Andrew Gowers
27. Interview, Peter Mandelson
28. Interview, Paul Everitt
29. Interview, Vince Cable
30. Gordon Brown, speech at Mansion House, London, 22 June 2006
31. The phrase was coined by the Princeton economist, Roland Benabou
32. George Osborne, speech to Credit Today conference, 12 May 2006
33. Interview, George Osborne
34. Interview, John Eatwell
35. Mervyn King, evidence to Treasury select committee, 26 February 2009
36. Interview, Andrew Gowers
37. Martin Arnold, 'Tax rate is lower than cleaner's', *Financial Times*, 4 June 2007
38. Conversation, minister
39. *Servants of the People*, Chapter 3
40. Interview, senior Treasury official
41. *Newsnight*, BBC2, 12 February 2009
42. Interview, John Gieve
43. Interview, senior Treasury official
44. Interviews, John Gieve and Steve Robson
45. Interview, Steve Robson
46. Interview, John Gieve
47. Interview, senior Treasury official
48. Interview, senior Treasury official
49. Interview, member of Monetary Policy Committee
50. Interview, Cabinet minister
51. Conversation, minister
52. Ed Balls, speech to British Bankers Association, 11 October 2006
53. Interview, Steve Robson
54. Interview, John Gieve
55. *The Love of Money*, BBC2, 17 September 2009
56. Adair Turner, evidence to Treasury select committee, 25 February 2009
57. Mervyn King, evidence to Treasury select committee, 26 February 2009
58. Interview, Bank of England official
59. Interview, senior Treasury official
60. Interview, senior Treasury official
61. Interview, senior Treasury official
62. Interviews, Bank of England and Treasury officials

63. Gordon Brown, evidence to Liaison Committee, 12 February 2009
64. Interview, member of Monetary Policy Committee
65. Interview, senior Treasury official
66. Interviews, Bank of England officials
67. Interview, Bank of England official
68. 'The nationalisation of Northern Rock', National Audit Office report, 20 March 2009
69. Gordon Brown, evidence to Liaison Committee, Q8, 12 February 2009
70. Interviews, Bank of England and Treasury officials
71. Interview, senior Bank of England official
72. Todd Purdum, 'Henry Paulson's longest night', *Vanity Fair*, October 2009
73. Brummer, p. 38
74. Interview, John Eatwell
75. Interview, Alistair Darling
76. Interviews, Treasury officials
77. Interview, John Eatwell
78. Interview, Bank of England official
79. Interview, Chairman of retail bank
80. Interview, Steve Robson
81. Interview, Bank of England official
82. Interview, Bank of England official
83. Interview, John Gieve
84. Interview, John Gieve
85. Interview, Steve Robson
86. Interview, Irwin Stelzer
87. BBC News, 11 August 2007
88. Interview, Chairman of retail bank
89. Interview, Director of Santander
90. Interview, John Gieve
91. Interview, senior Treasury official
92. Interviews, Treasury officials
93. Interview, Bank of England official
94. Interviews, Treasury officials
95. Interview, Chairman of retail bank
96. Interview, member of MPC
97. Interview, senior Treasury official
98. Interview, Bank of England official
99. Interview, senior Treasury official
100. Interview, member of MPC
101. Interview, Steve Robson
102. Interview, Chairman of retail bank
103. Mervyn King, letter to Treasury select committee, 12 September 2007
104. Interview, George Mudie
105. Interviews, members of Bank's Court
106. Interviews, Treasury officials
107. Interviews, Treasury officials and bank directors
108. Interview, Irwin Stelzer
109. Interview, Hazel Blears
110. Interview, senior Treasury official
111. Interview, Nick Brown
112. Interview, minister
113. Interview, Christine Lagarde
114. Interview, Chairman of retail bank
115. Interview, Alistair Darling

116. Interviews, Bank and Treasury officials
117. Interview, John Gieve
118. Interview, senior Treasury official
119. Interview, Nick Brown
120. Interviews, Number 10 and Treasury officials
121. Alistair Darling, news conference, HM Treasury, 17 September 2007
122. Interview, John Gieve
123. Interview, senior Treasury official
124. Who do you trust to deal with economic problems? Brown and Darling, 56 per cent; Cameron and Osborne, 18 per cent: Populus for *The Times*, 17 September 2007
125. Interview, Peter Hain

29. The Election That Never Was

1. Interview, Cabinet minister
2. Interviews, Brown inner circle
3. Interview, Gordon Brown
4. Labour, 40 per cent; Tories, 33 per cent; Lib Dems, 19 per cent: ICM for the *Sunday Telegraph*, 15 July 2007. Labour, 41 per cent; Tories, 35 per cent; Lib Dems, 15 per cent: Ipsos-MORI for the *Observer*, 22 July 2007
5. *Daily Mail*, 24 July 2007
6. Private interview
7. Interview, Cabinet minister
8. Interview, Brown inner circle
9. Interview, Cabinet minister
10. Interview, Brown inner circle
11. Interview, Brown inner circle
12. Interview, Michael Gove
13. Interview, minister
14. Conversation, member of Shadow Cabinet
15. Interview, member of Shadow Cabinet
16. www.number10.gov.uk, 'PM brings Margaret Thatcher back to No 10', 13 September 2007
17. Conversation, Cabinet minister
18. Interview, Harriet Harman
19. Interview, Jacqui Smith
20. Interview, Nick Brown
21. Interview, Jack Dromey
22. Interview, Jack Straw
23. Interviews, Cabinet ministers
24. Interview, Alistair Darling
25. Interview, Geoff Hoon
26. Interview, Peter Hain
27. Interview, Murray Elder
28. Interviews, Brown inner circle
29. Conversation, Cabinet minister
30. Interview, Brown inner circle
31. Interviews, Brown inner circle
32. Interview, Sunder Katwala
33. Interview, John Kampfner
34. Interview, Peter Hain
35. *The Times*, 24 September 2007
36. *Daily Mirror*, 24 September 2007
37. *The Sunday Edition*, ITV1, 23 September 2007
38. Interview, Jack Straw
39. Gordon Brown, speech to Labour conference, Bournemouth, 24 September 2007
40. Gordon Brown, speech to Labour conference, Bournemouth, 24 September 2007
41. Interview, Brown aide
42. Gordon Brown, speech to Labour conference, Bournemouth, 24 September 2007

43. Interview, Jon Cruddas
44. 'Brown's winning ways will take some beating', *Daily Telegraph*, 24 September 2007
45. *Sun*, 25 September 2007
46. Interview, Danny Finkelstein
47. Gordon Brown, speech to Labour conference, Bournemouth, 24 September 2007
48. Comment Central, www.timesonline.co.uk, 26 September 2007
49. Philip Webster and Sam Coates, 'Gordon Brown and his rehash speech', *The Times*, 27 September 2007
50. Interview, Brown inner circle
51. Interviews, Brown inner circle
52. Interview, Brown inner circle
53. Interview, Mariella Frostrup
54. Gordon Brown, remarks at conference Q & A, Bournemouth, 26 September 2007
55. *World at One*, BBC Radio 4, 26 September 2007
56. Interview, Cabinet minister
57. Interview, Cabinet minister
58. Interview, Hazel Blears
59. Interviews, Peter Hain and others
60. Interview, Jon Cruddas
61. Interview, Frank Field
62. *Guardian*, 27 September 2007
63. Interview, member of Number 10 Policy Unit
64. Interview, Cabinet minister
65. Interview, Cabinet minister
66. Labour, 41 per cent; Conservatives, 34 per cent; Lib Dems, 16 per cent. Best leader in a crisis? Brown, 60 per cent; Cameron, 13 per cent. Win election? Labour, 71 per cent; Conservatives, 12 per cent: Ipsos-MORI for the *Observer*, 30 September 2007
67. Conversation, member of Shadow Cabinet
68. Conversation, member of Shadow Cabinet
69. Conversation, member of Shadow Cabinet
70. About 6 per cent of estates, HM Treasury
71. Interview, Labour strategist
72. Interviews, Brown aides and Treasury officials
73. Interviews, Treasury officials
74. Interviews, Cabinet ministers and Treasury officials
75. Interviews, Labour officials
76. Interview, Cabinet minister
77. Gordon Brown, remarks to reporters in Baghdad, Iraq, 2 October 2007
78. *Today*, BBC Radio 4, 2 October 2007
79. David Cameron, speech to Conservative conference, Blackpool, 4 October 2007
80. Interview, Hazel Blears
81. Labour, 40 per cent; Tories, 36 per cent; Lib Dems, 13 per cent: YouGov for Channel 4, 4 October 2007
82. Labour, 39 per cent; Tories, 36 per cent; Lib Dems, 14 per cent: Populus for *The Times*, 5 October 2007
83. Labour, 38 per cent; Tories, 38 per cent; Lib Dems, 16 per cent: ICM for the *Guardian*, 5 October 2007
84. Interview, Brown aide
85. Interview, Cabinet minister
86. Interview, Brown inner circle
87. Interviews, Brown inner circle

88. Interview, Brown inner circle
89. Interview, Cabinet minister
90. Interviews, Brown inner circle
91. Interviews, Brown inner circle
92. Conversation, Cabinet minister
93. Conversation, Cabinet minister
94. Interview, Jon Cruddas
95. Interviews, Vince Cable and Michael Gove
96. Conversations, Conservative officials
97. Interview, BBC executive
98. Interview, Number 10 official
99. Conversation, Cabinet minister
100. Conversation, Cabinet minister
101. Conversation, Cabinet minister
102. Conversation, member of Shadow Cabinet
103. *Sunday Times*, 7 October 2007
104. Interviews, Number 10 officials
105. Gordon Brown, news conference, Number 10, 8 October 2007
106. Interview, Michael Gove
107. Conversation, member of Shadow Cabinet
108. Interview, Vince Cable
109. Interview, Nick Brown
110. Interview, Peter Hain
111. *Daily Telegraph*, 8 October 2007
112. Ibid.
113. *Today*, BBC Radio 4, 8 October 2007
114. Gordon Brown, news conference, Number 10, 8 October 2007
115. Hansard, 10 October 2007
116. Interview, Treasury minister
117. Interview, Cabinet minister
118. Interview, Cabinet minister
119. Interview, Alistair Darling
120. Hansard, 9 October 2007
121. Interview, Irwin Stelzer
122. Interview, Jon Cruddas
123. *Daily Telegraph*, 10 October 2007
124. Interview, Alistair Darling

30. It Eats My Soul

1. Interview, Alistair Darling
2. Interviews, Number 10 officials
3. Interviews, Brown aides
4. Conversations, Cabinet ministers
5. Hansard, 20 November 2007
6. *Daily Mail*, 21 November 2007
7. *Daily Mirror*, 21 November 2007
8. Interview, Jack Straw
9. Lords Hansard, 22 November 2007
10. Conversation, member of Shadow Cabinet
11. Interview, Jack Straw
12. Jonathan Oliver, 'Labour's third largest donor', *Mail on Sunday*, 25 November 2007
13. Political Parties, Elections and Referendums Act 2000
14. Michael White and Martin Wainwright, 'Labour in turmoil', *Guardian*, 27 November 2007
15. David Abrahams, 'All done in good faith', *Guardian*, 1 December 2007
16. Conversation, minister
17. Gordon Brown, Number 10 news conference, 27 November 2007
18. Interviews, Labour officials
19. Gordon Brown, Number 10 news conference, 27 November 2007
20. Patrick Wintour, 'Brown left exposed by donor row', *Guardian*, 29 November 2007

21. Ibid.
22. Gordon Brown, Number 10 news conference, 27 November 2007
23. Isabel Oakeshott, 'Brutal Brown sacrificed party chief', *Sunday Times*, 10 May 2009
24. Report by the Standards and Privileges Committee, 22 January 2009
25. Patrick Wintour and Michael White, 'Secret funder', *Guardian*, 1 December 2007
26. Conversation, Cabinet minister
27. Interview, Number 10 official
28. Interview, Matthew Taylor
29. Interview, Brown aide
30. Interviews, Brown inner circle
31. Interviews, Number 10 officials
32. Interview, civil servant
33. Interview, Brown inner circle
34. Interview, civil servant
35. Interview, civil servant
36. Interviews, Sue Cameron and civil servants
37. Interviews, civil servants
38. Interviews, civil servants
39. Private information
40. Hansard, 10 October 2007
41. Interviews, Number 10 officials
42. Conversations, Cabinet ministers
43. Interview, Murray Elder
44. Private interview
45. Conversation, Cabinet minister
46. Interview, Jacqui Smith
47. Interview, Matthew Taylor
48. Interview, Jack Straw
49. *Today*, BBC Radio 4, 30 April 2008
50. Interview, Number 10 official
51. Interview, Jack Straw
52. Interview, Jon Cruddas
53. Interview, senior civil servant
54. Interview, Geoff Hoon
55. Conversation, Number 10 official
56. Interview Irwin Stelzer
57. Interview, Alistair Darling
58. Interview, Harriet Harman
59. Interview, Murray Elder
60. Interview, Jack Straw
61. Interview, Sue Cameron
62. Interview, Number 10 official
63. Interview, civil servant
64. Interview, Cabinet minister
65. Interview, Murray Elder
66. Conversation, Cabinet minister
67. Interview, Vince Cable
68. Conversation, adviser to Cabinet minister
69. Interviews, civil servants
70. Interviews, civil servants
71. Conversation, Cabinet minister
72. Interview, civil servant
73. Interview, Matthew Taylor
74. Interview, John Kampfner
75. Interview, Sue Cameron
76. Conversations, Brown inner circle
77. Interview, minister
78. Conversation, Cabinet minister
79. Interview, Phil Collins
80. Interview, Brown aide
81. Interview, minister
82. Interview, Vince Cable
83. Hansard, 28 November 2007
84. Interview, Hazel Blears
85. Interview, Jack Straw
86. Interview, Vince Cable
87. Interview, Murray Elder

31. The Penny Drops

1. Interview, Nick Brown
2. Interview, Jon Cruddas
3. See Chapter 28
4. Interviews, Treasury officials
5. Conversations, ministers and Treasury officials
6. Interview, Irwin Stelzer
7. Interview, John McFall
8. Interviews, civil servants
9. Interview, senior civil servant
10. *Daily Mail*, 16 January 2008
11. Interview, Jack Straw
12. Interview, Alistair Darling
13. Interviews, Treasury officials
14. Interview, Treasury official
15. Interview, Alistair Darling
16. Interview, Alistair Darling
17. Interviews, Cabinet minister and Treasury officials
18. Darling, news conference, HM Treasury, London, 17 February 2008
19. Interview, senior Treasury official
20. Interviews, Treasury officials
21. Interview, Alistair Darling
22. Interview, Ken Purchase
23. Interviews, ministers
24. Interview, Treasury official
25. Interview, Alistair Darling
26. Halifax Index, 8 April 2008
27. Interview, Bank of England official
28. Hansard, 12 March 2008
29. Interview, John McFall
30. Interview, Labour strategist
31. Interview, Brown aide
32. See Chapter 26
33. Interview, Alistair Darling
34. Interview, Cabinet minister
35. Interviews, Labour MPs
36. Interview, minister
37. Interviews, Labour MPs
38. Report on the Budget, Treasury select committee, 7 April 2008
39. Interviews, Labour MPs
40. Interviews, Labour MPs
41. Interview, Nick Brown
42. Interview, Brown aide
43. Conversation, Cabinet minister
44. Polly Toynbee, 'This buffeted prime minister must stop scrambling at every puff of wind', *Guardian*, 11 April 2008
45. CBS News, 15 April 2008, cited on Nick Robinson's Newslog, BBC, 16 April 2008
46. *Good Morning America*, ABC, 16 April 2008
47. Anne McElvoy, 'Brown was put on earth . . .', *Evening Standard*, 17 April 2008
48. Interview, Mariella Frostrup
49. Interview, Vince Cable
50. Interview, Kathy Lette
51. Interview, Alistair Darling
52. Interview, Shami Chakrabati
53. *New Woman*, June 2006
54. *GQ*, October 2006
55. Interview, Matthew Taylor
56. Interviews, Brown aides
57. Conversation, minister
58. Interview, Jon Cruddas
59. BBC News, 20 April 2008
60. Interviews, Number 10 officials
61. Philip Webster, Sam Coates and Greg Hurst, 'I share your pain', *The Times*, 22 April 2008
62. Conversations, Labour MPs
63. Conversation, Cabinet minister; the Poll Tax was a major cause of the fall of Margaret Thatcher in 1990

64. Interviews, Labour MPs; Patrick Wintour and Nicholas Watt, 'You're dragging us to the edge', *Guardian*, 22 April 2008
65. Interviews, Cabinet ministers
66. Interview, Frank Field
67. Hansard, 23 April 2008
68. Conversations, Cabinet ministers
69. Hansard, 23 April 2008
70. *The Ten O'Clock News*, BBC1, 23 April 2008
71. *Daily Mail*, 24 April 2008
72. *The Times*, 24 April 2008
73. Interview, Peter Hain
74. Interview, Ken Livingstone
75. Conversation, Cabinet minister
76. Interview, Ken Livingstone
77. Interview, Nick Brown
78. Philip Webster, 'Brown bloodied in May Day massacre', *The Times*, 3 May 2008
79. Doing bad job as Prime Minister, 75 per cent; good job, 20 per cent: PHI 5000, www.politicshome.com, 11 May 2008
80. Interview, Brown aide

32. An Enemy in Need

1. ITV News, 27 March 2008
2. Interview, Irwin Stelzer
3. Interview, Kathy Lette
4. Interview, Alan West
5. Interview, Brown aide
6. Gordon Brown, 'On Liberty', speech at University of Westminster, London, 29 October 2007
7. Conversation, minister
8. Interview, Number 10 official
9. Interview, Brown aide
10. Interview, Brown aide
11. Interviews, Brown aides
12. Interview, Matthew Taylor
13. Interview, Murray Elder
14. Interviews, senior civil servants
15. Interviews, Number 10 officials
16. Interview, Number 10 official
17. Interviews, Number 10 officials
18. Interview, Brown aide
19. Private information
20. Interview, Brown aide
21. Interview, Brown aide
22. Interview, senior civil servant
23. Interview, Brown aide
24. Interview, Brown aide
25. Interview, senior civil servant
26. Interview, civil servant
27. Interview, Labour peer
28. Interview, Cabinet minister
29. Interview, civil servant
30. Interview, civil servant
31. Interview, senior civil servant
32. Interviews, Number 10 officials
33. Interview, Cabinet minister
34. Gordon Brown, 'On Liberty', speech at University of Westminster, London, 29 October 2007
35. Hansard, 3 July 2007
36. Interview, Sue Cameron
37. Interview, minister
38. Interview, Gordon Brown
39. Interview, Shami Chakrabati
40. See Chapter 20
41. Interview, Jon Cruddas
42. *Today*, BBC Radio 4, 14 November 2007
43. Interview, Alan West
44. Interview, Alan West
45. Interview, Brown aide
46. Interview, senior civil servant
47. Interview, Privy Counsellor
48. Interview, Brown aide
49. Interview, Labour MP

50. Interview, Labour peer
51. Interview, Brown aide
52. Interviews, Number 10 officials
53. Interviews, Number 10 officials
54. Interviews, Number 10 officials
55. Interviews, Number 10 officials and senior civil servants
56. Interviews, Neil Kinnock and others
57. Private interview
58. Peter Mandelson, Alcuin Lecture, Cambridge, 8 February 2008
59. Interview, Brown aide
60. Interview, Peter Mandelson
61. Interview, minister
62. Interview, Philip Gould
63. Interview, Brown aide
64. BBC News, 27 April 2008
65. *Servants of the People*, Chapter 12
66. Conversation, Cabinet minister
67. Interview, Brown aide
68. Interview, Brown aide
69. Private information

33. Assassins in the Shadows

1. *Hamlet*, Act III, scene ii
2. 'Cameron starts to look like a real leader', *Daily Mail*, 17 July 2008
3. Interviews, Brown inner circle
4. John Mason, speech at Tollcross Leisure Centre, Glasgow, 25 July 2008
5. Conversation, former Cabinet minister
6. BBC News, 28 July 2008
7. Conversation, Cabinet minister
8. Interview, Cabinet minister
9. Interview, minister
10. Barack Obama, remarks in Downing Street, 26 July 2008
11. Interview, Cabinet minister
12. Conversation, former Cabinet minister
13. Conversation, Cabinet minister
14. Interview, Peter Mandelson
15. Interviews, Cabinet ministers
16. Interviews, Cabinet ministers
17. Interview, Cabinet minister
18. Interviews, Cabinet ministers, former ministers and Labour MPs
19. David Miliband, 'A platform of change', *Guardian*, 30 July 2008
20. Conversation, Miliband ally
21. Interview, Brown aide
22. Interview, Brown aide
23. Joe Murphy and Nicholas Cecil, 'Brown's furious attack on "immature" Miliband', *Evening Standard*, 30 July 2008; Macer Hall and Gabriel Milland, 'Brown furious over Miliband "treachery"', *Daily Express*, 31 July 2008; Andy McSmith, James Macintyre and Nigel Morris, 'The smile of an assassin?', *Independent*, 31 July 2008
24. *Jeremy Vine Show*, BBC Radio 2, 31 July 2008
25. Interview, Cabinet minister
26. Interview, former Cabinet minister
27. Interviews, Cabinet ministers
28. Interview, Murray Elder
29. Interview, Mariella Frostrup
30. Simon Walters, 'Now will they let Gordon play?', *Mail on Sunday*, 18 June 2006
31. Private information

32. Interview, Brown aide
33. Interview, Brown inner circle
34. Interview, Number 10 official
35. Interviews, ministers and officials
36. Interview, Brown inner circle
37. Interview, Cabinet minister
38. Interviews, Treasury officials
39. Interview, Bank of England official
40. Interview, Number 10 official
41. Interview, Decca Aitkenhead
42. Decca Aitkenhead, 'Storm Warning', *Guardian Weekend*, 30 August 2008
43. Interview, Decca Aitkenhead
44. Decca Aitkenhead, 'Storm Warning', *Guardian Weekend*, 30 August 2008
45. Andrew Porter, 'Chancellor paints bleak picture', *Daily Telegraph*, 30 August 2008
46. Interview, Alistair Darling
47. Interviews, Treasury officials
48. BBC News, 30 August 2008
49. Interview, Nick Cohen
50. Interview, Treasury official
51. *The Times*, 1 September 2008
52. Interview, Treasury official
53. Private interview
54. Interview, Number 10 official
55. Interview, Cabinet minister
56. Interviews, Cabinet ministers
57. Interview, Brown inner circle
58. Interviews, senior civil servants
59. Interview, Brown aide
60. Interview, Brown aide
61. Ivan Lewis, 'We should tax the rich, not the middle class', *Sunday Times*, 17 August 2008
62. Ian Kirby and Sophy Ridge, 'Txt pest shame of Minister', *News of the World*, 7 September 2008
63. Glen Owen, 'Minister: "I'm sorry for sending suggestive texts to girl aide, 24"', *Mail on Sunday*, 7 September 2008
64. Interview, minister
65. Toby Helm, 'Vicious attack deepens Labour rift', *Observer*, 7 September 2008
66. Nick Cohen, 'Call off your Mafioso aides, Mr Brown', *Observer*, 14 September 2008
67. Interview, Number 10 official
68. Interview, Cabinet minister
69. *New Statesman*, 4 September 2008
70. *Today*, BBC Radio 4, 4 September 2008
71. Interviews, Cabinet ministers
72. Simon McGee and Brendan Carlin, 'The biggest question', *Mail on Sunday*, 14 September 2008
73. Interview, Cabinet minister
74. Interviews, Cabinet ministers and former Cabinet ministers
75. Interviews, Cabinet ministers
76. Newsnight, BBC2, 16 September 2008
77. Barry Gardiner, 'Brown's blown it', *Sunday Times*, 14 September 2008
78. Patrick Wintour, 'Rebels try to oust Brown', *Guardian*, 16 September 2008
79. Philip Webster, 'Minister quits in Brown challenge', *The Times*, 17 September 2008
80. Interviews, Number 10 officials
81. Patrick Wintour and Allegra Stratton, 'Ministers fuel talk of anti-Brown challenge', *Guardian*, 15 September 2008
82. Interview, Cabinet minister

83. Interviews, Cabinet ministers
84. Anne McElvoy and Joe Murphy, 'Brown humiliated as Ministers ignore him', *Evening Standard*, 17 September 2008
85. Patrick Wintour, 'Cabinet fury over complacency undermines PM', *Guardian*, 18 September 2008
86. Interview, Brown aide
87. Interview, former Cabinet minister
88. Interview, former Cabinet minister
89. Interview, Frank Field
90. *World at One*, BBC Radio 4, 16 September 2008
91. BBC News, 16 September 2008
92. See Chapter 34
93. Interview, Cabinet minister
94. Interviews, Cabinet ministers
95. Interview, Labour MP
96. Interview, Brown aide
97. Interview, Brown inner circle
98. Gordon Brown, speech to Labour conference, Manchester, 23 September 2008
99. Interviews, Cabinet ministers
100. Philip Webster, 'Brown digs in with attack on the novices', *The Times*, 24 September 2008
101. BBC News, 23 September 2008
102. *New Statesman*, 29 September 2008
103. Interviews and conversations, Cabinet ministers and former Cabinet ministers
104. Interview, Peter Mandelson
105. Interview, Peter Mandelson
106. Interview, friend of Peter Mandelson
107. Peter Mandelson, remarks in Downing Street, 3 October 2008
108. An exception is Donald Macintyre, Mandelson's biographer, who had long ago suggested it might happen
109. Conversation, Cabinet minister; *Daily Mail*, 4 October 2008
110. 'Gambling on Mandelson', *Guardian*, 4 October 2008
111. 'Mandelson rises from political dead', *Financial Times*, 4 October 2008
112. Gordon Brown, Number 10 news conference, 3 October 2008
113. Conversation, Cabinet minister
114. Conversation, Cabinet minister
115. Interview, James Purnell
116. Interviews, Cabinet ministers
117. Conversation, Cabinet minister
118. Interview, Cabinet minister
119. Interview, minister

34. The Great Escape

1. Interview, minister
2. Conversation, Cabinet minister
3. Interview, Alistair Darling
4. Interview, John Gieve
5. Interviews, Alistair Darling and Treasury officials
6. James Stewart, 'Eight Days', *New Yorker*, 21 September 2009
7. Interview, Alistair Darling
8. Interview, Alistair Darling
9. Interviews, Treasury officials
10. Interview, John Gieve
11. Interview, John Eatwell
12. Interview, Steve Robson
13. Interview, John Gieve
14. Interview, John Eatwell
15. Interview, Alistair Darling
16. Interview, Chairman of retail bank

17. Interview, Alistair Darling
18. Siobhan Kennedy, *The Times*, 22 September 2008
19. Interview, Alistair Darling
20. Interview, senior Treasury official
21. Interview, Chairman of retail bank
22. The Banking Act 2008
23. Interview, senior Treasury official
24. BBC News, 1 October 2008
25. Interview, Alistair Darling
26. Interview, senior civil servant
27. Interview, Alistair Darling
28. Interview, minister
29. Interviews, ministers
30. Interviews, ministers and officials
31. Andrew Porter, 'Brown Air', www.telegraph.co.uk, 24 September 2008
32. Gordon Brown, speech to UN General Assembly, New York, 25 September 2008
33. Conversation, Cabinet minister
34. Interview, senior civil servants and ministers
35. Interview, Number 10 official
36. Interviews, ministers and officials
37. Interview, senior Treasury official
38. Peter Thal Larsen, 'Goodwin's undoing', *Financial Times*, 25 February 2009
39. Interview, John Eatwell
40. Interview, George Osborne
41. Interview, Peter Mandelson
42. Interview, minister
43. Interview, Alistair Darling
44. Interview, Paul Myners
45. Interviews, ministers and officials
46. Interviews, Treasury officials
47. Interview, senior Treasury official
48. Interview, Chairman of retail bank
49. Interview, Alistair Darling
50. Interview, Treasury official
51. Interview, John Gieve
52. Interview, Paul Myners
53. Interview, Alistair Darling
54. Interviews, Nick Cohen and Alistair Darling
55. Interviews, ministers and Number 10 officials
56. Peston's Picks, www.bbc.co.uk/blogs/thereporters/robertpeston, 0700, 7 October 2008
57. Interview, Chairman of retail bank
58. Interview, senior Treasury official
59. Interview, Chairman of retail bank
60. Interview, Chairman of retail bank
61. Interviews, Treasury officials
62. Interviews, Treasury officials
63. Interview, Christine Lagarde
64. Interview, Christine Lagarde
65. Interview, Alistair Darling
66. Interviews, Treasury officials
67. Interviews, Alistair Darling and others
68. Interviews, ministers and officials
69. Interview, senior civil servant
70. Interview, Paul Myners
71. Interview, senior Treasury official
72. Interview, John Gieve
73. Interview, senior Treasury official
74. Interviews, ministers and officials
75. Interview, Alistair Darling
76. Interview, senior Treasury official
77. Interview, John Gieve

78. Interview, Treasury official
79. Interview, Treasury official
80. *The Love of Money*, BBC2, 24 September 2009
81. Interviews, ministers and Number 10 officials
82. *The Love of Money*, BBC2, 24 September 2009
83. Interview, minister
84. Interview, Paul Myners
85. Gordon Brown, news conference, Number 10, 8 October 2008
86. Interviews, Number 10 and Treasury officials
87. Interviews, Bank of England and Number 10 officials
88. Hansard, 8 October 2008
89. Gordon Brown, ad lib at Powerlist 2008 dinner, Foreign Office, London, 8 October 2008
90. Interview, minister
91. Interviews, ministers and officials
92. Reuters, 11 October 2008
93. Interview, Paul Myners
94. Gordon Brown, Number 10 Podcast, 10 October 2008
95. Interview, John Gieve
96. Interview, Alistair Darling
97. Interviews, senior Treasury officials
98. Interview, John Eatwell
99. Interview, Alistair Darling
100. Interview, Paul Myners
101. Interview, John Gieve
102. *The Times*, 14 December 2008
103. Interview, John Eatwell
104. Interview, Alistair Darling
105. Interview, senior Treasury official
106. Interviews, senior Treasury officials
107. Interview, senior Treasury official
108. Interviews, Treasury officials
109. Interviews, Treasury officials
110. Heather Stewart et al., 'The biggest bet in the world', *Observer*, 12 October 2008
111. Communiqué, G7 Finance Ministers, Washington, 11 October 2008
112. Tom Fletcher cited in George Parker, 'His finest moment', *Financial Times*, 14 October 2009
113. Francis Elliott and David Wighton, 'How Brown took the credit', *The Times*, 18 October 2008
114. Interview, minister
115. Paul Krugman, 'Has Gordon Brown saved the world financial system?', *New York Times*, 12 October 2008
116. Interview, Paul Myners
117. Interview, senior Treasury official
118. Interview, John Gieve
119. Interview, Director of retail bank
120. Interview, senior Treasury official
121. Interviews, John Gieve and others
122. Interview, senior Treasury official
123. Interview, minister
124. Paul Myners, evidence to Treasury select committee, 17 March 2009; Sir Tom McKillop, letter to Treasury select committee, 31 March 2009
125. Interview, minister
126. Interview, George Mudie
127. Interview, Paul Myners
128. Interview, Treasury official
129. Interviews, Alistair Darling, Bank of England officials and Treasury officials

130. Interviews, Alistair Darling and Treasury officials
131. Interview, Paul Myners
132. Interviews, Treasury officials
133. Interview, Alistair Darling
134. Interview, minister
135. Interviews, Paul Myners and others
136. Interview, minister
137. Interview, Paul Myners
138. Gordon Brown, Number 10 news conference, 13 October 2008
139. Interview, John Gieve
140. Interview, senior civil servant
141. Interview, Paul Myners
142. Interview, James Purnell
143. Interview, Peter Mandelson

35. Land Without Maps

1. Conversation, Cabinet minister
2. Interview, Peter Mandelson
3. Interview, Mark Malloch-Brown
4. Interview, Jon Cruddas
5. *Sunday Mirror*, 12 October 2008
6. *Journal du Dimanche*, 12 October 2008
7. Patrick Wintour, Saturday Interview, *Guardian*, 29 November 2008
8. Conversation, Brown aide
9. How has Gordon Brown been handling the crisis? Well, 61 per cent; badly, 33 per cent: ICM for the *Guardian*, 21 October 2008
10. Interview, Number 10 official
11. Conversation, Cabinet minister
12. Toby Helm, 'Resurgent Brown', *Observer*, 23 November 2008
13. Interview, Privy Counsellor
14. Alistair Darling, Mais Lecture, London, 29 October 2008
15. Gordon Brown, speech to CBI conference, 24 November 2008
16. Gordon Brown, speech to Council on Foreign Relations, New York, 13 November 2008
17. Conservative, 40 per cent (down 5); Labour, 37 per cent (up 7); Liberal Democrats, 12 per cent (down 2): Ipsos-MORI, 19 November 2008. Conservative, 37 per cent; Labour, 36 per cent; Liberal Democrats, 17 per cent: ComRes for *Independent on Sunday*, 30 November 2008
18. Interviews, Members of Shadow Cabinet
19. Martin Ivens, 'Mandelson damned PM to top Tory', *Sunday Times*, 5 October 2008
20. Letters to the editor, *The Times*, 21 October 2008
21. Better Prime Minister to deal with Britain's economy in recession? Brown, 52 per cent; Cameron, 32 per cent: Populus for *The Times*, 11 November 2008
22. House prices fell by 18.9 per cent in 2008 on the Halifax Index, *Observer*, 11 January 2009
23. Interview, John McFall
24. Interviews, Treasury officials
25. Interviews, Cabinet ministers, Number 10 officials and Treasury officials
26. Interview, Frank Field
27. Interview, Digby Jones
28. Interview, Paul Everitt
29. *Independent*, 25 November 2008
30. *Guardian*, 25 November 2008
31. *Daily Telegraph*, 25 November 2008

32. *The Times*, 25 November 2008
33. Hansard, 24 November 2008
34. *Newsweek*, 11 December 2008
35. Interview, Number 10 official
36. TF1, 5 February 2009
37. Interview, Christine Lagarde
38. David Cameron, speech at the London School of Economics, London, 9 December 2008
39. Hansard, 10 December 2008
40. Interviews, Treasury officials
41. Interview, John Eatwell
42. Interview, Alistair Darling
43. Interviews, bank executives and Treasury officials
44. Interview, Cabinet minister
45. Interview, Cabinet minister
46. Conversation, Cabinet minister
47. Conversation, Cabinet minister
48. Interview, minister
49. Interviews, minister and officials
50. Interview, Alistair Darling
51. Tony Blair, speech to New World Capitalism conference, Paris, 8 January 2009
52. Gordon Brown, speech in Davos, Switzerland, 31 January 2009
53. Gordon Brown, Number 10 news conference, 8 October 2008
54. Interview, Paul Myners
55. Interviews, Number 10 officials
56. Interview, Paul Myners
57. Gordon Brown, Number 10 news conference, 19 January 2009
58. Interview, Vince Cable
59. Conversation, Cabinet minister
60. HM Treasury; IMF; Cresc study, Manchester University
61. World Economic Outlook, IMF, 28 January 2009
62. *The Times*, 29 January 2009
63. *Independent*, 29 January 2009
64. Interview, Paul Myners
65. Interviews, Treasury officials
66. Patrick Hosking and Philip Webster, 'Bailed-out bankers set for millions in bonuses', *The Times*, 5 February 2009
67. Patrick Hosking and Philip Webster, 'Stampede by banks to beat bonus crackdown', *The Times*, 6 February 2009
68. *Observer*, 8 February 2009
69. Harriet Harman, speech to Labour regional conference, Sheffield, 7 February 2009
70. Conversations, Cabinet ministers
71. *GMTV*, 8 October 2008
72. Conversation, Cabinet minister
73. Interviews, Cabinet ministers
74. Interview, Cabinet minister
75. Interviews, ministers and Treasury officials
76. Interview, Digby Jones
77. Interview, Jon Cruddas
78. Evidence to Treasury select committee, 11 February 2009
79. David Cameron, speech in Davos, Switzerland, 30 January 2009
80. 89 per cent thought Government should have stopped bailed-out banks paying bonuses; 82 per cent wanted bonuses capped: Populus for *The Times*, 13 February 2009
81. Interview, Cabinet minister
82. Interview, Paul Myners
83. Jonathan Oliver et al., 'Payback time for culture of greed', *Sunday Times*, 1 March 2009
84. *Daily Mirror*, 26 February 2009
85. 'Dirty tricks as Darling dozes at

the wheel', *Daily Telegraph*, 27
February 2009
86. *Today*, BBC Radio 4, 26
February 2009
87. Number 10 briefing, 26
February 2009
88. Hansard, 26 February 2009
89. Jill Treanor and Patrick Wintour,
'RBS boss: minister approved
my pension and I'm keeping it',
Guardian, 27 February 2009
90. Andrew Rawnsley, 'Mandelson
shows he's ready for a fight',
Observer, 1 March 2009
91. *The Andrew Marr Show*, BBC1,
1 March 2009
92. Interviews, Cabinet ministers
and officials
93. Phillip Inman and Chris
Tryhorn, 'Fred finally shreds his
own pension', *Guardian*, 19
June 2009
94. Conversation, Brown aide
95. Interviews, Cabinet ministers
and officials
96. *Financial Times*, 12 January 2009
97. *Guardian*, 13 January 2009
98. Interview, Jon Cruddas
99. Interview, Hazel Blears
100. Heather Stewart and Hilary
Osborne, 'One family helped',
Guardian, 1 May 2009
101. Interviews, Cabinet ministers
102. Interview, Cabinet minister
103. Peter Mandelson, remarks to
Council on Foreign Relations,
New York, 17 February 2009
104. Jean Eaglesham, 'Flagship
scheme hit by delays', *Financial
Times*, 2 March 2009
105. Interview, Paul Everitt
106. Lords Hansard, 27 January
2009

107. Interview, Paul Everitt
108. Interviews, Paul Everitt and
Derek Simpson
109. Conversation, friend of Mandelson
110. Interview, Brown aide
111. Hansard, 25 February 2009
112. Ibid., 28 January 2009
113. Interview, Brown aide
114. Hansard, 4 February 2009
115. Interviews, Brown aides
116. Interview, minister
117. *Today*, BBC Radio 4, 23
January 2009
118. Alan Greenspan, testimony to
House Oversight Committee, 23
October 2008
119. Conversation, Cabinet minister
120. Interview, Cabinet minister
121. Sky News, 5 March 2009
122. Alistair Darling, evidence to
House of Lords Economic
Affairs Committee, 3 February
2009
123. *Daily Telegraph*, 3 March 2009
124. Gordon Brown, evidence to
Liaison Committee, 12 February
2009
125. Jackie Ashley, *Guardian*, 16
February 2009
126. Interview, Number 10 official
127. Interview, Brown aide
128. Private interview
129. Interviews, Cabinet ministers
130. Mervyn King, evidence to
Treasury select committee, 24
March 2009
131. Edmund Conway, '£150 billion
leap in the dark', *Daily Telegraph*, 6 March 2009
132. Conversation, Cabinet minister
133. ICM for the *Guardian*, 24
February 2009

36. Trillion Dollar Man

1. Interviews, Number 10 officials
2. Conversation, Number 10 official
3. Interview, Foreign Office official
4. Interview, Number 10 official
5. Interview, Mark Malloch-Brown
6. Interview, Number 10 official
7. See Chapter 12
8. Interview, Number 10 official
9. Conversation, Cabinet minister
10. Interviews, Number 10 officials
11. Brown–Obama news conference, White House, 3 March 2009
12. Interview, Number 10 official
13. Interview, Number 10 official
14. Interview, Number 10 official
15. Interview, Mark Malloch-Brown
16. Interviews, Brown aides
17. Gordon Brown, address to Congress, Washington, 4 March 2009
18. Interview, Number 10 official
19. Interviews, Number 10 officials
20. Interviews, Number 10 officials
21. Interview, Number 10 official
22. Interview, senior Treasury official
23. Brown–Obama news conference, White House, 3 March 2009
24. Gordon Brown, speech at Reuters HQ, Canary Wharf, London, 14 October 2008; news conference, Washington, 15 November 2008
25. Conversation, Cabinet minister
26. Interviews, Cabinet ministers
27. Interviews, Cabinet ministers and officials
28. Interview, senior civil servant
29. Interview, Mark Malloch-Brown
30. Gordon Brown, speech at the European parliament, Strasbourg, 24 March 2009
31. Mervyn King, evidence to Treasury select committee, 24 March 2009
32. Interview, Bank of England official
33. BBC News, 24 March 2009
34. Hansard, 25 March 2009
35. Interview, George Mudie
36. Gordon Brown, speech at the Plaza Hotel, New York, 25 March 2009
37. Conversation, Cabinet minister
38. Brown–Lula news conference, Brasilia, Brazil, 26 March 2009
39. Bachelet–Brown news conference, Santiago, Chile, 27 March 2009
40. BBC News, 27 March 2009
41. Interview, Peter Mandelson
42. Daniel Drezner, *Newsweek*, 30 March 2009
43. *Guardian*, 28 March 2009
44. Interview, Number 10 official
45. Interview, Mark Malloch-Brown
46. Conversation, Cabinet minister
47. Brown–Obama news conference, London, 1 April 2009
48. Private information
49. Merkel–Sarkozy news conference, London, 1 April 2009
50. OECD
51. Interviews, French and German diplomats
52. Brown–Obama news conference, London, 1 April 2009
53. Interview, Mark Malloch-Brown
54. Interview, Cabinet minister
55. YouTube, 1 April 2009
56. *Corriere Della Serra*, 3 April 2009

57. Interviews, Number 10 officials
58. *Financial Times*, 3 April 2009
59. Interview, British official
60. Interview, British official
61. Interview, Number 10 official
62. Interview, Number 10 official
63. Interviews, diplomats and officials
64. Interview, minister
65. Interviews, British officials
66. Interview, Mark Malloch-Brown
67. Interview, senior civil servant
68. Interview, Number 10 official
69. Interviews, Mark Malloch-Brown and others
70. Nicolas Sarkozy, news conference, ExCeL Centre, London, 2 April 2009
71. Interviews, ministers and officials
72. Interview, Number 10 official
73. Interview, British official
74. Interview, Mark Malloch-Brown
75. Interview, Peter Mandelson
76. *Libération*, 3 April 2009
77. Gordon Brown, news conference, ExCeL Centre, London, 2 April 2009
78. Final Communiqué, London Summit, 2 April 2009
79. Nicolas Sarkozy, news conference, ExCeL Centre, London, 2 April 2009
80. Barack Obama, news conference, ExCeL Centre, London, 2 April 2009
81. Angela Merkel, news conference, ExCeL Centre, London, 2 April 2009
82. Dmitry Medvedev, news conference, ExCeL Centre, London, 2 April 2009
83. *Newsnight*, BBC2, 2 April 2009
84. 'Bankers rage at G20 "witch hunt" against bonuses and buccaneers', *Guardian*, 4 April 2009
85. *Independent*, 4 April 2009
86. Interview, Brown aide
87. Conversation, member of Shadow Cabinet
88. Interview, Mark Malloch-Brown
89. Interview, Philip Gould
90. Tristram Hunt, *Guardian*, 4 April 2009
91. *The Times*, 3 April 2009
92. *Daily Telegraph*, 3 April 2009
93. *Financial Times*, 3 April 2009
94. *Washington Post*, 3 April 2009
95. *Le Monde*, 3 April 2009
96. *People's Daily*, 4 April 2009
97. Interview, senior civil servant
98. Interview, Brown aide
99. Interview, Mark Malloch-Brown

37. Chamber of Horrors

1. Interview, Cabinet minister
2. Interview, Peter Mandelson
3. 'Emails that toppled key Brown aide', *Sunday Times*, 12 April 2009
4. Damian McBride interview with James Robinson, *Media Guardian*, 20 July 2009
5. Interviews, Cabinet ministers
6. Interview, Brown inner circle
7. Interviews, Number 10 officials
8. Rachel Sylvester, 'Brown's loyal attack dogs always bite to order', *The Times*, 14 April 2009
9. Armando Iannucci quoted in the *Independent*, 15 April 2009
10. Steve Richards, 'This fiasco may have fatally damaged . . .', *Independent*, 14 April 2009

11. *Newsnight*, BBC2, 14 April 2009
12. Interview, Brown aide
13. Interview, Brown inner circle
14. Interview, Cabinet minister
15. Gordon Brown, remarks about McBride smears, Glasgow, 16 April 2009
16. Conversation, Cabinet minister
17. 'Lodger deal earns Jacqui Smith £100,000', *Mail on Sunday*, 8 February 2009
18. Jason Groves and Marco Giannangeli, 'Jacqui Smith puts adult films on expenses', *Sunday Express*, 29 February 2009
19. Kirsty Walker and Ryan Kisiel, 'Minister's £60,000 expenses for parents' home', *Mail on Sunday*, 22 March 2009
20. Interviews, Number 10 officials
21. Hansard, 30 April 2009
22. Interview, Number 10 official
23. Interviews, Cabinet ministers
24. Interview, minister
25. Interview, Cabinet minister; Philip Snowden, Labour's first ever Chancellor in 1924, and Chancellor again between 1929 and 1931, is generally regarded by historians as a disastrous holder of the office
26. Interview, Treasury official
27. Interviews, Treasury officials; Patrick Hennessy, 'How 50p split the Cabinet', *Sunday Telegraph*, 26 April 2009
28. Interview, Peter Mandelson
29. Interviews, Treasury officials
30. Treasury select committee report, 6 May 2009
31. Hansard, 27 April 2009
32. Interview, Liberal Democrat MP
33. Interviews, Cabinet ministers
34. Interview, Cabinet minister
35. Joanna Lumley, Evidence to Home Affairs committee, 5 May 2009
36. Conversations, Cabinet ministers
37. Interviews, Cabinet ministers
38. Hansard, 29 April 2009
39. Private information
40. Interview, Cabinet minister
41. BBC News, 29 April 2009
42. Hansard, 30 April 2009
43. Simon Carr, 'United only in despair', *Independent*, 1 May 2009
44. Hazel Blears, 'YouTube if you want to', *Observer*, 3 May 2009
45. Private information
46. Interview, Cabinet minister
47. *Daily Telegraph*, 8 May 2009
48. Interview, senior civil servant
49. *Daily Telegraph*, 8 May 2009
50. Ibid., 10 May 2009
51. Ibid., 8 May 2009
52. Ibid., 9 May 2009
53. Nicholas Watt, 'Ministers on defensive', *Guardian*, 9 May 2009
54. *Evening Standard*, 8 May 2009
55. *Question Time*, BBC1, 14 May 2009
56. Interviews, ministers and Number 10 officials
57. Interview, senior civil servant
58. Gordon Brown, Speech to the Royal College of Nursing, 11 May 2009
59. *Daily Telegraph*, 12 May 2009
60. Ibid., 21 May 2009
61. Ibid., 12 May 2009
62. Interviews, Cabinet ministers
63. Interview, Cameron aide
64. David Cameron, news conference, London, 12 May 2009

65. David Cameron, news conference, London, 12 May 2009
66. *Daily Telegraph*, 13 May 2009
67. *Guardian*, 13 May 2009
68. *The Times*, 13 May 2009
69. Who has handled expenses scandal best? Cameron, 57 per cent; Brown, 11 per cent; Clegg, 11 per cent: YouGov, 17 May 2009. Which leader most badly damaged? Cameron, 5 per cent; Brown, 62 per cent; Clegg, 1 per cent; All equally, 25 per cent: Populus for *The Times*, 30 May 2009
70. Interviews, Cabinet ministers and aides
71. Sky News, 12 May 2009
72. The money came from her husband's savings towards a new motorbike
73. *This Week*, BBC1, 14 May 2009
74. For the Hansard Society, cited in the *Financial Times*, 23 May 2009
75. Figures released by Fees Office, 18 June 2009
76. Andrew Grice, 'The married couple who took taxpayers for £282,731', *Independent*, 15 May 2009
77. *Daily Telegraph*, 14 May 2009
78. Andrew Sparrow, '"Sullied" members suspend two peers', *Guardian*, 21 May 2009
79. Interviews, Cabinet ministers
80. Interview, Number 10 official
81. Gordon Brown, news conference, Downing Street, 19 May 2009
82. Interview, Cabinet minister
83. Philip Webster, 'Smith and Blears likely to carry can', *The Times*, 11 May 2009
84. Interview, Number 10 official
85. Interview, friend of Blears
86. Interview, Number 10 official
87. Hansard, 3 June 2009
88. *Daily Mail*, 4 June 2009
89. *Financial Times*, 4 June 2009
90. 'Labour's dilemma', *Guardian*, 3 June 2009
91. Patrick Hennessy, 'Darling could replace Smith in nuclear option reshuffle', *Sunday Telegraph*, 10 May 2009; George Parker, 'Brown considers Mandelson for Foreign Secretary after June polls', *Financial Times*, 21 May 2009; Isabel Oakeshott, 'PM wants Balls as Chancellor', *Sunday Times*, 31 May 2009; Patrick Wintour and Nicholas Watt, 'Beleaguered Darling faces reshuffle axe', *Guardian*, 2 June 2009
92. Interviews, civil servants
93. Hansard, 3 June 2009
94. BBC News, 1 June 2009
95. Interview, Treasury official
96. Interviews, Cabinet ministers
97. Interviews, Cabinet ministers and officials
98. Interviews, Cabinet ministers and officials
99. Interviews, Cabinet ministers
100. Interviews, Cabinet ministers
101. Allegra Stratton, 'Life after Cabinet', *Guardian*, 18 July 2009
102. Interview, Tessa Jowell
103. Interviews, Cabinet ministers
104. Interviews, Cabinet ministers and officials
105. *Sun*, 5 June 2009
106. Interview, Number 10 official
107. Interviews, Cabinet ministers

108. Private information
109. Interview, Cabinet minister
110. Interviews, Cabinet ministers and former Cabinet ministers
111. Gaby Hinsliff and Carole Cadwalladr, 'Angry Flint in fresh attack', *Observer*, 7 June 2009
112. Interview, Cabinet minister
113. Interview, Cabinet minister
114. Interview, Cabinet minister
115. Interview, Cabinet minister
116. Interviews, Cabinet ministers
117. Interview, Cabinet minister
118. Interview, Barry Sheerman
119. Gordon Brown, news conference, Downing Street, 5 June 2009
120. BBC News, 5 June 2009
121. Interview, Tessa Jowell
122. Conversation, Labour MP
123. Interviews, Labour MPs
124. Interview, former Cabinet minister
125. Hansard, 10 June 2009
126. Interviews, Labour MPs

38. No Time to Lose

1. Gordon Brown, remarks at Camp Bastion, Afghanistan, 29 August 2009
2. Interviews, Number 10 officials
3. Jim Pickard, 'Mandelson met Gaddafi's son', *Financial Times*, 17 August 2009
4. Text released by Number 10, 22 August 2009
5. Gaby Hinsliff, 'Brown in new storm over freed terrorist', *Observer*, 23 August 2009
6. Interviews, Number 10 officials
7. Interview, senior civil servant
8. Interview, Number 10 official
9. Andrew Alderson, Patrick Hennessy and Colin Freeman, 'The Libyan connection', *Sunday Telegraph*, 23 August 2009
10. See Chapter 14
11. Jason Allardyce, 'Lockerbie bomber "set free for oil"', *Sunday Times*, 30 August 2009
12. Mary Riddell, 'Straw admits oil link', *Daily Telegraph*, 5 September 2009
13. Brown–Netanyahu news conference, Number 10, 25 August 2009
14. Interview, Cabinet minister
15. BBC News, 1 September 2009
16. Gordon Brown, statement on al-Megrahi, Birmingham, 2 September 2009
17. Dominic Lawson, 'The Prime Minister's silence is eloquent', *Independent*, 25 August 2009
18. Only 16 per cent thought Brown was doing a good job as PM: YouGov for the *Sun*, 3 September 2009
19. Interviews, Number 10 officials
20. Eric Joyce, resignation letter to Prime Minister, 3 September 2009
21. Barack Obama, speech to military veterans, 17 August 2009
22. 53 per cent thought British troops should not have been deployed to Afghanistan: ICM for National Army Museum, 9 September 2009; 68 per cent wanted troops withdrawn immediately or within a year: Populus for the *Times*, 14 October 2009; 57 per cent

thought the mission could not succeed: YouGov for *Channel 4 News*, 5 November 2009

23. *Servants of the People*, p. 159
24. *Sun*, 6 October 2009
25. Lords Hansard, 6 November 2009
26. See Chapter 3
27. See Chapter 23
28. Interview, Alan West
29. Kim Sengupta, 'Afghan critic quits', *Independent*, 25 September 2009
30. *Economist*, 30 January 2009
31. Mark Townsend, 'British troops put Taliban on the run', *Observer*, 1 June 2008
32. Ewen MacAskill and Nicholas Watt, 'US commander calls for hearts and minds', *Guardian*, 1 September 2009
33. Figures released by MoD
34. Gordon Brown, speech to International Institute for Strategic Studies, London, 4 September 2009
35. Kim Sengupta, 'Killed by the enemy within', *Independent*, 5 November 2009
36. Gordon Brown, speech to Royal College of Defence Studies, London, 6 November 2009
37. GFK NOP for the *Independent*, 11 November 2009
38. Gordon Brown, speech to Lord Mayor's Banquet, Guildhall, London, 16 November 2009
39. BBC News, 22 October 2009
40. *Daily Politics*, BBC2, 14 October 2009
41. *Channel 4 News*, 14 October 2009
42. *Daily Mail*, 23 September 2009
43. Patrick Wintour, 'Obama snubs Brown', *Guardian*, 24 September 2009
44. Toby Helm, Gaby Hinsliff and Heather Stewart, 'Labour has "lost the will to live"', *Observer* 27 September 2009
45. Peter Mandelson, speech to Labour conference, Brighton, 28 September 2009
46. *Observer* conference interview, Andrew Rawnsley with Peter Mandelson, Brighton, 28 September 2009
47. Interviews, Brown aides
48. Interview, minister
49. 'Sarah Brown section', www.number10.gov.uk
50. Interviews and conversations, Brown aides and Cabinet ministers
51. Sarah Brown, remarks to Labour conference, Brighton, 29 September 2009
52. Gordon Brown, speech to Labour conference, Brighton, 29 September 2009
53. Peter Mandelson, speech to Labour conference, Brighton 28 September 2009
54. *Sun*, 30 September 2009
55. Interview, minister
56. Tom Newton Dunn, 'Bloody shameful', *Sun*, 9 November 2009
57. Conversations, Brown aides
58. Tom Newton Dunn, 'PM couldn't even get our name right', *Sun*, 9 November 2009
59. Interviews, Number 10 officials
60. Interview, Brown aide
61. Gordon Brown, Number 10

news conference, 10 November 2009

62. Simon Hoggart, 'This should not be allowed', *Guardian*, 11 November 2009

63. 60 per cent of voters thought the *Sun* was unfair to Brown: ComRes for the *Independent on Sunday*, 15 November 2009

64. Interviews, Brown aides

65. Interview, Blair inner circle

66. Interview, Number 10 official

67. BBC News, 25 October 2009

68. Nigel Morris, Vanessa Mock and Tony Paterson, 'Support for Blair crumbles', *Independent*, 30 October 2009

69. *Süddeutsche Zeitung*, 30 October 2009

70. Andrew Grice, 'Blair happy to be out of the race', *Independent*, 21 November 2009

71. Conversations and interviews, Cabinet ministers and civil servants

72. George Parker, 'A tale of ambition and sheer desperation', *Financial Times*, 21 November 2009

73. Nicholas Watt and Ian Traynor, 'From obscurity to the most powerful woman', *Guardian*, 20 November 2009

74. 'A pitiful exercise in Euro-mini-malism', *Financial Times*, 21 November 2009

75. Conversations, Cabinet ministers

76. Philip Webster, David Charter and Francis Elliott, 'Brown went for second best', *The Times*, 21 November 2009

77. Peter Kellner, 'Labour's lost voters', *Progress*, October 2009

78. Interviews, Cabinet ministers

79. Conversation, Treasury Minister

80. Hansard, 3 November 2009

81. 32 per cent satisfied/62 per cent dissatisfied with Brown's performance as Prime Minister: Ipsos-MORI, 20 October 2009

82. Best Prime Minister. Cameron, 43 per cent; Brown, 20 per cent: ICM for *News of the World*, 27 September 2009

83. Interviews, Cabinet ministers and former Cabinet ministers

Broadcast and Published Sources

DOCUMENTARIES

The Rise and Fall of Tony Blair, written and presented by Andrew Rawnsley, BrookLapping for Channel 4, June 2007

The Blair Years, interviews by David Aaronovitch, Mentorn for BBC1, November 2007

The Undercover Diplomat, written and presented by Jonathan Powell, Juniper for BBC2, April 2008

Gordon Brown: Where Did It All Go Wrong?, written and presented by Andrew Rawnsley, BrookLapping for Channel 4, June 2008

Crash Gordon: The Inside Story of the Financial Crisis, written and presented by Andrew Rawnsley, BrookLapping for Channel 4, June 2009

The Love of Money, Money Programme for BBC2, September 2009

LITERATURE

Adams, Gerry, *Hope and History* (Dingle: Brandon, 2004)

Ahern, Bertie, *Bertie Ahern: The Autobiography* (London: Hutchinson, 2009)

Allawi, Ali, *The Occupation of Iraq* (Yale University Press, 2007)

Allen, Graham, *The Last Prime Minister* (London: Politico's, 2003)

Ashdown, Paddy, *The Ashdown Diaries, Volume I 1988–1997* (London: Penguin, 2000)

—, *The Ashdown Diaries, Volume II 1997–1999* (London: Penguin, 2002)

Atkinson, Dan and Larry Elliot, *Fantasy Island* (London: Constable Robinson, 2007)

Attlee, Clement, *As It Happened* (London: Heinemann, 1954)

Augar, Philip, *Chasing Alpha* (London: Bodley Head, 2009)

Bagehot, Walter, *The Collected Works* (Oxford: OUP, 1986)

Balls, Ed and Gus O'Donnell (eds.), *Reforming Britain's Economic and Financial Policy* (Basingstoke: Palgrave Macmillan, 2002)

Barber, Michael, *Instruction to Deliver* (London: Politico's, 2007)

Barker, Tony, *Ruling by Task Force* (London: Politico's, 1999)

Bartle, John and Anthony King (eds.) *Britain at the Polls 2005* (Washington: CQ Press, 2006)

Beckett, Francis, *Gordon Brown* (London: Haus, 2007)

Bew, John, Martyn Frampton and Inigo Gurruchaga, *Talking to Terrorists* (London: Hurst, 2009)

Blair, Cherie, *Speaking for Myself* (London: Little, Brown, 2008)

Blair, Tony, *New Britain* (London: Fourth Estate, 1996)

—, *The Third Way: New Politics for the New Century* (London: Fabian Society Pamphlet, 1998)

—, *The Courage of Our Convictions* (London: Fabian Society Pamphlet, 2002)

Blix, Hans, *Disarming Iraq* (London: Bloomsbury, 2004)

Blunkett, David, *On a Clear Day* (London: Michael O'Mara, 1995)

—, *The Blunkett Tapes* (London: Bloomsbury, 2006)

Bogdanor, Vernon, *The New British Constitution* (Oxford: Hart, 2009)

Boulton, Adam, *Memories of the Blair Administration* (London: Simon & Schuster, 2008)

Bower, Tom, *Gordon Brown* (London: HarperCollins, 2004)

Bremer, Paul, *My Year in Iraq* (New York: Simon & Schuster, 2006)

Brivati, Brian and Richard Heffernan, *The Labour Party: A Centenary History* (Basingstoke: Palgrave Macmillan, 2000)

Brown, Colin, *Prescott: The Biography* (London: Politico's, 2005)

Brown, Gordon (ed.), *The Red Paper on Scotland* (Edinburgh: EUSPB, 1975)

—, *Maxton: A Biography* (Edinburgh: Mainstream, 1986)

—, *Where There's Greed: Margaret Thatcher and the Betrayal of Britain's Future* (Edinburgh: Mainstream, 1989)

Brummer, Alex, *The Crunch* (London: Random House, 2008)

Burke, Jason, *Al-Qaeda: The True Story of Radical Islam* (London: Penguin, 2007)

Burton, John and Eileen McCabe, *We Don't Do God* (London: Continuum, 2009)

Callaghan, James, *Time and Chance* (London: Collins, 1987)

Campbell, Alastair, *The Blair Years* (London: Hutchinson, 2007)

Campbell, John, *Pistols at Dawn* (London: Jonathan Cape, 2009)

Clarke, Richard, *Against All Enemies* (London: Simon & Schuster, 2004)

Clausewitz, Carl von, *On War* (London: Everyman Library, 1993)

Clinton, Bill, *My Life* (London: Hutchinson, 2004)

Coates, David and Joel Krieger, *Blair's War* (Cambridge: Polity Press, 2004)

Cockburn, Patrick, *The Occupation, War and Resistance in Iraq* (London: Verso, 2006)

Cook, Robin, *The Point of Departure* (London: Simon & Schuster, 2003)

Cooper, Robert, *The Breaking of Nations* (London: Atlantic, 2003)

Coughlin, Con, *American Ally: Tony Blair and the War on Terror* (New York: Ecco, 2006)

Cowley, Philip, *The Rebels: How Blair Mislaid His Majority* (London: Politico's, 2005)

Crick, Michael, *In Search of Michael Howard* (London: Simon & Schuster, 2005)

Daalder, Ivo and James Lindsay, *America Unbound* (Washington: Brookings Institution Press, 2003)

Dell, Edmund, *The Chancellors* (London: HarperCollins, 1996)

Diamond, Patrick (ed.), *New Labour's Old Roots* (London: Imprint Academic, 2004)

Dyke, Greg, *Inside Story* (London: HarperCollins, 2004)

Egan, Dominic, *Irvine: Politically Correct?* (Edinburgh: Mainstream, 1999)

Elliot, Francis and James Hanning, *Cameron: The Rise of the New Conservative* (London: Fourth Estate, 2007)

Ferguson, Niall, *The Ascent of Money* (London: Penguin, 2008)

Filkins, Dexter, *The Forever War* (London: Bodley Head, 2008)

Frum, David, *The Right Man* (New York: Random House, 2003)

Galbraith, Peter, *The End of Iraq* (London: Simon & Schuster, 2006)

Garton Ash, Timothy, *Free World* (London: Penguin, 2004)

Godson, Dean, *Himself Alone: David Trimble and the Ordeal of Unionism* (London: Harper Perennnial, 2005)

Gordon, Michael and Bernard Trainor, *Cobra II* (New York: Atlantic Books, 2007)

Gould, Philip, *The Unfinished Revolution* (London: Little, Brown, 1998)

Greenberg, Stan, *Dispatches from the War Room* (New York: Thomas Dunne, 2009)

Greenspan, Alan, *The Age of Turbulence* (New York: Penguin, 2007)

Grey, Stephen, *Operation Snakebite* (London: Viking, 2009)

Hennessy, Peter, *The Prime Minister: The Office and Its Holders since 1945* (London: Penguin, 2000)

Hersh, Seymour, *Chain of Command* (London: Penguin, 2004)

Hiro, Dilip, *Secrets and Lies* (New York: Nation Books, 2004)

Hughes, Colin and Patrick Wintour, *Labour Rebuilt* (London: Fourth Estate, 1990)

Hyman, Peter, *1 Out of 10* (London: Vintage, 2005)

Jackson, General Sir Mike, *Soldier* (London: Transworld, 2007)

Jenkins, Simon, *Thatcher & Sons* (London: Penguin, 2007)

Jones, Seth, *In the Graveyard of Empires* (London: Norton, 2009)

Kagan, Robert, *Paradise and Power* (New York: Knopf, 2003)

Kampfner, John, *Blair's Wars* (London: The Free Press, 2003)

Kavanagh, Dennis and David Butler, *The British General Election of 2005* (Basingstoke: Palgrave Macmillan, 2005)

Keegan, William, *The Prudence of Mr Gordon Brown* (Chichester: John Wiley & Sons, 2003)

Kilfolye, Peter and Ian Parker, *Left Behind* (London: Politico's, 2000)

Kindleberger, Charles, *Manias, Panics, and Crashes* (New York: Basic Books, 1978)

King, Anthony, *The British Constitution* (Oxford: OUP, 2007)

— (ed.), *Leaders' Personalities and the Outcome of Democratic Elections* (Oxford: OUP, 2002)

Krugman, Paul, *The Return of Depression Economics* (London: Penguin, 2008)

Lawrence, Bruce, *Messages to the World: The Statements of Osama bin Laden* (London: Verso, 2005)

Le Grand, Julian, *Of Knights and Knaves* (Oxford: OUP, 2003)

Levy, Michael, *A Question of Honour* (London: Simon & Schuster, 2008)

Lipsey, David, *The Secret Treasury* (London: Viking, 2000)

Lloyd, John, *What the Media are Doing to Our Politics* (London: Constable, 2004)

MacDougall, Linda, *Cherie: The Perfect Life of Mrs Blair* (London: Politico's, 2001)

Macintyre, Donald, *Mandelson and the Making of New Labour* (London: Harper-Collins, 2000)

Mandelson, Peter, *The Blair Revolution Revisited* (London: Politico's, 2002)

Mason, Paul, *Meltdown: The End of the Age of Greed* (London: Verso, 2009)

McCarthy, Rory, *Nobody Told Us We are Defeated* (London: Chatto & Windus, 2006)

McDonald, Henry, *Trimble* (London: Bloomsbury, 2000)

McSmith, Andy, *Faces of Labour* (London: Verso, 1997)

Meyer, Christopher, *DC Confidential* (London: Weidenfeld & Nicolson, 2005)

Mitchell, George, *Making Peace* (London: Heinemann, 1999)

Moloney, Ed, *A Secret History of the IRA* (London: Penguin, 2003)

—, *Paisley* (Dublin: Poolbeg Press, 2008)

Morgan, Piers, *The Insider* (London: Ebury Press, 2005)

Mowlam, Mo, *Momentum* (London: Hodder & Stoughton, 2002)

Mulgan, Geoff, *Good and Bad Power* (London: Penguin, 2006)

Mullin, Chris, *A View from the Foothills* (London: Profile, 2009)

Naughtie, James, *Rivals* (London: Fourth Estate, 2002)

Obama, Barack, *The Audacity of Hope* (New York: Crown, 2006)

Oborne, Peter and Simon Walters, *Alastair Campbell* (London: Aurum, 2004)

Owen, David, *In Sickness and in Power* (London: Methuen, 2008)

Packer, George, *The Assassins' Gate* (London: Faber and Faber, 2006)

Peston, Robert, *Brown's Britain* (London: Short Books, 2005)

Pimlott, Ben, *Harold Wilson* (London: HarperCollins, 1992)

Pollard, Stephen, *David Blunkett* (London: Hodder & Stoughton, 2005)

Powell, Colin with Joseph Persico, *My American Journey* (New York: Random House, 1995)

Powell, Jonathan, *Great Hatred, Little Room* (London: Vintage, 2009)

Prescott, John with Hunter Davies, *Prezza, My Story* (London: Headline Review, 2008)

Price, Lance, *The Spin Doctor's Diary* (London: Hodder & Stoughton, 2005)

Rai, Milan, *War Plan Iraq* (London: Verso, 2002)

Ramesh, Randeep (ed.), *The War We Could Not Stop* (London: Faber and Faber with Guardian Newspapers, 2003)

Rashid, Ahmed, *Taliban: The Story of Afghan Warlords* (London: Pan, 2001)

Rawnsley, Andrew, *Servants of the People* (London: Hamish Hamilton, 2000, and rev. edn Penguin, 2001)

Rentoul, John, *Tony Blair, Prime Minister* (London: Little, Brown, 2001)

Ricks, Thomas, *The Gamble* (New York; Penguin, 2009)

Riddell, Peter, *Hug Them Close* (London: Politico's, 2003)
—, *The Unfulfilled Prime Minister* (London: Politico's, 2005)
Risen, James, *State of War* (London: The Free Press, 2006)
Robinson, Linda, *Tell Me How This Ends* (New York: Public Affairs, 2008)
Rogers, Simon (ed.), *The Hutton Inquiry and Its Impact* (London: Politico's with Guardian Newspapers, 2004)
Routledge, Paul, *Gordon Brown: The Biography* (London: Simon & Schuster, 1998)
Sands, Philippe, *Lawless World* (London: Penguin, 2006)
Sassoon, Donald, *One Hundred Years of Socialism: The West European Left* (London: Tauris, 1996)
Scott, Derek, *Off Whitehall* (London: Tauris, 2004)
Seldon, Anthony, *Blair* (London: The Free Press, 2004)
—, *Blair Unbound* (London: Simon & Schuster, 2007)
Shawcross, William, *Allies* (London: Atlantic Books, 2003)
Short, Clare, *An Honourable Deception?* (London: The Free Press, 2004)
Smith, Jon, *Election 2005* (London: Politico's, 2005)
Soros, George, *The New Paradigm for Financial Markets* (London: Public Affairs, 2008)
Stelzer, Irwin, *Neoconservatism* (New York: Atlantic Books, 2005)
Stephens, Philip, *Tony Blair: Making of a World Leader* (New York: Viking, 2004)
Stewart, Rory, *Occupational Hazards* (London: Picador, 2006)
Stothard, Peter, *Thirty Days* (London: HarperCollins, 2003)
Stuart, Mark, *John Smith: A Life* (London: Politico's, 2005)
Suskind, Ron, *The One Percent Doctrine* (London: Simon & Schuster, 2006)
Synnott, Hilary, *Bad Days in Basra* (London: Taurus, 2008)
Tenet, George, *At the Center of the Storm* (New York: HarperCollins, 2006)
Tett, Gillian, *Fool's Gold* (London: Little, Brown, 2009)
Toynbee, Polly and David Walker, *Better or Worse?* (London: Bloomsbury, 2005)
Unger, Craig, *The Fall of the House of Bush* (London: Simon & Schuster, 2007)
Wheatcroft, Geoffrey, *Yo Blair!* (London: Politico's, 2007)
Woodward, Bob, *Bush at War* (New York: Simon & Schuster, 2002)
—, *Plan of Attack* (New York: Simon & Schuster, 2004)
—, *State of Denial* (New York: Simon & Schuster, 2006)
—, *The War Within* (New York: Simon & Schuster, 2008)
Young, Hugo, *This Blessed Plot* (London: Macmillan, 1998)
—, *The Hugo Young Papers* (London: Penguin, 2008)

MANIFESTOS, REPORTS AND WHITE PAPERS

New Labour Because Britain Deserves Better, Labour manifesto, 3 April 1997
Modern Forces for the Modern World, The Strategic Defence Review, Cm 3999, Ministry of Defence, 8 July 1998

Abstract of National Statistics, Office of National Statistics, 2000–2009

Budget and Pre-Budget Report Analyses, Institute for Fiscal Studies, 2000–2009

Budgets and Pre-Budget Reports, HM Treasury, 2000–2009

Register of Donations to Political Parties, Electoral Commission, 2000–2009

Ambitions for Britain, Labour manifesto, 16 May 2001

Securing Our Future Health: The Wanless Review, Derek Wanless for HM Treasury, November 2001 and April 2002

Iraq's Weapons of Mass Destruction: The Assessment of the British Government, HM Government, 24 September 2002

The Future of Higher Education, White Paper, Cm 5735, Department of Education, January 2003

Iraq, Its Infrastructure of Concealment, Deception and Intimidation, 'the dodgy dossier', Number 10, February 2003

UK Membership of the Single Currency: An Assessment of the Five Economic Tests, Cm 5776, HM Treasury, June 2003

Inquiry into the Circumstances Surrounding the Death of Dr David Kelly, transcripts of evidence and report of inquiry by Lord Hutton, HC 247, 28 January 2004

An Independent Review of Government Communications, Bob Phillis for HM Government, February 2004

Public Service Agreements 2005–2008, Spending Review, Cm 6238, HM Treasury, July 2004

US Intelligence Community's Pre-War Intelligence Assessments on Iraq, US Senate Committee on Intelligence, 7 July 2004

Review of Intelligence on Weapons of Mass Destruction, Report of a Committee of Privy Counsellors Chaired by Lord Butler of Brockwell, HC 898, 14 July 2004

The 9/11 Commission Report, National Commission on Terrorist Attacks upon the United States, 22 July 2004

An Inquiry into an Application for Indefinite Leave to Remain, Sir Alan Budd for the Home Office, 21 December 2004

It's Time for Action, Conservative manifesto, 11 April 2005

Britain Forward Not Back, Labour manifesto, 13 April 2005

Higher Standards, Better Schools for All, White Paper, Cm 6677, Department of Education, 25 October 2005

Power to the People, independent inquiry into Britain's democracy chaired by Helena Kennedy for the Joseph Rowntree Reform Trust, February 2006

The Price of Dishonour, Chris Philp for The Bow Group, 22 July 2006

The Governance of Britain – Constitutional Renewal, Consultation Papers, Cm 7170 and 7342, Ministry of Justice, 2007–2008

Report on the Treatment of Fourteen 'High Value Detainees' in CIA Custody, International Committee of the Red Cross, February 2007

Building on Progress: Public Services, Strategy Unit, Cabinet Office, March 2007

Future Strategic Challenges for Britain, Strategy Unit, Cabinet Office, February 2008

Internal Audit Review of Supervision of Northern Rock, Financial Services Authority, 26 March 2008

Growing Unequal: Income Distribution & Poverty in OECD Countries, OECD, October 2008

The Road to the London Summit, HM Government, February 2009

The Nationalisation of Northern Rock, National Audit Office, 20 March 2009

Public Expenditure Statistical Analyses, HM Treasury, April 2009

The Global Credit Boom, Michael Hume and Andrew Sentance for MPC External Unit, Bank of England, June 2009

The Culture of Churn, Hugh Cleary and Richard Reeves, Demos paper, 12 June 2009

From Rescue to Recovery, International Monetary Fund, 16 July 2009

An Alternative Report on UK Banking Reform, CRESC, University of Manchester, 29 September 2009

Report on MPs' Expenses and Allowances, Sir Christopher Kelly, Cm 7724, Committee on Standards in Public Life, November 2009

Index

Page references for notes are followed by n and
the note number, e.g. 716n92